Current Biography Yearbook 2014

H. W. Wilson

A Division of EBSCO Information Services

Ipswich, Massachusetts

GREY HOUSE PUBLISHING

SEVENTY-FIFTH ANNUAL CUMULATION—2014

International Standard Serial No. 0084-9499

International Standard Book No. 978-1-61925-430-5

Library of Congress Catalog Card No. 40-27432

Current Biography Yearbook, 2014, published by Grey House Publishing, Inc., Amenia, NY, under exclusive license from EBSCO Information Services, Inc.

PRINTED IN CANADA

CONTENTS

LIST OF BIOGRAPHICAL SKETCHES

LIST OF OBITUARIES

Current Biography Yearbook 2014

Marina Abramović

Born: November 30. 1946
Occupation: Performance artist

Controversial performance artist Marina Abramović has presented her art internationally, winning acclaim in Europe, Japan, and the United States. She is also a renowned teacher; from 1994 until 2001 she was a professor for performance art at the Hochschule für Bildende Künst (University of Art) in Braunschweig, Germany. The Art Institute in Chicago, the University of Plymouth, and Willams College each awarded her honorary doctorates in 2004. After a visit to Sri Lanka and Laos in the late 1990s when she observed people who pushed the limits of the body, Abramović told Janet A. Kaplan for *Art Journal* (Summer, 1999), "My whole research in this piece is to find the limit. How can a Western body have this experience, and how can an Eastern body push much farther into an area unknown for us? I am interested in this because for me performance is a means of research to find mental and physical answers." Abramović has become a cultural icon, a fact confirmed when her work was spoofed in a sixth-season episode of the popular HBO series *Sex and the City*. Abramović has worked for most of her career to make performance art part of the history of the art world through re-performing the works of others as well as her own pieces. As she told Jeffrey Brown for PBS (Apr. 2011), "[Performance art] has never been mainstream art. And it took for [sic] so many years for me to fight for that position. . . . All my really [sic] life really was to make performance mainstream art."

EARLY LIFE AND EDUCATION

Abramović was born in Belgrade, Serbia, to a Communist family. Her parents met while fighting as Partisans in Josip Tito's resistance army during World War II. Vojo, her father, was a general in the army and a national hero; her mother, Danica, was a major in the army and friends with the Yugoslavian dictator, Tito. Abramović recalls that her parents slept with weapons under or near the bed and were often in uniform. Her father continued in the Yugoslav Air Force after the war. Abramović later used her parents' related war experiences as part of her *Balkan Baroque* (1999). Danica, whose father was a priest in the

Wirelmage

Serbian Orthodox religion, was also the director of the Museum of the Revolution and Art in Belgrade. Her parents divorced when Marina was eighteen. She has a brother, Velimir, who is six years younger than she and who has a doctorate in philosophy. Her parents, now both deceased, were considered Serbian national heroes.

Abramović attributes her need to perform and her own willingness to inflict pain on herself during performance, whether by cutting her flesh or sitting for many hours, to the lack of love she felt from her parents. Her mother was severe, waking her in the middle of the night if the sheets were rumpled because Marina was not sleeping straight. Her parents were physically and emotionally abusive to each other and to their children. As MoMA curator Klaus Biesenbach explained to Elizabeth Greenwood for *Atlantic*, "Marina is never not performing. The audience is fuel to her, in effect, a lover."

Abramović began as a painter and first exhibited her work at the age of twelve. Yugoslavia allowed greater freedoms than many of the Communist-controlled nations of Eastern Europe, so Abramović was able to travel throughout Europe, though she continued to live with her mother, who imposed a 10:00 p.m. curfew until Abramović moved out when she was twenty-nine. She attended the Academy of Fine Arts in Belgrade, then went to Croatia for further study at the Academy of Fine Arts in Zagreb from 1965–70. Hired in Serbia in 1973 to teach at the Academy of Fine Arts in Novi Sad—her mother sent an application form to Britain, where Abramović was living—she first focused on painting. Gradually she began pioneering performance art with sound being a major feature of her early work.

ABRAMOVIĆ AND ULAY

From 1975 until 1989, Abramović and Frank Uwe Laysiepen (Ulay) were partners both personally and professionally, performing jointly as Abramović/Ulay. They met in Amsterdam, Ulay's home base. Their work examined the polarization of East/West and male/female. In nearly all cases, however, they did not stress political polarization. The couple shared a November 30 birthday, though Ulay was born in Nazi Germany and Abramović in Communist Yugoslavia; he is three years her senior.

In 1977, the couple created a performance piece titled *Imponderabilia* during which they stood naked, facing each other in the main entrance of a major museum in Bologna, Italy. People wishing to enter were forced to face one artist or the other as they squeezed between the bodies, thus forcing physical contact. Although the piece was scheduled to run for three hours, the police broke it up after ninety minutes. (Abramović reperformed the piece in 2010 with several other artists at the Museum of Modern Art in New York City.) In 1979, feeling they had reached the limits of what they could do with performance art, the couple travelled to the Gobi, Sahara, and Thar deserts as well as the Australian outback. As Abramović told Kaplan, "Going to nature was a way to recharge. . . . We found new energy for performance, but now less physical and much more mental. We came from the Aborigines with this idea for the *Nightsea Crossing* piece, in which we just sat for long periods of time opposite each other at a table in the museum. The pair sat facing one another, absolutely immobile, for seven hours' duration. They repeated the performance ninety times in twenty-two countries between 1981 and 1986.

In 1988, the two embarked on what became their final project, *The Lovers: The Great Wall Walk*, three months of walking on the Great Wall of China. Ulay began from the west, Abramović from the east. When they came together at the same spot on the Wall, they ended their collaboration and their relationship. Afterward, Abramović became involved with the fashion industry, grew her hair long, and continued to exhibit performance art. All this, according to Greenwood, was as a result of what Abramović referred to as being "40, fat, ugly, and unwanted" following her breakup with Ulay.

PERFORMANCE ART

Performance art reached the United States in the 1970s. As Sarah Lyall, writing for the *New York Times* (19 Oct. 2013) defines performance art, "[It] refers, broadly, to live experimental pieces that are not theater and that tend to emphasize the direct, unmediated relationship between artist and audience. There are no rules or boundaries to the form."

Abramović, now in her sixties, is glad to be "the grandmother" of performance art, as she terms herself. Most of her early contemporary artists moved on to another field of art or are not physically able to perform. She, however, has always focused on the physical body, even when trying to transcend it in extreme circumstances. As she told Kaplan, "The only idea I have always had is the human body. That's the only thing I have always been interested in. It's a large area to be explored, and I always feel that I'm just at the beginning."

Although she claims to be fearful about many things in her personal life, Abramović incorporates pain and suffering in her work but insists she is not masochistic. "The aggressive acts I do to myself I would never dream of doing in my own life," she explained to Judith Thurman for the *New Yorker* (8 Mar. 2010). She went on to explain that "the sense of purpose I feel to do something heroic, legendary, and transformative; to elevate viewers' spirits and give them courage. If I can go through the door of pain to embrace life on the other side, they can, too."

Abramović often reperforms her work, but many critics and performers alike believe that because of that unmediated relationship, performance art cannot be reperformed. Using video or still photography to capture the performance or employing another artist to reenact the performance is anathema to many artists. Abramović, however, has championed the practice and likens it to an artist performing a piece composed by Bach or an actor reperforming a Shakespearian play. It is not the original, but it keeps the original alive.

SEVEN EASY PIECES

Nothing better expresses Abramović's commitment to reperformance than *Seven Easy Pieces*, which she performed for seven days in 2005 at the Guggenheim Museum in New York City. With permission, Abramović recreated earlier works of other performance artists, many of whom were no longer working in the medium. The pieces included *Body Pressure* by Bruce Nauman, originally performed in 1974; the 1972 work *Seedbed*, first performed by Vito Acconci;

Valie Export's *Action Pants: Genital Panic* of 1969; *The Conditioning*, originally performed in 1973 by Gina Pane; Joseph Beuys's *How to Explain Pictures to a Dead Hare* from 1965; Abramović's 1975 performance, *Lips of Thomas*; and finally, *Entering the Other Side*, Abramović's 2005 "living installation," which was created for the final night.

Reperforming these works presented certain challenges. As Abramović put it in an interview with Nancy Spector in the book *7 Easy Pieces* (2007), "It is a very big problem that when certain performance works were made, the artists never left a set of instructions or clue, because they didn't think it necessary at the time."

Abramović's reperformance pieces in *Seven Easy Pieces* were honored in 2006 at the Guggenheim's International Gala and received the AICA-USA (International Association of Art Critics, United States) award for Best Exhibition of Time Based Art in 2007.

THE ARTIST IS PRESENT

In 2010, New York City's Museum of Modern Art (MoMA) served as the venue for the retrospective *The Artist Is Present*. The work was conceived after more than a month at an Ayurvedic retreat in south India during the winter of 2008–9.

Defending the idea of works of long duration, Abramović told Linda Yablonsky for *Art News* (1 Dec. 2009), "The one thing we don't have anymore is time. As life gets shorter, art has to get longer. We can't do anything about the past, and we don't have the future. We only have the present." For nine hours each day, from November 15 to December 21, 2002, Abramović sat impassively facing museum visitors who chose to sit across from her at a table, some of them repeatedly. Some, for reasons that are unclear, wept. It was the longest duration of time for a single piece at MoMA.

Several other performance artists took part in the event, giving the first live re-presentation in a museum setting of Abramović's major works. The exhibit also included records of Abramović's four-decade career using sound pieces, video, photographic stills, solo performances, and collaborative performances made with Ulay. A documentary, *Marina Abramović: The Artist Is Present*, which followed Abramović as she prepared for the retrospective, premiered in 2012 at the Sundance Film Festival. In June of that same year, the documentary was broadcast on the cable television network HBO, and the following year, it won the network's Peabody Award, one of several awards for which it was nominated.

MARINA ABRAMOVIĆ INSTITUTE

In 2013 Abramović announced plans to open an institute that would be a sort of Bauhaus for performance art. The 33,000-square-foot space in Hudson, New York, will offer students and artists an opportunity to engage in mind-body cleansing exercises. Abramović referred to it as a cultural spa, as Lyall's interview notes. "I knew long duration was the answer to everything for me. And, with this, came the idea of the institute in the most clear form. . . . My work is not my work anymore. It's about culture in general, about changing the consciousness of human beings on this planet."

Abramović turned to the online funding platform Kickstarter for financing the initial construction costs, which are estimated at $600,000. Her hope is to open in 2014.

PERSONAL LIFE

Although Abramović claims that one's mind is all-important, she takes excellent care of her body. She does not smoke, drink, or take drugs, and she has cleansing routines to clarify her mind before a new performance and also works with a personal trainer. "I feel I'm in my third act," she told Yablonsky, "and I want it to go nicely." She has also overcome her early dissatisfaction with her nose, which, at fourteen, she wanted to resemble that of Bridgette Bardot. An early attempt to break her own nose so that it would need reconstruction failed.

Abramović married her first husband, a student from the Belgrade Academy of Arts, in 1977. In 1997 she met Italian artist Paolo Canevari, a video artist and sculptor who was seventeen years younger than she. They were together for twelve years before marrying and divorcing in 2009. Following the divorce, she learned to drive. In keeping with her belief that a woman must choose between a domestic life and an artist's life, she has never had children.

In addition to the property in Hudson, New York, Abramović and Givenchy designer Riccardo Tisci share living space in a New York City townhouse; Abramović has the three lower floors, while Tisci has the top two.

In December 2013, Abramović, in conjunction with the Elton John AIDS Foundation (EJAF), released a limited edition of prints to be sold at $1,000 each in order to raise funds for both EJAF and the Marina Abramović Institute. The photograph, titled *The Current*, is of Abramović against a pink background, eyes closed, wearing a white shirt, with her hair pulled back.

SUGGESTED READING

Brown, Jeffrey. "Conversation: Marina Abramović." *PBS Newshour: Art Beat.* MacNeil/Lehrer Productions, 8 Apr. 2011. Web. 13 Jan. 2014.

Greenwood, Elizabeth. "Wait, Why Did That Woman Sit in the MoMA for 750 Hours?" *Atlantic.* Atlantic Monthly Group, 2 July 2012. Web. 6 Jan. 2014.

Kaplan, Janet A. "Deeper And Deeper: Interview with Marina Abramovic." *Art Journal* 58.2 (1999): 6. Print.

Lyall, Sarah. "For Her Next Piece, a Performance Artist Will Build an Institute." *New York Times*. New York Times, 19 Oct. 2013. Web. 3 Jan. 2014.

Thurman, Judith. "Walking Through Walls." *New Yorker*. Condé Nast, 8 Mar. 2010. Web. 9 Jan. 2014.

Yablonsky, Linda. "Taking It to the Limits." *Art News*. ARTnews, 1 Dec. 2009. Web. 6 Jan. 2014.

SELECTED WORKS

Rhythm 10, 1973; *Lips of Thomas*, 1975; *Imponderabilia* (with Ulay), 1977; *Nightsea Passage* (with Ulay), 1981–86; *The Lovers: The Great Wall Walk* (with Ulay), 1988; *Balkan Baroque*, 1997; *The House with the Ocean View*, 2002; *Seven Easy Pieces*, 2005; *The Artist Is Present*, 2010; *The Life and Death of Marina Abramović*, 2011

—*Judy Johnson*

Getty Images

John Luther Adams

Born: January 23, 1953
Occupation: Composer

John Luther Adams is considered one of the most respected and original composers in America today, but his work, often inspired by nature, did not always have widespread recognition. It took Adams a number of decades, beginning in the 1970s, to carve out a place for himself and his work in the music world. Over the years as he slowly built a reputation for his compositions, he has been asked to teach at numerous prestigious universities and serve as composer in residence with respected musical ensembles. Now in his sixties, Adams is still composing for chamber ensembles, orchestras, percussion, and electronic media, and he has earned a host of awards including the 2014 Pulitzer Prize for music for his composition *Become Ocean*.

After winning the Pulitzer, Adams told Tom Huizenga in an interview with NPR (14 Apr. 2014), "I never thought much about career. I'm an artist. You know, I moved to Alaska in my twenties. I never studied with the right people at the right schools. Early on I didn't win the right prizes. It seems that every time I had the opportunity to make the right career choice, I made the wrong career choice, which in the long run turned out to be the right artistic choice. And now, after forty years or more of doing this, it seems like maybe there's a larger audience for the work and that's profoundly gratifying."

EARLY LIFE

John Luther Adams was born in 1953 in Meridian, Mississippi. Because of his father's career with telecom giant AT&T, the family moved frequently throughout Adams's formative years. As a teenager he lived outside of New York City in Millburn, New Jersey, where he came to love rock music and joined several bands as a drummer. In an interview with Ivan Hewett, a music critic for the *Telegraph* (3 July 2013), Adams recalled his early musical influences: "If it weren't for the Beatles we wouldn't be having this conversation. When I was fifteen I wanted to be John Lennon. I had a whole string of bands, one of which [Pocket Fuzz, which was the opening act for the Beach Boys at a concert in New Jersey] was quite successful. We used to hang out in record stores, and that's how I discovered modern music. There was an LP of Edgar Varèse, which just blew our minds." (Adams had only learned of Varèse thanks to the liner notes in Frank Zappa's 1966 album *Freak Out!*) His fascination with European and American avant-garde postwar music soon extended to Karlheinz Stockhausen, Iannis Xenakis, Henry Cowell, Charles Ives, Morton Feldman, and, most significantly, John Cage.

In 1969, Adams and his family moved to Macon, Georgia, where he was enrolled in Westminster Academy, a prestigious boarding school. His behavior, however, didn't mesh well with the rigid environment, and he dropped out before graduating.

FIRST MARRIAGE AND EARLY MUSIC EDUCATION

In addition to his ever-developing fascination with composing avant-garde music, Adams had become enamored with a girl named Margrit von Braun. Margrit was the younger daughter of Wernher von Braun (1912–77), the famed scientist who had helped to develop the V-2 rocket for Germany during World War II and, after becoming an American citizen, designed rockets for the early US space program, including the Saturn V, which took American astronauts to the moon in the late 1960s and early 1970s. The aspiring composer and the respected scientist did not get on well, and despite the elder von Braun's reservations, Adams married Margrit. The couple subsequently moved to Los Angeles, California, in 1971, so Adams could study music at the California Institute of the Arts (CalArts), from which he graduated in 1973.

At CalArts, Adams came into contact with a number of musicians who would greatly influence his development as a composer. Among them was the composer James Tenney, who was his teacher and mentor. His greatest influence, however, may have been the New York composer Morton Feldman, whose work *Piece for Four Pianos*, in which four pianists play the same music at different rates, inspired him like no other. Alex Ross, writing for the *New Yorker* (12 May 2008), noted, "That work galvanized Adams, teaching him that music could break free of European tradition while retaining a sensuous allure. One of his first characteristic pieces, for three percussion players, bears the Feldmanesque title 'Always Very Soft,' although the seamlessness of the construction—accelerating and decelerating patterns overlap to create a single, ever-evolving sonority—hints at a distinct sensibility."

MOVE TO ALASKA

The time Adams spent in California exposed him to the burgeoning environmental movement, which in turn would ultimately motivate him to move to Alaska. His entry into environmentalism came through the efforts to save the California condor, which was on the brink of extinction. During visits to the Los Padres National Forest to see some of the last condors living in nature, Adams became inspired to write some of his first nature music, including *Songbirdsongs*. "That piece is a sort of miracle," Adams remarked to Hewett. "I'd just finished my musical studies in California, and I needed to find a place I could call home. I've always been attracted to things that are singular, in every sphere of life—in art, and music, and places."

By the mid-1970s, Adams was fully immersed in the conservation movement and was working with a number of groups, including the Wilderness Society. At the time, the Society sought to preserve large sections of Alaska from exploitation by oil companies and other industries by lobbying the US government to pass the Alaska Lands Act, which was signed into law by President Jimmy Carter in 1980. Adams first visited Alaska in 1975 and then returned to the Arctic two years later. In that latter year, Wernher von Braun died and Adams's marriage to Margrit von Braun ended. In 1978, Adams moved to Alaska in part because he had fallen in love with a fellow environmentalist.

Adams's second wife Cynthia had worked alongside him during the run-up to the passage of the Alaska Lands Act. Throughout the 1980s, which was also the first ten years of their marriage, the couple lived apart—she with their son Sage in Fairbanks, Alaska, and Adams in a small, rough cabin in the woods outside the city—so he could work on his music in the rural Alaskan silence. During his time in the wilderness, Adams earned a living as a timpanist (one who plays the kettledrums in an orchestra) and as principal percussionist for the Fairbanks Symphony Orchestra and Arctic Chamber Orchestra as he struggled to perfect his singular style as a composer. Cynthia's patience with their nontraditional living arrangement wore thin in 1989 when she asked Adams to live with his family full-time or go his own way. Adams decided to leave the cabin and return to Fairbanks.

RISE TO PROMINENCE

Adams began to find his way as a composer during the 1990s with works that were largely inspired by the natural world. "Nature is that culture in which all human culture takes place," Adams told Hewett. "Everything we do is owed to the world of which we are part. So yes, nature is my culture." *Earth and the Great Weather* (1994) is an avant-garde classical collection that Adams wrote about the Alaskan wilderness. The compositions employ English, Latin, and native Alaskan languages to describe places and the changes in seasons. Also in 1994, Adams became the composer in residence with the Anchorage Symphony Orchestra, and the Alaska Public Radio Network, positions he held until 1997.

Adams writes compositions for orchestra, chamber ensembles, percussion, and electronic media, and his recorded works include *In the White Silence*, a seventy-five-minute piece written in 1998 for harp, celesta, vibraphones, and strings, which was released in 2003 on New World Records. Among his other recordings are *Clouds of Forgetting, Clouds of Unknowing* (1997), which was written for his father; *The Light that Fills the World* (2002); *Winter Music* (2004); *Strange and Sacred Noise* (2005), an almost seventy-five-minute percussion piece comprised of drums, gongs, sirens, and bells; *Red Arc/Blue Veil* (2007), and *The Place We Began*

(2009). As Ross wrote, "Adams's major works have the appearance of being beyond style; they transcend the squabbles of contemporary classical music, the unending arguments over the relative value of Romantic and modernist languages."

As his reputation grew, Adams's works began to be performed by major orchestras, including the Chicago Symphony Orchestra, the Radio Netherlands Philharmonic Orchestra, the California E.A.R. Unit chamber ensemble, the Percussion Group Cincinnati, and New Music America, among others.

ACHIEVING ACCLAIM

Adams began earning awards and fellowships for his work from institutions like the National Endowment for the Arts, the Rockefeller Foundation, the Rasmuson Foundation, Opera America, and the Foundation for Contemporary Performance Arts, among others. In 2006 he was chosen as one of the first Fellows of the United States Artists, and in 2010 he was named the winner of the Michael Ludwig Nemmers Prize in Music Composition, which carried a cash award of $100,000 and is administered by Chicago's Northwestern University Henry and Leigh Bienen School of Music. As part of the award, Adams served a two-year residency at the prestigious music school. "When I learned I'd been chosen to receive the 2010 Nemmers Prize, I was stunned," Adams explained to Judy Moore for *Northwestern University News* (29 Apr. 2010). "For most of my creative life I've worked in relative isolation. It's deeply gratifying to know that my music resonates in the larger world. And since few things make me happier than working with young musicians, I'm especially looking forward to my residencies at the Bienen School of Music."

In the early 2000s, Adams began to further develop his music as installations and electronic compositions. A 2005 installation, *Veils*, is three "soundscapes" that Adams created to be heard either simultaneously or sequentially. It toured venues across the United States and Europe and used a virtual choir of ninety polyphonic voices. *The Place Where You Go to Listen*, a sound-and-light installation that opened in 2006 at the University of Alaska Fairbanks, was controlled electronically by real-time natural events such as meteorological, seismic, and geomagnetic data. Adams also saw some of his major works, including *Dark Waves* (2007), a piece written for a large orchestra and electronic sounds, performed around the globe. *Inuksuit* (2013) is a percussion piece for up to ninety-nine musicians and has been performed across Canada, Australia, and the United States, including in New York City venues like Morningside Park and the Park Avenue Armory.

BECOME OCEAN

Adams received considerable critical acclaim for *Become Ocean*, a forty-two-minute piece for a large orchestra. It was commissioned by the Seattle Symphony and was performed in June 2013. In recent years Adams, who has lived in the Alaskan interior since the 1970s, began spending more time near the Alaskan coast and was inspired to write the piece while viewing the Pacific Ocean. The work, which is intended to give the listener the sense of a surging tidal wave and inspire fear of rising sea levels due to climate change, pleased many critics. Alex Ross wrote in a July 8, 2013, *New Yorker* article, "There are shocks of beauty, shocks of feeling, shocks of insight. Such were the virtues of John Luther Adams's 'Become Ocean.' . . . Like the sea at dawn, it presents a gorgeous surface, yet its heaving motion conveys overwhelming force. Whether orchestras will be playing it a century hence is impossible to say, but I went away reeling."

In April 2014 *Become Ocean* won the Pulitzer Prize in music. Adams learned of the prize while at Michigan Technological University (Michigan Tech) where he was in residence. "I was taking a nap between classes and the phone rang," Adams recalled to Michael Cooper in the *New York Times* (14 Apr. 2014). "Talk about a wakeup call!" Adams was unable to hear the piece performed during its premiere with the Seattle Symphony, but he was in the audience when it had its New York premiere at Carnegie Hall the following May.

OTHER ACCOMPLISHMENTS

Adams has taught at Bennington College, Harvard University, the Oberlin Conservatory, and the University of Alaska, and he has served as president of the American Music Center and as executive director of the Northern Alaska Environmental Center. He is also the author of two books, *Winter Music* (2004), a collection of short pieces reflecting on his life and work in Alaska, and *The Place Where You Go to Listen*, a 2009 work describing his installation at the Museum of the North.

SUGGESTED READING
Cooper, Michael. "A Pulitzer Today, and in May, a New York Premiere." *New York Times*. New York Times, 14 Apr. 2014. Web. 15 Apr. 2014.
Herzogenrath, Bernd, ed. *The Farthest Place: The Music of John Luther Adams.* Boston: Northeastern UP, 2013. Print.
Hewett, Ivan. "John Luther Adams, Interview." *Telegraph*. Telegraph Media Group, 3 July 2013. Web. 9 Apr. 2014.
Huizenga, Tom. "Alaskan Composer Wins Pulitzer for 'Become Ocean.'" *NPR Music*. NPR, 14 Apr. 2014. Web. 15 Apr. 2014.

"John Luther Adams: Bio." *Johnlutheradams.com*. John Luther Adams, n.d. Web. 9 Apr. 2014.

Ross, Alex. "Water Music." *New Yorker* 8 & 15 July 2013: 92–93. Print.

SELECTED WORKS

Earth and the Great Weather, 1994; *The Light that Fills the World*, 2002; *In the White Silence*, 2003; *Winter Music*, 2004; *Red Arc/Blue Veil*, 2007; *The Place We Began*, 2009; *Become Ocean*, 2013

—*Christopher Mari*

Tunde Adebimpe

Born: February 25, 1975
Occupation: Actor and musician

Tunde Adebimpe is best known in the music world as the cofounder and front man of the rock band TV on the Radio. The group got their first taste of popularity and major critical acclaim after the 2006 release of their second full-length studio album, *Return to Cookie Mountain*, which was followed by *Dear Science* (2008) and *Nine Types of Light* (2011). In particular, *Dear Science* was heralded by various music critics as one of the best albums of the year, if not the decade. The unique use of doo-wop, dance, punk, Afrobeat, vocal harmonies, and jazz elements gave the band its distinct sound and loyal following. Adebimpe has also appeared in several movies, most notably the indie comedy *Jump Tomorrow* (2001) and the major motion picture *Rachel Getting Married* (2008).

EARLY LIFE

Babatunde Omoroga Adebimpe was born on February 25, 1975, in Saint Louis, Missouri. His father, psychiatrist Victor Adebimpe, had traveled to the United States from Nigeria in 1973 to complete a medical residency; his mother, Folasade Olunemi, was a pharmacist. The family later moved from Saint Louis to Pittsburgh, Pennsylvania, where Adebimpe spent the rest of his younger years.

Growing up, Adebimpe was exposed to African and Indian music, as well as classical music and jazz. In an interview with Lauren Mechling for the *Wall Street Journal* (20 Sept. 2008), he said that although his parents had careers outside the world of art and music, he experienced a great variety of art growing up; his father was a painter, writer, and musician, and his mother, he said, was "one of the best storytellers I know." His sister later became a gospel and opera singer, and his brother (who has since died) was a writer.

Tim Mosenfelder/Getty Images

"DO EVERYTHING"

Adebimpe left Pittsburgh for New York City in 1993 to study film at the Tisch School of the Arts at New York University. Even in his early days, Adebimpe was somewhat of a Renaissance man; in an interview with Brandon Kim for IFC TV (5 Mar. 2009), he looked back on his first years in New York and his multiple artistic pursuits: "I feel like I was really fortunate to run into a lot of working artists when I moved to New York in the mid-'90s, and the single piece of advice that all these people seemed to be giving me was, 'Do everything that makes sense to you to do, and a couple of things that don't. Do everything.' And this was when I honestly just wanted to be a cartoonist. I met people who did illustration, made large-scale artworks, films, videos, and performance as well."

In 2001 Adebimpe starred in the film *Jump Tomorrow* as George Abiola, a character that film critic Roger Ebert described on his website (27 July 2001) as a "serious, dutiful Nigerian who always wears glasses and usually wears a suit and needs to learn to listen to his heart." In the film, which Ebert called a "low-key screwball comedy," George comes to the United States to marry a Nigerian woman as part of an arranged marriage. However, his plans are thrown into disarray when he meets a beautiful Hispanic woman named Alicia and falls in love. The film was generally well received, though by no means was it a hit. Although Adebimpe appeared in several short films after that, he did not return to the big screen until 2008, by which time TV on the Radio was well known and beloved by indie-rock fans and critics.

In *Rachel Getting Married* (2008), Adebimpe plays Sidney, the groom-to-be, who is a musician. Rachel, the bride-to-be, is played by Rosemarie DeWitt, and Anne Hathaway plays Kym, Rachel's sister. Writing for the *Wall Street Journal* (3 Oct. 2008), Joe Morgenstern ended his review by pointing out that "because Sidney is a musician, many of his friends perform at the wedding, and music . . . is the force that drives the drama once the ceremonies get under way."

TV ON THE RADIO

In 2001, when Adebimpe was still an animator and unknown actor, he started experimenting with music. Guitarist and keyboardist Dave Sitek, who lived in the same building as Adebimpe in the New York City borough of Brooklyn, became his main collaborator. Although Sitek was a musician and had played in various bands in high school, at the time he met Adebimpe, he was trying to establish himself as a painter. As Adebimpe has said in numerous interviews, painting and animation often take a long time, and neither provided the two of them with the fun and immediate sense of accomplishment that music could.

There was another factor as well: "After September 11th, there was a collective unspoken decision to not go outside very much anymore and stay inside and work on things that really meant something then," Adebimpe told Devin Gordon for *GQ* magazine (Nov. 2011). "I think that was, oddly, a really, really focusing time as far as music went. The *Young Liars* EP came out of that—out of that time of not really being very certain about what was happening around you, and of wanting to fabricate a platform to stand on." In the same interview, Adebimpe confessed that their first live shows were "really terrible," but they were never bored—and they got better.

The title of the duo's first recording, the eighteen-track demo *OK Calculator*, is a reference to Radiohead's major album *OK Computer* (1997). The demo was never officially released; the band produced their own discs in 2002 and left them in various locations around New York. In 2003 they released the EP *Young Liars*, featuring Yeah Yeah Yeahs members Nick Zinner and Brian Chase, on the label Touch & Go. At this time, TV on the Radio began to expand its lineup, adding guitarist and vocalist Kyp Malone.

In 2004 TV on the Radio released its first full-length studio album, *Desperate Youth, Blood Thirsty Babes*, to critical acclaim. In a review of the album for the website AllMusic, Heather Phares opened with a mini-review of *Young Liars*, writing that "its alchemy of strange sonic bedfellows like post-punk and doo wop, and powerful vocals and experimental leanings, into songs that were challenging and accessible was no small feat; indeed, *Young Liars* was such an accomplished EP that it begged the question—and ratcheted up the expectations—of what TV on the Radio could do over the course of an entire album." Phares went on to describe *Desperate Youth, Blood Thirsty Babes* as a "deeper, darker, denser version of the band's already ambitious sound" and wrote that "Adebimpe in particular continues to prove himself as a distinctive and captivating voice, both musically and lyrically." The band's unique blend of soul, jazz, gospel, rock, noise, and doo-wop impressed music fans as well as critics, and the album eventually reached number eleven on the Billboard Top Independent Albums chart.

RETURN TO COOKIE MOUNTAIN

The following year, TV on the Radio released the political song "Dry Drunk Emperor," a criticism of then-president George W. Bush, for free on its website. The song was followed by the album *Return to Cookie Mountain* (2006), which was more polished and less aggressive than *Desperate Youth*, featuring sweeter vocals and earning the band comparisons to 1960s pop groups such as the Beach Boys. In a glowing review on the music website Pitchfork (5 July 2006), Chris Dahlen concentrated on the sound of the record, specifically complimenting Adebimpe. "When I try to explain TV on the Radio to people who aren't into them, the first thing on the checklist is singer Tunde Adebimpe, a stoic romantic who falters but never whimpers," he wrote. "He's got about the best set of pipes in indie rock, yet on *Return to Cookie Mountain* his greatest strength lies in how well he stands back and blends in." Dahlen gave *Return to Cookie Mountain* a nearly perfect score of 9.1 out of 10. The record was also the band's first major commercial success, reaching number forty-one on the Billboard 200 chart.

With the success of *Return to Cookie Mountain*, the band signed to Interscope, a large record label. Though TV on the Radio continued to be categorized as indie rock, the members did not want their fan base to remain small. In an interview with Dahlen for Pitchfork (2 Oct. 2006), Sitek explained why the band moved to a major label: "We don't want to be hidden behind some shroud of secrecy. I don't think that TV on the Radio is some dark mysterious band that no one can know about. We write music because it's an immediate form of communication. We're able to put on record what's happening in our times, and we want that message to be heard by the most amount of people."

MAINSTREAM SUCCESS

TV on the Radio's 2008 album, *Dear Science*, peaked at number twelve on the Billboard 200 chart. In an interview for the *AV Club* (13 Oct. 2008), Adebimpe explained that the album's title stems from the idea that for all the good science has done, it has also created a lot of death and destruction. "It's about the questionable faith that we put in science," he said. "You know, we're allegedly able to live longer because of scientific advancement, but we're doing so in a world that might be getting hurt in the process."

Adebimpe also reflected on how the experience of recording *Cookie Mountain* was "something that none of us really wanted to experience over again." He described how the mood during the recording process was often quite dark, with band members sometimes leaving the studio for days after a disagreement. During the recording of *Dear Science*, Adebimpe told the *AV Club*, the band decided to use a metaphorical "loving fast-forward button" that let them skip arguments that had the potential to spiral out of control; if they had a disagreement about some piece of music or sound, they would skip it and move on to the next task, coming back to the area of disagreement at a later time.

Dear Science is a happier record as a result. As with its previous effort, the band made greater use of attention-grabbing hooks and polished structure. As the album's intense focus on rhythm suggests, TV on the Radio had set out to make a percussion-heavy record that was also danceable. The result was the band's biggest commercial success at the time, and it led to appearances on a variety of television shows, including the *Late Show with David Letterman*, *The Colbert Report*, and *Saturday Night Live*. Various publications, including *Rolling Stone*, named *Dear Science* the best album of 2008. Then, following a great deal of critical and commercial success, the band went on hiatus.

LOSS AND REDEMPTION

In April 2011, TV on the Radio released its second major-label album, *Nine Types of Light*. Like the previous record, it reached number twelve on the Billboard 200 chart. At the same time, the band's bassist, Gerard Smith, who had been with TV on the Radio since 2005, died of lung cancer at the age of thirty-six. Smith's death prompted the band to cancel several concerts, but they eventually returned.

Nine Types of Light was recorded at Sitek's home studio in Los Angeles, California (at the time Adebimpe still lived in Brooklyn), and the locale is woven into the fabric of the album. At least two of the songs written by Adebimpe, "Forgotten" and "Caffeinated Consciousness," refer to his exhaustion with Los Angeles. Critics raved about how much more accessible the album was than anything the band had done before; references were made to the Pixies and Prince. In a review for Pitchfork (12 Apr. 2011), Stuart Berman wrote, "*Nine Types of Light* is unquestionably TV on the Radio's most patient, positive recording to date, taking its cues as much from *Dear Science*'s serene ballads . . . as its brassy workouts." He concluded his review by stating, "In the past, TV on the Radio have tried to undercut their more rockist ambitions with dissonant textures and queasy atmospherics, or lace their prettiest ballads with subversively ominous lyrics. But *Nine Types of Light* shows how TV on the Radio's transmissions can be just as effective and affecting when delivered free of static and noise."

Adebimpe married cartoonist and illustrator Domitille Collardey in June 2011. In early 2014, after living in New York City for two decades, he relocated to Los Angeles. Before making the move he briefly toured with his musical side project, Higgins Waterproof Black Magic Band.

SUGGESTED READING

Adebimpe, Tunde. "Just Asking . . . Tunde Adebimpe." Interview by Lauren Mechling. *Wall Street Journal*. Dow Jones, 20 Sept. 2008. Web. 14 July 2014.

Adebimpe, Tunde. "Taking a Break with Tunde Adebimpe." Interview by Brandon Kim. *IFC*. IFC TV, 5 Mar. 2009. Web. 14 July 2014.

Adebimpe, Tunde. "Tunde Adebimpe of TV on the Radio." Interview by Devin Gordon. *GQ*. Condé Nast, Nov. 2011. Web. 14 July 2014.

Adebimpe, Tunde. "TV on the Radio's Tunde Adebimpe." *AV Club*. Onion, 13 Oct. 2008. Web. 14 July 2014.

SELECTED WORKS

Desperate Youth, Blood Thirsty Babes, 2004; *Return to Cookie Mountain*, 2006; *Dear Science*, 2008; *Nine Types of Light*, 2011

—*Dmitry Kiper*

Ben Ainslie

Born: February 5, 1977
Occupation: Competitive sailor

Sir Charles Benedict Ainslie, currently Britain's most well-known competitive sailor, has won five Olympic medals—four gold and one silver—in sailing. He is one of a handful of people in the world to win medals at five Olympic Games. Among his other accolades are eleven world titles in sailing, won first in Laser and then in Finn class. He was asked to be the first Olympic

Associated Press

torchbearer in 2012 prior to the London Games, and in addition, he carried the British flag in the closing ceremony. One of Ainslie's greatest honors is a knighthood, bestowed on him by Queen Elizabeth II in 2013 for services to the world of sport. He is a patron of the National Maritime Museum in Cornwall, to which he has donated many of his winning boats. His autobiography, *Close to the Wind*, was published in 2012. His next challenge and great hope is winning the American's Cup on a British team. As he explained to Donald McRae for the *Guardian* (12 Dec. 2013), "It's a strange psychology and it becomes very simple. You either win the race or go home."

EARLY LIFE AND EDUCATION

Ainslie grew up in southwest England in the county of Cornwall. With the support of his parents, Rod and Susan Ainslie, he began sailing at age eight in Restronguet Creek. Rod Ainslie was himself an avid sailor; in 1973, Rod sailed a yacht in the first Whitbread Round the World Race.

Ainslie was educated at Truro and Terra Nova Schools and later attended Peter Symonds College. During his early teenage years, he suffered from a sun allergy that caused his skin to blister and break out in a rash, and he became the target of bullying. "They never gave me a break," he wrote in his autobiography. "It made me ferociously determined to be good at something to prove to myself that I could be a success and that there was more to life than school and being picked on." Ainslie soon began to prove

that he was a success at sailing. He won the Yachting Journalist's Association's British Yachtsman of the Year award in 1995 and 1999 and the International Sailing Federation's World Sailor of the Year award in 1998.

THE OLYMPIC GAMES

As Ben's career advanced, his parents sold their home to help finance his first Olympic bid. At nineteen, Ainslie raced in the 1996 Olympics, in Atlanta, Georgia. Competing in Laser class, which requires a single-handed dinghy, he took home a silver medal for second place. It wasn't good enough for Ainslie. Four years later, in the same competition, in Sydney, Australia, he advanced to gold. However, his efforts to cut out the Brazilian sailor Robert Scheidt, who had won the gold in 1996, gained him the promise of police protection during the awards assembly—Brazilians' feelings of resentment were strong and death threats had been issued against him.

For the Athens 2004 games, held at the Agios Kosmas Olympic Sailing Centre, Ainslie gained more than thirty pounds of muscle on a diet of protein shakes and steak. His goal was to make the optimum weight for competing in the heavyweight Finn class. He again won gold in that class. For the 2008 games in Beijing, China, he raced in the same class with the same results, even though he had been ill a few days before the competition.

Ainslie feared he would be disqualified from the 2012 Olympics because of his behavior during the 2011 World Championships, held in Perth, Australia. Believing that a media dinghy was checking his progress, he got into the water and physically wrestled with that boat's crew, trying to hijack it. He was subsequently disqualified from that race for his actions, although Britain did not remove him from the Olympic team.

Ainslie lost the first six of eleven competitions in the 2012 Games to a Danish sailor. Furious because he felt the Danish and Dutch sailors were "ganging up on him," Ainslie famously stated, as reported by Simon Usborne for the *Independent* (26 Sept. 2013), "They've made a mistake, because I'm angry. And they didn't want to make me angry." He came from behind to win gold. Following the 2012 Olympics, Ainslie retired from Olympic competition, having suffered several injuries, particularly to his back, during his career.

AMERICA'S CUP

Days after the conclusion of the London Games, Ainslie headed to San Francisco Bay to compete in the America's Cup World Series, the oldest and most prestigious of sailing races. One of his lifelong dreams had been to win that race, which is held in various locations and times at the prerogative of the winning team. J.P. Morgan, his long-term sponsor for whom he races under the name J.P. Morgan Bar, also sponsored him for that competition.

Only three teams challenged the United States for the Cup in September 2013, perhaps in part due to new rules that took effect. The rules were changed from requiring a forty-five feet catamaran to one that was seventy-two feet long, making the competition even more expensive to enter. In addition, rather than mandating five competitions to win the Cup, the new protocol set out two races per day, requiring nine wins to become the ultimate victor. The 2013 competition was also the first to be held on inland waters.

To be more certain of winning the race, Oracle Team USA, owned by wealthy businessman Larry Ellison, held a preliminary race to determine which of two boats and crews would compete in the race. As part of an international team, Ainslie helmed the boat that won that race. Unfortunately, as the Cup race proceeded, Oracle Team fell behind and the challenging Emirates Team New Zealand pulled ahead. Then, after a timeout, Ainslie was shifted to the position of tactician. In an amazing upset, Oracle Team won the thirty-fourth America's Cup 9–8.

Some credit Ainslie, who assumed the position of tactician after the fifth race, for that comeback. Ainslie had never before handled that role, and found the software difficult to master. However, he studied the night before he began and had the support of the previous tactician. When he took the position, the Oracle team was already down 4–1. They lost the next two races as well. But they won the next seven, bringing the score to 8–8 and forcing a runoff, which the Oracle Team managed to win by a mere forty-four seconds. As Ainslie told Hannah Jane Parkinson for the *Guardian* (27 Dec. 2013), "No one gave us a prayer at 8–1 down. It truly was one of the great sporting comebacks and felt like an absolutely huge moment in my career. . . . To come back from where we were, it's one of the most amazing things I've ever been a part of."

HONORING A LOST FRIEND
By helping to pull off the Oracle Team USA win, Ainslie became the first Briton to sail a winning boat in the America's Cup since 1903, when Charlie Barr competed. Despite the astonishing victory, it was a bittersweet day for Ainslie, whose friend Andrew "Bart" Simpson had died the previous May while preparing for the race with a Swedish team on their sailboat, *Artemis*. The two men had together hoped to sail a British ship to victory in America's Cup. As Ainslie told Donald McRae for the *Guardian* (13 Dec. 2013), "After we crossed the line there were immediate celebrations on the boat. We had pulled off a remarkable win and were so happy. But soon after the bedlam died down I thought about

Bart. We had to sail the boat back to our base and this meant we were in the very stretch of water where the *Artemis* capsized. I could not stop thinking about Bart."

Partly to pay homage to his close friend, Ainslie aims to pursue the dream that they had both held and to win the America's Cup with a British team for the first time in the 163 years of that race. As Ainslie explained to Owen Gibson for the *Guardian* (8 Jan. 2014), "It was very hard. Even now. It was a sad, terrible moment for all of us and one that marked the year. We try and move on and do the best we can in his memory."

In addition to pursuing the America's Cup goal, Ainslie has found multiple ways to honor his friend. He has joined others in establishing the Andrew Simpson Sailing Foundation, whose purpose is to support young people in sailing. He is also one of the event ambassadors for a global sailing event fundraiser, initially proposed by Simpson's sister, Amanda. Called Bart's Bash, it is scheduled for fall 2014. The goal is to break the Guinness World Record for largest sailing event in the world.

PREPARING FOR THE NEXT WIN
In order to develop and maintain a British America's Cup team, fundraising is imperative. The cost of a team is about a hundred million US dollars; the money is used over several years to build a catamaran and train a crew. Ainslie hopes to raise about half that sum from private backers; several people, including Sir Keith Mills and Charles Dunstone, have been financially supportive. Both Dunstone and Mills had earlier supported a failed attempt at a British team. The rest of the money will come from corporate sponsorships.

Ainslie is optimistic about raising the needed monies within the three to five years before the next race, which he expects to be held in San Francisco. He is aware of the impact of his amazing win for the US team on the likelihood of establishing a British team. As he told Gibson, "Realistically, we wouldn't be able to get to where we are now—we still have a way to go but we've had a huge amount of support—if the Cup hadn't been the success it was."

Ainslie is carefully courting the Formula One designer Adrian Newey, though he is quick to point out that he is not trying to take Newey away from Formula One, where his work for the Red Bull team has led to a string of successes. As he put it to Gibson, "I'm certainly not sitting here trying to lure him away from Christian Horner, who I also have a huge amount of respect for. If we could get Adrian involved in any way that would be amazing for us but we also understand and appreciate his ties to Formula One." Ainslie did meet with Newey in Abu Dhabi to discuss matters in late 2013, as well as with J.P. Morgan in New York.

In 2014 Ainslie is competing in a number of short races in the Extreme Sailing series. Singapore and Oman were the first two venues for these international inland competitions; in May 2014 Ainslie raced in the third venue, Qingdao Bay in China. J.P. Morgan is once again sponsoring him and a team that includes Olympic medalists Paul Goodison and Pippa Wilson. Participating in Extreme Sailing, Ainslie feels, will provide an opportunity for his ideas about the right mix of designers and sailors for an America's Cup bid to gel. He is clear, however, that he will not enter the 2017 competition unless he perceives a viable chance of winning.

He is pleased by the increased attention given to sailing as a result of his recent career, telling McRae, "Ten years ago people looked down at sailing as one of those odd sports that no one really understood or cared about. Now, especially in the wake of the America's Cup, sailing has become quite cool."

CHARITABLE WORK

In addition to his competitive sailing, Ainslie has thrown his support behind a number of different charities. For example, he is an ambassador for the Prince's Trust, an organization set up to assist the large number (about 20 percent) of Britain's unemployed youth. The trust provides assistance with job training and ideas for new business ventures.

To offer support to those in his own profession, Ainslie works with the John Merricks Sailing Trust. Established in the memory of Olympian John Merricks, the trust offers training and assistance for those under twenty-five. As a patron of the group, Ainslie wrote on their website, "I am honoured to be the first patron of the John Merricks Sailing Trust and delighted to have been asked to support a charity that helps young sailors in the UK. John was not only a great sailor but his attitude to the sport was a terrific example to all young sailors of the future."

Ainslie is also involved in Sail4Cancer, an organization begun in 2001 by dedicated sailors who had lost family or friends to cancer. The group makes respite care available for those in Britain dealing with the disease, as well as for their families, providing cruises of a few days or weeks. The group also donates to cancer care centers and sponsors research related to ways in which exercise can aid in recovery.

Beginning in 2012, Ainslie has supported ShelterBox. This relief organization provides temporary housing and other necessities in the wake of a disaster or a humanitarian crisis. Along with a tent, the group offers items such as solar lamps, blankets, groundsheets, water storage and purification equipment, and mosquito nets.

Ainslie also works with Sported, founded by Keith Mills. The group, based in Britain, supports community organizations involved in Sport for Development, a program that provides aid to young people through sports. Sported was one of the major supporters of the 2012 Olympic and Paralympic Games.

PERSONAL LIFE

Ainslie's interest in sports is broad and includes cricket, football, and golf. He is also a fan of Formula One racing, seeing parallels between auto racing and sailboat racing related to speed, physicality, and performance. Like auto racers, he perseveres against great odds; in fact, he believes his greatest strength in his sailing career has been his refusal to give up.

Ainslie previously dated fellow Olympian sailor, Marit Bouwmeester. In 2013, he began a romantic relationship with Georgie Thompson, a British sports broadcaster currently based in the United States. When Wollaston asked if Ainslie could imagine himself teaching his children to sail, the thirty-six year old Ainslie responded, "Yeah, that would be amazing. I better sort that out at some stage soon. I'm getting a bit old, turning into a bit of a wrinkly old seadog."

SUGGESTED READING

Gibson, Owen. "Sir Ben Ainslie's Fundraising for America's Cup Bid 'in a Good Place.'" *Guardian*. Guardian, 8 Jan. 2014. Web. 24 April 2014.

McRae, Donald. "Ben Ainslie: Winning America's Cup in a British Boat Is Final Hurdle." *Guardian*. Guardian, 12 Dec. 2013. Web. 28 April 2014.

Parkinson, Hannah Jane. "Memorable Moments of 2013: Ben Ainslie Masterminds America's Cup Win." *Guardian*. Guardian, 27 Dec. 2013. Web. 22 April 2014.

Usborne, Simon. "Amazing Ben Ainslie." *Independent*. Independent, 26 Sept. 2013. Web. 29 April 2014.

Wollaston, Sam. "Ben Ainslie Interview: 'I Used to Turn into a Bit of a Monster on the Water.'" *Guardian*. Guardian, 4 Oct. 2013. Web. 24 April 2014.

—*Judy Johnson*

Haifaa Al Mansour

Born: August 10, 1974
Occupation: Filmmaker

Haifaa Al Mansour is a Saudi Arabian filmmaker who directed her award-winning film *Wadjda* (2012) from inside a van, via two-way radio. The distance, Al Mansour told Dan Zak for the *Washington Post* (19 Sept. 2013), was a precaution. Al Mansour also wrote the film—the first feature film shot entirely in Saudi Arabia—about a

Matt Crossick/PA Photos/Landov

young Saudi girl who enters a Qur'an memoriza-
tion contest in the hope of buying a green bicycle with the cash prize. Because bicycles were at
that time implicitly forbidden for women in the
country, this is no ordinary goal. A woman giving orders to a man is also forbidden—thus, the
importance of Al Mansour's van. If she had been
seen directing her cast on the streets of Riyadh,
"people would've stopped the shooting, because
they don't like it," she told Zak. "In Saudi, it's not
against the law, because there's no law, but it's
against the social conduct. People don't do that."

Al Mansour's first film, *Women without Shadows* (2005), was a documentary about Saudi
women. According to Al Mansour, Saudi Arabia,
among the world's top oil producers and exporters, is a bit of a contradiction. "It's conservative,
but it is rich," she told Katie Van Syckle for *New
York Magazine* (20 Sept. 2013). "People have
access to a lot of things and still cling a lot to
the tradition." In Saudi Arabia, citizens live according to Shari'a law, Islam's strict moral code.
In public spaces, women must be accompanied
by a male chaperone, and they must wear a full-
body black cloak known as an abaya. They are
not allowed to drive cars and are still not allowed
to vote. (They will be granted that right in 2015.)
Women were only recently given permission to
ride motorcycles and bicycles for leisure.

Since the Islamic revival of the 1980s, there
have been no movie theaters in Saudi Arabia.
Saudis routinely travel to neighboring countries like Bahrain to see movies from the United
States, Egypt, and India's Bollywood. When
Wadjda was shown in Dubai, United Arab Emirates, Saudis flocked to see it, causing a traffic
jam in the city; it was the first time Saudis were

able to see a film about their own country made
by one of their own. Though the film enraged
staunch conservatives, it inspired many members of the nation's large population of moder-
ates who had never seen the streets of Riyadh
depicted on film. "My veiled sister loved it.
And she's my target audience," Al Mansour told
Horatia Harrod for the *Telegraph* (19 July 2013).
"She's educated but she's still conservative, and
she really saw her life in the film."

EARLY LIFE AND EDUCATION

Al Mansour was born the eighth of twelve children on August 10, 1974. She grew up in Al-
Hasa (also spelled Al-Ahsa) on the east coast of
Saudi Arabia where her father, the late Abdul
Rahman Mansour, worked as a legal consultant but also wrote poetry. Unlike many homes
in Saudi Arabia, Al Mansour's had an extensive
library. She read Agatha Christie and loved the
Jackie Chan and Disney movies that her father
brought home for her from the video store. Al
Mansour recalls her more progressive family as
outsiders in their conservative town. She and her
sisters didn't cover their hair, and Al Mansour
even had her own green bicycle—though she
was allowed to ride it only in her family's private
courtyard. "My father . . . and my mother gave us
a lot of space to grow as individuals," Al Mansour
told Liz Hoggard of the *Guardian* (13 July 2013).
"I never felt I couldn't do anything because I was
a girl."

Al Mansour was the only one of her classmates to attend college abroad at the American
University in Cairo, Egypt, where she studied
comparative literature and learned to drive. Back
home, her friends told her that because of her
education, she would never find a husband. After graduation, Al Mansour returned to Saudi
Arabia and took a job as the director of media
relations at an oil company. As a single woman,
Al Mansour had a difficult time establishing herself in her home country. Her father had to sign
for her rental apartment, and she had to hire a
driver to shuttle her back and forth from work.
Often, Al Mansour told Harrod, her driver slept
in or didn't show up. (She bought him an alarm
clock, she said, but he sold it.) "I felt, 'I'm so invisible, nobody cares and I am no one,'" she said.
"I wanted to have a voice, and I wanted to say
something."

EARLY FILM CAREER

Al Mansour began making films as a kind of
therapy. Without a budget, she made shorts using only her camera and her family as cast and
crew. One of her first films, *Who?* (2003), is a
seven-minute short, based on a Saudi Arabian
urban myth in which a man dresses in the abaya
and niqab, or face veil, and murders women. According to Emily Jones, writing for the University of Sydney website in Australia (30 Jan. 2013),

Who? was the first narrative film of any kind to come out of Saudi Arabia. When her shorts were recognized in local competitions, Al Mansour decided to make a full-length film. In 2005 she shot a documentary called *Women without Shadows* about women living in her hometown of Al-Hasa. "[W]omen in Saudi Arabia are very much aware of the camera and they're afraid," Al Mansour told Liz Shackleton for *Screen International* magazine (5 Aug. 2010) of her decision to interview women in the city where she was born. "So I thought if they know me and know my mother, they would be more at ease and would trust me."

Many of the women told her that before the 1970s oil boom, they had lived in small villages in the mountains where women enjoyed more freedoms. Oil drew their families to the cities "where people were afraid of their neighbors," Al Mansour explained to Shackleton, "and a lot of Islamist movements emerged." The Islamic revival steered the country toward a new conservatism that changed the nature of the women's lives. The abaya, and particularly the niqab, Al Mansour suggests, rob Saudi women of their identity. In the film, Al Mansour interviews a cleric, Sheikh Ayed al-Qarni, who says that there is nothing in Islamic teachings that specifically states that a women must cover her face as well as her hair. After the film was released, he retracted his statement. (In 2004 al-Qarni said that there was nothing in Islam that specifically forbade a woman from driving a car. After an angry backlash, he retracted that statement as well.)

In 2006 *Women without Shadows* won prizes at the Muscat Film Festival in Oman and Abu Dhabi's Emirates Film Competition, but public opinion among Saudis was divided. Many women, most of whom had not even seen the film, applauded Al Mansour for raising issues that are generally considered too taboo for public debate. A woman named Fatima told Najah Alosaimi for Saudi Arabia's *Arab News* (21 Apr. 2005), "We need to be clear about the real purpose of 'hijab' and differentiate what is our culture and what are Islamic rules." Other Saudis criticized Al Mansour's film for what they perceived to be ignorance of Islamic teachings. "What gives her the right to pass judgment on such matters?" Norah, an Islamic culture teacher, told Alosaimi. "She isn't an Islamic scholar; she's a film director!"

FUNDING *WADJDA*

After the success of *Women without Shadows*, Al Mansour moved to Australia to study directing and film at the University of Sydney. She began writing *Wadjda* as a part of her thesis, and then—to get the film made—launched into five years of "charming and hustling," she told Catherine Armitage for the *Sydney Morning Herald* (22 Mar. 2014). In 2009 she pitched the script at the Circle Conference in Abu Dhabi, where she described *Wadjda* as a cross between the quirky and gently subversive film *Juno* (2007) and *The Kite Runner* (2007), a film based on a best-selling book about a young Afghan boy. Camille Alick, the program director for a nonprofit organization, Muslims on Screen and Television (MOST), praised the script as an ideal window into a conservative and closed society and helped Al Mansour refine her sales pitch. The jury at the conference awarded Al Mansour the $100,000 Shasha grant to develop the project.

In 2009 *Wadjda* was chosen as a project for the Sundance Institute's RAWI Middle East Screenwriters Lab in Jordan, but the largest hurdle for the film remained: Al Mansour could not find anyone to produce it. She e-mailed every arts funding organization in the Middle East and every production company in Europe. No one was biting. Finally, Al Mansour teamed up with Gerhard Meixner and Roman Paul of the German production company Razor Films—the same company that produced the award-winning Israeli animated feature *Waltz with Bashir* (2008) as well as *Paradise Now* (2005), a Golden Globe–winning film from Palestine. Al Mansour also received funding from Rotana, a film production company run by the billionaire Saudi prince, Al-waleed Bin Talal. A strong advocate for women's rights who encourages his female staff members to shed the veil, Prince Talal is perhaps the most progressive member of the royal family.

FILMING *WADJDA*

Al Mansour's producers assumed that it would be impossible to shoot the film in Saudi Arabia, but Al Mansour was determined to give her film an accurate sense of place. She secured the proper permissions and permits, though she was forced to direct her cast from the safety of a van and often had to pick up and move to avoid citizens who wanted to shut her down. When asked why she didn't choose to work out in the open in protest, Al Mansour told Armitage, "I wasn't trying to clash with people. I was trying to make a film. I'm making a film in Saudi Arabia—I'm a woman—about a young girl who wants a bicycle. That's enough." The film boasts an all-Saudi cast, including Reem Abdullah, a well-known Saudi television actress, who plays Wadjda's mother. But Al Mansour had difficulty casting her lead. Without casting calls, information about the auditions spread through word of mouth, but most parents forbade their daughters to try out. A week before principal shooting began, twelve-year-old Waad Mohammed showed up in the casting room. Mohammed wore jeans and Chuck Taylor sneakers (just as Wadjda does in the film) and listened to Justin Bieber on her headphones. Mohammed's family permitted her to appear in the film because she was not yet a woman. "They've told her that she can act until she's sixteen," Al Mansour told Harrod.

The film itself is semiautobiographical, but the character of Wadjda, Al Mansour insists, is based on her niece as well as the girls she knew in school who never had the chance to claim their own independence. Al Mansour describes her adolescent self as much more shy than the feisty Wadjda, who wants nothing more than to own a bicycle so that she can beat her friend Abdullah, a boy, in a race. The bicycle is a nuanced symbol of freedom—a legitimate mode of flight but also a toy. Elsewhere in the film, Al Mansour works to upend stereotypical notions about life in Saudi Arabia. For instance, she made a deliberate effort to show the two faces of both Saudi men and women—the public face and the private one. At home, Al Mansour told Armitage, Saudis "sing and flirt and laugh and eat," while in public, the women are veiled and the men "have this more serious kind of look that can hide how warm and kind they are." It was also important to Al Mansour to show how, perversely, women can act as the gatekeepers of conservative culture. In the film, Wadjda's female teacher comes down hard on the fun-loving girl. "A woman's voice is her nakedness," she snaps, when Wadjda is heard talking too loudly at school.

Wadjda premiered at the Venice Film Festival in 2012 and was released in the United States in 2013. It won numerous awards at independent festivals around the globe and made Al Mansour a legitimate name in the film industry. In 2014 the US film production company Gidden Media announced that Al Mansour would direct a film called *A Storm in the Stars*, about the nineteenth-century marriage of poet Percy Shelley and *Frankenstein* author Mary Wollstonecraft. Producer Amy Baer told Nancy Tartaglione for *Deadline Hollywood* (28 Feb. 2014), "From the minute I read the script, I was hoping to find a female director who would realize what Emma [Jensen, the author] was trying to say— that Mary Shelley's story is . . . about female empowerment and . . . about a young girl chafing against the norms of her society as she tries to be true to herself."

PERSONAL LIFE
Al Mansour's husband, Bradley Niemann, is an American diplomat. They met at a screening of *Women without Shadows* when Niemann was working in Saudi Arabia as the American cultural attaché. The couple married in 2007. Flouting Saudi's ban on women driving cars, Al Mansour drove a golf cart to her wedding. Al Mansour and Niemann lived in Australia for two years (while Al Mansour completed her master's degree in Sydney) before moving to Bahrain, an island country off the coast of Saudi Arabia in the Persian Gulf. Al Mansour wanted to be close to her family, but also to give her two young children, Adam and Hailey, a very different life from the one she experienced during her own childhood.

SUGGESTED READING
Armitage, Catherine. "*Wadjda*'s Saudi Director Says: 'Conservatives Don't Want to See Women Being Filmmakers.'" *Sydney Morning Herald*. Fairfax Media, 22 Mar. 2014. Web. 30 July 2014.
Harrod, Horatia. "Haifaa al-Mansour: I Wanted to Have a Voice." *Telegraph*. Telegraph, 19 July 2013. Web. 29 July 2014.
Hoggard, Liz. "Haifaa al-Mansour: 'It's Very Important to Celebrate Resistance.'" *Guardian*. Guardian, 13 July 2013. Web. 28 July 2014.
Jones, Emily. "Haifaa Al Mansour: Saudi Arabia's First Female Filmmaker." *University of Sydney Home Page: News and Events*. University of Sydney, 30 Jan. 2013. Web. 29 July 2014.
Shackleton, Liz. "Haifaa Al Mansour." *Screen International*. Media Business Insight. 5 Aug. 2010. Web. 29 July 2014.
Van Syckle, Katie. "Meet Saudi Arabia's Groundbreaking Filmmaker." *New York Magazine*. New York Magazine, 20 Sept. 2013. Web. 29 July 2014.
Zak, Dan. "*Wadjda*'s Director Haifaa Al Mansour Gives Female Perspective of Life in Saudi Arabia." *Washington Post*. Washington Post. 19 Sept. 2013. Web. 28 July 2014.

—*Molly Hagan*

Hashim Amla

Born: March 31, 1983
Occupation: Cricketer

Hashim Amla, a South African cricket player of Indian descent, earned the ranking of world's number-one batsman in 2013. Despite his success, he has been fairly immune to the spotlight, keeping a low profile off the field. As a practicing Muslim—he sports a full beard and does not wear endorsements for alcohol brands on his uniform—he has encountered ignorance and discrimination from some and veneration and admiration from others. As a boy, he played cricket for an integrated high school in South Africa and continued to improve after turning professional at the age of seventeen. Although he displayed an early talent for cricket, Amla played professionally for about six years before he began to shine, and it took him a few more years to get to the top. He eventually became the first player of Indian descent to play "test" cricket for South Africa.

EARLY LIFE AND EDUCATION
Hashim Mahomed Amla was born on March 31, 1983, and grew up in Tongaat, South Africa. Amla is from a middle-class family and is the youngest of three children: he has a sister and

Aman Sharma/Reuters/Landov

a brother, Ahmed, who was the first in the family to become a professional cricket player. The family's roots reach to India's state of Gujarat, from which his grandparents emigrated. Amla's parents are doctors, but his father did not push him to pursue a medical career; instead, he supported the boy's passion for and apparent talent at cricket. In an interview with Saj Sadiq for the website *Cricket Country* (18 May 2013), Amla said that his father had the biggest influence on his career: "He sacrificed much of his time and effort in taking me to practice, matches, and any other cricket commitments that would come up. My parents and entire family's support in and out of the game is something I could never repay. My father also never put any pressure on me to perform and instead allowed me to just play cricket and enjoy myself."

Unlike his older brother, Ahmed, who played high school cricket for an all-Indian school, Amla attended Durban High School beginning in 1996, by which point the school had been integrated. Because of the national policy of apartheid in place for much of the second half of the twentieth century, South Africa was a segregated society in which nonwhite citizens were openly discriminated against. However, starting in the early 1990s, apartheid began to fall apart and integration began to occur. Amla was a direct beneficiary of the change in South African political and social life.

At Durban High School, Amla's cricket talent caught the eye of coaches and players alike.

The fact that Amla did not attend an all-Indian school was a factor in how he viewed his future and his potential for playing professionally, according to his brother. In an interview with Sriram Veera for the ESPN cricket website *Cricinfo* (17 May 2009), Ahmed said that because he attended an all-Indian school, he felt a greater pressure than his brother to pursue a "proper" career. "When I went to school, I only played with the Indian kids," Ahmed said. "Integration hadn't occurred yet. But when Hash came along, the system had changed so rapidly. That really helped him. He studied in an integrated school, played with and against white and other coloured kids. It does have a huge impact on the personality." He added, "In an Indian school . . . you have to become a doctor! Even today, older relatives ask me, 'What do you do besides cricket?' I might be earning more than them, but . . . the Indian culture is not going to change. Most guys in school studied to become doctors, engineers, accountants." The school environment had a significant effect—and thereby made for significant differences—on how the brothers perceived a potential future in cricket. But there was another factor involved, said Ahmed: "When Hashim was under fifteen and showing promise, Natal cricket people [of the professional team KwaZulu-Natal Dolphins] said he had the potential to play higher. When I was playing in school, you never looked beyond the next game. All you are worrying about is which university you are going to. So he was always focused, more talented and more disciplined than I was." In other words, the combination of freedom—the younger Amla knew he could pursue cricket on a professional level if he so desired—along with his extraordinary abilities allowed him to reach the next level.

TEAM CAPTAIN

Although Amla grew up playing various sports, including soccer, rugby, and table tennis, by the time he was in high school, he knew that cricket was his strongest sport. He was inspired by his coaches and took playing and practice very seriously. He also learned from various challenges and setbacks. For example, in eleventh grade, when he was captain of his high school cricket team, the team did not have a good year. In an interview with the magazine *SA School Sports* (13 Dec. 2013), looking back on his school days, Amla said he remembered thinking at the time, "You know what, maybe I am not captaining very well." He was doing well as a player, he said, but he was disappointed that he could not improve his team's performance by inspiring them as team captain. Nonetheless, there were good times that year. When his high school team toured the United Kingdom, they won all twelve games they played; it was a "very proud moment and great memory," Amla said in the interview.

His toughest challenge, however, came not when he was playing for his school but when he was playing club cricket—alongside much older players—when he had just started high school. In the interview with *SA School Sport* magazine, Amla recalled, "I remember playing a club game when I was still at school and I received the worst abuse I have ever had in my life. . . . I was playing against thirty and forty year olds, seasoned club players and along comes this little kid and they did not hold back. But that experience of taking a player out of their comfort zone really builds character."

RULES OF THE GAME

Although cricket is a popular sport in many countries across the globe—including England, India, South Africa, and Bangladesh—it is little known in the United States. Because the game involves pitching a hard ball to a player with a bat, an analogy to baseball may be tempting to make, but such a comparison is ultimately misleading. Cricket is played between two teams consisting of eleven players each. Two umpires watch the game on the field and make calls, while an umpire off the field reviews decisions that are too close to call via video replay.

Three wickets, or long vertical stumps, stand on both sides of the playing area, on both sides of the pitch (where the batter, or batsman, and pitcher stand). Two horizontal bails sit on top of the wickets. The pitcher, known as the bowler, stands behind the wickets on his side and pitches the ball in the direction of the batter, who stands in front of the wickets on his side of the playing area. The batting team has two players on the field—a striker, the one trying to hit the pitch, and a nonstriker, who stands on the other side of the playing area waiting to run if the striker hits the ball. If the ball is hit, the two teammates run to the opposite ends of the pitch. The batter is out if the opposing team catches the ball before it bounces; if the bowler hits a stump and knocks off a bail, which is resting on top of the wicket; if a fielder knocks a bail from a stump when the batters are going for a run; or if the ball hits the batter but would have otherwise (according to the umpire) hit the wicket. If a batter hits the ball successfully, he in fact switches places with the other batter, and they can continue to score runs until the opposing team gets them out. Hitting a ball within the boundary of the field earns the batting team four runs, and hitting it out of the field boundary gives six runs. An inning is complete when everyone on the team has batted. Each team plays only one inning, and the team with the most runs wins. However, the long-form game of cricket, known as test cricket, lasts four innings, and those games often last four or five days.

BATTER RISING

After graduating from high school at seventeen, Amla joined the Dolphins, a national team in South Africa. In 2000 and 2001, he toured New Zealand with the South African Under-19 team and served as captain during the 2002 Under-19 World Cup. In 2004, after he made only thirty-six runs in a test game against England, Amla's batting technique was criticized. But he was undeterred. Although at the end of 2006 his average was an unimpressive twenty-two runs, it went up to thirty-two runs the following year. In 2007, he was awarded a national contract for the first time. The year after, his average improved to forty runs. In 2009, he was signed by Essex, an English team, for part of the season—because it was winter in South Africa, he was able to take time off to play in England. Writing for the website of the South African television channel Super Sport (20 July 2009), Jason Humphries observed that Amla made an "immediate impact for English county side Essex after he became the highest scoring debutant for the county."

Back in South Africa, Amla continued to improve. In 2011, he was appointed vice-captain of the Dolphins. The following year, he scored the third-most runs against England in a single inning (Don Bradman and Brian Lara scored more, while Amla's 311 runs tied Bob Simpson). With 311 runs, he became the first South African to score a test triple hundred, as it is called in cricket argot. Talking about the record to Paul Weaver of the *Guardian* (22 July 2012), Amla was as humble as always: "I'm happy, surprised, really excited that I managed to do something that has never been done before as a South African. . . . With my scoring rate 300 is usually a very long way away, so it didn't cross my mind until I'd got to 250. I'm overwhelmed. It's a lovely feeling." By this point, Amla had become one of the leading cricket batsmen in the world.

CONTROVERSY

On the field Amla looks different, not only because of his unique batting style and incredible poise but also because he has a thick, long beard, which is an expression of his faith. As an observant Muslim, Amla also does not wear logos advertising alcohol on his uniform. Although he occasionally encountered various hateful remarks throughout his career, he was not prepared for what an announcer said on air one day during an August 2006 test match between South Africa and Sri Lanka. During the match Dean Jones, an Australian cricketer turned commentator, wrongly assuming that the game was on a commercial break, said, "The terrorist has got another wicket," referring to Amla. The comment was heard all over the world.

Two years later, in an interview with Donald McRae for the *Guardian* (7 July 2008), Amla gave his side of the story. "I got off the field and went to my room and checked my messages. A friend of mine texted me and said, 'Listen there's a big thing back home, one of the commentators called you a terrorist.' I thought he was kidding. . . . But when I went down for supper the manager told me what Dean Jones [had] said. There were going to be lots of questions and SA Cricket had already released a statement. . . . At around quarter to ten I remember taking this call. It was from Dean Jones and he apologised and I said 'no problem.' I thought that was the end of it. But obviously there were implications . . . Coming from South Africa, which is very sensitive to stereotyping, it was a big thing . . . It was a lesson to everybody who has hidden stereotypes." In his interview with McRae, Amla said he forgave Jones, but he admitted that the comment hurt. However, Amla decided to turn the negative statement into an opportunity by engaging those who ask him about his faith or his beard.

BEST YEAR EVER
The year 2013 was by far the most significant in Amla's career to date. It included a change of teams and world ranking. In the spring, he left the Dolphins to join the Cape Cobras, a team based in Cape Town, South Africa. He made it clear in various interviews that the decision was not an easy one, but after much discussion with family and friends, he decided to opt for change. Then in the summer, the British cricket team Surrey County Cricket Club signed Amla on a short-term basis, to play in the season's last six County Championship matches. At that point, Amla was the highest-ranked test batsman in the world: out of seventy test matches, he had 5,785 runs. In fact, early in 2013, Amla had become not only the world's number-one test cricket batsman but also the highest-ranked one-day batsman. That made him the first cricket player since 2007 to hold both rankings simultaneously.

Amla is married and has a child.

SUGGESTED READING
Amla, Hashim. "Interview with Hashim Amla: My School Days!" *SA School Sports*. SA School Sports, 13 Dec. 2013. Web. 15 Apr. 2014.

Amla, Hashim. "I Use the IPL Period to Rest and Spend Time with My Family: Hashim Amla." Interview by Sadiq Saj. *Cricket Country*. India.com. 18 May 2013. Web. 15 Apr. 2014.

Essa, Azad. "Hashim Amla: A Quiet Hero." *Aljazeera English*. Aljazeera, 1 Aug. 2012. Web. 15 Apr. 2014.

Roebuck, Peter. "The Unbreakable South African." *Crickinfo*. ESPN Sports Media, 29 Jan. 2009. Web. 15 Apr. 2014.

—Dmitry Kiper

Laurie Halse Anderson
Born: October 23, 1961
Occupation: Writer

The author of best-selling books for young adults and children, Laurie Halse Anderson is, in the words of Suhana Jagadesan for the *Reading (Pennsylvania) Eagle* (18 Oct. 2011), "known for her uncanny ability to take any subject and relate to it, in a way that her readers, especially young adults, find incredible." In a career that has spanned more than two decades, Anderson has published young-adult novels and works of historical fiction as well as numerous picture books and chapter books for children. She is best known for her debut young-adult novel, *Speak* (1999), about a teenage girl's recovery following her rape. The book was a 1999 National Book Award finalist. Anderson's novels often grapple with challenging issues faced by teenagers, such as depression, peer pressure, eating disorders, and mental illness. "Being a teenager," Anderson explained to Carol Fitzgerald and Marisa Emralino for *Teenreads* (Aug. 2005), is "hard and confusing and few adults have the guts to talk about it honestly. That's my job. I try to write books that show teenagers struggling with all kinds of stuff; from the deadly serious to the lighter, day-to-day pressures. I want to show my readers that there really is a light at the end of the tunnel."

EARLY LIFE
Anderson was born Laurie Beth Halse on October 23, 1961, in Potsdam, a town in northern New York, near the Canadian border. She and

her younger sister, Lisa, grew up in Syracuse, New York. Her father, Frank, was a Methodist minister at Syracuse University, and her mother, Joyce, worked in management. Both of Anderson's parents wrote poetry and instilled in her a love of reading and writing. Anderson has cited her father as a major influence on her decision to pursue a writing career, which began in second grade after she learned how to write haiku. In an interview with Thomas J. Brady for the *Philadelphia Inquirer* (26 Apr. 2000), Anderson called her father "a great storyteller" and said that her "love of words comes from him."

Anderson developed a knack for storytelling as a young girl. Growing up, she often sneaked out of bed at night to eavesdrop on her parents and their friends relating stories to each other. "Their tales not only grounded Anderson in her own history," Patricia Newman wrote for the magazine *California Kids!* (Mar. 2005), "but subliminally implanted literary devices liked pacing, hooks, and dialogue." Anderson also became a voracious reader at an early age, making regular trips to the central branch of the Syracuse library, which was her "sanctuary," as she told Debbi Michiko Florence for *Book Friendly* (2003). Laura Ingalls Wilder's *Little House on the Prairie* book series sparked an early interest in historical fiction, while the books of J. R. R. Tolkien introduced her to science fiction and fantasy.

EDUCATION

Anderson attended Fayetteville-Manlius High School, a public school in the town of Manlius, located just outside of Syracuse. During her time there, she mostly "hid in books," as she told Fitzgerald and Emralino. She was a member of the school's swim and track teams during her sophomore and junior years. After joining the American Field Service student exchange program, Anderson, who by then had developed a growing interest in foreign cultures and languages, spent her senior year abroad in Denmark with a family that lived on a pig farm. During her stay in Denmark, she learned much about the language and customs of the country.

After graduating from Fayetteville-Manlius in 1979, Anderson took a brief hiatus from school, working a minimum-wage job at a clothing store before enrolling at Onodaga Community College in Syracuse. She received an associate's degree in liberal arts from the college in 1981. Afterward, she transferred to Georgetown University in Washington, DC, where she earned a bachelor's degree in languages and linguistics in 1984. During college, Anderson had aspirations of becoming a doctor and shied away from taking English classes out of disdain for analyzing books.

EARLY WRITING CAREER

After graduating from college, Anderson relocated to the Philadelphia area to start a family with her first husband, Greg Anderson. The couple had two daughters, Stephanie and Meredith, and later divorced but remained friends. Anderson continued to write while raising her children, but only as a hobby. She began working as a freelance journalist and writer in 1989, writing for various local papers before becoming a freelance reporter for the *Philadelphia Inquirer*. It was while covering local high schools that Anderson grew interested in writing about issues and problems related to teenagers.

Anderson developed an interest in fiction writing in the early 1990s, after her children began elementary school. "The day my youngest got on the bus for first grade," she recalled to Florence, "I took a solemn oath that I would try to get a children's book published in five years." By then, Anderson had started checking out "grocery sacks" of library books to read to her children, which she used "as textbooks for studying the craft of writing," according to Newman. Anderson's early experiences as a fiction writer were humbling. She received hundreds of rejection letters before having her first book published. It was during this time that she joined the Society of Children's Book Writers & Illustrators (SCBWI), which helped her further hone her writing craft.

Anderson found success in 1996, when her first children's book, *Ndito Runs*, was published. Featuring illustrations by Anita Van Der Merwe and drawing inspiration from a National Public Radio (NPR) piece about Kenyan marathon runners, the book tells the story of a young Kenyan girl who runs miles to and from school each day. Newman wrote that the book—which was later translated into several African languages—combined Anderson's "journalistic talent for research with her innate sense of fiction." Later in 1996, Anderson published *Turkey Pox*, a picture book about a girl named Charity who breaks out with chicken pox on Thanksgiving Day. Charity also served as the protagonist of her next picture book, *No Time for Mother's Day*, which was published in 1998. That year, Anderson stopped freelancing in order to focus on writing books.

SPEAK AND BREAKOUT SUCCESS

Anderson's debut young-adult novel, *Speak*, was published in 1999. The novel is set in Syracuse and is told from the perspective of a fourteen-year-old girl, Melinda Sordino, who becomes mute after being raped by an older boy at a party the summer before her freshman year at the fictional Mayweather High School. The story follows Melinda as she struggles to cope with and recover from this experience. Upon its publication, *Speak* received unanimous praise from critics, many of whom praised Anderson for her poignant handling of a difficult subject. A reviewer for *Publishers Weekly* (25 Oct. 1999) commented that "the book's overall gritty realism and Melinda's hard-won metamorphosis will leave readers touched and inspired."

Speak became a *New York Times* bestseller and received numerous awards and honors. It was a finalist for the 1999 National Book Award for young people's literature and the 2000 Edgar Allan Poe Award for best young-adult novel and was recognized as a 2000 Michael L. Printz Honor Book. It also won the 2000 Golden Kite Award for fiction and the 2000 American Library Association (ALA) Award for best fiction for young adults. *Speak* became part of the standard English curriculum at many schools around the United States and was adapted into a made-for-television movie in 2004. The movie stars Kristen Stewart, who would later become famous for her starring role in the *Twilight* films, as Melinda.

Since its release, *Speak* has been the subject of controversy and many attempts at censorship for its depiction of Melinda's rape, and it was included in the ALA's list of the hundred books most frequently banned or challenged between 2000 and 2009. Anderson, who came up with the idea for the book after having a nightmare about a girl screaming, has spoken out against such censorship. "*Speak* is not about rape," she explained to Peta Jinnath Andersen for the online magazine *PopMatters* (1 Oct. 2010). "*Speak* is about the struggle to find the courage to speak up when something terrible has happened."

FEVER 1793 AND CATALYST

Anderson's first work of historical fiction for young adults, *Fever 1793*, was published in 2000. The book, which Anderson began researching and writing in 1993, centers on fourteen-year-old Mattie Cook, who is forced to put her dreams on hold when the infamous yellow fever epidemic of 1793 wreaks havoc on her hometown of Philadelphia. Like *Speak*, *Fever 1793* was released to much critical acclaim and received a number of national and state awards. It was also added to the English curriculums of schools nationwide. A stage play adapted from the book debuted at the Gifford Family Theater in Syracuse in 2004.

In 2002, Anderson published her first historical-fiction picture book, *Thank You, Sarah! The Woman Who Saved Thanksgiving*, for which she drew inspiration from the American writer and editor Sarah Hale, who famously lobbied President Abraham Lincoln to make Thanksgiving a national holiday. That year also saw the publication of Anderson's second young-adult novel, *Catalyst* (2002), about high school senior Kate Malone, whose life revolves around getting accepted into the Massachusetts Institute of Technology (MIT). Like *Speak*, *Catalyst* is set at Mayweather High, but the two novels are otherwise quite different. Anderson told Florence, "I wanted to write about a kid who looks like she has it all together, as opposed to [Melinda] . . . who is obviously falling apart." *Catalyst* won the ALA Award for best book for young adults in 2003.

OTHER YOUNG-ADULT NOVELS

Anderson made use of a lighter approach for her third young-adult novel, *Prom* (2005), which tells the story of Ashley Hannigan, a high school senior from a low-income family who reluctantly agrees to help plan and organize her prom. The novel made the *New York Times* bestseller list and was nominated for the ALA Award in 2006. *Prom* was followed by the weightier novels *Twisted* and *Wintergirls*, published in 2007 and 2009, respectively. *Twisted* is told from the perspective of a male protagonist who is transitioning into manhood. *Wintergirls* focuses on an eighteen-year-old girl who is struggling with anorexia. Both *Twisted* and *Wintergirls* appeared on the *New York Times* bestseller list and won ALA Awards, among many others.

Anderson's sixth young-adult novel, *The Impossible Knife of Memory*, was published in 2014. It follows the story of a seventeen-year-old girl named Hayley Kincaid, a teenager trying to adjust to traditional high school after years of homeschooling by her father, Andy, an Iraq War veteran who suffers from alcoholism and post-traumatic stress disorder (PTSD). For the novel, Anderson drew on personal experiences with her own father, a veteran of World War II who suffered from PTSD. In a review (21 Oct. 2013), *Publishers Weekly* called the novel "a tough, absorbing story of the effects of combat on soldiers and the people who love them."

SEEDS OF AMERICA AND VET VOLUNTEERS SERIES

Throughout her career, Anderson has continued to write historical fiction. In 2008, she published the novel *Chains*, which centers on a thirteen-year-old runaway slave during the American Revolutionary War. The novel received wide acclaim and became the first of three books in the Seeds of America series. *Chains* was a finalist for the 2008 National Book Award and won the 2009 Scott O'Dell Award for historical fiction. The second installment of the trilogy, *Forge*, about a fifteen-year-old escaped slave who fights with the Continental Army at Valley Forge during the winter of 1777–78, was published in 2011. The final installment in the series is titled *Ashes* (2014).

In addition to her young-adult and historical-fiction novels, Anderson produced a children's series called the Vet Volunteers, which chronicles the adventures of a group of children who volunteer at a veterinary clinic. Books in the series include *Fight for Life* (2007), *Homeless* (2007), *Trickster* (2008), *Manatee Blues* (2008), *Say Good-Bye* (2008), *Storm Rescue* (2008), *Teacher's Pet* (2009), *Trapped* (2009), *Fear of Falling* (2009), *Time to Fly* (2009), *Masks* (2012), and *End of the Race* (2012).

OTHER WORK AND HONORS

Anderson's other books include *Independent Dames* (2008), a picture book about women who contributed to the American Revolution, and *The Hair of Zoe Fleefenbacher Goes to School* (2009), a children's book about a first-grade girl with a riotous mane of hair. In recognition of her contributions to young-adult literature, Anderson was awarded the Assembly on Literature for Adolescents (ALAN) Award in 2008. She received a Margaret A. Edwards Award in 2009 for her novels *Speak*, *Fever 1793*, and *Catalyst*. The latter award, presented by the Young Adult Library Services Association (YALSA), "recognizes an iconic and classic storyteller who in her character development has created for teens a body of work that continues to be widely read and cherished by a diverse audience." "If there's anything that you can take away from my body of work," Anderson told *PopMatters*, "it's that I think people should talk about things. I don't think anything gets better by avoiding talking about it. And I would like to think that we can all be civilized and find a way to talk about things that we disagree about."

PERSONAL LIFE

Anderson lives in the village of Mexico, in northern New York, with her second husband, Scot Larrabee, who is a carpenter. In addition to her two daughters, Anderson's family includes her husband's two children from a previous relationship, Jessica and Christian. Anderson does all of her writing in a woodland cottage near her home that was specially designed and built by her husband. She is a frequent user of Twitter and maintains a blog on her website. In her spare time, Anderson enjoys running, hiking, gardening, and spending time with her family.

SUGGESTED READING

Andersen, Peta Jinnath. "Speak Loudly: A Conversation with Laurie Halse Anderson on Topics Subject to Book Banning." *PopMatters*. PopMatters Media, 1 Oct. 2010. Web. 12 Nov. 2013.

Deutsch, Lindsay. "Laurie Halse Anderson Tackles Alcoholism, PTSD in Book." *USA Today*. Gannett, 12 Aug. 2013. Web. 12 Nov. 2013.

Fitzgerald, Carol, and Marisa Emralino. "Author Profile: Laurie Halse Anderson." *Teenreads*. Book Report, Aug. 2005. Web. 12 Nov. 2013.

Hadaway, Nancy L., and Terrell A. Young. "Good Storytelling Brings History Alive: An Interview with Laurie Halse Anderson." *Reading Today* Oct./Nov. 2012: 16–17. Print.

Jagadesan, Suhana. "Laurie Halse Anderson Takes Unflinching Look at Tough Topics." *Reading Eagle* [PA]. Reading Eagle, 18 Oct. 2011. Web. 12 Nov. 2013.

SELECTED WORKS

Ndito Runs, 1996; *Speak*, 1999; *Fever 1793*, 2000; *Catalyst*, 2002; *Prom*, 2005; *Twisted*, 2007; *Chains*, 2008; *Wintergirls*, 2009; *Forge*, 2011; *The Impossible Knife of Memory*, 2014

—Chris Cullen

Elena Arzak

Born: July 4, 1969
Occupation: Culinary alchemist

Elena Arzak is a Spanish chef and culinary alchemist who was named the world's best female chef in 2012. Her restaurant, Arzak, in the city of San Sebastián, located in the northern Basque region of Spain, is a family business that boasts three coveted Michelin stars. Her father, Juan Mari Arzak, a legend of contemporary Basque cuisine, put the restaurant on the culinary map in the 1970s, but the Arzak tradition reaches back much further. The restaurant itself has been in the family for over 116 years. Still, it was out of her father's shadow that Elena Arzak emerged, becoming a pioneer of an even newer

Juan Herrero/EPA/Landov

and more innovative new Basque cuisine that combines the traditional flavors of the region with modernist cooking techniques.

Arzak, who knew she wanted to be a chef at her family's restaurant since she was a child, works side by side with her father. Prior to this partnership, Arzak trained abroad for six years. When she returned, she spent another four years working through each station in the Arzak kitchen, honing her craft and re-learning her roots. She found the local bounty in San Sebastián— hot and sweet peppers, fresh fish, and cheese— just as inspiring as the complicated cooking techniques she had learned abroad. "After four years," she told Allan Jenkins for the *Guardian* (18 Aug. 2012), "I had found my voice."

In 2014, the restaurant Arzak was ranked eighth on the list of the World's 50 Best Restaurants. Arzak is one of only two female chefs on that year's list and the only woman in the top ten. Other awards include the Chef de l'avenir, Cofradía de la Alubia de Tolosa in 2002, Swedish Seafood Award, and La Gran Noticia Del Año Gastronomika.

THE FIRST ARZAK AND NEW BASQUE CUISINE

Arzak's great-grandparents opened their restaurant in 1897 as a tavern where the residents of San Sebastián could gather, and over one hundred years later, the restaurant is still a place to congregate and celebrate. Howie Kahn, who was in San Sebastián to write about Arzak for the *Wall Street Journal* (28 June 2013), reported that his cab driver's parents were married at the restaurant. It's appropriate that patrons feel at home at the restaurant; the structure itself is actually an old house. (For many years it was solely supported by an enormous tree that now informs that whimsical shape of its upstairs wine storage room.) The restaurant was passed down to Elena's grandparents, and her father, Juan Mari, was born there in a room directly above the kitchen. After the death of her husband, Juan Mari's mother, Paquita, became the sole proprietor. Juan Mari was nine, and as he recalled to Jenkins, "the restaurant was different then." He explained, "Our bedroom opened on to the dining room, there was my mother, my grandmother among five cooks, not the thirty now, serving traditional food." As an adult, he took over as head chef.

In the 1970s, Juan Mari Arzak and another several other local chefs led a gastronomic revolution, which was, as Tejal Rao explained for *T*, the *New York Times* style magazine (29 Apr. 2014), "inspired by the lighter beauty of 1970s [French] nouvelle cuisine." New Basque cuisine is an art form, and with San Sebastián's small-bite tradition (and local ingredients, such as olive oil, parsley, and fish) in mind, Juan Mari became a leader and founding father of an elevated and slightly avant-garde culinary renaissance in Spain. New Basque cuisine, or *nueva cocina vasca*, was described by Patricia Wells for the *New York Times* (24 July 1994) as "the lighter, fresher, more seasonal modern cooking that nonetheless maintains the traditions of Basque cuisine."

New Basque cooking made San Sebastián a world-renowned food destination, and that legacy continues. Today, the city is Spain's gastronomic capital, second only to metropolitan Barcelona.

A CHEF IN TRAINING

Elena Arzak was born on July 4, 1969, in San Sebastián. She knew that she wanted to be a chef from a very early age. Her father recalls taking her, at five years old, to one of the best restaurant in San Sebastián. "She asked for her meat 'less well-done but warm,'" he told Jenkins. "I was embarrassed. Even as a child, she was always showing others what to do." She was a zealous pupil and loved watching her family work in the kitchen. In one of her earliest memories, she told Kahn, she was looking up at an enormous stockpot on the stove, watching her family boil crabs. The experience "was like a fantasy," she told him, remembering the bustle of the kitchen and the intense smell of the stock. (Arzak's sensory memory is strong. She remembers smelling her first truffle when she was eight.)

For Arzak, cooking is a family affair, though her sister chose another path. Marta Arzak, who is one year older, is now the director of education for the Guggenheim Museum in Bilbao, Spain. "My parents were happy with any choice we made," Arzak told the Indian chef Geeta Bansal for California's *OC Weekly* (18 Feb. 2013), but added, "Of course it made them happy when I chose gastronomy." By the time she was eleven, Arzak was allowed to spend only two hours a day in the kitchen during school holidays; without the restriction, she would have never left.

FERRAN ADRIÀ AS MENTOR

After completing school at eighteen, Arzak formulated her own chef's education. She learned to speak French, German, and English in addition to Spanish and her regional Basque. She attended the Schweizerische Hotelfachschule, a hotel management school in Luzern, Switzerland, and for the next six years, she trained at various restaurants throughout Europe. In 1989, she spent six months at chef Albert Roux's Le Gavroche, a Michelin-starred French restaurant in London (now run by Albert's son Michel Roux) and from there went on to train with such culinary greats as Michel Troisgros at Maison Troisgros in Roanne, France; Pierre Gagnaire in Paris; Alain Ducasse at Le Louis XV in Monte Carlo; and Claude Peyrot at Le Vivarois in Paris. But perhaps her most formative work experience outside of her family's restaurant was at the modernist restaurant elBulli, working under renowned chef Ferran Adrià, in 1994.

Adrià's restaurant, elBulli, which he closed in 2011, was located in Roses, Spain, a tiny resort town less than two hours north of Barcelona. The year that Arzak trained there, Adrià was just beginning to include a savory white bean foam, or light mousse, with sea urchin in his recipes. The foam was a revelation in 1994, though today it is one of the most imitated tropes in molecular gastronomy (the term given to high-tech cooking techniques, though Adrià prefers the term *avant-garde cuisine*). Adrià was also experimenting with deconstruction, which refers to taking apart a dish or a drink and reassembling it in a profoundly different and nontraditional way. His deconstructed martini, which was described by food writer Jay McInerney for *Vanity Fair* (1 Oct. 2010), requires diners first to eat a gelatinous olive-colored sphere, which explodes "in the mouth to unleash a bath of intense olive-flavored liquid." Following that, a gin and vermouth mixture is sprayed from a silver atomizer directly onto the tongue. Arzak was inspired by Adrià's vision and his enthusiasm for experiments. At elBulli she was able to exercise "what Adrià calls her *fuerza mental*," Rao reported, and "a kind of unrelenting brainy stamina."

A FATHER AND DAUGHTER PARTNERSHIP

Arzak was a changed woman when she returned home after six years abroad, but she spent another four years honing her craft. "I had a cocktail of ideas, but I had to find my identity at Arzak, otherwise I wouldn't be useful," she told Jenkins. "I worked in each station of the kitchen to relearn what happens in my house. I also studied many books of Basque cooking to learn more about my roots." Still, creative synergy between father and daughter took time. It began when Elena created her first plate for her father when she was nineteen, a salad of vegetables and tuna. He liked the salad, she recalled, but not the dressing. Years later, their negotiations took on a new intensity. "My father risked very much with the ideas he started to make with me," Arzak told Jenkins. But Juan Mari's trust in his daughter outweighed his reservations. "I think my father thought, 'If I don't allow Elena to make her new things she will get bored and leave,' but he also knew that if I introduced a tandoor, ginger, a mole from Mexico, it would work with the tastes of my region."

Over eighteen years later, their partnership proceeds in a similar give-and-take fashion in two workshops located above the restaurant. One room is a small test kitchen; the other is something called a flavor library—a place, Rao wrote, that "seems straight out of a Roald Dahl story." The library's walls are lines with nearly two thousand small plastic boxes that contain exotic ingredients such as Vietnamese green rice and dried seaweed and are archived by color, texture, flavor, and aroma.

Creative juices flow fast and furious at Arzak. Along with deputy chefs Igor Zalakain and Xabier Gutiérrez, the Arzaks create some fifty new dishes each year. Still, both father and daughter must approve a dish before it becomes a part of the Arzak menu. (According to Jenkins, Elena holds a bit of a grudge against her father for a sea urchin gratiné he rejected some fifteen years ago.) The dishes that do make the cut are supremely imaginative. A fish course with sole, for example, is served on a glass plate on top of a digital screen that loops images of waves crashing against the San Sebastián shore. Arzak's well-known crispy cromlechs are stuffed with onion, green tea, and creamy foie gras. A tasting menu might include gooseberry and potato chip skewers served with coconut steam (created with the aid of dry ice), fresh sardines with strawberries, and a dessert of yellow pistachio and beetroot stone. Arzak has maintained its three Michelin stars, awarded by the prestigious Michelin restaurant guide, since 1989.

THE PINTXOS OF SAN SEBASTIÁN

San Sebastián, sometimes called by its Basque name, Donostia, is a small city—about 180,000 citizens—on the coast of the Bay of Biscay, with a long gastronomic history. Residents and tourists delight in roaming from bar to bar, eating one or two pintxos at each establishment. Pintxos are a Basque version of Spanish tapas (snacks) and are bite-sized morsels that are often served on a skewer and are meant to be eaten without using utensils. Some bars serve traditional pintxos of tortillas made from potatoes and onions, while others serve pintxos that are seafood-based— the classic being Gilda, a skewer of guindilla peppers, olives, and salted anchovies—or are simply a slice of slightly salty, Spanish Manchego cheese, ham, or a few marinated wild mushrooms. Arzak, as with many San Sebastián bars and restaurants, has begun experimenting with innovative combinations in its pintxos selections. Combining marinated fish with fresh strawberries or deep-frying traditional Spanish codfish mousse within a shell of vermicelli are approaches that meld the offerings of the Basque region with a new approach to cuisine. Arzak is rooted and intertwined in the region and in the city's love of food and eating.

AMETSA WITH ARZAK INSTRUCTION

The Arzaks have also served as consultants for a restaurant called Ametsa with Arzak Instruction in London's Halkin hotel. (Arzak Instruction is the name of their consultancy, and *ametsa* is Basque for "dream.") It is their first culinary venture outside of the main Arzak restaurant, and it opened in March 2013. They chose London, Arzak has said, because they view it as similar in character to San Sebastián: both cities maintain tradition while embracing modernity.

Early reviews of Ametsa were mixed, and going forward it will be a challenge for the Arzaks to adapt their Spanish vision to an English patronage. "We don't understand when people say, 'I have just one hour for lunch,'" deputy chef Zalakain told Kahn in reference to Londoners. "But that's what they have, one hour for lunch, so we're changing the menu to make the experience shorter." Even critics recognize the skill of the Arzaks present in Ametsa. "Ametsa is already a worthy restaurant," Edward Schneider wrote in his largely positive *New York Times* (9 July 2013) review of the newly opened establishment. "It has the potential to be a terrific one."

PERSONAL LIFE

Arzak is married to Manu Lamosa, an architect. Lamosa designed the wine cellar and kitchen at Arzak. They have two children, a daughter named Nora and a son named Mateo. Like her own parents, Arzak wants her children to pursue whatever career they choose. But, she told Bansal, "If one of them decides to be a chef I will be very happy."

SUGGESTED READING

Jenkins, Allan. "Elena Arzak: The Best Female Chef on the Planet." *Guardian*. Guardian News and Media, 18 Aug. 2012. Web. 11 June 2014.

Kahn, Howie. "Chef Juan Mari Arzak's Heirlooms." *Wall Street Journal*. Dow Jones, 28 June 2013. Web. 11 June 2014.

McInerney, Jay. "It Was Delicious While It Lasted." *Vanity Fair*. Condé Nast Digital, 1 Oct. 2010. Web. 11 June 2014.

Rao, Tejal. "Food Matters: The New New Basque Cuisine." *T*. New York Times, 29 Apr. 2014. Web. 11 June 2014.

Vines, Richard. "Top Woman Chef Arzak Says It Won't Be Man's World Forever." *Bloomberg*. Bloomberg, 19 Sept. 2013. Web. 11 June 2014.

Wells, Patricia. "Choice Tables: The Nueva Basque Cuisine of San Sebastian." *New York Times*. New York Times, 24 July 1994. Web. 11 June 2014.

—*Molly Hagan*

Courtesy of Malin Fezehai

Reza Aslan

Born: 1972
Occupation: Writer and scholar

Acclaimed nonfiction writer Reza Aslan is an Iranian American religious scholar and associate professor of creative writing at the University of California, Riverside. Born in Iran, he left with his family during the 1979 revolution, when the shah was deposed and a theocracy instituted. Aslan is known for his books that explain religious ideas and conflict in a readable way. Writing is a calling that Aslan decided to follow when he was in high school. As he told Amy Crawford for the *Smithsonian* (Fall 2007), "You can't win a battle against an idea with guns and bombs, you have to win it with words. Words become the greatest tools." Aslan's writing has appeared in a number of newspapers and magazines. His nonfiction books *No god but God* (2005), *How to Win a Cosmic War* (2009), and particularly *Zealot: The Life and Times of Jesus of Nazareth* (2013) have garnered widespread attention.

Aslan is also a member of the Council on Foreign Relations, the Pacific Council on International Policy, and the Los Angeles Institute for the Humanities. In 2013 his alma mater, Harvard Divinity School, recognized him among the inaugural recipients of the Peter J. Gomes Memorial Honors for outstanding contributions to his field.

EARLY LIFE

Aslan was born in Tehran, the capital of Iran, into an upper-middle-class, intellectual family. His parents, Hassan and Soheyla, met as college students but could not pursue a relationship because Hassan had been betrothed by his parents to someone else since childhood. When Hassan returned home to marry, he discovered his fiancé had eloped with someone else, so he was also free to marry. Thus, even before Aslan was born, his family was not bound by tradition.

The family—Aslan, his parents, and his younger sister—was among the last to leave Iran for the United States before the airports closed in the chaos that followed the deposing of the shah. Aslan's father was an atheist who regarded Islam as inherently violent. At the time the Aslans left Iran, they considered the departure temporary, taking only a suitcase each. Aslan was only seven and was formed by his arrival in a country where feminism had a greater footing than it did in Iran, where women were meant to be subservient. The family first lived in Oklahoma before moving to California. His mother took a job in a software company and was soon earning more than his father; eventually, however, Aslan's father formed his own successful business.

Because of the anti-Iran prejudice following the hostage crisis, in which Iranian revolutionaries held fifty-two United States citizens from the embassy for 444 days between 1979 and 1981, Aslan faced persecution as a child. Living in an immigrant community in northern California, he learned Spanish and pretended to be Mexican to avoid being bullied. As he explained to Terry Gross on National Public Radio's *Fresh Air* (15 July 2013), "I spent a lot of time just kind of backing away from my culture, my ethnicity, and certainly my religion. And really in my household, particularly from my father, there was an enormous amount of resentment against the ayatollahs, who had, in his view, taken over the country and destroyed it and forced him to flee his home."

CONVERSIONS

At fifteen Aslan attended a summer camp run by the evangelical Christian youth group Young Life, where he first encountered the evangelical Christian faith. Wanting to be thoroughly American, Aslan converted, attended a Christian church, and even began to proselytize to his family. Eventually both his sister and his mother converted as well, though his sister did not remain in the Christian faith.

During his freshman year of college at Santa Clara University, a Jesuit school, Aslan began to study the New Testament and early Christianity more seriously. His doubts grew, based on the disconnect he saw between the Jesus of the Gospels and what he heard of Jesus the Christ in church. Ironically, it was a priest at Santa Clara who suggested he reexamine Islam in his search for a viable faith. Eventually Aslan did embrace Islam, finding the Sufi tradition most compatible with his own worldview. He told Manuel Roig-Franzia for the *Washington Post* (8 Aug. 2013), "It's not [that] I think Islam is correct and Christianity is incorrect. It's that all religions are nothing more than a language made up of symbols and metaphors to help an individual explain faith." The metaphors of Islam made sense to him, particularly because of the focus on God as unity.

After completing his bachelor's degree in religion, Aslan earned a master's degree in theological studies from Harvard in 1999 and then a doctorate from the University of California, Santa Barbara. Aslan has been criticized for claiming his degree was in sociology of religions or history of religions. The university does not offer these degrees; his doctorate is officially in sociology.

FROM NOVEL TO NONFICTION

The following year Aslan was accepted into the famed Iowa Writers' Workshop, where he completed a master of fine arts degree and was named the Truman Capote Fellow in fiction. Concurrently, he was visiting assistant professor of Islamic and Middle Eastern studies at the University of Iowa. While there, he acquired a literary agent. Although he had completed a novel, the agent asked if he had other projects planned. When he mentioned that he was considering a book on Islam, she suggested they move ahead with that project first. It was only two years after the attack on the World Trade Center and the Pentagon, and interest in Islam was high.

Aslan told Amy Crawford for the *Smithsonian*, "It became very clear to me not only that there was this great need for someone who could provide a bridge between the West and the Islamic world, who understood both and could communicate one to the other, but also that I didn't have a choice in the matter." One of the points that Aslan emphasizes is that true Islam is a religion of peace, of pluralism, and of tolerance.

NO GOD BUT GOD

The impetus for Aslan's first book on Islam, *No god but God*, published in 2005, was to give some perspective on the background of the faith. By the time the book was updated in 2011, he recognized that interpersonal relationships—not facts and data—were the only thing that would change people's perceptions. He likens the current period in Islam to the Protestant Reformation, when differing opinions in Christianity about what constituted both right belief and right practice were being debated.

The work has been translated into thirteen languages and been named among the one hundred most important books of the decade. It was shortlisted for the Guardian First Book Award in the United Kingdom and nominated for a PEN USA award in research nonfiction. But one of the greatest accolades that Aslan received came from his father, who read the book three times, despite his antipathy toward religion. Aslan told Crawford that his father ultimately said, "'I think

I really get it, I think I get what you're saying. It makes a lot of sense.' That was a wonderful moment for me."

No god but God became so successful that Random House, Aslan's publisher, requested a second nonfiction work. That book was *How to Win a Cosmic War: God, Globalization, and the End of the War on Terror*, which came out in 2009 and was reprinted in paperback as *Beyond Fundamentalism: Confronting Religious Extremism in the Age of Globalization* the following year. Aslan's premise is that cosmic wars cannot be won, that the way to win a religious war, which he contends is currently being fought, is to refuse to fight.

Aslan is alarmed by the increased anti-Muslim sentiment he perceives ten years after the attack on September 11, 2001. As he wrote in the preface to the 2011 edition of his first book, "Simply put, Islam in the United States has become *otherized*. . . . Across Europe and North America, whatever is fearful, whatever is foreign, whatever is alien and unsafe is being tagged with the label 'Islam.'" He considers this tendency only to be expected, noting that Muslims are merely the latest to hear the sort of rhetoric that Catholic and Jewish immigrants heard during the early twentieth century.

TABLET & PEN
The online publisher Words Without Borders persuaded Aslan to put together a collection of literature of the Muslim world. Aslan refined the idea, expanding to the Middle East and limiting the literature to the twentieth century. The work is arranged chronologically, covering 1910 to 2010. Works were translated into English from Urdu, Turkish, Persian, and Arabic.

Aslan contacted colleagues with expertise in literature for recommendations, and spent about nine months simply reading. He included geographical regions beyond the bounds of what most westerners consider the Middle East, a term Europeans first coined. Aslan wanted to depict the commonalities of places such as Turkey and South Asia with the geographical area known as the Middle East. The nations shared the experience of colonialism and imperialism.

Part of the impetus for such a work is the perception Aslan senses that Islam is becoming "other" in the United States. With the economy performing not as well as hoped, some people are seeking a scapegoat and find it in the idea that the United States is becoming "Islamized." As Aslan told people gathered at a bookstore to promote his book, reported by Kianoush Naficy for the *Washington Report on Middle East Affairs* (Mar. 2011), Islam is "becoming a receptacle into which Americans are throwing all of their fears and anxieties, whether about the economy, or political instability, or the changing racial landscape in this country."

Aslan is hopeful that the book, published in 2011, will build greater understanding of the Middle East and perhaps lead to better relationships as a result. As he explained to Scott Esposito for *Publishers Weekly* (11 Oct. 2010), "Cultural bridges are built through literature and the arts. Those are universal. Israelis and Palestinians who cannot stand each other still read each other's books, watch each other's movies. It is only through the arts that we will ever understand one another."

ZEALOT: THE LIFE AND TIMES OF JESUS OF NAZARETH
With Random House still reluctant to publish his fiction, but eager for more nonfiction books in religion, Aslan inked a deal that required the publishing company to bring out his novel after one further nonfiction work. That book was *Zealot: The Life and Times of Jesus of Nazareth*, published in 2013; it offers a history of Jesus without relying exclusively on the New Testament sources. The work provides a detailed look at the social background of the era and the unrest in the Roman Empire, especially in Judea, that was part of the fabric of Jesus's life.

Some have criticized Aslan, wondering if a Muslim could write accurately about the Christ of Christianity, although, as numerous sources have pointed out, these same critics have no problem with a Christian writing about Islam. Lauren Green, a religion writer for Fox News, interviewed Aslan on July 26, 2013, after the book debuted. That conversation, ten minutes of questioning Aslan's bona fides rather than discussing the book, went viral with more than five million hits. Some consider it a case of religious persecution because Green was among those who had difficulty accepting the idea that a Muslim would write a book on the man whose life became the foundation of Christianity. The popular website Buzzfeed asked whether it was the most embarrassing interview Fox had ever done. Response to the interview led to Random House, Aslan's publisher, printing an additional 180,000 copies of the book. Debuting at number thirty on the *USA Today* best-seller list, the book moved up to number twenty-seven the week after the interview. It moved from number four to number one on the *Times* best-seller list.

Explaining his interest in religion, whether Christianity or Islam, Aslan told Terry Gross, "I think that if you believe that our experience of the world goes beyond just the material realm, that there is something beyond, that there is a transcendent presence that one can commune with, then it's only natural to want to reach out to this transcendent presence, to want to experience it in some way. That's what religion does."

MEDIA VENTURES

Aslan founded BoomGen Studios as a consulting firm, working with scripts, publicity, and marketing. As Aslan told Ed Leibowitz for the *Los Angeles Magazine* (Dec. 2010), "Movies have the power to not just change people's minds but to change the narrative with which people understand the world and their place in it." For this project, Aslan deliberately seeks funding only from Muslims, noting that many young Muslims in the tech world have a great deal of money.

Aslan also created AslanMedia Initiatives, a nonprofit organization, to provide Internet content for Muslims in the United States. The website is "working to break the mainstream chokehold on the public discourse about the Middle East," as its home page proclaims. Aslan-Media works through social media outlets such as Facebook, Tumblr, and Twitter. On the website GoodReads, AslanMedia hosts a book club. It also hosts a weekly podcast, Intersection. The site is particularly interested in giving young people another perspective, seeking to compress news of the Middle East into 140-character Twitter feeds. The team of volunteers writing for and monitoring the site is international. Editors focus on their areas of interest, such as fashion, arts and culture, music, and film.

The Writer's Room with Reza Aslan debuted in June 2014 at DBA, a West Hollywood nightclub. The series features Aslan interviewing writers, with musical groups performing before the interviews begin. According to Saba Hamedy of the *Los Angeles Times* (5 June 2014), Aslan told the crowd at the premier interview with B. J. Novak, "If you're going to have literary series in LA with an LA feel, it's got to be lively, it's got to be fun, it's got to be a party."

PERSONAL LIFE

Aslan intended to be a novelist before September 11, 2001, and continues to be drawn to the form. He explained his frustration with the work he has done to Ed Leibowitz for *Los Angeles Magazine*, saying, "I could write a dozen books and do a hundred interviews on every media channel in the world, and I am not going to shape the way people think as effectively as I would if I could just focus on what I really want to do, which is storytelling."

His wife, Jessica Jackley, is a writer and entrepreneur who was a cofounder of Kiva Microfunds. On their first date, the couple determined that their values were the same, despite their religious differences. They have twin sons and live in Hollywood Hills.

SUGGESTED READING

Aslan, Reza. "Building Bridges: PW Talks with Reza Aslan." Interview by Scott Esposito. *Publishers Weekly* 11 Oct. 2010: 25. Print.
Aslan, Reza. "Christ in Context: 'Zealot' Explores the Life of Jesus." Interview by Terry Gross. *NPR*. NPR, 15 July 2013. Web. 11 Aug. 2014.
Aslan, Reza. "Faith Healer." Interview by Amy Crawford. *Smithsonian* Fall 2007: 76. Print.
Hamedy, Saba. "Reza Aslan Kicks off Writer's Room Series with B. J. Novak." *Los Angeles Times*. Los Angeles Times, 5 June 2014. Web. 6 Aug. 2014.
Leibowitz, Ed. "Think Again." *Los Angeles Magazine* Dec. 2010: 106. Print.
Naficy, Kianoush. "Reza Aslan Promotes Tablet and Pen." *Washington Report on Middle East Affairs* 30.2 (2011): 56–57. Print.
Roig-Franzia, Manuel. "Reza Aslan: A Jesus Scholar Who's Hard to Pin Down." *Washington Post*. Washington Post, 8 Aug. 2013. Web. 5 Aug. 2014.

SELECTED WORKS

No god but God, 2005; *How to Win a Cosmic War*, 2009; *Tablet and Pen*, 2011; *Zealot: The Life and Times of Jesus of Nazareth*, 2013

—Judy Johnson

Alex Atala

Born: 1968
Occupation: Chef and restaurateur

Alex Atala, a world-renowned Brazilian chef, has made it his mission to introduce his native cuisine to the world and advance it as a source of pride for his country. "We are so proud of our soccer, our models, our music, our graffiti artists. Why is no one excited about Brazilian food?" Atala, who owns the world-class São Paulo–based restaurant D.O.M., told Jenny Barchfield for the Associated Press Worldstream (16 Oct. 2013). "Brazilian food is so amazingly diverse, and we have to celebrate that."

Atala is particularly interested in issues of sustainability and in preserving the use of indigenous ingredients found deep in the Amazonian wilderness—some even few Brazilians know of. Discussing his cookbook, *D.O.M.: Rediscovering Brazilian Ingredients*, he remarked to Barchfield, "It's funny that in Brazil, people know so much about different kinds of pasta and can tell you all the different properties of different sorts of flour . . . I'd say the average Brazilian has never tasted at least 50 percent of the ingredients in this book." Those ingredients are absolutely vital to his work, however. "The fare at D.O.M. could be seen as a culinary spin on a magical-realist novel about Brazil," Jeff Gordinier wrote for the *New York Times* (22 Oct. 2013), "and its connection to native ingredients runs so deep that conjuring

Paulo Whitaker/Reuters/Landov

up Mr. Atala's food without them would qualify as an empty gesture."

EARLY LIFE

The chef was born Milad Alexandre Mack Atala in 1968 in São Paulo. His father, also named Milad, was of Palestinian descent. His mother, Otavia, was the granddaughter of a British expatriate and explorer, Arthur Claude Brizzard Brink, whom family lore states was poisoned after challenging an alleged embezzler to a duel in the Amazon. Atala lived with his parents in the working-class neighborhood of São Bernardo do Campo, on the outskirts of São Paulo. His mother was a skilled seamstress, and the factory where his father worked produced compression stockings. At one point in their careers, Atala's parents joined forces to make dressings for neighboring burn victims.

The family loved to explore remote areas of the countryside, although Atala sometimes wondered why they could not simply visit the beach like other people seemed to do in their spare time. From Otavia's father, who was of British and Irish descent, he learned to hunt, and his father taught him to fish. Atala was exposed to the elder Milad's Palestinian heritage when they would visit an old family friend who had opened a Middle Eastern restaurant and were plied with Arab sweets and such entrees as rooster testicles and raw kibbe (a ground-meat dish).

A TURNING POINT

As a teen, Atala, in time-honored tradition, began to rebel, fashioning his hair into a tall, bright-red Mohawk and piercing not only his ears but also his neck and cheeks. A fan of punk rock, he became a DJ at a popular São Paulo punk club, and he fought as an amateur welterweight boxer on the side. Perhaps unsurprisingly, given his milieu, he began using drugs. "Problems, drugs,

fights," Atala admitted to Howie Kahn for the *Wall Street Journal* (14 Feb. 2013). "I looked like a real junkie—stick thin, punk rock style. We didn't have so much heroin in São Paulo. Cocaine, though, a lot. And it was the time when ecstasy first came out, which was strong."

In 1989 Atala decided to embark on an extended trip to Europe to backpack and check out the music scene. He earned money as he traveled around the continent by painting houses. Enjoying himself and wanting to stay, he searched for a way around the visa requirement. Becoming a student provided a solution. Although he had no real interest in cooking, when a friend recommended that he enter the École Hôtelière Provinciale de Namur (Provincial Hotel School of Namur) in Belgium, he agreed.

STARTING A CULINARY CAREER

Atala discovered that he had an aptitude in the kitchen, thanks in some part to his skills in hunting and fishing. He was already comfortable, he reasoned, with cleaning fish and butchering fowl. After graduation, however, when he approached the famed Parisian chef Joël Robuchon for a job, he was turned away; according to Atala, Robuchon simply found the idea of a Brazilian trained in Belgium (rather than at one of the more prestigious schools in France) not up to his exacting expectations. He had better luck with Bernard Loiseau, a traditional French chef trying to stem the tide of fusion cuisine and other such trends in the 1990s. Although Loiseau had published numerous cookbooks, formulated a line of frozen foods, ran several restaurants, and been decorated as chevalier (knight) of the French Legion of Honor, he is unfortunately now most remembered for committing suicide after a journalist reported that he was about to lose a Michelin star. (*The Michelin Guide*, the longest published and most respected European hotel and restaurant reference book, awards a system of stars to establishments its judges have visited. One star means "a very good restaurant in its category," while two indicates "excellent cuisine" that is "worth a detour" to experience. The coveted three-star rating identifies a place with "exceptional cuisine . . . worth a special journey.")

In 1993 Atala moved to Milan, Italy, where he worked at Sancho Panza, an *osteria*, or tavern. He had decided to focus on smaller, less demanding restaurants so that he would still have ample time for his leisure pursuits. Despite the advantages of that type of job, Atala was not fully content. Harking back to the way Robuchon had made him feel like an outsider during his ill-fated job application, he felt similarly detached from his Italian colleagues. He considered quitting but changed his mind when he was given the title of sous chef. (A sous chef is second in command in a restaurant kitchen, working directly under the chef de cuisine or head chef.) The promotion reinvigorated his commitment to a culinary career—he had briefly considered opening a bar and music venue instead—and he remained for a year.

RETURNING HOME

Atala had never severed his ties to Brazil, and throughout his time in Europe, he returned there regularly to see family, go camping, and reconnect with friends. In 1994—by then a new father and wanting to raise his son in Brazil—he moved back on a permanent basis and took a job at a trendy São Paulo eatery called Sushi Pasta. From there he completed stints at Filomena and 72, both well-regarded Italian restaurants.

Observers unfamiliar with that era's restaurant scene in Brazil might be excused for wondering why Atala was focusing on Italian food. Seth Kugel explained in the *New York Times* (12 May 2009), "The abundant praise for São Paulo's dining scene has historically focused on its global range. Brazilian food, meanwhile, is what you eat at home or in rural roadside pit stops or at restaurants serving dirt-cheap, starch-heavy lunch specials known as 'pratos feitos' (literally, 'made plates')."

There were several reasons for this lack of home pride. As Barchfield elucidated, "The colonial legacy of this former Portuguese colony, which traditionally valued imported European foods . . . looked down on native ingredients. To this day, the most ubiquitous fish on Brazilian menus remains cod, which is caught off the icy waters of Scandinavia, salted and shipped to Brazil—a country with its 7,500 kilometers (4,660 miles) of coastline." Moreover, decades of high tariffs under dictatorship prevented Brazilians from obtaining coveted European imports, leading to a huge fad once the regime gave way and more liberal international trade policies were implemented. Barchfield further notes that "regulations on the interstate transport of cheese between Brazil's 26 states have stymied the development of what Atala called a 'world-class cheese' from the central Minas Gerais state." Atala quipped to her, "If Parmesan was born in Minas Gerais, it would be an unknown cheese today."

RESTAURANTS OF HIS OWN

In late 1998, Atala opened his first dining establishment, a casual restaurant called Namesa, selling his car to raise the needed funds. Seating sixteen patrons around a single, convivial table, he initially served such continental dishes as chicken milanese and duck.

He was, however, becoming increasingly fascinated by Amazonian culture and cuisine. (At Filomena, he had been able to experiment with *farofa*, or cassava flour, adding passion fruit pulp to the traditional Brazilian ingredient, and he

discovered that patrons enjoyed the fresh, tangy flavor as an accompaniment to meat dishes.) On frequent trips into the wilderness, he began engaging in close discussions with native inhabitants, quizzing them about their typical meals.

One fishing trip, undertaken the year he opened Namesa, took a particularly unsettling turn. Accompanied by a friend and a group of native guides on the Araguaia River in Mato Grosso, Atala was enjoying the spectacular scenery and catching the large freshwater fish swimming alongside the boat. At one point the friend, a documentary filmmaker, asked the guides if they would be willing to appear on tape. They agreed in exchange for a new outboard motor. This angered a group of guides from a rival tribe, and the two men were taken hostage and held at gunpoint. Atala was eventually allowed to leave to procure the second motor, while the filmmaker remained with his captors. So remote was the area that it took him several days and sleepless nights of navigating the winding, rocky river before he could return and negotiate the release of his friend.

D.O.M.

That hair-raising experience did little to quell Atala's interest in native Brazilian cooking, however, and when he opened his second, more ambitious restaurant, D.O.M., in 1999, he was determined to showcase his new knowledge. "I had worked in France and Italy and I perceived that I would never cook [those cuisines] as well as an Italian or a Frenchman," he told Joseph Leahy for the *Financial Times* (12 Apr. 2013). "But on the other hand, I realized that no one could cook Brazilian food better than me."

Atala hit upon the name for the restaurant after noticing the initials displayed on the doors of several churches. A cleric explained to him that they stood for *Deo Optimo Maximo*, Latin for "to God, most good, most great," and that Benedictine monks had marked their monastery doors in that way to indicate to travelers that here was a welcoming place to eat and drink.

Friends predicted failure for D.O.M., which Atala housed in a shuttered Japanese restaurant on a dismal dead-end side street that seemed to have quite a large share of homeless people. They were also unsure of Atala's mission—to create a high-end cuisine using obscure Brazilian ingredients.

In his review, Kugel warned of the prices on the menu, writing, "It is expensive in a way that puts it out of reach of most Brazilians. I may have been the first person in São Paulo history to receive a confirmation call from D.O.M. while riding squashed in a crowded public bus. (Sixty-five reais, the cost of the cheapest menu item during my visit, a risotto, gets you 28 bus rides.)" He went on to describe, however, the wonders that commanded those prices, among them a salad of "thin, cozily curved slices of abobrinha squash dotted with tiny flower petals; crayfish hiding out underneath, and an extended ellipsis of pastel-orange passion fruit dots serving as an underline" and "baby pork ribs and forbidden rice [a purple-black heirloom variety] with catupiry . . . a creamy cheese that is a sort of national spread."

D.O.M. quickly landed on lists of the best restaurants in the world. In 2013, in the World's 50 Best Restaurants, a respected annual list compiled by *Restaurant* magazine and voted upon by more than nine hundred industry experts from around the world, it landed at the number-six spot. (D.O.M. was also named the second-best restaurant in Latin America.) He has cooked for three Brazilian presidents and numerous celebrities. Lunch and dinner are now routinely booked months in advance, making a reservation nearly impossible to obtain for those who can afford one.

NEW VENTURES
Atala's restaurant Dalva e Dito, which opened in early 2009, serves simple and homey Brazilian dishes. "In essence, the prix-fixe executive lunch for 47 reais (about $22 at 2.2 reais to the dollar) is a prato feito of rice, beans and meat at about eight times the price and a hundred times the quality," Kugel asserted. The success of Dalva e Dito led Atala to set up a market next door in 2012 to sell to-go versions of the dishes served in the restaurant as well as bakery items, preserves, and cheeses.

Another establishment, this one a jazz bar called Riviera, opened in September 2013. A collaborative effort between Atala and entrepreneur Facundo Guerra, the new Riviera is a remake of a popular hangout that had enjoyed its heyday among leftists in the 1940s and become a favorite among moviegoers and intellectuals in the 1970s, but slowly declined until its closing in the mid-2000s. Atala intends to play off the city's nostalgia in the venue's food offerings, reviving old favorites.

SUSTAINABILITY
Atala, who travels deep into the Amazon region several times a year to conduct research, is deeply concerned with the ecosystem in Brazil and the sustainability of his ingredients. "Back [when I was young] I was always against something," he explained to Kahn. "Now I use that same energy to fight for something. My main idea is to show local people how important these ingredients can be for them." In 2012 he launched the nonprofit ATÁ Institute, a think tank that advocates for the production and consumption of sustainably harvested ingredients from throughout Brazil, promotes trade in the Amazon, and aims to improve the lives of its indigenous residents. (*Atá* means "fire" in the Tupí language.)

Particularly concerned about deforestation, he recently purchased almost sixty thousand acres of rainforest in order to protect it. He remains a staunch advocate of responsible hunting and has been known to kill a chicken during cooking demonstrations in order to stress to the audience the connection between living creatures and the food on their plates.

ACCLAIMED COOKBOOK
In 2013 Atala, who was included on *Time* magazine's list of the hundred most influential people that year, wrote the lavishly illustrated cookbook *D.O.M.: Rediscovering Brazilian Ingredients*. Its recipes feature such ingredients as *priprioca*, an aromatic herb that reportedly tastes like a combination of vanilla and oak and that had been used mainly in the perfume and cosmetics industry before Atala discovered a culinary use for it; coconut apple, a spongy growth that forms when the coconut is sprouting; and *jambu*, an herb that the book states "creates a short circuit of our taste buds," as quoted by Barchfield. Among the most buzzed-about pages in the volume is one that features a glowing photo of a *saúva* ant (said to taste naturally of cardamom, lemongrass, and ginger), perched atop a chunk of pineapple. The accompanying recipe states simply, "Place a piece of pineapple on top of a serving dish and top with an ant. Serve immediately," as quoted by Brickman. While most reviewers conceded the impossibility of obtaining saúva ants or priprioca in the United States, the book was widely hailed as one of the loveliest and most intriguing of the year.

PERSONAL LIFE
Atala and his first wife, Cristiana, have one son, Pedro. He and his second wife, Marcia, have twins, Joana and Tomas. He maintains a wide circle of friends, including fellow chefs David Chang and René Redzepi. That trio appeared on the cover of several international editions of the November 18, 2013, issue of *Time* magazine, whose editors dubbed them the Dudes of Food and praised their good-natured machismo and physical prowess. The theme of the issue as a whole was "The Gods of Food: Meet the People Who Influence What (and How) You Eat."

Journalists almost always make reference to Atala's many tattoos, which include skulls, tribal markings, and an equation in comic-strip format that he says encapsulates his life: the first half consists of an unhappy face with a punk hairstyle, a plus sign, and a boiling pot. The solution to the equation, following an equal sign, is a happy face sporting a chef's toque.

SUGGESTED READING
Barchfield, Jenny. "Brazilian Hopes to Introduce World to His Food." Associated Press

Worldstream. Associated Press, 16 Oct. 2013. Web. 12 Nov. 2013.

Brickman, Sophie. "The Best Chef in Brazil Visits Queens." *New Yorker*. Condé Nast, 17 Oct. 2013. Web. 12 Nov. 2013.

Gordinier, Jeff. "In Manhattan, Alex Atala Offers a Sense of São Paulo." *New York Times*. New York Times, 22 Oct. 2013. Web. 12 Nov. 2013.

Kahn, Howie. "The Year of Cooking Dangerously." *Wall Street Journal*. Dow Jones, 14 Feb. 2013. Web. 12 Nov. 2013.

Kugel, Seth. "In São Paulo, Brazilian Cuisine Is Back on the Table." *New York Times*. New York Times, 12 May 2009. Web. 12 Nov. 2013.

Leahy, Joseph. "Chef Talk: Alex Atala." *Financial Times*. Financial Times, 12 Apr. 2013. Web. 12 Nov. 2013.

—Mari Rich

WireImage

Avicii

Born: September 8, 1989
Occupation: DJ, record producer

By the end of 2013, Swedish DJ Tim Bergling, who goes by the moniker Avicii, had a number-one hit in sixty-three countries with his catchy pop-folk-electronic song "Wake Me Up." The song was everywhere. With its infectious folk-rock guitars and vocals and a pulsating electronic beat, the song appealed to fans of numerous genres, including rock, country, pop, and dance. That year *Forbes* magazine placed Avicii on its list of the world's highest-paid DJs, listing his income at $20 million. Avicii was touring nonstop, playing more than two hundred shows a year and earning a reported $250,000 per show. Prior to the success of "Wake Me Up," Avicii had been DJing at dance-music venues and various festivals for about five years, producing such hits as "Levels" and "I Could Be the One." *True*, his first full-length album—featuring "Wake Me Up" as its first single—was released in the second half of 2013. The album won praise for its unique approach to anthemic dance music and its use of folk and bluegrass. In recognition of his success as a DJ and recording artist, Avicii has been featured in numerous music blogs and various magazines, including *Rolling Stone* and *GQ*.

MAKING MUSIC IN HIS BEDROOM

Tim Bergling was born on September 8, 1989, in Stockholm, Sweden. He was uninterested in music until the end of his high school years, when he began making and remixing tracks on his laptop in his bedroom. He created electronic house music influenced by acts such as Daft Punk, Steve Angello, Laidback Luke, Tocadisco,

Axwell, and Swedish House Mafia. Avicii started posting his melodic, high-energy tracks on music blogs, particularly in the comments sections. It did not take long for him to be noticed. In a profile of Avicii for *GQ* (Apr. 2013), Jessica Pressler told of how Avicii's "ear for melody caught the attention of Ash Pournouri, an ambitious then twenty-six-year-old club promoter who could see the electronic-music boom coming and wanted in on it." The young promoter, wrote Pressler, requested a meeting: "Pournouri asked the eighteen-year-old to coffee, figuring at least he could use his connections to help him get some club gigs. But after Tim warily ambled up, all disheveled-Viking hipster, a grander vision began to take shape." Pournouri, according to Avicii, promised to make him the biggest DJ in the world in two years. Pournouri could see that Avicii was talented, but he had only been making music on his laptop and did not know how to DJ until Pournouri taught him how. Bergling chose the name Avici—"a friend told him it was a level of Buddhist Hell," Pressler explained—but because that name was taken on the social-networking site MySpace, he added the extra *i*.

STAR RISING

From the beginning, Avicii did not limit himself to any one subgenre of house or electronic dance music (EDM). His high-energy beats, engaging melodies, and use of catchy vocals led him to become a recognizable name and made him a rising star on the European EDM scene. His early tracks—"Sound of Now," "Manman," and "Ryu"—confirmed his potential, the latter making the Beatport Top 20 and staying in the Beatport Top 30 for more than four weeks. "Manman" was released on Pete Tong's Bedroom Bedlam label and won the Pete Tong Fast Trax prize, receiving an impressive 70 percent of the total vote. Soon after the song's release, Avicii was contacted by various promoters, labels, and bookers. He also created remixes for various artists, including Roger Sanchez, Jose Nunez, Livin Joy, Phonat, Little Boots, Paul Thomas, Tim Berg, and Richand Grey & Erick Morillo. He performed alongside the likes of DJ A-Track, Laidback Luke, Bart B More, and Chocolate Puma and the Party Squad. In fact, Laidback Luke mentioned Avicii by name on his MySpace page, congratulating him on winning the Fast Trax prize and writing that he "left many contesters behind in their dust." In 2009, the French DJ magazine *Only for DJs* (May 2009) named Avicii "The Swedish Future," replacing Swedish House Mafia, one of Avicii's early influences.

MAINSTREAM SINGLES

Avicii's first mainstream release, "Seek Bromance"—with its clear melody and intensely pounding bass—became a hit in Europe and eventually made its way to audiences in the United States. However, it was the 2011 song "Levels," with its feel-good Etta James sample, that made the name Avicii recognizable to dance music fans across the globe. That year, without any notable promotion, Avicii reached the sixth spot in the *DJ Mag* Top 100 poll. The following year, he had another hit with "Silhouettes," the lyrics of which proclaim, "We've taken a big step forward," and "We will never get back to the old school." The latter lyric was a clear declaration to critics and fans that Avicii was not nostalgic for the good old days and sounds of EDM; he was making something new and original. In a 2012 interview with *DJ Mag*, Avicii elaborated on the song, saying that it is "definitely a track with significance behind it." He added, "The lyrics stand for my incredible journey in growing as a person and as an artist. However, I also feel it applies to the development of EDM at the moment and I guess I've just been in the right place at the right time, thanks to my team. My sound seems to connect with people in the United States. They really connect with the music and go crazy for it!"

Avicii was not just bragging. The interview with *DJ Mag* took place not long after he played Radio City Music Hall, the New York City music venue where numerous rock musicians as well as such greats as Tony Bennett and Leonard Cohen have performed. Toward the end of the year he released yet another hit, "I Could Be the One," a collaboration with Nicky Romero. The accolades kept on coming. In 2012, he was named a top DJ by *DJ Mag*. His song "Sunshine," a collaboration with David Guetta, was nominated for a Grammy, and "Levels" was nominated for

an MTV Video Music Award. His fan base kept growing too. To celebrate reaching two million followers on Facebook, Avicii released the song "2 Million" in the spring of 2012; the following year, he released "3 Million" to celebrate his next milestone.

FAME AND CONSEQUENCES

Avicii's popularity continued to grow throughout 2013, and a great deal of money and fame came with it. He continued to tour almost nonstop, and his DJ gigs and songs continued to generate substantial sums of money. Avicii placed sixth on *Forbes* magazine's list of the world's highest-paid DJs, with an income of $20 million. At twenty-three, he was the youngest artist on the *Forbes* list that year.

Avicii's rising popularity and grueling tour schedule of more than two hundred shows per year ultimately led to exhaustion, which he tried to cope with by smoking cigarettes and consuming energy drinks. He also began drinking alcohol excessively. "You are traveling around," Avicii told Pressler, "you live in a suitcase, you get to this place, there's free alcohol everywhere—it's sort of weird if you don't drink." He confessed that he drank in part because he did not expect his popularity to last. But it did last, Pressler wrote, and "soon he had a serious habit: champagne at night, Bloody Marys at the airport, wine on the plane, repeat." Avicii told Pressler, "I was so nervous. I just got into a habit, because you rely on that encouragement and self-confidence you get from alcohol and then you get dependent on it." Avicii's alcohol use led to serious health problems. In January 2012, he developed intense abdominal pains and was hospitalized in New York for a week and a half. Avicii admitted to Pressler, about a year after the hospitalization, that he still drinks more than he should.

With fame also came criticism. Some criticized Avicii for modeling for Ralph Lauren, being too mainstream, and making a remix for Madonna—all things he considered great accomplishments. The *GQ* profile by Pressler—who spent nearly a week traveling with Avicii and his entourage on tour—greatly irritated the artist. On his Facebook page, he stated that the article was filled with "little truth and misquotations." He took issue with how the reporter portrayed people in the EDM scene—as being unattractive, uneducated, and on drugs, among other unflattering descriptions—and what Pressler wrote about his DJ sets. In the profile, Pressler quoted Avicii as saying that DJing is "mostly before work" and that he prepares most of his set list and transitions between songs before he gets onstage. She also quoted him as saying that the only thing he does onstage while DJing is adjust the volume and occasionally the faders, all the while gyrating his body and pumping his fists to get the crowd going. In his reply, Avicii wrote, "I would never cheat my fans like that. . . . I want the entire night to progress seamlessly and when I have to adapt the energy on the fly for the crowd on any given night, I can do so with harmonic mixes that I've practiced over and over again. I am far from the only DJ that does this and it's something I take pride in being able to do." Because Avicii has over three million followers on Facebook and over a million followers on Twitter, news of his reply spread quickly, making its way to music blogs and print publications such as the *Los Angeles Times*.

TRUE

Avicii had been so busy making singles and touring that he had no time to release a full album until about five years into his music career. As a result of his popularity, expectations were high, but the DJ had a card up his sleeve. His first album came to be considered a crossover record between EDM, pop, and—most surprisingly, at least to many fans and critics—folk music. The album, simply titled *True*, was released in late 2013. The first single, "Wake Me Up," featuring singer Aloe Blacc, debuted a few months prior and became a global hit. It also gave people a clear musical view of Avicii's new direction. The song is undeniably electronic, but it features acoustic guitar and a soulful, pop-country voice. The song's electronic beat has an up-tempo country and bluegrass feel. The song "Hey Brother" similarly starts out with very soulful country vocals by bluegrass singer Dan Tyminski. After an electronic beat comes in to support the singing, the track goes back and forth between an electronic country sound and an anthemic dance sound appropriate for a music festival. The list of musical guest stars on the album is impressive. Mac Davis, a songwriter in his seventies—who wrote, among other hit songs, "A Little Less Conversation" and "In the Ghetto" for Elvis Presley—wrote for Avicii the song "Addicted to You." The track features a soulful performance by singer Audra Mae. Much of the material on *True* is energetic EDM that employs varying sonic touches. Whereas the song "Dear Boy" is Avicii-style house music, "Lay Me Down," featuring Adam Lambert on vocals, sounds like contemporary disco with a twist. The song was coproduced by Nile Rodgers, the guitarist and composer for the 1970s disco-funk band Chic.

In his review of the album for *Spin* (12 Sept. 2013), Philip Sherburne pointed out that the album's "eclecticism and its surprisingly tight execution are likely due, at least in part, to the fact that Avicii worked with such a staggeringly large (and diverse!) array of musicians." Sherburne, who gave the record a score of eight out of ten, also wrote, "It may be a sprawling hodgepodge, but all this works more often than you'd expect." He added, "It turns out that [Avicii is] a smart, fun, and persuasive pop songsmith, closer in spirit to Bruno Mars than Swedish House Mafia." The album received largely positive reviews from publications such as *Rolling Stone*, the *Huffington Post*, and the *New York Times*. In November 2013, Avicii won the award for best electronic musician at the MTV Europe Music Awards, beating out such big names in the genre as Calvin Harris, Skrillex, and—one of his longtime musical heroes—Daft Punk.

SUGGESTED READING

Caramanica, Jon. "Global Pop, Now Infused with Country." *New York Times*. New York Times, 18 Sept. 2013. Web. 14 Jan. 2014.

Doyle, Patrick. "Avicii's Rave New World." *Rolling Stone*. Wenner Media, 16 Aug. 2013. Web. 14 Jan. 2014.

Pressler, Jessica. "The King of Oontz Oontz Oontz." *GQ*. Advance, Apr. 2013. Web. 14 Jan. 2014.

Sherburne, Philip. "EDM Superstar Avicii Made a Kazoo-Heavy Kinda-Country Record with 'True,' It's Awesome." *Spin*. Spin Media, 12 Sept. 2013. Web. 14 Jan. 2014.

—*Dmitry Kiper*

Iggy Azalea

Born: June 7, 1990
Occupation: Rapper

Iggy Azalea seems to many observers to be an unlikely rap artist. "Iggy Azalea's ascent into the rap pantheon is little short of miraculous," Ian Gittins wrote for the *Guardian* (15 Oct. 2013). "[She] has somehow become one of US hip-hop's most touted female rising stars, despite the considerable practical and geographical handicaps of being a white, middle-class rapper raised in an obscure New South Wales outpost named Mullumbimby."

Other commentators believe that Azalea's rise to prominence signals a natural progression in rap's evolution. While acknowledging that "the majority of the conversation in hip-hop is and has always been about the actions, thoughts, feelings, and ethos of black men," cultural critic Touré wrote for the *New York Times* (23 Dec. 2011) that "this hegemony cannot last forever. Eventually the throne will have to be shared." Touré added, "If a group of white teenage boys conspired to construct their dream white female rapper they might come up with Iggy Azalea . . . a sexy rapper with long blond hair, a model's enticing looks, and the detached, hyperconfident air of a dominatrix. She has an aggressive vocal approach and a silky flow. . . . If the white women of the world can possibly

Redferns via Getty Images

produce one superstar rapper, Iggy Azalea could be it."

Like Touré, many commentators have focused on Azalea's physical appearance, and she is often referred to as a "blond bombshell." Early in her career, she was frequently told that she should model rather than pursue a career as a recording artist. When asked by Aimee O'Neill for *Interview* magazine (30 July 2012) if she ever felt that her beauty overshadowed her music in the eyes of critics, Azalea replied, "Yeah, I do. I guess it's my fault. I guess I should make better music so it doesn't overshadow it." Yet despite critics' fixation on her looks, Azalea's music has spoken for itself. Following the release of her debut full-length album, *The New Classic* (2014), Azalea's first two chart hits simultaneously held the top two spots on the Billboard Hot 100, a feat not achieved by any recording artist since the Beatles in 1964.

EARLY LIFE

Iggy Azalea was born Amethyst Amelia Kelly on June 7, 1990, in Sydney, Australia. She has two younger siblings, a sister named Emerald and a brother named Mathias. When she was young, her family moved to the small town of Mullumbimby in New South Wales. Describing Azalea's small hometown, Caroline Ryder wrote for the online arts-and-culture magazine *Dazed* (2 Apr. 2012), "Mullumbimby's 3,129 patchouli-loving denizens enjoy three pubs, proximity to Nimbin (home to MardiGrass, the biggest weed festival in the world), and a crystal shop called The Laughing Buddha, where Iggy once worked." Confirming the countercultural flavor of the

place, Azalea said to Ryder, "It's like, dreadlocks, no shoes, lots of weed-smoking, hemp clothing, a lot of tie-dye s—— going on, that kind of thing."

Azalea's parents married while still in their teens. Her father, Brendan Kelly, a cartoonist and oil painter, built their family home in Mullumbimby by hand out of mud bricks on twelve acres of land. He often tried to interest his daughters in art and literature, and Azalea has recalled, with some exasperation, being quizzed by him on various artists.

Azalea's parents split up when she was about nine years old, and her mother, Tanya, made a living by substitute teaching and cleaning vacation homes and hotel rooms in the nearby tourist town of Byron Bay. At a young age, Azalea began cleaning houses and hotel rooms as well.

BUDDING INTEREST IN RAP

Azalea traces her love of rap music to hearing Tupac Shakur's "Baby Don't Cry (Keep Ya Head Up II)" at a friend's house when she was about twelve years old. As she later explained in an interview with Michael Nguyen for *Complex* magazine (12 Oct. 2012), "Everything subconsciously influences you, but 2Pac influences me [to be] vulnerable in your music and be unapologetic about contradicting yourself. He showed he was human and people loved him." She became somewhat obsessed with the late rapper, plastering her bedroom wall with his photos. She especially loved the rebelliousness exhibited in rap culture and was drawn to the flashy clothing and jewelry worn by her favorite recording artists.

By the time Azalea was thirteen years old, she had procured a fake ID and was going to dance clubs with groups of friends. Soon she was coming up with her own raps. She often took the hour-long bus ride to Lismore, which had a large population of Sudanese refugees. "All the people from Sudan liked hip-hop and I liked hip-hop, so we would all be at the cipher zone," she recalled to Ryder. "That's where they play a beat, and then everybody's standing around and it's like, I say my rap, and you have to say your rap." At one point, she and two other girls formed a group inspired by the American hip-hop/R&B trio TLC. Calling themselves Baby Laydee, they rehearsed together only a short time before disbanding over creative differences.

Azalea came up with her stage moniker after commissioning a necklace with the name of her pet dog, Iggy. "I really loved that dog. He was a tough, cool, determined fighter. He had all the characteristics I admire in people," she told Alex Scordelis for *Paper* magazine (30 Sept. 2013). "When he got put down, I got a nameplate necklace with his name. People started calling me that, too." The nickname stuck. She later added the name of the street where she had once lived,

Azalea Street, in order to make her stage name sound more feminine.

SIXTEEN IN MIAMI

When she was thirteen years old, Azalea visited the United States with her grandmother. "It was like the movies, but real. I wanted to live in America ever since I visited," she told Scordelis. She added, "I just knew that this is where hip-hop is from. And all I wanted to do is become a rapper. I had to be in the States." She dropped out of high school when she was fifteen and carefully saved up the money she had earned from her cleaning jobs. Azalea initially told her mother that she intended only to take a vacation with a friend, but she had no intention of returning to live in Australia.

With the money she had earned from cleaning and other odd jobs, Azalea first settled in Miami, Florida, where she spent much of her time hanging around the pool at her apartment complex and recording videos of herself rapping, which she then posted to the social-media website MySpace. She soon caught the attention of a rapper and producer known as Mr. Lee, who encouraged her to move to Houston, Texas, to try her hand at the music scene there. Feeling adrift after breaking up with a boyfriend in Miami, she agreed. Just a few months after she arrived in Texas in 2008, however, the state was hit by one of the deadliest and costliest storms in its history. "Hurricane Ike came and blew everything I owned into the street, just as the financial crash came and the Australian dollar went down to 54 cents US," Azalea recalled to Nick Aveling for *Time Out London* (7 Oct. 2013). "All of a sudden my money was worth half as much and I didn't own s——."

In January 2009 Azalea moved to Atlanta, Georgia, where she met Shawna Peezy, who became her best friend and manager. She also signed a production contract that allowed her to attend Marvelous Enterprises Artist Development Center, a boot camp of sorts run by industry insider Marvin L. McIntyre. To her dismay, she found that because of her physical appearance, the instructors there wanted her to emulate blond pop stars such as Britney Spears rather than pursue her interest in rap. In 2010 she switched gears and moved to Los Angeles with Peezy, still focused on having a career on her own terms.

Although she was determined to make her home in the United States, Azalea had to travel back to Australia every three months because of her visa situation. Luckily, her stepfather worked for an airline, so she was able to fly cheaply when necessary.

EARLY MUSIC CAREER

Once in Los Angeles, Azalea continued to film music videos, which she posted on the video-sharing website YouTube. One such video, for a song called "Pu$$y," featured her licking an ice-cream cone in a suggestive manner while rapping about the desirability of her body. One morning in September 2011, she awoke to find that Perez Hilton, a popular blogger who covers celebrity gossip and entertainment news, had posted the video on his heavily trafficked site.

By noon of that day, the music video had been viewed more than sixty thousand times, bringing Azalea the most widespread attention she had ever received at that point. Not all of the attention was positive; some commentators excoriated her for hugging a little boy in the video as she raps about her sexual prowess. Azalea has explained that the boy appears only because a friend who was helping her shoot the video could not find a babysitter that day.

Shortly after the video went viral, Azalea released her debut mixtape, *Ignorant Art*, which contained nine tracks, including "Pu$$y," "My World," "The Last Song," and "Treasure Island." As she explained in an interview for the music magazine *Rap-Up* (13 Oct. 2011), "I made *Ignorant Art* with the intent to make people question and redefine old ideals." In a review for *Complex* (27 Sept. 2011), Anthony Osei wrote that the mixtape proved that Azalea was "ready to really make her mark on the game" and instructed his readers to "load up *Ignorant Art* onto your iTunes and let Ms. Azalea's machine-gun flow win you over."

The major label Interscope Records quickly began showing interest in signing Azalea, but a firm deal never came to fruition. Speaking about her decision to break off the deal, she told O'Neill, "I think a lot of people looked at it like, 'Why would you do that? It's Interscope! It's a giant!' but you also have to be happy in the place that you work. I was in a bunch of studios that cost way too much money and I was getting served warm cookies when I walked in the door. It was too far out of my comfort zone."

GRAND HUSTLE RECORDS

After turning down Interscope, Azalea signed a deal with the Atlanta-based record label Grand Hustle, founded by the hip-hop artist Clifford Joseph Harris Jr., better known by his stage name, T. I. "I felt like I was just floating around in a big ocean. I got picked up and caught by a label [Interscope], and it was very impersonal," Azalea told O'Neill. "It felt like I was a product. When I met [T. I.] and everybody else over at [Grand Hustle], it felt like I was with real people again. He cared about me as a friend, not just as a check." Just a few weeks earlier, in February 2012, she had appeared on the cover of the Freshman Class issue of the respected rap magazine *XXL*, sometimes referred to as a "hip-hop bible." She was the first woman to be featured in the magazine's eagerly anticipated annual survey of new talent.

Azalea released her EP *Glory* on the Grand Hustle label in July 2012. In October she released a second mixtape, titled *Trap Gold*, also on Grand Hustle. In a review for BET.com (16 Oct. 2012), Calvin Stovall wrote, "Once you overcome the gray area between Iggy's musical persona and her actual life, it's hard to discredit the quality of the music. . . . Azalea's latest release, *Trap Gold*, is one of the better mixtapes released this year."

THE NEW CLASSIC

For the release of her first full-length album, Azalea signed with the UK–based Mercury Records and the American label Island Def Jam. The album, *The New Classic*, was released in April 2014 and peaked at the number-three spot on the Billboard 200 chart. It includes the much-talked-about lead single "Work," which contains semiautobiographical lyrics about Azalea's move to the United States as a young woman with little money; "Bounce," which is accompanied by a lavish Bollywood-style video; "Change Your Life," in which she sings, "I'm a new classic, upgrade your status / From a standby to a frequent flyer / Pop out your past life, and I'll renovate your future"; and "Fancy," which reached the number-one spot on the Billboard Hot 100.

Azalea, who toured with the singer Beyoncé on the Australian leg of the American superstar's Mrs. Carter Show World Tour in October and November 2013, is sometimes criticized for employing a southern American accent while rapping. In an interview for *Complex* (16 Sept. 2013), Justin Monroe asked her how she felt about people calling her fake based on her race and nationality. Azalea responded, "The Rolling Stones go to America, play 'black' blues music, and nobody has a f——ing issue with it or thinks it's weird. But here we are, fifty years later, in the twenty-first century, and people are like, 'This is so weird that you're white, from another country, and you like black music.' Why is it not weird for Keith Richards or Mick Jagger, but it's so weird and taboo for me?" She added, "This is the entertainment industry. It's not politics. You should be more concerned about the message, not the voices saying it."

PERSONAL LIFE

Azalea's romantic life has been a subject of some fascination in the press. While dating fellow rapper Rakim Mayers, better known by his stage name, A$AP Rocky, she got the words "Live, Love, A$AP" tattooed on her finger; when the relationship ended, she had the last portion of the tattoo crossed out. In November 2013, Azalea began dating Los Angeles Lakers basketball star Nick Young, with whom she was featured in a March 2014 *GQ* magazine fashion spread.

Six years after moving to the United States, Azalea was issued a five-year O-1 visa, which is granted to an individual "who possesses extraordinary ability in the sciences, arts, education, business, or athletics, or who has a demonstrated record of extraordinary achievement in the motion picture or television industry and has been recognized nationally or internationally for those achievements." "I cried when I got it," she told Simone Amelia for the website BossLady.tv (20 Feb. 2013). "A visa meant more to me than my own label deal."

SUGGESTED READING

Azalea, Iggy. "Iggy Azalea Goes for Glory." Interview by Aimee O'Neill. *Interview*. Interview, 30 July 2012. Web. 18 June 2014.

Azalea, Iggy. "Iggy Azalea Interview: 'Sometimes I Feel Like Australians Can Go F—— Themselves.'" Interview by Nick Aveling. *Time Out London*. Time Out Digital, 7 Oct. 2013. Web. 19 June 2014.

Azalea, Iggy. "Iggy Azalea: 'The Low End Theory.'" Interview by Justin Monroe. *Complex*. Complex Media, 16 Sept. 2013. Web. 18 June 2014.

Ryder, Caroline. "Iggy Goes Pop." *Dazed*. Dazed Digital, 2 Apr. 2012. Web. 18 June 2014.

Scordelis, Alex. "Gettin' Iggy wit' It." *Papermag*. Paper, 30 Sept. 2013. Web. 18 June 2014.

Touré. "Challenging Hip-Hop's Masculine Ideal." *New York Times*. New York Times, 23 Dec. 2011. Web. 18 June 2014.

SELECTED WORKS

Ignorant Art, 2011; *Glory*, 2012; *The New Classic*, 2014

—Mari Rich

James Balog

Born: July 15, 1952
Occupation: Photographer

Though he began his career as a photojournalist with a passion for mountaineering, James Balog's real work of over thirty years has been to examine and document the relationship between people and the environment. His early photography captured the different ways that humans see animals and trees, but his shift to focus on ice in 2005 led to the work for which he is best known. With the creation of the Extreme Ice Survey (EIS) and its mission to document the rapidly changing glaciers of the Arctic, Balog provided shocking visual evidence of climate change through time-lapse images. The related 2012 documentary, *Chasing Ice*, further shared

© Lynn Goldsmith/Corbis

Balog's stunning study of disappearing ice and brought the immediacy of the problem to international attention.

In addition to his projects, Balog has photographed such momentous events as the eruption of Mount St. Helens in 1980, the Indian Ocean Tsunami in 2004, and the Deepwater Horizon oil spill in 2010. He has presented his work to bodies such as the United Nations and the White House, while continuing to lecture and work with his nonprofit, the Earth Vision Trust. "I believe photography is one of the most powerful mediums of communication ever invented," Balog told Claire Sykes for *Photographer's Forum* (2009). "Too much of the time, it's squandered on trivialities. I'd like to see us aspire to the angels of our higher nature. If we can pull our minds and hearts together to use the medium to its full power, we can make an important impact on the world."

CHILDHOOD AND EDUCATION

James Balog was born on July 15, 1952, in Danville, Pennsylvania—a state where both of his grandfathers had worked as coal miners. The family later moved to Watchung, New Jersey, and then New York City, where his father worked as a Wall Street financier while his mother stayed at home. Growing up in the suburbs, and later the city, Balog developed an early interest in nature and the outdoors. "Somehow back then, I fixated on the natural forces and hazards of nature, feeling small within its power and being

fascinated with that," he told Sykes. He joined the Boy Scouts and, when he was eighteen, went to Colorado for an Outward Bound course. Balog attended a private Catholic high school and his first job was working as a counselor at a summer camp.

After high school Balog attended Boston College, where he started as a history major, but changed to study photography and filmmaking. During this period of his life he also continued to develop his interest in hiking and mountain climbing, often traveling to New Hampshire's White Mountains. He graduated with a bachelor's degree in communications and secondary education in 1974. Though he studied communications, Balog had always nursed an interest in the earth's tectonics and the environment.

After college Balog moved to Boulder, Colorado. There, he continued to pursue photography—along with rock and ice climbing—while getting his master's degree in geography, specializing in geomorphology, from the University of Colorado in 1977. He researched the 1976 Big Thompson River flash flood for his dissertation. He told Jascha Hoffman for *Nature* (Sept. 2012): "When I was finishing my thesis, I remember looking at a stack of manila punchcards and deciding that I'd rather see the world through a camera than through data analysis." He added: "The data are incredibly important, but my calling is to understand the world through art."

EARLY CAREER

Though he had initially anticipated working as a consultant, Balog ultimately went in a different direction. In discussing his career path, Balog told Dennis Nishi "I didn't want to spend my career sitting in front of a computer screen doing mathematical models" (*Wall Street Journal* 26 Nov. 2009). Rather than work at a desk, Balog traveled to such places as Alaska, the Swiss Alps, and the Himalayas, bringing his camera along to document his trips. By the late 1970s his interests and education began to coalesce, and he was able to use his love of photography, his knowledge of the environment, and his comfort in the outdoors to begin work as a photojournalist. He began to read a great deal about photography, as well, and his first serious assignment was an article on avalanche control for *Smithsonian*.

Though he had to occasionally find side work as a mountaineering instructor or soils scientist, by 1978 Balog was able to make a living from writing magazine articles and creating photo-essays for publications such as *Mariah* (now *Outside*), *Time*, and *Life*. In a 2013 interview with the American Society of Media Photographers (ASMP) he noted, "I had no friends or mentors in documentary photography as a profession, but I wanted to work for the big, glossy, color-picture magazines." He added, "Naïveté, a willingness to take risks, good luck, the determination of a Clydesdale plus a unique combination of mountaineering skills and earth science background carried me forward." These factors carried Balog through until 1980, where documenting the eruption of Mount St. Helens was a life-changing event. For the next few years Balog continued to refine his skills and home in on the intersection of humans and nature in what he has referred to as the leitmotif of his entire career.

ANIMAL TANGENT

In the early 1980s Balog embarked on what he has called his "animal tangent" while in conversation with Sheila Roberts, for *Collider* (4 Dec. 2012). "It was sort of my furry period, you could say, and I did a lot of animal work for eight or ten years." Inspired by war photography, he began to take pictures with his 35-mm. camera of animals being stalked, hunted, and killed. He published his first book, *Wildlife Requiem*, in 1984 and in 1986 exhibited these pictures at the Museum of Contemporary Photography of Columbia College under the same title. "It was a study of big-game hunting in the Rockies. They're bloody pictures and gruesome," he explained to Nishi. "War photography had a long tradition of turning a glass eye onto horror and ugliness. I wanted to do the same here." The collection included images of a pick-up truck bed filled with animal bodies and a bear being skinned.

After the publication of *Wildlife Requiem,* Balog shifted to a portrait photography approach to animals. The result was the 1990 book *Survivors: A New Vision of Endangered Wildlife.* He was inspired with the idea for the book while taking a picture of a rhinoceros for a magazine article. "We always look for picturesque places to photograph them that make it look like they have these idyllic lives," he told Nishi. "Looking up close made me realize that this species is almost extinct. I wanted to put them in a setting that showed the alienation of that species from nature." *Survivors* featured sixty-two images of animals, such as a Florida panther, shot in the style of fashion photography.

A third work that came from Balog's "furry period" was 1993's *Anima*, a collection of photographs from 1991 to 1993 that examines the intimate relationship between humans and chimpanzees. During the mid-1990s he also developed the collection *Humans & Technology*, which consisted of pictures of what Balog calls "techno-sapiens"—people intersected with machines. The collection included a diver in a scuba suit, a camouflaged sniper, and a man with a prosthetic arm.

Balog became the first photographer to be commissioned by the US Postal Service to create a full plate of stamps. Released in 1996, Balog's stamps showcased wildlife species that were endangered in the United States.

TREE AND CHANGING FORESTS

Starting in 1998, Balog shifted his focus toward trees, where it remained for several years. He initially tried to create portrait studios in the forest, but found it limiting so he changed his approach. "I noticed that light, subject, moment, weather, scale, mood, and a hundred other variables always seemed in flux," he told the ASMP. "An eclectic range of visual treatments, it seemed, would better reflect the chameleon reality." These visual treatments utilized Balog's unique style and methods to compose and present the shots. Some images were close-ups of leaves, branches, and trunks, rearranged for presentation. Other images were taken while Balog was suspended from climbing ropes, hundreds of feet up in a redwood; to capture some of these massive trees he took over eight hundred exposures, creating a mosaic through this multi-frame approach. He also shifted between film format, color, and black-and-white. "With good light, proper technique, and some luck, the photo will be an easily understood celebration of the tree."

Balog published *Tree: A New Vision of the American Forest* in 2004. The collection was praised for its innovative approach and the diversity of trees included.

EXTREME ICE SURVEY

Balog spent time in 2005 and 2006 working on long-term projects for *National Geographic* and the *New Yorker* to photograph changing glaciers. "The real story wasn't the beautiful white top," he told Nishi. "It ended up being at the terminus of the glacier where it's dying. That idea gestated in my mind for a year and eventually turned into the 'Extreme Ice Survey' in 2006." The Extreme Ice Survey (EIS), based in Boulder, Colorado, eventually became a massive, multi-year project for photographing the ever-shrinking glaciers in the Arctic.

Balog explained his motivation for the project to the ASMP: "Glaciers can disappear in hours or days—with not a single human present to witness the change, let alone preserve a memory of what is gone." He went on the note, "When these metaphorical trees in the forest fall and no one is there to hear, a collective 'natural amnesia' sets in. Ultimately, we hope our art not only touches the human spirit but shifts perception of humanity's relationship to the natural environment, vital to sustainable living on a finite planet."

Balog's EIS team included experts Jason Box, Daniel B. Fagre, and Tad Pfeffer, along with mountaineer Conrad Anker. They set up time-lapse cameras using batteries and solar panels, but not without facing many challenges unique to the harsh environment. He told Hoffman "We had to tackle deep snow, torrential rain and falling rocks. Off-the-shelf gear wasn't robust enough, and it took six months of experimenting to come up with a reliable time-lapse system." Over time, the project grew to have forty-eight cameras on twenty-four different glaciers in locations in Greenland, Iceland, Alaska, the Rocky Mountains, and even on Mount Everest. The cameras took pictures in every hour of daylight and were combined to create stunning videos of the retreating ice.

The ongoing videos showed astonishing glacial melt and caught massive shelves of ice—some miles wide—collapsing into the sea. These calving events shocked the public and provided jarring images of climate change. This powerful evidence of melting polar ice caps gave Balog the opportunity to inform people about the ice he had grown to love decades earlier. His work was even featured in a 2009 NOVA/PBS television documentary called *Extreme Ice*, along with a book published that year, *Extreme Ice Now*. Balog's oft-repeated mission is "to show geological changes happening on a human time scale," a mission which he furthered in 2010 by founding the Earth Vision Trust, a nonprofit organization for educating the public about climate change.

CHASING ICE
Balog and the EIS team joined forces with film director Jeff Orlowski to turn their work into a documentary. Produced by Orlowski, Jerry Aronson, and Paula DuPré Pesmen, *Chasing Ice* premiered at the Sundance Film Festival in January 2012. *Chasing Ice* shows the team's expeditions to the Arctic and their struggles to deploy their camera equipment. Included is footage of the calving event at Greenland's Jakobshavn Glacier; the scenes are taken from the seventy-five-minute event, the biggest of its type to be recorded. Other scenes come from three years of the receding Columbia Glacier in Alaska, which changed so dramatically that the EIS team had to move the camera to keep the glacier in the shot.

Even more so than the EIS images, *Chasing Ice* shocked audiences with the scale of how climate change was affecting the glaciers. Balog did not shy away from showing the harsh truths of global warming. "We need to be grown-up enough as artists to look at this stuff with eyes wide open," he told Sam Moulton for *Outside* (4 Dec. 2012). "And if audiences can't take it, too bad."

Chasing Ice won over thirty awards from film festivals across the globe, including an award at Sundance for excellence in cinematography, as well as the award for best documentary from the Environmental Media Association. It also won a 2013 achievement award from the Renewable Natural Resources Foundation and was shortlisted for the Academy Award for best original song of 2012.

In 2012 Balog published the book *Ice: Portraits of Vanishing Glaciers*. In his interview with the ASMP, Balog generalized his efforts saying, "I feel a great obligation to preserve a pictorial memory of vanishing landscapes for the people of the future." Through the EIS, *Chasing Ice*, the Earth Vision Trust, and his continued work in photojournalism, Balog is a major figure in creating this pictorial memory, and has no plans to stop his work because, as he told to ASMP, "I have to believe that there is still time."

ANTHROPOCENE IN ACTION
In 2013 Balog was working on a project with the University of Colorado surveying hydrology patterns in the western United States and how they are being affected by climate change. He was also documenting the effect of sudden aspen decline (SAD)—a blight that kills aspen trees—for the nonprofit For the Forest, as well as filming the effect of bark beetles on ponderosas and whitebark pines. This is all part of what Balog calls "the Anthropocene in action," the theory that the Holocene epoch is ending and being replaced by the Anthropocene epoch. Balog's goal is to document the changes in action for review by geology experts who will decide if the epoch has indeed changed. In September of 2013 Balog also won the Ansel Adams Award from the Sierra Club for conservation photography.

PERSONAL LIFE
Balog married Karen Breunig, an artist, in 1976, but the two split in 1990. Balog lives in the Rocky Mountains near Boulder, Colorado, with his wife, Suzanne, and their daughter Emily, who was born in 2002. Balog's older daughter, Simone, was born in 1988, and graduated from Boston College in 2010.

Among many other accolades, Balog won the 2010 Heinz Award for his innovative contributions to the environment. He was also the first ever winner of the League Award from the International League of Conservation Photographers, an organization that he helped to found. Balog presented at the United Nations Climate Change Conference in 2009 and spoke on behalf of NASA, the World Wildlife Fund, and the US State Department. In 2010 Balog also presented his findings to the White House Office of Energy and Climate Change.

SUGGESTED READING
Balog, James. Interview. *American Society of Media Photographers*. American Society of Media Photographers, 2013. Web. 25 Sept. 2013.

Balog, James. "Q&A: Archivist of Ice." Interview by Jascha Hoffman. *Nature* 13 Sept. 2012: 206–7. Print.

Balog, James. "Turning a Lens to Climate Change." Interview by Dennis Nishi. *Wall Street Journal* 24 Nov. 2009: D8. Print.

Daniel, Joseph E. "James Balog Pushes the Limits of Eco-Photography—Again." *Earth Journal* 6.1 (1993): 32–34. Print.

Goodyer, Jason. "On the Ice." *Engineering & Technology* 7.11 (2012): 44–47. Print.

Moulton, Sam. "Disappearing Act: James Balog's Quest to Capture Climate Change in Action." *Outside*. Mariah Media Network, 4 Dec. 2012. Web. 25 Sept. 2013.

Sykes, Claire. "James Balog's Extreme Ice Survey." *Photographer's Forum* 31.3 (2009): 37–46. Print.

SELECTED WORKS

Wildlife Requiem, 1984; *Survivors: A New Vision of Endangered Wildlife*, 1990; *Anima*, 1993; *Tree: A New Vision of the American Forest*, 2004; *Extreme Ice Now*, 2009; *Ice: Portraits of Vanishing Glaciers*, 2012

—*Kehley Coviello*

Getty Images

Marcia Barbosa

Born: ca. 1960
Occupation: Physicist

Marcia Barbosa has been a professor of physics at the Universidade Federal do Rio Grande do Sul since 1991. Her research into the behavior of water has yielded results that have been applied to life and environmental sciences, and her strong advocacy and activism on the issue of women in science has led to greater understanding of the challenges and discrimination women have faced—and continue to face—in scientific fields, and physics in particular. Her cause has led her to speak and write widely on the topic in a number of countries besides her native Brazil. Barbosa is international councilor for the American Physical Society for the period of 2013 to 2015.

EARLY LIFE AND EDUCATION

Marcia Cristina Bernardes Barbosa was born in Rio de Janeiro, Brazil. After attending high school at Colegio Marechal Rondon in Canoas, Rio Grande do Sul, Brazil, she went on to study at the Universidade Federal do Rio Grande do Sul (UFRGS) in Porto Alegre. She received her bachelor of science degree in physics from the university in December 1981. Barbosa remained at UFRGS for her graduate studies. She received her master's degree in physics, under adviser W. K. Theumann, in October 1984 and earned her doctoral degree in science, also under Theumann, in July 1988.

Barbosa pursued her postdoctoral studies in the United States, at the University of Maryland. She was part of the research group of Michael E. Fisher, an award-winning physicist. From September 1988 to September 1990, Barbosa served as a research associate for Fisher at the University of Maryland. She returned to her home country after completing her postdoctoral work. In 1991 Barbosa was offered the permanent position of professor at UFRGS, a position she still holds.

FLUID KNOWLEDGE

Water is essential to life. Thus, to understand life, and how to improve it, it is essential to understand water. The chemical makeup of water seems simple (H_2O: two parts hydrogen, one part oxygen), but it is much more complex than appearances suggest. This ubiquitous liquid—water makes up a majority of the Earth's surface as well as a majority of the human body—can act in ways that are unusual and hard to predict. Barbosa has spent years studying the strange and exciting ways water behaves, and her work has tremendous implications for a great variety of disciplines, including physics, chemistry, biology, and geology.

Barbosa's studies of the properties of water were initially theoretical, but as her career has progressed, she has focused increasingly on practical applications. Her work has helped to explain water's interactions with biological molecules (such as DNA, proteins, and fats) and geological processes and has contributed to ongoing research into genetic vaccines, oil recovery, and ethanol production.

This research has made Barbosa a respected figure in the physics community and has earned her positions on a number of national and international commissions in the field. In addition to the American Physical Society, Barbosa is a member of the Grant Committee of the International Council for Science, the Grand Jury of the Descartes Prize of the European Commission, and Brazil's National Council of Science and Technology. She was elected vice president at large of the International Union of Pure and Applied Physics (IUPAP) in 2008 and was named chair of the Committee for Physics of the National Council of Science and Technology in 2011. Barbosa's membership in these organizations reflects the importance she places on international cooperation between scientists; as she wrote in a statement for the American Physical Society's website, her connections with researchers around the world have helped her to understand the "obstacles for physics to become genuinely 'without borders'" and work to overcome them.

WOMEN IN SCIENCE

Barbosa is a strong advocate for the equal representation of women in science in general and physics in particular. She has been involved in this advocacy since 1998. Her belief is that equal representation not only is a matter of fairness and justice but also is essential for the development of science. "By excluding female researchers, we are limiting the available pool of talented people to half of humanity and eliminating diversity," she wrote in an article for *Physics World* magazine (July 2003). "Physics needs women to survive."

Aside from her scientific publications, Barbosa has written several articles on the topic of women in science, both in Portuguese and in English. In a review of the book *Out of the Shadows: Contributions of Twentieth-Century Women to Physics* for *Physics World* (Jan. 2007), Barbosa began with a question: why have so few women been awarded the Nobel Prize in physics? The prestigious award was first granted in 1901, but between 1901 and 2014, only two out of more than one hundred Nobel laureates in the field were women. Barbosa first pointed out the traditional line of thinking on this: few women in math and science were allowed a university education until the late 1800s, so there were fewer eligible female candidates. The book, according to Barbosa, shows this line of thinking to be demonstrably false. *Out of the Shadows*, edited by Nina Byers and Gary Williams, tells the stories of forty women in science in the twentieth century, and the stories prove, Barbosa argued, that there were, in fact, women who deserved to win the Nobel Prize but were turned away or ignored because of prejudice.

In the book review, Barbosa noted a few examples, such as British physicist, mathematician, and engineer Hertha Ayrton (1854–1923), who had various patents for film projectors and searchlights; she even became the first woman to be nominated for membership to the Royal Society but was denied membership because married women were declared ineligible. Similarly, the first person to observe the recoil of a decaying nucleus, Harriet Brooks (1876–1933), had to resign her post at Barnard College, in New York City, after it became known that she was getting married. The men in charge considered it inconceivable for a woman to be married or have children and simultaneously pursue rigorous scientific research. German mathematician Emmy Noether (1882–1935) was not allowed to become a professor for the sole reason that she was a woman. Women in the "wrong" ethnic group, Barbosa wrote in her review, faced double discrimination. During World War II, Austrian nuclear fission pioneer Lise Meitner (1878–1968) was not acknowledged for her work by her coresearcher, Otto Hahn, because she was Jewish; as a result, when Hahn won the Nobel Prize for chemistry in 1944, Meitner received no credit. Barbosa made the case that ignoring important contributions women made to science "hurts science itself." As an example she offered English mathematician Mary Lucy Cartwright (1900–1998), whose work—if acknowledged by the scientific community—could have led to the birth of chaos theory in the early 1940s as opposed to the early 1960s. In the second half of the twentieth century, women were allowed more opportunities, yet they still had to "create two masterpieces to be recognized for one," as Barbosa put it. For example, medical physicist Rosalyn Sussman Yalow (1921–2011) and her research partner, Solomon Berson, were expected to win the Nobel Prize in physics, but after Berson died in 1972, Yalow's name was removed from consideration. She would go on to win the Nobel Prize in physiology or medicine in 1977. In the conclusion of her review, Barbosa wrote, "So, if anyone asks me why there are so few female Nobel laureates, my answer is that many female scientists have deserved the prize but they were invisible to the community."

PROPOSING SOLUTIONS

Despite some significant progress for women in the twentieth century, women in the twenty-first century are still underrepresented in physics, to an even greater extent than they are in other sciences. Besides the early discouragement that girls interested in physics tend to receive, the field suffers from what Barbosa, in her 2003 *Physics World* article, calls a "leaky pipeline," with a high proportion of female physicists dropping out of the field at each stage of their career. That fact was and continues to be the root from which Barbosa's activism grows. In 2000 she became the first chair of the Working Group in Women in Physics for IUPAP. In 2002 she took part in IUPAP's International Conference on Women in Physics, the first such conference ever held by the organization, which brought together more than three hundred participants from sixty-five countries. Barbosa presented a paper titled "Women in Physics in Brazil," in which she discussed the all-too-familiar obstacles for women—such as the relatively recent availability of higher education to women, pressure to focus more on family affairs, and a lack of women on the boards of grant agencies—and proposed some solutions, such as teaching physics in a way that does not emphasize it as a "male activity" and creating working groups at universities that help address issues unique to women in science. In her 2003 *Physics World* article, Barbosa pointed out that some progress had already been made since the previous year's conference: for example, the delegates from that conference became part of a network of about sixty-five national working groups, and some of those delegates were involved in organizing talks on women in science at local or international conferences in their fields. However, Barbosa wrote, "increasing awareness about the problem is not enough." Some change must be made, she argued, both in practice and in perception. She called for greater transparency in hiring standards and promotion decisions as well as for rewarding women and men equally for traits such as persistence, rather than seeing persistent men as "tough" and persistent women as "pushy."

True to her word, Barbosa has worked to make a tangible difference in the lives of female scientists in Brazil. While working on the National Council of Science and Technology's grant program, Barbosa succeeded in convincing the council to provide three months of paid maternity leave to the scientists it funds, so that the women who managed to secure grants would have less pressure to choose between starting a family and continuing their research. She also performed several studies that brought attention to the fact that women were not only underrepresented among the scientists bankrolled by the council but also held to a higher standard than men—the female scientists given grants at the postdoctoral level had, on average, nearly twice as many publications as their male counterparts.

Along with fellow scientist Elisa Saitovitch, Barbosa organized the Latin American Women in Exact and Life Sciences conference, which was held in Rio de Janeiro in November 2004. The event, which lasted three days, had more than one hundred participants, not only from various fields of science and technology—such as math, physics, biology, and engineering—but also from the fields of sociology, journalism, and public policy. Barbosa also continues to be involved with IUPAP and has presented her latest findings and ideas to the organization as recently as 2013.

AWARDS AND HONORS

Barbosa has received various honors and awards for her efforts to improve the lot of women in science. Some of them include the 2013 L'Oreal-UNESCO Award for Women in Science and the 2009 American Physical Society Dwight Nicholson Medal for Outreach. In her home country, she has also gained some attention outside of the science world; in 2013 she won the Premio Claudia, an annual award that recognizes the contributions of Brazilian women in a variety of fields.

SUGGESTED READING

Barbosa, Marcia. "Equity for Women in Physics." *Physics World* July 2003: 2–3. Print.
Barbosa, Marcia. "A Secret History." Rev. of *Out of the Shadows*, ed. Nina Byers and Gary Williams. *Physics World* Jan. 2007: 4. Print.
"Marcia Barbosa." *American Physical Society*. Amer. Physical Soc., n.d. Web. 15 May 2014.

—*Dmitry Kiper*

Cornelia Bargmann

Born: 1961
Occupation: Scientist

In the world of science Cornelia Bargmann is best known for her research on a millimeter-long roundworm, *Caenorhabditis elegans*. But the significance of her research reaches far beyond the worm, which she chose to focus on in her postdoctoral days. The neurological makeup of *C. elegans* is relatively simple, compared to that of a human being or even a mouse, which enables it to be studied with greater precision. Having already earned a reputation as a gifted scientist for her lab work at the Massachusetts Institute of Technology (MIT), the University of California San Francisco (UCSF), and Rockefeller University, Bargmann was chosen in 2013 as one of only two scientists to head the Brain Research through Advancing Innovative Neurotechnologies initiative. The BRAIN initiative, as it is commonly known, has the highly ambitious objective of mapping out the human brain with the goal of understanding it better and making further advances in treating such conditions as Alzheimer's disease and traumatic brain injuries. Also in 2013 Bargmann was one of eleven winners of the Breakthrough Prize in Life Sciences for her work on the genetics of neural circuits and behavior as well as synaptic guidepost molecules. Each Breakthrough Prize winner received $3 million, more than twice the amount granted for the Nobel Prize.

© Heeun Jang

EARLY LIFE AND EDUCATION

Cornelia Isabella Bargmann, who also goes by Cori, was born in Virginia in 1961. Her parents were born in Germany and grew up in Berlin. After the end of World War II, they met in Nuremburg, Germany, where Bargmann's father served as a translator at the Nuremburg trials—during which various members of the Nazi leadership were prosecuted by the Allies—and her mother worked as a translator for the American government. Bargmann's father later immigrated to the United States, followed by her mother a few years later.

When she was five years old, Bargmann and her family moved to Athens, Georgia, where she grew up. In a short autobiography on the Kavli Prize website, Bargmann described her childhood home as "an academic household." She continued, "We all read, we all played piano, we all sang. My most pleasant memories of my childhood are of falling asleep listening to my father play Beethoven sonatas far into the night." Her father spent a few years working at the technology company IBM and then went on to become a professor of statistics and computer science at the University of Georgia, in Athens. "My mother's humanistic and artistic passions," Bargmann wrote in the Kavli autobiography, "mirrored my father's love of math." Her mother often read to Bargmann and her sisters, Monika, Eve, and Dorie. By the time Bargmann was in high school, she loved Latin and chemistry most of all—a combination that seems not at all surprising given the diverse range of arts and sciences to which she was exposed at home.

LOVE OF LABS

As an undergraduate, Bargmann studied biochemistry at the University of Georgia. She started out with what she described to Melissa Marino for *PNAS Online* (1 Mar. 2005) as "the world's most menial summer job—making fly food for a population biology lab" when she was seventeen years old. Wyatt Anderson, the head of the lab, introduced the young student to the bacterial geneticist Sidney Kushner, of the genetics department, for whom Bargmann would work during her junior and senior years. At Kushner's laboratory, Bargmann studied bacterial genetics, RNA metabolism, and molecular biology. "I went into science because I loved the labs," Bargmann told Nicholas Wade for the *New York Times* (20 June 2011). In his article, Wade observed, "She liked the machines and instruments, the fun of building things with one's own hands, of learning what no one else knew." In 1981, Bargmann graduated with a degree in biochemistry from the University of Georgia, where she was class valedictorian and elected to Phi Beta Kappa. It was an "incredibly exciting time" for molecular genetics, Bargmann told Wade, and she decided to pursue her doctoral studies at MIT, in Cambridge, Massachusetts.

SCIENCE STAR RISING

In 1981 Bargmann began her doctoral program at MIT, and it did not take long for her to be recognized for her talent and intellect. Working in the MIT lab of top cancer biologist Robert A. Weinberg, Bargmann worked on helping to isolate cancer-causing genes by cloning a rat gene by the name of neu. That research, according to Marino, "turned out to have surprising clinical relevance." Marino continued, "Although the rodent neuroblastoma model was considered an interesting experimental model system, no human correlate was known, making its relevance to human cancer dubious." Although Bargmann and her colleagues knew that there was a small chance that their research would be relevant to human cancers, they continued their studies. Eventually, the research paid off. According to Wade, the human version of neu, called HER-2, a few years later would be found to be "amplified" in breast cancer. That would lead to the creation of an important breast cancer drug, Herceptin. While Bargmann was not involved in the development of the drug itself, her research was crucial to its creation.

According to *Vogue*'s Rebecca Johnson (Oct. 2013), at one point in the 1980s, the science writer Natalie Angier went to the MIT lab where Bargmann worked; Angier later wrote that Bargmann "may well be the brightest student at MIT." In her short autobiography, Bargmann gives significant credit to Weinberg, calling him a "terrific mentor." Aside from his creativity and acumen, Bargmann wrote, Weinberg was a family man, which showed by example that one can be both a great scientist and a good person. "In that respect," Bargmann wrote, "he was a role model . . . for everyone in science."

Bargmann disliked one aspect of her work, however: giving rats and mice deadly cancer tumors. Although mice are frequently used for those kinds of studies, it upset Bargmann to hurt the creatures. "In Weinberg's lab," she told Wade, "I would start to cry every time I had to do anything with a mouse." Bargmann elaborated on the topic to Johnson, saying, "I will defend to my grave the importance of animal studies. You cannot study metastasis"—the spread of disease-producing cells—"in a dish. Nevertheless, I personally found it hard to do."

FOCUS ON *C. ELEGANS*

Bargmann received her PhD from MIT in 1987 and chose to remain at MIT to do her postdoctoral research. Bargmann's profound interest in the biology of behavior—combined with her aversion to experiments on mice—would lead her to the area of research where she would make her greatest mark. She chose to study a tiny worm called *Caenorhabditis elegans*. These nearly invisible creatures feed on rotting vegetation, and Bargmann believed she could study their behavior to gain insight into the behavior of humans. Despite being mute, deaf, and nearly blind, these worms manage to pass on their genes like all creatures do, by eating and reproducing. The advantage of studying such worms was how relatively simple their neurological makeup was compared to that of human beings. Whereas a human has about 10 billion neurons in the brain, the *C. elegans* has only 302. The relatively simple neurological structure of the worm could, and would, lead to a better understanding of the relationship between genes, behavior, and the environment.

In 1986, the year before Bargmann received her PhD from MIT, she saw the publication of the complete wiring diagram of the nervous system of *C. elegans* mapped out by John White. During her postdoctoral research period at MIT, Bargmann worked at Bob Horvitz's lab at the university, where she began mapping sensory neurons and the worms' behavior—as well as how they responded to different environments. Bargmann confirmed that despite various sensory limitations, the tiny worms had senses of smell and taste that allowed them to detect and track chemicals in their environment. As a result of experiments in which she removed sensory neurons one by one using a laser beam, Bargmann created a diagram of what each of the neurons does. Different neurons are responsible for the worm's sensing abilities, while others lead the worm to go into hibernation when there is not enough food or too much competition for resources. About her success, Bargmann told Wade, "Horvitz told me that my great strength as a scientist was that I could think like a worm." Horvitz himself praised her ability to "think like very few other people in a rigorous and creative

way," which has led her to "repeatedly [develop] new kinds of approaches."

UNIVERSITY OF CALIFORNIA, SAN FRANCISCO

In 1991 Bargmann, as an investigator for the Howard Hughes Medical Institute, moved to the West Coast to start her own lab at UCSF. She started out as an assistant professor in the anatomy department. She was promoted to professor in 1998, and the following year Bargmann served as vice chair of the department of anatomy. She would remain at UCSF until 2004.

In her lab at UCSF, Bargmann found that 2,000 genes in *C. elegans* are involved in the sense of smell—twice as many as in a rat, according to Wade. (*C. elegans* has a total of 22,000 genes, nearly as many as a human being.) Because the worm is so limited in its other senses, it uses its sense of smell to move about and react to its environment. Bargmann later determined which odor receptor recognizes which odor, something that had not been done before with such precision. She also studied how the worm's genes affect not only its behavior but also its learning process, which is significant for understanding the worm's behavior and human behavior as well.

"It may seem a quirky choice to study the brains of worms," Bargmann wrote in her short autobiography, "but from a genetic perspective, it was a smarter choice than anyone would have guessed at the time. . . . The genomes of humans and worms share more genes than any of us expected, including most classes of genes that are important in the nervous system. . . . The basic functions of those genes are similar in all animals, so if we view one goal of biology as building a 'dictionary' containing the meaning of each gene, we can assemble definitions in that dictionary from any animal, with a good chance that the definitions and grammar will apply across all animals and humans."

THE BRAIN INITIATIVE

In 2004 Bargmann left UCSF for New York City to join Rockefeller University as head investigator of the Lulu and Anthony Wang Laboratory of Neural Circuits and Behavior. At Rockefeller University, Bargmann is free to focus on her research without also teaching medical students or running a hospital.

In April 2013, President Barack Obama announced that his administration would dedicate $100 million to an initiative called Brain Research through Advancing Innovative Neurotechnologies (BRAIN). The BRAIN initiative would take on the immensely ambitious goal of mapping out the human brain. The project, which was set to involve both government agencies and private institutions, would "require the development of new tools not yet available to neuroscientists and, eventually, perhaps lead to progress in treating diseases like Alzheimer's and epilepsy and traumatic brain injury," John Markoff and James Gorman wrote for the *New York Times* (2 Apr. 2013). As part of the initiative, there would also be studies regarding the ethical implications of new neuroscientific advances.

When Bargmann was asked to help head the BRAIN initiative, she was initially reluctant, according to Johnson. Bargmann explained her reluctance, saying, "It's more pressure, it's very public, and I have been very happy under the radar." She eventually decided to join the initiative, which she believed would be good for her field and for humanity. According to Johnson, making Bargmann cohead of the BRAIN initiative was a wise decision by Frances Collins, the director of the National Institutes of Health. (The other cohead of BRAIN is William Newsome, a neurobiologist at California's Stanford University.) Bargmann's appointment, wrote Johnson, served "to quiet the critics, not just because she's a brilliant scientist but because she also has a reputation for being a stellar person."

AWARDS AND RECOGNITION

Bargmann is a member of the National Academy of Sciences (2003) and the American Academy of Arts and Sciences (2002). Among her many honors, she has received the 2013 Breakthrough Award in Life Sciences, the 2012 Kavli Prize in Neuroscience, the 2012 Dart/NYU Biotechnology Achievement Award, the 2009 Richard Lounsbery Award from the US and French National Academies of Sciences, the 2004 Dargut and Milena Kemali International Prize for Research in Basic and Clinical Neurosciences, the Searle Scholar Award (1992–95), and the Lucille P. Markey Award (1990–95).

Bargmann has been a member of the editorial boards of such scientific journals as *Cell, Neuron, Genes and Development*, and *Current Biology*. From 2011 to 2013, Bargmann appeared three times on *Charlie Rose* on PBS, along with other scientists, to discuss her research and the human brain.

PERSONAL LIFE

Bargmann's first marriage ended in divorce. In 2007 she wed her second husband, the Nobel Prize–winning Columbia University neuroscientist Richard Axel, in Paris. Bargmann and Axel live in New York City, where they frequently attend the opera and ballet performances and dine out nearly every night, usually quite late in the evening.

SUGGESTED READING

Johnson, Rebecca. "New Frontier." *Vogue* Oct. 2013: 178+. Print.

Marino, Melissa. "Biography of Cornelia I. Bargmann." *PNAS Online*. National Academy of Sciences, 1 Mar. 2005. Web. 14 Mar. 2014.

Markoff, John, and James Gorman. "Obama to Unveil Initiative to Map the Human Brain." *New York Times*. New York Times, 2 Apr. 2013. Web. 14 Mar. 2014.

Wade, Nicholas. "In Tiny Worm, Unlocking Secrets of the Brain." *New York Times*. New York Times, 20 June 2011. Web. 13 Mar. 2014.

—*Dmitry Kiper*

Paolo Basso

Born: October 31, 1966
Occupation: Sommelier

While it can be intimidating for an average person to order wine in a fine restaurant, a good sommelier, or wine steward, can help. Paolo Basso is not merely a good sommelier, however; in 2013 the Italian-born Swiss wine expert was named the best sommelier in the world at a renowned triennial contest sponsored by the Association de la Sommellerie Internationale (ASI).

"To be the best sommelier in the world you must be able to do several things, and to do them swiftly and perfectly," Jason McBride wrote of the contest, sometimes referred to as the Sommelier Olympics, for the Canadian newsmagazine *Maclean's* (15 Mar. 2013). "You must not only be able to blindly identify thousands of different kinds of wine, you must comprehensively describe their flavor profiles, pinpoint where and when the grapes were grown, and state the most appropriate foods with which to pair them. . . . Your knowledge of every other kind of spirit, from absinthe to vodka, and even nonalcoholic

Yoshikazu Tsuno/AFP/Getty Images

beverages like tea and mineral water, will be similarly tested." Describing the intense pressure of the competition's dining service simulation, he continued, "A single spilled drop, or the incorrect fold of a napkin, may cost you points. And you must do it all with an audience of five thousand watching." The segments of the competition are timed, and each entrant must compete in a language other than his or her mother tongue.

Basso's duties have gone far beyond providing individual guidance to restaurant patrons. Over the course of his career, he has also managed the million-bottle cellars of large distributors, served as a judge on wine-tasting panels, and run an eponymous consultancy.

EARLY YEARS AND EDUCATION

Paolo Basso was born on October 31, 1966, in the countryside of Besnate, located in the Lombardy region of northern Italy. He lived in close proximity to several beautiful lakes and mountains, "but no vineyards," as he told *Current Biography*. He was not far from Piedmont, the area bordering Switzerland and France that is known for its stellar appellations (a geographical designation with which a winegrower is legally authorized to identify and market wine), including Gattinara, Boca, and Lessona.

Basso, who has described his childhood as idyllic, explained to *Current Biography* that although no one in his immediate family was involved in the food or beverage industries, his grandfather maintained a well-stocked wine cellar. "It was a place full of charm, with all those bottles resting in the cool and dark," he recalled. "It was a fascinating place for a child not authorized to explore it without the accompaniment of an adult."

Basso, who has one sister nine years his senior, was always a studious person. He has said that this is an absolute prerequisite for becoming a sommelier and entering international competitions because the training is so arduous. "Of course," he admitted to *Current Biography*, "it is easier if you are voluntarily studying a topic you like."

While in secondary school, Basso studied French with a teacher who conducted a cooking class for the student in order to introduce them to French cuisine. Intrigued, he decided to study hotel management. He attended a school in the historic and picturesque Italian municipality of Sondalo. The program was an especially rigorous one that demanded great discipline, "so much so that when I later joined the army, I seemed to be on vacation," Basso quipped to *Current Biography*.

Part of the school's curriculum involved learning about wine, and Basso found that an area of particular fascination. He subsequently entered the well-regarded school affiliated with the ASI in Switzerland.

WHAT A SOMMELIER DOES

The word *sommelier* derives from the Middle French word for a royal court official in charge of the transportation of supplies and later evolved to mean the member of court responsible for stocking and maintaining the monarch's store of wine, beer, and spirits, as well as serving the appropriate beverages with the royal meals. Modern restaurants (as public places where food and drink are ordered from a menu) originated in France, at around the time of the French Revolution, and restaurateurs soon adopted the royal practice of employing sommeliers.

Sommeliers are still generally found in the finest and most upscale restaurants. Their duties include explaining the wine list to those who are interested, making suggestions based on their own vast knowledge of the available wines (which they themselves have curated for the restaurant in many cases), and helping diners match their chosen meals with an appropriate beverage. Basso explained to Ellen Wallace for *Geneva Lunch* (2 June 2013) that patrons are well advised to "leave it to the sommelier. Introduce yourselves. Then put a little pressure on him. Tell him you trust him, you have confidence in him because you know he's passionate about wine and knows a lot about it." For those who might be reluctant to discuss price lest they appear overly frugal, he added, "Don't be afraid to do that. Buying wine is like buying any other product or service. It's like asking for an estimate." Similarly, he cautioned Wallace that a diner should not be afraid to introduce personal preference into the equation. "Do you like classic wines or big fat reds?" Wallace wrote. "Do you want to try something completely new? Tell the sommelier; it will help him select something suitable for you."

The stereotype associated with the sommelier is that of a pretentious, aloof older man who does little to disguise his disdain for the uninformed diners seeking his guidance. While still a familiar trope in films and books, that caricature is rapidly disappearing in real life, as women and a broader cross-section of men enter the profession. At first glance, Basso might mistakenly be thought to fit that old image: he is multilingual and cuts an elegant figure in a tuxedo. His manner, however, is anything but haughty. "Basso has a ready smile and confident manner," Wallace wrote. "Despite the [best-sommelier] title he is not intimidating: he comes across as friendly, down to Earth, sophisticated yet approachable."

Basso has also pointed out that today's sommeliers have a wide variety of options when choosing a professional path—as his own wide-ranging career shows—with restaurant service being just one of them.

EARLY CAREER

Upon graduating from his ASI sommelier program, Basso began working in a gourmet French restaurant in Switzerland. Like most novices, he initially found the high-pressure and fast-paced atmosphere difficult to contend with. Within a few months, however, he had proven his mettle and felt comfortable in the fast-paced environment.

In 1998 Basso began an affiliation with Conca Bella, a restaurant attached to a small family-run hotel in Vacallo, Switzerland. Opened in 1984 by Rocco and Ruth Montereale, the restaurant, not far from Lake Como, boasts a wine cellar with a reported 9,000 bottles on display, representing 1,250 different labels. Although no longer its sommelier, Basso now serves as Conca Bella's wine director and holds several tasting events each year at the atmospheric location. He recalled to *Current Biography*, "When the owner hired me, he said, 'Your goal is to put on the wine list all the best new wines. You have no limits.' It was a great experience."

From 1999 to 2005 Basso lent his expertise to Cantine e Distillerie Badaracco, a Swiss-based distributor of Bordeaux wines that had been founded in 1879 and whose cellars in Melano are said to hold more than a million bottles. He then remained in Melano, which is situated in the Swiss canton of Ticino, to serve until 2006 as a director at the well-regarded Swiss company ARVI, one of the largest traders of fine and rare wines in the world. (ARVI also fills a valuable niche by allowing clients to store their own wine collections in the company's carefully monitored cellar.) "I have had the opportunity to taste most of the legendary wines in the world as a result of my work," Basso told *Current Biography*.

THE WINE CONSULTANT

In 2006 Basso took on the title of chief sommelier consultant at the Swissôtel Métropole, a five-star luxury hotel in the heart of Geneva, and he has retained that affiliation in addition to his other duties. The following year he also began an ongoing relationship with Ceresio Vini (Ceresio Wines), a Lugano-based enterprise that recommends and sells a carefully chosen selection of vintages for serious wine connoisseurs. Since 2010 he has been the director of that company, which is now called Paolo Basso Wines.

Basso has said that there is no such thing as a typical day for him. "I might spend an entire day tasting, as a consultant for making blends, to discover new wines, or to prepare an opinion for a wine guide or magazine," he explained to *Current Biography*. "Other times I will be planning a wine matching for a dinner or compiling a wine list for one of my customers. Sometime, I could be traveling to visit a certain wine region or to teach a course. There is certainly no time to be bored."

Asked if there is any advice he could give to aspiring sommeliers hoping to follow in his footsteps, he said simply, "You must have a love of nature and geography, and you must be prepared to study continually."

COMPETITIONS

Preparing for ASI sommelier competitions takes an enormous amount of study and preparation, and when speaking to journalists, Basso frequently credits his family for allowing him the time and freedom to do so. In 1997 he was named the best sommelier in Switzerland, and in 2000, he came in at second place in the worldwide competition, behind Olivier Poussier of France. Basso racked up additional second-place finishes in 2007 (behind Sweden's Andreas Larsson) and 2010 (behind Gérard Basset, a French native who was representing his adopted England that year).

He fared better in 2010 at the European-wide contest, coming in first. Thirty-five sommeliers vied for the title of best sommelier in Europe that year, including semifinalists Andreas Jechmayr of Austria, David Biraud of France, Matteo Ghiringhelli of Italy, Merete Bo of Norway, Julia Gosea of Romania, Matthieu Longuère of the United Kingdom, and Arvid Rosengren of Sweden. The highly demanding competition required the entrants to serve a jeroboam (four-quart bottle) of champagne properly, decant a magnum of Alsatian pinot noir, blind taste and identify several wines, correct a written wine list, and demonstrate excellence in their attitude and foreign-language skills.

Basso, who had competed in the European competition in 2004, 2006, and 2008, only to finish in second place each time, told the assembled journalists, "Finally, I win the title, and you are asking me how I feel? I am just happy, it is as simple as that! I have been preparing for these international competitions for years. . . . Years of hard work and sacrifices. . . You know, I think that the level [of competition] is higher and higher [each year] and it is even tougher to succeed!"

In 2013 Basso accomplished one of the crowning achievements of his career, when he triumphed at the worldwide contest, held that year in Tokyo. In front of a cheering crowd of almost four thousand spectators, he was awarded a cherrywood corkscrew, a gold medal, and a massive silver trophy in the shape of a jeroboam of Moët & Chandon. The results were announced by ASI president Shinya Tasaki, who was joined onstage by every best-sommelier laureate from 1969 to 2010.

PERSONAL LIFE

Basso told *Current Biography* that his wife, Elena, is "not interested in wine as much as I am. She does drink good wine with pleasure though."

He has said that the best, most memorable bottle of wine that he has ever had the pleasure of opening was the one served at their wedding: an eighteen-liter bottle of Isole e Olena Chianti Classico.

The couple have a daughter, Chiara, who was eight years old at the time Basso won the world title. "Of course she was very proud of me," Basso told *Current Biography*. Asked if she might also want to become a sommelier one day, given the increasing number of women entering the profession, Basso said that while Chiara very much enjoys elegant restaurants and hotels and is now a seasoned traveler, she has no professional aspirations as yet. "She does show signs of having a great nose," Basso said, using a term that implies the ability to judge a wine by its aroma. "Surprisingly, most children do."

SUGGESTED READING

Basso, Paolo. "An Exclusive Interview with the World's Best Sommelier." Interview by Alain Wursching. *Karaf Magazine* May 2013: 56–59. Digital file.

Basso, Paolo. "The Sommelier Tastes, the Customers Drink." Interview by Chandra Kurt. *Swiss Universe* Dec. 2013: 108–11. Digital file.

McBride, Jason. "Why the Sommelier Olympics Is Serious Business." *Maclean's*. Rogers Media, 15 Mar. 2013. Web. 10 Apr. 2014.

Miller, Rupert. "Paolo Basso Named World's Best Sommelier." *Drinks Business*. Union Press, 3 Apr. 2013. Web. 10 Apr. 2014.

Stimpfig, John. "Paolo Basso Crowned World's Best Sommelier." *Decanter.com*. Decanter, 2 Apr. 2013. Web. 10 Apr. 2014.

Wallace, Ellen. "Tips on Leaning on the Sommelier, from the World's Best One." *GenevaLunch.com*. Geneva Lunch, 2 June 2013. Web. 10 Apr. 2014.

—*Mari Rich*

Joy Bauer

Born: November 6, 1963
Occupation: Author, dietician, television personality

Joy Bauer is the resident nutrition and health expert on NBC television's *Today* show, where she also hosts the program's "Joy Fit Club" series. Every week, Bauer spotlights the newest member of the club who has lost one hundred pounds or more through diet and exercise alone. From 2011 to 2012, she cohosted with Broadway and television actress Florence Henderson a half-hour program called *Good Food, Good Deeds*. The program was produced in partnership with

Peter Kramer/NBC/NBC NewsWire via Getty Images

the Meals on Wheels Association of America. In June 2014, Bauer was the host of the PBS special *Joy Bauer's Food Remedies*.

Bauer has authored over eleven books including *Slim and Scrumptious: More Than 75 Delicious, Healthy Meals Your Family Will Love* (2010); *Joy Bauer's Food Cures: Eat Right to Get Healthier, Look Younger, and Add Years to Your Life* (2011); and *The Joy Fit Club: Cookbook, Diet Plan & Inspiration* (2012). She is also a monthly columnist for *Women's Day* magazine and a regular contributor to *Parade* magazine and *USA Today*. In 2014, Bauer launched her own subscription-based food line called Nourish Snacks. "My whole mission is to help people feel comfortable in their skin," Bauer told Danielle Cantor for *Jewish Woman* magazine (2010). "Obviously, I want people to be healthy, but I want them to focus on being fit and healthy [rather] than feel pressured to be skinny."

Growing up, Bauer was an aspiring gymnast who hoped to own her own gym and train elite athletes. After serious foot injuries derailed her dream, she became interested in medicine and then nutrition and entered the graduate nutritional program at New York University.

In 1993, Bauer left her job as the director of a successful nutrition program at Mount Sinai Hospital to open a private practice as a nutrition consultant. She began in her two-bedroom New York apartment, but by 2010, she had opened the Joy Bauer Nutrition Center in Manhattan and Westchester, New York, which is one of the largest nutrition centers in the country. Bauer is also the nutritionist for the New York City Ballet and the American Ballet Theatre, and teaches at Columbia University. She received the 2010 National Media Excellence Award from the Academy of Nutrition and Dietetics and the 2012 Science Media Award from the American Society of Nutrition.

EARLY LIFE AND EDUCATION

Bauer was born Joy Schloss on November 6, 1963, in Brooklyn, New York, and grew up as part of a close-knit Jewish family in the nearby suburb of Tappan, New York. Bauer's parents, Artie and Ellen, both came from kosher households, but with four children of their own to raise (Bauer has two brothers, Dan and Glen, and a sister, Debra), the childhood eating habits of Bauer and her siblings were less strict. "I grew up in a family that loves to eat, loves to cook," Bauer told Cantor. Bauer fondly remembers her grandmother's matzo ball soup, stuffed cabbage, chicken noodle soup, and cheese pancakes. "My grandmother was all about food and feeding us and her secret recipes," she told Cantor. (Bauer uses her grandmother's matzo recipe today, though she has made a few healthful adjustments.)

As a child, Bauer played softball and basketball, and when she was in junior high, she developed a passion for gymnastics. By the seventh grade, she was spending five hours a day at the gym. A serious athlete from a young age, she thought a lot about how food affected her body and performance. She didn't know anything about nutrition, but she loved experimenting with different recipes that she concocted herself. As she explained to Dianne Patterson for *Prime Women*, "[I enjoyed] trying to figure out how foods made me feel. . . . I was much more interested in broccoli than Barbies!" By the time she was in high school, she had branched out to foreign cuisine and was making exotic meals for her family to enjoy.

Bauer had dreams to own her own gym and train elite athletes, and after earning a gymnastics scholarship to James Madison University in Virginia, she seemed well on her way. But her athletic career abruptly ended after she sustained serious injuries to her feet during her freshman year. Years of hard landings had taken their toll. Bauer underwent several reconstructive surgeries on both of her feet and was eventually told by doctors that she would be unable to compete again in gymnastics. Bauer decided to change her focus to science and considered becoming a pediatrician. She transferred to the School of Public Health at the University of Maryland where she majored in kinesiology, which is the study of human movement. She received her bachelor's degree in 1986. After graduation Bauer decided to wait to take the

MCATs, the standardized test required for entry to medical school, and instead entered the master's program in nutrition at New York University (NYU). "From the very first class, it was a revelation to me," Bauer told Patterson. She decided to forgo her original plan to study pediatrics and concentrate on nutrition instead. She explained to Robin Carol of the *Tufts Daily*, "With my first class, the light bulb went off and I [realized] . . . I have a passion for health, I love working with people, I care about the way I look, and I love to eat! You put all those things together and I was supposed to be in the field of nutrition." Bauer graduated with a master's degree in nutrition from NYU in 1989.

EARLY CAREER

During graduate school, Bauer worked as a personal trainer and exercise instructor at several upscale health clubs in New York City. After graduation she became a clinical worker at Mount Sinai Hospital where she was quickly promoted. "My very first job was a dream job," Bauer told Patterson, referring to her position as the Director of Nutrition and Fitness for Heart Smart Kids, a program she helped develop for underprivileged children at the hospital's department of pediatric cardiology. In this position, Bauer visited area schools where she taught students in kindergarten through twelfth grade. Working with children and their parents, she was pleased to see that she could affect change in other people's lives.

Bauer also worked as a clinical nutritionist with Mount Sinai's neurosurgical team and volunteered with the American Heart Association. It was in that capacity that Bauer began writing articles about nutrition for various magazines, which led a number of doctors to refer their patients to Bauer as a nutritional counselor. Since she didn't have an office at the time, she met with clients in her home, in her second bedroom, or in her living room. She soon decided to rent an office space that she shared with a psychologist two days a week, but her practice blossomed, and eventually she left her position at Mount Sinai in order to accommodate her growing list of clientele. Bauer's practice now includes the Joy Bauer Nutritional Center, which has locations in Manhattan and Westchester, New York. The center employs its own doctors and registered dieticians who work with clients hoping to lose weight and clients with health problems such as cardiovascular disease, kidney disease, eating disorders, Crohn's disease, and cancer. Bauer told Judith Lerner for the *Berkshire Eagle* (28 Dec. 2011) that she has learned a lot about her job along the way. She used to pass out lists detailing what to eat and what to buy based exactly on what she had learned in school, but "I've since learned that taste matters," she said. "Taste matters most."

TODAY AND THE "JOY FIT CLUB"

In 1996, Bauer landed a deal—"which I was so, so excited about," she recalled to Cantor—to write a book called *The Complete Idiot's Guide to Total Nutrition*. After the first edition of the book was published in 1999, Bauer began getting calls from television producers at daytime talk shows like *The View* and *Regis & Kelly*. Bauer was the resident nutrition expert on *The View* for two years before she received a call from NBC's *Today*. Bauer was a big fan of the long-running program, and when *Today* producers offered to bring her on the show for a segment, she jumped at the chance. "The first segment I ever did with Katie Couric was out on the plaza; she came from Studio 1A and came out to meet me where I had all my props," she told Cantor. "I was so, so excited when she came that I practically lunged at her." Bauer became a regular on the show, discussing everything from healthy recipes to the latest in exercise gadgetry. In 2008, she launched a biweekly segment called "The Joy Fit Club," in which she challenged viewers to lose weight by leading healthier lives rather than using diet pills, fad diets, fasting, or undergoing weight-loss surgery. Every other week, Bauer inducts a new member into the club who has lost one hundred or more pounds through diet and exercise alone. Bauer told Carin Lane of the Albany *Times Union* (22 May 2012) that she chose one hundred pounds as a threshold because it was inspirational milestone. "If these individuals can accomplish such a significant transformation, it's possible for anyone to follow in their footsteps," she said and recalled one member of the club who came back from a suicide attempt to walk off more than four hundred pounds. The segment was so popular with audiences that in 2012 Bauer published a book called *The Joy Fit Club: Cookbook, Diet Plan & Inspiration*. As the title suggests, the book compiles success stories, recipes, and a full weight-loss plan for dieters looking to lose as little as ten pounds or one hundred or more.

OTHER BOOKS AND PROJECTS

In 2009, Bauer published a book called *Joy's LIFE Diet: Four Steps to Thin Forever*. The book became a bestseller and was subsequently republished as *Your Inner Skinny: Four Steps to Thin Forever* (2010). The "LIFE" acronym in the original title stands for Look Incredible, Feel Extraordinary. Bauer claimed that her diet was not just about losing weight; it was about living better. Suzanne Farrell for the Academy of Nutrition and Dietetics (2009) recommended Bauer's LIFE diet saying that "[dieters] could be successful with this plan as long as you follow it as directed and commit to the plan. " *Your Inner Skinny* is one of Bauer's most popular books, as is *Joy Bauer's Food Cures: Eat Right to Get Healthier, Look Younger, and Add Years to Your Life* (2011). *Food Cures* addresses weight loss, but it is a more comprehensive look at overall health and wellness than Bauer's more diet-oriented books because Bauer discusses how food affects not only specific health concerns such as irritable bowel syndrome (IBS) or celiac disease but also more common issues such as quality of one's vision, skin, and memory health.

In 2014 Bauer launched a subscription-based snack food company called Nourish Snacks that delivers to customers portable snacks, none of which need refrigeration. Each box contains five snacks that are all rich in fiber and protein and contain less than two hundred calories. When first launched, the company offered dark chocolate chia-oat clusters, cinnamon-spiced crispy chickpeas, and chewy dried bananas and walnuts. Bauer also has her own brand of nutrition bars that are called Joy Bauer Bars. Each bar is all natural, low calorie, and high in fiber and protein.

PERSONAL LIFE

Bauer is married to Ian Bauer. The couple has three children: daughters Jesse and Ayden Jane, and a son, Cole. The Bauers are an active family and enjoy hiking, biking, skiing, and swimming. They are also very musical. Bauer herself is an accomplished pianist, though she had to stop taking lessons when her life became too hectic. Bauer is also very close with her siblings, telling Cantor, "We're all best friends with each other's spouses, too." The extended family enjoys visiting Bauer's parents' home in the Berkshires nearly every weekend. They dubbed the house, which her parents bought in the early 2000s, Castlebridge because the family name Schloss means "castle" in German. Bauer and her family live in Westchester, New York.

SUGGESTED READING

Cantor, Danielle. "Discovering Our Path to Healthy Living, With a Little Help from Joy." *Jewish Woman Magazine*. Jewish Women International, 2010. Web. 15 Sept. 2014.

Carol, Robin. "Nutrition Expert and 'Today Show' Personality Gives Advice at Tufts." *Tufts Daily*. Tufts Daily, 8 Mar. 2010. Web. 17 Sept. 2014.

Farrell, Suzanne. "Book Review: *Joy's LIFE Diet: Four Steps to Thin Forever*." *Eat Right*. Acad. of Nutrition and Dietetics, 2009. Web. 15 Sept. 2014.

Lane, Carin. "Book Review: '*The Joy Fit Club: Cookbook, Diet Plan & Inspiration*.'" *Times Union*. Hearst, 22 May 2012. Web. 15 Sept. 2014.

Lerner, Judith. "TV Celebrity Joy Bauer Joins Family for New Year in Stockbridge." *Berkshire Eagle*. Berkshire Eagle, 28 Dec. 2011. Web. 15 Sept. 2014.

Pace, Gina. "Eats Beat: 'Today Show' Nutrition Expert Joy Bauer Debuts Snack Subscription Service." *Daily News.* NY Daily News, 16 May 2014. Web. 15 Sept. 2014.

Patterson, Dianne H. "Interview with Joy Bauer, R.D. of NBC's *Today* Show and PBS's *Joy Bauer's Food Remedies*." *Prime Women.* Women in Their Prime, 20 June 2014. Web. 17 Sept. 2014.

SELECTED WORKS

The Complete Idiot's Guide to Total Nutrition, 2005; *Your Inner Skinny: Four Steps to Think Forever*, 2010; *Slim and Scrumptious: More Than 75 Delicious, Healthy Meals Your Family Will Love*, 2010; *Joy Bauer's Food Cures: Eat Right to Get Healthier, Look Younger, and Add Years to Your Life*, 2011; *The Joy Fit Club: Cookbook, Diet Plan & Inspiration*, 2012

—Molly Hagan

John Walker/MCT/Landov

Rick Bayless

Born: November 23, 1953
Occupation: Chef, television personality

Rick Bayless is an award-winning professional chef, cookbook author, and television personality who is best known for his meticulous study of authentic Mexican cuisine. Bayless was a doctoral student in anthropological linguistics when he and his wife embarked on the six-year tour of Mexico that inspired his classic 1987 book *Authentic Mexican: Regional Cooking from the Heart of Mexico*. That same year, the couple opened the Frontera Grill, a contemporary Mexican restaurant, in Chicago. When most Americans associated Mexican food with more prevalent Tex-Mex and Southwestern dishes, Bayless made a serious effort to educate home cooks in the art of authentic and accessible Mexican cuisine. "I'm not a museum cook," he told Todd S. Purdum for the *New York Times* (3 May 1995). "The only way to have a truly authentic Mexican meal is to be in Mexico, cooking with Mexican ingredients and have it eaten by Mexicans. I'm mostly looking for what is the soul of a dish." Bayless culled the recipes he included in *Authentic Mexican* from a number of Mexican home chefs and grouped the recipes according to the predominant regional flavors of each dish.

EARLY LIFE AND EDUCATION

Rick Bayless was born on November 23, 1953. His older brother, John "Skip" Bayless, is a popular sports commentator on ESPN, and his sister is a special education teacher in Oklahoma. His great-uncles owned Jones Brothers grocery stores, and his grandfather ran a drive-in restaurant in the 1950s. Bayless's parents, John and Levita Bayless, owned a restaurant called Hickory House in Oklahoma City. Although Hickory House closed in 1986, Bayless began working in the restaurant at the age of seven. "I loved it. I hung out there. . . . I did dishes, worked on the prep line, bused tables—whatever," he told Michael W. Sasser for the online magazine *Distinctly Oklahoma* (1 July 2009).

Inspired by the restaurant and his family's love of growing food, Bayless became fascinated by cooking and the "emotional experience" of a good meal, he told Marcia Froelke Coburn for *Chicago Magazine* (27 Feb. 2012). As a kid, he saved up his money and took a bus across town to eat at an upscale French restaurant. When he graduated from grade school, his parents gave him a copy of Julia Child's classic cookbook *Mastering the Art of French Cooking*. Every evening one summer, Bayless cooked a complete meal from its pages for his family.

Bayless attended Northwest Classen High School where he studied Spanish. He took his first trip to Mexico with his family when he was fourteen. Bayless studied Spanish and Latin American culture at the University of Oklahoma and graduated at the age of twenty. He then pursued a graduate degree in anthropological linguistics at the University of Michigan (U of M), where he met his future wife, Deann Groen. He opened his own catering business in Ann Arbor to make extra money and earned his master's degree in 1975. Bayless and Groen moved to Mexico so that Bayless, who was pursuing a PhD, could work on his dissertation, but after their arrival, he had a revelation: "I loved the language, the culture, and the way they interacted; the way that languages revealed culture," Bayless told Sasser. "However, what I loved and was most fascinated with was the way that culture was reflected in food."

Bayless stopped working on his PhD, and the couple moved to Cleveland, Ohio, where Bayless became the executive chef at a Southwestern/Mexican restaurant called Lopez. He also worked as a cooking instructor. In 1978, he won an audition to host twenty-six episodes of a television series for the PBS affiliate WBGU in Ohio called *Cooking Mexican*. The show's success inspired Bayless to return to Mexico and study the cuisine.

AUTHENTIC MEXICAN

Bayless moved to Mexico in 1980 and used the research methods he learned from his work in anthropology while he travelled the country sampling the food of each region. He prepared each dish and tested each recipe with three different cooks or families in order "to grasp every nuance, every approach, every ingredient," Evan Hansen for *LSA Magazine* (Spring 2012) wrote. Bayless wrote the first draft of his cookbook *Authentic Mexican: Regional Cooking from the Heart of Mexico* over the course of six years, and in 1986, he and his wife moved to Chicago with dreams of opening a restaurant. Within six months of securing a space, they opened Frontera Grill, and their first copy of *Authentic Mexican* arrived the same day.

Frontera Grill was billed as a contemporary Mexican eatery featuring cuisine from central and southern Mexico. Much like Bayless's book, it was an overnight success. Craig Claiborne, the late legendary food critic of the *New York Times* gave *Authentic Mexican* glowing praise. Bayless and his wife were grateful for the response, and in 2009 Bayless told Sasser, "Thankfully, we've had a line outside that door for twenty-two years."

In 1989, Bayless and his wife opened Topolobampo next door to the Frontera Grill, describing it as "Frontera's dressier sister." Topolobampo is known for its Mexican seafood specialties, raw bar, and award-winning wine selection. It has twice been nominated as one of the country's most outstanding restaurants by the James Beard Foundation.

Bayless's most recent restaurant venture, Xoco, which is pronounced "SHOW-coh" and means "little sister" in Aztec, opened in Chicago in 2009. Xoco is a no-frills cafe where patrons order their food and pay before taking a seat. The soups, sandwiches, and desserts are variations on Mexican street food. It was a particularly risky venture for Bayless who hadn't opened a new restaurant in twenty years and was enjoying new-found mainstream recognition, but the risk has paid off and has yielded both satisfied customers and positive reviews. All three restaurants are located on the same city block.

MORE COOKBOOKS, AWARDS, AND RECOGNITION

Bayless's second cookbook, *Rick Bayless's Mexican Kitchen: Capturing the Vibrant Flavors of a World-Class Cuisine* (1996), won the International Association of Culinary Professionals (IACP) National Julia Child Cookbook of the Year Award. His fourth book, *Rick Bayless Mexico One Plate at a Time*, which was published in 2000 and is a companion to his television show, was recognized as the best international cookbook by the James Beard Foundation in 2001. The book contrasts classic and contemporary Mexican dishes. His other books include *Salsas That Cook: Using Classic Salsas to Enliven Our Favorite Dishes* (1998), and *Rick and Lanie's Excellent Kitchen Adventures: Chef-Dad, Teenage Daughter, Recipes and Stories* (2004), published with his then fourteen-year-old daughter, Lanie Bayless. Bayless has also written and published several cookbooks with his wife Deann Groen Bayless.

Bayless has won numerous industry awards, including several prestigious James Beard awards such as best American chef in 1991, national chef of the year in 1995, and the James Beard Foundation's humanitarian of the year award in 1998. In 2007, Bayless's Frontera Grill earned the James Beard award for outstanding restaurant. Additionally, *Food & Wine* magazine dubbed him the best new chef of 1988, and *Bon Appétit* magazine named him cooking teacher of the year in 2002. In 2010, the White House asked Bayless to prepare the meal for a presidential dinner honoring Mexico's then president Felipe Calderón. According to Jenn Scott for the *Oklahoma Gazette* (23 Jan. 2013), Calderón told Bayless that his black mole, a spicy sauce, was one of the best he had ever eaten.

Bayless is no stranger to professional kitchen life. "I am fourth generation restaurant people," he told Edward Lewine for the *New York Times* (17 Feb. 2008). An essay he wrote about his parents' popular Oklahoma City eatery Hickory House was first published in *Saveur* magazine and was later anthologized in *Best Food Writing 2005*.

In 2012, Bayless appeared in a play called *Cascabel* at Lookingglass Theatre Company in Chicago. In a fine-dining interpretation of traditional dinner theater, audience members paid between $200 and $250 for a three-course meal and a play. Bayless prepared the food onstage in front of the audience.

CHARITY WORK AND TELEVISION APPEARANCES

In 1996, Bayless teamed up with Kraft Foods to create the Frontera Foods brand, a purveyor of gourmet Mexican food products including salsas and marinades. His charity, the Frontera Farmer Foundation, provides grants to small-scale sustainable farms in the Chicago area.

Bayless's PBS show *Mexico: One Plate at a Time* premiered in 2000, and his interest in presenting food and recipes from an anthropological viewpoint set him apart from other professional chefs: Bayless takes time during each episode to discuss and explain Mexico's history and culture. The show is part cooking tutorial and part travelogue as Bayless and his small crew travel between cities in Mexico and Chicago. The cooking portions of the show are shot at Bayless's Chicago home with one camera following him around the kitchen. "I was very much looking to get away from the format of the camera being on the other side of the counter," Bayless told Kristin Eddy for the *Chicago Tribune* (17 May 2000). "It creates a distance and a barrier. I wanted the sense that you were in my kitchen standing beside me when I cook the dish." The show aims to teach viewers to cook authentic Mexican cuisine using U.S. appliances and ingredients available in local grocery stores. Bayless was nominated for a 2012 Daytime Emmy Award for outstanding culinary host.

In 2009, Bayless appeared on the first season of Bravo's *Top Chef Masters*, which pits world-renowned chefs against one another to win challenges and earn money for charity. Bayless outperformed more than twenty-four contestants over the course of ten episodes and won the finale, in part, with a dish featuring his signature Oaxacan black mole. He was awarded $100,000 for his charity, the Frontera Farmer Foundation.

In 2003, Bayless appeared in a promotional TV ad for Burger King's new chicken sandwich, which drew criticism from food connoisseurs. As Bayless explained to Marcia Froelke Coburn for *Chicago Magazine*, Burger King was using natural and seasonal flavors in this new sandwich, which he believed "was a step in the right direction and deserved some recognition." Bayless donated his $300,000 fee to charity.

PERSONAL LIFE
Bayless and his wife have a daughter named Lanie and live in a converted tavern in the Bucktown neighborhood of Chicago. In addition to filming episodes of his television show at his home, Bayless grows about $25,000 worth of produce in his backyard for his restaurants. Bayless told Levine that although he cooks for pleasure, he never cooks Mexican food at home.

SUGGESTED READING
Eddy, Kristin. "Bringing Mexico Home: Chef Rick Bayless Introduces Classic South-of-the-Border Cuisine to TV on 'One Plate at a Time.'" *Chicago Tribune A&E*. Tribune Company, 17 May 2000. Web. 6 Aug. 2013.

Lewine, Edward. "Midwest Mex." *New York Times Magazine*. New York Times Co., 17 Feb. 2008. Web. 6 Aug. 2013.
Purdum, Todd S. "Cooking in Mexico with a Master Chef." *New York Times*. New York Times Co., 3 May 1995. Web. 6 Aug. 2013.
Scott, Jenn. "Born in OKC, Celebrity Chef Rick Bayless Reflects on his Long and Luscious Career." *Oklahoma Gazette*. Gazette Media, 23 Jan. 2013. Web. 6 Aug. 2013.

SELECTED WORKS
Authentic Mexican: Regional Cooking from the Heart of Mexico, 1987; *Rick Bayless's Mexican Kitchen: Capturing the Vibrant Flavors of a World-Class Cuisine*, 1996; *Mexican Everyday* (with Deann Groen Bayless), 2005; *Fiesta at Rick's: Fabulous Food for Great Times with Friends* (with Deann Groen Bayless), 2010; *Frontera: Margaritas, Guacamoles, and Snacks* (with Deann Groen Bayless), 2012

—Molly Hagan

Tzeporah Berman
Born: February 5, 1969
Occupation: Ecoactivist

Tzeporah Berman is a Canadian environmental activist and author. Her commitment to the environment has led her on a two-decade journey from a radical protestor blockading Vancouver Island's Clayoquot Sound to a savvy executive who works with corporations to stem the tide of man-made climate change. "Berman represents the rapid evolution—and increasing split—under way in the environmental movement both here and abroad," James Glave wrote for *Vancouver Magazine* (1 Nov. 2009). As a leader of the Clayoquot Sound protest in 1993—the largest act of civil disobedience in Canadian history—and then as the founder of a San Francisco–based nonprofit called ForestEthics, Berman focused on reforming the logging industry and protecting endangered forests. But a trip to the United Nations Climate Change Conference in Bali, Indonesia, in 2007 inspired her to make a drastic change. "I came home embarrassed, and outraged, and scared," Berman told Glave. "I decided to change my entire work and everything I do."

In 2008, mere weeks before the global market crash, Berman launched a new initiative called PowerUp Canada, which lobbies lawmakers and citizens to change destructive policies that contribute to the changing climate. Not all of Berman's followers supported her broader vision; some of the projects she was suggesting

© Mario Anzuoni/Reuters/Corbis

in the name of energy efficiency would have a negative impact on the very rivers and valleys she had worked so long to protect. But for Berman, who has pointed to one estimate for a looming tipping point for the world's climate in 2020, the implications of climate change are too urgent to ignore. "Wars have been lost," Berman told Glave, "because the generals were still fighting the last war."

In 2010, Berman was appointed by Greenpeace International to co-direct its major climate and energy campaign. She accepted the position despite a nasty campaign against her, and moved her family to Copenhagen, Denmark, only to step down in the spring of 2012 and move back to Vancouver. In 2011, she published her first book, written with Mark Leiren-Young, called *This Crazy Time: Living Our Environmental Challenge*.

EARLY LIFE AND EDUCATION

Susanne Faye Tzeporah Berman was born to a middle-class Jewish family in London, Ontario, on February 5, 1969. She has two older sisters, Corinne and Wendy, and a younger brother named Steven. Both of her parents ran small businesses. She enjoyed an average Canadian childhood—the family volunteered at synagogue and spent summers with Berman's mother's family in Lake of the Woods—but all of that changed when Berman was fourteen. That year, her father died during a heart-bypass operation, and less than two years later, Berman's mother died of cancer. Berman's oldest sister, Wendy,

was twenty and managed to hold the family together until she turned twenty-one and assumed legal guardianship of her siblings. The foursome survived on their parents' life insurance policies, part-time jobs, and the sale of nearly all of their parents' assets. "I think that's where the part of my talent as an organizer came from," Berman told Glave. "We used to have family meetings every Friday night. We'd decide what to spend money on, and who'd do what. We ran our household as a council."

After high school, Berman moved to Toronto to study fashion design at Ryerson University's prestigious arts design program. She began to go by her Hebrew name—Tzeporah—which means "bird." She excelled in the competitive program and garnered praise from Canadian retailer Harry Rosen. But a freshman-year trip to Europe, where she hiked through a German forest destroyed by acid rain, made Berman reconsider her ambitions.

VANCOUVER ISLAND

When Berman returned to Canada, she dropped out of Ryerson and enrolled in the environmental studies program at the University of Toronto. The next summer she volunteered as a researcher in the temperate rainforest on Vancouver Island. "I loved that place," she told Christine Langlois for *Reader's Digest* (1 Nov. 2009), referring to the Carmanah and Walbran Valleys, which boast spruce trees that are over eight hundred years old. She spent the next two summers tracking the movements of the marbled murrelet, a small seabird that nests in old-growth forests, but when she returned for her third summer in 1992, she discovered that her patch of forest—with its Sitka grove, pristine waterfall, and murrelet nest—was gone.

In her book *This Crazy Time* (2011), Berman describes the horrible discovery, stating that she was hoping to show her friends her old campground. After driving around for hours, lost, Berman realized they were covering familiar ground. They parked their truck by a new clear-cut area. (Clear-cutting is a controversial process by which all trees in an area of forest are uniformly chopped down. It is particularly devastating to the surrounding ecosystem.) The razed field, with a small patch of trees in the middle, was all that was left of the ancient Sitka grove. The once steep waterfall and clear pool trickled next to a logging road. The murrelet nest was gone. Berman had envisioned a future of studying old-growth forests, but when she saw the extent of the destruction caused by logging, she knew that she needed to do something more.

CLAYOQUOT SOUND PROTEST

In 1993, just a day after discovering her fallen forest, Berman joined up with a small group called Friends of Clayoquot Sound (FOCS).

Clayoquot Sound, located on the western coast of Vancouver Island, is a global rarity. It is a temperate rainforest that is host to an ecologically diverse population of plants and animals. FOCS was founded in 1979 to preserve the area and protect it from companies looking to exploit its resources. In 1993, Berman took charge of a FOCS campaign to blockade the sound to prevent MacMillan Bloedel, one of Canada's largest forestry companies, from chopping down trees for pulp. She had never been to a protest, but suddenly found herself the leader of one that called not just for an end to clear-cutting at Clayoquot Sound, but an end to the practice in forests across Canada.

Announcement of the campaign attracted attention from media all over the world, and from celebrity protestors like the Australian rock band Midnight Oil and American activist Robert Kennedy Jr. Berman became the face of the protest, and a photograph of her hoisting a fist in the air appeared on the cover of the Toronto *Globe and Mail*. All told, some ten thousand people showed up to support the group, and of that number, around nine hundred were arrested. Berman was arrested and charged with a dizzying 857 counts of "aiding and abetting" every protestor that was arrested over the course of the summer. She faced six years in prison, but after five days of trial the judge decided that he had no legal reason to lock her away.

GREENPEACE
Greenpeace, the world's largest environmental organization, hired Berman at the end of that summer in 1993. The protests had made her a national celebrity, but her new high profile was taking its toll. She was surprised and hurt when Jack Munro, head of the International Woodworkers of America (IWA), called her a "menace to society," and in her book she describes one incident in which a logger tried to run her off the road while she was driving her car. "I would go out to a restaurant, and people would either spit on me or hug me," she told Glave. She also found negotiating a compromise in regard to clear-cutting to be more difficult than she had ever imagined. In her book, she describes her interactions with leaders of First Nations (native Canadians) who brought their own grievances to the table.

The Clayoquot protests made history as Canada's largest act of civil disobedience ever, though negotiations with "MacBlo" lasted for another five years. The company finally agreed to pass its logging rights on the Clayoquot Sound to a First Nations–controlled company, who in turn agreed to leave the first-growth (i.e., virgin or old-growth) forests intact. The protest pitted activists and corporations firmly against one another, and it ultimately had no effect on first-growth logging elsewhere in the country. According to a

Greenpeace poll cited by Doug Sanders for the *Globe and Mail* (5 Aug. 2012), only 14 percent of Canadians supported the deal. "I was sure the issue was pretty black and white: I was on the side of the angels, and they were bad people," Berman told Saunders. The reality, as Berman would continue to find, turned out to be far more complicated.

FORESTETHICS
Berman stayed with Greenpeace throughout the 1990s, working on campaigns all over the world. In 1999, she cofounded ForestEthics in San Francisco, California. The organization works to protect endangered forests. In its early years, instead of blockading logging companies, ForestEthics pressured major companies to stop buying pulp from old-growth forests for their print catalogs. One of their first targets was the lingerie company Victoria's Secret, which was churning out millions of catalogs printed on paper from endangered forests. ForestEthics launched the "Victoria's Dirty Secret" campaign in 2000, and on January 1, 2001, the group ran a full-page advertisement in the *New York Times*, featuring a lace-clad model wielding a chainsaw. It was a bold move on Berman's part: she shelled out $30,000—half of the group's campaign budget—for the ad. But the exposure was invaluable. The ad drew attention to the rallies, protests, and letters that followed, and within six months, Berman was meeting with the company to discuss environmentally friendly alternatives. "[Berman] helps people identify themselves as part of the solution," Avrim Lazar, former president of the Forest Products Association of Canada, told Langlois. In 2006, ForestEthics announced that Victoria's Secret, Dell, and Williams-Sonoma had pledged to buy more recycled and sustainably harvested paper.

The success of the "Victoria's Dirty Secret" campaign, Berman wrote in her book, was critical to the success of the Canadian Boreal Forest Agreement (CBFA), signed on May 18, 2010. The CBFA, signed by nine environmental organizations, including ForestEthics, and twenty-one forest product companies, became the world's largest conservation agreement. It placed a three-year moratorium on logging on over seventy million acres of Canada's boreal forest and began long-term conservation efforts to preserve another 175 million acres. (Boreal forest, a vast coniferous forest region that stretches across northern North America and Eurasia, is home to caribou, also known as reindeer, and many other species threatened by logging activity.) In 2013, ongoing negotiations between the two opposing coalitions broke down after disagreements with one forestry company called Resolute Forest Products. Greenpeace Canada withdrew from the agreement in December 2012, and a sustainable forestry group called Canopy quickly followed suit, citing the lack of any tangible result of the agreement after three years of talks. Negotiations among the remaining groups have continued, but Lazar, in an interview with Canadian Press reporter Bruce Cheadle (25 Sept. 2013), conceded, "It's just more complex than anyone imagined."

POWERUP CANADA

In 2007, Berman was invited to Bali, Indonesia, to speak about logging and climate change at the United Nations Climate Change Conference. On December 3, 2007—a date of enlightenment she has referred to specifically—she listened to UN Secretary General Ban Ki-moon give his opening remarks and experienced something akin to both an epiphany and a vision of a dystopian future. Ban stressed the extreme urgency of the climate crisis: if human consumption continues at its current rate, humans will face a global tipping point, after which any effort to reverse climate change will be ineffective. Scientists have identified dates for such a tipping point, based on a number of different factors, falling between 2020 and 2050.

Berman was horrified by the data, but also embarrassed by fellow delegate John Baird, Canada's former federal environmental minister and head of the Canadian delegation at the conference, who seemed to be doing everything he could to avoid any hard commitment to reducing climate change. She had faced similar predicaments before: talks led to negotiation, and negotiations could drag on for years without result. Upon returning to Canada, Berman decided that this time things would be different. They would have to be—the stakes were just too high. So, Berman made the controversial decision to make climate change her sole focus and founded PowerUp Canada, a national lobbying initiative, in 2008. PowerUp is a bit like ForestEthics, but instead of focusing on corporate policy, it focuses on government policy. "We've changed our light bulbs," she told Langlois, "now we have to change our law."

Berman is an effective evangelist for the cause. She told Langlois that climate change is "the moral challenge of our age," and in 2009, she was appointed by the premier of British Columbia to make recommendations for developing renewable energies in the province. In 2010, Greenpeace International hired her as co-director of its Global Climate and Energy program in Amsterdam. However, the announcement spawned a petition and campaign against her called "Save Greenpeace." The protestors cited a decision Berman made in 2009 to present an award to a Canadian politician at the UN Climate Change Conference in Copenhagen as evidence of her willingness to compromise her environmental principles. Berman has argued that her intent was to spotlight positive change, such

as, in this particular case, support for a carbon tax that would make companies pay for their pollution. Berman stepped down from her position with Greenpeace in 2012, and returned to her position as the executive director of PowerUp Canada.

PERSONAL LIFE

In 2007, Berman appeared in the 2007 global warming documentary *The 11th Hour*, produced and narrated by actor Leonardo DiCaprio. In her review of the film for the *New York Times* (17 Aug. 2007), Manohla Dargis praises *The 11th Hour* as "unnerving" and "surprisingly affecting." For its horror, but also for its hope, she touts it as "essential viewing." In 2013, Berman was awarded an honorary doctorate from the University of British Columbia.

Berman met Christopher Hatch in 1993 at the Clayoquot protests. They were married in June 2000 on a beach in Clayoquot Sound. The couple has two children, Forrest and Quinn.

SUGGESTED READING

Cheadle, Bruce. "Environmentalists, Loggers Seek Consensus as Boreal Forest Agreement Hits Reset." *CTV News*. Bell Media, 25 Sept. 2013. Web. 13 Jan. 2014.

Dargis, Manohla. "Helpful Hints for Saving the Planet." Rev. of *The 11th Hour*, dir. Nadia Connors and Leila Conners Petersen. *New York Times* 17 Aug. 2007: E8. Print.

Glave, James. "Tzeporah Berman's Green Idea." *Vancouver Magazine*. Transcontinental Media, 1 Nov. 2009. Web. 13 Jan. 2014.

Langlois, Christine. "The Queen of Green." *Reader's Digest* Nov. 2009: 46–53. Print.

Sanders, Doug. "Greenpeace: Tactics Not So Clear Cut Anymore." *Globe and Mail* [Toronto] 5 Aug. 2012. Web. 13 Jan. 2014.

—*Molly Hagan*

Manoj Bhargava

Born: 1953
Occupation: Entrepreneur

"Some people say that they don't want to toil in obscurity," Manoj Bhargava, the billionaire entrepreneur who created the popular energy shot 5-Hour Energy, told Daniel Duggan for *Crain's Detroit Business* (19 Feb. 2012). "I don't mind that. I'd be fine if I were to toil in obscurity." The Indian-born Bhargava is an unusual figure among CEOs; he not only works to stay out of the spotlight—he agreed to his first press interview (with *Forbes*) in 2012—but also gives away 90 percent of his wealth to charity. Bhargava lived as a monk throughout most of his twenties,

Courtesy of Mskabich, via Wikimedia Commons

engaging in silent meditation and daily chores in an ashram in India. He began his multibillion-dollar company, Living Essentials, after officially retiring from his previous company, Prime PVC, Inc., in 2000. In 2003 Living Essentials launched a product called 5-Hour Energy, a two-ounce "shot" of energy drink containing B vitamins, taurine (a substance similar to an amino acid), and the amount of caffeine found in a cup of coffee. It purports to increase concentration, energy, and even athletic performance for five hours. Unlike other energy drinks, it does not contain sugar, which is why Living Essentials—and satisfied customers—can claim that drinkers will not experience a crash, or period of exhaustion, later on.

By far the most popular shot on the market, 5-Hour Energy has earned profits estimated in the billions, but scientists and health professionals remain wary. "These are caffeine delivery systems," Dr. Roland Griffiths, a researcher at Johns Hopkins University, told Barry Meier for the *New York Times* (1 Jan. 2013) "of energy drinks like 5-Hour Energy, Red Bull, and Rockstar." Referring to a well-known caffeine tablet, he added, "They don't want to say this is equivalent to a NoDoz because that is not a very sexy sales message." Indeed, 5-Hour Energy boasts B vitamins, including B12—8,333 percent of the recommended daily allowance, in fact—that allows it to sell at a higher price than a product such as NoDoz, which retails for about thirty cents per tablet. 5-Hour Energy costs three dollars a bottle. Whether the shots are actually dangerous has yet to be determined, though in 2012, Meier reported for the *New York Times* (14 Nov. 2012) that 5-Hour Energy was cited in thirteen official death reports. The Federal Drug Administration (FDA) is investigating the deaths but has yet to provide a direct connection between a specific death and 5-Hour Energy.

EDUCATION AND LIFE IN THE MONASTERY
Bhargava was born in Lucknow, India, in 1953. His parents were wealthy, and Bhargava spent his early years in a lush villa surrounded by servants. In 1967 the family moved to the United States so that Bhargava's father, an academic publisher, could get a PhD in business at the University of Pennsylvania's Wharton School. Bhargava was fourteen. They settled in a shabby, third-floor walk-up in Philadelphia, where the impoverished family split a can of Coca-Cola four ways as a treat. But Bhargava was scrappy and smart; he excelled at math and won interviews to top Philadelphia schools by offering to take math tests to prove his superior skills. (Later, he compared himself to the fictional mathematical genius played by Matt Damon in the 1997 movie *Good Will Hunting*.) At seventeen he bought a 1953 Chevy dump truck for $400, hoping to turn around his investment by clearing debris from a low-income neighborhood in North Philadelphia that was being razed. He made $600 and then resold the truck for $400. The anecdote is indicative of Bhargava's mindset. "He didn't care if the work was unglamorous," Clare O'Connor wrote for *Forbes* magazine (8 Feb. 2012). "It was profitable."

He won a full scholarship to the prestigious Hill School in Pottstown, Pennsylvania, in 1970. He graduated in 1972 and enrolled in Princeton University, but he found the Ivy League culture did not suit him and left after one year. He wanted to examine his life "from a clearer perspective," he told Rachel Feintzeig for the *Wall Street Journal* (18 Oct. 2013). He explained, "The purpose of our life has been trained into us, from our parents: you go to school, you go to college, you get a job, you get a family. You assume, 'Yes, that's the purpose of life.' You work hard and after that you die. It's an assumption. Well my thought was, 'Why?'"

His parents were not pleased with his decision but welcomed him into their new home in Fort Wayne, Indiana. His father owned a plastics company, but elsewhere, "there were no jobs," Bhargava told O'Connor. After reading a book about a Hindu saint, Bhargava decided to go on his own spiritual quest. He moved to India in 1974. For the next twelve years, Bhargava traveled among monasteries operated by the Hanslok order in New Delhi. He compared his time there to living in a commune: he performed daily chores, helped run a printing press, worked construction for Hanslok, and spent hours in silent meditation. He hoped to master one technique, "the stilling of the mind," during his time there, he told O'Connor,

EARLY BUSINESS CAREER
Bhargava occasionally returned to the United States during his years in India to work odd jobs such as driving a cab in New York City. In 1990 he moved back for good, at his parents' behest, to help his father in the plastics business. He acquired the company Prime PVC, Inc. and spent

ten years, as O'Connor put it, "dabbling in RV armrests and beach chair parts." Bhargava was not particularly interested in plastic, but he approached the business with the same zeal of the dump truck operation he had run as a teenager. He focused on buying small and struggling regional companies and turning them around. By 2000 his company had built up $25 million in sales. In his late forties, he decided to retire and sold his business to a private equity firm, but the life of leisure did not suit him. He immediately began looking for opportunities to invest.

Bhargava was interested in chemicals. "Basically, you mix a bunch of stuff together and you can sell it for more than you bought it for," he told Duggan of the industry. "I can mix two nickels together and sell it for a dollar. It's a business where things aren't sold based on what they cost, it's based on what they do." In 2000 he created Chemicalpartners.com, an outfit that connected corporations seeking new ideas with inventors. Bhargava communicated with thousands of inventors and noticed patterns of behavior. He saw that inventors often did not want to part with their ideas, and he saw that companies, even those with billions of dollars at their disposal, frequently failed to bring a new product to market. The perverse logic that wealthier companies often had a harder time helping a product succeed was explained thus by David Brophy of the University of Michigan's Ross School of Business to Duggan: "Someone with too much money isn't going to be as dependent on the success of a product like someone who is worried about starving or going broke."

5-HOUR ENERGY
In the spring of 2003 Bhargava attended a trade show for natural products in Anaheim, California. He stopped at one booth handing out samples of a sixteen-ounce energy drink. Its makers claimed that it would boost productivity for hours. Bhargava took a sip, and for the next six or seven hours, "I was in great shape," he told O'Connor. "I thought, 'Wow, this is amazing. I can sell this.'" He approached the makers with an offer, but they turned him down. So Bhargava set out to make the product on his own. (He made a mental note of the elixir's ingredients and replicated it with his own team.) Bhargava made a smart decision very early—he would not, as the drink's makers had done, market his product as a sixteen-ounce beverage. He did not want to compete with popular energy drinks such as Red Bull and Monster. He later reasoned to O'Connor, "If I'm tired, am I also thirsty?" In other words, if he was looking for a product to give him energy, did it have to be a full beverage? He decided to sell 5-Hour Energy in two-ounce bottles, but crucially, and riskily, he sold those smaller bottles at the same retail price as their sixteen-ounce brethren. It was a gamble that

played out in Bhargava's favor. "Nobody pays three dollars twice," he told O'Connor.

In its now well-recognized red and black bottle, 5-Hour Energy became available in stores six months after Bhargava had attended the trade show. Stores were initially leery of the product's safety, but the health chain GNC decided to give it a chance in 2004. Walgreen's, Rite Aid, and Sheetz followed, but the company's real coup was Wal-Mart. O'Connor reported that an estimated 15 percent of 5-Hour Energy's sales come from the Wal-Mart checkout aisle.

As of 2012 it was estimated that 5-Hour Energy controlled 90 percent of the US energy shot market, although there is no way to know an exact percentage because Living Essentials does not report revenue or profits. All published estimates are made by independent data groups and sources close to the company. Bhargava keeps a cheeky "graveyard" of failed competitors— 6-Hour Power, 8-Hour Energy—in a glass case in his office. "In front of each [bottle] are little placards with a skull and crossbones drawn in felt-tip pen," O'Connor wrote. Today, 5-Hour Energy is offered in a variety of flavors, though even its most enthusiastic supporters admit that it tastes terrible: "Chalky cough syrup is more like it," O'Connor, who became hooked on the shots while writing about Bhargava, reported.

OTHER INVESTMENTS AND PHILANTHROPY
After the success of 5-Hour Energy, Bhargava is looking to invest in other sectors through Stage 2 Innovations, a $100 million tech venture fund. Bhargava hired Tom LaSorda, the former CEO of Chrysler Group, to run the operation. According to its website, the fund is interested in companies working in clean energy, water purification, medical technology, and "benefitting mankind." One company that Stage 2 has invested in removes salt from water (a process known as desalination) at a significantly reduced cost compared to the current method. "The last fifty years were about oil," Bhargava told Duggan. "The next fifty years will be about water. Maybe you're responsible for something that can help, really impact, a billion people around the world." Another company builds indoor hydroponic gardening systems that offer increased production and allow for year-round farming. Bhargava is also interested in diesel fuel and a company that extracts mercury from coal.

As for his philanthropy, Bhargava's transactions are complicated. He deals with a charity called Rural India Supporting Trust, which in turn gives many of its grants to the nonprofit Hans Foundation, which was also founded by Bhargava. The Hans Foundation employs twelve people who seek out Indian schools and hospitals in need. "The foundation has funded more than four hundred charity projects in India," Bhargava told a reporter for India's *Economic*

Times (10 Apr. 2012). Several reporters have pointed out that the larger, complex structure of his charitable giving, which exploits a loophole linking donated stock and capital gains tax, has earned him a hefty tax break—a charge he does not deny. "Look, for me to not save tax would be stupid okay, then I would be called 'stupid rich man,'" he told the Economic Times. He sees his mission as keeping his money out of the hands of the government so that he can distribute it as he sees fit. "The biggest challenge is always the governments," he told the Economic Times, "they try to stop all good things. I try to stay away from them as much as I can, as I know if someone can destroy something good, it's the government!"

PERSONAL LIFE

Bhargava still considers himself a member of the Hanslok order and meditates for an hour each day. He has a wife and a son. He moved to the Farmington Hills neighborhood of Detroit, to be closer to his wife's family, during his short-lived retirement in the early 2000s and continues to make his home there.

SUGGESTED READING

Duggan, Daniel. "Wizard of Odds." Crain's Detroit Business. Crain Communications, 19 Feb. 2012. Web. 27 June 2014.

Feintzeig, Rachel. "Living Essentials CEO: 'I Wanted Something Different.'" Wall Street Journal. Dow Jones, 18 Oct. 2013. Web. 27 June 2014.

"Manoj Bhargava, Richest Indian in US Commits 90 Percent Earnings to Charity." Economic Times [India]. TimesInternet, 10 Apr. 2012. Web. 27 June 2014.

Meier, Barry. "Caffeinated Drink Cited in Reports of Thirteen Deaths." New York Times. New York Times, 14 Nov. 2012. Web. 27 July 2014.

Meier, Barry. "Energy Drinks Promise Edge, but Experts Say Proof Is Scant." New York Times. New York Times, 1 Jan. 2013. Web. 27 July 2014.

O'Connor, Clare. "The Mystery Monk Making Billions with 5-Hour Energy." Forbes. Forbes, 8 Feb. 2012. Web. 27 June 2014.

—Molly Hagan

Andrew Bird

Born: July 11, 1973
Occupation: Multi-instrumentalist and songwriter

Andrew Bird is a musician, singer-songwriter, professional whistler (by his own account), and classically trained violinist. Born and raised in Chicago, Bird spent years on the Chicago cult

music scene, traveling from venue to venue with his violin, his looping station, and a batch of his CDs. Bird now enjoys an international following and released his eleventh studio record, an album of cover songs called Things Are Really Great Here, Sort Of . . . , in 2014. Bird's sound is eclectic. "His songs are swelling and orchestral, the legacy of years spent studying classical violin," wrote Jonathan Mahler for the New York Times (2 Jan. 2009). "But Bird's sound is also distinctly American, part of a new wave of folk. . . . His songs have a pastoral, homespun feel, but they also have a darkness and emotional complexity not typically associated with folk rock."

Bird is inspired by everything from overheard words and phrases to the patterns the wind creates on the fields at his family farm near Elizabeth, Illinois. Bird moved to the farm in 2002, after recording three critically acclaimed albums with his first band, Andrew Bird's Bowl of Fire. But the band was more popular with critics than audiences, and Bird sequestered himself in a converted barn on the farm to take stock of his career. He experimented with unusual sounds in his solitude, recording and layering them using a looping station. In the winter of 2002, the Handsome Family, a folk and alt-country band, asked Bird to open for them at a local dance hall. The other members of Andrew Bird's Bowl of Fire were not available, but Bird agreed to play the show alone. He brought only his violin and a looping pedal, and in a desperate attempt to hold the audience's attention he whistled for the first time onstage. "I was worried they were all thinking: Where's the band?" Bird explained to Mahler.

The short performance was a hit and laid the foundation for Bird's solo career. He released his

first solo album, *Weather Systems*, in 2003. "In his first couple of albums,"—with Andrew Bird's Bowl of Fire—"you can hear a lot of his influences," Andrea Troolin, Bird's manager, told Mahler. "I think it was a matter of him getting that out of his system in some ways and figuring out what an Andrew Bird song sounds like."

CLASSICAL BACKGROUND

Andrew Wegman Bird was born on July 11, 1973, in Chicago, Illinois. Bird, the second youngest of four siblings, grew up in Evanston and then Lake Bluff, to the north of Chicago. Bird's mother is an artist who creates copperplate etchings, and she encouraged Bird to begin taking music lessons at the age of four. He learned to play the violin using the intuitive Suzuki method, which is based on the principles of language acquisition and teaches students to play by ear at a young age. Still, Bird's earliest career ambition was not musically related at all. At the age of ten, he wanted to become a psychiatrist. When he was fourteen, his mother enrolled in graduate school for art therapy—Bird attributed her decision to his oldest brother, who has severe autism. When his mother took psychology classes, Bird was her study partner.

Bird was a shy child but, ironically, he enjoyed performing. As he recalled to Laura Barton for the *Guardian* (2 Dec. 2007), he was more comfortable presenting a book report in front of his elementary school classmates than interacting with them. Bird continued to study the violin through high school. While his friends were listening to rock bands like the Smiths and the Cure, Bird was busy practicing Mozart and Bach. After graduating from Lake Forest High School in 1991, he enrolled in the prestigious conservatory program at Northwestern University in Evanston, Illinois, just outside of Chicago. In college, he developed a distaste for the conservatory mindset and longed to improvise and create his own work. "There is something comforting about going into a practice room, putting your sheet music on a stand and playing Bach over and over again," Bird told Mahler. "But at the same time, it's not demanding much of you." When he was nineteen, he joined a punk-ska band called Charlie Nobody, hoping to branch out musically. "I was really desperate to find people that I liked and that I had a chance to hang out with," he told Hugo Lindgren for *New York* magazine (25 Jan. 2009).

Bird graduated with a degree in violin performance in 1996, and he then moved to Chicago. He was able to support himself by playing his violin at bars, weddings, and funerals. Bird even got a gig as a "fiddling knave," he told Lindgren, at a Renaissance fair in Wisconsin. He was playing the violin eight to ten hours a day, and he developed tendinitis in his hand. It occurred to him that one day, he might not be able to play anymore at all. He began writing songs as a second musical outlet and self-released a jazz- and folk-inspired album called *Music of Hair* in 1996. Between 1996 and 1998, Bird performed with the jazz and swing band Squirrel Nut Zippers, playing violin on three of their albums.

ANDREW BIRD'S BOWL OF FIRE

Soon after the release of *Music of Hair*, a young executive at Rykodisc Records named Andrea Troolin stumbled across Bird's demo. She signed him in 1997, and Bird organized a band called Andrew Bird's Bowl of Fire to record the group's first album that year. (Troolin later left Rykodisc and became Bird's manager.) Throughout his twenties, Bird explored a variety of musical genres, including swing, calypso, and folk. His diverse musical interests informed his work as well as his working style. When Andrew Bird's Bowl of Fire traveled to a recording studio in New Orleans, Bird insisted that the entire ensemble crowd around one microphone—just like the early American jazz greats whom he so admired. It made the process all the more difficult—requiring the entire band to play each song until everyone got it right on the same take—but the anecdote is indicative of Bird's exacting standards and exhausting work ethic in the studio. The group finished recording the album in just five days.

In 1998, Andrew Bird's Bowl of Fire released *Thrills*, an album that enjoyed popularity amid the short-lived swing revival of the late 1990s. Over the next four years, the group released two more albums: *Oh! The Grandeur* in 1999 and *The Swimming Hour* in 2001. A reviewer for the *A.V. Club* (24 Aug. 1999) praised Bird's ability to transcend the hype of *Thrills* with his deeper (and stranger) sophomore album, which combined pop, jazz, classical, folk, and blues influences. The *A.V. Club* review commended Bird for "choosing to follow his own vision rather than capitalize on cash cows." Joe Tangari, reviewing *The Swimming Hour* for the influential indie music website *Pitchfork* (3 Apr. 2001), rated the album an impressive nine out of ten points. Tangari wrote that Bird had advanced from a "stylist" of disparate nostalgic genres to a much more nuanced "chemist" of sound. Andrew Bird's Bowl of Fire, he wrote, is "one of the only bands out there who have decided to treat the whole past as a single body of work to draw freely from, rather than restricting themselves to an era or a style." Despite their critical success, Andrew Bird's Bowl of Fire did not sell many records, much less sell out any shows. "We'd roll into town, and there would be no posters advertising our show and no radio stations playing our songs," Bird told Mahler. "Forty people would show up, and we'd get paid $500, if we were lucky." By 2002, Bird decided it was time to reassess his career.

He moved out of his Chicago apartment and into an old barn on his family's rural Illinois farm.

EARLY SOLO CAREER

At the farm, Bird experimented with an electronic device called a looping station. The device allows musicians to record their music live and then play snippets of these recordings back on a loop. The result, particularly when one uses the machine to layer as many instruments and sounds as Bird does, is a tapestry or, as Bird prefers to call it, a "sculpture" of sound. The loop allows him to manipulate the "block of sound I can visualize between me and the audience," he told Jessica Curry for *Chicago Life* magazine (18 Feb. 2009). "I add some bass or cello with another analog pedal that drops it an octave. I can get seven or eight tracks going. It's a pretty amazing tool. People think it must be a lot to think about onstage, but it's actually a very intuitive device. Because the violin is a linear instrument, you really can't do much counterpoint with it. It's also up against your throat, so it's hard to sing. So it was really an ideal tool." After his opening performance for the Handsome Family in 2002, Bird applied his new looping techniques while recording his first solo album, *Weather Systems*, which was released in 2003.

Reviewing *Weather Systems* for *Pitchfork* (30 Oct. 2003), Tangari wrote that Bird had successfully "managed to synthesize his myriad influences to the point where you can't hear any of them distinctly anymore." He was developing his own signature sound, but even so, Bird had to hustle to keep his career afloat. He started touring again, opening for more famous artists such as the singer-songwriter Ani DiFranco. Bird called these shows "guerrilla attacks" in his interview with Mahler. "I would play for 30 minutes for 2,000 people, none of whom knew who I was." And when he got off the stage, he rushed out to the lobby to sell copies of his album at his own merchandise table. His fan following grew with his second solo album, *Andrew Bird & the Mysterious Production of Eggs*, which was released in 2005. (Little did fans know that the meticulous Bird had scrapped two full cuts of the album before recording a third from scratch.) The album pairs Bird's dense, image-laden lyrics with complex tunes that David Raposa described as "ebullient" in a review for *Pitchfork* (10 Mar. 2005).

Bird's third solo studio album, *Armchair Apocrypha*, was released in 2007 and features sweeping and guitar-driven music. Tangari wrote (23 Mar. 2007) that "the biggest criticism you could level at it is that it's not better than the three albums that came before it—but that scarcely matters when you're actually listening to it, because *Armchair Apocrypha* is ultimately another object of strange and unique beauty from this inventive songwriter and performer."

NOBLE BEAST

Bird embraced an entirely different ethos for his next album, *Noble Beast*, which he released in 2009. Instead of feeding his desire for more and more complexity, he challenged himself to embrace simplicity. Some of the tracks are downright poppy (or as poppy as one can get with lyrics like "From proto-Sanskrit Minoans to por-to-centric Lisboans"), leading many critics, for better or worse, to dub it the most "mainstream" album in Bird's oeuvre. When Curry asked him what he would have thought of *Noble Beast* back when he was twenty-two years old, Bird said, "I had very different tastes in some ways back then. I was more impatient. I might have found some things I'm doing now as being boring, whereas now I see it as being patient. I found a lot of indie rock or pop music just repetitive and boring when I was 22. Now I get it a little more. I understand space. Back then I was all jacked up ready to express myself."

The album was popular with his fans and even garnered him some new ones, but the experience of creating it and then touring had exhausted Bird. "I was burned out, and I didn't really want to go home to Illinois," Bird told Barton for the *Guardian* (7 Mar. 2012). Instead of retreating to his farmhouse, he rented a house in Venice Beach, California, where he recharged by writing a few songs for the movie *The Muppets* (2011). A song called "The Whistling Caruso" was the only one of Bird's contributions to appear on the film's soundtrack. That same year, he covered Kermit the Frog's iconic song "Bein' Green" for a Muppets tribute album called *The Green Album*, which also featured such artists as Weezer, OK Go, the Fray, and My Morning Jacket. It was not Bird's first foray into film scores; he wrote the majority of the songs on the soundtrack for the 2010 indie film *Norman*.

BREAK IT YOURSELF AND OTHER RECENT WORK

Bird returned to the farm and gathered his band to play some of the new material he had been working on during his California sojourn. The mood was happy, and the gatherings were less rehearsals than they were "jam sessions," Bird told Barton (7 Mar. 2012). "I was just in a good place in my head after a long time of not being," he added. After eight days of jamming, Bird and his band had, almost unintentionally, recorded the bulk of his new album, *Break It Yourself*, which peaked at number ten on the Billboard 200 following its release in 2012. Reviewers described the record as mellow but rich. "*Break It Yourself* is a quiet, careful grower," Stephen Thompson wrote for NPR (26 Feb. 2012). "Give it time, though, and it blooms into something beautiful." Bird's next album, *Hands of Glory*, came only a few months later, in October 2012. The album harkens back to Bird's early American influences. The album included original songs, heavy with backwoods imagery, and covers of the Handsome Family's "When That Helicopter Comes" and the late singer-songwriter Townes Van Zandt's "If I Needed You."

In 2014, Bird released *Things Are Really Great Here, Sort Of . . .*, an entire album of Handsome Family cover songs. The husband-and-wife team behind the band, Brett and Rennie Sparks, are close with Bird. He told Abby Johnston for the *Austin Chronicle* (16 June 2014) that he was first drawn to the Americana duo when he heard Rennie's enigmatic lyrics. Bird tries to take the same approach in his own songwriting, explaining to Johnston, "You only have three minutes [in a song], and there's no hope in answering any questions in three minutes, so it's best to just start a conversation."

In June 2014, Bird's song "Pulaski at Night" was featured in the season two premier of the Netflix series, *Orange Is the New Black*. The song is the title track of Bird's 2013 seven-track EP, *I Want to See Pulaski at Night*.

PERSONAL LIFE

Bird met Katherine Tsina, a fashion designer and former dancer, in 2008. The couple married in 2010. Her clothing collection, Avion Feminin, expanded to include clothes for men in 2012, and Bird became the model and public face of the men's clothing line, Avion Homme. They have one son and live in New York.

SUGGESTED READING

"Andrew Bird's Bowl of Fire: *Oh! The Grandeur.*" *A.V. Club*. Onion, 24 Aug. 1999. Web. 7 July 2014.

Barton, Laura. "Andrew Bird's Frog Chorus." *Guardian*. Guardian News and Media, 7 Mar. 2012. Web. 7 July 2014.

Curry, Jessica. "Ornithology: An Interview with Andrew Bird." *Chicago Life*. Chicago Life, 18 Feb. 2009. Web. 7 July 2014.

Johnston, Abby. "Virtuosic Violinist Gets Handsome at the Paramount Tonight." *Austin Chronicle*. Austin Chronicle, 16 June 2014. Web. 7 July 2014.

Lindgren, Hugo. "Influences: Andrew Bird." *New York*. New York Media, 25 Jan. 2009. Web. 7 July 2014.

Mahler, Jonathan. "Andrew Bird Discovers His Inner Operatic Folkie." *New York Times*. New York Times, 2 Jan. 2009. Web. 7 July 2014.

SELECTED WORKS

Weather Systems, 2003; *Andrew Bird & the Mysterious Production of Eggs*, 2005; *Armchair Apocrypha*, 2007; *Noble Beast*, 2009; *Break It Yourself*, 2012; *Hands of Glory*, 2012; *Things Are Really Great Here, Sort Of. . .*, 2014

—Molly Hagan

Mark Boal

Born: January 23, 1973
Occupation: Screenwriter

When Mark Boal turned his experience as an embedded journalist with a US Army bomb-disposal unit in Iraq into the 2008 feature-length war thriller *The Hurt Locker*, directed by Kathryn Bigelow, little did he know that the film would change his life. Boal, who began his journalism career in the mid-1990s writing for such publications as the *Village Voice*, *Rolling Stone*, and *Playboy*, coproduced and wrote the original script for the film, which received widespread praise from critics and won numerous awards, including the Academy Award for best picture. *The Hurt Locker* earned Boal his first Academy Award for best original screenplay and instantly catapulted him from obscure journalist to leading Hollywood screenwriter.

Boal teamed up with Bigelow for a second time to coproduce and write the original screenplay for *Zero Dark Thirty* (2012), which dramatizes the real-life CIA hunt for al-Qaeda terrorist leader Osama bin Laden. The well-received film garnered him his second Academy Award nomination for best original screenplay. Speaking of his unlikely path toward becoming a screenwriter, Boal told Claudia Eller for the *Los Angeles Times* (11 Feb. 2010), "Hollywood has always been the promised land when you're an ink-stained wretch in New York City. It was always a dream that seemed pretty unrealistic."

EARLY LIFE AND EDUCATION

Mark Boal was born on January 23, 1973, in New York City. His father, William Stetson Boal Jr., who died in 2010, was an educational film producer. His mother, Lillian Firestone, is an author, educator, publisher, and scholar of spiritual teacher George Gurdjieff. His brother, Christopher Stetson Boal, is a playwright and screenwriter.

Boal grew up in New York City's Greenwich Village in a Jewish, "leftie, counterculture-y, sandals-wearing, granola-crunching" household, as he described to Naomi Pfefferman for the *Jewish Journal* (25 Feb. 2010). His interest in journalism was sparked at an early age by his father, who read the *New York Times* every day. Boal fondly remembers reading the *Times* sports pages with him and "discuss[ing] the game from the point of view of whoever was writing about it," he told Shauna Siggelkow for the *Oberlin Review* (27 Sept. 2010). Boal added, "I really grew up loving that whole world. . . . I wanted to see if I could be a part of it."

Boal attended the prestigious Bronx High School of Science, a New York City public school that requires prospective students to complete a competitive entrance examination in order to

Adrees Latif/Reuters/Landov

be admitted. He excelled academically and was a standout member of the speech and debate team, ranking among the top ten debaters in the country as a senior. Boal is regarded as one of the best debaters in Bronx Science history, and as of 2010 he still ranked among the school's top fifty debaters.

After graduating in 1991, Boal attended Oberlin College, a private liberal arts institution in Oberlin, Ohio, famous for its progressive politics. He has credited Oberlin with helping to shape his political point of view and leading him to develop "a kind of intellectual skepticism," as he said to Siggelkow. He graduated from Oberlin in 1995 with an honors degree in philosophy.

JOURNALISM CAREER

Upon graduation, Boal, following the advice of Oberlin's then-president S. Frederick Starr to carve out a unique niche for himself in the world, returned to New York and embarked on a journalism career. After struggling to find steady work, however, he moved to Europe and found work as a copy editor for the *Budapest Sun*, a now-defunct English-language newspaper in Budapest, Hungary. Boal held the position for a year and a half, after which he returned to New York. He wrote for several small circulars before being hired as a writer for the *Village Voice*, the largest and most influential alternative news-weekly in the United States, in 1998.

Boal's work for the *Village Voice* included an acclaimed series of articles chronicling American surveillance tactics. The series helped him land a weekly column for the paper called the *Monitor*. During his time at the *Voice*, Boal worked closely with the paper's former long-time executive editor, Richard Goldstein, whom he has cited as a major influence on his career

as a journalist. Another one of Boal's editors at the *Voice*, Hillary Rosner, remembered him to Jordan Michael Smith for the *Nation* (14 June 2013) as "a good muckraking journalist."

The course of Boal's career as a journalist was shifted by the terrorist attacks of September 11, 2001, when members from the militant Islamist group al-Qaeda hijacked four commercial airliners and deliberately flew two into the World Trade Center towers, destroying them and killing thousands. At the time, Boal, who was living in an apartment in New York City, specialized in stories on youth culture for the *Voice* and various other national publications, including *Mother Jones* and *Rolling Stone*. Boal lost a number of friends in the attack, and the harrowing experience immediately prompted him to switch his journalistic focus to more military-themed stories. "For weeks after 9/11 you could smell the dust and pulverized concrete in New York, and the National Guard came in, so there was a military presence on the streets. . . . After that, I became keenly interested in national security issues, the birth of the war on terror, and the invasion of Iraq," he recalled to Sheila Johnston for the *Telegraph* (25 Aug. 2009).

MOVE INTO SCREENWRITING

Boal's growing interest in US military affairs led him to write a series of articles about the war on terror for *Playboy* magazine. The first, "Death and Dishonor," was featured in the magazine's May 2004 issue and centered on US Army specialist Richard T. Davis, who was inexplicably murdered by fellow soldiers in Columbus, Georgia, just two days after returning from Iraq. The article served as the inspiration for the 2007 film *In the Valley of Elah*, which was written and directed by Paul Haggis and starred Tommy Lee Jones in an Academy Award–nominated performance. Boal shared a screen story credit with Haggis, whom he has credited with teaching him the ins and outs of screenwriting.

Boal next convinced *Playboy* to send him to Iraq for a story about the harsh realities of the war. In late 2004 he was accepted as an embedded journalist with the US Army's 788th Ordnance Company, a specialized unit made up of elite bomb-squad technicians, and spent two weeks with the unit in the Iraqi capital of Baghdad. "It was eye-opening to see the tidal wave of bombs erupting all over the city and the everyday courage and professionalism of the people trying to deal with it," Boal told Johnston.

Upon returning from Iraq, Boal wrote an article for *Playboy* titled "The Man in the Bomb Suit," which focused heavily on the leader of the bomb-squad company, Sergeant Jeffrey S. Sarver. The article was published in the magazine's September 2005 issue and helped provide the inspiration for *The Hurt Locker*, an original screenplay Boal had already started writing about his experiences and observations in Iraq. He was persuaded to write the screenplay by director Kathryn Bigelow, best known at that time for helming action-driven films such as *Point Break* (1991) and *Strange Days* (1995), whom he had met several years earlier when she developed a Fox television series based on one of his articles.

THE HURT LOCKER

Inspired by such seminal and influential war films as *The Deer Hunter* (1978), *Apocalypse Now* (1979), and *Platoon* (1986), Boal set out to write a traditional, character-driven "war movie that takes place in a combat situation and puts the audience in the soldiers' shoes," as he told Johnston. After writing numerous drafts, Boal worked together with Bigelow to sell his *Hurt Locker* script to studios. The duo's efforts ultimately proved futile, however, as their script was in competition with at least forty other Iraq-themed projects. As a result, Boal and Bigelow, whose desire to cast relatively unknown actors also impeded their chances at securing financing, decided to produce the film on their own.

Shot mostly in Jordan over forty-four days, *The Hurt Locker* tells the story of Bravo Company, a three-man US Army Explosive Ordinance Disposal (EOD) unit in 2004 war-torn Iraq. It follows EOD team leader Sergeant First Class William James, played by Jeremy Renner, as he recklessly puts his and his team members' lives at risk in order to satisfy his thirst for adrenaline. After completing his tour of duty with Bravo Company, James returns home to his wife and infant son, but his boredom with daily civilian life eventually leads him back to Iraq for another tour.

The Hurt Locker had its world premiere at the Venice International Film Festival in September 2008, where it was greeted by many critics with rapturous praise. After being screened at other prominent film festivals around the world, the film was picked up by Summit Entertainment for distribution in the United States, where it received a limited release in June 2009. Despite playing in only five hundred theaters, *The Hurt Locker* was a box-office success, grossing $49 million on a budget of $15 million, and won widespread critical acclaim. Richard Corliss, in a representative review for *Time* (4 Sept. 2008), proclaimed it to be "a near-perfect war film" and commented that Boal and Bigelow "have pooled their complementary talents to make one of the rare war movies that's strong but not shrill, and sympathetic to guys doing an impossible job."

The Hurt Locker received numerous awards, including six Academy Awards and six British Academy of Film and Television Arts (BAFTA) Awards. Boal won the Academy Award for best original screenplay and shared the Academy Award for best picture with fellow producers Bigelow, Nicolas Chartier, and Greg Shapiro. He also won BAFTA Awards for best original screenplay and best picture and earned a Golden Globe nomination, among other honors. Bigelow, meanwhile, won the Academy Award for best director, becoming the first woman ever to receive the award.

ZERO DARK THIRTY

Boal next coproduced and wrote the original screenplay for *Zero Dark Thirty*, which marked his second collaboration with Kathryn Bigelow. The film chronicles the real-life, decade-long hunt for al-Qaeda terrorist leader Osama bin Laden after the September 11 terrorist attacks. It centers on the obsessive efforts of a young CIA operative, Maya Lambert (Jessica Chastain), to track down the elusive terrorist leader. Reportedly made with unprecedented cooperation from CIA, Pentagon, and White House officials, *Zero Dark Thirty* features more than one hundred speaking parts and includes a painstakingly detailed final sequence depicting the elite Navy SEAL team's raid on Osama bin Laden's compound in Abbottabad, Pakistan, which resulted in his death on May 2, 2011.

Despite receiving heavy criticism for its propagandistic tone and graphic scenes of enhanced interrogation techniques such as waterboarding, *Zero Dark Thirty* was met with wide critical acclaim and became a box-office hit, taking in $138 million worldwide. The film earned Boal a second Academy Award nomination for best original screenplay and another Academy Award nomination for best picture, shared with coproducers Bigelow and Megan Ellison. Commenting on the divisive response to the depiction of torture in *Zero Dark Thirty*, Boal explained to Pat Sierchio for the *Jewish Journal* (11 Feb. 2013), "The political point [of the film] is that this work was carried out by people without regard to politics one way or another. It was carried out by civil servants, not by Republicans or Democrats. . . . The real point is that the country and Washington have to face that they're culpable for what they did."

In 2014 Boal partnered with his *Zero Dark Thirty* coproducer Megan Ellison, the founder of Annapurna Pictures, and Hugo Lindgren, the former editor of the *New York Times Magazine*, to form Page 1, a journalism-based movie and television production company. "The goal is to dig out substantive stories that tell us something about who we are as a people and as a nation," Boal said, as quoted by Brooks Barnes for the *New York Times* (6 May 2014).

Boal lives in Los Angeles, California. In June 2014, he teamed up with Bigelow once again for a movie about US Army soldier Sergeant Bowe Bergdahl, who was a Taliban prisoner of war in Afghanistan for five years, from 2009 to 2014.

SUGGESTED READING

Boal, Mark. *"The Hurt Locker* Had Explosive Effect on Mark Boal's Screenwriting Career."' Interview by Claudia Eller. *Los Angeles Times.* Los Angeles Times, 11 Feb. 2010. Web. 21 July 2014.

Boal, Mark. "Off the Cuff: Mark Boal, Oscar Winner." Interview by Shauna Siggelkow. *Oberlin Review.* Oberlin Coll., 27 Sept. 2010. *Internet Archive.* Web. 21 July 2014.

Johnston, Sheila. *"The Hurt Locker:* Interview with Mark Boal." *Telegraph.* Telegraph Media Group, 25 Aug. 2009. Web. 21 July 2014.

Pfefferman, Naomi. "Oscar Watch: *The Hurt Locker's* Mark Boal." *Jewish Journal.* Tribe Media, 25 Feb. 2010. Web. 21 July 2014.

Sierchio, Pat. "Mark Boal's Journey from Journalism to Movie Chronicler of the Middle-East Wars." *Jewish Journal.* Tribe Media, 11 Feb. 2013. Web. 21 July 2014.

Smith, Jordan Michael. "The Many Faces of Mark Boal." *Nation.* Nation, 14 June 2013. Web. 21 July 2014.

SELECTED WORKS

In the Valley of Elah, 2007; *The Hurt Locker,* 2008; *Zero Dark Thirty,* 2012

—*Chris Cullen*

Courtesy of UNESCO/Michel Ravassard

Irina Bokova

Born: July 12, 1952
Occupation: Director-general of UNESCO

First elected in 2009 and then reelected in 2013, Irina Bokova is the first woman to serve as the director-general of the United Nations Educational, Scientific and Cultural Organization (UNESCO). During her tenure, she has championed such causes as the education and empowerment of women, the safety of journalists, and freedom of expression. Bokova has been scrutinized for her family's connections to communism in Bulgaria, but she has stressed that her history informed her professional path as her country and family emerged from the Cold War. She has advocated for greater intra-European collaboration and the embracement of pluralism in the modern nation-state.

Headquartered in Paris, UNESCO supports efforts to build strong foundations for sustainable development, poverty eradication, and lasting peace through international cooperation in areas such as education, the sciences, information, communication, and culture, including the preservation of the nearly one thousand World Heritage sites around the world. World Heritage sites are chosen based on their cultural or environmental significance; the list includes such sites as Australia's Great Barrier Reef and the Great Wall of China. Sometimes these sites are in the line of fire of military conflicts, as is the case in northern Mali, which has experienced several separatist uprisings since 2012, and in Syria, a country enmeshed in a destructive civil war. One such site in Syria, the three-thousand-year-old Sumerian and Amorite city of Mari on the Euphrates River, marks the birthplace of one of the earliest urban civilizations. "Let's be clear," Bokova wrote in an op-ed article for the *New York Times* (2 Dec. 2012). "We are not just talking about stones and building. This is about values, identities, and belonging."

Bokova's tenure as director-general has been marked by her and the organization's efforts to protect UNESCO sites from challenges posed by mass tourism, uncontrolled urbanization, and climate change as well as conflict situations, a task that has grown increasingly difficult since the organization lost financial support from the United States.

EDUCATION AND GOVERNMENT CAREER

Bokova was born on July 12, 1952, in Sofia, Bulgaria, to an elite Bulgarian family during the era of Soviet influence. Like many countries in eastern Europe, Bulgaria is ethnically diverse, and Bokova grew up in a small town that was predominantly Muslim. Her father, Georgi Bokov, was the well-known editor in chief of a newspaper called *Rabotnichesko Delo* ("workers' cause" or "workers' deed"), the mouthpiece of the Bulgarian Communist Party (BCP). Bokova and her brother, Filip Bokov, attended the country's best English-speaking school and, like many other children of the party elite, eventually studied at Moscow's State Institute of International Relations in the former Soviet Union. Bokova has been criticized for taking advantage of the privileges afforded to her by her family's ties to the BCP.

Bulgaria began its transition from a Communist regime to a democracy in 1989, but many former Communist leaders and their offspring—such as Bokova and her brother, who recently served as a principal adviser to former Bulgarian president Georgi Parvanov—remained in power. "I am from this Cold War generation that lived through this period; we didn't choose it," Bokova told Dan Bilefsky for the *New York Times* (23 Sept. 2009). "All my life I have shown I supported the political transformation of my country. I have nothing to be ashamed of." She graduated from university in 1976 and joined Bulgaria's Ministry of Foreign Affairs in 1977.

As third secretary at the Ministry of Foreign Affairs, Bokova concentrated on human-rights issues, particularly women's rights. In 1989 she completed postgraduate studies in US foreign policy as a Ford Foundation fellow at the University of Maryland. After 1989 the BCP became the Bulgarian Socialist Party (BSP), and Bokova was elected as a BSP candidate to Bulgaria's seventh Grand National Assembly in 1990, in which role she helped draft Bulgaria's democratic constitution, adopted in 1991.

Bokova ran unsuccessfully for vice president in 1996, then served as the Bulgarian minister of foreign affairs from November 1996 to February 1997. In 1999 she attended the Leadership and Economic Development program at Harvard University's John F. Kennedy School of Government. Later she was elected to Bulgaria's thirty-ninth National Assembly, where she served as a member of parliament from 2001 to 2005. Prior to becoming the director-general of UNESCO, Bokova was also Bulgaria's ambassador to France, Monaco, and UNESCO and the personal representative of the president of Bulgaria to the Organisation internationale de la Francophonie (OIF).

THE UNITED NATIONS AND THE 2009 ELECTION

Bokova joined Bulgaria's permanent mission to the United Nations in New York City in 1982. As third secretary of the mission, she was in charge of political and legal affairs. Throughout the 1980s and 1990s, she was also a member of the Bulgarian delegation at the UN conferences on the equality of women.

Bokova announced that she was running for director-general of UNESCO in 2009. There were nine candidates in the race, including painter and Egyptian culture minister Farouk Hosny, who was at the time considered the favorite to win. However, support for Hosny waned when allegations surfaced that he had once publicly threatened to burn any Israeli book he could find in Egypt's recently rebuilt Library of Alexandria. UNESCO voters were also wary of his close ties to Egypt's then president Hosni Mubarak, who supported censorship and other policies considered antithetical to the organization's mission. By the fall of 2009, a number of other candidates had dropped out of the race, but the voting in September was still fraught with political tension. Hosny apologized for his remarks about Israelis, but a large contingent of voters remained unimpressed, while Bokova gained popularity late in the race and was heralded, as Alfred de Montesquiou wrote for the Associated Press (22 Sept. 2009), as a "consensus figure."

Standard protocol for the director-general position is for members to vote by secret ballot, with the first candidate to receive a majority of the votes winning the election. If a majority cannot be determined by the fourth round of voting, the fifth round is limited to the two candidates with the most votes. Hosny and Bokova tied in the fourth round, and Bokova won with a final vote of 31–27 in the fifth, becoming both the first woman and the first eastern European to be elected to the position. Previous directors-general have served a maximum of two terms; Bokova, who replaced Koichiro Matsuura of Japan, began her second term after being reelected in 2013.

Following her election in 2009, Bokova did her best to quell the hostilities that had arisen among the member countries. She reached out to Egypt and to the larger Arab world, promising a renewed commitment to multiculturalism. "[Bokova] is a conciliatory politician who prefers to be behind the scenes," Assen Indjiev, a Bulgarian television journalist, told Bilefsky. "No one in Bulgaria believed that she would make it, because we are a small and poor country, but she was determined and she succeeded." Still, Bulgarians were divided about her new post. Another Bulgarian citizen, a political blogger named Ivo Indzhev, told Bilefsky, "Those who dislike Communism in this country are not happy about her promotion. For people in this region, her appointment sends the message that the West can swallow someone's Communist past very easily but can't abide an Arab who is anti-Israel."

UNESCO'S HISTORY AND MISSION

UNESCO is a specialized agency of the United Nations, established shortly after the founding of its parent organization in 1945. In an interview with *Leaders* magazine (July 2012), Bokova described the organization's mission:

"UNESCO's role lies in bridging the gaps in global governance by fostering international cooperation in education, the sciences, culture, and communication. UNESCO does not deliver development financial aid, but we craft the conditions for development. The organization does not itself keep the peace, but works to make it last." Ongoing projects include the United Nations' Millennium Development Goals, a pledge drafted in 2000 that includes such goals as reducing poverty, improving maternal health, and fighting AIDS/HIV. The goals are also tied to the larger mission of UNESCO's Education for All program. In 2012 Bokova told *Leaders* that approximately 16 percent of the world's population was illiterate—close to 792 million adults, most of them women.

Critics of UNESCO say that the organization is unfocused, with too many goals and not nearly enough funding to realize them. UNESCO operates on a relatively paltry budget; in 2009 Mort Rosenblum reported for the news website *GlobalPost* (15 Oct. 2009) that UNESCO's annual budget was $325 million, scarcely more than it was in the 1980s. UNESCO is considered one of the UN's most influential agencies, but frustrations with the organization are not new. It was plagued by mismanagement in the 1970s and 1980s, and in 1984, during Ronald Reagan's presidency, the United States withdrew from UNESCO for nearly twenty years, although it maintained a relationship with the organization during this time. The United States rejoined UNESCO in 2003, when the George W. Bush administration was preparing to invade Iraq. Like the UN itself, UNESCO has had to contend with an increasingly complex web of international and domestic politics.

THE UNITED STATES AND UNESCO

In 2013 the United States lost its vote in UNESCO's General Conference after failing to pay dues for two years, an automatic provision established in the organization's official rules. In the early 1990s Congress had passed laws prohibiting the United States from giving money to any United Nations agency that accepted Palestine as a full member; in 2011 UNESCO member states voted to give Palestine full membership, and consequently the United States began withholding dues. The same year, Bokova traveled to Washington, DC, to lobby lawmakers to change the legislation, a move supported by President Barack Obama's administration, but the proposal died in Congress. Prior to 2011, contributions from the United States had accounted for nearly 22 percent of UNESCO's budget. The organization was forced to reduce costs by cutting or delaying some of its programs and redeploying staff. In 2012 Bokova created an emergency fund and solicited contributions from various countries, including Saudi Arabia, Qatar, Gabon,

and Norway, but these funds failed to make up for the nearly $144 million lost. "There is still an enormous shortfall," Bokova told Steven Erlanger for the *New York Times* (11 Oct. 2012). "I can't think of a single program that was not affected."

The United States' unwillingness to amend its laws regarding Palestine took some lawmakers by surprise; Congress had passed the laws with little fanfare at a time when the Palestine Liberation Organization (PLO) was considered a terrorist organization and before it recognized Israel's right to exist in 1993. The Obama administration has supported rejoining UNESCO, but Congress largely supports the cutoff. In congressional testimony given in March 2012, former American ambassador to the United Nations Susan Rice argued that the cutoff was actually harming American interests abroad and that the relevant laws "run counter to US national security interests because they enable the Palestinians to determine whether the United States can continue to fund and lead in UN agencies that serve a wide range of important American interests," as reported by Erlanger. Rice continued, "A law that was intended to deter is failing to deter and then boomeranging on us."

PROTECTING SYRIAN SITES

In March 2014, UNESCO received reports of looted World Heritage sites in Syria, casualties of the country's ongoing civil war. These sites are pockmarked with bullet holes and show evidence of illegal digging for mosaics and ancient coins. The artifacts of Syria's rich and ethnically varied history are threatened by a modern political quagmire; how people treat the sites is complicated by their relationship with the Syrian government, which technically controls the sites. From afar, archaeologists and scholars mourn the tremendous loss of both Syrian lives and relics of history.

Cultural artifacts have long been at the front lines of modern warfare, from the bombing of Europe during World War II to the looting of the National Museum of Iraq in Baghdad following the US invasion in 2003. After the reports from Syria, Bokova, in her *New York Times* op-ed piece, proposed making the protection of cultural heritage a priority of international security. She argued that places like Mari in Syria could serve as pillars of peace, though she conceded that this is not by itself enough. "It is true that culture alone is not enough to build peace," she wrote. "But without culture, peace cannot be lasting."

PERSONAL LIFE

In addition to her native Bulgarian, Bokova is fluent in English, French, Spanish, and Russian. She holds state distinctions from numerous countries, including Bulgaria's highest state distinction, the Order of Stara Planina with ribbon, awarded in 2014.

Bokova is married to Kalin Mitrev, the director of the European Bank for Reconstruction and Development for Bulgaria, Albania, and Poland. Her first marriage, to Bulgarian journalist Lubomir Kolarov, ended in divorce. She has two adult children and lives in Paris.

SUGGESTED READING

Bilefsky, Dan. "Bulgarian Who Is to Lead UNESCO Advocates Political Pluralism." *New York Times*. New York Times, 23 Sept. 2009. Web. 4 June 2014.

Bokova, Irina. "Crafting the Conditions for Development." *Leaders*. Leaders Magazine, July 2012. Web. 4 June 2014.

Bokova, Irina. "Culture in the Cross Hairs." *New York Times*. New York Times, 2 Dec. 2012. Web. 4 June 2014.

de Montesquiou, Alfred. "Irina Bokova Wins UNESCO Race, Defeats Controversial Egyptian Farouk Hosny." *Huffington Post*. TheHuffingtonPost.com, 22 Sept. 2009. Web. 4 June 2014.

Erlanger, Steven. "Cutoff of US Money Leads UNESCO to Slash Programs and Seek Emergency Aid." *New York Times*. New York Times, 11 Oct. 2012. Web. 4 June 2014.

Rosenblum, Mort. "Analysis: Bokova Will Need Goodwill at UNESCO." *GlobalPost*. GlobalPost, 15 Oct. 2009. Web. 4 June 2014.

—*Molly Hagan*

Katherine Boo

Born: 1964
Occupation: Journalist and author

Katherine Boo, a *New Yorker* reporter and Pulitzer Prize winner, is not a typical journalist. In an interview with Clayton Moore for *Kirkus Reviews* (7 Feb. 2012), she stated, "My interest as a writer is in more ordinary low-income people, particularly women and children, and in seeing how their experiences over time illuminate the infrastructure of opportunity in their societies." Boo uses both audio- and video-recording devices as she works, which gives her the ability to go back and review her written notes. As she explained to Moore, "For me, good nonfiction writing begins with good reporting. The more thoroughly I document something, the more able I am to evoke it on the page." She also records her emotional responses so that she can recall them clearly when she begins writing the final piece.

Boo has earned numerous honors over the course of her career, including the 2004 National Magazine Award for feature writing for

Getty Images

her article "The Marriage Cure," which examines the idea of marriage as a cure-all for the ills of poverty. She was a senior fellow at the New America Foundation, a public-policy institute, from 2002 to 2006 and a Haniel Fellow at the American Academy in Berlin for the 2006–7 semester. In 2012 she received the Columbia Journalism School's most prestigious award, the Columbia Journalism Award, and spoke at the school's commencement ceremony. Of her own method of journalism, she wrote in the author's note of her book *Behind the Beautiful Forevers: Life, Death, and Hope in a Mumbai Undercity* (2012), "When I settle into a place, listening and watching, I don't try to fool myself that the stories of individuals are themselves arguments. I just believe that better arguments, maybe even better policies, get formulated when we know more about ordinary lives."

EDUCATION AND EARLY CAREER

Katherine Boo was born to Minnesotan parents who had moved to Washington, DC, when her father became an aide to Eugene McCarthy, then a member of the House of Representatives. Their last name is an Anglicization of the Swedish surname Bö. Boo enjoyed reading books as a child, especially those in which good triumphed over evil. The Encyclopedia Brown series was a favorite of both her and her sister.

Since her late teens, Boo has suffered from rheumatoid arthritis. She is able to write only because her 2002 MacArthur Fellowship helped cover the cost of an operation on her right hand. A native of Washington, DC, Boo took the civil service exam and worked as a typist for the General Services Administration after she graduated from high school. She stopped working for a time after becoming ill, then became a typist for the Federal Election Commission while attending college at night.

Boo received her bachelor's degree from Barnard College, part of Columbia University, in 1988, graduating summa cum laude. By that time, aged twenty-five, she knew what she wanted to do. While at Barnard she had typed and written editorials for the *Columbia Daily Spectator*, Columbia's daily student newspaper. A story she wrote about how budgets were allocated for DC public parks was published in a local magazine, the *Washington Monthly*, and caught the attention of Jack Shafer, then the editor of the *Washington City Paper*, an alternative weekly. Shafer hired Boo as a writer and later promoted her to his second in command, giving her editorial duties as well. As he told Charles McGrath for the *New York Times* (8 Feb. 2012), "She had the soul of a poet but the arm strength of an investigative reporter."

INVESTIGATIVE REPORTING

Not long after her promotion, Boo was hired as an editor at the *Washington Monthly*, where she focused on issues of poverty. In 1993 she joined the staff of the *Washington Post*, first writing for the newspaper's Sunday Outlook section before joining the investigative reporting team in 1994. While at the *Post*, Boo and editor Jodie Allen formed what they called the Self-Loathing Club; their "meetings" consisted of sharing drinks at the Jefferson Hotel near the newsroom and each praising the other's work while denigrating her own.

Boo began contributing to the *New Yorker* in 2001 and became a staff member two years later; her articles typically appear under the heading "Letter from . . ." or "A Reporter at Large." Her personal credo for investigative reporting, as she told an interviewer for the *New York Times'* By the Book feature (10 Feb. 2013), is, "It's OK to feel like an idiot going in as long as you don't sound like an idiot coming out." Her work for the *New Yorker* has covered topics such as the effects of Hurricane Katrina, a charter school in Boston, and the loss of manufacturing jobs in Texas.

WINNING THE PULITZER

The *Washington Post*'s 2000 Pulitzer Prize for public service was awarded for Boo's two series detailing the mistreatment of developmentally disabled residents of group homes in Washington, DC. She was thirty-five at the time and had spent thirteen months investigating DC's system of caring for people with such disabilities. The original series and its follow-up, separated by nine months, brought the residents' poor treatment to light and, according to the Pulitzer Board, "forced officials to acknowledge the conditions and begin reforms."

The series began when Boo, who does not drive, accepted the offer of a ride home after working on a story about a housing project.

An infamous asylum, Forest Haven, had been closed in the early 1990s, and its thousand-plus residents were placed in smaller residences and group homes. Boo's driver visited one such home on the way in order to meet with the staff; Boo joined him inside, where she found the house was completely dark. She emerged with cockroaches on her clothes and a determination to learn more.

Boo's original series, "Invisible Lives: DC's Troubled System for the Retarded," details the facts: oversight was lacking, records were not kept, and those supposed to be in authority colluded in a variety of unsavory situations, including rape, virtual slave labor in so-called training programs, and preventable deaths. Using the Freedom of Information Act as well as interviews, funeral home records, and cemetery databases, Boo recovered the names of forty-seven people who died between 1993 and 1999 for whom there were no official death records or explanations. Their names were printed as a sidebar in her follow-up series, "Invisible Deaths: The Fatal Neglect of DC's Retarded," in an article titled "System Loses Lives and Trust." The *Washington Post*'s investigations editor, Jeff Leen, told Ellen Liburt for *Editor & Publisher* (17 Apr. 2000), "Kate wanted to do a more rounded, textural approach, incorporating more the sights, sounds, and emotions of the material. This is a hard thing to marry with factual findings that are extremely serious and troubling."

THE GENIUS GRANT

Boo was also the recipient of a John D. and Catherine T. MacArthur Fellowship, nicknamed the Genius Grant, in 2002. Boo joined a select group; of the 635 people awarded the grant between 1981, when the program began, and 2002, she was only the fourteenth whose principal focus was in journalism. The citation included mention of her "expansive research, elegant presentation, and empathy for her subjects." The grant, however, is not a response to past work; rather, it is an investment in future endeavors.

The fellowship awards a $500,000 grant, paid over five years, with no strings attached; Boo planned first to purchase a digital camera to allow her to photograph places she visited and people about whom she was writing. The award, she told Carla Correa for the *American Journalism Review* (Nov. 2002), offered "a security that for five more years I can afford to do this and afford to take chances I might not otherwise afford to take."

When Boo was notified of the award by phone, she had just returned from a trip to a housing project in Oklahoma City and had difficulty hearing because of all the sirens in her neighborhood that night. She told Correa that she thought, "What if I'm just imagining this?

What if it's a fantasy? What if it's Joe Arthur from DC Auto?" and added, "I had him say it twice."

MOVE TO INDIA

After nearly twenty years spent reporting on poverty in the United States, Boo turned her attention to her husband's native country. As she spent more time in India, particularly Mumbai, she wondered how residents of the nearby slums could lift themselves from poverty. Although she knew none of the several languages spoken in the region, she traveled to the area in November 2007 and she spent over three years practicing her trademark immersive journalism.

Unlike many works that focus on poverty, Boo's *Behind the Beautiful Forevers* does not rely on statistics or charts; rather, it tells the stories of several people Boo observed and interviewed. In general, she neither makes judgments nor draws conclusions. With the aid of several women who served as translators, Boo focused her attention on Annawadi, a slum housing about three thousand residents, built on reclaimed swampland near Mumbai International Airport and five luxury hotels. Six of the residents had permanent jobs; the rest made quilts or marigold necklaces or searched through trash for materials that could be recycled or sold.

India would seem a strange choice for someone with Boo's health issues. In addition to her arthritis, she suffers from other immunological disorders and eye problems. Her conditions are best treated with immunosuppressants, making life in a slum where tuberculosis is prevalent risky. However, Boo felt that not telling the story would be too great a sacrifice. She writes in *Behind the Beautiful Forevers* about the night she decided to take the risk: "Tripping over an unabridged dictionary, I found myself on the floor with a punctured lung and three broken ribs in a spreading pool of Diet Dr Pepper, unable to slither to a phone. . . . Having proved myself ill-suited to safe cohabitation with an unabridged dictionary, I had little to lose by pursuing my interests in another quarter . . . where the risk of failure would be great but the interactions somewhat more meaningful."

BEHIND THE BEAUTIFUL FOREVERS

Although at first cautious about the presence of a forty-something blond American woman, the residents of Annawadi adjusted to her being there. As Boo told a reporter for *Rolling Stone* (7 June 2012), "I'd just show up and show up and show up. I tried to stay out of the way of their making a living, and people were cool with me hanging out." The first piece of published writing to result from her visit, a 2009 article she wrote for *New Yorker*, also enhanced her credibility. The article, which contrasts her observations of India's slums with their portrayal in the 2008 movie *Slumdog Millionaire*, was picked up

and translated by a Marathi-language newspaper, and the Annawadians saw that she understood their lives.

Asked by Moore about her tendency to omit herself from the narrative—she does not appear as "I" in *Behind the Beautiful Forevers* until her author's note at the end—Boo responded, "As a writer I've embraced my subject by choice. I can get off the sweaty bus and walk away. My hope is to devote whatever limited space a reader might grant me to conveying what life is like for the people who can't get off and walk away."

Behind the Beautiful Forevers won the National Book Award for nonfiction in 2012. In response, Boo said, as quoted by Stephan Lee for *Entertainment Weekly* (23 Nov. 2012), "A book like mine, which is about people buying and selling garbage in a Mumbai slum, is not sexy. If people read it, that makes publishers more receptive to the next three writers who are trying to write about unsexy, difficult topics." The book has won several other awards as well, including the 2013 PEN/John Kenneth Galbraith Award for nonfiction, which came with a $10,000 cash prize. Also in 2013 London's National Theatre announced plans to produce a dramatic version of the novel, adapted for the stage by David Hare and scheduled to debut in fall 2014.

PERSONAL LIFE AND INFLUENCES

Boo is married to Sunil Khilnani, a former Johns Hopkins University professor whom she met in 2001. He is based in London, where he is the director of the India Institute at King's College London; Boo lives in Washington, DC. In November 2007 she was elected to the Pulitzer Prize board.

Boo neither sugarcoats what she sees nor offers a Hollywood ending to her first book. As she told McGrath, "Very little journalism is world changing. But if change is to happen, it will be because people with power have a better sense of what's happening to people who have none." She reads fiction to learn techniques for writing concisely and working with multiple story lines. In addition, she credits Roberto Bolaño's novels *The Savage Detectives* (1998) and *By Night in Chile* (2000) for pulling her from a depressive state several years before she published *Behind the Beautiful Forevers*.

SUGGESTED READING

Boo, Katherine. "By the Book: Katherine Boo." *New York Times* 10 Feb. 2013, Sunday Book Review sec.: 8. Print.

Boo, Katherine. "Tales of the Unwritten Mumbai." Interview by Clayton Moore. *Kirkus Reviews*. Kirkus Media, 7 Feb. 2012. Web. 3 Mar. 2014.

Chotiner, Isaac. "Poverty as Destiny." Rev. of *Behind the Beautiful Forevers*, by Katherine Boo. *New Republic* 1 Mar. 2012: 32–35. Print.

Correa, Carla. "Betting on Her Future." *American Journalism Review* Nov. 2002: 11. Print.

Goldenberg, Kira. "Katherine the Great." *Columbia Journalism Review* July–Aug. 2012: 44–45. Print.

Liburt, Ellen. "Light amid Shadows." *Editor & Publisher* 17 Apr. 2000: 24–25. Print.

McGrath, Charles. "An Outsider Gives Voice to Slumdogs." *New York Times*. New York Times, 8 Feb. 2012. Web. 3 Mar. 2014.

—*Judy Johnson*

Scooter Braun

Born: June 18, 1981
Occupation: Talent manager

Scott "Scooter" Braun is a talent manager who is best known for discovering and subsequently managing the career of pop superstar Justin Bieber. In 2008, Braun stumbled upon a YouTube clip of a twelve-year-old Bieber singing at a local talent competition in early 2007. Braun arranged for Bieber and his mother to travel to Atlanta, Georgia, where Bieber had a chance meeting with famed R & B singer Usher. Braun and Usher subsequently worked out a production deal for Bieber, forming Raymond Braun Media Group. Braun and Usher then connected Bieber to Island Def Jam, which offered Bieber a recording contract. Bieber's debut album sold five million copies worldwide, and by 2012, *Forbes* magazine listed Bieber as the third most powerful celebrity in the world.

During those early years, Braun wielded more influence over Bieber than any other person in Bieber's life, including his doting single mother. Braun has been characterized as both an exacting manager and an indulgent parent, but if anecdotes about the relationship are true, it might be more accurate to say that Braun represents a little bit of both. For better or worse, Braun has played a significant role in shaping Bieber into the star and person that he is today. When Bieber began making tabloid headlines for illegal and reckless behavior in his late teens, Braun responded like a worried father. "I'm usually up pretty much all night until I know Justin is in," he told Shirley Halperin in an interview for the *Hollywood Reporter* (20 Nov. 2013).

Of course, Bieber is not Braun's only client. Braun owns School Boy Records, which signed Canadian singer Carly Rae Jepsen and Korean singer and rapper Psy. Many of Braun's clients have found enormous success through viral videos. The phenomenon speaks not only to Braun's skills as a marketer but also to his opportunist frame of mind. Of the music industry, he told

Landov

Lizzie Widdicombe in an interview for the *New Yorker* (3 Sept. 2012), "This isn't a dying business, this is a changing business." Braun is invigorated by the challenge. He routinely inks retail, product endorsement, and movie deals for his clients—deals that other talent managers might shy away from—to make up for the money they are theoretically losing in traditional record sales. "People can get taken advantage of in the music industry, but then we can also take advantage of the music industry," Bieber explained to Halperin (20 Nov. 2013). "That's what me and Scooter are doing."

EARLY LIFE

Scott Samuel Braun was born on June 18, 1981, and raised in Greenwich, Connecticut. His father, Dr. Ervin Braun, is a dentist who was born in Hungary, where Braun's Jewish paternal grandparents narrowly escaped the Holocaust. The family fled to the United States in 1956 during the Hungarian Revolution. Braun's mother, Susan Schlussel, worked as an orthodontist before retiring to teach dentistry. (She briefly returned to orthodontics in 2010 to give a fifteen-year-old Bieber invisible braces.) She instilled in Braun a sense of moral responsibility. "My mom is the most moral woman I know," Braun told Chris Hodenfield for *Greenwich Magazine* (Dec. 2010). "I know my compassion for others came from my mother. Since I was a little boy we spent Christmas at the soup kitchen. I'm Jewish, and my mother would say, 'We're not going to celebrate it, we might as well help people who need it.'"

Braun has two biological siblings, Adam and Liza, and two adopted brothers, Sam Manhanga and Cornelio Gouibunda, from Mozambique. Manhanga and Gouibunda, both former members of the Mozambique national basketball team, were thirteen and fifteen (Braun had just finished high school) when they came to live in Greenwich. Braun's parents became their legal guardians so that they could continue to study in the United States.

Braun earned the nickname Scooter when he was in the first grade. He attended a friend's birthday party, and a balloon magician who was entertaining the party guests coined the nickname. "I hated it," Braun told Halperin (22 Nov. 2010). "And my brother found that so he kept calling me Scooter. . . . My sophomore year in high school, I started my first basketball game and my brother was standing there with all my friends holding signs that say 'Ride the Scooter to Victory!' And all my friends chanting 'Scoooter.'" After that, the nickname stuck with him, and Braun ultimately came to embrace it.

EDUCATION

As a thirteen-year-old student at Central Middle School, Braun made a short film about the persecution of Jews in Hungary during the Holocaust and submitted the film to a school contest for National History Day. To Braun's delight and surprise, his ten-minute documentary, titled *The Hungarian Conflict*, advanced through the regional and state divisions, ultimately winning third place at the nationals. His grandmother sent a copy of the film to famed director Steven Spielberg. Braun later received a heartfelt letter from Spielberg, who in turn sent the film to the Holocaust Museum in Washington, DC. Braun told Hodenfield that the museum still shows the film, but it was the letter that had the biggest impact on him. "I still have the letter hanging on my wall, to this day. It was one of the most inspirational moments—it made me believe. *I can do this.*" Braun eventually met Spielberg at the White House decades later, in 2010. "I look over and see Steven Spielberg standing there, and I get star-struck. I get star-struck for people like [producer] David Geffen and Steven Spielberg, not celebrities," he said. "I get star-struck for people *who make it happen.*"

Braun was the class president and a basketball star at Greenwich High School. This is unsurprising given his father's love of the game, which was so strong that he founded a local league and built his children a basketball gymnasium in the family's backyard. After graduating from high school, Braun enrolled at Emory University in Atlanta, Georgia, where he played basketball. In a new city, far from home, Braun was free to reinvent himself. He did not like to admit that he came from cushy Greenwich, so he told people he grew up in Queens, giving them his father's childhood address.

PARTY KING

While in college Braun got involved selling fake IDs and began organizing parties for Emory students at nightclubs. "I got eight hundred kids at my first party," he told Widdicombe. He began throwing a party every week. Several months later, he quit the basketball team. As he devoted more of his time to party promotion, he realized that he could make more money from club owners if he chose a different club to host a party every week. Braun was a shrewd manager; he never drank at his parties, choosing instead to seek out strategic partnerships with Atlanta hip-hop talent and music-industry insiders. Braun ultimately dropped out of Emory in order to pursue party promotion full time.

When Braun's hard-working, middle-class parents found out that he had stopped going to school and given up his spot on the basketball team, they were devastated. When they heard that he did it to focus on throwing parties, they were furious. Braun's father traveled to Atlanta to investigate and happened to arrive on the weekend of the NBA All-Star Game, a big event for both basketball players and celebrities. When he arrived at his son's party, he was shocked to see basketball players and music-industry bigwigs climbing out of stretch limousines and waiting in line to get in. Braun saw his father and ushered him in, introducing him to everyone at the party. "I look at this and think, jeez, this is amazing," Braun's father recalled to Hodenfield. "That's when it dawned on me that he's a heavy hitter. And it finally hit me that he wasn't going to parties—he was *working.*"

Braun developed relationships with all of the big names coming out of Atlanta at the time, including Lil Jon, Ciara, Chingy, and CeeLo Green. He began throwing parties for 'N Sync, Britney Spears, Ludacris, and Shaquille O'Neal; he was even asked to arrange parties in Miami and London. Then one day, Braun met producer and rapper Jermaine Dupri, who told him, "You're never going to get to living in mansions by throwing parties," Braun recalled to Widdicombe. Dupri offered Braun a marketing position at his label, So So Def, and Braun was quickly promoted to executive director of marketing.

EARLY MUSIC MANAGEMENT CAREER

That trajectory was short-lived, however. A few years later, Braun was fired from So So Def, allegedly after a dispute over the direction of the company. He began working as a freelance consultant. "I knew the right people in the industry," he explained to Hodenfield. "But I wanted equity in something. I said the only way I'm going to get that is to get the same kind of control I had over my parties. And I'm going to take what I learned as a businessman doing the parties and institute it." In order to arrange one endorsement deal, Braun procured the names of several executives at Pontiac by pretending to be a college reporter writing a story about the car company's marketing strategy. Then he cold-called those executives and arranged a multimillion dollar endorsement deal with Ludacris and the Pontiac Solstice.

Shortly after that, he set up his own management company. His first client was a rapper named Asher Roth whom he had discovered on MySpace. Braun paid for Roth, who was from Pennsylvania, to move to Atlanta. Braun came up with a development and marketing plan for Roth, who released his first hit single—the slurred-sounding, stoner anthem "I Love College"—in 2009. The song was platinum certified.

Braun's fledgling company, which he founded in 2007, was called SB Projects. It was an umbrella organization that included his record label, School Boy Records, but it was still looking for its first big act. In 2008, while consulting for the recording artist Akon, Braun found a video of a young Justin Bieber singing a Ne-Yo song at a talent show in his hometown of Stratford, Ontario. As it happened, Braun was looking for a young Michael Jackson type—someone like the then enormously popular boy band the Jonas Brothers, with more polished chops. For Braun, Bieber was just that musician, but his general manager, Allison Kaye, was not so sure. She did not see a future with the twelve-year-old Canadian, but Braun did, and he was determined to sign him. "He sees the big picture," Kaye later conceded in an interview with Hodenfield. "A lot of managers lose the forest for the trees, but he's always eight steps ahead and you've got to catch up." Braun scoured the Internet for the name of the theater where Bieber had performed, and then he found Bieber's school online and began calling school board members and begging them to put him in touch with Bieber and his mother.

MANAGING JUSTIN BIEBER'S CAREER
Pattie Mallette, Bieber's mother, was initially wary of Braun (she saw her son as a budding Christian musician) but consented to come to Atlanta, where Bieber could record some demos. But Braun had a more detailed plan for Bieber. He wanted to build Bieber's YouTube following and had him and his mother produce home videos of him singing covers of R & B songs and playing a variety of instruments. The "homemade" videos attracted more than fifty-four million views. Buoyed by Bieber's new Internet following, Braun took him to meet record executives in New York and Los Angeles, but they all turned him down. Because Bieber was so young, they said, he needed a solid platform, such as the Disney Channel, to back him up, or

a singing competition show, such as *American Idol*, to boost his profile. Braun decided to try a different tack; he pitched Bieber to R & B singer Usher and pop star Justin Timberlake. Both stars expressed interest in working with Bieber, and Braun ignited a bidding war between them, which he played up in the press. Bieber eventually signed with Island Def Jam, which arranged a profit split between Island Def Jam and the Raymond Braun Media Group (RBMG), formed by Usher (whose last name is Raymond) and Braun. The chair of Island Def Jam, Barry Weiss, commented to Widdicombe that "between YouTube and Usher, Scooter created a platform that basically hadn't existed."

Braun and Usher became the dominant forces in Bieber's early career. The men saw themselves as keepers of a fragile talent. Bieber was good natured, but he was young. It was not all smooth sailing. Braun was tough on his charge and worked hard to control Bieber's image, even when that meant controlling Bieber himself. Braun prepped him for every interview and cajoled him into taking a myriad of business deals, even putting Bieber's name on a line of women's perfumes. But the relationship was a strong, and oddly public, one. Bieber looked up to Braun, and Braun welcomed Bieber into his own family while simultaneously cultivating his celebrity status as his manager. While Bieber was still a minor, Braun also set up a fund with a board of advisers to manage Bieber's finances, which are estimated to be worth more than $130 million. The board includes a business manager, two portfolio managers, a lawyer, Bieber's mother, and Braun himself, who coached Bieber on finances weekly.

OTHER PROJECTS
As Bieber got older, Braun gave him more power within SB Projects. When Braun signed Carly Rae Jepsen, a pop singer from Canada, he gave Bieber a 50 percent cut. Bieber agreed to go on tour with Jepsen and even shot a video of himself and several friends dancing to Jepsen's single "Call Me Maybe," which spawned a number of copycat videos during the summer of 2012 and helped to shoot the song to the top of the charts. Braun remains an important figure in Bieber's life, but their relationship has suffered as Bieber has gotten older and more independent. "Scooter was like the father figure in my life," Bieber told Halperin in 2013. "But when I started to grow up, it was hard for him to have to listen to my input. I want to be me, to show everybody who I am as an individual. I don't want to just be a puppet."

In addition to Jepsen and Bieber, Braun manages an English boy band called the Wanted and singer Ariana Grande. Braun has also been active in diversifying his company, SB Projects, into areas beyond music and talent management, establishing a film and television division, a publishing division, and a technology investment unit. He is an executive producer of the film *The Giver*, released in the United States in August 2014.

PERSONAL LIFE

Braun has invested heavily in several Silicon Valley companies. Two of his most successful investments are the ride-sharing service Uber and the streaming-music service Spotify. In January 2014, he became engaged to longtime girlfriend Yael Cohen, the founder and chief executive of the health organization and charity F—— Cancer. The couple married on July 6, 2014. Braun himself supports several philanthropic causes, including Pencils of Promise, which was founded by his brother Adam to build schools in underserved communities around the globe. Braun lives in Los Angeles.

SUGGESTED READING

Halperin, Shirley. "Justin Bieber Reveals Will Smith Counsels Him Weekly in Rare, Raw Interview." *Hollywood Reporter*. Hollywood Reporter, 20 Nov. 2013. Web. 15 May 2014.

Halperin, Shirley. "The Brains behind Bieber: A Conversation with Scooter Braun." *Hollywood Reporter*. Hollywood Reporter, 22 Nov. 2010. Web. 15 May 2014.

Hodenfield, Chris. "Brains & Braun." *Greenwich*. Greenwich Magazine, Dec. 2010. Web. 15 May 2014.

Widdicombe, Lizzie. "Teen Titan: The Man Who Made Justin Bieber." *New Yorker*. Condé Nast, 3 Sept. 2012. Web. 15 May 2014.

—*Molly Hagan*

Jim Breyer

Born: 1961
Occupation: Venture capitalist

Jim Breyer is an investor and venture capitalist who is managing partner of Accel, a firm based in Palo Alto, California. His estimated worth is $2 billion and he was ranked number one on the Forbes Midas List of top tech investors for three consecutive years. (He lost his rank in 2014 to Jim Goetz of Sequoia Capital. Goetz, who used to work for Accel, invested in the text messaging application WhatsApp, which Facebook bought for a staggering $19 billion in February.) Breyer is best known as an early investor in the social network Facebook. In 2005, a year after Mark Zuckerberg launched Thefacebook.com in his Harvard dorm room, Breyer and Accel invested $12.7 million in the social network, valuing it at nearly $100 million. At the time of Facebook's

Bloomberg via Getty Images

initial public offering in May 2012, Accel was one of the largest shareholders—at one point, the second largest, after Zuckerberg himself—in the company. The investment reinvigorated the firm, which was still smarting from losses suffered during the tech bust in 2001, and made Breyer a billionaire, as well as raising his stature among venture capitalists. In early 2014, after raising two Accel funds totaling nearly $1.5 billion, Breyer decided to minimize his role at the firm to focus on investing his own money through the newly created Breyer Capital.

Venture capital (VC) firms raise funds through a number of investors. They then invest those funds in fledgling companies. Theoretically—due to the number of investors involved in any given fund—risk is diversified, but investing with VC firms is an inherently high-risk business. Of course, as with any high-risk endeavor, venture capital investments also hold the possibility of high returns. Accel specializes in technology start-ups, and Breyer himself has said that he has a special fondness for companies in the nascent stages of their growth. He told Nicole Perlroth for *Forbes* magazine (6 Apr. 2011) about a visit to the San Francisco Museum of Modern Art, where he is a board member. A curator there wrote that of "every ten artists I pick, nine of them will end up failing. But that one out of ten becomes the next Picasso." Breyer told Perlroth, "That's the venture capital business! You're not going to get them all right. But if you stop taking chances, stop discovering, you're never going to figure out who the next Picasso or Gerhard Richter is."

In February 2013, Breyer took a position on Harvard University's corporation board, and the board of 21st Century Fox, a part of News Corporation. Breyer joined the board at News Corp in 2011, just after it was made public that the company had hacked the phones of celebrities and a murder victim. He once sat on the boards of Facebook, Walmart, and Dell, but resigned all three positions in May 2013. It was an abrupt end for three long-serving roles; Breyer sat on the board of Facebook for eight years, the board of Walmart for twelve years and Dell's board for four years. But Breyer has said it was simply time for him to go. Meanwhile, Accel has extended its reach far outside of Silicon Valley, with partners in Beijing, India, and London. The firm also enjoys a successful partnership with the International Data Group (IDG) in China. In fact, Accel is doing a huge chunk of its business in the country. "It's not the US as the hub and China as the satellite anymore," Breyer told Perlroth. "Perhaps China becomes the hub and we in the US become the satellite."

The move toward global investment marks a shift in venture capital akin to the shift that took place between the tech bust and the Facebook era. How well a firm can adapt to the change—or better yet, anticipate the change—is an indicator of how well the firm will perform in the long run. Accel focuses on keeping with their investment thesis, Perlroth reported, which means that individual associates must keep a "prepared mind." The "new-age maxim," Perlroth wrote, "boils down to defining who you are and who you're not and investing accordingly." To put the concept in context, it means doing the opposite of what many investors did in the early 2000s. Accel cofounder, Jim Swartz told Perlroth: "A lot of people in the business get caught up in momentum investing. That's a good way to get killed."

EARLY LIFE AND EDUCATION

James W. Breyer was born in 1961 in New Haven, Connecticut. His parents were Hungarian immigrants who fled Budapest after the revolution in 1956. They settled in Vienna and began studying at the University of Vienna, but Breyer's father, an engineer, received a scholarship to Yale University. They moved to New Haven, with only five dollars to their name, in 1957. Breyer spent his early years living in a funeral home in New Haven. The family later moved to Natick and Weston, both in the Boston area. Breyer's mother, Eva, is a mathematician who worked for Honeywell and later ran their design automation group. His father, John, left Honeywell to work for the International Data Group (IDG). His position at IDG would later prove useful to his son.

For college, Breyer was accepted to both Yale and Stanford University in California. His parents lobbied for Yale because it was closer to home, but Breyer chose Stanford because he wanted to study economics and computer science, and because of the school's proximity to Silicon Valley. He enrolled in 1979. During the summer and fall of 1981, his junior year, Breyer worked for Hewlett-Packard's data systems division in Cupertino doing product management and some technical work. "I came away from the experience with enormous respect for HP," Breyer told Udayan Gupta for the book *Done Deals: Venture Capitalists Tell Their Stories* (2000). "One event stands out: the time I had the audacity to schedule a lunch with John Young, HP's CEO. To his credit, he met with me, and I offered him my opinions on what HP should be doing differently in the computer business." Breyer told him about an innovative company called Apple, and suggested HP get into the personal computer business. "I smile when I look back on what he must have been thinking during that lunch," Breyer said.

WORKING AT APPLE

Breyer was an ambitious college student, and in 1981, the same year he worked for HP, he saw Steve Jobs on the cover of *Time* magazine and became enamored of the computer company Apple. He sent Jobs a resume, and Jobs passed it along to his director of marketing. Breyer worked part-time at Apple while going to school, and full-time during the summer of 1982. Breyer recalled the excitement of the time, and told Gupta that 1982 was "one of the defining years in the computing business." IBM entered the market and Apple's stock rose from eleven dollars to sixty dollars during the span of the summer months. Apple was a young company with young employees; Breyer was twenty-one, and few of his colleagues were much older. He was happy to work for Apple, in the charged, almost spiritual atmosphere presided over by the guru-like Jobs. Still, he decided to apply to business school.

HARVARD BUSINESS SCHOOL

He was accepted at Harvard, but decided to spend two years working for the consulting firm McKinsey & Company in New York before enrolling. In more ways than one, McKinsey was a world away from Apple and the computer companies of Silicon Valley. The executives traveled in limousines, and one day, after a series of presentations ending at nine o'clock at night, his boss asked him to hand deliver copies to each of the ten higher-ups who would be attending the meeting the next morning. Driving through New York, New Jersey, and Connecticut that evening, Breyer might have been thinking what he later told Gupta: "I was absolutely convinced I didn't want to be a management consultant."

"I was at Harvard Business School from 1985 to 1987, a period when Wall Street mania was ubiquitous," Breyer told Gupta. "There was very little interest in technology." Breyer estimated that about a third of his graduating class went directly to a Wall Street firm. Still, he remained focused on the computer industry—more so than venture capital. He credits Harvard professor Bill Sahlman and Mitch Kapor, the founder of the pioneering Lotus Development Corporation, for sparking his interest in venture capital. Kapor also inspired Breyer's early fascination with the Internet. Breyer was advised to spend five to ten years working for a technology company before working with a VC firm.

ACCEL PARTNERS

After graduating from Harvard Business School in 1987, Breyer was recruited by Tom Siebel of the tech company Oracle. Breyer was poised to become the company's director of product management. But Siebel knew that Breyer also had his eye on a career in venture capital. In his conversation with Gupta, he recalled Siebel's pitch: "Jim, you can come work for me for ten years, and you'll be investing your own money—not someone else's." Breyer also received several offers from VC firms, and ultimately chose Accel Partners in San Francisco. Accel Partners was founded by Jim Swartz and Art Patterson in 1984, and Breyer joined as an associate in 1987. He planned to stay only a few years before starting his own investment firm, but of course, things turned out a little differently.

Breyer worked closely with Swartz and Patterson, and thrived under Accel's focus on technology companies. From the beginning, Breyer told Gupta, Accel was "a tremendous fit." He grew to view Swartz and Patterson as mentors. "Venture capital is still an apprenticeship business," he told Gupta, "and mentorship is at the heart of learning the venture capital business." He was paid far less at Accel than he would have made working for Oracle, but he was happy. He notes however, that due to the market crash of 1987, people were squeamish about the VC business. Venture capitalists were leaving the business in droves; for Gupta, Breyer cited a 20 percent drop in both individual venture capitalists and VC firms in the late 1980s. The limited base made competition fierce.

TECH BOOM

By contrast, the 1990s—the late 1990s, in particular—were characterized by the bluster of the tech boom. In 1993, Breyer invested $2 million in UUNET, one of the earliest commercial Internet providers. Before Facebook came along, it was often cited as one of his biggest deals. In 1996 alone, Accel invested in Redback Networks (sold to Ericsson for $1.9 billion in 2007); Foundry Networks (sold to Brocade for

$3 billion); and Portal Software (sold to Oracle for $220 million in 2006). But the good fortune wouldn't last. Breyer—who spoke with Gupta in 2000, as the tech bubble reached its peak—said: "Today there is euphoria—in many cases a mania—that will inevitably come to an end. In today's environment, it is easy to confuse brains with a bull market." Despite Breyer's prescience, he and Accel were hit hard by the bust and weren't able to bounce back as quickly as other VC firms. Harvard, Princeton, and the Massachusetts Institute of Technology (MIT) all cut Accel from their portfolios in 2004, but as Perlroth noted, their decision could not have come at a worse time. (Of the Ivies investing with Accel, only Stanford remained.) Breyer was just then struggling to raise a fund called Accel IX, which would become "the best performing venture capital fund—ever."

FACEBOOK INVESTMENT

In 2005, Accel partners gathered to discuss their investment thesis. Part of that thesis reaffirmed their growing interest in social media, so Breyer tasked a principal named Kevin Efrusy with exploring the social media realm. Fortuitously, Chi-Hua Chien, a graduate student at Stanford who was working part-time at Accel, showed Efrusy a site called Thefacebook.com. Zuckerberg refused to meet with Efrusy despite many dogged attempts on Efrusy's part to set up communication. Finally, Efrusy met with Sean Parker, the founder of Napster and Facebook's first president. He found out that Zuckerberg was interested in making a deal with Donald Graham at the Washington Post Company. At that point, everyone at Accel was focused on Facebook. "The statistics were so spectacular, you didn't need to be a genius to know it was a great project," Patterson told Perlroth.

Breyer tried to reach out to Graham to get in on the deal, but Graham, unsurprisingly, was not interested. The same night, he invited Zuckerberg and his team to dinner. The dinner has become a well-known story in itself. Breyer ordered a bottle of expensive wine for the table, but Zuckerberg, who was not yet twenty-one, drank Sprite. When it became clear that it would be a smarter move to partner with Accel than the Washington Post Company, Zuckerberg reportedly wept in the restaurant bathroom at the thought of dealing the blow to Graham. The next day, Zuckerberg signed a deal with Breyer and Accel.

There is some dispute about Breyer's fame resulting from the Facebook deal. Perlroth wrote that some venture capitalists believe that Breyer took undue credit for the deal, credit that was reinforced when he invested $1 million of his own money into the company. Still, Breyer's role in persuading Zuckerberg—whom he quickly identified as the one who needed persuading—clinched the deal.

In April 2005, Accel invested $12.7 million in Facebook, valuing the site at $98 million. It was a triumph for Accel, but also, Breyer told Perlroth, incredibly controversial. Valuing Facebook at nearly $100 million, on the surface, seemed ludicrous. Other sites like Friendster and MySpace were losing steam. And while Facebook was the day's hot ticket, the company had only ten employees, 700,000 users and no business model. "Investors thought we had grossly overpaid," Breyer told Perlroth. So far, this hasn't proved to be the case. When Facebook made its initial public offering in May 2012, Accel sold $2.1 billion worth of shares. Breyer alone made $81.1 million.

PERSONAL LIFE

While Breyer doesn't consider himself "particularly talented as a writer," he told Gupta, he loves writing short stories. Before beginning business school, he spent several weeks at Cambridge University, writing. Breyer divorced in 2004 and has three children.

SUGGESTED READING

Gupta, Udayan. *Done Deals: Venture Capitalists Tell Their Stories.* Cambridge: Harvard Business School P, 2000. Print.
Levy, Ari. "Accel Facebook Bet Poised to Become Biggest Venture Profit." *Bloomberg.* Bloomberg, 18 Jan. 2012. Web. 14 Apr. 2014.
Morgenson, Gretchen. "A Director with Irons in So Many Fires." *New York Times.* New York Times, 26 May 2012. Web. 14 Apr. 2014.
Perlroth, Nicole. "The Comeback Kid." *Forbes.* Forbes, 6 Apr. 2011. Web. 14 Apr. 2014.

—*Molly Hagan*

Nancy Brown

Born: ca. 1963
Occupation: Chief executive officer of the American Heart Association

Nancy Brown became the first female chief executive officer of the American Heart Association (AHA) in 2009. The AHA is the oldest and largest volunteer-based health organization dedicated to fighting cardiovascular disease in the United States. The AHA's team of employees and volunteers works to educate the public about heart disease and to advance initiatives designed to reduce the number of lives claimed by the disease every year. The AHA also raises funds for scientific research and treatment and lobbies for better public health policies at the local, state, and federal levels. Heart disease—also known as cardiovascular disease or coronary heart disease—is the leading cause of death in

Bloomberg via Getty Images

the United States and worldwide. It is an umbrella term that describes a number of conditions that arise from atherosclerosis (clogged arteries), arrhythmia, or heart valve problems.

At the AHA, Brown has led a number of ongoing initiatives to improve heart health, including the START! campaign, a program to promote workplace walking groups; Power to End Stroke, a public awareness campaign about stroke risks and prevention; Alliance for a Healthier Generation, a health and fitness campaign targeted at children; and Get with the Guidelines, a program created for hospitals and health providers caring for patients with heart disease. Brown has worked with the AHA since 1986 and served as its chief operating officer (COO) for eight years before becoming its chief executive. As COO, she helped draft the AHA's 2010 Impact Goal in 1998, which aimed to reduce deaths related to coronary heart disease and stroke by 25 percent by 2010. The success of the 2010 Impact Goal prompted the AHA to propose an even broader goal for 2020, focusing not only on mortality reduction but on improving individual cardiovascular health, as well.

EDUCATION AND EARLY CAREER

Nancy Brown was born in Port Huron, Michigan, and grew up in Marysville, a small town on the border between Michigan and Ontario, north of Detroit. She took her first job at the age of fifteen, scooping ice cream at Stroh's Ice Cream Parlor in St. Clair. She was a competitive swimmer at Marysville High School and graduated in 1981. Growing up, Brown was interested in communications and debate and considered a career in broadcast journalism, but she chose to study marketing and communications at Central Michigan University in Mount Pleasant. By the time she earned her bachelor's degree in 1985, her desire to become a television news anchor had faded. "I realized that the opportunities for me would be broader if I focused on broad business and marketing," she told Kristy J. O'Hara for *Smart Business* magazine (31 May 2011).

Her first job out of college was at the Mount Carmel Mercy Hospital in Detroit. As the special events director, Brown worked to raise money for the hospital. She discovered that she enjoyed working for a mission-driven nonprofit organization and developed a passion and skill for fundraising. She next served as the director of development and deputy director of the endowment campaign for the Michigan Cancer Foundation.

Brown was hired as the Metro Detroit director in the Michigan affiliate of the American Heart Association in 1986. For the next fifteen years, she served various roles in the organization, including executive vice president for the Massachusetts affiliate, executive vice president for the New England affiliate, and national executive vice president for science operations. She was named the COO of the AHA at its headquarters in Dallas in 2001.

HEALTH INITIATIVES AT THE AMERICAN HEART ASSOCIATION

As COO, Brown led many of the AHA's health initiatives, including Go Red for Women, which increases public awareness about women's heart health and raises funds for heart disease research and treatment. The initiative was launched in 2004. In 2005, Brown and the AHA teamed up with the William J. Clinton Foundation to launch the Alliance for a Healthier Generation, a program designed to reduce the prevalence of childhood obesity and to teach children about health and fitness. The alliance's first initiative, called the Healthy Schools Program, was launched in 2006 and focuses on a number of school-based wellness initiatives, such as improving the nutritional value of public school lunches, increasing after-school program time dedicated to physical activity, and removing junk food options from school vending machines. As of 2014, more than twenty thousand schools across the United States had joined the Healthy Schools Program.

The AHA has also supported the passage of several ordinances and laws that promote healthy nutrition in school lunches at the local and state level. The START! campaign, a group walking initiative, and Power to End Stroke, both founded in 2006, are two of the many Brown-helmed programs that encourage people to adopt healthier lifestyles in the name of heart health. Power to End Stroke is an education and awareness campaign of the AHA and its affiliate organization the American Stroke Association.

Brown has also been a part of major in-house initiatives at the AHA, including the American Heart University, an intensive training program for staff and volunteers established in 2008. AHU offers both online classes and face-to-face workshops in subjects such as fundraising, advocacy, communications, and science and research. It is not an academically accredited institution, but AHU equips employees and volunteers with professional development opportunities to better help the AHA reach its impact goals.

Brown has also led the You're the Cure volunteerism initiative. The program seeks to promote health-related policy initiatives and laws through a grassroots network of volunteers. She also created the Vision for Volunteerism initiative, which seeks to create more opportunities for volunteer service based on the volunteers' specific interests. Brown explained the importance of a strong volunteer network in an interview with Shashana Pearson-Hormillosa for the *Dallas Business Journal* (10 Sept. 2009), saying, "When you work in the not-for-profit sector, you depend on volunteers to build the organization. What I realized and learned very quickly is that organizations like the American Heart Association are only as strong as the volunteer leaders they attract."

CHIEF EXECUTIVE OFFICER

After serving as COO for eight years, Brown was named the CEO of AHA in 2008, but she did not officially assume the position until January 2009. She replaced the outgoing chief executive Cass Wheeler, who had headed the AHA for eleven years. Working out of the AHA headquarters in Dallas, Brown oversees the organization's 2,700 employees and nearly twenty-three million volunteers. "As COO, I was focused on operations, making sure the organization delivered on finances, science, etc." Brown told Pearson-Hormillosa, but she noted that her objectives as CEO are quite different. "As CEO, the buck stops with me. I get to spend a lot of time externally building relationships to help further the mission of the organization. I spend a lot of time working with individuals and corporations who support our work," she said.

Brown is the public face of the AHA and works hard to establish collaborative arrangements with businesses and corporations to promote heart-healthy policies and products. She also seeks to inspire the American public to live healthier lives; she has her work cut out for her in this regard—one in every three Americans are affected by some form of cardiovascular disease—but she believes that people can take simple steps to reduce their risk. In addition to the health column that she writes for the *Huffington Post*, Brown speaks on behalf of the AHA whenever an issue touching on heart health is in the news. She is vocal in her support of advances in heart health, such as the adoption of graphic cigarette warning labels; criticizes setbacks, such as the current e-cigarette trend; and clarifies misinformation through her column and other outreach initiatives. As CEO, Brown has focused on prevention—promoting exercise, smoking cessation, and a healthy diet as the building blocks of a disease-free life. "Despite being the number-one killer of all Americans, cardiovascular disease is largely preventable through lifestyle choices such as increased physical activity and better nutrition," she told Rachel Horn in an interview for the *Atlantic* (6 Apr. 2011). "It is deceptively simple. The big challenge is in motivating people to make lifestyle changes and removing environmental barriers that hinder them."

In 2011, under Brown's leadership, the AHA launched a program called the Guideline Advantage in collaboration with the American Cancer Society and the American Diabetes Association. Guideline Advantage, which is a broader version of Brown's Get with the Guidelines program, is a data collection program for physicians, hospitals, and other health care providers.

2020 HEALTH IMPACT GOAL

During Brown's tenure as COO, the AHA met a portion of its 2010 Impact Goal—to reduce deaths from coronary heart disease and stroke by 25 percent—two years ahead of schedule. Despite the outstanding success of the 2010 Impact Goal in reducing deaths from cardiovascular diseases and strokes, Brown and her associates at the AHA were deeply concerned by the increasing prevalence of obesity and sedentary lifestyles—two major risk factors for heart disease and stroke. In response to these growing concerns, the AHA began looking for ways to craft an even more ambitious impact goal for 2020. "Having a bold goal the entire organization rallies around is one way that we've been able to really propel the organization and grow our revenue as well as grow our mission impact," Brown told O'Hara. Soon after her appointment as chief executive, the AHA announced its 2020 Impact Goal—to improve the cardiovascular health of all Americans by 20 percent and to reduce deaths caused by heart disease and stroke by 20 percent by 2020.

The 2020 Impact Goal is significant—and also unusual—in that it focuses on individual heart health as well as the usual metric of total annual deaths from heart disease and stroke. The 2020 goal finds specific ways to focus on improving individual cardiovascular health—a trickier concept in terms of measurement than simply calculating the number of deaths per year. In order to achieve this goal, the AHA's volunteer scientists created a unique metric designed to define and measure cardiovascular health based on seven key health factors: blood pressure, physical activity, cholesterol, diet, weight, smoking status, and blood glucose.

The 2020 Impact Goal was a product of Brown's Innovation Think Tank, an in-house initiative that she helped to establish after becoming CEO. The think tank is comprised of both staff members and volunteers. Brown knew that she wanted the AHA to rally around one goal, and the think tank generated more than one hundred ideas to accomplish that objective. To narrow down the list, Brown cited her priorities, explaining to O'Hara how the AHA "looked at what might have the biggest impact toward our mission and biggest possibilities for revenue, and that's how we prioritized our ideas." The think tank has fostered a culture of innovation that has worked in the AHA's favor. "Think about who the best and brightest minds are who are willing to be open and that will have significant expertise to contribute to your business goals, and make it informal," Brown told O'Hara. "Don't create another bureaucracy. Make it that they are truly a think tank providing advice and guidance and thinking."

ANTISMOKING EFFORTS

The AHA, along with a number of other health organizations, has been locked in a legal battle with tobacco companies for decades. Brown and the AHA continue to actively campaign in collaboration with antitobacco groups. According to the AHA, about one-third of smoking-related deaths are linked to cardiovascular disease and stroke. The rise of e-cigarettes, marketed as a healthy alternative to cigarettes, has presented a slew of new problems for health and antismoking organizations. In 2010, the AHA—in support of the Federal Drug Administration (FDA)—lost a battle to regulate e-cigarettes as drugs in the District of Columbia. The FDA argues that e-cigarettes, which are smokeless but deliver nicotine through vapor, are just as harmful as cigarettes. (Many harmful chemicals can be found in e-cigarettes, even in the absence of tar.) The devices deliver nicotine, the highly addictive substance in cigarettes, and the FDA has tried to ban them or regulate them more strictly as a drug, rather than a tobacco product. After the 2010 ruling, Brown spoke to Duff Wilson for the *New York Times* (7 Dec. 2010) about the dangers of unregulated drug products and the marketing promise that e-cigarettes are healthy or will help smokers quit. "The appeals court has cleared the way for the industry to peddle these products to consumers without any scrutiny as to their safety or efficacy," she said. "There is no scientific evidence that e-cigarettes are effective smoking cessation devices and, until they undergo rigorous evaluation by the Food and Drug Administration, they should be pulled from the marketplace. With this ruling, e-cigarette manufacturers will continue to make misleading claims that their products can help smokers quit." Despite this setback, the AHA continues to work closely with the US Centers for Disease Control and Prevention and the Center for Tobacco Products to implement the Tobacco Control Act and to promote other antismoking initiatives.

ONGOING EFFORTS TO IMPROVE HEART HEALTH

In a more positive development, the AHA has supported the passage of the Affordable Care Act, which expanded health care coverage to a majority of Americans. In 2013, an estimated 7.3 Americans with cardiovascular disease were uninsured. Uninsured individuals are far less likely to receive appropriate and timely care, leading to poor medical outcomes and higher mortality rates. The quality and cost of health care in the United States has always been a concern of the AHA, and the organization has long advocated for health care reforms to improve access to affordable coverage and has opposed policies that seek to scale back eligibility or reduce benefits. The Affordable Care Act, Brown told Horn, "is revamping a broken healthcare system that too often didn't meet the needs of patients." The new law bans lifetime limits on coverage and requires insurance companies to provide coverage for people with preexisting conditions. "A year after the Affordable Care Act was enacted, the prospects for a healthier future have improved dramatically for heart disease and stroke patients," Brown told Horn.

As heart disease becomes an increasing health concern worldwide, the AHA has sought to extend its mission, "to build healthier lives, free of cardiovascular disease and stroke," to a global reach. In 2013, Brown represented the AHA and other nongovernmental organizations devoted to fighting heart disease at a summit on noncommunicable diseases at the United Nations. The AHA was subsequently granted Special Consultative Status in collaboration with the World Health Organization to share expertise and resources in the global effort to reduce cardiovascular diseases and stroke, which are the leading causes of death not only in the United States but worldwide. This designation is critical in expanding the AHA's mission and outreach globally. "This designation is a tremendous opportunity for us to leverage our volunteers' expertise to save and improve lives around the world," Brown stated in a press release by the AHA (11 Sept. 2013).

PERSONAL LIFE

Brown is married to Gary Brown—who shares her maiden name though not a familial connection. They live in Plano, Texas, with their bichon frise dog, Zoe.

In addition to her work at the AHA, Brown is chair-elect of the National Health Council, cochair of the Coalition to Transform Advanced Care, and a member of the executive committee and board of directors of Research!America. She is also a board member of the Campaign for Tobacco-Free Kids and the Alliance for a Healthier Generation. She serves on the Qualcomm Life Advisory Board (Qualcomm is a telecommunications company), the Corporate Advisory Board of the Healthcare Business Association, and the FasterCures Advisory Council for the Research Acceleration and Innovation Network (TRAIN).

SUGGESTED READING

Horn, Rachel. "A Conversation with Nancy Brown, CEO of the American Heart Association." *Atlantic*. Atlantic Monthly Group, 6 Apr. 2011. Web. 10 Feb. 2014.

O'Hara, Kristy J. "How Nancy Brown Engages Employees to Improve the American Heart Association." *Smart Business*. Smart Business Network, 31 May 2011. Web. 10 Feb. 2014.

Pearson-Hormillosa, Shashana. "Beating the Odds." *Dallas Business Journal*. American City Business Journals, 10 Sept. 2009. Web. 10 Feb. 2014.

Wilson, Duff. "E-Cigarettes Win Court Ruling." *New York Times*. New York Times, 7 Dec. 2010. Web. 10 Feb. 2014.

—*Molly Hagan*

Luke Bryan

Born: July 17, 1976
Occupation: Country singer

After Luke Bryan won the coveted Entertainer of the Year award at the 2012 Academy of Country Music (ACM) Awards, which were held in April 2013, some critics sniped. In a piece for the *New York Times* (16 Aug. 2013), Jon Caramanica wrote somewhat derisively that Bryan's win "says far less about him—there is perilously little to say about Mr. Bryan—than it does about the spectrum of country music, which has moved so far away from rural modes that its stars need no longer code their familiarity with them." Bryan's defenders have pointed out that the *New York Times*, which is sometimes perceived to be elitist, rarely covers the country-music world but had been forced to pay attention to the rising star because of his overwhelming popularity; notably, in January 2014, he sold out a performance at Madison Square Garden—one of New York City's largest and most iconic venues—within five minutes of tickets going on sale.

However, even critics and publications more amenable to his charms sometimes feel the need to question Bryan's popularity. "Why does Bryan—a 36-year-old Nashville crooner with

Debby Wong/Landov

father, Tommy, was a peanut farmer who also ran a chemical fertilizer business.

Bryan was reportedly a fussy, sickly infant, and to soothe him, his mother, LeClaire, frequently sang him the gospel tune "Rock of Ages." "He could literally hum 'Rock of Ages' before he could talk," she recalled to Amy Robach for the news show 20/20, as reported by Janice Johnston, Emily Whipp, and Alexa Valiente for the ABC News website (4 Nov. 2013). When he was slightly older, Bryan's parents gave him records by country artists Ronnie Milsap, Merle Haggard, and Conway Twitty, while his older brother and sister introduced him to pop music. "*Thriller* [by Michael Jackson] was my first cassette; that was like currency," he recalled to Matt Hendrickson for *Parade* (5 Apr. 2014). "At school I could moonwalk all the way to the pencil sharpener and back." He was, he has admitted, relatively unenthusiastic about his academic studies, and because he was consistently the youngest and smallest in his class, he never excelled at sports, although he did enjoy them.

GROWING INTEREST IN MUSIC

Bryan, who worked during the summers sweeping and stocking shelves at a local grocery store, sang in the choir at Leesburg's First Baptist Church. He also performed in occasional school productions, including *Annie Get Your Gun*, in which he portrayed sharpshooter Frank Butler. When he was fourteen, his parents purchased him his first guitar; his mother particularly loved to hear him play songs by George Strait, who has been called the "King of Country."

When he was not practicing his music, Bryan loved to hunt and fish, and he could often be found at nearby Muckalee Creek. The locale later inspired some of his songs, most notably the popular "Muckalee Creek Water," whose nostalgic lyrics read in part, "Daddy brought me down here when I was a kid / Taught me how to bait a crawfish basket / From the time I was old enough to walk / He had me running down squirrels and rabbits."

Soon after getting his guitar, and before he could legally drink in any of the area clubs, Bryan began sitting in with country bands from around the region. At age sixteen, he started writing his own songs and dreaming that he might one day move to Nashville to earn a living as a musician. Two local songwriters who had found a small measure of professional success encouraged him and allowed him to sit in on their writing sessions.

CHANGE OF PLANS

In 1996, after he graduated from high school, Bryan began making firm plans to move. Then, on October 27 of that year, while he was visiting a girlfriend in the nearby town of Valdosta, he received word that his older brother, Chris, had

solid-though-not-spectacular vocals, whose songs are relentlessly catchy but tackle standard country fare—elicit such hysteria?" Emily Yahr wrote for the *Washington Post* (19 May 2013). "It could be because of the dynamic dual character he has created through his music. On one hand, he's the ultimate guy's guy, dedicating about half his material to drinking beer with buddies, partying on spring break, and watching girls in bikinis. Then, a minute later, he is the ultimate Romeo, wanting nothing more than to take the love of his life out to the country for some romantic off-roading or a picnic for two in the woods." In a similar vein, Nancy Wilson wrote for the *Dayton Daily News* (6 Sept. 2013), "Why is Luke so popular? Ladies, if you've watched [his YouTube dance video] by now, you'll know he can dance. But it's not just that. It's not his voice, which is very nice, but not at Vince Gill level. It's not necessarily his writing skills—most of his songs aren't very deep and are about having a good time." Her answer was simple: a Luke Bryan performance, she wrote, is just "a backward-hat-wearing good time." "Above all that," she continued, "he is a genuinely nice guy."

CHILDHOOD

Thomas Luther Bryan was born on July 17, 1976, in the small town of Leesburg, Georgia, which boasts some three thousand residents. Journalists have remarked on the town's main strip, which features a quintessentially American combination of barber shops, bail bonds offices, gun stores, and auto parts outlets. While many residents work in nearby factories and warehouses—MillerCoors Brewing, Procter & Gamble, and Mars Chocolate all maintain facilities in the area—Bryan's been killed in a car accident. "Man, I've had a billion emotions around all that. You never quite get over it," he said to Hendrickson. "But I do believe that when my brother was born, God allocated him twenty-six years. It was his time." Wanting to remain at home to lend emotional support to his family, Bryan scrapped his plans to move to Nashville and instead enrolled at Georgia Southern University, where he studied business administration. In the evenings and on weekends, he played with his band at fraternity parties and bars near campus.

Bryan graduated with an associate's degree in 1999 and, still feeling the need to be close to his family, began working alongside his father on the farm and in the fertilizer business. After about a year and a half, however, his father gave him an ultimatum: follow his long-held dream or be fired from the family business. "I said, 'You know, if you're going to pursue your music career, you need to pack your truck up and move to Nashville,'" Tommy Bryan recalled to Robach, according to Johnston, Whipp, and Valiente. Bryan's parents ended up divorcing soon thereafter, a turn of events most sources attribute to the difficulties of dealing with Chris's death.

NASHVILLE

On September 1, 2001, Bryan took his father's advice and left Georgia to head to the city that has long been synonymous with the country-music industry. Within a few months he had earned a contract with a publishing house and was penning hits for such stars as Travis Tritt, for whom he wrote the title track to the 2004 album *My Honky Tonk History*. When he was not writing, Bryan played at various Nashville clubs, where a scout from Capitol Records saw him perform a set of original material and signed him to a recording deal.

Bryan has referred to himself as a "late bloomer" because his first widely distributed album, *I'll Stay Me*, was not released until 2007, when he was thirty-one years old. (He had previously recorded an independent album, which he sold at the side of the stage when he had a gig, but the Capitol release is generally referred to as his debut.) Bryan wrote or cowrote all but one of the tracks on the album, which had a relatively positive reception. Two tracks, "All My Friends Say" and "Country Man," landed in the top ten on the country singles chart.

ANOTHER TRAGEDY

The same year his debut album was released, Bryan was invited to perform at the famed Grand Ole Opry, which has for decades been home to a weekly concert series and radio broadcast featuring a wide array of legendary performers and up-and-comers. His sister, Kelly, a teacher, excitedly organized more than one hundred family members, friends, and Leesburg neighbors for a trip to Nashville to attend the performance together. Just a few days after they returned, Kelly, who was married and had two young children, unexpectedly died while at home in her kitchen. Although Bryan has not publicly discussed the details of her death, most sources report that she suffered from an aneurysm.

Bryan often sings his 2013 single "Drink a Beer"—which includes the lines "So long, my friend, until we meet again / I'll remember you / And all the times that we used to / Sit right here, on the edge of this pier / And watch the sunset disappear / And drink a beer"—in tribute to his lost siblings. "My sister was drink-a-few-beers-on-the-back-porch perfect," he said to Hendrickson. "So many people have been right there. Sitting on a dock drinking a beer with your dad or granddad—it's such an honest connection."

CONTINUED SUCCESS

Bryan's sophomore effort, *Doin' My Thing* (2009), peaked at number two on the country-album chart and spawned three number-one hit singles: "Do I," "Someone Else Calling You Baby," and "Rain Is a Good Thing." He followed up in 2011 with *Tailgates & Tanlines*, which debuted at number one on the country-album chart and sold approximately 150,000 copies within days of its release. It featured the track "Country Girl (Shake It for Me)," which quickly became something of an anthem for Bryan's fans. In a review of the album for *American Songwriter* magazine (9 Aug. 2011), Eric Allen wrote, "The lead-off track, which surely everyone has heard by now, has prompted country girls to shake it collectively over the long, hot summer." Allen concluded, "*Tailgates & Tanlines* is, for the most part, exactly what the title implies: a soundtrack for fun and sun, along with an instantaneous cure for the summertime blues. However, it's the moments when Bryan digs deeper, such as on Radney Foster's emotionally charged 'I Knew You That Way' and the somber 'You Don't Know Jack,' warning against the dangers of alcohol abuse, when he really shines. These brief instants trump the fluffier material and hint at the kind of greatness Bryan is capable of delivering on future albums."

In 2013 Bryan released *Crash My Party*, and most critics were lukewarm. "The majority of the record is given over to 'Party' games we've heard Bryan—and many others in contemporary country—play before," Sarah Rodman wrote for the *Boston Globe* (12 Aug. 2013). Joseph Hudak, writing for *Country Weekly* (14 Aug. 2013), had hoped for more: "In the future, it'd be nice to see Luke . . . grow out of the fields he's so clearly comfortable in. But for now, if the soil is still bearing fruit, you can't blame him for continuing to plow ahead." As Hudak implied, fans seemed to have no quibbles with Bryan's new songs, and the album broke at number one on both the country and the Billboard 200 charts. It sold five hundred thousand copies during its first week of release and spawned three number-one singles: the title track, "My Kind of Night," and "Drink a Beer."

In addition to his full-length studio recordings, Bryan releases annual spring-break-themed EPs, which have proven exceptionally popular with his young fans. In 2013 these songs were compiled into the album *Spring Break . . . Here to Party*.

RECOGNITION
In recent years, Bryan has amassed a slew of awards. In 2010 he was named Top New Artist of the Year and Top New Solo Vocalist of the Year at the 2009 ACM Awards; in 2012 he won the American Music Award for Favorite Country Male Artist, a feat he repeated the following year. Also in 2012 Bryan swept the American Country Awards program, which bills itself as "the show for the next generation of country music fans," winning top prize in nine categories, including Artist of the Year; Album of the Year (for *Tailgates & Tanlines*); and Single of the Year, Music Video of the Year, and Most Played Radio Track (for "I Don't Want This Night to End"), among others.

In April 2013 Bryan achieved what was arguably the greatest honor of his career to date when he was named 2012 Entertainer of the Year at the ACM Awards, beating out more seasoned competitors such as Blake Shelton and Taylor Swift. Speaking of his bemusement at the win, he later told Chris Talbott for the Associated Press (13 Aug. 2013), "I won entertainer of the year and I ain't really been an entertainer yet." He was nominated for the same award the following year but ultimately lost to George Strait.

PERSONAL LIFE
In 2006 Bryan married Caroline Boyer, who he met while both were attending Georgia Southern University; she was a patron at the bar Dingus Magee's, as they often recall to journalists, and he was playing a gig there. The couple have two sons: Thomas Boyer, born in 2008, and Tatum Christopher, born in 2010. They live outside of Nashville.

SUGGESTED READING
Caramanica, Jon. "Luke Bryan, the Leading Gentleman of Country." *New York Times*. New York Times, 16 Aug. 2013. Web. 11 Aug. 2014.

Hendrickson, Matt. "Luke Bryan Takes You Home to Leesburg, Ga.: 'I Loved Growing Up Here.'" *Parade*. Parade, 5 Apr. 2014. Web. 11 Aug. 2014.

Johnston, Janice, Emily Whipp, and Alexa Valiente. "Luke Bryan Opens Up about the Two Tragedies That Nearly Broke Him." *ABC News*. ABC News, 4 Nov. 2013. Web. 11 Aug. 2014.

Paxman, Bob. "Luke Bryan and Family: Life's Good Things." *Country Weekly*. Amer. Media, 19 July 2013. Web. 11 Aug. 2014.

Talbott, Chris. "Luke Bryan Releases Album amid High Expectations." *Big Story*. Assoc. Press, 13 Aug. 2013. Web. 11 Aug. 2014.

Yahr, Emily. "Luke Bryan Masters the Two Sides of His Country-Music Persona at WMZQ Fest." *Washington Post*. Washington Post, 19 May 2013. Web. 11 Aug. 2014.

SELECTED RECORDINGS
I'll Stay Me, 2007; *Doin' My Thing*, 2009; *Tailgates & Tanlines*, 2011; *Crash My Party*, 2013

—Mari Rich

Bob Burnquist
Born: October 10, 1976
Occupation: Skateboarder

Bob Burnquist is a Brazilian American skateboarding icon and one of the most influential figures in the history of his sport. Known particularly for his versatility and unrivaled technical prowess, he is widely credited with being one of the first true switch-stance skateboarders, which refers to the ability to ride with either foot forward. The skill is often likened to being able to successfully pitch a baseball with either hand. Burnquist is a master of the two primary type of skateboarding: street and vert

Danny Moloshok/Reuters/Landov

(short for "vertical") skating, which entails riding a skateboard on any type of ramp or incline, and he and his close friend and fellow professional skateboarder Danny Way are known as the pioneers of mega ramp, or "Big Air," skateboarding (a technique where skaters perform tricks at extreme heights from large-format vert ramp structures). The two are co-owners of the southern California company MegaRamp Events LLC, which builds and produces mega ramp events worldwide. Burnquist owns one of the world's few permanent mega ramps and is famous for his death-defying stunts, the most notable of which came in 2006 when he launched himself off a ramp and then BASE jumped (parachuted) into the Grand Canyon. Skateboarding legend Tony Hawk said to Josh Dean for *Outside* magazine (29 July 2009) about Burnquist, "Besides creating tricks previously thought impossible, he's taking existing moves and doing them at dangerous heights and over frightful distances." He added that the switch-stance skater is unique because "his motivation is progression; not fame or fortune."

Burnquist's lifelong emphasis on progression has resulted in numerous "firsts" in professional skateboarding. Since bursting onto the scene as a teenager in the early 1990s, he has captured most of street and vert skating's biggest titles, he has competed in every Summer X Games since the preeminent extreme sports event began in 1995, and he has captured a record twenty-six medals. Burnquist, who was inducted into the Skateboarding Hall of Fame in 2010, is well-known for his many pursuits outside the world of skateboarding, which include piloting airplanes, skydiving, organic farming, playing music, and championing a number of social causes. "What I do is live my life, do my thing, and try to make progress toward something," he explained to Dean. "I do more than the average guy, but I definitely need to do more."

EARLY LIFE

The second of three children, Robert "Bob" Dean Silva Burnquist was born on October 10, 1976, in Rio de Janeiro, Brazil, to an American father, Dean, and a Brazilian mother, Dora. Burnquist, who broke his first bone when he was just nine months old, grew up mostly in the city of São Paulo, but he attended kindergarten in Pleasanton, California, where his father, a coffee exporter, worked for a year; his parents later divorced. It was in São Paulo where Burnquist first discovered skateboarding. As he recalled to Mackenzie Eisenhour for *Transworld Skateboarding* (Dec. 2012), " I had let my friend borrow a soccer ball and he had lost it. So he was like, 'Well, I don't have the ball anymore but you can take my skateboard.'"

When Burnquist was eleven years old, his father gave him his first pro-grade skateboard.

He was already involved in sports such as soccer and baseball, but severe asthma kept him from enjoying them. Burnquist first learned how to ride on a vert ramp at around age twelve, when the first wooden ramp in Brazil opened at a skate park three blocks from his home. It was here that he first came across American skating videos and industry magazines such as *Transworld* and *Thrasher*, and he soon developed what would become his signature switch-stance style by mimicking what he saw in those videos and magazines. He was particularly influenced by skaters Danny Way and Colin McKay, both of whom were among the first practitioners of switch-stance skateboarding.

Burnquist's switch-stance style took on a more aggressive form in his teens when the skate park closed and he was forced to transition to street skating. He skated almost exclusively on cement and grew accustomed to experiencing, and enduring, painful injuries. Street skating exposed Burnquist to Brazil's bleaker realities, however, and he soon began to sniff glue and use cocaine. Burnquist would spend much of his teenage years trying to stay clean. "I realized I couldn't be the best skater if I was partying all night," he told Zev Borow for *ESPN Magazine* (14 Aug. 2002), adding, "I got to a point where it was like, what do I want? To get high, or to skate?"

BREAKING INTO THE SCENE

Burnquist turned professional at age fourteen, and by the early 1990s, he was regularly winning skateboarding competitions around Brazil. He remained largely unknown in the United States until 1994, when Jake Phelps, the editor of *Thrasher*, traveled to Brazil with a group of American professional skateboarders to survey the country's skateboarding scene. Upon arriving in São Paulo, they met Burnquist, who offered to serve as their guide and translator. "He was a dirty skate rat dude with two different shoes on," Phelps recalled to Matt Higgins for the *New York Times* (1 Nov. 2006). Despite his disheveled appearance, Burnquist quickly impressed the Americans with his progressive repertoire of tricks, which was "light years ahead of what people were doing then," Phelps told Higgins. "With his switch riding, he had a go-for-it mentality— 'Make it, or take me to the hospital.'"

During the summer of 1994, Burnquist, at the urging of Phelps, visited San Francisco, California, to experience firsthand the American skateboarding scene. After staying there for a month, he returned to Brazil at his parents' behest to finish high school. Despite his initial intentions, however, Burnquist left school before graduating in order to focus on his fast-rising skateboarding career. He then moved to the United States and completed his GED (general educational diploma) at a city college.

Burnquist's profile in the skateboarding world rose considerably in 1995, when, at eighteen, he competed as a virtual unknown in his first international competition, the Slam City Jam in Vancouver, British Columbia. He beat out some of the world's top skateboarders to capture first place in the vert event. In an interview with Matt Higgins for *Sports Illustrated for Kids* (Aug. 2002), Burnquist called the win "the turning point" of his career and said that helped to realize that if he expanded on his switch-stance skating, he "could progress skateboarding in a way that hadn't been approached before on vert." During the summer of 1995, Burnquist showcased his innovative skating style at the first X Games, which was broadcast on ESPN and held in Newport, Rhode Island.

CEMENTING HIS LEGACY

Since 1995, Burnquist has established himself as the most progressive skateboarder in the world by creating and executing numerous skateboarding tricks such as the Burntwist (or eggplant revert), the one-side backside Smith grind, and the fakie 5-0 kickflip. From 1996–99, he was a sponsored rider for Antihero Skateboards, an American board company founded by professional skateboarder Julian Stranger, and he debuted new maneuvers in such skating videos as *Transworld* magazine's *Interface* (1997), and Antihero's *Anti Hero* (1998). In the 2000s he filmed progressive video segments for other sponsors, including sports clothing manufacturer Hurley, éS Skateboarding, eyewear manufacturer Oakley, and Flip Skateboards. In 2005 he was featured in a documentary, *The Reality of Bob Burnquist.*

Meanwhile, Burnquist became a mainstay of the X Games and other major skateboarding competitions. In 1996 he took home his first X Games medal, a bronze in vert. The following year Burnquist was recognized as *Thrasher* magazine's Skater of the Year, becoming the first Brazilian to receive the honor, and in 1998 he won first place, beating legend Tony Hawk, at the Vans Triple Crown skating series championship. That same year Burnquist won another X Games bronze in the vert doubles event and captured the vert title at the Grand Prix of Skateboarding event in Lausanne, Switzerland. Burnquist won his first X Games gold in 2000, when he won the vert best trick contest. That year he earned the World Cup Skateboarding's number-one world ranking for vert, after he captured four of the discipline's biggest titles.

Burnquist drew attention at the 2001 X Games in Philadelphia, Pennsylvania, where he won gold in the vert competition with a final run that Tony Hawk noted to Borow was "the best we've ever seen." Unveiling a bevy of new, complicated tricks, Burnquist beat out two-time defending champion Bucky Lasek with a

near-perfect score of ninety-eight, the second-highest score ever awarded in an X Games skateboarding event. He also won a bronze for vert best trick. By 2002 Burnquist had won more than fifty professional competitions and become one of skateboarding's most popular personalities.

BIRTH OF MEGARAMP AND X GAMES HISTORY

It was in 2002 that close friend Danny Way built the world's first mega ramp in Aguanga, California, which he prototyped in 2003 in the film *The DC Video.* Captivated by Way's innovative creation, Burnquist soon learned how to skate the ramp himself, and shortly thereafter the two formed a mega ramp building company called MegaRamp Events LLC. In 2004 organizers of the X Games added a mega ramp to their event lineup for a new skateboarding discipline called Big Air. Way won the inaugural Big Air title, while Burnquist placed sixth that year.

In 2006 Burnquist, with considerable funding from Hurley and Oakley, designed and built a $280,000 mega ramp in his backyard. It stands 75 feet high and 360 feet long and is the first permanently installed mega ramp in the world and became a frequent destination for world renowned skateboarders and their film crews.

Also in 2006 Burnquist performed one of his most daring stunts, which involved a mini–mega ramp, a BASE jump, and the Grand Canyon. The stunt required him to ride his skateboard down a forty-foot-high mega ramp, ride his board along a forty-foot rail that jutted out over the Grand Canyon, and then BASE jump 1,600 feet to the bottom. His outrageous feat was later featured on an episode of the Discovery Channel show *Stunt Junkies.* "When I'm risk-taking, I feel like I'm alive," Burnquist told Higgins for the *New York Times.*

Burnquist's backyard mega ramp set him up for dominance at the X Games, where he captured his first mega ramp Big Air title in 2006, receiving a bronze medal. He then won the gold in 2008, and in 2010 he received another gold and a silver in two other X Game mega ramp events. Burnquist continued to score wins in mega ramp events throughout 2011 and 2012, and when the 2013 Summer X Games were held in four different countries—Brazil, Spain, Germany, and the United States—Burnquist won the Big Air mega ramp gold medal in three of them: Brazil, Spain, and Germany. The close of the 2013 season brought Burnquist's all-time X Games medal wins to twenty-six. He is one of just three athletes to compete at every Summer X Games. Commenting on the often overlooked subtlety of Burnquist's skating, Chris Stiepock, X Games general manager, remarked to Dean, "The things that he's able to do from a technical standpoint are really what makes him spectacular."

OTHER ENDEAVORS AND PERSONAL LIFE

"In the adrenalized world of the X Games, where athletes tend to be tattooed, caffeinated, and more concerned with their style of footwear than their carbon footprint," Dean wrote, "Bob is an anomaly." One of his sport's more iconoclastic personalities, Burnquist is known for pursuing endeavors that do not fit the traditional mold of a skateboarder: He is the founder of the Bob Burnquist Foundation, which strives to educate people about organic farming, and a cofounder of the Action Sports Environmental Council, a nonprofit organization dedicated to promoting awareness and advocacy for global warming and climate change. He also co-owns Burnquist Organics, an umbrella company that controls many of his business interests, and a production company called Zoobamboo Entertainment.

In addition to the mega ramp, Burnquist's twelve-acre compound in Vista, California, which he refers to as "Dreamland," features numerous skate ramps and contraptions, such as a conventional vert ramp and bowl and a loop-de-loop with a retractable top.

Burnquist's interests outside of skateboarding include flying, skydiving, and BASE jumping. He has had a pilot's license since 2003 and has completed more than five hundred skydives and more than a dozen BASE jumps. He also enjoys surfing, and plays drums in indie-rock band Escalera with Danny Way.

Burnquist is married to Veronica Nachard, a physical therapist from Brazil. The couple have a daughter, Jasmyn, who was born in 2007. Both have daughters from previous relationships. Burnquist was previously in a relationship with the professional skater Jen O'Brien, with whom he had his first daughter, Lotus, in 2000.

Burnquist's many honors include serving as an official torch bearer for the 2004 Olympics in Athens, Greece, and being inducted into the Skateboarding Hall of Fame in 2010.

SUGGESTED READING

Blakely, Brian. "Bob Burnquist: 2013 Mega Ramp." *Skateboarder.* GrindMedia, 31 July 2013. Web. 7 Apr. 2014.

Borow, Zev. "Full Circle." *ESPN Magazine.* ESPN Internet Ventures, 10 July 2012. Web. 24 Feb. 2014.

Dean, Josh. "Skateboarder Bob Burnquist's Far-Out Dreams." *Outside.* Mariah Media, 29 July 2009. Web. 24 Feb. 2014.

Eisenhour, Mackenzie. "Pioneer: Bob Burnquist, Full Interview—Antihero to the Mega." *Transworld Skateboarding.* GrindMedia, Dec. 2012. Web. 7 Apr. 2014.

Higgins, Matt. "Ramped Up." *Sports Illustrated for Kids* 14.8 (2002): 27. *MasterFILE Complete.* Web. 7 Apr. 2014.

Higgins, Matt. "A Skateboarding Ramp Reaches for the Sky." *New York Times.* New York Times Company, 1 Nov. 2006. Web. 24 Feb. 2014.

Phelps, Jake. "The Sincerest Apologies of Bob Burnquist." *Thrasher.* High Speed Productions, 1 Nov. 2009. Web. 24 Feb. 2014.

—*Chris Cullen*

Sarah Burton

Born: August 19, 1974
Occupation: Fashion designer

"It had been one of the most eagerly anticipated dresses of the decade, and when it was finally unveiled on the steps of Westminster Abbey, Kate Middleton's wedding gown did not disappoint," Alice Wyllie wrote for the *Scotsman* (30 Apr. 2011) following the marriage of Catherine "Kate" Middleton to Prince William, an heir to the British throne. The ivory satin garment, which featured intricate lace sleeves, a full skirt, and a form-fitting bodice, had been created by designer Sarah Burton, who was catapulted instantly into a global spotlight thanks to the millions of viewers watching the televised ceremony on April 29, 2011.

Although the royal nuptials marked her debut with the general public, Burton was already known within the fashion world. The previous year, after the suicide of famed designer Alexander McQueen, Burton, his longtime assistant, became the head of the fashion house he founded. In the wake of her ascension, industry observers avidly watched to see in which direction she would take the company, which was celebrated for its edgy, unconventional designs and meticulous craftsmanship. Most were relieved when she expressed a desire to retain her predecessor's target clientele and mission while still making her own creative mark.

Pool/Reuters/Landov

"There will always be those McQueen elements, but at the same time, you can never stay still and you have to stay true to yourself," she told Harriet Quick for *Vogue* (Feb. 2011). "That's what [McQueen] drummed in to me: you have to be able to stand behind your work." Speaking with Sarah Jessica Parker for *Interview* magazine (Mar. 2012), she reiterated her intention. "There'll always be a McQueen woman," Burton, who has designed clothing for First Lady Michelle Obama and pop star Lady Gaga, asserted. "She is a strong woman and she is a powerful woman, and when she puts a McQueen jacket on, she feels different. The way she stands is different. The way she moves is different. It's almost like the clothes are slightly empowering. There's this emotion that goes into the clothes." She concluded, "You know, [McQueen] was such a genius that I can never pretend to be him, but I am very aware that I'm designing for a house that he created, and I try to keep it as true to that as possible."

EARLY LIFE AND EDUCATION

Sarah Burton was born Sarah Heard on August 19, 1974, to Anthony Heard, an accountant, and Diana Heard, then a music teacher. She grew up in the village of Prestbury, England, and attended the Withington Girls' School, a highly regarded day school in Manchester, where she was widely considered a solid student. "Withington Girls' School was very academic—not the best for fashion, but if you have the talent, then you will shine," her mother told the *Macclesfield Express* (4 May 2011). "Her art teacher was great, her artwork was always on display." That art teacher, Diane Connell, who taught Burton for several years, told an interviewer for the BBC (29 Apr. 2011) that her former student possessed "amazing creativity." Connell asserted, "Even from an early age you could tell she'd be doing something in the creative arts. She was very easy going, cheerful, very modest about her abilities and it's obviously carried through." Her artistic ability made Burton something of an anomaly in her musically inclined family. Of her four siblings, two went on to professional music careers: one brother is an oboe player, and a sister is an opera singer.

After graduating from Withington in 1993, Burton entered Manchester Metropolitan University, which had changed its name from Manchester Polytechnic the previous year. There she completed a foundation course and cemented her decision to focus on a career in fashion. (She had briefly considered studying fine art at the University of Oxford's Ruskin School.)

In 1994 Burton moved to London to attend the Central Saint Martins (CSM) College of Art and Design, a constituent school of the University of the Arts London. Among the highly competitive college's other noted alumni are fashion designers John Galliano, Zac Posen, Stella McCartney, and Alexander McQueen.

While studying textile design at CSM, Burton impressed a print-and-dye instructor named Simon Ungless, who, despite minor misgivings, helped her approach McQueen to ask for an internship. "I just really wondered about the gentle side of her," he explained to Cathy Horyn for the *New York Times* (4 May 2011). "There's a kind of profile for a Saint Martins student—it's turn your clothes upside down and look as bonkers as you want to look. It's not about the work necessarily. And she wasn't like that." Still, he continued, "she could draw, which is a really unusual thing for a student these days. She was also really passionate about research—but more, she knew how to turn it into something." McQueen agreed to take on the soft-spoken and modest Burton, and she began her internship in 1996. They had in common, as Horyn wrote, "a love of work, craft, history, art and films." (He had also reportedly been impressed by her affirmative answer to his question about whether she believed in UFOs—a response he took as a sign of her imagination and faith.)

WORK AT ALEXANDER MCQUEEN

Lee Alexander McQueen—known professionally as Alexander and to his friends as Lee—left school at sixteen to apprentice on Savile Row, the iconic Mayfair street known for its many custom tailor shops. He later earned a master's degree in fashion from CSM; his entire graduation collection was purchased by an influential stylist, an unusual accomplishment for a student. (That stylist, Isabella Blow, continued to follow his career and soon became a mentor and friend.) McQueen subsequently worked for several years at Givenchy; his own eponymous label ultimately became part of the Gucci Group stable. A four-time winner of Designer of the Year honors at the British Fashion Awards, McQueen was known for his brash, attention-grabbing garments. He was often referred to in the press as a "bad boy" or "provocateur."

"McQueen, though indisputably a great talent and a visionary, was also a taskmaster who had his own demons to battle," Harriet Quick wrote for *Harper's Bazaar* (Mar. 2013). "Psychologically, one needed a strong backbone to endure the storms at McQueen headquarters and roll with the creative highs and lows." Burton, despite her mild manner, had the required backbone, and after completing her internship and graduating from CSM, she remained with McQueen, becoming his trusted assistant and close confidante. "It's like studying somewhere you never want to leave," she told Quick. "Everything I know I learnt here," she once said, as quoted by Helen Wigham for British *Vogue* (June 2011). "If you didn't know how to do something, Lee made you take on the challenge and would teach you how, or leave you to figure out how to do it yourself. He once handed over a bias-cut houndstooth dress and said, 'Now, put a zip in it,' then left for the weekend!"

Burton was appointed head of the label's womenswear division in 2000 and was universally regarded as McQueen's right-hand person. She was, according to Bryan Appleyard for the *Economist*'s lifestyle and culture magazine *Intelligent Life* (May/June 2013), "the ultimate backroom girl at the London atelier of Alexander McQueen, the quiet sensible big sister to a wayward punk couturier."

CREATIVE DIRECTOR

In early February 2010 McQueen—still reeling from the 2007 suicide of Isabella Blow and despondent over the recent death of his mother—committed suicide in his London home. In May of that year, Burton was chosen by executives at Gucci to succeed him as creative head of the label. She was initially intimidated by the idea of stepping into his shoes. "I thought: 'How would I ever begin to begin?' Lee's mind was so different to anyone else's," she recalled, as quoted by Wigham.

McQueen died shortly before Paris Fashion Week, an annual event during which new collections are shown, and Burton, although devastated by the death of her friend and employer, ensured that his designs were completed and shown as he had planned. "I had no idea of the size of the job," she admitted to Parker. "I had no idea of the other sorts of pressures that he must have faced."

The new creative head showed her own first collection in the fall of 2010. "In an extraordinarily beautiful show, Burton succeeded in both being faithful to the late designer's distinctive design ethos while taking the label into a new era," Imogen Fox wrote for the London *Guardian* (5 Oct. 2010), going on to praise a dress created from hand-painted feathers, a pantsuit made from leather crafted into the shape of ivy leaves, and wedge shoes carved into butterflies and lacquered to resemble porcelain. "As the first model wearing a white tailcoat with frayed edges walked down a catwalk of bare wooden planks with mossy grass poking through the cracks, the audience were in no doubt this was a McQueen show," she explained. "But as it progressed, it became apparent that this was a new, softer McQueen collection. There was none of the angst and aggression of previous catwalks; this was an altogether more feminine McQueen woman."

THE ROYAL WEDDING

In November 2010, as soon as William, the son of Prince Charles and the late Princess Diana, announced his engagement to Middleton, his longtime girlfriend, speculation began swirling as to who would design the royal wedding dress.

As had long been tradition, however, the British royals took every precaution to keep the identity of the designer a secret. Even some of those who worked alongside Burton were not told for whom the dress was intended; anyone who did know was bound by a confidentiality agreement.

Certain that Middleton—a down-to-earth young woman known for buying clothing off the rack and wearing her favorite outfits on multiple occasions—would select a British designer, as was expected of royal brides, many guessed that Burton might be chosen. Almost daily, articles appeared in the press, weighing in on the issue and putting forth conjecture and assorted rumors. When an unidentified woman was seen rushing into the Goring Hotel, where Middleton and her family were staying the night before the wedding, sharp-eyed observers discerned that it was Burton, who had tried in vain to conceal her long blond hair and had neglected to take off a distinctive studded leather belt that she frequently wore.

As Middleton appeared at Westminster Abbey on the morning of April 29, 2011, most viewers were rapturous. "It was a moment of Cinderella magic: the future queen, emerging from a Rolls Royce in a slim ivory-and-white satin gown with a dramatic neckline, sheer lace sleeves, and a train that followed her straight into fashion legend," an Associated Press reporter wrote on April 30. "The dress, perhaps the most closely guarded secret of the royal wedding, became an icon from the moment it was broadcast around the world. . . . Fashionistas swooned. Some people cried." An extraordinary amount of work and care had gone into the garment's creation. The lacework incorporated hundreds of individual, hand-cut, embroidered flowers, and the members of the Royal School of Needlework who worked on it were required to wash their hands every thirty minutes and sharpen their needles every three hours. Middleton's sister, Pippa, her maid of honor, was also attired in a Burton creation, this one a form-fitting sheath that led to nonstop tabloid coverage during the ensuing days.

Burton, released from her vow of secrecy, issued a short press release after the wedding that stated, in part, "Alexander McQueen's designs are all about bringing contrasts together to create startling and beautiful clothes and I hope that by marrying traditional fabrics and lacework, with a modern structure and design we have created a beautiful dress for Catherine on her wedding day. The last few months have been very exciting and an incredible experience."

SUBSEQUENT COLLECTIONS

Burton's subsequent collections have been received well. Her spring 2013 show, for example, was staged in Milan's lavish central train station, and while most critics opined that the grandeur of the setting might have diminished the work of other designers, her woven golden jacquard suits and printed silk blouses proved opulent enough to fit their surroundings.

Calling Burton "a voice of her generation," Quick wrote, "When McQueen died, it could have heralded the end of the Great British fashion adventure—an era defined by romance, vision, and a devil-may-care attitude. . . . Instead, Burton continued to make her mark on the house—and the world—through her love of storytelling. She has feminized and lightened the codes of fetishism, historicism, and romanticism that McQueen made his leitmotifs."

PERSONAL LIFE

Burton is married to the fashion photographer David Burton. They live in St John's Wood, a tony district of London that borders Regent's Park. They are the parents of twins, born in early 2013.

Among Burton's many honors are the 2011 Designer of the Year title at the British Fashion Awards and inclusion in *Time* magazine's 2012 list of the hundred most influential people in the world. In 2012 she was also named an Officer of the Order of the British Empire (OBE) for her service to the country's fashion industry.

SUGGESTED READING

Burton, Sarah. "Sarah Burton." Interview with Sarah Jessica Parker. *Interview*. Interview Magazine, Mar. 2012. Web. 16 Apr. 2014.
Horyn, Cathy. "Into the Spotlight, Gently." *New York Times*. New York Times, 4 May 2011. Web. 16 Apr. 2014.
Johnston, Robert. "McQueen's Perfect Fit." *GQ*. Condé Nast, 5 Oct. 2012. Web. 16 Apr. 2014.
Mower, Sarah. "New Order." *Vogue*. Vogue, Jan. 2011. Web. 16 Apr. 2014.
Quick, Harriet. "Fashion's Queen Bee: Alexander McQueen's Sarah Burton Is Setting the World Abuzz." *Harper's Bazaar*. Harper's Bazaar, Mar. 2013. Web. 16 Apr. 2014.
Wyllie, Alice. "All Hail a Style Queen." *Scotsman*. Scotsman, 10 Dec. 2011. Web. 16 Apr. 2014.
Wyllie, Alice. "Less Diana, More Grace Kelly: The Dress of the Decade." *Scotsman*. Scotsman, 30 Apr. 2011. Web. 16 Apr. 2014.

—*Mari Rich*

Ian Callum

Born: July 30, 1954
Occupation: Automotive designer

Ian Callum, the design director of the luxury car brand Jaguar, is widely recognized as one of the foremost automotive designers in the world. A native of Scotland and an alumnus of London's

Royal College of Art, Callum began his career with the Ford Motor Company in 1979. After spending eleven years with Ford, he joined Tom Walkinshaw Racing (TWR), a Kidlington, England–based boutique automotive design firm, as chief designer in 1990. As TWR's chief designer, Callum designed the iconic Aston Martin DB7, which was released in 1993 and helped catapult him to fame in the automotive industry.

Callum oversaw the design and development of cars for other TWR clients, including Ford, Volvo, and Nissan, before becoming the design director of Jaguar in 1999. Since stepping into that role, Callum has been credited with transforming Jaguar's design aesthetic from one that relied heavily on retro-conservative styling into one that has come to represent twenty-first century technology and innovation. Callum is responsible for designing such all-new 2000s Jaguar models as the XK, XF, XJ, and the F-Type, all of which have helped revitalize the company's brand image as a maker of "fast, beautiful cars." In an interview with Tim Pollard for the British motoring magazine *Car* (3 Apr. 2009), Callum said, "I want people to notice Jaguars and admire them."

EARLY LIFE

The second of the four children of Stuart and Sheila (Wood) Callum, Ian Stuart Callum was born on July 30, 1954, in Dumfries, Scotland. He has a brother, Moray, and two sisters, Helen and Iona. With his siblings, Callum enjoyed a modest upbringing; his father was a solicitor, his mother a housewife. From the age of four, Callum knew that he wanted to become a car designer. He developed that desire after being granted an opportunity to sit in a neighbor's luxury car, a Bentley Silver Cloud, which, he told Jamie Merrill for the London *Independent* (30 Mar. 2013), "was the first time that I realized that a piece of nothingness can actually be very beautiful."

Callum, who displayed artistic talent at an early age, began drawing cars as a boy. He grew up idolizing the legendary Scottish Formula One race car driver Jim Clark and became a devoted reader of car enthusiast magazines like the iconic American monthly *Hot Rod*. His grandfather helped encourage his growing interest in cars by giving him books on the subject, including renowned British artist Frank Wootton's *How to Draw Cars* (1949). Callum passed down his interest in cars to his brother Moray, who is four years younger. (Moray has become a highly distinguished car designer in his own right. In November 2012 he was appointed vice president of design for Ford Motors.) The two wrote letters to local car dealers posing as potential customers to get brochures on new models; they used the brochures to decorate the room they shared. On one occasion, a salesman for the esteemed British luxury car manufacturer Rolls-Royce showed up at the Callum brothers' house to give their father a test drive of the then-new Silver Shadow, first released in 1965.

Callum grew up in a family that, at times, did not even own a car. He told Ali Howard for the Glasgow *Herald* (7 Nov. 2011) that it was this "sense of the exotic or unattainable" that gave him the impetus to pursue his dream of becoming a car designer. Callum inherited a strong work ethic and drive to succeed from his father, who, despite not being particularly interested in cars, would take him and his brother to watch motor races at the Ingliston race track, on the outskirts of Edinburgh, Scotland. There, Callum dreamed of making it big outside of Dumfries, which "was like the little town in the film *American Graffiti*—but without the hot rods," he told Phil Patton for the *New York Times* (25 Oct. 2006).

EDUCATION IN DESIGN

In 1968, when he was fourteen years old, Callum sent a letter, along with some car sketches, to William Heynes, Jaguar's legendary vice chairman of engineering, inquiring about how he should go about becoming a car designer. Heynes, who was responsible for designing the company's famous XK six-cylinder engine, quickly replied with a letter offering advice, stressing among other things that he study technical drawing in college. At the time, Callum told Nancy Durrant for the London *Times* (13 July 2013), Jaguar was "the car company that I admired the most; the car company that I wanted to work for at that age." By then, Jaguar had established its reputation in the automotive industry as a maker of sleek and sexy luxury sports cars that relied heavily on innovation and a compelling design ethos, following the release of such iconic models as the Mark II, E-Type, and XJ, in 1959, 1961, and 1968, respectively.

After graduating from secondary school, Callum attended Lanchester Polytechnic's (now Coventry University's) School of Transportation Design, in Coventry, England, where he studied transport design. He then took a foundation course at University of Aberdeen, in Aberdeen, Scotland, before enrolling at the Glasgow School of Art in 1972. Upon receiving a bachelor's degree in industrial design from Glasgow, Callum passed up an opportunity to further his education in the United States in order to continue his studies at London's Royal College of Art (RCA), known for its prestigious automobile design program. He completed a two-year master's degree in automobile design from RCA in 1978.

FORD MOTOR COMPANY

After graduating from RCA, Callum was immediately recruited to work as a junior designer for Ford Motor Company, headquartered in the Detroit suburb of Dearborn, Michigan. He went on to spend eleven years with the company, during which he held various roles while working in design studios in England, the United States, Germany, Japan, and Australia. Before designing any cars, however, Callum was mostly relegated to working on auxiliary car parts like steering wheels, side mirrors, and door handles. "I soon realized that I wasn't going to be jumping in and designing the next [Ford] Capri or Escort," he recalled to Mike Duff in an interview for the automotive enthusiast magazine *Car and Driver* (Apr. 2010). "You didn't get a chance to design cars until you'd earned your place." That kind of entry-level work notwithstanding, Callum worked on such signature Ford models as the Fiesta, the Mondeo, the Ford RS200 mid-engine sports car, and the Escort RS Cosworth, among others.

During his last two years at Ford, from 1988 to 1990, Callum served as design manager for the Ghia design studio, a Ford subsidiary located in Turin, Italy. In that role, he oversaw the design and development of such Ford auto show concepts as the Ghia Via mid-engine sports car, the Ghia Zig compact two-seat sports car, and the Ghia Zag multipurpose van. In 1990 Callum left Ford to join Tom Walkinshaw Racing (TWR), a boutique automotive engineering and consultancy firm based in Kidlington, near Oxford, England. Upon joining TWR, which was founded by the late Scottish race car driver Tom Walkinshaw in 1976, Callum was appointed the firm's chief designer. Nonetheless, the move confounded many of his colleagues from Ford at the time. "They thought I was utterly mad," Callum said, as quoted on his website. "But I was happy as could be, I was doing something I wanted to do."

TWR TENURE AND DESIGN OF THE ASTON MARTIN DB7

One of Callum's first projects at TWR was designing a new car for the luxury British sports car maker Aston Martin. "At the time, Aston was in a really precarious position, selling tiny numbers of very expensive cars," Callum told Duff, adding, "There was a huge opportunity to turn it around by getting a new product out there, something that was more affordable—but most importantly, beautiful." The result was the DB7, a six-cylinder grand tourer that revived Aston Martin's legendary DB series of cars, made famous by the James Bond series of spy films and named after the British entrepreneur David Brown, who served as head of the company from 1947 to 1972. The DB7 succeeded the DB6, which had stopped being produced in 1971, and debuted at the Geneva Motor Show in Switzerland in 1993; it was made available as either a two-door coupe or convertible. The car became the highest-production Aston Martin model ever, with more than seven thousand built (in various forms) during its ten-year production run from 1994 to 2004.

With the DB7, Callum was instantly catapulted to the forefront of the automotive design world. In 1995 he was honored with the Jim Clark Memorial Award for his styling work on the car. In his interview with Howard, Callum described the car as "a huge turning point—my first number one record. If you have so much energy to make something happen, no matter how wrong it goes, you'll get it right." The success of the DB7 led to Callum becoming an in-demand designer for other TWR clients, including Ford, Volvo, and Nissan, among others. In the late 1990s he contributed to the design and development of the Ford Puma sports coupe, the Volvo C70 coupe-convertible, and the Nissan R390 GT1 mid-engine racing car, the latter of which was made specifically for the 24 Heures du Mans (24 Hours of Le Mans), the oldest and most famous endurance sports car race in the world, held annually since 1923 near the city of Le Mans, France.

BECOMING JAGUAR'S DESIGN DIRECTOR

Callum's professional relationship with Jaguar began in 1999, when he was appointed design director of the company, which had recently become a subsidiary of Ford Motors. (In 2008 Ford sold Jaguar, which is part of Jaguar Land Rover, to Tata Motors of India.) He succeeded the veteran designer Geoff Lawson, who had died suddenly that year of a stroke. Upon arriving at Jaguar, Callum was charged with overhauling the design aesthetic of the company, which had been suffering from a "decades-long over-indulgence in heritage and retro," according to Edward Niedermeyer for the automotive website *The Truth about Cars* (4 Jan. 2010). Despite emerging as one of the hippest car brands of the 1960s, Jaguar had established a reputation in subsequent decades as "the old man's car company" for releasing traditional-looking cars that sported antiquated features like vinyl door panels and wood-trim interiors. "It was too retro and old-fashioned," Callum told Howard. "When I was growing up, Jaguar was a very cool brand."

Wanting to reestablish Jaguar as a maker of fast and beautiful cars, Callum immediately set a design program in place for the company that threw "away the rulebook," as he told Niedermeyer, and looked ahead to the twenty-first century. The first Jaguar design of Callum's to reflect his future vision for the company was the R-Coupe, an eight-cylinder four-seat concept car that debuted at the Frankfurt Motor Show in Germany in 2001. The car retained Jaguar's signature design features, such as beautiful lines and flawless proportions, while sporting a bold, modern look. Callum followed up the R-Coupe with another concept car, the RD-6, a compact, six-cylinder four-seater, in 2003. The following year he put his influence on two Jaguar models from the Lawson era, giving a facelift to the mid-sized S-Type and designing a five-door station wagon version of the X-Type, which was first produced as a compact executive car.

ASTON MARTIN AND JAMES BOND

During his early tenure at Jaguar, Callum continued to design cars for Aston Martin. In 2001 he designed the Vanquish, a twelve-cylinder grand tourer that replaced the company's decade-old Virage series of eight-cylinder cars. The car became famous when it was featured as the official James Bond car in the film *Die Another Day* (2002), the twentieth installment of the Bond series. Callum also played a vital role in the design of another twelve-cylinder grand tourer, the DB9, which succeeded the DB7 and went into production as both a coupe and convertible in 2004. Many observers would later find striking design similarities between Callum's Aston Martin and Jaguar models. Callum told Duff that while his designs for the two car brands share similar values, Jaguars are "much more voluptuous" while Aston Martins "are more muscular—strength in a tailored suit."

JAGUAR XK SERIES

The first all-new Jaguar model of Callum's to go into production was the XK, an eight-cylinder sports coupe that was first unveiled at the Frankfurt Motor Show in 2005. The following year the convertible version of the car was unveiled at the North American International Auto Show in Detroit. The Jaguar XK succeeded the XK8, which was launched in 1996, and features a sleek and curvaceous exterior that Callum said was inspired by the British actress Kate Winslet. "She is naturally a very shapely woman, very British with an underlying integrity and ability," he said in 2006, as quoted by Laura Roberts for the London *Daily Mail* (22 Apr. 2008). "Like a car, she has got substance." The XK retains some of Jaguar's classic design elements, such as an oval chrome grille inspired by the 1961 E-Type, but it also incorporates modern, high-tech features like an all-aluminum body structure.

The car, which has a top speed of 155 miles per hour, received a facelift in 2009, with the introduction of an enhanced 5.0 liter, eight-cylinder engine. It received another facelift in 2011, when styling changes were made to both its interior and exterior. Faster, supercharged versions of the car, which has drawn comparisons to the Aston Martin DB9, include the XKR and the XKR-S, which were launched in 2007 and 2008, respectively.

XF AND XJ MODELS

Callum followed the XK with the XF, a four-door mid-size sport sedan that was launched at the Frankfurt Motor Show in 2007 and went into production in 2008. The car, offered with a range of six- and eight-cylinder engines, replaced the Jaguar S-Type model line, which was first introduced in 1963. It features a sleek and modern exterior and a state-of-the-art interior that includes pale-blue backlighting and a one-touch glove compartment. "I saw the XF as being the new Mark II," Callum told Pollard, referring to Jaguar's iconic 1960s sedan. He added, "I took all the values of the Mark II and translated them into the 21st century." In 2011 the Jaguar XF received a facelift that included subtle revisions to both its interior and exterior. Other versions of the car include the XFR and the XFR-S, which were released in 2009 and 2013, respectively.

Callum's third all-new Jaguar model, the XJ, a four-door full-size luxury sedan, was unveiled during a special ceremony at London's Saatchi Gallery in 2009; it went into production in 2010. The critically acclaimed car marked a significant stylistic departure from its 1968 predecessor, featuring a low-slung, forward-looking design. For Callum, the new XJ, offered in a number of different models and engines, completed the first phase of Jaguar's twenty-first century revival. Modified versions of the car, which received an update in 2011, have been used to transport members of the British royal family as well as British Prime Minister David Cameron.

CONCEPT CARS AND THE F-TYPE

Following the XJ, Callum oversaw the design and development of two Jaguar concept cars, the C-X75 and the C-X16. The former is a hybrid-electric two-seat sports car that boasts a top speed of more than 200 miles per hour. It debuted at the 2010 Paris Motor Show, where it was honored with the Car of the Show Award. Despite plans to build a limited production of

the C-X75, Jaguar was forced to stop production in 2012 due to the global economic recession. The C-X75 was followed by the C-X16, another hybrid-electric two-seat sports car that was unveiled at the 2011 Frankfurt Motor Show.

The C-X16 provided the inspiration for Callum's next all-new production vehicle for Jaguar, the F-Type, which was launched at the Paris Motor Show in 2012. The two-seat convertible sports car features a compact, all-aluminum body structure and a supercharged six-cylinder engine; it also comes with a supercharged eight-cylinder engine. It is the successor to Jaguar's legendary E-Type and the company's "most important car in a generation," according to Merrill. The convertible version of the F-Type went into production in 2013, while a coupe version of the car was planned for production in 2014. Other models expected to be released by Jaguar include a compact sedan, a small saloon, and a "baby" luxury sport utility vehicle (SUV). Callum told Rory Mackenzie for the Edinburgh *Scotsman* (22 June 2013), "We're progressing towards a bigger car company, there's no doubt about that." In his interview with Callum, Niedermeyer describes Callum's tenure at Jaguar "as nothing less than one of the most significant in the history of automotive design."

HONORS AND PERSONAL LIFE

Callum has been awarded five honorary doctorate degrees from academic institutions around the world for his contributions to car design. He has also received a number of awards, including the Royal Designer for Industry Award from the Royal Society of Art (RSA) in 2006, the inaugural Person of the Year Award from the British motoring magazine *Auto Express* in 2009, and the Man of the Year Award from *Top Gear* magazine in 2012.

Callum lives near the Jaguar design studios in Coventry, England. He has two adult sons, Fraser and Alistair, with his first wife, Lesley, who is a former teacher. A self-described American car fanatic, Callum boasts a personal collection that includes a 1932 Ford Model B, a 1956 Chevrolet Two-Ten, and a 1990 BMW Mini Cooper.

SUGGESTED READING

Callum, Ian. "Interview: Ian Callum, Jaguar Car Designer." Interview by Rory Mackenzie. *Scotsman* [Edinburgh]. Johnston Pub., 22 June 2013. Web. 7 Jan. 2014.

Howard, Ali. "The Scot Who Transformed Jaguar." *Herald* [Glasgow]. Herald & Times Group, 7 Nov. 2011. Web. 7 Jan. 2014.

Merrill, Jamie. "Wheels of Fortune: Jaguar Updates Its Iconic E-Type with the Launch of the F-Type Sports Car." *Independent*. Independent.co.uk, 30 Mar. 2013. Web. 7 Jan. 2014.

Patton, Phil. "A Golden Touch That Runs in the Family." *New York Times*. New York Times, 25 Oct. 2006. Web. 7 Jan. 2014.

—*Chris Cullen*

Gail Carriger

Born: 1976
Occupation: Archeologist, steampunk author

Science-fiction and fantasy authors are not often known for their humor. Apart from some notable exceptions, such as Douglas Adams and Terry Pratchett, few writers have managed to combine vivid world building and rich characterization with clever comedic touches. Enter Gail Carriger, whose best-selling Parasol Protectorate series has been hailed as one of the funniest and most inventive sci-fi series published in the past few years. Her achievement is even more notable because she is most often identified with the steampunk subgenre, which, apart from being known for its steam-driven retro technology, is often dystopian in nature. Since 2009, with the publication of *Soulless*, the first volume in the Parasol Protectorate series, Carriger has charmed critics and readers alike with her witty dialogue and wonderfully imaginative inventions set in an alternate-universe England where vampires and werewolves are out in the open and very much part of the British Empire. Carriger concluded the series after five novels

Getty Images

but has continued to write about that world in *Etiquette & Espionage* (2013) and *Curtsies & Conspiracies* (2013), the first two volumes in a new series aimed at the young adult set. She is also working on a new Parasol series for adults, the Parasol Protectorate Abroad.

Carriger, who holds degrees in archeology and has worked as an archeologist for a number of years, is a popular guest at book events and conventions, known for her vintage outfits and her obsessive love of tea. She also maintains a large online presence, via Livejournal, Blogspot, Twitter, Goodreads, and Facebook, as well as her own website—all done in an effort to keep in contact with her growing legion of fans, whom she wants to entertain more than anything. In an interview with Jason Henninger for *Tor.com* (28 May 2010), she remarked, "I don't want my writing to be work to read. My main goal is completely shameless entertainment. I want people to smile and giggle and enjoy the book. I'm not trying to save the world through literature."

EARLY EDUCATION AND CAREER

Gail Carriger is the pen name of Tofa Borregaard, who was born in 1976 in Bolinas, California. In a brief biography posted on her official website, she has playfully described her mother and father as, respectively, "an expatriate Brit and an incurable curmudgeon." She grew up with a great love of reading and is an admirer of the works of Jane Austen, Charles Dickens, and P. G. Wodehouse in particular. As an undergraduate at Oberlin College in Oberlin, Ohio, she did her first work in field archeology in 1996 but quickly switched over to laboratory work after discovering her specialization through what she refers to as a fortunate accident. The accident left her unable to do fieldwork, and she was consequently assigned to the field laboratory for a classical site in Tuscany whose artifacts included mostly ceramics. She recalled in her interview with Henninger that her colleagues quickly discovered she had a knack for the work: "They could put a potsherd in front of me and I could ID it without being taught anything. Like, this piece has wheel striation marks, this was thrown, that one was hand-built and that one is a cooking vessel." She found that she preferred working in the field lab, especially because she "got to look at the best artifacts without digging through the dross first!" Her experience compelled her to switch her focus to the technology of ceramic production rather than a specific time and geography.

Carriger completed her undergraduate degree at Oberlin in 1998 and went on to earn her MS in archeological materials at the University of Nottingham, a public research university in Nottingham, England, in 2000. She earned another master's degree, in anthropology with a focus on archeology, from the University of

California Santa Cruz in 2008. Between earning those two degrees, she worked in field laboratories all over the world, studying ceramic technological development. Her particular specialties were paste/glaze interaction and early kiln technology. One of her notable kiln projects was the Northern California Experimental Firing Group (NCEFG), which she founded in 2003 with fellow archeologist Dave Walker. According to its official website, the group was formed "to understand more about pottery production in historic and prehistoric periods by building pottery kilns and firing pottery within them." The kiln they built was based on Romano-British and medieval up-draught kilns and was capable of reaching temperatures up to 1,100 degrees Celsius (2,012 degrees Fahrenheit).

DIVING INTO FICTION

While working as an archeologist, Carriger wrote fiction on the side, specifically young adult fiction with a fantastical element. Her first story was published in 1998. She also enjoyed making historical costumes and going to science-fiction conventions. Her varied interests eventually helped her develop a story idea about an alternate Victorian England, one in which vampires, werewolves, ghosts, and other supernatural creatures had been directly involved with world history for millennia.

Before long, Carriger had created a unique world made up of several subgenres of fiction: romance, comedy, urban fantasy, and steampunk. Urban fantasy typically employs mythological or magical elements, such as magicians or vampires, in a contemporary or historical city, while steampunk is a subgenre of science fiction that uses nineteenth-century technology in either an alternate history or futuristic setting where steam-driven mechanisms once again have widespread use. Steampunk fiction might, for example, describe a society in which the time machine from H. G. Wells's groundbreaking science-fiction novel *The Time Machine* (1895) had really been built, or one in which British inventor Charles Babbage had really been able to build his analytical engine (a mechanical computer) in the mid-1800s, as he had wanted to.

In an interview with Kristin Centorcelli for *My Bookish Ways* (6 Feb. 2013), Carriger described the widespread appeal of the steampunk subgenre, elements of which can be found in art, film, video games, and music, in addition to literature: "Steampunk is a unique movement in that it isn't entirely literary—it has ties to the green movement, the maker community, historical reenactment societies, and the fashion world. I believe it has immense escapist appeal. With the economy in chaos, steampunk offers up an alternative lifestyle of sedate civilized behavior where everyone (whether truthfully or not) knows where they belong."

THE PARASOL PROTECTORATE SERIES

Soulless, the first book in Carriger's Parasol Protectorate series, was published in 2009 by Orbit Books, a division of Hachette Book Group. It follows the adventures of Alexia Tarabotti, a stubborn and "unmarriageable" twenty-five-year-old Victorian woman who lives in a London filled with ghosts, vampires, and werewolves. Alexia is also "soulless"—she literally does not have a soul—a rare condition that is considered an embarrassment in her society and something to be kept hidden. (In Carriger's universe, there are some people, however, who have an "excess" of soul, which allows them to survive being bitten by a vampire.) In her interview with Henninger, Carriger explained how she fell upon this idea of having a quantifiable amount of soul: "I took Victorian scientific thought, looking at the theories and practice around in 1873, and made it—at least in possibility—true. . . . Some scientists had this very strange notion that the soul was physical and could be weighed. An American scientist took to weighing people who were terminally ill and then again when they died. A very separatist idea of life and soul."

In the first novel, Alexia kills a vampire at a party with her parasol and must work with Lord Conall Maccon, an impetuous werewolf from Scotland to whom she takes an immediate dislike (and he to her), to solve a supernatural secret with the help of Alexia's best friend, vampire Lord Akeldama. *Soulless* met with critical acclaim upon its publication; a reviewer for *Publishers Weekly* (24 Aug. 2009) wrote "Carriger debuts brilliantly with a blend of Victorian romance, screwball comedy of manners and alternate history. . . . This intoxicatingly witty parody will appeal to a wide cross-section of romance, fantasy, and steampunk fans." A commercial success upon publication, the novel also earned nominations for the Compton Crook, Campbell, and Locus awards and won the Alex Award, which is presented annually by the American Library Association (ALA) to the authors of ten adult books that have a special appeal to teenagers.

Two sequels appeared in rapid succession in 2010. *Changeless* and *Blameless* both quickly secured places on the New York Times Best Sellers list. *Heartless*, the fourth book in the series, was published in 2011 and was also a New York Times Best Seller. By this point in the series, Alexia is married to Lord Maccon and still verbally jousting with him. Despite being eight months pregnant, she is still ready to face any challenges that come her way, including zombie porcupines, threats to her unborn child, and a ghost that wants her to protect Queen Victoria. The Parasol Protectorate concluded with the fifth book in the series, *Timeless* (2012), which introduces Alexia's daughter, Prudence, in addition to wrapping up storylines for the main characters. Like its predecessors, *Timeless* was also a New York Times Best Seller.

The Parasol Protectorate has also been adapted into a graphic novel series in the manga comic style that first became popular in Japan. Illustrated by the artist Rem, the first two volumes, *Soulless Vol. 1* (2012) and *Soulless Vol. 2* (2012), became best sellers; the third book was published in November 2013.

FINISHING SCHOOL SERIES AND UPCOMING BOOKS

Much to her publisher's dismay, Carriger decided to conclude her best-selling series after five novels. But the author was not yet done with the world she had created. She proposed instead two new series: Finishing School, a young adult series featuring a new heroine named Sophronia that takes place more than twenty years before the Parasol Protectorate series, and another adult series, the Parasol Protectorate Abroad, featuring Alexia's daughter, Prudence, after childhood. "When Gail came to us suggesting a series with Alexia's daughter, Prudence, how could we resist?" Devi Pillai, senior editor at Orbit, told Gabe Habash for *Publishers Weekly* (30 Sept. 2011). The first two titles in the series, *Prudence* and *Imprudence*, are expected to be released in 2015 and 2016, respectively.

The Finishing School series was sold to another Hachette division, Little, Brown Books for Young Readers, in a four-book deal. The first title of the series, *Etiquette & Espionage*, was published in February 2013; the second, *Curtsies & Conspiracies*, was published in November of that year. The series is off to a terrific start, with *Etiquette & Espionage* becoming both a New York Times Best Seller and a critical success just months after its initial publication. *Etiquette & Espionage* introduces readers to Sophronia, a fourteen-year-old girl far better at climbing trees and taking apart clocks than curtseying. As the novel opens, she is unhappy to learn she is being sent to finishing school, away from all she has known. Her sadness disappears, however, when she learns that Mademoiselle Geraldine's Finishing Academy for Young Ladies of Quality is a far cry from any finishing school she might have imagined. The school, which is housed in an enormous airship that floats above the moors, teaches its students not only how to be proper ladies but also how to "finish" anyone, including through assassination. A reviewer for *Publishers Weekly* (14 Jan. 2013) wrote, "Effortlessly blending Victorian, paranormal, and steampunk elements, Carriger offers a feast of words (flywayman, mechanimals) and names (Dimity Ann Plumleigh-Teignmott, Phineas B. Crow) to lunch on in her YA debut. . . . Carriger deploys laugh-out-loud bon mots on nearly every page . . . and Sophronia is a capable and clever heroine."

Carriger, who is at work on the third book in the Finishing School series, *Waistcoats & Weaponry*, is a frequent guest at book events and conventions and is, according to her official biography, "overly fond of tea."

SUGGESTED READING

Habash, Gabe. "Hachette Looks to Broaden Reach for Gail Carriger." *Publishers Weekly*. Publishers Weekly, 30 Sept. 2011. Web. 14 Aug. 2013.

Herz, Henry. "Interview with NY Times Bestselling 'Finishing School' Author Gail Carriger." *San Diego Examiner*. Clarity Digital Group, 6 Aug. 2013. Web. 11 Oct. 2013.

Northern California Experimental Firing Group. "About the NCEFG." *Northern California Experimental Firing Group*. Northern California Experimental Firing Group, n.d. Web. 15 Aug. 2013.

Schmitz, S. L. "Gail Carriger: Building a Steampunk Empire, One Parasol at a Time." *Charlotte Examiner*. Clarity Digital Group, 23 July 2013. Web. 11 Oct. 2013.

Williford, John. "No Soul, But Plenty of Spirit." *Miami Herald*. Miami Herald Media, 1 June 2012. Web. 11 Oct. 2013.

SELECTED WORKS

Soulless, 2009; *Blameless*, 2010; *Changeless*, 2010; *Heartless*, 2011; *Timeless*, 2012; *Soulless: The Manga* (with Rem), 2012– ; *Etiquette & Espionage*, 2013; *Curtsies & Conspiracies*, 2013

—Christopher Mari

Jessica Chastain

Born: March 24, 1977
Occupation: Actor

Jessica Chastain has been recognized as one of the premier actors of her generation. She has also been named to many lists, including *Time* magazine's 100 Most Influential People list for 2012 and the International Best-Dressed List compiled that year by *Vanity Fair*. She is the face of Manifesto, an Yves Saint Laurent scent. Photographed by the renowned Annie Leibovitz for a *Vogue* cover profile, she re-created artworks by Gustav Klimt, René Magritte, and Vincent van Gogh. Despite the awards she has been nominated for and won, Chastain told Nicole Frehsee for *Rolling Stone* (31 Oct. 2011), "My personal life hasn't changed. I think only three people have come up to me in the past six months. Which is too bad, because I love to meet people. I wouldn't be mean to them."

FilmMagic

EARLY LIFE AND EDUCATION

Jessica Michelle Chastain was born on March 24, 1977, in Sacramento, California, to a sixteen-year-old high school student, Jerri Chastain, and a twenty-year-old rock star hopeful, Michael Monasterio, whose name was not listed on her birth certificate. Chastain's parents separated soon after her younger sister, Juliet, was born. After her mother married Michael Hastey when Chastain was in eighth grade, life grew easier. Chastain eventually had two brothers and two sisters in a family she describes as average and middle class. Her mother is a vegan chef, and Hastey is a firefighter.

When Chastain was seven, her grandmother took her to a live production of *Joseph and the Amazing Technicolor Dreamcoat*, a musical by Andrew Lloyd Webber and Tim Rice. Chastain told Margy Rochlin for the *New York Times* (24 Aug. 2011), "It's so embarrassing; you think, 'That's the reason I'm an actor?' But that was the moment that I realized acting is a job and that it was what I was supposed to do." At nine she discovered the world of dance, joining a troupe four years later. Her grandmother gave her ballet tutus for Christmas, as well as ballet lessons.

Chastain performed in school productions at El Camino Fundamental High School, and after graduating, she attended Sacramento City College for a short time. In 1998 she starred in a Silicon Valley production of William Shakespeare's *Romeo and Juliet*. She later performed one of Juliet's monologues as part of her audition for the Juilliard School, a prestigious performing

arts college in New York City. Recalling her monologue, she told Lynn Yaeger for the *New York Times* (13 Apr. 2012), "Most people do it so precious and sweet, a girl just married, but she is going to be a woman, and 'he shall die' means orgasm! It was crazy. I was on the ground by the end of the audition. When I finished, the admissions panel was like, 'Who is this little redheaded girl coming in here?'" She was offered a scholarship, funded by comedian and Juilliard alumnus Robin Williams, to attend Juilliard and became the first in her family to go to college. Her grandmother flew to New York when Chastain moved to help her settle into the dorm.

BEGINNING A CAREER

In 2003, during her senior year at Juilliard, Chastain caught the attention of John Wells, the producer of *The West Wing* and *ER*, who signed her for a twelve-month contract; she later appeared in a small role in an episode of *ER*. She performed opposite veteran actor David Strathairn in an Off-Broadway production of *Rodney's Wife* in 2004 and also appeared in guest roles in television shows such as *Veronica Mars* and *Law and Order: Trial by Jury*.

Veteran actor Al Pacino gave Chastain her first big break in 2006, casting her as Salomé opposite his King Herod in Oscar Wilde's *Salomé*. Chastain told interviewers that Pacino effectively became her acting coach for a year. Impressed by her performance, he retained her in the title role when the play was later made into a film, *Wilde Salomé* (2011).

Pacino gave Chastain two pieces of advice for her first major film. First, he told her that the camera sees more deeply than the partner in the scene will. Second, the camera will know if an actor is lying, so actors should not lie. Chastain told Tom Shone for *Vogue* (Dec. 2013) that the role of Salomé—a young woman who dances before the biblical monarch Herod and demands the head of John the Baptist on a platter as her reward—was a challenge, and not only because it was her first major role. "I did not feel like a beautiful woman that people would kill each other for," she explained. "Jessica—who I am in my personal life—I'm very shy, I feel very awkward, I don't feel like a femme fatale at all."

Chastain made her feature film debut in 2008, starring in the independent film *Jolene*. The following year, she played Desdemona in a New York stage production of Shakespeare's *Othello*. These early experiences helped form her ideas about her profession. She told Shone, "Acting is about exploring things I don't understand in myself."

A VERY BIG YEAR

In 2011, Chastain appeared in seven films and garnered her first award nominations. A modern adaptation of Shakespeare's *Coriolanus*, starring

Ralph Fiennes and Vanessa Redgrave, premiered at the Berlin Film Festival in February. In May *The Tree of Life*, in which she stars alongside Brad Pitt and Sean Penn, opened. Two very different films opened in the United States in August: *The Debt*, in which Chastain plays a Mossad agent tracking down Nazi war criminals, and *The Help*, in which she portrays an awkward white woman who befriends her black maid. *Wilde Salomé*, which is both a film of and a backstage documentary about Wilde's play, premiered in Venice, Italy, in September. That same month *Take Shelter*, which features Chastain as the wife of a man having apocalyptic visions, was released, and the crime thriller *Texas Killing Fields* premiered the following month.

The release of seven films in a year was unplanned; studio reschedules and delays in production brought about the box office bounty. Those delays actually worked in her favor, as Chastain explained to Frehsee: "It was frustrating, but the lag was good for my career. Directors hadn't seen my work, so I could go into auditions and not carry the baggage of past performances."

Chastain regarded filming *The Help* with Octavia Spencer, who played her character's maid, as one of the best on-set experiences of her life. The film became Chastain's greatest financial success to date and earned both Chastain and Spencer Academy Award nominations for best actress. (Chastain ultimately lost the award to Spencer.) Her performances resonated with audiences, in part because of her focus on authentic emotions. Chastain explained to *Take Shelter* costar Michael Shannon in a piece for *Interview* (Dec. 2011/Jan. 2012), "I think that with any emotion—fear, love, nervousness—if the actor's feeling it, then the audience feels it. I'm gonna have to be in a place where my heart's beating fast and I have a physical reaction to what I'm feeling."

To reach that place, Chastain prepares carefully for each role. Cast as Pitt's wife in *The Tree of Life*, she spent hours at the Metropolitan Museum of Art in New York, looking at the Madonnas that Italian Renaissance artist Raphael had painted, to develop a sense of the grace she felt the role demanded. For *The Debt*, Chastain spent three months looking at Holocaust photographs. In one scene, her character is looking at photographs and learning about the experiments the Nazis performed on children and pregnant women; she allowed the crew to film her first reactions, having not seen those particular photographs ahead of time. Chastain proved her versatility through those diverse roles, holding her own against the stars with whom she shared the screen.

FURTHER WORK
Chastain voiced Gia the jaguar for the animated film *Madagascar 3: Europe's Most Wanted*

in 2012. That year also saw the release of the controversial *Zero Dark Thirty*, a film directed by Kathryn Bigelow about the search for Osama bin Laden. Although Chastain's agents had declined the role of CIA agent Maya on her behalf, Megan Ellison, the producer of the 2012 Chastain film *Lawless*, gave Bigelow the actor's phone number. Bigelow called her directly, and Chastain ultimately accepted the role.

Continuing to expand her portfolio, she appeared in the horror film *Mama*, produced by Mexican filmmaker Guillermo del Toro, who spoke to Shone about Chastain's private nature. "She is never guarded, but she is very protective of not having to be an open book," he explained. "The crew loves her, the cast loves her, but that doesn't mean that she has to cook a dinner for twenty-five people every Friday." During the weekend of January 18–21, 2013, two of Chastain's films—*Zero Dark Thirty* and *Mama*—were the top-grossing box office hits. That weekend marked the first time in nearly half a century that a leading lady had two films at the top.

Chastain made her Broadway debut in 2012 in the title role of Catherine Sloper in *The Heiress*, again working with Strathairn, who played her father. Based on the Henry James novel *Washington Square*, the play was written in 1947 by Augustus and Ruth Goetz. Although it is relatively rare for a film actor to take time out of a busy career to perform on Broadway, Chastain explained to Evgenia Peretz for *Vanity Fair* (2012), "I had a connection to [Catherine]. She's painfully uncomfortable and I used to be that."

To prepare for the role, Chastain asked the wardrobe department to outfit her from day one of rehearsals with something similar to the costume she would wear. She wanted to get used to the shoes, corset, and long skirt a nineteenth-century woman would wear, as well as her wig. Director Moisés Kaufman noted that Chastain remained completely in character even during breaks, when she sat embroidering, because needlework was what Catherine did. Chastain also visited Merchant's House, a National Historic Landmark and New York museum, with Kaufman. In that preserved nineteenth-century home, she learned how a woman of that era would carry herself. For example, she always held up her skirt with both hands when going up the stairs. The lessons also included such details as when to curtsy and how to hold a fan or handkerchief.

During the Broadway run of *The Heiress*, Chastain purchased a co-op apartment in Greenwich Village to be near the theater. The show closed a day early so that Chastain could attend the British Academy Film Awards (BAFTA) ceremony in London. She had been nominated for a BAFTA for *The Help*.

AWARDS

Explaining her method of choosing roles, Chastain told Andrea Mandell for *USA Today*, "I believe that it's come from not following the money. The people I work with, I'm such a fan of. I've seen other things that they've directed and acted in, and I want to be there because I want to learn from them." That strategy has brought her a large measure of success.

For her role in *Zero Dark Thirty*, Chastain won a Golden Globe for best actress. The award came while she was performing on Broadway. She was also nominated for an Academy Award and a BAFTA for her role in that film. In addition, she won the first Gucci Award for Women in Cinema for *The Tree of Life*. At the 2013 Maui Film Festival, she received the Nova Award for the range of characters she has brought to life. A number of regional and state film associations—among them the Dallas-Fort Worth Critics Association, the Florida Film Critics Circle, and the Los Angeles Film Critics—have also granted her awards.

PERSONAL LIFE

Chastain is a notoriously private person, in part because of her desire to protect her younger half-siblings from media attention. Her sister Juliet committed suicide in 2003, and her biological father, Michael Monasterio, died in 2013 at the age of fifty-five.

A lover of food and cooking, Chastain is vegan. She practices yoga and begins the day with a 5:30 a.m. workout. She also plays the ukulele.

Chastain began a relationship with Gian Luca Passi de Preposulo, an Italian fashion executive, in 2013, but keeps it out of the limelight. She strives to keep her head despite her newfound fame. She told Frehsee in 2011, "I know this is all gonna go away. I'm not some naive twenty-year-old trying to cling to this amazing year. Because a year like this . . . it's just not normal."

SUGGESTED READING

Chastain, Jessica. Interview by Michael Shannon. *Interview* Dec. 2011–Jan. 2012: 116–25. Print.
Morris, Alex. "The Rituals of Jessica Chastain." *New York* 22 Oct. 2012: 103–7. Print.
Naoreen, Nuzhat. "Oscar Style." *Entertainment Weekly* 9 Mar. 2012: 43–46. Print.
Peretz, Evgenia. "Angel on Horseback." *Vanity Fair*. Condé Nast, Sept. 2012. Web. 13 May 2014.
Shone, Tom. "Jessica Chastain: Hollywood's Most Versatile Star." *Vogue*. Condé Nast, Dec. 2013. Web. 13 May 2014.

SELECTED WORKS

Coriolanus, 2011; *The Tree of Life*, 2011; *The Debt*, 2011; *The Help*, 2011; *Take Shelter*, 2011; *Texas Killing Fields*, 2011; *Zero Dark Thirty*, 2012; *Mama*, 2013

—Judy Johnson

Perry Chen

Born: 1976
Occupation: CEO of Kickstarter

"I believe that everyone has some kind of creative project that they think about—whether it's something small they'd like to do over a weekend with friends, or it's the film they've always wanted to make. . . . Our goal is to meet everybody at his or her level," Perry Chen, the cofounder of Kickstarter, told Hallie Davison for the *Economist: Intelligent Life* (22 Oct. 2010). Chen's seeming nonchalance and thoughtful demeanor might seem inconsistent with his role as the CEO of the paradigm-shifting "crowdfunding" website that has impacted both art and the American economy, but they are key attributes of his success.

Though he may seem aloof to some and an outsider within the tech industry—headquartering his company in Brooklyn as opposed to Silicon Valley and refusing to offer an IPO that would make him and his team wealthy—Chen aligns himself with the struggling artist and those on the fringes of popular culture, stressing

Robert Pitts/Landov

that Kickstarter's mission is a selfish endeavor at its core. "We would like it to be a fundamental tool for the liberation or the acceleration of our own creativity," he explained to Om Malik for the website *GigaOM* (22 May 2012). Nonetheless, many have argued that Kickstarter is essentially altruistic, enabling both artists to express themselves and communities to band together in support of meaningful expression outside of a prescribed set of boundaries.

EARLY LIFE AND EDUCATION

A Chinese American, Chen was born in 1976 and raised in New York City, growing up on Roosevelt Island, a small strip of land two miles long and approximately eight hundred feet wide that sits in the East River between Manhattan and Queens. Life on Roosevelt Island—technically part of, but isolated from, Manhattan—may have nurtured Chen's eccentricities or given him the sense of isolation that has partially informed his lifestyle and creative vision. Chen's father was a schoolteacher, and his mother a social worker, and Chen exhibited intellectual gifts from an early age. He was accepted to Hunter College High School but, while there, was an average student who had a difficult time concentrating on his studies.

Chen attended and graduated from Tulane University's Freeman School of Business in 1998. He returned to New York after graduating, briefly opening an art gallery in Brooklyn; he then returned to New Orleans, a city for which he has great affinity, and was living there in 2001 when he first developed the idea for Kickstarter. "I had the idea, and then I was like, 'That's a good idea. Now, back to my regularly scheduled life,'" he told Malik. "I did expect that, in six months or one year or two years, I was just going to turn on the TV or go on the web one day and somebody was going to send me a link and be like, 'Oh, check this thing out,' and I would be like everybody else, 'Oh, I had that idea.'"

A REVOLUTIONARY IDEA

Having worked as an art curator, waiter, preschool teacher, and musician, Chen has held numerous jobs outside the mainstream; Kickstarter emerged from his desire to fund his own musical endeavors and, specifically, his inability to finance an electronic-music show in New Orleans. In 2001, Chen attempted to hire Kruder & Dorfmeister, DJs from Austria, to make an appearance at the New Orleans Jazz and Heritage Festival, and he contacted the pair directly. Unable to front or acquire the necessary funds (about twenty thousand dollars) that the band requested to make an appearance, Chen was discouraged, but the failure started the wheels spinning in his mind. "I had this feeling that this was a problem that should be solvable," he informed Max Chafkin for *Fast Company* (18 Mar.

2013). "There was a possibility that the artists would have a great show and everybody would have a great time. But none of that could happen because the decision had to be made by me—based on my own resources. There was an inherent flaw in that."

After spending time in New Orleans, Chen eventually returned to New York, working as a waiter and distancing himself from mainstream culture. "I wanted to focus on dropping out of society," he told Chafkin. While he was waiting tables he struck up a friendship with Yancey Strickler, editor in chief of eMusic and a frequent patron of the restaurant at which Chen worked. Soon, Chen shared his vision of Kickstarter with Strickler, though he was initially skeptical. Strickler thought the platform seemed like an unlikely one for producing exceptional art and could, in fact, fund mediocre projects. Chen eased Strickler's mind: "What about someone like a sculptor in some small town in the middle of nowhere? They have no way to get into a gallery. No one around them appreciates what they're doing—but the Internet could," reports Rob Walker for the *New York Times* (5 Aug. 2011). Strickler was onboard, and soon they hunted for a website designer, eventually adding Charles Adler as the third cofounder.

In 2006, the trio began looking for investors, and received funds from comedian David Cross, who promised to use Kickstarter—as the company was originally known—to fund one of his projects. Kickstarter eventually received $10 million from venture capitalists that included Union Square Ventures, Vimeo's Zach Klein, and Flikr's Caterina Fake. The company launched in 2009, initially as an invite-only opportunity for artists, and grew quickly into a multimillion-dollar operation.

NEW SPIN ON AN OLD SYSTEM

"Everything comes from somewhere," Chen explained to *T* (the *New York Times* style magazine) on May 30, 2013. "I didn't even know this till later on, but we found out that Mozart and Beethoven and [Walt] Whitman and a lot of 19th-century authors used pre-Internet models like Kickstarter . . . not just going to rich patrons or the Medici or the Church to get the big check, but . . . going to dozens or even hundreds of people to fund a creative work." This bit of historical knowledge seems to give Chen confidence that his creation is an almost intuitive process, thus giving it the strength to survive and to flourish. In a way, he sees himself as the gatekeeper for the unfiltered creative process, and Kickstarter is a reflection of the notion that if an audience enjoys a particular work of art, it will patronize the artist.

"Artists have always been extremely creative people both in art and in talking to audiences, and in hustling to get the things that they want done," Chen explained to Malik. "A lot of the things that you're seeing on the web now, from YouTube to Twitter, and what we're doing, are really just the tools so that creative people can get their things done and connect with other people. They don't create the creativity." The Kickstarter interface is as simple as the concept—which allows artists, musicians, and inventors (within reason and subject to approval) to host fundraising drives for specific amounts of money and durations of time (usually a month). Each artist or group page usually has explanatory videos and monetary donation levels that generally coincide with a prize (such as free album downloads). Both supporters and the general public can chart the progress of a project by viewing the amount of money already pledged and the amount of time left in the campaign. Other than approving or rejecting each submitted project, the Kickstarter staff takes a hands-off approach, acting as facilitator. The company does take a 5 percent cut of each project, and Amazon, which handles payments, takes an addition 3 to 5 percent.

Though Chen points to the past when discussing the idea of the "subscription artist" (GigaOM), such as Mozart, Kickstarter has also inspired creativity in unlikely sectors and has encouraged artists without mainstream financial resources to both create and promote their art. He told Malik: "We're reaching this bursting point of creativity. People are embracing their own creativity more and more. It's now OK to be an accountant during the day, but at night you're a writer or you're a painter or you're a DJ. We don't have to be one thing anymore." Kickstarter may be working from an age-old model, but it is not too much of a stretch to say it is also affecting the economy, representing a paradigm shift in which artists can control their creative endeavors apart from a "studio" system (the Hollywood film industry, for example).

SUCCESS AND BACKLASH

Kickstarter began as a platform for relatively small-scale creative projects—to help a local band record an album, for example—and was essentially backed by built-in communities of family, friends, and fans. The company still hosts such projects, but along the way, well-known artists and entertainers realized they could also use Kickstarter to their advantage.

One of the most publicized examples of Kickstarter being used for a large-scale project is the saga of Veronica Mars, a cult television program that aired from 2004 to 2007. For years, producer Rob Thomas had attempted to make a film based on the series but was perpetually rebuked for funding by Warner Bros. In 2013, however, the creators of Veronica Mars decided to use Kickstarter as their fund-raising venue. As star Kristen Bell explained in Time magazine (18 Apr. 2013), "I don't know much about studio financing models, but I do know they weren't working for Veronica Mars." She added that Kickstarter was fun and easy to use, noting: "There's something so smart and magical about that idea—connecting consumers with creators and letting them vote with their own money." The project greatly exceeded its $2 million funding goal, collecting more than $5.5 million from more than ninety thousand contributors.

Some have criticized well-known artists and entertainers for using Kickstarter, insisting that the practice diminishes the projects by unknown artists and represents a potential opening for scams, but Chen sees the situation differently: "Those large projects draw attention," he told Malik. "They draw new people to the site and they're rallying points for people to find out more about the site." In Chen's view this is essentially beneficial for the company, the model, and for any creative person that hopes to launch a project. Chen understands the criticism but insists that Kickstarter's function is to facilitate endeavors and not necessarily draw a line between known and unknown artists or high and low art. It is neither his nor the company's job to make value judgments on the types of works that are being funded, though they still possess veto power over any project before it is launched.

The largest Kickstarter projects to date include the Pebble "smartwatch," which raised more than $10 million after the creators were unable to finance the project via traditional routes. Several video games have raised millions of dollars, as did the film Wish I Was Here, cowritten and directed by Zach Braff. A successful Hollywood actor, Braff received considerable condemnation for his choice to fund his film through Kickstarter, as many believed the film could have received financial backing from a major studio. Such denunciation seems counterintuitive to Chen, whose primary goal is to ensure creative projects can be funded, regardless of scale. "We focus on a middle ground between patronage and commerce. People are offering cool stuff and experiences in exchange for the support of their ideas. People are creating these mini-economies around their project ideas. So, you aren't coming to the site to get something for nothing," he explained to Davison.

THE COMMON GOOD

Chen seems to have captured a notion that was floating in society's collective consciousness—a logical progression from the entrenched economy into a world in which personal creativity and industriousness can fashion an individual life. As Malik insists: "Kickstarter is not just a startup—it's part of an important shift away from the industrial manufacturing era and toward the maker economy." Though Chen does not exactly agree with this assessment, insisting that the "industrial creative complex" is a relatively new phenomenon, it is clear that Kickstarter, and other crowdfunding sites such as Indiegogo and GoFundMe, represents a new era in audience consumption and artistic endeavors. Though Kickstarter has the potential to be abused—a primary reason why Chen and his colleagues vet every submitted project—it also has transformative potential, emboldening artists and designers to rethink how they conduct business and set up their communities, both virtual and physical, what Chen dubs "purposeful infrastructure" (T magazine).

The idea that Kickstarter has the potential to promote "social good" is an intention that others have attached to the concept, often because of projects they may have created with help from the Kickstarter platform. Chen insists, however, that he never saw larger social ramifications when he brainstormed the concept or created the company. "I was just scratching my own itch," he told T. "I wanted something like this to exist in the world, and I thought other people would, too. I wasn't calibrating how much good it was going to do." Nonetheless, projects such as Landfill Harmonic, the goal of which is to fashion musical instruments from trash, resonate with communities and represent creative ways of using the environment to address social issues. Such projects have provoked Chen to think about ways in which Kickstarter can benefit physical communities and urban settings, and he feels that Kickstarter might be able to help change that model.

WHAT THE FUTURE HOLDS

"I definitely do think of Kickstarter as my baby. . . . But I also certainly know it's bigger than me," Chen told Malik. "I think even before it became big, there was this moment where I just felt like I was the shepherd of the idea." Chen's focus on shepherding the concept has meant the company has not grown the way other tech start-ups have.

Though the company moved into new, sprawling headquarters in 2013, its plans for expansion are minimal. Unlike other tech companies that offer an IPO then take the money and run, Chen envisions a steady course that does not divert from the original mission of the company. "Did you know there are companies in Japan that have been around for a thousand years?" he asked Chafkin. "It's weird: In the Internet industry, you're basically a custodian of your own idea for maybe three to five years and then you're supposed to sell. That's insanity." Though Kickstarter has been the guardian of nearly $550 million in pledges for close to one hundred thousand projects, Chen clearly wants to maintain a reasonable semblance of control over the idea that has sparked what some deem to be no less than an artistic revolution. Despite his quick rise, Chen remains an iconoclast.

SUGGESTED READING

Bell, Kristen. "Perry Chen." *Time*. Time, 18 Apr. 2013. Web. 24 Sept. 2013.

Chafkin, Max. "True to Its Roots: Why Kickstarter Won't Sell." *Fast Company*. Fast Company, 18 Mar. 2013. Web. 24 Sept. 2013.

Chen, Perry. "The Q&A: Perry Chen, Kickstarter." Interview by Hallie Davison. *Economist: Intelligent Life*. Economist Newspaper, 22 Oct. 2010. Web. 24 Sept. 2013.

Roettgers, Janko. "Kickstarter CEO Perry Chen: We Don't Ever Want to Sell This Company." *GigaOM*. GigaOM, 5 Nov. 2012. Web. 24 Sept. 2013.

Walker, Rob. "The Trivialities and Transcendence of Kickstarter." *New York Times*. New York Times Co., 5 Aug. 2011. Web. 24 Sept. 2013.

—Christopher Rager

Brian Chesky

Born: August 29, 1981
Occupation: Founder and CEO of Airbnb

In September 2007, roommates Brian Chesky and Joe Gebbia were short on their rent. In a last-ditch effort to raise funds, they decided to rent out their small San Francisco home to three people who were in town for a design conference and could not find hotel rooms. Chesky and Gebbia did not even have extra beds, but they had air mattresses, and they charged eighty dollars per night for their "Airbed and Breakfast." In the years that followed, the simple idea proved to be successful—so astronomically and profoundly successful that it spawned a multibillion-dollar home-rental business and a new concept: the sharing economy. Today, Chesky is the CEO of Airbnb, a company that facilitates rentals of not only airbeds but also castles, yurts, igloos, trailers and recreational vehicles, water towers, lighthouses, tree houses, and private islands. Yet the bulk of Airbnb's listings are still regular apartments and houses, scattered across the globe. The company, which was valued at over $10 billion in 2014, offers more than 600,000 listings, representing more than 34,000 cities in 190 countries.

Navigating safety concerns, tax codes, and rental laws has been a learning curve for the company. Unlike hotels, Airbnb hosts do not pay an occupancy tax, which raises the complicated question of whether Airbnb hosts should be treated like hotel corporations. The answer to this question will have consequences for the burgeoning notion of the sharing economy. In 2014, Airbnb went to court in New York for violating a 2010 law prohibiting New York City

Bloomberg via Getty Images

professional hockey, ran RISD's hockey team, the Nads (as in "Go, Nads!"), while Gebbia founded the school's basketball team, the Balls. Despite the sophomoric names, Chesky told Austin Carr for *Fast Company* (17 Feb. 2012) that the teams presented serious marketing challenges for the two men to overcome. "These were basically our first startups," he said, summarizing the problem with the question, "How do you get art school students to a sporting event on a Friday night?" Successful tactics included free beer, outrageous halftime shows, and a mascot named Scrotie. At graduation in 2004, Chesky, who was scheduled to give the commencement address, ripped off his robes to reveal a white tuxedo and moonwalked to the microphone to the sound of Michael Jackson's song "Billie Jean."

RAISING RENT
After earning his degree in industrial design, Chesky moved to Los Angeles to work at a small design firm, due in part to his mother's plea that he find a job that offered health insurance. But Chesky did not enjoy the work and quit after three years. In September 2007, he packed his belongings into his Honda Civic and drove to San Francisco to move in with Gebbia, who had also quit his job and had been pestering Chesky to start a company with him since graduation. The same week that Chesky moved in, however, Gebbia's landlord raised their rent by 20 percent.

"Unfortunately, my share came to $1,150 and I only had $1,000 in the bank, so I had a math problem—and I was unemployed," Chesky told Thomas L. Friedman in an interview for the *New York Times* (20 July 2013). But Chesky had an idea. San Francisco was hosting the ICSID/IDSA World Design Congress (cosponsored by the International Council of Societies of Industrial Design and the Industrial Designers Society of America) in October, and all the hotels on the conference website were booked. Chesky and Gebbia decided to rent out their shared living space, despite the fact that they had no spare beds. They inflated an air mattress in the living room and called themselves the "Airbed and Breakfast." "We created a simple site and promoted it by emailing a few top design blogs," Gebbia wrote for *Fast Company* (7 Nov. 2011). "After they wrote about it, we received so much interest that we had to buy two more air mattresses." That week, Chesky and Gebbia welcomed three guests and charged them each eighty dollars per night for the air mattress, breakfast, and local tips. The modest profits they made were enough to cover their rent.

CEREAL-BOX BEGINNINGS
It was clear that Chesky and Gebbia had found a workable business model, but finding investors proved much harder than they had anticipated. They brought in a third cofounder, Nathan

residents from renting out their apartments for less than a month at a time, intended to crack down on slumlords and the proliferation of illegal hotels. "We're not against regulation, we want fair regulation," Chesky told Andy Kessler for the *Wall Street Journal* (17 Jan. 2014). "We're trying to help take this from an activity that existed under the table with Craigslist and bring it out of the shadows. We want to work with cities to streamline the process for hosts to pay occupancy taxes. . . . It turns out that in cities like New York, you can't just pay the tax, you can't just send them a briefcase of money, you have to change the laws first."

EARLY LIFE AND EDUCATION
Brian Chesky was born on August 29, 1981, in Niskayuna, New York. Both of his parents were social workers. In school, his interests lay in art rather than business; in 1999 he was the winner for his district of the Congressional Art Competition, an annual contest that recognizes the best artwork by high school students throughout the country, and his work was displayed in the United States Capitol in Washington, DC, for one year.

After graduating from Niskayuna High School, Chesky attended the prestigious Rhode Island School of Design (RISD), where he met fellow student Joe Gebbia. Both men were known for their cheeky, entrepreneurial verve; Chesky, a former bodybuilder who once dreamed of playing

Blecharczyk, in 2008. Blecharczyk is an engineer who specializes in computer coding, a fact that Chesky and Gebbia hoped would endear them to Silicon Valley investors. It did not. Fifteen major investors passed on the idea, citing the team's overall lack of experience in business or technology and objecting to Chesky and Gebbia's background in design. "They thought we just made things pretty," Chesky told Carr in an interview for *Fast Company*'s 2012 list of the top innovative companies (7 Feb. 2012).

On their own, Chesky, Gebbia, and Blecharczyk launched a basic version of their website in anticipation of the 2008 South by Southwest (SXSW) music and media festival in Austin, Texas. The site attracted only fifty listings and two bookings—one of which was Chesky. They spent the spring adding an online payment system, to avoid the awkward hand-to-hand exchange of cash, and generally making the website easier to use. By the summer of 2008, the company, still called Airbed and Breakfast, was bringing in only a few hundred dollars a week; worse, it owed over $20,000 to various credit-card companies. Chesky told Kessler that he simply moved to a new card each time one was maxed out. Once again they were desperate for cash, and once again Chesky and Gebbia had an idea: they would go into the cereal business.

Inspired by the "Breakfast" component of their company's name, Chesky and Gebbia decided to design branded cartoon cereal boxes commemorating the 2008 presidential election. The cereals were named Obama O's and Cap'n McCains, for candidates Barack Obama and John McCain. They found a small Berkeley-based manufacturer, a fellow RISD alumnus, who agreed to manufacture the cartons in exchange for a cut of the royalties. Chesky and Gebbia poured generic store-bought cereal into the cartons and sealed them with a hot-glue gun. Each box cost forty dollars. Miraculously, sales of the boxes took off; Chesky and Gebbia were featured on CNN and *Good Morning America*, and singer Katy Perry auctioned off an autographed box to her fans. In the end, the company netted $30,000 from the cereal boxes—just enough to keep them in business until they met Paul Graham, a venture capitalist who also had a RISD connection.

Graham, the cofounder of the San Francisco–area seed-capital firm Y Combinator, gave Airbnb $20,000 in early 2009. A few months later, the venture-capital firm Sequoia Capital invested $600,000 in the company. Airbnb grew exponentially from there. In 2011 the company saw $500 million worth of transactions and was valued at $1.3 billion; in 2013, more than ten million people rented Airbnb accommodations, earning the company $250 million in revenue and a $2.7 billion valuation. In 2014 it was valued at $10 billion, making the company worth more than the hotel chain Hyatt. According to Carr, venture capitalist Fred Wilson, who passed on Airbnb, keeps a box of Obama O's in his office conference room as a reminder never to make such a costly mistake again.

HOW AIRBNB WORKS

Airbnb guests have a variety of options in terms of privacy; they can rent either a room in a house or a private apartment (or private island, or yurt). To rent accommodations, the guest contacts the owner and arranges a date. Guests pay for their stay on the Airbnb website, with Airbnb charging service fees of about 9 percent to the guest and 3 percent to the host. As Friedman points out, the process is the opposite of anonymous: guests and hosts alike can verify driver's licenses, passports, and other personal information. Regardless of whether or not guest and host ever meet, they must arrange their own key swap. After the experience (Chesky's preferred term) is over, guests can rate their stay on Airbnb's website, giving star ratings for cleanliness, location, and value, among other things. As with sites such as Yelp and TripAdvisor, they can even write reviews. Airbnb has expanded the listings portion of the site to include sprawling neighborhood guides for major cities, with descriptors such as "trendy," "residential," "nightlife," "touristy," and "loved by locals." One of the site's most popular features allows users to create themed wish lists.

All three founders regularly use the site, which in the past has helped them solve problems in an unusually straightforward manner. For example, in 2009, when Chesky was commuting between San Francisco and New York trying to rally investors, he noticed that listings in New York City, a major potential market, were stagnating. Chesky and Gebbia quickly identified the problem. "The photos [on the website] were really bad," Gebbia told Carr for the Most Innovative Companies 2012 profile. "People were using camera phones and taking Craigslist-quality pictures. Surprise! No one was booking because you couldn't see what you were paying for." So the two men took it upon themselves to rent a $5,000 professional-quality camera and go door to door, photographing as many apartments as they could. When the photos were posted on the site a month later, bookings in New York City doubled.

Now Airbnb offers hosts free professional photography services from over two thousand freelance photographers across the globe. The program sounds unsustainable, but Chesky and Gebbia have found that the benefits of the improved aesthetics far outweigh the cost of the photographers. "When we fixed the product in New York," Gebbia told Carr, "it solved our problems in Paris, London, Vancouver, and Miami." Chesky says it is all part of his very un–Silicon Valley maxim: "Do things that don't scale." He explained to Carr, "We start with the perfect experience and then work backward. That's how we're going to continue to be successful."

CREATIVE PROBLEM SOLVING

Chesky is notorious for finding solutions to problems through art and design. In 2012 he commissioned a Pixar animator to draw storyboards of trip experiences he had created from the perspectives of a guest, a host, and a prospective Airbnb employee. Chesky believes that the storyboards, which hang in the Airbnb offices, keep the company focused on individual experience.

To that end, Chesky considers Chip Conley, a former boutique hotelier, to be his principal mentor. Conley represents the anticorporate wing of the travel industry because, Chesky believes, he understands why people travel in the first place. Chesky approached Conley in 2013 and persuaded him to come out of semiretirement to work at Airbnb. Conley has since become Chesky's most trusted adviser. Among his contributions to the site are hospitality standards and a Dublin-based "hospitality lab" that offers free training for hosts.

Chesky also plans to roll out an Airbnb-helmed cleaning service, and there is talk of an airport transportation service as well. Chesky insists that it all makes for a better experience. "There is a whole generation of people that don't want everything mass produced," he told Friedman. "They want things that are unique and personal."

Like any savvy tech company, Airbnb is focusing much of its efforts on mobile devices. "One thing that we're doing is trying to shift every host to mobile," Chesky told Derek Thompson in an interview for the *Atlantic* magazine (13 Aug. 2013). "We'll eventually get to a place where every booking is insta-book." The company's insta-book feature allows customers to reserve a property with a single click. "In our business, if a seller has a mobile device, it could simulate the responsiveness and the up-to-dateness of a hotel," he explained. "This is why mobile is transformational for our business. It means a seller can act like a company, in the best possible way."

THE SHARING ECONOMY

Airbnb has faced its share of problems, but thus far Chesky has shown great aplomb in navigating them. In 2011 a guest robbed a host's apartment. Within weeks Chesky had instituted a $50,000 liability guarantee, voice and video verification systems, and a 24-7 customer-support hotline. As a result, customer trust actually improved.

Friedman, an economist as well as a *New York Times* op-ed columnist, has offered his endorsement of the sharing economy. He thinks that empowering entrepreneurship on individual terms will encourage people to use their own unique

skills, rather than seek to obtain skills that may or may not help them find jobs in the existing market. "In a world where, as I've argued, *average is over*—the skills required for any good job keep rising—a lot of people who might not be able to acquire those skills can still earn a good living now by building their own branded reputations, whether it is to rent their kids' rooms, their cars, or their power tools," Friedman wrote in his *New York Times* interview with Chesky. From the car-sharing company Lyft to Vayable, a company that offers customizable local tours, companies modeled on Airbnb are cashing in on the sharing economy in droves. But as evidenced by Airbnb's problems in New York City, these companies will also have to determine exactly what a sharing economy means in legal terms and how such a profoundly different economic structure can survive and flourish in the future.

SUGGESTED READING

Carr, Austin. "Most Innovative Companies 2012: 19_Airbnb." *Fast Company*. Mansueto Ventures, 7 Feb. 2012. Web. 17 June 2014.

Carr, Austin. "Watch Airbnb CEO Brian Chesky Salute RISD, Whip Off His Robe, Dance Like Michael Jackson." *Fast Company*. Mansueto Ventures, 17 Feb. 2012. Web. 17 June 2014.

Carr, Austin, and Joe Gebbia. "Starred: The Email That Launched Airbnb." *Fast Company*. Mansueto Ventures, 7 Nov. 2011. Web. 17 June 2014.

Chesky, Brian. "Airbnb CEO Brian Chesky on Building a Company and Starting a 'Sharing' Revolution." Interview by Derek Thompson. *Atlantic*. Atlantic Monthly, 13 Aug. 2013. Web. 17 June 2014.

Friedman, Thomas L. "Welcome to the 'Sharing Economy.'" *New York Times*. New York Times, 20 July 2013. Web. 17 June 2014.

Kessler, Andy. "Brian Chesky: The 'Sharing Economy' and Its Enemies." *Wall Street Journal*. Dow Jones, 17 Jan. 2014. Web. 17 June 2014.

—*Molly Hagan*

Priyanka Chopra

Born: July 18, 1982
Occupation: Actor

Priyanka Chopra is an award-winning Indian actor, singer, and model. While still in high school, she won the Miss World 2000 beauty competition and was able to leverage her popularity to launch a successful acting career. She has appeared in over forty Bollywood films since 2002. Today, she is one of the most famous and highest

Jason Merritt/Getty Images

paid actors in India. In 2013 Chopra was named the spokesmodel for the American clothing brand Guess and is the first Indian "Guess girl" in the company's history. She has released several pop singles in the United States. Her first, "In My City" (2012), was used as the theme song for the 2013 Thursday night professional football games on television.

Chopra spent four years in the United States as a teenager, and she has dreams of one day winning over the country that she calls her second home. "In one part of the world, I'm one of the top actors in the country, and in another part of the world, I'm a complete newcomer," Chopra told Sheila Marikar for the *New York Times* (7 Feb. 2014). But Chopra considers herself a hybrid rather than a crossover and hopes to acquire the same credibility as a singer in the United States that she has built up as an actor in India. Still, she plans to keep one foot in Bollywood as she embarks on her musical career in the west.

In addition to her work in the entertainment industry, Chopra is also a philanthropist, a UNICEF Goodwill Ambassador, and an advocate for women's rights. She has spoken out against child marriage (nearly half of Indian women are married before they turn eighteen) and the practice of female genital mutilation (FGM). Chopra has also contributed to the *Times of India* as a columnist. In one famous column (19 Aug. 2012), Chopra responded to the grisly attempted rape and subsequent murder in 2012 of a Mumbai lawyer named Pallavi Purkayastha. The incident was one of a number of attacks on women in the city, and as a famous and independent

Indian woman, Chopra's opinion carried a unique weight. She recalled living alone in bustling Mumbai where she "never felt scared" taking a taxi at four in the morning or living alone. She pointed out, however, that the magnitude of Purkayastha's murder "can perhaps only truly be understood by a woman" because "in the blink of an eye, every woman in Mumbai no longer feels safe." Chopra called for action and protection by the government, law enforcement, and housing facilities and she encouraged "all women across [India] . . . to reflect on this incident, learn from it, and then move forward in a constructive manner, finding ways to protect ourselves, not just individually but as a community."

EARLY LIFE AND EDUCATION

Chopra was born on July 18, 1982, in the city of Jamshedpur in the Indian state of Jharkhand (then Bihar). Her late father, Dr. Ashok Chopra, was a surgeon in the Indian army, and the family, which includes her brother Siddharth who is seven years younger, moved nearly every two years. Chopra's father had once dreamed of having a music career, and he pushed his daughter to take singing lessons at the age of three. Because Chopra's parents worked much of the time, her maternal grandmother, Madhu Jyotsna Akhauri, was an important figure in her childhood. Chopra attended La Martiniere Girls' School in Lucknow and St. Maria Goretti College in Bareilly. (Chopra considers the city of Bareilly in Uttar Pradesh to be her hometown.) When she was thirteen, Chopra visited her mother's sister in Cedar Rapids, Iowa, and, on a whim, decided to remain there and attend school with her cousin. The family moved to Indianapolis; Queens, New York; and Newton, Massachusetts, and along the way, Chopra's high school classmates were often less than welcoming. Chopra was shy, but she says that she was also picked on for being brown. "I would pick up a packet of chips and go to the bathroom and eat because I was so afraid to go to the cafeteria where everyone had their own friends and cliques," she told Marikar. But Chopra took refuge in her love of music, particularly American hip-hop and the rapper Tupac Shakur, who was killed in 1996. "I wore black to school for ten days after [Tupac] died," she told Sameer Pandya for *Spin* magazine (12 Oct. 2012).

MISS INDIA AND MISS WORLD

When Chopra returned to India at seventeen, beauty pageants were the furthest thing from her mind. "I wanted to be an aeronautics engineer," Chopra told Sally Holmes for *Elle* magazine (29 Apr. 2014). "I wanted to make planes. And I was an academic. . . . And going from being a geek to a geek's fantasy is really strange."

Chopra was a senior in high school when her mother sent a few glamour shots to the Miss India pageant officials who then asked Chopra to participate. She won the title of Miss India in 2000 and went on to win the Miss World pageant the same year—though she told Marikar that she felt terribly out of place. "I was petrified," she said, years later. "I didn't know how to walk in heels and wear a massive gown. I just wanted it to be over." The Miss World pageant, which was held in London's Millennium Dome, was celebrating its fiftieth anniversary that year, and it was wildly popular in India. The BBC estimated that 96 percent of India's available television audience watched the Miss World pageant in 2000.

Chopra, who was by then eighteen years old, was a favorite going into the competition, and she won despite a gaffe during the interview portion of the competition. In answer to the question, "Who do you think is the most successful woman living today?" Chopra responded, "Mother Teresa" (who had died three years before in 1997). Still, Chopra managed to best ninety-four other contestants for the title of Miss World 2000 and was the second consecutive Indian to win the crown. Chopra quit school to pursue the pageant, but after she won, she advised other women against following the same path. At the time she told reporters that she planned to return to her studies after her year-long reign, but she never did.

ACTING AND A SUCCESSFUL BOLLYWOOD CAREER

Although Chopra was awarded $100,000 for winning the Miss World title, the estimated two billion viewing audience was perhaps her largest prize because the exposure and resulting popularity helped to propel her into acting and land her first film role in *Thamizhan* in 2002. Her first Bollywood film, *The Hero: Love Story of a Spy*, was released in 2003.

In the same year that Chopra appeared in *The Hero*, she also starred in the romantic musical *Andaaz*. Chopra performed the vocals herself, which is unusual, as most Bollywood actors lip-synch their songs. Her performance earned her a 2004 Filmfare Award for best debut of a female actor. Chopra was nominated for another Filmfare Award the following year, this time as best actor in a negative role for the 2004 thriller *Aitraaz*. In 2006, she landed a starring role in the Bollywood superhero franchise *Krrish* and reprised the role in 2013 for *Krrish 3*. She also starred in the box office hit *Don* in 2006 and its sequel *Don 2* in 2011.

In 2008, Chopra won the prestigious National Film Award for best actress for her starring role in *Fashion*, and in 2012 she demonstrated her dramatic range when she played an autistic runaway in the film *Barfi!* "This is a film made with love, bolstered by wonderfully etched vignettes," Anupama Chopra wrote for the *Hindustan Times* (15 Sept. 2012) who added that

Chopra's portrayal as a charming deaf-mute "surprised" her because "[Priyanka Chopra] abandons the props of glamour and costumes and puts in a sincere effort to make you forget that you're watching Priyanka Chopra."

In 2014, Chopra starred in the biopic *Mary Kom*, which is about an Indian Olympic boxer from a poor family in Manipur. Kom, whose real name is Mangte Chungneijang, won a bronze medal at the 2012 London Olympic Games. She is also a five-time world amateur boxing champion and a mother of three. Chopra trained for six hours a day for nearly two years in order to play the role. "I'm exhausted," Chopra told Nova Lorraine for the *Huffington Post* (14 May 2014). "The reward will be once people watch the movie. This story is about every girl out there that is going to say, 'I'm not going to be limited.'" The film was politically significant in its inspiring and nontraditional story about a strong and independent Indian woman. It also caused controversy in highlighting India's northeastern state of Manipur, which is home to several ethnic minorities who have been marginalized by much of Indian Hindi culture. Some critics of the film voiced their disapproval in casting Chopra in the lead role rather than an actor from northeastern India. Many felt that the casting decision reinforced certain cultural stereotypes of the northeastern Indian people. Chopra addressed this topic in her interview with Shashank Chouhan for Reuters (4 Sept. 2014) and explained that a "commercially viable actor" was needed to play the role but that many northeastern residents were cast in other roles in the film, which Chopra hopes will prompt movie goers to become more aware and accepting of the "various cultures and people [in India]" and that this will prompt regional stereotypes to begin to change. The political regime in Manipur, however, has banned Bollywood films since 2000, and despite pleas from Kom herself, the film was not released in Manipur.

MUSICAL CAREER

Chopra signed a global recording contract with Interscope Records/ Desi Hits and 2101 Records in 2011. However, her debut album, which is produced by Moroccan American producer and music executive RedOne, is not scheduled to be released until late 2014. Chopra took her time with the album because, as she explained to Lee Hawkins in an interview for *WSJ Video* (10 Jan. 2013), she didn't want the record to be a collection of "doctored songs that I'd been given to sing." For help in creating the album, she worked closely with Interscope head Jimmy Iovine as well as Troy Carter, then a member of Lady Gaga's management team.

Chopra released her first single in the United States in 2012. "[The single] 'In My City' is very close to my heart," Chopra told Dibyojyoti

Baksi for the *Hindustan Times* (7 Sept. 2012). "It celebrates the contribution of all these cities to my life making me the nomad that I am." The song sold about 200,000 copies within the first thirty days of its release in India—a rarity in an age of Internet downloads. Chopra told Hawkins that she was happy with the reception, particularly because it was so unexpected. "It was overwhelming," she said. "In My City" was chosen as the theme for Thursday night NFL football games in 2013, despite Chopra and the National Football League receiving a deluge of hate mail and negative online comments from fans who felt that Chopra should not be representing an American sport. Some called her an "Arab terrorist," she told Hawkins (18 Jan. 2014). "Why is every Arab person a terrorist?" Chopra said, "Why, just because I'm brown, am I a terrorist?"

Chopra's other singles include "Exotic," which features rapper Pitbull, and "I Can't Make You Love Me," which debuted in the United Kingdom in 2014 and is an electronic cover of Bonnie Raitt's 1991 country ballad by the same name. The video for "I Can't Make You Love Me" features Chopra and *Heroes* star Milo Ventimiglia, who in one scene in the video throw colored powder paint at one another, mimicking an Indian springtime tradition called Holi, or festival of colors.

Chopra is committed to displaying her own Indian roots proudly and dispelling the stereotypes that cling to Indians in the United States. "We don't talk like Apu from *The Simpsons*," she told Nosheen Iqbal for the London *Guardian* (12 May 2014), "and there's more to the world's biggest democracy than henna and sparkly clothes."

SUGGESTED READING

Baksi, Dibyojyoti. "Priyanka Chopra First Single Inspired by Her Life." *Hindustan Times*. HT Media, 7 Sept. 2012. Web. 10 Sept. 2014.

Chopra, Priyanka. "No Woman in Mumbai Feels Safe Any Longer." *Times of India*. Bennett, Coleman, 19 Aug. 2012. Web. 11 Sept. 2014.

Chouhan, Shashank. "Representing Manipur: Priyanka Chopra on Playing Mary Kom." *Reuters*. Thomson Reuters, 4 Sept. 2014. Web. 10 Sept. 2014.

Hawkins, Lee. "Bollywood Star Priyanka Chopra Goes Global." *Wall Street Journal*. Dow Jones, 10 Jan. 2013. Web. 11 Sept. 2014.

Hawkins, Lee. "Priyanka Chopra: I Was Called a Terrorist by NFL Fans." *WSJ Video*. Dow Jones, 18 Jan. 2014. Web. 11 Sept. 2014.

Holmes, Sally. "Priyanka Chopra on Her New Country Single and Shattering Indian Stereotypes." *Elle*. Hearst Communications, 29 Apr. 2014. Web. 10 Sept. 2014.

Marikar, Sheila. "The Move from Celebrity to Ubiquity." *New York Times*. New York Times, 7 Feb. 2014. Web. 10 Sept. 2014.

SELECTED WORKS

The Hero: Love Story of a Spy, 2003; *Andaaz*, 2003; *Krrish*, 2006; *Fashion*, 2008; *Don 2*, 2011; *Barfi!*, 2012; *Mary Kom*, 2014

—Molly Hagan

Clayton Christensen

Born: April 6, 1952
Occupation: Professor and consultant

Clayton Christensen is a Kim B. Clark professor of business administration at the Harvard Business School, best known for his 1997 book *The Innovator's Dilemma*, which inspired a generation of business and technology leaders. Larissa MacFarquhar, in her profile of Christensen for the *New Yorker* (14 May 2012), called him the "most influential business thinker on earth." Christensen introduced the concept of "disruptive innovation," a term, some argue, that has come to mean both everything and nothing. Disruption has become the battle cry of entrepreneurs in Silicon Valley, where the popular TechCrunch Disrupt conference encourages start-ups to compete for a $50,000 prize and the coveted Disrupt Cup. More recently, the term has cropped up in other sectors, such as health care and higher education. The University of Southern California website tells prospective business students, "The degree is in disruption." "Ever since *The Innovator's Dilemma*, everyone is either disrupting or being disrupted," Jill Lepore, a historian at Harvard, wryly noted for the *New Yorker* (23 June 2014).

Courtesy of Evgenia Eliseeva

Christensen's research began with one question: why is success so difficult to sustain? He found that, for established companies, the difficulty was not because managers made mistakes, but because they did not make mistakes. According to Christensen's research, managers at established companies played by the rules, and therein lay the innovator's dilemma: "doing the right thing is the wrong thing." Established companies failed, Christensen found, because their pace of innovation was disrupted by smaller companies making inferior goods. The theory itself goes something like this: Large firms ignored the smaller companies (because their goods were inferior), but, as MacFarquhar explained, "the new products were usually cheaper and easier to use, and so people or companies who were not rich or sophisticated enough for the old ones started buying the new ones, and there were so many more of the regular people than there were of the rich, sophisticated people that the companies making the new products prospered." By the time the old companies caught up, the new companies were producing a better product, putting the old companies out of business. Christensen dubbed these low-end products "disruptive technologies."

Disruption—and its various co-opted definitions—had few public critics until Jill Lepore wrote a critique of the doctrine nearly twenty years after the term was coined. Christensen readily admits that the term is overused, but Lepore questions the original research on which Christensen based his theory as well as the theory itself. She argues that the concept has been applied to industries and arenas (such as public schools, churches, museums, and hospitals) whose values are at odds with those of the profit-driven businesses to which Christensen's theory was originally applied. When these industries are encouraged to disrupt themselves, rather than focusing on what Christensen calls "sustaining innovations," they may short-change the people they are intended to serve. Instead of focusing on incrementally improving their product—whether it be a computer or a college education—they scrap a thing that works for something that might not. To paraphrase Kevin Rose's critique for *New York Magazine* (16 June 2014), disruption lends credence to the idea that all change is good change. Lepore, who argues her point from the perspective of a historian, alleges worse, writing that many of the firms Christensen held up in his research have failed, while some of the less innovative firms he claimed had been toppled by disruption are still going strong. "Disruptive innovation is a theory about why businesses fail. It's not more than that. It doesn't explain change. It's not a law of nature. It's an artifact of history, an idea, forged in time; it's the manufacture of a moment of upsetting and edgy uncertainty," Lepore wrote, referring to

the tech boom and bust of the late 1990s and early 2000s. "Transfixed by change, it's blind to continuity. It makes a very poor prophet."

EARLY LIFE AND EDUCATION

Clayton M. Christensen was born on April 6, 1952, the second of eight children in a poor Mormon family living on the west side of Salt Lake City. Both sides of his family have been involved with the church almost since its founding in the nineteenth century. In fact, his paternal great-grandfather, a resident of Denmark, was converted in the 1850s by one of the first groups of Mormon missionaries to travel to Europe. Christensen's great-grandfather travelled by boat and rail to Iowa where he piled his belongings in a handcart and walked to Salt Lake City, the Mormon mecca, in Utah. Christensen's mother, Verda Mae Fuller Christensen, grew up in Canada and attended Brigham Young University (BYU) in Salt Lake City. She graduated at nineteen and went on to write for radio and television and to anchor a television show for farmers. She met a grocery store worker named Robert Christensen, Christensen's father, at a church function after World War II. With two working parents—his mother quit her job when she had children but continued to write scripts at night—Christensen learned to be self-sufficient, making his own food and mending his own socks. His parents were active church participants as well as vehement Republicans. Christensen remembers going door-to-door handing out political flyers before each election. (He told MacFarquhar that he didn't realize that "dumb Democrat" was two words until he got to high school.)

In high school, Christensen earned good grades and made all-state in basketball. He was even elected student body president. He dreamed of going to Harvard or Yale, and got into both though his mother wanted him to go to BYU. After much fasting and prayer, MacFarquhar wrote, "he discovered that God agreed with his mother."

During his senior year, Christensen won a Rhodes Scholarship to study economics at Oxford University in England. By this time, he had already served his mandatory two-year mission in South Korea. (College-aged Mormon men are required to act as missionaries for the Church of Jesus Christ of Latter-day Saints in an assigned location.) But at Oxford he had a crisis of faith. He spent an hour each night reading the Book of Mormon and praying. "One evening in October 1975," he later wrote, as quoted by MacFarquhar, "I felt a marvelous spirit come into the room and envelop my body. I had never before felt such an intense feeling of peace and love . . . I knew then, from a source of understanding more powerful than anything I had ever felt in my life, that the book I was holding in my hands was true." After that, according to MacFarquhar,

Christensen claimed that he was granted special powers, including healing the sick and seeing into the future. He graduated from BYU in 1975 and earned a master's degree in applied econometrics from Oxford in 1977. Christensen earned his MBA with high distinction from Harvard Business School in 1979, graduating as a George F. Baker Scholar. He served as a White House fellow assisting US Transportation secretaries Drew Lewis and Elizabeth Dole from 1982 through 1983.

RESEARCH AT HARVARD

Christensen worked as a consultant and then, in 1984, founded a business called Ceramics Process Systems (CPS) Corporation with several professors from the Massachusetts Institute of Technology (MIT). Three months after the company went public in 1987, the market crashed and Christensen was fired. Thankfully, he had already decided the life of an executive was not for him. He entered the doctoral program at Harvard Business School in 1989, and earned his DBA and joined the faculty in 1992. For his doctoral thesis, Christensen wanted to study an industry that had experienced a similar phenomenon to the one he had seen during his time at CPS, a company which, despite the market crash, successfully occupied a niche market where other larger companies had failed. A colleague suggested hard-disk drives, Craig Lambert wrote for Wired (1 July 2014), "for the same reason that geneticists study fruit flies: their life spans are brief and new generations appear quickly."

The hard-disk drive weighed nearly a ton when it was invented by IBM in 1955, but throughout the late 1970s and 1980s, disk drives gradually decreased in size from 14 inches to 1.8 inches. Christensen categorized the incremental improvements in the industry, writing that 5 disk drives could be considered disruptive innovations, while the other 111 were sustaining innovations. The 5 disk drives in question, he wrote, as quoted by Lepore, were "slower and had lower capacity than those used in the mainstream market," but their size made them a valuable part of the trend towards smaller and smaller machines, and the companies that adopted those drives were upstarts that put old firms out of business. Christensen introduced the concept of a disruptive innovation in his 1995 paper "Disruptive Technologies: Catching the Wave." He earned full professorship and tenure at Harvard in 1998.

INNOVATOR'S DILEMMA

Christensen published The Innovator's Dilemma in 1997. In the book, he applied his theory about the hard-disk drive industry to mechanical excavators, the steel industry, and department stores. A few established department stores, like F. W. Woolworth and Dayton-Hudson, saw the coming tide of discount stores early; they opened Woolco and Target respectively, of which only Target has survived. Christensen argued that Woolco failed because Woolworth ran the store within its existing structure. "Two models for how to make money cannot peacefully coexist within a single organization," he wrote in the book. Like Dayton-Hudson and Target, Christensen argued, big companies should set up small companies to investigate "disruptive" possibilities, while the company as a whole maintains their original focus and pace of innovation. Years later, this directive would spawn the now cliché "disrupt or be disrupted" ethos of Silicon Valley.

One of Christensen's most famous acolytes, the former CEO of Intel, Andy Grove, heard about Christensen even before The Innovator's Dilemma was published. A woman in Intel's engineering department had read one of Christensen's articles and brought it to Grove's attention. When the two men met, Grove asked Christensen if he should set up a company to compete with two microprocessor companies edging in at the low end of the market. Christensen refused to say, but pointed again to his theory. "Instead of telling him what to think, I told him how to think," Christensen told Jeff Howe of Wired (12 Feb. 2013). Grove's competitor company was enormously successful, and in 1999, Grove appeared alongside Christensen on the cover of Forbes magazine after Grove called The Innovator's Dilemma the most important book he had read in ten years. The endorsement effectively launched Christensen's career as a business guru. Steve Jobs, the late CEO of Apple and a guru in his own right, jumped on the disruption bandwagon, as did businessman and former mayor Michael Bloomberg and Microsoft's Bill Gates. However, Apple never invited Christensen to speak—as many other companies did—which was just as well, MacFarquhar pointed out, because Christensen was once convinced that the iPhone would be a failure. (It wasn't until later, when Christensen saw that the high-end phone was actually disruptive to laptops, that he realized where his prediction had gone awry.)

The book itself became a best seller thanks in part to Christensen's straightforward yet meaty writing style. Several years after it was published, Fred Andrews for the New York Times (19 Oct. 2003) wrote that the book "has a strong claim as the best business book of the '90s." In Lepore's critique, she agreed, writing that the theory is a product of its time. Disruptive innovation, she argued, is characterized by the confusion of the dot-com era followed by the uncertainty of the war on terror. "[T]he rhetoric of disruption—a language of panic, fear, asymmetry, and disorder—calls on the rhetoric of another kind of conflict, in which an upstart refuses to play by the established rules of engagement, and blows things up," she wrote. "Disruptive innovation is competitive strategy for an age seized by terror."

OTHER WORK

Based on the predictive capabilities of his theory, Christensen launched the Disruptive Growth Fund with a broker named Neil Eisner in 2000. The fund fared poorly that year, as the tech bubble burst and the stock market crashed in 2001. The fund was quickly liquidated. In 2001, Christensen founded a consulting firm called Innosight with fellow Harvard grad Mark Johnson, and in 2003, he published a book called *The Innovator's Solution: Creating and Sustaining Successful Growth* with Michael E. Raynor. The book, Andrews wrote, coaches "companies in how to generate a consistent flow of disruptive innovations"—a feat, Christensen and Raynor added, that has never been accomplished. In 2007, Christensen, Michael Horn and Jason Hwang founded a think tank called the Clayton Christensen Institute for Disruptive Innovation. The men then applied Christensen's disruption theory to the education system and health care: Christensen, Horn and Curtis Johnson published *Disrupting Class: How Disruptive Innovation Will Change the Way the World Learns* in 2008; and Christensen, Hwang, and Dr. Jerome Grossman published *The Innovator's Prescription: A Disruptive Solution for Health Care* in 2009. Christensen published *The Innovative University: Changing the DNA of Higher Education From the Inside Out* with Henry J. Eyring in 2011.

Despite his Harvard affiliation, Christensen is excited about the way online classes are disrupting the current higher education model. He envisions a future where online learning is king. As for institutions like Harvard, or any other university looking to survive, he told Howe, they "will evolve hybrid models" in which they "license some courses from an online provider like Coursera but then provide more-specialized courses in person." A few years prior to 2012, Christensen got a call from the University of Phoenix, an online, for-profit higher education provider. They asked if he would let them film one of his lectures. With the dean's blessing, Christensen agreed. When he arrived at the rented space, he encountered about fifty "beautiful people," he told MacFarquhar. It turned out that the "students" were really models, hired to be attentive listeners. Still, Christensen was and is excited about the prospect of reaching hundreds of thousands of students online—though he acknowledges the inherent risk for professors that the endeavor presents. The Harvard Business School—one of the first established universities to pursue a separate online program—no longer teaches accounting, Christensen claimed in his interview with Howe, "because there's a

guy out of BYU whose online accounting course is so good."

After a life-changing medical scare in 2010, Christensen published a book called *How Will You Measure Your Life?* with James Allworth and Karen Dillon in 2012. The book applies Christensen's theory of disruption to self-help; instead of asking why good companies fail, Christensen (and his coauthors) asked why good people are led astray. His new book, called *The Capitalist's Dilemma*, is slated for publication in 2014.

After Lepore's critique of disruption was published in June 2014, Christensen responded in a short interview with Drake Bennett for *Businessweek* (20 June 2014). Initially, he said, he was pleased that his colleague (whom he has never met, though they both teach at Harvard) was critical of the ubiquity of the word "disruption." "I was delighted that somebody with her standing would join me in trying to bring discipline and understanding around a very useful theory," he said. But after a few pages, he realized that she took issue with the theory itself. The interview, in which he refers to himself in the third person, got a bit heated. In a "stunning reversal," he said, Lepore tries "to discredit Clay Christensen, in a really mean way. And mean is fine, but in order to discredit me, Jill had to break all of the rules of scholarship that she accused me of breaking—in just egregious ways, truly egregious ways," he said, adding, "I hope you can understand why I am mad that a woman of her stature could perform such a criminal act of dishonesty—at Harvard, of all places."

PERSONAL LIFE

Christensen met his wife Christine Quinn during his freshman year at BYU. They have five children. He founded a boutique investment firm called Rose Park Advisors with his son Matthew in 2007.

In late 2009, Christensen was misdiagnosed with a terminal form of cancer. He did have cancer, but it turned out that it was a type that could be treated. He underwent chemotherapy and went into remission, but a few months later, in 2010, he suffered a stroke while giving a talk to a church group. He lost nearly all of his linguistic abilities, but worked twelve hours a day to relearn how to speak English.

SUGGESTED READING

Andrews, Fred. "On the Shelf: First the Dilemma, Now the Solution." *New York Times*. New York Times, 19 Oct. 2003. Web. 7 July 2014.

Bennett, Drake. "Clayton Christensen Responds to *New Yorker* Takedown of 'Disruptive Innovation.'" *Businessweek*. Bloomberg, 20 June 2014. Web. 7 July 2014.

Howe, Jeff. "Clayton Christensen Wants to Transform Capitalism." *Wired*. Condé Nast, 12 Feb. 2013. Web. 7 July 2014.

Lambert, Craig. "Disruptive Genius." *Harvard Magazine*. Harvard U, 1 July 2014. Web. 7 July 2014.

Lepore, Jill. "The Disruption Machine: What the Gospel of Innovation Gets Wrong." *New Yorker*. Condé Nast, 23 June 2014. Web. 7 July 2014.

MacFarquhar, Larissa. "When Giants Fail: What Business Has Learned from Clayton Christensen." *New Yorker*. Condé Nast, 14 May 2012. Web. 7 July 2014.

Rose, Kevin. "Let's All Stop Saying 'Disrupt' Right This Instant." *New York*. New York Media, 16 June 2014. Web. 7 July 2014.

—*Molly Hagan*

Jared Cohen

Born: November 24, 1981
Occupation: Geopolitical adviser

"There is a canyon dividing people who understand technology and people charged with addressing the world's toughest geopolitical issues, and no one has built a bridge," geopolitical adviser Jared Cohen and former Google CEO Eric Schmidt wrote in their 2013 book, *The New Digital Age: Reshaping the Future of People, Nations and Businesses*. The quandary, as quoted by Janet Maslin for her *New York Times* review (25 Apr. 2013), is central to Cohen's career: a Google executive and former State Department official, Cohen is helping to shape a burgeoning form of diplomacy known as "twenty-first-century

Getty Images Entertainment

statecraft." The term, which comes from former secretary of state Hillary Clinton, refers to the use of digital and social media in diplomacy, and its applications are manifold.

Cohen, whose actions during the 2009 Iranian protests gave rise to the State Department's foreign policy in the digital realm, believes in the relationship between social media and social change. In addition to his work for the State Department, which he left in 2010, Cohen is the cofounder of a human rights organization called Movements.org. In 2012 the organization merged with another group called Advancing Human Rights, founded by publisher and activist Robert L. Bernstein. Cohen cofounded Google Ideas, the Internet company's think tank, in 2010. He now serves as the director of Google Ideas. He is also an adjunct senior fellow at the Council on Foreign Relations.

EARLY LIFE

Cohen was born on November 24, 1981, and raised in Weston, Connecticut. His father, Donald Cohen, is a family therapist and his mother, Dee, is a former children's book illustrator and real estate agent. Cohen's childhood home was filled with art and political memorabilia, a combination of interests that shaped his formative years. Growing up, Cohen was a serious artist—one of his paintings, an interpretation of the Rwandan genocide modeled after Pablo Picasso's *Guernica*, hangs in the home of one of his college professors. Cohen played soccer in high school and also whetted his appetite for international travel. He took a trip to Africa and, upon his return to Connecticut, found a tutor to teach him Swahili. Cohen is fluent in the African language and conversant in a couple of regional African languages, as well as Arabic, Farsi, Spanish, and Korean. After high school, Cohen enrolled at Stanford University in California.

EDUCATION

Cohen spent the summer of his freshman year, 2001, in Kenya, where he and two classmates lived in a dung hut and studied the culture of the Masai (or Maasai) people, a seminomadic group living in southern Kenya and northern Tanzania. Cohen then traveled to Rwanda for the purpose of tracking gorillas but ended up seeking accounts of that country's 1994 genocide, in which Hutus murdered over 800,000 Tutsis and raped and maimed thousands more. Crossing into the Congo, Cohen managed to interview three Hutu perpetrators of the violence, and his collected interviews and research comprised his undergraduate thesis. He graduated from Stanford in 2004 with a bachelor's degree in history and political science and a minor in African studies, and his senior thesis was eventually published in 2007 as the book *One Hundred Days of Silence: America and the Rwanda Genocide*. In a review of the book for the *African Studies Review* (1 Apr. 2008), Omar McDoom wrote that the book was notable for its exploration and detailed indictment of US inaction in 1994. "The book's chief strength is Cohen's understanding of the inner workings of the US government machinery; we learn as much about the decision-making process and culture of the individual bureaucracies as we do about the genocide," McDoom wrote. He further noted, "In fact, Cohen does what he argues the US should have done during the genocide: he names and shames those responsible."

During his time at Stanford, Cohen interned at the State Department and was named a consultant on a PBS *Frontline* documentary about the Rwandan genocide. He also founded a campus publication called *Six Degrees: A Journal of Human Rights*. In 2003 he was awarded a Rhodes Scholarship and began his fully funded graduate studies at Oxford University in England in 2005.

UNCOVERING IRAN'S YOUTH CULTURE

As a first-year graduate student at Oxford, Cohen traveled to Iran to conduct interviews with members of the country's political opposition. He was writing a paper about US–Iran relations in the wake of the attacks of September 11, 2001, but he came across a different subject, the character of which was even closer to home. As Timothy Dumas put it for *Greenwich Magazine* (1 Apr. 2011), "It dawned on him he had come to study the wrong opposition." Cohen had stumbled upon the underground youth culture of Tehran. He found that within Iran's restrictive Islamist society existed an exploding population of people under thirty who meet at secret alcohol-fueled parties (alcohol consumption is illegal in Iran, so young people make their own), listen to Western music, and watch American television shows. Out in the street, they interact with each other covertly, using reappropriated Bluetooth technology. (When Cohen asked one Iranian if he was afraid he might be caught communicating about illicit social activities via cell phone, the young man replied that no one in Iran over thirty knows what Bluetooth is.) He found that Iranian young people were remarkably similar to young people in America when they were free to speak what was on their mind. Cohen wrote, "For Iranians, this was their democracy after dark."

CHILDREN OF JIHAD

Cohen next traveled to Beirut, Lebanon, where he stayed at a fraternity brother's apartment. The underground parties were much the same, but Cohen, who is Jewish, also managed to forge relationships with young members of Hezbollah, an Islamic militant group. Later, he interviewed General Mounir Maqdah, a military commander of the Palestinian political party Fatah. The general had survived numerous assassination attempts, and Cohen had to be led through a complex series of passageways to reach his secret chamber. Cohen also visited Mia Mia, a Palestinian refugee camp, where he ran into a group of young supporters of Hamas, a militant Palestinian Islamic group based in the Gaza Strip. Engaging them in conversation, Cohen pressed past their anti-Jewish sentiments to get to their real concerns: lack of education, lack of opportunity, and boredom.

From Lebanon, Cohen traveled to Syria, where young people walked miles to chat at Internet cafes and, as in Iran, used Bluetooth to organize dance parties and other opportunities for illicit social connection. He then spent time in Iraqi Kurdistan during the US–led occupation, choosing the northern part of the country because it was less affected by the violent insurgency then in full swing in Iraq. When Cohen hired a taxi to drop him at the Turkish border, across which he had entered the country, the driver instead took him through war-torn Mosul to the Syrian border along one of the country's most dangerous roads. When they reached the border, US troops were incredulous.

Cohen's encounters in Iran, Lebanon, and Syria inspired his 2007 book *Children of Jihad: A Young American's Travels among the Youth of the Middle East*. A reviewer for *Kirkus* (1 Sept. 2007) wrote that *Children of Jihad* was "riveting from start to finish" and noted Cohen's keen observations on the ways in which the Internet and even cable television were changing the lives of young Middle Easterners. The intersection of two worlds—oppressive regimes and the rise of the technology-savvy generation within them—became Cohen's unlikely area of expertise.

"TWENTY-FIRST-CENTURY STATECRAFT"

Cohen was invited by Secretary of State Condoleezza Rice to join the State Department in 2006, during the administration of President George W. Bush. At twenty-four years old, he was the youngest person on Rice's policy planning staff, but he had met Rice several years before that, when he was able to land a meeting with her when she was national security adviser. He was only twenty-two. "He had insights into Iran that frankly we didn't have in the government," Rice told Jesse Lichtenstein for the *New York Times* (16 July 2010). "He was so articulate about it, I asked him to write up a memo that I could send to the president." In 2006 Rice put Cohen to work in the areas of youth outreach, counter-radicalization, and counterterror. Two years later, in February 2008, over two hundred protests against the Revolutionary Armed Forces of Colombia (FARC), a terrorist group based in Colombia, occurred worldwide. The protests were organized on Facebook and Skype. "It was the largest protest against a terrorist organization in history," Cohen told Lichtenstein. Cohen contacted a group he found on the Internet called One Million Voices Against FARC and began collecting antiterrorist groups in a larger social network.

After President Barack Obama's election in 2008, Cohen remained in the State Department and was, according to Lichtenstein, "walking on eggshells," hoping to keep his job. Alec Ross, who had run day-to-day operations for Obama's tech policy during the 2008 campaign (and whose job title was "senior adviser for innovation"), read Cohen's work and was impressed. The two men became partners under Secretary of State Hillary Clinton and the public face of e-diplomacy. Cohen and Ross became an interesting breed of political celebrity: on Twitter in 2010 they were the two most-followed people in politics after the president and Senator John McCain. They traversed the Middle East and Silicon Valley on diplomatic missions (tweeting all the while) and even let actor Ashton Kutcher tag along on a trip to Russia. In January 2010 they led the State Department partnership with James Eberhard of mobile-platform company Mobile Accord to create Text Haiti 90999 in the wake of the earthquake in Haiti. The program raised over forty million dollars for the Red Cross through ten-dollar donations sent via cell phone.

IRANIAN PROTESTS AND TWITTER CONTROVERSY

In June 2009 Iran was roiling with protests as citizens claimed that President Mahmoud Ahmadinejad had stolen the country's presidential election from opposition candidate Mir Hossein Mousavi. The demonstrations in Tehran were the largest Iran had seen in a decade, and Iranians took to Twitter and YouTube (the government had blocked text-messaging capabilities) to communicate with each other and with the outside world. Cohen, then twenty-seven, was monitoring the situation online. The Obama administration had vowed to stay out of the election and its aftermath, but a post on Mousavi's Twitter feed spurred Cohen to act. The site was scheduled to shut down for routine maintenance. It would be only for a few hours in the middle of the night in the United States, but the shutdown would silence hundreds of thousands of Iranians during the height of the protests. So Cohen e-mailed Jack Dorsey, one of Twitter's founders, asking him to postpone the scheduled maintenance because of the information streaming out of Iran. He did not ask permission from his boss, Secretary Clinton, nor did he stop to think of what the e-mail might mean alongside the Obama administration's pledge of neutrality. Dorsey complied, and when the New York Times broke the story, the Iranian government was furious, accusing the United States of meddling

in the election. But the administration stood behind Cohen—whose e-mail to Dorsey made CNN's list of the top ten most important moments of the decade—arguing that the United States has always supported free expression. Thus, the Obama administration gave fitful birth to foreign policy in the modern age. In effect, two foreign policies, one for the physical world and one for the online world, now exist unofficially between the United States and countries like Iran and China that censor Internet content, a concept further explored in Cohen and Schmidt's book.

Of course, opening the floodgates of information in repressive countries poses ethical questions about what recipients of that information should do with it. During those 2009 protests, the world witnessed the death, captured from multiple angles on cell phone video, of a young woman named Neda Agha-Soltan, who was shot. While this did not change its outcome, it shamed Iran and horrified viewers. "The entire world was forced to make a comment on [the video]," Cohen told an audience at Fairfield University in Connecticut in November 2011, as quoted by Dumas. "That's a change in policy."

THE NEW DIGITAL AGE

Cohen left the State Department in 2010 to cofound Google Ideas, an interdisciplinary arm of Google devoted to improving the world through technology. He currently serves as the organization's director. In April 2010 he led Google to donate three million dollars to create a database system connecting sixty-five independent hotlines for reporting human trafficking. In 2013 Cohen and Google chair Eric Schmidt published The New Digital Age: Reshaping the Future of People, Nations and Businesses. Maslin, in her review of the book, wrote that the book was "prescient and provocative" in its visions of the future. The book touches on everything from smart houses to drone warfare to diplomacy. "We fundamentally believe that states will have two foreign policies and two domestic policies: one for the physical world, and one for the cyber world," Cohen, referring to himself and Schmidt, told J. P. O'Malley for the conservative British magazine the Spectator (8 May 2013). "And they won't always look the same." Cohen cites China and the United States, which he says are ultimately allies in the physical world but adversaries in cyberspace.

In 2013 Cohen and Schmidt traveled to North Korea, where the government has very successfully blocked all Internet access. Upon their return, Cohen told a reporter for National Public Radio's All Things Considered (23 Apr. 2013), "North Korea is the last stop. . . . All they have to do is turn it on a little bit, and they can't turn it back. Once the ideas are in, you cannot kick them out of the country."

Cohen married Rebecca Zubaty, a lawyer, in 2012. They live in New York City.

SUGGESTED READING
Cohen, Jared. "Interview: Jared Cohen and the New Digital Age." Interview by J. P. O'Malley. *Spectator*. Spectator, 8 May 2013. Web. 9 May 2014.

Lichtenstein, Jesse. "Digital Diplomacy." *New York Times*. New York Times, 16 July 2010. Web. 9 May 2014.

Maslin, Janet. "Formatting a World with No Secrets." Rev. of *The New Digital Age: Reshaping the Future of People, Nations and Businesses*, by Eric Schmidt and Jared Cohen. *New York Times*. New York Times, 25 Apr. 2013. Web. 9 May 2014.

SELECTED WORKS
Children of Jihad: A Young American's Travels among the Youth of the Middle East, 2007; *One Hundred Days of Silence: America and the Rwanda Genocide*, 2007; *The New Digital Age: Reshaping the Future of People, Nations and Businesses* (with Eric Schmidt), 2013

—Molly Hagan

FilmMagic

Lauren Conrad

Born: February 1, 1986
Occupation: Entrepreneur and television personality

Lauren Conrad is an entrepreneur, author, and former reality television star. As a teenager in tony Laguna Beach, California, Conrad was chosen to star in the MTV reality series *Laguna Beach: The Real Orange County* in 2003. Then known by the nickname LC, Conrad proved popular with viewers, and she went on to star in a spin-off series, *The Hills*, following her departure from *Laguna Beach*. *The Hills* aired for six seasons (Conrad appeared in five) and followed Conrad through her fashionable post–high school life as a student at the Fashion Institute of Design and Merchandising in Los Angeles and an intern for the magazine *Teen Vogue*. While *Laguna Beach* and *The Hills* were far from the first reality shows, they were two of the first series to blur the line between fact and fiction with their slick cinematography. Many viewers debated the veracity of the series' storylines, and Tim Stack for *Entertainment Weekly* (19 Aug. 2008) described the shows' approach as "scheduled reality," with producers choosing storylines based on actual conflicts in each player's life. Regardless of their truthfulness or lack thereof, both shows became a hit with audiences, particularly with young women.

It was clear from the outset that Conrad had larger ambitions. While many of her costars fell into obscurity or infamy following their time on the shows, Conrad has managed to parlay her unusual fame into successful ventures in retail, design, and even publishing. She is quick to paint reality television as a distant part of her past, but at the same time she acknowledges how her time on television has shaped her life. "It turned out to be such a cool experience," she wrote of her *Laguna Beach* years on her website, as quoted by television critic Virginia Heffernan for the *New York Times* (22 Jan. 2007). "I feel very fortunate to have my own personal video yearbook of those great times."

EARLY LIFE
Lauren Katherine Conrad was born in Laguna Beach, California, on February 1, 1986. Her parents, Jim and Kathy, are both architects. The oldest of three siblings, Conrad has a younger sister named Breanna, who starred in the third season of *Laguna Beach*, and a younger brother named Brandon. Growing up, Conrad knew that she wanted to work in fashion, though she has often described her young self as a tomboy. This is one of a handful of contradictions inherent in Conrad's persona; perhaps the most prominent among them is the fact that she spent many of her formative years in front of a camera but remained far more reserved than any of her costars.

"She was always much more wary and anxious than a pretty teenager should have any cause to be," Heffernan mused in the *New York Times* (31 May 2006). In an interview with Lola Ogunnaike for the *New York Times* (11 June 2006), the *Times* reporter lamented the difficulty of getting Conrad to talk about her life. "She internalizes a lot, so with [Conrad] it's all about reading her face," Tony DiSanto, an MTV executive producer, told Ogunnaike. "If you look at her face you can always tell what she's thinking and feeling."

Conrad attended Laguna Beach High School. Before she began her senior year, she signed on to appear in a new MTV reality television show chronicling the lives of well-to-do teens living in Laguna Beach.

LAGUNA BEACH

The idea for *Laguna Beach: The Real Orange County* was originally developed by Liz Gateley, who would become the show's creator and executive producer. She approached MTV in 2003 with a pitch for a show that played on the mean-girl dynamics found in the dark comedy *Heathers* (1988). Gateley, who grew up in Palos Verdes, California, was familiar with the kind of wealthy upbringing she wanted to capture on the show. "I think the biggest hesitation [for MTV] was, 'Can you tap into a clique of friends and have them all be interesting and beautiful?'" Gateley recalled to Margy Rochlin for the *New York Times* (30 Aug. 2005). "I told them, 'They're a dime-a-dozen in Southern California. They're everywhere.'" The show additionally capitalized on the success of *The O.C.* (2003–7), a primetime drama series that focused on the lives of teenagers in California's Orange County.

In a cast interview with MTV, Conrad recalled that her costar and longtime friend Lauren "Lo" Bosworth had excitedly told her that MTV was camped in the school's front office, holding auditions for a new show. Conrad decided to audition, later telling MTV that she did so because she had always been shy and wanted to become more comfortable with herself. The casting process was fairly involved; Conrad participated in multiple interviews and auditions and filled out a lengthy questionnaire. In the end she was chosen as the focal point of the first season of *Laguna Beach*.

Conrad spent much of the first season, which chronicled her senior year of high school, pining after Stephen Colletti, her childhood friend and on-again, off-again beau. Her feelings for him often brought her into conflict with the show's pseudovillain, Kristin Cavallari, a junior who also dated Colletti. Unlike *The O.C.*, which explored such serious issues as death, divorce, and alcoholism, *Laguna Beach* focused primarily on the friendships and romances of its cast members, and the Conrad-Colletti-Cavallari love triangle was the height of the show's drama.

Conrad graduated from Laguna Beach High at the end of the show's first season and moved to San Francisco to study fashion at the Academy of Art University. Homesick, she returned to her hometown—and *Laguna Beach*—after one semester. Conrad left the show after the conclusion of the second season.

THE HILLS

After *Laguna Beach*, Conrad decided to appear in another MTV reality show, *The Hills*, which premiered in May 2006. Distancing herself from her former show, Conrad put the kibosh on the nickname LC. She told Ann Oldenburg for *USA Today* (30 May 2006), "That was just a high school nickname, and nobody refers to me like that anymore." Producers of *The Hills* promoted the series as a reality version of *Sex and the City*, with four "main girls" who have "different ideals," Conrad told Oldenburg. The early episodes of *The Hills* saw Conrad studying at the Fashion Institute of Design and Merchandising and interning for *Teen Vogue* in Los Angeles, where the show took place. According to Lisa Love, *Vogue*'s West Coast editor, Conrad won the coveted position with the magazine without the show's sway. "I hadn't seen the show before, so I didn't know what to expect, but she was a very good interview. She knew photographers, she knew magazines, she knew why she wanted to work at *Teen Vogue*," Love told Ogunnaike. "If I didn't like her, she definitely would not have gotten an internship, regardless of what the cameras wanted."

The Hills was tremendously popular with audiences, making Conrad and her three main costars—Audrina Patridge, Whitney Port, and Heidi Montag—national celebrities. Their rising fame, however, soon became a new source of conflicts, among them a bitter rivalry between Conrad and Montag. A conflict that likely would have led to an amicable parting of ways in a less public setting became prime fodder for the show, which fed their toxic relationship for another four seasons. In season three, Conrad believed that Montag had started a rumor about the existence of a sex tape starring Conrad. As Heffernan pointed out in the *New York Times* (13 Aug. 2007), such a rumor would rightfully distress any woman, but Conrad also had to worry about attention from the tabloids and protect her contract with MTV—concerns that fell outside the scope of her documented "reality." "The hysteria that often informs friendships among young women shouldn't have to bump up against subjects like money, television channels, careers, and libel," Heffernan wrote. Though Conrad recalls the time as a low period in her life, her conflict with Montag made *The Hills* the most-watched MTV program of the year. In fact, the show was so popular that in 2008, presidential candidate Barack Obama quipped to David

Letterman, "My first act as president will be to stop the fighting between Lauren and Heidi."

In part due to friction with Montag and her boyfriend (later husband), Spencer Pratt, Conrad left the show in 2009, halfway through its fifth season. Years in the public eye had left her exhausted, and she told Stack that she often woke up in the middle of the night, certain she was being filmed. Despite her success to that point—which included endorsement deals with Avon cosmetics and AT&T—some warned that Conrad's departure from *The Hills* could mark the end of her career. "Everybody told me to stay on TV," she told Ned Martel for *Marie Claire* (11 June 2013). "*Nobody* wanted me to leave." Despite those warnings, Conrad remained determined to launch a new phase of her career—one with fewer cameras.

BUILDING A BRAND

Even prior to quitting reality television, Conrad began to establish herself as a shrewd entrepreneur. In 2006 she found an agent to help negotiate all of her deals toward the ultimate goal of running her own business. The following year Conrad, with the financial backing of MTV and Tangerine Promotions, launched a line of women's clothing called the Lauren Conrad Collection. Consumers balked at the relatively high prices, and the line was largely unsuccessful. In 2009 Conrad partnered with Kohl's, a department store chain, to manufacture the affordable clothing line LC Lauren Conrad. According to Stephanie Rosenbloom for the *New York Times* (22 Apr. 2009), Kohl's introduced Conrad's "casual California-inspired clothing line for young women" on its website and into three hundred of its stores that October. "Now that the economy's not doing so well, I think it's everybody that's looking for bargains," Conrad told Rosenbloom. The LC Lauren Conrad line has since expanded to include shoes, jewelry, and bedding. Conrad is also the designer and co-owner of the boutique women's wear company Paper Crown.

Conrad has also found success as a writer. In 2009 she published a young adult novel titled *L.A. Candy*, the first book in a semiautobiographical trilogy about a young woman named Jane Roberts who stars in a Los Angeles–based reality show. Conrad published the first installment in another trilogy, *The Fame Game*, in 2012. Her novels became *New York Times* best sellers, and though many celebrity authors employ a ghostwriter (often uncredited), Conrad insists that she does not. She has also published two beauty and fashion guides: *Lauren Conrad Style* (2010) and *Lauren Conrad Beauty* (2012).

In 2013 Conrad launched a lifestyle website, LaurenConrad.com. Featuring everything from recipes and fitness advice to fashion tips and a book club, the site, Conrad told Joshua David Stein for the *New York Times* (13 Nov. 2013),

serves "as a hub for [her] brand." Later that year Conrad launched the e-commerce company The Little Market, cofounded with Human Rights Watch advocate Hannah Taylor Skvarla. The Little Market sells crafts made by women in developing countries in order to support struggling artisans through fair-trade commerce. "We've been to Bali and El Salvador and Africa and India and Nepal," Conrad told Martel. "Hannah is good about educating me about not just the beautiful places we go to but also the issues people there face. I think when you've been fortunate, you have a moral obligation to do things for others."

PERSONAL LIFE

Conrad became engaged to William Tell, a law student and musician, in October of 2013. The two met on Valentine's Day in 2012. Conrad told Martel that Tell "has experience in the entertainment industry, so he understands a lot of things that people don't always get." The couple expect to marry in the summer of 2014.

Conrad owns several homes in the Los Angeles area, including homes in Brentwood, Beverly Hills, and her hometown, Laguna Beach.

SUGGESTED READING

Heffernan, Virginia. "Learning from Lauren: Smells Like Teen Spirit, Looks Like Hard Work." *New York Times*. New York Times, 22 Jan. 2007. Web. 14 Mar. 2014.

Martel, Ned. "Lauren Conrad: Golden Girl." *Marie Claire*. Hearst Communications, 11 June 2013. Web. 14 Mar. 2014.

Ogunnaike, Lola. "Shopping with: Lauren Conrad and Heidi Montag, Blond Ambition Comes in Flats or Heels." *New York Times*. New York Times, 11 June 2006. Web. 14 Mar. 2014.

Stack, Tim. "'The Hills': They Shoot, Lauren Conrad Scores." *Entertainment Weekly*. Entertainment Weekly, 19 Aug. 2008. Web. 14 Mar. 2014.

SELECTED WORKS

L.A. Candy, 2009; *Sweet Little Lies*, 2010; *Lauren Conrad Style* (with Elise Loehnen), 2010; *Sugar and Spice*, 2011; *The Fame Game*, 2012; *Starstruck*, 2012; *Lauren Conrad Beauty* (with Elise Loehnen), 2012; *Infamous*, 2013

—*Molly Hagan*

Bryan Cranston

Born: March 7, 1956
Occupation: Actor

Bryan Cranston is an Emmy Award–winning actor best known for his role as Walter White, a high school chemistry teacher turned drug kingpin, in

Danny Moloshok/UPI/Landov

the AMC drama *Breaking Bad*. Cranston enjoyed a stable if somewhat static career acting in television shows and commercials before winning the lead role in *Breaking Bad* in 2007, at the age of fifty-one. It was, in both its complexity and its exposure, the role of a lifetime for Cranston, and Walter White became the ultimate antihero in an age of carefully shaded bad guys on television. Created by writer and director Vince Gilligan, *Breaking Bad* leads White down an increasingly dark path from pushover to killer, or as Gilligan famously said, referring to the beloved fictional schoolteacher created by James Hilton and the ruthless drug dealer portrayed by Al Pacino, from "Mr. Chips to Scarface."

Given the extent to which White surrenders to his darkest impulses, Cranston seemed an odd choice for the part. His most prominent role prior to *Breaking Bad* was that of Hal, the bumbling husband in the Fox sitcom *Malcolm in the Middle*. (Gilligan later said that he liked the association because it turned the image of a hapless father on its head.) But Gilligan, who sought out the actor specifically, was mostly thinking of a role that Cranston played in 1998, when he appeared in an episode of the sci-fi mystery show *The X-Files*. Gilligan was working on the show at the time and wrote an episode called "Drive" that featured a character whom Gilligan described to Brett Martin for *GQ* (1 Aug. 2013) as an anti-Semitic "redneck creep." The episode's conceit was based on two characters driving in a car together, with the knowledge that when the car stopped, the villain would die. Gilligan worked hard to make the second character the most unpleasant human being imaginable, yet the structure of the episode required the audience to feel empathy for him when he died. It was a tall order for an actor to fill in a single, one-hour episode,

and Gilligan interviewed a number of strong actors for the role, though none of them seemed to fit the bill. The search ended when Gilligan hit upon Cranston, who imbued the character with subtle traits suggesting his vulnerability, such as a tremble in his hands or a flash of fear in his eyes. For Gilligan, it was as though Cranston could magically embody good and bad, or perhaps more accurately, humanity and evil, at the same time. "Casting bad guys is easy," Gilligan told Martin. "Casting a bad guy you feel sympathy for is much harder."

EARLY LIFE AND EDUCATION

Bryan Lee Cranston was born on March 7, 1956, and grew up in Canoga Park, in Los Angeles's San Fernando Valley. The second of three children, he has an older brother named Kyle, who is also an actor, and a younger sister, Amy. His parents, Joe Cranston and Peggy Sell, were both actors, and Joe Cranston had appeared in such television shows as *Dragnet* and *My Three Sons* as well as a handful of B movies. The couple separated when Cranston was twelve years old. "My dad wanted desperately to be successful, and he wasn't, and it just brought him to his knees," Cranston told Tad Friend for the *New Yorker* (16 Sept. 2013). His mother struggled with depression and alcoholism after they lost the family house to foreclosure, and for a time, Cranston and his brother were sent to live with their maternal grandparents. When the siblings were reunited with their mother a year later, the family subsisted on food stamps, living in a house with several boarders.

Cranston appeared in his first play, a school production called *The Time Machine*, when he was in the fifth grade. As the lead, Mr. Flipnoodle, Cranston had a line that read, "President Lincoln will finish writing the Gettysburg Address when he returns to the White House." But instead of "White House," the young Cranston said "White Front," the name of a local department store chain. The audience was practically weeping with laughter, but Cranston was mortified. "The experience probably had something to do with me pushing away from performing for a long time," he told Friend. Considering a career as a police officer, the teenage Cranston joined the LAPD Law Enforcement Explorers and rose to the top of his class of more than one hundred cadets. Cranston also wrote for the Canoga Park High School newspaper and, as *Breaking Bad* fans have gleefully noted, was a member of the school's chemistry club.

After graduating from high school in 1974, Cranston attended Los Angeles Valley College with the aim of becoming a police officer. Required to choose an elective, he fortuitously chose acting. In his interview with Martin, Cranston insisted that he simply chose the first class on the alphabetically arranged list.

"If acting had been called *shmacting*," he said, "I may have wound up taking archery." He completed his two-year degree in police science in 1976, though notably, he did not attempt to join the force right away or pursue a bachelor's degree in police science as he had initially planned.

EARLY ACTING CAREER

The summer following his graduation, Cranston and his brother embarked on a cross-country motorcycle trip. The brothers traveled more than 140,000 miles in two years, working odd jobs to pay for food and gas. In Daytona, Florida, they worked at a Hawaiian restaurant as waiters and at a pool, selling suntan lotion and other products to tourists. At this time, Cranston began performing at the Daytona Playhouse. During one performance of *The King and I*, Cranston started tearing up when the Vaseline underneath his stage makeup began to melt into his eyes. "It was a total accident, but I got so much praise," Cranston told Friend. "And I realized that in acting—unlike in high school—if you show vulnerability, you become attractive. It's like you've suddenly got a grenade: power was at hand!" Around the same time, Cranston found himself absorbed in Norwegian playwright Henrik Ibsen's play *Hedda Gabler*, which he read while taking shelter at a rest stop off the Blue Ridge Parkway in Virginia during a six-day downpour. The play solidified Cranston's new path: he would become an actor. "I understood that this is what I should be doing with my life," Cranston told Friend. "I came up with this motto: 'Find something you love and hopefully become good at' as opposed to 'Find something you're good at and hopefully fall in love with.'"

Cranston moved back to Los Angeles, where he studied a host of different acting techniques and even tried his hand at standup comedy. After a few years, he began landing guest roles in popular television shows such as *Murder, She Wrote* and *Matlock*, in which he usually played a forgettable victim or equally forgettable criminal with few to no lines. He appeared in a handful of soap operas as well, though he made most of his money from commercials, hawking everything from Coffee-Mate to Preparation H. "I had that everyman look—nonthreatening, nondistracting, no facial hair," he told Friend. "I fit in." But by his account, he fit in too well. As the 1980s wore on, Cranston became increasingly frustrated. He was making a decent living, but his career did not seem to be going anywhere.

A CHANGE IN ATTITUDE

A major turning point in Cranston's career came after he worried to his wife that he was "stuck on the junior varsity," as quoted by Friend. She arranged for him to attend several private sessions with the self-help guru and life coach Breck

Costin. With Costin's guidance, Cranston began to see the exhausting slog of auditioning in a new light. Instead of focusing on his competition, he began to focus on his own craft. "It incrementally came to me that when I audition I'm not trying to get a job, but to give them something, my acting," he explained to Friend. "The victory is not 'Did I beat that other guy out?' but 'Did I present that character as believably as I could?' That was the turning point."

His new attitude paid off in the mid-1990s, when he landed a recurring role in *Seinfeld*, playing the dentist Tim Whatley. In 1996, Cranston appeared in an episode of the Dick Van Dyke procedural *Diagnosis Murder*. The role, as it was written, was not particularly demanding, but Van Dyke was so impressed by the performance that he sang Cranston's praises to anyone who would listen.

After that, many of the roles the actor won were a matter of luck. Cranston himself relayed to Martin a lesson he learned from watching the disillusionment of his father: "It doesn't matter if you're good. If you're just good, you won't succeed. If you have patience and persistence and talent and that's it, you will not have a successful career as an actor. The elusive thing you need is luck." But luck for Cranston was less random than it is for others; his was the accumulation of years of postcards sent to casting directors and a consistently high level of commitment to even the smallest roles.

MALCOLM IN THE MIDDLE

A stroke of luck came when Cranston was cast as astronaut Buzz Aldrin in the 1998 HBO miniseries *From the Earth to the Moon* because the actor who was originally cast in the role was too large to fit into his spacesuit. Cranston's role as the hapless father, Hal, in the comedy *Malcolm in the Middle* derived from similarly serendipitous beginnings. According to Jane Kaczmarek, who was cast as Hal's wife, Lois, Cranston got the part two days before production started "after all the hairy fat guys didn't work out," she told Friend.

Creator Linwood Boomer admitted to Martin that the role was woefully underwritten; the thrust of the show was clearly the antics of the couple's children and Kaczmarek's outspoken character. Cranston's audition was a scene that mostly consisted of Lois fighting with one of their sons. But Cranston's interpretation of Hal in that moment—he pulled out a pipe and watched the volleys as if at a tennis match—made Boomer fall off his chair with laughter. "People say that, but I literally *fell off* my metal chair," Boomer emphasized in an interview with Martin. "He just had this vast inner life going on. You realize, 'This guy looks like he's listening, but he's actually building a rocket ship in his head.'" When Cranston won the role, the show's writers rose to his talent, offering Hal meatier storylines and even challenging Cranston physically: the pilot opens with Lois shaving tufts of hair off Hal's back while he stands in his underwear, and in another episode, Hal is completely covered in twenty-five pounds of live bees. (Martin wrote that the latter stunt was the final chapter of a game the show's writers played, called "What won't Bryan do?")

Malcolm in the Middle ran from 2000 to 2006, during which time Cranston was nominated for the Emmy Award for outstanding supporting actor in a comedy series three times.

BREAKING BAD

The idea for *Breaking Bad* occurred to Gilligan in 2004, when his friend Thomas Schnauz, who later became one of the show's writers, told him about a news story he had read about a local meth manufacturer. Both writers were out of work, and, according to a profile on Gilligan by David Segal for the *New York Times* (6 July 2011), it was a "fallow period" for the creator, whose career seemed to have dried up after the end of *The X-Files* in 2002. Gilligan decided to run with the idea in a new pilot about a middle-aged man, his career seemingly all dried up, who starts cooking meth.

The circumstances under which Walter White breaks bad (a Southern phrase akin to *raising hell*) are markedly different from any previous premises in Gilligan's writing career. White is a fifty-year-old high school chemistry teacher (though had he seized any number of earlier opportunities, his career might very well have been much more) who works part time at a carwash to support his pregnant wife and a teenage son with cerebral palsy. Within the first twenty minutes of the pilot episode, White is diagnosed with terminal lung cancer.

White's foray into meth cooking is born of financial necessity—a need for a nest egg for his family when he dies and a way to pay for his own medical bills—as well as some amalgamation of a midlife crisis and a parting shot at the world that had killed his spirit. He teams up with a former student named Jesse Pinkman (Aaron Paul), a young drug dealer who failed White's class in high school. The unlikely duo botch a number of early jobs, the dark humor of which is the show's signature. (According to Friend, Gilligan asked his team if he should submit the first season of the show to the awards committees as a drama or a comedy.) What set *Breaking Bad* apart from other shows was Gilligan's determination to test his audience's allegiance to White through a series of irreversibly bad decisions made, ostensibly, in the name of protecting White's family. "Walter White progresses from unassuming savant to opportunistic gangster—and as he does so, the show dares you to excuse him, or find a moral line that you deem a point of no return," Segal wrote.

BECOMING WALTER WHITE

Cranston dove into his role with characteristic zeal. "He's telepathic," Gilligan gushed to Martin. "I can't tell you how much dialogue we've cut out of this show over the years in the editing room, stuff that we wrote and really liked, that when we got to the editing room we said to ourselves, 'You know, we don't really need this line. It's not necessary, because I see exactly what he's thinking.'" Cranston created pages of backstory for White, and he instructed the show's makeup artist to give White a mustache that looked "impotent." For Cranston, White was a study in burden and heartbreak and the slow wearing down after a lifetime of disappointments; somewhat chillingly, Cranston told Martin that he modeled White's physicality after his own father. "We didn't have Walt stand erect until he became Heisenberg," Cranston told Martin, referring to White's drug kingpin alter ego.

Breaking Bad premiered in January 2008 and, over the course of its five seasons, gained a fervent and loyal fan base. Cranston began serving as a producer of the show during the fourth season, and he directed three episodes of *Breaking Bad* himself. In the weeks leading up to the finale, the show was the dominant subject of cultural conversation, with a slew of parodies on *Saturday Night Live* and late-night television talk shows. *Breaking Bad* far surpassed the expectations of its creators while demonstrating the mass appeal of intelligent and complex characters. For his part, Cranston won three consecutive Emmy Awards for outstanding lead actor in a drama series during the show's run, becoming the first actor to do so since Bill Cosby won three consecutive Emmys for his performance in *I Spy* in the mid-1960s. As the show was brought to a close, Cranston accepted a number of other jobs, including roles in the Academy Award–winning film *Argo* (2012) and the upcoming feature film *Godzilla* (2014).

PERSONAL LIFE

Cranston married writer Mickey Middleton in 1979, but the couple divorced two years later. He met his current wife, actor Robin Dearden, in 1986 on the set of *Airwolf*, a sci-fi adventure show. The two married in 1989, and Dearden gave birth to their daughter, Taylor, in 1993. The family lives in Los Angeles.

SUGGESTED READING

Friend, Tad. "The One Who Knocks." *New Yorker*. New Yorker, 16 Sept. 2013. Web. 4 Dec. 2013.

Martin, Brett. "The Last Stand of Walter White." *GQ*. Condé Nast, 1 Aug. 2013. Web. 4 Dec. 2013.

Segal, David. "The Dark Art of 'Breaking Bad.'" *New York Times*. New York Times, 6 July 2011. Web. 4 Dec. 2013.

SELECTED WORKS
Seinfeld, 1994–97; *Malcolm in the Middle*, 2000–2006; *Breaking Bad*, 2008–13

—*Molly Hagan*

Amy Cuddy

Occupation: Social psychologist

Social scientist Amy Cuddy is best known to general audiences for her 2012 Technology, Entertainment, and Design (TED) Talk, called "Your Body Language Shapes Who You Are." In the inspirational talk, which has been viewed over 9 million times to date, Cuddy presented her findings on how posture and body language can shape not only how people are perceived by others but also how people perceive themselves by affecting their hormonal levels. Cuddy offered what she called a free "life hack" tip to the audience, encouraging people to "power pose" privately before entering challenging situations. Cuddy—who struggled with self-confidence as a young professional—has said that she hopes her power pose research can help average people who lack confidence take control of their lives. Her research generally focuses on the ways in which people perceive and react to one another. Often collaborating with her former graduate advisor, Susan Fiske, Cuddy has produced numerous influential studies about how people's perceptions of two core traits in others, warmth and competence, affect judgment and behavior in a variety of settings and social contexts. Cuddy was named a *Time* magazine Game Changer in 2012 and one of *Business Insider*'s 50 Women Who Are Changing the World in 2013.

EARLY LIFE AND EDUCATION

Amy J. C. Cuddy grew up in the small farming town of Robesonia, Pennsylvania, which was populated almost entirely by Protestant German Americans. In an interview with the *Association of Psychological Science Observer* (29 Dec. 2011), Cuddy said of her hometown, "You couldn't imagine a more homogeneous place." Cuddy was a bright student who had always been told that she had gifted intelligence. She trained as a ballet dancer and was also interested in theater and singing. As a high school student, her goal was to be a broadcast journalist.

When Cuddy was nineteen years old and a student at the University of Colorado at Boulder, she was involved in a serious car accident.

Astrid Stawiarz/Getty Images

The driver of the car she was a passenger in fell asleep at the wheel while traveling at ninety miles per hour. Cuddy suffered a severe head injury. Doctors told her that she had lost about two standard deviations of her IQ and that she was not likely to graduate from college.

Cuddy was initially devastated by the prognosis, especially because she had so identified with being intelligent—even gifted. But instead of giving up, she worked hard to regain the brain functioning she had lost after her accident, attending therapy sessions, studying more hours than other students, and even listening to classical music. "I finally decided the doctors just were wrong," she said in an interview for a March 19, 2012, *Time* magazine video. "I didn't have to accept things as they appeared to be."

When she returned to college at the age of twenty-two, Cuddy had regained her IQ and was able to dance again. Cuddy's experiences led her to major in psychology. After finding a position in a neuropsychology lab to be a little dull, she decided to focus on social psychology. She continued to struggle in school, however, and dropped out of college twice before finally graduating magna cum laude in 1998—four years after her peers.

STRUGGLES AS A GRAD STUDENT

After receiving her undergraduate degree, Cuddy sought out a mentor and found one in Susan Fiske, a social psychologist known for her research on social cognition, particularly emotional prejudices, such as pity, contempt, envy, and pride. Cuddy worked for several years as an assistant to Fiske at the University of Massachusetts at Amherst. Both women then moved to Princeton University, where Cuddy began her graduate work. She received a master's degree from Princeton in 2003 and was accepted into a doctoral program at Princeton as a Woodrow Wilson Scholar, which included a full scholarship.

Despite all her hard work and success, throughout graduate school Cuddy struggled with a lack of confidence and an overwhelming sense that she did not belong in such a prestigious program. Before delivering her required first-year talk to twenty other students, she almost quit the program. When she told Fiske about her insecurities and her plans to quit, Fiske responded with a piece of advice that would have an enormous impact on Cuddy's career—and her future research. "You're going to stay, and this is what you're going to do. You are going to fake it. You're going to do every talk that you ever get asked to do. You're just going to do it and do it and do it, even if you're terrified . . . until you have this moment where you say, 'Oh my gosh, I'm doing it. Like I have become this. I am actually doing this,'" Fiske said, as Cuddy recalled during her 2012 TED Talk. The advice proved true, and two years later, in 2005, Cuddy completed her doctorate. Her research explored the ways in which people's perceptions and prejudices about out-groups—groups that are distinct from one's own—affect their emotions and behavior in a variety of contexts. Cuddy told the *American Psychological Science Observer* that she was drawn to studying stereotypes in part because she came from such a homogeneous background. "When I moved away to college, I was wide-eyed and eager to make the world a better place," Cuddy said. "I was sort of shocked to see the range and scope of suffering, and so when I became interested in social psychology, studying prejudice was just a natural fit."

THE WARMTH/COMPETENCE MODEL

Most of Cuddy's research on social perception and prejudice, including her dissertation, has incorporated a framework called the warmth/competence model. Developed by Cuddy and her colleagues Fiske and Peter Glick, the model is based on the finding that warmth and competence are the two primary characteristics people assess in one another and use to make judgments. Cuddy explained to the *American Psychological Science Observer* that this tendency is likely rooted in "the evolutionary need to make correct survival decisions: What are this person's intentions toward me? and Is this person capable of acting on those intentions?"

During her graduate studies, Cuddy and her colleagues conducted a series of studies on warmth and competence. They found significant relationships between the way people were perceived, in terms of their warmth and competence, and the attitudes and behaviors those elicited in others. People who were perceived as warm and competent consistently sparked admiration in others and evoked behaviors including helping and cooperating. In contrast, people perceived as cold and incompetent caused others to feel contempt and elicited two different behaviors: passive harm, such as neglect, or active harm, such as harassment. The poor—especially the homeless—are consistently viewed this way, according to Cuddy. "They're blamed for their misfortune," she told Craig Lambert for a 2010 article in *Harvard Magazine*. "They are both neglected and, at times, become the targets of active harm."

Cuddy's research also showed that the other two groups in the model sparked emotional and behavioral responses that were more ambiguous. Groups perceived as cold and competent—often the case with Asian Americans, career-oriented women, and African American professionals—sparked envy in others, an ambivalent emotion that can cause people to feel either respect or resentment toward the person. People considered warm and incompetent—which includes the elderly and, often, mothers—also evoke an ambivalent emotion, pity, which can lead others to feel compassion or sadness.

Using this model, Cuddy was able to draw many conclusions about the ways people stereotype others. For example, she observed that people often view warmth and competence as inversely related: if a person is warm, he or she is believed to be incompetent and vice versa. Cuddy's dissertation, titled "The BIAS Map: Behavior from Intergroup Affect and Stereotypes," which included these and many other findings about warmth and competence, was published in the *Journal of Personality and Social Psychology* in 2007.

SELECTED RESEARCH

Cuddy and her colleagues have used the warmth/competence model to study the perceptions and treatment of numerous out-groups, such as Asian Americans, working mothers, and prisoners. In a 2004 study published in the *Journal of Social Issues*, Cuddy found that women were generally viewed as less competent in the workplace after they became mothers, while men who became fathers were viewed as warmer but equally as competent as they were before. The study also concluded that employers were significantly more likely to hire and promote childless employees or fathers than working mothers. Cuddy has pointed out that basing business and hiring decisions on stereotypes is not beneficial to a company. "When facing personnel decisions, managers should push themselves to be aware of how they form impressions," Cuddy wrote in a 2009 article for the *Harvard Business Review*.

In November 2004, in the wake of the Abu Ghraib prison abuse scandal, in which members of the US military and CIA were revealed to have physical and sexually abused prisoners at the Baghdad prison, Cuddy and her colleagues published a study in the journal *Science*, titled "Why Ordinary People Torture Enemy Prisoners." The study analyzed 25,000 past studies involving eight million participants that pointed to the same conclusion: almost everyone is capable of committing cruel acts to a "dehumanized outgroup" under certain conditions, especially if they are ordered to do so by a respected authority. The report concluded, "Abu Ghraib resulted in part from ordinary social processes, not just individual extraordinary evil."

After Hurricane Katrina, Cuddy coauthored a 2007 study on the way people perceived the emotional states of in-group and out-group victims in the southern United States. Two weeks after the storm, white and nonwhite participants were asked to infer the emotional state of white and nonwhite victims and to report their own intentions to help the victims. Cuddy found that participants believed that out-group victims experienced fewer human emotions, such as anguish and mourning, than in-group victims. The more a participant believed a victim suffered from such emotions, the more likely the participant was to state his or her intention to help the victim.

In recent years, Cuddy has coauthored numerous other studies focused on social perception and stereotyping. Some of these have explored the overlap between gender and race stereotypes, the role of racism in affirmative action, the stereotyping of people who are biracial, the connection between expansive postures and dishonest behavior, and the relationship between economic inequality in a country and the population's ambivalence toward its poor.

POWER POSES

After earning her doctorate, Cuddy taught at Rutgers University from 2005 to 2006 before joining the Kellogg School of Management at Northwestern University as an assistant professor. There she continued her research on social perception and stereotyping, while teaching in the Management and Organizations Department. She then became an assistant professor at Harvard Business School, teaching courses on negotiation, power, and influence.

While teaching future business leaders, Cuddy observed different body language in the people who were thriving in her class (where participation counted for half the grade) compared

to those students who were struggling in class. Those who were doing well—and were more likely to speak in class—were striking poses known to convey a sense of power and respect. They occupied more space in the room, were spread out in their seats, and had good posture. In contrast, those who were struggling—and less willing to speak in class—were using postures that conveyed a sense of weakness. That is, they were making themselves small, crossing their legs, folding their arms, and slouching.

Though specific postures and poses are known to convey a sense of power and respect, affecting the way a person is perceived by others, Cuddy wondered whether such postures—dubbed "high power poses"—could actually affect people's internal states and make them *feel* more powerful. To determine this, Cuddy and her colleagues Dana Carney and Andy J. Yap, both at Columbia University, took forty-two subjects and had them hold two high power poses or a low power pose for one minute per pose. After the subjects held the poses, their hormone levels were measured and compared to their baseline levels.

The study, published in 2010 in *Psychological Science*, found that in the high-power posing people, testosterone increased by 20 percent and the stress hormone cortisol decreased by 25 percent. That hormone profile is associated with power, dominance, higher risk-taking behaviors, adaptability, and even disease resistance. The lower power poses led people to experience a 10 percent decrease in testosterone and a 15 percent increase in cortisol levels. Participants were also asked to take part in a gambling game after the poses; the high power posers turned out to be more likely to take risks in the game than the low power posers. *Psychology Today* named the study one of its Top 10 Psychology Studies of 2010.

FOLLOW-UP STUDY

To test the practical applications of the finding, Cuddy, Carney, and Caroline Wilmuth conducted a follow-up study in which sixty-one people stood in high or low power poses for two minutes and were then asked to interview for a job. The evaluators consistently rated the people who prepared with high power poses as more hirable—even though they were no more competent, qualified, or even necessarily articulate than the low-power posing group. The authors of the follow-up study, a 2012 Harvard Business School Working Paper, concluded, "This experiment demonstrates that preparatory power posing affects individuals' presence during a job interview, which in turn affects judges' evaluations and hiring decisions."

Based on these findings, Cuddy has recommended that people use power poses to help them prepare for important meetings and events. She suggests standing in a power position in the privacy of an office or a bathroom stall for a couple of minutes. She told the *Toronto Star* (1 Oct. 2010), "Your body, your mind, your hormones will be in line and you will be ready to go."

2012 TED TALK

In October 2012, Cuddy delivered a talk at the TED Global event. In her speech, Cuddy presented her findings about power posing, presenting it as a free, simple "life hack," a way for people to improve their lives. To demonstrate the importance of body language, she showed the crowd a series of photos of notable people in seemingly revealing poses. These slides included images of powerful people, such as President Barack Obama and Oprah Winfrey, adopting power poses, sitting back in their chairs or standing tall and square. Explaining that such power poses convey strength across the animal kingdom, she also showed pictures of animals in similar postures.

Cuddy linked her research about power poses to her own personal struggles: her traumatic brain injury and her lack of confidence early in her career. She recalled the advice she was given by her advisor, who encouraged her to keep trying over and over again until she became successful: "Fake it till you make it." Cuddy explained that power poses are one tool people can use to remove obstacles in the way to becoming their best selves. She concluded by saying, "And so I want to say to you: don't fake it till you make it. Fake it till you *become* it."

Cuddy's TED Talk became enormously popular. It was voted by TED employees as the most inspiring TED Talk of 2012, and it is one of the most viewed talks of all time, with more than nine million views to date. In 2013 it made the *Guardian*'s 20 Online Talks That Could Change Your Life list. Her findings on power posing went on to be cited in numerous articles. Cuddy herself has received thousands of messages from people around the world about how power posing has helped them overcome a challenge, ranging from engaging in school to securing a job to leaving an abusive relationship. "I'm moved beyond words by these strangers' willingness to share such personal stories of vulnerability," she wrote in an October 28, 2012, article for CNN, "and I'm humbled and astounded to see how this research has resonated with people outside my science."

PERSONAL LIFE

Cuddy has been an associate professor at Harvard University Business School since 2012. A serious ballet dancer early in her life, she continues to take dance classes. She has said that her interest in physical expression is rooted in this early passion.

SUGGESTED READING

Cuddy, Amy. "Act Powerful, Be Powerful." *CNN.* Cable News Network, 28 Oct. 2012. Web. 15 Jan. 2014.

Cuddy, Amy. "Just Because I'm Nice, Don't Assume I'm Dumb." *Harvard Business Review.* Harvard Business, Feb. 2009. Web. 15 Jan. 2014.

Lambert, Craig. "The Psyche on Automatic: Amy Cuddy Probes Snap Judgments, Warm Feelings, and How to Become the 'Alpha Dog.'" *Harvard Magazine.* Harvard Magazine, Nov./Dec. 2010. Web. 15 Jan. 2014.

Murphy, Kate. "The Right Stance Can Be Reassuring." *New York Times* 5 May 2013, Style Desk: 10. Print.

"Rising Stars." *Association for Psychological Science Observer.* Assoc. for Psychological Science, May/June 2011. Web. 15 Jan. 2014.

SELECTED WORKS

"When Professionals Become Mothers, Warmth Doesn't Cut the Ice," *Journal of Social Science*, 2004 (with S. Fiske and P. Glick); "Why Ordinary People Torture Enemy Prisoners," *Science*, 2004 (with S. Fiske and L. T. Harris); "The BIAS Map: Behaviors from Intergroup Affect and Stereotypes," *Journal of Personality and Social Psychology*, 2007 (with S. Fiske and P. Glick); "Your Body Language Shapes Who You Are," TEDTalk, 2012

—*Margaret Roush Mead*

Benedict Cumberbatch

Born: July 19, 1976
Occupation: Actor

In 2013, Benedict Cumberbatch went from being a well-respected actor best known for playing a modern-day Sherlock Holmes in the critically acclaimed BBC series *Sherlock* to a household name for his captivating performances in such major motion pictures as *Star Trek Into Darkness*, *The Fifth Estate*, *12 Years a Slave*, and *August: Osage County*. At thirty-eight, he is a bit older than most breakout superstars—an odd thing considering that he has been earning critical acclaim for his work on British stage and screen since 2004, when he was hailed for his performance as physicist Steven Hawking in the television film *Hawking*. Yet the praise he has been receiving from all corners recently comes as no surprise to his large and devoted (and largely female) fan base, which made him something of a cult sex symbol since he began work on *Sherlock* in 2010. Although his atypical looks have made

Matt Crossick/PA Photos/Landov

him an unlikely heartthrob, his clear talents as an actor—portraying characters from a tormented genius to a period-piece dandy to a genetic superman to a rapist—have garnered him a host of rave reviews from film critics and fans alike. His popularity earned him a cover story on the international edition of *Time* in 2013, the same year he was tweeted about more than 700,000 times. "It's one of the more bizarre levels of success," he said of the *Time* cover—which he first assumed was fake—in an interview with Sarah Lyall for the *New York Times Style Magazine* (7 Mar. 2014). "Someone sent me a photograph of it and I thought, 'Some fan has got hold of a photo and done one of those neat apps where they impose your head on something.'" In April 2014 *Time* featured Cumberbatch in its 100 Most Influential People list.

EARLY LIFE AND EDUCATION
Benedict Timothy Carlton Cumberbatch was born in London, England, on July 19, 1976, the only son of actors professionally known as Wanda Ventham and Timothy Carlton. (His paternal family name is Cumberbatch; one of his ancestors was a consul for Queen Victoria.) Although his parents were devoted to their chosen profession, they had little interest in having their offspring follow in their footsteps. To that end, they sought to lead him away from acting by giving him the best possible education they could provide at the Harrow School, an elite all-male British boarding school, which he began attending on an arts scholarship as an adolescent. "It suited me down to the ground," he recalled, as quoted by Alice-Azania Jarvis for the *Independent* (29 Jan. 2011). "I fell in love with the place."

While there, Cumberbatch developed his budding passions for both painting and performing on stage. As an actor he demonstrated a willingness to take on almost any part, including the roles of such famous Shakespeare heroines as Titania in *A Midsummer Night's Dream* and Rosalind in *As You Like It*. His drama teacher, Martin Tyrell, told Amanda Mitchison for the *Guardian* (16 July 2010) that he was "the best schoolboy actor I've ever worked with." After spending a year in Tibet, and despite his family's concerns, Cumberbatch decided to study drama at the University of Manchester. When asked why he chose Manchester, he told Mitchison, "I needed to be out of the danger of tying a cashmere jumper round my neck. I wanted something a bit more racy, a bit more different, a bit more egalitarian. I had a thoroughly healthy—and unhealthy—mix of friends." He then took another year to complete his master's degree at the London Academy of Music and Dramatic Art. His studies paid off: by the time he graduated, he already had an agent.

EARLY CAREER ON STAGE AND SCREEN
Cumberbatch's early acting career consisted of a mix of roles on British stage and television. He appeared regularly onstage at such venues as Regent's Park Open Air Theatre, the Almeida, the Royal Court, and the National, and in such television movies and series as *Fields of Gold* (2002), *Tipping the Velvet* (2002), *Silent Witness* (2002), *Cambridge Spies* (2003), *MI-5* (2003), *Fortysomething* (2003), and *Heartbeat* (2000–2004).

His breakout television performance, however, came in the 2004 television movie *Hawking*, in which he played Stephen Hawking, the famed physicist who suffers from Lou Gehrig's disease, at a period in his life when he is just beginning his major scientific work and then learns of his diagnosis. For his performance, Cumberbatch was nominated for a 2005 British Academy of Film and Television Arts (BAFTA) Award for best actor. He followed this with a celebrated performance in the 2005 BBC adaptation of British author William Golding's seafaring trilogy *To the Ends of the Earth*, portraying protagonist Edmund Talbot in all three parts of the miniseries, "Fire Down Below," "Close Quarters," and "Rites of Passage." In 2010, he again portrayed a troubled genius after being cast as the great Dutch painter Vincent Van Gogh in the television movie *Van Gogh: Painted with Words* (2010).

Cumberbatch's leading roles on British television afforded him entry into big-screen filmmaking. His earliest roles in major motion pictures were typically key, but supporting, parts. He played, for example, Prime Minister William Pitt the Younger in *Amazing Grace* (2006), a biopic about the life of the British parliamentarian and abolitionist William Wilberforce; Paul

Marshall, the rapist in the 2007 adaptation of Ian McEwan's novel *Atonement*; and William Carey, the arrogant husband in the 2008 adaptation of Philippa Gregory's historical novel *The Other Boleyn Girl*. Part of his success in playing a wide range of parts, many critics agree, has to do with his unique looks. Lyall wrote, "Tall and lean, he has an other-century look about him, with his long, narrow face, his mop of crazy hair (he keeps it shorter off-duty) and bright, far-apart, almond-shaped blue eyes that on-screen can play intelligent, ardent, manic, or insane, depending on the job."

SHERLOCK

Cumberbatch went from respected actor to household name in 2010. It was in this year he starred as Sherlock Holmes, Sir Arthur Conan Doyle's legendary detective, in the first season of *Sherlock*, a BBC television adaptation set in modern London and developed by Mark Gatiss (who also plays Sherlock's brother, Mycroft) and Steven Moffat, two veteran writers for the long-running British sci-fi series *Doctor Who*. A year prior to landing the plum role of Holmes, Cumberbatch had been nearly chosen by *Doctor Who* show-runner Moffat to replace David Tennant, who was then leaving the role of the Doctor on the series, but the role ultimately went to actor Matt Smith. Moffat remembered Cumberbatch well, however, and offered him the assignment of bringing Holmes into the modern world—to which Cumberbatch readily agreed. The actor told Mitchison, "There's a great charge you get from playing him, because of the volume of words in your head and the speed of thought—you really have to make your connections incredibly fast. He is one step ahead of the audience, and of anyone around him with normal intellect. They can't quite fathom where his leaps are taking him. Zip zip zip."

Costarring Martin Freeman as Dr. John Watson, Holmes's longtime sidekick, the series takes classic Holmes stories penned by Conan Doyle during the late nineteenth and early twentieth centuries and brings them into the modern age, adding modern technologies and crime-solving techniques but never dispensing with the key element of those tales: the incredible deductive mind of Holmes. Cumberbatch's Holmes is cold, impatient, and superior with others; when bored and without a case to work on, he can be infuriating to Watson and his other cohorts or self-destructive by binging on illicit drugs. Although brilliant and technologically savvy, he has such an inability to behave within societal norms that he seems to be manifesting the symptoms of a condition akin to Asperger syndrome. And he is seemingly well aware of it: Cumberbatch's Holmes often corrects others who would dub him a psychopath by reminding them he is in fact a "high-functioning sociopath," as quoted by

Alessandra Stanley for the *New York Times* (17 Jan. 2014).

Each episode of the series is ninety minutes long—about the length of a television movie—and each season, of which there have been three thus far, is just three episodes long. The unusual scheduling allows the writers to develop each episode the way they would a feature film and also gives the series' lead actors time to work on other projects. (Both Cumberbatch and Freeman are involved with Peter Jackson's trilogy of films based on J. R. R. Tolkien's *The Hobbit*, in which Freeman plays Bilbo Baggins and Cumberbatch voices the motion-capture characters of the Necromancer and Smaug.) *Sherlock* is a megahit in Great Britain and abroad due in large part to the show's high-caliber writing and production, the talents of its two leads, and the devotion of its millions of fans worldwide.

2013: A BUSY YEAR

Although Cumberbatch was an emerging star in the United Kingdom—and was well known among American television viewers via *Sherlock*, which airs on PBS in the United States—2013 would prove to be the year he became an international superstar. In addition to his work on *Sherlock* and in the first two parts of *The Hobbit* trilogy (released at the end of 2012 and 2013, respectively), Cumberbatch found himself starring in four major motion pictures, in either leading or key supporting roles, in 2013. The films included *12 Years a Slave*, based on the memoir of Solomon Northup, in which Cumberbatch plays a somewhat sympathetic slave owner; *The Fifth Estate*, a biopic in which he portrays WikiLeaks founder Julian Assange; *August: Osage County*, in which he has a small part in an ensemble cast featuring such esteemed players as Meryl Streep and Julia Roberts; and *Star Trek Into Darkness*, in which he portrays the greatest nemesis Captain James Kirk and the crew of the USS *Enterprise* have ever faced.

In interviews Cumberbatch has admitted that his success at this point in his career is beyond his wildest imaginings. "I knew when I started out that I wanted something very different from what Mom and Dad had anyway, but I didn't know quite what—I didn't know how it would manifest—but even they look at it and go, 'Whoa,'" Cumberbatch remarked to Ann Hornaday for an interview published in the *Washington Post* (11 Oct. 2013). "It's beyond everyone's sort of expectation. But also the workload and everything, it's different to their game."

HIGH-PROFILE FILMS

Cumberbatch received particularly impressive accolades for his work in *The Fifth Estate* and *Star Trek Into Darkness*, despite the fact that the former film did not do well at the box office and many longtime *Star Trek* fans criticized the latter.

In *The Fifth Estate*, Cumberbatch portrays Julian Assange from his days as a computer hacker to his time as editor-in-chief of the whistle-blowing website WikiLeaks, which published an enormous hoard of classified US diplomatic and military documents supplied by Chelsea Manning. As of April 2014, Manning is in military prison serving a thirty-five-year sentence for her role in the affair, and Assange is living in political asylum at the Ecuadorian embassy in London, having fled there to escape extradition to Sweden on rape charges, which he claims have been fabricated. Of Cumberbatch's take on Assange, Decca Aitkenhead wrote in the *Guardian* (13 Sept. 2013), "Cumberbatch's performance doesn't so much evoke as inhabit his character, and the accuracy of the voice, physicality, and mannerisms is uncanny. He captures Assange's extraordinary capacity to charm and beguile, to intoxicate and manipulate, while offering glimpses of his isolation."

Cumberbatch reportedly wrote a letter to Assange before filming started on *The Fifth Estate*. Hillary Busis for *Entertainment Weekly* (11 Oct. 2013) reported that Assange responded to the actor in a January 2013 letter that WikiLeaks made public just ahead of the film's US release on October 18, 2013. In the letter, Assange asks Cumberbatch to stop working on the film, writing that though he admires Cumberbatch's previous work, the movie is "based on a deceitful book by someone who has a vendetta" against Assange and WikiLeaks. Cumberbatch responded to Assange's letter, as quoted by Busis, "To have the man you are about to portray ask you intelligently and politely not to do it gave me real cause for concern . . . . I believe that the film, quite clearly, illuminates the great successes of [WikiLeaks] and its extraordinary founder [Julian] Assange."

STAR TREK INTO DARKNESS

In *Star Trek Into Darkness*, the second outing for a new cast of actors, including Chris Pine and Zachary Quinto, in roles forged in the popular consciousness by William Shatner and Leonard Nimoy beginning in the 1960s, Cumberbatch portrays a genetic superman from a more barbaric period of Earth's history, who has been awoken in the twenty-third century as part of a plot to undermine Starfleet. Though some critics were frustrated by the film's convoluted plot and reliance on iconic moments in earlier *Star Trek* films, they were united in their praise of Cumberbatch's star turn as the antagonist. In the *Spectator* (11 May 2013), David Blackburn wrote, "Benedict Cumberbatch . . . is brilliant as the villain. Cumberbatch follows the Richard Burton School of Acting in Trash and approaches the film as if it were serious. He delivers even the most cartoonish lines as if Christopher Marlowe had written them."

PERSONAL LIFE

In 2004, while filming *To the Ends of the Earth* in South Africa near the Mozambique border, Cumberbatch and two of his costars were carjacked by six gunmen. The men bound the actors with their own shoelaces, dumped them in the trunk of their car, and then drove them around for two-and-a-half hours. Finally the gunmen took Cumberbatch out of the trunk and prepared to shoot him. As he told Stuart McGurk for *British GQ* (31 Dec. 2013), at that moment he thought, "No matter how loved you are in this life, you will die alone." Cumberbatch said that he tried to convince the men not to carry out the murder; after a while the kidnappers left the scene, leaving the actors free to go. Following that near-death experience, the actor took to daring sports, including hot air ballooning and skydiving. In interviews he has said that he believes the experience helped him evolve as a human being and as an actor, making him far more willing to take risks.

Cumberbatch was in a twelve-year relationship with the actor Olivia Poulet, which began when they were both at the University of Manchester and ended amicably in 2011. Currently single but interested in settling down and having a family, he enjoys traveling to New York City and Los Angeles but is most at home in his neighborhood near Hampstead Heath in London. "I go running and swimming there, it's fantastic," he told Hornaday. "It's a beautiful, neighborly part of the world as well—families, it's quiet, especially during the night, it's gorgeous. It's a really nice place to go home to."

SUGGESTED READING

Hornaday, Ann. "Benedict Cumberbatch, Just as Lovely as You Think He Is." *Washington Post.* Washington Post, 11 Oct. 2013. Web. 10 Apr. 2014.

Jarvis, Alice-Azania. "Benedict Cumberbatch: Success? It's Elementary." *Independent.* Independent, 29 Jan. 2011. Web. 10 Apr. 2014.

Lyall, Sarah. "The Case of the Accidental Superstar." *New York Times Style Magazine.* New York Times, 7 Mar. 2014. Web. 10 Apr. 2014.

McGurk, Stuart. "The Many Lives of Benedict Cumberbatch." *British GQ.* Condé Nast UK, 31 Dec. 2013. Web. 10 Apr. 2014.

Mitchison, Amanda. "Benedict Cumberbatch on Playing Sherlock Holmes." *Guardian.* Guardian, 16 July 2010. Web. 10 Apr. 2014.

Stanley, Alessandra. "The Logical Sherlock for Our Time." *New York Times.* New York Times, 17 Jan. 2014. Web. 10 Apr. 2014.

SELECTED WORKS

Hawking, 2004; *Atonement*, 2007; *Van Gogh: Painted with Words*, 2010; *Sherlock*, 2010– ; *The Hobbit: An Unexpected Journey*, 2012; *Star Trek*

Into Darkness, 2013; *12 Years a Slave*, 2013; *The Fifth Estate*, 2013; *August: Osage County*, 2013; *The Hobbit: The Desolation of Smaug*, 2013

—Christopher Mari

Missy Cummings

Born: December 2, 1966
Occupation: Aeronautical and aerospace engineer

In addition to being an associate professor of aeronautics, astronautics, and engineering systems at the Massachusetts Institute of Technology (MIT) and a visiting associate professor at Duke, Missy Cummings is the director of MIT's Humans and Automation Lab (HAL) and a program officer for the Office of Naval Research. She studies interactions between humans and automated machines, focusing much of her research on the development of unmanned aerial vehicles (UAVs), more commonly known as drones. Cummings prefers the former term to the latter, she told Jon Stewart on the *Daily Show* (23 Jan. 2013), because "the word *drone* [connotes] a kind of stupidness, and they're definitely getting smarter." She approaches the use of UAVs from a scientific perspective, though she is not deaf to the raging ethical debate that surrounds their use, particularly as weapons of war.

In early 2013, Cummings appeared in an episode of the PBS documentary series *Nova* called

Larry Busacca/WireImage for Wired/Getty Images

"Rise of the Drones." In his review of the episode, Mike Hale wrote for the *New York Times* (22 Jan. 2013) that the program "argues, convincingly, that the move to remotely piloted aircraft is inevitable and accelerating," noting that "the Air Force is training more drone pilots than cockpit pilots." Elsewhere, Cummings has discussed the many practical applications of UAV technology, including facilitating humanitarian aid and disaster relief, and made headlines for developing a prototype for a small-scale drone that could be operated by a smartphone. Given the range of applications, Cummings and others have tried to direct public debate away from the question of whether UAV technology should continue to be used in the future and toward the more pertinent questions of how, why, and for what purpose.

Innovations in UAV technology are making pilots safer, Cummings told Morgan Bettex for *MIT News* (5 Apr. 2010). During her decade-long career in the US Navy, Cummings flew the F/A-18 Hornet fighter jet. "I can't tell you how many friends died because of bad designs," she told Bettex. Though she left her military career on unhappy terms following years of harassment, she has since dedicated her research to developing safer aerial vehicles.

EARLY LIFE AND MILITARY EDUCATION

Mary Louise "Missy" Cummings was born on December 2, 1966, in Memphis, Tennessee. She has two brothers. Her mother, Janella (née Butler), taught eighth grade, and her father, Clyde Cummings, served in the US Navy for thirty years. The family moved several times, though Cummings spent most of her childhood in Memphis. Her father was a quintessential military man, she wrote in her 1999 book *Hornet's Nest: The Experiences of One of the Navy's First Female Fighter Pilots*, and "ran [the] household like a little platoon." He showed his children war movies on Sunday afternoons, usually quizzing them about the contents afterward, and Cummings was riveted. "I was a soldier from the time I was five," she wrote.

While she was in high school, Cummings's father encouraged her to consider joining the United States Air Force because he felt that it was more welcoming to women, but she chose the navy. At the time, she did not realize that women could be pilots, and she entered the United States Naval Academy in Annapolis, Maryland, with aspirations of becoming an intelligence officer. She graduated with a BS in mathematics in 1988.

Cummings, who was selected by *Glamour* magazine as one of its top ten college women of 1988, found out that women were being trained to fly high-performance aircraft while earning her bachelor's degree. It was the era of *Top Gun*, the popular 1986 film about navy fighter pilots, she told Stewart, and Cummings daydreamed about dropping bombs and dogfighting (a form of aerial combat). After graduation, she began the grueling first stage of her flight training, known as aviation indoctrination (AI), at the naval air station (NAS) in Pensacola, Florida. She then reported to NAS Corpus Christi in Texas, where her father was stationed following her parents' divorce in 1985, to begin primary training.

A student's first solo flight is a major milestone in primary training, and it is commemorated by a symbolic tie cutting ceremony. Cummings's tie cutting, she wrote, "was [her] first glimpse into the darker side of naval aviation and how the guys really felt about women." She was the first woman in her class to have her tie cut, and during the ceremony, the men booed and jeered. She dismissed the incident, but more serious abuses followed. It was clear early on, she wrote, pointing to an initiation ceremony in which a female lieutenant went along with having her underwear cut off in front of the whole squadron, that "to be a successful female naval aviator, the women must either act just like the guys, or sit and watch in silence."

EARLY MILITARY CAREER

Cummings reported to a jet training base in Meridian, Mississippi. She was overjoyed about her assignment, as the navy allows only the highest-ranking flight students to train to fly jets. In 1989, Cummings completed another milestone in a pilot's training: she successfully landed a fighter jet on an aircraft carrier. It was both terrifying and exhilarating, particularly because the carrier, a World War II carrier called the USS *Lexington*, had the smallest landing area of any carrier in use. But one of Cummings's fellow trainees was not so lucky. Shortly after Cummings made her landing, another pilot was killed during a landing attempt, along with four maintenance personnel, in one of the US Navy's worst training carrier accidents ever.

Cummings earned her wings—became a full-fledged pilot—in 1990. Students with the highest marks received the best assignments, and according to Cummings, everyone wanted to fly the fighter jets, the F/A-18s and the F-14s. Even though she finished second in her winging class, Cummings knew she would not be assigned to the fighters because at the time, women were still barred from piloting aircraft that might be used for combat. After a short stint at the Naval Air Technical Training Center (NATTC) in Memphis, she was assigned to a squadron in the Philippines.

In her book, Cummings describes the debauched after-hours life of military men in the Philippines, where, Cummings wrote, sex was both social currency and a male bonding exercise. She spent her time there alternately trying to remain above the fray and pretending to play

along after being reprimanded for not being a "team player." She loved piloting and excelled in her post as a lieutenant, but, mostly for the aforementioned reasons, she decided to leave her squadron and pursue a graduate degree in 1992.

THE HORNET'S NEST

Cummings enrolled in the Naval Postgraduate School in Monterey, California, where she began studying to become an astronaut. In 1993, the combat exclusion law instituted by the Women's Armed Services Integration Act of 1948 was repealed, and Cummings set her space dreams aside to become a fighter pilot. She petitioned to fly the F/A-18 Hornet, a premier fighting jet. Her request was granted, and she finished her master's degree in astronautical engineering six months early, in 1994. Her excitement initially blinded her to the backlash of the repeal. She was chastised by her male classmates, who accused her of not earning her position, even though, as a top-ranked student in flight school, the only thing that had stood between her and an F/A-18 assignment was the exclusion law.

Cummings reported to Jacksonville, Florida, to join her new squadron, VFA-106. Early on in her training, one woman died in an accident after a botched landing on a carrier. The incident shocked the squadron and was held up as evidence that women were not fit to fly fighter aircraft. The environment in Jacksonville became more hostile, and the squadron's ready room was plastered with antiwomen posters and articles. Though the exclusion law had been repealed, whether women belonged in combat was still an active debate within the military at the time; integration was still in its earliest stages, and many seemed to think that the decision could be reversed.

In 1995, Cummings was asked to report to a body called the Field Naval Aviator Evaluation Board (FNAEB), which heard testimony about her piloting and social abilities from the pilots in her squadron. They told the board that Cummings was "aggressive" and did not "fit in." The FNAEB recommended dismissing her from the squadron. With the endorsements of a number of allies, Cumming appealed the ruling. At the same time, she was undergoing surgery for a tumor on her ovary, and she has described the ordeal as one of the lowest points in her life. She was redeemed by a higher board that declared the FNAEB decision invalid and wiped it from her record. But in a strange effort to punish her superiors for their mistreatment of her, she was sent back to the same squadron in Jacksonville. She returned to treatment so inhospitable that she tendered her resignation soon after.

The US Navy issued a statement saying that Cummings's case was a lamentable example of "professional distancing"—in other words, she had been intentionally ostracized by many of the men, including her superiors, within her own squadron. Officially, the incident was chalked up to the growing pains of integrating the sexes. Still, her reputation was effectively shattered; the false testimony of her peers, including one statement about her love of bubble baths, later appeared in another book about fighter pilots during that era. Cummings finished her career in the navy as a Reserve Officers' Training Corps (ROTC) instructor at Pennsylvania State University.

UNMANNED AERIAL VEHICLES

After leaving the navy, Cummings earned a PhD in systems engineering from the University of Virginia in 2003 and went on to pursue a career in research. As the majority of naval crashes are the result of human error, Cummings seeks to develop systems that are more intuitive, more precise, and more autonomous—meaning they would rely on error-prone humans as little as possible. "I'm not trying to take automation and replace humans," she told Karen Weintraub for the *Boston Globe* (21 Jan. 2013). "My research is how to develop collaborative systems so that automation is enabling people to do their jobs better." If a system is capable of performing certain skilled tasks, such as a military drone operating the zoom on a camera, then operators are free to perform knowledge-based tasks or any task that involves uncertainty or the unpredictable, such as accurately identifying a target. For many, the word *drone* connotes a military weapon, but in reality the term can be applied to any flight-capable object that is controlled remotely and can be switched to some form of autonomous flight.

HUMANS AND AUTOMATION LAB

Cummings is the director of the MIT Humans and Automation Lab (HAL), which she founded in 2004. "I realized . . . that technology was quickly outpacing human abilities, and that dedicated research was needed in the joint space between humans and automation," she told *Laboratory News* (1 Sept. 2010). At HAL, Cummings looks at the design of the technology and the mind of the system's operator to strengthen the relationship between human and machine. As an engineer, she has developed machines that are easier to use, and as a researcher, she has studied ways to circumvent the most common human errors that lead to accidents and mistakes.

Working in conjunction with the Seattle-based company Boeing and the US Office of Naval Research in Washington, DC, Cummings and her team of graduate and undergraduate MIT students developed a small UAV that can be piloted by a smartphone. The goal of the project was to make a device that is easy to use and requires minimal training. The iPhone UAV has more intuitive controls; a pilot need only tilt the phone in the direction he or she wants the UAV to move. According to Cummings, "pilots" can be trained to fly the UAVs with less than three minutes of instruction. The device, which is not widely available, is little more than an app and uses the iPhone's existing GPS technology. The military currently spends millions of dollars training drone operators, but Cummings asserts that anyone, for good or ill, can pilot a drone.

Even when UAVs are easy to use, there are a number of human factors that complicate their operation, including stress, distraction, and boredom. The latter in particular has been a serious problem for people such as pilots of commercial airplanes, nuclear power plant operators, and, perhaps most chillingly, UAV pilots in the military. "UAV pilots get very bored," Cummings told *Laboratory News*, "especially when they loiter for hours watching a target below." To combat this problem, Cummings and her team look for ways to keep operators engaged. In one experiment, her team gathered a group of drone pilots, gave them personality tests, and recorded video of them performing simulated missions in four-hour shifts. The simulation required human input only 5 percent of the time—similar to an actual drone mission, in which long periods of inactivity are punctuated by short bursts of activity. Cummings and her group found that pilots were performing more tasks than they needed to in an effort to stay alert. The personality test yielded stranger results; Cummings found that while those pilots who scored as the most conscientious stayed the most alert, they were also the ones who hesitated the most about firing their weapon. The goal of the investigation is to create optimal conditions for patience and performance.

ETHICAL IMPACT OF UAV TECHNOLOGY

Cummings also studies the ethical implications of living in what Jefferson Morely, in an article for *Salon* (3 Apr. 2012), called "a surreal moral universe." For military drone pilots, even the smallest mistake can be a deadly mistake, though this is not reflected in their surroundings. The experience is strangely akin to playing video games in a darkened basement; pilots report to trailers in the Nevada desert for shifts that can last as long as twelve hours.

With drones, the military has found a technology that keeps men and women out of combat, but drone pilots seem to be exhibiting similar levels of post-traumatic stress as their colleagues on the ground. "You shoot a missile, you kill a handful of people," Cummings told Morely, "and then, this is what is strange, you go home. Your shift is over. You get in your car and drive thirty minutes to the northern suburbs of Las Vegas and you mow the lawn, talk to your kids, you go to church." Unsurprisingly, Morely reported that as of 2012, retention rates for drone pilots were low. UAV technology in warfare is not a completely new concept, but for cost and security reasons, it is becoming more prevalent. Through her multifaceted research, Cummings hopes to allow for more control over this burgeoning field.

Cummings has a young daughter and lives in Cambridge, Massachusetts. She was pleased to discover that there is an Australian racing horse named Missy Cummings in her honor.

SUGGESTED READING

Bettex, Morgan. "In Profile: Missy Cummings." *MIT News.* MIT, 5 Apr. 2010. Web. 9 Aug. 2013.

Cummings, Missy. "As Era of Drones Takes Off, She's at the Controls." Interview by Karen Weintraub. *Boston Globe.* New York Times, 21 Jan. 2013. Web. 9 Aug. 2013.

Cummings, Missy. *Hornet's Nest: The Experiences of One of the Navy's First Female Fighter Pilots.* San Jose: Writer's Showcase, 1999. Print.

Hoshaw, Lindsey. "The Sky's the Limit." *Boston Globe.* New York Times, 18 July 2011. Web. 9 Aug. 2013.

Morely, Jefferson. "Boredom, Terror, Deadly Mistakes: Secrets of the New Drone War." *Salon.* Salon Media Group, 3 Apr. 2012. Web. 9 Aug. 2013.

—*Molly Hagan*

Kaley Cuoco-Sweeting

Born: November 30, 1985
Occupation: Actor

Kaley Christine Cuoco-Sweeting is an actor who began her career at a young age and transitioned to adult roles in film and television, eventually becoming a fixture on prime time television. Just before turning eighteen, she won the Teen Choice Award for choice female TV breakout star in 2003 for her work in the sitcom 8 *Simple Rules.* After that series ended, Cuoco-Sweeting landed the role of Penny in the popular CBS sitcom *The Big Bang Theory,* which premiered in 2007. In 2013, she hosted the Academy of Television Arts and Sciences Hall of Fame gala, which honored inductees such as Ron Howard and Leslie Moonves. After five years with Queen Latifah at the helm, Cuoco-Sweeting took over as the host of the fan-driven People's Choice Awards for both 2012 and 2013.

For her increasingly creative portrayal of the vibrant Penny in *The Big Bang Theory,* Cuoco-Sweeting also tied for the Critics' Choice Television Award for best supporting actress in a comedy series in 2013 and took home the favorite comedic TV actress award at the People's

Jon Kopaloff/FilmMagic

Choice Awards ceremony in 2014. Commenting on the success of *The Big Bang Theory,* Cuoco-Sweeting told Lynette Rice for *Entertainment Weekly* (21 Sept. 2012), "Every week is different! That's what makes it fun to read each new script. The writers just don't know."

Still in touch with her acting roots in television commercials, Cuoco-Sweeting began appearing in advertisements for Priceline in 2013; she played William Shatner's daughter. The company was seeking to appeal to a younger audience than the octogenarian could reach.

EARLY LIFE AND CAREER

Cuoco-Sweeting was born to Gary Cuoco, a real estate agent, and Layne Ann Wingate, a stay-at-home mom, on November 30, 1985, in Camarillo, California. Her father is of Italian descent; the name Cuoco means *cook* in Italian. Her mother's ancestors are German and English. She has a younger sister, Briana, who has made a guest appearance on *The Big Bang Theory.* Cuoco-Sweeting's first screen appearances occurred when she was still a child and she also began modeling. Starting at age six, she starred in several commercials for Barbie dolls and appeared in an advertisement for Oscar Mayer products. According to Cuoco-Sweeting, her parents encouraged her to maintain a balanced lifestyle. About her well-rounded youth, she told Erin Bried for *Self* (Jan. 2013), "When I was growing up, my parents' rule was don't do just one thing. So if I was auditioning, I had to play tennis or go to art camp, too." Cuoco-Sweeting, who graduated with her diploma at sixteen, was homeschooled on the set and never attended a traditional high school.

Cuoco-Sweeting's first movie appearance was in the 1992 made-for-television film

Quicksand: No Escape, with Donald Sutherland and Tim Matheson. In 1994 she had guest appearances on television shows such as *Northern Exposure* and *My So-Called Life*. On the latter, she played a younger version of lead character Claire Danes, a role that cemented her love of acting. As she told Carita Rizzo for *Variety* (19 Jan. 2012), "It gave me a sense of what it was like to be on a set, and I fell in love with it. I knew it was the life for me." She also notably played a younger version of Ellen DeGeneres on the *Ellen* show in 1996.

In 1995 Cuoco-Sweeting appeared in the action movie *Virtuosity* with Russell Crowe and Denzel Washington. Two years later she had a small role in the romantic comedy film *Picture Perfect*, starring Jennifer Aniston. In 1998 she had a leading role in the television miniseries adaptation of Dean Koontz's novel by the same name, *Mr. Murder*. She then appeared on *Don't Forget Your Toothbrush* and also had a role in the 2000 television movie *Growing Up Brady*, based on the earlier, successful television program *The Brady Bunch*.

8 SIMPLE RULES

Cuoco-Sweeting's first major television series was the 2002 ABC show *8 Simple Rules for Dating My Teenage Daughter*, playing one of two daughters of star John Ritter's character Paul Hennessey. Although Cuoco-Sweeting had been out of work for some time, she was encouraged to audition for the role of the older sister. She was ultimately cast in that role, even though her on-screen younger sister, Amy Davidson, was actually six years her senior. As the rebellious Bridget Hennessey, Cuoco-Sweeting's often flirtatious and lascivious performance became a motif of the show.

The series experienced a tragic setback when Ritter died unexpectedly in 2003. Five weeks after Ritter's death, shooting for the show had resumed with the new title *8 Simple Rules*. Cuoco-Sweeting told *People* (1 Dec. 2003) that the atmosphere on the set was not somber, however, as the actors chose to remember fond times with Ritter: "When you think of John, you can't be sad." She continued, "People are laughing because we'll think of something John would have said or a face he would have made." One year after Ritter's death, the cast gathered at his grave in Forest Lawn, from which the sound stage for *8 Simple Rules* on the Disney/ABC lot can be seen. They also visited Disneyland, one of Ritter's favorite places, having decided that John would want them to enjoy themselves. In 2004 Ritter was nominated posthumously for an Emmy Award for outstanding lead actor in a comedy series, but did not receive the award.

Veteran actors James Garner, Suzanne Pleshette, and David Spade soon joined the cast. However, the show ended in 2005, lost

without Ritter. Cuoco-Sweeting still credits Ritter for his role in helping shape her career and her sense of comedy. Explaining her adoration for the late actor to Frazier Moore for the Associated Press, she said, (14 Nov. 2012), "Working with him showed me that I loved sitcoms." She went on, "I love silliness. That's who I am at heart, and I know I can do it. If my career path takes me elsewhere, that's great. But comedy is my forte."

After *8 Simple Rules* ended, ideas for a spin-off show for Cuoco-Sweeting's character, Billie, did not materialize. Other opportunities did come her way in 2005, however, including some voice-over work for animated features. She returned to television in the final season of *Charmed* (2005–6) and was also cast in the Lifetime movie *To Be Fat Like Me* (2007). Based on the 2003 ABC television news special *Fat Like Me*, the role called for Cuoco-Sweeting to don a fat suit that made her appear to weigh 250 pounds. The film was shot in a high school, and Cuoco-Sweeting had a new experience—people ignored her, refused to make eye contact with her, or made hateful remarks to her. The goal of the film was to increase empathy and awareness of the body image issues of young women.

THE BIG BANG THEORY

In 2007 Cuoco-Sweeting was cast in what would be the biggest role of her career thus far. *The Big Bang Theory*, a half-hour sitcom, debuted on Monday nights in 2007. On it, Cuoco-Sweeting plays Penny, a waitress and hopeful actor living across the hall from two physicists, played by actors Jim Parsons and Johnny Galecki. The latter plays Penny's love interest; the two actors secretly dated off-set for almost two years. The sitcom depicts the unlikely friendship between Penny and the young scientists as they try to relate to each other, deriving comedy from their contrasting backgrounds, social skills, and intellects. As written, Penny is the character with which most viewers can identify; though sometime portrayed as a so-called dumb blonde, the character displays depth and common sense when dealing with her cerebral neighbors. When describing her multidimensional character, Cuoco-Sweeting told Moore, "The producers never made her ditzy. Maybe she doesn't always get what the guys are talking about. But in that way she represents most of the world."

Though the show received mixed reviews from critics when it premiered, it quickly became a hit with audiences, achieving consistently high ratings. It later moved to the Thursday night lineup, which has been a prime slot, especially for sitcoms, since *The Cosby Show*. Thursday is also the biggest day for advertisers. Though never a hit with critics, the show was nominated for best comedy series for the 2011,

2012, and 2013 Emmy Awards; Parsons has won four Emmys for lead actor for his role of Sheldon Cooper.

In its fourth season, *The Big Bang Theory* was television's highest rated comedy. The three stars in the series—Cuoco-Sweeting, Parsons, and Galecki—reportedly earned $200,000 per episode by 2010. Cuoco-Sweeting commented to Rice, "I would be lying if I said I couldn't do Penny with my eyes closed." She added, "It's such second nature to me now. But if I ever do get those moments of 'God, this feels the same,' I just read those articles about how much money I make and think, 'You know, it's not so repetitive anymore!'" Salaries continued to rise; by the end of 2013, the three actors were earning $350,000 per episode. As season eight began production toward the fall of 2014, after tense negotiations, the three had reached an agreement of $1 million per episode for three seasons. With that near tripling of her salary, Cuoco-Sweeting remains one of the highest-paid female actors on television.

FORMULA FOR SUCCESS

Explaining his formula for his successful sitcoms, *The Big Bang Theory*'s cocreator Chuck Lorre, as quoted by Adam K. Raymond in *New York*, said, (4 May 2014), "Stories should be about these characters trying to make it through the day. The obstacles in [their] path—that's where the comedy comes from. You can start any story with the seven deadly sins. We all fall prey to those."

In addition to its Thursday night schedule, being a CBS show has also helped the series; the network is the number one television network. Demographic studies for the show indicate that it is number one (excluding sports) among a range of age groups: teens aged twelve to seventeen, adults aged eighteen to thirty-four, adults aged eighteen to forty-nine, and adults aged twenty-five to fifty-four. Part of the appeal is the pacing of the humor, with an average of over four jokes per minute.

As for Cuoco-Sweeting's role in the cast and in this formula for success, the show's once sole female star is thrilled to be a part of it; during the show's fourth season two additional women were cast as regulars. Describing her gratitude regarding this milestone in her career, Cuoco-Sweeting told Matt Webb Mitovich for *Vegas* magazine (Sept. 2011), "After 8 *Simple Rules*, I didn't think I'd strike gold again, but I did. Now I'm holding on for dear life and enjoying it." Lorre himself has lauded Cuoco-Sweeting's performance and inherent comedic talent. "Kaley is that rare epitome—crazy pretty while also being naturally funny and honest as an actress. . . . Personally, I think we're seeing the beginning of a long and great career," Lorre said, as quoted by Mitovich.

PLAYING AGAINST TYPE

At the same time, like many actors, Cuoco-Sweeting has to fight against being typecast; others sometimes see her only as a bubbly blonde and a comedic actor. This is not her perception, however. As she told Moore regarding *The Big Bang Theory*, "I know this sounds like it's not true . . . but as huge as the show is, it's just part of my life—not my whole life." For example, Cuoco-Sweeting has also worked as a voice actor, providing the voice of characters such as Sam O'Hare in the 2011 animated feature *Hop*.

Getting the role of Stacy Peterson opposite Rob Lowe in a Lifetime movie, *Drew Peterson: Untouchable*, proved challenging. When her agent called casting for the show, the response was not encouraging. Based on a true story, *Drew Peterson* tells the story of a Chicago police officer whose third wife is found dead, a mystery that remains unsolved as Peterson moves on to wife number four, Stacy, who is half his age. She disappears after marrying Peterson, leaving behind her own children as well as Peterson's older children.

Proving the casting folks wrong pleased Cuoco-Sweeting. As she told Rizzo for *Variety* (13 June 2012), "That's why I really wanted to do it. I didn't think anyone thought I could, so it meant a lot to me to be able to play that role." Landing the role moved her further toward her goal of being considered a well-rounded actress. She added, "I need to keep pushing myself because it's easy to get stuck." *Drew Peterson* was the most-viewed made-for-cable movie of 2012, with about six million viewers.

PERSONAL LIFE

Once engaged to addiction specialist Josh Resnik, Cuoco-Sweeting married tennis pro Ryan Sweeting on New Year's Eve 2013 at the Hummingbird Nest Ranch in Santa Susana, California. The two had been dating for only a few months. The theme of the wedding was "fire and ice" and Cuoco-Sweeting wore a pink Vera Wang gown. Her hyphenated last name began appearing on *The Big Bang Theory*'s credits later in January; she is credited as Kaley Cuoco in previous productions as well as in *The Wedding Ringer* and *Burning Bodhi*, two movies due to be released in 2015.

Horseback riding is another one of Cuoco-Sweeting's passions; she began riding horses at age fifteen and has ridden almost daily ever since. After a serious accident in 2010 when she fell off of her horse, she nearly lost her leg, which now has two metal bars above her foot. She was also a nationally ranked amateur tennis player, a sport she began at age three. An animal lover, she sang "Somewhere over the Rainbow" with then-boyfriend Christopher French to raise funds for animal adoption on behalf of the Humane Society. Despite her success, she told Bried, "I judge myself all the time. It takes a huge effort to look this way, and I *still* think I could lose five pounds. . . . [Y]ou wake up some days and feel ugly. When that happens, I accept that I'm not perfect, and it's OK; I can start over again tomorrow."

SUGGESTED READING

Cuoco, Kaley. "*The Big Bang Theory's* Kaley Cuoco: My Theories on Life." Interview by Erin Bried. *Self.* Condé Nast, Jan. 2013. Web. 4 Sept. 2014.

Mitovich, Matt Webb. "Kaley Cuoco's *Big Bang Moment.*" *Vegas.* Niche Media, Sept. 2011. Web. 4 Sept. 2014.

Moore, Frazier. "Kaley Cuoco Gets a Bang out of 'Big Bang Theory.'" Associated Press. Associated Press, 14 Nov. 2012. Web. 22 Aug. 2014.

Raymond, Adam K. "Why Are 23.4 Million People Watching *The Big Bang Theory*?" *New York.* New York Media, 4 May 2014. Web. 12 Aug. 2014.

Rice, Lynette. "'The Big Bang Theory': Making a Bigger Bang." *Entertainment Weekly.* Time, 21 Sept. 2012. Web. 12 Aug. 2014.

Rizzo, Carita. "Cast Confessions: 'The Big Bang Theory' 100th Episode." *Variety.* Variety Media, 19 Jan. 2012. Web. 21 Aug. 2014.

Rizzo, Carita. "Femmes Push Themselves with Out-of-Comfort-Zone Roles: Road to the Emmys 2012; The Actress." *Variety.* Variety Media, 13 June 2012. Web. 21 Aug. 2014.

SELECTED WORKS

Quicksand: No Escape, 1992; *Virtuosity,* 1995; *Growing Up Brady,* 2000; *8 Simple Rules,* 2002–2005; *Charmed,* 2005–2006; *To Be Fat Like Me,* 2007; *The Big Bang Theory,* 2007– ; *Drew Peterson: Untouchable,* 2012

—*Judy Johnson*

Jack Dalrymple

Born: October 16, 1948
Occupation: Farmer and politician

Jack Dalrymple, who served ten years as North Dakota's lieutenant governor, was elected governor of North Dakota in 2012. He first assumed the post in 2010, when Governor John Hoeven resigned to become a US senator. Dalrymple serves as the chair of the National Governors Association Natural Resources Committee and previously served as chair of the North Dakota Trade Office and the Governor's Commission on Education Improvement.

Dalrymple, who enjoyed a long and prosperous career as a farmer before becoming a

Mike Theiler/EPA/Landov

politician, is a dyed-in-the-wool North Dakotan—his family farm in Casselton dates to 1875. The western part of the state is currently in the midst of an oil boom likened in its prosperity to the nineteenth-century gold rush in California. At a time when much of the country is still smarting from the 2008 recession, North Dakota boasts a budget surplus and a shortage of labor, meaning there are too many jobs and not enough people to fill them. Dalrymple acknowledges, however, that prosperity brings its own set of problems. "Everybody needs to realize that we are a unique state in the United States right now. We are a rapidly growing state, unlike almost any other in the nation," he told Kent Brick for *North Dakota Living* magazine (1 Jan. 2013). "Our economy is very strong. We have financial reserves. And we have the lowest unemployment in the United States. That means we have challenges that no other state has right now." He hopes to invest the extra cash in much-needed infrastructure improvements. But Dalrymple's tenure has not been marked only by good problems. Oil exploration in North Dakota has raised a number of environmental and social concerns, and in 2011, the state—whose largest industry is agriculture—was devastated by floods. Most recently, Dalrymple, a staunch Republican, caused political controversy in March 2013, when he signed into law the toughest abortion restrictions in the United States.

EARLY LIFE AND FARMING CAREER

John Stewart Dalrymple III was born on October 16, 1948, in Minneapolis, Minnesota. He was raised at Dalrymple Farm in Casselton, North Dakota, founded as a wheat farm by his great-grandfather in 1875. His father, John Dalrymple Jr., was a successful farmer; his mother's name was Mary. Dalrymple has three sisters named Florence, Susan, and Judy. Describing his childhood, he told Brick, "I grew up on the farm—it was a true farm, rural upbringing. Even though we weren't that far away from Fargo—just twenty miles away in Casselton—we didn't go to Fargo very often. We would work six days a week and on Saturday night, we would stay home at the farm." (He later gave his four daughters a similar childhood on the same farm.) He attended the Blake School in Hopkins, Minnesota, from fourth to eighth grade, and finished his high school education at a boarding school. A longtime hockey player, Dalrymple played on the varsity team at Yale University with current Minnesota governor Mark Dayton. (Dayton also attended the Blake School, though he is a year older.) Dalrymple graduated with honors with a bachelor's degree in American studies in 1970.

After graduation, Dalrymple returned to Casselton. He took up management of the Dalrymple Farm, and in 1983, he was named an Outstanding Young Farmer of the United States by the US Junior Chamber (Jaycees). He served on the Casselton Jobs Development Commission and helped found Share House, Inc., a residential treatment and recovery center for alcoholics and drug addicts, in Fargo. In 1991, he became a founding board chairman of the Dakota Growers Pasta Company. The company's purpose was to add value to durum wheat; farmers bought delivery rights for their wheat to be turned into pasta, which is worth more than raw durum. The company began with 1,100 North Dakota durum wheat producers. "I think that we started our life as a cooperative . . . and that was the right structure for us," Dalrymple told Emily Coleman for the Bismarck Tribune (26 June 2010). The company, one of the nation's largest pasta manufacturers, officially became a corporation in 2004. For his work with the Dakota Growers, Dalrymple earned the Ernst and Young Midwest Master Entrepreneur of the Year Award in 2007. He left his position on the board in 2010. The same year, the company was sold to a Canadian firm for about $240 million. All told, Dalrymple made about $3.8 million from the sale.

POLITICAL CAREER

Dalrymple was elected to the North Dakota state legislature in 1985 and served eight terms, including six years as the chair of the House Appropriations Committee. He had decided to retire from politics when gubernatorial candidate John Hoeven asked him to be his running mate in 2000. Hoeven won, and Dalrymple served as lieutenant governor under Hoeven for ten years. In 2000, North Dakota faced an entirely

different set of problems than it would a decade later. "When I was first elected governor in 2000, we were one of only three states losing population," Hoeven recalled to Nick Smith for the Bismarck Tribune (23 Dec. 2013). "I set out to get the economy going and create jobs." Dalrymple kept out of the spotlight during his three terms as lieutenant governor. Lauren Donovan for the Bismarck Tribune (22 Nov. 2002) observed, "Jack Dalrymple doesn't get his name in the paper much." Donovan went on to note that Dalrymple's role as lieutenant governor was more focused on crafting policy than making public appearances. After all, Hoeven forged the partnership for Dalrymple's extensive agricultural knowledge and legislative experience. "All that moving around, handshaking and ribbon cutting," Dalrymple told Donovan in 2002, "I don't think that's my bag."

After Hoeven won a seat in the United States Senate in 2010, Dalrymple was sworn in as North Dakota's thirty-second governor in December. Dalrymple's ninety-four-year-old mother was present for the swearing-in ceremony. His first act as governor was to appoint US Attorney Drew Wrigley as lieutenant governor. Dalrymple has been popular and widely credited with the state's financial good fortune. He kicked off his campaign for his first full term as governor in 2011, promising to manage the state's abundant resources wisely. (The state surplus currently hovers around $1 billion.) Dalrymple announced plans to spend the money on public safety and housing, both urgent issues as North Dakota's population is stretched to its limits. His opponent in the race was Ryan Taylor, a Democrat and state senator. Dalrymple defeated Taylor, 63 percent to 34 percent. Returning to office, he retained a large portion of Hoeven's staff.

FLOOD EMERGENCY

When Dalrymple took over Hoeven's term in 2011, he was immediately confronted with historic flooding in the city of Minot and the Souris River Valley. That winter, there was record snowfall in the Rocky Mountains and the Northern Plains states. Spring came late, and the snow melted rapidly and, compounded by the unusually high rainfall that year, caused devastating floods in central North Dakota, including in Minot, North Dakota's fourth-largest city. Based on early reports for the season, Dalrymple declared a flood emergency in February, and the Souris River damaged some three to four thousand homes—around eight hundred of them beyond repair—in Minot in late May. Many residents blamed the US Army Corps of Engineers. The engineers that managed the Garrison Dam were forced, for the first time ever, to open the dam's spillway gates to release floodwaters due to the unprecedented runoff. Residents had less than a week to evacuate.

NORTH DAKOTA OIL BOOM

The western part of North Dakota is in the middle—or, according to some estimates, the very beginning—of a massive oil boom. It began in earnest in 2009, and the state has not been the same since. At the center of the boom is the Bakken shale deposit. Its location—two miles below ground in northwestern North Dakota—has been known for decades, but new technology has allowed access to the oil and an economic payoff unlike any North Dakotans have seen before. In an incredibly short period of time, the state has been completely transformed. Clay Jenkinson wrote for the *Bismarck Tribune* (18 Nov. 2012), "Wages are up. Land values are up. The long nightmare of rural decline and outmigration has not only been halted, but reversed in a breathtaking way." North Dakota has experienced oil booms in the past, but this one is significant because oil is selling high, and methods such as hydraulic fracking are yielding unprecedented amounts of it.

The boom is regulated by the North Dakota Industrial Commission, which is composed of Dalrymple, the state attorney general, and the agriculture commissioner. Regulation is difficult, as the state produces more than one million barrels of oil a day—more than any other state except Texas. Environmental and social concerns about such methods as fracking are more prevalent elsewhere than they are in North Dakota. Dalrymple is a firm supporter of fracking and, additionally, has called on the administration of President Barack Obama to approve the proposed Keystone XL oil pipeline, which would run past the southwest corner of the state and to which the state could build a feeder pipeline.

EFFECTS OF THE BOOM

Since the beginning of the oil boom, tens of thousands of people—mostly young men—have flocked to the state, and local populations have exploded. In Watford City, Ken Barcus reported for National Public Radio (29 Jan. 2014), the census counted about 1,500 residents in 2010. By early 2014, Watford's population was over 10,000. The increase in traffic is taking its toll on North Dakota's roads (many are literally crumbling under the weight of trucks transporting oil and equipment), social services, and longtime residents. The scarcity of resources despite the influx of cash has brought with it unusual and often dangerous consequences. Jude Sheerin and Anna Bressanin for the BBC (12 Mar. 2014) noted that some oil workers with no degree and little to no experience can nevertheless expect to make more than six figures. Still, many are living in so-called "man camps" due to the lack of affordable or available housing. Runaway prices on everything from groceries to rent are making life in the geographically isolated boomtowns difficult.

Crime rates have also skyrocketed. Drug-related crimes and assault are common, as are domestic abuse and sexual assault. The latter crimes have been attributed to the disproportionate ratio of males and females in boomtowns. Sheerin and Bressanin reported that men often outnumber women ten to one. The frantic pace of life in the oil rush is wearying for some. "We need something now so these people can keep a job. . . . They want a life, not a gold rush," resident Florenda Holen told Brian Gehring for the *Bismarck Tribune* (22 Aug. 2013).

RESTRICTING ABORTION

Dalrymple, who governs a deeply red state, has other issues on his agenda as well. In 2013, Dalrymple signed into law three bills that banned most abortions in North Dakota. The bills were nationwide news, and a group called Stand Up for Women organized a protest outside the state capitol in Bismarck in March to try to stop Dalrymple from signing them into law. Rallies also took place in Fargo, Grand Forks, and Minot. The three bills, which are being challenged in the state court, ban abortions after the point where a fetal heartbeat can be detected—as early as six weeks into a pregnancy, if invasive transvaginal ultrasounds are used. Dalrymple acknowledged that the laws are efforts to test the limits of *Roe v. Wade*, the 1973 Supreme Court decision legalizing abortion prior to about twenty-four weeks of pregnancy—the point where a fetus is viable outside the womb. "Although the likelihood of this measure surviving a court challenge remains in question, this bill is nevertheless a legitimate attempt by a state legislature to discover the boundaries of *Roe v. Wade*," Dalrymple said, as quoted by John Eligon and Erik Eckholm for the *New York Times* (26 Mar. 2013).

Dalrymple was named the chair of the National Governors Association's Natural Resources Committee in October 2013. Dalrymple married Betsy Wood in 1971. They have four grown daughters and live in Casselton.

SUGGESTED READING

Barcus, Ken. "Oil Boom: See a Modern-Day Gold Rush in Motion." *National Public Radio.* NPR, 29 Jan. 2014. Web. 14 Apr. 2014.

Brick, Kent. "Gov. Jack Dalrymple, First Lady Want Us to 'Create the Future.'" *North Dakota Living.* NDAREC, Jan. 2013. Web. 9 Apr. 2014.

Coleman, Emily. "How Dakota Growers Pasta Came to Be Sold." *Bismarck Tribune.* Bismarck Tribune, 26 June 2010. Web. 13 Apr. 2014.

Donovan, Lauren. "Lieutenant Governor High on His Low Profile." *Bismarck Tribune.* Bismarck Tribune, 22 Nov. 2002. Web. 13 Apr. 2014.

Eligon, John, and Erik Eckholm. "New Laws Ban Most Abortions in North Dakota." *New York Times*. New York Times, 26 Mar. 2013. Web. 9 Apr. 2014.

Gehring, Brian. "After the 'Gold Rush.'" *Bismarck Tribune*. Bismarck Tribune, 22 Aug. 2013. Web. 13 Apr. 2014.

Jenkinson, Clay. "The 2012 Election in ND: A Resounding Endorsement of Oil Development." *Bismarck Tribune*. Bismarck Tribune, 18 Nov. 2012. Web. 13 Apr. 2014.

Sheerin, Jude, and Anna Bressanin. "North Dakota Oil Boom: American Dream on Ice." *BBC News*. BBC, 12 Mar. 2014. Web. 14 Apr. 2014.

Smith, Nick. "How the Governor Spends His Time." *Bismarck Tribune*. Bismarck Tribune, 23 Dec. 2013. Web. 13 Apr. 2014.

—*Molly Hagan*

AFP/Getty Images

Aliko Dangote

Born: April 10, 1957
Occupation: Business magnate

Aliko Dangote, a Nigerian business magnate, is the richest person in Africa. *Forbes* magazine ranked him forty-third on its annual list of the world's richest people in March 2013; by December 2013 his personal fortune was worth $22 billion. His conglomerate Dangote Group manages eighteen subsidiaries, with plants that refine sugar, mill flour, process salt, and produce cement. Dangote Cement is the group's most successful subsidiary; with operations in eight countries, it is sub-Saharan Africa's largest cement manufacturer. The year 2013 was a busy and lucrative one for Dangote, who announced plans to build new cement plants in Kenya and Niger as well as a $9 billion private petroleum refinery in Nigeria.

Nigeria is one of the world's biggest exporters of crude oil, but its state-run refineries are inadequate and the country must import most of its fuel. The Nigerian government pays subsidies to those importers to keep fuel costs artificially low. Officials tried to remove the subsidy in 2012, but the move sparked violent protests after fuel prices doubled, literally overnight. The subsidy was quickly reinstated, but it was later discovered that the Nigerian government had lost an estimated $6.5 billion in 2012 in a fuel subsidy scam. Corruption in Nigeria is common, particularly in conjunction with its oil. In an article for the *Wall Street Journal* (27 Dec. 2013), Drew Hinshaw cites the Economist Intelligence Unit, which reported that Nigeria has received $1.3 trillion in oil revenue since 1980—yet a majority of Nigerians live in grinding poverty,

in some areas on less than one dollar a day. The government claims that nearly one-sixth of its total output, or 400,000 barrels of oil a day, are "pilfered from pipelines by bandits," Hinshaw wrote. "Most of the stolen crude is loaded onto barges at night and shipped abroad." Nigerian President Goodluck Jonathan and Dangote have expressed the hope that the projected plant will turn the country's fortunes around. If it is built, it will be the largest of its kind in Africa. According to Dangote, it would also quintuple his wealth, making him one of the five richest people in the world.

Given Nigeria's turbulent business climate over the years, Dangote's sustained success is impressive. He began making money during the country's cement armada of the 1970s and expanded the Dangote Group against the backdrop of three separate military coups in the 1980s and 1990s. He is unapologetic about his own ambitions. According to William Wallis for *Financial Times* magazine (11 Oct. 2013), Dangote one day hopes to become the richest man in the world. Based on his dominance in the Nigerian marketplace, he told Wallis, soon "his companies will be contributing as much as 10 percent of Nigeria's gross domestic product"—which would be, Wallis notes, "proportionately far more than J. D. Rockefeller did for the US economy in his early 20th-century heyday."

Dangote is a complicated figure; he is boastful yet self-effacing, breathtakingly ambitious yet outwardly humble. He is held up as the hero of his own success story yet fields accusations that his dominance is due to his cozy relationships with corrupt politicians and his willingness to strong-arm competitors out of the marketplace through predatory pricing. Alexis Okeowo for *Bloomberg Businessweek* (7 Mar. 2013), notes that Nigeria has no antitrust legislation. Dangote has denied those accusations. Businessman Bismarck Rewane, Dangote's friend, defended him in an interview with Okeowo, saying: "Is this economy better off for having Aliko Dangote investing and creating capital? Yes. Is this economy stifled by monopolistic tendencies? Yes, but Aliko has moved from having a monopolistic mind-set to that of a very aggressive competitor."

EARLY LIFE AND EDUCATION

Alhaji Aliko Dangote was born to a wealthy Muslim family on April 10, 1957, in the northern city of Kano, Nigeria. His ancestors have a long history of business success in West Africa. His maternal great grandfather, Alhassan Abdullahi Dantata, built a prosperous business importing kola nuts from Ghana and shipping groundnuts from Nigeria during the first half of the twentieth century. Groundnuts, or peanuts, were a major export for Nigeria until the discovery of oil in the 1950s; when Abdullahi died in 1955, he was reportedly the wealthiest man in Nigeria. He passed the business down to Dangote's grandfather, Alhaji Sanusi Dantata, who gave Dangote the name Aliko, which means "the victorious one who defends humanity." Dangote's mother, Sanusi's daughter, is Mariya Dantata, and his father, Mohammed Dangote, was a businessman. Business, Dangote told Okeowo of his family, is "in our blood." But he has been careful to point out that his own success is self-made. "I started everything by myself through hard work and didn't inherit a dime," he told Okeowo. Dangote received an inheritance when his father died in 1965, but he donated it to charity. After his father's death Dangote's grandfather and maternal uncle, Usman Amaka Dantata, became the paternal figures in his life.

When Dangote was eight years old, he sold boiled sugar sweets to his primary school classmates. He went on to study business at Al-Azhar University in Cairo, Egypt, and graduated in 1977. He started his first business with a $3,000 loan—worth about 500,000 Nigerian naira—from his uncle. Dangote traded food products, and he was able to pay back the loan within six months. Beyond this anecdote, there are various accounts about the early days of Dangote's trading business. He procured a government import license and entered the cement business in the mid-to-late 1970s during an incident that became known as Nigeria's "cement armada." The country was enjoying an oil boom, and the government ordered the import of sixteen million metric tons of cement for development projects with the revenues. The amount of cement needed was wildly overestimated and ships weighted with cement clogged the Lagos harbor for years.

Some sank because of their cargo, while others were awarded huge demurrage fees as compensation for the wait; of course, plenty of people took advantage of the fees, parking their boats in line just to receive payment. According to Tim Cocks for Reuters (11 Sept. 2012), Dangote bought trucks and began a transportation firm, importing goods in bulk, including cement.

DANGOTE GROUP

After reinvesting the profits of his successful trading outfit, Dangote was able to begin manufacturing. His conglomerate, Dangote Group—with interests in sugar, flour, salt, textiles, real estate, cement, oil, and gas—was born in 1981. Part of Dangote's success through turbulent times has been in his diversification. When the market was flooded with cement, Dangote had other basic commodities to turn to. In 1997, Dangote Group began producing pasta, salt, sugar, and flour. His sugar refinery in Lagos became the second largest in the world. Dangote himself lived for a time in Atlanta, Georgia, and returned to Nigeria with plans to begin manufacturing cement in 1998.

In 2000, after the 1999 election of Olusegun Obasanjo, Nigeria's government privatized Benue Cement Company (BCC), a defunct, state-owned cement company in Gboko in Benue state. Dangote invested in the company and expanded its operations, increasing its capacity from 900,000 tons per year to three million metric tons per year. Over the next ten years, Dangote expanded his cement production across the region. His Obajana Cement in Kogi state is the largest cement plant in sub-Saharan Africa. Obajana has a capacity of over five million metric tons annually. In 2010, Dangote Group acquired a controlling stake in a South African company called Sephaku Cement. Plans have been underway to construct plants in Iraq and Burma.

Dangote Cement was listed on the Nigerian Stock Exchange in 2010. Dangote announced plans to list 20 percent of the company on the London Stock Exchange in 2014, pricing it so that the company's value would be between $35 and $40 billion. If he pulls it off, it would make Dangote Cement the world's top cement firm and Africa's top stock.

AN INFLUENTIAL CONGLOMERATE

Dangote Group wields extraordinary power in Nigeria, which is Africa's second largest economy. According to Cocks, its annual turnover contributes nearly one percent of the country's gross domestic product (GDP). The conglomerate employs 26,000 Nigerians, and Dangote's publicly traded subsidiaries account for 30 percent of Nigeria's stock exchange. In 2013, those companies made $1 billion by September—a 43 percent increase from 2012. This meteoric rise is exciting but also troubling. In an opinion piece for the Lagos-based *Vanguard* (9 Jan. 2014), Is'haq Modibbo Kawu asks if such growth can sustain itself and ultimately pull the 112.5 million Nigerians living in poverty up into the middle class. Dangote—and a small, thriving class of Nigerian billionaires—has benefited from Nigeria's largely unregulated marketplace, making most of his money after the country's transition to civil rule. But according to Kawu, who cites the Nigerian Bureau of Statistics, most Nigerians have only gotten poorer: in 2004, 54.4 percent of Nigerians lived in poverty; in 2010, that number rose to 69 percent.

The frustration of many Nigerians is palpable. Kawu wrote about violence, crime, and drug use among the disillusioned and mostly unemployed ranks of the poor. Criticizing *Forbes*'s celebration of Dangote and others, Kawu wrote: "So the uber-capitalist magazine, *Forbes* has again revealed the nature of the society that is being built in Nigeria. When these annual reports began coming out a couple of years ago, it became clear that we have arrived at a new pass in Nigeria, the pass of the fetishism of money and the lionizing of the super rich."

POLITICAL CONNECTIONS AND MARKET CONTROL

Dangote supported his friend Olusegun Obasanjo in his successful bid for the presidency in 1999. After taking office, Obasanjo provided Dangote with exclusive import rights to cement, sugar, and rice. In a 2007 diplomatic cable that appeared on the WikiLeaks website in 2011, Brian Browne, then US consul general in Lagos, suggested that Dangote was given preferential treatment in exchange for funding Obasanjo's re-election campaign in 2003. "It is no coincidence that many products on Nigeria's import ban lists are items in which Dangote has major interests," Browne wrote, as quoted by Cocks. Dangote dismissed the cable, telling Cocks in response: "[Dangote Group has] been close to almost all the presidents that have passed." He added, "We have never taken advantage . . . and we were not even always treated fairly."

In the same interview Dangote also referred to his relationships with Nigeria's military dictators preceding President Obasanjo, among them Muhammadu Buhari (1983–85), Ibrahim Babangida (1985–93), and Nigeria's most controversial ruler, Sani Abacha (1993–98). (When Abacha died of a heart attack in 1998, Nigerians celebrated, calling it a "coup from heaven.") Dangote is a member of President Jonathan's economic management team and sits on Nigeria's job creation committee. In November 2011, Jonathan awarded Dangote the Grand Commander of the Order of the Niger, the country's second-highest honor. Dangote is the first nongovernment figure to receive the distinction.

According to numerous accounts, Dangote has no problem wielding his economic power to frighten his competitors. In 2010, one of Dangote's biggest rivals, the French multinational company Lafarge, opened a packing plant in Ogun state and Dangote dropped his prices for a few weeks, just enough to make his competitor squirm. He also admitted that he crashed the price of sugar when Sani Abacha's children entered the market. "Not because of wickedness," he told Wallis. "It was part of business." In 2012 and 2013, Dangote sued Dangote Cement competitor Cletus Ibeto, claiming that Ibeto's company received illegal tax breaks. According to Okeowo, however, Dangote himself has received a five-year tax holiday, unlike many of his competitors.

DANGOTE'S ROLE IN NIGERIA'S FUTURE

Nigeria's population is exploding, but there are a number of factors—political instability, corruption, a crumbling infrastructure, chronic housing and fuel shortages, and mass unemployment, to name a few—that prevent it from attaining its projected mantle as one of the world's largest economies. "When you look at most of what we're consuming today, these are things that are being imported," Dangote told Okeowo. Nigeria's population is predicted to crack 200 million by 2020. "We want to make sure that our people are self-sufficient in terms of producing more," Dangote said. "The market is there for us to take, but the production is not there." With this in mind, Dangote announced plans in December 2013 to invest $16 billion into Nigeria's infrastructure within the next five years. It is a risky move, but one that Dangote believes will yield big dividends—for himself as well as for Nigeria as a whole.

The idea of a Nigerian businessman rebuilding Nigeria has captured the nation's popular imagination; Dangote's success has become popular lore. Author Peter Anosike published a book called *Dangote's Ten Commandments of Money: Lessons on How to Make Money from One of the World's Richest Men* in 2011, and there is a Nigerian pop song called "Aliko Dangote Special."

PERSONAL LIFE

As a philanthropist, Dangote and his Dangote Foundation have given generously to education and social causes in Nigeria. In 2011, he reportedly gave $600 to each person displaced by the widespread violence following the presidential elections that year. In 2013, he announced plans to build a one thousand–bed state-of-the-art hospital wing named after his mother at Murtala Muhammad Specialist Hospital in Kano.

Dangote, who owns various properties around Lagos, has been married twice and has three daughters and five grandchildren, as well as a number of nieces and nephews. He reportedly took his family to Walt Disney World in 2012. It was his first vacation in seventeen years.

SUGGESTED READING

Cocks, Tim. "Special Report: In Nigeria, a Concrete Get-Rich Scheme." *Reuters*. Reuters, 11 Sept. 2012. Web. 10 Jan. 2014.

Hinshaw, Drew. "Africa's Richest Man Bets Big on Oil Refinery." *Wall Street Journal*. Dow Jones, 27 Dec. 2013. Web. 10 Jan. 2014.

Kawu, Is'haq Modibbo. "Nigerian Billionaires and the Nigerian Condition." *AllAfrica: Vanguard*. Vanguard/AllAfrica Global Media, 9 Jan. 2014. Web. 12 Jan. 2014.

Okeowo, Alexis. "Africa's Richest Man, Aliko Dangote, Is Just Getting Started." *Bloomberg Businessweek*. Bloomberg, 7 Mar. 2013. Web. 10 Jan. 2014.

Wallis, William. "Aliko Dangote Africa's Richest Man." *Financial Times*. Financial Times/Pearson, 11 Oct. 2013. Web. 10 Jan. 2014.

—Molly Hagan

Bill de Blasio

Born: May 8, 1961
Occupation: Mayor of New York City

On January 1, 2014, Bill de Blasio took office as the 109th mayor of New York City. For many New Yorkers the election of a progressive Democrat to that office was considered a welcome change after nearly a dozen years of governance by Republican Michael Bloomberg, a multibillionaire who had held the office of mayor for three consecutive terms since his election in 2001. Throughout his campaign, de Blasio emphasized efforts to curb the rising levels of inequality in the city. At a campaign event in Brooklyn, de Blasio asserted, "We are living in a tale of two cities, and ignoring it isn't going to move us forward," as quoted by Edith Honan for Reuters (7 Sept. 2013). During a postprimary lunch, de Blasio commented on his ability to identify and connect with voters: "I have displayed already an ability to connect with the people. . . . The sweep of our victory in the primary across all sorts of demographics says that something got felt. So I hope that what I do, what I say, who I am, is something that people can connect with," as quoted by John Cassidy for the *New Yorker* (27 Sept. 2013). De Blasio continued, noting that the primary results demonstrate how New York City voters "wanted leadership that connected to their reality. . . . They wanted leadership that could relate to them."

It is not only New York City residents who are waiting to assess the changes the de Blasio administration might bring. "Liberals across the country are looking to Bill de Blasio . . . to morph New York City's municipal machinery into a closely watched laboratory for populist theories of government that have never before been enacted on such a large scale," Michael M. Grynbaum wrote in an article for the *New York Times* (31 Dec. 2013). "The elevation of an assertive, tax-the-rich liberal to the nation's most prominent municipal office has fanned hopes that hot-button causes like universal prekindergarten and low-wage worker benefits—versions of which have been passed in smaller cities—could be aided by the imprimatur of being proved workable in New York."

FAMILY BACKGROUND AND CHILDHOOD

The youngest of three sons, Bill de Blasio was born on May 8, 1961, in Manhattan to Warren Wilhelm and Maria de Blasio Wilhelm. His name at birth was Warren Wilhelm Jr., and he was often called Bill or Billy by his family and childhood friends. Both branches of the family highly valued education. The son of a Harvard-educated author, de Blasio's father graduated with honors from Yale in 1939 and subsequently earned a master's degree in economics from Harvard. His mother was one of two students of Italian descent to graduate from the Smith College in 1938, a time when discrimination against Italian Americans was common.

De Blasio's father volunteered for military service in 1942 and lost his leg in the Battle of Okinawa, one of the fiercest battles of World War II. His mother served at the Office of War Information and later penned the book *The Other Italy: The Italian Resistance in World War II* (1988). De Blasio's parents met before the war while both were working at *Time* magazine—he as a business reporter and she as a researcher—and they married after Warren returned from combat.

In 1950 de Blasio's parents were both caught up in Joseph McCarthy's Red Scare and were investigated for alleged communist sympathies. These allegations hampered Warren's government career trajectory, and he soon entered the private sector. He ultimately became Texaco's chief international economist, but embittered by the accusations against him and the loss of his limb during the war, he descended gradually into alcoholism.

A few years after de Blasio was born, the family moved to Cambridge, Massachusetts, so that his father could accept a job at Arthur D. Little Inc., a consulting firm in Boston.

With their marriage deteriorating because of Warren's drinking, de Blasio's parents divorced in 1969. De Blasio rarely saw his father after that, and when he was compelled to do so, he tried to visit early in the day, before his father had drunk too much. In 1979, terminally ill with lung cancer, de Blasio's father committed suicide. "[I've had] anger and sadness and very, very powerful personal lessons in terms of how to live life and what not to do," de Blasio explained in an interview with Anna Sale for WNYC News (30 Sept. 2013). "It's tough stuff to make sense of to this day."

EDUCATION

At his high school, Cambridge Rindge and Latin, de Blasio took part in what was called the Pilot School, a less-regimented alternative program located on the Harvard campus. "It was a very collaborative-learning, call-your-teacher-by-their-first-name, sit-on-the-desk-with-bare-feet kind of place," Nora Burns, a fellow classmate of de Blasio, recalled in an interview with Michael Levenson for the *Boston Globe* (30 Sept. 2013). There de Blasio was heavily involved in student government, and Burns explained to Levenson how students "went to Bill to get it done." De Blasio, influenced by the "very progressive grounding" he received in Cambridge, was deeply concerned about social issues at a young age. "Decades before his surprising political success, he was making his mark on a smaller stage, as a student activist in this proudly left-leaning city that helped shape his values," Levenson wrote. "At an age when many of his peers were sneaking into rock concerts, de Blasio was revamping school disciplinary codes, fielding student grievances, and decrying the unequal treatment of minorities."

De Blasio graduated from Cambridge Rindge and Latin in 1979 and enrolled at New York University (NYU), where he majored in metropolitan studies. As in high school he became known for his activism while at NYU. He participated in antinuclear rallies, protested against tuition hikes (even though he had won a full scholarship

and paid no tuition), and demanded that a student be placed on NYU's board of trustees. Once, he was threatened with expulsion for his part in a demonstration at NYU's Bobst Library, but he nevertheless earned the respect of his peers and professors. Ann Meyerson, former director of NYU's metropolitan studies program, in an interview with Greg B. Smith for the *New York Daily News* (6 Oct. 2013), recalled how de Blasio "really stood out as one of the brightest students—very engaged, wanting to do things. . . . He was a star."

After graduating from NYU in 1983, de Blasio petitioned to change his legal name to Warren de Blasio-Wilhelm, a version he had been using informally since high school to honor his mother's family for their role in raising him. (He later shortened his name to its current form, Bill de Blasio, making that second change legal in 2002.)

EARLY CAREER

After graduating de Blasio became part of the Urban Fellows Program for the New York City Department of Juvenile Justice. The highly selective fellowship is aimed at giving aspiring public servants meaningful experience in policy, urban planning, and government operations.

In 1987 de Blasio completed a master's degree at Columbia University's School of International and Public Affairs, where he studied Latin American politics, and he then accepted a job as a political organizer for the Quixote Center, a Maryland-based grassroots organization focused on social justice issues. In that capacity, he traveled to Nicaragua for ten days to help distribute food and medicine during the Nicaraguan Revolution. He ardently supported the Sandinista government at the time—a fact that detractors still bring up to paint him as a radical.

De Blasio then worked as a volunteer coordinator for Democrat David N. Dinkins's 1989 mayoral campaign. After Dinkins won the election, de Blasio worked at city hall as a junior aide before being promoted to the post of assistant for community affairs. (Dinkins would be the last Democratic mayor of New York City until de Blasio himself was elected.) In 1997, during Bill Clinton's presidency, de Blasio served as regional director of the US Department of Housing and Urban Development for New York and New Jersey, where he worked under future New York governor Andrew Cuomo, who was then housing secretary. In 2000 former First Lady Hillary Rodham Clinton, who was vying for a seat in the US Senate, tapped de Blasio to serve as her campaign manager.

ELECTED OFFICE

In 2001, with Clinton victorious in her Senate bid, de Blasio began focusing on his own political career. He was elected to the New York City

Council that year to represent Brooklyn's Thirty-Ninth District, which includes the diverse neighborhoods of Borough Park (home to a large Orthodox Jewish population), Carroll Gardens (a rapidly gentrifying Italian enclave), Gowanus (an industrial zone), and Park Slope (a relatively affluent area with blocks of historic brownstones and a thriving retail and dining scene). He was reelected to two additional terms, in 2003 and 2005, each time by a wide margin. As a city council member, de Blasio earned a reputation as a tireless advocate for tenants' rights, helping pass legislation that prevents landlords from discriminating against those with federal housing subsidies and improving housing services for those living with HIV/AIDS. He was also instrumental in the passage of laws banning housing discrimination based on gender or sexual orientation.

On November 3, 2009, de Blasio defeated Republican candidate Alex Zablocki by a three-to-one-margin to become the public advocate of New York City. As described on the official city website, the post, whose holder is second in power only to the mayor, "serves as a direct link between the electorate and city government, effectively acting as an ombudsman, or 'watchdog,' for New Yorkers by providing oversight for city agencies, investigating citizens' complaints about city services and making proposals to address perceived shortcomings or failures of those services."

Public advocate de Blasio frequently butted heads with Mayor Michael Bloomberg, especially on issues such as education spending and housing policy. Even the relatively liberal *New York Times* sometimes criticized de Blasio for grandstanding or engaging in political opportunism, but Michael Grynbaum and Javier C. Hernández nevertheless praised de Blasio's efforts as public advocate in an August 31, 2013, article for that paper: "Despite a meager budget and a small staff of 40, his office has handled some 20,000 complaints from residents, helping tenants avoid eviction and assisting small-business owners with disputes over utility charges and city fees."

CITY HALL

As the public advocate, de Blasio sometimes addressed contentious causes such as campaign-finance reform, which seemed to have little to do directly with his mission but raised his political visibility greatly. Thus, few were surprised when he announced his intention to run for mayor in January 2013; observers believed he had been readying himself for the city's top office for years. Although early polls placed de Blasio behind several other candidates, he emerged at the head of a crowded field in the Democratic primary, beating such high profile candidates as city council speaker Christine Quinn, former US

representative Anthony Weiner, and former city comptroller Bill Thompson to win the nomination—even without the expected runoff.

Campaigning on a platform that included an expansion of universal prekindergarten education, an end to the New York Police Department's use of controversial stop-and-frisk tactics, and more affordable housing, de Blasio painted a picture of a divided city with a widening income gap between its wealthiest citizens and the rest of its inhabitants. "For all his reliance on his well-worn 'tale of two cities' metaphor, Mr. de Blasio has already united New York," the editorial board for the *New York Times* asserted in an October 26, 2013, article endorsing his candidacy. "Voters across the boroughs support him overwhelmingly. He promises to be a mayor who listens instead of scolds, who calms fears instead of inciting them. If he combines his populist touch with attentive, courageous leadership, he will have earned the city's support; he already has ours."

In the November general election, de Blasio defeated Republican Joe Lhota, the former chair of the Metropolitan Transportation Authority and deputy mayor under Rudolph Giuliani, in a landslide victory, earning more than 73.3 percent of the vote. On January 1, 2014, he was sworn into office by Bill Clinton, with whom he has long maintained ties. In his inaugural address de Blasio declared, "We see what binds all New Yorkers together: an understanding that big dreams are not a luxury reserved for a privileged few, but the animating force behind every community, in every borough. The spark that ignites our unwavering resolve to do everything possible to ensure that every girl and boy, no matter what language they speak, what subway line they ride, what neighborhood they call home . . . has the chance to succeed."

In a Quinnipiac University poll carried out in the month following the inauguration, 53 percent of respondents approved of de Blasio's performance and 67 percent expressed optimism about the next four years.

PERSONAL LIFE

In 1994 de Blasio married Chirlane McCray, an African American woman he met in 1991 while they were both working for the Dinkins administration. McCray, a poet and activist, identified as a lesbian at the time of their meeting but put "aside the assumptions I had about the form and package my love would come in," upon getting to know de Blasio, as she told Linda Villarosa for *Essence* magazine (9 May 2013). "He felt like the perfect person for me," she explained. "For two people who look so different, we have a lot in common. We are a very conventional, unconventional couple." The two have announced their intention to work closely together in city hall, eliciting comparisons to the political partnership forged by Bill and Hillary Clinton.

McCray and de Blasio have two children: a son, Dante, and a daughter, Chiara. With the approval of her father's office, in December 2013 Chiara released a video describing her former struggles with substance abuse and depression. She said, "Getting sober is always a positive thing, and by no means is it easy—it's the hardest thing I've ever done—but it's so worth it." In a public statement released with the video, her parents stated, "As parents, our instinct has been to protect our daughter and privately help her through a deeply personal struggle. . . . But not only has Chiara committed to her own health, she is also committed to helping young people everywhere who face similar challenges."

Although de Blasio had considered remaining in his modest Park Slope home after taking office, security concerns made that impossible, and de Blasio relocated with his family to the mayor's official residence, Gracie Mansion, on the Upper East Side of Manhattan.

SUGGESTED READING

Cassidy, John. "De Blasio: I'll Be a Different Type of Mayor." *New Yorker*. Condé Nast, 27 Sept. 2013. Web. 6 Mar. 2014.

Corasaniti, Nick, and Mark Suppes. "Analyzing de Blasio's Inaugural Address." *New York Times*. New York Times, 1 Jan. 2014. Web. 6 Mar. 2014.

Grynbaum, Michael M. "De Blasio Draws All Liberal Eyes to New York City." *New York Times*. New York Times, 31 Dec. 2013. Web. 6 Mar. 2014.

Hernández, Javier C. "From His Father's Decline, de Blasio 'Learned What Not to Do.'" *New York Times*. New York Times, 13 Oct. 2013. Web. 6 Mar. 2014.

Levenson, Michael. "NYC Mayoral Favorite Bill de Blasio Has Massachusetts Roots." *Boston Globe*. Boston Globe Media Partners, 13 Sept. 2013. Web. 6 Mar. 2014.

Smith, Chris. "The 99% Mayor." *New York*. New York Media, 27 Oct. 2013. Web. 6 Mar. 2014.

—*Mari Rich*

Courtesy of Jeff Dean

outsized and ridiculous attributes and accomplishments. On April Fool's Day in 2007, Google engineers created a website of Dean "facts" that mirror, or parody, those attributed to Norris; however, most of Dean's facts—"Compilers don't warn Jeff Dean. Jeff Dean warns compilers"—are unintelligible to nonprogrammers. Despite its satirical nature, the website was inspired by Dean's reputation as a programming genius.

In 1999 Dean, who had just finished his PhD, decided to join Google, then a fledgling technology company. At the time Google had only about twenty employees. Dean's earliest contributions included MapReduce, BigTable, and Spanner, all of which made Google one of the most innovative companies in Silicon Valley. While the names of the programs are not "ones most Google users associate with the company," Oremus said, they are "the kind that made Google—and, consequently, much of the modern Web as we know it—possible." Dean is now hard at work on a revolutionary project involving "deep learning," with profound implications for technology, science, and business.

Jeffrey Dean

Born: July 23, 1968
Occupation: Computer scientist

As Will Oremus wrote for *Slate* magazine (23 Jan. 2013), engineers at Google consider Jeffrey Dean the Chuck Norris of computer programming, a tongue-in-cheek association with the American martial artist and actor who has become a pop-culture phenomenon credited with

EDUCATION AND EPI INFO

Dean was born on July 23, 1968. He moved around often growing up; as he explained to Edward Z. Yang for *XRDS* magazine (2012), "I went to eleven schools in twelve years in lots of different places in the world." In the early 1980s his father, Dr. Andrew Dean, a physician and computer programmer, was the chairman of the Council of State and Territorial Epidemiologists. (His mother also works in the medical field.) In 1984 Dr. Dean joined the Centers for Disease

Control and Prevention (CDC) and made plans for the creation of a series of programs called Epi-Aids to help epidemiologists track and understand the AIDS epidemic. Meanwhile, Dean was a student at Paideia High School in Atlanta, Georgia. In 1985 he was working as an intern at an insurance company, but he told his father that he wished to be doing more challenging work. He had already expressed an interest in coding, and the elder Dean asked him to create a data-entry program for epidemiologists. In the summer of 1986, the year Dean graduated from high school, he adapted a program he had used to put the game Dungeons & Dragons on a microcomputer, developing a software system used by the CDC.

Dean enrolled in the University of Minnesota to pursue an undergraduate degree in computer science and economics, but he continued to collaborate with his father and another programmer from the CDC named Tony Burton. He traveled to Geneva, Switzerland, home of the Global Programme on AIDS at the World Health Organization (WHO), where he wrote several subsequent versions of Epi Info and created Epi Map. Epi Info was created to handle troves of data, and Dean told Oremus that his version of the software was "26 times faster" than what epidemiologists had previously been using. He graduated summa cum laude in 1990, and before entering the PhD program in computer science at the University of Washington, he spent a year working for the WHO. At the University of Washington, he studied under Craig Chambers, a new professor at the time who now works with Dean at Google. Dean was interested in optimizing compilers—a program that translates source code into object code, which computers can execute. "It was great, a small research group of three or four students and [Chambers]," Dean told Yang. "We wrote this optimizing compiler from scratch, and had fun and interesting optimization work." Optimizing compilers became the subject of Dean's thesis. He earned his PhD in 1996.

DIGITAL EQUIPMENT CORPORATION

After completing his PhD, Dean joined the staff at the Western Research Lab, run by the Digital Equipment Corporation (DEC), in Palo Alto, California. He often collaborated with programmer Sanjay Ghemawat, who worked at another DEC lab a few blocks away. Together they built a compiler for the Java programming language and a system profiler. At the time, DEC, which had its own search engine called Alta Vista, employed some of the brightest minds in the business. According to Steven Levy, the author of the book *In the Plex: How Google Thinks, Works, and Shapes Our Lives* (2011), DEC already had a digital music player comparable to the iPod in development a full two years before Apple. But

the company's products were quickly becoming outmoded. In 1998 Compaq acquired DEC, merging with Hewlett Packard four years later. "DEC labs were going through a bit of a rocky period after the Compaq acquisition," Dean told Cade Metz for *Wired* magazine (8 Aug. 2012), "and it wasn't exactly clear what role research would have in the merged company." So most of those engineers, including Dean, left the company.

Dean went to a start-up called mySimon, a shopping site that offered price comparisons, like a search engine for retail goods, but the work did not interest him. He learned that Urs Hölzle, a computer programmer and a former professor at the University of California, Santa Barbara, had recently joined another start-up called Google. He knew of Hölzle because his graduate adviser at Washington had studied with him, making Hölzle, Metz noted, Dean's "academic uncle." So Dean e-mailed Google looking for a job, and cofounder Larry Page hired him. At the time Google was an unknown entity, but Dean's hiring signaled both the seriousness and the potential of the company. "It was like some basketball team playing in an obscure minor league grabbing a player who was first-round NBA material," Levy wrote. Levy also noted that the feeling was, in many ways, mutual. Dean was supposed to begin work at Google in August of 1999, but he was so excited that he began showing up at Google offices in July after putting in full days at mySimon.

EARLY CAREER WITH GOOGLE

Ghemawat joined the company shortly after his friend Dean, and the two men resumed their collaboration. Dean started out building an ad system for Google, but he quickly moved to what Levy calls the "war room"—a designated area where programmers and other Google employees gathered to tackle software, storage, and other issues. In the late 1990s and early 2000s, the web was growing exponentially, and Google's core search technologies were having trouble keeping up with the sheer volume of information. Star engineers such as Dean recognized that there was a fundamental difference between what Google was doing and what other search engines, such as DEC's Alta Vista, were doing. "Google eclipsed AltaVista in large part because it turned [DEC's] model on its head," Metz explained. "Rather than using big, beefy machines to run its search engine, it broke its software into pieces and spread them across an army of small, cheap machines." But in 2000 the machines were breaking down every few days, and Google instated the "war room" to find a way to support the system.

Where other companies have sought out existing technologies, Google has always opted to create its own, and in 2003 Ghemawat led the team that built the Google File System (GFS), the company's first major breakthrough in storage and indexing. The GFS addressed the fundamental issue of scalability—how could Google continue to accommodate an ever-expanding web? It was a common problem, but Google was the first company to address it "head-on," Sean Gallagher wrote for the technology news website Ars Technica (26 Jan. 2012). The GFS works in tandem with one of Dean's programs called MapReduce. "As Google crawled the world's web pages, grabbing info about each, it could spread this data over tens of thousands of servers using GFS, and then, using MapReduce, it could use the processing power inside all those servers to crunch the data into a single, searchable index," Metz explained. Dean devised another high-capacity storage system called BigTable in 2006 and followed it with Spanner in 2012. Google has replaced the GFS with a program called Colossus, and pieces of MapReduce have been used to create a system called Caffeine.

EXPERIMENTING WITH DEEP LEARNING

Dean's current projects may turn out to be just as revolutionary as the ones he introduced earlier in his tenure. Dean and the research department at Google have been testing the bounds of the artificial intelligence (AI) subfield known as "deep learning." "Deep-learning software attempts to mimic the activity in layers of neurons in the neocortex, the wrinkly 80 percent of the brain where thinking occurs," Robert Hof explained for the *MIT Technology Review* (23 Apr. 2013). "The software learns, in a very real sense, to recognize patterns in digital representations of sounds, images, and other data." The concept has been around for decades, but Google—because of its vast resources and mammoth infrastructure—has been leading the field in deep-learning discovery.

Through deep learning, computers can be "taught" how to recognize patterns in sounds and images. In 2012 Dean and Andrew Ng of Stanford University led a deep-learning experiment in which sixteen thousand computer processors, functioning as a collective network, taught themselves to recognize a cat. As Dean told John Markoff for the *New York Times* (25 June 2012), this was no small feat. The scientists presented the computers with ten million random digital images found on YouTube and let the data speak for itself. "We never told it during the training, 'This is a cat,'" Dean explained to Markoff. "It basically invented the concept of a cat." Like children, the computers learned to identify the animal through repetition. Such technology could lead to improvements in image search, speech recognition (an example of which is Apple's Siri), and machine-language translation—perhaps even a machine modeled

after the human visual cortex or a machine that could teach itself. But Ng and Dean are careful to qualify their successful experiment. "It'd be fantastic if it turns out that all we need to do is take current algorithms and run them bigger," Ng told Markoff, describing a self-teaching machine, "but my gut feeling is that we still don't quite have the right algorithm yet."

APPLYING DEEP LEARNING

In 2013 Google hired Ray Kurzweil, a noted inventor and machine-intelligence futurist, a year after Dean and Ng completed their deep-learning experiment. The Google deep-learning system performed twice as well as any previous deep-learning technology ever engineered. The successful outcome was largely thanks to Dean and his previous work for the company. "Deep learning has . . . benefited from the company's method of splitting computing tasks among many machines so they can be done much more quickly," Hof wrote. He cited Dean's work in making this infrastructure possible. "It vastly speeds up the training of deep-learning neural networks as well, enabling Google to run larger networks and feed a lot more data to them."

The research has already been put to good use. Dean and his team reconfigured Google's Android software based on deep-learning models, resulting in much more accurate speech recognition. With the help of Dean's programming, Google has a steady platform on which to explore the intricacies of deep learning. "Deep learning," Dean told Hof, "is a really powerful metaphor for learning about the world."

PERSONAL LIFE AND PROFESSIONAL RECOGNITION

Dean met his wife, Heidi Hopper, a psychologist, as a freshman at the University of Minnesota. The couple established a computer science and engineering fellowship at the University of Washington—where they both earned PhDs—in 2006. They live in Palo Alto.

Dean is a Google senior fellow, one of the highest-ranking positions at the company. In 2009 he was both elected to the National Academy of Engineers and named a fellow of the Association for Computing Machinery (ACM). In 2012 Dean and his longtime collaborator Ghemawat shared the ACM SIGOPS Mark Weiser Award and the ACM Infosys Foundation Award in the Computing Sciences.

SUGGESTED READING

Gallagher, Sean. "The Great Disk Drive in the Sky: How Web Giants Store Big—And We Mean *Big*—Data." *Ars Technica*. Condé Nast, 26 Jan. 2012. Web. 4 May 2014.
Hof, Robert. "10 Technology Breakthroughs of 2013: Deep Learning." *MIT Technology*

Review. MIT Technology Review, 23 Apr. 2013. Web. 4 May 2014.

Levy, Steven. *In the Plex: How Google Thinks, Works, and Shapes Our Lives*. New York: Simon, 2011. Print.

Markoff, John. "How Many Computers to Identify a Cat? 16,000." *New York Times*. New York Times, 25 June 2012. Web. 12 May 2014.

Metz, Cade. "If Xerox PARC Invented the PC, Google Invented the Internet." *Wired*. Condé Nast, 8 Aug. 2012. Web. 2 May 2014.

Oremus, Will. "The Optimizer: How Google's Jeff Dean Became the Chuck Norris of the Internet." *Slate*. Slate Group, 23 Jan. 2013. Web. 2 May 2014.

Yang, Edward Z., and Robert J. Simmons. "Profile Jeff Dean: Big Data at Google." *XRDS* 19.1 (2012). 69. Print.

—Molly Hagan

Courtesy of Barbara Demick

Barbara Demick

Born: ca. 1957
Occupation: Journalist

Barbara Demick is an award-winning journalist and book author, including the book *Nothing to Envy: Ordinary Lives in North Korea* (2009). Her first book, *Logavina Street: Life and Death in a Sarajevo Neighborhood*, was published in 1996. She has worked for the *Philadelphia Inquirer* and the *Los Angeles Times*, reporting from cities across eastern Europe, the Middle East, and Asia. Demick's work focuses on the stories of individuals and the ordinariness of human life despite extraordinary circumstances. For *Logavina Street*, she wrote about the siege of Sarajevo during the Bosnian War from the perspective of the people living on a single street. Of her intention when writing *Nothing to Envy*—about the former inhabitants of Chongjin, a city in North Korea—she told Scott Martelle for *Publishers Weekly* (26 Oct. 2009), "My point in doing this book was not to write another political book about the rogue regime or why you should fear a North Korean missile." Instead, Demick was driven by two questions, as told to Meehan Crist for the National Book Foundation website in 2010: "What happens to people living in the most totalitarian of regimes? Do they lose their essential humanity?"

Demick's reporting in Asia has earned her awards from Stanford University, the Asia Society, the Overseas Press Club, and the American Academy of Diplomacy. *Nothing to Envy* has been translated into twenty languages and was a finalist for the National Book Award in 2010. The book won the International Book Award on Human Rights in 2012. Demick's work in Sarajevo earned her the George Polk Award and the Robert F. Kennedy Award, and she was a finalist for the Pulitzer Prize in international reporting in 1995.

EARLY LIFE AND EDUCATION

Barbara Demick was born in Ridgewood, New Jersey, in about 1957. She graduated from Ridgewood High School in 1975 and attended Yale University, where she studied nonfiction writing with John Hersey, the legendary author of the book *Hiroshima* (1946), about survivors of the atomic bomb dropped on the Japanese city in 1945. Hersey, who died in 1993, was a Pulitzer Prize–winning novelist and pioneer of new journalism, a style of the 1960s and 1970s that hemmed closely to the narrative rules of fiction. Demick told Crist that she used *Hiroshima* as a model for her book *Nothing to Envy*, though she admitted that she received a lower grade in Hersey's class than she could have earned because she failed to finish her last paper. She was "disorganized" as a college student, she said, and suffered from intense bouts of writer's block. "Hersey told me at the end of the semester to send him something later," Demick told Crist. "If he were still alive, I'd send him the book."

Demick earned a bachelor's degree in economic history in 1982. In 1984, she was among a handful of men and women to receive the prestigious Bagehot Fellowship (now known as the Knight-Bagehot Fellowship) at Columbia University. Recipients of the fellowship spend one year studying economic and business journalism through the school's journalism and business graduate programs. Later in her career, Demick studied Korean at Yonsei University Language Institute in Los Angeles.

BEGINNINGS OF A NEWSPAPER CAREER

Demick began her career as a journalist in 1981 as a city-hall reporter for the now defunct *Hudson Dispatch* in Union City, New Jersey. The paper, which was taken over by its competitor the *Jersey Journal* in 1991, was known for its aggressive coverage of city corruption in the 1970s and early 1980s. Demick left the *Dispatch* in 1983. From 1984 to 1985, the year of her Bagehot Fellowship, Demick worked as an investigative reporter for the *Jersey Journal* and as a business reporter for the *Dallas Times Herald*. She joined the staff of the *Philadelphia Inquirer* in 1986 and, after working a handful of other beats, became a foreign correspondent in Eastern Europe and then the Middle East.

Demick moved to the *Los Angeles Times* in 2001. "There is something to be said for a craft (yes, I'll call it a craft) that requires the writer to be clear, direct, accessible," Demick told Crist of her career writing for newspapers. "This is a discipline. A newspaper article has to be written with the assumption that the reader has no prior knowledge of the subject and all essential information is contained within." Demick would apply these same principles to the writing of her books.

SIEGE OF SARAJEVO

Demick was working in the United States in 1991, the year that the Soviet Union crumbled and left the former Soviet bloc to climb out from under the rubble. The Eastern European countries, unalike but bound together by nearly half a century of Soviet rule, embraced their individual nationalism in different ways. Yugoslavia was made up of six republics, and shortly after the fall of the Soviets, those republics began to pull away from one another and declare their own sovereignty. Bosnia, a diverse republic of Serbs, Croats, and Muslims, declared independence in 1992. Ethnic unrest in the regions that make up the former Yugoslavia can be traced to ancient times, and without the stifling oppression of the Soviets, old hatreds resurfaced with a vengeance. Serb nationalists wanted to form their own republic, and with the support of President Slobodan Milošević in Serbia, set out to eradicate the entire Muslim population from the land that they had claimed. This directive precipitated Europe's worst genocide since the Holocaust. Beginning in 1992 and then continuing for three and a half years, Serb nationalists held the capital city of Sarajevo under siege.

"A whole generation of war correspondents cut their teeth covering Bosnia," Demick wrote in an article about the siege for the London *Guardian* (3 Apr. 2012) twenty years later. "It was so difficult to get in and out of Sarajevo that a huge press corps simply moved into the Holiday Inn and became part of the story." One of those reporters was Demick, who arrived in Bosnia in January 1994 with a photographer named John Costello. (The Holiday Inn became a target for attacks and was constantly peppered with mortar shells. Demick was never hurt, though she is still haunted by the sound of explosions.) She had been a foreign correspondent for only a few months, but her editors at the *Inquirer* wanted her and Costello to cover the siege from a human perspective. The editors made a suggestion: what if they chose a street in the city and profiled the people who lived there?

THE RESIDENTS OF LOGAVINA STREET

Demick immediately set her sights on a beautiful street called Logavina, and she developed relationships with residents who endured a constant barrage of bullets, food and water shortages, and a lack of heat for three and half years. Among them were Delila Lacevic and her younger brother Berin. Delila was nineteen when Demick first met her in 1994 and had witnessed the gruesome deaths of her parents when the family traveled to a brewery for water in 1993. Mortar shells exploded into the walls of the brewery, sending bricks and shrapnel flying. Berin was taken in by a family in Kansas, and Delila, who was badly injured in the shelling, joined him soon after. Demick later reported that Delila returned to Logavina Street in 2007; she had planned to spend two weeks showing her American husband and mother-in-law where she grew up, but insisted that they return to the United States after five days. There were also several Serbs living on Logavina Street, including Jovan Divjak, who was born in Belgrade but became a general in the Bosnian army. In her book Demick makes clear that the war was really fought between those who believed in a peaceful multiethnic state and those who did not.

At the time of the siege, Sarajevo boasted a population of about five hundred thousand people. The number of Sarajevans who died was placed somewhere between ten and twelve thousand, according to the BBC, with more than sixty thousand citizens wounded. In her review of the 2012 edition of *Logavina Street*, Miriam Laufner wrote for the *DC Spotlight* (3 Sept. 2012), "Logavina Street in 1990s Sarajevo is a microcosm for the question being asked around the globe today, from the still-fragile former Yugoslavia to the European Union to Washington, D.C.: Is it possible to maintain a stable, integrated multiethnic society? Is it, as Demick suggests, even worth fighting for?"

LOGAVINA STREET

In 1995, a ceasefire and then the war's end made it possible for Demick to move out of the Holiday Inn and into an apartment around the corner. Later, she lived with a couple named Jela and Zijo Džino. In her book, Demick describes their marriage and family as "mixed": the husband a Muslim, the wife a Catholic Croat, and their son-in-law a Serb.

Demick wrote a series of articles for the *Inquirer* for which she was named a finalist for the Pulitzer Prize. The articles became the basis for her 1996 book *Logavina Street: Life and Death in a Sarajevo Neighborhood*, which won a number of awards in its own right. Demick returned to Sarajevo several times after the book was published and kept in touch with many of the former residents of Logavina Street. In 2012, on the twentieth anniversary of the beginning of the siege, she published a new edition of the book with an added preface, final chapter, and epilogue. She considered rewriting the entire book—she even told Jon Thurber of the *Los Angeles Times* (16 May 2012) that when she reread the book, she thought some of her writing sounded naïve. "I was shocked by things I perhaps wouldn't find as surprising now; for example, that snipers would target civilians in the middle of Europe while journalists and U.N. peacekeepers looked on." Ultimately, Demick decided to keep the book the same. "My innocence was in fact part of the story and . . . to inject the cynicism of an older reporter wouldn't improve the book," she told Thurber.

REPORTING ON NORTH KOREA

Demick moved to the Middle East as a correspondent for the *Inquirer* in 1997 and joined the staff of the *Los Angeles Times* in 2001, where she was assigned to cover the Korean Peninsula at the newspaper's bureau in Seoul, the bustling capital of South Korea. Demick knew early on that she wanted to write about the everyday lives of people living in North Korea, but it took her some time to find her subjects. North Korea, or the Democratic People's Republic of Korea, was an old ally and beneficiary of the Soviet Union, but the North Korean economy collapsed with the USSR in 1991. Famine killed millions of citizens, and electricity was cut off throughout the entire country.

Demick has written that to look at satellite images of North Korea is to stare into a void. Foreign visitors are hardly ever allowed into North Korea, and when they are, they remain under constant supervision. (Demick was finally granted a visa in 2005, but her visit to Pyongyang gave her little insight into life in the country; she and her colleague were never without their government-mandated chaperones.) North Korea's totalitarian government maintains a viselike grip on all media, and its citizens' access to the Internet is severely limited. As a result, the world outside knows little to nothing about North Koreans, and judging from Demick's book, most North Koreans seem to know less than nothing about life in the outside world.

Demick applied for a visa shortly before President George W. Bush implicated North Korea in his famous "axis of evil" speech in 2002,

but it was already clear that she would not be visiting the country any time soon. "I became obsessed," she told Crist. "I felt if I couldn't get inside their country, I'd get inside their heads." Demick began interviewing North Korean defectors in South Korea, those men and women who escape the regime. Demick considered the fact that defectors might (reasonably) give a skewed account of what life was like in North Korea; after all, defectors risk their own lives, as well the lives of the family members and friends they leave behind, when they flee the country. So, in 2004, Demick decided that she would find defectors who had all lived in the same town, so that she would be in a better position to cross-check their stories and weed out any untruths.

NOTHING TO ENVY

For her focus, Demick chose Chongjin, a large city in North Korea's North Hamgyong Province. During the economic instability of the 1990s in North Korea, many Chongjin citizens died of starvation. Demick interviewed more than thirty former residents of the city over a few years. The stories unfolded over time, she told Zhang Yiqian for the *Global Times* (13 Dec. 2012): "For example, the older woman in the book, Mrs. Song, I knew her for maybe two years before she told me how her son had died from starvation." The resulting narratives were collected and published in a two-part series of articles for the *Los Angeles Times* in 2005.

When Demick decided she wanted to collect the stories in a book, she chose to focus on only six interviewees. One of them, a woman named Mi-ran, was a defector who left her North Korean boyfriend without saying good-bye. Their love story provides a larger framework for the book. "This is not the sort of thing that shows up in satellite photographs," Demick says of the relationship in the book (excerpted by the *New York Times*, 27 Jan. 2010). Most Americans, and outsiders in general, are more concerned about North Korea's nuclear-arms program and its potential threat to other countries than with the everyday lives of North Korean citizens. "They don't stop to think that in the middle of this black hole, in this bleak, dark country where millions have died of starvation, there is also love," she states.

Demick titled her book *Nothing to Envy: Ordinary Lives in North Korea* after a song that North Korean schoolchildren are taught to sing called "We Have Nothing to Envy in This World."

REPORTING IN BEIJING

Demick moved to China to work as a correspondent for the *Los Angeles Times* in 2007. Though she is based in Beijing, China's capital, she prefers to report from the country's rural provinces. In 2009, she traveled to the Guizhou Province to interview women about a child trafficking story on which she was working. What she found surprised her. The resulting story was much more complex than the existing narrative of corrupt government officials stealing children for profit. But complexity is not always so easy to convey, particularly when readers are used to stories with clearly defined good guys and bad guys, Demick told Zhang. "For a news story, it's hard to say this victim is not so innocent and this culprit isn't that guilty."

Demick told Zhang that reporting in China can be tricky. The Chinese government goes out of its way to keep foreign journalists out of the country's affairs even though, on several occasions, according to Demick, the real story ended up showing the government in a positive light. Still, Demick told Zhang, "It's not the journalists' role to praise the government. . . . We are trained to be watchdogs."

In 2010, Demick received the Samuel Johnson Prize for Non-Fiction for *Nothing to Envy*, and in 2011, her book was a finalist for both the National Book Critics Circle Award for nonfiction and the National Book Award for nonfiction. She lives in Beijing with her son, Nicholas.

SUGGESTED READING

Demick, Barbara. "Life and Death on My Street in Sarajevo." *Guardian.* Guardian News and Media, 3 Apr. 2012. Web. 18 Dec. 2013.

Demick, Barbara. "*Nothing to Envy: Ordinary Lives in North Korea.*" Interview by Meehan Crist. *National Book Foundation.* National Book Foundation, 2010. Web. 18 Dec. 2013.

Demick, Barbara. "Sarajevo with Tears: Another Walk down Logavina Street." Interview by Jon Thurber. *Los Angeles Times.* Los Angeles Times, 16 May 2012. Web. 18 Dec. 2013.

Laufner, Miriam. "Book Review: *Logavina Street*—Revisiting a Country Divided by Ethnicity." Rev. of *Logavina Street: Life and Death in Sarajevo Neighborhood*, by Barbara Demick. *DC Spotlight.* DC Spotlight Newspaper, 3 Sept. 2012. Web. 18 Dec. 2013.

Martelle, Scott. "PW Profiles: Barbara Demick." *Publishers Weekly.* PWxyz, 26 Oct. 2009. Web. 18 Dec. 2013.

Zhang Yiqian. "Correspondent Calling." *Global Times.* Global Times, 13 Dec. 2012. Web. 18 Dec. 2013.

—*Molly Hagan*

Toi Derricotte

Born: April 12, 1941
Occupation: Poet and professor

Toi Derricotte, poet and professor of English and creative writing at the University of Pittsburgh, has been writing verse about some of the most

© Lawrence Schwartzwald/Splash News/Corbis

pressing and personal subjects in American poetry since the early 1970s. As a light-skinned African American woman of Creole descent, she focused in much of her early work on her feelings of alienation and guilt for passing as a white woman. In raw yet accessible language, her poetry explores the issues of race, racism, identity, gender oppression, family dynamics, abuse, and grief. *Publishers Weekly* (11 Aug. 1997) has praised Derricotte, noting that "her work reaches out into the black and white and comes up with meaning that is often complex and rich—in short, gray. . : . Derricotte delivers frankness and hope through her thoughtful probing of encounters with complex racial and sexual relations."

Derricotte has been the recipient of the PEN/Voelcker Award for Poetry, the Pushcart Prize, two National Endowment for the Arts fellowships, the Paterson Poetry Prize, and the Anisfield-Wolf Book Award for nonfiction. She is also the cofounder, with poet Cornelius Eady, of the Cave Canem Foundation, a Brooklyn-based workshop for African American poets. Founded in 1996, Cave Canem has grown from a small organization to a network of more than three hundred fellows with a biennial publication and an annual writers retreat.

EARLY LIFE

Toi Derricotte was born Antoinette Webster in Hamtramck, Michigan, on April 12, 1941. Her grandparents owned and operated a funeral home in Detroit, and her father, Benjamin

Sweeney Webster, worked as an undertaker. Her mother, Antonia (Baquet) Webster Cyrus, was a Creole woman from Louisiana. Derricotte was an only child until the birth of her half brother, Benjamin Jr., the son of her father and his second wife.

Derricotte started writing at an early age, keeping diaries and journals in which she recorded the breakup of her parents' marriage, her father's abuse, and her grief at her beloved grandmother's death. "I started writing when I was ten or eleven years old—and I think that my journals, my diaries, my poems were ways that I addressed the things that I couldn't talk about in my everyday relationships," she told Charles Rowell in an interview for the literary journal *Callaloo* (31 Mar. 1991). "My feelings—especially of grief, anger, and fear—were as real as, maybe more real than, my relationships. I felt that I had to give some kind of shape to them."

Derricotte attended Girls Catholic Central High in Detroit, where she was heavily influenced by Catholic imagery. "There was an abundance of images of death and punishment everywhere—the crucifixion, saints, martyrs, in the Old Testament and the prayers of the Mass," she told Rowell. Her childhood experiences in her grandparents' funeral home would also have a major impact on shaping her later poetry. "My grandparents owned a funeral home; they lived on top, and often when I stayed overnight, there'd be bodies downstairs. I was three, four, five years old and my grandparents were as casual as if they had owned a grocery store." Inspired by these influences, her early poetic efforts often focused on death and morbidity.

Derricotte kept her early poems a secret until she was about fourteen years old. She recalled to Rowell, "A cousin who was in medical school took me to [a] Chicago museum to show the embryos from conception to birth and so I thought, 'Oh my god. This man is really into the secret, the hidden.' And I showed him some poems and he said, 'Oh, these are morbid.'" Although she was dejected by her cousin's reaction to her work, Derricotte recommitted herself to her writing. "I could have said something is wrong with me and stopped writing, or I could have continued to write but written about the things I knew would be acceptable, or I could go back underground," she said of her decision to continue writing poetry, as quoted by James W. Richardson Jr. in *The Concise Oxford Companion to African American Literature* (2001).

EDUCATION

After graduating from Girls Catholic Central in 1959, she enrolled in Wayne State University in Detroit. While still a college student, Derricotte became pregnant. She gave birth to a son, Anthony, in a home for unwed mothers in 1962. She later married Anthony's father,

Clarence Reese, on July 5, 1962, but their marriage was brief and ended in divorce in 1964. In 1965, Derricotte completed her bachelor's degree in special education at Wayne State and began teaching children with developmental disabilities in Detroit-area schools. On December 30, 1967, she married Bruce Derricotte. (They would go on to separate in the late 1980s but remain friends.) The newlywed couple relocated to New York City, where they moved into a predominantly white neighborhood. Far removed from her hometown and her family ties, Derricotte truly began to develop her poetic voice.

Derricotte began to attend poetry workshops and readings, which exposed her to poets, genres, and themes she had never before encountered. "I went into a writers' workshop and I read Sylvia Plath's poem 'Daddy.' And I thought, 'Damn, she's really mad.' And I never knew that in art, you could express anger. I always thought art was very contained and very intellectual, and removed, like it was an object in a museum," she explained to Eastman. Derricotte soon began exploring more personal and darker subject matter in her poetry. In 1972, she had her first poem published in the *New York Quarterly*, after which she began publishing more extensively.

Derricotte and her husband moved from New York to Upper Montclair, New Jersey, in 1974, becoming the first African American family to settle in the area. Beginning in 1974, Derricotte served as the poet in residence for the New Jersey State Council on the Arts, a position she would hold until 1988. In 1978 her first collection of poetry, *The Empress of the Death House*, was published by Lotus Press, a Detroit-based publisher of African American poets. Derricotte's poems in *The Empress of the Death House* deal with her childhood traumas and her relationships with her parents and grandmother. In "The Grandmother Poems," Derricotte focuses specifically on her fear of death and her memories of her grandparents' funeral home. In 1984, Derricotte completed her master's degree in English literature and creative writing at New York University.

EARLY WORK

Derricotte's second volume of poetry, *Natural Birth*, was published by the Crossing Press in 1983. (The volume was reissued by Firebrand Books in 2000 with a new preface by the author.) The collection focuses on the birth of Derricotte's son sixteen years prior and details Derricotte's decision to go through labor and delivery without anesthesia. In a review of the reissued edition for *African American Review* (2001), critic Pinkie Gordon Lane praised the collection for taking its readers on "an amazing journey into the depths of agony, of wonder—surrealistic in treatment, unrelenting in the frank and open disclosure."

In raw and vivid prose poetry, Derricotte tells of learning of her unplanned pregnancy at a time when out-of-wedlock births were still taboo, writing, "It was as if my body had betrayed me, became evidence against me. My flesh and bones pressed out showing what I so wanted to hide." Critic Eileen Robinson, in her review of the book for *Black Issues Book Review* (Sept. 2000), praised the collection's "powerful rhythm that seeps into your pores and settles just beneath the skin like unseen pins incessantly pricking the skin until the dance is done" and added, "*Natural Birth* is a triumph of one woman's spirit that will appeal to readers who are looking for depth, emotion, originality and truth."

In 1989, Derricotte's third collection of poetry, *Captivity*, was published by the University of Pittsburgh Press. In this volume, Derricotte shifts her focus from her personal recollections to the broader issues of racism and discrimination. Poet Rita Dove positively reviewed *Captivity* for the *Washington Post* (23 Dec. 2001), writing, "Something elusive keeps sending you back to the page; and with each new reading, another layer of mystery will gently exhale and open up. Much like a favorite grandparent's parable-disguised-as-an-anecdote, the poem will unfold when you need it but least expect it, illuminating its revelations as you grow into the lessons life has to offer." *Captivity* earned the Columbia Book Award from the Poetry Committee of Greater Washington, DC. The University of Pittsburgh Press issued second and third reprints of *Captivity* in 1991 and 1993. After holding teaching positions at Old Dominion University and George Mason University in Virginia, Derricotte joined the faculty of the University of Pittsburgh as an associate professor of English in 1991.

CAVE CANEM

In 1996, Derricotte cofounded Cave Canem, a workshop for African American poets, with Cornelius Eady. Derricotte had wanted to found such an organization since the early 1980s, when she was attending poetry workshops and was often the only African American poet in the group. However, she was unable to secure the funding to make her dream a reality until she partnered with Eady and his wife, Sarah Micklem, and the three decided to start the organization with their own money. Speaking to Elizabeth Hoover in an interview for *Sampsonia Way* (18 June 2010), Derricotte explained how many African American poets felt when they were the only black poet in a workshop: "They felt like their work was exoticized and that there were certain expectations that made them uncomfortable." She told Eastman, "You never read [African American or female poets] in books. I didn't read them in high school. I didn't read them in college. I didn't read them in graduate school. When I

asked my professor, he said, 'We don't go down that low.'"

Cave Canem held its first retreat in Esopus, New York, and attracted twenty-six poets in its first year. Since its founding, Cave Canem has grown into an influential foundation with more than three hundred fellows, a biennial publication of the fellows' work, and an annual writing retreat at the University of Pittsburgh at Greensburg. Derricotte explained to Hoover, "Cave Canem gives poets a chance to talk about these types of experiences and form their own community. This way they know they are not alone and they are much more comfortable even in situations where they are the only person of color." Derricotte continues to serve as president of the board of Cave Canem and occasionally teaches classes at the foundation's headquarters.

THE BLACK NOTEBOOKS

W. W. Norton published Derricotte's first volume of nonfiction, *The Black Notebooks: An Interior Journey*, in 1997. Derricotte had begun writing the material that would become *The Black Notebooks* in 1974, shortly after she and her husband moved to Upper Montclair, New Jersey. Feeling extremely isolated and uncomfortable as the only African American woman in the neighborhood, Derricotte began chronicling her experiences of race and racism in a journal. "I began writing this book in the middle of a severe depression," she wrote in an article for *Callaloo* (1997). "Living in a neighborhood in which I was inescapably weighted and bound by race, in which I was the known 'black' person, felt entirely different from my previous experience in the white world, a world in which I am usually invisible." Derricotte ultimately returned to her journals and diaries and began working toward publishing her work. "*The Black Notebooks* took twenty-five years," she told Eastman. "And probably about fifteen of those years were spent trying to piece it together to take the really important parts that absolutely were essential, but not repeating anything twice, to pare it down to the minimum."

The Black Notebooks garnered Derricotte widespread critical acclaim and earned the 1998 Anisfield-Wolf Award in nonfiction from the Cleveland Foundation and the 1997 nonfiction award from the Black Caucus of the American Library Association. The book was also nominated for the PEN Martha Albrand Award for the art of the memoir. Sapphire, author of the 1996 best-selling novel *Push*, reviewed Derricotte's book, writing, "*The Black Notebooks* is the most profound document I have read on racism in America today. . . . It is not just one of the best books on race I have ever read but just simply one of the best books I have ever read." In an equally laudatory review for the *New York Times* (2 Nov. 1997), which named the book one of the most notable of the year, critic Benjamin De-Mott wrote, "The book's achievement lies in the telling light it casts on how white skin functions in a multiracial world, what whiteness sees and can't see. . . . There's no social science, no media analysis, little lecturing in the book; the bitter story is told mainly through poignantly realized details of feeling." Following the success of *The Black Notebooks*, Derricotte began experimenting more often with prose and nonfiction writing, and two of her essays were later included in the anthologies *The Best American Essays 2006* and *The Best American Essays 2011*.

LATER WORK

Derricotte's fourth collection of poetry, *Tender*, was also published in 1997. In a review of *Tender* for the *Women's Review of Books* (1 May 1998), Melanie Kaye Kantrowitz, wrote that "Derricotte's language feels, as usual, fresh and urgent, but *Tender* is a highly crafted volume, with poems lodged in an intricate structure. . . . Derricotte's range of diction, form, and subject is grand." *Tender* received the 1998 Paterson Poetry Prize, and Derricotte also received the Pushcart Prize that year.

In her next collection, *The Undertaker's Daughter* (2011), Derricotte revisited her early childhood traumas and the physical abuse of her father, subjects she had not dealt with extensively in her poetry since the publication of *Empress of the Death House* in 1978. Natasha Trethewey, United States poet laureate, reviewed *The Undertaker's Daughter*, calling it "a courageous act of healing and redemption." In 2012, Derricotte received the PEN/Voelcker Award for Poetry and the Paterson Award for sustained literary achievement for previous winners of the Paterson Poetry Prize.

Derricotte continues to teach English and creative writing at the University of Pittsburg and has lectured at a number of other colleges and universities, including New York University, the College of Charleston, and the University of Southern Florida. She has also contributed poems and essays to several prestigious publications, including *Pequod*, *Northwest Review*, *American Poetry Review*, *Massachusetts Review*, *Ploughshares*, and *Feminist Studies*.

SUGGESTED READING

DeMott, Benjamin. "Passing: A Black Poet and Teacher Chronicles Life in a White World." *New York Times*. New York Times, 2 Nov. 1997. Web. 10 Oct. 2013.
Derricotte, Toi. "Beyond Our Lives." Interview by Charles H. Rowell. *Callaloo* 14.3 (1991): 654–64. Print.
Derricotte, Toi. "We Are Not Post-Racial." Interview by Elizabeth Hoover. *Sampsonia Way*. Sampsonia Way Magazine, 18 June 2010. Web. 10 Oct. 2013.
Derricotte, Toi. "Writing *The Black Notebooks*." *Callaloo* 20.1 (1997): 195–201. Print.
Richardson, James W., Jr. "Derricotte, Toi." *The Concise Oxford Companion to African American Literature*. Ed. William L. Andrews, Frances Smith Foster, and Trudier Harris. Oxford: Oxford UP, 2001. 107–8. Print.

SELECTED WORKS

The Empress of the Death House, 1978; *Natural Birth*, 1983; *Captivity*, 1989; *The Black Notebooks: An Interior Journey*, 1997; *Tender*, 1997; *The Undertaker's Daughter*, 2011

—Mary Woodbury Hooper

Persi Diaconis

Born: January 31, 1945
Occupation: Mathemagician

Persi Diaconis was a teenager when he dropped out of school, cut ties with his family, and hit the road as a magician's assistant. "I took some decks of cards and some socks," he told Jeffrey R. Young for the *Chronicle of Higher Education* (16 Oct. 2011) of his departure. His work in magic led him to mathematics, and as a young assistant professor at Stanford University in California, he hid his unusual past while studying probability and chance as it applies to cards and gambling. Early in his mathematics career, Diaconis stumbled upon the work of Paul Lévy, a French mathematician who studied a phenomenon known as the perfect shuffle. A perfect shuffle can be achieved by dividing a standard deck of cards exactly in half and precisely shuffling it eight times, at which point the cards return to the exact order at which they began. Diaconis's own studies revealed that when a standard deck of cards is shuffled imperfectly seven times, the cards reach optimal randomization. His influential paper on the subject, "Trailing the Dovetail Shuffle to Its Lair," written with Columbia University mathematician Dave Bayer, was published in the *Annals of Applied Probability* in 1992.

Diaconis specializes in statistics, probability theory, and a subdiscipline of mathematics called combinatorics but occasionally ventures outside of his own field in search of answers to deeper questions. In 2011, he began talking to physicists about a complex subfield of physics known as fluid dynamics. Diaconis's appetite for knowledge across disciplines—and his unusually social mode of working—are well known at Stanford. "He brings groups of people together who weren't talking to each other," David Aldous, a mathematics professor at the University of California, Berkeley told Young. "He straddles

Courtesy of Linda A. Cicero / Stanford News Service

statistics and mathematical probability and pure mathematics—and he's one of the few people who straddles all of these things." Diaconis's wife, Susan Holmes, also a Stanford professor, traces her husband's desire to bring people together to his early days as a magician. "He was already used to sitting around in coffee shops and bars, exchanging ideas with these old magicians," she told Esther Landhuis for the *Stanford Report* (7 June 2004). "He just transported that idea to mathematics. Why can't we sit around in a coffee shop and talk mathematics?" The recipient of a MacArthur Foundation Fellowship, Diaconis is also a fellow of the American Academy of Arts and Sciences and a member of the National Academy of Sciences. He was named Mary V. Sunseri Professor of Statistics and Mathematics at Stanford in 1998.

EARLY LIFE

Persi Warren Diaconis was born in New York City on January 31, 1945. His father worked as a cook and housepainter and also played the mandolin. His mother was a music teacher. Diaconis described his early childhood as unhappy to Young but did not elaborate. He learned to play the violin at an early age and won a scholarship to study the instrument at a youth program at the prestigious Juilliard School of Music. (Diaconis quit playing for good when he ran away from home, and claims that he can no longer even read sheet music.) But Diaconis's overwhelming interest was magic. He showed an aptitude

as a young teen, when two of his card tricks were published in *Scientific American* magazine. Martin Gardner, the magazine's famous mathematical games columnist, later called the submissions two of the world's ten best card tricks. Gardner, whom Diaconis met when he was thirteen, served as his introduction to the world of mathematics, though he did not fully realize it at the time.

Diaconis often spent time at Tannen's Magic Shop, which was then located in the former Wurlitzer Building in bustling Times Square. (Now considered the city's oldest magic store, Tannen's has since relocated to Herald Square.) Tannen's was a gathering place for the masters of the trade, and Diaconis delighted in watching magicians perform for one another. Among the magicians he met there was Dai Vernon (born David Frederick Wingfield Verner). According to Karl Johnson, author of *The Magician and the Cardsharp: The Search for America's Greatest Sleight-of-Hand Artist* (2005), it is difficult to overstate Vernon's reputation among fellow magicians. Vernon was "certainly the single most influential" magician of the twentieth century, if not the greatest, Johnson told Barry Gordemer for National Public Radio's *Morning Edition* (18 Aug. 2006). He was affectionately known as "The Professor" and billed himself as the magician who had once fooled famed magician and escape artist Harry Houdini with one of his card tricks. "There's not a magician today who was not influenced by his methods and his theory," Johnson said.

APPRENTICESHIP

Diaconis became Vernon's assistant, and in 1959, at the age of fourteen, he dropped out of George Washington High School to join the magician on the road. Diaconis did not even tell his family he was leaving. He reconnected briefly with his parents in his late twenties, after starting graduate school, but did not reestablish a relationship with them. "The magic community was my family," he explained to Young. "And mathematics became a family in the same way."

Vernon was in his sixties when Diaconis met him and spent most of his time collecting tricks from card sharks in dive bars and clubs across the country. There was no itinerary for their travels, Diaconis told Morris H. DeGroot for the magazine *Statistical Science* (1 Aug. 1986). "If we heard an Eskimo had a new way of dealing the second card with snow shoes, we would be off to Alaska," he said. Vernon was also working on an annotated version of the 1902 book *The Expert at the Card Table*, by the pseudonymous S. W. Erdnase. Vernon was a performer, but not a showman; he preferred a bare-bones kind of magic, reliant on the seemingly effortless sleight-of-hand outlined in Erdnase's influential work. Diaconis served as Vernon's researcher on the project and later wrote the book's introduction. After two years, the two men parted ways, but they remained friends until Vernon's death in 1992.

THE SHORT CAREER OF PERSI WARREN

In 1962, at the age of seventeen, Diaconis embarked on his own magic career as Persi Warren. (He used his middle name, Warren, as his last name because he believe it was easier to pronounce.) He traveled around the globe, securing gigs in Europe and South America and spending several years performing on Caribbean cruise ships. Early in his career, he sought to outsmart a crooked Caribbean gambling house that he believed was shaving its dice to improve house odds. "I was never a star in the sense of making a great living," he told DeGroot of his career as a magician, "but I lived OK." After several years, Diaconis was tired of show business, and prompted by his struggle to read and understand William Feller's classic textbook *An Introduction to Probability Theory and Its Applications* (1950), he enrolled in the City College of New York (CCNY) to study math.

TRAINING IN MATHEMATICS

Diaconis, who never finished high school, had been slated to graduate a year after he left home. Later, he learned that he had actually received his diploma—his teachers had met after he dropped out and decided to graduate him anyway. "I took it and ran," Diaconis told DeGroot. Tony D'Aristotile, the professor who taught him advanced calculus at CCNY, recalled to Landhuis that Diaconis was "nothing special" where math was concerned, but he was gutsy. "Barely six to nine months after he struggled with my advanced calculus course, he was applying to the finest graduate schools to continue his study," D'Aristotile said. Diaconis earned his bachelor's degree in mathematics from CCNY in 1971 and was determined to go to Harvard for graduate school. His professors refused to write him recommendation letters—no CCNY graduate had ever gotten into the Harvard mathematics department—so Diaconis contacted his old friend Martin Gardner at *Scientific American*, who wrote a letter to Fred Mosteller, a Harvard statistics professor with an affinity for magic. Mosteller welcomed Diaconis into the statistics department at the prestigious school but advised him to keep his card tricks out of the classroom. "He said, 'The kids end up thinking you're a performer, and they stop believing you're a scholar,'" Diaconis recalled to Young. Diaconis earned his master's degree in 1972 and his doctorate in 1974, after which he joined the faculty of Stanford University as a statistics professor. He went on to teach at Harvard, the Massachusetts Institute of Technology, and Cornell University before returning to Stanford in 1998.

COINCIDENCE AND CHANCE

Throughout the 1980s, Diaconis and Mosteller collaborated on a study of coincidences. "All of us feel that our lives are driven by coincidences," Diaconis told Gina Kolata for the *New York Times* (27 Feb. 1990). "Who we live with and where we work, why we do the things we do often rest on slim coincidences." They defined a coincidence, Diaconis told Kolata, as "a surprising concurrence of events, perceived as meaningfully related, with no apparent causal connection." With that definition in mind—alongside the presumption that coincidences are not caused by forces that exist outside the realm of science—the two sought to differentiate among so-called coincidences and discover their hidden causes.

In the early 1980s, Diaconis and Mosteller asked friends to share surprising coincidences from their own lives. They received an overwhelming response. The men collected the stories in notebooks and file folders and organized the stories into groups for analysis. In Kolata's article for the *Times*, Diaconis and Mosteller talked about a then-recent coincidence in which a New Jersey women won the lottery twice in four months. At the time, it was reported that the likelihood of such an event was one in seventeen trillion. Narrowly defined, this is true, but on a broader level, the event could be explained by the existing Law of Truly Large Numbers. The law states that if an event has a one-in-a-million chance of happening, it will eventually happen given a large enough sample. "It's the blade-of-grass paradox," Diaconis told Kolata. "Suppose I'm standing in a large field and I put my finger on a blade of grass. The chance that I would choose that particular blade may be one in a million. But it is certain that I will choose a blade."

Other categories of coincidence—two people sharing the same birthday, for example, or the phenomenon of learning a new word and then seeing that word everywhere—offered similar statistical explanations. Diaconis and Mosteller published their influential paper "Methods for Studying Coincidences" in the *Journal of the American Statistical Association* in 1989.

MAGICAL MATHEMATICS

In addition to studying coincidence, Diaconis spent many years writing a book with mathematician Ron Graham, a former juggler and acrobat. With the book, *Magical Mathematics: The Mathematical Ideas That Animate Great Magic Tricks*, the two men hoped to demonstrate the link between magic and mathematics. The book was finally published in 2011, with a foreword by Gardner. It is aimed at a general audience but contains a number of advanced equations. When Diaconis first pitched the book, his publisher suggested the subtitle "Revealing the Secrets of the World's Great Magic Tricks," but Diaconis was careful not to offend his magician friends by exposing too many of their secrets. (Revealing how a trick is performed is frowned upon in the magic community.) Rather than debunk the trade, Diaconis aimed "to show people that tricks have a lot of substance in them—that magic is an art, and it has its own depth and breadth," he told Young. Writing for the *Wall Street Journal* (10 Dec. 2011), Alex Stone called the book "a dazzling tour of math-based magic tricks." He concluded, "While exposing magic secrets in a book intended for the general public may raise hackles among some old-guard magicians, exploring the math behind these tricks will, in truth, only deepen the mystery. For, as the authors remind us, sometimes the methods are as magical as the tricks themselves."

Diaconis is married to Susan Holmes, a professor of statistics and mathematical approaches to biology at Stanford. They have two daughters, Camille and Emma.

SUGGESTED READING

DeGroot, Morris H. "A Conversation with Persi Diaconis." *Statistical Science* 1.3 (1986): 319–34. Print.

Gordemer, Barry. "A Magician's Quest for the Perfect Card Cheat." *NPR Books*. Natl. Public Radio, 18 Aug. 2006. Web. 11 Aug. 2014.

Kolata, Gina. "1-in-a-Trillion Coincidence, You Say? Not Really, Experts Find." *New York Times*. New York Times, 27 Feb. 1990. Web. 11 Aug. 2014.

Landhuis, Esther. "Lifelong Debunker Takes on Arbiter of Neutral Choices." *Stanford Report*. Stanford U, 7 June 2004. Web. 11 Aug. 2014.

Stone, Alex. "Pick a Card, Any Card." *Wall Street Journal*. Dow Jones, 10 Dec. 2011. Web. 11 Aug. 2014.

Young, Jeffrey R. "The Magical Mind of Persi Diaconis." *Chronicle of Higher Education*. Chronicle of Higher Education, 16 Oct. 2011. Web. 11 Aug. 2014.

—*Molly Hagan*

Peter Diamandis

Born: May 20, 1961
Occupation: Chairman and CEO of the XPRIZE Foundation

In 1992, Peter Diamandis, an entrepreneur, aeronautics enthusiast, and, later, the founder of the XPRIZE Foundation, came to the sad conclusion that the American space program was never going to be able to maintain the progress it had made during its heyday in the 1960s and 1970s. Diamandis, who is also an author and a nonpracticing medical doctor with a degree from Harvard Medical School, was an energetic

© James Leynse/Corbis

entrepreneur who spoke of intergalactic travel with an earnestness that seemed out of place approaching the new millennium. Americans did not view space travel with the same excitement—or urgency—that they once did, and NASA's budget suffered (and continues to suffer) accordingly. Diamandis would not give up on his childhood dreams, however, and decided that commercial space tourism could pick up where NASA left off. He began in 1993, with a company he cofounded called Zero Gravity (Zero G) Corporation. The company would allow customers to experience the weightlessness of space on parabolic airplane flights—though Zero Gravity would not make its first flight for another eleven years.

During the interim, Diamandis funded, or found funding for, a number of other projects to draw capital to space exploration under the guiding principle that both tourism and the promise of valuable resources drive progress. The latter part of this principle, one that in the nineteenth century spurred the construction of the railroads and the California gold rush, is particularly important to Diamandis's idea of mining asteroids with a company he founded called Planetary Resources. Many have dismissed the idea—a reaction not unusual for Diamandis—but astrophysicist Neil deGrasse Tyson was intrigued—as were Google's Larry Page, film director James Cameron, and former presidential candidate Ross Perot, who are among the company's backers. In an interview for *Star Talk Radio Show with Neil deGrasse Tyson* (28 Apr.

2013), Diamandis pointed out that many of the resources that humans fight over on Earth are found in abundance in space. "The Earth," he told Tyson, "is a crumb in a supermarket filled with resources and if we can gain access to those resources, it uplifts everybody." The comment is characteristic of Diamandis, who is the coauthor of the book *Abundance: The Future Is Better Than You Think* (2012) and is famous for his unbridled optimism. According to Diamandis, entrepreneurs are driven by such incentives, and incentive drives innovation: "I'm trying to start a gold rush," he told Brian Caulfield for *Forbes* (26 Jan. 2012).

EARLY LIFE AND DREAMS OF SPACE

Diamandis was born to Greek immigrant parents on May 20, 1961, and grew up in Long Island, New York. He was obsessed with rockets and space. The premiere of the sci-fi television show *Star Trek* and the golden age of NASA—particularly the Apollo 11 moonwalk in 1969 and the harrowing journey of Apollo 13 in 1970—only fueled his obsession. He fantasized about traveling to other planets and spreading humanity throughout the galaxy. The young Diamandis was a dreamer, but he was also a pragmatist. "[W]hen I was eight years old, I sat my parents down and gave them a lecture on the Apollo program," he told Ted Greenwald for the UK edition of *Wired* magazine (17 July 2012). "My dad gave me $5—the first money I ever earned in aerospace."

Diamandis enjoyed a childhood that was markedly different from that of his parents. His father grew up picking olives on the Greek island of Lesbos and later became a successful obstetrician-gynecologist—a professional path Diamandis felt pressure to follow. But Diamandis showed a startling aptitude for aeronautical engineering from an early age. At twelve, he won first place in the Estes Rocket Design Competition for building a model automated launch system capable of launching three rockets at once. He excelled as a student at Great Neck High School and spent his spare time performing rocket experiments that would make any parent cringe. "If I did anything close to what I did back then I would be flagged as a terrorist," he said to Caulfield. Ordering pounds of potassium chloride and magnesium through the mail, Diamandis and a friend once threw a homemade bomb into the friend's family pool to see how big the resulting splash would be. The explosion cracked the pool. Later, he and another friend built a four-stage rocket that they named *Mongo*. The two tested the rocket on Long Island's Roosevelt Field, the launching place of the *Spirit of St. Louis*, though the experiment did not fare very well. The timing of the ignition was off, and Diamandis and his friend ended up running from *Mongo*.

EDUCATION

Diamandis graduated from high school in 1979 and enrolled at the Massachusetts Institute of Technology (MIT). He studied premed at the behest of his parents but also founded a successful group called Students for the Exploration & Development of Space, or SEDS. SEDS was more than an extracurricular activity for Diamandis. He managed the organization, which opened chapters at Princeton and Yale, and gained his first experiences in serious fundraising. "When I got my first $5,000 donation [for SEDS] it felt like a million-dollar check," he told Caulfield. SEDS now boasts chapters in universities across the United States and in Asia, the United Kingdom, and the Middle East. Despite his busy schedule outside the classroom, Diamandis won several awards for his research in life sciences and was accepted to Harvard Medical School after graduating from MIT with a bachelor's degree in molecular biology in 1983.

While completing his medical degree at Harvard, Diamandis went on leave to earn a master's degree in aeronautical engineering at MIT. There, he and two colleagues founded the International Space University (ISU) in 1987. ISU began as a summer program for graduate students interested in space exploration on MIT's campus. The university is now a full-fledged research institute located in Strasbourg, France.

ENTREPRENEURIAL BEGINNINGS

Diamandis graduated from Harvard Medical School in 1989 and began his own firm called International Microspace the same year. The company raised $2.5 million in the hopes of building a microsatellite launcher and won a $100 million contract with the Defense Department through the Pentagon's Strategic Defense Initiative, also known as the "Star Wars" program. Ultimately, the company was unable to launch a rocket, and Diamandis sold International Microspace after the Star Wars program was scrapped under the Bill Clinton presidential administration.

Diamandis did not want to give up his dreams of space, but at the same time, he saw NASA struggling to fund its projects. In 1992, the five hundredth anniversary of the voyage of Christopher Columbus, the George H. W. Bush presidential administration considered an initiative to refocus the country on space travel in the spirit of exploration—but that effort never came to fruition. "That's when I got it: this was never going to happen. Any time a new Congress came in, it would cut NASA's budget," Diamandis told Greenwald, concluding: "Commercial industry was the only way to generate long-term funding." In 1993, Diamandis teamed up with former NASA scientist Ray Cronise and astronaut Byron Lichtenberg to found Zero Gravity Corporation, a for-profit venture that would allow customers to experience the weightlessness of space travel in parabolic flight. The men raised $500,000, but the California Space Authority would not allow the company to do a parabolic flight without the passengers wearing seatbelts. It took Zero Gravity eleven years to get permission from the Federal Aviation Administration. The company performed its first flight in October 2004 in a modified Boeing 727. Since then, for about $5,000 a piece, thousands of people have gotten a glimpse of what it's like to be an astronaut, including the famous astrophysicist Stephen Hawking, who suffers from amyotrophic lateral sclerosis (ALS), a neural disease that has left him almost entirely paralyzed. It took Diamandis another six months to secure the proper permissions for Hawking's flight.

XPRIZE FOUNDATION

Incentive is the driving force behind the XPRIZE Foundation, of which Diamandis is the founder and chairman. In 1994, a friend of Diamandis gave him a copy of Charles Lindbergh's famous 1953 memoir *The Spirit of St. Louis*, named after his single-engine plane, hoping it would encourage him to get his pilot's license. However, after reading the book, Diamandis was more inspired by wealthy hotelier Raymond Orteig, who had offered to pay $25,000 to the first pilot who could successfully complete a transatlantic journey. Diamandis realized that Lindbergh's historic solo flight from New York to Paris was not, originally, the aviator's own idea. It took an innovative entrepreneur to help make Lindbergh's flight a reality. "Aviation didn't get easier, but [Lindbergh's] flight changed people's belief in what was possible," Diamandis told Greenwald. "Getting the public to change its beliefs is the underpinning of an X Prize."

The idea for the XPRIZE came to Diamandis almost immediately; he told Greenwald that he wrote "X Prize" in the margins of Lindbergh's book while he was reading it. (He also scrawled the words "suborbital flight.") The "X" stands for "experimental," the name of the benefactor, which changes depending on the goal of the prize, and also for the Roman numeral 10 because each XPRIZE, no matter the challenge, is worth $10 million. Diamandis chose to base his fledgling organization in St. Louis and, on May 18, 1996, announced the creation of the XPRIZE under the city's famous arch alongside Apollo 11 astronaut Buzz Aldrin. He courted the city's investors, some of them the aviator's own descendants, just as Lindbergh did in the 1920s. His early supporters included local businessmen, the science-fiction writer Sir Arthur C. Clarke, and Lindbergh's grandson Erik Lindbergh. Diamandis had both critics and advocates, but he did not have the prize money. Diamandis hoped that a relatively modest goal like a suborbital flight—which Dan Brekke described for *Wired*

(1 Jan. 2000) as "something more like the Coney Island Cyclone than a full-on, 17,500-mph orbital cruise"—might spur a new era of aeronautical development, just as Orteig's challenge had ushered in a new era in aviation.

THE ANSARI XPRIZE

By 2001, those close to Diamandis were beginning to worry about him. After five years, he was still working himself to the bone looking for a backer willing to make a large enough investment to raise the promised $10 million. The same year, Diamandis read about a woman named Anousheh Ansari, the former CEO of Telecom Technologies, who said in an interview that one day she hoped to travel to space. Ansari gave Diamandis $1 million, and the prize became the Ansari XPRIZE. Her investment opened the door to others, and by 2004, Diamandis and the XPRIZE Foundation were able to award Burt Rutan and Paul Allen, the latter the cofounder of Microsoft, $10 million after the successful flights of *SpaceShipOne*, the first reusable spacecraft to carry people in suborbital flight, doing so twice within two weeks. After completing its historic flight on October 4, 2004, *SpaceShipOne* was hung in the Smithsonian's National Air & Space Museum next to *The Spirit of St. Louis*.

The twenty-six teams competing for the Ansari XPRIZE invested more than $100 million in research and development—spurring just the kind of commercial space race for which Diamandis was looking. The same scenario was true of Orteig's challenge and in many ways, Diamandis sees the future of the XPRIZEs as tied to the success of Orteig and Lindbergh.

XPRIZE EXPANSION

Diamandis still considers space and space exploration his deepest passion, but the foundation has expanded to other industries ripe for innovation. Larry Page, the cofounder of Google, joined the XPRIZE board and funded the organization to address more of what Diamandis called "humanity's grand challenges" in his interview with Greenwald. Paul Jacobs of Qualcomm Incorporated is sponsoring the Qualcomm Tricorder XPRIZE, offering $10 million to a person that can create a real-life version of the *Star Trek* tricorder—a device that would accurately diagnose fifteen different disease states with a cough or skin prick. Bill and Melinda Gates are sponsoring a prize for a device to better detect tuberculosis. Still, the XPRIZE has a number of critics, many of whom argue that it would be more beneficial to offer entrepreneurs money up front to develop their ideas rather than rewarding the entrepreneurs after those ideas are already made manifest. But defenders of the prize argue that the real innovators are just the type of people to be incentivized by the XPRIZE.

SINGULARITY UNIVERSITY AND BEYOND

In 2008, Diamandis and the futurist, inventor, and Google engineer Ray Kurzweil founded Singularity University (SU) in Mountain View, California. Caulfield described the ten-week graduate program as "entrepreneurial basic training," but for Diamandis, SU is much more than that. Each year thousands of applicants compete for a handful of slots to hear lectures from leading tech wizards and thinkers on topics such as artificial intelligence, robotics, and synthetic biology; Diamandis hopes that SU graduates will be the world's next generation of innovators. (SU also offers a course for business executives, though the application process is no less competitive.) The university's name is a tribute to Kurzweil and his theory of the coming "singularity"—the term he uses to describe a time in the near future when humans and machines will be one and the same. Kurzweil, who has been in the public eye for decades, has his own detractors, but he has also been able to accurately predict the advent of current technologies such as the Internet and smartphones almost to the year. In an interview with Andrew Goldman for the *New York Times* on January 25, 2013, he predicted, that by 2029, "computers will have emotional intelligence and be [as] convincing as people." Together, Kurzweil and Diamandis represent the dual offerings of Singularity U: inspiration to think big and practical entrepreneurial advice in a world of rapid technological change. "A lot of people who are dreamers anticipate things happening," Diamandis told John H. Ostdick for *Success* magazine (1 Apr. 2013). "But there is a point where you realize that you are going to have to make something happen."

In 2012, Diamandis and journalist Steven Kotler published a book called *Abundance: The Future Is Better Than You Think*. In the book, Diamandis writes that coming exponential advances in technology will benefit humanity in ways that humans might now think are impossible, arguing that problems plaguing the world's poorest citizens—water scarcity, lack of electricity, and lack of health care, for example—can be solved by renegade entrepreneurs (as opposed to big companies) harnessing new technologies. When Diamandis talks about "abundance," however, he does not mean a world in which every human being lives in luxury; rather, he sees a future in which all are provided "a life of possibility."

SUGGESTED READING

Brekke, Dan. "Who Needs NASA?" *Wired*. Condé Nast Digital, 1 Jan. 2000. Web. 16 Oct. 2013.

Caulfield, Brian. "Peter Diamandis: Rocket Man." *Forbes*. Forbes.com LLC, 26 Jan. 2012. Web. 16 Oct. 2013.

Diamandis, Peter. "Eureka! Asteroid Mining." Interview by Neil DeGrasse Tyson. *Star Talk Radio Show with Neil DeGrasse Tyson* 28 Apr. 2013. Web. 16 Oct. 2013.

Diamandis, Peter. "Peter Diamandis Launched the X Prize, Now He Plans to Mine Asteroids." Interview by Ted Greenwald. *Wired*. Condé Nast UK, 17 July 2012. Web. 16 Oct. 2013.

Ostdick, John H. "Abundantly Clear: Peter Diamandis Looks to the Future." *Success*. Success Magazine, 1 Apr. 2013. Web. 16 Oct. 2013.

Vance, Ashlee. "Merely Human? That's So Yesterday." *New York Times*. New York Times Co., 12 June 2010. Web. 16 Oct. 2013.

—Molly Hagan

Mark Dimunation

Born: April 1952
Occupation: Rare books curator

"Many book collectors and curators would give all their first editions for Mark Dimunation's job," Sarah L. Courteau wrote for *Fine Books and Collections* magazine (July 2009). Dimunation—the head of the Rare Book and Special Collections Division of the Library of Congress—oversees holdings that include more incunabula (items printed before 1500) than any other library in the Western Hemisphere; a copy of the first book ever printed in what is now the United States, *The Bay Psalm Book* (1640); volumes from the personal libraries of Adolf Hitler, Sigmund Freud, Harry Houdini, and other notable figures; and one of the only three complete Gutenberg Bibles printed on vellum in existence.

Courtesy of Mark Dimunation

Although part of his job involves showing visiting celebrities and world leaders—including the monarchs of Norway and Spain—around the collections, Dimunation is quick to point out that the Library of Congress is a public facility, and anyone who wishes can come to Room 239 of the library's Thomas Jefferson Building to see some of the more than 850,000 items housed in his division.

EARLY YEARS

Mark Dimunation was born in April 1952 in Minnesota. His parents, John and Olga, were both the children of immigrants from the Ukraine. "The story of my family is in many ways a typical American tale," Dimunation told *Current Biography*. Near the turn of the twentieth century, Dimunation's paternal grandparents settled in North Dakota, where they built a sod home and earned a living as farmers. (Because lumber was expensive and difficult to obtain, many new immigrants to the region constructed such homes, using sturdy, flexible squares of sod cut from the prairie for walls and roofs.) Olga, whose father was a stonecutter in Winnipeg, was one of eight children. Both of Dimunation's parents attended college—John to study engineering and Olga to become a teacher. Although the institution she enrolled in would now be called a teachers' college, it was known then as a "normal" school, because it focused on inculcating teaching standards or norms.

After their marriage and the birth of Dimunation's older brother, John Michael, the couple built a home in St. Anthony Village, Minnesota. (The website of the village historical society notes that in 1803, the area had been a part of the Louisiana Purchase negotiated between Thomas Jefferson and France and that by the end of World War II most residents had abandoned farming for more cosmopolitan pursuits.) John found work as a pneumatic engineer. "I don't know all the details," Dimunation explained to *Current Biography*, "but he was involved somehow with the high-speed vehicles used on the Bonneville Salt Flats, which actually subjected their drivers to G-forces." While Olga stayed home to raise the two boys, she eventually returned to the workforce and was employed in various capacities well into her eighties. Dimunation's brother, who is older by four years, has undertaken a range of occupations, including farming and accounting, but has remained firmly rooted in Minnesota.

Dimunation was a conscientious student who played the clarinet in the school band and was active in a variety of activities. He loved the theater, and during his senior year at St. Anthony Village High School, he played Professor Henry Higgins in a production of *My Fair Lady*. That year he was also named Minnesota state oratory champion. "Among the smartest things I did as a student was to become involved in speech and debate," Dimunation told *Current Biography*. "It gave me the ability to speak my mind and make my case in an articulate way. In my job, I'm often called upon to give lectures, and those experiences in high school have proven invaluable."

COLLEGE AND POSTGRADUATE EDUCATION

Upon graduating from high school in 1970, Dimunation entered St. Olaf College, a Lutheran-affiliated school in Northfield, Minnesota. Founded in 1874, the school, according to its mission statement, "stimulates students' critical thinking and heightens their moral sensitivity; it encourages them to be seekers of truth, leading lives of unselfish service to others; and it challenges them to be responsible and knowledgeable citizens of the world." Dimunation credits the school with giving him a solid foundation and shaping him as a person. "My midwestern ethos, my sincerity . . . a lot of what I am was nurtured at St. Olaf," he says.

Attending college at a time when political protests were common on campuses across the country, he was once part of a group of protesters who occupied the St. Olaf administration building. The school's president engaged the students in a dialogue, and the demonstration was peacefully disbanded shortly thereafter. "Before we left the building, we cleaned up," Dimunation recalled to David Hawley for the Spring 2007 issue of *St. Olaf Magazine*, an alumni publication. "To me, that defines the St. Olaf experience. We had our demonstration, made our point and reached a consensus. Then we tidied things up in the president's office and left it as we found it."

Dimunation, known around campus for his unruly hair and love of theater and music, attended St. Olaf's "paracollege," a special program that allowed students to design their own course of study with the close guidance of a faculty advisor. A history major, he spent a semester in England in 1973, studying Tudor history at the University of Oxford's Christ Church College.

Dimunation graduated from St. Olaf College in 1974 and entered the University of California, Berkeley, intending to earn a doctoral degree in American history. To fund his graduate studies, he took a job in the university's library system. Although he was originally assigned to work in the physics section, he was later moved to the Bancroft Library, which houses the university's special collections. (The library was founded in 1905, when historian Hubert Howe Bancroft donated his massive collection to the school. Although his volumes focused on the history of California and the American West, the library is now home to several other special collections.)

Dimunation found that he preferred the congenial, scholarly atmosphere of the library to the environment of academia, and in 1981 he earned a master's degree in library and information science (MLIS) from Berkeley.

BUILDING A LIBRARY CAREER

From 1981 to 1983, Dimunation served as the assistant chief of acquisitions at the Bancroft Library, and he then accepted a post as the rare book librarian and assistant chief for special collections at Stanford University. The university is located in a famously earthquake-prone region, and the campus had suffered extensive damage in the 1906 San Francisco earthquake. On October 17, 1989, history seemed to repeat itself when a 15-second quake damaged some twenty Stanford buildings badly enough to force their closure—including the library in which Dimunation worked. (Luckily, an ambitious seismic bracing effort had taken place the year before, and while thousands of books tumbled to the ground and large cracks appeared in the structure, no one was seriously injured.) "For the next two years, I spent my time administering the library from a plywood box," Dimunation recalled to Hawley.

In 1991 Dimunation was hired by Cornell University, in Ithaca, New York, to serve as curator of rare books and associate director for collections. Given his deep love of the San Francisco Bay Area, Dimunation found it challenging to adapt to the slower pace of upstate New York, but the work proved gratifying, and he remained until 1998. That year, news reached him that the Library of Congress was seeking someone with exactly his qualifications.

THE NATION'S LIBRARY

The Library of Congress was founded in 1800, thanks to an act of Congress that called for a reference library containing "such books as may be necessary for the use of Congress—and for putting up a suitable apartment for containing them therein." Legislators earmarked $5,000 for the endeavor and housed the new collection in the Capitol. In 1814, however, invading British troops set fire to the building, destroying the contents. In response, statesman and former president Thomas Jefferson offered as a replacement his personal library of almost 7,000 books, which he had amassed over the course of fifty years. The collection included books in foreign languages and volumes on such topics as science and philosophy, and although some questioned whether items of those types belonged in a legislative library, Congress ultimately accepted the offer. Thus, as the library's website states, "the foundation was laid for a great national library." The site continues, "The Jeffersonian concept of universality, the belief that all subjects are important to the library of the American legislature, is the philosophy and rationale behind the comprehensive collecting policies of today's Library of Congress."

In addition to being the oldest federal cultural institution in the United States, the Library of Congress is also the world's largest library, with more than 155 million items on over 800 miles of bookshelves. Some 850,000 of those items are housed in the division Dimunation was hired in 1998 to oversee: Rare Books and Special Collections. "It's an extraordinary privilege to have access to these materials," he told Hawley. "Often the collections are of monumental books or are associated with grand figures in history. But many others tell stories of ordinary individuals and give us an understanding of what it was like, for instance, to live in the sixteenth century or to arrive in this country at a certain time. It's quite a sandbox to play in."

REPLICATING JEFFERSON'S COLLECTION

In a cruel twist of fate, most of Jefferson's original 6,487-volume library was destroyed in 1851—not by British troops this time, but in a blaze caused by a malfunctioning chimney flue. Upon assuming his new job, Dimunation was tasked with trying to replicate that collection. He was able to replace some of the volumes by looking through the Library of Congress's holdings and finding duplicates. Other were found and purchased on the antiquarian book market. Today, the project is almost complete, with only about 250 volumes still missing. "There's an Italian pamphlet on the pomegranate tree that I suspect is going to vex us for the rest of this project," Dimunation told Michele Norris for National Public Radio's *All Things Considered* (25 June 2008). "There are a couple things like that."

While journalists were intrigued by his years of work on Jefferson's collection, they seemed almost equally interested in a task Dimunation completed in the space of a few hours on January 4, 2007. On that day, Keith Ellison, a Democrat from Minnesota, made history by becoming the first Muslim member of Congress. After being elected the previous November, Ellison had announced his intention to take the oath of office using a Quran, and he had heard that Jefferson once owned a copy of the Muslim holy book. Upon contacting Dimunation's division, he found that the volume had survived the 1851 fire and asked for permission to use it. Dimunation, who had coincidently grown up in the Fifth Congressional District that elected Ellison, carried the leather-bound Quran to the Capitol and stood by until the ceremony was over. The event elicited a firestorm of criticism from the nation's conservative commentators, but others saw the move as a symbol of American diversity and acceptance. For his part, Dimunation told a reporter for the news site *Capitol Hill Blue* (4 Jan. 2007), "As a rare book librarian, there is something special about the idea that Thomas Jefferson's books are being walked across the street to the Capitol building, to bring in yet another session of governmental structure that he helped create."

PORTRAYAL IN *THE BAY PSALM BOOK*
Although he appears in the media on occasion, Dimunation is arguably best known among the general public in fictional form. In 2006 he served as the model for Jonathan DeHaven, a character in thriller writer David Baldacci's book *The Collectors*, which has now been published in more than thirty languages. To research the bestseller, Baldacci shadowed Dimunation for a week, ascertaining which books a thief would be interested in acquiring and which might even be worth committing murder to obtain. He settled upon *The Bay Psalm Book* and has been effusive in praising Dimunation and his staff for giving him the benefit of their expertise. "What better way to experience the Library than to have people who love it bring it to life by letting me absorb their knowledge, understanding and passion and thereby letting me transfer it onto the pages?," he said, as quoted by John Y. Cole for the *Library of Congress Information Bulletin* (April 2007). Asked by *Current Biography* how it felt to see himself fictionalized, Dimunation bluntly observed, "Well, I get killed on page 33."

TEACHING
In addition to his library duties, Dimunation has taught throughout his career. While in graduate school at Berkeley, he worked as a teaching assistant, and at Stanford, he taught in the Cultures, Ideas, and Values program that had replaced Western Civilization offerings as the university became more inclusive. At Cornell, he taught a course in culturally relevant literature to postgraduate students.

Dimunation is now a regular faculty member at the Rare Book School, offered each year at the University of Virginia. The school, which attracts librarians, academicians, and collectors, along with ardent book-loving laypeople, "combines the intensity of the seminar room, the nerdiness of a *Star Trek* convention and the camaraderie of a summer camp where people come back year after year," Jennifer Schuessler wrote for the *New York Times* (23 July 2012).

PERSONAL LIFE
Dimunation makes his home in Washington, DC, which he characterizes as "an ideal place to cultivate both friends and ideas." His commute to the Library of Congress takes him past the Washington Monument and the Supreme Court, and he has not lost his sense of delight at being in the nation's capital. Nor has he lost his wonder at the scope of his post. The library's collections "belong to the American people, and they tell our story," Dimunation explained to Courteau. "It's very infectious stuff. I know it

sounds like . . . what you would expect [someone from] a large national agency to say, but the experience of it all is captivating. Scratch any curator in this library and you will find that they fundamentally believe that."

SUGGESTED READING
Courteau, Sarah L. "Nation Building: At the Library of Congress, Mark Dimunation Collects for America." *Fine Books and Collections*. OP Media, July 2009. Web. 16 Jan. 2014.
Hawley, David. "The Nation's Caretaker." *St. Olaf Magazine* Spring 2007: 8–49. Print.
Orndorff, Amy. "Re-Created Library Speaks Volumes about Jefferson." *Washington Post*. Washington Post, 11 Apr. 2008. Web. 16 Jan. 2014.
Schuessler, Jennifer. "Peering into the Exquisite Life of Rare Books." *New York Times*. New York Times, 23 July 2012. Web. 16 Jan. 2014.
Thomas, Louisa. "David Baldacci Will Thrill You." *Newsweek*. IBT Media, 30 Mar. 2009. Web. 16 Jan. 2014.

—Mari Rich

Isabel dos Santos
Born: April 1, 1973
Occupation: Investor

Angolan investor Isabel dos Santos is Africa's only female billionaire, and its youngest. *Forbes* magazine estimated her net worth at $3.5 billion in November 2013—a huge increase from only one year before, when *Forbes* reported her net worth as $500 million. The oldest daughter of Angolan President José Eduardo dos Santos, dos Santos's swift rise into the ranks of Africa's growing billionaires' club is historic but also shrouded in secrecy. Dos Santos keeps an extremely low profile and hardly ever engages with the press; more often, her spokespeople speak for her. However, in a rare interview with Tom Burgis for the British *Financial Times* (29 Mar. 2013), she told him, "Most rumors you've heard [about me] are not true." Dos Santos was referring to compelling evidence—cited in *Forbes*, the *New York Times*, the *Financial Times* and the *Guardian*, among other publications—that she has made her fortune at the expense of Angola, a poor but resource-rich country located on the southwestern coast of Africa. After Angola won its independence from Portugal in 1975, it immediately plunged into a destructive and bloody twenty-seven-year civil war. José Eduardo dos Santos became president on September 21, 1979 when Isabel dos Santos was only six years old; he is one of the longest-ruling nonroyal leaders in the world.

© Tiago Petinga/epa/Corbis

Angola's civil war ended in 2002 with the death of rebel leader Jonas Savimbi. Savimbi financed the opposition with revenue from diamonds mined in rebel-controlled territories. (Angola is the world's fourth-largest diamond producer.) His death and the end of the war was a cause for celebration in Angola and abroad. In an editorial on March 20, 2002, the *New York Times* wrote that Savimbi's death presented the "possibility of finally ending the fighting, introducing more accountable government and using oil revenues to build a better life for Angola's people." During the war, which at the time had been going on for the entirety of dos Santos's presidency, the Angolan government used the country's instability as an excuse for holding no elections, postponing development, eschewing transparency, and claiming a lion's share of Angola's sizeable oil revenues, the *Times* editors wrote. "Now that Mr. Savimbi is gone, so too are the government's excuses."

A formerly Communist regime, dos Santos's ruling MPLA party has embraced capitalism, though most Angolan citizens have yet to benefit from the country's lucrative partnerships with international companies. Nepotism and corruption are rampant in Angola because President dos Santos enjoys complete control over the country's state institutions, major businesses, and single national newspaper—and it appears that he has no problem rigging the system to benefit his own family. "It's clear through documented work that the ruling party and the president's inner circle have a lot of business interests. The source of funds and corporate governance are very murky," Peter Lewis, an African studies professor at Johns Hopkins University, told Kerry A. Dolan for *Forbes* (23 Jan. 2013). "The central problem in Angola is the complete lack of transparency." In 2011, the International Monetary Fund (IMF) found that $32 billion, a

staggering 25 percent of the country's gross domestic product, went missing between 2007 and 2011. The funds were never fully and accurately accounted for. In 2013, the global anticorruption organization Transparency International ranked Angola 153rd out of 177 countries on its Corruption Perceptions Index.

There is no clear picture of Isabel dos Santos's financial holdings, even after a yearlong investigation led by Kerry A. Dolan for *Forbes* magazine and Rafael Marques de Morais, an Angolan journalist and founder of the anticorruption website *Maka Angola*. Dolan wrote (14 Aug. 2013), "As best as we can trace, every major Angolan investment held by dos Santos stems either from taking a chunk of a company that wants to do business in the country or from a stroke of the president's pen that cut her into the action." Dos Santos has denied this and similar accusations, but has failed to answer any direct question regarding her stake in major Angolan companies. Investigations into dos Santos's wealth as well as Angola's government corruption are ongoing but dangerous: one month after publishing the article about Isabel dos Santos in *Forbes*, Marques was arrested and beaten in Angola's capital city, Luanda.

EARLY LIFE AND EDUCATION

Dos Santos was born on April 1, 1973, in the Soviet Union, in what is now the Republic of Azerbaijan, located on the Caspian Sea with inland borders touching Georgia and Armenia, also former Soviet republics. Her father was studying oil engineering at a Soviet university in the Azerbaijani capital of Baku, where he met her mother, Tatiana Kukanova, a fellow engineering student and local chess champion. The two were married but later divorced. Kukanova, now a British citizen, lives in London. Dos Santos's father returned to Angola, and her early years were marked by the guerilla war for independence. José Eduardo dos Santos was a member of the Movimento Popular de Libertação de Angola (People's Movement for the Liberation of Angola, or MPLA), a Soviet-backed liberation movement that ultimately succeeded, taking power in 1975. Dos Santos was six years old in 1979 when Angola's founding president and MPLA leader Agostinho Neto died and her father took office. The family moved to the presidential palace in Luanda, where she attended a state school. Marques told David Smith for the *Guardian* (25 Jan. 2013), "She was very humble. People liked her because she was very simple and down to earth and didn't want to be seen as the privileged one." By other accounts, dos Santos enjoyed a childhood fit for a royal. Her family's penchant for expensive things earned her the nickname "the princess."

When dos Santos's parents separated, she moved to London with her mother. (She has seven siblings born of her father's other marriages.) She attended St. Paul's Girls School in West London and later, King's College, London, where she studied electrical engineering and business management. Being the daughter of a powerful political figure didn't make her schoolwork any easier, she suggested in her interview with Burgis. "You have about 23 hours of classes per week, plus the labs, plus doing the reports, so you're not going to be partying," she said.

EARLY BUSINESS VENTURES

She returned to Angola in 1992 when there was a pause in the country's civil war. Dos Santos took a job with a German recycling company and later started a trucking business. In 1997, when dos Santos was twenty-four, she partnered with Rui Barata as an owner of a Luanda bar and restaurant called Miami Beach; it remains popular with wealthy locals and tourists. The same year, dos Santos and her mother set up a company called Trans Africa Investment Services (TAIS) in Gibraltar, a British territory on the southern tip of the Iberian Peninsula. Dos Santos held 75 percent of the company's shares and her mother the rest. Two years later, in 1999, President dos Santos engineered a joint venture with Angola's state-owned diamond company Endiama, TAIS, and a trio of Israeli diamond merchants that included Soviet-born billionaire Lev Leviev. The new company was called the Angolan Diamond Selling Corporation or Ascorp, and dos Santos ended up with a 24.5 percent stake in it through TAIS. According to Dolan and Marques, the company yielded "millions of dollars in dividends per month," but, after Angola's diamond trade came under scrutiny in the mid-2000s, dos Santos transferred her shares of TAIS (renamed Iaxonh Limited) to her mother.

TELECOM AND BANKING INVESTMENTS

In the early 1990s, dos Santos took an interest in the developing walkie-talkie system in Angola, a technology that would lay the groundwork for a mobile phone network years later. (Today, Africa is one of the world's fastest growing regions for cell phone users.) In 1999, the Angolan government entered into a joint venture with a private mobile phone operator called Unitel. Unitel is one of only two mobile phone providers in Angola, and dos Santos managed to garner a 25-percent stake in the company. A year after she became a shareholder, Portugal Telecom purchased a 25-percent stake in Unitel for $12.6 million. Though dos Santos's spokespeople have said that she also contributed capital to the company to earn her stake, which has a value estimated at over $1 billion, they have declined to specify how much. According to Marques, dos Santos was serving on Unitel's board of directors as of 2012, but it is unclear how she came to hold the position. With 9 million subscribers

and $2 billion in revenue, Unitel was the country's largest private company in 2012.

In 2005, dos Santos garnered a 25 percent stake of Banco Internacional de Credito, or BIC, through a partnership with Portuguese billionaire Americo Amorim and Fernando Teles, a Portuguese banker and former CEO of an Angolan bank. When asked to comment about her role in the bank, dos Santos's spokespeople said that she was a founder and invested her own money in the venture. "Regardless," Dolan and Marques wrote, "BIC was a hit, in large part because of a deal to lend money to . . . the Angolan government." Dos Santos's stake in the bank is valued at $160 million.

OIL AND CEMENT INVESTMENTS

Documents also suggest that dos Santos has a hand in Amorim's oil subsidiary, Amorim Energia, possibly through a Netherlands holding company called Esperaza Holding BV. Amorim Energia reportedly has ties to Sonangol, Angola's hugely profitable state-owned oil firm. Angola is the second-largest oil producer in Africa and joined the Organization of Oil Producing Companies (OPEC) in 2007. According to Victoria Eastwood and David McKenzie for CNN (29 Nov. 2012), about 90 percent of Angola's total revenue comes from its oil production. But those revenues are filtered through the state. There are no available records of how the money is used, though executives at Sonangol vaguely suggest that it goes to the Angolan people—if this is the case, it appears to have gone only to the country's elite. Angola is one of the fastest growing economies in the world, and its capital, Luanda, was recently named the most expensive for expatriates, yet most Angolans lack basic electricity service. When asked if he thought that the revenues were being stolen, Elias Isaac, an activist with Open Society Initiative for Southern Africa, told Eastwood and McKenzie, "To say that it's not being stolen would not be true to the situation, because if the oil money was not being stolen, we could have better social services in this country. Someone is taking it."

Dos Santos also owns a significant stake in an Angolan cement company called Nova Cimangola. According to his report for the European Parliament, Marques wrote that in 2006, the Angolan government bought 49 percent of the shares in Nova Cimangola for $74 million. "Soon after those shares were transferred to her business portfolio," he wrote, referring to dos Santos, "the state lost what it had invested."

PORTUGUESE INVESTMENTS

Dos Santos has a growing number of business interests in Portugal. She has been the face of a partnership between Angola and Portugal that, superficially at least, has turned their mutual history on its head. The Portuguese economy took a huge hit during the 2008 global market crash and has been soliciting investments from Angola's wealthy elite. It is an odd role reversal for the former colony and its former colonizer, but the power structure of their new partnership can be deceiving, Marques told Adam Nossiter for the *New York Times* (19 Nov. 2011). He cited Angola's crumbling infrastructure and grinding poverty—many Angolans live on less than two dollars a day. "There is still the colonial mentality in Portugal. They just want to extract resources and plunder the country. The only difference is this time they didn't take them by force."

In 2013, Smith reported that dos Santos was the largest shareholder in ZON Multimedia, a Portuguese cable television company. She owns 28.8 percent of the conglomerate's stock, worth $385 million. She also owns 19.5 percent of Banco BPI, one of Portugal's largest publicly traded banks. Her stake is worth about $465 million. She has another sizeable stake in Galp, a Portuguese energy company. In 2013, dos Santos announced a partnership with the Portuguese conglomerate, Sonae. She plans to open five new food hypermarkets—a term for a retail superstore that could be described as a grocery store–department store hybrid—in Angola. The first hypermarket is scheduled to open in 2015.

PERSONAL LIFE

Dos Santos married a Congolese businessman and art collector named Sindika Dokolo in 2003. The multimillion-dollar ceremony and reception reportedly boasted a choir flown in from Belgium and two charter planes of food delivered from France. They have three children and divide their time among Luanda, London, Lisbon, and Johannesburg. Dos Santos is also the president of the Angola Red Cross.

SUGGESTED READING

Burgis, Tom. "Lunch with FT: Isabel dos Santos." *Financial Times*. Financial Times, 29 Mar. 2013. Web. 20 Jan. 2014.
Dolan, Kerry A. "Isabel Dos Santos, Daughter of Angola's President, Is Africa's First Woman Billionaire." *Forbes*. Forbes.com, 23 Jan. 2013. Web. 20 Jan. 2014.
Dolan, Kerry A., and Raphael Marques de Morais. "Daddy's Girl: How An African 'Princess' Banked $3 Billion in a Country Living on $2 a Day." *Forbes*. Forbes.com, 14 Aug. 2013. Web. 19 Jan. 2014.
Eastwood, Victoria, and David McKenzie. "The Billion-Dollar Question: Where Is Angola's Oil Money?" *CNN*. Cable News Network, 29 Nov. 2012. Web. 25 Jan. 2014.
Nossiter, Adam. "Fortunes, and Tables, Turn for Portugal and Angola." *New York Times*. New York Times, 19 Nov. 2011. Web. 24 Jan. 2014.
Smith, David. "Isabel dos Santos, Dubbed 'Princess,' Named Africa's First Female Billionaire."
Guardian. Guardian News and Media, 25 Jan. 2013. Web. 19 Jan. 2014.

—*Molly Hagan*

Gabby Douglas

Born: December 31, 1995
Occupation: Artistic gymnast

Gabby Douglas is an Olympic gold medal–winning artistic gymnast. She made history during her Olympic debut in the 2012 London Games at the age of sixteen, winning a gold medal in the team competition as well as the coveted gold medal in the individual all-around competition, in which athletes compete on the vault, uneven bars, balance beam, and floor exercise. Douglas's bubbly personality and incredible physical strength captivated audiences; she emerged from the games not only an Olympic champion but also a star.

The first woman of color and first African American to win the individual all-around, Douglas is also only the fourth American woman to take Olympic gold in that category, and her road to London was not a smooth one. She showed an astonishing aptitude for gymnastics as a toddler, and at the age of fourteen, she moved halfway across the country to train with Liang Chow,

Wirelmage

former coach of Olympic gold medalist Shawn Johnson, in West Des Moines, Iowa. As Meghan O'Rourke for the *New Yorker*'s Culture Desk blog (6 Feb. 2014) wrote, demands on elite gymnasts have become more rigorous in the United States. "Women's gymnastics continues to be a sport of incredible paradoxes—a crucible for both sheer athleticism and delicate grace, in which gymnasts who can do full-twisting double-backs can also be penalized for having messy hair," O'Rourke noted. "Today's élite gymnasts face pressures to learn ever more difficult moves— ones that were routinely considered impossible a few short years ago." That ever-growing competitive pressure, paired with the relatively short career of most gymnasts, can be isolating even before a gymnast is required to leave home and live in a strange place.

Douglas moreover remains one of only a few African American gymnasts in a sport dominated by white women. Despite these and other obstacles, Douglas competed with amazing focus and grace in the 2012 Olympic Games. She told Juliet Macur for the *New York Times* (2 Aug. 2012) that focus was once a nagging problem for her: she had succumbed to her nerves in competition in the past and had been scolded by her coaches for looking at the crowd before her balance beam routine. But when she arrived in London, after beating a rival for a spot on the Olympic team, she was confident that she would win gold. "It was just an amazing feeling," she told Macur. "I was just like, Believe, don't fear, believe."

EARLY LIFE AND TRAINING

The youngest of four children, Gabrielle "Gabby" Douglas was born to Natalie Hawkins and Timothy Douglas on December 31, 1995, in Newport News, Virginia. Her mother works as a debt collector, and her father is an Air National Guard staff sergeant who has served several tours in Afghanistan. According to her autobiography, *Grace, Gold and Glory: My Leap of Faith* (2013), she spent her early months in Tulsa, Oklahoma, where her family was briefly homeless. Another early challenge was Douglas's branched chain ketoaciduria, a rare congenital blood disorder that almost killed her as an infant. As she grew older, her father became a distant figure; he and Hawkins separated in 2007 and divorced in 2011. (He later surprised Douglas by traveling to London during the Olympics but was unable to watch her compete.)

It was Douglas's older sister Arielle who first introduced her to gymnastics. A gymnast and competitive cheerleader herself, Arielle taught her then three-year-old sister how to do a cartwheel. Douglas was soon turning one-armed cartwheels across the family's house. When Douglas was six Arielle convinced their mother to enroll her in a proper training facility. Two years later Douglas joined the elite program at the local gym, Excalibur, in Virginia Beach. Not long after she was named Virginia's 2004 gymnastics state champion. It was clear that Douglas had a special talent, and her siblings gave up their own sports and hobbies so that she could afford to train at an elite level.

EXCALIBUR AND BEYOND

Douglas trained at Excalibur for seven years. During that time, she told Oprah Winfrey in an interview for *Oprah's Next Chapter* (26 Aug. 2012), she was ostracized as the elite gym's only African American gymnast. She put up with racist jokes and comments, such as when a teammate said that Douglas should be the person to scrape the bars with chalk because "she's our slave." After such incidents, Douglas would go home and cry. "I definitely felt isolated. Why am I deserving this? Is it because I'm black?—those thoughts were going through my mind," she explained to Winfrey. There was another component to her isolation as well. Hawkins told Winfrey that she thought that Douglas's coach kept her apart from the group because of her potential—maybe he did not want their bad habits to rub off on Douglas, she said—but it all contributed to a sense of not belonging. When she was fourteen, Douglas told her mother that she would rather quit the sport than stay with the same coach and gym.

Douglas was named to the US junior team in 2010. That July Liang Chow, a former Chinese national gymnast and personal coach of Olympic gold medalist Shawn Johnson, came to Excalibur to hold a clinic. In the 2008 Beijing Olympics, Johnson won women's gold in the balance beam and silver in the all-around, floor exercise, and team events. Douglas had watched the games and soon became obsessed with the idea of working with Chow. Chow told Blythe Lawrence for *espnW* (21 Nov. 2011) that he was impressed by Douglas's warm-up at the clinic and asked a trainer at the gym what kind of vault she could do. The trainer replied that Douglas could do a double-twisting Yurchenko, but Chow thought Douglas was capable of the much more difficult Amanar vault.

According to Rachel MacGrath, writing for the Couch Gymnast blog (11 Sept. 2012), any Yurchenko vault begins with "the gymnast doing a round-off onto the springboard and jumping backwards to place her hands on the vault." Douglas was already pulling off two twists in the air before landing on the mat, but the Amanar requires two-and-a-half twists. It is one of the most difficult vaults currently being performed in competition. "Adding another twist is a much, much bigger feat than it sounds," MacGrath wrote. "It requires more power, so you have more time in the air to compete the extra half twist. It requires good aerial awareness. It requires you to land forward, which is a 'blind' landing, in that the gymnast does not see the mat before she hits it."

Later that day Chow asked Douglas to try her Yurchenko with an extra half twist. After fifteen minutes she had completed her first Amanar.

MOVE TO IOWA

Douglas begged her mother to move to West Des Moines, Iowa, so that she could train at Chow's Gymnastics and Dance Institute, which is located in the middle of an old cornfield. Hawkins lobbied for Texas, where they had family and Douglas could train with Valeri Liukin, father and coach of American gymnast Nastia Liukin, who won the all-around in 2008. But Douglas had her heart set on Chow. She won the support of her sisters, and the family called a meeting. Douglas's sisters, Arielle and Joyelle, presented their mother and brother Johnathan with a list. Hawkins recalled to Lawrence, "They said, 'Here are the pros' . . . The only con was: 'We're going to miss her.'" Hawkins relented. In Iowa, Chow was reluctant to separate Douglas from her mother, but an unusual offer from a local family made Chow reconsider. After the 2008 Olympic Games, Missy and Travis Parton, who have four young daughters, told Chow that they would be willing to host a gymnast with Olympic aspirations in the event that the gymnast's family could not afford to move to Des Moines.

Douglas arrived in Iowa in February 2011 and moved in with the Partons after spending several weeks with other host families. According to Hawkins, the match could not have been better. "They literally took her in as if she were their own daughter," she told Alice Park for *Time* magazine (19 July 2012). Douglas, for the first time in her life, took on the mantle of oldest sibling. It was a role she relished, helping her much younger Parton sisters with homework and dance routines. The Partons became a second family to Douglas, and Missy and Travis later traveled to London to cheer her on in the Olympics.

ROAD TO LONDON

Things did not go as smoothly for Douglas at the gym. Her first major competition with Chow was the US national championships in St. Paul, Minnesota, in August 2011. Her nerves got the best of her, she told Park, and she took three falls from the balance beam during her ninety-second routine. She placed a disappointing seventh in the all-around, though she managed a third-place finish in the uneven bars. In October she joined Team USA at the world championships in Tokyo, Japan. She was the youngest member of the team and was included for her strength on the uneven bars. Her performance during the team finals earned her the nickname the Flying Squirrel. Douglas

reluctantly accepted the cloyingly cute nickname, bestowed by team coordinator Marta Karolyi. "I was like, Why can't it be Superwoman or something like that?" she told Park. "But I like it." Team USA earned their third team gold at the meet. Douglas had only participated in one event, but insiders began to talk about her Olympic potential—a discussion that seemed unthinkable just a few short months before. Her teammate Alicia Sacramone, who competed at the 2008 Olympics but did not make the 2012 Olympic team, said that something clicked for Douglas in Tokyo. "It was a point where she had to prove herself, and she did really well," Sacramone told Chrös McDougall for the Team USA website (1 Aug. 2012). "I think before she was a little more timid about going 100 percent, and now she is going full-force."

Douglas's family visited Iowa for her sixteenth birthday. Seeing them made Douglas homesick, and she told her mother in January 2012 that she wanted to come home. She planned, she wrote in her book, to work at Chick-fil-A and run track. To her family's relief she eventually changed her mind, telling her mother, "I'm going to stay and fight," Hawkins recalled to McDougall. True to her word, Douglas competed at the AT&T American Cup in New York City in March, scoring highest in the all-around and thus beating teammate and reigning titleholder Jordyn Wieber. Wieber bested her at the Visa Championships in St. Louis in June by 0.2 points, but Douglas rallied and won the event again at the Olympic Trials a few weeks later.

FIERCE FIVE

As a member of the American women's artistic gymnastics team, Douglas competed at the 2012 London Olympics alongside Wieber, McKayla Maroney, Alexandra "Aly" Raisman, and Kyla Ross. Nicknamed the Fierce Five, the group was favored to win gold. Their early lead on the vault only grew as the competition wore on—Douglas competed in all four Olympic events—and by the time Raisman completed her nearly flawless floor exercise, the Fierce Five had won by the largest margin in over five decades. The historic win came after preliminaries for the individual all-around. Douglas and Raisman earned high enough scores to represent the United States (each country can send only two team members to the event), but Wieber, the reigning world champion, did not make the cut.

Douglas was certainly one of the top athletes in the event, but her performances were inconsistent, and those lingering doubts made her somewhat of an underdog. She had proved herself in the team all-around finals—just as she had proved herself before that at the world championships—but Karolyi, among others, questioned her ability to continue to perform under such extraordinary pressure. But

Douglas, who had once struggled to find her focus, entered the event with a determination those around her had never seen before. She was ahead of the field after the vault, the first event, and was able to maintain that lead through the competition, finishing ahead of Viktoria Komova of Russia by 0.259 points. From Douglas's perspective, her victory was a whirlwind, and it took a while for its historical significance to dawn on her. "Someone mentioned that I was the first black American [to win the all-around gold], and I said, 'Oh yeah, I forgot about that!' I feel so honored," she told Kelly Whiteside for USA Today (3 Aug. 2012).

During the second week of the games, Douglas competed unsuccessfully for an individual medal on the uneven bars, her signature event. She attributed her lackluster performance to exhaustion. "I'm kind of disappointed in myself, could have fought a little harder, could have pulled a little harder. But I don't know, you just get to that, you know, mentally you're just so tired," she told Macur for the New York Times (6 Aug. 2012), adding that she felt like she lost her rhythm halfway through the routine. "I made a little mistake," she said, "but, you know, I'm human."

ALL-AROUND GOLD MEDALIST

To say that Douglas's rise to superstardom was meteoric would be an understatement; she appeared on the cover of a Kellogg's Corn Flakes cereal box fewer than eighteen hours after winning the all-around. Her favorite rapper, Lil Wayne, posted a tweet about her calling her an icon, and strangers stopped her in the street for photographs. She even got her first taste of controversy. During the competition Douglas's hair, which she wore gelled and pinned back into a ponytail like her fellow teammates, became an unexpected topic of conversation among African American women on Twitter. "It hurt a little bit," Douglas told Winfrey of the critical response. Shortly thereafter Douglas hired renowned hair stylist Ted Gibson to style her hair for upcoming television appearances.

Following the Olympics, Douglas remained in the public eye. With Michelle Burford, a founding editor of O magazine, she wrote an autobiography titled Grace, Gold and Glory: My Leap of Faith (2012). She published a book of photos and facts for young readers, titled Raising the Bar, in 2013. A television movie based on Douglas's life, The Gabby Douglas Story, aired on Lifetime on February 1, 2014. Douglas and her mother were executive producers.

In September 2013 Douglas left the Partons and Chow in Iowa and moved to Los Angeles, California, to join her family, who had moved there from Virginia Beach. She reports that she is training on her own in preparation for the 2016 Olympic Games in Rio de Janeiro, Brazil.

SUGGESTED READING

Lawrence, Blythe. "Gymnast Gabrielle Douglas Making Her Mark." ESPNW. ESPN Internet Ventures, 21 Nov. 2011. Web. 10 Mar. 2014.

Macur, Juliet. "A Very Long Journey Was Very Swift." New York Times. New York Times, 2 Aug. 2012. Web. 10 Mar. 2014.

Macur, Juliet. "Her Energy and Smile Flagging, Douglas Surrenders Stage." New York Times. New York Times, 6 Aug. 2012. Web. 10 Mar. 2014.

McDougall, Chrös. "Gabby Douglas Flies from under the Radar." Team USA. United States Olympic Committee, 1 Aug. 2012. Web. 10 Mar. 2014.

Park, Alice. "Gabby Douglas: Team USA's Flip Artist." Time. Time, 19 July 2012. Web. 10 Mar. 2014.

—Molly Hagan

Rackstraw Downes

Born: 1939
Occupation: Realist painter

Though often called a "realist landscape painter," Rackstraw Downes does not consider himself one, and neither do his paintings cover the traditional landscape subjects of sweeping vistas and breathtaking scenes of natural beauty. Downes, rather, is best known for his large painted works documenting the unsightly necessities of modern civilization—rural drainage ditches, power lines, industrial waste-churned rivers, sooty highway underpasses, and even garbage dumps. But critics give Downes credit for producing remarkably lifelike depictions of—and finding the beauty in—these atypical panoramas. Of his subject matter, the artist remarked to David Yezzi in an interview for the December 2005 issue of New Criterion, "Yeah, it is garbage. I think art without any sense of mischief about it tends to get a little prim or something. So there's a little mischief going on at the dump."

Downes has spent decades under the mainstream radar, racking up dozens of exhibitions and earning the respect of his peers while remaining generally unknown to the public at large. Since winning the John D. and Catherine T. MacArthur Foundation Fellowship in 2009, however, Downes has seen his work garner even greater recognition as he himself begins to be ranked among the great American artists working today. The MacArthur Foundation's official website notes, "In painting the American landscape as it is, not as it has been idealized, Downes imbues seemingly ordinary subjects with extraordinary power. His artistry is deeply rooted in the history and thought of painting. . . .

Courtesy of the John D. & Catherine T. MacArthur Foundation

Considered one of the most distinctive representational painters of his generation, Downes is challenging familiar conceptions of realist painting in works of formal rigor and quiet, yet stunning, beauty."

EARLY LIFE AND EDUCATION

The artist was born in Kent, England, in 1939. As a teenager he became interested in illuminated manuscripts and calligraphy. A sample of his handwriting was presented on television in the mid-1950s, which he later admitted to Dorothy Spears for the *New York Times* (21 July 2010) "was the beginning of visual art for me." Around that time he attended a preparatory school in Connecticut, where his growing interest in jazz flourished. He also became fascinated with modernist abstract painting, of which he had seen very little in Great Britain. He visited the Museum of Modern Art (MoMA) in New York City and the Arensberg Collection at the Philadelphia Museum of Art in Pennsylvania, and was completely captivated.

After earning his bachelor's degree in English literature from Cambridge University in England in 1961, he returned to the United States on an English-Speaking Union Traveling Fellowship, where he entered Yale University's School of Art in New Haven, Connecticut, during the 1961–62 school year. There he studied alongside such fellow students such as Richard Serra and Brice Marden and worked under the noted abstract painter Al Held, who was known for his boldly colored, hard-edge paintings. Held was so influential on the young painter that Held, on a visit to Downes's studio, concluded that his student was far too influenced by his own work.

In 1964 Downes earned his bachelor and master degrees of fine art in painting from Yale and took on a postgraduate fellowship at the University of Pennsylvania for the 1964–65 school year. He would go on to teach painting at the University of Pennsylvania from 1967 to 1979. In the 1960s, however, he had become disenchanted with abstraction and, as he has admitted in interviews, gave it up completely. As he searched around for a new style to work in, Downes kept coming back to the work of Fairfield Porter, a realist landscape painter whose lectures he had attended at Yale.

REINVENTING HIMSELF

Downes's reinvention of himself began in the summer of 1965, when he and his wife, Janet Fish, had rented a house in Maine. As Fish and one of her friends went out to paint landscapes, he painted abstract works in the garage. Soon thereafter he purchased a thousand-acre farm in the state with money left to him in his father's will and thought he would paint abstractions in the barn on that property. But he soon began to feel stifled by his artistic framework. He told David Yezzi for their interview in the *New Criterion*: "I felt trapped in a set of stylistic decisions. I went into a painting knowing every edge was going to be hard, and every color was going to be an absolute color, and that I would have to look for a long time for a subject made out of these ingredients." Slowly but steadily, he began to reshape his artistic efforts from abstractions to realism and representation.

While not teaching at the University of Pennsylvania, Downes would be at his farm in Maine, developing his new style. It was difficult for Downes to learn how *not* to draw hard edges, even on something like bushes, and it took him an entire summer to retrain his hand and eye. He recalled to Yezzi: "[The bushes] flickered in the breeze, and the colors were infinitely subtle. There was no hard edge at all, and I needed to introduce this tremble, which was terribly difficult to do. . . . by the end of the summer, I was making drawings that trembled, where there was shimmering foliage, where there was no longer just this static shape."

No one witnessed Downes's slow artistic transformation. Having separated from his wife, he worked in isolation, against not only the initial limitations of his own ability, but also against the prevailing artistic styles of the era. In the late 1960s and 1970s minimalism and abstraction were the popular means of expression in the artistic world; his traditional landscapes were completely out of fashion.

In 1972 and 1973 Downes traveled through Belgium and the Netherlands to study the works of those nations' artists, who were world famous for their remarkable attention to detail. In Rotterdam he was particularly entranced with Pieter

Bruegel the Elder's *The Tower of Babel*, for its breathtaking detail. Of it, Downes raved, "Bruegel's alert curiosity and relish for the whole observable world, in which the minute is the natural component, not enemy, of the grand," as quoted by Stephen Maine for *Art in America* (Nov. 2010).

FINDING THE RIGHT SCALE

By the late 1960s Downes had grown comfortable enough with his new style to allow his landscapes to be exhibited in small commercial galleries and at universities. Among the first places his work was displayed in solo exhibitions were Swarthmore College in Swarthmore, Pennsylvania (1969); the Marlin McLeaf Gallery in Philadelphia, Pennsylvania (1969); the Kornblee Gallery in New York City (1972, 1974, 1975 and 1978); and the Swain School of Design in New Bedford, Massachusetts (1978). The landscapes on display in these exhibitions demonstrated Downes's fascination with the built environment, particularly with those parts of cities not often painted—exposed ductwork, highway overpasses, dumps, and ventilation towers—as well as his interest in obscure rural settings such as farm buildings, ditches, and radio towers. Though he is often called a "landscape" painter, Downes does not consider himself as such, but as simply a painter of his environment. Unlike some other artists, he does not go out and scout sites first with a camera; rather he stumbles upon them by chance. In rural areas he typically arrives at them by car; in New York City he often finds them by taking public transit to different neighborhoods.

One aspect of Downes's paintings that most critics remark on is their size. Often their width is three to four times their height. He told David Yezzi: "I remember abandoning something saying, 'It should be smaller or it should be a little bigger.' Getting that scale and the relationship of the mark to the surface of the painting till the mark began to disappear became a very major, major consideration for me in my work." An example of his work in this period is *The Dam at Fairfield* (1974), which is 12.5 inches by 46.5 inches. Although a realistic landscape, depicting the way fishermen are being forced off the river by logs being sent downstream to a paper mill, the painting's perspective is distorted and not a true depiction of the dam; in fact, half the painting looks downstream, the other upstream. Stephen Maine writes of the painting in *Art in America*: "Downes is uninterested in traditional perspective, that Renaissance construct for creating an orderly space predicated on a stationary vantage point. He embraces disorder and messiness, and would rather include all relevant details than exclude any. In his works from the '70s, those details are frequently social or economic in significance."

STYLE, SUBJECT, AND METHOD

Critics often remark on the perspective, subject matter, and restrained expression in Downes's work. They note that his paintings tend to exaggerate the curvature of the earth, because he employs a perspective that tends to give his paintings a "fish-eye" look. Relying on his own eye and his sketches, he will paint for two three-hour sessions each day and use several angles of operation, moving his easel this way and that to ensure that he get down every detail of his subject. While working, he takes just a few basic supplies—his box easel with brushes and paints, a hammer, cords and metal tent pegs to keep his work anchored, his lunch, and a small weather radio and compass to prevent him from being caught in the rain.

The subjects of Downes paintings are typically manmade landscapes, or more specifically, the landscapes humans remake. From the underside of a highway overpass to the debris strewn about a garbage dump, the paintings show how humans have shaped their environment, but very infrequently do any people actually appear in the paintings apart from the occasional car or faceless figure. One example of this is *The Mouth of the Passagassawaukeag at Belfast, ME, Seen from the Frozen Foods Plant* (1989), which depicts the river at low tide under some overpasses, with industrial buildings and cars to one side, but no people. Another, *At the Confluence of Two Ditches Bordering a Field with Four Radio Towers* (1995), is also empty of people, apart from buildings in the distance and hints of a road. The piece is particularly notable for its exaggerated curvature, especially in the power lines that occupy the top part of the canvas. Downes seems interested in the tucked-away parts of human activity, as exemplified by *Snug Harbor, Metal Ductwork in G Attic* (2001), which as the title suggests, portrays the functional workmanship found in a building's attic. He frequently works in series, with several panels or paintings depicting the whole scope of a given scene. Two such multipanel works are the triptychs *Farm Buildings near the Rio Grande* (2008) and *Under the Westside Highway at 145th Street* (2008).

Since winning a MacArthur Fellowship in 2009, Downes has found himself in greater demand, and more ardently praised, than ever before in his career. Writing for the *Brooklyn Rail* (6 May 2014), Hearne Pardee proclaimed: "Downes's restrained expression is welcome in an age when emotions are often over-exposed and trivialized in social media. . . . Both [Downs and his teacher Al Held] rejected Abstract Expressionist spontaneity in favor of complex, labor-intensive arts of spatial construction and subdued passion." Richard B. Woodward said of Downes for the *Wall Street Journal* (14 July 2010): "He may be the only member of a Hudson River School who prefers to paint the infrastructure that has grown up beside it." Woodward continued, "His is a cool-headed realism that almost never turns coldly academic. . . . In his egalitarian view of things, garbage scows and old tires deserve the same attention and weight—no more, no less—granted to patches of sky, earth, water, and architecture."

AWARDS AND ACHIEVEMENTS
The work of Rackstraw Downes has been seen at more than two-dozen solo exhibitions as well as in numerous group exhibitions across the United States. Many of his paintings are part of the public collections of the most respected museums in the world, including the Museum of Fine Arts in Boston, the National Gallery of Art in Washington, DC, the Museum of Fine Arts in Houston, and the Art Institute of Chicago. His paintings also hang in New York City's three greatest art museums: the Metropolitan Museum of Art, the Museum of Modern Art, and the Whitney Museum of American Art.

Inducted into the American Academy and Institute of Arts and Letters in 1999, he has also been the recipient of numerous awards. In 1980 he received a National Endowment for the Arts grant. He was later presented with the 1989 Academy-Institute Award from the American Academy and Institute of Arts and Letters. In 1998 he won a Guggenheim Fellowship. More recently, in 2009, he was asked to deliver the Ninth Annual Raymond Lecture for the Archives of American Art and received the MacArthur Fellowship. Downes divides his time between his homes in Presidio, Texas, and New York City.

SUGGESTED READING
Bui, Phong. "Rackstraw Downes: In Focus." *Brooklyn Rail*. Brooklyn Rail, 8 July 2010. Web. 15 Sept. 2014.

Maine, Stephen. "Rackstraw Downes Infrastructures." *Art in America* Nov. 2010: 166–71. Print.

Pardee, Hearne. "Rackstraw Downes." *Brooklyn Rail*. Brooklyn Rail, 6 May 2014. Web. 15 Sept. 2014.

"Rackstraw Downes." *Art21*. ART21, n.d. Web. 15 Sept. 2014.

Spears, Dorothy. "Street Life as Still Life." *New York Times*. New York Times, 21 July 2010. Web. 15 Sept. 2014.

Woodward, Richard B. "Landscape's Grittier Aspects." *Wall Street Journal*. Dow Jones, 14 July 2010. Web. 15 Sept. 2014.

Yezzi, David. "A Conversation with Rackstraw Downes." *New Criterion* Dec. 2005: 48–52. Print.

SELECTED WORKS
The Dam at Fairfield, 1974; *The Mouth of the Passagassawaukeag at Belfast, ME, Seen from the Frozen Foods Plant*, 1989; *At the Confluence of Two Ditches Bordering a Field with Four Radio Towers*, 1995; *Snug Harbor, Metal Ductwork in G Attic*, 2001; *Farm Buildings near the Rio Grande*, 2008; *Under the Westside Highway at 145th Street*, 2008

—Christopher Mari

Lena Dunham
Born: May 13, 1986
Occupation: Filmmaker and actor

Lena Dunham is the award-winning creator of the HBO television show *Girls*. Dunham writes, directs, and stars in the show as Hannah Horvath, a girl in her mid-twenties, who is making a life for herself in New York City. Dunham won the 2012 Golden Globe for best actress in a television series comedy and has been nominated for seven Emmy Awards since the show premiered in 2012. *Girls* won a Golden Globe for best television show for comedy in 2012. Dunham is young—about the age of Horvath—but as a writer, actor, and director, she has been exceptionally prolific. In addition to her work on *Girls*, her early films and a slew of script commissions, she has also written a handful of essays for the *New Yorker*. (A book of essays, *Not That Kind of Girl: A Young Woman Tells You What She's Learned*, is slated for publication in fall 2014.) Dunham and her work have inspired both vicious criticism and glowing praise, but the divisiveness that marks any mention of the writer seems almost beside the point in light of

FGA/Landov

her ubiquity in contemporary culture since her low-budget second film, *Tiny Furniture* (2010). The film—which featured female members of her real-life family, each playing a version of herself—was a surprise hit. In her positive review, Manohla Dargis for the *New York Times* (11 Nov. 2010) called it "one of the bigger itsy-bitsy movies to hit this year." Dunham wrote, directed, and starred in the film that caught the attention of Judd Apatow, the writer, director, and producer behind such movies as *The 40-Year-Old Virgin* (2005) and *Knocked Up* (2007). Apatow is now an executive producer on *Girls*, the third season of which will air beginning in January 2014.

EARLY LIFE AND EDUCATION
Lena Dunham was born in New York City on May 13, 1986. Her father is the artist Carroll Dunham and her mother, Laurie Simmons, is an artist and photographer. Carroll "Tip" Dunham is best known for his cartoonish and sexually-explicit paintings. Simmons is known for her fascination with scale and photographs of dollhouse furniture; Dunham's film *Tiny Furniture* is conceptually based on Simmons's work. The family—which includes Dunham's younger sister, Grace, a poet—is very close. Dunham was prescribed medication for obsessive-compulsive disorder (OCD) as a child and had few friends her own age growing up. She was happiest with her parents and other adults. "She had her own adult world," Simmons recalled to Calvin Tomkins for the *New Yorker* (10 Dec. 2012). "Lena would say, 'Parents, what are we doing this weekend?,' and I'd say there was an opening at the Sonnabend gallery, and she'd say, 'Great!'"

Dunham grew up in Manhattan and Brooklyn, surrounded by artist friends of her parents such as Cindy Sherman, the famous conceptual portrait artist and Simmons's close friend. It would be safe to say that, from a young age, Dunham was better versed in feminist art than she was in classic sitcoms, though she did watch the television show *Sex and the City* as a young adolescent. She attended Saint Ann's, a competitive independent school in Brooklyn Heights, where she met Jemima Kirke, who appears in *Tiny Furniture* and plays the character Jessa on *Girls*. Her parents' artistic sensibilities and circle of friends had a strong influence on Dunham and her view of her own future. She was interested in playwriting and art films in high school and told Meghan O'Rourke, a former St. Ann's classmate, for *Slate* (15 June 2012) that she saw herself writing, teaching feminist studies, and, like many in the fine arts, finding "an unorthodox way to cobble my life together." At the same time, particularly as an undergraduate at Oberlin College, a liberal arts school in Ohio, Dunham was somewhat bored within the confines of the insular art world. "I thought that there was something poppier about my

sensibility that other people didn't understand," she told O'Rourke. (Take, for instance, a video short Dunham made of herself in a bikini, bathing in a public fountain, influenced by a gender studies class and the television show *Jackass*.) Of her work to date, Dunham told O'Rourke, "[it] very much exists in a place between going into a white box with my parents and watching video art and being at the roundtable punch-up for a sitcom," she told O'Rourke.

DELUSIONAL DOWNTOWN DIVAS
Dunham moved back to New York City after graduating with a degree in creative writing from Oberlin in 2008. In 2009, she developed a web series, *Delusional Downtown Divas*, for the now-defunct *Index* magazine. The project started out as a low-budget webisode—the association with *Index* was unpaid—which Dunham cowrote, directed, produced, and acted in alongside friends Isabel Halley (daughter of Peter Halley, the artist who published *Index*) and Joana D'Avillez. The three women are all children of artists, and *Delusional Downtown Divas* was a satirical take on how the art world has become more focused on celebrity and status than art. Summing up the essence of the project, which was, amusingly, lauded by the art world, Dunham told Jada Yuan for *New York* magazine (16 Aug. 2009), "Now you have people who are like, *Yeah, I'm going to be in a band, but if that doesn't work out, I'm probably going to make my living as a painter.* There's this illusion all of a sudden that it's this financially viable industry to enter into, whereas it used to be that if you decided to be an artist, you were basically deciding to live in an attic and get TB and die." There are twenty episodes of the show—filmed "renegade" style, the girls told Yuan—over two seasons.

CREATIVE NONFICTION
Dunham made *Creative Nonfiction*, her first feature film, as a twenty-two-year-old college student. She wrote, directed, and starred in it as Ella, a liberal arts student writing a screenplay. Dunham and her tiny crew shot the film in four weeks, but editing and postproduction took almost two years. In 2009, *Creative Nonfiction* was selected for screening at the South By Southwest film festival in Austin, Texas. Around the same time, Dunham discovered the diaries that her mother had kept as a young woman in the 1970s. Reading about her mother's struggles to make it as an artist was an important moment in Dunham's own career path. "Finding those diaries of my mother's was a real watershed moment for me because, you know, I've always known her, my entire life she's been someone with—who's sort of been doing the impossible, which is supporting herself in a family in a career doing what she wants to do, sort of that holy grail of having a job that's also sort of some kind of catharsis

and self-expression," Dunham told Terry Gross for NPR's *Fresh Air* (6 Dec. 2010).

After graduation and with her budding success as a filmmaker, Dunham's parents made her an offer: they would help finance graduate school or the making a feature film. Dunham chose the latter, though Simmons was actually the first family member to make a movie; her art film, *The Music of Regret*, was produced in 2005 and screened in 2006 at the Museum of Modern Art, the Whitney Museum, and the Metropolitan Museum of Art. It was a forty-five-minute puppet musical—featuring family friend Meryl Streep—and cost more to make than *Tiny Furniture*. But the process of making the movie was exciting and, by some accounts, spurred Dunham's interest in the field.

TINY FURNITURE

Filmed in only eighteen days in the fall of 2009, *Tiny Furniture* is semiautobiographical; Aura (Dunham) is a recent college graduate who moves back in with her artist parents after a bad break-up. She is depressed but also self-involved; the film's tagline is "Aura would like you to know that she's having a very, very hard time." Dargis wrote that Aura "stirs your sympathy even as she routinely tests your patience, oscillating between likable and dislikable." Grace Dunham plays Aura's younger sister, Kirke plays her best friend, and Simmons plays Siri, Aura's artist mother who photographs dollhouse furniture (thus the title). The only family member not to appear in the movie is Dunham's father, who Dunham described to Gross as supportive but a "decidedly private person." Many events in the movie, as with all of Dunham's work, are drawn from her own life. (In one scene, Aura discovers the diaries her mother wrote when she was in her twenties.) Other aspects of the plot are embellished to create conflict and drive the narrative forward, though the story, as Dargis wrote, "unfolds leisurely, almost listlessly." She continued: "Part performance piece, part thought experiment, 'Tiny Furniture' only looks like a straightforward coming-of-age narrative. But this isn't a formulaic representation of a life that has been neatly packaged into a happy or sad tale. It is instead a documentation of the drip drip drip of existence." *Tiny Furniture* won South by Southwest's 2010 award for best narrative feature and an Independent Spirit Award for best first screenplay in 2011.

GIRLS

Girls premiered on HBO on April 15, 2012, and quickly became one of the most talked-about shows of the season. In the pilot episode, viewers meet Hannah, a recent college graduate with a creative writing degree who is working an unpaid internship while being supported by her parents. But when Hannah's parents come to visit from Michigan, they have an announcement for her: she is being cut off—no more money. (This is actually an episode drawn from Simmons's life.) Hannah, an aspiring memoirist, sputters about being the voice of her generation—"or, at least, *a* voice of *a* generation"—but with no sympathy from her college professor parents. She sulks to her quasi-boyfriend, the deeply conflicted Adam Sackler (Adam Driver), who is, at first glance, the very picture of a complete jerk. Viewers also meet the ambitious Marnie Michaels (Allison Williams), Hannah's roommate and best friend who seems to have it all together but who is sick of her long-time boyfriend, Charlie. Meanwhile, the virginal Shoshanna Shapiro (Zosia Mamet) welcomes her willfully free-spirited and globetrotting cousin Jessa Johansson (Kirke) back to New York from a stint abroad. Like Aura before them, Hannah and her friends are depressed and self-involved, alternately likeable and unlikeable.

At its heart, *Girls* is a comedy and a send-up of everything from unpaid internships to the literary world and the tech industry to wealthy New York culture. But it is also something more unusual and melancholy; sometimes, this is a bit disorienting, as with the recurrence of Hannah's self-destructive OCD in season 2. In this sense, Emily Nussbaum wrote for the *New Yorker* (11 Feb. 2013), *Girls* is television "in a more modern mode: spiky, raw, and auteurist." "During the past fifteen years, the medium has been transformed by bad boys like Walter White [of *Breaking Bad*] and sad sacks like Louis C.K. [of *Louis*]," Nussbaum wrote. "'Girls' is the crest of a second, female-centered wave of change, on both cable and network, of shows that are not for everyone, that make viewers uncomfortable."

But the most satisfying thing about the first season of *Girls*, from Dunham and Apatow's perspective at least, was that it was not just girls who were watching. The most popular television shows to date—*The Sopranos*, *Mad Men*, *Breaking Bad*—all feature male protagonists navigating a largely male environment. Women are used to this and were a large part of the viewership that made those shows popular, but it has long been assumed that the reverse—a show that asks a man to identify with a female protagonist—would never work. The demographics of *Girls*, however, seem to prove this theory wrong. Large demographics included men over fifty as well as men and women outside of New York City.

CRITICAL RECEPTION

Dunham has been criticized for writing characters that are white and born into privilege (i.e., spoiled). In response to the race critique, Dunham responded quickly and profusely, and season 2 soon introduced Hannah's new black boyfriend Sandy (Donald Glover), with whom she spars about race-related issues. Even from within the narrow world she has evoked, Dunham has been able to capture the complexities—and vulnerabilities—of her main characters in surprisingly deft ways. The show's premise could easily be described in so many clichés—what it means to be an adult, what it means to be in control of your own life—but in the same way, Dunham manages to defy tropes in this regard, too. Elaine Blair, writing for the *New York Review of Books* (7 June 2012), described a scene in the first season in which Shoshanna, who is in many ways *Girls'* most childlike character, explains *Sex in the City* to her cousin Jessa, who claims to have never seen it. (It is common for fans of *Sex in the City* to describe themselves in terms of one of the characters of the show, each of whom represents a particular set of traits—"I'm a Carrie, I'm a Charlotte"—like flavors of ice cream.) "'I think I'm definitely a Carrie at heart, but sometimes'—her smile widens into a stiff grimace and she stammers—'sometimes Samantha kind of comes out,'" Blair wrote, quoting the show. Samantha is the show's most promiscuous character. "The moment when Shoshanna stammers that 'sometimes Samantha comes out' is a brilliantly excruciating depiction of a young person assuming an ill-fitting mantle of sexual sophistication," Blair wrote. There is a lot of sex on *Girls*, but not of the wholly prurient variety. Intimate scenes between characters—both sexual and platonic—are unexpectedly frank and often uncomfortable, even funny. Dunham approaches the female friendships on the show with the same knowing, comedic eye but without diluting any of the inherent "romance in female friendship" as Claire Danes put it in *Interview* magazine (11 Apr. 2012).

PERSONAL LIFE

Much of Dunham's personal life—whether it be anecdotal or her actual family members and friends—appears in her work. "To my own detriment, everything that happens to me becomes fodder," Dunham told a reporter for *Fast Company* (15 Jan. 2013). "Sometimes I wonder if I would be a bit happier if I were more in the moment, and less trying to translate the moment into a piece of writing or a piece of film. I have never known another way to express myself . . . It's just the way that I think."

Dunham is currently dating Jack Antonoff of the band Fun. She lives in Brooklyn.

SUGGESTED READING

Blair, Elaine. "The Loves of Lena Dunham." *New York Review of Books*. NYREV, 7 June 2012. Web. 18 Nov. 2013.
Danes, Claire. "Lena Dunham." *Interview*. Interview, 11 Apr. 2012. Web. 18 Nov. 2013.
Dargis, Manohla. "Girl Undefined: Post-College but Pre-Real World." Rev. of *Tiny Furniture*, by Lena Dunham. *New York Times*. New York Times Co., 11 Nov. 2010. Web. 18 Nov. 2013.
Gross, Terry. "Lena Dunham's Big Dreams Rest on 'Tiny Furniture.'" *Fresh Air*. Natl. Public Radio, 6 Dec. 2010. Web. 18 Nov. 2013.
Nussbaum, Emily. "Hannah Barbaric." *New Yorker*. Condé Nast, 11 Feb. 2013. Web. 18 Nov. 2013.
O'Rourke, Meghan. "A Conversation with Lena Dunham." *Slate*. Slate Group, 15–17 June 2013. Web. 19 Nov. 2013.
Tomkins, Calvin. "A Doll's House: Laurie Simmons's Sense of Scale." *New Yorker*. Condé Nast, 10 Dec. 2012. Web. 18 Nov. 2013.

SELECTED WORKS

Delusional Downtown Divas, 2009; *Creative Nonfiction*, 2009; *Tiny Furniture*, 2010; *Girls*, 2012

—*Molly Hagan*

James Dyson

Born: May 2, 1947
Occupation: Industrial designer and founder of Dyson Ltd.

James Dyson, most famous for inventing the popular Dyson bagless vacuum cleaner, which utilizes cyclonic separation technology (and which took more than five years and five thousand prototypes to perfect), has single-handedly altered the vacuum industry in much the same way the Hoover company changed the floor-care business in the early twentieth century. In fact Dyson relays in his 1997 autobiography, *Against the Odds*: "I lay no claim to the epithet 'household word', though I harbour a secret dream of synonymity, and occasionally imagine a time . . . when 'dyson' replaces 'hoover', [and] pulls that cunning stunt . . . becomes a noun, a verb, out there on its own and detached from me to such an extent that most people will have no idea that there ever was a man called Dyson."

Not only is "Dyson" on its way to becoming a household word, Dyson's vacuum cleaner in some ways parallels the shift in gender roles that has taken place in the postindustrial world, in which increasing numbers of men find themselves contributing to their families' housework. "Dyson brought a level of excitement to housekeeping that's usually reserved for cell phones and plasma televisions," Hannah Clark wrote for *Forbes* magazine (1 Aug. 2006). "Vacuuming has now joined grilling as the one household chore men can get excited about, perhaps because the Dyson, with its bright yellow cylinders, is designed like a cool kid's toy. And it actually works."

© Axel Heimken/dpa/Corbis

After the dual cyclone vacuum cleaner was rejected by several major companies, Dyson decided to manufacture and market it himself in 1993. Now he controls a significant portion of the worldwide vacuum market and is said to have a net worth more than four billion dollars.

EARLY YEARS

James Dyson was born on May 2, 1947, in the coastal town of Cromer in Norfolk, England. He has an older sister, Shanie, and an older brother, Tom. Their father was a classics teacher at Gresham's, a well-regarded independent school in the town of Holt, and the family lived in a rambling Victorian home near the school's sports fields. (Causing some confusion for Americans, tuition-charging institutions like Gresham's are referred to as "public" schools in the United Kingdom.)

Dyson's father, an avid amateur actor who regularly directed school plays, died of cancer in 1956. At the time of his death, he had been preparing to accept a job at BBC Television. "Seeing him thwarted by death in that way, having done something else for so long, made me determined that that should never happen to me," Dyson wrote in *Against the Odds*. "I would not be dragged into something I didn't want to do." While Dyson's mother received no formal pension from Gresham's, her sons were given scholarships to attend the school, and she supported the family by dressmaking and private tutoring. (She also went back to school herself, studying English at the University of Cambridge.)

EDUCATION AND EARLY CAREER

By his own account Dyson was far from an accomplished student; he passed only seven O levels—and those just barely. (O, or "ordinary" levels, were the tests of subject material then required for graduation in England.) He took up the bassoon when he was ten and often recounts to journalists the tale of volunteering to learn the instrument for the school orchestra and then being horrified the first time he saw it—with its "eight feet of pipes and millions of keys." He nonetheless eventually mastered the

instrument; he was also a skilled runner. He has said that those pursuits—training to win races and practicing the bassoon—taught him the value of perseverance and determination. Dyson also loved painting, and he once won a transistor radio—then a much-coveted item—in a student art competition.

Those skills did not readily suggest a future profession, however. He briefly contemplated medicine and acting before deciding, in 1966, to enter the Byam Shaw Art School in Kensington. There he studied drawing, painting, and printmaking, and after a year he moved on to the Royal College of Art (RCA). Although RCA was a prestigious graduate-level school, Dyson was accepted thanks to a special program that he characterizes in his book as an "experiment in educational anti-elitism." He spent the first year there filling in the gaps in his arts education, taking courses in furniture design, filmmaking, sculpting, industrial design, and architecture. He took a course with structural engineer Anthony Hunt, famed for his work on Waterloo Station, and became enamored with the work of the visionary designer Buckminster Fuller and Isambard Kingdom Brunel, a mechanical and civil engineer who built several innovative bridges and tunnels. He has cited those two men as inspirations, for their iconoclastic natures and willingness to question conventional wisdom.

To earn pocket money Dyson sold unlabeled wine that a friend had imported from Spain to students and staff members. He also completed a three-month internship with the Conran Design Group, then the only such design consultancy in England, and counted himself lucky to be making a small salary. There he worked on designing such projects as banquette seating, a headrest, and a children's chair. While he found the experience valuable, he knew that he would not enjoy a career as a consultant. "I didn't want to put the icing on other people's creations," he wrote in *Against the Odds*. "I wanted to make things."

Dyson, who graduated from RCA in 1970, earned his first paid commission while still a student, designing an auditorium for the Roundhouse theater in north London. The project introduced him to businessman Jeremy Fry of the Rotork Engineering Company, who would play a major role in Dyson's future.

THE SEATRUCK AND THE BALLBARROW

Impressed by the work Dyson had done on the theater project, Fry hired him in 1968, while he was still at RCA, to help design and build a high-speed fiberglass watercraft. The finished product, dubbed the Seatruck, could carry a load of three metric tons (about nearly seven thousand pounds) and travel at speeds of up to fifty miles per hour. It proved particularly popular in the oil and construction industries, and it was sold for military use as well. (The Egyptian army employed several of the vessels during the 1973 war with Israel.)

After graduating Dyson signed on to work full time on the Seatruck. "Having realized at college that I wanted to change the world by building extraordinary things, and shaking people up, I suddenly saw that it was genuinely possible," he wrote in *Against the Odds*. He continued to work with Fry until 1974, when, tired of seeing his efforts enrich the coffers of Rotork's shareholders rather than his own and eager to strike out independently, he left to focus on what he called the Ballbarrow, a portmanteau of "ball" and "wheelbarrow."

Dyson had gotten the idea for the Ballbarrow while renovating an old farmhouse he had purchased in the Cotswolds. His conventional wheelbarrow, he noticed, was unstable when carrying heavy loads, prone to sinking in soft ground and leaving ruts, and difficult to clean after being filled with a messy substance, such as cement. He replaced the narrow wheel with an indestructible plastic ball, fashioned an easy to tip out and clean bucket, and widened the feet of the back portion so that when placed on the ground, the weight of the load was spread out, making the unit less likely to sink.

Dyson received financial backing from a group that included his brother-in-law to manufacture and market the item, which sold well. Within a few years, however, differences in business philosophy emerged, and Dyson was ousted by his partners, who then sold the rights to the Ballbarrow to another company. Hurt, he did not speak to his sister and brother-in-law for almost a decade, and he vowed never again to assign a patent to another person or company. Losing his invention, he has told journalists, felt like losing a limb.

A NEW TYPE OF VACUUM

The tale of how Dyson got the idea for his bagless vacuum has become the stuff of company legend. His old Hoover Junior vacuum had long been a source of frustration for him, and although money was tight at the time, he invested in a new canister model that was advertised as the most powerful on the market. When that machine also proved less than satisfactory, Dyson—still part of the Ballbarrow enterprise at that point—disassembled it and discovered that the pores of the vacuum bag were clogging with dirt almost immediately. "I was furious," he wrote in *Against the Odds*. "I felt the same anger towards the vacuum cleaner as I had towards the wheelbarrow." He continued, "The most powerful vacuum cleaner ever produced . . . was essentially just as useless as the old one."

He found the answer to the clogging problem in an unlikely place. At the Ballbarrow factory, an epoxy powder was sprayed on the frame of each

unit in order to strengthen it; the excess powder was collected for disposal by means of a cloth screen, which clogged regularly, causing production to halt while it was cleaned. When Dyson approached the manufacturers of the spraying equipment, he learned that other clients employed a "cyclone," a large cone that spun the excess powder out of the air by centrifugal force, rather than a cloth screen. He fashioned one for the Ballbarrow factory out of sheets of steel and found that it worked perfectly.

Armed with that knowledge, he then fashioned a miniature cyclone out of cardboard for his old Hoover Junior. It worked well, but Dyson spent years perfecting his invention, ensuring that it could trap both the finest dust and the largest pieces of detritus. Each night he trudged from his workshop, exhausted and demoralized, wondering if he would ever hit upon a marketable version. He ultimately made 5,127 prototypes before being satisfied. He then "set off, like a traveling vacuum cleaner salesman of old, to tackle the fire-belching giants of British industry," as he quipped in his book.

DYSON LTD.

Those industry giants expressed little interest, but finally in 1983, Apex, a Japanese company, licensed his design and marketed the G-Force, a striking pink-and-purple vacuum that sold for more than one thousand dollars and became a status symbol.

Using the proceeds from the G-Force, Dyson set up an eponymous company and set about marketing a series of cyclonic vacuums. The models generally featured bright-yellow components and transparent containers for the dust, so that consumers could see that the machines were working. Although industry insiders initially mocked his designs, eventually brightly colored components, transparent containers, and internal cyclones became widely copied features. (Dyson has been embroiled in several patent infringement suits, most notably with Hoover, which was forced to pay him several million dollars in damages in 1999.) The motor on his newest model, the DC59, rotates at 110,000 revolutions per minute—about five times faster than that of a high performance race car.

Although Dyson had long been vocal about the need for Great Britain to invest in technology and business development, in 2002 he moved his production facilities from Wiltshire to Malaysia, causing a spate of bad publicity. He recently announced, however, that he would be doubling the size of his Wiltshire-based research facilities and expected to hire up to three thousand new engineers in the coming years.

In addition to vacuums, the company produces the Dyson Airblade, a hand dryer found in many public bathrooms. The futuristic-looking Airblade produces a stream of air at speeds of more than four hundred miles per hour and dries a patron's hands in about ten seconds. Even more futuristic is Dyson's Air Multiplier, a bladeless fan that works by drawing a large quantity of air per second in through its base and forcing it through an outlet in the upper portion of the device.

Among Dyson's few high profile failures was the Contrarotator, a washing machine with two drums, which he claimed gave it superior cleaning power. The expensive machine never caught on with the public, however, and was discontinued in 2014.

PHILANTHROPY

In 2002 Dyson launched an eponymous foundation, with the aim of supporting design and engineering education. Among its most popular initiatives is the Education Box, which contains several learning activities and is provided free of charge to any teacher who requests one. The foundation also sponsors the James Dyson Award, which is given annually to the engineering student (or student team), who submits the most viable, inventive design. The 2013 winner, for example, was the Titan Arm, a lightweight, inexpensive exoskeleton meant to help users lift heavy objects. Another award, for the best design and technology teacher of the year, is also given. Dyson has endowed a building at RCA, where he serves as provost, that houses dozens of incubators and encourages British invention, and he has funded scholarships at Northwestern University in the United States.

In addition to his educational mission, Dyson gives generously to medical causes. In November 2013 he donated £750,000 (about $1.3 million) to the Royal United Hospital in Bath to fund the Dyson Centre for Neonatal Care and contributed £4 million (about $7 million) for the launch of a new cancer center, citing the fact that both his parents had died of the disease.

PERSONAL LIFE

Since 1968 Dyson has been married to the former Deirdre Hindmarsh, whom he met while both were students at RCA. She can be seen modeling in the original advertising brochures for the Ballbarrow. During the years when Dyson was struggling to perfect his vacuum prototype, she supported the family with her wages as an art teacher. The couple have three children: Emily, who works in the fashion industry; Jacob, who is a product designer specializing in lighting; and Sam, a musician.

Although there were many years when Dyson was deeply in debt and nearing bankruptcy, he is now worth $4.4 billion, according to *Forbes*, and is one of the three hundred richest people in the world. He and his wife live at Dodington Park, a three-hundred-acre estate in Gloucestershire, and also own a townhouse in London and a

château in France. His ninety-one-meter yacht, *Nahlin*, is one of the largest British-owned vessels in the world.

In 1996 Dyson was appointed a commander of the Most Excellent Order of the British Empire, and he was made a knight bachelor in 2007. He holds an honorary doctoral degree in engineering from the University of Bath, and in 2005 he was elected a fellow of the Royal Academy of Engineering.

Despite his vast wealth, Dyson is still actively engaged in developing projects and seeking innovations. "We have to embrace failure and almost get a kick out of it. Not in a perverse way, but in a problem-solving way," he told Nadia Goodman for *Entrepreneur* (5 Nov. 2012). "Life is a mountain of solvable problems and I enjoy that."

SUGGESTED READING

Dyson, James. "James Dyson Cleans Up." Interview by Hannah Clark. *Forbes*. Forbes.com, 1 Aug. 2006. Web. 21 Jan. 2014.

Dyson, James. *Against the Odds: An Autobiography*. London: Orion, 1997. Print.

Dyson, James. "James Dyson on Using Failure to Drive Success." Interview by Nadia Goodman. *Entrepreneur*. Entrepreneur Media, 5 Nov. 2012. Web. 7 Mar. 2014.

Hardy, Frances. "Partners in Grime." [London] *Daily Mail*. Associated Newspapers, 27 Feb. 1999. Web. 21 Jan. 2014.

Kelley, Raina. "How James Dyson Revolutionized the Vacuum." *Newsweek*. Newsweek, 3 Jan. 2011. Web. 21 Jan. 2014.

Onderko, Patty. "The Ever Tinkering Engineer." *Success*. Success Magazine, 1 Nov. 2013. Web. 21 Jan. 2014.

—*Mari Rich*

Caterina Fake

Born: June 13, 1969
Occupation: Entrepreneur and businesswoman

Caterina Fake is a technology entrepreneur whose most recent venture is a location-based website called Findery. Findery allows its users to leave notes for themselves or for other users about locations they have visited. On October 2, 2013, Fake herself took to the site to post a note about the chestnut tree in the middle of a traffic circle in the Prospect Park neighborhood of Brooklyn. Fake is also the cofounder of the photo-sharing website Flickr as well as the cofounder of Hunch, a website that generates recommendations for users based on individual "taste graphs." Fake is chair of the board at Etsy and serves as a consultant and investor

Maria J. Avila/MCT/Landov

for numerous technology companies. She is a founding partner of Founder Collective, a venture capital fund that provides crucial seed money for start-ups.

For all of her success, one might imagine that Fake set out to make her fortune in technology. Rather, she is an artist and writer who taught herself how to write computer code in the hope of making enough money to fund her artistic dreams. In technology she found a new passion. "I'm an accidental business person," Fake told Nick Bilton for the *New York Times* (6 Oct. 2010). "I just love the medium. I love the Internet. If you looked at my résumé in the years leading up to Flickr, I worked in a dive shop in landlocked Arkansas, I was a starving artist. I just arrived at the thing I love to do accidentally."

EARLY LIFE AND EDUCATION

Caterina Fake was born on June 13, 1969, in Pittsburgh, Pennsylvania. Her mother, a pharmacist, is from Manila, and Fake has a number of relatives in the Philippines. Her father, Peter Fake, is a book lover who worked as an insurance executive. Fake and her sister grew up in a wealthy New Jersey suburb, and as a child, she dreamed of becoming a writer and artist. She recalls selling her drawings to her parents when she was five years old "for ten cents or a quarter, depending on the size," she told Teri Evans for *Entrepreneur* magazine (28 Mar. 2011). Fake's father and grandfather were natural storytellers and shared with Fake and her sister tales of imaginative travels to places such as the Pirate Islands and the Kingdom of Mice. Their stories

encouraged Fake's creativity and her wanderlust later in life and were, along with the myths and fairytales she read growing up, her primary source of entertainment.

Fake attended high school at Choate Rosemary Hall in Wallingford, Connecticut, and graduated in 1986. She then attended Smith College and later transferred to Vassar College, where she studied English literature and graduated in 1991. After college, she backpacked across Central and South America, Europe, Syria, and Lebanon. She spent another year painting in New York City.

Fake moved to San Francisco in 1995 and lived with her sister while she taught herself HTML, the main language for creating web pages, and worked as an art director for Salon. com. In 1997, she began managing community forums for the computer services company Netscape. In 2002, she and her then-husband Stewart Butterfield founded Ludicorp and created the online role-playing game Game Neverending, or GNE. "The game," Fake told Devin Leonard for *Wired* (28 July 2010), "is just an excuse. It's a framing device . . . to hang out and smoke cigars and gossip." Fake and Butterfield then worked on a handful of other projects, including a photo-sharing website called Flickr, which they launched in 2004.

CREATING FLICKR

Flickr, which Fake originally wanted to call Flicker before learning that the domain name was already taken, is a true rags-to-riches story. Fake and Butterfield had set out to create another game and had hired staff to create it, but they "only had money for one last shot" and realized that they "could deploy Flickr faster than the game," Fake told Michael Fitzgerald for *Inc.* magazine (1 Dec. 2006). The team took a vote, and Flickr was born. It was not the first photo-sharing website, but it was the first to encourage users to interact with each other by following and tagging photos. Fake and Butterfield also worked hard to foster the positivity of an actual community; the site's tone was, as Leonard described it, "playful," and Fake often left long, supportive comments on users' photographs, hoping to dispel the toxic commentary that was pervading so many sites. She believes that the efforts to keep Flickr friendly led to its quick rise; six months after the site debuted, it had over 250,000 users. Flickr is considered an important part of the Internet's history because it inspired a slew of other sites devoted to user-generated content. Search engines had been the focus of the early Internet era; Flickr marked the beginning of the age of social media. "One of the overarching goals of my career has been to make technology more human," Fake told Leonard. "You should be able to feel the presence of other people on the Internet."

SELLING FLICKR

Technology companies Google and Yahoo both made advances toward acquiring Flickr, but Yahoo won the bidding war in 2005 and bought the site for $35 million. Fake and Butterfield were overnight tech celebrities, and they soon appeared on the covers of both *Time* and *Newsweek*. The following year, however, Butterfield admitted to Fitzgerald that he felt they might have sold the company too soon. A number of factors came into play when the team decided to sell, he explained, including the illness of a close friend and investor as well as fear of another market crash, but the regret did not cut too deep. Reid Hoffman, cofounder of the professional networking site LinkedIn and an early Flickr investor, told Fake and Butterfield that with the money they earned from the deal, they would have another chance to make history. Hoffman told them, "You'll be able to be entrepreneurs the rest of your lives," Fake recalled to Fitzgerald. Fake and Butterfield followed Flickr to Yahoo, where executives hoped they would breathe new life into the company. "They were the vanguard of a new movement," Bradley Horowitz, tech entrepreneur and vice president of product management for Google+, told Leonard. "Yahoo executives very much wanted their mojo to rub off on them."

Fake signed a three-year contract with Yahoo. During her tenure with the company, she advised executives and organized hack days, which gave a fun and competitive platform for Yahoo employees to present new ideas for programs and applications. Fake left Yahoo in 2008 when her contract expired, and although she was part of a larger exodus of Yahoo executives, including Butterfield, Fake maintains that she left because she had developed other interests, and she wanted to start a new business and take some time off to reassess her future. Despite this, Fake was hounded by offers from venture capitalist firms and start-ups. Before leaving Yahoo, she met with Chris Dixon, a tech entrepreneur and investor, who was starting a recommendation site called Hunch.

HUNCH

Hunch is a website that provides customized recommendations to its users, but unlike sites such as Amazon, which offer recommendations based on prior purchases, Hunch offers information and suggestions that are based on the answers users provide to multiple-choice questions. Dixon's original idea for the site worked with an existing concept called collaborative filtering, which had been used in the mid-1990s to make music recommendations by matching users who had similar musical tastes. Dixon believed the concept could work more efficiently and function in a way that allowed users to feel as if they were receiving advice from a close friend.

Hunch relies on queries that users answer in a feature called "Teach Hunch About You." The questions vary across topics, and the more questions a user answers, the more complete his or her profile becomes. From that profile, Hunch creates a "taste graph," which offers users their personalized recommendations.

While the idea drew significant attention initially, there was a problem, because in order for Hunch to function, it required users to begin making recommendations. When Fake met with Dixon in the spring of 2008, she suggested a solution. As she explained to Leonard, she began to reflect on her work at Yahoo and realized "if you could create a search engine that could learn from the input of users, you would have the magic recipe." Fake joined Hunch as the site's chief product officer and cofounder in June 2008.

Hunch attracted users as soon as it made its public debut in 2009. It was Fake's idea to reward users with badges known as banjos for participating on the site and allow users to track how many banjos they had accumulated in comparison with others. Fake was also responsible for the "Teach Hunch About You" feature, which helped to make the questions fun to answer and mildly addictive. As Fake explained to Leonard, answering the questions is "one of those things where you can't stop and you don't know why, but it's fun."

In 2011, the online auction site eBay purchased Hunch for a reported $80 million.

FINDERY

Fake explained to Dan Schawbel for *Forbes* magazine (11 Sept. 2012) that the idea for Findery came from an idyllic camping trip she took with her daughter. The two were hiking in a northern California forest in 2010 and stopped to take a nap among a circle of redwood trees. Fake envisioned a social network that would allow her to "remember that moment forever and mark that spot" and, as she told Emily Brennan for the *New York Times* (4 Dec. 2013), to "leave a note in this place, so . . . this moment will be preserved." Findery aims to create narratives through its notes. The site is not about recommendations, Fake told Brennan. Instead, it allows its users to make maps of their own memories. Fake clarified to Brian Patrick Eha for *Entrepreneur* magazine (2 Apr. 2013) that she is "deeply steeped in the humanities," and because of that, she envisions Findery as a "kind of a liberal arts paradise" where users can read about another's firsthand experience at a faraway location but also benefit from an expert's perspectives of events at the location or knowledge of its unique history.

Findery launched in public beta in October 2012 and released its mobile app in early 2014. Fake explained to Eha that she believes the mobile app will expand the site's usability, because then people can log into Findery "while lounging at home—'the armchair traveler experience'—and while exploring the world outside." The site is still building its user base, but Fake explained to Schawbel that releasing the Findery website prior to the mobile app was purposeful. "We want[ed] to avoid the 'empty restaurant' problem of many location-based apps," she said. "It takes a long time to build a body of participatory media." In the meantime, Fake and her Findery team, which is based in the Hayes Valley neighborhood of San Francisco, are preparing a number of features for the app, including audio and video capabilities. She also hopes to feature hidden notes on the site that will be available only to users in specific locations.

WORK HABITS

Fake is often asked about her tremendous productivity in light of her dedication to and success with so many projects. She explained to Schawbel that it could be partially attributed to her sleeping schedule: she sleeps each night from 10 p.m. to 2 a.m. and then from 5 a.m. to 8 a.m. "I have an extremely productive few hours in the middle when I get most of my mental and creative work done," she said.

Surprisingly, Fake is also a committed user of pencil and paper. She explained to Tessa Miller for *Lifehacker* (15 Aug. 2012) that she takes notes in a steno notebook and uses a small, spiral-bound notebook to record her ongoing, numbered to-do list. She is also an admitted "pencil snob" and uses a specific brand of wooden pencil, and because she makes "a lot of mistakes," she also has a supply of extra erasers.

Fake believes that people work more productively in an environment that resembles their home than they do in cubicles under fluorescent lighting. Her group's office in Hayes Valley is therefore full of natural light, plants, and furniture gleaned from flea markets rather than from trendy, sleek furniture stores.

HONORS AND DISTINCTIONS

In 2005, Fake received a Best Leader award from *Business Week* for creating Flickr, was listed on *Forbes*'s e-Gang (its list of technology trendsetters), and appeared on *Fast Company* magazine's Fast 50 list, which recognized the year's fifty most notable "leaders, innovators and technology pioneers." The following year, Fake was included in *Time* magazine's list of the world's hundred most influential people. She has received an honorary doctorate from the Rhode Island School of Design and in 2013 received the Symons Innovator Award from the National Center for Women and Information Technology.

Fake is chair of the board of Etsy, an e-commerce website specializing in handmade and vintage items. She is a board member of Creative Commons, which advocates for increasing and supporting creative work that can then be built upon and shared without the constraints of copyright issues. Fake is also on the board of advisors for the School of Information at the University of California, Berkeley, which is a graduate program devoted to increasing access to information while improving its reliability and maintaining its security.

PERSONAL LIFE

Fake married Stewart Butterfield in 2002, and in 2007 she gave birth to their daughter, Sonnet Beatrice. After Fake and Butterfield divorced in 2008, Fake moved with their daughter to San Francisco. She also has a home in New York City.

SUGGESTED READING

Bilton, Nick. "One on One: Caterina Fake, Flickr and Hunch." *New York Times*. New York Times, 6 Oct. 2010. Web. 6 Feb. 2014.

Brennan, Emily. "Story First, Maps Second." *New York Times*. New York Times, 4 Dec. 2013. Web. 6 Feb. 2014.

Evans, Teri. "Caterina Fake on Stepping into the Unknown." *Entrepreneur*. Entrepreneur Media, 28 Mar. 2011. Web. 6 Feb. 2014.

Fitzgerald, Michael. "How We Did It: Stewart Butterfield and Caterina Fake, Co-Founders, Flickr." *Inc*. Mansueto Ventures, 1 Dec. 2006. Web. 6 Feb. 2014.

Leonard, Devin. "What You Want: Flickr Creator Spins Addictive New Web Service." *Wired*. Condé Nast, 28 July 2010. Web. 6 Feb. 2014.

Schawbel, Dan. "Caterina Fake on Launching Her Third Startup 'Findery.'" *Forbes*. Forbes.com, 11 Sept. 2012. Web. 6 Feb. 2014.

—Molly Hagan

Negin Farsad

Born: 1978
Occupation: Comedian and filmmaker

The Iranian American comedian and filmmaker Negin Farsad, who is known for her irreverent humor and high-pitched delivery, has established a reputation as one of the leading practitioners of social justice comedy. As one of the few female Muslim comedians in a male-dominated profession, Farsad has used humor as a vehicle to combat negative cultural stereotypes, particularly those about her Iranian heritage. She began her stand-up career in the early 2000s while a graduate student at Columbia University and worked briefly as a public policy adviser for the city of New York before launching a full-time career in the entertainment industry in 2006. Farsad has since enjoyed success not only as a stand-up act but also as a writer, director, producer, and performer for television and film.

Getty Images

She is best known for her critically acclaimed, feature-length documentaries *Nerdcore Rising* (2008) and *The Muslims Are Coming!* (2013), the latter of which centers on the issue of Islamophobia in the United States. She has also written and developed original content for such television networks as Comedy Central, MTV, Public Broadcasting Service (PBS), and the Independent Film Channel (IFC). Discussing her experiential approach to comedy, she explained to Kathleen Daminger for the *Lancaster (Pennsylvania) New Era* (27 Jan. 2013), "When you're the daughter of immigrants, you see through a different lens that might be [a] bit more international and a little more sensitive to the plight of minorities."

EARLY LIFE AND EDUCATION
The younger of two children, Negin Farsad was born in New Haven, Connecticut, in 1978. Her Iranian immigrant parents, Reza and Golnaz, and brother, Ramin, who is thirteen years older, had come to the United States in 1972, when her father was admitted to a medical residency program at Yale University in New Haven. When Farsad was seven years old, her family settled in the wealthy resort enclave of Palm Springs, California, where her father began working as a surgeon. She and her brother were raised in a traditional Muslim household and grew up speaking Farsi and Azeri, a Turkic language prevalent in the country of Azerbaijan.

As an Iranian American in a predominantly white community, Farsad has recalled feeling like an outsider growing up, which in turn sparked an early interest in social change. One

of Farsad's childhood dreams was to become the first female Muslim president. She told Daminger, "I wanted to end racism." That desire notwithstanding, Farsad was subject to constant teasing as a girl because of cultural restrictions that forbade her from shaving her legs.

Farsad attended Palm Springs High School, where she was reportedly one of only two Iranian students. Despite being painfully shy, she found her niche in the drama and debate clubs. For Farsad, a turning point came when she starred as a kitchen wench in a school production of Hans Christian Andersen's *The Princess and the Pea*. "That's what changed my life," she told Melissa Pandika for the news and culture site *Ozy* (11 Apr. 2014). "The sort of freedom you get in a creative zone opens you up in a different way." Farsad, who was an exceptional student, went on to star in other student productions—including playing God in a production of the Neil Simon comedy *God's Favorite*—and became president of the debate club.

DUAL PASSIONS
After graduating from Palm Springs High in 1994, Farsad attended Cornell University in Ithaca, New York, where she majored in both theater and government. As a freshman she auditioned for and earned a spot in the Cornell sketch-comedy group the Skits-O-Phrenics, which was then devoid of female members. Farsad performed with the group throughout college, during which she honed her comedic skills. Still, she viewed her comedic exploits as nothing more than a hobby and remained committed to a career in politics. "I was eventually going to run for Congress in my district," she told journalist Omar Bilal Akhtar (2 Apr. 2012), "end up in the White House and end the racial divide."

Upon earning a bachelor's degree in theater arts and government from Cornell in 1998, Farsad enrolled at Columbia University in New York. There, she earned her master's degree from Columbia's School of International and Public Affairs. During her time at Columbia, Farsad interned for longtime Harlem congressman Charles Rangel and New York senator Hillary Clinton. She also founded a sketch-comedy group called Three Jews and a Persian with former Skits-O-Phrenics colleagues Geoff Kirsch, Jason Reich, and Alex Zalben. The foursome performed at venues all over New York and served as an opening act for Tina Fey and Rachel Dratch's sketch-comedy duo.

In 2005 Farsad started working as a public policy adviser for the New York City Campaign Finance Board. She held that position for roughly a year and a half, during which she moonlighted as a stand-up comic, performing at open-mike nights and comedy clubs. Torn between her passion for public service and her love of comedy, Farsad has said that her friends began to stage interventions to convince her that the latter profession was her true calling. Comedy "started taking over all aspects of my life," she recalled to Daminger. "But I struggled with it because I thought it wasn't going to help change the world, and that bummed me out."

BREAKING INTO TELEVISION AND NERDCORE RISING

Taking her friends' advice, Farsad left her public policy job in 2006 to focus on her burgeoning comedy career, thus beginning what she has called "the Era of Parental Disappointment." By then, she had already started developing an irreverent stand-up routine that riffed on her Muslim Iranian heritage, public policy, and social justice issues. Farsad spent the next year refining her routine at comedy clubs around the country, during which she earned very little money. Nonstop touring, however, left her exhausted. In an attempt to ground her creative efforts, Farsad founded her own production company, Vaguely Qualified Productions, and began to focus on writing and directing.

In 2007 Farsad began writing, directing, producing, and performing for the Comedy Central web series The Watch List, which was the first American show to feature all Arab American comedians. Cocreated by Dean Obeidallah and Max Brooks, son of legendary comedian Mel Brooks, the series, which poked fun at international politics, generated some of the highest web traffic on the Comedy Central site.

Farsad next directed and produced her first feature-length film, Nerdcore Rising (2008). The film—a documentary that examines the genre of hip-hop known as nerdcore, which expounds on topics related to nerds—chronicles the history of the genre and follows its founder, Damian Hess, better known by the stage name MC Frontalot, as he embarks on his first national tour. It also features other nerdcore artists, such as MC Chris and the Seattle-based group Optimus Rhyme, and interviews with celebrities such as parody pioneer Weird Al Yankovic. In an interview with Karen Eng for the TED (Technology, Entertainment, Design) blog (27 Sept. 2013), Farsad said that her goal with the film was to "make a real-life thing funny, without being funny at people's expense."

Nerdcore Rising made its world premiere in March 2008 at the South by Southwest (SXSW) Film Festival in Austin, Texas, where it received wide critical acclaim. In a review for Film School Rejects (12 Mar. 2008), Neil Miller called the film "electrifying and arresting" and commented that it was "a well-edited, wonderfully presented look at a movement that speaks to everything geek." Nerdcore Rising screened at other festivals around the world and received a wide release on DVD in September 2009.

Later in 2008, Farsad wrote and directed a short film, Hot Bread Kitchen, about bakery owner Jessamyn Waldman Rodriguez. The film won the Lifetime Network's Every Woman's Filmmaker Competition.

THE MUSLIMS ARE COMING STAND-UP TOUR

In 2009, after the success of The Watch List and Nerdcore Rising, Farsad landed jobs writing and developing projects for a number of television networks. That year, she wrote for and developed MTV's web and television show Detox, which mocked MTV programming, and signed on as a writer for the PBS animated series 1001 Nights, which was coproduced by the Iranian-born entrepreneur Shabnam Rezaei. Farsad served as a tech correspondent for IFC News at the 2010 South by Southwest festival.

In the midst of her busy web and television career, Farsad continued doing stand-up at night, mostly around New York. During the spring and fall of 2011, she took her stand-up act on the road as part of a national, multicomedian US tour called The Muslims Are Coming, which used comedy to break down negative stereotypes about Muslims. For Farsad, the idea for the tour arose from the tide of Islamophobia and anti-Muslim violence that swept across the country in the wake of the 2008 presidential election, when President Barack Obama was accused of secretly following Islam. "It was bothering me that being a Muslim became an accusation," she told Pandika.

On the tour, Farsad was joined by a diverse group of Muslim comedians, including Dean Obeidallah, who is of Palestinian and Italian descent; Kareem Omary, who is half Syrian and half Peruvian; Preacher Moss, an African American; Maysoon Zayid, a Palestinian with cerebral palsy; and Omar Elba, an Egyptian-born comic from Los Angeles. They performed free comedy shows throughout the American South and Southwest, traveling to traditionally "red" states such as Tennessee, Georgia, Mississippi, and Arizona.

At each stop on the tour, Farsad and her fellow comics organized Muslim-centric public stunts as a way to interact with locals. Such stunts included setting up an "Ask a Muslim" booth, holding up "Hug a Muslim" signs, arranging a "Bowl with a Muslim Day," and playing a game called "Name That Religion." Commenting on the goal of the stunts, Farsad explained to Eng, "We wanted to shatter the links in mainstream American consciousness with Muslims as violent people. . . . We wanted to come up with new stereotypes—such as Muslims are all hilarious and they're really bad at bowling."

THE MUSLIMS ARE COMING! DOCUMENTARY AND OTHER WORK

With Obeidallah, Farsad codirected the filming of the tour. The two subsequently edited nearly three hundred hours of footage into the feature-length docucomedy *The Muslims Are Coming!* (2013), which includes clips from the comedians' stand-up acts, footage from their public stunts, and interviews with a host of celebrities, including comedians Jon Stewart, Lewis Black, and Janeane Garofalo and political commentators Rachel Maddow and Soledad O'Brien. The film tackles various issues associated with the Islamic community, from religious fanaticism to the role and rights of women, comments on the proliferation of anti-Muslim fervor, and argues for comedy as a unifying force. "Humor tends to open people up," Farsad said in her interview with Daminger. "It tends to make sense of things while not making people feel like they're being accused."

The Muslims Are Coming! premiered to a sold-out crowd in October 2012 at the Austin Film Festival, where it received the Comedy Vanguard Audience Award. The film was released theatrically in select cities in September 2013 and released on Netflix in January 2014. It elicited mixed responses from reviewers. In a representative review for the *Los Angeles Times* (12 Sept. 2013), Annlee Ellingson concluded that Farsad and Obeidallah "try to keep it light, even a little cheesy, in the face of at-times infuriating anti-Muslim attitudes—an approach that best serves their goal of giving America 'this big Muslim hug.'"

In 2014, Farsad began preproduction work on her third feature-length documentary, *3rd Street Blackout*, which takes a comedic look at the power outage caused by Hurricane Sandy. The film is codirected by Jeremy Redleaf and features Janeane Garofalo.

In addition to her film, television, and stand-up work, Farsad has made a wide array of web videos, advertisements, and public-service announcements for organizations such as MoveOn.org, Healthy Americans Against Reforming Medicine—a satirical organization mocking the anti–health care reform movement—and the American Federation of Labor and Congress of Industrial Organizations, among others. In 2008, she made a video for Queen Rania of Jordan about Arab stereotypes called *Don't Call Me That*. The video was featured as a part of web series that later won the first ever YouTube Visionary Award.

Farsad lives in New York. In 2011 she was named one of the *Huffington Post*'s favorite female comedians and was also named a TED Fellow. She gave a talk about her brand of social justice comedy at the 2013 TED Conference in Long Beach, California.

SUGGESTED READING

Daminger, Kathleen. "Muslim Comedian Hopes to Change World with Laughs." *Lancaster Online*. LancasterOnline, 27 Jan. 2013. Web. 7 May 2014.

Eng, Karen. "The Muslims Are Coming!: Fellows Friday with Negin Farsad." *TED Blog*. TED Conferences, 27 Sept. 2013. Web. 7 May 2014.

Herzog, Brad. "Make 'em Laugh." *Cornell Alumni Magazine*. Cornell Alumni Association, Mar./Apr. 2013. Web. 7 May 2014.

Pandika, Melissa. "Hugging Muslims: A Comedic Primer." *Ozy*. Ozymandias, 11 Apr. 2014. Web. 7 May 2014.

—*Chris Cullen*

Arash Ferdowsi

Born: October 7, 1985
Occupation: Cofounder and CTO of Dropbox

Arash Ferdowsi met Drew Houston, another Massachusetts Institute of Technology student, in 2007 through a mutual friend, Kyle Vogt. This friend, like Ferdowsi, was from Kansas; he and Houston were members of an entrepreneurs' club. Houston had the idea for an Internet file hosting service, but needed a partner. Ferdowsi told Angus Loten for *Wall Street Journal* (14 March 2012) that Houston calls their partnership "a shotgun marriage, because we had two or three meetings and didn't spend more than five hours together before deciding to jump into the business together. And we never looked back." Working from a Cambridge, Massachusetts, apartment, the two men founded Dropbox, a cloud computing application that permits access to files from any computer at any time, without the need to transfer files to a flash drive. Some

Contour by Getty Images

have referred to it as an Internet file cabinet. The company launched in mid-2007, at which point Ferdowsi dropped out of college. The two moved to San Francisco, where they currently have an office employing more than one hundred people. As chief technology officer, Ferdowsi stays in the background, letting Houston be the frontman while he does back-end work. Dropbox was honored as best overall startup at the Crunchies (a Silicon Valley tech award) in 2012. In July 2013, the company hosted DBX, its first tech conference, at Fort Mason in San Francisco, designed to be a creative event among programmers and engineers. Because the need that Dropbox fills is so great, the company has not formally advertised; its user base has grown through word of mouth and media exposure.

EARLY LIFE AND EDUCATION
Ferdowsi was an only child, born to Gholam and Tahminah (Tammy) Ferdowsi, His father had come from Tabriz, Iran, to the United States in 1978 to study at Central Missouri State; when the shah of Iran was deposed in an Islamic revolution the following year, Gholam, now a mortgage broker, chose to remain in the United States. He met Tammy, another Iranian, at the University of Missouri–Kansas City in 1984. They gave Arash, who was born in 1985 and grew up in Overland Park, Kansas, an unusual amount of say in family decisions, including where to vacation and what furniture to purchase. When only five or six years old, after studying blueprints for the house being built for the family, Arash caught a mistake in the placement of a staircase that his father had not noticed.

His interest in technology, especially computers, began when he was very young. "He was always interested in how they worked," according to Tammy Ferdowsi, in an article by Eric Adler for the *Kansas City Star* (20 Feb. 2013). "I think he was nine or ten when he put his own computer together. We ordered the pieces for him and he assembled the hard drive." He attended Harmony Middle School and graduated from Blue Valley Northwest High School as valedictorian. Unlike many tech whiz-kid narratives, Ferdowsi was known as a nice kid, not an arrogant geek. As he told Adler, "People would probably point to me as someone who was likely to be—how do I phrase this? A kind of a go-to person if you needed help with math or computers or science or anything like that and, just generally, hopefully, a nice person. I would say that people felt I was friendly and generally tried to help people."

Because of his superior academic performance in high school, Ferdowsi had scholarship offers from several universities, including Harvard and Stanford, but chose the Massachusetts Institute of Technology, where he was a computer science major. As did many other young people at the time, he hoped to become a programmer for a newer technology company, such as Google. The company was smaller then, and such a position was not easy to come by. As he learned more about the emerging tech world, he switched his focus to a desire to work for Facebook.

AN IMPORTANT CONNECTION
Meanwhile, Dropbox cofounder Drew Houston was frustrated by the need to remember his flash drive in order to work on a computer away from home. Having forgotten it yet again, he sat down and wrote code that would allow for the kind of sharing of data that had been available at MIT. He wanted a program that would work equally well for a Mac or a PC.

Paul Graham of the business incubator Y Combinator became Houston's first investor, but advised him that he needed a collaborator to form a successful company. Houston then met Ferdowsi through Kyle Vogt, a young serial entrepreneur also from Kansas City. Speaking of Vogt, Ferdowsi told Adler, "He dropped out [of MIT] his sophomore year to start a company. He was getting all sorts of awesome press and working on really cool, exciting problems. I kind of pointed to him and saw him as a little bit of a role model."

A programmer fascinated by how things work, Ferdowsi was the perfect counterpart for the more outgoing Houston. "Drew kind of has this amusing analogy," Ferdowsi told Adler about running the company together. "It's kind of like raising a kid as a single parent. You can do it, but it's so much harder."

With only one semester of coursework left until graduation, Ferdowsi dropped out of MIT in 2008, certain that he could return if Dropbox did not succeed. Along with Houston, who had already graduated, he spent three months in Cambridge, writing code in a small office, working until dawn and sleeping until noon. The pair moved to California in September to be nurtured by Y Combinator.

LAUNCHING DROPBOX
Venture capital to fund Dropbox came from several sources: Accel Partners, Sequoia Capital, and Y Combinator. The lattermost, which investor Paul Graham began in 2005, invests smaller seed money grants twice a year in startup companies focused on technology. The companies' principals are invited to Silicon Valley for an intense three months of preparation before launching a public quest for investors. The conclusion of the incubator period is Demo Day, a pitch to a group of investors. YC, as the company calls itself, continues to offer support after the conclusion of the three-month period. The company has founded more than 550 start-ups.

Like other tech start-ups such as Facebook, Google, and Twitter, Dropbox began as a simple one-string company to fill a need—in this case, for simple, elegant digital file storage. While the company was still in beta testing, the founders posted their Demo Day video demonstration on the news aggregator website Digg. It went viral; that three-minute demo caused the beta testing list (the people applying to try the software) to go from 5,000 to 75,000 in a single day. Steve Jobs, then head of Apple, approached the two about buying the service. However, Jobs did not envision Dropbox as a separate company. The co-founders turned him down, because, as Ferdowsi told Angus Loten for the *Wall Street Journal* (14 Mar. 2012), "The problem that we're trying to solve is a problem that only an independent company can solve. . . . It isn't a problem any of those larger companies is going to be as inclined to solve in the same way we are."

The company opened an office in China Basin, a section of San Francisco, in 2011, moving from their first 12,000-square-foot office into an 87,000-square-foot one. No one has an enclosed office, in line with the flat hierarchy style of Internet start-ups. The new location features not only a cafeteria and gym, but also a conference room fully equipped with Legos. Friday night jam sessions occur in the music room, which is equipped with a piano and guitars. Houston was part of a band while in college.

WHAT DROPBOX OFFERS

The service focuses on solving real-world problems. By 2011, 60 percent of adult computer users had at least two Internet connected devices. At the other end of the spectrum, some 3 percent of users had nine different devices to coordinate. With tablets, smartphones, work and multiple home computers, reaching that figure is not difficult. Dropbox offers a way to access all of these technologies. "Our vision is to simplify millions of peoples' lives," Drew Houston told Verne G. Kopytoff for the *New York Times* (5 June 2011). "You don't have to worry that you have some files on your Mac, some stuff on your work computer and then some more on your iPhone."

A major advantage to online storage is synchronization, or sync. By allowing changes to be made to the documents that are accessible in every storage device or platform, file sharing among colleagues or sending photos to friends or family becomes easy. Using the service eliminates the fear of a hard drive crash—documents and photos are stored in the cloud (a large number of servers connected via the Internet), accessible from any computer or mobile device. The goal of the company is to create a service that seamlessly allows uploads from smartphones, cameras, tablets, and computers of any platform. It has added a camera-upload feature, so that any photo taken can automatically go to a Dropbox account.

By July 2013, Dropbox had more than 175 million users, less than five years after it launched. More than a billion files are synchronized on Dropbox daily. As Ferdowsi and Houston blogged, "Keeping devices and apps synced with your most up-to-date info has gone from 'nice-to-have' to essential, which creates a real challenge for the people developing apps."

The basic service is free; customers who want more than two gigabytes of storage pay for premium service. A referral system also gives users more storage space. Most clients, perhaps as many as 95 percent, rely on the basic service alone. A small percentage of users pay extra for more gigabytes of storage capacity. Recognizing a need among their users—as many as half of their clients—living outside the United States, the service is available not only in English but also in Chinese, French, German, Indonesian, Japanese, Malay, Polish, Russian, and Spanish.

CAPITAL AND CONCERNS

In 2011, Dropbox netted $250 million in venture capital, based on a company valuation of $4 billion. Index Ventures led this round of funding, which included several new investors. These included Benchmark Capital, Goldman Sachs, Greylock Partners, Institutional Venture Partners, RIT Capital Partners, and Valiant Capital Partners. The money from that round of funding was to be used for acquisitions, growth, and partnerships. Earlier funding efforts had landed $7.2 million, making this a significant step forward.

Security is an ongoing concern for the company. The Federal Trade Commission received a complaint against Dropbox for the way it encrypted files; the complaint alleged that Dropbox employees could access private data. Houston referred to the critique as a "rite of passage," and assured users that Dropbox took security seriously.

As with all tech start-ups, Dropbox's long-term prospects are unclear. Cloud storage has become a competitive market, with Apple's iCloud, Google Drive, Microsoft's SkyDrive and any number of smaller startups having entered the field. As Ferdowsi's childhood friend Jon Ying, now Dropbox's chief of design, told Eric Adler for the *Kansas City Star*, "It's definitely very dreamlike, and I think it's always going to seem dreamlike. We joke it is like we flipped a coin 10,000 times and it turned up heads every time."

GROWING A YOUNG COMPANY

With its latest infusion of venture capital, Dropbox began making purchases of other tech start-ups. In February 2012, they purchased Cove, a start-up begun by two former Facebook engineers, a married couple known for their experience and technical expertise. Ruchi Sangh-vi, who oversaw Facebook's news feed, was Facebook's first female engineer. Her husband, Aditya Agarwal, served as Facebook's director of engineering and was chosen to lead Drop-box's team of engineers. Sanghvi became head of operations and recruiting. The pair started Cove only in January 2011 with funding from Facebook founder Dustin Moskovitz. Along with Cove's technology, Dropbox gained an additional two other Cove employees with expertise gained at Hewlett-Packard and Facebook.

In March 2013, Dropbox acquired the iPhone e-mail application Mailbox for a reported $100 million. The app provided an answer for people frustrated with trying to access mail from tablets and other devices. Mailbox needed more resources to match its rapid growth; more than 1.5 million users were sending 100 million e-mails daily. Gentry Underwood, the chief execu-tive officer of Mailbox, told Jessica Guynn for the *Los Angeles Times* (23 May 2013), "Our priority is basically to try to get Mailbox in the hands of as many people who want it. There are so many more places where we can ease the pain around e-mail. There is a sea of opportunity there, and the challenge is figuring out strategically where to put our resources first. It's like trying to boil the ocean. There is just so much to do." One of their priorities is to make it easier to use e-mail on mobile devices.

In July 2013, Dropbox added Endorse, a mo-bile coupon app, to its roster of young-company acquisitions. Begun in 2010 with venture capi-tal from SV Angel and Accel, Endorse first was a Web application. It then moved to mobile de-vices with an app for iPhone. Most of Endorse's team—about a dozen employees—migrated with the company. This is important for Drop-box, which is competing with many tech start-ups for a finite pool of talent. The company has hired employees away from Facebook, Google, and Instagram.

PERSONAL

As a native of the Kansas City area, Ferdowsi is a fan of the Kansas City Chiefs football team. He is also a serious player of the video game *Dance Dance Revolution*. In 2011, Ferdowsi and Hous-ton were named to the Fortune 40 under 40 list of most influential younger business executives as well as to the annual Inc. 30 under 30 list of top young entrepreneurs. Both men were also listed among Wealth-X's 2013 top ten wealthiest tech entrepreneurs (or "technopreneurs") under thirty. Ferdowsi occupied the number-seven slot with an estimated net worth of $400 million, while Houston came in fourth at $610 million. Unsurprisingly, Ferdowsi has also been named one of Silicon Valley's top ten most eligible tech-nology bachelors. Wealth and fame have not gone to Ferdowsi's head, however. He does not

own a car; instead, he rides a Dropbox shuttle to work, where he continues to put in twelve-hour days. As Ying told Adler for *Kansas City Star*, "Arash isn't motivated by money. He has purchased himself a home, but that's about it."

SUGGESTED READING

Adler, Eric. "Meet the Richest Area Native You've Probably Never Heard Of." *Kansas City Star*. Kansas City Star, 20 Feb. 2013. Web. 12 Sept. 2013.

Barret, Victoria. "Dropbox: The Inside Story of Tech's Hottest Startup." *Forbes*. Forbes.com, 18 Oct. 2011. Web. 12 Sept. 2013.

Guynn, Jessica. "Mailbox Hits Send on New iPad App." *Los Angeles Times*. Los Angeles Times, 23 May 2013. Web. 12 Sept. 2013.

Kopytoff, Verne G. "Data Grows, and So Do Storage Sites." *New York Times*. New York Times, 5 June 2011. Web. 12 Sept. 2013.

Loten, Angus. "Dropbox Seeks Big Solutions." *Wall Street Journal*. Dow Jones, 14 Mar. 2012. Web 12 Sept. 2013.

—*Judy Johnson*

Nikky Finney

Born: August 26, 1957
Occupation: Poet and professor

Nikky Finney is an award-winning poet and the John H. Bennett Jr. Chair in Southern Letters and Literature at the University of South Caro-lina in Columbia. In 2011 Finney won the Na-tional Book Award for her poetry collection *Head Off & Split*, and her acceptance speech, of which she reportedly wrote thirty-nine drafts, became a viral sensation. At the podium, Finney first read out loud the penalty for teaching slaves to read or write, as stipulated by the slave code of South Carolina in 1739. Then she began a spoken-word poem: "The ones who longed to read and write, but were forbidden, who lost hands and feet, were killed, by laws written by men who believed they owned other men. Their words de-voted to quelling freedom and insurgency, imagi-nation, all hope; what about the possibility of one day making a poem?" She concluded, "If my name is ever called out, I promised my girl-poet self, so too would I call out theirs."

Finney's poems often find their heart in her activist upbringing—both of her parents were involved in the civil rights movement in the 1960s—and many draw from historical fig-ures and experiences from her own life. (One poem, "Dancing with Strom," about her mother dancing with virulent racist and former senator Strom Thurmond at her brother's wedding, is a surreal blend of the two.) As a student, Finney

Associated Press

2013, she began working on a collection of autobiographical essays called *The Sensitive Child*.

ACTIVIST UPBRINGING

Lynn Carol Finney was born on August 26, 1957, in Conway, South Carolina, and grew up in Sumter. Her father, Ernest A. Finney Jr., was a civil rights attorney who later became a judge. In 1994, he was elected the state's first African American chief justice since Reconstruction. Finney's mother, Frances Davenport, worked as an elementary school teacher. Finney has two brothers, Ernest A. Finney III and Jerry Leo Finney, both attorneys.

Finney was very close to her maternal grandmother, Beulah Butler Davenport, who she says taught her the importance of honesty. "The big thing she taught me—a lie was equal to murder," Finney told Cara Dees for Vanderbilt University's *Nashville Review* (1 Apr. 2013). "If you couldn't tell the truth in life then you were taking up space and you should go do something else." Finney took this advice to heart and later applied it to her poems. She always loved writing and began keeping a journal when she was ten years old. "My love for poetry started in the fifth or sixth grade when I started trying to compose stanzas and things like that," she told Joshua Barnes for *Sampsonia Way* (14 Aug. 2012). She distinctly recalls composing her first poem while sitting on the bus. It was at that moment, she told Barnes, that she knew she wanted to write poetry for the rest of her life.

Finney, who grew up during the 1960s, recalls not being allowed into the Sumter County Library, a Carnegie library that was replaced with a newer building in 1968. When the laws changed and she was finally allowed to enter, she discovered that it held no books by black authors; she would not have the chance to read the work of African American poets such as Langston Hughes and Claude McKay until she was in college.

Encounters with South Carolina's hostile and humiliating segregation laws are some of Finney's earliest memories, and those memories have had a profound impact on her writing and her worldview. Her parents and the adults in her community were deeply involved in the civil rights movement, and Finney, even as a child, felt the need to contribute. "So I started to be a witness," she told Barnes. "I started writing down and documenting what I saw: Mr. Brown, the electrician, making signs; Reverend Scott, the preacher in our church, driving someone to a march. That was one level. The other level was that I couldn't understand how human beings could be so mean to each other."

A WRITER'S EDUCATION

Finney graduated from Sumter High School in 1975 and left home to attend Talladega College,

studied African American literature; as a poet, she honed her craft under the tutelage of the late Toni Cade Bambara, a writer who was influential in the Black Arts movement of the 1960s and 1970s. Bambara, who died in 1995, was a significant figure in Finney's life. When the two women met, Finney was a graduate student and aspiring poet who had never been to a school that offered a creative writing class. "I didn't know it then," Finney wrote in an essay titled "Ambrosia," anthologized in *Shaping Memories: Reflections of African American Women Writers* (2009), "but there were very few writing workshops being taught at any of the historically Black colleges. Creative writing as a discipline was seen as something special but nothing integral." Bambara, who was also a professor, turned in a creative writing syllabus at Spelman College in Atlanta, but the department rejected it. Undeterred, Bambara held the workshop in her own living room. It was Finney's first creative writing class.

Finney herself later became a professor and taught at the University of Kentucky in Lexington for over twenty years. She was named the Guy Davenport Endowed English Professor at the school in 2012, but the following year she decided to move back to her home state of South Carolina to be closer to her aging parents. In the fall of 2013, she began her position at the University of South Carolina, a joint appointment in the Department of English Language and Literature and the African American Studies Program. Finney is also a founding member of the Affrilachian Poets, a Lexington-based writers' group. In a historically black college in Talladega, Alabama, where she majored in English. There, she read the work of Toni Morrison, Alice Walker, and Zora Neale Hurston. She still wanted to be a poet, and a professor named Gloria Wade Gayles encouraged her to continue her academic career in graduate school. Finney wrote her senior thesis on a writer named Toni Cade Bambara; at graduation, Gayles surprised her by giving her Bambara's address and phone number on a notecard.

Finney chose to study African American literature at Atlanta University in Georgia because the famous writer W. E. B. Du Bois had once taught there. She began her graduate studies in 1979 but was too shy to initiate a meeting with Bambara, who was teaching at Atlanta University and several other Atlanta colleges at the time. Nevertheless, during her first year, Finney was helping to organize a writer's conference with the newly formed Southern Collective of African American Writers when she recognized Bambara among the crowd of volunteers. "I could hardly look up," Finney wrote in "Ambrosia." "The room had changed. The boring work had changed. And soon, very soon, my life would change."

When Finney worked up the courage to speak to her, Bambara was livid; she had spoken to Gayles and was irked that Finney had not contacted her sooner. (Finney claims that Bambara would not fully forgive her for the slight for another two years.) Still, she invited Finney to attend a monthly writing workshop in her living room. She called it the Pamoja Writing Workshop, *pamoja* being the Kiswahili word for "unity."

Finney thrived in the workshop, and the ritual of trekking to Bambara's house on the first Sunday of every month became sacred. One Sunday, Finney came armed with the most beautiful poem she had ever written. In "Ambrosia," she described it as "one beautiful metaphor after the other." The gathered writers were duly impressed, but Bambara was not, saying, "So you can write pretty, so what? What does all that pretty stand for?" Finney was hurt, but it was a watershed moment in her writing life. She later wrote of Bambara, "She taught me strategy and mindfulness long before I knew what to call it."

After about two years, Finney made a risky decision: she quit graduate school and left Atlanta. She had excelled in her classes, but she was tired of studying the work of others; she wanted to create her own. She returned to Alabama, where she took a job as campus photographer at Talladega College, and made plans to finish her first book of poems.

AN UNEXPECTED INVITATION

Finney's first book of poems, *On Wings Made of Gauze*, was published in 1985. "I have some burn marks with William Morrow and the way they handled my book," Finney told Tara Betts for *Mosaic* magazine (1 Sept. 2001) of her first publisher, which later became an imprint of HarperCollins. She vowed to take more control over the production of her work in the future.

After her first book, Finney moved to Oakland, California, where she worked the late-night shift as a manager at Kinko's. In 1989, the University of Kentucky in Lexington offered her a one-year visiting professorship. Despite being wary of entering academia, Finney accepted, largely because her exhausting schedule left her little time to write. She was amazed by the amount of writing she was able to accomplish in such a short time; when the year was over, she returned to California and her old job with a completed first draft of her second book of poems, *Rice*. Before long, Finney got a call asking her to come back. Finney initially took the position for the health care and financial security but soon found that she genuinely loved teaching.

RICE AND OTHER WORK

While walking around Lexington one day, Finney discovered the Carnegie Center for Literacy and Learning, which reminded her of the Carnegie library in her hometown. She staked out a study carrel in the quiet building to use as an office, and it was there that she finished work on *Rice*, published in 1995 by the Toronto-based Sister Vision: Black Women and Women of Colour Press. A collage of family poems and family photos, *Rice* is Finney's most personal book, though its format was inspired by the late poet Lucille Clifton. When Finney was twenty-three years old, she was perusing New York City's cavernous Strand Bookstore and came across Clifton's *Generations* (1976), a book of prose and photographs. "It just opened up my head about the possibility of thinking outside the box," she told Dees.

Rice tells the history of African Americans in South Carolina in an urgent, vital voice. One of the poems, "The Afterbirth, 1931," is about Finney's father, who was delivered by a drunken white doctor and walks with a limp as a result. According to Finney's aunts, the doctor had convinced the family to hire him instead of a midwife. Finney was an adult when she first heard the story at a family reunion, and she immediately wrote it down. The resulting poem is astonishingly present for a tale so long buried. *Rice* earned Finney a Beyond Margins Award (now the PEN/Open Book Award).

Finney's next book was *Heartwood*, published in 1997 as part of the Kentucky Humanities Council's New Books for New Readers series. Books in the series are written at a fourth-grade reading level for adults in literacy programs. *Heartwood* consists of four interlocking short stories that revolve around the relationships between white people and black people in small-town Kentucky.

After *Heartwood*, Finney returned to poetry with *The World Is Round* (2003), which won a 2004 Benjamin Franklin Award from the Independent Book Publishers Association. She also edited *The Ringing Ear: Black Poets Lean South* (2007), an anthology of poems by writers from the Cave Canem Foundation, which was established by Toi Derricotte and Cornelius Eady in 1996 to support and promote African American poets.

HEAD OFF & SPLIT

The title of Finney's next poetry collection, *Head Off & Split* (2011), was inspired by her hometown fishmonger, who would ask his customers if they wanted their fish headless and gutted; Finney always said yes. As an adult, Finney returned to the fishmonger, and when he asked her the same question, she paused and then said no. She decided that she would take the fish home and dismember it herself. The significance of her decision is explored in the book's introduction, titled "Resurrection of the Errand Girl": "Not a girl any longer, she is capable of her own knife-work now. . . . She has come to use life's points and edges to uncover life's treasures. She would rather be the one deciding what she keeps and what she throws away."

The book includes a poem called "Red Velvet," about Rosa Parks; four poems about former secretary of state Condoleezza Rice, which Finney dubbed "concertos" and collected under the heading "The Condoleezza Suite"; and one about a woman who, after her home was destroyed by Hurricane Katrina, held up a sign for rescuers reading, "Pleas Help Pleas." Finney likes to plumb the histories of well-known people and events. A lesser writer might turn such material into didactic or wooden poems, but Finney imbues her subjects with the same anguish and tenderness bestowed upon members of her own family in *Rice*. The tone of the collection is characteristic of Finney, one she described to Noah Adams for NPR's *Weekend Edition* (8 Apr. 2012) as "where the beautifully said thing meets the really difficult to say thing."

Head Off & Split has won several awards, including the 2011 National Book Award for poetry and the 2012 GCLS Award for poetry. It was also nominated for a SIBA Book Award and an NAACP Image Award.

PERSONAL LIFE

Finney's partner, A. J. Verdelle, is an award-winning author of several novels, including *The Good Negress* (1995). She teaches creative writing at Lesley University in Cambridge, Massachusetts, and Finney has often cited her as an editorial influence. Finney and Verdelle lived in Lexington with their daughter until 2013, when Finney moved to Columbia to begin her new teaching position.

SUGGESTED READING

Adams, Noah. "The Beauty and Difficulty of Poet Nikky Finney." *NPR*. Natl. Public Radio, 8 Apr. 2012. Web. 14 May 2014.

Betts, Tara. "Country Grammar." *Mosaic*. Mosaic Lit. Mag., 1 Sept. 2001. Web. 14 May 2014.

Blackford, Linda B. "Poet Nikky Finney Hopes Prestigious Award Illuminates Arts' Role in Kentucky." *Kentucky.com*. Lexington Herald-Leader, 19 Nov. 2011. Web. 14 May 2014.

Butler, Jonathan. "A Woman with Keys: Nikky Finney's *Rice*." Rev. of *Rice*, by Nikky Finney. *Jasper*. Jasper, 17 Aug. 2013. Web. 14 May 2014.

Finney, Nikky. "Ambrosia." *Shaping Memories: Reflections of African American Women Writers*. Ed. Joanne Veal Gabbin. Jackson: UP of Mississippi, 2009. 142–51. Print.

Finney, Nikky. "An Interview with Nikky Finney." Interview by Cara Dees. *Nashville Review*. Vanderbilt U, 1 Apr. 2013. Web. 14 May 2014.

Finney, Nikky. "'So I Became a Witness': An Interview with Nikky Finney." Interview by Joshua Barnes. *Sampsonia Way*. City of Asylum/Pittsburgh, 14 Aug. 2012. Web. 14 May 2014.

SELECTED WORKS

On Wings Made of Gauze, 1985; *Rice*, 1995; *Heartwood*, 1997; *The World Is Round*, 2003; *Head Off & Split*, 2011

—Molly Hagan

Missy Franklin

Born: May 10, 1995
Occupation: Competitive swimmer

Missy Franklin has often been called the female counterpart of Michael Phelps, the American swimming phenomenon who won twenty-two Olympic medals during his career. Widely considered the best and most versatile female swimmer in the world, Franklin has amassed an unprecedented list of accomplishments for a swimmer of her age. In 2008, at thirteen, she became one of the youngest swimmers ever to compete at the US Olympic Trials, and by 2010, she had won her first national and international medals. In 2012, Franklin became the successor to Phelps as the face of American swimming when she took home five medals, including four golds, at the Summer Olympic Games in

© Jorge Silva/Reuters/Corbis

London. She added to her laurels in 2013 when she became the first female swimmer to win six FINA World Championship gold medals.

Unlike Phelps, who turned professional at age sixteen, Franklin has rejected lucrative endorsement deals to remain an amateur athlete and compete at both the high school and college levels. A Colorado native, she swam for the Denver-area Colorado Stars club team and Regis Jesuit High School before beginning her college career at the University of California, Berkeley (UC Berkeley) in the fall of 2013.

Franklin is known for her bubbly and infectious personality and for her preternatural physical attributes. Her strong frame and "lifetime of training at Colorado's high altitude make for an impressive physical package," Kelli Anderson wrote for *Sports Illustrated* (23 May 2011). Todd Schmitz, head coach of the Colorado Stars, told Anderson, "Missy has an innate ability to flip the switch between competitor and noncompetitor. . . . Up until about two heats before her race, she's goofing around and cheering on her teammates. As soon as her race is over, she's back to having fun. At practice, she's the one cheering teammates through a hard set."

EARLY LIFE
Melissa "Missy" Franklin was born on May 10, 1995, in Pasadena, California, the only child of Dick and D. A. Franklin. Shortly after Franklin was born, her Canadian-born parents moved to Colorado, settling in the Denver suburb of Centennial. Unlike other Olympic-level swimmers, Franklin, who has dual citizenship, does not have a swimming pedigree—though she does come from an athletic family. Her father, a director for a clean-energy firm, was a standout football lineman at Saint Mary's University

in Halifax, Nova Scotia, and the Toronto Argonauts of the Canadian Football League drafted him. He played in one exhibition game with the Argonauts before suffering a career-ending knee injury, after which he returned to Halifax and attended Dalhousie University, where he met Franklin's mother, a medical student who later became a family physician.

Growing up in Centennial's upscale Heritage Greens neighborhood, Franklin was just six months old when she took her first swim class with her mother, who has admitted to being afraid of the water. After going under the surface for the first time, "the other kids came up screaming," Franklin's mother recalled to Anderson, "but Missy came up with a huge smile on her face." Franklin started snorkeling with her father at the age of two, and by five, she was competing on her neighborhood summer league team in the Rocky Mountain Swim League. Also at five, she set her first record, in the six-and-under girls' twenty-five-yard backstroke. "She was born to be in the water," Franklin's father told Wayne Drehs for ESPN.com (26 June 2012).

SWIMMING PRODIGY
Franklin started swimming year round at the age of seven, when she joined the Stars. At that time, she began training under Schmitz, who immediately noticed her above-average size. "I really remember her blonde hair standing about six inches taller than the rest of the seven-year-olds who were there," Schmitz told Drehs.

When Franklin first started swimming for the Stars, she did not display exceptional technical proficiency in any of the four competitive strokes and was largely apathetic toward practice. However, her physical attributes and passion for competing quickly made her a standout in the pool. She blossomed under Schmitz, who became the Stars' head coach in 2008. He entered Franklin in events for every stroke, in an effort to improve her versatility as a swimmer. He also designed practices that offered a careful balance of fitness and fun, helping Franklin develop "an unabashed love of swimming," as John Henderson noted for the *Denver Post* (11 July 2013).

When Franklin was ten, she was regularly beating children two years older. Then, at twelve, she set three national age-group records at the 2008 Colorado fourteen-and-under short course State Age Group Swimming Championships. Franklin set two more national age-group records at the 2008 NCSA Junior National Swimming Championships in Orlando, Florida, with Olympic Trials–qualifying times in the two-hundred-meter individual medley (IM) and fifty-meter freestyle events. In 2008, just after turning thirteen, Franklin became the youngest swimmer to attend the US Olympic Trials in Omaha, Nebraska. She competed in three events but did not finish better than thirty-seventh place in any of them.

JOURNEY TO THE 2012 OLYMPICS

After the 2008 US Olympic Trials, Franklin and her family resisted the temptation to move to California, Texas, or Florida to train with other Olympic-bound swimmers in elite programs headed by more established coaches than Schmitz. Instead, Franklin remained in Colorado to continue training with the Stars, which, unlike most swim clubs, does not even have its own home pool. (The club rents practice lanes at five Denver-area facilities.)

Around this time, Schmitz outlined a big-picture strategy with Franklin's parents. "Credit goes to them and to her for sticking to it," he told Matthew Futterman for the Wall Street Journal (30 July 2012). Franklin thanks her parents, with whom she is extremely close, for providing her with an upbringing centered on unconditional love and support and for not pushing her to the brink of burnout, which is common among swimmers and other elite youth athletes. "Swimming is tough enough," she explained to Drehs in an article for ESPN magazine (28 June 2013). "The last thing you need is your parents asking you what went wrong. You need a hug. And my mom and dad have always been there with that hug."

One of the first major steps in Franklin's journey to the 2012 Olympics came in the summer of 2009, when Schmitz and Franklin's parents decided against entering her in the US National Swimming Championships, which also serves as the trials for the World Championship team. Instead, Franklin swam at that summer's Junior National Championships, where she was able to compete in a full slate of events against swimmers in her age range. At the meet, she recorded the sixth-fastest time ever in the women's hundred-meter freestyle, with a time of 54.03 seconds, which would have earned her a place on the US World Championship team.

In August 2009, Franklin began attending Regis Jesuit High School, an all-girls Catholic institution in Aurora. To ensure that Franklin would be able to swim for Regis Jesuit, Schmitz worked closely with her high school coach, Nick Frasersmith, to develop a training plan. "I wouldn't have a career without him," Franklin said of Schmitz to Henderson (11 July 2013). She added, "Todd and I have a relationship that's special. . . . We've always been more than athlete and coach."

MAKING HER MARK

As a freshman Franklin led Regis Jesuit to a second-place finish at the 2010 Colorado Class 5A state swimming championships, where she set state records in the fifty-yard freestyle and hundred-yard backstroke. In the summer of 2010,

she competed at the US Nationals, finishing second in the hundred- and two-hundred-meter backstroke. She placed in the top ten in all six of her individual events, en route to winning the Kiputh High-Point Award for the meet's top female swimmer. Franklin next swam at the 2010 Pan Pacific Swimming Championships, where, as the youngest member of the US team, she placed fourth in the hundred-meter backstroke. For her achievements, she was named the Breakout Performer of the Year at USA Swimming's seventh annual Golden Goggles Awards—the "Academy Awards of American swimming," as Kevin Fixler put it in an article for The Post Game (21 July 2011).

Franklin first made her mark on the international stage in December 2010, when she earned two silver medals at the FINA Short Course World Championships, placing second in the two-hundred-meter backstroke and four-hundred-meter-medley relay. Two months later, she led Regis Jesuit to the 2011 Colorado Class 5A state title, after breaking her own state records in the fifty-yard freestyle and hundred-yard backstroke and swimming on the school's first-place two-hundred-meter medley and four-hundred-meter freestyle relay teams. Afterward, she was inducted into the Colorado Sportswomen Hall of Fame, becoming, at fifteen, the youngest woman ever to receive the honor.

Franklin's cumulative performance at the seven-meet 2010–11 USA Swimming Grand Prix Series, in which she led all swimmers with seventeen gold medals and won the high-point award, caught the attention of none other than Phelps. In an interview with Amy Shipley for the Washington Post (15 May 2011), Phelps described Franklin as a "stud" and said that she "can get in and swim with anybody and it doesn't faze her." Franklin's Kiputh Award came with a prize of twenty thousand dollars, but she opted to forfeit the money to retain her amateur status.

Franklin became the breakout star of the 2011 World Championships in Shanghai, China, where she took home five medals, including three golds. One week after the World Championships, Franklin won her first career national titles at the US Nationals, finishing first in the hundred-meter freestyle and hundred-meter backstroke. Then, at a 2011 FINA Swimming World Cup meet in Berlin, Germany, she set her first short-course world record, doing so in the two-hundred-meter backstroke. At the Golden Goggle Awards she was named Female Swimmer of the Year.

DARLING OF THE 2012 LONDON GAMES

By the end of 2011 Franklin had turned down hundreds of thousands of dollars in winnings and endorsement deals to continue swimming with her high school team, an opportunity that she "couldn't put a price on," as she told Karen Crouse for the *New York Times* (9 Feb. 2012). "A lot of people think of swimming as an individual sport," she added to Crouse, "but I've always loved the team aspect." During her junior year, Franklin led Regis Jesuit to a second-place finish at the 2012 Colorado Class 5A state championships, establishing state records in the two-hundred-yard freestyle and hundred-yard backstroke.

Expectations were extremely high for Franklin at the 2012 US Olympic Trials in Omaha, Nebraska, where she entered five individual events. At the eight-day meet, which is "regarded as more pressure-packed than the Olympics themselves," as Beth Harris noted for the Associated Press (22 June 2012), only the top two finishers in each event qualify for the Olympic team. Franklin began the meet as a runaway favorite to make the 2012 Olympic team and as American swimming's "Next Big Thing," following Phelps's announcement that he would retire after the 2012 Games. Undaunted by such pressure, she qualified for four individual events at the trials to secure her first Olympic berth, placing first in the hundred-meter backstroke, with an American record–breaking time of 58.85; first in the two-hundred-meter backstroke; and second in the hundred- and two-hundred-meter freestyle events. Those finishes guaranteed her spots on all three relays in London.

At the 2012 Olympics, Franklin became the first female US swimmer to compete in seven events in one year at the Games, and she emerged as a national darling. On the opening night of swimming competition, she won her first Olympic medal, a bronze, as a member of the four-hundred-meter freestyle relay team, which set a new American record in the event. Two days later, she won her first gold medal in the hundred-meter backstroke, finishing with an American-record time of 58.33. Franklin then captured three more gold medals, in the eight-hundred-meter freestyle relay, two-hundred-meter backstroke, and four-hundred-meter medley relay; in the latter two events, she set world records. Meanwhile, she narrowly missed out on two more medals, missing third place in the two-hundred-meter freestyle by just one-hundredth of a second and placing fifth in the hundred-meter freestyle. At the end of the Games, Anderson declared in an article for *Sports Illustrated* (13 Aug. 2012) that Franklin had posted "arguably the greatest Olympic performance ever by an American female swimmer" and "unquestionably the most impressive Olympic debut by a US swimmer of either gender not named Phelps."

2013 WORLD CHAMPIONSHIPS AND UC BERKELEY

Following her performance at the 2012 Olympics, Franklin was recognized as the World Swimmer of the Year and American Swimmer of the Year by *Swimming World* magazine. Meanwhile, she declined an estimated $5 million in endorsement deals to swim her senior season of high school. Franklin led Regis Jesuit another state title, closing out her four-year high school career with a total of eight individual state titles. She graduated from Regis Jesuit in May 2013.

During the summer of 2013, Franklin made history again at the World Championships in Barcelona, Spain, when she became the first female swimmer to win six gold medals at a single World Championship meet. She also became just the fifth swimmer to capture six or more golds at either a world meet or an Olympics. During the competition, Franklin set a new World Championship record in the two-hundred-meter backstroke and an American record in the four-hundred-meter freestyle relay.

After the World Championships, Franklin rejected more lucrative professional opportunities to retain her college eligibility and swim for UC Berkeley, which she chose for its prestigious swim program. There, she began training under coach Teri McKeever, who served as the head coach of the US women's team at the 2012 Olympics. Franklin has announced plans to swim in college for two years before turning professional in the run-up to the 2016 Olympics in Rio de Janeiro, Brazil. Commenting on her decision to attend UC Berkeley, Franklin told Jane McManus for ESPNW.com (11 Dec. 2013), "If I had to make the decision to stay amateur again, I would make it one hundred times over."

PERSONAL LIFE

Franklin lives on the UC Berkeley campus. She is known for maintaining a close connection with her fans and has more than 350,000 followers on the social-networking service Twitter. "With her friendly smile and outgoing personality," McManus wrote, "she seems like the best friend you haven't met yet, a big sister down the hall in your dorm."

SUGGESTED READING

Anderson, Kelli. "Sweet 16." *Sports Illustrated.* Time, 23 May 2011. Web. 30 Dec. 2013.

Crouse, Karen. "Before the Olympic Trials, There's This Big High School Meet." *New York Times.* New York Times, 9 Feb. 2012. Web. 30 Dec. 2013.

Drehs, Wayne. "In Water, Franklin 'Can Do Anything.'" *ESPNW Summer Olympics.* ESPN Internet Ventures, 26 June 2012. Web. 30 Dec. 2013.

Futterman, Matthew. "Missy Franklin, Olympic Radical." *Wall Street Journal.* Dow Jones, 30 July 2012. Web. 30 Dec. 2013.

Henderson, John. "Missy Franklin Soon to Say Goodbye to Longtime Swim Coach Todd Schmitz." *Denver Post.* Denver Post, 11 July 2013. Web. 30 Dec. 2013.

McManus, Jane. "Impact 10: Missy Franklin." *ESPNW*. ESPN Internet Ventures, 11 Dec. 2013. Web. 30 Dec. 2013.

—*Chris Cullen*

Christian Frei

Born: 1959
Occupation: Filmmaker

The filmmaker Christian Frei is one of Switzerland's best-known and most celebrated documentarians. With a career that has spanned over three decades, Frei—who writes, directs, produces, and edits all of his own films—has created a body of work that has pushed the boundaries of the documentary genre. He is best known for his 2001 critically acclaimed feature, *War Photographer*, which offered a daring glimpse into the life and work of American photojournalist James Nachtwey, considered one of the most important and influential war photographers of the late twentieth century. Following Nachtwey into some of the world's most hostile regions, the film became an international success, winning prizes at twelve film festivals and earning Frei an Academy Award nomination for best documentary feature, a historic first for a Swiss filmmaker.

Frei's other feature-length documentaries include *Ricardo, Miriam y Fidel* (1997), *The Giant Buddhas* (2005), and *Space Tourists* (2009), the latter of which became the first Swiss film

Wirelmage

to receive an award at the prestigious Sundance Film Festival. His fifth feature, *Sleepless in New York*, is scheduled to be released in 2014. Discussing his approach to filmmaking, Frei said in an interview with Indiewire (15 Jan. 2006), "I like to work for the screen—being creative [and] bringing real people's emotions, dreams and conflicts on the big screen, bigger than life—far away from TV and journalism."

EARLY LIFE AND EDUCATION

Christian Frei was born in 1959 in Schönenwerd, a small town in northwest Switzerland. While Frei has made little mention of his upbringing and family life in interviews, it is known that his interest in film was sparked at a young age. As a high school student, Frei learned how to use a Super-8 film camera after attending a workshop on filmmaking conducted by Stephan Portmann (1933–2003), a cofounder and first director of the Solothurn Film Festival, one of the oldest and most important festivals for Swiss films.

At the age of seventeen, Frei used a Super-8 camera to shoot his first film, a documentary about the everyday lives of Capuchin monks. The forty-minute film was broadcast on Swiss television and helped inspire Frei's desire to become a filmmaker. "With a camera I could enter . . . a world which for me would not have been otherwise accessible," Frei explained in the Indiewire interview, "and I was fascinated by the pure documentary approach."

In the late 1970s Frei enrolled in the Department of Journalism and Communications at the University of Fribourg in Fribourg, Switzerland, where he studied visual media. One of his teachers at the university included Portmann, who taught him the intricacies of filmmaking. Though Frei has cited Portmann as a mentor, he has said that he ultimately left the university in an effort to extricate himself from Portmann's influence as well as the mode of thinking that "was too 'post-May '68' for my liking," as he explained to Norbert Creutz in a profile for *Swiss Films* (May 2006), referring to the volatile events of civil unrest in France during May 1968.

EARLY CAREER

After leaving the University of Fribourg, Frei began making corporate films for the Swiss pharmaceutical company Ciba-Geigy (which merged with another pharmaceutical firm in 1996 to become Novartis). He spent two years working at the headquarters in Basel, Switzerland, before returning to Solothurn in 1981. That year he directed his first documentary short, *Die Stellvertreterin*, which focuses on the unconventional teaching methods of a young female substitute teacher. Frei followed *Die Stellvertreterin* up with two other short films, *Fortfahren* (1982) and *Der Radwechsel* (1984), both of which were shot in the sixteen-millimeter format. *Fortfahren* centered on the renowned Swiss sculptor Schang Hutter and was made in collaboration with Ivo Kummer, a former director of the Solothurn Film Festival. *Der Radwechsel* was inspired by the German writer Bertolt Brecht's 1953 poem of the same name and offered a free-associative examination of car breakdowns as a metaphor for anxiety. *Der Radwechsel* was filmed in the United States and in Italy.

In 1984 Frei began working as an independent director and producer. Over the next eleven years he was commissioned to make approximately seventy films, many of which were educational films for Swiss television. Frei has described this period of his career as being invaluable in his development as a filmmaker. "I needed to earn a living and I looked on it as a training ground," he said in his interview with Creutz. "As a result, I acquired considerable technical expertise. . . . At the same time, it helped me free myself from my narcissistic tendencies, directing large teams of people or laying rails for tracking shots all over the place."

RICARDO, MIRIAM Y FIDEL AND SWISS TELEVISION

Frei's desire to take on more ambitious projects led him to turn his attention to feature-length documentary films. His first feature-length documentary, *Ricardo, Miriam y Fidel* (1997), took five years to complete and marked his first collaboration with his longtime cinematographer, Peter Indergand. Set against the backdrop of Cuba's revolutionary landscape and featuring a mixture of real and imagined situations, the ninety-minute film tells the story of Miriam Martínez and her father, Ricardo Martínez, a former Cuban rebel who helped to cofound Fidel Castro's famous Radio Rebelde. It follows Miriam and Ricardo in their struggle to remain committed to Cuba's elusive utopian ideals and chronicles Miriam's long and tortuous journey to immigrate to the United States with her family. *Ricardo, Miriam y Fidel* premiered in April 1997 at the Swiss film festival Visions du Réel, held annually in the town of Nyon, and was well received by critics. Creutz observed that the overall impact of the film was strengthened by Frei's "objectivity" and "attention to storytelling and aesthetics (from the quality of the photography to the sparing use of music)," all of which would become distinct hallmarks of his style.

Frei next made two hour-long documentaries for Swiss television. The first, *Kluge Köpfe* (1998), tackles the topic of prejudice experienced by child prodigies and focuses on three girls, aged four, nine, and twelve, with preternatural intellectual gifts and features an in-depth interview with the renowned Swiss psychologist Ulrike Stedtnitz. The second, *Bollywood im Alpenrausch* (2000), examines the decades-long trend of filming commercial Indian movies in the Swiss Alps. It centers on Jakob Tritten, a Swiss film organizer from the village of Zweisimmen in the canton of Bern, who started bringing Indian film crews to the picturesque area in the 1980s.

WAR PHOTOGRAPHER

Concurrently with the televised documentaries, Frei worked on his second feature-length documentary, *War Photographer* (2001), which marked a major breakthrough in his career. The film offers a portrait of the award-winning and internationally acclaimed American photojournalist James Nachtwey, whom Frei first learned about in 1997 while traveling to the Chicago Film Festival. Reminiscing to Hera Diani for the *Jakarta Post* (3 Nov. 2002) about photos he had seen in the German magazine *Stern*—photos that Nachtwey had taken in Afghanistan—Frei explained, "I was struck immediately by the outstanding photographs . . . and the fact that there was a man who was interested in [the 1990s Afghan civil war] while nobody was at that time."

Though Nachtwey turned down Frei's first proposal to make a film about him, he eventually agreed, and Frei spent two years tracking him in war-torn and poverty-stricken areas of Kosovo, Indonesia, and Palestine. Frei affixed a special micro-camera—the size of an index finger—to Nachtwey's camera, which allowed him to capture the photojournalist without being too intrusive to his work. Much of *War Photographer* includes footage taken from this camera, which creates an atmosphere of immediacy and allows viewers to see things from Nachtwey's perspective. The documentary also features interviews with Nachtwey's close friends and colleagues and addresses larger themes such as the role of the photojournalist in a violent world.

Premiering in November 2001 *War Photographer* received unanimous praise from critics and brought Frei worldwide recognition. A. O. Scott, in a review for the *New York Times* (19 June 2002), called the film "engrossing" and described it as "a sad and stirring testimony to [Nachtwey's] vision and to the quiet, self-effacing heroism with which [he] has pursued it." In another review for the *San Francisco Chronicle* (6 Dec. 2002), Edward Guthmann observed that the film "has a somber tone that seems as if it developed in proportion to [Frei's] regard for his subject" and called it "an act of spiritual faith—an eloquent, deeply felt meditation on the nature of compassion." *War Photographer* was invited to forty-one international film festivals, winning prizes at many of them, and received an Academy Award nomination for best documentary feature, becoming the first Swiss documentary to earn such an honor. The fifty-two-minute television version of the film, meanwhile, captured a

Peabody Award in 2003 and an Emmy nomination in 2004.

THE GIANT BUDDHAS

Frei's next feature-length documentary, *The Giant Buddhas* (2005), centers on the Taliban's destruction of the famous Buddhas of Bamiyan, which are located in the high-altitude valley of Bamiyan in central Afghanistan. For Frei, the destruction of the centuries-old sandstone Buddhas, which represented the Taliban's attempt to remove all non-Islamic statues, served "as a starting point for a cinematic journey, an essay on fanaticism and faith, terror and tolerance, ignorance and identity," as he explained in his Indiewire interview. Shot over a period of twenty-four weeks, the film traverses the globe, visiting not only the site where the Bamiyan Buddhas once stood, but also locations in China, Qatar, Europe, and Canada. It includes firsthand interviews with individuals who witnessed the destruction of the Bamiyan Buddhas, including an Afghan cave dweller and the famed Al Jazeera reporter Tayseer Allouni, as well as with those with intimate knowledge of the statues, such as the Afghan expatriate journalist Nelofer Pazira and Afghan archaeologist Zemaryalai Tarzi.

The Giant Buddhas premiered at Switzerland's Locarno International Film Festival in August 2005 and was screened in competition at the prestigious Toronto and Sundance film festivals, among others. The film elicited a positive response from critics and received several awards, including the Silver Dove at the 2005 International Leipzig Festival for Documentary and Animation Film in Leipzig, Germany. A reviewer for *Time* magazine (19 Sept. 2005) called *The Giant Buddhas* a "subdued, indeed Zen-like rumination on the things that war spoils." Robert Fulford wrote for Toronto's *National Post* (13 Sept. 2005), "Frei's account ranges from the horrifying to the comic, and in the process delivers as much fresh information as I've ever absorbed from a single documentary." In July 2006 Frei organized a special screening of *The Giant Buddhas*, which was held in Afghanistan's Bamiyan Valley at the site of the destroyed statues.

SPACE TOURISTS AND SLEEPLESS IN NEW YORK

Frei's fourth feature-length documentary was released in 2009, and examines the phenomenon of space tourism. Featuring stunning imagery from outer space and a minimalistic musical score, *Space Tourists* follows the journey of Anousheh Ansari, an Iranian American multimillionaire entrepreneur and philanthropist who became the world's first female space tourist in 2006. The narrative of Ansari, who paid twenty million dollars for a ten-day trip to the International Space Station, is used as a jumping off point to delve into various other stories related to the Russian space program, from rocket debris collectors in Kazakhstan to the formerly top-secret Baikonur Cosmodrome, the world's largest and oldest space launch facility. Commenting on his decision to structure the film as a series of interconnected stories, Frei explained to Brad Balfour for the *Huffington Post* (22 Feb. 2010), "The instinct of a documentary filmmaker is to find the economy behind phenomenons. If I were to do a film on the rollercoaster, I would not just film the passengers and the adrenaline; I would film the system. The workers, the problems, the struggle, the competition."

Space Tourists debuted at the Zurich Film Festival in October 2009 and premiered in North America at the Sundance Film Festival in January 2010. At Sundance, Frei became the first Swiss recipient of the World Cinema Documentary Directing Award. In a review for the *Hollywood Reporter* (26 Jan. 2010), Duane Byrge called *Space Tourists* "a multi-dimensional glimpse into dreams and obsessions. . . . Frei smartly interweaves the pride that many felt because of the space program's accomplishments while visualizing its down-to-earth, economic failings."

In 2010 Frei began preproduction work on his fifth feature-length documentary, *Sleepless in New York*, which is about the elusiveness of love. The film is scheduled to premiere in the spring of 2014.

Frei lectures at the University of St. Gallen, a prestigious Swiss research university, and has served as president of the Swiss Film Academy since 2010. He previously headed the Documentary Film Commission of the Swiss Ministry of Culture from 2006 to 2009.

Frei resides in Zurich, where his film production company, GmbH, is based.

SUGGESTED READING

Balfour, Brad. "Q&A: Former Oscar-Nominated Director Christian Frei Travels with the *Space Tourists*." *Huff Post Entertainment*. TheHuffingtonPost.com, 22 Feb. 2010. Web. 21 Jan. 2014.

Bodmer, Marc, and Sophie Schricker, eds. *GEO Edition Documentaries: The Tectonics of Humanity: Christian Frei Collection*. Zurich: Warner Home Video Switzerland, 2007. Digital file.

Creutz, Norbert. *Ciné-Portrait: Christian Frei*. Zurich: Swiss Films, 2006. Digital file.

Diani, Hera. "Christian Frei: Documentary Shows Authentic Moments." *Jakarta Post*. PT. Niskala Media Tenggara, 3 Nov. 2002. Web. 21 Jan. 2014.

"Park City '06: Christian Frei." *Indiewire*. SnagFilms, 15 Jan. 2006. Web. 21 Jan. 2014.

SELECTED WORKS
Die Stellvertreterin, 1981; *Ricardo, Miriam y Fidel,* 1997; *War Photographer,* 2001; *The Giant Buddhas,* 2005; *Space Tourists,* 2009

—Chris Cullen

Mike Segar/Reuters/Landov

Andrew Friedman

Born: November 13, 1976
Occupation: Baseball executive

Andrew Friedman is the award-winning executive vice president for baseball operations (effectively the general manager) of Major League Baseball's Tampa Bay Rays—formerly known as the Devil Rays (the team dropped "Devil" in 2008). A former investment banker and college baseball player, Friedman was hired from a private equity firm by Rays owner Stuart Sternberg, a Wall Street veteran, in 2004. Friedman began his finance career at the now defunct investment-banking firm Bear Stearns. Matt Silverman, the Rays' president, worked at Goldman Sachs with Sternberg. The men have built the Rays into a perennial contender—from a team that had finished near the bottom of its division for its first ten seasons—doing so through statistical strategies similar to those popularized by Billy Beane, the general manager of the Oakland Athletics (A's) and the subject of Michael Lewis's 2003 book, and the 2011 film, *Moneyball.*

The A's had a negligible budget but were able to assemble a contending team by taking a quantitative approach to scouting. Beane did this at the expense of instinctual, "old-fashioned" scouting, but the Rays' executives see their method as a healthy meeting of the two schools. "Andrew is an opportunist," Silverman told Jerry Crasnick for ESPN.com (21 Oct. 2008). "He's always looking to make improvements within the club. Some are major leaps and require risk, and others are things on the margin. Oftentimes, it's those decisions that make the difference in the end." In 2011, journalist Jonah Keri wrote a book about the Rays executives called *The Extra 2%: How Wall Street Strategies Took a Major League Baseball Team from Worst to First.*

EARLY LIFE AND EDUCATION
Friedman was born on November 13, 1976, in Harris County, Texas. He is one of five children. His father is a lawyer and former baseball player for Tulane University in New Orleans. His mother is a psychologist. As a child, Friedman asked his mother to drop him off early at the Houston Astrodome, then the home of the Astros, so he could watch batting practice before each game. He hung around the team so much that people often thought he was a son of one of the players.

As for his own baseball career, he played shortstop in Little League, but he switched to center field at Episcopal High School in Bellaire, Texas. He earned a baseball scholarship to Tulane University and was a member of the team that won the first ever Conference USA championship in 1996. A shoulder injury put an end to his baseball career. Tulane coach Rick Jones told Peter Finney for the New Orleans *Times-Picayune* (21 Oct. 2008) that Friedman was "one of those hard-nosed players with a passion for the game. He was hit on the wrist by a fastball as a freshman and suffered some broken bones, and the next year he dove headfirst trying to steal third and came away with a shoulder separation. That was Andrew as a player." He added of Friedman's current job, "He took those attributes, that passion, from the playing field and into the baseball business world."

BEAR STEARNS
Friedman became an intern with Bear Stearns in New York City after his junior year in college, on the advice of Tal Smith, an Astros executive and family friend. Friedman was already eyeing a job in baseball; according to a former boss at Bear Stearns, Friedman often asked people if they knew anyone in baseball. He said he was willing to start mopping floors, to work his way up. After graduating from Tulane in 1999, Friedman entered a two-year program to work as an analyst for Bear Stearns. In 2002, he was hired as an analyst by MidMark Capital, a private equity firm in Morristown, New Jersey. He was soon promoted to senior associate.

"You could tell from the very beginning that he was a very, very intelligent guy," Matthew Finlay, a managing director with MidMark, told Mike Vorkunov for the New Jersey *Star-Ledger* (12 Aug. 2011). "Not only was he an intelligent guy, but he knew how to use it to his advantage. An excellent negotiator. His instincts for negotiating are second to none." Friedman was on his way to becoming partner when he walked into Finlay's office in 2004 and announced, according to Vorkunov, that he was "going to the big leagues."

A LEAP FROM FINANCE TO BASEBALL

Friedman's leap from the finance world to the baseball world was a comfortable, if unbelievable, one for him. He was consulting on his brother's fantasy baseball league in Houston and following the box scores of his hometown Astros when he met Sternberg through his friend and former Wall Street buddy Matt Silverman in April 2003. Sternberg was in the process of buying the Devil Rays, a Major League Baseball team with an abysmal record. When the three men met at a diner near Sternberg's Rye, New York, home, Sternberg was impressed by Friedman's intelligence. "I sensed his passion," Sternberg told Joey Johnston for the *Tampa Tribune* (22 Oct. 2008). "His willingness to step away from a lucrative career meant an enormous amount to me." Friedman became Sternberg's soundboard as the deal went through, and in 2004, Sternberg offered him a job. Friedman signed on as the director of baseball development with the Rays in 2004. "Was there skepticism from others?" Sternberg told Johnston of the hire. "Yes, but [those] people didn't know Andrew."

TAMPA BAY DEVIL RAYS

The Tampa Bay Devil Rays became a major-league franchise in 1998. The team had ten consecutive losing seasons, losing ninety-one or more games in each of those seasons. In nine of those ten seasons, the Rays finished in last place. Sternberg, and five former Wall Street bankers, bought the team in the middle of this losing streak, in 2004. According to *Forbes* magazine, the Rays were ranked last among major-league teams in terms of value, but Sternberg, who left his job as a partner at Goldman Sachs in 2002 for a reported $400 million, was an obsessive baseball fan. He was determined to own the team and was, somewhat perversely, delighted by its horrible standing. "I'm a buy-low guy," Sternberg told Landon Thomas Jr. for the *New York Times* (2 Apr. 2006), "and if you pay the right price for something, I don't care what it is, you can't go very wrong." Sternberg was right about the Rays, but his wisdom would not be apparent for another four years.

Friedman was named executive vice president for baseball operations on November 3, 2005, at the age of twenty-eight. He quickly became known for shrewd trades that maximized the Rays miniscule payroll. In 2006, Thomas reported that the Devil Ray's entire payroll—$35 million—was one-fifth that of the New York Yankees, and $4 million less than the four-year contract the Yankees awarded to free-agent pitcher Carl Pavano in 2004. To compensate for a lack of funds, Friedman used principles that he learned on Wall Street, such as "mark-to-market" accounting (or "fair value" accounting). Friedman makes decisions based on what he reckons the team's real value is, over its physical payroll. In 2006, he estimated that the Rays' payroll was really worth about $50 million. He told Thomas that he applies the same principle to trading. "I am purely market driven," he said. "I love players I think that I can get for less than they are worth." Also in 2006, he signed twenty-year-old pitcher Scott Kazmir. Kazmir was on the payroll for $370,000, but according to Friedman, he was worth about $7 million.

CRITICAL DEALS

Friedman made a handful of critical deals during this period. With the third pick in the 2006 amateur draft, the Rays selected Evan Longoria, who has become a star, earning the American League Rookie of the Year award in 2008 and making the All-Star team three times. In 2007, Friedman signed first baseman Carlos Peña as a minor-league free agent. "As a small-revenue team, we don't have the luxury of one-dimensional players," Friedman told Crasnick. "We always liked Carlos as a hitter and what he brings defensively, so we felt like he was worth a shot. That's one of the benefits of not being very good . . . . : You're able to give chances to players when you like their profile." That season, Peña hit more home runs (forty-six) than any other player in team history. Also in 2007, with the number-one pick of the amateur draft, the Rays selected pitcher David Price. In November 2007, Friedman made a six-player trade, sending outfielder Delmon Young to the Minnesota Twins for pitcher Matt Garza and shortstop Jason Bartlett. Garza won the American League Championship Series (ALCS) most valuable player award in 2008.

NEW NAME, NEW LOOK, NEW BEGINNING

In 2008, the Devil Rays changed their name to the Rays—and updated their uniforms. The changes were strategic. Silverman told Joe Lapointe for the *New York Times* (16 June 2008), "We wanted to distance ourselves" from the previous decade. The Rays began the 2008 season as a 200-to-1 long shot to win the World Series, but after thirty-eight games, they had their best record (22–16) in franchise history. In June they took opponents by surprise, sweeping teams such as the defending World Series champion Boston Red Sox, and by early July, they were in first place in the American League East Division. The 2008 Rays were a young team, but functioned powerfully as a unit, not relying on one player or a handful of individuals; only three Rays players (Longoria, Kazmir, and Dioner Navarro) made the 2008 All-Star roster and none of them were starters. (By contrast, the Cubs, who led the National League, sent eight players to the All-Star game.)

Despite injuries to Longoria and other key players, by the end of August, the Rays had guaranteed their first ever winning season. In September, they had earned a playoff spot, becoming the only team since the 1991 Atlanta Braves to reach the postseason after having the league's worst record the previous season. In 2007, the Rays' record was 66–96. In 2008, their record was 97–65. The stunning thirty-one-game improvement was the third best in American League history, behind the improvements of the 1946 Boston Red Sox and the 1989 Baltimore Orioles. Troy Percival, the Rays' closer, played for the World Series–winning Anaheim Angels (now the Los Angeles Angels of Anaheim) in 2002, the first time the Angels had reached the postseason in sixteen years. In comparing the rise of the two teams, Percival told Pete Williams for the *New York Times* (1 Oct. 2008), "There might be a little more excitement [with the Rays] because we're talking about a team that suffered nearly 1,000 losses in a 10-year span. The Angels had good teams over the years. This is unprecedented."

In October, the Red Sox pushed the Rays into a seventh game in the ALCS, but the unstoppable Rays pulled out a 3–1 victory, earning a trip to the World Series to meet the Philadelphia Phillies. Unfortunately, the Rays won only one game in the series, losing in five games. Nonetheless, the year had been a tremendous one for the team, in no small part because of Friedman, who, at thirty-one, was the youngest person ever to be named the Sporting News Executive of the Year.

In 2009, the Rays finished third in the American League East with an 84–78 record. The team returned to the postseason in 2010, notching a season record of 96–66, but they lost the ALCS to the Texas Rangers. They returned to the postseason in both 2011 and 2013, losing to the Rangers in the former year and to the Red Sox in the latter.

BOLD MOVES

Since 2008, Friedman has engineered some bold trades, Jose de Jesus Ortiz wrote for the *Houston Chronicle* (3 July 2013), including sending Kazmir to the Angels in the middle of the 2009 season and Garza to the Cubs in January 2011. Entering the 2014 season, Friedman faced the challenge of continuing to field a winning team and conforming to the parameters of the franchise's limited budget; the payroll is the highest it has ever been, and there has been widespread speculation that the team will trade its star pitcher, Price, because of his impending free agency. "We can't be afraid to make bold moves," Friedman told Ortiz. "It's almost become a cliché, but

we operate with one eye on the present and one eye on the future . . . right now we're trying to walk the extremely fine line of remaining competitive while continuing to retool to be able to sustain that over the long haul."

Friedman met his wife, Robin, when he was a student at Tulane. They married in 2009 and have a son named Ethan. The family lives in Tampa.

SUGGESTED READING

Crasnick, Jerry. "Rays' Astute Moves Take Them from Cellar to Summit." *ESPN.com*. ESPN Internet Ventures, 21 Oct. 2008. Web. 8 Feb. 2014.

Johnston, Joey. "Passionate, and Tough as Nails." *Tampa Tribune*. Tampa Media Group, 22 Oct. 2008. Web. 10 Feb. 2014.

Lapointe, Joe. "The Rays Are Putting Their Dismal Past in the Past." *New York Times*. New York Times, 16 June 2008. Web. 10 Feb. 2014.

Ortiz, Jose de Jesus. "Rays' Friedman Shows Astros How to Achieve Success with Less." *Houston Chronicle*. Hearst, 3 July 2013. Web. 9 Feb. 2014.

Thomas, Landon, Jr. "Case Study: Fix a Baseball Team." *New York Times*. New York Times, 2 Apr. 2006. Web. 8 Feb. 2014.

Vorkunov, Mike. "Tampa Bay Rays GM Andrew Friedman Went from Private Equity to the Big Leagues." *Star-Ledger* [New Jersey]. New Jersey On-Line, 12 Aug. 2011. Web. 8 Feb. 2014.

Williams, Pete. "Last to First, Few Teams Compare to the Rays." *New York Times*. New York Times, 2 Oct. 2008. Web. 10 Feb. 2014.

—*Molly Hagan*

Diana Gabaldon

Born: January 11, 1952
Occupation: Author

There are few modern authors harder to label than Diana Gabaldon, the former academic and comic book writer who shot to literary stardom in 1991 with her genre-bending novel, *Outlander*. In the book, a nurse from the mid-twentieth century falls back in time to eighteenth-century Scotland, where she meets the love of her life, a Highlands gentleman and soldier. The novel spawned an ongoing series, over the course of which the duo has traveled across time to right wrongs and save the day. Gabaldon has been celebrated for her devotion to historical accuracy, sharp attention to detail, and ability to take various strands of convoluted plots and weave them into page-turning stories of more than a thousand pages in length.

Getty Images

The success of *Outlander* and its sequels has enabled Gabaldon to pen another equally genre-bending series: historical mysteries with a gay lead character, Lord John Grey, who plays a minor role in Gabaldon's original series. The idea that none of her writing can be easily labeled appeals to Gabaldon, who released the eighth book in the *Outlander* series, *Written in My Own Heart's Blood*, in 2014. Gabaldon once told a reporter for the *Montreal Gazette* (6 Oct. 2007): "So far I've seen my books sold as fiction, historical fiction, historical non-fiction (because they're very accurate), science fiction, fantasy, romance, mystery, military history, gay and lesbian, and horror. It sort of doesn't matter what you call my books, but I do prefer to have them shelved in fiction. Because they do have something to offer anyone regardless. No matter where your tastes lie."

EARLY LIFE AND EDUCATION

The older of two daughters, Diana Gabaldon was born at the Williams Hospital in Williams, Arizona, during a blizzard on January 11, 1952. Her parents, Antonio "Tony" Gabaldon and the former Jacqueline Sykes, had been married just thirteen months on the night their daughter was born. They were both twenty-one years old and, by Diana's account, madly in love.

Despite their love for each other, Diana's parents had been pressured to give up their relationship. Jacqueline was the daughter of the mayor of Flagstaff, of English ancestry, and descended from the early settlers of the town; Tony, although ambitious, hardworking, and intelligent, had a major strike against him in the eyes of

many at the time: he was a Mexican American, born in Belen, New Mexico. Gabaldon recalled on her official website: "In 1949, in a small Arizona town, this was miscegenation—or so everyone said. My mother's friends said so. Mrs. X, her English teacher, said so, telling her firmly that she couldn't possibly marry a Mexican; her children would be idiots. The parish priest who refused to marry them said so; such a marriage would never last. The 'interested parties' who took out a public petition against the match said so; it was a scandal. Her parents said so—and at last she was persuaded, and reluctantly broke the engagement."

Jacqueline's parents sent her to the University of Arizona in Tucson to "forget" Tony, but a few months later, in December, she called him and asked him to come get her. He did just that. They were married the next morning by a priest from a neighboring parish. Tony, who would go on to serve as an Arizona state senator for sixteen years, had many happy years with Jacqueline, who died in 1970. (Tony Gabaldon died in 1998.)

Tony also encouraged his daughter to get an education. Following her father's advice, Diana earned a bachelor of science in zoology from Northern Arizona University in 1973, a master of science in marine biology from the Scripps Institution of Oceanography at the University of California, San Diego, in 1975, and a PhD in quantitative behavioral ecology from Northern Arizona University in 1978.

A VARIED EARLY CAREER

One day, while Gabaldon was doing her postdoctoral work at the University of California, Los Angeles (UCLA), she stopped in a store on her way to work and picked up a Walt Disney comic. Her mother had taught her to read with such comics and she continued to enjoy them into her adulthood. But the comic she picked up that day infuriated her because she found it to be very badly written. After tracking down the editor, she wrote him a pointed letter saying that she had been a fan of these comics for many years and believed she could write a better story than the one she had just read. Gabaldon recalled the response she received in an interview with Stephan Lee for *Entertainment Weekly* (26 Oct. 2011): "Luckily, [the editor] had a sense of humor and he wrote back, 'Okay, try.' He sent me a couple of layout sheets so I could see how a story was constructed by the company guidelines, so I wrote him a story. He didn't buy it, but he did something much more valuable: He told me what was wrong with it. He did buy my second story, which was my first fiction sale ever. I continued to write for him for the next three years until the Disney Company said well we've got forty years worth of Carl Barks in the files, why are we buying more stories?"

Around the time her freelance work with Disney dried up, Gabaldon was teaching environmental science at Arizona State University's Center for Environmental Studies, a position she would hold for the next dozen years. During her tenure there she became an expert in the then emerging field of scientific computation. She wrote on her website: "I started and ran a scholarly journal called *Science Software* for several years. See, I started using computers for scientific analysis in the early '80s, just when microcomputers were getting started. It occurred to me that there should be a venue for other scientists who did what I did (not many, back then) to share their work. The journal took off, and took over—within a year, I was doing virtually nothing else; I ran the journal, did training seminars for scientists wanting to get into computers and lab automation, wrote texts and manuals and so on."

Gabaldon's work on the journal enabled her to write on assignment for the mainstream computer press. She typically was able to procure freelance jobs by sending copies of *Science Software* and her Disney comics to editors, who warmed to a pitch coming from someone who was versatile enough to do such different types of writing.

BREAKING THROUGH WITH *OUTLANDER*

Although Gabaldon's freelance writing career provided her with steady work, she was inspired to write a novel—a "practice" novel, she thought, something she would never show another living soul. She wanted to see if the experience of reading novels for more than thirty years would translate into the ability to write one of her own. She set out with no plan apart from the fact that she wanted her setting to be eighteenth-century Scotland—and that was only due to the fact that she had been inspired to write about a Highlands gentleman after seeing a rerun of an old *Doctor Who* episode featuring Frazer Hines as Jamie MacCrimmon, the Doctor's Scottish, kilt-wearing traveling companion. Gabaldon's hero—Jamie Fraser, a young swashbuckling soldier seeking to defend Scotland from the British in 1743—is even named after the actor and his character. His companion on these adventures is an English nurse named Claire Beauchamp Randall, who arrived in eighteenth-century Scotland after walking through a cleft stone in the year 1945. The time-crossed duo become romantically involved as they attempt to stop "Black Jack" Randall from crushing the fledgling Scottish rebellion.

Gabaldon was surprised to discover that *Outlander* found a receptive professional audience. She succeeded in getting a literary agent, through whom she procured a three-book contract—all from a book she considered practice and about a place she had never seen personally.

After getting her contract, she did travel to Scotland and has since returned many times. She recalled to Jean Brittain for *Scottish Memories* (May 2009): "I still remember standing on the Bar, in front of a white stone monolith that has 'England' carved on one side, 'Scotland' on the other, looking out over this vast, undulating green countryside, rolling up and up before me, and thinking simply, 'Home.'"

Outlander was a critical and commercial hit upon its publication in 1991. A reviewer wrote of *Outlander* in *Publishers Weekly* (3 June 1991): "Absorbing and heartwarming, this first novel lavishly evokes the land and lore of Scotland, quickening both with realistic characters and a feisty, likable heroine. . . . Scenes of the Highlanders' daily life blend poignant emotions with Scottish wit and humor."

Since that first outing, Gabaldon has written several additional volumes in the series, which continue Claire and Jamie's adventures. The novels, with more than twenty million copies in print around the world, are now published in twenty-six countries in twenty-three languages. Each novel in the series is about one thousand pages long and takes the author about two and a half years to write. Other titles in the *Outlander* series include: *Dragonfly in Amber* (1992), *Voyager* (1994), *Drums of Autumn* (1997), *The Fiery Cross* (2001), *A Breath of Snow and Ashes* (2005), *An Echo in the Bone* (2009) and *Written in My Own Heart's Blood* (2014). She has also penned *The Outlandish Companion* (1999), a nonfiction work that gives fans a better understanding of the characters and backgrounds of the series, as well as insights into the author's research and writing process, and *The Exile* (2010), a graphic novel illustrated by Hoang Nguyen that looks at the events of the series from Jamie's point of view.

Gabaldon has been lauded for the intricate plots of each of her novels, which has led to speculation that she has some overarching master plot for what she predicts will be a nine-book series. She claims, however, that each book can be read on its own merits and that the entire series can be read out of chronological order (though she doesn't recommend the latter, owing to all the time traveling). "I don't plan books ahead of time," Gabaldon said in her *Montreal Gazette* interview. "I don't write with an outline. And I don't write in a straight line. I write in bits and pieces where I see things happening and eventually they will form a structure for me."

A television show based on her best-selling *Outlander* series is scheduled to premiere on the Starz network in August 2014. The executive producer of the series is Ronald D. Moore, the award-winning screenwriter and producer celebrated for his provocative reimaging of *Battlestar Galactica* (2003–9).

THE LORD JOHN SERIES

The world Gabaldon has created is so rich, in fact, that she was able to spin an entirely different series out of it, based on Lord John Grey, one of the minor characters in the *Outlander* series. The character, who pops up only occasionally in the main series, fascinated his creator, both because he is a continually troubled nobleman and army officer and because he is a closeted gay man in an era when same-sex sexual activity is a capital offense.

The series came about when Gabaldon wrote a short story about Lord John for a British anthology. She began to write another short story about Lord John, but the story soon grew into a full novel. After submitting the first volume, *Lord John and the Private Matter* (2003), she had a contract for three Lord John books, each a historical mystery taking place in the 1700s. There have been three additional titles in the best-selling series: *Lord John and the Hand of Devils* (2007), *Lord John and the Brotherhood of the Blade* (2007), and *The Scottish Prisoner* (2011), in which Lord John again teams with Jamie Fraser.

Like Gabaldon's *Outlander* series, the Lord John books have met with considerable critical praise. In a review for *Publishers Weekly* (15 Sept. 2003), a critic wrote of *Lord John and the Private Matter*: "Grey is a competent and likable sleuth, and Gabaldon's prose is crisply elegant. Her many fans will be happy to learn that this is the first in a series about the travails of Lord John Grey." Reviewing *Lord John and the Brotherhood of the Blade* for the *Washington Post* (17 Sept. 2007), Patrick Anderson wrote: "Gabaldon provides a rich, abundantly researched, entirely readable portrait of life among the English upper classes in the 1750s. From London's literary salons and political intrigue to fearsome battle scenes in the Seven Years' War, her writing is always vivid and often lyrical. . . . Lord John's adventures are first-rate popular history."

PERSONAL LIFE

Diana Gabaldon and her husband, Douglas Watkins, have three adult children and live primarily in Scottsdale, Arizona, but maintain the family home in Flagstaff, a place where Gabaldon especially enjoys writing. Gabaldon gave up teaching after her second book was finished. At the time she told her husband that she would like to again enjoy sleeping more than four hours a night.

SUGGESTED READING

Anderson, Patrick. "A Man's Man." *Washington Post*. Washington Post, 17 Sept. 2007. Web. 12 June 2014.

Brittain, Jean. "The Outlander Lady (Interview)." *Scottish Memories*. Scottish Memories, May 2009. Web. 3 June 2014.

"From Academia to Steamy Fiction." *Montreal Gazette*. Canada.com, 6 Oct. 2007. Web. 12 June 2014.

Kirch, Claire. "BEA 2013: Diana Gabaldon: Wrinkles in Time." *Publishers Weekly*. Publishers Weekly, 1 June 2013. Web. 12 June 2014.

SELECTED WORKS

Outlander, 1991; *Dragonfly in Amber*, 1992; *Voyager*, 1994; *Drums of Autumn*, 1997; *The Fiery Cross*, 2001; *Lord John and the Private Matter*, 2003; *A Breath of Snow and Ashes*, 2005; *Lord John and the Brotherhood of the Blade*, 2007; *Lord John and the Hand of Devils*, 2007; *An Echo in the Bone*, 2009; *The Scottish Prisoner*, 2011; *Written in My Own Heart's Blood*, 2014

—Christopher Mari

Andrew Garfield

Born: August 20, 1983
Occupation: Actor

When it was announced that Andrew Garfield, an American-born British actor relatively unknown in the United States, had been cast as the iconic title character in *The Amazing Spider-Man*, a 2012 revival of the beloved franchise, fans exploded with indignation. Blogs and online discussion boards were rife with missives questioning his build (too slim and boyish), his background (too British), and even his eyebrows (too bushy). Despite that inauspicious

Getty Images

start, in mid-2011 Garfield won over superhero aficionados when he appeared on a panel at Comic-Con International: San Diego, an annual four-day convention that draws more than one hundred thousand fans of comic books, video games, and other forms of popular media. Garfield took to the floor in the guise of an ordinary convention-goer, dressed in a cheaply made Spider-Man costume, before removing the mask to give a heartfelt speech about his longtime love and respect for the character he would be portraying in the big-budget blockbuster. "[Spider-Man creator] Stan Lee says that the reason why Spidey is so popular is because all of us can relate to him, and I agree," Garfield told the audience. He added, "I think that we all wish we had the courage to stick up for ourselves more, to stick up for a loved one more, or even a stranger you see being mistreated, and [Spider-Man] has inspired me to feel stronger. He made me, Andrew, braver."

Garfield was greeted with tumultuous applause, and the fan and critical response to his casting improved further following the film's premiere in the summer of 2012. In a review echoed by several other critics, Hugh Hart wrote for *Wired* (2 July 2012), "When your movie's called *The Amazing Spider-Man*, it is going to rise or fall on the shoulders of its title character. Garfield gets it done. He's in nearly every scene of the two-hour, eighteen-minute movie, and we never get tired of watching him. That, in itself, is pretty amazing." Although Garfield has earned praise for his work on a variety of other projects—including the Academy Award–winning 2010 film *The Social Network* and a critically acclaimed 2012 revival of the play *Death of a Salesman*—he became best known for his interpretation of the web-slinging superhero, a role he would go on to reprise in 2014's *The Amazing Spider-Man 2*.

EARLY LIFE

Andrew Russell Garfield was born on August 20, 1983, in Los Angeles, California. He has one older brother, Ben, who is now a doctor. Their father, Richard, was an American, and their mother, Lynn, hailed from Essex, England. Richard and Lynn ran a small interior-design firm but later switched careers, Richard becoming a swimming coach and Lynn taking a job as a nursery-school teacher. When Garfield was three years old, the family left California for Lynn's native United Kingdom, and Garfield was raised in the county of Surrey, in southeastern England.

Although he enjoyed a comfortable middle-class childhood with caring parents, Garfield's early years were not entirely happy. Because of his slight frame, he was often bullied. "Every school has their bullies, and when you're a kid you wish you had the power to fight them and protect other people—and yourself," he told Baz Bamigboye for the *Daily Mail* (7 Jan. 2011). "Kids can be incredibly cruel. On certain days [I] would come home and think, 'Today was really horrible.'" Garfield attended the Priory Preparatory School in the town of Banstead and went on to the City of London Freemen's School, a tradition-rich institution that placed a strong emphasis on sports such as rugby and cricket.

As a child, Garfield enjoyed swimming, and he also participated in gymnastics. He gave up the latter activity, he told journalists, after a traumatic experience involving a heavyset boy who sat on him while he was attempting to do a split. He briefly thought he might like to pursue a career in music, but two years of stultifying classical guitar lessons dissuaded him from that idea.

ACTING LESSONS AND DRAMA SCHOOL

In his teens Garfield suffered from depression, a fact that he has been open about in interviews. "Certain days would be great, I'd have everything figured out," he told Danny Leigh for *Radio Times* (3 July 2012). "Other days, I wouldn't." He has admitted that on occasion he still feels like that floundering adolescent. "I'm unsure, insecure, awkward in my body," he told Leigh. "I definitely haven't shed that skin." In an interview with Isabel Albiston for the *Telegraph* (27 Oct. 2007), Garfield posited that sibling rivalry was at least partially to blame for his period of discontent. "I was very sensitive and didn't cope very well," he explained. "My brother is super-intelligent and a pretty sorted guy. He's an overachiever and was head boy at school. . . . We were very competitive."

As a possible antidote to his depression, his parents suggested that he take acting lessons. Garfield agreed, found that he enjoyed the pursuit, and began appearing regularly in local stage productions. At the age of seventeen, he left Surrey to attend the University of London's Central School of Speech and Drama at the suggestion of Phil Tong, the drama teacher at the Freemen's School. Upon arriving in the city, Garfield moved into a house in the neighborhood of Golders Green and found a job at a nearby Starbucks. He later told journalists that he had a romanticized notion of what it would be like to work in a coffee shop and had harbored hopes—which remained unfulfilled—of meeting a succession of brainy, quirky women. Garfield ultimately earned a bachelor's degree in acting from the University of London, graduating with honors in 2004.

EARLY CAREER

During his third year at the Central School of Speech and Drama, Garfield attracted the attention of an agent, and he was soon cast in a production of the comedic play *Mercy* at the Soho Theatre in London. His performance in the coming-of-age drama *Kes* at the Manchester Royal Exchange Theatre earned him the title of most promising newcomer at the Manchester Evening News Theatre Awards. In 2006 Garfield won the Milton Shulman Award for outstanding newcomer at the Evening Standard Theatre Awards for his performances in a trilogy of plays about young people—*Burn*, *Chatroom*, and *Citizenship*—mounted at the National Theatre. The Milton Shulman Award additionally recognized his performances in *The Overwhelming*, a drama about the Rwandan genocide that had also been a National production, and *Beautiful Thing*, a production of Jonathan Harvey's 1993 play at the Sound Theatre.

After seeing Garfield perform at the National, film director Stephen Daldry arranged a meeting between Garfield and a casting director who happened to be working on *Lions for Lambs*, a 2007 film directed by and starring veteran actor Robert Redford. Garfield loved the script, a multitextured drama dealing with the ramifications of the United States' wars in the Middle East, but felt there was little chance of being cast in the role for which he auditioned, that of a disaffected student who is mentored by a professor played by Redford. "I thought, I'm not going to get it," he recalled to Albiston. "This [character] is the president of his college fraternity; he's got to look like an Abercrombie & Fitch model and he's got to have big biceps." Confounding his expectations, he was cast in the film, which also starred Tom Cruise and Meryl Streep. Working with such Hollywood heavyweights was both a heady experience and an educational one, he told interviewers, recalling to Albiston that he had the opportunity to fly in Redford's private jet as well as to watch the director edit portions of the film.

TELEVISION AND FILM WORK
Garfield made several television appearances in 2007, including in two episodes of the hit British science-fiction series *Doctor Who*. Broadening his audience even further, that year he also starred in the made-for-television film *Boy A*, a drama based on the 2004 novel by Jonathan Trigell. "[This is] television at its most painful and compulsive: a portrait of a young man who, egged on by a schoolfriend, had committed a brutal murder as a child," Chrissy Iley wrote for the *Guardian* (21 Apr. 2008). "Andrew Garfield's performance as the twenty-three-year-old, released from prison and struggling to adjust to a new life with a new identity, is rare and mesmerising." Many other critics agreed, and Garfield won the British Academy Television Award for best actor for his performance. Garfield's next major television project, an adaptation of David Peace's Red Riding series of noir novels, which deal with murder and police corruption in Yorkshire, aired in 2009.

Though initially best known in the United Kingdom, Garfield soon found international success through a series of high-profile films. In 2009 he portrayed a member of a traveling theater troupe in *The Imaginarium of Doctor Parnassus*, directed by Terry Gilliam. The film was overshadowed by the death of one of its stars, Heath Ledger, midway through the filming, and most media coverage and reviews focused on that fact rather than on the performances of Garfield and his fellow cast members. The following year Garfield starred in the film *Never Let Me Go*, based on a novel by Kazuo Ishiguro, alongside British actors Keira Knightley and Carey Mulligan.

In 2010 Garfield appeared in perhaps his most publicized film to date, *The Social Network*, which chronicles the founding of the social-networking site Facebook. Garfield was cast as Facebook cofounder Eduardo Saverin, a college friend of Facebook CEO Mark Zuckerberg (Jesse Eisenberg) and one of the company's first financial backers. Garfield's performance earned him praise from critics as well as a nomination for the Golden Globe Award for best actor in a supporting role, and the film itself was nominated for eight Academy Awards.

BECOMING SPIDER-MAN
In early 2010, Sony Pictures announced its plans to reboot the Spider-Man film franchise in 2012. The three previous Spider-Man films, directed by Sam Raimi and starring Tobey Maguire, had been both critically and commercially successful, but a number of factors led the development of the next film in the series, *Spider-Man 4*, to be canceled. The studio instead opted to bring in a new director and cast to rejuvenate the franchise. In July 2010, Sony announced that Garfield had been cast in the lead role of high school student Peter Parker, better known as the masked superhero Spider-Man. Although some fans were skeptical, Garfield soon won over many with his personal connection to the character and commitment to capturing his energy and spirit—and a photograph, released to the media by his parents, of a very young Garfield wearing a homemade Spider-Man Halloween costume.

When the film opened in the summer of 2012, critics praised Garfield's physical agility, which he attributed to his childhood gymnastics training, as well as the depth and sensitivity of his portrayal of Parker, a teenage orphan who struggles with his newfound responsibility after gaining superpowers from a spider bite. While some observers argued that a reboot of the franchise was unnecessary, as *Spider-Man 3* had been released only five years before, the movie ultimately grossed more than $700 million worldwide, largely on the strength of Garfield's performance and that of costar Emma Stone. A sequel, *The Amazing Spider-Man 2*, was scheduled for the spring of 2014.

OTHER PROJECTS

Shortly before the premiere of *The Amazing Spider-Man*, Garfield spent several months on Broadway, performing in a revival of the Arthur Miller play *Death of a Salesman*. The play starred the late Philip Seymour Hoffman as the iconic salesman Willy Loman, while Garfield played the part of Biff, Willy's conflicted son. "It's a wrenching performance, exquisitely calibrated," David Rooney raved for the *New York Times* (10 May 2012) about Garfield's portrayal of the character, suggesting that Garfield had perhaps taken the role in order to "showcase his dramatic range before being thrown into the popcorn machine with the release of *Spider-Man*." Garfield, however, told Rooney, "It was more of an antidote to the previous experience [of filming in Hollywood]. . . . I wanted to balance it out somehow. Plus, any mention of Miller, I'm sold." In recognition of his work, Garfield was nominated for the Tony Award for best performance by a featured actor in a play.

By early 2014 Garfield had multiple projects in various stages of production, including the contemporary drama *99 Homes* and the Martin Scorsese–helmed historical film *Silence*, in which he was cast as a seventeenth-century Jesuit priest who travels to Japan to spread the gospel of Christianity.

PERSONAL LIFE

While *The Amazing Spider-Man* was filming, rumors began to swirl that Garfield was romantically involved with Stone, who plays his on-screen love interest. Although the pair initially refused to discuss the matter with interviewers, they eventually acknowledged that they were a couple and, as of April 2014, have been dating about three years.

Garfield was described by Rooney as "intense and observant, without the slightest trace of cockiness." The actor has expressed great ambivalence about achieving international stardom and told Rooney, "[Fame is] not something I take to naturally. I still have to find my comfort zone within it where I can protect myself and be good to the people around me."

SUGGESTED READING

Bamigboye, Baz. "From Web Nerd to Spider-Man: Andrew Garfield Talks about School Days." *Daily Mail*. Associated Newspapers, 7 Jan. 2011. Web. 6 Mar. 2014.

Hart, Hugh. "How Andrew Garfield Spins *Amazing Spider-Man* Forward." *Wired*. Condé Nast, 2 July 2012. Web. 6 Mar. 2014.

Rooney, David. "His Own Network of Tortured Souls." *New York Times*. New York Times, 10 May 2012. Web. 6 Mar. 2014.

SELECTED WORKS

Boy A, 2007; *Lions for Lambs*, 2007; *The Imaginarium of Doctor Parnassus*, 2009; *The Social Network*, 2010; *The Amazing Spider-Man*, 2012; *The Amazing Spider-Man 2*, 2014

—*Mari Rich*

Kenneth Goldsmith

Born: June 4, 1961
Occupation: Poet and conceptual artist

"My books are better thought about than read," Kenneth Goldsmith told Dave Mandl for the *Believer* (Oct. 2011). "I mean, do you really want to sit down and read a year's worth of weather reports or a transcription of the 1010 WINS traffic reports . . . every ten minutes over the course of a twenty-four-hour period? I don't. But they're wonderful to talk about and think about, to dip in and out of, to hold, to have on your shelf. In fact, I say that I don't have a readership, I have a *thinkership*. I guess this is why what I do is called 'conceptual writing.' The idea is much more important than the product."

Goldsmith's work includes such books as *Fidget* (2000), in which he exhaustively chronicles every physical movement he makes over the course of several hours; *Soliloquy* (2001), which documents every single utterance he made in a week; and *Day* (2003), a word-for-word transcript of the contents of one issue of the *New York Times*. He is also the author of a trilogy comprising *The Weather* (2005), *Traffic* (2007), and *Sports* (2008), equally faithful transcriptions of, respectively, a year of weather reports, twenty-four hours' worth of traffic bulletins, and the running commentary from an entire Yankees–Red Sox baseball game.

Getty Images

Mandl asserted that Goldsmith's work "is simultaneously among the most mundane and the most maddeningly provocative writing being done today" and wrote, "[He] forces a drastic rethinking of what a book or text can be." On the other end of the spectrum are critics who deride Goldsmith for exhibiting no originality and even condoning plagiarism at times. Embracing an ethos he calls "uncreative writing," he explained in a piece for the *Chronicle of Higher Education* (11 Sept. 2011), "In 1969 the conceptual artist Douglas Huebler wrote, 'The world is full of objects, more or less interesting; I do not wish to add any more.' I've come to embrace Huebler's idea, though it might be retooled as: 'The world is full of texts, more or less interesting; I do not wish to add any more.'" He continued, "It seems an appropriate response to a new condition in writing: With an unprecedented amount of available text, our problem is not needing to write more of it; instead, we must learn to negotiate the vast quantity that exists. How I make my way through this thicket of information—how I manage it, parse it, organize and distribute it—is what distinguishes my writing from yours."

EARLY YEARS AND EDUCATION

Goldsmith was born on June 4, 1961, in Freeport, New York, on the South Shore of Long Island, an area he has termed a "suburban wasteland." His father worked in a garment business founded by his own parents but longed to be a social worker—a situation that resulted in his suffering from periodic depression. The family, while Jewish, was not observant, and Goldsmith and his sister were sent to left-leaning camps and schools that emphasized Jewish culture and progressive social values rather than religion.

"I had absolutely no contact with art or media or poetry," Goldsmith told John Jourden for *Archinect* (26 June 2007). "[Except for an occasional Broadway show,] all I knew was the television. I grew up in a house that was bereft of culture entirely." He has told other interviewers, however, that his upbringing was not exactly as conventional as might be assumed from his references to suburbia and television. "My parents were early adopters of New Age," he recalled to Ruth Saxelby for the arts-and-culture magazine *Dazed* (June 2013). "So our whole family grew up doing Transcendental Meditation, eating vegetarian food and practicing holistic health. Of course, when I was a teenager I shoveled as many drugs into my body as was humanly possible as a form of rebellion."

Another point of departure from the conventional was Goldsmith's grandfather, Philip Field, an attorney who invested heavily in Cuban sugar fields, only to lose all of his earnings when Castro came to power. He later began drinking heavily, lost his practice, and ended up working as a rent-collector in the Hell's Kitchen section of Manhattan. Despite those travails, Field amassed an impressive library of rare books, which absorbed Goldsmith for hours as a child and which he ultimately inherited.

After graduating from Paul D. Schreiber High School in 1979, Goldsmith began his undergraduate studies at New York University (NYU). He has explained that in his freshman year he took a drawing class and emerged with an entirely new outlook. "A car was no longer a car; instead it was an amalgam of color, shape and form," he told Saxelby. "I never did drugs again and dedicated myself to art."

He left NYU in 1980, spent a year at the Parsons School of Design, and then followed a favorite teacher to the Rhode Island School of Design (RISD), where he earned a bachelor of fine arts degree in sculpture in 1984. He supported himself during his college years by mold making and casting; after graduating he moved back to New York City to sculpt.

ART CAREER

As a student, Goldsmith had experimented with stacking hundreds of random items into assemblages, and he continued to explore that technique as a professional. At the suggestion of one curator, he carved a stack of wooden books, and when that piece sold quickly, he began carving individual volumes with detailed pages and provocative titles. A 1989 exhibit of the work at New York City's White Columns Gallery established him as an artist to watch, and he was soon being considered a force in the art world.

Although the sculptures sold well, Goldsmith eventually found himself discontented. "I was bothered by the fact that the idea of what to put on the books came in a flash, but then the execution could take up to several months of work to realize," he recalled to Marjorie Perloff for *Jacket* (Feb. 2003). "In response, I began to question what I was more interested in—the objects themselves or the words on the objects—and chose the latter. I stopped making sculpture and began simply putting words on large pieces of paper." He called the pieces "text art," and they marked a shift from one world to another. "My long transition from the visual to the verbal . . . has been an incredibly idiosyncratic and personal journey," he told Perloff. "I never could have anticipated, some twenty years out of art school, that I would think of myself as a writer." He has acknowledged the seeming folly of his career trajectory. "Choosing to be a poet is like choosing to have cancer," he admitted to Saxelby. "No one in their right mind would do that. But it chose me."

WRITING

Understanding the difficulties inherent in making a living as a poet, Goldsmith learned to code HTML and do programming; he worked in the dot-com world from about 1993 until 2002 as he concurrently produced chapbooks and other volumes. Most critics consider 73 *Poems* (1993) to be his first serious literary foray. The pieces (a representative line reads, "gain weight / jail bait / soul mate / hesitate / penetrate / Watergate") are printed in black and gray graphite on parchment-colored rag paper, and the limited-edition book is packaged with a CD by singer Joan La Barbara, who used the text as inspiration for a series of avant-garde tracks.

In 1997 Goldsmith released the collection *No.111 2.7.93–10.20.96*, which its publisher described as a work of "conceptually uncategorizable brilliance by one of New York's most unpredictable young artists." As preparation, Goldsmith spent three years collecting phrases ending in *r* sounds. He ultimately organized his findings into a 606-page book that begins with single-syllable words, moves on to two-syllable words in the second section, and continues from there to increase by one syllable in each subsequent section. "*No. 111* excels at startling juxtapositions of obscenity, pop cultural references, idiosyncratic slang, and generational buzzwords," a description on the website of the University of Pennsylvania's Center for Programs in Contemporary Writing states. "Amazingly comprehensive and wide-ranging in its references (including the just-emerging Internet culture and its lingo) *No. 111* is . . . the last significant epic poem of the twentieth century." In one widely quoted assessment, a writer for *Publishers Weekly* (19 Jan. 1998) called it "perhaps the most exhaustive and beautiful collage work yet produced in poetry."

Goldsmith followed that with *Fidget* (2000), a tribute to James Joyce's *Ulysses* that critics did, indeed, often describe as Joycean. To prepare the text, he used a Dictaphone to keep a verbal record of every physical movement he made during his waking hours on June 16 (known as Bloomsday in literary circles) in 1997. "Most of the time, the actual prose is not the point: 'Facial muscles relax. Back tingles. Chills emerge. Right hand moves to top of head. Fingernail scrapes scalp. Thumb meets each successive fingertip. Rubs,'" a reviewer for *Publishers Weekly* (30 May 2001) wrote. "This is another important book from Goldsmith, pointing the way to a rapprochement between poetry and conceptual and performance art—avant-gardists and art lovers of all stripes will want to experience its near-hypnotic pleasures."

Of *Soliloquy* (2001), which documents every word Goldsmith spoke from the moment he woke up one Monday morning until he fell asleep the following Sunday night, he told Mark Gurarie for *Publishers Weekly* (12 Apr. 2013): "[Preparing it] made me aware of just how disjunctive, challenging and curious our normative speech patterns are. After that book, I was never able to hear language in quite the same way."

Goldsmith's most recent book is *Seven American Deaths and Disasters* (2013), in which he transcribes archival radio and television coverage of the assassinations of President John F. Kennedy and iconic musician John Lennon; the explosion of the space shuttle *Challenger*; the shootings at Columbine High School; and the terrorist attacks of September 11, 2001, among other tragedies. "It knocks the air from your lungs," Dwight Garner wrote for the *New York Times* (18 June 2013). "His book is about the sounds our culture makes when the reassuring smooth jazz of much of our broadcast media breaks down, when disc jockeys and news anchors are forced to find words for events that are nearly impossible to describe."

In addition to his own writing, Goldsmith is a coeditor of *Against Expression: An Anthology of Conceptual Writing* (2011).

TEACHING AND OTHER ACTIVITIES

Since 2004 Goldsmith has been a faculty member of the University of Pennsylvania, where he now teaches a workshop on "uncreative writing." He explained to Jourden, "Creativity is such a bankrupt concept in our culture and such an over-used cliché, and yet something held so highly esteemed, still, that in order to truly be creative and truly find a way out of that we need to employ a strategy of opposites—we need to be uncreative, we need to be boring, we need to be everything that the culture claims creativity isn't." His workshop, he asserts, "is a way of going against the tendency toward MFA creative writing programs, which don't really teach you how to be creative at all. They're truly uncreative. They're teaching you how to yet write another short story of the rise of a hero and his even more dramatic downfall. Or a poem that is work-shopped to death and that is written by committee."

Goldsmith spends a portion of his time administering UbuWeb, an Internet resource devoted to what he terms the "radical distribution" of avant-garde visual art, literature, and music. He founded the site in 1995, well before personal computers became ubiquitous. "I get e-mails from people like one from a girl in Texas, who said 'Thank you for what you put up on Ubu-Web. And the type of materials you offer there certainly are not available to a girl living in a small town in Texas,'" he told Jourden. "It really is about free and unfettered access for people to materials that were relegated to museums or relegated to specialists."

Additionally, Goldsmith hosted a radio show, *Unpopular Music*, on the alternative New York

City station WFMU from 1995 to 2010, wrote music criticism for the New York Press from 1998 to 2001, and served as a National Public Radio (NPR) commentator from 1999 to 2004.

In 2013 he served as the poet laureate of the Museum of Modern Art in New York City. In that capacity, he brought over one hundred poets, novelists, essayists, and others to the museum to present works. His other honors have included an Anschutz Distinguished Fellow Professorship in American Studies at Princeton University (2009–10) and residencies at such places as Canada's Banff Center for the Arts and France's Château de Bionnay.

On May 11, 2011, he was invited to the White House to read his work during an event called "A Celebration of American Poetry," which also featured more mainstream writers like Billy Collins and Rita Dove. Public reaction to his inclusion on that occasion was decidedly mixed: Linh Dinh, a fellow poet with left-leaning political views, for example, accused him of performing for mass murderers, while some right-wing talk-show hosts opined that his invitation to the White House was a sign of the decline of Western civilization.

PERSONAL LIFE

Goldsmith has been married to the artist Cheryl Donegan since 1989. She is known for such conceptual pieces as "Head," for which she filmed herself drinking a milky liquid from a plastic spout, and "Kiss My Royal Irish Ass," in which she is shown dipping her buttocks in green paint and using them to press shamrock shapes onto paper.

They have two sons, Finnegan and Cassius, and live in the Chelsea section of New York City.

SUGGESTED READING

Garner, Dwight. "The Words We Heard as Horrors Sank In." *New York Times*. New York Times, 18 June 2013. Web. 8 Apr. 2014.

Gurarie, Mark. "The Transcribed Life: *PW* Talks with Kenneth Goldsmith." *Publishers Weekly*. Publishers Weekly. 12 Apr. 2013. Web. 8 Apr. 2014.

Jourden, John. "UbuWeb Vu: Kenneth Goldsmith." *Archinect*. Archinect. 26 June 2007. Web. 8 Apr. 2014.

Mandl, Dave. "Kenneth Goldsmith: Poet." *Believer*. Believer. Oct. 2011. Web. 8 Apr. 2014.

Perloff, Marjorie. "A Conversation with Kenneth Goldsmith." *Jacket*. Jacket. Feb. 2003. Web. 8 Apr. 2014.

Saxelby, Ruth. "Kenneth Goldsmith." *Dazed*. Dazed. June 2013. Web. 8 Apr. 2014.

SELECTED WORKS

No. 111 2.7.93–10.20.96, 1997; *Fidget*, 2000; *Soliloquy*, 2001; *Day*, 2003; *I'll Be Your Mirror:*

The Selected Andy Warhol Interviews 1962–1987, 2004; *The Weather*, 2005; *Traffic*, 2007; *Sports*, 2008; *Uncreative Writing: Managing Language in the Digital Age*, 2011; *Seven American Deaths and Disasters*, 2013

—Mari Rich

Selena Gomez

Born: July 22, 1992
Occupation: Actor and singer

Selena Gomez first came to widespread attention as the lead in the hit Disney Channel sitcom *Wizards of Waverly Place*, which aired from 2007 to 2012. The popular television show catapulted her to fame and helped launch her broader career on the big screen and in the recording studio. Like many other stars of her generation, Gomez is a fixture in the tabloid press, and her romance with pop singer Justin Bieber has been the source of particularly obsessive media coverage.

In a profile for the *Guardian* (13 July 2013), Olly Richards called Gomez "one of the most successful of the Disney Channel alumni . . . the new breed, who are primped and propagated like prize roses; toothy munchkins given TV shows and then slapped on backpacks, pencil

© Xavier Collin/Retna Ltd./Corbis

cases and, if they can carry a tune without significant wobble, album covers." Richards explained, however, "Where the Miley Cyruses of this world try cropping their hair off and gyrating semi-naked in order to be seen as adults, or the likes of Lindsay Lohan and Amanda Bynes lose all semblance of a plan and spin off into pitiable tabloid notoriety, Gomez's transition [into adult stardom] has been rather smarter." Gomez has frequently acknowledged the difficulties of forging an adult career after years as a Disney star. "It doesn't feel good to be rejected, to hear that directors want Mila Kunis, not a Disney girl," she lamented to Carrie Rickey for the *Philadelphia Inquirer* (26 June 2011). "The [mistaken] perception is of somebody who probably overacts, probably has no sincerity, probably thinks of acting as a job rather than a skill."

While still generally careful to not shock or offend her tween fans, Gomez starred in *Spring Breakers*, a 2012 R-rated film that went into wide release in 2013. In the film, her character and three friends decide to rob a bank in order to fund a hedonistic trip to Florida, where they fall in with a drug-dealing rapper. Noting that her costars included fellow "Disney and *Teen People* princesses" Vanessa Hudgens and Ashley Benson, critic Scott Foundas wrote for the *Village Voice* (13 Mar. 2013) that the group members "don't so much toy with their good-girl images as set them ablaze."

CHILDHOOD

Selena Marie Gomez was born on July 22, 1992, and grew up in Grand Prairie, Texas, a suburb of Dallas. Her mother, Amanda "Mandy" Cornett Teefey, was sixteen years old when Gomez, who was named for popular Tejano singer Selena Quintanilla, was born. Teefey, a stage actress who sometimes appeared in local productions, split from Gomez's father, Ricardo Gomez, about five years after her daughter's birth. The future singer endured a difficult childhood. "I remember when my parents broke up I didn't understand it," Gomez told Chloe Melas for *Hollywood Life* (28 June 2011). "I blamed my mom a lot . . . because I wanted a family so bad. I wanted to have my dad and my mom together." Money was often in short supply. "I can remember about seven times when our car got stuck on the highway because we'd run out of gas money," Gomez told an interviewer for *Elle* (July 2012). Still, she continued, Teefey, who now works as her manager, "saved up to take me to concerts. She took me to museums, aquariums, to teach me about the world, about what's real." Later, in 2006, Teefey remarried, and by all accounts Gomez enjoys a good relationship with her stepfather, Brian Teefey. She has a half-sister, Gracie Elliot Teefey, who was born on June 12, 2013.

Gomez—who was homeschooled and earned her high school diploma in 2010—imagines that her life would have taken a very different turn had she remained in Texas. "I'm terrified of what I would have become if I'd stayed there," she explained to Kyle Buchanan for *Glamour* (Dec. 2012). "I'm sure I'd have two children by now."

EARLY SCREEN CAREER

Mandy Teefey had little intention of allowing her daughter to repeat her own youthful follies, however, and she encouraged Gomez, then ten years old, to try out for a role on the children's show *Barney & Friends* (2002–4). Gomez was hired for the recurring part of Gianna, one of the human youngsters who interacted with the title character, a large purple dinosaur with a jovial grin and a voice that many adult critics found saccharine and irritating. Each show features a simple storyline that finds the anthropomorphized character and his human friends dancing and singing childhood tunes.

Gomez portrayed Gianna during the seventh and eighth seasons of the show and was then let go on the grounds that she was getting too old to appear on a show aimed at preschoolers. She considers those two years a valuable experience, however. "I was very shy when I was little," she recalled to Michelle Tan for *People* (26 May 2008). "I didn't know what 'camera right' was. I didn't know what blocking was. I learned everything from Barney." Learning along with her was Demi Lovato, who would also later become a teen star; the two have remained friends throughout their careers.

Gomez landed a bit part (credited as Waterpark Girl) in the 2003 movie *Spy Kids 3-D: Game Over*, the penultimate entry in a big-screen franchise about a pair of young secret agents, but roles were difficult to find once she left *Barney & Friends*. After two years of unsuccessfully auditioning for various projects, she was cast in the 2005 television film *Walker, Texas Ranger: Trial by Fire*, which starred martial artist Chuck Norris as a Texas lawman. The following year she portrayed Emily Grace Garcia, an intrepid girl who investigates mysterious happenings at her local library, in the 2006 television short *Brain Zapped*.

DISNEY

The year 2006 proved something of a turning point for the young actress. In addition to *Brain Zapped*, she appeared in her biggest role to date, guest-starring in the hit Disney Channel show *The Suite Life of Zack and Cody*, which follows the adventures of a pair of towheaded tweens who live at the hotel where their mother is employed as a lounge singer.

Having caught the attention of Disney executives, Gomez next played the role of the evil nemesis Mikayla in the runaway hit *Hannah*

Montana. That series starred Miley Cyrus as an average teen who, unbeknownst to most of her fellow students, moonlights as a pop star. As Mikayla, Gomez was featured in a handful of episodes in 2007 and 2008. Gomez and Cyrus are close in age, and because their careers have taken such disparate turns, media observers often compare and contrast the two—with most praising Gomez as a role model for her fans and chastising Cyrus for her sexually charged performances and scanty clothing.

Gomez landed her first starring role on Disney Channel, as Alex Russo, a teenage wizard in the sitcom *Wizards of Waverly Place*. The series, which centers on Alex and her two siblings, aired from 2007 until 2012. During that time it won a slew of accolades, including the Primetime Emmy Award for outstanding children's program in 2009 and 2012 and numerous Kids' Choice Awards; Gomez herself won five consecutive Kid's Choice Awards for favorite television actress for her role on the show.

While starring in the show Gomez took on a variety of other projects. She did voice-over work in the animated 2008 feature *Horton Hears a Who!* and later that year she starred in the romantic comedy *Another Cinderella Story*, a modern take on the classic fairy tale. She also made two television movies under the Disney Channel Original Movie banner: *Princess Protection Program* (2009), which costarred her friend Demi Lovato, and *Wizards of Waverly Place: The Movie* (2009), based on her hit series.

FEATURE FILMS

Gomez costarred as Beezus Quimby in *Ramona and Beezus* (2010), a feature film based on author Beverly Cleary's popular children's book series. Roger Ebert echoed the sentiments of other reviewers when he wrote on RogerEbert.com (21 July 2010), "This is a featherweight G-rated comedy of no consequence, except undoubtedly to kids . . . Joey King and the Disney star Selena Gomez are both appealing, and the movie is wisely populated with grownups who are content to play straight men."

Gomez followed that with another comedy, *Monte Carlo* (2011), in which her character is mistaken for an heiress and takes advantage of that confusion to briefly indulge in a jet-setting lifestyle. While most reviewers dismissed the film entirely, Stephanie Merry wrote for the *Washington Post* (1 July 2011) that "starry-eyed girls and rabid fans of Gomez will probably go gaga for the movie. It is ultimately a sweet story, after all, and a few scenes might even make them LOL."

Unlike many of her fellow Disney stars, Gomez did little to tarnish her image—a fact that some credited to her close relationship with her mother, who managed her career and kept a watchful eye on her. "I really haven't changed

any rules for her. If she wasn't allowed to do it in Texas, she's not allowed to do it here [in Hollywood]," Teefey told Michelle Tan. "Selena knows who she is, and I am around to make sure she doesn't change." Once *Wizards of Waverly Place* stopped filming, however, Gomez did feel free to appear in racier films, including *Spring Breakers*, which features Gomez, Vanessa Hudgens (of *High School Musical* fame), Ashley Benson, and Rachel Korine on a crime spree to fund a wild vacation in Florida. Gomez's next non-Disney role was that of a young woman who teams with a former race-car driver (played by Ethan Hawke) to save his kidnapped wife in the thriller *Getaway* (2013), which did poorly at the box office and was ignored by most critics.

Despite her desire to expand her oeuvre, Gomez has had only fond words for Disney. (She returned to the channel for 2013's *The Wizards Return: Alex vs. Alex*, in which she played not only her original character but an evil version of her, as well.) "I had an incredible four years [being] a part of Disney, it was my family, it was the reason I got to do everything that I loved," she told Mark Worgan for the website EntertainmentWise.com (2 Apr. 2013). Gomez's next projects include star turns in the drama *Rudderless* and the comedy *Behaving Badly*, both set for release in 2014.

MUSIC

Concurrent with her on-screen career, Gomez has enjoyed success as a recording artist. She has released three albums with her band, Selena Gomez & the Scene: *Kiss & Tell* (2009), *A Year Without Rain* (2010), and *When the Sun Goes Down* (2011). Reviews of the albums were generally mixed or lukewarm; some reviews seemed colored by the writer's attitude toward Disney. "Following Miley Cyrus and Demi Lovato, we now have the debut album from Selena Gomez, star of the TV show *Wizards of Waverly Place*," Michael Hann wrote in a review of *Kiss & Tell* for the *Guardian* (14 Apr. 2010). "There will be naysayers, but once again a Disney act has produced a hugely likable and at times inspired collection—these are never cheap cash-in efforts, as the quality of the songwriting attests." In another representative review of *When the Sun Goes Down*, Jody Rosen wrote for *Rolling Stone* (2 Aug. 2011): "At just 18 years old, Selena Gomez is a showbiz vet, with a decade-plus in the game. . . . So it's no surprise that Gomez's third album is a very professional affair. . . . The songs are swathed up-to-minute Top 40 sounds—perky electro-pop, tuneful balladry—and they hit the expected notes."

In 2013 Gomez released her first solo album, *Stars Dance*, meant to convey a more mature, professionally evolved sound. In a review for *Billboard* (23 July 2013), Andrew Hampp described it as "11 shinily produced pop songs that find Gomez trying on a series of different personalities with her slight-yet-capable vocals." The album sold 97,000 copies in its first week and bumped Jay Z's *Magna Carta Holy Grail* from the number-one spot on the Billboard 200 chart. Gomez has since announced her intention to stop recording and focus on her acting career.

PERSONAL LIFE AND PHILANTHROPY

Gomez once dated teen heartthrob Nick Jonas, from the band the Jonas Brothers. Because he had also been romantically involved with Miley Cyrus, rumors swirled that the two young women were bitter rivals. (Gomez has denied feeling any such animosity.) Since 2011 she has been engaged in an on-again, off-again relationship with pop star Justin Bieber. Tabloid journalists nicknamed the pair "Jelena" and frequently speculated about what the dutiful Gomez sees in Bieber, who is known for his bad behavior, including insulting his fans, smoking marijuana, and driving recklessly. Discussing the media's interest in her, Gomez told Lauren Waterman for *Teen Vogue* (June/July 2011), "A lot of times the paparazzi will try to use [my fans]. They'll say, 'Your fans want this.' And it's frustrating because my fans are amazing: They love me, they support me. . . . But the press? They don't care about me. They just want something on me that they can use. They just want to get that shot."

Although Gomez has reportedly been diagnosed with lupus—an autoimmune disease that causes fatigue, headaches, and joint pain—she made no mention of the condition when she canceled thirteen shows during her early 2014 *Stars Dance* tour in Asia and Australia. In a statement released on December 20, 2013, Gomez said that though her fans are important to her "it has become clear . . . that after many years of putting my work first, I need to spend some time on myself in order to be the best person I can be," as reported by Cavan Sieczkowski for the *Huffington Post* (20 Dec. 2013). Since 2009 she has served as a UNICEF ambassador and at the time of her appointment she was the youngest person in the United States to hold the title.

SUGGESTED READING

Buchanan, Kyle. "Selena Gomez: The Independent Spirit." *Glamour*. Condé Nast, Dec. 2012. Web. 18 Mar. 2014.

Richards, Olly. "The Wonderful World of Selena Gomez." *Guardian*. Guardian News and Media, 13 July 2013. Web. 18 Mar. 2014.

Rickey, Carrie. "Selena Gomez: Teen Disney Celebrity on the Cusp of Adult Stardom." *Philadelphia Inquirer*. Interstate General Media, 26 June 2011. Web. 18 Mar. 2014.

Sieczkowski, Cavan. "Selena Gomez Cancels Tour of Asia, Australia to 'Spend Some Time on Myself.'" *Huffington Post*. TheHuffingtonPost.com, 20 Dec. 2013. Web. 18 Mar. 2014.

Tan, Michelle. "Is Selena Gomez the Next Miley Cyrus?" *People*. Time, 26 May 2008. Web. 18 Mar. 2014.

Waterman, Laura. "Her Magic Moment: Selena Gomez." *Teen Vogue*. Condé Nast, June/July 2011. Web. 18 Mar. 2014.

SELECTED WORKS

Wizards of Waverly Place, 2007–12; *Another Cinderella Story*, 2008; *Princess Protection Program*, 2009; *Wizards of Waverly Place: The Movie*, 2009; *Ramona and Beezus*, 2010; *Monte Carlo*, 2011; *Spring Breakers*, 2012; *Getaway*, 2013

—*Mari Rich*

Gotye

Born: May 21, 1980
Occupation: Musician

Belgian Australian singer, songwriter, producer, and multi-instrumentalist Gotye has often drawn comparisons to Sting and Peter Gabriel for his impassioned, reedy voice and unique, multilayered sound. Jason Treuen, writing for *Rolling Stone Australia* (Nov. 2011), called him "a tinkering troubadour, an eccentric outsider that revels in post-modern pop." Since launching his music career in the early 2000s, Gotye has independently released the studio albums *Boardface* (2003), *Like Drawing Blood* (2006), and *Making Mirrors* (2011), and a remix album, *Mixed Blood* (2007). He is known particularly for his meticulous approach to making music, which revolves around the innovative use of samples and found sounds. "I tend to just do whatever I want on an album and try to make it work," Gotye explained to Craig Mathieson for the *Sydney Morning Herald* (30 Sept. 2011). He added, "I want to see how far I can push things."

Gotye's signature sample-based recordings, though unorthodox in nature, have struck a chord with the masses. The single for which he is best known, 2011's "Somebody That I Used to Know," off *Making Mirrors*, became a worldwide phenomenon and helped propel him to fame. It topped the charts in more than two dozen countries and became the best-selling single of 2012. Gotye solidified his place in music history in 2013, when he won three 2012 Grammy Awards, marking the first Grammy wins of his career.

EARLY LIFE

Gotye was born Wouter De Backer on May 21, 1980, in Bruges, Belgium. When he was two years old, he and his family moved to the northern Melbourne suburb of Montmorency. His

Wirelmage

he had developed adoration for legendary British synth-pop band Depeche Mode. Inspired in particular by the group's multi-instrumentalist songwriter Martin Gore, he began teaching himself chord progressions on the piano and writing lyrics. De Backer soon formed a Depeche Mode–inspired band with three of his high school friends called Downstares, which he described to Marlow Stern for the *Daily Beast* (31 Mar. 2012) as "a rock-synth-pop hybrid." He sang and played drums in the band, which, in addition to Depeche Mode, covered songs by such seminal grunge bands as Nirvana, Alice in Chains, and Soundgarden. The band played shows mostly around Melbourne's northeastern suburbs.

After graduating from Parade College in 1998, De Backer attended the University of Melbourne. He initially pursued a dual degree in law and arts, along with Japanese language, before switching his focus to cultural studies. In 2001 De Backer's parents left the family home in Montmorency and moved to a remote, thirteen-acre rural property on the Mornington Peninsula in southwest Australia. He continued to live in the family home to focus on his studies and eventually completed a bachelor of arts degree.

While attending college De Backer and his fellow Downstares members parted ways, prompting him to embark on a solo career. He turned his attention specifically to electronic music after a friend introduced him to the work of American sampling pioneer DJ Shadow. De Backer bought his first DJ and recording equipment and started collecting albums of all kinds, in hopes of being able to find sounds that he could integrate into new, self-produced songs. "I just loved discovering old culture and discarded things, thinking maybe I could make them relevant again," he told Jonah Weiner for *Rolling Stone* (3 May 2012).

father worked as a computer engineer, and his mother was a French teacher. In Australia he was called Walter or Wally. Early on Gotye's mother began calling him Gaultier, a nickname derived from the French translation of his Flemish birth name. He later adopted a phonetic variation of that name as his stage name.

De Backer's attraction to music began early in life. As a child he combed through his parents' record collection, which was made up mostly of classical, folk, and world music. One of the few pop records in their collection was the Beatles' *Abbey Road* (1969), which De Backer has cited as being a favorite album while he was growing up. The first musical instrument he took up was the drums, at about age fifteen or sixteen, when he received his first proper drum kit.

De Backer's first experiences with sampling also date back to his childhood. Because his parents limited the amount of time he could watch television, he would use a portable tape recorder to record snippets from his favorite shows, which included the educational children's programs *Sesame Street* and Australia's *Play School*. De Backer's early "sampling curating," as he described it to Brian Mansfield for *USA Today* (20 Feb. 2012), and preoccupation with found sound led to his interest in such sample-heavy acts as influential British acid house duo the KLF, French electronica producer Jean-Jacques Perrey, and German-born American synth music pioneer Gershon Kingsley.

HIGH SCHOOL AND COLLEGE YEARS

By the time De Backer entered Parade College, an all-boys Catholic high school in Bundoora,

EARLY SOLO WORK AND THE BASICS

De Backer began creating tracks made almost entirely of samples culled from his ever-growing record library. He produced a series of four- and five-track EPs and sent copies to radio stations all over Australia in an attempt to build an audience for his music. The meticulously crafted EPs were well received, particularly by the influential youth-centric Australian radio station Triple J, and helped Gotye, as he began calling himself, land a distribution deal with the independent label Creative Vibes. He subsequently compiled eleven tracks from his EPs for his first full-length album, *Boardface*, which was released in 2003 through his own Samples 'N' Seconds label. The album received positive critical notice, with several of its tracks gaining steady airplay on Triple J. Its success enabled Gotye to acquire a manager, Danny Rogers of Lunatic Entertainment.

While working on his early solo recordings, Gotye met fellow singer-songwriter Kris Schroeder. Bonding over shared musical tastes, the two formed an indie-pop band called the Basics and soon began performing around Melbourne, with Gotye (billed as Wally De Backer) on drums and Schroeder on acoustic guitar. The duo eventually became a trio, with the addition of electric guitarist Michael Hubbard (at which point Schroeder moved to bass guitar), and they independently released their debut album, *Get Back*, in 2003. The following year Hubbard was replaced by Tim Heath, who solidified the band's lineup.

The Basics toured Australia nonstop over the next decade, during which they released ten more digital albums and a compilation set. In an interview with Iain Shedden for the *Australian* (12 Sept. 2013), Gotye described the Basics' music as "stripped back rock 'n' roll with three instruments." He insisted that the group was as important a project for him as his solo work is, explaining, "I like to think that anything I do, I do it to the best of my abilities and with focus."

LIKE DRAWING BLOOD AND RISE TO FAME

Gotye's second full-length studio album, *Like Drawing Blood*, was released in 2006. The album's title refers to the many obstacles he faced while making the record. For a time after his parents sold the Montmorency home in 2004, he led a peripatetic lifestyle, moving from home to home in Melbourne as he worked a number of odd jobs, including that of a library assistant and data entry clerk, to support his music career. As a result, many of the tracks on *Like Drawing Blood* were recorded in different acoustic environments, giving the album an expansive and eclectic sound.

For Gotye, the arduous experience of making *Like Drawing Blood*, which was mixed and mastered by François Tétaz, ultimately proved fruitful. Upon release, it found critical and commercial success. Two of its singles, "Hearts a Mess" and "Learnalilgivinanlovin," quickly received heavy radio airplay, peaking at number eight and ninety-four, respectively, on the Triple J Hottest 100 list. *Like Drawing Blood* was voted the number-one album of the year in a Triple J listeners' poll and earned Gotye the most outstanding independent artist award at the first-ever Australian Independent Record Chart Awards. The album was also nominated for an Australian Recording Industry Award (ARIA Award, the Australian equivalent of a Grammy) for best independent release and short-listed for the 2006 Australian Music Prize. In a review for the Melbourne *Age* (9 June 2006), Andrew Drever wrote that Gotye "bravely tackles a mind-boggling array of musical styles with conviction and flair" and declared that the album "highlights the arrival of an important new talent."

In 2007 Gotye released the follow-up album *Mixed Blood*, which features remixes of songs from his first two albums performed by various artists. The album received six ARIA Award nominations, with Gotye winning for best male artist. As a result of exposure from the awards, *Like Drawing Blood* experienced a significant increase in sales, eventually becoming certified platinum in Australia after selling more than 70,000 copies. *Like Drawing Blood* was recognized as the iTunes album of the year 2008 in the United Kingdom and was officially released on CD in the United States in 2012.

MAKING MIRRORS

The success of *Like Drawing Blood* instantly made Gotye one of Australia's biggest music artists. More importantly, it brought him the financial security to quit his day job and focus on his music career full-time. He bought a home in Melbourne and set up a permanent recording studio in a barn built by his father on the family's thirteen-acre estate on the Mornington Peninsula. It was there where Gotye started recording tracks for his third studio album.

Unlike his two previous albums, which relied heavily on samples from other artists, Gotye approached what would become *Making Mirrors* with the intention of using only original found sounds and instruments. Though continuing to stay within a sample-based framework, he explained to Elisa Bray for the London *Independent* (17 Feb. 2012), "I wanted to set myself a new method of working. I was like, 'what if I can take it a step further and make more sounds from scratch.'"

Gotye offered fans a glimpse of his new sound in October 2010, when he released the single "Eyes Wide Open," which features a bass line constructed from samples of an aboriginal musical fence in the Queensland outback. The complexly layered, pop-tinged track served as the lead single off *Making Mirrors*. It quickly caught on with listeners, reaching number fifty-five on the ARIA singles chart and number twenty-five on the Triple J Hottest 100 list. In an article for *Billboard* (13 Apr. 2012), Richard Smirke described "Eyes Wide Open" as "a stadium-sized, feel-good number reminiscent of Peter Gabriel's finest cuts."

Gotye's perfectionist nature resulted in him spending months tinkering with other tracks that would end up on *Making Mirrors*. Unsatisfied with his initial mixes of songs, he suffered depressive periods and, at one point, even considered scrapping the album altogether, believing his creative output was not good enough. Gotye told Jason Treuen, "It was one of the first times in my life that I felt I could completely devote myself to my career and creativity, without having any barriers like finance or a studio, but

I'd wake up a lot of mornings unable to make a choice about what to do."

Making Mirrors was finally released in August 2011, after taking more than two years to complete. Distributed in Australia on the independent label Eleven (licensed through Samples 'N' Seconds), the twelve-track album reached number one on the ARIA Top 50 Australian Albums chart and charted inside the top ten in twenty-three other countries. It peaked at number six on the Billboard 200 album chart and topped Billboard's alternative albums chart. *Making Mirrors* subsequently earned triple-platinum status in Australia, Poland, France, and Belgium, and gold certification in the United States, United Kingdom, Canada, New Zealand, and the Netherlands.

Making Mirrors, which featured the singles "Somebody That I Used to Know," "I Feel Better," "Easy Way Out," and "Save Me," received widespread praise from critics. *Rolling Stone*'s Jonah Weiner described the album as "a pleasantly schizophrenic set" and called Gotye's voice "a reedy but powerful instrument that can sound uncannily like Sting's." Meanwhile, in a review for the *Music Network* (19 Aug. 2011), Caitlin Welsh commented that the album was "just as rich, cheeky and steeped in pop history and musicality as its predecessor [*Like Drawing Blood*]" and wrote that "it will cement Wally de Backer as the oddball, everyman genius of Australian pop."

"SOMEBODY THAT I USED TO KNOW"

Making Mirrors' success was spurred by its breakout hit, "Somebody That I Used to Know," which was released as the album's second single in July 2011. Despite taking more than six months to make, the song became one of the biggest and most successful songs in Australian music history. Described by Gotye to Jason Treuen as "a curated reflection of multiple past relationships," "Somebody That I Used to Know," which features vocals from the New Zealand singer Kimbra, revolves around a sample of a two-note guitar riff from Brazilian bossa nova guitarist Luiz Bonfá's 1967 instrumental recording "Seville," a syncopated xylophone line, and other sparse instrumentations. During the course of the slow-burning, four-minute song, Gotye and Kimbra engage in a vocal interplay, playing two former lovers who trade barbs over an acrimonious breakup.

"Somebody That I Used to Know" quickly became a mainstay on Australian pop radio and reached the top spot on the ARIA Top 50 Australian Artists Singles chart. Thanks to its crossover appeal and enthusiastic Twitter endorsements from such celebrity tastemakers as Ashton Kutcher, Katy Perry, and Lily Allen, the song achieved global success, eventually reaching number one in more than twenty other countries. It spent eight consecutive weeks atop the Billboard Hot 100 chart, making Gotye the first Australian artist to reach number one in the United States since Savage Garden in 2000. Meanwhile, the accompanying video for the song, directed and produced by Australian filmmaker Natasha Pincus, and featuring Gotye and Kimbra covered in body paint via stop-motion animation, became a YouTube phenomenon. By June 2013 "Somebody That I Used to Know" had sold more than thirteen million copies worldwide. As of May 2014 its video had been viewed more than a half billion times on YouTube.

AWARDS AND DISTINCTIONS

For *Making Mirrors*, Gotye earned a number of awards and accolades. In 2012 he took home four ARIA Awards: album of the year, best pop release, best male artist, and best Australian live act. Then in 2013 he received his first three Grammy Awards in the categories for best alternative music album, record of the year 2012, and best pop duo/group performance, the latter two for "Somebody That I Used to Know." Also that year Gotye was listed among the top fifty most influential Australians in the arts by the *Australian* newspaper.

Gotye lives in Melbourne, where he shares a home with his longtime girlfriend, the Australian singer-songwriter Tash Parker.

SUGGESTED READING

Mathieson, Craig. "Man in the Mirror." *Sydney Morning Herald*. Sydney Morning Herald, 30 Sept. 2011. Web. 12 May 2014.

Shedden, Iain. "Time for Gotye to Get Back to Basics." *Australian*. Nationwide News, 12 Sept. 2013. Web. 12 May 2014.

Smirke, Richard. "Gotye's Smash Hit Almost Didn't Happen." *Billboard*. Billboard, 13 Apr. 2012. Web. 21 Apr. 2014.

Weiner, Jonah. "Inside Gotye's Weirdo Aussie Pop That's Invading Your Radio." *Rolling Stone*. Rolling Stone, 3 May 2012. Web. 21 Apr. 2014.

SELECTED RECORDINGS

Boardface, 2003; *Like Drawing Blood*, 2006; *Making Mirrors*, 2011

—*Chris Cullen*

Jehmu Greene

Born: June 22, 1972
Occupation: Political commentator and organizer

Jehmu Greene is a political commentator and social activist, though she prefers to describe herself as an "evangelist for disenfranchised and vulnerable communities." Greene became

Jeff Kravitz/FilmMagic, Inc

a regular contributor to the Fox News Channel in 2010, but before that she served as the president of the Women's Media Center, which was founded by Jane Fonda, Robin Morgan, and Gloria Steinem in 2005. She also served as an adviser and national surrogate for Hillary Clinton's 2008 presidential campaign. Greene was named the first African American president of Rock the Vote, a nonprofit organization that registers young voters, in 2003, just before the 2004 presidential election. Rock the Vote registered a record number of young voters that year, but Greene's motivation was personal. She herself had been registered to vote by a Rock the Vote volunteer at the University of Texas, Austin, campus just before the 1990 election. She was a politically minded eighteen-year-old and planned to cast her first vote for one of her idols, governor-elect Ann Richards. When she showed up on voting day, Greene recalled in an interview with Leslie Zaikis for *Levo League* (20 June 2013), she was told her name was not on the list and was turned away. "I broke down," Greene said. "I cried like a baby." She went on, "Something happened to me that day where I really determined to myself and made a life mission that, you know, as far as I was concerned other young people, other people who wanted to be engaged in the process, other people who didn't have a voice, that my situation, that was not going to happen to them."

Greene, whom Secretary of State Clinton appointed to serve on the US National Commission for UNESCO in 2010, is a lifelong Democrat and a feminist—characteristics that make her an odd match for the staunchly conservative Fox News. For Greene, however, engaging with people who do not share her views is essential to her work. "I know I'm connecting with individuals out there," Greene told Zaikis, "and changing their minds, engaging them in new ways, and making them think differently." Greene is the owner of JSG Strategies, a consultancy firm for nonprofits, corporations, and individuals. She is also the cofounder of Define American, an organization that, according to its website, uses "the power of story" to change the conversation about immigration and citizenship in the United States.

EARLY LIFE AND EDUCATION

Greene was born in Washington, DC, on June 22, 1972. Both of her parents are Liberian immigrants, she told Chloe Angyal for the blog *Feministing* (5 Dec. 2009). "I definitely understand and appreciate the immigrant experience, as the daughter of immigrants who's gotten to live the American dream," she said. Greene's family moved to Austin, Texas, when she was five years old so that her father could get his PhD. He hoped to run for political office in Liberia.

At the time Austin had recently elected its first female mayor. Texas, Greene told Angyal, is "the home of [former governor] Ann Richards and [congressional representative] Barbara Jordan, so I feel like I come from a place where, as Ann Richards would say, 'a woman's place is in the dome,'" Greene said, referring to a quip homemaker-turned-politician Richards made about Austin's capitol building when she was elected the state's first female governor in 1990. Greene graduated from Stephen F. Austin High School in 1990. As a high schooler, Greene ran for prom queen and won. She affectionately refers to her candidacy as her first encounter in campaigning. As an undergraduate student at the University of Texas in Austin, Greene worked on Richards's reelection campaign in 1994. Richards lost the election to George W. Bush, son of George H. W. Bush, whom she had once famously jibed was "born with a silver foot in his mouth."

DEMOCRATIC NATIONAL COMMITTEE

In 1995 Greene, who had once dreamed of running for office herself, was inspired to pack up her car, leave her family and boyfriend in Austin, and work for President Bill Clinton's successful 1996 reelection campaign in Washington, DC. She had no job and only ten dollars in her pocket. A friend gave her a card the night she left and instructed Greene not to open it until she was halfway through her road trip. When Greene opened the card, she found that her friend had enclosed fifty dollars. Without it, Greene later said, she would not have been able to pay for gas. "I didn't know anyone in DC," she told Zaikis. "I didn't have any real national political connections—I just knew that I wanted to be a part of this movement to re-elect President Clinton and I was fearless" in a way that she, looking back, often tries to recapture. "Taking that risk is the best thing I ever did," she said. Greene went on to work on more than twenty political campaigns and to serve as the director of women's outreach and the Southern political director of the Democratic National Committee (DNC). During her time there, she told Zaikis, she relied on her fears to drive her career forward. In 1998 someone came looking for a representative from the DNC to appear on a local news channel. When no one else volunteered, Greene raised her hand. She knew nothing about television interviews or talking points—"I think I repeated the same points twenty times in one interview," she told Zaikis of one of her early television appearances.

ROCK THE VOTE

Feeling burnt out at the DNC, Greene joined the staff at the nonpartisan, nonprofit organization Rock the Vote in 2000. Rock the Vote, which is dedicated to registering young voters, was founded in Los Angeles in 1990—the same year that Greene was registered to vote by a Rock the Vote volunteer.

Rock the Vote built relationships with such music superstars as Madonna, and MTV, when the network was in its heyday. In the 2000 presidential election, according to Charles Duhigg for the *Los Angeles Times* (7 Feb. 2006), youth voting was down by 9 percent from 1992. That year registration numbers for young people reached a thirty-year low. Later Greene said that she saw voter apathy among youths as a symptom of a larger problem. "The candidates aren't reaching out to young people," Greene told Susannah Rosenblatt for the *Los Angeles Times* (11 Aug. 2003). "The political parties don't include young voters as a primary target as far as where they spend their resources. If we really look at it, then democracy is facing a crisis when generations are opting out of participating. . . . [Voter participation] is not going to immediately increase as we grow older. It's not a youth problem, it's an American problem."

Greene was named president of Rock the Vote in 2003. In 2004, when Senator John Kerry challenged the deeply unpopular President George W. Bush, youth voting grew by a whopping 11 percent. Of the 20 million ballots cast by young people that year, Rock the Vote had registered 1.4 million of them. The organization's success was largely thanks to a massive online registering campaign and partnerships with popular musical acts, such as Lenny Kravitz and the Dixie Chicks, a female country music trio that criticized President Bush and the war in Iraq at a concert in 2003. The recorded quip—lead singer Natalie Maines told a London crowd that she was ashamed that the president was from Texas, her home state—effectively killed the Chicks' career in the conservative country music industry but made them the liberal heroes of the 2004 election. Rock the Vote was all too happy to cash in on the Chicks' rebellious image. The Chicks also helped fund Rock the Vote's registration website and massive Internet campaign.

Rock the Vote's success in 2004 came at a cost, however. The organization had gained a much larger profile— in her capacity as president and spokesperson for Rock the Vote, Greene appeared on CNN, MSNBC, FOX, NBC News, and ABC Radio—but it emerged from the election deeply in debt. Shortly after the election Greene left Rock the Vote amid a dispute about the direction of the organization.

WOMEN'S MEDIA CENTER (WMC)

In 2008 Greene worked on Senator Hillary Clinton's presidential campaign in the Democratic primary, and in 2009 Greene was named president of the Women's Media Center (WMC). During her yearlong tenure as president, the WMC launched the Name It, Change It campaign to fight sexism against female political candidates, something Greene was familiar with from her time working on the Clinton campaign. The Name It, Change It campaign encouraged participants to call out such sexism in media and broadcast their discontent. Greene also oversaw the expansion of the Progressive Women's Voices program, a media training and leadership program, and the development of the Not Under the Bus campaign against anti-choice measures in health-care reform. According to a WMC press release from September 2010, Greene resigned as president for personal reasons, but in her interview with Zaikis, Greene says that she was fired by the board of directors. "It was really hard because at that point in my life I was used to overwhelming success," she said. It took her some time to process the blow.

FOX NEWS

Greene joined the channel as a commentator in 2010 and told Zaikis that she considers Roger Ailes, the president of Fox News, to be one of her most influential and supportive mentors. "If I had . . . been intimidated by our differences," she said of their relationship, "I wouldn't be where I am now." Despite her respect for Ailes, the atmosphere on the air at Fox is generally less welcoming to different viewpoints, and Greene quickly found herself involved in some fairly heated debates. In 2012 Fox viewers lobbied the channel to fire Greene after she called her

Caucasian copanelist, Carlson, "a bow-tying, white boy" in a heated debate on the Fox program *America Live* about the heritage of Senator Elizabeth Warren (who is part Cherokee). The comment came after Carlson suggested that Warren, a former Harvard professor, had been awarded her job at the university because of her racial status. Greene retorted that that characterization of Warren's career would appeal to voters like Carlson, who is indeed famous for wearing bow ties. Host Megyn Kelly, who is white, apologized for Greene's comments at the end of the show calling Greene's words "inappropriate" and "not consistent with our standards" at Fox, Noah Rothman reported for the news website *Mediaite* (4 May 2012). Fox spokespeople reported that Greene called Carlson after the show to apologize and that he accepted her apology, but the incident stuck in the craw of Fox viewers, who called her a racist and demanded that she be fired. Though Fox declined to take any action against Greene, the brief affair has taken on a life of its own, dominating Internet searches for Greene and serving as a battle cry for viewers who would prefer to see the network remain more uniform in its views.

HONORED SOCIAL ACTIVIST

"In many ways, I think that I have always been an activist," Greene told Zaikis, from lobbying for more female representation in her high school clubs to working for the DNC. In her interview with Zaikis, Greene emphasized how important it is for her to have fun and enjoy her work. She makes "sure that I am as fulfilled in my organizing as the communities that I'm trying to engage," she said. Of late Greene has been working with her Define American campaign, which she cofounded with Jose Vargas, a journalist formerly of the *Washington Post* who revealed that he was an undocumented immigrant in 2011. "We have a strong desire to shift the conversation from the very typical twenty-four-hour news cycle coverage of immigration that currently exists, to use all of Jose's expertise as a journalist, and to bring support from his colleagues, to change how they cover it as an issue and not have it be so polarizing," she told Keach Hagey for *Politico* (22 June 2011). "So we are sharing Jose's story as an effort to get others to share their stories."

Greene is also a member of the board of directors for the *American Prospect* magazine, a communications group called Green Media Toolshed, Planned Parenthood of New York Action Fund, and a New York–based mentoring program called Petals-n-Belles. *Essence* magazine has reportedly included her on its list of forty women under forty shaping the world as well as its thirty-five most beautiful and remarkable women in the world. She has also been the recipient of the National Conference for Community and Justice (NCCJ) Community Service

Award, the American Association of University Women's Women of Distinction Award, and the Women Making a Difference Award from the National Council for Research on Women.

Greene loves performing and singing country music. She lives in New York City.

SUGGESTED READING

Angyal, Chloe. "The Feministing Five: Jehmu Greene." *Feministing*. Feministing, 5 Dec. 2009. Web. 16 Sept. 2014.
Duhigg, Charles. "Rock the Vote Is Stuck in a Hard Place." *Los Angeles Times*. Los Angeles Times, 7 Feb. 2006. Web. 16 Sept. 2014.
Greene, Jehmu. "Office Hours with Jehmu Greene." Interview by Leslie Zaikis. *Levo League*. Levo League, 20 June 2013. Web. 16 Sept. 2014.
Hagey, Keach. "Jose Vargas Story Turned Down by Washington Post." *Politico*. Politico, 22 June 2011. Web. 16 Sept. 2014.
Rosenblatt, Susannah. "Rock the Vote Picks Up the Beat." *Los Angeles Times*. Los Angeles Times, 11 Aug. 2003. Web. 16 Sept. 2014.
Rothman, Noah. "Jehmu Greene Calls Tucker Carlson A 'Bow-Tying White Boy,' Megyn Kelly Apologizes." *Mediaite*. Mediaite, 4 May 2012. Web. 16 Sept. 2014.

—*Molly Hagan*

Glenn Greenwald

Born: March 6, 1967
Occupation: Political commentator and journalist

Glenn Greenwald became one of the best-known journalists in the world in mid-2013 when he helped break the story of the National Security Agency (NSA) and its widespread and indiscriminate surveillance programs—some of which targeted US citizens. His work was based largely on a cache of top-secret documents provided to him by an ex-NSA contractor named Edward Snowden. Even before Snowden approached Greenwald with what has been called in journalistic circles "the story of the century," Greenwald had gained a reputation as both a tireless crusader for press freedom and as a contrarian unafraid of excoriating his fellow journalists. A "suffocating constraint on how reporters are permitted to express themselves produces a self-neutering form of journalism that becomes as ineffectual as it is boring," he complained to Bill Keller in an online dialogue for the *New York Times* (27 Oct. 2013). He further explained that a "failure to call torture 'torture' because government officials demand that a more pleasant euphemism be used, or lazily equating a demonstrably true assertion with a demonstrably false

AFP/Getty Images

one, drains journalism of its passion, vibrancy, vitality and soul."

Greenwald has famously referred to his colleagues working in the nation's capital as "courtiers," and he told Erik Wemple for the *Washington Post* (24 June, 2013), "They are far more servants to political power than adversarial watchdogs over it, and what provokes their rage most is not corruption on the part of those in power (they don't care about that) but rather those who expose that corruption, especially when the ones bringing transparency are outside of, even hostile to, their incestuous media circles."

In the wake of the Snowden story, many of those mainstream journalists questioned Greenwald's motives for disseminating classified government documents and suggested that he was using his informant for his own self-aggrandizing purposes. Some even asserted that Greenwald should be tried for treason. For his part, Greenwald takes such criticisms in stride. "Some of what is driving this hostility . . . is personal bitterness," he told Wemple. "Some of it is resentment over my having been able to break these big stories not despite, but because of, my deliberate breaching of the conventions that rule their world."

EARLY YEARS AND EDUCATION
Glenn Greenwald was born on March 6, 1967, in the New York City borough of Queens. He was raised in the working-class neighborhood of Lauderdale Lakes, Florida, where his parents, Arlene and Daniel, had moved shortly after his birth. The couple eventually divorced, and Arlene supported Greenwald and his

younger sibling by working as a McDonald's cashier, among other jobs.

Greenwald's major role model was his paternal grandfather, L. L. Greenwald, who served as a Lauderdale Lakes city councilman from 1976 to 1980 and was known for his advocacy on behalf of the poor who were being displaced as luxury condos were built throughout the region. "The most important thing my grandfather taught me was that the most noble way to use your skills, intellect and energy is to defend the marginalized against those with the greatest power—and that the resulting animosity from those in power is a badge of honor," Greenwald told Janet Reitman for *Rolling Stone* (4 Dec. 2013).

As a child, Greenwald attended council meetings with his grandfather, and when he was eight, he held an honorary seat on the city's recreation advisory board. From 1980 to 1984 Greenwald was the only teenager ever to sit on the county's parks and recreation board. When he was seventeen and still a student at Nova High School, Greenwald ran unsuccessfully for a city council seat. While he drew only 6.6 percent of the vote, he claimed not to be disappointed and instead focused on the fact that at such a young age he had convinced seven hundred people that he would be a good councilman. His teachers and school administrators might not have been among those seven hundred: Greenwald, who happened to be a star member of the debate team, was frequently sent to detention or was suspended for arguing about school policy and what he perceived to be unjust rules. Greenwald has explained that some of his combativeness was due to being a gay teen in a relatively unenlightened age. "I decided to wage war against this system and institutional authority that had tried to reject and condemn me," he told Reitman.

A CAREER IN LAW
After graduating from high school, Greenwald attended George Washington University in Washington, DC. After earning a bachelor's degree in 1990 and getting almost perfect scores on the LSATs, he entered New York University's School of Law. There he led a successful drive to ban Colorado-based firms from recruiting on campus because voters in that state had passed an amendment overturning an already-adopted set of anti-discrimination laws.

Completing law school in 1994, Greenwald took a job as a litigator at the high-powered firm Wachtell, Lipton, Rosen & Katz, whose client base included such corporate giants as Bank of America and AT&T. Although he made an enviable salary, Greenwald found the work thankless and soul-crushing, and in early 1996, he opened his own practice and focused primarily on civil liberties and constitutional law. Among his clients were several neo-Nazis, and Greenwald has said that while he found their views reprehensible, they had the same First Amendment rights as any other citizen and deserved legal representation.

In 2005 Greenwald travelled to Brazil on vacation and fell in love with a man he had met on the beach. He decided to relocate to that country permanently. Unable to practice law there, he began to consider other ways to earn a living.

BECOMING A WRITER

Greenwald had been an early aficionado of computer message boards and delighted in sparring with those of a more conservative bent. He became especially active in debates about the US–led war on terror following the terrorist attacks of September 11, 2001. He came to the conclusion that the Internet was an ideal forum in which to engage in political debate, and upon settling in Brazil he decided to try his hand at blogging.

"Political bloggers in general have two important roles," he explained to an interviewer for *PR Week* (23 Apr. 2007). "One is they represent a line of opinion that believes that the political system in Washington—the entire structure of both political parties, the consulting class, the media class—is just deeply corrupt and that the entire system is flawed in a fundamental way. The other aspect is that the nature of blogging just enables much deeper analysis and thought about the various facts." He added, "I felt like there were issues that were being insufficiently discussed and covered in general, and really wanted a platform to be able to bring attention to those issues."

One of the early posts on his blog, which he had titled *Unclaimed Territory*, deals with the case of Valerie Plame, a CIA operative whose identity had been leaked. The editors of the *New Republic* linked to the piece, sending thousands of readers to Greenwald's fledgling blog.

In 2007 he joined the staff of the online magazine *Salon*, whose editors guaranteed him complete freedom to write whatever he chose. His subjects ranged from Islamophobia to the curative powers of the Internet to the George W. Bush administration's program of warrantless wiretapping and beyond, and his pieces regularly attracted hundreds of reader comments.

Greenwald left *Salon* after five-and-a-half years to join the staff of the London *Guardian*. In his *Salon* farewell piece, posted on July 19, 2012, he wrote: "Even when influential political and media figures vehemently complained about the criticisms I wrote, *Salon*'s editors unfailingly stood behind my work. Throughout my time here, *Salon* always evinced an unyielding belief in publishing a wide range of views without fear of offending orthodoxies or establishments." He added, "The *Guardian* affords the opportunity to reach a new audience, further internationalize

my readership, and be reinvigorated in a different environment."

BOOKS

Once Greenwald had decided upon a career as a political writer, he penned a handful of books in addition to his magazine articles. In 2006 he released *How Would a Patriot Act? Defending American Values from a President Run Amok*, which is a blistering indictment of the Bush administration. In the book, Greenwald argues against what he perceives to be the president's unlimited and unchecked power as evidenced in the imprisonment and torture of terror suspects, who had not been formally charged with a crime or who did not have legal representation, as well as the warrantless wiretapping the administration had authorized in the wake of the September 11 attacks.

Greenwald followed *How Would a Patriot Act?* with *A Tragic Legacy: How a Good vs. Evil Mentality Destroyed the Bush Presidency* in 2007, which is an in-depth look at the failings of the George W. Bush administration. In a review for the *Daily Kos* (1 July 2007), Susan Garner observes that Greenwald "wrestles with much more significant and amorphous material [in his sophomore effort] as he attempts to trace the dangerous, stark philosophy underlying the most pernicious policies of the current administration and to tease out their implications for the character of this nation. To say that he succeeds is a massive understatement."

Greenwald subsequently wrote *Great American Hypocrites: Toppling the Big Myths of Republican Politics* (2008), a no-holds-barred look at the GOP, and *With Liberty and Justice for Some: How the Law Is Used to Destroy Equality and Protect the Powerful* (2011), a historic overview that includes Greenwald's take on Watergate, the Iran-Contra scandal, and recent presidential pardons.

THE STORY OF THE CENTURY

In December 2012, soon after he had begun writing for the *Guardian*, Greenwald received an e-mail asking for his public encryption (PGP) key, a computer program that allows for exceptionally secure communications. Despite being a seasoned journalist who had written widely on the issue of national security, Greenwald was unaware of how to obtain or install such a program and he ignored the request.

The writer was subsequently sent step-by-step tutorials on encryption, which he also ignored. Finally, six months later, Greenwald heard from the anonymous source again, this time through a friend, documentary filmmaker Laura Poitras, whom the source had also e-mailed. In June Poitras, Greenwald, and the former NSA contractor Edward Snowden—their anonymous source—met secretly in

Hong Kong. There, Snowden showed them thousands of highly classified documents that comprised, as Reitman wrote, "a mother lode laying bare the architecture of the national-security state . . . exposing the seemingly limitless reach of the National Security Agency, and sparking a global debate on the use of surveillance—ostensibly to fight terrorism—versus the individual right to privacy."

Greenwald was astounded at the sheer number of documents as well as their scope: they covered the war in Afghanistan, the drone program, NSA operations involving allied countries, and much more. On June 5, 2013, Greenwald's first piece on Snowden's material appeared in the *Guardian*—an exposé of a secret court order issued the previous April that called for telecommunications giant Verizon to hand over extensive consumer data to the NSA. Other pieces followed in quick succession detailing the existence of a widespread clandestine data-mining program, stating that the United States had spied on German chancellor Angela Merkel and other heads of state, and revealing that American operatives had hacked into Arab broadcasting system Al Jazeera. "The thing people most did not know is just how limitless the NSA's goals are when it comes to spying," Greenwald told Brian Stelter for CNN's *Reliable Sources* (1 Sept. 2013). "What they're really doing is creating a spying system that literally has as its goal the elimination of privacy worldwide."

BACKLASH FROM POLITICIANS AND THE MEDIA

Snowden was charged with several felonies, some of which fell under the Espionage Act, and was forced to flee the country. Several politicians and some of Greenwald's fellow journalists called for Greenwald to face criminal charges. When Greenwald appeared on the show *Meet the Press* in late June 2013, host David Gregory accused him of aiding the fugitive Snowden and asserted that there was no reason he should not also be considered a criminal. Caroline Bankoff for *New York Magazine* quoted Greenwald's vehement reply: "It's pretty extraordinary that anybody who would call themselves a journalist would publicly muse about whether or not other journalists should be charged with felonies."

A book-length account of the NSA scandal by Greenwald, titled *No Place to Hide: Edward Snowden, the NSA, and the U.S. Surveillance State*, has been planned for publication in mid-2014.

A NEW MEDIA OUTLET

In October 2013 Greenwald announced that he would be leaving the *Guardian* to join a planned news organization backed by eBay founder Pierre Omidyar. His fellow editors at the news organization, First Look Media, include Poitras and Jeremy Scahill of the *Nation*. "They are people who are willing to put themselves out there and be transparent about it, not just spouting opinions without any kind of basis," Omidyar explained to David Carr for the *New York Times* (20 Oct. 2013). "We want to do a better job bringing important investigative stories or deep human stories that tend to be overlooked to a broader audience." First Look Media's first publication, *The Intercept*, went live online on February 10, 2014.

PERSONAL LIFE

Greenwald lives in Rio de Janeiro with his Brazilian partner, David Michael Miranda. Miranda became the subject of intense media attention in August 2013 when he was detained by British authorities at Heathrow airport as he was returning from a visit to Poitras made at Greenwald's behest. His electronic devices were confiscated under the pretext of the Terrorism Act, and he was questioned for nine hours before being released. The couple later filed a lawsuit, alleging that the British had misused the Terrorism Act as a means of intimidation.

Reporters visiting the couple in their light-filled, wood-and-glass house often comment that it seems incongruous that the hard-edged Greenwald has a pronounced soft spot for dogs and lives with almost a dozen strays he has rescued.

SUGGESTED READING

Bernstein, Fred. "Glenn Greenwald: Life Beyond Borders." *Out*. Here Media, 18 Apr. 2011. Web. 10 Dec. 2013.

Greenwald, Glenn. "Interview with Glenn Greenwald." Interview by Brian Stelter. *Reliable Sources*. CNN Transcripts. Cable News Network, 1 Sept. 2013. Web. 10 Dec. 2013.

Keller, Bill, and Glenn Greenwald. "Is Glenn Greenwald the Future of News?" *New York Times*. New York Times, 27 Oct. 2013. Web. 10 Dec. 2013.

Omidyar, Pierre. "An Interview with Pierre Omidyar." Interview by David Carr. *New York Times*. New York Times, 20 Oct. 2013. Web. 10 Dec. 2013.

Reitman, Janet. "Snowden and Greenwald: The Men Who Leaked the Secrets." *Rolling Stone*. Rolling Stone, 4 Dec. 2013. Web. 10 Dec. 2013.

Wemple, Erik, and Glenn Greenwald. "Greenwald: Beltway Media Types Are 'Courtiers to Power.'" *Washington Post*. Washington Post, 24 June 2013. Web. 10 Dec. 2013.

SELECTED WORKS

How Would a Patriot Act?, 2006; *A Tragic Legacy*, 2007; *Great American Hypocrites*, 2008; *With Liberty and Justice for Some*, 2011

—*Mari Rich*

Robert Griffin III

Born: February 12, 1990
Occupation: Football player

After only two seasons in the National Football League (NFL), Robert Griffin III, the quarterback for the Washington Redskins, has established himself as arguably the most exciting player in the league. Brendan Vaughan, writing for *GQ* magazine (Sept. 2013), made note of Griffin's "elusiveness and unpredictability" and his "lethal combination of improvisational brilliance and unflappable calm," declaring that "at any moment you might see him do something that no QB has ever done before."

A quintessential dual-threat quarterback with a cannon for an arm and Olympic-caliber speed, the six-feet-two, 220-pound Griffin, who enjoyed a three-year college career at Baylor University that culminated with him winning the 2011 Heisman Trophy, emerged as one of the new faces of the league in 2012. After being selected by the Redskins as the number-two overall pick in that year's draft, Griffin enjoyed one of the most dazzling rookie seasons ever. He set NFL rookie records for passer rating (102.4), touchdown-to-interception ratio (4:1), and rushing yards by a quarterback (815). He earned his first Pro Bowl selection in December 2012 and was named the 2012 Associated Press (AP) NFL Offensive Rookie of the Year. Meanwhile, he revived a moribund Redskins franchise by leading the team to a surprising 10–6 record, helping them clinch their first National Football Conference (NFC) East division title since 1999 and first postseason berth since 2007.

After suffering a devastating knee injury in the first round of the 2012–13 NFL Playoffs, Griffin significantly regressed in his sophomore season. Nevertheless, he entered the 2014 season as the clear-cut franchise quarterback for the Redskins. While his dynamic style of play has left him more susceptible to injury, many believe Griffin has a chance to leave a lasting legacy on the league with his rare combination of skills.

EARLY LIFE

Robert Lee Griffin III was born on February 12, 1990, in Okinawa, Japan, to Robert Griffin Jr. and Jacqueline (Ross) Griffin. Both of Griffin's parents are retired US Army sergeants; his father was a petroleum supply specialist and his mother a personnel specialist. Due to his parents' military careers, Griffin had a peripatetic childhood, growing up on military bases across the United States with his two older sisters, Jihan and De'Jon.

Griffin was three years old when his family moved from Japan to Fort Lewis, Washington, where they lived for three years before Griffin's parents were deployed to separate bases in

Patrick McDermott/Getty Images

South Korea. The children then went to live with their grandparents and relatives in New Orleans, Louisiana, and after a fourteen-month tour in Korea, Griffin's parents returned to the United States and moved the family permanently to Copperas Cove, Texas, near Fort Hood, in 1997.

Early in his childhood, it was apparent that Griffin was blessed with extraordinary athletic ability. His first love was basketball, which he started playing at the age of seven. He grew up aspiring to be like his idol, NBA legend Michael Jordan, who is widely regarded as the greatest basketball player of all time. Both of Griffin's parents recognized his potential and became intimately involved in his athletic development. They trained and coached him based on military principles, stressing the importance of discipline, hard work, and education. Griffin's father, a basketball and track star in high school, ran him through a rigorous daily regimen of conditioning drills, while his mother shuttled him to school, practices, and games. "My dad was tough, pushed me, always looking for ways to make me better," Griffin told Rick Maese for the *Washington Post* (21 Apr. 2012). "My mom was caring."

MAN OF THE HOUSE

Griffin was already outshining his peers in basketball when, at the age of eleven, he started running track and playing football. He became a standout hurdler on an Amateur Athletic Union (AAU) track team organized and coached by his father, who had his son study videos of the four-time Olympic sprint champion Michael

Johnson. Meanwhile, on the gridiron, Griffin played quarterback; despite his blistering speed, his father molded him into a player who threw first and ran second. Griffin tried to model his style of play after that of his favorite NFL quarterback, Denver Broncos Hall of Famer John Elway, who was known as much for his powerful arm as his ability to run.

Griffin's development as a football player took a slight detour on his thirteenth birthday in 2003, when his father unexpectedly received news that he would be deployed to Kuwait to serve in the Iraq War. Griffin was instructed by his father to look after his mother and sisters, to keep them away from the television set and news reports of the war, and to continue following the workout regimen he had designed for him. "He told me I was the man of the house," Griffin recalled to Maese. "So I had to try to stick as much as I could to the plan he set out." Robert Griffin Jr. returned home safely after six months in Iraq and retired from the military shortly thereafter. Griffin's mother was granted a medical retirement from the military in 1998.

HIGH SCHOOL CAREER

Griffin attended Copperas Cove High School, where he was a three-sport star in football, basketball, and track and field. He played on Copperas Cove's freshman football team before earning a spot on the varsity squad as a backup quarterback during his sophomore year. Griffin became Copperas Cove's starting varsity quarterback as a junior after impressing head coach Jack Welch with his speed, arm strength, work ethic, and leadership ability. In his junior and senior seasons, he threw a combined 3,300 yards, rushed for 2,161 yards, and amassed a total of seventy-three touchdowns. He earned first-team all-district honors both years (2006 and 2007), posting a 25–4 record as a starter and helping to lead Copperas Cove to back-to-back Class 4A Division I state title games.

Meanwhile, Griffin was also the starting point guard on the school's varsity basketball team and was racking up achievements in track. As a junior, he set state records in the 110- and 300-meter hurdles and came within one-hundredth of a second of the national high school record in the 300-meter hurdles. Griffin also posted the fastest time in the 400-meter hurdle event that year among juniors worldwide and was named the 2007 Gatorade Texas Boys Track and Field Athlete of the Year. Along with his athletic achievements, Griffin served as class president and excelled academically, graduating from Copperas Cove a semester early and ranking seventh in his class. "The only thing Robert did was homework and play ball," Jack Welch told Sally Jenkins for the *Washington Post* (11 Mar. 2012). "He was very grounded, very rooted."

Rated among the top five dual-threat quarterbacks in the nation, Griffin was heavily recruited to attend the top football colleges across the country. Many of those schools, however, expressed their desire to convert him from quarterback to a receiver or defensive back, positions they felt would better complement his world-class speed. Determined to realize his dream of becoming an NFL quarterback, Griffin accepted an offer to attend Baylor University in nearby Waco, Texas, after Art Briles, the school's incoming head football coach, guaranteed him an opportunity to compete for the starting quarterback position. "I was looking for a guy who could run," Briles recalled to Pablo S. Torre for *Sports Illustrated* (26 Sept. 2011), "but the first time I saw Robert throw, I said, Man, this guy's special."

BAYLOR UNIVERSITY AND OLYMPIC TRIALS

Griffin arrived at Baylor in January 2008 and began taking classes during the spring semester in order to become eligible for the track-and-field team. In addition to his NFL plans, he dreamed of representing the United States in the 400-meter hurdles at the 2008 Summer Olympics in Beijing, China. That spring, Griffin placed first in the 400-meter hurdles at both the Big 12 Conference Championships and the National Collegiate Athletic Association (NCAA) Midwest Regional Championships and earned All-American honors after finishing third in that event at the NCAA Outdoor Championships. He qualified and competed in the 400-meter hurdles at the 2008 US Olympic Team Trials, where he advanced to the semifinals and finished eleventh overall.

Despite failing to earn a spot on the Olympic team, Griffin became Baylor's starting quarterback as a freshman after outperforming incumbent junior Blake Szymanski in off-season workouts. He began his Baylor tenure in auspicious fashion, setting an NCAA record by throwing 209 passes at the start of his career before his first interception. As the nation's youngest starting quarterback, Griffin started eleven of twelve games and set Baylor freshman records for quarterback rushing yards (843) and rushing touchdowns (thirteen). He was named the Baylor Most Valuable Offensive Player and received Big 12 Freshman of the Year honors from a number of media outlets. Though the Baylor Bears tied for last place in the Big 12 Conference with a 4–8 record, Griffin fully dedicated himself to reviving the school's program and bringing it back to prominence by quitting track to focus solely on football.

Griffin's ambitious plans came to a screeching halt just three weeks into his sophomore season when he tore the anterior cruciate ligament (ACL) in his right knee in a game against Northwestern State. The injury required surgery and forced him to miss the rest of the season. "It could have easily been a sob story—'Robert Griffin stops running track, dedicates all his time to football, gets hurt in football, never plays again,'" Griffin said to Maese. "I didn't want it to be that."

After months of intense rehabilitation, Griffin entered the 2010 season with greater accuracy and arm strength. He started in all thirteen games and established Baylor single-season records for passing yards (3,501) and passing touchdowns (twenty-two), among others. He led Baylor to a 7–6 record and a berth in the Texas Bowl, marking the school's first postseason appearance since 1994. In the Texas Bowl, Baylor lost to the Illinois Fighting Illini 14–38, but Griffin nonetheless earned Big 12 Offensive Player of the Year and Comeback Player of the Year honors for his regular-season performance.

HEISMAN TROPHY WINNER AND 2012 NFL DRAFT

Griffin followed his stellar 2010 season with an even more remarkable one in 2011, when he emerged as the best college player in the country. In thirteen starts for Baylor that year, he set school single-season records in completion percentage (72.3), passing yards (4,293), touchdown passes (37), and yards in total offense (4,992). He earned All-American status and was named the Big 12 Offensive Player of the Year. Griffin became the first Baylor player to win the coveted Heisman Trophy as well as the Davey O'Brien Award and the Manning Award. Meanwhile, he led Baylor to a 10–3 record, a 2011 Alamo Bowl victory, and a number-twelve final Bowl Championship Series (BCS) ranking.

Two weeks after the Alamo Bowl, Griffin announced that he intended to forgo his final year of eligibility to enter the NFL Draft. He finished at Baylor as the school's all-time leader in twenty offensive categories. In addition to his accomplishments on the football field, Griffin made the honor roll all eight semesters of his collegiate career and graduated in just three years, earning a bachelor's degree in political science in December 2010. He subsequently enrolled in graduate school at Baylor and pursued a master's degree in communications. Baylor track-and-field director Clyde Hart remarked to Torre, "You can put limitations on even the great ones. With Robert, you can't do that. He's . . . different."

Analysts and scouts projected Griffin to be the number-two pick of the 2012 NFL Draft. However, the St. Louis Rams, who held the number-two pick in that year's draft, already had an incumbent franchise quarterback in Sam Bradford, whom they had selected with the number-one overall pick in the 2010 NFL Draft. Consequently, the Rams exchanged their pick with the Washington Redskins for four high-value draft picks. Expectedly, the Redskins used the pick to select Griffin, who

was immediately christened the franchise quarterback. During the summer of 2012, Griffin signed a four-year contract with the Redskins worth $21.1 million.

EARLY SUCCESS WITH THE REDSKINS

Griffin's arrival rejuvenated a loyal but long-suffering Redskins fan base that had endured a string of underachieving seasons. Redskins head coach Mike Shanahan and his son Kyle, the team's offensive coordinator, designed an offense that was tailor-made for Griffin's unique dual-threat abilities and surrounded him with talented playmakers. Following Griffin's first full-squad workout with the Redskins, wide receiver Pierre Garcon remarked to Howard Fendrich for the Associated Press (21 May 2012), "He's always alive. The play is always on, no matter what happens. . . . He can make plays with his feet and then turn it into passes."

In Griffin's NFL debut on September 9, 2012, he completed nineteen of twenty-six passes for 320 yards, two touchdowns, and no interceptions, while adding forty rushing yards in a dramatic 40–32 upset victory over the New Orleans Saints. He was named NFC Offensive Player of the Week and became the first rookie quarterback to receive that honor in his first game. He then won the NFC Offensive Rookie of the Month Award for September, after amassing 750 passing yards, 192 rushing yards, and six touchdowns (two passing and four rushing) in his next three games.

Though the Redskins got off to a slow 3–6 start, Griffin, who was voted a cocaptain by his teammates at midseason, led the team on a seven-game winning streak to finish the season with a 10–6 record. The Redskins clinched their first NFC East title since 1999 and first playoff berth since 2007. Griffin set numerous Redskins records and established NFL rookie records for passer rating (102.4), touchdown-to-interception ratio (4:1), and rushing yards by a quarterback (815).

In the NFC wild-card playoff round, the Redskins were defeated by the Seattle Seahawks, 24–14. Griffin was limited to eighty-four yards passing and just twenty-one yards rushing in the game after tearing two major ligaments in his right knee. Despite suffering the injury early in the game, he insisted on playing until the fourth quarter. Commenting on that decision, Griffin explained to Vaughan, "I'm a team guy. . . . I wasn't doing that for self-fame. I was doing that for the team. I wanted to show that I'll do anything for them." Three days after the game, Griffin underwent major reconstructive knee surgery.

2013–2014 SEASON

Many fans and pundits questioned whether Griffin would be ready for the start of the 2013 regular season after it was projected that he would need a minimum of seven to nine months of rehabilitation to recover from his injury. Despite missing the entire preseason, Griffin returned in time for the season opener, in which he passed for a career-high 329 yards in a 27–33 loss to the Philadelphia Eagles.

Still, he was unable to duplicate the success of his rookie year in his sophomore season. Griffin started in the first thirteen games of the season and passed for a career-high 3,203 yards and sixteen touchdowns and rushed for 489 yards. However, he was controversially benched by head coach Mike Shanahan, with whom he had fallen out of favor, for the season's final three games and was replaced by second-year backup quarterback Kirk Cousins. The Redskins finished with a disastrous 3–13 record, marking the team's worst season since 1993, resulting in the firing of Shanahan and the majority of his staff at the conclusion of the regular season. Shanahan was replaced by Cincinnati Bengals offensive coordinator Jay Gruden.

After working with quarterback guru and former NFL coach Terry Shea during the off-season, Griffin entered the 2014 season with renewed confidence and optimism in the hopes of returning to his rookie form. Griffin was sidelined again however, this time with a dislocated left ankle, in mid-September. Although it is unclear exactly how long his recovery will take, he is expected to return to finish the season.

PERSONAL LIFE

With his infectious smile and personality, Griffin has become one of the most popular and marketable players in the NFL. He had the highest-selling jersey in the league in 2012 and has landed sponsorship deals with a number of prominent companies, including Adidas, Subway, Gatorade, Nissan, and Castrol Motor Oil.

On July 6, 2013, Griffin married his college sweetheart, Rebecca Liddicoat, in a ceremony in Denver, Colorado. The couple lives in Loudoun County, Virginia.

SUGGESTED READING

Jenkins, Sally. "Robert Griffin III: Poised to Handle the Pressure." *Washington Post.* Washington Post, 11 Mar. 2012. Web. 14 Aug. 2014.

Maese, Rick. "NFL Draft: Robert Griffin III Embarks on Pro Career, and Washington Redskins Fans Await." *Washington Post.* Washington Post, 21 Apr. 2012. Web. 14 Aug. 2014.

Torre, Pablo S. "Back of All Trades." *Sports Illustrated* 26 Sept. 2011: 56–60. Print.

Vaughan, Brendan. "The Second Coming of RG3." *GQ.* Condé Nast, Sept. 2013. Web. 14 Aug. 2014.

—*Chris Cullen*

Grimes

Born: March 17, 1988
Occupation: Artist and musician

Grimes is a one-woman musical act who came to prominence following the 2012 release of her third album, *Visions*. Without any formal musical training, she taught herself to record music using Apple's GarageBand and released her debut effort, *Geidi Primes*, in 2011. By 2012, her music was being named to best-of lists by music critics for the *Guardian* and *Pitchfork* magazine. "Her music is like a seven-layer cake," Kayne Lanahan told Laura M. Holson for the *New York Times* (7 Mar. 2012). "After repeated listening, it doesn't get stale." Citing influences as diverse at Hildegard of Bingen, Aphex Twin, and Mariah Carey, Grimes described her sound as "ADD music" in an interview with Fan Zhong for *W* magazine (June 2012) and noted, "I go through phases a lot."

Taking on nearly every possible role in the production of her music, Grimes not only writes and records her music herself but also creates her album art and directs her music videos. "Grimes is all about image-branding, but DIY image-branding," she told Lizzy Goodman for *New York* magazine (22 Apr. 2012). "I was like, 'It would be so awesome if there were an actual pop star who was like a sick super-experimental producer.' And then I was like, 'I'll just do that.'"

Steven C. Mitchell/EPA/Landov

In fact, she initially wanted to be a behind-the-scenes producer because of her intense shyness. "I have forced myself to confront my worst fears," she told Chitra Ramaswamy for the *Scotsman* (6 May 2012). "I used to have panic attacks if I was around too many people. . . . The rate at which you can achieve things is amazing. If you are constantly confronting your worst fears you zoom through life."

EARLY LIFE

Grimes was born Claire Boucher on March 17, 1988, in Vancouver, British Columbia. Her mother worked as a public relations consultant, and her father was a banker. Grimes has two younger biological brothers and two stepbrothers; her oldest stepbrother grew up to become a rapper known as Jay Worthy. Grimes studied ballet for eleven years as a child before becoming interested in visual arts. "From an early age I knew I would be unhappy if I wasn't doing something creative," she told Sam Richards for the *Guardian* (27 Apr. 2012). "I was always really into painting but I didn't feel like I would be able to do anything new, whereas with music there's still so much to be explored." She was about eleven years old when the file-sharing website Napster became popular. "I went through my adolescence having this revelatory experience—I can have any music I want and I can get it immediately. For me and for a lot of people I know, there's this musical eclecticism that happened." She would later cite such diverse musical influences as twelfth-century composer Hildegard of Bingen and modern artists Mariah Carey, Enya, and Aphex Twin, among many others.

Grimes was raised in a strict Catholic household, but she was drawn to Vancouver's alternative scene. As a teenager, she spent a few years addicted to drugs. Her parents pulled her out of high school and sent her to a boot camp, which helped put her back on course. Grimes was eager to leave Vancouver, and after graduating from Lord Byng Secondary School in 2006, she enrolled in the prestigious McGill University in Montreal.

EDUCATION

At McGill University, Grimes held a double major in philosophy and psychology and a double minor in Russian language and electroacoustics. In an interview with Kendah El-Ali for *Filter* (13 June 2012), Grimes explained the electroacoustics minor as "a neuroscience-orientated study" that focused on "how the brain processes music." However, Grimes soon became involved in Montreal's underground music scene through her university friends. About one year after moving to Montreal, she began spending time at Lab Synthèse, a performance space housed inside an old textile warehouse. Her friend Devon Welsh, who records music as Majical Cloudz, asked her to provide backing vocals for one of his tracks. While working with him, she asked him to teach her to use the software he was using, Apple's GarageBand. "I just kind of got addicted to it. it was just like a thing I sort of started doing and as soon as I realized I could do it, I didn't really want to do anything else," she told Marsha Lederman for the *Globe and Mail* (30 July 2012). As she became more involved in Montreal's music scene, she moved farther north from McGill, settling in the Parc-Ex neighborhood.

Without any prior formal musical instruction, Grimes began experimenting with looping vocals on GarageBand. "There was sort of a moment of realization," she told Hermione Hoby for the *Observer* (28 Jan. 2012). "One day, I was listening to music and it suddenly made sense to me how it was constructed." She also began to expand her musical interests, opening herself to mainstream pop music. "In 2007 or 2008, I started listening to R&B on this road trip with my dad because we couldn't agree on anything else," she told Carrie Battan for *Pitchfork* (16 Feb. 2012). When she first heard Mariah Carey's 1995 hit song "Fantasy," she said she "felt something [she had] never felt before." In a post to her Tumblr account (6 Feb. 2013), she explained, "The first time I heard Mariah Carey it shattered the fabric of my existence." She dedicated herself to recording under her stage name, which she derived from the name of visual artist Ken Grimes.

DEBUT EPS

In the summer of 2009, Grimes embarked on an adventure with her friend William Gratz. She and Gratz traveled to Bemidji, Minnesota, where they constructed a pontoon houseboat on a friend's property. With a copy of Mark Twain's *Adventures of Huckleberry Finn* on board, they launched the boat from Minneapolis with the intention of floating down the Mississippi River to New Orleans. However, their boat's engine failed shortly after launch. They were dogged by police and park rangers for several weeks for repeatedly docking without a permit before their boat was impounded by police and they were forced to cancel their plans.

After returning to Montreal, Grimes began focusing more intensively on producing music. "My friends started Arbutus Records and asked me if I would be on it even though I had no music at all," she said in an interview with François Marchand for the *Vancouver Sun* (18 Feb. 2012). She uploaded her early bedroom recordings to her MySpace page before releasing her debut EP, *Geidi Primes*, on cassette tape through Arbutus in January 2010. The album's title and songs are peppered with references to Grimes's favorite book, Frank Herbert's 1965 science-fiction novel *Dune*. "When I wrote *Geidi Primes*, I thought, 'Oh, no one will ever hear this, it doesn't matter,'" she told Henry Farmery for the *Stool Pigeon* (30 Aug. 2011). "That decision has kind of haunted me," she added, referring to the amount of attention and acclaim her debut EP generated. In a laudatory review of *Geidi Primes* for *Pitchfork* (7 Sept. 2011), Lindsay Zoladz wrote, "Even though it clocks in at a slight thirty minutes, *Geidi Primes* is a wholly immersive listen. The melodies are hooky and sweet, but each track has a throbbing undercurrent of menace that pulls you in like a riptide."

Grimes's second EP, *Halfaxa*, was released by Arbutus in October 2010. The album was widely acclaimed by critics. Even though she had been performing as Grimes for less than two years, her unique mash-up of sounds and genres launched her into a new arena. As she became more involved in recording and performing music in Montreal, she skipped nearly a year's worth of classes at McGill, prompting the school to expel her in December 2010. "I was done," she told Battan. "Now, I'm working on music all the time."

RISE TO FAME

In early 2011, Grimes traveled to the South by Southwest music festival in Austin, Texas. "I quit my job right before that and dropped out of school in December. I decided I might as well take a risk. It was a crazy journey sleeping on random people's floors," she told Marchand for the *Vancouver Sun*. "My manager would carry my keyboard and I would carry everything else and we would sprint from venue to venue." She ultimately played eleven live shows in three days. Her appearances at South by Southwest garnered Grimes widespread attention on music sites and fan blogs.

Grimes recorded a split LP with her friend Chris d'Eon called *Darkbloom*, which was released jointly by their two labels, Arbutus Records and Hippos in Tanks, in April 2011. In an interview with Steve Kerr for *Dummy* magazine (9 May 2011), d'Eon explained, "We don't jam with other people very much, so that's why we did the split, rather than a collaboration, because it would just be too stressful to compromise." Grimes worked with photographer Sadaf Hakimian to design the LP's cover art, and she directed the music video for the song "Vanessa" after being displeased with the video for "Crystal Ball," which was directed by Tim Kelly. "I felt powerless," she said of the "Crystal Ball" video in an interview with Laura M. Holson for the *New York Times* (7 Mar. 2012). "I need to feel like I'm really involved." For the "Vanessa" video, Grimes took control. "The budget was $60, which all went to alcohol," she told Battan. "We literally planned it the night before."

With her popularity soaring, Grimes's original cassette-only release, *Geidi Primes*, was rereleased on CD and vinyl by the London-based label No Pain in Pop in the summer of 2011. Beginning in May 2011, she was the opening act for Swedish singer Lykke Li's North American tour. "It forced me to become a musician," Grimes told Battan. "Previously I was playing shows for thirty people, and then it turned into three thousand people. So I practiced a lot and made everything more coherent. Before that, it was kind of jammy—I would improvise a lot." Grimes recorded her next album during a nonstop, three-week solo session. "I'd been reading a lot about medieval approaches to art, cloistering, and fasting," she explained to Ramaswamay. "So I decided to go for it. I wanted to do something extreme."

VISIONS

Grimes's third solo album, *Visions*, became her most accomplished effort to date, both technically and lyrically. "Early Grimes releases showed hazy promise, even if they felt a little too much like scenester in-jokes," wrote Holson for the *New York Times*. As Grimes turned to more personal source material for her musical inspiration, her songs became more relatable, relevant, and wrenching.

Grimes wrote and recorded *Visions* in a three-week session, in which she cloistered herself in her parents' basement and recorded nonstop, using amphetamines to carry her through days without sleep. "Once you hit day nine, you start accessing some really crazy s——," she told Richards. "You have no stimulation, so your subconscious starts filling in the blanks. . . . It was like I knew exactly what to do next, as if my songs were already written." For *Visions*, Grimes used a Roland Juno-G workstation keyboard, a Line 6 M9 vocal processor, and a BOSS VE-20 vocal processor as well as the production software Logic.

The lyrics on *Visions* are much more personal and provocative than those on her first EPs. "*Visions* was an extremely cathartic album to make. I went through a period a few years back when I was really addicted to drugs. . . . I never really dealt with all that, but I eventually realized that by making songs I could work through these things that had been plaguing me for years," she told Richards. The song "Oblivion" deals with a violent assault Grimes had endured a few years prior. "It can totally be a party album, which is hilarious to me because it's so tortured," she explained to Richards. "But because it's about sloughing off that pain, there is a kind of joy in the way it takes you from utter depression to utter ecstasy."

Visions became Grimes's best-reviewed album to date when it was released in January 2012. The *Guardian* and *Pitchfork* magazine listed *Visions* among the best new albums of 2012. "Propulsive, heady, beat-driven synth music, its unspooling psychedelia is made all the more intoxicating by Boucher's extraordinary voice," Battan wrote in her review of the album for *Pitchfork* (16 Feb. 2012). Whereas *Geidi Primes* and *Halfaxa* are accomplished yet slightly amateurish debuts, *Visions* is the work of an artist who is just coming into her prime. "Those other two albums were literally the first music I ever made. They were just practice," Grimes told Battan. "I don't hate them, but instead of actually making what I wanted to make, I was making what I was able to make." With Grimes just hitting her stride on *Visions*, fans and music critics are eager to see what the musician will produce next.

SUGGESTED READING

Adams, Gregory. "Sound Says Most to Grimes." *Straight*. Vancouver Free Press, 25 May 2011. Web. 7 Oct. 2013.

Grimes. "Grimes of the Heart." Interview by Durga Chew-Bose. *Interview*. Interview Magazine, n.d. Web. 7 Oct. 2013.

Grimes. Interview by Carrie Battan. *Pitchfork*. Pitchfork Media, 16 Oct. 2011. Web. 7 Oct. 2013.

Grimes. Interview by Chitra Ramaswamy. *The Scotsman*. Johnston Publishing, 6 May 2012. Web. 7 Oct. 2013.

Holson, Laura M. "Claire Boucher Mines Beauty from the Dark Side." *New York Times*. New York Times Co., 7 Mar. 2012. Web. 7 Oct. 2013.

Richards, Sam. "Grimes: Nine Days without Food, Sleep or Company Gave Me *Visions*." *Guardian*. Guardian News and Media, 27 Apr. 2012. Web. 7 Oct. 2013.

SELECTED WORKS

Geidi Primes, 2010; *Halfaxa*, 2010; *Darkbloom* (with Chris d'Eon), 2011; *Visions*, 2012

—*Mary Woodbury Hooper*

Chen Guangcheng

Born: November 12, 1971
Occupation: Civil rights activist

Chen Guangcheng, a lawyer and human rights activist from China, was tried and convicted in 2006 on charges of destroying property and disrupting traffic. The charges were concocted by Chinese government officials to obscure what many believe was Chen's real crime—for agreeing to represent a group of women who had accused the Chinese government of forcing them to have abortions in adherence with China's one-child policy. Sentenced to fifty-one months of prison time and released in 2010, Chen was

© Ron Sachs/Corbis

placed under house arrest, during which he and his wife were routinely beaten. Chen made a harrowing escape to the US embassy in Beijing in April 2012, and then, through the intervention of US Secretary of State Hillary Clinton, he and his family fled to New York City in May 2012. He was offered a position as a visiting fellow at the New York University (NYU) School of Law and became a lauded symbol of defiance against China's oppressive government. But from the moment Chen arrived in the United States, various political groups have vied for his support and attention. For Chen, trying to remain above the fray became increasingly difficult. After a public falling out with NYU in 2013—in which he accused the school of bowing to pressure from the Chinese government to remove him—he accepted a position with the Witherspoon Institute, a conservative think tank known for its opposition to abortion, and the left-leaning Lantos Foundation for Human Rights and Justice as a senior distinguished adviser. He is also a visiting fellow at the Catholic University of America's Institute for Policy Research and Catholic Studies in Washington, DC.

Chen is not the first foreign dissident to have trouble navigating American domestic politics, as Andrew Jacobs pointed out in an article for the *New York Times* (10 July 2013). "Chen often told me he had no interest in siding with the Democratic or Republican Party, but that he was on the side of democracy and freedom," Hu Jia, a Chinese dissident explained in an interview, as quoted by Jacobs. "I think that maybe he got in over his head."

EARLY LIFE

Chen was born to a poor family on November 12, 1971, in a rural area of China's Shandong province. He went blind after a fever in his infancy damaged his optical nerves. Growing up in the remote farming village of Dongshigu, Chen's career options were limited—discrimination against persons with disabilities is common in rural China. According to Evan Osnos's June 17, 2013, entry in the *Letter from China* blog for the *New Yorker*, 90 percent of blind workers in China work in massage therapy or acupuncture. Chen did not start school until he was in his late teens, and he attended the Qingdao High School for the Blind from 1994 to 1998. After graduation he entered the Nanjing University of Chinese Medicine to study traditional massage. But Chen was not interested in becoming a masseur; he wanted to be a lawyer. As a student at Nanjing, he attended law lectures in his spare time and took it upon himself to study the law and jurisprudence.

A "BAREFOOT LAWYER"

In 2001 Chen returned to his hometown, where he became a sought-after "barefoot lawyer." Chen represented peasants in local pollution cases and became an inspirational success story. As Jamil Anderlini noted for the *Financial Times* (21 Sept. 2012), "The only one of a large family of peasant farmers to attain anything beyond rudimentary education, he and his story would be highly unusual even were he not blind." Chen became a full-time legal activist, taking on cases involving government corruption, pollution, and discrimination against the poor and persons with disabilities. His work garnered worldwide attention in 2005 when he brought a class-action lawsuit against authorities in Linyi on behalf of a number of women who said they had been forcibly sterilized and subjected to forced abortions under China's one-child policy. The details of Chen's investigation were gruesome and appeared in several human-rights reports, as well as in an article for *Time* magazine (12 Sept. 2005). Government officials were embarrassed by the case and placed Chen under house arrest from September 2005 until he was formally tried in the summer of 2006.

By this time, Chen was already an international figure. A number of activists and journalists tried unsuccessfully to visit Chen at his home in Dongshigu in 2005. "I got no further than the front yard before plainclothes police and their proxies moved in," Osnos wrote of his own attempt to see Chen that year in an April 18, 2012, *Letter from China* blog entry. "They pushed me into a taxi, sent me away, and tailed the car to the county line." In August 2006 Chen was sentenced to fifty-one months in prison on trumped-up criminal charges of "destroying property" and "assembling a crowd for the purpose of disrupting traffic."

IMPRISONMENT AND ESCAPE

Chen served his sentence but again faced house arrest after his release from prison in 2010. Chen and his wife—and, at one time, his young daughter—lived under the constant threat of abuse. In 2011 Chen and his wife secretly recorded a video that was smuggled out of their home and uploaded to the Internet, but they were severely beaten when their captors found out. As in 2005 several journalists and activists tried to visit Chen to no avail. In December 2011 American actor Christian Bale and a television crew from CNN were attacked by guards in their attempt to see Chen. (According to Chen, there were plainclothes guards stationed inside and directly outside his house and more guards blocking the road to his house and the entrance to his village.) After Chen escaped, he recorded a video detailing his captivity. In it, Chen details other abuses and addresses China's prime minister, Wen Jiabao, directly. "Prime Minister Wen, you owe the people an explanation," he said, as quoted by Andrew Jacobs and Jonathan Ansfield for the *New York Times* (27 Apr. 2012). "Are these atrocities the result of local officials violating the law or a result of orders from the top leadership?"

One night in April 2012, Chen managed to slip past the guards stationed outside his home. He broke his ankle when he tumbled over the wall of his farmhouse, but with the help of a network of activists, he trekked three hundred miles to the US embassy in Beijing. The timing of his escape was fortuitous; the week after Chen arrived in Beijing, Secretary of State Hillary Clinton and other US officials were scheduled to gather in the city for the annual Strategic and Economic Dialogue. Clinton was aware of Chen's story and had publicly discussed his plight prior to her arrival in China, but she was eager to avoid controversy. After Chen made a plea to American lawmakers, Clinton, Clinton's aides, and NYU professor Jerome Cohen crafted what Jonathan Allen described as a "diplomatically elegant solution" in an article for *Reuters* (25 Nov. 2013). They arranged for Chen and his family to move to New York City, where Chen was offered a position as a visiting scholar at the NYU School of Law.

ARRIVAL IN THE UNITED STATES

Chen and his family moved into an apartment provided by NYU in Greenwich Village in May 2012, where Chen held his first press conference amid a crowd of supporters and journalists. (Chen, who does not speak fluent English, relies on the aid of a translator.) Cohen, a respected professor of Chinese law, stood beside Chen at that first appearance. He was one of

Chen's closest advisers, guiding him through his transition to the United States and overseeing his scholarship at the university. They were also joined by Bob Fu, a Chinese dissident himself and the founder a Texas-based evangelical Christian organization that advocates for religious freedom in China called ChinaAid. Fu and Chen had a lot in common. Their wives were from neighboring villages, and they had both been imprisoned by the Chinese government. Fu and his wife had fled China in 1997 after she became pregnant without the approval of the family planning authority. Fu had also been involved in the efforts to call international attention to Chen's plight while he was still under house arrest by helping to circulate Chen's video in which he described the horrible conditions of his imprisonment.

Fu and Cohen represented two opposing forces in Chen's life. Cohen was concerned that Chen might unwittingly step into political hot water, particularly concerning the debate about abortion rights in the United States. Chen was already an icon among pro-life supporters for his work exposing forced abortion in China, but access to legal abortion in the United States was, of course, a separate issue altogether. Cohen saw enormous potential in Chen and remarked that Chen could be "a potential Gandhi figure for Chinese society," as quoted by Isaac Stone Fish in an article for *Foreign Policy* (10 Jan. 2014). Cohen was not the only one to see leadership potential in the firm but soft-spoken Chen. "In the dissident community, someone with his kind of stature doesn't come along every day," John Kamm, director of the Dui Hua Foundation, which supports Chinese political prisoners, explained, as quoted by Jacobs. "His face, with those sunglasses, is the kind of Che Guevara–like image you can stick on a T-shirt."

Relations between Fu and Cohen soured during Chen's first weeks in New York. Fu and his wife gave Chen and his family an iPhone and an iPad, which Cohen suspected were bugged with tracking devices. (Fu denies this.) Fu, for his part, suspected similar transgressions perpetrated by Cohen and NYU. He told Allen, "I felt Chen was being watched." He cited an incident in which C. J. Huang, Chen's aide and translator, dropped in on a meeting between Fu and Chen and appeared to be taking notes on their conversation on her laptop. These competing suspicions likely colored their interactions with Chen.

POLARIZING POLITICAL PRESSURE

Fu told Allen that he was, perhaps, "a little naïve" about the abortion debate in the United States, explaining, "I was not very conscious of how strong the battle with the pro-life group is, the almost irreconcilable differences." Fu did help to set up other partisan inroads for Chen. Early

on he arranged a meeting for Chen with Viet Dinh, a Republican lawyer who offered Chen pro bono legal advice about negotiating his book deal, after Cohen suggested that Chen write a book about his ordeal as a way to share his story and financially support his family. In July 2012 Republican congressional representative Chris Smith, who had lobbied on Chen's behalf prior to his arrival in the United States, asked Chen to testify before the House Committee on Foreign Affairs. Cohen staunchly disagreed with this proposal. "Whether the requests came from Chris Smith, Bob or various other groups, my view was that Chen should take some months to learn about American life and should not allow himself to be injected into the presidential election campaign, whether in favor of or critical of either political party," Cohen told Allen. Cohen advised Chen against accepting Smith's request. The ordeal was the breaking point for Chen. He felt pressured to accept the invitation because Smith had played an important role in his departure from China, and he was irked by the pressure from Cohen and other NYU administrators to refuse. He felt that people at NYU were condescending in their suggestion that he did not understand American politics—in this complaint, Chen found an ally in Fu.

With the help of his colleagues at NYU, Chen visited Washington, DC, in August. After meeting with politicians from both parties, he gave a short speech to lawmakers and journalists in which he again addressed the Chinese government, calling on them to investigate the ill treatment of his family in China. When he returned from Washington, NYU officials approached Chen to discuss his plans after leaving the university. Chen believed that the discussion was a direct result of his decision to go to Washington and speak against the Chinese government. He also believed that NYU officials were being pressured by Chinese government officials to distance themselves from him. The latter assumption, several sources have suggested, might have something to do with plans for NYU's new campus in Shanghai. NYU denies this.

SPLIT WITH NYU

Chen drew closer to Fu because he increasingly felt that his NYU colleagues were trying to control him. In the fall of 2012, Cohen told Chen that he had arranged a possible position for him with the Committee to Support Chinese Lawyers through the Fordham Law School in Manhattan. It was one thing on which all of Chen's advisers seemed to agree. Cohen explained to Allen how he thought Chen "would do better in a more neutral, academic setting, especially one that focused on the plight of Chinese lawyers." Still, Smith arranged a meeting for Chen to speak with Luis Tellez, the founder and president of the conservative research center

Witherspoon Institute in Princeton, New Jersey. Tellez did not know who Chen was, but he was interested in his views on abortion. Chen, with Fu acting as his translator, met with Tellez, but Chen expressed a desire to be affiliated with a university. On June 2, 2013, David Pilling and Demetri Savastopulo reported for the *Financial Times* that Chen was talking to both Fordham and Witherspoon. In the article, Cohen was quoted saying: "If he takes the Witherspoon position that would diminish his stature in the US." The quote outraged Fu, and most certainly got back to Chen.

The same month the *New York Post* ran a story suggesting that NYU was dumping Chen, whose fellowship was scheduled to end that month, to remain in China's good graces amid their Shanghai expansion. Three days later, without Cohen's prior knowledge, Chen released a statement in which he announced his departure. He thanked NYU but also accused the university of colluding with the Chinese government. "In fact, as early as last August and September, the Chinese Communists had already begun to apply great, unrelenting pressure on New York University," Chen said, as reported by several sources. "So much so that after we had been in the United States just three to four months, NYU was already starting to discuss our departure with us." Dinh circulated the statement to the press. For their part, the Chinese government was confused by the claim, while Chen's NYU colleagues were hurt. Several days later, Fordham withdrew its offer to Chen.

HUMAN RIGHTS FELLOWSHIPS

In September 2013 Chen made another announcement. He was taking on a position as a senior fellow in human rights at Witherspoon and a visiting fellow at Catholic University's Institute for Policy Research and Catholic Studies. In the name of political neutrality, he also became an adviser for the Lantos Foundation for Human Rights and Justice, a left-leaning organization. "I believe human rights supersede partisan politics, and it's greater than national borders," Chen said in a news conference, as quoted by Allen, after accepting his new posts. Through the Witherspoon Institute, the Catholic University of America, and the Lantos Foundation, Chen has continued his efforts to advocate for human rights in China.

PERSONAL LIFE

Chen's brother, Chen Guangfu, and his elderly mother have only recently obtained visas to visit Chen in the United States, after being denied multiple times. His nephew, Chen Kegui, and his nephew's wife were brutally beaten by a gang of government thugs after it was discovered that Chen had escaped from his home in April 2012. When the gang returned to Kegui's home, he was able to stab three of his assailants with a kitchen knife. No one was killed, but Kegui was detained on charges of attempted homicide and sentenced to more than three years in prison. Like Chen in 2005, Kegui was given a government lawyer to defend him in court.

In his *New York Times* op-ed (29 May 2012), Chen called on the Chinese government to investigate the mistreatment of his family and other human rights violations in China. Despite the country's efforts to reform its judiciary practices, Chen wrote that lawlessness is still a huge problem in China. "Any serious investigation of the injustices that we and hundreds of thousands of others have suffered must determine who is beating, kidnapping, disbarring and prosecuting these lawyers and threatening their families, and why defendants are compelled to accept the nominal legal assistance of government-employed lawyers instead of counsel of their choosing," Chen stated.

Chen married his wife, Yuan Weijing, in 2003. They have two young children.

SUGGESTED READING

Allen, Jonathan. "Friends Like These." *Reuters*. Thomson Reuters, 25 Nov. 2013. Web. 14 Feb. 2014.

Anderlini, Jamil. "Lunch with FT: Chen Guangcheng." *Financial Times*. Financial Times, 21 Sept. 2012. Web. 14 Feb. 2014.

Beech, Hannah. "Enemies of the State?" *Time*. Time, 12 Sept. 2005. Web. 14 Feb. 2014.

Chen Guangcheng. "How China Flouts Its Laws." *New York Times*. New York Times, 29 May 2012. Web. 14 Feb. 2014.

Jacobs, Andrew. "After Epic Escape from China, Exile Is Mired in Partisan U.S." *New York Times*. New York Times, 10 July 2013. Web. 14 Feb. 2014.

Osnos, Evan. "Chen Guangcheng's Journey." *New Yorker*. Condé Nast, 28 Apr. 2012. Web. 14 Feb. 2014.

Osnos, Evan. "N.Y.U., China, and Chen Guangcheng." *New Yorker*. Condé Nast, 17 June 2013. Web. 14 Feb. 2014.

—*Molly Hagan*

Mohsin Hamid

Born: 1971
Occupation: Writer

The Pakistani-born novelist Mohsin Hamid has been hailed as "one of his generation's most inventive and gifted writers," by Michiko Kakutani for the *New York Times* (23 Feb. 2013). The author of three innovative and critically acclaimed novels—*Moth Smoke* (2000), *The Reluctant*

© Dimitris Legakis/Splash News/Corbis

Fundamentalist (2007), and *How to Get Filthy Rich in Rising Asia* (2013)—Hamid has won the Betty Trask Award (2001), the Anisfield-Wolf Book Award (2008), and the Ambassador Book Award (2008), among other laurels. In his work, he draws upon his own experience moving between the disparate worlds of his native Pakistan and the West to craft compelling and memorable tales that, like Hamid himself, transcend boundaries and defy easy categorization. The tension between East and West is a recurring theme in both his work and his identity. As such, he describes himself as "geographically transgendered," according to Ruby Cutolo for *Publishers Weekly* (23 Nov. 2012), stating, "I've seen these worlds, I've felt these pressures, but I've taken a different path."

CHILDHOOD

Mohsin Hamid was born in 1971 in Lahore, Pakistan. At a very young age, he moved with his family to the United States, to the San Francisco Bay Area, where his father entered a PhD program at Stanford University. It was a difficult adjustment. Hamid spoke only Urdu and the other children in the campus housing development where the family lived made fun of him at first. As a consequence, "I didn't speak for a month," Hamid wrote for the *Guardian* (30 Apr. 2011). "And when I next spoke, much to [my parents'] surprise, it was in English, in complete sentences, and with an American accent."

He didn't speak Urdu for the next six years. Instead he immersed himself in American culture, developing an interest in science fiction and the role-playing game Dungeons & Dragons. At the age of nine, Hamid moved back to Pakistan with his family, which now included his younger sister. Resettled in Lahore, Hamid had to reacclimatize himself to his homeland and his native language, a task made easier by

his extended Pakistani family. The English he had picked up in the United States, meanwhile, came in handy during his time studying at the American School in Lahore.

EDUCATION

After completing high school, Hamid returned to the United States to attend Princeton University, in Princeton, New Jersey. There he stumbled into his passion for writing. "I fell in love with it," he recalled to Shivani Vora for the *New York Times* blog *India Ink* (18 Mar. 2013). After taking a couple courses with the renowned author Joyce Carol Oates and a long fiction seminar with the Nobel Prize–winning novelist Toni Morrison during his senior year, Hamid began to think about writing as a calling.

After graduating in 1993 with a degree in international relations, he went back to Pakistan for a year before returning to the United States to take up studies at Harvard Law School in Cambridge, Massachusetts. The decision to become a lawyer was partly a financial one. Though he wanted to write, he was not convinced it would pay the bills. "I had to make a living," he explained to Vora. "I didn't know how I was going to support myself as a writer. I still wonder about it." Though he was a student at one of the most exclusive law schools in the country, Hamid soon concluded that he might not be cut out for a legal career. "I discovered quickly that I didn't want to be a lawyer," he told Vora, "but found my way back to writing and am lucky I got support along the way."

During his third and final year at Harvard, Hamid approached his advisor, Professor Richard Parker. Rather than write a final thesis like his classmates, he asked if he could instead produce a novel about a trial. Parker approved the project, and Hamid started working on the manuscript that would become his debut novel, *Moth Smoke*.

MOTH SMOKE

Hamid graduated from Harvard Law in 1997. From there, he went to work as a management consultant for McKinsey and Company in New York City. But he remained committed to his writing, working out an agreement with his employer that allowed him to take time off each year to focus on finishing *Moth Smoke*. "When I went to McKinsey," he recalled to Vora, "I asked if I could consult for nine months and take three months off to write which my bosses agreed to." Hamid would work long days for McKinsey, then write at night and on weekends from his home on Cornelia Street in Manhattan's West Village. During his time off, he would head back to Pakistan to write from there.

Published by Farrar, Straus and Giroux in 2000, *Moth Smoke* is a "brisk and absorbing novel," Jhumpa Lahiri observed for the *New York*

Times (12 Mar. 2000). Set in Lahore over the course of a summer fraught with nuclear tensions between India and Pakistan, *Moth Smoke* tells the story of Darashikoh "Daru" Shezad, a striving but low-level banker with a short fuse and grandiose dreams of wealth and influence. After he loses his job, he descends into a hedonistic haze of drugs and excess. He begins an affair with a wealthy friend's wife and witnesses the same friend kill a teenager in a hit-and-run accident, a crime for which Daru ends up taking the fall.

For a debut novel, the work was a critical hit. "*Moth Smoke* is a steamy (in both senses) and often darkly amusing book about sex, drugs, and class warfare in postcolonial Asia," Richard Gehr wrote for the *Village Voice* (25 Jan. 2000), describing it as "a subtly audacious work and prodigious descendant of hard-boiled lit and film noir." Lahiri offered a similarly positive assessment, hearing in *Moth Smoke* echoes of the F. Scott Fitzgerald masterpiece *The Great Gatsby* (1925). "Hamid steers us from start to finish with assurance and care," she remarked. "Like Fitzgerald, Hamid writes about the slippery ties between the extremely wealthy and those who hover, and generally stumble, in money's glare." Named a New York Times Notable Book of the Year in 2001, *Moth Smoke* won the Betty Trask Award and was a finalist for the PEN/Hemingway Award that same year.

THE RELUCTANT FUNDAMENTALIST

Despite the success of *Moth Smoke*, Hamid kept his job at McKinsey in New York but soon embarked on his second novel. By September 2001, he had completed the first draft of a story about a Pakistani expatriate working in corporate America who decides to return home. Then, while Hamid was staying in London during a trip to Europe, the September 11, 2001, terror attacks unfolded. "I was in a gym at that time, and I remember hearing that the planes had hit the towers," Hamid recalled to Amitabh Pal for the *Progressive* (May 2013). "Being a writer, I watched everybody, and I noticed that some people were smiling as they saw the television coverage." Hamid could not tell if the expressions he saw were a product of emotional overstimulation or actual glee at seeing trauma inflicted upon the United States.

As the post–September 11 world took shape, Hamid realized he would have to completely rewrite the novel, taking into account the changes the events had wrought. As attitudes shifted and security tightened at airports and elsewhere, Hamid, a multicultural and well-traveled Pakistani, was in a unique position to observe, and his revelations helped inform the novel. Soon after the September 11 attacks, he decided to move to London, where he took up work as a brand consultant. His employers agreed to allow him to work part-time so he could also stay focused on his writing.

The Reluctant Fundamentalist, published by Harcourt in 2007, takes place in Lahore several years after September 11. The Pakistani protagonist Changez recounts his life in the time before and after the attacks in a prolonged monologue over tea with an American stranger in a Lahore cafe. A Princeton graduate, Changez worked as a financial analyst in New York City. As he describes his attempts to achieve the American dream on Wall Street, he also reminisces about a love affair with a troubled New Yorker named Erica. Despite his successes in the United States, Changez's efforts to assimilate, to fit in, only go so far. When the attacks occur, unbidden and to his complete surprise, a smile plays out across his face. He realizes that at his core, his sense of belonging is illusory, a notion only confirmed by how the heightened security situation, his objection to American foreign policy, and the suspicion with which he is viewed by others affect him in the aftermath of the attacks. Increasingly alienated, he decides to return to Pakistan. "At its core, this is a story of someone who is in love with America, in love with an American woman, who finds he has to leave," Hamid explained to Jane Perlez for the *New York Times* (13 Oct. 2007). What Hamid sought was to invert the usual American immigrant narrative. "The traditional immigrant novel is about coming to America," he told Perlez. "I wanted to do the twenty-first-century polarity when the magnet switches and pushes them away."

A New York Times Best Seller, the work was well-received by reviewers. "The courage of *The Reluctant Fundamentalist*," Laila Halaby declared for the *Washington Post* (22 Apr. 2007), "is in the telling of a story about a Pakistani man who makes it and then throws it away because he doesn't want it anymore." In a similarly superlative critique, Andrew Anthony wrote for the *Observer* (22 Dec. 2012), "One of the novel's notable achievements is the seamless manner in which ideology and emotion, politics and the personal are brought together into a vivid picture of an individual's globalised revolt." The book was shortlisted for the Man Booker Prize and earned the Anisfield-Wolf and the Ambassador book awards, among other honors.

A film adaptation of the novel directed by Mira Nair and starring Kate Hudson and Riz Ahmed, debuted at the Venice Film Festival in August 2012. It received mixed reviews and did poorly at the box office.

HOW TO GET FILTHY RICH IN RISING ASIA

With the success of *The Reluctant Fundamentalist*, Hamid soon felt secure enough to leave his day job and focus on writing full-time. But his third novel still took many years to craft. The work was inspired by a conversation

Hamid had with a friend in New York. The two were joking about how every novel is, in effect, a self-help book, since the act of reading a novel is broadly seen as a form of self-improvement. So Hamid became fascinated with the idea of crafting a literary novel told in the form of a self-help manual and set about writing *How to Get Filthy Rich in Rising Asia*.

Adhering to the self-help style, the book uses a second person narration. The "you" addressed by the narrator is an anonymous peasant in a vast unnamed Asian city. The narrator is a wealthy man who describes how he climbed out of rural poverty to build a fortune in the big city by repackaging and selling boiled tap water as fancy mineral water. The book, published in 2013 by Riverhead Books, unfolds in twelve chapters, each illuminating a lesson the narrator learned and deployed in his ascent, among them "Get an Education," "Don't Fall in Love," and "Befriend a Bureaucrat."

Like Hamid's two earlier works, the novel earned widespread praise. His fusion of the self-help form with the coming-of-age story, in particular, resonated with critics. "The marriage of these two curiously compatible genres," Parul Sehgal observed for the *New York Times* (29 Mar. 2013), "is just one of the pleasures of Mohsin Hamid's shrewd and slippery new novel, a rags-to-riches story that works on a head-splitting number of levels." Sehgal was not as impressed with some of the book's more serious musings on such topics as mortality and storytelling, however. Edmund Gordon, on the other hand, offered unqualified praise in a review for the *Telegraph* (22 Mar. 2013), describing the work as "a vital and affecting portrait of a teeming and globally significant, but largely unrecorded culture. It is a bold formal experiment contained within an elegant novella. It is moving and charming and funny. When you reach the end, you want to go straight back to the beginning."

PERSONAL LIFE

Hamid holds dual citizenship in the United Kingdom and Pakistan, but makes his home in Lahore. He has been married to his wife, the former Zahra Khan, a Pakistani television actress and classical singer, since 2005. The two actually grew up just a few houses apart in Lahore, but only met years later in a London bar. Together they have two children.

Hamid's novels have been translated into over thirty languages. He has contributed articles and short fiction to such publications as the *Guardian*, the *New Yorker*, *Granta*, and the *New York Times*. While writing *How to Get Filthy Rich in Rising Asia*, Hamid found himself stuck at various points, uncertain where to take the novel. To break out of the rut, he took up walking first thing every morning as a way to draw inspiration, a practice he has kept up in the years

since. Though a renowned novelist, Hamid prefers to stay out of the public eye while writing. "I spend my time with my friends and my family," he explained to Anis Shivani for the *Los Angeles Review of Books* (14 July 2013). "And then, once every six or seven years, I step out into full-blown publicity."

SUGGESTED READING

Cutolo, Ruby. "The Meeting of East and West." *Publishers Weekly*. PWxyz, 23 Nov. 2012. Web. 14 Mar. 2014.

Hamid, Mohsin. "Once Upon a Life." *Guardian*. Guardian News and Media, 30 Apr. 2011. Web. 14 Mar. 2014.

Pal, Amitabh. "I'm Very Comfortable as a Hybridized Mongrel." *Progressive*. Progressive Magazine, May 2013. Web. 14 Mar. 2014.

Perlez, Jane. "A Pakistani Voice in Search of a True Home." *New York Times*. New York Times, 13 Oct. 2007. Web. 14 Mar. 2014.

Vora, Shivani. "A Conversation With: Pakistani Author Mohsin Hamid." *New York Times: India Ink*. New York Times, 18 Mar. 2013. Web. 14 Mar. 2014.

SELECTED WORKS

Moth Smoke, 2000; *The Reluctant Fundamentalist*, 2007; *How to Get Filthy Rich in Rising Asia*, 2013

—*Paul McCaffrey*

Rachel Haot

Born: August 15, 1983
Occupation: Chief digital officer and deputy secretary of technology for New York State

Rachel Sterne Haot was named New York State's first deputy secretary for technology by Governor Andrew Cuomo in December 2013. She previously served as New York City's chief digital officer under Mayor Michael Bloomberg, a newly created job that she earned at the age of twenty-seven. One of her major initiatives updated New York City's website and broadened access to the city's 311 help line. The job, as Haot told Javier C. Hernandez for the *New York Times* (31 July 2011), was "not just about a Twitter account. It's about evolving government. It's about doing a better and better job of serving New Yorkers." Haot, who interned for the United Nations, has a passion for public policy, but her background more closely resembles those of the leaders of the private-sector tech companies she partners with than of her colleagues in Albany. At twenty-two, Haot launched a journalism start-up called

EARLY LIFE AND EDUCATION

Haot was born Rachel Gorelick Sterne on August 15, 1983, and raised in the Park Slope neighborhood of Brooklyn, where she first flexed her entrepreneurial muscles by running stoop sales in front of her family's brownstone. Her family moved to Dobbs Ferry in Westchester, New York, when she was eight. Her mother, Anna Sterne, is a registered nurse and the director of patient services at the nonprofit St. Mary's Community Care Professionals in Elmhurst, Queens. She ran for New York State Assembly in the Ninety-Second District in 2010. Haot's father, Paul L. Sterne, was the managing director for corporate development at IBM in Armonk, New York. After retiring from IBM he became the president of anti-virus software seller RAE Internet in 2010, and he oversees Haot's first project, the citizen-journalist-driven news website GroundReport, as trustee. Haot has three younger siblings: Erica, Kate, and Ben.

It could be said that Haot and the Internet came of age at the same time. She owned her first Macintosh computer when she was seven years old—she was surrounded by technology growing up, she has said in various interviews, because her father worked for IBM—and created her first website at age thirteen. In high school, Haot and her friends tried to launch a start-up called Constellation. Though unsuccessful, it was indicative of Haot's ambitions. She graduated from Dobbs Ferry High School in 2001 and enrolled at New York University (NYU), where she majored in history. Haot took numerous opportunities to work outside of the city, spending a summer in France as an au pair and volunteering on an American Indian reservation in Montana. In New York, she interned for former Manhattan city councilman Alan Gerson.

UNITED NATIONS INTERNSHIP AND LIMEWIRE

Haot graduated from NYU in 2005 and that same year spent four months working as a political intern for the United States Mission to the United Nations, where she reported on daily UN Security Council meetings. During her time there, then general secretary Kofi Annan urged the council to take action in Darfur, Sudan, where a mass genocide was taking place. Haot was moved by Annan's plea and frustrated that others, including the US government, were not spurred to act. "If more people knew that this was happening and they could hear about [it] in the voice of people who are experiencing it, instead of a dry, third-party report from a wire service, then maybe they'll feel that sense of urgency too and they will urge their elected, our elected, officials to do something about it," Haot told Budd Mishkin for NY1 (27 Feb. 2012).

Haot left the UN in April 2005 and shortly after, in June, began working for a file-sharing start-up called LimeWire. The substance of the

GroundReport, and less than two years later founded a digital consulting firm called Upward Strategy.

When Haot was hired by the city in January 2011, her pedigree spoke to Mayor Bloomberg's desire to make New York the next hub of the technology world. Almost six months later, the mayor announced plans to support and partially finance a state-of-the-art technology and engineering campus on Roosevelt Island. The mayor's office accepted proposals from a number of schools, and the bid ultimately went to Cornell University in Ithaca, New York. "We understand that we will not catch up to Silicon Valley overnight," Bloomberg said when he announced plans for the school, as reported by WCBS's Peter Haskell (19 July 2011). He added, "The new campus will help us build a critical mass towards our ultimate goal—reclaiming our title as the world's capital of technological innovation." In the meantime, Bloomberg asked Haot to court up-and-coming companies. She already had close ties with executives at Facebook, Foursquare, and Tumblr, and she spent a good amount of time building on those relationships on behalf of the New York City Economic Development Corporation.

Haot, who taught classes in social media as an adjunct professor at Columbia Business School during the 2010–2011 school year, has been listed as one of *Forbes*'s "30 under 30" (2011, 2012) as well as *Fortune*'s "40 under 40" (2013). In 2009, *BusinessWeek* (now *Bloomberg Businessweek*) named her one of "America's Most Promising Social Entrepreneurs."

work was vastly different from her work reporting on the Security Council, but she realized that the tools she was learning to use at LimeWire could be useful in policy making. With this as her guiding principle, Haot invested her personal savings and some money from her family into a news website called GroundReport, which she launched in 2006.

GROUNDREPORT

GroundReport is a platform that crowdsources its content, which means that anyone, anywhere, can write a story about or upload a photo or video of a particular event, and GroundReport in turn edits and aggregates those stories for the website. The quality of the reportage on the site is high; many of GroundReport's contributors are professional writers and journalists, breaking stories such as the terrorist attacks in Mumbai in 2008. As Rich McCormick wrote for the *Verge* (18 Dec. 2013), the site publishes "local stories for international audiences."

GroundReport has fared much better than other start-ups, but it never generated the traffic or the income to match its buzz. By 2008, Haot had reached a crossroads. She did not know how she was going to sustain the company or herself. "My hopes for GroundReport had been that it would take off wildly and be this new news platform," she told the *Atlantic* in an interview (9 Oct. 2013). In the same interview, she talked about the "serial failures" in the life of an entrepreneur. GroundReport was certainly not a failure—according to Hernandez, the site boasts ten thousand contributors—but it has not been the success Haot had envisioned either. Haot founded Upward Strategy in April 2008, a digital consulting firm that she ran along with GroundReport until late 2010. Haot still wanted to combine her love of policy with her love for technology, and as she was contemplating her next move, she came across an ad for a new job with the city of New York.

NYC CHIEF DIGITAL OFFICER

Mayor Bloomberg appointed Haot as the city's first chief digital officer in January 2011. The administration had created the job six months earlier, but at the time Haot was hired, the nature of her position was still hazy. She was offered a sizeable salary but, initially at least, no separate staff and no budget. Her office was under the mayor's Office of Media and Entertainment.

The tech community applauded Haot's appointment. Andrew Rasiej, the chairman of NY Tech Meetup, a nonprofit that fosters the technology community in New York, called her "an inspired choice," as reported by Patrick McGeehan for the *New York Times* (24 Jan. 2011). Tech entrepreneurs, who had long complained that the city provided an unfriendly environment for technology, saw Haot, an entrepreneur herself,

as one of their own. "I can't think of anybody who captures the zeitgeist of New York's resurgence as a technology and media capital better than Rachel," Rasiej told McGeehan. This response was likely Bloomberg's intention. From the beginning, Haot's directive was twofold: bring New York into the twenty-first century through the use of social media and forge partnerships with successful tech companies.

Haot produced a sixty-two-page report called *Road Map for the Digital City* after her first ninety days on the job. The document contained forty initiatives, all of which were completed by the time she left office. One of her first projects for the city was a blog called the *Daily Pothole*, which, as its name implies, tracks potholes across the five boroughs. A more major accomplishment was the redesign and relaunch of the city's website, NYC.gov, which had not received a makeover since 2003. To brainstorm ideas for its new look, Haot proposed hosting a "hackathon." In tech jargon, the term refers to a sustained period of intense collaboration; Facebook is famous for holding twenty-four-hour adrenaline-fueled coding hackathons. When Haot pitched the idea to her colleagues at City Hall, however, she had to explain that this hackathon "would not pose a security threat," Hernandez wrote.

NYC.GOV, WE ARE MADE IN NY, AND OTHER PROJECTS

The new NYC.gov, designed by the Brooklyn-based firm Huge, was unveiled in September 2013. The new site is easy to use, and its home page features clear notices about public transit, parking, garbage collection, and school closings, alongside buttons that allow residents to pay parking tickets or property taxes. There are also a number of places on the site to file complaints through the city's help line, 311. The help line itself has its own Twitter account, with over sixty thousand followers. Haot also worked to bring free Wi-Fi coverage to various public spaces in the city, including libraries, parks, and even a number of pay-phone booths, which remain active but are rarely used. The Wi-Fi project, part of a larger exploration of the feasibility of a city-wide Wi-Fi network, was an ingenious way to marry New York's outdated infrastructure with new technology.

Haot also took the lead on an initiative called We Are Made in NY, launched in early 2013. The initiative is an ambitious campaign to highlight local start-ups and foster jobs in technology. We Are Made in NY connects companies with job seekers through its interactive digital jobs map and holds meet-ups and seminars to teach job seekers practical computer skills. It also offers funding for aspiring entrepreneurs and employee training. During Haot's two years on the job, the Bloomberg administration's proactive policies seemed to be paying off. In an article for the *Huffington Post* (23 Feb. 2013), Haot, citing data from the *Crain's New York Business* website, wrote that tech acquisitions totaled $8.3 billion in 2012, putting the city second in the nation after Silicon Valley.

CRITICISM OF BLOOMBERG'S VISION

Not everyone shared Bloomberg's, and by extension Haot's, vision for a new New York, however. According to Gerry Smith for the *Huffington Post* (10 Oct. 2012) and the New York City Housing Authority (NYCHA), 40 percent of New York City's public-housing residents lack Internet access. The growing wealth disparity in the city has become a major cause for concern. Bloomberg's successor, Bill de Blasio, won overwhelming support for his anti-Bloomberg election campaign, which painted a vivid picture of a city divided by class and race. Doug Frazier, head of an organization called the Digital Divide Partnership, which brings Internet service to low-income neighborhoods, told Smith of Haot, "She's the chief digital officer, but not for the poor people."

While providing poor New Yorkers with Internet access was not Haot's directive and, with only five staffers in her office when she left—tackling the digital divide amidst the technological upgrade that the city's services so desperately needed would have been a Herculean undertaking—Haot was frank about the problem and tried to address it through seminars and Internet hubs around the city. "We always need to be doing more," she told Smith. "It doesn't matter how great all these innovations are if people can't take advantage of them."

CHIEF DIGITAL OFFICER FOR NEW YORK STATE

In December 2013, a month before Bloomberg left office, New York governor Andrew Cuomo announced that Haot would become the state's first chief digital officer and deputy secretary for technology. "The governor made a very smart hire here," Bloomberg said in a statement as reported by Thomas Kaplan for the *New York Times* (18 Dec. 2013). Haot is the first person to fill the role. According to the governor's office, she will be tasked with updating the state's website and streamlining its social-media accounts through partnerships with private tech firms. In the same statement, Bloomberg added, "Rachel helped us set the standard for how a municipal government can engage the people it serves through digital platforms, and her work has made New York City the digital model for cities across the country and around the world."

PERSONAL LIFE

Outside of her work, the six-foot-tall Haot is known for her fashionable taste, and she was profiled in *Vogue* in 2011. She married Maxime Haot, the chief executive officer of Internet video-streaming company Livestream, in July 2012. The couple live in Brooklyn.

SUGGESTED READING

Hernandez, Javier C. "A Digital Matchmaker for the City and Its Public." *New York Times* 31 July 2011: MB1. Print.

McGeehan, Patrick. "City Picks Entrepreneur to Lead Digital Efforts." *New York Times*. New York Times, 24 Jan. 2011. Web. 13 Jan. 2014.

Mishkin, Budd. "*One On 1 Profile*: NYC Chief Digital Officer Rachel Sterne Brings City Government into 21st Century." *NY1*. Time Warner, 27 Feb. 2012. Web. 13 Jan. 2014.

Smith, Gerry. "Rachel Haot, New York's Tech Czar, Is the Woman behind Bloomberg's Digital Vision." *Huffington Post*. TheHuffingtonPost.com, 10 Oct. 2012. Web. 13 Jan. 2014.

Sterne, Rachel. "We Are Made in NY: Tech Thrives in NYC." *Huffington Post*. TheHuffingtonPost.com, 23 Feb. 2013. Web. 13 Jan. 2014.

—*Molly Hagan*

Tom Hardy

Born: September 15, 1977
Occupation: Actor

The British actor Tom Hardy has drawn comparisons to Marlon Brando for the brooding intensity and unflinching realism he brings to his acting roles. Like the late Hollywood screen legend, Hardy is known for completely immersing himself in his characters and for his uncanny ability to steal every scene in which he appears. Don Steinberg noted for the *Wall Street Journal* (17 Apr. 2014) that Hardy "builds his characters using real people as models, borrowing an accent from one, a demeanor from another, a posture from a third."

After beginning his career with minor supporting roles in the HBO miniseries *Band of Brothers* (2001), produced by Steven Spielberg and Tom Hanks, and the war film *Black Hawk Down* (2001), directed by Ridley Scott, Hardy was cast as the villain Shinzon in *Star Trek: Nemesis* (2002) and was promptly hailed British acting's next big thing until alcoholism and drug addictions nearly derailed his career. After entering rehab and kicking his addictions in 2003, Hardy delivered a number of acclaimed performances on the stage and television before starring in the eponymous role in director Nicolas Winding Refn's *Bronson* (2008). Hardy was catapulted into the mainstream with roles in two Christopher Nolan–helmed blockbusters, *Inception* (2010) and *The Dark Knight Rises* (2012). Meanwhile, he earned widespread critical attention for his

FGA/Landov

Hardy's predilection for delinquent behavior turned more serious in his teens, when he began drinking, experimenting with drugs, and committing petty crimes. At age fifteen he was arrested for riding in a stolen Mercedes and possessing a gun. Nonetheless, in 1998, at the age of twenty, Hardy entered and won a "Find Me a Supermodel" contest on the UK show *The Big Breakfast* and briefly landed a contract with Britain's leading agency Models 1. Later that year he enrolled at Richmond Drama School in southwest London to study acting, a discipline he felt would allow him to channel his personal demons. Hardy, who grew up idolizing his future costar Gary Oldman, explained to John Hiscock for the *Telegraph* (25 Aug. 2011) that he "fell into acting because there wasn't anything else I could do, and in it I found a discipline that I wanted to keep coming back to, that I love and I learn about every day."

At Richmond Drama School, Hardy learned all the facets of the acting trade, most importantly how to analyze and break down a script. He was eventually kicked out of that school, too, but his commitment to acting was such that he continued his education at the prestigious Drama Centre London. There, he studied method acting under renowned instructor Christopher Fettes.

EARLY CAREER AND ADDICTION STRUGGLES
Hardy left the Drama Centre in 2001, when he landed his first screen role as US Army Private John Janovec in HBO's ten-part World War II miniseries *Band of Brothers*. He appeared in two episodes of the critically acclaimed, award-winning series, which was coproduced by Steven Spielberg and Tom Hanks and featured an ensemble cast of largely unknown actors. Later in 2001 Hardy made his feature film debut playing another American soldier, Specialist Lance Twombly, in Ridley Scott's harrowing war drama *Black Hawk Down*, which also featured a large ensemble cast.

Hardy then landed the role of the villain Shinzon, a clone of USS *Enterprise* Captain Jean-Luc Picard (Patrick Stewart), in Stuart Baird's *Star Trek: Nemesis*, the tenth installment of the Star Trek film franchise. Though the film was poorly received by critics, Hardy was singled out for giving a standout performance and was widely heralded as British acting's next big thing. His promising acting career was soon derailed, however, by escalating addictions to alcohol and crack cocaine, which he used to relieve his "low self-esteem and raging ego," as he told Tom Junod for *Esquire* (22 Apr. 2014).

Hardy's drinking and drug abuse came to a head one day in 2002, when he awoke in a pool of blood and vomit on Old Compton Street in London's Soho district after a crack binge. Afterward, he entered rehab and began attending

well-rounded and carefully nuanced performances in the films *Tinker Tailor Soldier Spy* (2011), *Warrior* (2011), *Lawless* (2012), and *Locke* (2013). Director George Miller described Hardy to Nicole Sperling for *Entertainment Weekly* (4 July 2014) as an actor who is "utterly abandoned in his work" with "a sense of unpredictability" unmatched by his peers.

EARLY LIFE AND EDUCATION
An only child, Edward Thomas "Tom" Hardy was born on September 15, 1977, in Hammersmith, a district in west London, England. His father, Edward "Chips" Hardy, is a Cambridge-educated comedy writer and creative director of an advertising firm; his mother, Anne (Barrett) Hardy, is an artist and painter. Hardy enjoyed a middle-class upbringing in East Sheen, an affluent suburb of London.

Despite his privileged upbringing, Hardy, by his own admission, was a poor student and troublemaker in his youth and adolescence. "From a very young age I was flagrantly disobedient," he told Nick Curtis for the *London Evening Standard* (7 Nov. 2006). "I got involved in anything that was naughty. I wanted to explore all the dark corners of the world." Hardy first attended Reed's School, an independent boarding school for boys in Surrey. He was expelled from the school, however, for stealing. Afterward, he studied at the Tower House School in London.

regular psychotherapy sessions. "I went entirely off the rails and I'm lucky I didn't have some terrible accident or end up in prison or dead—because that's where I was going," Hardy explained to Gareth McLean for the *Guardian* (22 June 2009). "Now I know my beast and I know how to manage it."

RISE TO ACTING PROMINENCE

After getting out of rehab, Hardy reestablished his career on the British stage, "a place you can totally humiliate yourself and explore a character," as he put it to Steinberg. In 2003 he won the London Evening Standard Theatre Award for outstanding newcomer for his performances in Stephen Adly Guirgis's play *In Arabia, We'd All Be Kings* at the Hampstead Theatre and Lars Norn's *Blood* at the Royal Court Theatre. Also that year he costarred in the Jeff Noon drama *The Modernists* at the Crucible with Jesse Spencer, Paul Popplewell, and Orlando Wells.

Over the next several years, Hardy worked steadily in a wide variety of roles as a television, film, and stage actor. In 2005 he portrayed Robert Dudley, Earl of Leicester, in the BBC four-part miniseries *The Virgin Queen*, about the life of Queen Elizabeth I. The following year he costarred in the BBC television movie *A for Andromeda*, a remake of the 1961 science fiction series of the same name, and he cofounded his own repertory company, Shotgun Theatre Company, directing a play written by his father called *Blue on Blue*. Meanwhile, Hardy appeared as a dapper henchman in Matthew Vaughn's high-octane British crime thriller *Layer Cake* (2004), a sarcastic aristocrat in Sofia Coppola's stylish period drama *Marie Antoinette* (2006), and an awkward young man in Ed Blum's ensemble comedy *Scenes of a Sexual Nature* (2006).

In 2007 Hardy played the title character in the BBC drama *Stuart: A Life Backwards*, an adaptation of the biography by Alexander Masters about his friend Stuart Shorter, a homeless drug addict and criminal who suffered from muscular dystrophy. For his portrayal of Stuart, Hardy, who shed nearly thirty pounds in a month to obtain an emaciated appearance, received a best actor nomination from the British Academy of Film and Television Arts (BAFTA) in 2008.

Hardy played the part of a gay gangster, Handsome Bob, in Guy Ritchie's slick, London-based crime film *RocknRolla* (2008), which starred Gerard Butler, Tom Wilkinson, and Idris Elba. That same year, Hardy underwent another dramatic physical transformation to play Britain's most notorious prisoner, Michael Gordon Peterson, who is better known by his boxing name Charles Bronson, in Danish director Nicolas Winding Refn's provocative biopic *Bronson* (2008). Hardy shaved his head, grew a handlebar mustache, and packed on thirty pounds

of muscle for the role, which proved to be his breakthrough. His bravura performance earned him a British Independent Film Award for best actor and brought him to the attention of Hollywood. "He wants to be your instrument," Winding Refn said of Hardy's willingness to inhabit roles to Junod. "He wants you to be part of him, he wants you to devour him, he wants you to use him up."

MAINSTREAM STARDOM

In 2009 Hardy received critical acclaim for his starring roles in two British television productions, *The Take*, a four-part Sky 1 series based on crime novelist Martina Cole's 2005 book of the same name, in which he plays a psychotic East End gangster named Freddie Jackson, and *Wuthering Heights*, an ITV adaptation of Emily Brontë's classic novel, in which he plays the tormented romantic hero Heathcliff.

Hardy's profile rose considerably in 2010, when he appeared in Christopher Nolan's mind-bending psychological thriller *Inception*. In the film, Hardy plays a debonair, wisecracking British forger named Eames, who is part of a group of mercenary dream thieves assembled by main character Dom Cobb, portrayed by Leonardo DiCaprio. He was singled out by critics for his comic, scene-stealing turn in the film, which, in addition to DiCaprio, featured an all-star cast that included Ken Watanabe, Ellen Page, Joseph Gordon-Levitt, Marion Cotillard, Cillian Murphy, Tom Berenger, and Michael Caine. *Inception* won four Academy Awards and grossed more than $800 million worldwide, making it one of the most commercially successful films of all time.

The year 2010 also saw Hardy make his American stage debut in the Brett C. Leonard play *The Long Red Road*, which was directed by the late Academy Award–winning actor Philip Seymour Hoffman and staged at Chicago's Goodman Theatre. He won rave reviews for his riveting portrayal of Sam, a chronic alcoholic living a hopeless existence. "I think the experience that people had in the 1950s of seeing Marlon Brando on stage experienced the exact same thing as seeing Tom Hardy on stage," Robert Falls, the artistic director at the Goodman Theatre, opined to Steinberg. Falls added that Hardy brought "a sort of sensitivity [to the role], like Brando, where he was both extraordinarily masculine but in touch with a feminine side as well."

In 2011 Hardy played a rogue agent opposite Gary Oldman in Tomas Alfredson's *Tinker Tailor Soldier Spy*, an adaptation of the 1974 spy novel of the same name by John le Carré. Hardy also costarred in Gavin O'Connor's mixed martial arts film *Warrior* (2011), as a troubled ex-Marine who enters the same fighting competition as his estranged older brother, played by Joel

Edgerton. Both *Tinker Tailor Soldier Spy* and *Warrior* received widespread praise from critics, most of whom wrote glowingly of Hardy's performances. Commenting on those performances in an article for *GQ* magazine (16 Dec. 2011), Tom Carson stated that Hardy has "a way of making movies curl around him for however long he's on-screen . . . no kind of movie is alien to him."

THE DARK KNIGHT RISES AND OTHER ROLES
Hardy reunited with Nolan a second time in 2012, when he played menacing supervillain Bane in *The Dark Knight Rises*, the third and final installment in the director's Batman film trilogy. For his portrayal of the masked antagonist, Hardy again transformed his body, shaving his head and gaining thirty pounds of muscle. He also created a voice modeled after that of real-life Irish Traveler bare-knuckle fighter Bartley Gorman, "a voice—intense in its artificiality, its almost Elizabethan resonance, and its menace," Junod wrote. Like *Inception*, *The Dark Knight Rises* was a box-office juggernaut, grossing more than $1.1 billion worldwide, making it the tenth highest-grossing films of all time. Bane, meanwhile, became one of Hardy's most famous film roles.

Also in 2012 Hardy gave a standout performance as Virginia bootlegger Forrest Bondurant in John Hillcoat's *Lawless*, a violent, Prohibition-era drama that costarred Shia LaBeouf, Jason Clarke, Jessica Chastain, Guy Pearce, and Gary Oldman. In addition, he starred opposite Chris Pine and Reese Witherspoon in the romantic comedy *This Means War* (2012).

In 2013 Hardy delivered his "most unvarnished performance yet," according to Kyle Buchanan for *Vulture* magazine (25 Apr. 2014), as Welsh construction manager Ivan Locke in the ambitious thriller *Locke*, written and directed by Steven Knight. The eighty-five-minute film consists solely of Hardy driving alone in his car and talking to various people on the phone via Bluetooth in a Welsh accent inspired by Richard Burton. *Locke* opened to rave reviews at that year's Venice Film Festival and was later screened at the 2014 Sundance Film Festival; it was released in the United States and Britain in April 2014.

In 2013, Hardy began filming for *The Drop* (2014), in which he appears as Brooklyn bartender Bob Saginoski opposite the late actor James Gandolfini (in his final feature film role), a crime drama directed by Michael R. Roskam and written by Dennis Lehane.

Hardy was married to producer Sarah Ward from 1999 to 2004 and is now married to the British actress Charlotte Riley, his costar in *The Take* and *Wuthering Heights*. He has a son, Louis, from a previous relationship with Rachael Speed.

SUGGESTED READING
Carson, Tom. "GQ's New Favorite Hardy Boy." *GQ*. Condé Nast, 16 Dec. 2011. Web. 3 Sept. 2014.
Conrad, Peter. "'Maybe Feeling Alive Is Only Possible in the Presence of Death.'" *Observer*. Guardian News and Media, 22 Sept. 2007. Web. 3 Sept. 2014.
Fisher, Alice. "Tom Hardy: The Rake's Progress." *Observer*. Guardian News and Media, 3 July 2010. Web. 3 Sept. 2014.
Hiscock, John. "Tom Hardy: Real-life Blows That Shaped My Acting." *Telegraph*. Telegraph Media Group, 25 Aug. 2011. Web. 3 Sept. 2014.
Junod, Tom. "Hey, Isn't That Tom Hardy, the Greatest Actor of His Generation?" *Esquire*. Hearst Communications, 22 Apr. 2014. Web. 3 Sept. 2014.
McLean, Gareth. "'I Want Adulation.'" *Guardian*. Guardian News and Media, 22 June 2009. Web. 3 Sept. 2014.
Steinberg, Don. "Tom Hardy on His Upcoming Roles and Acting Inspirations." *Wall Street Journal*. Dow Jones, 17 Apr. 2014. Web. 3 Sept. 2014.

SELECTED WORKS
Band of Brothers, 2001; *Black Hawk Down*, 2001; *Star Trek: Nemesis*, 2002; *Stuart: A Life Backwards*, 2007; *Bronson*, 2008; *Inception*, 2010; *The Long Red Road*, 2010; *Warrior*, 2011; *Lawless*, 2012; *The Dark Knight Rises*, 2012; *Locke*, 2013

—Chris Cullen

Calvin Harris
Born: January 17, 1984
Occupation: DJ and record producer

Scottish DJ and music producer Calvin Harris is among a group of artists widely credited with popularizing electronic dance music (EDM) in mainstream America. Like many DJs, Harris began by making music at home before being discovered on the social-networking site MySpace in 2006, the year he landed his first major recording contract. He burst onto the music scene the following year, with the release of his debut full-length album *I Created Disco* (2007), which featured the electro-pop hits "Acceptable in the 80s" and "The Girls." Harris's next album, *Ready for the Weekend* (2009), spawned the number-one hit "I'm Not Alone" and debuted at number one on the UK albums chart. After transitioning from a live solo act and vocalist to a DJ cum

Jeff Spicer/Alpha/Landov

music producer in 2010, Harris began making a name for himself in the American music scene as a top-notch songwriter and producer. He was catapulted to fame in 2011 after writing and producing the pop singer Rihanna's international smash hit "We Found Love." The song was included on Harris's third studio album, *18 Months* (2012), which broke the UK chart record for most Top 10 singles from one album.

In addition to Rihanna, Harris has written, produced, and remixed tracks for such artists as All Saints, Kylie Minogue, Dizzee Rascal, Shakira, Katy Perry, and Sophie Ellis-Bextor. "He is the go-to producer for many pop stars," the legendary British DJ and producer Dave Seaman told John Dingwall for the Glasgow, Scotland *Daily Record* (24 July 2013). "Everybody wants a Calvin record because he is very good at the sound of electronic dance music, which is the sound of the zeitgeist at the moment." In 2013 Harris was listed by *Forbes* magazine as the highest-earning DJ in the world.

EARLY LIFE AND EDUCATION

Calvin Harris was born Adam Richard Wiles on January 17, 1984, in Dumfries, a town in southwest Scotland. (He created the stage name Calvin Harris from the combination of the names of R&B singer Calvin Richardson and producer Andre Harris.) His father, David, is a biochemist, and his mother, Pamela, is a homemaker. Harris is the youngest of three children. An avid soccer fan growing up, he initially aspired to be a professional soccer player before turning his attention toward music. Harris first became

drawn to electronic dance music in his early teens and was an early fan of such artists as the pioneering British DJ-producer Fatboy Slim (the stage name of Norman Cook) and the legendary French house duo Daft Punk.

At fourteen Harris began experimenting with music production on an antiquated Amiga 500 computer. He used sounds from computer games to create minimalist dance tracks and soon started sending out hundreds of demos to record producers and DJs. "I just got obsessed with it and spent all my time trying to make songs," Harris told Guy Raz in an interview for National Public Radio's news program *All Things Considered* (7 Dec. 2012), also admitting that his newfound passion took precedence over his studies at Dumfries High School. "I was doing it instead of going to high school, which I don't recommend," Harris explained.

SELF-TAUGHT DJ TO MYSPACE SENSATION

After finishing high school, Harris bypassed university to pursue his burgeoning music career. He took on a number of odd jobs to finance new DJ gear and equipment. He first stocked shelves at a series of local supermarkets and then worked at a fish market. By the time he was eighteen, Harris had released his first two singles, "Da Bongos" and "Brighter Days," under the moniker Stouffer, on the Prima Facie label.

In 2003, with around £4,000 in savings, Harris left Scotland and moved to London, England, in an attempt to make it in the music industry, as he told Craig McLean for the London *Independent* (2 Aug. 2009). The bold endeavor, however, proved to be short-lived: the city's high cost of living combined with the ultra-competitive music scene in London forced Harris to move back home with his parents after a year. During that time he released only one song, "Let Me Know," with the Jordanian singer Ayah Marar, which was featured on the Unabombers' 2004 compilation album *Electric Soul 2*. Upon returning home, Harris recalled to Ryan Mac for *Forbes* (14 Aug. 2013), "I was . . . just thinking like, 'That's probably it, that's my attempt.'"

Harris turned his fortunes around after he joined the social-networking site MySpace, which helped to bring his music to a wider audience. Harris's big break came in 2006, when he was discovered on MySpace by the Brooklyn-based DJ and producer Tommie Sunshine. Soon afterward, Harris landed recording and publishing deals with Sony BMG and EMI, respectively. He also acquired a manager, Mark Gillespie, who quickly signed him to his newly formed entertainment company Three Six Zero Group. By the end of 2006, Harris had begun working on his first full-length album and lending his talents to other artists, including the British girl group All Saints.

I CREATED DISCO AND RISE TO FAME

Harris's popularity rose considerably in 2007 with the release of the hit electro-pop anthems "Acceptable in the 80s" and "The Girls," both of which made the Top 10 on the UK singles chart, reaching number ten and three, respectively. In June of that year, he released his debut full-length album, *I Created Disco*, which settled on the UK charts at number eight and sold more than 200,000 copies. The album featured fourteen tracks, all of which were exclusively written, produced, and performed by Harris and characterized by "old-school house rhythms and funky basslines," as Adrian Thrills noted for the London *Daily Mail* (6 Aug. 2009). In addition to "Acceptable in the 80s" and "The Girls," the album included the singles "Vegas," "Merrymaking at My Place," and "Colours," which was used in television advertisements for the British furniture retailer DFS and the South-Korean auto manufacturer KIA Motors. The cover of the album, which showed a black and white image of Harris's face juxtaposed against a bright yellow background, was used in a US advertising campaign by Apple to promote the fourth-generation iPod Nano in 2008.

Though *I Created Disco* received a largely tepid critical response, the album's commercial success helped Harris land touring gigs as an opening act for such electronic headliners as Groove Armada and Faithless. It also brought Harris to the attention of artists such as Australian pop sensation Kylie Minogue, who hired him to write and produce two songs, "Heart Beat Rock" and "In My Arms," for her 2007 comeback album *X*. "Heart Beat Rock" incorporated elements of synthpop, retro, and modern dance music, which reached number ten on the UK charts.

Harris next produced and contributed vocals to the Mercury Prize–winning Ghanaian-British artist Dizzee Rascal's hit single "Dance wiv Me," which featured Dizzee's signature rhymes over an infectious dance beat. Released in June 2008, the song, which also featured guest vocals by the British R&B singer Chrome, reached number one on the UK singles chart, holding the top spot for four consecutive weeks and selling over 600,000 copies. That success suddenly made Harris "a bona fide pop star," according to Craig McLean, and helped him secure a deal with the US electronic dance music label Ultra Records.

READY FOR THE WEEKEND AND COLLABORATOR TO THE STARS

Unhappy with the rushed nature of *I Created Disco*, Harris approached his sophomore album with the intention of making "a big, commercial record" that featured "classic dance music in a modern environment," as he told Adrian Thrills. The much-anticipated album, *Ready for the Weekend*, was eventually released in August 2009 and debuted at number one on the UK albums chart, holding the top spot for two consecutive weeks; it peaked at number twelve on the *Billboard* dance/electronic albums chart and sold over 100,000 copies in the UK. The album was preceded by the release of the hit singles "I'm Not Alone" and the title track "Ready for the Weekend," which reached number one and three, respectively, on the UK charts. It also included the singles "Flashback" and "You Used to Hold Me" and an extended remix of the song "Dance wiv Me." Another song, "Yeah Yeah Yeah La La La," was used in a European ad campaign for Coca-Cola in 2009. In a review of *Ready for the Weekend* for the AllMusic website, John Bush commented that the album boasted "more energy, more hooks, more professionalism, and, in places, a little more sincerity" than Harris's debut, and called it "an enjoyable amalgam of dance energy and pop focus."

Harris spent most of 2009 touring in support of *Ready for the Weekend*, performing as a solo act with a full live band at gigs and festivals throughout Europe and the United States. During this time he became an in-demand producer, songwriter, and remixer, working on songs for some of the biggest names in the music industry. In the summer of 2009, Harris teamed up with Dizzee Rascal again to produce and write Rascal's single, "Holiday," which, like their previous collaboration, reached number one on the UK charts. That summer Harris provided vocals and cowrote the song "Century" for Dutch musician, DJ, and producer Tiësto. The song appeared on Tiësto's fourth studio album *Kaleidoscope* (2009). Harris also remixed songs for Colombian singer/songwriter Shakira ("She Wolf") and American performer Katy Perry ("Waking Up in Vegas").

CAREER TRANSFORMATION AND "WE FOUND LOVE"

Harris reached a turning point in his career in mid-2010 after wrapping up his *Ready for the Weekend* tour. Wanting to move away from his live shows and singing responsibilities, he turned his attention to DJ sets and music production. "I just want to make things that I enjoy creating," Harris said in an interview with Simon Hampson for the Australian music and arts magazine *Beat* (1 Dec. 2010). "They should be tunes that make me happy, make others happy and make them want to dance." Mark Gillespie later explained to Ryan Mac that Harris "felt more comfortable behind a set of turntables than on a stage. He made what felt to everybody . . . like a natural evolution at the perfect time."

Harris made his career transformation at a time when EDM was beginning to enjoy unprecedented mainstream popularity in the United States. While it had long been a part of Europe's mainstream culture, it remained largely an underground phenomenon in North America until the late 1990s. However, with the rise of technology, social media, and superstar DJ-producers like Tiësto and Frenchman David Guetta in the 2000s, pop and R&B artists began experimenting with electronic music. Harris began using his DJ sets to debut new material while continuing to do production work for other artists. He produced the track "Time Machine" for the British rapper Example's second studio album *Won't Go Quietly* (2010) and "Off & On" for British singer Sophie Ellis-Bextor's fourth studio album *Make a Scene* (2011).

Harris's most fruitful musical collaboration came in 2011 when he worked on material for Barbadian singing sensation Rihanna. Harris wrote and produced the dance-powered electro-house track "We Found Love," which appeared on Rihanna's sixth album *Talk That Talk* (2011). The album spent ten nonconsecutive weeks atop the Billboard Hot 100 chart, became a worldwide hit, and sold over five million copies in the United States. The video for "We Found Love," which Harris appeared in, won Video of the Year at the 2012 MTV Video Music Awards ceremony, where Harris also served as the house DJ. One year after the song's release, Allison Stewart wrote for the *Washington Post* (29 Oct. 2012) that "We Found Love" was "to EDM crossover songs what T-Rex was to dinosaurs."

18 MONTHS

"We Found Love" was one of fifteen tracks featured on Harris's long-awaited third studio album, *18 Months*, which was released in October 2012. In addition to Rihanna, the album featured collaborations with the American R&B singers Kelis and Ne-Yo, Example, Dizzee Rascal, Florence Welch from the indie rock band Florence + The Machine, and the British dance-pop singer Ellie Goulding. The album debuted at the top of the UK albums chart and also reached the top spot on the Billboard dance/electronic albums chart; it peaked at number nineteen on the Billboard 200 album chart. The album's release was preceded by five singles—"Bounce" and "Feel So Close" in 2011 and "Let's Go," "We'll Be Coming Back," and "Sweet Nothing" in 2012—all of which reached the Top 10 on the UK singles chart. Subsequent singles "Drinking from the Bottle," "I Need Your Love," and "Thinking About You" also reached the Top 10. Harris became the first artist in UK chart history to have nine Top 10 singles from one album, surpassing Michael Jackson's previous record of seven Top 10s from his 1991 album *Dangerous*. By late 2013, *18 Months* had sold over 650,000 copies in the UK and more than twenty-five million singles worldwide.

Critical reception to *18 Months* was mixed to positive. In a review for the *New York Times* (2 Nov. 2012), Jon Caramanica observed that the album featured "bits of trance and big beat and progressive house and other king-size dance genres of the last 15 years" but concluded that it was mostly comprised of "style-agnostic club music, beholden to a structural blueprint than to a particular set of finishes." Allison Stewart commented, "Harris's beats are basic and repetitive, which is different than saying they're bad. There's a giddy urgency to even his middling material and a heavy reliance on collaborations." Tim Sendra further noted for the AllMusic website that the whole album was largely characterized by "melancholy and romantic lyrics, impassioned vocal build-ups, and pounding techno beats all coated with layers of shiny synths," it showed "Harris to be a solid producer with an easily identifiable sound."

AWARDS AND DISTINCTIONS

Harris received a number of awards and distinctions in 2013. In February he won in the best short form video category for "We Found Love" (shared with Rihanna) at the 55th Annual Grammy Awards ceremony, marking the first Grammy win of his career. In April he became the first DJ-producer in history to win the prestigious Songwriter of the Year award at the Ivor Novello Awards. Also that month Harris became the first resident DJ at the MGM Grand Hotel & Casino's newly opened nightclub and restaurant complex Hakkasan Las Vegas, where he was scheduled to play a total of forty-six dates. In July 2013 Harris ranked first on *Forbes* magazine's second annual list of the highest-earning DJs in the world, with an estimated $46 million in earnings over the previous twelve months. He was also listed by *Forbes* as the fourth-highest celebrity earner under the age of thirty, behind Lady Gaga, Justin Bieber, and Taylor Swift. Commenting on his future aspirations, Harris, who commands up to $300,000 per DJ gig, told Ryan Mac, "I like to think I don't have an ego [that's] like you need to be number one—the best, the DJ of all time. I want to be the number one songwriter-producer guy of all time."

In 2009, Harris founded the vanity music label Fly Eye Records through which he has released and sold his own and other artists' new music. He has been romantically linked to the British-Albanian singer Rita Ora since May 2013.

SUGGESTED READING

Hampp, Andrew. "Hey, Mr. DJ." *Billboard* 21 Apr. 2012: 22–23. Print.

Hampson, Simon. "Calvin Harris." *Beat*. Furst Media, 1 Dec. 2010. Web. 4 Nov. 2013.

Kaufman, Gil. "Calvin Harris' Road to the VMAs: From the Bedroom to the Big Show." *MTV.com*. Viacom International, 3 Sept. 2012. Web. 4 Nov. 2013.

Mac, Ryan. "EDM's $46 Million Man: How Calvin Harris Became the World's Highest-Paid DJ." *Forbes*. Forbes.com, 14 Aug. 2013. Web. 4 Nov. 2013.

McLean, Craig. "Calvin Harris: How the Non-Dancing, Foul-Mouthed, Anti-Social Scot Became the 'Caledonian Justin Timberlake.'" *Independent*. Independent.co.uk, 2 Aug. 2009. Web. 4 Nov. 2013.

Raz, Guy. "Calvin Harris On Dance-Pop as a 'Futuristic Experiment.'" *NPR*. NPR, 7 Dec. 2012. Web. 4 Nov. 2013.

SELECTED WORKS
I Created Disco, 2007; *Ready for the Weekend*, 2009; *18 Months*, 2012

—*Chris Cullen*

Getty Images

Kamala Harris

Born: October 20, 1964
Occupation: Attorney

Kamala D. Harris was elected attorney general of California in 2010, becoming both the first African American woman and the first Asian American woman to hold the position. She is a rising star in the Democratic Party and is often cited as a potential gubernatorial or presidential candidate, though by early 2014 she had not yet announced plans to run for either office. In 2013, Harris was included in *Time* magazine's list of the world's one hundred most influential people for her progressive vision of California.

The foundation of Harris's reputation was built in the courtroom. As a prosecutor, she was known for taking tough cases, such as child sexual abuse, to trial. She is motivated by a lifelong yearning for social justice and wants to change people's perceptions of how the Democratic Party deals with crime. "Democrats often give the impression that we just want to open the jailhouse door and let everybody out," she told Karen Breslau for *More* magazine (6 Apr. 2009). "The public wants to know that we can keep them safe. If it's always the Republicans or conservatives who come up with the plan, we will lose the debate. The old paradigm isn't working: 'Are you soft on crime or hard on crime?' We should be asking, 'Are you smart on crime?'" In 2009, Harris published a book called *Smart on Crime* about her experiences as a prosecutor.

For Harris, being "smart on crime" means changing the nature of the criminal justice system—the relationship between law enforcement and those who break the law. As the district attorney for San Francisco, a position she held from 2003 to 2010, Harris reached out to at-risk teens through preventative initiatives and placed a new emphasis on protecting crime victims over simply incarcerating criminals. In 2005, she created a reentry program for nonviolent first-time drug offenders called Back on Track. The program was created in response to what she described in the *Huffington Post* (9 Nov. 2009) as a "sad cycle" of repeat low-level drug offenders shuffling in and out of an already bloated prison system.

Back on Track costs taxpayers about $5,000 per offender, versus county jail, which costs $35,000 per offender per year. It is a more measured approach to crime and criminals than California's existing "three strikes" law, which was enacted in 1994 and mandates a minimum sentence of twenty-five years to life for third-time felons. The law flooded the prison system and, according to a study published in the *California Journal of Politics and Policy*, had no effect on the crime rate. The Back on Track program has been successful because it seeks to address the underlying causes of criminal behavior. "A district attorney will usually not take the lead on prevention," Joan Petersilia, codirector of the Stanford University Criminal Justice Center, told Phil Willon for the *Los Angeles Times* (20 Oct. 2010). "Historically, they are putting people in prison, not keeping people out of prison, and that's what makes [Harris] unique."

EARLY LIFE AND EDUCATION
Kamala Devi Harris was born on October 20, 1964, in Oakland, California. Her father, Donald Harris, was an immigrant from Jamaica who later became an economist and professor at Stanford. Her mother, Dr. Shyamala Gopalan, was an Indian-born breast cancer researcher whose

father, Harris's grandfather, served as joint secretary for the Indian government. "He was one of the original freedom fighters in India," Harris told Bob Egelko for the *San Francisco Chronicle* (7 Nov. 2012). "He would talk all the time about the importance of honest government." According to Steve Kaplan for the magazine *Super Lawyers* (Aug. 2010), Gopalan's mother, a progressive feminist, used to drive around Indian villages with a bullhorn, telling women to use birth control. Harris's parents divorced when she was five years old, and she and her younger sister, Maya, were both raised by their mother. Maya later served for five years as vice president for democracy, rights, and justice at the Ford Foundation before becoming a senior fellow at the Center for American Progress.

Harris was profoundly influenced by her early participation in the civil rights movement. Her parents had met through the movement while they were both graduate students at the University of California, Berkeley; when Harris was a toddler, her mother took her to rallies in a stroller. "My early memories are of a sea of legs marching around the streets and the sounds of shouting," she wrote in her book, *Smart on Crime*. During her early teens, she lived in Montreal for a few years while her mother worked at the Jewish General Hospital and taught at McGill University. While there, the thirteen-year-old Harris organized the other children in their housing complex in protest against a ban on children playing in the courtyard.

Lawyers, Harris told Sam Whiting for the *San Francisco Chronicle* (14 May 2009), "were the heroes growing up. They were the architects of the civil rights movement. I thought that that was the way you do good things and serve and achieve justice." From an early age, she admired figures such as Thurgood Marshall, the lawyer who successfully argued the landmark *Brown v. Board of Education* case before the Supreme Court and later became the court's first African American justice, and Constance Baker Motley, the activist who became the first African American female federal judge. Harris attended Howard University, a historically black college in Washington, DC, where she protested South African apartheid, worked for California then-senator Alan Cranston and polling consultant Peter D. Hart, and volunteered for Walter Mondale's 1984 presidential campaign. She earned her bachelor's degree in 1986 and went on to the University of California's Hastings College of Law in San Francisco, where she was president of the Black Law Students Association and volunteered for Jesse Jackson's 1988 presidential campaign. She earned her juris doctorate in 1989.

EARLY CAREER

In 1990, Harris began working as a deputy district attorney in Alameda County in San Francisco's East Bay. She cut her teeth prosecuting sex crimes against children and established a solid reputation for winning over juries. Harris told Peter Byrne for *SF Weekly* (24 Sept. 2003) that prosecuting child abuse cases was particularly difficult because jurors tend to take the word of an adult over the word of a child. Of her closing argument strategy, she told Kaplan, "You should always show the jury the math, and let them arrive at the sum, instead of arguing the sum and telling them to bring the verdict to that sum." In 1994, she took a six-month leave of absence to join the Unemployment Appeals Board.

In 1998, Harris left Alameda County to work for Terence Hallinan, the district attorney of San Francisco. She managed the career-criminal unit, focusing on cases in which the offense was a third strike, and personally prosecuted three cases, one of which was a homicide. She excelled in her work but saw Hallinan's office as overly politicized and inept. In 2000, Harris and a few of her colleagues attempted to oust Hallinan's chief deputy, Darrell Salomon, but failed.

Harris quit her job and found a position in the San Francisco city attorney's office, where she headed a division that dealt with cases of domestic violence, child abuse, building-code enforcement, and public health. In 2003, at age thirty-nine, Harris challenged her old boss for his job as district attorney. Hallinan was a popular two-term incumbent, but Harris painted him as an incompetent, far-flung lefty, more focused on legalizing marijuana and demonizing the police force than on fighting crime. (Both Harris and Hallinan are Democrats.) Harris's shrewd tactics were effective. During the campaign, the powerful San Francisco County Democratic Central Committee voted not to endorse either candidate in the race. It was the first time the committee had chosen not to endorse an incumbent.

In December 2003, Harris beat Hallinan 56 to 44 percent in a run-off election. In her victory speech, as quoted by Demian Bulwa for the *San Francisco Chronicle* (10 Dec. 2003), she vowed to make the district attorney's office "an office we can be proud of and an office that takes seriously prosecuting crime and rehabilitating offenders."

DISTRICT ATTORNEY OF SAN FRANCISCO

Harris got her first taste of political controversy early in her career as San Francisco's district attorney. In April 2004, a twenty-nine-year-old undercover police officer named Isaac Espinoza was shot to death by a gang member. Several days after the killing, Harris publicly announced that, in accordance with the philosophical beliefs on which she based her campaign, she would not seek the death penalty for Espinoza's accused killer. Among her loudest critics were the mayor and the state attorney general at the time, Jerry Brown and Bill Lockyer, as well as US senator Dianne Feinstein—not to mention the public, the San Francisco police force, and Espinoza's family. "She made the decision after just three days," said Carol Espinoza, the victim's mother, as quoted by Willon. "My son wasn't even in the ground yet."

Despite overwhelming pressure, Harris defended her position and even took the same stance when another grisly case garnered public support for the death penalty in 2008. "I feel it's a flawed system," Harris told Willon. "With the advent of DNA, we know that people have been convicted and sentenced to death who later proved not to be guilty of the crime. That's at the top of the list of my concerns." Espinoza's killer was ultimately convicted of second-degree murder and sentenced to life in prison.

In 2005, Harris introduced the successful Back on Track program, which offered first-time offenders a new way to make their reentry into society. Instead of being given a bus ticket and a bit of cash on their way out of jail, offenders facing their first felony conviction were given an immediate choice: agree to a strict "personal responsibility plan" or go to prison. The plan requires participants, who tend to be in their twenties, to earn a high school equivalency certificate, maintain a steady job, complete classes in life skills such as finance and parenting, and meet with a judge every other week for a year. Upon successful completion of the program, the felony charge is cleared from the offender's record. Participants who are unsuccessful in the program serve time. "For this population, the recidivism (or reoffense rate) is typically 50 percent or higher," Harris wrote in the *Huffington Post*. "Four years since the creation of this initiative, recidivism has been less than 10 percent among Back on Track graduates."

During her time as San Francisco's district attorney, Harris raised the city's conviction rate to just over 70 percent. She also placed greater emphasis on prosecuting environmental and financial crimes. In 2007, she ran for a second term unopposed.

ATTORNEY GENERAL

In 2010, Harris ran for state attorney general against Los Angeles County district attorney Steve Cooley, a Republican. It was a hard-fought race on both sides. According to Willon, Cooley portrayed Harris as "a 'radical' too concerned about the welfare and rights of criminals whom many California voters would rather leave behind bars." He rekindled the ire surrounding her views on capital punishment and used another incident during her career, in which she had failed to disclose information about a scandal involving a laboratory technician with the San Francisco Police Department, as ammunition against her. The race was one of the closest statewide races in California history. Cooley actually declared victory on election night, only

to retract his speech the next day. Three weeks later, in late November, Harris was declared the winner.

During her time as California's state attorney general, Harris has focused on cases of human trafficking. She also secured an $18 billion settlement for California homeowners following the bank foreclosure crisis. In November 2013, she announced the launch of a statewide initiative to reduce recidivism, based on the successful Back on Track program she had established in San Francisco.

PERSONAL LIFE

Harris was an early supporter of President Barack Obama, and *More* magazine followed her through a neighborhood in Des Moines as she campaigned for him on the afternoon of the 2008 Iowa caucus. In 2012, the president was criticized for referring to Harris as the "best-looking attorney general in the country" at a Democratic National Committee luncheon in Atherton, California. Many felt that the remark belittled her professional achievements, which he had touted moments before. The president quickly apologized for his gaffe.

In 1994, Harris dated former San Francisco mayor Willie Brown, who was at the time the speaker of the California Assembly. Harris dumped him after his mayoral inauguration in 1995, but the relationship caused her an enormous amount of grief during her 2003 campaign. Asked alternately to defend or distance herself from him, Harris was furious. "His career is over; I will be alive and kicking for the next forty years," she told Byrne of Brown, who left office in 2004 after reaching the limit of his mayoral term. "I do not owe him a thing."

Harris began dating Los Angeles lawyer Douglas Emhoff in 2013. In April 2014, Harris announced the couple's engagement and said that she and Emhoff would maintain homes in both San Francisco and Los Angeles.

SUGGESTED READING
Breslau, Karen. "'Female Obama' Wins in California." *More*. Meredith, 6 Apr. 2009. Web. 8 Apr. 2014.

Egelko, Bob. "Kamala Harris Mixing Idealism, Political Savvy." *SFGate*. Hearst Communications, 7 Nov. 2012. Web. 8 Apr. 2014.

Garchik, Leah. "California Attorney General Kamala Harris Engaged." *SFGate*. Hearst Communications, 7 Apr. 2014. Web. 8 Apr. 2014.

Harris, Kamala. "Brilliant Careers." Interview by Steve Kaplan. *Super Lawyers*. Thomson Reuters, Aug. 2010. Web. 8 Apr. 2014.

Harris, Kamala. "Finding the Path Back on Track." *Huffington Post*. TheHuffingtonPost. com, 9 Nov. 2009. Web. 8 Apr. 2014.

Harris, Kamala. "Kamala Harris Grew Up Idolizing Lawyers." Interview by Sam Whiting.

SFGate. Hearst Communications, 14 May 2009. Web. 8 Apr. 2014.

Willon, Phil. "Kamala Harris Is a Different Kind of Prosecutor." *Los Angeles Times*. Los Angeles Times, 20 Oct. 2010. Web. 8 Apr. 2014.

—Molly Hagan

Imogen Heap

Born: December 9, 1977
Occupation: Singer and composer

Imogen Heap is a twenty-first-century musical pioneer who finds innovative ways to make, distribute, and stretch the boundaries of her music. Over the course of four solo albums and her work in the duo Frou Frou with Guy Sigsworth, she has sought to push the edge of electronic music beyond the expectations of both professional music critics and her fans. The result has been an eclectic, layered, and nuanced style of electronic music that remains markedly unique, in large part because she often makes everyday sounds serve as the foundations for her songs. In addition to collaborating online with her fans in the creation of her songs, she has developed the Mi.Mu gloves, wearable-tech gloves that allow her to create and manipulate music with hand gestures. Believing that anyone can be musical, Heap hopes that the gloves will eventually be mass marketed.

Despite years of hard work as an independent musician who is not signed with a record label, Heap continues to enjoy the process of making her music and selling it online. This work was rewarded in 2010, when her third solo album, *Ellipse* (2009), won the Grammy Award for best nonclassical engineered album. Her latest album, *Sparks*, was released in August 2014, but singles she wrote for it had been released online over the previous three years, thanks to fans who have contributed "sound seeds" to the songs' production. A natural optimist, Heap remains committed to creating her kind of music on her terms, despite any obstacles that might get in her way. She told Stuart Dredge for the *Guardian* (3 June 2014), "Many times in my career I've been really frustrated, but usually some good comes from it, maybe a couple of months or even a whole year afterwards. A label might mess me over, but it'll give me an opportunity. Often, when something's gone bad, it's because it's reached a natural end and really wasn't working. I like finding solutions."

EARLY LIFE AND CAREER

Imogen Heap was born in Havering, a borough of London, England, on December 9, 1977. She was raised in Essex and studied at the BRIT

© Frank Trapper/Corbis

School for Performing Arts and Technology in South London. Through her mother—who had named her Imogen after the cello-playing daughter of famed composer Gustav Holst—she gained a passion for music during her childhood. She told Geary Yelton for *Electronic Musician* (Oct. 2009), "I learned the piano, so I learned harmony [and] counterpoint through that. And then I learned the clarinet [and] cello, so I understood different parts of the orchestra and how they work with each other. And I studied composition and arrangement, not to a great degree, not even to a degree level, just for the love of it." While attending boarding schools, she branched out from classical music when she discovered Europop, electronica, and alternative rock.

She also developed an early fascination with the confluence of music and technology. After receiving a keyboard when she was eight years old, she began recording herself with her brother's tape recorder. At twelve, she discovered that she could play her compositions directly into her Atari computer via Musical Instrument Digital Interface (MIDI) without having written them down first. At nineteen, her purchase of a looping machine showed her that she could record a piece and be more than one musician on an individual song. But by that time, she was well on her way to becoming a professional musician.

Heap's debut album, *I Megaphone*—released by Almo Sounds in 1998—immediately earned comparisons to the records of Kate Bush, Annie Lennox, and Björk for its alternative rock stylings. Her experience on that first album brought her into contact with three notable record producers, David Kahne, Dave Stewart, and Guy Sigsworth, who worked with Heap on various tracks. She felt a particular musical connection with Sigsworth, with whom she continued to work following the release of the record. Before long, the duo was collaborating so frequently that they had recorded enough material to fill an album. *Details* (2002), which they released as the pop duo Frou Frou, was unlike Heap's solo record, as the group's sound used a variety of electronics to create a very nuanced atmosphere. The record was met with considerable praise upon its release. James Roberts wrote for *Music Week* (11 May 2002), "It is one of the most commercially viable albums of the year and the best excuse in years for executives at their label Universal to be excited about a UK release."

SOLO ARTIST REDUX

Frou Frou's *Details* produced two singles: "Breathe In" and "Let Go," the latter of which became very popular two years after the album's release, having been included on the soundtrack for *Garden State* (2004), a film directed by Zack Braff and starring Braff and Natalie Portman. Heap recalled in an interview with Andrew Williams for *Metro* (23 Oct. 2006), "Zach put one of our songs in a really major scene in his film *Garden State*. We'd already split up at that point and lost our deal. That film came out and we ended up selling another 100,000 records just because of it. They used 'Let Go' in the trailers. I met him at a gig in LA. I thought I knew him so I ran up to him and gave him a hug and realized I'd never met him before."

Braff would insert another of Heap's songs, "Hide and Seek," into his film *The Last Kiss* (2006). That song, an a cappella piece with a digital harmonizer, was a single off Heap's second solo album, *Speak for Yourself* (2005), which also produced the single "Goodnight and Go." Like its predecessor, the album earned many warm words from professional critics. A writer for *Music Week* (6 May 2006) noted that her "sophomore solo effort sounds not a million miles away from *Details* . . . but that's no bad thing. It is clear from stunning opener 'Headlock' that the dulcet-toned Brit has taken the textured and layered approach of Frou Frou and advanced it to wonderful effect." Heap toured the United States on the back of this record and received rave reviews from music critics, including Laura Sinagra for the *New York Times* (13 Jan. 2006), who wrote, "Ms. Heap delivered a rendition of 'Hide and Seek' that could have made a robot weep."

EXPERIMENTAL AND COLLABORATIVE MUSIC

Although Heap has experimented with electronic music throughout her career, she took her efforts to an entirely new level while recording her third solo LP, *Ellipse*, which debuted in 2009. Two years prior to its release, she had purchased her childhood home in Essex, a two-century-old elliptical house, and converted her former childhood playroom into a high-tech recording studio that both was warm and inviting and reflected her idiosyncratic personality. In order to produce the music she would use on the album, she began to record various everyday sounds from around her home—including tap water dripping into her kitchen sink and her fingers running over wine glasses. Because she does not like the idea of being confined to her studio during the recording process, she also traveled to countries such as China, Japan, and Thailand in order to get more noises to provide a rich and nuanced sound. Throughout the recording process, she would go online to ask her fans what they thought of each song's progress, as she played with and tweaked sounds through her software. "I like music I can listen to over and over again," she told Geary Yelton for *Electronic Musician*. "I don't listen to my own music, but that's the kind of stuff I like, with details, and lots and lots of parts going on, but at the same time trying to keep a focus." *Ellipse* would go on to win the Grammy Award for best nonclassical engineered album in 2010. (At the awards ceremony, she wore a dress that flashed messages from fans across it; she called it the "Twitdress.")

When Heap began working on her fourth solo album, *Sparks*, in 2011, she again went online to the website SoundCloud, this time to solicit "sound seeds" from her fans. She asked them to provide their own samples of everyday sounds to help her with producing the first single from that LP, "Lifeline." The recording of *Sparks* allowed Heap to be innovative in a number of ways beyond asking fans to help produce the record's sound. She also raised money for the recording by crowdfunding on the website PledgeMusic and used the video site Vokle to audition musicians for a tour. Thirteen songs were recorded for *Sparks* over a three-year period, and the complete album was released in August 2014.

MI.MU GLOVES

During the production of *Sparks*, Heap worked with a development team led by an electronics designer named Tom Mitchell from the University of the West of England to design a pair of gloves that employ sensors, gyroscopes, and small microphones so she can control sounds by simply using hand gestures. She told Caspar Llewellyn Smith for the *Guardian* (23 Feb. 2012), "I can make things louder, I can make them quieter, stretching, I make drum beats, I can stretch sounds . . . I wanted to change the way that these things come across on stage, so I can record and loop sounds and then throw them across the stage." She had been inspired to create such wearable-tech gloves because she wanted electronic music to be as expressive and free as more traditional forms of music, by allowing electronic musicians to be uninhibited by their keyboards and consoles. Although the Mi.Mu gloves are, at the moment, an expensive prototype, she hopes they will someday enable virtually anyone to make their own music. She told Dredge, "I don't want [the gloves] to be a gimmick, because it just adds to the noise out there. Maybe they will, partly, but also become this incredible tool for people to feel free and get closer to that sound that's in their head, or the performance they want to give, without being hindered by that thing that's in front of them." With the goal of eventually developing the gloves beyond the prototype stage and making them affordable enough to market, Heap started a Kickstarter crowdfunding drive in the spring of 2014. While she was unable to raise the amount required to fund the project fully, she remains committed to her goal. In the meantime, the gloves challenge and excite her own musical creativity.

INSPIRATION AND FRUSTRATION
Making music digitally inspires Heap as much as the occasional technological glitches irritate her. She looks forward to a time when new and evolving technologies will be able to speak to older ones flawlessly, in the same way that various musical instruments developed in different eras can work together seamlessly in a band or orchestra. "It's the frustration of technology: we're at this point where there's lots of new software and new platforms being developed all the time, but the common language isn't quite there yet," Heap said in her interview with Dredge. "Eventually, there'll be almost an Esperanto for technology that will mean nothing has to be defunct or obsolete any more: things will continue to grow and learn and feed each other, like the semantic web. People have to be better at making things speak to one another."

INTERNET FOLLOWING
Heap has used the Internet not only to communicate with her fans but also to gauge their interest in the various pieces or songs she is composing, as well as to sell her music. By July 2014 she had more than two million followers on Twitter and maintained a robust presence on other social media and music websites, including Facebook, SoundCloud, and Myspace. Of her numerous fans, she says about three thousand of them are deeply involved with the production of her music, giving her creative feedback throughout every step of the process. In 2012 she conducted an online poll of her fans to learn more about them: 65 percent were under thirty-five; 52 percent were male, and 48 percent were female; 58 percent were musicians; and 41 percent had recorded a song. Heap's own music, which she releases on her own record label, is widely available for download on her own website, Imogenheap.com, as well as on iTunes and through streaming services such as Spotify and Pandora. Her music has been featured on the soundtracks of such television shows as *Six Feet Under*, *The O.C.*, and *The Vampire Diaries* and in films such as *The Chronicles of Narnia: The Lion, the Witch and the Wardrobe* (2005), *The Holiday* (2006), and *The Town* (2010). Heap hopes that her partnerships with corporate sponsors such as the audio company Sennheiser will enable more people to be exposed to her music.

SUGGESTED READING
Block, Melissa. "Imogen Heap." *All Things Considered/NPR.org*. NPR, 1 Sept. 2009. Web. 17 June 2014.

Dredge, Stuart. "Imogen Heap Talks Tech: 'Make It Glitch, and Then Suddenly That's Your Sound.'" *Guardian*. Guardian, 3 June 2014. Web. 17 June 2014.

Pareles, Jon. "A 21st-Century Geek Getting Her Loop On." *New York Times*. New York Times, 4 Dec. 2009. Web. 17 June 2014.

Roberts, James. "A Masterpiece from the Post-Digital Era." *Music Week* 11 May 2002: 8. Print.

Sinagra, Laura. "With Her Sythesizer, She Mesmerizes." *New York Times*. New York Times, 13 Jan. 2006. Web. 17 June 2014.

"Speak for Yourself." *Music Week* 6 May 2006: 22. Print.

Yelton, Geary. "The Elliptical World of Imogen Heap." *Electronic Musician* Oct. 2009: 24–28. Print.

SELECTED WORKS
I Megaphone, 1998; *Details* (with Frou Frou), 2002; *Speak for Yourself*, 2005; *Ellipse*, 2009; *Sparks*, 2014

—*Christopher Mari*

Kristofer Helgen
Born: March 14, 1980
Occupation: Zoologist

Kristofer Helgen is the curator in charge of the Division of Mammals at the Smithsonian Institution's National Museum of Natural History. He has become renowned for his discovery of previously unknown species—more than one hundred as of 2014. "Most people don't realize this," Helgen told Natalie Angier for the *New York Times* (25 July 2009), "but we are smack-dab in the middle of the age of discovery for mammals."

Among his most celebrated discoveries was the olinguito, a carnivorous animal that looks, as

Courtesy of Ulla Lohmann

many journalists have pointed out, like a cross between a house cat and a teddy bear. (The word "adorable" featured heavily in headlines reporting the finding.) "The discovery of the olinguito shows us that the world is not yet completely explored, its most basic secrets not yet revealed," Helgen said, as quoted in an article on the *Smithsonian Science* website (15 Aug. 2013). "If new carnivores can still be found, what other surprises await us? So many of the world's species are not yet known to science. Documenting them is the first step toward understanding the full richness and diversity of life on Earth."

EARLY YEARS

Helgen was born on March 14, 1980, in Fridley, Minnesota. As a child, he moved with his mother, Kari, and father, Howard, a lawyer, to the town of Coon Rapids, a suburb of Minneapolis. Helgen's parents recalled that as a toddler, he often carefully lined up his stuffed animals around his crib. He said in an interview for the National Geographic Explorers website (2009), "Even then, my excitement revolved around figuring out how many different kinds [of animals] there were."

In fifth grade, Helgen contracted mononucleosis and spent weeks recuperating on the sofa. Although he was too ill to move, he propped his geography book next to him and memorized whole passages; his mother stood by to turn each page as he finished. He also read almost obsessively about animals, especially mammals. "I loved how beautiful and different they could be," he told Siri Carpenter for *Science* journal's Science Careers website (6 Feb. 2009). "From bats to whales to dogs, it's one coherent group, but there's so much difference in form and biology."

Helgen was particularly fascinated by the question of how many different types of mammals exist. "It seemed like something you should be able to look up in a book, and I tried to do that my whole childhood," he said to Carpenter. "I kept lists of the mammals I found out about, but it was only as I started working in museums that I found out that there is no place to go to for that information. We're so far from a good answer."

Helgen's intense curiosity made a career in zoology a natural choice. "I think it's in my blood. It's just something that has always been," he said to Sarah McCann for the Minneapolis *Star Tribune* (22 Feb. 2006). "It's perhaps the luckiest thing in my life because I've just never had to second-guess or think about what it is I want to do with my life." Helgen graduated from Coon Rapids High School in 1997 and entered Harvard University. He was excited at the prospect of studying and working at the school's celebrated Museum of Comparative Zoology, which was founded in 1859 and contains an estimated twenty-one million invertebrate and vertebrate specimens.

An issue of the *Harvard Crimson* from May 14, 1999, jokingly describes an unusual research project Helgen undertook for an anthropology course: studying men's choices of urinals in crowded public restrooms. He discovered, unsurprisingly, that most men, when given a choice, prefer the urinal farthest from the one another man is using. Helgen earned his bachelor's degree from Harvard in 2001 and traveled to Australia to attend a graduate program at the University of Adelaide.

DISCOVERIES IN THE LOST WORLD

Helgen began his graduate studies as a Fulbright Fellow and later won a variety of scholarships. He was especially interested in the mammals of the Melanesian area, which reaches from the western end of the Pacific Ocean to the Arafura Sea and east toward Fiji. As a doctoral candidate, he took part in expeditions to Borneo and Timor, among other places.

Shortly before earning his PhD in zoology in 2006, Helgen traveled to the Foja Mountains, an isolated range in Indonesia's Papua Province, on the island of New Guinea. He and his fellow researchers, who hailed variously from Australia, the United States, and New Guinea itself, spent almost a month at their base camp in the tiny lowland village of Kwerba, which had just two hundred inhabitants. One team then made its way up the mountains on foot, while others, including Helgen, took a helicopter to a lake bed near the range's highest point. "The first bird I saw when I stepped out of the helicopter was a honeyeater with an orange face, which turned out to be a new species," Helgen told Tiffany Chaparro for *Scholastic News* (27 Mar. 2006). "This is the first new bird discovered on the island of New Guinea since the Second World War."

The bird was just one of the exciting discoveries made by Helgen and his colleagues. "It was the concentration of new findings that really blew us all away," Helgen told McCann. He added, "The animals up there didn't seem to know what people were. It is just so astonishingly rare to find a place the whole globe over where there are just no people living whatsoever." There was, in fact, so little evidence that the 3,700-square-mile rainforest has ever been inhabited by humans that the area is commonly known as the "Lost World." Villagers from Kwerba explained to the scientists that while they hunt game and collect medicinal herbs from the periphery of the forest, they do not venture into its interior. In the 1970s geographer Jared Diamond became the first Westerner to explore the Foja range, but he did not visit the section where Helgen and his colleagues would later be working.

In addition to the honeyeater, the group ultimately found more than twenty new species of frog (including one only a half-inch long), several new varieties of butterfly, and—most excitingly for Helgen—a golden-mantled tree kangaroo, the first of its kind ever seen in Indonesia.

THE NATIONAL MUSEUM OF NATURAL HISTORY

After receiving his doctoral degree, Helgen moved to Washington, DC, to conduct postdoctoral research at the Smithsonian Institution's National Museum of Natural History, which was founded in 1910 and contains more than 126 million natural-science specimens and cultural artifacts. In 2008 he was hired by the institution as a research zoologist and curator of mammals; the following year he was named curator in charge of his division.

Helgen remained fascinated by New Guinea, and in 2009, near Mount Bosavi, an extinct volcano on the Great Papuan Plateau, he made another thrilling discovery: one of the largest rats in the world, later provisionally dubbed the Bosavi woolly rat. "It is a true rat, related to the same kind you find in the city sewers, but a heck of a lot bigger," Helgen told Paul Revoir for the *Daily Mail* (7 Sept. 2009). "I had a cat and it was about the same size of this rat." The rodent was exceptionally tame, he added. "It just sat next to me nibbling on a piece of leaf. It won't have seen a human being before," he enthused. "The crater of Mount Bosavi really is the lost world."

The expedition was being filmed by the BBC Natural History Unit, but the involvement of a television crew did not make the trip any easier or more luxurious, and the researchers often worked in chilly and rainy conditions. Helgen found it well worth the effort. "It was an unbelievably exciting moment," he said of the discovery, as quoted in a press release from the Smithsonian Institution (11 Sept. 2009). He continued, "Discoveries like this should remind us how much of the world is still left to explore and how much stands to be lost when any rainforest is threatened." The expedition also found almost fifty potentially new species of frog, gecko, fish, insect, and spider, as well as a new subspecies of marsupial that Helgen dubbed the Bosavi silky cuscus.

Not every discovery is made in the field. "Though I go looking for mammals in some of the most remote corners of the globe, sometimes the most startling finds are right under our noses," Helgen said in a Q&A for the Smithsonian Journeys website, a museum-sponsored travel service. "Three years ago I 'discovered' a fantastic new species of bat from Papua New Guinea and the Solomon Islands—not out in the rainforest, but in museum cabinets at the Smithsonian." In addition to the Smithsonian specimen—which dates back to World War II, when US troops were stationed in the South Pacific—Helgen also found examples of the species in museums in Sydney, Chicago, and Honolulu. The large, distinctive bat has a monkey-like face, piercing red eyes, a massive wingspan, and bigger teeth than any other known bat in the world. Helgen observed, "You might think that such a conspicuous bat could not go overlooked in museums for so long, but there you have it."

Helgen has explained that oversights of this type are a common occurrence. "An expert can go into any large natural history museum and identify kinds of animals no one knew existed," he said in the National Geographic Explorers interview. He added, "Collections build up over centuries. It's virtually impossible to fully interpret that wealth of material. Every day brings surprises."

THE OLINGUITO

Among the most high-profile discoveries of Helgen's career was that of the olinguito. The story behind the discovery, which was officially announced in 2013, is one of mistaken identity and serendipity. An olinguito had actually lived at the National Zoological Park in Washington, DC, for several years. Zookeepers, who named the creature Ringerl, believed her to be an olingo, a carnivore from the family Procyonidae. They repeatedly tried to mate her to olingos from other zoos, with no luck. As it turned out, Ringerl was not simply being recalcitrant; she was from an entirely different species, as Helgen discovered while examining pelts and skeletons in the museum. Olinguitos are smaller than olingos, with shorter tails, rounder faces, smaller ears, and bushier fur.

Helgen next embarked on a field trip to South America to find live olinguitos. "I could have simply described it as a new species based on the specimens in the museum," he told the

National Geographic Explorers interviewer. "But I wanted to go a step further and find it in the wild. We brought back film, photographs, and a much better understanding of how and where it lives." The olinguito's habitat is being decimated by development, and Helgen hopes that the publicity generated by his discovery will help preserve it. "The cloud forests of the Andes are a world unto themselves, filled with many species found nowhere else, many of them threatened or endangered," he said, as quoted in the Smithsonian Institution press release announcing the find (15 Aug. 2013). "We hope that the olinguito can serve as an ambassador species for the cloud forests of Ecuador and Colombia, to bring the world's attention to these critical habitats."

Not only is the olinguito the first newly discovered carnivorous species in the Americas in almost four decades, but at least three subspecies were found to exist. "This is extremely unusual in carnivores," Helgen said, as quoted by Joseph Stromberg for *Smithsonian* magazine (15 Aug. 2013). "I honestly think that this could be the last time in history that we will turn up this kind of situation—both a new carnivore, and one that's widespread enough to have multiple kinds."

OTHER ACTIVITIES
Helgen has appeared in multiple BBC documentary series, including *Lost Land of the Volcano* (2009), which was filmed on Mount Bosavi, and *Wild Burma: Nature's Lost Kingdom* (2013). He has also explored how African environments and wildlife have changed since US president Theodore Roosevelt, an avid hunter and naturalist, went on an ambitious expedition to Africa in 1909 and 1910, shortly after leaving office.

In addition to his other activities, Helgen, who was named in *Business Insider's* 2013 list of the world's most innovative people under the age of forty, is the editor of the respected database *Mammal Species of the World* and sits on the editorial board of the peer-reviewed journal *ZooKeys*. He is an affiliate professor of environmental science and policy at George Mason University and a member of the Genome 10K Community of Scientists, a group that aims to assemble what they call a "genomic zoo"—a collection of DNA sequences representing the genomes of ten thousand vertebrate species.

PERSONAL LIFE
On January 21, 2006, Helgen married Lauren Elizabeth Johnston, an evolutionary biologist and a fellow graduate of the University of Adelaide. She works as a research collaborator at the National Museum of Natural History. Although she focuses on mammalian taxonomy, she has also engaged in the study of marine invertebrates and moths. Helgen and his wife reside in Arlington, Virginia.

SUGGESTED READING
Angier, Natalie. "New Creatures in an Age of Extinctions." *New York Times*. New York Times, 25 July 2009. Web. 8 July 2014.

Carpenter, Siri. "Darwin's Legacy: Rich Collections, Deep Expertise." *Science Careers*. Amer. Assoc. for the Advancement of Science, 6 Feb. 2009. Web. 8 July 2014.

Chaparro, Tiffany. "In the News: Kristofer Helgen." *Scholastic News*. Scholastic, 27 Mar. 2006. Web. 8 July 2014.

"Kristofer Helgen, Zoologist." *National Geographic Explorers*. Natl. Geographic Soc., 2009. Web. 8 July 2014.

McCann, Sarah. "Scientist's World Is an Animal Planet." *Star Tribune*. Star Tribune, 22 Feb. 2006. Web. 8 July 2014.

Revoir, Paul. "The Rat That's the Size of a Cat: BBC Team Discovers 40 New Species in 'Lost World.'" *Mail Online*. Assoc. Newspapers, 7 Sept. 2009. Web. 8 July 2014.

Stromberg, Joseph. "For the First Time in 35 Years, a New Carnivorous Mammal Species Is Discovered in the Americas." *Smithsonian*. Smithsonian Inst., 15 Aug. 2013. Web. 8 July 2014.

—*Mari Rich*

Peter Hessler

Born: June 14, 1969
Occupation: Writer and journalist

"To many China watchers, [Peter] Hessler represents a kind of gold standard for intimately reported pieces on lesser-known people and parts of the country," William Wan wrote for the *Washington Post* (23 Sept. 2013). Hessler gained that reputation over the course of almost two decades in the Far East, arriving in China as a Peace Corps volunteer in 1996, becoming the Beijing correspondent for the *New Yorker*, and penning four well-regarded books about his time there: *River Town: Two Years on the Yangtze* (2001), *Oracle Bones* (2006), *Country Driving* (2010), and *Strange Stones: Dispatches from East and West* (2013). "In each book I've written about China, there is a level of really significant personal involvement and connection," Hessler told Patrick Brzeski for the website *Time Out Hong Kong* (13 Apr. 2010). "For me being in China had a great deal of meaning. As a writer, I found it very fulfilling."

Despite his close links to that country, in 2011 Hessler moved to Egypt, where he became an eyewitness to the Arab Spring and other developments, and where he continues to write and report for the *New Yorker*, *National Geographic*, and other publications. Explaining his decision

Courtesy of the John D. & Catherine T. MacArthur Foundation

to leave China, he told Wan, "It wasn't because I was burnt out or sick of the place. I think I was still learning a lot, getting better as a writer and researcher. [But] I did also feel I didn't want to reach a point where I was tired of it, where I felt I knew everything, no longer appreciating it with a fresh eye."

In 2011 Hessler won a John D. and Catherine T. MacArthur Foundation Fellowship, more commonly known as a "genius grant," for his ability, according to the foundation's website, "to weave multiple narrative threads into richly illuminating depictions of people and places confronted with a staggering pace of change."

EARLY YEARS
Peter Hessler was born on June 14, 1969 in Pittsburgh, Pennsylvania, but at an early age he moved with his parents and three sisters to Columbia, Missouri. His father, Richard, was a sociology professor at the University of Missouri (MU), and his mother, Anne, taught history at nearby Columbia College. The family lived not far from MU's bucolic campus. "It was a wonderful place to be a kid," Hessler recalled to Nancy Moen for the school's online publication, *Mizzou Wire* (14 May 2013). "The university was so close that it essentially became my back yard."

From the time he was in third grade until he entered high school, Hessler rose at five in the morning to deliver the *Columbia Missourian*, a daily newspaper published by professionals affiliated with MU's School of Journalism. He subsequently became an avid newspaper reader and also enjoyed MU's literary journal, the *Missouri Review*.

During the academic year 1977–78, Hessler lived with his family in Sweden, where his father was taking a sabbatical. He told Rolf Potts in an undated interview for the online publication *Vagabonding*, "My family always traveled a fair amount when I was growing up—long driving trips to different parts of America, the sort of travel that is familiar to many Midwestern childhoods. . . . But apart from that experience [in Sweden] I saw little of the world outside of America."

PRINCETON AND OXFORD
After graduating from Hickman High School in 1988, Hessler entered Princeton University, where he studied English and creative writing and where Joyce Carol Oates and Russell Banks served as his thesis advisers. He credits a course he took his junior year with renowned writer John McPhee with encouraging him to focus on nonfiction writing.

The summer before he graduated from Princeton, he accepted a job as a researcher for the Kellogg Foundation, whose mission is to promote the health, education, and welfare of disadvantaged children. As part of his duties, he wrote an ethnography focused on the small city of Sikeston, Missouri, which was later published in the *Journal for Applied Anthropology*.

In 1992, after earning his bachelor's degree from Princeton, Hessler won a Rhodes Scholarship and began studying English language and literature at Mansfield College, a constituent school of Oxford University. "That was really the start of my international experiences," he recalled to Potts. "I lived cheaply at Oxford and picked up odd jobs and the occasional freelance writing gig, and this allowed me to travel extensively in Europe and Asia. During those two years I visited something like 30 countries—Oxford was very generous with its vacation time, and I traveled cheaply, using rail-passes and camping a lot."

EARLY CAREER
When Hessler completed his studies at Oxford in 1994, he decided to travel home via a spontaneous, circuitous route, starting in Prague, and then through Russia, China, and Thailand. One particularly memorable experience—a journey from Moscow to Beijing partly via the Trans-Siberian Railway—formed the basis for an article published by the *New York Times* in 1995, thus marking his first foray into professional travel writing. "I was surprised because I knew nobody there [at the *Times*] and just sent it to a name on the masthead," he told Potts. He subsequently published several other pieces in that paper. "Publishing those travel pieces in the *Times* was a way of reminding me that there was a writing world out there," he continued. "And I was fortunate because the *Times* was very patient with the logistical difficulties—I had no Internet access and had to take a bus into town to get a fax. In retrospect I'm surprised they were patient enough to work with me, even sporadically."

In 1995 Hessler received a Stratton Fellowship from the nonprofit group Friends of

Switzerland and used it to spend two months hiking across the Alps, from France to Italy. In between travels, he returned to Missouri, where he tutored at MU's writing center and taught occasional sessions of English composition.

IN CHINA WITH THE PEACE CORPS

Hessler had applied to the Peace Corps while still at Princeton and was on track to be sent to Africa, but after winning the Rhodes Scholarship, he had abandoned the idea. In 1996, however, he reapplied, hoping to be sent to China. He had become interested in the country during his trip on the Trans-Siberian Railway. "I really had no interest [before that] in China itself," he told Angilee Shah during an interview posted on the website of the Asia Society (3 July 2012). "I wanted to take that train, and I wanted to pass through Mongolia, and unfortunately China was the only terminus. I had heard mostly bad things about China from other travelers. I figured I'd spend as little time as possible there and continue on to southeastern Asia, which sounded more appealing. In those days China wasn't yet seen as a place where so much was changing. The popular image was still very much connected to the Tiananmen protests and crackdown." He continued, "After [a] long and strange trip, Beijing was a revelation. There was so much energy in the city; it was clear that something significant was happening in this country."

Hessler was accepted into the Peace Corps and as part of one of the first groups sent to China, he was assigned to teach English at a small college in Fuling, a remote town on the Yangtze River. "The Peace Corps in China can be a very tough two years," he told Wan. "Everywhere you go in your town, you've got a mob of people following you and talking about 'the foreigner,' and there's just a lot of stuff that doesn't work well. . . . In the end you sorta think, well, I got myself into this. If I didn't want to be in a place like this, where I've got twenty people watching me eat a bowl of noodles, I shouldn't have signed up for the Peace Corps."

Hessler and one other volunteer were the first foreigners to live in the city for some five decades. While they earned $120 a month—a princely sum by local standards—"we caught a lot of the same diseases local people had, and our electricity would get turned off when everyone else's electricity got turned off," as he recalled to Wan. Hessler's two-year stint in the organization formed the basis of his first book, *River Town: Two Years on the Yangtze*, which he wrote with the encouragement of his old professor John McPhee.

CHINA CORRESPONDENT

Hessler had become fluent in Mandarin while in Fuling, and although he had gone back to Missouri to pen *River Town*, he was determined to return to China to establish himself as a freelance writer there. He did so in early 1999, writing pieces for a variety of publications. He was accredited for a short time as the *Boston Globe*'s correspondent in Beijing, and in 2000 he became the *New Yorker*'s first full-time correspondent since the Communist Revolution. Based in Beijing, he produced regular "Letters from China" on a wide array of topics, including the basketball player Yao Ming, factory workers, and the Three Gorges Dam. He also wrote about such personal experiences as being robbed on the border between China and North Korea.

There were certain challenges for Hessler—besides being robbed—to living and working in Communist-controlled China. "I speak decent Chinese, and I also have a Chinese driver's license," he told Potts. "So things like language and culture aren't major problems. Instead, the biggest hassles are political." He explained that in China, in order to be a full-time resident journalist, he needed a special accreditation and visa, which went into his passport. Thus, every time he registered at a Chinese hotel, they knew a journalist was in the vicinity and reported his presence to the local police. On multiple occasions, he was kicked out of town. "In those situations it's particularly frustrating because my research wasn't in any sense critical or unfair," he recalled to Potts. "In general I try to write about everyday life in China and I'm less concerned with politics than most journalists." Hessler, who also writes regularly for *National Geographic*, remained in China until 2007.

BOOKS

River Town, Hessler's widely praised 2001 debut, garnered the Kiriyama Prize for outstanding nonfiction book about the Pacific Rim and South Asia and was shortlisted for the Thomas Cook Travel Book Award. In sentiments echoed by numerous other reviewers, Adam Goodheart wrote for the *New York Times* (11 Feb. 2001), "*River Town* is an important work of reportage, and not just because of the peculiar historical moment it describes—a moment when Hessler's students can speak of their sincere admiration for the Communist ideals of Chairman Mao, then go off after graduation to seek their fortune in the tumultuous prosperity of China's southern cities. It's also a window into a part of China—the province of Sichuan—that has rarely been explored in depth, even though, as Hessler notes, it is home to one out of every 50 people on earth."

Hessler's next book, *Oracle Bones* (2006), a National Book Award finalist, won similar acclaim. The title of that sophomore effort is derived from artifacts found in and around the city of Anyang that date from the second millennium BCE. Hessler first became interested in the oracle bones—made from the flat lower carapace of tortoises—while writing an article on archaeology for *National Geographic*. (Ancient diviners would heat a carapace until its surface cracked, and the resulting patterns were thought to reveal future truths to the questioner.) Critics appreciated the structure of the book, which interspersed tales of modern China (revisiting some of the students from *River Town* and describing how Hessler went undercover at Falun Gong demonstrations in Tiananmen Square) with stories about the past. He tells, for example, of one scholar, Chen Mengjia, who committed suicide during the Cultural Revolution.

Hessler followed *Oracle Bones* with *Country Driving* (2010), for which he embarked on an ambitious road trip that followed the Great Wall across northern China in order to report on the rapidly changing social and economic conditions in the country. His latest book, *Strange Stones: Dispatches from East and West* (2013), consists of a series of pieces originally published in the *New Yorker*. The most discussed article in the collection chronicles Hessler's willingness to eat rat meat at restaurants specializing in the preparation of the rodents, which are considered a delicacy in certain locales.

LIFE AFTER CHINA
In 2007, after leaving China, Hessler and his wife, fellow journalist Leslie Chang, moved to Ridgeway, Colorado. Although they knew that many people in their situation would settle in a more cosmopolitan locale, they sought quiet and anonymity. He appreciated the fact that when talking to his new neighbors, they evinced little interest in the fact that he was a writer. "If I was in New York or San Francisco it would be very different. And that's partly why my wife and I didn't move to one of those cities," he told Wan. "I felt like, in a way, I would still be in China, but not in China. If I was in New York, I would know all these people connected to China and would always be asked to go to dinners or give talks about China, and I kinda just wanted something different."

Their American interlude did not last long. In 2011 the family—which by then included twin girls, Ariel and Natasha, born the previous year—moved to Cairo. The couple took an immersive Arabic language course before they left, and Hessler, who now regularly reports on Egypt for the *New Yorker*, among other publications, hopes to one day work without a translator, as he did in China.

SUGGESTED READING
Brzeski, Patrick. "The Unabridged Peter Hessler Interview." *Time Out Hong Kong*. Time Out Group, 13 Apr. 2010. Web. 8 July 2014.
Moen, Nancy. "Hessler's Homecoming." *Mizzou News*. University of Missouri, 14 May, 2013. Web. 8 July 2014.
Richardson, Lloyd Macauley. "China, Taken Personally." *Policy Review*. Hoover Institution, June–July 2001. Web. 8 July 2014.
Spence, Jonathan. "Letters from China." *New York Times*. New York Times, 30 Apr. 2006. Web. 8 July 2014.
Wan, William. "In China, It's Never Like This." *Washington Post*. Washington Post, 23 Sept. 2013. Web. 8 July 2014.

SELECTED WORKS
River Town: Two Years on the Yangtze, 2001; *Oracle Bones*, 2006; *Country Driving*, 2010; *Strange Stones: Dispatches from East and West*, 2013

—*Mari Rich*

Mazie K. Hirono
Born: November 3, 1947
Occupation: United States Senator

When longtime politician Mazie K. Hirono won election to the United States Senate in 2012, she became the first Japanese-born US senator, the first Buddhist senator, and the first female Asian American senator. She also became the first female senator to represent Hawaii. Born in the Fukushima prefecture of Japan, Hirono and her family settled in Hawaii in the 1950s and Hirono learned to speak English while attending Honolulu public schools. "I know what

Joshua Roberts/Reuters/Landov

it feels like to be discriminated against, to feel powerless, to have landlords who threaten to kick you out, and not having a place to go. So, equality and fairness, equal opportunities are driving principles for me," Hirono told Kevin Dayton for the *Honolulu Advertiser* (4 Sept. 2002).

Hirono was first elected to public office in 1981, after winning election to the Hawaii House of Representatives, where she served for more than a decade. She was then elected to serve two terms as lieutenant governor of Hawaii, earning a reputation as a strong pro-labor and pro-consumer advocate. After a failed bid to be elected to the governorship, Hirono dedicated herself to establishing a political action committee that supports the political campaigns of other Democratic women. In 2006, Hirono was elected to the US House of Representatives, where she advocated for improvements to early childhood education and defended abortion rights. She served three terms in the House before she was elected to the Senate in 2012. Hirono was sworn into office on January 3, 2013, joining nineteen other female senators—the most at any point in US history.

EARLY LIFE

Mazie Keiko Hirono was born in Fukushima, Japan, on November 3, 1947. Despite being born in Japan, Hirono was able to attain US citizenship because her mother, Laura Chie Hirono, had been born in Waiphahu, Hawaii, in 1924 and therefore retained her US citizenship. Before the outbreak of World War II, Hirono's mother and maternal grandparents returned to Japan, where her mother married veterinarian Matabe Hirono and settled in Fukushima. Laura and Matabe Hirono had three children, Roy, Mazie, and Wayne, before separating in 1951. "After six years, I just couldn't take it anymore," Laura Hirono told Rod Ohira for the *Star-Bulletin* (8 May 1999). "He just drank and gambled. Sometimes he didn't come home for days. . . . There was no food or money in the house. He sold all of our things to gamble."

Laura Hirono left her abusive husband and took her three young children to her parents' home, where they stayed for four years. After deciding to relocate to the United States, Laura Hirono left her youngest child, Wayne, in the care of her parents and traveled in steerage with Roy and Mazie on the *President Cleveland* from Yokohama to Honolulu, where they moved into a rooming house on Kewalo Street. Laura Hirono found work at the Japanese-language newspaper *Hawaii Hochi* as a typesetter, and she catered on the side to make ends meet. "It took a lot of courage to come here with three kids to start a new life, not knowing how it would turn out. But she kept the family moving forward," Hirono told Ohira (8 May 1999). "My mother is in a class by

herself. She's a risk-taker who has a lot of guts. I learned risk-taking from her."

Mazie Hirono arrived in Hawaii in 1955 at the age of eight and became a naturalized US citizen in 1959, the same year Hawaii attained statehood. Knowing only Japanese, Hirono learned English at public schools in Honolulu and Kaimuki. Her maternal grandparents, Hiroshi Sato and Tari Shinoki Sato, and her little brother, Wayne, joined them in the United States a few years later. The Hirono family was poor and moved around to new apartments frequently. Hirono attended Ka'ahumanu Elementary School, Koko Head Elementary, Niui Valley Intermediate, Jarrett Intermediate, and Kaimuki High School. "I had responsibilities at home that other kids didn't have; I had to help take care of the family, so I didn't do a lot of things with the other kids. I was a serious kid," Hirono told Dan Boylan for *MidWeek* (21 Mar. 2007). She took on her first job in elementary school, working as a student cashier during lunch hours. At Kaimuki High, Hirono was an honors students and coeditor of the school newspaper, the *Kaimuli Bulldog*.

EDUCATION

Hirono enrolled in the University of Hawaii at Manoa to major in psychology. In the summer of 1968, she was one of several students chosen by the Young Women's Christian Association (YWCA) to work with at-risk youth in Waimanalo. "They were all activists and war protesters," she told Boylan. "Nine of them had been arrested during the famous Bachman Hall sit-in," in which students overtook the University of Hawaii's main administration building to protest the Vietnam War. Hirono cites her experience that summer as heavily influencing her decision to pursue politics. Kate Stanley, a former staff member of the Department of Education, was volunteering for Service to America in Waimanalo that year. "That summer Mazie saw a whole bunch of people she had never seen before," Stanley told Boylan. "Remember, she had gone to Koko Head Elementary, which was a good, upper-middle-class school, but right around the curve in Waimanalo was a different world. And Mazie stood out in that group of university students. You could tell she wasn't there just to have fun." Following her experience volunteering for the YWCA, Hirono took an active interest in politics and began actively protesting the US military's involvement in the Vietnam War.

Hirono earned her bachelor's degree in 1970, graduating Phi Beta Kappa. She spent the five years following graduation working at the Hawaii legislature and assisting with political campaigns. Through her campaign work, Hirono made the acquaintance of David Hagino, who decided to run for the Hawaii House of Representatives in 1970 and asked Hirono to head his campaign. Although Hagino lost that race, Hirono became increasingly active in the Young Democrats and she was a staff member for the House campaigns of Anson Chong in 1972 and Carl Takamura in 1974.

Hirono then enrolled at the Georgetown University Law Center in Washington, DC, to study public interest law. She graduated with a law degree in 1978 and returned to Hawaii to work as a deputy attorney-general. "I was in the office's new anti-trust division," she told Boylan. "I had a terrific anti-trust professor at Georgetown, and I enjoyed my time in the AG's office." She worked in the attorney-general's office for two years before leaving to campaign for a seat in the Hawaii House of Representatives.

HAWAII STATE POLITICS

In 1980, Hirono ran for and won a seat in the Hawaii House of Representatives that had been vacated by Hagino. She took office, representing Hawaii's twelfth House district, on January 3, 1981. After serving one two-year term, Hirono ran again to represent Hawaii's twentieth district, following statewide redistricting. After another round of redistricting, Hirono was elected in 1984 to represent Hawaii's thirty-second district, where she served for four terms, until January 1993. From 1987 to 1992, she chaired the House Consumer Protection and Commerce Committee, where she developed a reputation for being strongly pro-labor. "I've always been pro-consumer . . . pro the working people," she told Boylan. "The political path Hirono chose was left-of-center and close to organized labor," Kevin Dayton wrote for the *Honolulu Advertiser* (4 Sept. 2002). As a state representative, Hirono also helped to form a bipartisan women's caucus, which was able to advance unpaid family leave laws and childcare tax credits. In 1993 Hirono took office representing the state's twenty-second district, where she served one term before stepping down to run for statewide office.

In 1994, Governor John D. Waihee III had reached the end of his two-term limit as governor of Hawaii. Ben Cayetano, Waihee's lieutenant governor, mounted a campaign for the 1994 gubernatorial election, and Hirono announced her candidacy for lieutenant governor. Hirono beat out state representative Jackie Young in the primaries, 65 percent to 26 percent, to secure the Democratic nomination. Hirono was elected to the lieutenant governorship on November 3, 1994, becoming the first immigrant woman of Asian ancestry in US history to be elected to statewide office. She and Cayetano ran for re-election in 1998. Although she was challenged in the primary by Nancy L. Cook, Hirono won easily, 89 percent to 11 percent. The results of the general election were tighter, but Hirono defeated Republican state senator by a difference of approximately five thousand votes.

Hirono clashed somewhat with Governor Cayetano, telling Boylan for *MidWeek*, "It was a challenge to work with him. Ben takes up all the oxygen in a room, so mine was the plight of most vice presidents and lieutenant governors. I had my disagreements with him, but I didn't take potshots at Ben. It was not my role to do that." Instead, she focused her efforts on workers' compensation issues reform and other issues.

2002 GUBERNATORIAL ELECTION

After reaching the end of her term limit as lieutenant governor, Hirono set her sights on the 2002 gubernatorial election. After a tight contest with state representative Ed Case in the primaries for the Democratic nomination, which Hirono won by some 2,600 votes, she faced off against Republican Laura Lingle, the former mayor of Maui, for the governorship.

Throughout her campaign for governor of Hawaii, Hirono drew criticism for Cayetano's administration, with Lingle blaming Hirono and Cayetano's policies for Hawaii's lagging economy. "All of a sudden it's the Cayetano-Hirono administration," Hirono vented to Dayton for the *Honolulu Advertiser* (27 Oct. 2002). "You could call it that if I had half of the appointments, if I had half of the decision-making power, if I could veto bills, but that's not how that works." Instead, Hirono emphasized her political experience, explaining that "the role of the lieutenant governor is really to support the governor and to be part of the team. And, yes, I had disagreements with the governor, but my value is not about putting the governor down. I know how tough the job is."

The race between Lingle and Hirono was only the second gubernatorial contest in US history between women from the two major parties, the first being the 1986 gubernatorial campaign between Republican candidate Kay Orr and Democrat Helen Boosalis in Nebraska. In one of Hawaii's closest gubernatorial elections, Lingle's better-funded campaign secured the election with 51 percent of the vote. "It was a tough time to carry the water for the Democrats," Hirono told Boylan. "The unions didn't get involved. Some were running around trying to get a man to run. . . . I'm surprised I came as close as I did. But I'm still here."

UNITED STATES CONGRESS

Following her failed gubernatorial campaign, Hirono remained active in Hawaii state politics by founding a political action committee, the Patsy T. Mink Political Action Committee, to assist and fund the campaigns of state-level Democratic women who support and advance abortion rights. When US representative Ed Case announced his decision to challenge Senator Daniel Akaka in the Democratic primary for the US Senate in 2006, Hirono began raising money to campaign for Case's vacated seat in the US House of Representatives. She ultimately raised $1.4 million and beat out nine other Democratic candidates in the primary. "Money plays an important role in politics," Hirono said to Boylan (21 Mar. 2007). "I had to call those contributors one-by-one. I had to reach out to new voters and overcome the baggage of the Cayetano years."

In the general election, Hirono easily defeated Republican state senator Bob Hogue to represent Hawaii's second congressional district, which covers all the Hawaiian Islands except for the urban part of Oahu, which is in the first district. Hirono became the first Asian immigrant women to serve in Congress. Hirono pledged to dedicate herself to improving health care, Social Security, and early education. She served on the Committee on Education and the Workforce, the Committee on Transportation and Infrastructure, and the Committee on Ethics. Hirono won reelection to a second two-year term in 2008 with more than 75 percent of the vote and to a third term in 2010 with 72 percent of the vote.

In 2011, junior senator Daniel Akaka announced his intention to retire after completing his third term in the Senate in 2012. Hirono jumped into the race to fill Akaka's vacated Senate seat, winning the Democratic primary on August 11, 2012. Hirono's former opponent Laura Lingle earned the Republican nomination and ran a campaign that painted Hirono as an ineffective legislator for never having one of her own bills signed into law. Hirono's platform focused on spurring job creation, improving tourism, strengthening early childhood education, reforming immigration law, and raising funds for infrastructure projects. Both major-candidates raised approximately five million dollars for their campaigns, but Hirono ultimately beat Lingle, earning more than 62 percent of the vote. Hirono was sworn into the Senate on January 3, 2013, becoming the first female senator from Hawaii, the first Asian American female United States senator, and the first Buddhist senator. Hirono lives in Honolulu with her mother, Laura, and her husband, Leighton Kim Oshima, who is an attorney.

SUGGESTED READING

Boylan, Dan. "The Immigrant Congresswoman." *MidWeek*. MidWeek, 21 Mar. 2007. Web. 1 Oct. 2013.
Dayton, Kevin. "Labor, Consumer Advocate Tries to Connect with Business." *Honolulu Advertiser*. Honolulu Advertiser, 27 Oct. 2002. Web. 1 Oct. 2013.
Koh, Yoree. "Hirono Becomes First US Senator Born in Japan." *Wall Street Journal*. Dow Jones, 6 Nov. 2012. Web. 1 Oct. 2013.
Ohira, Rod. "Lieutenant Governor Reflects on the 'Bookends' of Her Life." *Honolulu Star-Bulletin*. Honolulu Star-Bulletin, 8 May 1999. Web. 1 Oct. 2013.

—*Mary Woodbury Hooper*

Freeman A. Hrabowski III

Born: August 13, 1950
Occupation: Educator

Freeman A. Hrabowski III is the president of the University of Maryland, Baltimore County (UMBC). Since taking office in 1992, Hrabowski has made UMBC a top research institution for graduates, particularly low-income and minority students, in the fields of math and science. In 2010, 41 percent of UMBC's undergraduate students completed bachelor's degrees in science, math, and engineering, a figure that is significantly higher than the national average of 25 percent. These fields—science, technology, engineering, and mathematics—are referred to by the acronym STEM. "You have to appreciate the importance of STEM education," Brian Kelly, editor of the *US News and World Report*, told Childs Walkers in an interview for the *Baltimore Sun* (1 Sept. 2012). "This is a huge national issue of competitiveness; it's a crisis. One of the questions is, can you get African-American students to thrive in a science environment? Some people would tell you no, but Freeman is proof that yes, you can." Throughout the United States, many students begin majors in the STEM fields, but a large number either switch to another major or do not graduate at all. Hrabowski is determined to reverse this trend. "We have to teach Americans of all races, from all backgrounds, what it takes to be the best," Hrabowski told Byron Pitts in an interview for the television program *60 Minutes* (13 Nov. 2011). The secret, he says, is simple: hard work. As he said to Pitts, "Nothing,

AFP/Getty Images

I don't care how smart you are. Nothing takes the place of hard work." UMBC offers undergraduates research opportunities traditionally reserved for grad students, and Hrabowski has introduced a number of initiatives aimed at success, such as the Meyerhoff Scholars program, which began with the goal of providing support to black men in science and engineering fields.

Hrabowski "manages to steal A students away from far more famous schools because he recruits brainiacs the way some schools recruit quarterbacks," Kim Clark wrote in an article for *US News and World Report* (19 Nov. 2008). He is a charismatic figure with an inspiring personal history, having earned his PhD in statistics at the age of twenty-four. Hrabowski has become a superstar among administrators, but the foundation of his sterling reputation is his relationships with his students, who call him "Doc." He has been the president of UMBC for more than twenty years—despite lucrative offers for more high-profile positions—and believes that he can affect more profound change by forging meaningful relationships with individual students.

EARLY LIFE
Freeman A. Hrabowski III was born on August 13, 1950, and raised in a segregated neighborhood in Birmingham, Alabama. His surname derives from his paternal grandfather, who was a Polish slave master in rural Alabama, and his first name comes from his grandfather, who was the first man in his family to be born free from slavery. Education is an important part of Hrabowski's family history; both of his grandmothers saw Booker T. Washington, the famous African American educator and author, speak about the importance of education in the black community. Thus, both of Hrabowski's parents graduated from Alabama State College at a time when most of their peers did not study past high school. "I was fortunate to grow up in a middle-class home with two hardworking parents who enjoyed both reading and mathematics," Hrabowski explained in an interview for the *Washington Post* (27 July 2010). His father, Freeman Hrabowski Jr., was a former schoolteacher who worked three jobs and earned additional money tutoring his less-educated white supervisors in reading and writing. His mother, Maggie Geeter Hrabowski, taught in Birmingham public schools from 1952 until 1978 and sold insurance as a side job. Hrabowski had an early interest in mathematics. "My mother was an English teacher who decided to become a math teacher, and she used me as a guinea pig at home," Hrabowski recalled, as quoted by the *Washington Post* (27 July 2010).

Hrabowski was naturally precocious, and his parents encouraged him to learn facts from the daily newspaper and to read the works of Langston Hughes, Emily Dickinson, and Fyodor Dostoevsky. He jokingly described his young self to Walker as a "fat kid who loved math." He attended Ullman High School in Birmingham, where he was inspired by the school principal, George Bell, a mathematician who presented a difficult math problem on the blackboard every day for his students to solve. By the time he was twelve years old, Hrabowski had skipped ahead to the ninth grade.

THE CHILDREN'S CRUSADE
In 1963, Hrabowski attended a civil rights meeting with his parents at church, where he heard Martin Luther King Jr. call for participants at an upcoming demonstration to protest racial segregation in Birmingham. In an interview with Kim Lawton for WGBH (26 Apr. 2013), Hrabowksi recalled, "I'll never forget listening . . . and hearing a man say, if the children participate in this demonstration, in this peaceful demonstration, all of America will see that even children understand the difference between right and wrong and that children want the best possible education." Despite his enthusiasm, his parents initially forbade him to join the march, which was led by students and later dubbed the Children's Crusade. They feared that their son would be attacked by police dogs, sprayed by high-powered fire hoses, or arrested. They supported dissent, but they feared the consequences of allowing him to join the protest. (They were not alone in their opinion; Malcolm X reportedly opposed the march because it exposed children to violence.)

Hrabowski told his parents they were being hypocritical and, after much thought, they ultimately allowed him to join the march. The city's public safety commissioner, Eugene "Bull" Connor, did indeed release police dogs and open up fire hoses on the protestors—nearly all of whom were young children and teenagers. On *60 Minutes*, Hrabowski recalled to Pitts how Connor approached him at the march: "He asked me, 'What do you want little negro?' I was so scared . . . and I said, 'We want to kneel and pray.'" Connor then picked up the twelve-year-old Hrabowski, spat in his face, and threw him in the paddy wagon to take him to jail. The brutal police response to the nonviolent protest sparked national outrage and marked a major turning point in the civil rights movement. Still, Hrabowski spent five days in jail, sharing a cell with actual criminals.

His experience in jail changed the course of his entire life. While Hrabowski and the other student demonstrators were still in prison, King led a march of parents to the jail and said to the children protestors, "What you do this day will have an impact on generations as yet unborn," as Hrabowski recalled in his interview with Clark. Hrabowski never forgot King's words, saying, "The experience taught me that the more we expect of children, the more they can do."

EDUCATION AND EARLY CAREER

After his release from prison, Hrabowski was often asked to speak about his experience in the Children's Crusade. The requests kindled in him a love of oration, which was fostered by one of his early mentors, a man named John Porter, who was the pastor at Sixth Avenue Baptist Church. Porter taught the young Hrabowski to be prepared. "Always have a paragraph in your head," he advised, as Hrabowski told Walker. Porter's wife, Dorothy, played an important role in Hrabowski's life, as well, broadening his horizons by taking him to high-end restaurants and the symphony. He spent a summer at the Tuskegee Institute, a historically black university in Alabama, where, for the first time, he felt challenged by math problems. The dean suggested that Hrabowski aim to acquire a PhD, explaining that it is "the highest degree you can get," which became Hrabowski's singular goal, as he explained to Walker.

He earned acceptance to Morehouse College in Atlanta when he was only fourteen years old, but his mother made him wait another year before attending college. He then enrolled at Hampton Institute in Virginia and graduated with highest honors and a bachelor's degree in mathematics at the age of nineteen. He then enrolled at the University of Illinois at Urbana-Champaign, where he earned his master's degree in mathematics in 1971 and completed his PhD in higher education administration and statistics in 1975. From 1976 to 1977, he served as the associate dean of graduate studies at Alabama A&M University before taking a faculty position at Coppin State College in Baltimore in 1977. He served as the dean of arts and sciences at Coppin State from 1977 to 1981, when he became the vice president of academic affairs there. His colleagues at Coppin State bestowed upon him the derogatory nickname "boy dean." He was certainly young, but the word "boy" had pointed racial implications at the historically black university. "There was some opposition to him, being as young as he was," Coppin State president Calvin W. Burnett, who had hired Hrabowski, told Walker. "He's ambitious, so that may have offended some people. But whatever they had to say wouldn't have much weight, because he deserves whatever it is he gets."

MEYERHOFF SCHOLARS PROGRAM

Hrabowski became the vice provost at the University of Maryland, Baltimore County (UMBC) in 1987. In 1988, he teamed up with billionaire philanthropist Robert Meyerhoff to launch the Meyerhoff Scholars program. Both Hrabowski and Meyerhoff were concerned that African American men were being shut out of careers in math and science because of a lack of opportunity and not due to a lack of interest or talent. (Their concerns were certainly warranted. In the decade before Hrabowski arrived at UMBC, the college had graduated fewer than twenty black students with degrees in science.) The Meyerhoff program was aimed at providing those opportunities through scholarships, research opportunities, and strict academic guidelines. Hrabowski did not just want black men to graduate, he wanted them to excel in difficult subjects and become leaders in their field.

The first year, Hrabowski identified twenty freshman students for the program. In the program's second year, it expanded to admit women as well as men. In 1996, the program began accepting scholars of all races, and the Meyerhoff Scholars now accept sixty to seventy students each year. According to Pitts, 90 percent of Meyerhoff's nearly one thousand graduates have gone on to graduate school. "It's by far the greatest thing I've ever done, and it's all Freeman Hrabowski," Meyerhoff told Walker. "I talk to people who can't understand why it hasn't been replicated in other places, and I say it's because they don't have Freeman Hrabowski."

Incoming Meyerhoff freshmen participate in a summer boot camp that boasts some surprisingly strict behavioral restrictions: no cell phones, no social media, and no electronics. Scholars are forced to bond and collaborate, even in their downtime. Collaboration is one of Hrabowski's highest principles. He believes that if students support each other that they will succeed. The structure of the Meyerhoff program also reinforces team-building skills as an effective way to solve problems. "It's commonplace in athletic teams, but in math and science, we tend to make people feel like they have to compete against each other, and not help each other so much," Hrabowski explained to David Firestone for the *New York Times* (10 Dec. 2013). "We can be more effective in problem solving when we learn to collaborate, ask good questions, explain with clarity, use the technology, and build that community in an effort to become even more proficient in the work." Students learn to complement each other in their abilities and to work together for a common goal without feeling intimidated by another group member's skill set.

UMBC PRESIDENT

In 1990, Hrabowski became the executive vice president of UMBC, a school that has nearly 12,500 students. From 1992 to 1993, he served as the interim president of the university, and has now held the position of UMBC president for more than two decades. It is uncommon for a university president to remain in office for as long as Hrabowski has, but he sees his own destiny as tied to the destinies of UMBC students. In his 2013 convocation address, he told his incoming students, "Our goal is to make sure all of you graduate. And we don't intend to fail." In addition to his work as president, it is clear that

Hrabowski also sees himself as a motivator in chief. "To understand UMBC's success story," Walker wrote, "you have to watch Hrabowski with students, to hear them speak of how he has animated their dreams and kept them on track." He spends hours a day chatting with students, but when he takes someone under his wing, he expects a lot from them. Recalling his own early guidance in public speaking, he will often ask students to speak extemporaneously in front of large groups of people. He explained to Walker that privileged students tend to be comfortable speaking in front of large audiences or important people. "But I want my middle-class and working-class students to be comfortable in front of anyone," he told Walker.

Hrabowski has initiated a number of policies that make UMBC the school it is today, but not all of those policies have been instantly popular. He reportedly rejected a proposal to start a football team at the school, choosing to siphon potential athletic funds into academic scholarships and the school's extracurricular pride, its chess team. Still, his decisions have captured the attention of other schools looking to draw more students to math and science. Before Hrabowski became president, UMBC was a little-known commuter school. Even Baltimore residents often mistook it for a community college. Now, UMBC is known as one of the most innovative research universities in the country, with major institutions such as Harvard rushing to implement Hrabowski's policies on their own campuses. Furthermore, since Hrabowski took on the role of UMBC president, the university's endowment has risen from $1 million to more than $60 million in 2012, and its research funding has increased from $10 million to more than $90 million.

The Meyerhoff program is definitely a major component of the school's success, but Hrabowski has also orchestrated high-level research opportunities for his undergraduate students, who can find jobs and internships with technology start-ups located directly on UMBC's campus. Research is all about encouraging curiosity in students, Hrabowski told Pitts. Students, he said, "should not be allowed to sit back and be bored."

PERSONAL LIFE
His wife, Jacqueline "Jackie" Coleman Hrabowski, is a retired T. Rowe Price executive. They met as students at Hampton Institute when he was fifteen and she was eighteen. According to Walker, Hrabowski told Jackie that he had found his "future bride" when he discovered that she had scored higher than him on a math exam. They have one son named Eric. Hrabowski and his wife live in Owings Mills in Baltimore County.

Hrabowski is a board member at the spice company McCormick and Company, the Constellation Energy Group, and the Maryland Business Roundtable for Education. He also serves as a consultant to the National Science Foundation, the National Institutes of Health, and the National Academies. Since 2012, he has served as the chair of the President's Advisory Commission on Educational Excellence for African Americans. Hrabowski also holds more than twenty honorary degrees from such prestigious institutions as Harvard, Duke, Princeton, and Johns Hopkins University. As for his downtime, he does not consider himself exempt from his own exacting standards; he told Walker that he works eighty to ninety hours and reads three books each week.

SUGGESTED READING
Clark, Kim. "America's Best Leaders: Freeman Hrabowski, University of Maryland-Baltimore County." *US News and World Report*. US News and World Report, 19 Nov. 2008. Web. 17 Mar. 2014.
Firestone, David. "Q. & A. with Freeman Hrabowski." *New York Times*. New York Times, 10 Dec. 2013. Web. 17 Mar. 2014.
Pitts, Byron. "Hrabowski: An Educator Focused on Math and Science." *60 Minutes*. CBS News, 13 Nov. 2011. Web. 17 Mar. 2014.
Rotherham, Andrew J. "100 Most Influential People: Freeman Hrabowski, Educator." *Time*. Time, 18 Apr. 2012. Web. 17 Mar. 2014.
Walker, Childs. "Freeman Hrabowski's UMBC Legacy Grows as He Celebrates 20 Years as President." *Baltimore Sun*. Baltimore Sun, 1 Sept. 2012. Web. 17 Mar. 2014.

—*Molly Hagan*

Chris Hughes
Born: November 26, 1983
Occupation: Entrepreneur, publisher

Many people develop close relationships with their college roommates for the relatively brief period they live together, while others form lifelong friendships. Arguably, few, if any, housing assignments have had as much effect on the world as that of Chris Hughes, Dustin Moskovitz, and Mark Zuckerberg, who once shared a small suite in Harvard University's Kirkland House and who founded the now ubiquitous social-networking site Facebook in 2004.

A humanities major thrown in with a group of zealous computer coders, Hughes became, as Carl Swanson wrote for *New York* magazine (2 Dec. 2012), Facebook's "minister of external affairs and chief liaison to the human race." Swanson continued, "He acted as

Bloomberg via Getty Images

spokesperson, sounding board, and right-brain brainstormer among the coders, for whom even normal social interaction (of the kind they were trying to map onto the web) was a public-relations adventure."

"The story about how we got started in Facebook is not particularly exciting," Hughes admitted to Rebecca Davis O'Brien for the *Daily Beast* (8 Sept. 2010). "In general, in our room, we were always talking about what people were doing on the Web, what people needed to do to make their lives work better. . . . [Existing sites like Friendster and MySpace hadn't] really figured out how to make people feel comfortable sharing information in a trusted, controlled environment. [That] has been one of Facebook's defining features." So comfortable did users eventually become with sharing information and connecting on the web, that when Barack Obama ran for US president in 2008, he made social media a centerpiece of his campaign, and Hughes left Facebook to oversee that effort. Hughes is widely credited with ensuring that Obama overwhelmingly won the youth vote—and with fundamentally changing the way that all political candidates now reach out to the public.

Despite being deeply immersed in the online world, Hughes recently purchased the venerable print magazine the *New Republic*, which he aims to invigorate. "I have been fascinated by this idea of how serious journalism would survive in this digital era," he said, explaining the purchase to Swanson. "It's important. If people don't support

this type of journalism, I feel like we'll have a less cultivated citizenry and it's less likely for democracy to flourish."

EARLY YEARS AND EDUCATION

Chris Hughes was born in Hickory, North Carolina, a town previously best known as home to one of the oldest furniture manufacturers in the United States. His parents, Brenda and Arlyn "Ray" Hughes, were Evangelical Lutherans; Ray was a sales manager at Hickory's Snyder Paper Company, and Brenda taught math at a high school in the nearby town of Newton. Hughes often felt alienated from his surroundings. "I didn't feel like I was necessarily in sync with a lot of people I was around," Hughes told Swanson, who was also more vehemently informed by an acquaintance of Hughes, "He hates where he's from with a passion."

When he was in his early teens, Hughes searched the Internet for the best high schools in the country and learned of Phillips Academy, in Andover, Massachusetts, which counts actor Humphrey Bogart and President George W. Bush among its many famed alumni. Without informing his family, he filled out the application and was not only accepted but managed to win a generous financial aid package.

At the academy, Hughes set about a process of self-transformation. He rid himself of his heavy Southern accent and came out as gay. He also underwent something of a political awakening. "When I was 17, I went to India for six weeks and had what, at the time, was a very challenging trip," he recalled to Laura M. Holson for the *New York Times* (4 May 2012). "You walk down the street and you see lepers and beggars. . . . It was sort of like, why should one person have so many challenges and another person not? To me the dissonance between the levels of opportunity, it just doesn't make sense."

In 2002, after graduating from Phillips Academy, where he had served as president of the Young Democrats club and worked on the school paper, Hughes entered Harvard. There, thanks to a generous scholarship he received, he studied history and literature, and in his sophomore year he moved into the dorm that would soon become a major part of Facebook's founding legend.

FACEBOOK

Before meeting Hughes, Mark Zuckerberg had already written the code for a website he called Facemash, which allowed players to compare two student photos and vote on who was "hot" and who was "not." Because he had accessed the pictures by hacking into Harvard's computer network and copying the images from student IDs, the site was swiftly shut down by college administrators who then accused him of copyright violation and breach of security and threatened to expel him. The charges were eventually dropped.

In those few days before the shutdown, Facemash received more than twenty thousand hits, and Zuckerberg realized the need for a dynamic online community at Harvard. Enlisting the help of his roommates, who would later be joined by fellow students Eduardo Saverin and Andrew McCollum, he unveiled Thefacebook. com in February 2004. "In creating Facebook," O'Brien wrote, "Zuckerberg had hit on the school's weakness. Harvard does a lot of things. . . . But Harvard could not manufacture community. Facebook could."

During their summer break in 2004, Moskovitz, Zuckerberg, and Hughes traveled to California's Silicon Valley in search of venture capital. They attracted the support of investor Sean Parker, founder of the music-sharing site Napster. While Zuckerberg and Moskovitz remained in Palo Alto to focus on the company, which soon changed to Facebook, Hughes was reluctant to drop out of Harvard and returned to the East Coast to complete his studies. He had few financial resources outside of his scholarship money on which to rely, and besides, as he told Holson, he considered his courses to be "a prism to better understand and see how the world works today."

Still, Hughes remained involved in the company, conferring by phone and e-mail on ways to make Facebook more user-friendly and intuitive and spending his breaks in Palo Alto to work with his former roommates. Because of his people-centered contributions, coworkers nicknamed him "the Empath," and while some in the tech community have derided him as being less significant than the original coders, most observers of Facebook history acknowledge his contributions to its success.

In 2006, Hughes graduated from Harvard magna cum laude with a bachelor's degree in history and literature. He subsequently moved to Palo Alto to manage product development for the now booming website.

MY.BARACKOBAMA.COM

In the fall of 2006, a few months after Hughes moved to the West Coast and prior to the midterm elections in the United States, Facebook began allowing political candidates to set up profile pages. Barack Obama, then freshman Illinois senator, was encouraged by aides to be an early adopter, and when he approached the company, Hughes became his point person.

The two shared a strong conviction that the Internet could be an effective means of connecting citizens to the political process, and after a perfunctory interview with Obama's head of hiring in 2007, Hughes decided to sign on as a new-media strategist. Zuckerberg

was incredulous that his former roommate was leaving Facebook, which had grown by then to a reported ten million users and which had attracted lucrative buyout offers from Viacom and Yahoo!, among other high-profile companies. "He kept saying, 'Really?' But I wouldn't have left Facebook for any other person or at any other time," Hughes recalled to Ellen McGirt for *Fast Company*.

Hughes worked with Obama to create, as McGirt wrote, "the most robust set of Web-based social-networking tools ever used in a political campaign, enabling energized citizens to turn themselves into activists, long before a single human field staffer arrived to show them how." My.BarackObama.com, as the site was named, allowed supporters to plan events, raise campaign contributions, and connect with one another. Thanks in large part to Hughes's work, Obama was able to reach out to supporters efficiently and cheaply. By the 2008 presidential election, more than 2 million profiles had been posted by enthusiastic fans; 200,000 offline events, such as house parties and rallies, had been planned; and some $30 million had been raised.

The night Obama was declared the winner, campaign workers at the Chicago headquarters raced to the prearranged trolley that would take them and a group of Secret Service escorts to Grant Park where Obama was delivering his acceptance speech. Hughes stayed behind for a few extra minutes to send victory e-mails and texts to supporters. He missed the trolley and was forced to run to the park.

NEW REPUBLIC

Hughes's 1 percent stake in Facebook was said to be worth some $600 million in the wake of the company's May 2012 Initial Public Offering. He had not imagined such a windfall. "We started Facebook, because this was a fascinating idea, something that could be useful at Harvard, and something that could change the world," he told Nathaniel Mott for the September 26, 2013, edition of *PandoDaily*, an online publication that covers the world of start-up companies. "It wasn't like there was some market analysis, and we weren't making it for a fast exit or a high valuation." That year he used part of his wealth to purchase a majority share in the *New Republic*, a Washington, DC–based print magazine first published in 1914; the exact terms of the deal were not disclosed. Hughes assumed the titles of editor-in-chief and publisher and set about revitalizing the financially struggling periodical, which covers politics and culture from a slightly left-leaning point of view. During a March 9, 2012, broadcast, Hughes told National Public Radio's Mark Memmott that he appreciated the *New Republic*'s "liberal values. And by that I mean values that embrace the core American ideals of freedom, equality and an American responsibility to make the world a better place."

Hughes received some criticism from industry insiders who questioned his qualifications and expressed distaste for what they considered his hubris. Within a year, however, he had revamped its iPad and mobile applications, redesigned its website, and tripled the magazine's online readership. Readership of the print edition had also increased by almost 50 percent. At a panel discussion held at the 2013 American Magazine Media Conference, he asserted, "Print is an underestimated technology because it's light, it's colorful, it's cheap, it's all these important things. There's a reason it's lasted as long as it has. That immersive experience and the consumer who prizes that immersive experience is why magazines, in particular print and tablet magazines, still have a pretty rosy future."

PHILANTHROPY AND ENTREPRENEURSHIP

Hughes has been involved in a variety of entrepreneurial and philanthropic enterprises. In March 2009, for example, he was named Entrepreneur in Residence at General Catalyst Partners, a Massachusetts-based venture-capital firm, and in 2010 he founded Jumo, a social-networking site that allowed users to find and support nonprofit causes. Jumo was acquired the following year by the media company GOOD. Also in 2010 Hughes joined the newly formed High Level Commission on HIV Prevention, which was launched by UNAIDS, the Joint United Nations Programme on HIV/AIDS.

In 2012 Hughes joined the board of Give-Directly, a philanthropic group that transfers donations electronically to a specific recipient. Additionally, he is an investor in Upworthy, a news-aggregation site designed to promote socially meaningful yet mass appealing content. The site is drawing wide attention for its catchy, clickable headlines, which link to important stories rather than the ephemeral or humorous fodder so prevalent on other aggregators.

ACTIVISM AND PERSONAL LIFE

Hughes is deeply involved in the fight for gay rights and marriage equality. He and his husband, Sean Eldridge, are major donors to the national group Freedom to Marry. Eldridge, who had dropped out of Columbia University's law school to work for civil rights for same-sex couples, once served as a director of that group, and he is currently hoping to win election to New York's Nineteenth Congressional District seat in the November 2014 race where he will face incumbent Chris Gibson, a moderate Republican.

The couple had met through a mutual acquaintance in 2005 when Hughes was still at Harvard and Eldridge was working in the customer-service department of a moving company. Hughes proposed to Eldridge on New Year's Eve in 2010 while they were vacationing in Thailand. They married in late June of 2012 at their shared home in Garrison, New York. They had been heavily criticized for purchasing the $2 million residence, which some cynical observers characterized as merely a political move enabling them to claim residency in the Nineteenth District. Gibson's supporters have been quick to depict Eldridge as an interloper who actually cares little for the region. The couple also owns a loft in the SoHo section of Manhattan, where they are known for hosting lavish fundraisers.

SUGGESTED READING

Holson, Laura M. "A Powerful Combination." *New York Times*. New York Times, 4 May, 2012. Web. 12 Dec. 2013.

Karpel, Ari. "Forty Under 40: Chris Hughes and Sean Eldridge." *Advocate*. Here Media, 11 Apr. 2011. Web. 12 Dec. 2013.

McGirt, Ellen. "How Chris Hughes Helped Launch Facebook and the Barack Obama Campaign." *Fast Company*. Mansueto Ventures, 1 Apr. 2009. Web. 12 Dec. 2013.

Solomon, Brian. "Facebook Co-Founder Chris Hughes Marries Longtime Boyfriend." *Forbes*. Forbes.com, 2 July, 2012. Web. 12 Dec. 2013.

Stelter, Brian. "The Facebooker Who Friended Obama." 7 July 2008. *New York Times*. New York Times, 9 Mar. 2012. Web. 12 Dec. 2013.

Swanson, Carl. "Chris Hughes Is About to Turn 100." *New York*. New York Media, 2 Dec. 2012. Web. 12 Dec. 2013.

—*Mari Rich*

Daniel Humm

Born: 1976
Occupation: Chef and restaurateur

Swiss chef Daniel Humm is one of the world's brightest up-and-coming culinary talents. He is the executive chef and co-owner of Eleven Madison Park, a three-Michelin-star restaurant in New York City's Flatiron district. Since taking over the kitchen at Eleven Madison Park in 2006, Humm, who received culinary training at some of Switzerland's top hotels and restaurants, has been credited with redefining New York's ultracompetitive fine-dining scene with his innovative and inventive cuisine, which draws from influences all over the world. Under his leadership, Eleven Madison Park has won a number of awards and honors and established a reputation as "one of the most elegant and esteemed restaurants in New York City," according to Jeff Gordinier for the *New York Times* (28 July 2012). The restaurant, which has retained three Michelin stars since 2011, has also become an

Getty Images for Mercedes-Benz

international culinary destination. Its rank in the highly influential World's 50 Best Restaurants list, annually organized and compiled by the British trade magazine *Restaurant*, has risen steadily since 2010 and in 2014 was ranked number four.

In 2012 Humm, at age thirty-five, became one of the youngest-ever recipients of the James Beard Foundation's prestigious Outstanding Chef Award. That year he and business partner Will Guidara, Eleven Madison Park's general manager, opened their second Manhattan restaurant, NoMad, in the NoMad Hotel. Humm has refused to rest on his laurels, however. "You're only as good as your last meal," he told Susan Jung for the *South China Morning Post* (15 Mar. 2013). "The pressure is in satisfying every guest every night."

EARLY LIFE

Daniel Humm was born in 1976 in Strengelbach, a small village located about an hour outside of Zurich, Switzerland. His father, Roland, is an architect, and his mother, Brigitte, is a homemaker. Humm has described his mother as an excellent cook and has credited her with sparking his interest in and appreciation for food. He has fondly recalled coming home from school as a boy to observe his mother prepare both lunch and dinner. In an interview with Frank Bruni for the *New York Times Diner's Journal* (7 Aug. 2006), Humm said that his mother taught him early on the importance of cooking seasonally and locally, "using the best ingredients, shopping at markets or farms, or finding the freshest rabbit in town. It was never anything fancy but it was always simple, fresh, and cooked from the heart."

Humm was around eight years old when he decided to pursue a culinary career. He arrived at this decision after eating with his family at the legendary Swiss chef Frédy Girardet's self-named, three-Michelin-star restaurant in

Crissier, Switzerland. Girardet, who is widely regarded as one of the most influential chefs of the twentieth century, prepared Humm a spaghetti dish with tomatoes and lobster, which left a lasting impression on him. Soon afterward Humm started working at a local farmers' market frequented by his mother.

Despite his culinary aspirations, Humm was urged to follow in his father's footsteps and become an architect. Before he even reached his teens, his father had begun securing him internships at various architectural firms around Zurich. It was not long, however, before Humm realized that architectural work was not for him. Humm has nonetheless credited his father with instilling in him a strong sense of design and structure that he would later apply to his cooking, as well as with encouraging him to follow a vocation that he enjoyed and where he could excel.

Another obstacle standing in the way of Humm's culinary dreams was a burgeoning athletic career. He grew up playing soccer and racing mountain bikes, and as a teenager, he became a member of the Swiss junior national mountain biking team. Though good enough to consider entering the professional cycling ranks, Humm too often found himself coming up short against Europe's top cycling talents. "The guys who were beating me were on another level," he told Anne E. McBride for the quarterly food and culture journal *Gastronomica* (2012). "I felt that I could never beat them. . . . So I stopped cycling and started cooking."

EARLY COOKING CAREER

In 1990, at the age of fourteen, Humm left school to begin a three-year apprenticeship at the Hotel Baur au Lac, an internationally renowned five-star hotel restaurant in Zurich. There, he learned the basics of formal cooking, receiving training as a garde-manger, or pantry chef, and in such disciplines as baking and butchering. "I started cooking because I really loved being in the kitchen," he told McBride. "I loved the atmosphere, loved the ingredients and the fact that I could create something with them."

After working at a series of other Swiss luxury hotel restaurants, Humm landed a job at Gérard Rabaey's Le Pont de Brent, a highly acclaimed, three-Michelin-star restaurant in Brent. He worked there for about three years, during which he became a protégé of Rabaey, whom he has cited as a mentor. Rabaey, known for his demanding and uncompromising approach to cooking, "embodied perfection and consistency on all levels, with the fewest possible—yet perfect—ingredients," Humm told Bruni. "I learned from him the philosophy behind cooking and about understanding how the dish comes together and why ingredients work." During his time at Le Pont de Brent, Humm worked exhausting eighteen-hour days and performed an array of menial tasks, from separating vegetables into five different sizes to cleaning the ceilings of the restaurant's kitchen with Q-tips.

In the early 2000s Humm left Le Pont de Brent to accept his first executive chef position at Gasthaus zum Gupf, a forty-five-seat restaurant located in the Swiss mountain village of Rehetobel. Within months, he transformed the remote mountain establishment into a world-renowned dining destination. At age twenty-four Humm received his first Michelin star, becoming the youngest chef in Europe to earn one, and in 2002 he was named Discovery of the Year by the influential French restaurant guide Gault Millau.

CAMPTON PLACE

Humm saw his profile in the culinary world rise in May 2003, when he became executive chef of Campton Place, an upscale fine-dining hotel restaurant in San Francisco. Paul Zuest, a prominent Swiss hotelier who was then serving as Campton Place's general manager, recruited Humm to helm the eponymous restaurant inside the hotel after its previous incumbent, the Michelin-starred French chef Laurent Manrique, left to take over the San Francisco restaurant Aqua. Upon arriving there, Humm was immediately presented with the challenge of leading an overhaul of the restaurant, which had opened in 1982. "It was a turning point for me," he told Roberta Naas for *Gotham* magazine (Nov. 2013). "I entered an unfamiliar world where I spoke no English and was essentially starting from the ground up."

Four months after Humm took over its kitchen, *San Francisco Chronicle* food critic Michael Bauer awarded Campton Place three and a half stars, the highest possible rating for a restaurant with a new chef. In his review for the *Chronicle* (31 Aug. 2003), Bauer called Humm a "miracle worker" and praised his "contemporary brand of European cuisine." Campton Place received enthusiastic reviews from other critics, most of whom lauded Humm for his innovative and sophisticated French cuisine. Humm was nominated for a Rising Star Chef award by the James Beard Foundation in both 2004 and 2005 and was recognized as one of *Food & Wine* magazine's Best New Chefs in 2005. That year Bauer upgraded Campton Place to a perfect four-star rating. His updated review of the restaurant for the *Chronicle* (4 Sept. 2005) touted Humm as "the brightest star to land in Northern California since Thomas Keller opened the French Laundry in Yountville."

ELEVEN MADISON PARK

In January 2006 Humm left Campton Place to become executive chef of Eleven Madison Park, an elegant and spacious high-ceilinged restaurant in the Flatiron neighborhood of Manhattan. He was hired by the famed New York restaurateur Danny Meyer, whose Union Square Hospitality Group first opened the restaurant as a brasserie in 1998. Meyer "wasn't happy with the restaurant and wanted to change directions," Humm told Jung. "He wanted to bring me in to make the food more refined; he thought the dining room had so much potential." Several months after he took the helm, Humm brought in a new general manager, Will Guidara, who had opened restaurants for Meyer at New York's Museum of Modern Art, and the two began transforming the then two-star brasserie into a unique and contemporary fine-dining establishment. As a model for their changes, they initially drew inspiration from other top-rated restaurants.

Situated on the ground floor of the Metropolitan Life North Building, a historic thirty-story art deco skyscraper, the newly revamped Eleven Madison Park opened to rave reviews and quickly developed a reputation as one of the best restaurants in New York City. In a notable, three-and-a-half-star review for the *New York Observer* (24 Apr. 2006), Moira Hodgson wrote that Humm is "a star" and that "there's a purity and directness to Mr. Humm's dishes (which are also visually stunning)." She concluded, however, that the restaurant "needed a bit of Miles Davis." Hodgson's Miles Davis line caught the attention of Humm and Guidara, who started researching the legendary jazz trumpeter to understand its meaning better. They subsequently came up with a list of eleven words—in honor of Eleven Madison Park—that best describe Davis and his music, such as *cool*, *forward-moving*, *reinvention*, and *collaborative*, and began using the list as part of their new mission statement for the restaurant. In his interview with McBride, Humm explained, "If you want to create something unique, I think it's important that you take inspiration from something outside of your own world. Because otherwise, you're just going to become like any other restaurant."

RISE TO INTERNATIONAL PROMINENCE

In 2007 Eleven Madison Park earned its first three-star rating from the *New York Times*. In his review (10 Jan. 2007), Bruni, then the paper's chief restaurant critic, wrote of Humm's "opulent, inspired cooking" and noted that his meals "hit highs they never came close to in the past." Bruni elevated Eleven Madison Park's rating to four stars in 2009, making it one of only a handful of restaurants in the city to earn the rare honor; that same year the restaurant received its first Michelin star. More importantly, Bruni's four-star review helped Eleven Madison Park recover strongly from economic troubles caused by the 2008–9 financial crisis. Bruni told John Colapinto for the *New Yorker* (10 Sept. 2012) that the restaurant "just oozed from every one of its pores the fact that it was a place where a number of extraordinary young and talented people were determined to make their mark." He added that there "was a crackle of excitement to being there that you didn't feel" at other top high-end New York restaurants.

In 2010 Humm was named best chef in New York by the James Beard Foundation, and Eleven Madison Park debuted on *Restaurant* magazine's annual World's 50 Best Restaurants list, coming in at number fifty. That year, in an effort to evolve and create a better all-around experience for patrons, Humm removed thirty-four seats from the dining room and replaced the restaurant's traditional à la carte menu with an innovative grid of sixteen main seasonal ingredients, which patrons built their courses around. The grid menu, Humm told McBride, gave patrons the freedom to "choose their favorite things and then be surprised."

Humm's bold, innovative changes helped Eleven Madison Park climb to number twenty-four on the World's 50 Best Restaurants list in 2011. That year also saw the restaurant receive a James Beard Award for outstanding restaurant and earn three stars in the Michelin Guide, a rating it has since retained. In October 2011 Humm and Guidara teamed up with investors to purchase Eleven Madison Park from Meyer, in part so they could pursue other restaurant ventures. Around this time they formed a new restaurant group, called Made Nice.

NOMAD AND OTHER ENDEAVORS

Humm and Guidara's highly anticipated second Manhattan restaurant, NoMad, opened in the NoMad Hotel in March 2012. Located just four blocks away from Eleven Madison Park, the restaurant features five separate but connected dining spaces and a contemporary menu of European and American dishes. Humm has said that NoMad, which serves breakfast, lunch, and dinner as well as room service for hotel guests, was inspired by the legendary British rock band the Rolling Stones. He has billed the restaurant as a more casual and cheaper alternative to his flagship. Within its first year of opening, the restaurant earned three stars from the *New York Times* and one from Michelin.

Two months after NoMad debuted, Humm was named the top chef in the United States by the James Beard Foundation, and Eleven Madison Park moved up to number ten on the annual World's 50 Best Restaurants list. In the fall of 2012, Humm and Guidara instituted more changes at Eleven Madison Park, remodeling the restaurant to a more modern décor

and redesigning its menu to offer only one option for lunch and dinner: a $195 twelve-course tasting menu inspired by the food and history of New York. The participatory four-hour meal "integrates haute cuisine with a playful, street-smart sense of performance and theater," Andy Battaglia wrote for *Nation's Restaurant News* (12 Nov. 2012). "You've got to listen to your guests," Humm explained to Gordinier. "And our guests are telling us that they want this unique experience and journey."

Humm's first cookbook, *Eleven Madison Park*, was published by Little, Brown and Company in November 2011. Coauthored with Guidara, the highly acclaimed book features 125 recipes that reflect the sophisticated cuisine of Eleven Madison Park. Humm and Guidara published their second cookbook, *I Love New York*, in April 2013. That month Eleven Madison Park rose to number five on the World's 50 Best Restaurants list, becoming the highest-ranked restaurant in the United States. Humm has said that he hopes to continue setting culinary trends. "I want it so that fifty years from now," he told Jung, "people will look back at this time and say, 'Wow, those guys at Eleven Madison Park were ahead of their time, they were doing something really cool.'"

PERSONAL LIFE

Humm lives in northern New Jersey with his wife, Geneen, and their two daughters, Vivienne and Colette. He is an avid marathon runner and a competitive mountain bike racer. He told Jacqueline Raposo for the *Serious Eats New York* food blog (27 Feb. 2012), "For me there are three things in life: I love my job and I love working. I love my family. . . . And I love running and biking."

SUGGESTED READING

Colapinto, John. "Check, Please." *New Yorker* 10 Sept. 2012: 58. Print.
Gordinier, Jeff. "A Restaurant of Many Stars Raises the Ante." *New York Times* 28 July 2012: A1. Print.
Humm, Daniel. "An Interview with Daniel Humm, Eleven Madison Park." Interview by Anne E. McBride. *Gastronomica* 12.2 (2012): 96–99. Print.
Humm, Daniel. "Q&A: Daniel Humm." Interview by Frank Bruni. *New York Times*. New York Times, 7 Aug. 2006. Web. 15 Jan. 2014.
Jung, Susan. "New York Chef Daniel Humm's Menu Is Inspired by Jazz Legend Miles Davis." *South China Morning Post*. South China Morning Post, 15 Mar. 2013. Web. 15 Jan. 2014.

—*Chris Cullen*

Bob Iger

Born: February 10, 1951
Occupation: Disney CEO

Bob Iger is the CEO of Disney, one of the world's great multinational corporations. Although at first regarded as an unlikely successor to former CEO Michael Eisner, Iger, vetted by the board of directors, took his position in 2005. Under Iger the company has expanded its overseas theme parks and made strategic purchases to strengthen its role in creating content, aimed primarily at children and tweens, across a variety of platforms. The former chair of ABC, Iger is a self-professed techno-geek who travels with two iPods and early on saw the potential of new media venues for Disney. Among other technological innovations, the company pioneered a new tracking device, Magic Bands, in 2013. The waterproof wristband serves as an admission ticket, hotel key, and credit card at Disney resorts. While some detractors are concerned about the device's privacy implications, for its proponents, the Magic Band enhances the customer service provided to guests. Park employees can even use the device to enable a costumed character to walk up to a child and call him or her by name. Under Iger Disney has purchased several big-name media companies, including LucasFilm for $4.06 billion in 2013, with plans to release a new Star Wars trilogy starting in 2015.

EARLY LIFE AND EDUCATION

Robert A. Iger was born on February 10, 1951. Iger's father worked in marketing and was a jazz trumpeter on the side; his mother worked as a librarian and cared for him and his younger sister in the Long Island middle-class suburb of Oceanside. As a child, Iger enjoyed watching the *Mickey Mouse Show* and wearing his *Davy Crockett* coonskin cap. In high school he was the sports editor of his school's paper and the varsity teams' radio announcer; he also acted a bit, portraying Francis Nurse in a production of Arthur Miller's *The Crucible*. He graduated magna cum laude with a bachelor of science degree in communications from Ithaca College, where he worked on *Campus Probe* for the college's ICB-TV show. Although he set his sights on a job as a news anchor, he worked as a weatherman briefly before joining the low ranks of ABC. He eventually moved to ABC Sports.

CAPITAL CITIES/ABC

In 1989 Iger became president of ABC Entertainment. Four years later he became president of ABC Television Network Group. In 1994, at forty-four, Iger was named president of Capital Cities/ABC, Inc. The move was a step toward taking the CEO position that his mentor there, Thomas Murphy, planned to leave. During this

period Iger was trained in what he terms the "Tom Murphy School of Management." He explained to Ronald Grover for *Business Week* (5 Feb. 2007), "You put good people in jobs and give them room to run." He added, "You involve yourself in a responsible way, but not to the point where you are usurping their authority. I don't have the time or concentration—and you could argue maybe even the talent—to do that."

The only flaw in Iger's plan was Michael Eisner's too-good-to-refuse offer to buy the company in 1996. Murphy sold the company for nineteen billion dollars. Iger spent most of the next decade as Eisner's right-hand man, serving as chair of ABC Group and president of Walt Disney International. In that position he consolidated the company's overseas operations.

Between 1996 and 2004 ABC had four different leadership teams. The new team in place in 2004, when relations between the board and Eisner became increasingly tense, was composed of Disney insiders. Yet at the end of 2002 ABC had slipped to rank fourth among the major broadcast networks. Analysts suggested part of the problem was the lack of clear leadership; each of the other major networks had a single head, while ABC was run by committee. Ratings and income improved enough, however, that Iger's work at ABC was not considered a black mark against him when the members of the board began the search for Eisner's replacement.

A NEW CEO FOR DISNEY

At the annual meeting in 2005, calls for Eisner to resign intensified. Roy Disney, the nephew of Walt Disney, was among Eisner's most vocal opponents. Iger was the only in-house candidate for the CEO position. Outside contenders included Peter Chernin of News Corp, Paul Pressler of Gap, Terry Semel of Yahoo, and Meg Whitman of eBay. During the vetting process, scrambling ensued when journalist James Stewart's book *DisneyWars* was published, charging that Iger knuckled under to Eisner and exhibited poor judgment. Asked by Patricia Sellers for *Fortune* magazine (7 Mar. 2005) about his fitness to take the position, Iger responded, "Do you ever know? I have much more authority than people believe."

In Iger's favor was his work with Hong Kong Disneyland, which was on the verge of opening as the decision was being made. The addition of such hit shows as *Desperate Housewives* and *Lost* to ABC's lineup and a profit turnaround were also his doing. Ultimately, the eleven-member board voted to offer Iger the position. Despite a move by the disaffected Roy Disney and Stanley Gold to nullify the offer, Iger became CEO. The two men withdrew their lawsuit and soon became firm Iger supporters.

DISNEY IN ASIA

Iger was influential in facilitating the opening of Hong Kong Disneyland, a 310-acre park located on Lantau Island. In contrast to Eisner, Iger saw international growth as key to the company's growth. Hoping to attract visitors from mainland China, Disney placed a Chinese version of the original California Disneyland in Hong Kong. A master in feng shui was consulted and his recommendations heeded; the front gate was rotated and boulders strategically placed for success.

Iger's Hong Kong Disneyland is culturally tailored in other ways as well. The restaurant menus reflect local preferences, including options such as seafood fried rice and dim sum. Murals in one restaurant are based on Disney's *Mulan*, a 1998 animated film based on a Chinese legend. Mickey Mouse sports a traditional-style red-and-gold suit. There is still a castle for Sleeping Beauty, but Mulan has her own pavilion. As Tom Morris, one of Disney's creative designers (known as "imagineers"), told Michael Schuman and Jeffrey Ressner for *Time* magazine (2005), "It's turn-of-the-century America, with a Disney overlay, with a Chinese overlay."

Iger was hoping for success similar to that of Tokyo Disneyland, which boasted some twenty-five million guests a year, rather than the kind of cultural mistake that had caused Euro Disney to do poorly in Paris. Disney wanted to reach the 1.3 billion residents of China, of whom 290 million were under the age of fourteen in 2005. Yet Iger was also a realist. "Our eyes are wide open to the fact that, while China is very exciting for us in terms of potential, it's filled with great challenges," he told Schuman and Ressner. Those challenges include frequent piracy of films and other content, the nearly forty-year ban of Disney under communism, and restrictions on media ownership that prevent the Disney Channel from being broadcast in China. Disney films are popular, however; in 1995 *The Lion King* was one of the first foreign films shown in the country, and by the opening of Hong Kong Disneyland, fifteen Disney animated features had been screened in China, no small feat in a country that permits just twenty foreign films to be shown annually. To facilitate its entry into modern China, Disney began opening English-language centers in 2008. With animated white boards, these thirty-plus schools are high-tech introductions to Disney music and songs, teaching children English through Disney's world.

The Hong Kong park finally turned a small profit in 2013, after seven years and a multimillion-dollar expansion that increased its size by about one-fourth. Annual attendance increased to 6.7 million, an increase of 13 percent. In addition, revenue grew by 18 percent. Seeking to expand further into the Chinese market, Disney has slated 2015 for the opening of a new park in Shanghai.

TAKING CHARGE

When Iger was named CEO of Disney in 2005, he was viewed as lacking experience for the job, despite Eisner's recommendation. As Eisner himself put it to Sellers, "I bought into the cliché of Bob—that because he didn't get on top of the table and rant and rave and act like a fool, he wasn't a creative, passionate person." Iger was also seen as Eisner's yes man. Iger told Richard Siklos for *Fortune* (19 Jan. 2009), "I don't know that I was necessarily on a mission to prove people wrong," noting that he "wanted very much to exceed expectations."

Iger has been called the Anti-Eisner. He has made Monday morning staff meetings more about conversation than pronouncements. To foster better communication, he added another door from his own office to a hallway with more traffic and moved key executives to the same floor. Most notably, division heads under Iger have regained and maintained much greater autonomy, a move out of the Tom Murphy management playbook that has proven a successful and lucrative business strategy.

In another first for the company, Iger put creative teams in such high-demand locations as China, India, and Russia to develop Disney-original content in the local language. As is true for most multinational retailers, overseas growth has been key to profit. Many of the initiatives that occurred as Iger began his tenure had been put in motion by his predecessor. As Iger told Ronald Grover, "It was because of [Eisner] that I was able to hit the ground running."

Although Mickey Mouse is the face of Disney, the company also owns ABC as well as 80 percent of ESPN, which generates nearly half of Disney's operating income and is so powerful that Iger phased out ABC Sports in 2006. Disney is also part owner of A & E Networks, which operates the cable channels A & E, Lifetime, and History. Perhaps the most significant purchase made by Disney, however, was made during Iger's tenure.

PURCHASING PIXAR

The same day he was named CEO of Disney in May 2005, Iger spoke to Apple founder Steve Jobs about acquiring the animation studio Pixar, which Apple owned. Disney had already been distributing Pixar films, but the deal, which was set to expire, was in jeopardy due to the tension between Eisner and Jobs. Jobs consented, not least because Iger shared his vision of distributing content across platforms, including the new ones Jobs was building at that point. The iPod (Iger has been known to travel with two) would soon carry Disney films and ABC shows.

That October Disney made Jobs the major individual shareholder, with 7 percent of the company's stock; the figure for purchase was $7.4 billion, which seemed high to some. Jobs reported that he was willing to make the deal because Iger, when first aware that he was going to become CEO, spent a day at Disneyland, riding every ride and attending every show; that day showed him that Pixar characters were the basis of the newest entertainment. Addressing concerns about a possible Apple-Disney merger, Jobs told Siklos, "I think there are some companies that transcend just being businesses. Disney is one of those very special companies, and I think it's very special companies that prosper in the long run. I've never worried about my investment. I know that it's going to be just fine. Family is a renewable resource."

The acquisition of Pixar led to a refocus of Disney brands, which had become tired. Disney was then seen as creating content for only the youngest children; rivals such as Viacom's Nickelodeon were appealing to tweens as well with some edgier content and attitude. A first move in this direction was the release, shortly after Iger became CEO, of the film *Pirates of the Caribbean: The Curse of the Black Pearl* (2003), Disney's first PG-13 movie, based on one of the most popular rides at Disney theme parks.

FRANCHISES AND MERCHANDISE

A second initiative that Iger began was in emphasizing the various Disney franchises and creating new ones. For Iger a franchise, as he defined it for Siklos, is "something that creates value across multiple businesses and across multiple territories over a long period of time." Disney's princess and fairy franchises, for example, have multiple consumer goods, publishing, and online tie-ins to delight consumers. The offerings include not only sheet sets and lunch boxes but also such high-end merchandise as a Mickey Mouse T-shirt from Dolce and Gabbana retailing for more than a thousand dollars. By 2009, three years after the first *Cars* movie was released, merchandising from the movie was bringing in an annual two billion dollars. In 2008 Disney acquired Marvel Entertainment for $4.3 billion, a move that attracted consumers already interested in well-known characters such as Captain America and Iron Man as well as new audiences and opened up further possibilities for product tie-ins.

LOOKING FORWARD

In December 2012 Disney announced that its content would be made available through the web-based video service Netflix, beginning with new films made in 2016. Pixar, Marvel, and Star Wars films, along with Disney's own family-friendly fare, are expected to boost Netflix, which had been struggling in comparison with competing providers such as Hulu and Amazon.

Although Disney's board in October 2011 set a departure date for Iger, only two years later they extended his contract through June 2016. The decision was based largely on the company's performance. Between September 2005 and the end of fiscal year 2013, shareholder returns increased by 193 percent. (By contrast, the Standard & Poor's average for the same period was 54 percent.) Stock prices increased by 80 percent under Iger, based in part on his decision to spend during the recession rather than pull back as some other entertainment companies did. Iger has said he will resign as CEO in early 2015 and remain chair of the board of directors until July 2016. Although he has not discussed any plans for his future, some speculate that he may have political aspirations.

PERSONAL LIFE

Iger is married to Willow Bay, senior editor of the *Huffington Post*. The couple have two sons. Iger also has two grown daughters from a previous marriage.

Having retained his childhood love of sports, Iger competes for the Disney Team in the Nautica Malibu Triathalon, a fundraiser for Children's Hospital Los Angeles. He is dedicated to remaining physically fit, working out with a trainer in his Brentwood home at 4:30 each morning. As an early arrival at the office, usually there by 6:45 a.m., he sometimes makes the first pot of coffee of the day.

Iger is a sailor and the owner of a fifty-two-foot Hinckley. He sometimes uses sailing analogies to describe his strategy for dealing with crises. "It sounds like a cliché, but I'm a sailor.

When you start overreacting to storm conditions, you're in peril," he told Sellers.

SUGGESTED READING

Grover, Ronald. "How Bob Iger Unchained Disney." *Business Week* 5 Feb. 2007: 74–79. Print.

Gunther, Marc. "Is Bob Iger Ready for His Close-Up?" *Fortune* 4 Apr. 2005: 76–78. Print.

Reingold, Jennifer, and Marilyn Adamo. "The Fun King." *Fortune* 21 May 2012: 166–74. Print.

Schuman, Michael, and Jeffrey Ressner. "Disney's Great Leap into China." *Time* 11 July 2005: 52–54. Print.

Sellers, Patricia. "The Two Faces of Bob Iger." *Fortune* 7 Mar. 2005: 23. Print.

Sherman, Jay. "Stuck in Eisner's Shadow." *Television Week* 23.9 (2004): 41–42. Print.

Siklos, Richard. "Bob Iger Rocks Disney." *Fortune* 19 Jan. 2009: 80. Print.

—*Judy Johnson*

Associated Press

Thomas R. Insel

Born: October 19, 1951
Occupation: Head of the National Institute of Mental Health (NIMH)

The psychiatric field has undergone a radical transformation in recent decades. For about a century, the treatment of mental illnesses and disorders was conducted through the lens of the psychoanalytic theories developed at the turn of the twentieth century by pioneering thinkers like Sigmund Freud, who believed that the unconscious and events in a person's past contribute greatly to mental afflictions. Since the 1990s, however, psychiatrists and other mental health professions have been aided in their treatment options by a better understanding of the biological origins of mental illnesses and disorders. Today, the field is seeking a new framework by which to diagnose patients, provide better treatment options, and improve the overall quality of care people are receiving.

Spearheading the US government's efforts in improving mental health is Thomas R. Insel, a psychiatrist and neuroscientist who, since 2002, has been the director of the National Institute of Mental Health (NIMH), which provides funding for a broad array of mental health research initiatives. Dr. Insel believes that the world is poised on the edge of a new era, one in which the recent discoveries of the varied ways the brain malfunctions will lead to new and far more effective treatments for mental disorders. In an article for *Scientific American* (Apr. 2010), Insel wrote: "From the scientific standpoint, it is difficult to find a precedent in medicine for what is beginning to happen in psychiatry. The intellectual basis of this field is shifting from one discipline, based on subjective 'mental' phenomena, to another, neuroscience. Indeed, today's developing science-based understanding of mental illness very likely will revolutionize prevention and treatment and bring real and lasting relief to millions of people worldwide."

EARLY LIFE AND EDUCATION

Thomas R. Insel was born on October 19, 1951, in Dayton, Ohio, to H. Herbert Insel and Ruth Insel. Both of Insel's parents were well educated—his father was an ophthalmologist and his mother a medical social worker who had attended New York University and later (on full scholarship) the Columbia University School of Social Work, from which she graduated in 1946. The year prior she had married Insel's father, with whom she shared a passionate devotion to aiding and preventing blindness in people living in developing nations. Later in her life she would serve as president of the Prevention of Blindness Society of Metropolitan Washington and as vice president of the Pan American Health and Education Foundation.

Thomas Insel and his three brothers would all go on to become doctors. Insel began taking college courses at age fourteen and matriculated at Boston University's College of Liberal Arts at age fifteen. Between the completion of his liberal arts courses and entering medical school as part of the university's combined BA-MD program, he decided to take time off to travel around the world. In 1969, eighteen-year-old Insel married Deborah Silber, and the two of them traveled together in Asia. While there, they worked at a tuberculosis clinic in Hong Kong and a Mennonite mission hospital in India. They returned to the United States in 1970, and Insel returned to Boston University. After completing his degree in 1974, Insel interned at Berkshire Medical Center in Pittsfield, Massachusetts, and was a resident at the Langley Porter Neuropsychiatric Institute at the University of California, San Francisco.

EARLY CAREER

In 1979, after Insel completed his residency, he joined the National Institute of Mental Health as a clinical neuropharmacology associate. NIMH is one of twenty-seven institutes of the National Institutes of Health (NIH), the US government's main agency responsible for medical research. The largest agency in the world for the study of mental illnesses and disorders, NIMH uses its roughly $1.5 billion annual budget to fund a wide variety of research programs through its grants to universities and other research organizations.

During his first stint at NIMH, which lasted until 1994, Insel was involved in two main areas of research. The first centered on some of the first treatment trials for people suffering from obsessive-compulsive disorder (OCD). During these trials he and his colleagues demonstrated how serotonin reuptake inhibitors help control the symptoms of OCD. The second area involved animal research. In this latter program, he and his colleagues sought to demonstrate how neurobiology affects complex social behavior in animals. "Using molecular, cellular, and pharmacological approaches, Dr. Insel's laboratory . . . demonstrated the importance of the neuropeptides, oxytocin and vasopressin, in maternal behavior, pair bond formation, and aggression," notes a NIH news release (10 Sept. 2002) announcing his appointment as NIMH director.

In 1994 Insel left NIMH to serve as director of Emory University's Yerkes Regional Primate Research Center in Atlanta, Georgia. According to the NIH news release, "As director of Yerkes, Dr. Insel built one of the nation's leading HIV vaccine research programs." Upon leaving the directorship of Yerkes in 1999, he became a professor of psychiatry at Emory and the founding director of the Center for Behavioral Neuroscience, an association of more than 150 neuroscientists that receives funding from the National Science Foundation (NSF). At the same time he was also director of the Center for Autism Research, which receives funding from the NIH to investigate the root causes of all aspects of autism spectrum disorder (ASD). During his time at Emory, Insel continued his research into the neurobiology of complex social behaviors—similar to the work he had been doing at NIMH.

DIRECTOR OF NIMH

In September 2002, Elias Zerhouni, who was then serving as NIH director under President George W. Bush, announced that Insel had been appointed director of the National Institute of Mental Health. Since becoming NIMH director, Insel has been responsible for allocating research grants to universities and institutions engaged in both basic science and clinical research that are aimed at improving existing treatments or developing new ones for mental illnesses and disorders. As director, he also oversees the in-house research efforts at the NIMH in Bethesda, Maryland, as well as implements studies aimed at better understanding and ultimately improving the way mental health services are provided across the United States.

Since taking on his responsibilities at NIMH, Insel has sought to move his agency toward funding research that will help mental health professionals better understand the role genetics and biology play in mental illnesses and disorders. Since Insel began his training in psychiatry in the 1970s, the field has undergone enormous changes. In the 1970s, psychiatric treatment was based mainly on psychoanalytic theory, with psychiatrists treating patients by trying to understand what in a person's individual background makes him or her, for example, depressed or obsessive-compulsive. Twenty-first century science, however, is revealing that many psychological disorders are in fact biological in nature and that some are caused by malfunctioning connections between different parts of the brain. This new and better understanding of neuroscience has required many mental health professionals to completely reevaluate their field as they learn more about the true causes of mental disorders. In an interview with PBS for its *Frontline* program (18 July 2007), Insel noted that psychiatry "largely has been swept by understanding that many of these disorders can be thought of in more biological terms; that psychiatric disorders are, at the end of the day, brain disorders."

BIOLOGY OF MENTAL ILLNESS

Some of the major disorders that Insel and other leaders in the field believe are more biological in nature than previously thought include depression (also known as major depressive disorder), OCD, and post-traumatic stress disorder (PTSD), which was formerly known as shell shock due to its prevalence among soldiers who had been under fire during wartime. Depression, as one example, affects an estimated 16 percent of all Americans, according to Insel ("Faulty Circuits," Apr. 2010); in the developed world, it is the main cause of mental affliction in people ages fifteen to forty-four. Research has indicated that a circuitry disorder in a tiny region of the brain's prefrontal cortex, called Brodmann area

25, is found in people suffering from major depressive disorder. In brain scans of people suffering from OCD, neurologists have discovered abnormal activity near the orbitofrontal cortex, a region of the brain that involves higher-level tasks like decision-making. Research has even shown that PTSD, a condition that typically has a clear environmental, or outside, trigger, may also be biological in nature. Neuroimaging studies of those afflicted with PTSD indicate that these individuals have reduced activity in the brain's ventromedial prefrontal cortex, an area that helps reduce anxiety related to memories of traumatic events.

Although researchers have yet to develop fully effective treatments for these disorders, the discoveries that these conditions have a biological basis gives hope to mental health professionals like Insel that, first, they may ultimately have a medicinal cure, and second, that in the short term, the societal stigmas associated with these diseases may end. As Insel wrote in *Scientific American*: "Perhaps the most immediate result of approaching mental disorders as brain circuit disorders will be changing public perception of these illnesses. In different generations, people with mental illness have been stigmatized as possessed, dangerous, weak-willed, or victimized by bad parents. Science supports none of this. A scientific approach to mental disorders could allow those who struggle with these illnesses to receive full acceptance and the high-quality care that they deserve."

As NIMH director, Insel has also been deeply involved in autism research, a field of study with which he has long been associated. He has significantly increased NIHM's funding into researching this pervasive developmental disorder, which greatly reduces a person's ability to fully communicate and interact with other people. Under his leadership, NIMH has also advanced the studies of other disorders that affect children and adults, including attention deficit hyperactivity disorder.

CRITICIZING THE *DSM*

In 2013 Insel received widespread media attention when he proclaimed that the psychiatric field's main guide to identifying mental conditions, the *Diagnostic and Statistical Manual of Mental Disorders* (DSM), suffers from a "lack of validity," according to an article by Pam Belluck and Benedict Carey published in the *New York Times* (7 May 2013). "As long as the research community takes the D.S.M. to be a bible, we'll never make progress," Insel told Belluck and Carey. "People think that everything has to match D.S.M. criteria, but you know what? Biology never read that book." Such bold statements sent shockwaves through the psychiatric field. For decades mental health professionals have used the *DSM* as a shorthand way for

psychiatrists to understand each other, when presented with specific patients with specific symptoms. Moreover, the *DSM* is published by the prestigious American Psychiatric Association and is revised only periodically; the 2013 edition is only the fifth edition and the first new one since 1994. Mental health professionals eagerly anticipate each newly revised edition because it is based on new research conducted since the last edition.

Insel believes the *DSM*, and particularly *DSM-5* as the 2013 edition is known, does not do enough to account for the complexity of mental disorders in the way it categorizes particular diseases. He also believes that it does not use objective, scientific measurements in defining or grouping mental disorders. Insel is not alone in his criticism of the *DSM*—his predecessor at NIMH, Steven Hyman, was also critical of it, believing its categories to be an invented common language—but he is one of the highest profile scientists to question its validity. As Gary Greenberg points out in the *New Yorker* (16 May 2013), "the D.S.M. has frustrated scientists, who note that the most common symptoms of mental disorder—sadness and worry, for instance, or delusions and hallucinations—appear as criteria for many different diagnoses; that many patients can be diagnosed with more than one disorder; and that the few solid findings about mental illness that have emerged from genetic and neuroscience studies indicate that the D.S.M's categories simply don't correspond to biological reality."

While Insel does not suggest that the mental health community immediately abandon the *DSM*, he believes that researchers should begin to move away from its categorizations and build a new framework through the investigation of the root biological causes of mental illnesses and disorders. To that end, he has asked any outside researchers seeking grants from NIMH to disregard *DSM* categories and instead focus on the neuroscience in their investigations.

RESEARCH DOMAIN CRITERIA

Under his directorship, NIMH also established a federal research initiative called the Research Domain Criteria (RDoC) in 2011, as a way to help researchers build a new foundation for studying mental afflictions by starting with what is already known about the brain's role in mental disorders. On its website, NIMH describes RDoC's purpose as "to define basic dimensions of functioning (such as fear circuitry or working memory) to be studied across multiple units of analysis, from genes to neural circuits to behaviors, cutting across disorders as traditionally defined. The intent is to translate rapid progress in basic neurobiological and behavioral research to an improved integrative understanding of psychopathology and the development of new and/or optimally matched treatments for mental disorders."

Despite NIMH's efforts, RDoC has yet to be fully embraced by researchers, according to Belluck and Carey, in part because most understand it will take a number of years before the new framework would be capable of being used to treat patients. Until that time, most mental health professionals agree, the *DSM* will remain the industry standard, for better or worse, because it is what is being used to treat patients. Despite this, Insel and other RDoC supporters remain optimistic that the new framework will ultimately provide more accurate categorization and improved treatment of mental illnesses and disorders.

PUBLICATIONS, MEMBERSHIPS, AND AWARDS

During his decades in the psychiatric field, Insel has published more than 250 scientific articles, as well as a number of books, including *The Neurobiology of Parental Behavior* (2003), which he coauthored with Michael Numan. He has received several awards for his contributions to his field, including, among others, the A. E. Bennett Award (1986), the Curt Richter Prize (1991), the Sachar Prize (2007), the Outstanding Alumnus Award from Boston University (2009), and the Ipsen Prize (2010). He is a member of the Institute of Medicine of the National Academy of Sciences.

Insel lives with his wife, Deborah. They have two children.

SUGGESTED READING

Belluck, Pam, and Benedict Carey. "Psychiatry's New Guide Falls Short, Experts Say." *New York Times* 7 May 2013: A13. Print.

Greenberg, Gary. "The Rats of N.I.M.H." *New Yorker*. *New Yorker*. Condé Nast, 16 May 2013. Web. 18 Nov. 2013.

Insel, Thomas R. "Faulty Circuits." *Scientific American* Apr. 2010: 44–51. Print.

Insel, Thomas R. Interview. *Medicated Child/Frontline*. PBS/WGBH Educational Foundation, 18 June 2007. Web. 18 Nov. 2013.

"Thomas R. Insel, M.D., Named New Director of the National Institute of Mental Health." *National Institute of Mental Health*. NIH, 10 Sept. 2002. Web. 18 Nov. 2013.

SELECTED WORKS

New Findings in Obsessive-Compulsive Disorder (editor), 1984; *The Psychobiology of Obsessive-Compulsive Disorder* (edited with Joseph Zohar and Steven Rasmussen), 1991; *The Neurobiology of Parental Behavior* (with Michael Numan), 2003

—Christopher Mari

Jessica Jackley

Born: 1977
Occupation: Entrepreneur

When asked to describe her nonprofit organization Kiva in fewer than ten words, Jessica Jackley told Erika Brown Ekiel for the Stanford Graduate School of Business website (7 May 2013), "Kiva reframes stories of poverty into stories of entrepreneurship." Jackley cofounded and launched Kiva (the word means "unity" in Swahili) with her first husband, Matthew Flannery, in October 2005. The organization is the world's first person-to-person microlending website. In her October 2010 TED talk "Poverty, Money—and Love," Jackley described microfinance as financial goods and services—such as those one might receive at a regular bank—"tailored to the needs of someone living on a few dollars a day." Kiva provides small loans to entrepreneurs across the globe. For example, in 2014, a Pakistani woman named Farzana requested a loan for approximately five hundred dollars to purchase a cow. Farzana sells milk, butter, and cheese. If she can acquire the money for another milk cow, she could greatly increase her production and improve her family's income. Since its founding, more than one million borrowers have utilized the Kiva website, which allows lenders to contribute as little as twenty-five dollars to any given loan request. The borrower receives the loan

Robert Pitts/Landov

when the full amount is fulfilled. (Borrowers, each of whom is vetted by local microfinance institutions affiliated with Kiva, work out their own repayment schedule. As of 2014, Kiva's repayment rate was nearly 99 percent.)

From an early age, Jackley saw the plight of the poor as her calling, but for years, she struggled with a nagging frustration that her community service and charitable giving were not enough. If the "poor would always be with us," she said, paraphrasing the words of the Bible in her TED talk, how could she possibly effect any change? Jackley traveled to poorest regions of Haiti in high school and spent part of her college career in Kenya and South Africa. But still, her quest to do good in the world felt toothless. "I gave, in general, when the negative emotions built up enough that I gave to relieve my own suffering not someone else's," she said.

In 2003, while working at the Business School at Stanford University, Jackley encountered Dr. Muhammad Yunus, a Nobel Peace Prize–winning economist and microfinancing pioneer. Offering a loan that would be repaid made giving a breeze for lenders, but more importantly, it offered borrowers a sense of dignity. "[Yunus] told stories about the poor that were different than any stories I had heard before. . . . He was talking about strong, smart, hardworking entrepreneurs who woke up every day and were doing things to make their lives and their family's lives better. All they needed to do that more quickly and to do it better was a little bit of capital."

EARLY LIFE AND EDUCATION

Jackley was born in 1977 and grew up in Franklin Park, a suburb of Pittsburgh, Pennsylvania. Her mother, Sandra, was a first-grade teacher, and her father, David, was a management consultant. She was raised in a middle-class Evangelical Christian household and volunteered with the local Orchard Hill Church. As a freshman, she was elected class president and served in that role all through high school. As a senior at North Allegheny High School, Jackley traveled to Haiti on a service mission. The trip proved to be a life-changing experience. "Realizing how ridiculously privileged I was compared to most of the world, I felt like I wouldn't know how to be a human being on the planet if I didn't [pay] attention to the lives of all the other people," Jackley told Doug Oster of the *Pittsburgh Post-Gazette* (9 Nov. 2008). "The vast majority [of people] have such a drastically different set of opportunities laid out before them." Jackley recalled returning to Pennsylvania with a nagging sense of unease. The next week at her senior prom, she recalled to Susan Katz Miller in an interview for the book *Being Both: Embracing Two Religions in One Interfaith Family* (2013), she burst into tears thinking about the starving children she had met.

Jackley graduated from high school in 1996 and enrolled at Bucknell University in Lewisburg, Pennsylvania. She studied philosophy, poetry, and political science and ran cross-country and track with the late coach Art Gulden. In an article for *Bucknell Magazine* (Winter 2013), Jackley wrote that Gulden, who died in 2001, taught her the importance of performing well "even in those moments when I feel like I can't." As the story goes, Jackley stayed up late finishing a paper and woke up the next morning with a low-grade fever and a sore throat. To her horror, when she arrived at practice, Gulden had devised an eight-mile run for the team through hilly Amish country. In tears, she told him that she could not complete the run. "Coach Gulden put his hands on my shoulders, looked straight into my eyes, and said, 'Jessica. You don't have to feel good to run good. You'll see. Now go.'" She kept up with the team and finished the run. During her college career, Jackley interned with World Vision, a Christian humanitarian organization that fights poverty. She also traveled to South Africa and Kenya during her junior year through the Semester at Sea program. Jackley graduated with a bachelor's degree in philosophy and political science in 2000.

MICROFINANCE AND THE VILLAGE ENTERPRISE FUND

Jackley met Matthew Flannery at the interfaith National Prayer Breakfast in Washington, DC, in 2000. At the time, she was a senior at Bucknell, and Flannery was a senior at Stanford studying symbolic systems. He was just about to begin a master's program in analytic philosophy at Stanford. Cynthia Haven for the *Stanford Alumni Magazine* (Nov. 2007) described the meeting as "love-at-first-sight." Jackley moved to California to be with Flannery in January 2001. She came with two suitcases, but "no car, no bike, no job," she told Haven. She hoped to find a job on Stanford's campus but was only able to land a temporary position in the Stanford Graduate School of Business. "I was disappointed, because I was a philosophy student and had never studied business," she told Ekiel. Eventually, Jackley joined the staff of the public management program, where she helped launch the Global Philanthropy Forum.

In 2003, Jackley attended a talk by Muhammad Yunus, a Bangladeshi economist and founder of Grameen Bank. Yunus, who was awarded the Nobel Peace Prize in 2007, helped to develop the concept of microcredit as a way to combat poverty in the 1970s. At the time, he was working as a professor of economics during a deadly famine in Bangladesh. "Nothing in the economic theories I taught reflected the life around me," he told a reporter for PBS (2005). "How could I go on telling my students make-believe stories in the name of economics? I needed to run away from these theories and from my textbooks and discover the real-life economics of a poor person's existence." Today, Grameen Bank initiates small loans, or "microloans," to poor borrowers in Bangladesh without requiring collateral. Yunus inspired Jackley to learn everything she could about microfinance. In that endeavor, she found a mentor in Brian Lehnen, the cofounder of the nonprofit Village Enterprise, an organization that provides grants and training to entrepreneurs in Africa.

Within six months, Jackley quit her job at Stanford and moved to East Africa, where she traveled through Kenya, Uganda, and Tanzania interviewing loan recipients. Jackley saw that when those small-time entrepreneurs had a little bit more money—even just one hundred dollars—their lives largely improved dramatically. Parents were able to send their children to school. People, for the first time, were able to purchase a mosquito net to protect against disease. No matter the benefit, the extra money was meaningful to the borrowers. "It was really humbling to see for the first time, to really understand that even if I could have taken a magic wand and fixed everything, I probably would have gotten a lot wrong," Jackley said in her TED talk. "Because the best way for people to change their lives is for them to have control and to do that in a way that they believe is best for them."

FOUNDING KIVA

Jackley and Flannery married in August 2003. While Jackley was working in Africa, Flannery was working as a programmer for TiVo. He had dreams of launching his own tech start-up, but his ideas never came to fruition. In March 2004, he traveled to Uganda, where he and Jackley met seven local entrepreneurs. They hatched a plan for a microlending website called Kiva. The couple built a beta website and, using their e-mail wedding guest list, managed to raise three thousand dollars in loans in a single weekend in 2005. The money went to the seven Ugandan business owners. In those early days, Jackley and Flannery had to deal with a myriad of laws, both domestic and international. Jackley recalled that no lawyer wanted anything to do with them. "One day I called forty-seven lawyers," she told Haven. "Finally, the forty-eighth would talk to me." Kiva became a nonprofit, and its website was officially launched in October 2005. That year, Kiva was able to facilitate about $500,000 in loans. The next year, Kiva raised $14 million. According to the Kiva website, 1.2 million Kiva lenders have organized more than $600 million in loans since the organization's founding, as of 2014. Kiva sets itself apart from other microlending organizations because it allows lenders to give as little as twenty-five dollars—other organizations deal in much larger loans. It also

functions like a social-networking site, allowing both lenders and borrowers to browse each other's profiles.

Kiva collaborates with microlending institutions across the globe that provide training to and manage relationships with borrowers and distribute the loans. (These institutions collect interest on the loans—Kiva does not.) Kiva screens each institution and awards ratings based on repayment history, so that lenders can assess their own risk. Loan terms range from about four to eighteen months, but Kiva's overall repayment rate is 98.8 percent. Most lenders, when they recoup their loan, choose to reinvest. Kiva counts borrowers in seventy-eight countries. The organization has been wildly successful, but Flannery warns that microfinance alone is not a cure-all for poverty. "Microfinancing alone cannot solve poverty. It will not build a road, build a hospital, relieve a community suffering a tsunami, or cure malaria," he told Haven. "Providing credit to the poor . . . addresses one need, not every need."

PROFOUNDER AND COLLABORATION FUND

Jackley, who received her master's in business administration from the Stanford Graduate School of Business in 2007, left Kiva in early 2009 to found a crowd-funding organization called ProFounder with Dana Mauriello. The website officially launched in 2010. ProFounder helped US-based start-up companies find investors in their communities, but the organization shut down operations in 2012 due to the regulatory hurdles to crowd-funding. During its brief life, one of Jackley's investors, a venture capitalist named Paige Craig, wrote a controversial article about how the news of Jackley's pregnancy (she was pregnant with twins at the time) gave him pause. The article, "VC Confession: 'I Have Doubts Once I Think of Women Founders Having Kids and Being Distracted from Work'" (19 Apr. 2011), was published on the website *Business Insider* and sparked a backlash. Jackley responded to Craig's article in *Forbes* (21 Apr. 2011) a few days later, writing that she would run her business and her life in any way she saw fit. "When my titles expand from just founder-CEO to founder-CEO-mom, I may have a different kind of load to bear than that of other entrepreneurs, especially if we're talking about the ones who fit the old Silicon Valley stereotypes. . . . I've tried forcing myself to fit more into this profile during other seasons of my life and would like to report that, shockingly, there's really no correlation between eating takeout everyday or skipping that thirty-minute jog again and great entrepreneurial success. If anything, I've found the opposite to be true," she wrote. "I have no desire to fit that old stereotype. I desire to live a life that is rich in relationships both in and outside of work."

Jackley is currently an investor and advisor with the Collaborative Fund, an organization that provides seed money for entrepreneurs.

PERSONAL LIFE

Jackley and Flannery separated in late 2008 and ultimately divorced. Jackley married Reza Aslan, a writer and scholar, in a ceremony officiated by Jackley's brother Adam, who is a pastor. Aslan, who teaches creative writing at the University of California, Riverside, is the author of the best-selling books *Zealot: The Life and Times of Jesus of Nazareth* (2013) and *No god but God: The Origins, Evolution, and Future of Islam* (2005). The Iranian-born Aslan is Muslim and Jackley remains a Christian, though she no longer identifies as Evangelical. Susan Katz Miller described their happy, interfaith marriage in her 2013 book *Being Both: Embracing Two Religions in One Interfaith Family*. As for the couple's young twin boys, Jackley and Aslan hope that they will grow up to choose a faith for themselves. "What we're going to teach our kids is the values, the beliefs, the activism, the worldview," Aslan told Miller in an interview for the *Huffington Post* (28 Sept. 2013). "And when it comes to the stories, we'll give them all of them," he said, adding that the meaning of the stories was most important.

In addition to her work in business, Jackley is a trained yoga instructor and enjoys surfing. She and her family live in Los Angeles.

SUGGESTED READING

Haven, Cynthia. "Small Change, Big Payoff." *Stanford Alumni Magazine*. Stanford University, Nov. 2007. Web. 10 Sept. 2014.

Jackley, Jessica. Interview by Erika Brown Ekiel. "Jessica Jackley: A Kiva Cofounder Discusses Stories of Poverty and Entrepreneurship." *Stanford Graduate School of Business*. Stanford Graduate School of Business, 7 May 2013. Web. 10 Sept. 2014.

Jackley, Jessica. "Poverty, Money—and Love." TEDGlobal 2010. *TED*. TED Conferences, July 2010. Web. 15 Sept. 2014.

Jackley, Jessica. "'Run Good' Anyway." *Bucknell Magazine*. Bucknell University, Winter 2013. Web. 10 Sept. 2014.

Miller, Susan Katz. "Reza Aslan and Jessica Jackley: A Muslim and Christian Interfaith Family." *Huffington Post*. TheHuffingtonPost.com, 28 Sept. 2013. Web. 10 Sept. 2014.

Oster, Doug. "Her Goal: End Poverty, One Loan at a Time." *Pittsburgh Post-Gazette*. PG Publishing, 9 Nov. 2008. Web. 10 Sept. 2014.

Springhetti, Joan. "Crowd Standout: Jessica Jackley Brings Together Entrepreneurs with Investors from their Communities." *Stanford Business* Autumn 2011: 14–17. Print.

—Molly Hagan

Omotola Jalade-Ekeinde

Born: February 7, 1978
Occupation: Actor and singer

Omotola Jalade-Ekeinde is a Nigerian actor, singer, and philanthropist whom fans refer to simply as Omosexy. She is a megastar in Nigeria, where she has acted in over three hundred Nollywood films. In 2012 her reality television show, *Omotola: The Real Me*, the first of its kind in Africa, pulled in a staggering 150 million viewers, and in 2013 she was the first African celebrity to receive one million "likes" on Facebook. Still she remains largely unknown in the United States. Those who have never seen a Nollywood film—or missed Jalade-Ekeinde's June 2013 US debut as R & B/hip-hop artist Akon's date on the VH1 drama series *Hit the Floor*—might recognize her as a former United Nations World Food Programme ambassador or as the head of the Omotola Youth Empowerment Project. In 2013 her philanthropy and activism landed her on *Time* magazine's list of the hundred most influential people in the world.

Nollywood is Jalade-Ekeinde's first love. Her acting career began when the industry was in its infancy, when directors shot films with handheld cameras and many films were shot, edited, and available for distribution within one single week. Today, Nollywood is the world's third-highest-grossing film industry behind Hollywood and India's Bollywood. It generated more than $250 million in revenues in 2013, according to *Time*. The industry is making strides toward a more

Getty Images

professional environment and higher quality films—yet it still lacks adequate infrastructure. Nollywood has no official studio. So, in early 2014, Jalade-Ekeinde announced plans to build a "film village," the first place in Nigeria that will function as a Nollywood studio. She is more excited about the industry's future than pursuing a Hollywood career, she told Vladmir Duthiers for the CNN program *Africa Voices* (10 Jan. 2014). Of her many causes, Jalade-Ekeinde is perhaps most passionate about the future prosperity of Nigeria and Africa. She believes that the success of Nollywood is a sign of a new era for the region. "We are growing something really major here," she said of Nollywood. "Maybe our films could be better . . . but we have the spirit, the willpower. We want to achieve something."

EARLY LIFE AND EDUCATION

Omotola Jalade-Ekeinde was born into a middle-class, Methodist family in Lagos, Nigeria, on February 7, 1978. Her father, Shola Jalade, managed the Lagos Country Club. Her mother, Oluwatoyin Amori Oguntade-Jalade, worked at a supermarket. Growing up Jalade-Ekeinde saw herself as one of the boys. She has two younger brothers, Tayo and Bolaji, and was very close to her father. "He was very enlightened," she told Ben Arogundade for the *Telegraph* (28 Aug. 2013). "He always asked me what I wanted, and encouraged me to speak up. He treated me like a boy." Shola Jalade died in an accident when Jalade-Ekeinde was twelve. When it happened, she was away at the Command Secondary School, a boarding school in Kaduna. Tasked with taking care of her brothers and her grief-stricken mother, Jalade-Ekeinde bottled up her own sadness. When she began acting, she used to think about her father's death during scenes that required her to cry. "The director would shout, 'Cut!' and I'd still be crying," she told Arogundade. "I could bring the tears, but I could not control them. In the end I had to stop using that technique."

Jalade-Ekeinde began modeling as a teenager to help her mother support the family. When she was fifteen, she accompanied a friend to a film audition and ended up winning the role herself. She was to play a mermaid, but her mother, superstitious, told her to turn the part down. The director came to Jalade-Ekeinde's house to try to convince her mother to let her act, but her mother chased him out of the house with a broom. When the same director was working on his next film, *Venom of Justice* (1995), he cast Jalade-Ekeinde again. This time around, he brought the entire cast and crew to her house to help him plead his case. Jalade-Ekeinde appeared in the film, but her mother was wary of early Nollywood. For her, acting, Jalade-Ekeinde told Matthew Bannister in a radio interview for the BBC *Outlook* (11 Sept. 2013), still bore the stigma of prostitution. Jalade-Ekeinde told Bannister that the social pressures of African widowhood had taken their toll on her mother. She was struggling just to make ends meet and did not want her daughter's acting career "to reflect badly on the family." But Jalade-Ekeinde was determined, and despite a few early beatings from her mother, she began to make a living through acting.

NOLLYWOOD

The Nigerian film industry was born in 1992. At the time the country was suffering under military dictatorship and the economy was tanking. There was no work for actors and camera crew, and movie theaters were shuttered because it was too dangerous to go out at night. Still, a man named Okechukwu Oguejiofor was desperate to make a movie. He did not have enough money to hire actors, so he cast his friends. He did not own expensive equipment, so he rented a handheld video camera and shot the script he had written himself in seven days. Through a chance meeting with a local television personality, Oguejiofor became acquainted with Kenneth Nnebue, an electronics merchant who had an overstock of blank cassettes and agreed to collaborate on Oguejiofor's project. The result was a movie called *Living in Bondage*, about a man who sells his soul for riches. *Living in Bondage*, released on videocassette, was a smash hit and ushered in an era of more democratic moviemaking in Nigeria. By 2005, the Nigerian film industry, which had been producing just a few films a year in the early 1990s, was outputting over twenty-five hundred features annually. By comparison, Hollywood and Bollywood make between one thousand and two thousand.

The budding industry continues to be characterized by its low production values and outsized stories. Melodrama, comedy, action, thriller—Nollywood films want to be everything at once. According to Andrew Rice for the *New York Times* (23 Feb. 2012), the industry's "bawdy humor—or fright or fantasy—appeals to a public seeking escape from depressing living conditions." Indeed, a majority of Nigerians live in grinding poverty, but Oguejiofor, who is often called Mr. Nollywood, bristles at such characterizations and disdains the term "Nollywood." He told Sunny Okim for the Heidelberg, Germany–based *African Courier* in 2012: "The name Nollywood actually came into existence in 1995 when some Americans looked at what we were producing and concluded that it was trash."

BREAKING INTO FILM

Jalade-Ekeinde made her Nollywood debut in 1995 with *Venom of Justice*. That same year she earned her breakthrough role in the movie *Mortal Inheritance* (1996), in which she plays a woman with sickle-cell disease. She won two acting awards for her portrayal. Since then Jalade-Ekeinde has averaged an exhausting sixteen films a year, though her direct-to-video days are fortunately over. Turnover for direct-to-video movies is high, and shooting schedules come in short, grueling bouts. "It is the fashion to shoot until you drop, night and day," Jalade-Ekeinde told Arogundade. But all of that is "old Nollywood," Jalade-Ekeinde told Bannister—on its way out in 2014. "New Nollywood" more closely resembles American Hollywood, with bigger budgets and cinema openings. In 2012 Jalade-Ekeinde starred in a New Nollywood thriller called *Last Flight to Abuja*, directed by Kunle Afolayan. The film was inspired by several plane crashes that took place between 2005 and 2006. It received an African Movie Academy Award (AMAA) for best African film by an African abroad because it was shot in part in the United Kingdom. Jalade-Ekeinde received an AMAA for best supporting actress in 2005, the first year the awards were given.

The film industry has become one of the largest private-sector employers in chronically underemployed Nigeria. Nollywood celebrities are prominent public figures. In 2012 they campaigned with President Goodluck Jonathan and lent support to the Occupy Nigeria protest in response to a hike in fuel prices. In short, Nollywood stars like Jalade-Ekeinde hold a lot of sway in a country where they so recently had none. "We started from nothing. The government in my country did not support us, so we started from just passion, sheer passion," Jalade-Ekeinde said to Bannister of her Nollywood beginnings. "Most of us were not trained but we knew what it should be. And we were pushing. We pushed so hard and now it is the third largest movie industry in the world. Nollywood, you see, so we've come a long way."

PHILANTHROPY AND ACTIVISM
Jalade-Ekeinde became a World Food Programme ambassador with the United Nations in 2005 and began working for Amnesty International in 2009. She has felt more at home with the latter organization, she said in a video interview for *Time* magazine (30 Dec. 2013), because it allows her a more active role. She has been able to go out into the world and campaign on issues that are important to her, such as the maternal mortality crisis in Sierra Leone in West Africa, where one in every eight women was at risk of dying while giving birth in 2009. In September 2009 Jalade-Ekeinde helped Irene Khan, then secretary general of Amnesty International, launch an effort to reduce maternal death in Sierra Leone. The campaign was aimed at raising awareness, but it also lobbied world leaders for increased health care funding for mothers in Sierra Leone and other poor African states.

Jalade-Ekeinde and four Sierra Leonean musicians even recorded a song about the crisis, "Bellé woman, dae suffer" ("Pregnant women are suffering").

Jalade-Ekeinde is also passionate about the Niger Delta, Nigeria's largest wetland region. Oil was discovered in the delta in 1958, and though the export has been at times a boon for the Nigerian economy, hundreds of oil spills ravage the region annually. In November 2013 Amnesty International reported that a number of oil companies, including Shell, have not been honest about the nature of the spills. The companies have claimed that the spills—which are destroying the environment and killing the people of the Niger Delta—are the result of theft and sabotage. However, Amnesty International found that corrosion and disrepair are to blame. Jalade-Ekeinde has expressed frustration that other oil spills have sparked public outcries, while the tragedy in the Niger Delta has continued to unfold. "Why is there so much silence?" she asked Duthiers. "Why is there no one helping these people?"

Up Creek without a Paddle, a movie about the Niger Delta in which Jalade-Ekeinde appears, was shot in 2012. "I went around for myself to see what was really going on and I understood really why these people are very angry," Jalade-Ekeinde told Duthiers about the situation. "I don't live there and I am really, truly angry."

In addition to her contributions to international activist organizations, Jalade-Ekeinde has established her own philanthropic foundation, the Omotola Youth Empowerment Project (OYEP). The foundation organizes various lectures, seminars, workshops, and fund-raising walks for the empowerment of Nigerian youths.

TELEVISION AND SINGING CAREER
Activism inspired Jalade-Ekeinde, already a huge movie star, to launch her singing career in 2005. "I wanted to speak out, I wanted to say more," she told Duthiers, "and there's so much you can just say with words." Her debut album, *Gba*, was released in 2006. Her follow-up album, *Me, Myself, and Eyes* was released in 2010 and features the pop single "Feel Alright." She reportedly began working on a third album in 2013. It is said to feature Akon and Grammy Award–winning producer Kendrick Dean, who has worked with Chris Brown and Mariah Carey.

Jalade-Ekeinde's reality television show, *Omotola: The Real Me*, premiered in December 2012 on M-NET's Africa Magic channel. The show is low key by American reality show standards. It follows Jalade-Ekeinde's daily life and features her husband and, on rare occasions, her four children. Still, the first episode drew the channel's highest ratings ever. The first season drew 150 million viewers—a larger viewership, Arogundade wrote, than that of the

Oprah Winfrey Show and that of the *Tyra Banks Show* at their respective peaks, combined. Jalade-Ekeinde has enjoyed filming the show but has expressed nervousness about continuing to film as her children become teenagers. "It was fun while it lasted," she told Duthiers of the show, "but I don't know if I want to do a season two."

PERSONAL LIFE

Jalade-Ekeinde met Matthew Ekeinde, an airline pilot ten years her senior, at church when she was sixteen. He would later say that it was love at first sight, but it took Jalade-Ekeinde some time to feel the same. He became a close friend of the family and a father figure to her brothers, and proposed when she was eighteen. At first her mother was against the partnership, arguing that Jalade-Ekeinde was too young. Ekeinde was undeterred. "He was very, very bold," Jalade-Ekeinde told Arogundade. "It was one of the things I found fascinating about him." The couple married in March 1996. They enjoyed a wedding ceremony on a flight from Lagos to the country of Benin in West Africa in April 2001.

Jalade-Ekeinde's loving relationship with her husband is an integral part of her appeal in conservative Nigeria. She is "Omosexy"—a nickname Ekeinde gave her—yet a religious, doting mother of four children: Meraiah, M. J., Princess, and Michael. Many Nigerian men wonder at Jalade-Ekeinde's marriage. Ekeinde, she told Arogundade, "gets a lot of invitations from various bodies to speak about how he copes as a modern Nigerian man in a relationship with a powerful working woman."

SUGGESTED READING

Arogundade, Ben. "'Omosexy': The Biggest Film Star You've Never Heard Of." *Telegraph*. Telegraph Media Group, 28 Aug. 2013. Web. 12 Jan. 2014.

Bannister, Matthew. "'Omosexy:' The Queen of Nollywood." *Outlook*. BBC, 11 Sept. 2013. Web. 12 Jan. 2014.

Jalade-Ekeinde, Omotola. "Omotola Jalade-Ekeinde." Interview by Vladmir Duthiers. *African Voices*. Cable News Network, 10 Jan. 2014. Web. 12 Jan. 2014.

Jalade-Ekeinde, Omotola. "Omotola Jalade-Ekeinde Talks to *TIME* about Nollywood, Activism and Africa." Interview. *Time100*. Time, 30 Dec. 2013. Web. 12 Jan. 2014.

SELECTED WORKS

Venom of Justice, 1995; *Mortal Inheritance*, 1996; *Last Flight to Abuja*, 2012

—*Molly Hagan*

Suzan Johnson Cook

Born: January 28, 1957
Occupation: Pastor, theologian, and former ambassador

Rev. Dr. Suzan Johnson Cook, or Sujay, as she is affectionately known, is a former ambassador and author, and a towering figure on New York City's religious landscape. She was the first woman chaplain of the New York City Police Department (NYPD), and has preached in neighborhoods and venues across the city, including her native Bronx, the legendary Apollo Theater in Harlem, and the Financial District in Lower Manhattan. Johnson Cook has made a name for herself as a mentor to fellow women pastors and a charismatic religious and political leader. "I'm going to make you love me," she said in a *New York Times* profile by Jane Gross (3 July 2002). "I'm going to hug you until you hug back."

Johnson Cook studied acting and worked as a television producer, but in her mid-twenties, she felt compelled to pursue a more pious Christian path. As a woman in the male-dominated African American church, it was an uphill battle for Johnson Cook, who nonetheless went on to become the first black woman to be named a senior pastor in the American Baptist Churches USA. She eventually became the first woman president of the multidenominational Hampton University Ministers' Conference, an influential gathering of more than seven thousand African American church leaders. She used her cachet to build what she calls a "new girl network," she told Samuel G. Freedman for the *New York*

Courtesy of AK Photo

Times (10 Mar. 2007), mentoring other aspiring black Christian women. Though black women are thriving members of church congregations, there are relatively few black women preachers—and not for lack of interest. Freedman reported that nearly half of black seminary students are women, "yet they are far less likely than men to lead a congregation." The long-standing bias was evident in Johnson Cook's own career, when upon leaving the seminary, she was turned down for every position she applied for, save an interim pastorship at Mariner's Temple, a failing and forgotten Baptist ministry in New York City's Chinatown.

Johnson Cook spent thirteen fruitful years at Mariner's Temple, growing the congregation exponentially while also accepting speaking engagements across the city, writing several books, and serving on President Bill Clinton's seven-member advisory panel on race relations. In 1996, she founded her own ministry, Bronx Christian Fellowship, in the Bronx. In 2010, President Barack Obama nominated her to serve as the US Ambassador-at-Large for International Religious Freedom. She was confirmed in the spring of 2011, and held the position until 2013.

EARLY LIFE AND EDUCATION

Suzan Denise Johnson was born on January 28, 1957, in New York City. She spent her early years in a Harlem neighborhood tenement building. Her mother, Dorothy C. Johnson, earned two master's degrees and worked as a school-teacher. Her father, Wilbert T. Johnson, was one of New York City's first black trolley car drivers. The family moved to the Gun Hill section of the Bronx in 1959, and Wilbert founded Johnson Security Bureau, a security guard company, in 1962. Church was an integral part of Johnson Cook's upbringing. Growing up, she and her older brother, Charles, attended Bible school at Eastchester Presbyterian Church in Gun Hill each Sunday, and then took the train to Harlem to meet their mother for the 11 a.m. service at Rendall Presbyterian. A few hours later, they joined their father at Union Baptist Church, ten blocks away.

By the time she was fourteen years old, Johnson Cook stood five feet ten inches tall, and spent most of her afternoons playing basketball with the boys at Mullaly Park in the South Bronx. After gaining acceptance on the court, Johnson Cook began bringing her female friend to games. The decision was indicative of Johnson Cook's larger feelings about giving women a place at the proverbial table. "Shooting hoops with the guys gave me a comfort level around them that I've never lost," she told Freedman. "I've always felt I deserved to be on the team. And it also gave me the understanding that having another sister around makes a difference."

The Johnsons were one of the first black families to live in their largely white, Jewish, and Italian neighborhood. Johnson Cook attended the predominantly white Riverdale Country Day School, where her parents organized a black parent-teacher association. In an interview with David Gonzalez for the *New York Times* (21 June 1997), Johnson Cook recalled the frustration of being a young girl and asking a white classmate to sit next to her on the bus: "She said, 'My mother said I can't sit next to a black person.' I told her I was brown, but that was it. The seeds of racism were already planted. In the life of every African-American there is a turning point when you recognize there is a difference."

Like her brother, the precocious Johnson Cook skipped grades at school, and at sixteen, she enrolled at Fisk University, a historically black college in Nashville, Tennessee. She soon transferred to Emerson College in Boston, where she studied acting and singing. (She once performed at the Apollo Theater's famed Amateur Night.) Her older brother, meanwhile, went to Dartmouth College and studied law at the University of California, Berkeley. Johnson Cook worked on his successful campaign for New York state assemblyman for the Seventy-Sixth District in the Bronx in the 1970s. After his political career, Charles Johnson joined the family security company in 1983. (He died in 2008.) Johnson Cook graduated from Emerson with a degree in speech in 1976. She then earned a master's degree in educational technology from Teachers College at Columbia University in New York in 1978. By the age of twenty-one, she was working as a television producer for public affairs programming on stations in Boston, Washington, and Miami.

CALL TO MINISTRY

In the early 1980s, she told Freedman, she felt the call to ministry. She was preaching in her dreams, and she called her family's pastor, the late Reverend Ollie B. Wells Sr. at Union Baptist, for advice. "She was frightened. . . . She just didn't know if she could put everything on the line," Wells recalled to Freedman in 2000. "I told her to go back to Miami and pray on it. And if your faith is real, you've gotta do what Peter did. Which is step out onto the water." So, Johnson Cook opted to pursue ordination, though her decision was not without push-back. Her practical-minded mother questioned her choice, knowing that the road for a female Baptist minister would be long and hard. In December 1980, Wells licensed Johnson Cook as a minister, the first step toward her ordination. In 1981, she entered New York's Union Theological Seminary, and Wells appointed her youth minister. On March 6, 1982, halfway through her studies, Wells ordained her under the aegis of the mostly white

American Baptist Churches of Metropolitan New York/USA—notably not the black National Baptist Convention. As Freedman reported for *New York* magazine (15 May 2000), major black denominations have "few formal restrictions on women in the ministry," though in practice, the distinction was clear: "the pulpit was a man's place and the pew was a woman's." (The Baptist Ministers' Conference, which Johnson Cook now regularly attends, barred women until the mid-1990s.)

MARINER'S TEMPLE

Johnson Cook earned her master of divinity degree in 1983. The same year, she was invited to serve as interim pastor at Mariner's Temple in the Chinatown neighborhood in Lower Manhattan. Mariner's Temple boasted an impressive history: founded in 1795, it was the oldest Baptist church in New York. But when Johnson Cook stepped up to the pulpit her first Sunday, there were only fifteen worshippers in the pews. The church was deeply in debt, and as Freedman pointed out, it was "a black church in a neighborhood without blacks." Many men auditioned for the permanent job of pastor, but took one look at the church and walked out the door. To make matters worse, many fellow ministers were unsupportive of Johnson Cook, some openly voicing their disapproval of female ordination.

Johnson Cook focused her energy on drumming up attendance at Mariner's Temple. She went door-to-door to find worshippers, and six months later, with the support of 150 parishioners, she was officially voted the church's senior pastor. The appointment made her the first black woman senior pastor in the 200-year history of the American Baptist Churches denomination. In an effort to further grow her fellowship, Johnson Cook began preaching tailored services, like the Wednesday "Lunch Hour of Power." Over the years, Johnson Cook would also host "Wonderful Wall Street Wednesdays" services at the downtown John Street United Methodist Church; a nondenominational worship series called "Harlem Hallelujah" at the Apollo Theater in Harlem; and an early morning power walk in the Bronx called "Fine, Fit and Fabulous." Her handful of books—among them, *Too Blessed to Be Stressed: Words of Wisdom for Women on the Move* (1998), *A New Dating Attitude: Getting Ready for the Mate God Has for You* (2001) and *Moving Up: Dr. Sujay's Ten Steps to Turning Your Life Around and Getting to the Top!* (2008)—similarly straddle spirituality and self-help. She told Freedman for *New York* magazine, "My whole theological understanding of Jesus is that His ministry was holistic, that it was about mind, body, *and* spirit. Many times, faith traditions have focused just on the spirit. But what happens after Sunday is that people have to face the realities—their bodies, their minds. So yes, my ministry does concentrate on black health and wealth. We can't just talk about what we're going to have as a people. We must achieve it."

NYPD CHAPLAIN AND OTHER APPOINTMENTS

Johnson Cook earned her doctor of ministry from the United Theological Seminary in Dayton, Ohio, in 1990, the same year she was appointed the first woman chaplain of the NYPD. From 1990 to 1992, she served as an associate dean and professor at Harvard Divinity School, where she was a Sam Proctor Fellow (1990) and President's Administrative Fellow (1991). She also served as professor at New York Theological Seminary from 1988 to 1996. In 1993, she was a White House Fellow in urban policy, and was tempted to remain in Washington and accept a position as an assistant secretary to the secretary of housing and urban development. She turned the offer down, though she served as an advisor for the department's faith-based initiatives from 1994 to 1997. In 1997, Johnson Cook was the only religious leader appointed to President Bill Clinton's Initiative on Race and Reconciliation.

By the mid-1990s, her career was booming, as was her congregation at Mariner's Temple, which grew to more than a thousand during her thirteen-year tenure, but in 1996, she decided to leave that church and found her own.

RETURN TO THE BRONX

In 1996, Johnson Cook founded a ministry called Bronx Christian Fellowship in a former bank at 161st Street and the Grand Concourse near the old Yankee Stadium—though at the time she preached her last sermon at Mariner's Temple in June, her new church did not have a physical home. (At Mariner's Temple, she was succeeded by another female preacher.) In an interview with Nadine Brozan for the *New York Times* (25 June 1996), she compared starting a ministry to giving birth—in this case, a second birth. "You can give birth to a new ministry, mold it and develop it with joy and love," she said. "Because I'm a seasoned pastor I will start out with a level of skill this time." In an effort to build her new fellowship, Johnson Cook appeared in a television commercial appealing to middle-class African Americans, whom she believed were losing their connection to the church. Johnson Cook, who was named president of the Hampton University Ministers' Conference in 2002, worked hard to tailor her services to the larger community as well. She is fluent in Spanish, and used her language skills to draw Hispanic worshippers to the church. She even hosted career-training programs, for which, in 2000, she received a $100,000 grant.

AMBASSADOR-AT-LARGE FOR INTERNATIONAL RELIGIOUS FREEDOM

In 2010, President Barack Obama nominated Johnson Cook to serve as the third United States Ambassador-at-Large for International Freedom, a position created under the 1998 International Religious Freedom Act. Despite the support of a Democratic majority within the Senate Foreign Relations Committee, the first step in her confirmation process, Republicans blocked her appointment, and her nomination died in December. The next month, Freedman reported for the *New York Times* (14 Jan. 2011) that one senator, likely Republican senator Jim DeMint of South Carolina, had stymied her nomination through a privilege known as a hold-over letter, in which one politician can force the entire committee to delay its vote. By exercising a hold-over letter in December, DeMint (who neither confirmed not denied that he had been the senator in question) ensured that Johnson Cook's nomination would expire. DeMint later said that he had concerns that Johnson Cook did not have enough international experience for the job. President Obama nominated her for the position again in the spring of 2011. She was confirmed in April as the first African American, woman, and pastor to hold the job.

During her tenure as ambassador-at-large, Johnson Cook visited twenty-seven countries, but was criticized for not speaking out about high-profile incidents like the persecution of Coptic Christians in Egypt and attacks by the militant group Boko Haram in Nigeria. She maintained that the restrictions of her job did not allow her to do more. "She had very few resources she could employ to develop strategies to advance international religious freedom," Thomas Farr, a professor of religion and international affairs at Georgetown University told Lauren Markoe for *Religion News Service* (28 Oct. 2013). Johnson Cook resigned the position in October 2013, citing the cost of her sons' college tuition. "The reality is, for them to be able to pursue their dreams, I can't do it on a government salary," she told Markoe. She said she planned to sit on corporate boards, relaunch her Charisma Speakers speakers' bureau, and act as a consultant to nongovernmental organizations. She also said she does not expect to return to the pulpit. "I did 32 years, three decades, in inner city New York City," she told Markoe. "Never say never, but I believe that season is complete."

PERSONAL LIFE

Johnson Cook married Ronald Cook, then the coordinator of the Convent Avenue Baptist Church, at Riverside Church in New York City on October 11, 1991. They met during a Lenten fast at Cook's church. The couple has two sons, Samuel David and Christopher Daniel. They live in Washington, DC, and Long Island.

SUGGESTED READING

Freedman, Samuel G. "An Almost Ambassador Encounters a Congressional Dead End." *New York Times*. New York Times, 14 Jan. 2011. Web. 7 Aug. 2014.

Freedman, Samuel G. "The Gospel According to Sujay." *New York*. New York Media, 15 May 2000. Web. 7 Aug. 2014.

Freedman, Samuel G. "Pastor Leaves Door Ajar for Other Black Women." *New York Times*. New York Times, 10 Mar. 2007. Web. 7 Aug. 2014.

Gonzalez, David. "Old Rebuffs Spur Efforts on Racism." *New York Times*. New York Times, 21 June 1997. Web. 7 Aug. 2014.

Gross, Jane. "Public Lives: Preaching Everywhere, Even in Her Dreams." *New York Times*. New York Times, 3 July 2002. Web. 7 Aug. 2014.

Markoe, Lauren. "Suzan Johnson Cook Defends Her Work on Religious Freedom and Explains Why She Left." *Religion News Service*. Religion News, 28 Oct. 2013. Web. 7 Aug. 2014.

—*Molly Hagan*

Calvin Johnson

Born: September 29, 1985
Occupation: Football player

Detroit Lions wide receiver Calvin Johnson has earned the nickname "Megatron," after the robotic villain of the Transformers franchise, for his seemingly superhuman capabilities on the football field. "At least once every Sunday, the [National Football League (NFL)] stops," Elizabeth Merrill wrote for ESPN (3 Sept. 2012). "Calvin Johnson does something, midair, in triple coverage or with his tiptoes glancing the chalk, that causes everyone to watch." The six-feet-five Johnson, who is known for his giant hands, blazing speed, and awe-inspiring leaping ability, has made a viable case for being the league's best all-around player since being drafted by the Lions in the first round of the 2007 NFL Draft.

In his first seven seasons with the Lions, Johnson helped transform the Lions from the laughingstock of the NFL to a playoff contender, teaming up with quarterback Matthew Stafford, the Lions' 2009 number-one draft pick, to form the most prolific quarterback-receiver tandem in the league. In 2012 Johnson posted arguably the greatest season by a receiver in NFL history, when he led the league in receptions and set league records for single-season receiving yards

Getty Images

and consecutive 100-yard games. He has earned four Pro Bowl selections (2010–13) and has been named to three All-Pro first teams (2011–13). "He's the best receiver I've ever seen," the Washington Redskins free safety Ryan Clark told Gerry Dulac for the *Pittsburgh Post-Gazette* (16 Nov. 2013) about Johnson. "He's a combination of all the greats in one. . . . As far as the totality of his game, he's like nothing we've ever seen before as a receiver."

EARLY LIFE

The second of four children, Calvin Johnson Jr. was born in Newnan, Georgia, on September 29, 1985, to Calvin Johnson Sr. and Arica Johnson. Along with his two sisters, Erica and Elan, and brother, Wali, Johnson was raised in Tyrone, Georgia, a suburb of the state capital of Atlanta. His father was a conductor for Southern-Pacific Railroad; his mother, who has a doctorate in education, worked as a project manager in the Atlanta public school system. Both of Johnson's parents instilled in him and his siblings the importance of family, education, and a strong work ethic, and they "wouldn't tolerate a lot of being foolish," as his father told Judy Battista for the *New York Times* (26 Apr. 2007).

Despite not having an athletic pedigree, Johnson demonstrated preternatural athletic ability from an early age. His first love was baseball, which he started playing at around age five. Growing up a fan of the hometown Atlanta Braves, Johnson dreamed of following in the footsteps of his childhood hero, perennial All-Star center fielder Ken Griffey Jr. He started playing football in seventh grade, after he finally convinced his mother, who forbade him from playing the sport in grade school out of fear that he would get hurt, to let him play.

HIGH SCHOOL CAREER

Johnson attended Sandy Creek High School in Tyrone, where he was a standout on the football and baseball teams. Already tall as a freshman—he stood around six feet—Johnson had a growth spurt during the summer before his sophomore year, which, by his own admission, helped transform him from a relatively unpolished athlete into a potential superstar. He became a starting wide receiver on Sandy Creek's football team as a sophomore, but it was as a junior that he first garnered attention from NFL scouts, when he caught thirty-four passes for 646 yards and scored ten touchdowns.

Johnson also emerged as a star center fielder and pitcher on Sandy Creek's varsity baseball team. Despite being good enough to draw attention from major-league scouts, he ultimately decided to make football his main focus heading into his senior season, largely due to his size and desire to pursue higher education. As a senior Johnson made forty receptions for 736 yards and eight touchdowns. His many end-of-season honors included being recognized as a first-team all-state selection by the *Atlanta Journal-Constitution* and universally rated among the top ten wide receivers in the nation.

Johnson was recruited heavily by football powerhouses all over the country, including the University of Georgia, the University of Oklahoma, and the University of Notre Dame, but he chose to attend the Georgia Institute of Technology, better known as Georgia Tech, because of the school's renowned engineering program. Johnson impressed scouts and recruiting analysts not only with his prototypical NFL size, blazing speed, and uncanny ability to make gravity-defying catches but also with his humility, work ethic, and character. His high-school coach, Rodney Walker, told Tom Kowalski for the Michigan news website MLive (20 Apr. 2008), "I don't think I'll ever coach anybody again who had that much ability and that much character. . . . Great players usually come with great problems, but you didn't have that with Calvin."

COLLEGE FOOTBALL STAR

At Georgia Tech, Johnson wasted little time showcasing his game-changing abilities. In only his second game, against Clemson University, he recorded two leaping touchdown catches in the final two minutes to help clinch a dramatic come-from-behind victory for the Yellow Jackets. Despite playing in a run-first offensive system, Johnson, under the guidance of head coach Chan Gailey, finished his freshman season with forty-eight catches for 837 yards and eight touchdowns. He was selected to the All-Atlantic Coast Conference (ACC) First Team and was honored with the ACC Rookie of the Year Award. Instead of resting on his laurels, however, Johnson used an early-season blowout 27–3 loss to the University of Miami, in which Miami cornerback and future NFL Pro Bowler Antrel Rolle limited him to just two catches for ten yards, as motivation to improve his strength and various aspects of his game, from his route running to his release against press coverage. "It made me understand that I was going to have to work harder, get stronger, and improve my technique a lot if I wanted to play with the big boys," he recalled to Austin Murphy for *Sports Illustrated* (30 Dec. 2013).

Johnson's improvements paid lasting dividends, and during his sophomore and junior seasons, he established himself as the top wide receiver prospect in the country. As a sophomore he made fifty-four receptions for 888 yards and six touchdowns, earning him All-ACC honors for the second straight year as well as first- and second-team All-America honors from various sports associations and media outlets. During his junior season, Johnson attained seventy-six catches, 1,202 receiving yards, and fifteen touchdowns. He was a unanimous first-team All-America selection and was named the 2006 ACC Player of the Year; he also received the 2006 Biletnikoff Award as the nation's top wide receiver.

By the end of his junior season, Johnson was already being hailed as a once-in-a-generation talent destined for NFL superstardom. As a result he opted to forgo his senior year to enter the NFL Draft. Johnson finished his career at Georgia Tech as one of the most accomplished players in school history, ranking as the school's all-time leader in career receiving yards (2,927), touchdown receptions (28), and 100-yard receiving games (13), and second in receptions (178). Buddy Geis, Georgia Tech's receivers coach during Johnson's tenure, said of his former pupil, as quoted by Murphy, "God touched him in so many different ways. But Calvin works like He didn't give him anything."

DETROIT LION

Johnson was unanimously projected to be a top-ten pick in the 2007 NFL Draft. His draft stock rose further after he participated in that year's NFL Scouting Combine, in which he completed the forty-yard dash in a blistering 4.35 seconds, the third-fastest time ever recorded at the event by a receiver. Johnson also impressed coaches, general managers, and scouts at a private workout held at Georgia Tech, where he posted a 42.5-inch vertical leap and a standing long jump of eleven feet seven inches. Blown away by his rare combination of skills, the Detroit Lions selected him with second overall pick in the draft's first round, signing the wide receiver to a six-year contract worth approximately $64 million.

Despite entering the league to high expectations, Johnson was not immediately greeted with open arms in Detroit. Upon his arrival in the Motor City, the Lions had just completed their sixth consecutive losing season and seventh without a postseason berth. The team had used three of their previous four top-ten draft picks on receivers, and all had failed to live up to expectations. Skepticism toward receivers notwithstanding, Johnson arrived at his first NFL training camp eager to fulfill the role of franchise savior and determined to improve upon his already-preternatural abilities.

Johnson made his NFL debut on September 9, 2007, as a reserve in the season opener against the Oakland Raiders, scoring his first NFL touchdown in a 36–21 Lions victory. He appeared in fifteen games for Detroit during his rookie season, making ten starts and forty-eight receptions for 756 yards and four touchdowns, despite being hampered by various injuries. The Lions, bolstered by Johnson's contributions, posted a promising 6–2 record during the first half of the season but lost seven of their final eight games to finish 7–9, missing out on the playoffs for an eighth straight year. Still, their record marked a four-game improvement from the previous season.

THE BIRTH OF MEGATRON

Johnson entered his sophomore campaign as the Lions' number-two starting receiver behind Roy Williams, who, during the 2007 season, bestowed upon him his now-famous nickname, "Megatron." "I've never seen anything like him," Williams said of his teammate to Brian VanOchten for the *Grand Rapids (Michigan) Press* (9 Sept. 2007). "He's a big, strong, physical, fast guy." Johnson's abilities notwithstanding, it was his mental toughness that was put to the test during the 2008 season, which saw the Lions regress in historic fashion.

Hampered by front-office woes, an inept offense, and a porous defense, the Lions became the first team in NFL history to lose all sixteen of their regular-season games. Johnson nonetheless proved to be one of the Lions' lone bright spots, leading the team in receptions, receiving yards, and touchdowns. He managed to post exceptional numbers despite playing with three different quarterbacks throughout the season. For his regular-season performance, Johnson was named a Pro Bowl alternate for the National Football Conference (NFC) squad. Meanwhile, the Lions, desperate to reverse their fortunes, cleaned house after the season, firing head coach Rod Marinelli and the majority of his assistants. Marinelli was replaced by Jim Schwartz, who had spent the previous eight seasons as the Tennessee Titans' defensive coordinator.

In efforts to maximize Johnson's potential, Schwartz hired former St. Louis Rams head coach

Scott Linehan as offensive coordinator and used the Lions' number-one draft pick on the University of Georgia quarterback Matthew Stafford. Heading into the 2009 season, Schwartz and Linehan implemented an offensive system that continually moved Johnson around to each of the three receiver positions (split end, flanker, and slot) as a way to create more pass-catching opportunities for him against opposing defenses.

Johnson subsequently spent most of the 2009 season trying to develop chemistry with Stafford, who, despite winning the Lions' starting quarterback spot out of training camp, missed several games as a rookie due to various injuries. Johnson himself sat out two games with a knee injury but still finished the season with sixty-seven receptions for 984 yards and five touchdowns. The Lions only marginally improved, finishing with a 2–14 record, the second-worst results in the league. Speaking of Johnson, Stafford said to Merrill, "He's so big and so fast. My rookie year, I had trouble just figuring it out. Some spots I can put [the ball], I've never been able to put it before and have the guy be able to go up and get it. And there were times he felt he was open and I didn't think he was open."

RESTORING THE ROAR

While Stafford was plagued by injuries again in 2010, playing in just three games before undergoing season-ending shoulder surgery, Johnson continued to grow into one of the league's most dangerous and versatile offensive threats. Teaming up mostly with backup quarterback Shaun Hill, he finished the 2010 season with seventy-seven receptions for 1,120 yards and twelve touchdowns. Johnson earned his first Pro Bowl selection, as a starting wide receiver for the NFC quad, and was selected to the AP All-Pro second team. Thanks to Johnson's weekly efforts and the addition of another talented first-round draft pick, defensive tackle Ndamukong Suh, the Lions improved their record to 6–10.

During the 2011 season, Johnson took his game to the next level, as he and a finally healthy Stafford developed into one of the NFL's most prolific quarterback-receiver tandems. Starting all sixteen games for only the second time in his career, Johnson made ninety-six receptions, led the league in receiving yards, and earned his second straight Pro Bowl selection and first AP All-Pro first-team selection. During the season, Lions wide receivers coach Shawn Jefferson, who had worked closely with Johnson on improving various aspects of his game since his rookie year, described his pupil to Jon Saraceno for *USA Today* (27 Oct. 2011) as "the Michael Jordan of football" and the kind of athlete who comes "around once every ten or fifteen years."

Johnson and Stafford were instrumental in restoring the Lions' so-called roar, as the team placed second in the NFC North Division with a record of 10–6 and advanced to the postseason for the first time since the 1999 season. The Lions were defeated by the New Orleans Saints in the wild-card play-off round, 45–28. In his play-off debut, Johnson caught twelve passes for a franchise-record 211 yards and two touchdowns.

MAKING HISTORY

In March 2012 Johnson signed an eight-year contract extension with the Lions worth approximately $132 million. The contract included $60 million in guaranteed money and made him the highest-paid receiver in the league. The following month he was voted by fans to appear on the cover of the popular video game *Madden NFL 13*, which was released in August 2012.

Instead of falling victim to the so-called Madden Curse, which refers to the large number of players who have suffered injuries or disappointing seasons after appearing on the cover of the game, Johnson lived up to his contract in spectacular fashion during the 2012 season. In sixteen starts, he led the NFL with a career-high 122 receptions and set the league single-season record for receiving yardage with 1,964, breaking Hall of Famer Jerry Rice's 1995 record of 1,848. He earned his third straight selection to the Pro Bowl, although an injury prevented him from participating, and was named to his second consecutive All-Pro first team. Despite Johnson's historic season, the Lions failed to return to the play-offs and finished with an underachieving 4–12 record.

Johnson further cemented his status as the league's most talented receiver in 2013, when he made eighty-four catches for 1,492 yards and scored twelve touchdowns in fourteen games. Johnson's most notable performance came during a week eight game against the Dallas Cowboys, when he made fourteen catches for a franchise-record 329 receiving yards, just short of Flipper Anderson's 1989 NFL single-game record of 336 yards. In the same game, which the Lions won 31–30, he tied the league record for most career games with at least two hundred yards receiving, with five. Following his performance, Lions running back Reggie Bush proclaimed, as quoted by Michael Rothstein for ESPN (27 Oct. 2012), "He's the greatest receiver in the history of the National Football League."

Two weeks after the Cowboys game, in a week ten matchup against the Chicago Bears, Johnson made his sixty-second and sixty-third career touchdown receptions, becoming the Lions' all-time leader in that offensive category. He earned his fourth consecutive Pro Bowl appearance and was named to his third straight All-Pro first team later in 2013. The Lions enjoyed a promising first half of the season, going 5–3, but lost six of their final eight games to finish with a mediocre 7–9 record. At the conclusion of the regular season, head coach Jim Schwartz was fired and replaced by former Baltimore Ravens offensive coordinator Jim Caldwell.

During the off-season, Johnson lives in a luxury condominium in Atlanta's Buckhead district. In 2009 he launched the Calvin Johnson Jr. Foundation, which is dedicated to helping at-risk youths stay out of trouble.

SUGGESTED READING

Battista, Judy. "Johnson Has No Baggage and a Seat in First Class." *New York Times*. New York Times, 26 Apr. 2007. Web. 16 July 2014.

Dulac, Gerry. "Detroit's Calvin Johnson Has No Peers Today, and Maybe Not in History." *Pittsburgh Post-Gazette*. PG Pub., 16 Nov. 2013. Web. 16 July 2014.

Kowalski, Tom. "Getting to Know Lions Receiver Calvin Johnson." *MLive*. MLive Media Group, 20 Apr. 2008. Web. 16 July 2014.

Merrill, Elizabeth. "Calvin Johnson Is Magic on Sundays." *ESPN*. ESPN Internet Ventures, 3 Sept. 2012. Web. 16 July 2014.

Murphy, Austin. "I Am (More Than) Robot Megatron." *Sports Illustrated*. Time, 30 Dec. 2013. Web. 16 July 2014.

—*Chris Cullen*

Jennifer Jones

Born: July 7, 1974
Occupation: Professional curler and lawyer

Jennifer Jones is one of Canada's most accomplished female curlers. Widely considered to be the best skip, or captain, in Canadian women's curling, Jones has compiled an impressive array of achievements since emerging on the professional curling circuit in the early 2000s. A typical curling game consists of eight or ten ends, which are similar to innings in baseball, with two teams of four taking turns delivering polished granite stones, known as rocks, across a sheet of ice toward a target area called the house, where points are scored.

As the longtime skip of a Winnipeg, Manitoba–based team, Jones has won six Manitoba women's provincial championships and four Canadian national championships, called the Scotties Tournament of Hearts, which is sanctioned by Canada's governing body of curling, the Canadian Curling Association (CCA). She also won a world title in 2008 and has amassed a record nine Grand Slam victories on the Women's World Curling Tour. Such achievements have led some to refer to Jones as "the Kevin Martin of women's curling," as fellow Manitoban skip Chelsea Carey described her to Paul Wiecek for the *Winnipeg Free Press* (30 Jan. 2012), referring

Mark Blinch/Reuters/Landov

to Canada's most famous and decorated curler. Jones's crowning achievement as a curler came in 2013, when she earned her first Olympic berth after leading her team to victory at the Canadian Olympic Curling Trials. Jill Officer, Jones's longtime friend and teammate, told the Canadian Press (26 Mar. 2010) that Jones "has a lot of drive and a lot of determination and a desire to be great at things. . . . Even at how good she is, I don't think she ever lets up on trying to be better."

Unlike other world-class curlers, whose countries pay them to train and play in tournaments all year round, Jones, a graduate of the University of Manitoba, has also managed to balance a successful career as a lawyer. Since 2005, she has worked as a corporate lawyer with Wellington West Holdings, now owned by the National Bank of Canada. "I think it's great to be in a situation where I can have both [careers]," Jones told Bob Weeks for the Toronto *Globe and Mail* (14 Nov. 2009). "When curling is over, I can go to my career."

EARLY LIFE AND EDUCATION

Jennifer J. Jones was born on July 7, 1974, in Winnipeg, the capital and largest city of Manitoba, Canada. With her sister, Heather, who is eighteen months older, she grew up in Winnipeg's Windsor Park neighborhood. Her father, Larry, was a sales professional, and her mother, Carol, worked as an oncology nurse at Concordia Hospital in Winnipeg. Jones's interest in curling was shaped by her parents, both of whom were curling enthusiasts and members of Winnipeg's St. Vital Curling Club. As a toddler Jones would routinely wander off from the curling club's day care center to watch her parents curl. "I remember being plastered against the glass and everybody always looking for me," she recalled to the Canadian Press (26 Mar. 2010), adding, "I loved it from the very beginning."

Jones attended General Vanier Elementary School and Windsor Park Collegiate High School. She began curling competitively in the St. Vital junior program at the age of eleven. Jones has credited her parents with encouraging and nurturing her passion for the sport. "They never missed one curling event and they often skipped holidays to take me," she told Sally Correia for *On Manitoba* (Dec. 2006), the alumni magazine of the University of Manitoba.

Heeding the example set by her parents, whom she described to Correia as "role models," Jones learned at an early age the value of making sacrifices in order to achieve athletic and professional goals. She also cultivated a strong work ethic and invaluable time-management skills that would pay dividends later in her adult life. As a teenager Jones not only curled for Windsor Park Collegiate, St. Vital, and other Winnipeg club teams but also was involved in volleyball, basketball, and baseball and worked a part-time job.

HIGH SCHOOL AND COLLEGE YEARS

While attending Windsor Park Collegiate, Jones established herself as one of the top junior curlers in Canada, where curling is considered a national pastime. In 1990, at age fifteen, she guided Windsor Park to a second-place finish at the Manitoba High Schools Athletic Association (MHSAA) provincial curling championships. Two years later, during her senior year, she led Windsor Park to the MHSAA provincial curling title.

Meanwhile, on the junior-level club circuit, Jones won her first Canadian provincial junior title in 1991, as a member of Winnipeg's Charleswood Curling Club. Her team represented Manitoba at that year's Canadian Junior Curling Championships, where they posted a 10–1 record in the preliminary round-robin before losing to New Brunswick in the final. "[The loss] made me work harder and made me more determined than ever to win one day," she said in an article posted on the website for the Whirlpool Corporation, an official sponsor of Canadian women's curling.

After graduating from high school in 1992, Jones enrolled at the University of Manitoba in Winnipeg. By that time she had become the skip of a formidable St. Vital junior women's curling team that included lead Dana Allerton (then Malanchuk), second Jill Officer, and third Trisha Baldwin. (In the sport of curling, a team, or rink, is made up of four players: the lead, the second, the third, and the skip, the latter of whom is responsible for deciding the strategy behind shot choices.)

Jones led her St. Vital team to Canadian provincial junior titles in 1993 and 1994 and helped it win a coveted Canadian junior title in 1994. She earned a bachelor's degree in psychology and economics from the University of Manitoba in 1996 and completed her law degree there in 1999.

BALANCING TWO CAREERS

Upon graduating from the University of Manitoba, Jones joined the law firm of Aikins, MacAulay & Thorvaldson in downtown Winnipeg, where she practiced law from 1999 to 2005. During this time she entered the Canadian professional curling circuit. Despite being discouraged from pursuing two full-time careers, Jones decided to follow her dreams of becoming both a professional curler and a lawyer. She has drawn strong parallels between the two professions. "The work world is a little different from the sports world, but then again, not really," she explained to Correia. "There are certain values that transfer . . . the biggest thing that sport has taught me is how to deal with pressure—this has definitely helped me in my career, especially when there is a time crunch."

Jones's ability to thrive in high-pressure situations would become her trademark as a curler. In 2001, Jones skipped her St. Vital team, which consisted of Allerton at lead and twin sisters Lynn Fallis-Kurz and Karen Porritt at second and third, respectively, to a runner-up finish at the Manitoba Scott Tournament of Hearts, the provincial women's curling championship. The following year she guided the same team to the Manitoba women's curling title, which helped them qualify for the 2002 Scott Tournament of Hearts, Canada's women's national championship. (Since 2007 Canada's national and provincial curling championship tournaments have been called the Scotties Tournament of Hearts.)

At the 2002 nationals, held in Brandon, Manitoba, Jones helped her team post an 8–3 record in the round-robin to advance to the playoffs, where they narrowly lost to Ontario, 7–6, in the quarterfinals. Jones, who uncharacteristically missed her last shot in that match, attributed the critical miss to putting too much pressure on herself. "After that, I learned to enjoy the moment," she explained to the Canadian Press (26 Mar. 2010). Jones's teams failed to qualify for the 2003 and 2004 national championships, after falling successively in the finals and quarterfinals of the Manitoba provincial championships.

BREAKTHROUGH

Jones was relatively unknown outside of curling circles until 2005, when she claimed both provincial and national titles. After winning the 2005 provincial title with her St. Vital team, which included lead Cathy Gauthier, second Officer, and third Cathy Overton-Clapham, Jones earned the right to represent Manitoba at the 2005 Scott Tournament of Hearts. There, her team finished the round-robin in first place with a 9–2 record before advancing to the playoffs and defeating Ontario, 8–6, in the championship final.

In the final, Jones defeated Ontario in dramatic walk-off fashion by making an extremely difficult shot known as an in-off, in which the delivered stone must deflect off another stone in order to redirect into the house for points. "The Shot," as it came to be known in the Canadian sports media, landed perfectly inside the button, or center of the house, to score the maximum of four points, thus clinching both the game and the tournament for Manitoba. It turned Jones into a household name in Canada and has since come to be regarded as "the most dramatic walk-off shot in Canadian curling history," according to Allen Cameron for the *National Post* (7 Nov. 2012).

By winning the Canadian title, Jones and her team automatically qualified for the 2005 World Curling Championships in Paisley, Scotland. The team finished the round-robin in third place with an 8–3 record but was eliminated from the tournament after being defeated handily by Norway, 12–5, in the opening playoff round. In December 2005, Jones's team, which now included the 2002 Olympic bronze medalist Georgina Wheatcroft as lead, competed at the Canadian Olympic Curling Trials in Halifax, Nova Scotia, where they compiled a disappointing 5–4 record in the round-robin, failing to reach the playoffs and missing out on the chance to represent Canada at the 2006 Olympics.

MOVE TO WELLINGTON WEST

One month before the 2005 Olympic Curling Trials, Jones joined Wellington West Capital, a privately owned wealth-management firm headquartered in Winnipeg. She was hired and personally recruited to the company by its founder, Charlie Spiring, who brought her on to serve as the company's first in-house counsel. "Going in we understood if we wanted her skillset as a lawyer, we had to work with her skills as a curler," Spiring explained to Marg. Bruineman for *Canadian Lawyer* (2 July 2013), referring to his decision to offer Jones flexibility that enabled her to develop in both professions. Jones's working arrangement at Wellington West allowed her to make her own schedule during the Canadian curling season, which typically runs from early fall to early spring.

As in-house counsel for Wellington West, Jones was responsible for drafting contracts and directing company processes and policies. She played a pivotal role in Wellington West's growth as a company and in preparing its $333 million sale to the Montreal-based National Bank of Canada in 2011. Jones, who has since moved to the bank's regulatory compliance office, has cited Spiring as a mentor and credited him with helping her achieve a rewarding work-life balance. "If you surround yourself with great people, you can do anything in life, business, and sport," she told the Wellington West client magazine *Inspired Thinking* (Spring/Summer 2008).

SCOTTIES THREE-PEAT AND FIRST WORLD TITLE

While working full time at Wellington West, Jones continued to rack up achievements as a curler. In 2006, as skip of Team Canada (designated to the national title winner from the previous year), she reached the finals of the Scott Tournament of Hearts, held in London, Ontario, before losing to a British Columbia team skipped by Kelly Scott. Later that year she skipped her regular Manitoba team to victory at the 2006 Players' Championship, which included a $100,000 purse.

In 2007, Jones captured her third career Manitoba provincial title, as skip of a team that included Overton-Clapham, Officer, and lead Janet Arnott. In February of that year, she skipped the same team at the Scotties Tournament of Hearts, leading them to the semifinals before losing again to Kelly Scott of British Columbia. The following month Jones won her first Canada Cup of Curling, with Dawn Askin at lead. She then closed out the 2006–7 curling season by winning her second consecutive Players' Championship, this time exacting revenge on Scott in the final.

During the 2007–8 season, Jones, with Overton-Clapham, Officer, and Askin, won her fourth overall and second straight Manitoba title and the first of three consecutive Scotties titles. She also won her first career world title after leading her team to a 7–4 victory over China in the gold-medal match of the 2008 World Curling Championship in British Columbia. Afterward, Jones landed a sponsorship deal with the Canadian facial tissue brand Scotties, for which she began appearing in commercials.

During the 2008–9 season, Jones won two Grand Slam events, the now-defunct Wayden Transportation Ladies Classic and the Players' Championship, and led a successful defense of her Scotties title. At the 2009 World Curling Championship in Gangneung, South Korea, Jones and her team narrowly missed out on a medal, losing to Denmark, 7–6, in the bronze-medal game. They would win the first Grand Slam event of the following season, the 2009 Autumn Gold Curling Classic, before competing at the 2009 Canadian Olympic Curling Trials. Despite entering the trials as the favorites to win, Jones and her team failed to reach the playoff round after posting a disastrous 2–5 record in the round-robin, thus again missing out on an Olympic berth.

Jones and her team bounced back at the 2010 Scotties Tournament of Hearts, which they won to secure their third straight national title. They then won a bronze medal at the 2010 World Curling Championship in Saskatchewan. That performance was considered another disappointment, however, after Jones and her team finished the round-robin with a tournament-best 10–1 record. Following the round-robin, they lost playoff games to Germany and Scotland before defeating Sweden, 9–6, in the bronze-medal game.

MORE CURLING TITLES AND FIRST OLYMPIC BERTH

Shortly after the 2010 world championships, Jones replaced her longtime third Overton-Clapham with the young rising star Kaitlyn Lawes, as a way "to shake things up," as she put it in an interview with the Canadian Press (24 Apr. 2010). During the 2010–11 season, Jones's revamped team won two Grand Slam events, the now-defunct Sobeys Slam and the Players' Championship. Meanwhile, on the CCA circuit, they finished as runner-up to Saskatchewan at the 2011 Scotties Tournament of Hearts. Later in 2011 Jones won her second Canada Cup of Curling, in British Columbia, after defeating a fellow Manitoban team skipped by Carey. The win earned her team automatic qualification into the 2013 Canadian Olympic Curling Trials.

In 2012, Jones won her fifth Manitoba title, captured a bronze medal at the Scotties Tournament of Hearts, and reached the semifinals of the Players' Championship. Shortly after the latter event, Jones had surgery for ligament damage in her right knee, after which she began extensive physiotherapy that kept her sidelined for the first half of the 2012–13 season. In November 2012, while still recovering from the injury, she gave birth to her first child, daughter Isabella, with partner Brent Laing, a Canadian curler who plays second for an Ontario team. In an interview with Wiecek for the *Winnipeg Free Press* (29 Nov. 2012), Jones called the birth of her daughter "the best thing that ever happened to me."

Jones returned to the ice just weeks after giving birth. In January 2013, she skipped her team to victory at the Manitoba Scotties Tournament of Hearts, claiming her sixth provincial title; in the following month, she helped the team reach the finals of the Scotties Tournament of Hearts. In the round-robin of the latter tournament, Jones and her team compiled a perfect 11–0 record, becoming the first team in nearly thirty years to accomplish such a feat. During the tournament, Jones recorded her hundredth Scotties victory, becoming only the second woman in Canadian curling history (behind six-time Canadian champion Colleen Jones) to record at least one hundred Scotties wins as a skip.

At the 2013 Canadian Olympic Curling Trials in Winnipeg, Jones defeated Sherry Middaugh of Ontario in the final, 8–4, to earn her first trip to the Olympics, representing Canada at the 2014 games in Sochi, Russia. Jones's team is the first team from Manitoba to do so. Commenting on the Olympic-clinching victory, Jones told Judy Owen and Scott Edmonds for the Canadian Press (8 Dec. 2013), "This is one of the best, if not the best, moments of our curling careers."

By the end of 2013, Jones had amassed nine career Grand Slam event victories, which is a record for a female skip. She divides her time between Winnipeg and Horseshoe Valley, Ontario, where her partner, Laing, is based. The couple plan on deciding where they will settle down to raise their daughter sometime after the 2013–14 season. Jones was previously married to Scott Labonte, whom she divorced in 2012.

SUGGESTED READING

Bruineman, Marg. "A Win-Win Career: Cross Examined." *Canadian Lawyer.* Thomson Reuters Canada, 2 July 2013. Web. 25 Nov. 2013.

Edmonds, Scott. "Jennifer Jones Back on Curling Circuit." *Globe and Mail* [Toronto]. Globe and Mail, 12 Dec. 2012. Web. 25 Nov. 2013.

Fitzgerald, Sean. "Jennifer Jones Soars into Elite Company with Undefeated Record, 100th Scotties Victory." *National Post.* National Post, 22 Feb. 2013. Web. 25 Nov. 2013.

"Nothing Like Curling for Jennifer Jones." *Canadian Press.* Rogers Media, 26 Mar. 2010. Web. 25 Nov. 2013.

Weeks, Bob. "Jones Keeps Things in Perspective." *Globe and Mail* [Toronto]. Globe and Mail, 14 Nov. 2009. Web. 25 Nov. 2013.

Wiecek, Paul. "Another One for Drama Queen." *Winnipeg Free Press* 30 Jan. 2012: C1. Print.

—*Chris Cullen*

Jónsi

Born: April 23, 1975
Occupation: Musician

The Icelandic singer and guitarist Jón Þór Birgisson, better known to the world as Jónsi, has earned a reputation for having "the most transcendent voice in popular music," according to Jason Killingsworth for *Paste* magazine (6 Apr. 2010). Jónsi is the frontman and leader of the critically acclaimed ambient rock band Sigur Rós, which has been frequently hailed as Iceland's second-biggest musical export after Björk. Since forming in 1994, the band has been known for Jónsi's ethereal falsetto vocals and for

Redferns via Getty Images

his equally distinctive guitar sound, created using a cello bow. Those distinct elements have featured prominently on most of Sigur Rós's seven full-length studio albums, the most notable of which, *Ágætis byrjun* (1999), helped propel the band to international fame. Jónsi has also won attention for singing a large number of Sigur Rós songs in a made-up language called "Hopelandic," which has further contributed to his band's mystique. In addition to his work with Sigur Rós, Jónsi has released two solo albums and contributed music to film soundtracks.

EARLY LIFE AND EDUCATION
Jón Þór "Jónsi" Birgisson was born on April 23, 1975, in Iceland. He grew up in the village of Mosfellsbær, located about seven miles east of the Icelandic capital of Reykjavik. His father worked as a blacksmith, and his mother was a nurse. He has three younger sisters, Lilja, Ingibjörg, and Sigurrós, the latter of whom, upon being born in August 1994, inspired Sigur Rós's band name. Born blind in his right eye due to a broken optic nerve, Jónsi has said that he was raised in a traditional family and enjoyed a carefree, innocent childhood in the Icelandic countryside.

Jónsi was exposed to music at an early age. He grew up listening to his parents' record collection, which included a number of Beatles albums. One of his earliest memories was playing the Beatles' 1963 cover of "Twist and Shout"

at double speed on his parents' stereo. As Jónsi grew older, his musical tastes evolved toward heavy metal bands such as Iron Maiden, Metallica, and AC/DC, as well as grunge music. He has recalled that during his youth, very few foreign bands ventured to Iceland to perform.

For his thirteenth birthday, Jónsi's father, recognizing his son's growing interest in music, bought him his first electric guitar. It was at that age that Jónsi bought his first record, Iron Maiden's 1981 album *Killers*. The first song Jónsi learned to play on guitar was that album's second track, "Wrathchild." Iron Maiden was also the first band he saw live. Jónsi has cited the group's lead vocalist, Bruce Dickinson, who is well known for his wailing, high-pitched voice, as an influence on his vocal style.

In his late teens, Jónsi's musical tastes branched out to more alternative forms of music, particularly ambient. By that time he had already started playing guitar in various school bands, one of which was a grunge band called Stoned. For Jónsi, who knew from a young age that he was gay but did not come out until he was twenty-one, music offered him an outlet to express himself. A career in music, however, seemed unlikely. Growing up in Iceland, he told Laura Studarus for *Under the Radar* magazine (3 May 2010), "you get a lot of English and American music and listen to a lot of music and play in a band . . . [but] never think that one day you're going to live off the music and play shows and concerts." He added that while his parents supported his musical aspirations, "they were always pressing about school."

FORMATION OF SIGUR RÓS
In the early 1990s, while attending a technical school in Reykjavik, Jónsi met bassist Georg Hólm and drummer Ágúst Ævar Gunnarsson. Sharing similar music tastes, the three teenagers became fast friends and decided to form a band that would make ambient music with a traditional rock bent. Formed in August 1994, the trio named themselves Sigur Rós, meaning "Victory Rose," in honor of Jónsi's youngest sister, Sigurrós, who was born around the same time. Their first song, "Fljúgðu" ("Fly"), was recorded in a mere six hours, but they spent roughly the next three years honing their sound and developing the material that would end up on their debut album, *Von* (1997; "Hope").

Released on the Icelandic label Smekkleysa (Bad Taste), *Von* was critically well received but went largely unnoticed, even in Iceland, where it initially sold just 313 copies. The album drew heavily on the band's early music influences, which included groups such as the Smashing Pumpkins, Spiritualized, and the Verve. Jónsi and his bandmates were ultimately dissatisfied with the album, which, because of its long gestation period, featured songs that sounded completely different from their original recordings. Scott Mervis, writing for the *Pittsburgh Post-Gazette* (19 Sept. 2013), described *Von* as "the type of creaky ambient record that could scare the little ones away from your house on Halloween." *Von* was followed by the Smekkleysa-distributed remix album *Von brigði* ("Variations on *Von*") in 1998. The album consisted of reworkings of songs from *Von* by various Icelandic artists, as well as one new song by Sigur Rós, "Leit af lífi" ("Search for life"). Originally intended to go on *Von*, the song reached number one on the Icelandic charts.

Two distinct elements of the Sigur Rós sound came about during this time. First, Hólm was given a violin bow by Gunnarsson as a birthday present. Hólm quickly grew unhappy with the sound it created on his bass, after which Jónsi started using it on his guitar and "found it worked very well for getting that floating ambient sound," as he recalled to a writer for the London *Mirror* (31 Oct. 2008). Shortly thereafter, Jónsi started experimenting with falsetto vocals and discovered that it not only expanded his voice but also gave him better control over it. The singer's androgynous, multilayered falsetto vocals and the use of bowed guitar eventually became Sigur Rós trademarks. The band's sound further evolved with the addition of Kjartan Sveinsson, a classically trained keyboardist and multi-instrumentalist who joined the band shortly after *Von*'s release.

ÁGÆTIS BYRJUN AND RISE TO INTERNATIONAL FAME

Sigur Rós's refined sound was showcased prominently on the band's second album, *Ágætis byrjun* ("A good beginning"), which was released on Smekkleysa in 1999. Around this time Gunnarsson left the band to pursue a career in graphic design; he was replaced by Orri Páll Dýrason. Featuring a collection of ten mostly lengthy, slow-burning songs, characterized by ethereal vocals sung in a combination of Icelandic and the imaginary language "Hopelandic," and elaborate orchestral and string arrangements, *Ágætis byrjun* marked the band's international breakthrough and earned them praise from critics. "Otherworldly," "heavenly," and "gorgeous" were some of the adjectives critics used to describe their sound, which many felt defied categorization. As noted by Marc Hogan for *Spin* (13 June 2013), one British journalist famously said that their music was "like God weeping tears of gold in heaven." At the time, Jónsi and his bandmates seemed to bask in such bombast, declaring on their website, "We are simply gonna change music forever, and the way people think about music. And don't think we can't do it, we will."

Ágætis byrjun resonated with music listeners in Iceland, where it spent several weeks atop the charts and achieved double-platinum status there after selling twenty thousand copies, the rough equivalent of twenty million in the United States. In 2000, Sigur Rós signed an international distribution deal with the British label Fat Cat Records, which helped generate more buzz for the album. The band spent much of that year touring, opening for popular bands such as Radiohead, whose frontman Thom Yorke cited *Ágætis byrjun* as an inspiration for Radiohead's landmark 2000 album, *Kid A*. Other celebrities who became devoted followers of the band included actor Brad Pitt; Metallica drummer Lars Ulrich, who wrote a letter of thanks to the band after watching them perform; and director Cameron Crowe, who used three of the band's songs in his 2001 science-fiction thriller *Vanilla Sky*.

In 2001, following a major bidding war among US record labels, *Ágætis byrjun* was released in North America through a distribution deal between Fat Cat, Smekkleysa, and PIAS. That year Sigur Rós famously turned down an opportunity to perform on *The Late Show with David Letterman* after only being allowed a four-minute time slot. (Most of the band's songs average seven to eight minutes in length.) Such bold career decisions, however, only added to the band's mystique. Later in 2001 *Ágætis byrjun* won the inaugural Shortlist Music Prize for Artistic Achievement in Music. The album would later receive increasingly breathless critical adulation. In a review for the music website Pitchfork (1 June 1999), which later ranked the album number eight on its list of the top two hundred albums of the 2000s, Brent DiCrescenzo called Sigur Rós "the first vital band of the twenty-first century."

( ) AND *TAKK . . .*

Following the success of *Ágætis byrjun*, Sigur Rós's third album, released in 2002, was received with much anticipation. Titled with a pair of parentheses, *( )*, and sometimes referred to as "the bracket album," it was recorded in the band's newly built Mosfellsbær recording studio, Sundlaugin, a converted 1930s swimming pool. Further pushing the boundaries of musical experimentation, *( )* featured eight tracks, all of which lacked titles and were sung entirely in Hopelandic, and came with a booklet of twelve blank pages. "The idea," Jónsi explained to Chris Campion for the London *Telegraph* (10 Oct. 2002), "is that filling in the space between the music and lyrics becomes a soundtrack to your own life." Campion described *( )* as "a record of two halves, contained but open-ended. Naïve sing-song melodies give way to epic tracks that negotiate an otherworldly musical landscape that veers from brittle to brutal." The album, in spite of its mystifying nature, received a positive response from critics. It also fared well commercially, reaching number one on the Iceland charts and number fifty-one on the US Billboard 200 album chart.

Sigur Rós's next album, *Takk . . .* (2005; "Thanks . . ."), was more accessible and marked a return to the band's distinctive sound. All of the album's eleven songs were titled, and most were sung in Icelandic. The album included the single "Hoppípolla" ("Hopping into puddles"), which became the band's biggest hit to date thanks to its widespread use in commercials, advertisements for the acclaimed BBC wildlife series *Planet Earth* (2006), and trailers for award-winning films such as *Children of Men* (2006) and *Slumdog Millionaire* (2008), among many others. "Hoppípolla" reached number twenty-four on the UK singles chart. In an article for the *Guardian* (25 Aug. 2005), Dorian Lynskey opined that *Takk . . .* was Sigur Rós's "most accomplished and affecting record yet." He added, "Although their songs suggest epic vistas, they are really about the small things."

SIGUR RÓS HIATUS AND JÓNSI SOLO CAREER

In 2007 Sigur Rós released the two-disc compilation *Hvarf/Heim*, which included studio versions of previously unreleased songs and live acoustic versions of songs already released. (The band translates *hvarf* as "disappeared" or "haven," while *heim* means "home.") The album was released in conjunction with the documentary film *Heima* (2007; "At home"), which followed the band as they toured around Iceland for two weeks during the summer of 2006. Sigur Rós's fifth studio album, *Með suð í eyrum við spilum endalaust* ("With a buzz in our ears we play endlessly"), was released in 2008. The pop-focused and guitar-heavy album was considered by many critics to be the band's most accessible. It included the songs "Gobbledigook" and "All Alright," the latter of which was the band's first to be sung in English.

Following a world tour in support of the album, Sigur Rós went on an indefinite hiatus, at which point Jónsi embarked on a solo career. His first project, a nine-track album of instrumental ambient music titled *Riceboy Sleeps*, was released in 2009 under the moniker Jónsi & Alex. The name refers to the artistic collaboration between Jónsi and his partner, Alex Somers, an American-born visual artist, producer, and musician. Tim Sendra, reviewing *Riceboy Sleeps* for the AllMusic website, likened the album's sound to that of Sigur Rós, writing that it "has all the majestic calm" of the Icelandic band "with none of the dramatic storm, all of the lull and none of the squall."

Jónsi's first solo effort under his name alone, *Go*, was released in 2010 on the British label XL Recordings. The album was made in collaboration with Somers, Finnish percussionist Samuli Kosminen, and American modern classical composer Nico Muhly, best known for his work with artists such as Philip Glass, Björk, and Antony and the Johnsons. Unlike *Riceboy Sleeps*, *Go* marked a departure from Jónsi's previous work, featuring nine songs primarily sung in English and characterized by acoustic, rock, and pop elements. "Much of the glacial, alien quality of [Jónsi's] earlier work with Sigur Rós has melted away to reveal a gorgeous collection of mostly brisk, summery jams," Jason Lamphier wrote for the *Advocate* (Apr. 2010). "*Go* sounds fearless, like the rush of falling in love."

During the spring of 2010, Jónsi launched a tour across North America and Europe in support of *Go*, which reached number twenty on the UK Albums Chart and number twenty-three on the Billboard 200 chart. Later that year the singer recorded a song, "Sticks and Stones," for the soundtrack to *How to Train Your Dragon* (2010), an animated film about a teenage Viking codirected by Chris Sanders and Dean DeBlois, the latter of whom also directed *Heima*. In 2011, Jónsi composed his first film score, for the Cameron Crowe comedy-drama *We Bought a Zoo*. "Jónsi is able to score the highs and lows of life while reminding you that there's exuberance to life itself," Crowe told Dave Karger for *Entertainment Weekly* (6 Jan. 2012).

VALTARI AND *KVEIKUR*

Jónsi rejoined Sigur Rós in 2012, when the band released its sixth studio album, *Valtari* ("Roller"). Featuring cover art by Jónsi's sisters Lilja and Ingibjörg, the album was a critical and commercial success, reaching number one in Iceland and debuting at number seven on the Billboard 200, marking the band's first top-ten entry on that chart. In an article for the music website Gigwise (7 May 2012), Michael Baggs called *Valtari* "a spectacular collection of ethereal soundscapes and haunting epics."

Following the release of *Valtari*, Sveinsson left Sigur Rós to focus on other endeavors. In the wake of his departure, Jónsi, Hólm, and Dýrason decided to carry on as a trio and reinvented their sound. That new sound was introduced on the band's seventh studio album, *Kveikur* ("Fuse"), which was released on XL Recordings in 2013. Mervis described the experimental, nine-track album, which excluded piano arrangements and placed less emphasis on Jónsi's vocals, as "a darker, dystopian record showcasing the explosive rhythm section and embracing more aggressive elements of electronic dance." In a review for *Electronic Musician* (Sept. 2013), Ken Micallef called the album "a mammoth production, with all the aggression of modern warfare and the ethereal beauty of a midnight mass."

Three months before *Kveikur*'s release, in March 2013, Sigur Rós achieved what Hogan described as the "crowning moment" of their illustrious career, when they played their first headline show at New York City's legendary Madison

Square Garden. Two months later, the band appeared in and contributed music to an Iceland-themed episode of *The Simpsons*, titled "The Saga of Carl." Jónsi and his bandmates appeared in the hit HBO series *Game of Thrones* on season four's second episode, "The Lion and the Rose," which first aired on April 13, 2014.

PERSONAL LIFE

Jónsi lives in Reykjavik with his partner, Alex Somers. In addition to their music collaborations, the couple have exhibited artwork at galleries around the world and released an online-only raw food cookbook featuring some of their homemade recipes. Jónsi is a longtime vegetarian, and Somers is a vegan; both are certified raw-food chefs and were previously raw-food vegans.

SUGGESTED READING

Campion, Chris. "Cool Band from a Cool Place." *Telegraph*. Telegraph Media Group, 10 Oct. 2002. Web. 14 Mar. 2014.

Hogan, Marc. "Speaking in Tongues: A Conversation with Sigur Ros' Jonsi." *Spin*. Spin, 13 June 2013. Web. 14 Mar. 2014.

Jónsi. Interview by Jason Heller. *AV Club*. Onion, 14 Apr. 2010. Web. 14 Mar. 2014.

Killingsworth, Jason. "The Unbearable Lightness of Being Jónsi." *Paste*. Paste Media Group, 6 Apr. 2010. Web. 14 Mar. 2014.

Lynskey, Dorian. "Strange? Us?" *Guardian*. Guardian News and Media, 25 Aug. 2005. Web. 14 Mar. 2014.

Mervis, Scott. "Preview: Icelandic Band Sigur Ros Brings Atmospheric Sound to Town." *Pittsburgh Post-Gazette*. PG, 19 Sept. 2013. Web. 14 Mar. 2014.

SELECTED WORKS

Von, 1997; *Ágætis byrjun*, 1999; ( ), 2002; *Takk . . .* , 2005; *Með suð í eyrum við spilum endalaust*, 2008; *Riceboy Sleeps*, 2009; *Go*, 2010; *Valtari*, 2012; *Kveikur*, 2013

—*Chris Cullen*

Sebastian Junger

Born: 1962
Occupation: Journalist and documentarian

Sebastian Junger is known for his gripping life-and-death stories and films. A surfer, he wiped out off Balston Beach on Cape Cod in 1994, losing his board and nearly drowning. That experience gave him firsthand knowledge of the physical realities of drowning that figure in his best-selling first book, *The Perfect Storm*. Other personal experiences informed some of his

subsequent books, including the essay collection *Fire*, the true-crime book *A Death in Belmont*, and *War*, which focuses on American soldiers' experiences of modern warfare.

Fellow journalist Scott Anderson commented to Adam Langer for *Book* (Sept.–Oct. 2001), "Things have gone very well and very smoothly for him. Whether it's prescience or luck, he's repeatedly in the right place at the right time." Junger has said that he is not interested in people who voluntarily put themselves in dangerous situations, such as mountain climbers. He explained to Langer, "If you write about someone who gets in trouble in a sailboat race or on a mountain, there's no implication for mankind. You write about a country where there's a preventable war, a stoppable war, there are implications. There's importance there."

EARLY LIFE AND EDUCATION

Sebastian Junger was born in 1962. Even as a child growing up in the Boston suburb of Belmont, Massachusetts, Junger wanted to be able to survive in the wild. He made bows and arrows as well as lean-tos in the nearby woods to which he would escape some nights. Junger was a misfit, uncomfortable with the comparative wealth of his home. His mother, artist Ellen Sinclair, told Langer, "He's always had troubles with the fact that this is the suburbs, and an elegant house in the suburbs is not what he likes." He and his family also traveled abroad several times, even briefly living in France with relatives when he was six. These and other such experiences would shape his later career.

When Junger was a baby, Sinclair added a studio to their home. One of the construction workers on that job was Albert "Al" DeSalvo, who later confessed to being the Boston Strangler. Junger later used the man's presence and the conviction of Roy Smith for the murders as the basis of his book *A Death in Belmont*. Miguel Junger, his father, is a physicist and former professor at the Massachusetts Institute of Technology; some of *The Perfect Storm* relies on Miguel's work with underwater acoustics engineering. Junger's sister, Carlotta, is a photographer and an art director for a London publisher.

David Smith, Junger's middle-school social studies and English teacher at Shady Hill School, recalled to Langer, "Sebastian was an incredibly enthusiastic writer and reader even back then, especially about topics relating to nature and the outdoors." After Shady Hill, Junger went to Concord Academy, a preparatory high school in the town nineteenth-century writer Henry David Thoreau made famous. There Junger added long-distance running to his accomplishments, running one hundred miles each week. By the time he attended Wesleyan University, he had dreams of making the Olympics and three times qualified for NCAA Division III Nationals. Fittingly, he conducted field research on and wrote his senior thesis about Navajo long-distance runners. Junger graduated in 1984 with a major in cultural anthropology.

TRAINING FOR WRITING

Following Junger's graduation from college, the shoe company Etonic sponsored him as he ran marathons. He was not quite fast enough, however; he could not break a four-minute mile. One day he simply stopped in the middle of a workout and walked back home.

Junger had done well in a solitary sport that demanded daily discipline. He explained to Christopher Busa for *Provincetown Arts* (2002–3), "From running, I learned that I know how to make myself suffer." Running became part of his training for a life of writing. He rejects the idea of writer's block.

To support his writing habit, Junger took on odd jobs, including waiting tables. He learned that by working for a tree-trimming company, he could work for two days and make enough money to live on the rest of the week, which he spent writing.

When a cut on his leg from a chainsaw put him out of the tree-trimming business, he determined to write about physically difficult and demanding jobs. He thought about firefighters and deep-sea fishermen, as well as other professions. Junger also became intrigued by the sinking of the *Andrea Gail*, a swordfishing boat from Gloucester, Massachusetts, when three storm systems converged on the Grand Banks on October 30, 1991. He had grown up only about thirty miles from Gloucester and in fact had been living in the town at the time of the storm.

Junger showed a book proposal on dangerous jobs, including tree-trimming, to his literary agent, Stuart Krichevsky, who told him to focus only on the *Andrea Gail* story. Junger, who considers himself a journalist, had other plans and left for the Balkans to write about the war correspondents covering the civil war in the former Yugoslavia. During the five months he spent there, he determined that if he could not sell a book, he could become a journalist. While still in Eastern Europe, however, Junger heard from his agent. *Outside* magazine wanted to publish the chapter on the *Andrea Gail*, and the publisher W. W. Norton was offering an advance of $35,000 for a book solely on the storm.

THE PERFECT STORM

Junger spent most of the next three years researching in Gloucester and working on the book at the family summer home on the Cape. Even there, he imposed hardship on himself: his "writing desk" was a plywood board nailed to a couple of sawhorses, and the house became so cold in winter that ice would form over the water in glasses. Of that time, his mother commented to Langer, "When he was working on that book on the Cape in a house with very little heat and no insulation, I think I have never felt so proud as I did. He was so focused, so dedicated to that story."

No trace had been found of the boat or its six-man crew. Junger believes that in admitting that no one knew what had really happened and that his viewpoint is a guess, the book, titled *The Perfect Storm* and published in 1997, is truthful. The finished book surprised Junger by selling more than half a million copies in hardcover and two million copies in paperback. He told Robert Pushkar for *Yankee* magazine (Sept. 2000), "By a factor of a thousand, it was more successful than people thought. The summer of 1997, when it came out, was a very disorienting time for me. I was completely unprepared and totally overwhelmed. It was as if suddenly I was voted president." The book has been translated into more than twenty languages. Junger also received recognition that few writers get: *People* magazine named him Sexiest Author in 1997.

A film adaptation of *The Perfect Storm* came out in 2000. Filmed on location, the Warner Bros. movie had no need to create storms; at times, the dangerous Gloucester weather had actors running for cover. Starring George Clooney, Diane Lane, and Mark Wahlberg, it was the fourth-highest-grossing film of that year, making more than $180 million. Although he consulted with both screenwriter William B. Wittliff and director Wolfgang Petersen on the script, Junger was displeased by its finale, which gave a definitive conclusion he avoided in the book itself.

Moreover, the money depressed Junger, who felt it took away any reason for him to continue working. So he invested in an eighteenth-century home on Cape Cod and, with Scott Anderson, bought an interest in the Half King, a Manhattan restaurant and bar named after a Seneca chief. The restaurant offers changing visual displays, often of photographs of war. Junger also bought a yacht and founded a nonprofit organization to educate the children of commercial fishermen like those he interviewed for *The Perfect Storm.*

WRITING ON WAR

Following his experiences covering the Bosnian War, Junger continued to go to dangerous areas, including Nigeria, Sierra Leone, and Bosnia, even after *The Perfect Storm* was published. He explained to Christopher Busa for *Provincetown Arts* (2002–3), "One reason I write about war is that, as a form of reporting, it is intense, demanding. I get gratification, challenging myself." He explained that as a citizen of the world's most powerful country, he believed that by bringing war to the attention of readers, he might move the United States to stop senseless wars, citing the efforts of the United States and NATO to end conflicts in Bosnia and Kosovo.

When *Men's Journal* assigned Junger to write about Western hikers who had been kidnapped in Kashmir, he persuaded the magazine that he needed to find the root of the issue. That quest led him to Afghanistan in the summer of 1996, just as the Taliban swept into the region. Thus, after the terrorist attacks of September 11, 2001, Junger was one of the few Americans who knew and could speak intelligently about Afghanistan.

His 2010 book *War* is based on his further observations in Afghanistan, where he served as an embedded journalist for *Vanity Fair* magazine on five occasions between June 2007 and June 2008. He lived with the thirty infantrymen of the 173rd Airborne Brigade Combat Team, experiencing the daily life of battles with men twenty-five years his junior. During his time with their division in Korengal Valley, he was in a Humvee that hit an improvised explosive device (IED) made from a pressure cooker. Because the IED went off under the engine block, Junger and the rest of the men survived. Junger's camera was recording during the entire experience.

When interviewed by David Lauterborn for *Military History* (1 Sept. 2010) about the war in Afghanistan, Junger commented that combat was a test of character. "Character is: Are you willing to make yourself do things you don't want to do, to put the interests of the group above your own interests? That's, essentially, being an adult. It's an extreme version of being a responsible and selfless adult."

Although as a journalist Junger sticks primarily with writing in third person, he will occasionally use first person. He explained to Adam Dunn for *Publishers Weekly* (24 Sept. 2001), "In really complex situations like Sierra Leone or Afghanistan, using a little bit of the first person helps bring the country you're writing about into focus. It's sort of a lens that helps the reader see more clearly. Once, I was getting shelled on this hilltop, I was absolutely miserable—without the first person it would be hard to communicate that. It really gives you the sense of what war is like."

A FRIEND LOST

Junger frequently traveled with Tim Hetherington, a British photojournalist who, according to Junger, focused on the quiet dignity that humans show during times of struggle. Hetherington wrote a book about his experiences in Afghanistan, *Infidel*, using his photographs to illustrate the text; Junger wrote the introduction. The two codirected a film, *Restrepo*, about their experiences following soldiers during the Afghanistan war between 2007 and 2008. Private First Class Juan Restrepo was a medic who had been killed shortly after the company's arrival and for whom the base camp was nicknamed.

Junger had no experience with filmmaking and acknowledges that he could not have made the film without Hetherington. The film was nominated for an Academy Award for best documentary in 2011. That same year at the Sundance Film Festival, it was awarded a grand jury prize.

Less than two months after the Oscars, Hetherington was killed in Libya while covering the uprising to topple Muammar al-Qaddafi. Junger subsequently made a film about Hetherington's work and life, *Which Way Is the Front Line from Here?* The film was televised on HBO in April 2013.

Junger credits Hetherington for opening his mind to visual communication. As he pondered the organization of *War*, his book about the battalion in Afghanistan, Junger tried to consider how his friend would have organized it. He concluded that a linear approach was not the right way and instead divided it into three thematic sections: "Fear," "Killing," and "Love." Junger told Michael Coffey for *Publishers Weekly* (19 Apr. 2010) about that structure, "I just thought very long and hard. And it really boiled down to those three—fear, killing, and love—and those dovetailed very nicely with this other agenda that I had, which was to try to understand neurochemically, psychologically, and sociologically what courage is."

AFTERMATH

Hetherington had been hit in the femoral artery with mortar shrapnel. Without medical care, he bled to death within five minutes in a truck racing to get him to a hospital. After Hetherington's death Junger started a training group, Reporters Instructed in Saving Colleagues (RISC). Although correspondents from major networks who travel to war zones receive basic medical training because insurance carriers demand they do so, freelancer reporters, who cover most of the combat reporting, often do not. RISC offers free first aid courses for journalists and also supplies freelance reporters with medical kits.

Hetherington's death had a profound influence on Junger, who decided he would no longer go to the front lines of war. He explained to Reed Johnson for the *Los Angeles Times* (9 June 2011), "I'm not going to do any more front-line reporting, because I don't want to put my wife through what I went through with Tim." He added, "It was a very obvious thought to come to in the wake of all this. Tim's death made war reporting feel like a selfish endeavor."

Junger also had to come to terms with a certain amount of survivor's guilt. He, too, had been scheduled to be in Libya, but his plans changed at the last minute. He told Terry Gross for National Public Radio's *Fresh Air* (18 Apr. 2013), "I thought had I gone maybe we wouldn't have been there, or if we had been there maybe I could've saved his life. I'd had a little bit of medical training from the combat medic out at Restrepo, as had Tim. I felt very, very guilty that I'd abandoned my friend and that I should've been there with him."

PERSONAL LIFE

Junger married Daniela Petrova, who is from Bulgaria, in 2005. After years of attempts to conceive a child, they did so in 2011. It was for the sake of that pregnancy that Junger did not go to Libya; however, a rare chromosomal abnormality ended the pregnancy prematurely not long before Hetherington's death. The two losses deeply affected Junger and his wife.

Junger refuses to attempt writing fiction, though he made a stab at it in his twenties. He explained to Johnson, "A bad novel is hard to write. A brilliant novel, like I don't even know how that happens. So that's why I don't do it. Writing fiction feels like it would be like going off the diving board into a swimming pool that has no water in it. Maybe one day I will, and the pool will be filled with water and it'll be nice, but right now it doesn't feel that way."

SUGGESTED READING

Busa, Christopher. "Sebastian." *Provincetown Arts* 17 (2002–3): 34–41. Print.

Coffey, Michael. "War of Emotion." *Publishers Weekly* 19 Apr. 2010: 26–28. Print.

Dunn, Adam. "PW Talks with Sebastian Junger." *Publishers Weekly* 24 Sept. 2001: 80. Print.

Gross, Terry. "Sebastian Junger: 'Which Way' to Turn after Hetherington's Death." *Fresh Air*. NPR, 18 Apr. 2013. Web. 13 Mar. 2014.

Langer, Adam. "Sebastian Junger." *Book* [Summit, NJ] Sept.–Oct. 2001: 33. Print.

Lybarger, Dan. "From the Valley of Fire: An Interview with Tim Hetherington and Sebastian Junger." *Cineaste* 35.4 (2010): 38–41. Print.

Pushkar, Robert. "After the Storm." *Yankee* Sept. 2000: 66. Print.

"Sebastian Junger: On Combat New and Old." *Military History* Nov. 2010: 14+. Print.

SELECTED WORKS

The Perfect Storm, 1997; *Fire*, 2002; *A Death in Belmont*, 2007; *War*, 2011; *A World Made of Blood*, 2012; *Which Way Is the Front Line from Here?*, 2013

—*Judy Johnson*

Scott Jurek

Born: October 26, 1973
Occupation: Ultramarathoner

Although he had long been something of a celebrity in the decidedly insular world of ultramarathons—a designation applied to any race longer than the standard marathon distance of 26.2 miles—Scott Jurek was only introduced to the wider public in 2009 in Christopher McDougall's book *Born to Run: A Hidden Tribe, Superathletes, and the Greatest Race the World Has Never Seen*. The best-selling volume describes Jurek's experiences racing in the 2006 Copper Canyon Ultra Marathon alongside Mexico's Rarámuri (or, in Spanish, Tarahumara) people. The Rarámuris, who are native to the northwestern state of Chihuahua, are

Associated Press

able to run hundreds of miles without resting and are said to be able to chase a deer until the animal falls from exhaustion. Although Jurek lost the fifty-mile race by six minutes to famed Rarámuri runner Arnulfo Quimare, he returned to Copper Canyon the following year and won, beating his nearest competitor by eighteen minutes. Of his association with the Rarámuris, Jurek wrote in his own book, *Eat & Run: My Unlikely Journey to Marathon Greatness* (2012), "Running can be a lonely activity. It can also introduce you to people [and] worlds beyond your imagining."

While Jurek and his fellow endurance runners often tout the physical and psychological benefits of their sport, they are used to being considered strange by those in the mainstream. "Men and women who race at distances longer than marathons . . . are by reputation and reality a strange, obsessive, and somewhat socially awkward lot," Steve Friedman wrote for *Runner's World* (24 Mar. 2010). In an article for the online magazine *Slate* (28 May 2013) titled "What Are Extreme Runners *Thinking*?," Lisa Palmer vividly described a common race situation: "Ultramarathon running god Scott Jurek has a deep, gnawing pain. The familiar assault begins thirty miles into a one-hundred-mile race. His legs feel like they've been beaten by a baseball bat, and his suffering will only increase over the next seventy miles. Sooner or later he'll contend with a pitiful triad: vomiting, dry heaves, and stomach pains from the stress of sweating, eating, and drinking while running continuously. And that's the best-case scenario."

Friedman's assertion and Palmer's titular question are echoed in almost all of the press surrounding Jurek, who has won the 100-mile Western States Endurance Run an astonishing seven times and the grueling Badwater Ultramarathon, a 135-mile race across Death Valley, twice. For a time he also held the national record for most miles run (165.7) in a twenty-four-hour period. He explained to Palmer, "When people look at it on paper, it doesn't make sense: 'Why do you put your body through all that, and your mind?' But I think [it is] because in the end, I come out a different person, and I look at life differently."

EARLY YEARS

Scott Jurek was born in Minnesota on October 26, 1973, and was raised just outside the small town of Proctor, near Duluth. His father, Gordon Jurek, was a veteran of the US Navy who held a variety of jobs, including pipefitter, boiler operator, and hospital maintenance worker. He was a strict disciplinarian, and Jurek has recalled to journalists that even as a young child, he was not allowed to play until his many chores, including hauling and stacking wood, were complete.

Jurek's mother, Lynn Swapinski, held a degree in home economics. In addition to her job as a substitute teacher, she worked for Litton Industries, developing recipes for the company's line of microwave ovens and demonstrating the then-new technology to consumers. She also acted as spokesperson for the Minnesota Egg Council, doing radio and television ads for the trade group, and eventually landed her own cooking show on a local cable station. However, when Jurek was still young, his mother began exhibiting symptoms of multiple sclerosis, and as her condition worsened, his list of chores grew exponentially. Soon he was cooking all of the family meals and caring for his younger siblings, Angela and Greg.

Money was perpetually tight, and the three siblings often sold lemonade and made pinecone wreaths to earn what little pocket money they could. The family's financial situation meant that Jurek could participate in few team sports, as they required expensive equipment and travel to other towns. Instead, he began spending time in the woods near his house, sometimes running, sometimes toting along a fishing pole or hunting rifle. "The trees didn't care how hard I worked, whether I stacked wood the right way, or how fast I was," Jurek wrote. "The sky wasn't depending on me to make sure my mom didn't get worse. The ground wasn't testing me."

OTHER SPORTS

A shy and skinny boy, Jurek was diagnosed with high blood pressure when he was twelve. Reluctant to take the medicine he was prescribed because he associated pills with his mother's illness, he learned to control his stress level by doing relaxation exercises. He also began playing basketball in a church league, which he was able to do because the church paid for the uniforms and travel expenses. Yet while Jurek enjoyed being on a team, he found it painful to see his mother, who by then had great difficulty walking, struggle to get from the car to the bleachers to watch him play.

Jurek's father had purchased him a used pair of downhill skis in the wake of his high-blood-pressure diagnosis, sparking an interest in all forms of skiing. During his sophomore year of high school, he joined the school's newly formed cross-country ski team, headed by a Norwegian coach named Glen Sorenson. Jurek discovered that he had an aptitude for the sport and soon became one of the top cross-country skiers in the state. Sorenson insisted that his athletes build up their endurance by running during the off-season, and Jurek excelled at that as well.

After graduating from high school in 1992, Jurek entered the College of St. Scholastica in Duluth. Inspired by one of his mother's caregivers, he studied physical therapy, paying his way by selling NordicTrack exercise machines at a nearby mall. One night toward the end of his first year, Jurek and his father fought after Jurek arrived home later than expected, and Gordon banished his son from the house. Jurek found refuge with friends and periodically snuck home to see his mother and siblings when his father was not there. During his sophomore year of college, he moved into a dorm.

LEARNING TO LOVE TO RUN
While Jurek briefly ran on St. Scholastica's cross-country team, he still thought of running mainly as a way to get in shape for the ski season. This began to change when he started training with fellow runner and skier Dusty Olson, an iconoclastic and free-spirited character whom Jurek had first met in high school. "Dusty would come by and knock on my dorm door, and I'd take a break from *The Brothers Karamazov*, or *War and Peace*, or upper-level physics and anatomy and physiology, and we'd head out. . . . We were running where deer bounded, where coyotes rambled," Jurek wrote. "We ran through calf-deep snow and streams swollen with spring melt so cold that after a while I couldn't feel my feet. Somewhere between my agonized, gasping high school forays . . . and now, running had turned into something other than training. It had turned into a kind of meditation, a place where I could let my mind—usually occupied with school, thoughts of the future, or concerns about my mom—float free."

In 1994 Olson asked Jurek to compete in the Minnesota Voyageur Trail Ultra, a fifty-mile endurance race. To Jurek's great astonishment, he came in second place to Olson's third; while Olson was unquestionably the stronger runner, he had lost a shoe during the final moments of the contest. Jurek realized that his talents for enduring extreme pain and for gaining speed when others were forced to drop out made him a force to be reckoned with. He had, as he has recalled to interviewers, found his calling in life. Early in his running career, Olson became his pacer—in running parlance, the person who helps a racer stay on track by maintaining a specific time per mile.

Jurek again placed second in the Voyageur the following year before finally winning in 1996. He repeated the feat in 1997 and 1998, setting a new course record of six hours and forty-one minutes in the latter instance. Also in 1998, Jurek completed his physical-therapy training and found work in South Dakota, where he ran ten to fifteen miles each weekday and twenty to thirty on the weekends. He occasionally flew out of state to races, racking up victories and setting course records in competitions such as the fifty-mile Zane Grey Highline Trail Endurance Run

and the fifty-kilometer (approximately thirty-one miles) McKenzie River Trail Run.

DOMESTIC VICTORIES
In 1999 Jurek ran in the Western States Endurance Run, better known as the Western States 100, for the first time. "Double the marathon . . . then double it again," Friedman wrote of the infamous race, which starts in Squaw Valley, California, travels through Emigrant Pass and the Granite Chief Wilderness, and ends in the town of Auburn. "Add steep climbs over rocky paths. . . . Turn up the heat, and plunge the course into frigid darkness. . . . Add shrieking headwinds, and dusty canyons and icy rivers and exposed mountain ridges and what you have is the Western States Endurance Run, a 100-miler that has 41,000 feet of ups and downs, and scores of men and women facing not just thirst, and hunger and fatigue and unforgiving terrain, but each other, and more daunting, themselves." Jurek finished in first place, completing the punishing course in seventeen hours and thirty-four minutes.

So focused had he been on winning that Jurek had not considered where he would stay once the race was over. Unable to afford a hotel room, he simply rolled his sleeping bag out near the finish line, a vantage point that allowed him to cheer on the other runners as they approached. This subsequently became his ritual, a practice that has earned him exceeding goodwill from the running community and a reputation as one of the nicest runners in the sport.

Jurek won his second Western States 100 the following year. The repeat victory made him something of a cult figure, as few non-Californians have ever won the iconic race even once. His third consecutive win, in 2001, catapulted him to the status of legend, especially since he ran much of the race with severely torn ligaments. Ultimately Jurek won the Western States an unprecedented seven consecutive times, from 1999 to 2005, setting a course record of fifteen hours and thirty-six minutes in 2004. The record stood until 2010, when Geoff Roes finished in fifteen hours and seven minutes.

In addition to his legendary Western States wins, Jurek has twice triumphed, in 2005 and 2006, at the Badwater Ultramarathon, an event that bills itself as the toughest footrace in the world. His 2005 win set a course record of twenty-four hours and thirty-six minutes, just weeks after he had won the Western States— an unheard-of feat of back-to-back victories. The Badwater route travels 135 miles from the Badwater lake bed in Death Valley to Mount Whitney in the Sierra Nevada, crossing three mountain ranges along the way for a cumulative vertical ascent and descent of 17,400 feet. Describing the 2006 contest, William Booth wrote for the *Washington Post* (27 July 2006), "Leave a credit card on the dashboard of a rental car in Death Valley, and it will melt. A freshly opened can of icy-cold soda turns into a kind of caramelized soup within eleven minutes. . . . When the National Park Service records the official daily maximum temperature, it takes the measurement in the shade. On Monday, it reached 123 degrees Fahrenheit."

INTERNATIONAL ACHIEVEMENTS

Among Jurek's high-profile international race wins have been three consecutive Spartathlon victories, from 2006 to 2008. The 153-mile Spartathlon takes place each year in Greece, and the course traces the route of Pheidippides, an ancient Athenian messenger who, according to legend, was sent to Sparta in 490 BCE to seek help in what would become the Battle of Marathon between the Athenians and the Persians. Jurek was the first North American ever to win the storied race, and his 2008 time of twenty-two hours and twenty minutes made him the second-fastest runner in the race's history; only the Greek runner Yiannis Kouros, who holds the record time of twenty hours and twenty-five minutes, has ever run it faster.

In 2010 Jurek set a new American record of 266.677 kilometers (approximately 165.7 miles) at the International Association of Ultrarunners (IAU) 24-Hour World Championship, where competitors run as far as they can within a twenty-four-hour period. The 2010 race was held in Brive-la-Gaillarde, France. (His record was broken in 2012 by Mike Morton, who ran 277.543 kilometers, or 172.5 miles, in Katowice, Poland.) In April 2014 Jurek and fellow runner Rickey Gates logged a time of twenty-three hours and forty-four minutes on the challenging Bob Graham Round, becoming the first two Americans to complete the race in less than twenty-four hours. The Bob Graham Round is a sixty-six-mile circuit of the forty-two highest summits in England's Lake District; runners who meet the twenty-four-hour cutoff are eligible to become members of the exclusive Bob Graham 24 Hour Club.

DIET

Perhaps no aspect of Jurek's life and training regime has attracted more comment than his strict vegan diet. "It is difficult for some to comprehend how this lifestyle is compatible with training weeks of 140 miles and more, 'easy' runs of forty miles and interval training that includes uphill three-mile repeats, all culminating in races that are often one hundred miles or more, sometimes through deserts or frozen wastelands or up and down mountains," Mark Bittman wrote for the *New York Times* (12 May 2010).

Jurek, raised on a conventional Midwestern diet heavy in meat and potatoes, was first introduced to how delicious and nourishing salads and vegetables could be while at a ski camp as a teenager. Later, under the influence of the woman who became his first wife, Leah Kangas, and a friend and health-food store proprietor known as "Hippie Dan," he began to gradually eliminate all animal products from his diet. He eats whole-grain pancakes or smoothies made of fruit and protein powder for breakfast; for lunch and dinner he has large salads, vegetables, and either beans, tofu, or tempeh. His 2012 book *Eat & Run* contains several of his own recipes.

"The whole issue is . . . getting enough calories," Jurek told Bittman—by his account, some five thousand to eight thousand a day, which he gets from plants and plant-derived foods. "None of this is weird," he explained. "If you go back three hundred or four hundred years, meat was reserved for special occasions, and those people were working hard."

PERSONAL LIFE

Jurek was married to his first wife from 1996 to 2008; he married his second wife, Jenny Uehisa, in 2013. He eventually reconciled with his father. His mother, who entered a nursing home in 1995, died in 2010.

Jurek has said that he cannot envision a time when he stops running altogether. "I want to have a healthy relationship with ultramarathons so I can keep giving back and keep going to events . . . to feel like this is fun too, that I don't need to win," he told Nick Mead for the *Guardian* (22 Oct. 2013). "I want to keep running for the rest of my life."

SUGGESTED READING

Bittman, Mark. "Diet and Exercise to the Extremes." *New York Times.* New York Times, 12 May 2010. Web. 14 Aug. 2014.

Booth, William. "Marathon Melt." *Washington Post.* Washington Post, 27 July 2006. Web. 14 Aug. 2014.

Friedman, Steve. "The King of Pain." *Runner's World.* Rodale, 24 Mar. 2010. Web. 14 Aug. 2014.

Jurek, Scott, and Steve Friedman. *Eat & Run: My Unlikely Journey to Ultramarathon Greatness.* New York: Houghton, 2012. Print.

Mead, Nick. "Scott Jurek: 'There Are So Many Great Races, Which Do You Make Your Last?'" *Guardian.* Guardian News and Media, 22 Oct. 2013. Web. 14 Aug. 2014.

Palmer, Lisa. "What Are Extreme Runners Thinking?" *Slate.* Slate Group, 28 May 2013. Web. 14 Aug. 2014.

—*Mari Rich*

Michael Kahn

Born: December 8, 1935
Occupation: Film editor

Though he may not be a household name, Michael Kahn is one of the most storied and acclaimed editors in the history of film. With eight nods from the Academy of Motion Picture Arts and Sciences, Kahn has received more Oscar nominations than any editor in history, and is tied for the most Oscar wins for film editing, with three. All but one of those nominations, and all three of his wins—for *Raiders of the Lost Ark* (1981), *Schindler's List* (1993), and *Saving Private Ryan* (1998)—were for his work on films directed by Steven Spielberg, the legendary Hollywood filmmaker with whom he has had a historic partnership for nearly four decades. Kahn began his editing career in television working on the military sitcom *Hogan's Heroes* (1965–71), before graduating to feature films in the early 1970s. His partnership with Spielberg began when the director hired him to assemble his third theatrical feature, the sci-fi masterpiece *Close Encounters of the Third Kind* (1977). Since then, Kahn has edited nearly every one of Spielberg's films, and their partnership has evolved into one of the most successful director-editor teams in the industry. In addition to the aforementioned films, their collaborations include *Empire of the Sun* (1987), *Jurassic Park* (1993), *A.I. Artificial Intelligence* (2001), *Catch Me If You Can* (2002), *Munich* (2005), *The Adventures of Tintin* (2011), *Lincoln* (2012), and the three Indiana Jones sequels.

Kahn, who has occasionally worked for other directors, was well known for being one of the last prominent editors to cut films on an old-fashioned Moviola machine. He and Spielberg used the machine exclusively on all of their collaborations until 2011, when the two switched to digital editing technology for the director's first 3-D animated feature, *The Adventures of Tintin*. Known for his intuitive style and strong sense of rhythm and pacing, Kahn explained to Michael Kunkes for *Editors Guild Magazine* (Jan.–Feb. 2006), "An editor is only as good as his contributions to the film. All editors bring ideas and a spirit of collaboration; what is important is how they present those ideas. An editor has to be more than just a visual typist."

EARLY LIFE AND EDUCATION

Michael Kahn was born on December 8, 1935, in the New York City borough of Brooklyn. He has a brother and a sister. Despite growing up with no intentions of working in the entertainment industry, let alone becoming a professional film editor, Kahn has said that he developed an affinity for movies at an early age. His favorite weekend pastime as a teenager was

The Washington Post/Getty Images

going to double features. "I'd see anything that was playing," he recalled to Peter Tonguette for *Cinema Editor* magazine (Mar. 2011), the official periodical of the American Cinema Editors (ACE), an honorary society to which Khan holds membership.

Kahn attended Abraham Lincoln High School, located in the Coney Island section of Brooklyn. During his high school years, he was involved in the Boy Scouts of America, eventually rising to the top rank of Eagle Scout. Kahn would later follow the Scouts' motto Be Prepared when embarking on his career as a film and television editor. Still, upon graduating from Abraham Lincoln High in the early 1950s, he was, admittedly, directionless and unsure about his future.

BREAKING INTO THE INDUSTRY

After high school Kahn started working as a messenger boy for the New York advertising agency Foote, Cone & Belding. He then landed a job in the television department of the Milton H. Biow Company, another New York advertising agency that produced commercials in California for iconic brands such as Pepsi-Cola and Philip Morris. Despite being nothing more than a "flunky" there, as he told Tonguette, Kahn was taken under the wing of his boss and eventually leaped at an opportunity to move out to California with him. It was while working on commercials in California that Kahn met Dann Cahn, the editorial supervisor for Desilu—a production company formed by Desi Arnaz and Lucille Ball, stars of the landmark television sitcom *I Love Lucy* (1951–57). Cahn hired him as an executive assistant in Desilu's editorial office, and soon afterward, helped him get into the editors union.

Upon joining the union, Kahn became an assistant to Desilu editor John Woodcock, with whom he worked on his first television series, *The Adventures of Jim Bowie*, which aired on ABC from 1956 to 1958. He subsequently worked as an apprentice on other Desilu-produced television shows, assisting editors such as Harry Harris and Bud Molin. Kahn graduated from assistant editor to editor in 1965, when his friend, Jerry London, offered him a job as his assistant on *Hogan's Heroes*, a World War II comedy series produced by Bing Crosby Productions. He assisted London on six episodes before being promoted to the series' regular editor when London became a director for the show. Kahn edited 130 episodes of the series over the next six years, during which he worked with an eclectic mix of directors. He explained to Michael Kunkes that "television was really where you learned how to cut. . . . I learned that once you have control of the film and feel confident enough, you can do anything you want to do."

MOVE TO FEATURE FILMS

Kahn's work on *Hogan's Heroes* brought him to the attention of the venerable, Oscar-winning actor George C. Scott. An unabashed fan of the show, Scott recruited Kahn to serve as editor of his theatrical directorial debut, *Rage* (1972), about a Wyoming sheep rancher whose peaceful existence turns upside down after he loses his livestock and his son to a military-related poison gas leak. By then, Kahn had already edited an independent film, *The Activist* (1969), and assisted in the editing of another feature, the cult western drama *A Man Called Horse* (1970), starring Richard Harris. *Rage* marked his first solo effort as an editor on a studio release.

Kahn next edited a series of blaxploitation films, in addition to several other low-budget pictures, before collaborating with Scott again on the adventure film *The Savage Is Loose* (1974). "It wouldn't matter what film it was," he recalled to Peter Tonguette. "Whatever came up, I did it." Kahn, meanwhile, continued to edit for television, serving as editor of the 1976 ABC movie *Eleanor and Franklin*, based on Joseph P. Lash's Pulitzer Prize–winning book of the same name about Franklin and Eleanor Roosevelt. His work on the film earned him both Primetime Emmy and ACE Eddie awards.

The year 1976 also saw Kahn edit the sequel to *A Man Called Horse*, *The Return of a Man Called Horse*, which was directed by Irvin Kershner and photographed by Owen Roizman. Impressed by Kahn's work on the film, both Kershner and Roizman recommended him to their close friend Steven Spielberg, who was then looking for an editor to work on *Close Encounters of the Third Kind*, a science-fiction film that would serve as his follow-up to *Jaws* (1975), the blockbuster thriller that instantly propelled him into the pantheon of Hollywood directors. During a brief interview for the job, Kahn was asked by Spielberg if he was a good editor, to which he replied by saying that he had no idea, but that all those with whom he had previously worked kept on asking him back. "The next thing I knew I was hired," he told Kunkes.

CLOSE ENCOUNTERS AND PARTNERSHIP WITH SPIELBERG

Close Encounters of the Third Kind tells the story of a disparate group of people whose lives become forever altered after chance encounters with unidentified flying objects. The film includes a breathtaking, thirty-minute finale, which depicts a surreal back-and-forth exchange between the humans and the alien mothership through an iconic five-note musical motif. To assemble the final sequence, Kahn and Spielberg had to go through thousands of feet of film. "Everything I did in television prepared me to work with a guy like Steven," Kahn explained to Trevor Hogg for *Post* magazine (1 Feb. 2011). "He moves quickly but . . . shoots a lot of coverage" and "gives us an endless amount of options."

Critics hailed *Close Encounters*, which opened in November 1977, as a groundbreaking technical achievement. In a representative review for the *Washington Post* (14 Dec. 1977), Gary Arnold called the film "a uniquely transporting filmgoing spectacle" and lauded Kahn and Spielberg's "bustling, incisive editing rhythms." Kahn earned his first Academy Award nomination, as well as the first of six British Academy of Film and Television Arts (BAFTA) Award nominations, for his work on the film, which grossed more than $300 million worldwide.

During the filming of *Close Encounters*, Kahn and Spielberg started an efficient routine that they would continue to follow on subsequent collaborations. "I run dailies with him on a KEM [flatbed editing machine]; he selects the performances he likes and gives me his ideas about how a scene should go," Kahn related to Michael Kunkes. "Then I'll put it together [on a Moviola] and show it to him . . . and any adjustments are made." Because Kahn edits Spielberg's films as they are shooting, he is normally able to assemble a rough cut of a film, which typically takes up to three months to complete, within a week after production has wrapped.

FIRST OSCAR WIN AND EXPLORING DIFFERENT GENRES

After *Close Encounters*, Kahn edited Spielberg's World War II comedy *1941* (1979), and then worked on the director's action-adventure epic

Raiders of the Lost Ark (1981), the first installment of the Indiana Jones franchise. While the
former film received a mixed critical response
and enjoyed only mild commercial success,
the latter became a cultural phenomenon and
was credited with redefining the action genre.
Highlighted by a twenty-minute-long, bravura
opening sequence, the film follows the fictional
globe-trotting archaeologist Indiana Jones—
famously portrayed by Harrison Ford—as he
races against Nazis to recover the hallowed Ark
of the Covenant. In a review for *Variety* (5 June
1981), Stephen Klain remarked that Kahn's
"crisp editing keeps the pace and energy unflag-
ging" throughout the duration of the film. Kahn
earned his first Academy Award for the editing.

Instead of working on Spielberg's next film,
the heartfelt sci-fi family drama *E.T.* (1982),
Kahn was commissioned by the director to work
on another project he was producing, the supernatural horror film *Poltergeist* (1982), which he
felt was the more difficult film to edit. Directed
by Tobe Hooper, the film was both a critical and
commercial success, but it was largely overshadowed by *E.T.*, which upon its release, became
the highest-grossing film of all time. *E.T.*, nonetheless, ended up being the last feature film of
Spielberg's to be edited by someone other than
Kahn.

Spielberg's willingness to explore new terrain
gave Kahn the opportunity to work consistently
in different genres. In addition to revisiting the
action genre for the sequels *Indiana Jones and
the Temple of Doom* (1984) and *Indiana Jones
and the Last Crusade* (1989), the two forayed
into period drama (*The Color Purple*, 1985), war
(*Empire of the Sun*, 1987), romance (*Always*,
1989), and fantasy (*Hook*, 1991). Kahn received
another Oscar nomination for his work on *Empire of the Sun*, which was based on J. G. Bal-
lard's same-titled, coming-of-age book about his
experiences as a prisoner of war in a Japanese
internment camp during World War II.

Concurrent with his Spielberg projects,
Kahn assembled films for other directors, most
notably Adrian Lyne on his psychological thriller
Fatal Attraction (1987), starring Michael Douglas as a married man who becomes involved in
an affair that goes horribly wrong. Kahn was
nominated for his work on that film (with coeditor Peter E. Berger) alongside *Empire of the Sun*
at the 1988 Academy Awards, but failed to take
home a golden statuette for either film. *Fatal Attraction*, however, earned him his first BAFTA
Award for film editing.

SCHINDLER'S LIST

Kahn and Spielberg were most lauded for their
work on two films released in the 1990s, both
of which centered on major historical events
from World War II. The first, *Schindler's List*
(1993), was based on the life of Oskar Schindler,
a German businessman who used his influence
and wealth to save nearly 1,200 Jews during the
Holocaust. For the 195-minute film—which was
shot in black and white to establish a feeling of
documentary authenticity—Kahn and Spielberg
used intercutting to heighten the dramatic impact, often alternating between scenes related
to Schindler's story and those related to Amon
Goeth, the brutal and sadistic German Nazi SS
officer who served as commandant of a forced
labor camp outside Kraków, Poland. "How you
intercut is so important because there's rhythm,
there's pace, there's emotional drama taking
place," Kahn explained to Bernard Weinraub for
the *New York Times* (20 Aug. 1998). "If you're on
something too long, then you lose power in the
next scene."

Despite its horrific subject matter, *Schindler's
List* was a box office success, and received almost unanimous praise from critics. The film
yielded Kahn his second Oscar for best editing
(as well as a second BAFTA) and Spielberg his
first Oscar for directing, and took home seven
awards in total, including best picture. "Michael
Kahn has edited with intensity and line, never
breathless, always fast," Stanley Kauffmann
wrote in a review for the *New Republic* (10 Dec.
1993), adding, "Spielberg has not used one trite
shot, one cheap tear-jerking assemblage." Kahn,
who, as *Schindler's List* was filming, simultaneously edited Spielberg's equally groundbreaking, box-office smash hit *Jurassic Park* (1993),
which preceded the Holocaust film's release by
six months, later called *Schindler's List* the most
difficult film he has ever worked on.

SAVING PRIVATE RYAN AND OTHER FILMS

Kahn and Spielberg landed their third and second Oscars, for editing and directing, respectively, for their efforts on *Saving Private Ryan*
(1998), a World War II film about a squad of soldiers charged with finding a paratrooper whose
three brothers have been killed in combat. The
film, which also took home three other Oscars
(five total), is particularly noted for its powerful and relentless, nearly thirty-minute opening
battle sequence, which depicts, in harrowingly
graphic fashion, the Allied D-Day invasion of
Normandy, France, on June 6, 1944. With his
third Oscar win, Kahn tied Daniel Mandell and
Ralph Dawson for the most wins for film editing.
(Thelma Schoonmaker matched them with her
third win for *The Departed* in 2006.)

In between *Schindler's List* and *Saving
Private Ryan*, Kahn edited two other films
for Spielberg—the historical drama *Amistad*
(1997), and the Jurassic Park sequel *The Lost
World* (1997), as well as Brad Silberling's family comedy *Casper* (1995), and Jan de Bont's
disaster drama *Twister* (1996). The latter film
marked Kahn's first experience using digital editing technology—in this case, an Avid digital

non-linear editing system—to cut a film. He later used an Avid system to cut Silberling's fantasy film *Lemony Snicket's A Series of Unfortunate Events* (2004).

SWITCH TO DIGITAL TECHNOLOGY

Despite the time-saving benefits of editing digitally, Kahn continued to cut Spielberg's films, at the director's insistence, on a Moviola well into the new millennium. In his interview with Michael Kunkes, Kahn described Spielberg as a "traditionalist" and said that he "likes to feel the film, see the film, touch the film." He added that he himself likes film "because, as an editor, you are forced to have a point of view and to make decisions that can only go one way at a time."

Consequently, Kahn used a Moviola to cut Spielberg's next seven films. They included the science-fiction thrillers *A.I. Artificial Intelligence* (2001), *Minority Report* (2002), and *War of the Worlds* (2005), the biographical crime drama *Catch Me If You Can* (2002), the hostage drama *Munich* (2005), and the hotly anticipated sequel *Indiana Jones and the Kingdom of the Crystal Skull* (2008). Kahn received his seventh Oscar nomination for *Munich*, which was based on the Israeli government's vengeful response to the massacre of Israeli athletes by Palestinian terrorists at the 1972 Olympic Games in Munich, West Germany.

Kahn and Spielberg collaborated on two films released in 2011: *The Adventures of Tintin*, a 3-D motion capture animated feature based on the comic series by Belgian cartoonist Hergé (Georges Remi), and *War Horse*, a World War I family drama adapted from British author Michael Morpurgo's 1982 children's novel of the same name. Both films marked the duo's first experiences working on an Avid together.

Kahn and Spielberg stuck with Avid for their next project, *Lincoln*, which was released in 2012. For his work on the film, Kahn received his eighth Academy Award nomination, thus making him the most-nominated editor in history.

Kahn, who has also earned ten ACE Eddie Award nominations for film editing and four awards, was the recipient of the ACE Career Achievement Award in 2011. He was further commended in 2013, when Spielberg honored their longtime partnership by establishing the Michael Kahn Endowed Chair in Editing at the USC School of Cinematic Arts.

Kahn, who is married with grown children, has been said to keep a humble attitude towards his many cinematic achievements. He is, however, intensely passionate about his craft. "When I was coming up as an editor," he told Peter Tonguette, "editing was a transitory stage. [Editors] wanted to be directors. I was one of the few who was happy as an editor. I just wanted to be the best that I could be at it."

SUGGESTED READING

Hogg, Trevor. "Editor Michael Kahn Reflects On His Work with Spielberg." *Post*. Post Magazine, 1 Feb. 2011. Web. 13 Feb. 2014.

Kunkes, Michael. "Munich, Mentoring & Moviolas: The Michael Kahn Interview." *Editors Guild Magazine*. Motion Pictures Editors Guild, IATSE Local 700, Jan.–Feb. 2006. Web. 13 Feb. 2014.

Tonguette, Peter. "A Beginner's Mind, A Professional's Craft." *CinemaEditor* Mar. 2011: 46. Print.

Weinraub, Bernard. "Hollywood's Kindest Cuts." *New York Times*. New York Times, 20 Aug. 1998. Web. 13 Mar. 2014.

SELECTED WORKS

Rage, 1972; *Close Encounters of the Third Kind*, 1977; *Raiders of the Lost Ark*, 1981; *Empire of the Sun*, 1987; *Fatal Attraction* (with Peter E. Berger), 1987; *Schindler's List*, 1993; *Saving Private Ryan*, 1998; *Munich*, 2005; *The Adventures of Tintin*, 2011; *Lincoln*, 2012

—*Chris Cullen*

Zoë Keating

Born: February 2, 1972
Occupation: Avant-garde cellist

Zoë Keating has been called a one-woman orchestra for her richly layered cello music, which she composes in an improvisational style by recording and looping samples of her riffs to create haunting works that have generated widespread crossover appeal. However, unlike recording artists who have signed to major labels and have the full promotional force of those labels behind them, Keating has taken a do-it-yourself (DIY) approach to her music, through which she has sold some sixty thousand copies of her self-recorded and self-released albums and garnered more than one million followers on Twitter. Although she knows it is not easy for an independent musician to find widespread critical and commercial success, she believes she would continue to make her music even without the success she has enjoyed. "I'm compelled to do what I do. I think that's true for a lot of artists. There are things we have to express. Creating cello music is the thing I'm driven to do. It makes me very satisfied," she remarked in a 2010 interview with Anil Prasad for the online magazine *Innerviews*. "It's like therapy. It helps me be okay with the world. The world is very imperfect and messy. I feel like my studio process of shaping and sculpting is adding to the order of the universe.

It's very mathematical, orderly, and controlled. It's my way of coping."

EARLY LIFE

Zoë Keating was born on February 2, 1972, and grew up in Guelph, Ontario. She began studying the cello at the age of eight and performed in classical concerts until she began to experience serious stage fright as a teenager. She told National Public Radio (NPR) correspondent Martina Castro (6 Sept. 2011), "Suddenly I'm like, 'How am I doing this? This seems really difficult. How am I doing it?' And then, soon enough, you wouldn't be able to play the cello and I would, like, falter. . . . Like, your brain works against you." Because the stage fright proved so severe—once she even dropped her bow during a performance—Keating gave up on her dreams of becoming a classical musician and performing with an orchestra. At Sarah Lawrence College in Yonkers, New York, where she earned her liberal arts degree with a concentration in music in 1993, she continued to play the cello in an improvisational way. She discovered that somehow the act of improvisation helped to eliminate her anxieties.

Keating's interest in experimenting with her instrument only grew after she moved to San Francisco, California, where she was exposed to a wide range of electronic music. As she explained to Castro, "I thought, wouldn't it be neat to make music that has that same production quality, but entirely acoustic?" After listening to what so many of the local deejays were doing by sampling bits of music, she decided to try

something similar by recording her cello on her computer and layering each beat and rhythm she liked with subsequent improvisations. Because she did not have anyone to record her playing, Keating recorded the parts she wanted to using foot pedals; her pedal taps would tell her computer to save particular recordings and to loop back what she had just played. The result was the early development of what would become her signature style of live-layered improvisational music. She continues to employ this recording technique—both live in concert and in her home studio—to this day.

INFORMATION ARCHITECT

During her twenties, Keating worked at a software company as an information architect. "I had never turned on a computer before I came to San Francisco," Keating remarked to Rory Williams for *Strings* magazine (July 2010). "It was an industry that allowed liberal arts majors to have a job. I fit in along with everyone else—it was like a second education." As she entered her thirties, however, she grew ever more dissatisfied with the idea of spending the rest of her working life sitting in front of a computer, even though, as she has noted in interviews, she did enjoy her work. She came to the conclusion that despite her fears of performing live, she would regret not having tried to make a living as a cellist. So in 2003, at the age of thirty-one, she quit her tech job to begin the next phase of her life as a musician. Her highest-profile success in those early days was with the rock band Rasputina, with which she recorded two albums, *Frustration Plantation* (2004) and *A Radical Recital* (2005).

SUCCESS AS A SOLO ARTIST

At the same time, Keating was hard at work developing a career as a solo artist. While not recording or performing with Rasputina, she was giving free concerts featuring her own compositions, which she recorded as an extended play (EP) record titled *One Cello x 16* (2004) and sold on her official website and at shows. As it became clear to her that a record label would not sign her because her music did not fit into any standard music industry category, Keating decided on a DIY approach in which she would record, market, and distribute her own albums.

At one time, going it alone without a major label's backing was a risky endeavor for a musician: a budding artist could spend a small fortune pressing a record to see it never sell enough to earn the investment back. Keating, however, was fortunate to embark on her solo career at the right time. "By the time I came along, the Internet was already changing the power dynamics of the music industry, but the most fundamental shift for me came in 2003, when iTunes opened its doors to unsigned artists," she recalled in an op-ed piece she wrote for the *Los Angeles Times*

(1 Sept. 2013). "Any artist could sell music and get the same percentage deal from Apple as the record labels. CD distribution was still difficult and the old problem of how to get anyone to pay attention wasn't solved, but an unsigned artist could now sell music alongside bestselling artists in the largest digital music store in the world."

FULL-LENGTH ALBUMS

By the time her first full-length album, *One Cello x 16: Natoma*, debuted in 2005, Keating had gotten some national media attention through NPR and other media sources. The album sold well and soon topped the classical charts on iTunes. It remained at the top of the iTunes classical and electronica charts for so long that the monthly payments from iTunes enabled Keating to purchase her car, her house, and health insurance, as well as enabling her to stop working for a time after her son was born in 2010. She also credits Twitter with helping to grow her fan base, particularly after Twitter's staff placed her on the site's "Suggested Users" list, which Twitter compiles to help its members discover interesting people to follow. "Around the time that I went on the Suggested User list, my CD went to number one on the iTunes classical chart, and it's stayed in the top twenty ever since," she told Evie Nagy for *Billboard* (30 May 2009). "I've also gotten a lot more sales from my website, and I get lots of fan mail that says, 'I found out about you from Twitter.'" As of November 2013, she has more than 1.2 million followers on Twitter.

Keating released a second full-length album, titled *Into the Trees*, in 2010. Like its predecessors, it has garnered considerable praise from music fans, who, for the most part, have discovered it thanks to the cellist's active online presence on Twitter and Facebook as well as her personal website. The album is a reflection of her transition from city life in San Francisco to her current home in a redwood forest. "Once I left my urban life in San Francisco and started making new music out here in the woods, I noticed certain themes were developing and I went with them," she remarked in her interview with Prasad. "I don't know if something creatively new was emerging or if it was about me getting in touch with my new environment. What I do know is I was trying to capture a feeling of motion, about moving towards or away from something, and that this thing is unknown. I think of this album as moving into an unknown world. Having been an urbanite for so long, the forest sort of represents that."

THE ECONOMICS OF MUSIC

In the years that Keating has earned a living as a professional musician, the music industry—and the model for making money from recorded music—has continued to evolve. Since the start of the twenty-first century, both record labels and unsigned independent artists such as Keating have seen ever-larger shares of their revenue streams come from digital downloads via iTunes and other websites rather than though the sale of CDs. Today, however, the digital download model looks to be giving way to another online format: streaming services, such as Spotify, Pandora, Songza, and YouTube, that pay recording artists a fee per play on the service. The difference between the payment for a streaming service and a digital download, however, is striking: a performer may receive anywhere from seven to ten cents on a ninety-nine-cent download, while the same artist might receive only a fraction of a cent per stream. (Spotify, for example, pays 0.4 cents per stream.)

Although she praises streaming services for the benefits they give listeners, Keating has been publicly critical of what these services pay artists, particularly as the royalty fees seem to favor very popular artists who are signed to record labels and can therefore generate massive amounts of streaming on those sites. She has made a decent living from sales of her CDs and digital downloads, with a significant portion of her sales coming from iTunes. But what she fears is that she and other artists like her will be unable to support themselves under the current streaming payment model. "In certain types of music, like classical or jazz, we are condemning them to poverty if this is going to be the only way people consume music," Keating told Ben Sisario for the *New York Times* (28 Jan. 2013).

In order to make people better understand the economics of being an independent musician in the digital age, Keating released records of some of her earnings as Google Doc spreadsheets on her Tumblr blog. Some of the spreadsheets cover the first six months of 2013 and detail how much tracks from her two earliest albums made on two streaming services during that period. As Keating described in her *Los Angeles Times* op-ed, it was not very much: "It would be unwise for an individual niche artist to count on streaming revenue to pay the bills. In the last six months, I've netted $808.01 from 201,412 streams on Spotify and $1,610 from 1,242,030 spins on Pandora. Because I own the copyrights of both my songs and my recordings, these amounts are almost double what an artist on a record label would receive for the same amount of streaming."

THE FUTURE OF STREAMING

Alone, Spotify, which launched in 2008, already has roughly twenty-four million users worldwide. Although listeners can listen to music on the site for free in exchange for viewing advertisements, nearly one-quarter of the site's users pay a membership fee of five to ten dollars a month to get their music without ads. To Keating, it seems unlikely that streaming services will fade from view anytime soon, which means she will have to find a way to make streaming a part of her revenue stream, despite its drawbacks. (One of her documents revealed that 97 percent of her income has come from selling, not streaming, her music.) As quoted by Stuart Dredge for the *Guardian* (19 Aug. 2013), she wrote, "Streaming is not yet a replacement for digital sales, and to conflate the two is a mistake. I do not see streaming as a threat to my income, just like I've never regarded file-sharing as a threat but as a convenient way to hear music. If people really like my music, I still believe they'll support it somewhere, somehow. Casual listeners won't, but they never did anyway." In February 2014 Keating published her 2013 recorded music earnings on Google Drive. According to her records, she earned just 8 percent, or $6,380, of her income from streaming services last year.

OTHER WORK AND AWARDS

In addition to her solo albums, Keating has contributed to a number of soundtracks to feature films and television series, including *I Am a Sex Addict* (2005), *Frozen Angels* (2005), *The Devil's Chair* (2007), *Ghost Bird* (2008), *The Secret Life of Bees* (2008), *Breaking Bad* (2010), *Desert Son* (2010), *Warrior* (2011), and *Elementary* (2012). She has also collaborated with numerous artists, including Imogen Heap, Amanda Palmer, Tears for Fears, DJ Shadow, Dan Hicks, Thomas Dolby, John Vanderslice, and Paolo Nutini, among others.

She was the recipient of an artistic development grant from the Belle Foundation in 2005 and a performing arts grant from Creative Capital Foundation in 2009. In 2005 she received an emerging artist award from the San Francisco Artsfest. Keating was named a young global leader at the World Economic Forum in 2011. She is a board member of the San Francisco chapter of the Recording Academy, the Magik Magik Orchestra, and CASH Music, a nonprofit that develops open-source digital tools for musicians and record labels. She and her husband, Jeff Rusch, live in the middle of a redwood forest about an hour and a half north of San Francisco with their son, Alex, who was born in May 2010. Keating is at work on a new album.

SUGGESTED READING

Dredge, Stuart. "Streaming Music Payments: How Much Do Artists Really Receive?" *Guardian.* Guardian News and Media, 19 Aug. 2013. Web. 11 Dec. 2013.

Keating, Zoë. "The Sharps and Flats of the Music Business." *Los Angeles Times.* Los Angeles Times, 1 Sept. 2013. Web. 11 Dec. 2013.

Keating, Zoë. "Zoë Keating's Radical Cello." Interview by Alex Chadwick. *My Fellow Americans.* NPR, 9 Dec. 2005. Web. 11 Dec. 2013.

Keating, Zoë. "Zoë Keating: A Symphony Unto Herself." Interview by Martina Castro. *NPR Music.* NPR, 6 Sept. 2011. Web. 11 Dec. 2013.

Sisario, Ben. "As Music Streaming Grows, Royalties Slow to a Trickle." *New York Times.* New York Times, 28 Jan. 2013. Web. 11 Dec. 2013.

SELECTED WORKS

One Cello x 16, 2004; *One Cello x 16: Natoma*, 2005; *Into the Trees*, 2010

—*Christopher Mari*

Clayton Kershaw

Born: March 19, 1988
Occupation: Baseball player

Los Angeles Dodgers pitcher Clayton Kershaw has frequently been compared to another Dodger legend, Hall of Fame pitcher Sandy Koufax. Like Koufax, Kershaw utilizes a silky-smooth left-handed delivery and is an unflappable competitor on the mound. Armed with a Koufax-like mid-nineties four-seam fastball and 12-to-6 curveball, as well as a slider and changeup, Kershaw has not only given credibility to such comparisons, but has also emerged in a class all his own since making his major league debut with the Dodgers in May 2008 at the age of twenty. In his first six seasons in the majors, Kershaw established himself as arguably the best pitcher in baseball. After compiling a 26–23 record and 3.32 earned-run average (ERA) in his first three seasons, Kershaw enjoyed a breakout year in 2011, winning the so-called "triple crown" of pitching by leading the National League (NL) in wins (21), ERA (2.28), and strikeouts (248). For his performance that season, he was awarded the NL Cy Young Award, given annually to the league's best pitcher.

USA Today Sports/Reuters/Landov

After finishing second in the NL Cy Young voting in 2012, Kershaw won his second career Cy Young in 2013, joining Koufax as the only Dodgers to win the award multiple times. That year, he led the NL in ERA for the third consecutive season and surpassed 200 innings and 200 strikeouts for the fourth straight year. Dismissing comparisons between himself, Koufax, and other Dodger pitching greats, Kershaw—who earned three consecutive All-Star selections from 2011 to 2013—explained to Dylan Hernandez for the *Los Angeles Times* (19 Sept. 2011), "I'm not trying to be anybody else. I've got expectations for myself that surpass anybody else's." Dodgers pitching coach Rick Honeycutt told Tim Kurkjian for *ESPN The Magazine* (9 June 2011), "He's a rare breed. He doesn't want to be good. He wants to be the best."

EARLY LIFE

Clayton Edward Kershaw was born on March 19, 1988, in Dallas, Texas, the only child of Marianne (Tombaugh) Kershaw, a graphic designer, and Christopher Kershaw, a musician. He grew up in the Dallas suburb of Highland Park, an affluent town often referred to as the "Beverly Hills of Texas" for its stately mansions and beautiful tree-lined streets. Kershaw's parents divorced when he was ten years old, after which he was raised by his mother, who is the niece of the late astronomer Clyde Tombaugh, best known for discovering the dwarf planet Pluto in 1930. Kershaw has seldom spoken about his father, who died of unknown causes at the age of sixty-three on April 28, 2013.

From an early age, Kershaw fostered dreams of becoming a professional baseball player. He grew up playing baseball year-round in Highland Park, largely because his mother chose to remain in the area after divorcing his father. This ensured that Kershaw remained in a school district with some of the best athletic programs in the country. "We didn't have a lot of money," he recalled to Ken Gurnick for MLB.com (2 Oct. 2013). "I don't know how she did it, but keeping me in that school district, that was huge."

Throughout his youth, Kershaw played baseball, soccer, football, and basketball. One of his closest childhood friends was quarterback Matthew Stafford, the top overall pick in the 2009 National Football League Draft. The two were frequent teammates on youth-level sports teams, playing together on a soccer team called the Blue Bombers, as well as on the same Little League baseball team.

HIGH SCHOOL CAREER

Kershaw attended Highland Park High School, a public school in nearby University Park known for its nationally renowned sports programs. Kershaw made Highland Park's varsity baseball team as a freshman. He also played on the school's junior-varsity football team. At that time Kershaw was overweight, not exceptionally tall, and his athletic abilities paled in comparison to those of Stafford, who would go on to be the most sought-after high school quarterback in the country. Kershaw stopped playing football after his freshman year to focus on baseball, while Stafford quit baseball after his sophomore year to focus on football.

Kershaw began to fill out physically after his freshman year. He started weight training and eventually underwent a growth spurt that left him six feet three inches tall. Kershaw first drew interest from major-league scouts during the summer after his sophomore season, thanks to his playing on a summer travel team, the Dallas Bats, which featured the future MLB pitchers Jordan Walden and Shawn Tolleson, both of whom were more highly regarded than Kershaw at the time. His coach, Ken Guthrie, said to Alan Matthews for *Baseball America* (24 May 2006), "If you wanted to put a number on them, you probably could say he was the No. 3 starter. But I always thought that he would go the furthest and be the closest to big league ready, just for his body type and frame."

Kershaw's stock rose the following summer when he was selected for the US junior national team. During the winter of 2005–6, Kershaw took a series of pitching lessons with Skip Johnson, then the head baseball coach at Navarro Junior College, to further improve and maximize his overall pitching potential. Under Johnson, he changed his delivery from a low three-quarters position to a standard over-the-top motion, which helped add more velocity to his fastball and improve the control of his breaking ball, which up until that point had been a mostly inconsistent pitch. Johnson explained to Gurnick that Kershaw's "aptitude and athleticism make him what he is. He has the ability to repeat his delivery, and he makes adjustments fast."

LOS ANGELES DODGER

When Kershaw entered his senior year, the one goal he hoped to achieve was "to get college paid for," as he told Hernandez in another article for the *Los Angeles Times* (2 May 2009). With that goal in mind, he went on to establish himself as the top high school pitching prospect in the country. That season Kershaw posted a perfect 13–0 record and an extraordinary 0.77 ERA, with 139 strikeouts in sixty-four innings. His performance helped Highland Park achieve a 31–7 overall record and an appearance in the Texas Class 4A Region II finals. At the end of the season, Kershaw was named Gatorade National Player of the Year and *USA Today*'s High School Baseball Player of the Year.

By the time Kershaw graduated, he was on the radar of several major-league teams, not only because of his physical ability but also because of his competitive character. He signed a letter of intent to attend Texas A&M University, but he ultimately turned down a scholarship to that school to enter the 2006 MLB Draft. The Dodgers selected Kershaw with the seventh overall pick in the draft and awarded him a contract that included a then franchise record $2.3 million signing bonus. Upon drafting him, Logan White, then the Dodgers scouting director and now the team's vice president of scouting, recalled to Jeff Passan for Yahoo! Sports (14 May 2008), "We hoped we got Sandy Koufax, because when you're out there drafting, you're praying."

THE NEXT KOUFAX

Kershaw quickly answered the Dodgers' prayers. He rose through the team's farm system in less than two years. In the summer of 2006, Kershaw pitched ten games for the Dodgers' now defunct Gulf Coast League team in Vero Beach, Florida, before moving up to the organization's single-A affiliate, the Great Lakes Loons of the Midwest League. Kershaw played with the Loons for most of the 2007 season, going 7–5 with a 2.77 ERA in twenty starts. He finished that season with the double-A Jacksonville Suns of the Southern League, for whom he made five starts. In his twenty-five combined starts with the Loons and Suns, he limited opposing batters to a .201 batting average.

Kershaw entered the 2008 season ranked by *Baseball America* as the Dodgers' best prospect. He lived up to that lofty ranking when he was invited to the Dodgers' annual spring training camp. In his second spring training appearance, on March 9, 2008, against the then reigning World Series champion Boston Red Sox, Kershaw earned widespread attention around the league for a curveball he threw to strike out the Red Sox first baseman Sean Casey. The devastating nature of the pitch, which "moved like a magic bullet," Passan noted, prompted the legendary Dodgers broadcaster Vin Scully to declare it "Public Enemy No. 1." Around this time, many people in the Dodger organization began comparing Kershaw to Sandy Koufax for his deadly fastball-curveball combination.

RISE TO THE ELITE

Koufax comparisons notwithstanding, the Dodgers—opting not to rush his development—assigned Kershaw back to the Jacksonville Suns to open the 2008 season. His stay in Jacksonville, however, was brief. Kershaw made just ten appearances for the club before earning his first call-up to the majors on May 25, 2008, in a game against the St. Louis Cardinals. At twenty years and two months, he became the youngest player in the majors and the fourth-youngest starting pitcher in Dodger history. He pitched six innings, allowing two runs on five hits, and earned a no-decision in a 4–3 extra-inning win for Los Angeles.

Following his debut, Kershaw appeared in seven more games for the Dodgers before being optioned back to Jacksonville. His return to Jacksonville lasted just three weeks, and on July 22, he was recalled by the Dodgers, with whom he remained through the end of the season. He finished his rookie year with a 5–5 record and 4.26 ERA in twenty-two games. Under first-year manager Joe Torre, the Dodgers finished first in the NL West Division with an 84–78 regular season record and advanced to the NL Championship Series (NLCS). In the series, the Dodgers lost to the Philadelphia Phillies in five games. Kershaw said to Kurkjian in the *ESPN The Magazine* article, "The Dodgers did me a huge favor calling me up as early as they did. I took my lumps [as a rookie], but I'm better off for it."

In 2009, his first full season in the majors, Kershaw became a permanent fixture in the Dodgers' rotation. Despite finishing that season with an 8–8 record, which was mostly attributed to poor run support, he held opponents to league lows in batting average (.200), slugging percentage (.282), and hits per nine innings (6.3), and posted an impressive 2.79 ERA with 185 strikeouts. Kershaw's strong pitching played a large role in the Dodgers successfully defending their NL West title. The team finished with a NL–best 95–67 record and advanced to the NLCS for the second straight year. However, the team was defeated once again by the Phillies. Kershaw made his first two career postseason starts for the Dodgers, including Game 1 of the NLCS.

Kershaw continued to build on his success in 2010. Though the Dodgers failed to return to the postseason, he compiled a 13–10 record with a 2.91 ERA and 212 strikeouts in 204.1 innings. Kershaw's improved performance was largely attributed to his adding an effective slider to his pitching repertoire. He had developed the pitch to use as an alternative to his big-breaking curveball, which was at times uncontrollable on the mound. "It was a point where he was maybe a little frustrated," the Dodgers pitching coach Rick Honeycutt told Scott Miller for CBS Sports (11 Sept. 2013). "It was a combination of him seeing where his misses were and more than anything, he's an intelligent guy."

FIRST AND SECOND CY YOUNG AWARDS

Kershaw's mastery of the slider and a refined changeup helped him transform from a merely good pitcher to a great one in 2011. That year, he made a career-high thirty-three starts and finished with a record of 21–5 in 233.1 innings. He tied for the NL lead in wins and was the sole league leader in ERA (a major-league-best 2.28) and strikeouts (248), thus making him the league's first pitching triple crown winner since Jake Peavy in 2007. He became only the third Dodger to accomplish the feat and the first since Koufax in 1966. In addition to earning his first career All-Star selection during the season, Kershaw received, among many other honors, the 2011 NL Cy Young Award, becoming the eighth Dodger to receive the award and the first since Eric Gagné in 2003.

Over the next two seasons, Kershaw laid a legitimate claim to being arguably the best pitcher in baseball. During the 2012 season, he led the majors in ERA (2.53) for the second straight year and finished second in the NL in strikeouts (229) and innings pitched (227.2), while earning his second career All-Star selection. After finishing as the runner-up to R. A. Dickey in the voting for that season's Cy Young Award, Kershaw returned in 2013 to lead the majors in ERA for the third consecutive season, with a career-best 1.83, which was the lowest since Pedro Martinez's 1.74 in 2000. He also led the NL in strikeouts (232) and finished second in the league in innings pitched (with a career-high of 236). Despite those numbers, Kershaw—who also earned his third career All-Star selection—finished the season with a deceiving 16–9 record, which was again attributed to poor run support.

As the ace on a pitching rotation that had the NL's second-best ERA (3.25), Kershaw helped the Dodgers win their first NL West title since 2009, with a 92–70 record. Under manager Don Mattingly, who had replaced Torre after the 2010 season, the Dodgers advanced to the NLCS, where they lost to the St. Louis Cardinals in six games. In November 2013, Kershaw won his second NL Cy Young Award in three seasons, falling just one vote shy of winning the award unanimously. He became the sixth pitcher in MLB history to finish in the top three in Cy Young voting in three consecutive seasons and became only the second Dodger (after Koufax) to win the award more than once.

A NEW CONTRACT

Prior to the 2014 season, Kershaw agreed to terms with the Dodgers on a record-setting seven-year, $215 million contract, the largest ever for a pitcher and the sixth largest for an MLB player. The deal has an average annual value of $30.7 million, the highest in baseball history, and runs through the 2020 season. As the long-term face of the Dodgers franchise, Kershaw has said that he holds a responsibility not only to fans, but also to teammates. He explained to Ramona Shelburne for ESPN Los Angeles (18 Oct. 2013), "Everything that I do is so that I don't have any regrets when I'm pitching and so I can look every one of these guys in the eye at the end of the day and know I did everything I possibly could."

PERSONAL LIFE AND PHILANTHROPY

On December 4, 2010, Kershaw married his high school sweetheart, Ellen Melson, in a ceremony in Dallas. They are both devout Christians and well known for their charity work, particularly in Zambia. In 2011 Kershaw and his wife founded Kershaw's Challenge, which helps raise funds for disadvantaged children and underserved communities in Zambia, Los Angeles, and Dallas. In 2012 the couple coauthored the book *Arise: Live Out Your Faith and Dreams on Whatever Field You Find Yourself.*

Kershaw has received many honors for his charitable activities, most notably the 2012 Roberto Clemente Award, baseball's top humanitarian honor. He received the Branch Rickey Award in 2013.

SUGGESTED READING

Gurnick, Ken. "Kershaw Not Afraid to Reach for New Heights." *MLB.com.* Major League Baseball, 2 Oct. 2013. Web. 17 Jan. 2014.

Hernandez, Dylan. "Clayton Kershaw Makes Those Sandy Koufax Comparisons Plausible." *Los Angeles Times.* Los Angeles Times, 19 Sept. 2011. Web. 17 Jan. 2014.

Kurkjian, Tim. "Clayton Kershaw Built to Just Be Great." *ESPN The Magazine.* ESPN, 9 June 2011. Web. 17 Jan. 2014.

Miller, Scott. "Kershaw Otherworldly as Historic Season Heads Toward October." *CBSSports. com.* CBS Interactive, 11 Sept. 2013. Web. 17 Jan. 2014.

—Chris Cullen

Rinko Kikuchi

Born: January 6, 1981
Occupation: Actor

The Japanese actor Rinko Kikuchi first received international acclaim for her performance in the film *Babel* (2006), in which she played a deaf teen. This nonspeaking role, for which she was nominated for an Oscar, drew attention to Kikuchi's ability to portray thoughts and emotions without uttering a word. Kikuchi has also starred in *Norwegian Wood* (2011), a film version of the best-selling Haruki Murakami novel of the same name; *Pacific Rim* (2013), a futuristic monster film directed by Guillermo Del Toro; the critically panned samurai movie *47 Ronin* (2013); and the critically beloved, touching, and curious independent film *Kumiko, The Treasure Hunter* (2014), in which she played a lonely young woman who is inspired by a scene in the film *Fargo* (1996) to travel to North Dakota from her native Japan.

Wirelmage

EARLY YEARS
Rinko Kikuchi was born Yuriko Kikuchi on January 6, 1981, in Hadano, Japan, about forty miles outside of Tokyo. Her father was a big fan of *chanbara* (samurai) films, and Kikuchi would often watch those films with him. As a child she was also a fan of *kaiju* movies, ones featuring monsters like Godzilla. She also watched silent films, particularly those of Buster Keaton, which influenced her own silent performances. In an interview with Kuriko Sato for MidnightEye. com (16 Jan. 2007), a website about Japanese cinema, Kikuchi recalled that by the time she was in junior high school, she started going to the movies by herself, just to watch any Hollywood blockbuster that happened to be playing. Around the age of sixteen, she began to develop an intense interest in the films of American actor-director John Cassavetes, who directed such realistic drama classics as *Husbands* (1970), *Minnie and Moskowitz* (1971) and *A Woman Under the Influence* (1974). The actor Gena Rowlands starred in the latter two films, and Kikuchi became fascinated by her acting. She told Sato: "I remember looking up at Gena Rowlands and thinking, 'Ah, I would really love to play a character like that!' She was so cool. Even when she was insane, she was beautiful. I don't know where it came from, why I had such a strong reaction to the film and to her, but anyway I was really attracted to them. Today I'm so glad that I discovered their films. It brought me where I am now. If I had taken another direction, I wouldn't be sitting here today."

Yet acting was not the first direction Kikuchi took. She recalled in the interview with Sato

that around the age of fourteen she began modeling. She wanted to act, but was "pushed" to do singing and modeling, with the reasoning that that would be a stepping stone to acting. After a point Kikuchi found modeling to be a "boring job" and quit. She also had no interest in becoming a singer. She was determined to pursue an acting career. For Kikuchi, films were not mere entertainment or distractions—they were about real life, including her own. She said to Sato, "Cinema is a kind of bible to me. I [learned] a lot from films—history, music, relationships between man and woman. I never did much studying in school. I was saved by cinema. So I figured that if I could enter the world of cinema, my life would be saved."

EARLY CAREER AND BREAKTHROUGH
Kikuchi was in her late teens when she began getting roles in films in her native Japan. After appearing in Kaneto Shindo's *Ikitai* (*Will to Live*, 1999), she had a more high-profile role in Kazuyoshi Kumakiri's *Sora no Ana* (*Hole in the Sky*, 2001), which received some attention at various film festivals around the globe. The next film she appeared in, Katsuhito Ishii's *Cha no Aji* (*The Taste of Tea*, 2004), also got a good deal of attention and praise at international film festivals, bringing Kikuchi greater international exposure, though her role was small. Though her performances in these offbeat independent films were well received, however, Kikuchi had difficulty breaking into mainstream Japanese film or television. "I think most Japanese directors like when you're more sweet or cute," she told Vanessa Lawrence for *W* (28 Oct. 2013). "I'm too tough."

She found more success abroad when she was cast in the film *Babel* (2006), directed by Alejandro González Iñárritu and written by Guillermo Arriaga. The film divided critics mostly into two camps: those who thought it was a beautifully told tale of miscommunication and violence in the contemporary world and those who thought it was a nonsensical and pretentions failure. The film tells four separate stories that have some relationship to one another. Kikuchi is the star of the storyline set in Tokyo, in which she plays a deaf teenager named Chieko Wataya trying to deal both with the death of her mother and the rejection she faces from the opposite sex. Kikuchi, who was up against a number of hearing-impaired actors for the role, learned sign language for the film, but that wasn't the only challenge she encountered; she told Sharon Swart for *Variety* (28 Sept. 2006), "the character was emotionally difficult, and that was hard."

In his review of the film for the *New York Times* (27 Oct. 2006), A. O. Scott gave the film a mostly positive review, calling it "an experience." Although throughout the review he qualifies his praise for *Babel*, he gives Kikuchi's acting and portrayal of her character unqualified praise: "Chieko's brazen attempts to solicit attention result, again and again, in humiliation, and Ms. Kikuchi's performance is an unnerving blend of sexual provocation, timidity and sheer rage. Of all the characters in *Babel*, she seems most surprising and least tethered to cultural stereotype (in spite of the short-skirted schoolgirl uniform she wears). And her story, unfolding without evident connection to the other three, does not seem quite as bound by the fatalism that is Mr. Arriaga's hallmark—as well as his limitation—as a storyteller." Kikuchi received an Academy Award nomination for her role in the film, which made her the first female Japanese actor to be nominated for an Oscar in over fifty years, as well as one of only five women of any nationality to be nominated for a role with no spoken lines.

INTERNATIONAL SUCCESS

Her next major film was an action-adventure heist comedy, *The Brothers Bloom* (2009), starring Adrien Brody and Mark Ruffalo as two brothers who decide to con a sad, rich, lonely woman, who is played by Rachel Weisz. Kikuchi plays a mostly mute character nicknamed Bang Bang, because she is a demolition expert. The film got mixed reviews, and even those critics who offered up positive reviews concluded that it sagged and disappointed toward the end. Writing for the *Onion*'s A.V. Club (14 May 2009), Keith Phipps, though unimpressed with the film overall, observed that Kikuchi "does brilliant mime work" and gives "able support" to the film. That same year Kikuchi starred in *Sideways* (2009), a Japanese remake of the 2004 Academy Award–winning American comedy-drama. Kikuchi plays the role originated by Sandra Oh in the American version, portraying one of the young women that the wine-loving protagonist encounters in California's Napa Valley.

Although Kikuchi's next major film was also in Japanese, it would get a good deal of attention internationally. *Norwegian Wood* (2010), by Vietnamese director Tran Anh Hung, is based on Haruki Murakami's 1987 novel of the same name, which sold more than ten million copies worldwide and was translated into more than thirty languages. Murakami had, for twenty years, refused to sell movie rights to the book, but in 2008, Tran Anh Hung finally got permission, after four years of back-and-forth correspondence with the author. For Kikuchi, being involved in bringing *Norwegian Wood* to life onscreen was a dream come true. She had loved the novel since she first read it at the age of seventeen, and insisted on being considered for the lead female role, despite the director's initial resistance to the idea.

The story, which takes place in Japan in 1967, is about a serious college student named Watanabe (played by Ken'ichi Matsuyama) who falls for a psychologically troubled young woman named Naoko (played by Kikuchi). Naoko was at one point the girlfriend of Watanabe's best friend, until that friend committed suicide by carbon monoxide poisoning, a memory which haunts both Watanabe and Naoko. Naoko disappears from Watanabe's life shortly after the two have sex for the first time, and is eventually found at a sanitarium in a rural part of Japan recovering from a mental breakdown. *Norwegian Wood* received mostly favorable notices from critics; in a generally positive review for the National Public Radio website (5 Jan. 2012), Mark Jenkins called the film "an impressive showcase for Kikuchi, playing a much more vulnerable character than *Babel*'s brassy deaf teenager."

HOLLYWOOD AND BEYOND

In 2013 Kikuchi appeared in two major Hollywood films: *Pacific Rim* and *47 Ronin*. The former, directed by Guillermo Del Toro, starred Idris Elba, Charlie Hunnam, Ron Pearlman, and Kikuchi. *Pacific Rim* is a sci-fi action movie set in a future where robots controlled by humans are used to fight giant alien beasts that are out to destroy the world. Kikuchi plays one of the pilots who control these robots. The film was generally well received by critics as an entertaining summer action blockbuster. Kikuchi next played a witch in *47 Ronin*, a samurai film starring Keanu Reeves, which was widely panned in both Japan and the United States and failed to recover its budget of $175 million.

Kikuchi's performance in the independent film *Kumiko, The Treasure Hunter* (2014), directed by David Zellner, won her a great deal of praise. Kikuchi stars as Kumiko, a twenty-nine-year-old woman who works as an assistant to a man she dislikes; she also has an overbearing mother, who hounds her for not having a man in her life. During a walk on the beach, Kumiko finds an old videotape. When she plays it, she sees a man, covered in blood, burying a briefcase full of money somewhere in North Dakota. The scene is, in fact, from the Coen Brothers film *Fargo* (1996), but Kumiko nonetheless decides to go to Fargo, North Dakota, and find the treasure. She takes a plane from Japan to Minnesota, where the second half of the film takes place, showing Kumiko's attempts to reach Fargo and some of the strange characters and situations she encounters along the way. "Kumiko seems lost in a melancholy haze, apart from everyone—apart, even, from herself," Scott Foundas wrote in *Variety* (24 Jan. 2014), reviewing the film after its debut at the Sundance Film Festival. "It's a marvelous role for Kikuchi, who has the intensity of the great silent film stars, and who's fascinating to watch even when Kumiko is doing nothing more than sitting solemnly by the window of her apartment eating ramen noodles as a rain begins to fall. At every turn, we can sense what's going on behind Kumiko's doleful, downcast eyes; Kikuchi pulls us deeply into her world."

As an actor, Kikuchi is always looking for the opportunity to try something new and difficult. Asked by Todd Gilchrist for the *Hollywood Reporter* (19 July 2012) about the diversity of character types she has taken on, Kikuchi said, "I like challenges. That's why if I read a script, and I feel 'Oh, I can't do this,' I'll take that role, because if I feel like 'Oh, I can do this,' I don't want to take that because I can't learn from that film." Or, as she told Swart for *Variety*, "In my opinion there is nothing an actor should never do or be. I think everything is a wonderful experience."

PERSONAL LIFE

Kikuchi lives primarily in New York City, though she travels frequently for her acting projects. Despite her early resistance to pursuing a modeling career, her distinctive fashion sense has garnered attention from designers, and she has appeared in several fashion magazines in the United States, Japan, and China. Her other hobbies include horseback riding, Japanese archery, and the swordplay-focused martial art known as *iai*, interests which were influenced by her childhood love of samurai films.

SUGGESTED READING

Foundas, Scott. "Sundance Film Review: 'Kumiko, The Treasure Hunter.'" *Variety*. Variety Media, 24 Jan. 2014. Web. 16 June 2014.

Lawrence, Vanessa. "Rinko Kikuchi: Tough Girl." *W*. Condé Nast, 28 Oct. 2013. Web. 16 June 2014.

Sakuma, Yumiko. "Rinko Kikuchi: And You May Find Yourself, But Will You Know Who You Are?" *Flaunt*. Flaunt Magazine, 20 Nov. 2013. Web. 16 June 2014.

Sato, Kuriko. "Rinko Kikuchi." *Midnight Eye*. Midnight Eye, 16 Jan. 2007. Web. 16 June 2014.

Swart, Sharon. "Rinko Kikuchi." *Variety*. Variety Media, 28 Sept. 2006. Web. 16 June 2014.

Wiseman, Eva. "Rinko Kikuchi: The Interview." *Observer*. Guardian News and Media, 26 Feb. 2011. Web. 16 June 2014.

SELECTED WORKS

Hole in the Sky, 2001; *The Taste of Tea*, 2004; *Babel*, 2006; *The Brothers Bloom*, 2008; *Sideways*, 2009; *Norwegian Wood*, 2010; *Pacific Rim*, 2013; *47 Ronin*, 2013; *Kumiko, The Treasure Hunter*, 2014

—*Dmitry Kiper*

Yuna Kim

Born: September 5, 1990
Occupation: Figure skater

The South Korean figure skater Yuna Kim, known as Queen Yuna to her countless fans around the world, is a cultural icon in her country and one of its best-known and beloved athletes. Since making her debut on the senior international circuit in 2006, Kim has established herself as the most dominant athlete in her sport. Aside from winning numerous international figure skating titles, Kim has achieved numerous firsts in South Korean figure skating history, the most important of which came at the 2010 Olympic Games in Vancouver, Canada, where she became the first South Korean to win an Olympic gold medal in figure skating. At the 2010 Games, Kim overcame enormous pressure and delivered a performance for the ages, setting world records in the short program, long program, and combined total, with 78.50, 150.06, and 228.56 points, respectively. "I have never seen a skater with such combination of artistry and athleticism," Michelle Kwan, a five-time world figure skating champion and two-time Olympic medalist, wrote for *Time* (29 Apr. 2010). Kwan added that Kim's "inspiring performances in Vancouver changed the face of figure skating forever."

In 2013, following a nearly two-year absence, Kim returned to competition at the International

Getty Images

Skating Union (ISU) World Figure Skating Championships, held in London, Ontario, Canada. There, she captured her second career world title—she won her first in 2009—with a dazzling performance that impressed commentators. Covering that event for the Associated Press (17 Mar. 2013), Nancy Armour wrote, "Kim is technically superior. She's like a bumblebee when she jumps, daintily going from flower to flower. Her spins are quick and tight, with intricate positions that don't seem humanly possible. But it is her presentation that makes her incomparable."

In 2014 Kim entered the Winter Olympics in Sochi, Russia, as an overwhelming favorite to defend her title. Already "viewed as one of the best female skaters in history," as Christine Brennan noted for *USA Today* (14 Mar. 2013), Kim announced that she planned to retire after competing in Sochi.

EARLY LIFE

Yuna Kim was born Kim Yu-na on September 5, 1990, in Bucheon, a city in the Gyeonggi province of South Korea, the second of two daughters. Korean names are traditionally listed with the family name first, followed by the given name; Kim's first name means *pretty girl* and often appears in print as "Yu-na." Her father, Kim Hyeon-seok, is a businessman, and her mother, Park Mee-hee, is a homemaker. Kim developed an interest in figure skating at the age of five, when an indoor rink opened near her home. She and her family started making regular excursions to the rink, which at the time was one of only a few in all of South Korea.

Kim's preternatural talent on the ice was evident early on. At about age six she caught the attention of a national figure skating coach, Ryu Jong-hyun, who suggested to her mother that she sign Kim up for figure skating lessons. Recognizing her enormous potential, Kim's mother immediately enrolled her in daily lessons and dedicated herself to her daughter's career, soon overseeing all facets of her skating activities. "I majored in Yu-na," Park wrote in a 2008 memoir that became a best-seller in South Korea, as quoted by Choe Sang-Hun for the *New York Times* (10 June 2009). "For Yu-na, I studied harder than when I was in school. I devoted myself to her more passionately than when I was in love."

Kim was seven years old when she first aspired to become an Olympic figure skater. She developed that desire after watching Michelle Kwan compete at the 1998 Winter Olympics in Nagano, Japan. Mesmerized by Kwan's silver medal–winning performance, Kim started emulating the legendary American figure skater's moves on the ice. "I followed her every day and watched her programs so closely I almost memorized everything," she told Helene Elliott for the *Los Angeles Times* (7 Sept. 2010).

Kim successfully completed her first triple jump, a triple toe loop, at the age of ten, and she was soon able to execute numerous other difficult skating maneuvers. During this time she was coached by Shin Hae-sook, who skated for the Korean national team at the 1980 Winter Olympics.

EARLY CAREER

Kim first came to national prominence in 2002, when she started competing at the novice level. That year she participated in her first international competition, the Triglav Trophy in Slovenia, where she claimed the gold medal in the novice competition. Kim again made history in 2003, when she became, at twelve, the youngest skater to win the South Korean Figure Skating Championships, a senior-level event. Later that year she won the novice competition at the Golden Bear of Zagreb, in Croatia, to claim her second international title.

By 2004, Kim had entered the junior ranks and started competing in events on the ISU Junior Grand Prix (JGP), a series of international competitions for top junior-level skaters. In the fall of that year, she won a gold medal in her first JGP event, in Budapest, Hungary, becoming the first South Korean skater to win a grand prix event. Kim then qualified for the 2005 JGP Final in Helsinki, Finland, where she won a silver medal, placing second behind longtime rival Mao Asada of Japan; she became the first South Korean skater to earn a podium placement in the competition, which pits the highest-ranking junior qualifiers against each other.

Meanwhile, Kim claimed two additional South Korean national titles in 2004 and 2005. After the latter competition, she competed at the 2005 World Junior Figure Skating Championships in Kitchener, Canada. She placed a disappointing sixth in the short program but bounced back to win the long program, more commonly known as the free skate, finishing second in the overall competition, once again behind Asada.

Age restrictions prevented the then fourteen-year-old Kim from competing at the 2006 Winter Olympics in Turin, Italy, and the 2006 World Figure Skating Championships in Calgary, Canada. As a result Kim competed on the junior grand prix circuit during the 2005–6 season, winning competitions in Slovakia and Bulgaria en route to a gold medal at that season's JGP Final, which marked another first by a Korean skater. She closed out 2006 with yet another gold medal at the South Korean championships, followed by a gold medal at the World Junior Championships in Ljubljana, Slovenia, where she finished ahead of silver medalist Asada by nearly twenty-five points.

ENTERING THE WORLD STAGE

After winning the junior worlds, Kim joined the women's senior international circuit. In 2006, she worked with the renowned Canadian choreographer David Wilson in Toronto. Charged with improving her emotional disposition on the ice, Wilson recalled to Juliet Macur for the *New York Times* (14 Feb. 2010) that Kim wanted "to be a happy skater." He added, "I remember even having to teach her how to hug me because she was so shy. She was always so stiff, like a telephone pole." It was through Wilson that Kim met Brian Orser, a two-time Canadian Olympic silver medalist who was the skating director at the rink where they trained. Orser, who was then just beginning his coaching career, began working with Kim on a part-time basis before eventually agreeing to become her full-time coach. He went on to serve as her coach from 2006 to 2010.

Under the tutelage of Wilson and Orser, Kim established herself as the best all-around skater in the world. At the 2006 Skate Canada International she made her senior international debut, winning the bronze medal. That performance marked the beginning of an unprecedented string of medals for Kim in international competitions. Kim's 2006–7 season also included gold medals at the Trophée Eric Bompard and Grand Prix Final competitions and a bronze medal at the 2007 World Figure Skating Championships in Tokyo, Japan. After that season, Kim moved to Toronto on a permanent basis to work regularly with Orser and Wilson—and in part to escape suffocating media scrutiny in her home country. "When you're with her in Korea, it's like you're traveling with Princess Diana; Yu-na's that famous there," Orser told Macur. "But here [in Toronto], things are obviously quieter. It gives her a chance for a normal life. She can focus on what she has to do."

During the 2007–8 season, Kim won gold medals at two prestigious Grand Prix events, the Cup of China and Cup of Russia, and defended her title at the 2007 Grand Prix Final. That season she won her second straight bronze medal at the World Championships. She added five more titles during the 2008–9 season, the most notable of which came at the 2009 World Championships in Los Angeles, California. Kim won her first world title with a combined total of 207.71 points, becoming the first female figure skater to break the 200-point barrier.

RECORD-BREAKING OLYMPIC PERFORMANCE

Kim entered the 2009–10 season as a favorite to win the gold medal at the 2010 Olympics. Leading up to the Olympics, she won gold medals in two Grand Prix events and captured her third Grand Prix Final title. In Vancouver, Kim lived up to gargantuan national expectations. During her short program, set to a medley of theme songs from the James Bond film franchise, she executed a wide variety of difficult jump combinations, including a triple Lutz-triple toe loop, a double axel, and a triple flip. For her performance, Kim received a score of 78.50, which led all skaters and set a new world record. She then turned in an even more impressive performance in her free skate program, which was set to George Gershwin's Concerto in F. "She was as electric as the stunning blue dress she wore," Jerry Brewer wrote for the *Seattle Times* (25 Feb. 2010), "flawlessly executing triple flips, triple Lutzes and double axels at full speed, landing so softly each time that it felt like you were watching a feather float to the ice."

Kim won the free skate portion of the women's singles competition with a score of 150.06, which shattered her earlier record of 133.95. Her combined total of 228.56 points also established a new world record, and she finished more than twenty points ahead of second-place finisher Asada. Brewer noted that Kim's accomplishment was "every bit as impressive as [Jamaican sprinter] Usain Bolt running 100 meters in 9.58 seconds." With her first-place finish, Kim became the first South Korean to win a Winter Olympic medal in a sport other than speed skating. "I have accomplished the biggest, most important goal in my life," Kim said after the win, as quoted by Macur for the *New York Times* (26 Feb. 2010).

COMPETITIVE HIATUS AND 2013 WORLD CHAMPIONSHIPS

Following the 2010 Olympics, Kim competed at the 2010 World Championships in Turin, Italy, where she won the silver medal, finishing second to Asada. She again won the silver medal at the 2011 World Championships in Moscow, Russia, this time finishing behind Japan's Miki Ando. Afterward, Kim took an almost two-year hiatus from skating competitions to focus on her future. "After winning the Olympics," she explained, as quoted by Brennan for *USA Today*, "I felt a bit empty because I had achieved my goal."

Kim made her triumphant comeback in March 2013, when she took part in the World Championships in London, Canada. She won both the short and free skate programs with a combined score of 218.31 points, more than twenty points ahead of second-place finisher and defending world champion Carolina Kostner of Italy. It marked the largest margin of victory since the ISU adopted its latest scoring system in 2004.

In January 2014 Kim participated in her final domestic competition at the South Korean national championships, finishing in first place. She was next scheduled to skate at the 2014 Olympics in Sochi, Russia, where she would attempt to become the first woman to defend an

Olympic figure skating title since Germany's Katarina Witt in 1988. Kim also announced that the Sochi Olympics would be her final competition, as she planned to retire from competitive figure-skating after the Games.

PERSONAL LIFE

Since 2010 Kim has served as the headline act in the *All That Skate* figure-skating show, which is organized and produced by her sports agency, All That Sports. She has appeared in numerous commercials in South Korea thanks to her many sponsors, which include Samsung Electronics, Hyundai Motor Company, Korean Air, and Nike. In 2013 she ranked sixth on *Forbes*'s annual list of the world's highest-earning female athletes, with an estimated $14 million in earnings.

Kim is also known for her many philanthropic efforts and has donated millions of dollars to various causes. In 2010 she was appointed a goodwill ambassador by the global humanitarian aid organization UNICEF and named one of the world's most influential people by *Time* magazine. In 2013 she received an achievement award as well as a bachelor's degree from Korea University.

SUGGESTED READING

Brennan, Christine. "Time Off Doesn't Slow Kim Yu-na, Leader at Worlds." *USA Today*. Gannett, 14 Mar. 2013. Web. 16 Jan. 2014.

Brewer, Jerry. "Captivating Figure Skater Kim Yu-na Wins Gold." *Seattle Times*. Seattle Times, 25 Feb. 2010. Web. 16 Jan. 2014.

Choe Sang-Hun. "Mother's Love Becomes Obsession for Some South Koreans." *New York Times*. New York Times, 10 June 2009. Web. 16 Jan. 2014.

Hersh, Philip. "Kim Yuna Is a Champion for All Time." *Los Angeles Times*. Los Angeles Times, 27 Feb. 2010. Web. 16 Jan. 2014.

Macur, Juliet. "Olympic Hopes Rest with Skating Favorite Kim Yu-na." *New York Times*. New York Times, 13 Feb. 2010. Web. 16 Jan. 2014.

—*Chris Cullen*

Jeff Kinney

Born: February 19, 1971
Occupation: Writer and game designer

Jeff Kinney is the creator of the *Diary of a Wimpy Kid* books, a joke-filled series designed to give the impression that it has been handwritten and drawn by a middle school student. The popular books, which follow the adventures of Greg Heffley—a scrawny preteen who must deal with tough bullies, mean teachers, and perplexing

Oliver Berg/DPA/Landov

girls as he navigates the halls of middle school—has spawned three live-action films and a host of imitators who "try to create similarly infectious blends of pen-and-ink illustrations and fast-paced, highly relatable narrative," in the words of Pamela Paul for the *New York Times* (15 Nov. 2011).

Publishers Weekly (21 Oct. 2013) estimates that more than 115 million Wimpy Kid books were printed between the series' debut in 2007 and the publication of the eighth book in 2013. The series has been translated into more than forty languages, albeit sometimes with some difficulty: in Germany, Kinney has explained to interviewers, there is no word for *wimpy*, and thus the first book in the franchise is known as *Gregs Tagebuch: Von Idioten umzingelt!* (Gregs Tagebuch: I'm surrounded by idiots!). He asserts that the concept of wimpiness is, however, vital to the success of the books. "To me, the definition of a wimp is somebody who feels powerless," Kinney told Michelle Tauber for *People* magazine (17 May 2010). "Everyone in fifth or sixth grade knows what it feels like to be powerless in the world."

EARLY LIFE

Jeff Kinney was born on February 19, 1971, at Andrews Air Force Base in Maryland, and he grew up in nearby Fort Washington. He enjoyed what he has characterized as a totally average childhood. His father worked at the Pentagon, and his mother ran a preschool. Kinney, the third of four children, has two brothers and a sister. "Though I look back fondly on my childhood I think that when you've got four siblings sharing the same resources and a single kids' bathroom, it's going to get a little tense at times," he told

Nick McGrath for the *Guardian* (30 Nov. 2012). "The conflicts tended to be me against the three of them. My younger brother was the new cute one and my two older siblings were the teens, so I was somewhere stuck in the middle."

Kinney, who believes that he suffered from an undiagnosed attention deficit disorder (ADD) as a student, attended Potomac Landing Elementary School and then went on to Eugene Burroughs Middle School. "I think that my middle school experience was more scary than Greg Heffley's middle school experience," Kinney recalled to Anna Weaver for the Capital News Service (26 Sept. 2012). "I felt like we went from the safe confines of the elementary school to the really scary, almost prison yard environment of middle school. So it was terrifying for me."

Always an avid reader, Kinney loved books by Judy Blume, and in the fourth grade he discovered science fiction and fantasy, methodically working his way through everything by Piers Anthony, Terry Brooks, and J. R. R. Tolkien. Like his father, he was a devoted fan of comics, and in addition to *Calvin and Hobbes* and *The Far Side*, Kinney's father introduced him to the work of Carl Barks, best known for creating *Donald Duck* cartoons from the 1940s to the 1960s. "Mr. Barks taught me that comics could be high art," Kinney told Paul, "and I consider his work to be the best storytelling I've experienced in any form."

EDUCATION
In 1989, after graduating from Bishop McNamara High School in Forestville, Maryland, Kinney entered Villanova University, in Pennsylvania, on an Air Force ROTC scholarship. There he began publishing his own comic strip, *Igdoof*, in the school paper. The strip's protagonist was an awkward freshman with a large nose and only a few hairs on his head—physical characteristics shared by Greg Heffley. Like Greg, the character loathed schoolwork and liked practical jokes. "A lot of the DNA of my *Igdoof* cartoons . . . made [its] way into my Wimpy Kid books," Kinney told Weaver. After a year, Kinney transferred to the University of Maryland in College Park, and there he also found an outlet for *Igdoof*, in the *Diamondback*, the university's high-circulation paper.

Having enjoyed tinkering with the Apple II computer his parents bought him as a teen, Kinney initially majored in computer science, but when he earned poor grades in those courses, he switched to criminal justice and interned at the Bureau of Alcohol, Tobacco, and Firearms (ATF) during his college breaks.

Meanwhile, *Igdoof* was proving exceptionally popular on the Maryland campus. "I knew that I was writing for 30,000 people each day, so it became the priority for me," Kinney told Kristi Tousignant for the *Diamondback* (1 Nov. 2009). "I

put an unhealthy amount of time into the strip." He began to harbor hope that he could get the strip syndicated after he earned his bachelor's degree in 1993.

A FLEDGLING CAREER
Kinney's hopes were dashed when newspaper after newspaper declined to publish *Igdoof*. "Nobody liked my work," Kinney recalled to Christopher Reynolds for the *Los Angeles Times* (9 Nov. 2013). "I didn't have the control or flair that was necessary to create something that didn't look childish." Discouraged, he took jobs as a software engineer and as a designer for a small Massachusetts newspaper. Eventually, however, he hit upon a way to make his lack of polished cartooning skills an asset. "I just could not draw like a professional cartoonist," he explained to Michelle Norris for National Public Radio's *All Things Considered* (29 June 2012). "I was like, 'I draw like a middle schooler, right?' And eventually this idea came to me. . . . Maybe if I act like I'm doing it on purpose, everybody will think that I was doing it on purpose, and they won't be able to reject me. That's where the idea of *Diary of a Wimpy Kid* came from."

For several years, Kinney worked on his project in private, creating a mock journal that chronicled the adventures of a typical sixth grader, much like his younger self. "I think I felt a lot like Greg Heffley as a kid," he told Norris. "You know, I did a lot of the same sorts of things that Greg did and I wasn't always the best kid. I was average but I wasn't always the best."

By 2004 Kinney was working as a game developer at Funbrain, a website published by Pearson's Family Education Network that features free educational games, online books, and comics for kids. He talked to the editors there about running *Diary of a Wimpy Kid* as a daily comic strip, and, seeking to boost traffic during the typically slow days of summer, they agreed. Soon the strip was attracting almost one hundred thousand visitors a day.

WIMPY KID BOOKS
In 2006 Kinney attended New York Comic Con, a massive annual gathering in New York City that brings together creators and fans of comic books, science fiction, fantasy, horror, anime, and video games. Although he was there mainly to scout possible content for the Family Education Network, he also brought along a sample of his mock journal, wondering if he could interest a publisher in releasing it as a nostalgic novelty book for adults. Trudging through the multifloor convention center, Kinney found most traditional publishers unimpressed by his online success and unwilling to consider what was then an unusual prose-cartoon hybrid. As he prepared to leave, however, he chanced upon the Abrams Books booth, manned by editor Charles

Kochman, who had previously worked at DC Comics and *Mad* magazine.

Kochman loved Kinney's concept and within months had secured him a publishing contract—with the proviso that the series be aimed at young readers rather than the nostalgic adults Kinney had envisioned. The first volume, *Diary of a Wimpy Kid*, was published in 2007—almost a decade after Kinney had begun doodling it in a small sketchbook—and immediately found an enthusiastic audience. The series went on to include *Roderick Rules* (2008), *The Last Straw* (2009), *Dog Days* (2009), *The Ugly Truth* (2010), *Cabin Fever* (2011), *The Third Wheel* (2012), and *Hard Luck* (2013), as well as *Diary of a Wimpy Kid: Do-It-Yourself Book* (2008), which features pages that can be filled in by the reader.

Asked why his work is so popular with fans, Kinney suggests that much of the reason is that he entertains without preaching or moralizing. "Kids can sniff out a moral," he explained to Reynolds. "They can feel the heavy hand of an adult." "Besides," he wrote in a July 18, 2011, essay for *Time*, "the conversations that a complicated character like Greg inspires in the classroom and at the dinner table are infinitely more interesting and educational than a baked-in moral."

Kinney's nonjudgmental attitude toward his fallible main character has, however, invited criticism. He wrote for *Time*, "It seems that when anything aimed at kids catches on, it causes the collective antennae of the older set to go up. As *Diary of a Wimpy Kid* gathered steam, I braced myself for the inevitable backlash. I consider my books to be harmless fun and wholesome entertainment, but somehow I ended up in the position of defending my writing to [interviewer] Barbara Walters. Later, a nationally televised news program ran a segment titled "'Wimpy Kid' with a Foul Mouth.' (My inclusion of the word dork didn't sit well with them.) But eventually the clouds passed—or perhaps just moved on to settle over [other books]."

THE WIMPY KID MOVIES

The books have given rise to a trio of live-action films: *Diary of a Wimpy Kid* (2010), *Diary of a Wimpy Kid: Rodrick Rules* (2011), and *Diary of a Wimpy Kid: Dog Days* (2012). More than twenty-five thousand young hopefuls had sent in audition tapes to a website set up by casting agents, IAmTheWimpyKid.com, before actor Zachary Gordon was chosen to star as Greg. The filmmakers had been seeking "physically unprepossessing" actors with "quirky, memorable faces" who were not "overly cute or precocious."

"*Diary of a Wimpy Kid* is a PG-rated comedy about the hero's first year of middle school, and it's nimble, bright, and funny," film critic Roger Ebert wrote on his eponymous website of the first big-screen installment (17 Mar. 2010).

"It doesn't dumb down. It doesn't patronize. It knows something about human nature. . . . Here is a family movie you don't need a family to enjoy." Ebert concluded, "The movie is inspired by the books of Jeff Kinney, and the titles reproduce his hand-lettering and drawing style. The movie reproduces his charm." Other critics were less charmed. "The pervasive doomed feeling of junior high is *too* accurate," Peter Hartlaub opined for the *San Francisco Chronicle* (19 Mar. 2010). "Who wants to pay money to relive that?"

Collectively, the films earned more than $165 million in domestic box-office receipts. In the tie-in book, *The Wimpy Kid Movie Diary: How Greg Heffley Went Hollywood* (2010), Kinney describes how a script is created, a location scouted, props created, and more. He has told interviewers that there will probably be no additional films in the series because Gordon and the other young cast members were getting too old to play middle school students.

POPTROPICA

Despite the demands of writing, drawing, and promoting his books, Kinney has continued to work for the Family Education Network. Since 2007 he has been the creative director of Poptropica, a virtual world in which a child can adopt an avatar in order to travel to various locales, solving mysteries, collecting objects, and learning fun facts. (Two of the locales, Wimpy Boardwalk and Wimpy Wonderland, feature characters from Kinney's books.) In September 2011, *Publishing Perspectives* reported that Poptropica had 75 million registered users and 10 million visitors monthly, while in January 2012, *Publishers Weekly* reported that the website had had more than 180 million readers since its launch in September 2007. According to a March 2014 corporate press release, the site has had hundreds of millions of visitors between 2007 and 2014.

PERSONAL LIFE

Kinney lives in Plainville, a small Massachusetts town with about eight thousand inhabitants. He and his second wife, Julie, have two sons, Will and Grant. Despite the fact that the Wimpy Kid franchise was said to be worth some $550 million in 2012, Kinney maintains a modest lifestyle. He serves as a Cub Scout leader and soccer coach, and even when traveling on book tours, he attempts to get home to fulfill those duties. His major personal expenditures have been to install a pool in his backyard for his sons and to purchase the house next door to his own, for use as an office space. He and his wife also plan to renovate an old building in Plainville, which will then serve as a community center.

Despite Kinney's relatively normal life, his work has involved some moments that he describes as surreal. "I've met three presidents, I've spoken at the Sydney Opera House, I've got to walk the Wimpy Kid balloon in the Macy's Day parade," he explained to Hannah Stephenson for the Cardiff, Wales, *Western Mail* (29 Dec. 2012). In 2009 *Time* magazine named him one of the hundred most influential people in the world because of his role in getting children to read. "That was strange," he told Stephenson. "I'm not even the most influential person in my own house."

SUGGESTED READING

McGrath, Nick. "Jeff Kinney: People Ask Me, Is Greg Really You?" *Guardian*. Guardian News and Media, 30 Nov. 2012. Web. 10 Apr. 2014.

Mehegan, David. "Story of the Weak." *Boston Globe*. Boston Globe Media Partners, 8 Apr. 2008. Web. 10 Apr. 2014.

Parker, James. "Revenge of the Wimps." *Atlantic*. Atlantic Monthly Group, May 2010. Web. 10 Apr. 2014.

Paul, Pamela. "Jeff Kinney's Favorite Books from Childhood." *New York Times: ArtsBeat*. New York Times, 15 Nov. 2011. Web. 10 Apr. 2014.

Reynolds, Christopher. "'Diary of a Wimpy Kid's' Jeff Kinney Hits the Middle School Road." *Los Angeles Times*. Tribune Newspaper, 9 Nov. 2013. Web. 10 Apr. 2014.

Tauber, Michelle. "Revenge of the Wimp." *People*. Time, 17 May 2010. Web. 10 Apr. 2014.

Thompson, Bob. "Get Out of Here!" *Washington Post*. Washington Post, 3 Mar. 2009. Web. 10 Apr. 2014.

SELECTED WORKS

Diary of a Wimpy Kid, 2007; *Diary of a Wimpy Kid: Roderick Rules*, 2008; *Diary of a Wimpy Kid: The Last Straw*, 2009; *Diary of a Wimpy Kid: Dog Days*, 2009; *Diary of a Wimpy Kid: The Ugly Truth*, 2010; *Diary of a Wimpy Kid: Cabin Fever*, 2011; *Diary of a Wimpy Kid: The Third Wheel*, 2012; *Diary of a Wimpy Kid: Hard Luck*, 2013

—*Mari Rich*

Nancy Knowlton

Born: May 30, 1949
Occupation: Marine biologist

Nancy Knowlton is the Sant Chair for Marine Science at the Smithsonian Institution. She is also the founding director of the Center for Marine Biodiversity and Conservation at the Scripps Institution of Oceanography at the University of California, San Diego (UCSD). A marine biologist, Knowlton is one of the world's leading experts on coral reefs—massive structures in the ocean, constructed over millions of years from

© Christian Ziegler

coral, sponges, and sometimes even stony seaweed—and has been studying them for more than thirty years.

Knowlton and her husband, ecologist Jeremy Jackson, have been called Drs. Doom and Gloom because of their dark outlook on the future of ocean life, but they are not alone in their assessment. Knowlton and Jackson have noted that biologists in their sixties and seventies have spent their careers cataloging the ocean's rapid decline. But Knowlton hopes to change that rhetoric for the next generation of scientists. "Such tales of doom and gloom—ecosystem collapse without recovery—have become the norm," she wrote for the website of SeaWeb, the oceanic conservation organization. "Those of us who study the health of the ocean sometimes feel less like PhDs and more like MDs. But medical doctors do not spend their careers writing ever-more-refined obituaries of their patients, and neither can we. Notwithstanding the media credo 'If it bleeds, it leads,' the public is tired of tragedy and craves solutions and successes."

With this in mind, Knowlton published a book for National Geographic called *Citizens of the Sea: Wondrous Creatures from the Census of Marine Life* (2010), a vividly photographed conclusion to the Census of Marine Life, a scientific endeavor ten years in the making. The book celebrates the ocean's array of living creatures, but also offers solutions to the problems plaguing the seas. Knowlton and her husband also host a series of seminars and events called Beyond the Obituaries: Success Stories in Ocean Conservation.

EARLY LIFE AND EDUCATION

One of four female siblings, Knowlton was raised in Darien, Connecticut. Her father, Archa Knowlton, worked in advertising. Her mother, Aline, was a homemaker. As a child, Knowlton spent summers with her grandparents on Long Island Sound. Her grandfather was a medical doctor who taught her how to fish. His love of science kindled Knowlton's curiosity for the natural world. When she was eight years old, she collected hundreds of snails for a project she called "Density dependent migration in an intertidal marine gastropod." At Darien High School, a teacher named Mr. Vazquez suggested she study biology. She graduated in 1967 and, instead of attending college immediately, worked for pioneering marine biologist Ruth Turner at Harvard University. Working with Turner, Knowlton found her passion for marine life. Discussing her admiration for Turner, Knowlton told *Current Biology* (26 Apr. 2011), "Like many women scientists of her generation, she had to struggle for her success—she was the first woman to go down in the Alvin submarine, and she inspired me to learn to SCUBA dive."

Knowlton studied biology at Smith College until 1969 and earned an AB in biology from Harvard University in 1971. She earned her doctorate in zoology at the University of California, Berkeley, in 1978, and she was a NATO Postdoctoral Fellow through the University of Liverpool and Cambridge University in 1979.

RESEARCH AND TEACHING CAREER

As a graduate student in the 1970s, Knowlton researched the flourishing coral reefs of the Caribbean. She spent most of her time at the research station at Discovery Bay, located on the north coast of Jamaica, which was among the most studied coral reefs on Earth. In August 1980 Hurricane Allen all but destroyed the reef, but Knowlton and Jackson, among others, persevered. Knowlton and another biologist tagged hundreds upon hundreds of surviving corals, hoping to track their growth. Jackson even wrote a paper in which he predicted that the reef would regenerate—but his predictions proved to be completely wrong. Because of overfishing, the area became overgrown with seaweed and algae. The corals never returned.

Knowlton taught at Yale University for five years beginning in 1979. In 1985, she began a long stint with the Smithsonian Tropical Research Institute in the San Blas Archipelago in Panama. In 1989, during the US invasion of Panama, Knowlton, her four-year-old daughter, and nine other researchers were taken hostage. "When your job description ends with '. . . and other duties as assigned,' somehow you never imagine being force marched at gun point, barefoot, over the continental divide, carrying your data and your daughter's favorite stuffed

animal," Knowlton told *Current Biology*. They were released after twenty-four hours, and no one was hurt.

THREATS TO CORAL REEFS

In her interview with Beth Py-Lieberman for *Smithsonian* magazine (Sept. 2008), Knowlton described ocean life as a naturally inverted pyramid. The plants on the reef and small fish are at the bottom of the pyramid, even though they reproduce and die quickly. Parrotfish and various types of sea urchins are particularly important because they eat seaweed, which grows ten times faster than coral and, unchecked, can smother a reef. After the hurricane at Discovery Bay, a disease killed nearly all of a certain species of sea urchin and the reef was overgrown with seaweed. According to Knowlton, about one-quarter of all marine life live on coral reefs. But Knowlton's subject is disappearing fast; overfishing, poor water quality, and an excess of carbon dioxide resulting from climate change all have contributed to the rapid decline of coral reefs around the globe.

The finality of the destruction at Discovery Bay troubled scientists. Corals have existed for millennia and have weathered much worse than hurricanes. Something more serious appeared to be happening. Knowlton told Py-Lieberman that, over the course of her career, 80 percent of the corals in the Caribbean have been destroyed. Corals in the Pacific are not faring much better. "This is a level of destruction that rivals the devastation of tropical rain forests," Knowlton told Py-Lieberman. "If people don't change the way they're doing things," Knowlton said, "reefs as we know them will be gone by the year 2050."

The first threat to the survival of coral reefs is overfishing. Humans mainly eat large predators—the sharks, snappers, and groupers at the top of the pyramid—but more and more humans are "fishing down the chain," as Knowlton told Py-Lieberman, and eating the small herbivores that protect corals. The second threat is declining water quality. Toxic materials and fertilizers are finding their way into the ocean and polluting the water. The third threat is an increase in carbon dioxide resulting from climate change. As it dissolves, carbon dioxide makes seawater more acidic, and the acid erodes the skeletons of corals. (The effect is similar to acidic soft drinks on one's teeth, Knowlton has said.) It also warms the temperature of the ocean, killing algae necessary to a coral's survival. "Over the long term, this is really the biggest threat," Knowlton told Margaret Wertheim for *Cabinet* magazine (2008). "Global warming is hard on reefs because they depend on a very delicate relationship with single-celled algae called zooxanthellae. Zooxanthellae live near their thermal maximum, so if the temperature rises one degree centigrade over normal maximum levels, it cripples their ability to photosynthesize." These threats also make corals more vulnerable to disease.

CONSERVATION EFFORTS

In 1996, Knowlton joined the faculty at UCSD as a professor in the Scripps Institution of Oceanography. She founded the Center for Marine Biodiversity and Conservation in 2001. The graduate program is research-based but also emphasizes collaboration and public outreach. Knowlton does not see science and science activism—particularly with regard to climate change—as two separate endeavors. Neither does Randy Olson, a Harvard-educated scientist who left his tenured teaching position to become a filmmaker. In 2009, Olson wrote a book called *Don't Be Such a Scientist*, and he talks about the importance of storytelling and humor in publicly addressing fraught topics such as climate change. Knowlton was inspired by Olson's message and, with her husband, launched a project called Beyond the Obituaries: Success Stories in Ocean Conservation. Environmental forecasts have grown increasingly bleak, but this is exactly the reason Knowlton decided it was time to try a new tack. "Doom and gloom stops being an effective motivator for people, for, not only scientists, but the public at large," she told Bruce Gellerman in a recorded interview for the magazine *Living on Earth* (23 Sept. 2011).

With their Beyond the Obituaries mission, Knowlton and Jackson hold events and seminars to educate people about threats to marine life but also focus on positive changes. Knowlton believes it is important to share success stories such as efforts currently being made to protect Australia's Great Barrier Reef. She told Kevin Dennehy for *Yale Environment 360* (13 Mar. 2012) that Australians are the "gold standard for reef protection." The Great Barrier Reef Marine Park Authority regulates fishing in the area to foster the biodiversity reefs need to flourish. (A perfect reef would be a part of a bustling ecosystem with plenty of both large predators and small herbivores.) Of course, it is not practical to ban fishing outright in certain regions—such as the areas surrounding the reefs that pepper New Guinea, Indonesia, and the Philippines—because people depend on the fish to survive. In many cases, it is "more about managing fishing than putting fishing off limits," Knowlton told Dennehy. Reefs are an important part of the ocean's ecosystem, but they benefit humans as well. They protect shorelines from hurricanes and tsunamis and can serve as boons for tourism. Knowlton encourages tourism because she believes that people feel more strongly about protecting coral reefs when they have the chance to interact with them. Additionally, some corals are even used for biopharmaceutical drugs.

THE SMITHSONIAN AND CENSUS OF MARINE LIFE

In 2007, Knowlton was named the Sant Chair for Marine Science at the Smithsonian Institution in Washington, DC. The position allows her to spend a good portion of her time interacting with the public. She was the scientific advisor to the Hyperbolic Crochet Coral Reef, a major art project from the Los Angeles–based Institute for Figuring that sought to re-create coral reefs in yarn. She even helped bring the project to the National Museum of Natural History in Washington, DC.

Knowlton was also a leader of the Census of Marine Life. The multimillion-dollar, ten-year project was the work of nearly three thousand scientists from more than eighty nations. The mission of the census was to describe the abundance, diversity, and distribution of the world's ocean life. The results of the census were reported in October 2010 and illustrated in Knowlton's book *Citizens of the Sea*. According to the census website, the project yielded many surprises, from the discovery of new species (some twelve hundred with a possible five thousand more) to the rediscovery of a Jurassic shrimp, thought to have been extinct for 50 million years. The census did not provide a concrete number of species living in the ocean, but it gave scientists an idea of the incredible scope of marine life, from tiny bacteria to giant squid. The data has already provided the basis for thousands of formal papers. The most sobering confirmation of the census was that climate change is already having a tremendous negative impact on the world's oceans.

Though Knowlton spends most of her time out of the lab, she has not given up research just yet. She told *Current Biology* that before she retires she hopes to figure out how many species live in the ocean, using next-generation sequencing.

PERSONAL LIFE

Knowlton's first marriage ended in divorce. She met Jackson at Discovery Bay in the 1970s and married him in 1983. They have a daughter named Rebecca; Jackson has a son named Stephen from his previous marriage. The family lives in Washington, DC, and Maine.

Knowlton serves on the national board of the American Association for the Advancement of Science and on the editorial board of the *Annual Review of Marine Science*. She and Jackson jointly received the Peter Benchley Ocean Award for excellence in science in 2009. In 2011, Knowlton received the Heinz Award and was honored as an environmental trailblazer.

SUGGESTED READING

Knowlton, Nancy. "Celebrating the Citizens of the Sea: From Doom and Gloom to Hope and

Change." *SeaWeb.org*. SeaWeb, n.d. Web. 29 Jan. 2014.

Knowlton, Nancy. Interview by Kevin Dennehy. "Interview: In Fight to Save Coral Reefs, Finding Strategies That Work." *Yale Environment 360*. Yale University, 13 Mar. 2012. Web. 29 Jan. 2014.

Knowlton, Nancy. Interview by Bruce Gellerman. "Heinz Awards Celebrate 'Environmental Champions.'" *Living on Earth*. World Media Foundation, 23 Sept. 2011. Web. 1 Feb. 2014.

Knowlton, Nancy. Interview by Beth Py-Lieberman. "Nancy Knowlton: The Renowned Coral Reef Biologist Leads Smithsonian's Effort to Foster a Greater Public Understanding of the World's Oceans." *Smithsonian*. Smithsonian, 1 Sept. 2008. Web. 29 Jan. 2014.

Knowlton, Nancy. Interview. "Q & A: Nancy Knowlton." *Current Biology* 26 Apr. 2011. Web. 1 Feb. 2014.

Knowlton, Nancy. Interview by Margaret Wertheim. "The Reef Builders: An Interview with Nancy Knowlton." *Cabinet*. Cabinet Magazine, 2008. Web. 29 Jan. 2014.

—*Molly Hagan*

Francis Specker/Landov

Kendrick Lamar

Born: June 17, 1987
Occupation: Rapper

In a June 25, 2014, *New York Times* profile, journalist Lizzy Goodman described Kendrick Lamar as a "future king" of hip-hop. In 2012, Lamar's major-label debut, *Good Kid, M.A.A.D City* (styled *good kid, m.A.A.d. city* or *GKMC* for short), sold more than 1.2 million copies and was nominated for four Grammy Awards. (He was nominated for a total of seven Grammys that year, though, controversially, took home none.) "His lyrical style and his background"—Lamar was born and raised in Compton, California, the West Coast mecca of hip-hop—"have shaped his reputation as the kind of old-school rapper you don't see much anymore, a street poet who has earned the affection of hip-hop purists as well as younger listeners," Goodman wrote. On one hand, Lamar, who is only twenty-seven, cuts a monastic figure for a celebrity. He does not smoke or drink and often works through the night after performances. Producer Pharrell Williams compared his skill and drive to that of iconic singer-songwriter Bob Dylan. "You can just see the kid's mind like a kaleidoscope over a beat," he told Goodman, and the flattering comparisons do not end there. More than one journalist has likened Lamar's debut album to the James Joyce classic *Ulysses*.

On the other hand, Goodman points out, Lamar's abstinence has more to do with his singularity of purpose than spirituality. Lamar is outspoken about his own ambitions, his formidable talent, and what he sees as the lamentably "soft" state of current hip-hop acts. "If my edge is dull, my sword is dull, and I don't want to fight another guy whose sword is dull. . . . Everybody that's in the industry has lost their edge," he told Goodman. In a famous 2013 guest verse for the single "Control" by rapper Big Sean, Lamar places himself in the company of Jay-Z, Nas, Eminem, and Andre 3000 of Outkast as one of the best MCs of all time. "There's a certain hunger that you can sense about Kendrick," Eminem told Goodman. "He raps to be the best rapper in the world. He competitive-raps. That's one of the things that's going to drive his career. He's going to be around for a long time."

EARLY LIFE AND EDUCATION

Kendrick Lamar Duckworth was born on June 17, 1987, in Compton, California. His parents, who are originally from Chicago, moved to Compton in 1984 with only five hundred dollars. His mother has fourteen siblings and his father has ten, and Lamar's parents paved the way for the whole family to move to Compton in the late 1980s and early 1990s. It was the era of crack cocaine in cities across the United States, and Compton was turning into a war zone. Family members ran drugs out of the projects apartment building where the family lived. When Lamar was five years old, he witnessed the murder of one of his uncles. "Everybody that I touched physically," Lamar told Goodman, "they ended up dead or in jail." Some of his earliest memories are of the 1992 Los Angeles riots. There was violence, Lamar has said of his childhood, but there were also holidays and birthdays, "which allowed me to actually be a kid," he told Grammy Award–winning singer-songwriter Erykah Badu, who interviewed Lamar for *Interview* magazine (9 May 2013). Gang life offered some protection—as well as a sense of power, he told Goodman, and "the sense of being wanted or being needed"—but Lamar was uninterested in leading such a life. He described himself to Badu as a "dreamer." Still, he was fired from the only job he held before his career took off. He was working as a security guard at a truck stop, but his boss thought Lamar and his friends were planning to "cause trouble," Goodman wrote.

Like a lot of poets, Lamar showed an early appreciation for words—though he confided to Goodman that he once had a stutter. "My first-grade teacher flipped out because I wrote the word 'audacity' in a story," he told Insanul Ahmed for *Complex* (1 Aug. 2014). "I knew the word only because I heard my auntie and uncles arguing, saying, 'You got the audacity to take my motherf——ing drink and pour it out?!' I learned all my words like that, so when I went to school it was in my head." Lamar was a good student who, unsurprisingly, loved studying English and poetry. He started rapping young and studied hip-hop culture with an academic zeal. He idolized Jay-Z, Nas, Notorious B.I.G., and Tupac Shakur. By his own account, he spent more time listening to records than writing. It was valuable training for his ear, he told Badu, but consequently, it took him awhile to find his own voice as a rapper. According to Dave Free, Lamar's manager and childhood friend, by the time the rapper was a student at Compton's Centennial High School, "nobody wanted to rap with him," he told Goodman. It seemed clear to the people around him that Lamar was destined for greater things.

TOP DAWG ENTERTAINMENT

Lamar met a manager named Anthony "Top Dawg" Triffith when he was still in high school and released his first mixtape in 2003 under the name K-Dot when he was sixteen. Eventually, Triffith launched Top Dawg Entertainment with Lamar—who quickly dropped the K-Dot moniker—as his top act. Lamar released *Kendrick Lamar EP* in 2009 and a digital-only mixtape, *Overly Dedicated* (also known as *O(verly) D(edicated)* or *O.D.*), which appeared on the Billboard R & B/hip-hop chart, in the fall of 2010. Sasha Frere-Jones of the *New Yorker* (29 Oct. 2012) later wrote of the *Overly Dedicated* mixtape that Lamar already "sounded preternaturally well rounded and professional."

Top Dawg released Lamar's first independent album, *Section.80*, in 2011. Shortly after that, he signed with Aftermath, Dr. Dre's Interscope Records imprint. It was an especially meaningful moment for Lamar; not only is Dre a Compton celebrity, but when Lamar was nine years old, he saw Dre and Tupac filming the second "California Love" video in the city. "My pops had seen him and ran back to the house and got me, put me on his neck, and we stood there watching Dre and Pac in a Bentley," he told Badu. "I'll never forget this moment—it was probably about a year and some change before Pac died." When he met with Dre for the first time fifteen years later, Lamar recalled to Badu, he could not get the scene out of his head.

GOOD KID, M.A.A.D CITY (2012)

Lamar was meticulous about his major-label debut, *Good Kid, M.A.A.D City*, which was released in 2012. He recorded sixty or seventy songs, which he later whittled down to a lean fifteen. Notably, Lamar did not recruit major names to carry his debut—though the album features Dre and Drake—and he did not overtly market himself on social media. Still, the album sold 242,122 copies during its first week—the best-selling debut for a male artist that year. The album's title refers to Compton, which he told Rebecca Haithcoat for *LA Weekly* (20 Jan. 2011), is his "mad city." The record is structured as a day in the life of a seventeen-year-old artist, who reckons with friends, enemies, and the streets of Compton while pursuing a girl named Sherane. Recordings and voicemails from Lamar's parents, with whom he is close, provide interludes throughout the record. Lamar plays on a lot of familiar hip-hop tropes, but his perspective is more meta. In "The Art of Peer Pressure," Lamar deflates a classic gangsta rap image. "Look at me," he raps with almost sarcastic bravado, "I got the blunt in my mouth." Badu wrote that Lamar recognizes the tension between the reality and "mythology" of Compton in real time. She quotes a verse from the song "Compton": "Harsh realities we in made our music translate / To the coke dealers, the hood rich, and the broke n——s that play . . . Roll that kush, crack that case, ten bottles of rosé / This was brought to you by Dre . . . In the city of Compton / Ain't no city quite like mine." Lamar has always seen himself as more of an "observer," he told Goodman. His verses, Frere-Jones wrote, are "reportage rather than confession," and sometimes that reportage takes on an astonishing empathy for its characters.

Critical reception for the record was unanimously positive and unusually rich. Ahmed called it "a landmark event, a modern masterpiece." Jon Caramanica for the *New York Times* (28 Oct. 2013) wrote that the album required "ways of listening that went out with the Clinton presidency or with the advent of the seven-inch single. There are almost no obvious entry points, nothing bite-size to latch onto." Lamar's raps are lyrically dense, but critics say that (much like Joyce's prose) there are rewards in that depth. Words often come fast and furious to Lamar, lending the impression of having so much to say and not enough time to say it. "I put my energy into making music," he told Goodman, "That's how I get my thoughts out, instead of being crazy all the time." The album is a vivid portrait of a city—Lamar pointedly features Compton legend MC Eiht on the track "m.A.A.d. city"—but Ta-Nehisi Coates argued in a piece for the *New York Times* (6 Feb. 2013) that Lamar's vision of Compton carries a troubling universality for cities across the United States. "Hip-hop originates in communities where such hazards are taken as given. Rappers generally depict themselves as masters, not victims, of the attending violence," he wrote. "'Good Kid' is narrative told from behind the mask. Fantasies of rage and lust are present, but fear pervades Lamar's world. He pitches himself not as 'Compton's Most Wanted' but as 'Compton's Human Sacrifice.' He loves the city, even as he acknowledges that the city is trying to kill him."

ACCOLADES AND CONTROVERSIES

In 2013, Lamar was nominated for seven Grammy Awards, including album of the year and best new artist, but he went home empty-handed. Macklemore, a white rapper, swept the hip-hop categories that year, taking home best new artist, best rap album, best rap song, and best rap performance. (Daft Punk's *Random Access Memories* won album of the year.) "For fans on Twitter and members of the media (including *Complex*), Macklemore's wins and Kendrick's snubs served as a watershed moment for cultural appropriation in rap," Ahmed wrote. Even Macklemore was uncomfortable with the outcome and sent a text message of apology to Lamar that read in part, "I robbed you." Macklemore took a picture of the text before he sent it and posted it to his Instagram account, adding more fuel to the media maelstrom. Months later, Lamar told Ahmed, "It wasn't really a huge deal for me. Macklemore deserves the accolades. That's still my partner regardless. He probably didn't need to Instagram the text. But what's done is done."

The Grammy snub seemed to matter less to hardcore fans than the "Control" verse earlier that year, when Lamar threw down the proverbial gauntlet in a song by Big Sean. In the one-upmanship culture of rap, Lamar called out popular rappers—including Big Sean and Drake, who appear on *GKMC*—and crowned himself "the king of New York." (Lamar is from the West Coast. The phrase was intentionally provocative.) The guest spot was big music news in the summer of 2013. The hip-hop magazine *XXL*, Goodman wrote, went as far as to call it "the verse that woke up the rap game."

In late 2013, *GQ* named Lamar their rapper of the year, but the accompanying article—written by Steve Marsh and published in the magazine's December issue—though positive, was tone-deaf. The write-up miffed Lamar's label boss and led him to make a public statement. Triffith took issue with the article's racial overtones—Marsh relied on hazy stereotypes of black rappers to illustrate Lamar's character—and its focus on hip-hop's violent past. Marsh rightly noted that Lamar deconstructs rap clichés, and, as Spencer Kornhaber wrote for the *Atlantic* (18 Nov. 2013), "that's why it's all the more frustrating to see [Marsh] lean on those clichés."

FUTURE PROJECTS AND PERSONAL LIFE

In 2014, Lamar opened for Kanye West on a leg of his Yeezus tour. The partnership, which was initiated by West himself at the 2013 MTV Video Music Awards, is indicative of Lamar's artistic ascendency. As of fall 2014, Lamar was feeling the pressure to produce a worthy follow-up record. "Kendrick shook up the rap game, so anticipation for his second offering is through the roof," Nas told Ahmed. "Kendrick's an album guy and the album artist has a whole different kind of value. Kendrick is going to be one of the most important writers of our time; dude's a rhyming animal." Manager Free, meanwhile, takes a different tack. He insists that, in terms of stories to tell, Lamar has barely scratched the surface. "There's still so much to be said," Free told Ahmed. "The question is, is he gonna say it?" According to Ahmed, Lamar has already recorded thirty to forty new songs for his next album.

Lamar has a longtime girlfriend named Whitney Alford. As for his home base, he told Badu that he lives on his tour bus. When he is not on tour, he added, he lives in the studio.

SUGGESTED READING

Ahmed, Insanul. "Turn the Page." *Complex*. Complex Media, 1 Aug. 2014. Web. 14 Sept. 2014.

Badu, Erykah. "Kendrick Lamar." *Interview*. Interview, 9 May 2013. Web. 14 Sept. 2014.

Coates, Ta-Nehisi. "Hip-Hop Speaks to the Guns." *New York Times*. New York Times, 6 Feb. 2013. Web. 14 Sept. 2014.

Frere-Jones, Sasha. "California King." *New Yorker*. Condé Nast, 29 Oct. 2012. Web. 14 Sept. 2014.

Goodman, Lizzy. "Kendrick Lamar, Hip-Hop's Newest Old-School Star." *New York Times*. New York Times, 25 June 2014. Web. 14 Sept. 2014.

Kornhaber, Spencer. "Kendrick Lamar Has a Right to Be Mad at *GQ*." *Atlantic*. Atlantic Monthly Group, 18 Nov. 2013. Web. 14 Sept. 2014.

Marsh, Steve. "Kendrick Lamar: Rapper of the Year." *GQ*. Condé Nast, 1 Dec. 2013. Web. 14 Sept. 2014.

—*Molly Hagan*

Eric Lander

Born: February 3, 1957
Occupation: Mathematician and geneticist behind the Human Genome Project and the Broad Institute

Eric Lander is a professor of biology at the Massachusetts Institute of Technology (MIT) and a professor of systems biology at Harvard Medical School, though he is perhaps best known as one of the principal leaders of the Human Genome Project. Lander is the founding director of the Broad (rhymes with "code") Institute, a research institution that studies genetics and applies the fruits of the successful Human Genome Project, completed in 2003, to medical research and other areas of discovery. In 2009, President Barack Obama appointed Lander cochair of the President's Council of Advisors on Science and Technology.

Lander earned his doctorate in pure mathematics but left that solitary and exclusive world behind to head what Gina Kolata for the *New York Times* (3 Jan. 2012) calls a "biology empire." This is unusual considering that Lander never studied biology; he simply saw the field's enormous potential for progress and, after fortuitously meeting a biologist with a statistics problem,

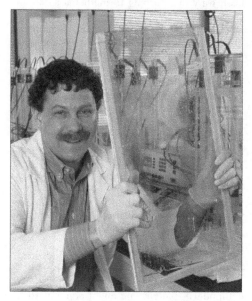

© Roger Ressmeyer/Corbis

realized that he had unique skills to contribute to that progress. "He was super smart, but so what?" Paul Zeitz, a childhood friend of Lander who teaches mathematics at the University of San Francisco, told Kolata. "Pure intellectual heft is like someone who can bench-press a thousand pounds. But so what, if you don't know what to do with it?"

A former Rhodes Scholar, Lander was awarded the MacArthur Foundation's "genius" grant in 1987 at the age of thirty. He has also received the Max Delbrück Medal (2001), the Canada Gairdner International Award (2002), the AAAS Award for Public Understanding of Science and Technology (2004), the Albany Medical Center Prize in Medicine and Biomedical Research (2009), and the New York Academy of Medicine Medal for Distinguished Contributions in Biomedical Science (2009). Lander is an elected member of the US National Academy of Sciences, the US Institute of Medicine, and the American Academy of Arts and Sciences.

EARLY LIFE AND EDUCATION

Eric Steven Lander was born on February 3, 1957, and was raised in the working-class Flatlands neighborhood of Brooklyn, New York. His parents were both lawyers. His father, Harold, died of multiple sclerosis when Lander was eleven. After that, Lander and his younger brother, Arthur, were raised by their mother, Rhoda. As children, the two boys had divergent interests: Arthur loved music, and Eric loved math and numbers. Lander aced the entrance exam to Manhattan's prestigious Stuyvesant High School, an elite high school focused on mathematics and science, and enrolled his freshman year. He joined the math team and quickly became its captain.

There is a stereotype, particularly among high school students, that people who excel at math are quiet and shy, but Lander was neither. He was popular among his classmates for his friendly and outgoing attitude. "Forty kids considered him their best friend," Lander's former teammate Francis Barany, a microbiology professor at Cornell University, told Aaron Zitner for the *Boston Globe* (10 Oct. 1999). "That's how inclusively he was in treating people."

ACHIEVEMENTS IN MATHEMATICS

Lander spent several summers studying and later teaching at a math camp at Hampshire College in Amherst, Massachusetts, where talented high school students spent full days working math problems. During his senior year of high school, Lander earned the second-highest score on a nationwide math test and landed a spot on the United States' team for the 1974 Mathematics Olympiad.

The Olympiad began as a competition among the countries within the Soviet bloc, and 1974 was the first year in which the United States participated in the contest. Lander and the team spent a summer preparing at Rutgers University in New Jersey and ultimately placed second, after the Soviet Union. Lander graduated from Stuyvesant in 1974 with the highest grades in his class. The same year he won the Westinghouse Science Talent Search prize for a paper he wrote on "quasi-perfect" numbers.

After high school, Lander enrolled in Princeton University to study mathematics. He also took a course in creative nonfiction writing from the author John McPhee, one of the biggest names in the then-budding genre, and wrote for the school newspaper. Lander graduated as the valedictorian of his class in 1978 and was awarded the prestigious M. Taylor Pyne Prize for academic excellence and community service. He then earned a Rhodes Scholarship to study pure mathematics at Oxford University in England, where he completed his PhD in two years. His doctoral thesis, *Symmetric Designs: An Algebraic Approach*, remains a widely read text in the field.

EARLY CAREER

Despite Lander's interest and talent in mathematics, he began to have some misgivings about his chosen career path. "I began to appreciate that the career of mathematics is rather monastic," he told Kolata. "Even though mathematics was beautiful and I loved it, I wasn't a very good monk." After earning his PhD, Lander took a job that he felt better utilized his people skills: assistant and later associate professor of managerial economics at the Harvard Business School. At age twenty-four, he was scarcely older than his students, and he learned the course material as he went along. The job satisfied his desire to interact, but intellectually, it was less fulfilling. Unsure of his next step, he talked to his brother, a neurobiologist, who sent him some mathematical models of the brain. Lander was intrigued—though he told Kolata that he though the models were "hokey"—and began spending time at Harvard's fruit fly genetics laboratory.

A few years later, while taking a leave of absence from Harvard under the pretense of studying artificial intelligence, Lander ended up at the MIT worm genetics laboratory of Robert Horvitz, who would later win the Nobel Prize in physiology or medicine in 2002. Horvitz served as the intermediary to a more significant relationship in Lander's professional life; it was at Horvitz's lab that Lander met MIT geneticist David Botstein in 1985.

EARLY WORK WITH HUMAN GENETICS

For several years, Botstein and his colleagues had been working on a proposed method to map the human genome using restriction fragment length polymorphisms (RFLPs), or pieces of DNA "that have been sliced apart by restriction enzymes," as Bill Snyder explained in an article for Vanderbilt Medical Center's *Lens* magazine (Feb. 2007). After a group of researchers noticed that a specific RFLP is a different length in people with sickle-cell anemia than it is for people without the disease, Botstein posited that such slivers of information might make it possible to map the entire human genome.

It is unusual for a disease to correspond to one and only one faulty gene as in the case of sickle-cell anemia, however. Most diseases—and traits in general—are the result of a complex association of many genes. Biologist Richard Dawkins has a famous, and helpful, visual metaphor for this phenomenon. "Imagine a bed sheet hanging by rubber bands from 1,000 hooks in the ceiling," he wrote for the *London Evening Standard* (3 Apr. 2000). Rather than hanging neat and straight, the rubber bands "form an intricate tangle above the roughly horizontal sheet," which, in the case of the metaphor, represents the body. If cutting one rubber band were akin to a genetic mutation, the change in tension would not simply affect one part of the sheet—it would affect the tangle "and therefore the shape of the whole sheet."

Botstein wanted to understand the role that genes play in different diseases, which is, essentially, a statistics problem. "It became clear that what was needed was somebody to think about this problem who had mathematical tools beyond what I knew," Botstein told Snyder. Within a week of meeting each other, Lander and Botstein had outlined something resembling a solution to Botstein's problem. Lander had initially been wary of returning to mathematics in any capacity, but he was more than pleased with the partnership. "I got excited about it," Lander told Zitner, "and I entered human genetics and never looked back."

WHITEHEAD INSTITUTE

Lander left Harvard Business School in 1986 and moved to MIT, where he was awarded a fellowship at the Whitehead Institute for Biomedical Research. He also became an assistant and later full professor of biology at the university. The same year, at a meeting at Cold Spring Harbor Laboratory on Long Island, scientists held the first public debate about the possibility of sequencing the human genome. Lander was present—and talkative—at the meeting and was welcomed into the ranks of leading geneticists.

In 1987, Lander was awarded the prestigious MacArthur "genius" grant for his application of statistics to the field. Lander's statistical models—paired, one might argue, with his business acumen—were revolutionary because they allowed geneticists to "read" many genes simultaneously. "Lander has also become a kind of Henry Ford of genome research, pioneering some of the production-line technology that has made it possible to read the chemical sequence of DNA more quickly," Zitner wrote. "Where geneticists were once like safari hunters, bush-whacking for long distances to track an individual disease gene, they can now search more DNA more rapidly and at a lower cost."

HUMAN GENOME PROJECT

In 1990, the National Institutes of Health (NIH) and the Department of Energy launched the Human Genome Project (HGP), which endeavored to sequence the three billion bits of information encoded in every human cell. Lander received one of the project's first grants and became the founding director of the Whitehead/MIT Center for Genome Research. The institute became the flagship of the billion-dollar international project, with Lander as one of its principal leaders.

Every human being is different, but human genomes are 99.9 percent identical. The project aimed to create a resource map using pieces of the DNA of a number of different people. "The best analogy is to a GPS in a car," Eric Green, the director of the National Human Genome Research Institute, told Kolata for the New York Times (16 Apr. 2013). "It is nice to have a highway map, but you really want to know where is the shopping center, where is the gas station, the next park, a restaurant. We want to know where are the genes, the parts of the genome that code for proteins. Where are the places on the genome that people tend to vary? Where are the genes that code for diseases?"

In 1998, Lander and his team reassessed the timeframe of their mission after NIH scientist Craig Venter and his company, Celera, announced that they would sequence the human genome by 2001. The Human Genome Project was sequencing one "clone," or individual piece of DNA, at a time. This technique had been successful in sequencing the genome of the roundworm some years earlier. But Celera offered a different approach. Venter and his team used a process called "shotgun" sequencing, in which DNA is cut into smaller, random pieces. The latter takes less time to assemble, but it is also less accurate than the approach employed by the Human Genome Project. Nevertheless, with Celera closing in on the finish line, Lander and his team doubled down.

RESULTS OF THE HUMAN GENOME PROJECT

In June 2000, both Celera and the Human Genome Project announced rough drafts of the sequence; in the language of the race between them, the successful endeavor resulted in a tie. The final sequence was declared complete by HGP in April 2003, but there was still much work to be done. Sequencing the genome and understanding the genome are two very different things. The progress predicted by President Bill Clinton in 2000—he said that the information would revolutionize the treatment and diagnosis of disease within the next fifteen to twenty years—has been slower than expected. By the tenth anniversary of the sequencing of the human genome, medicine had changed little, but science had made enormous strides. In 2013, a person could have his or her genome sequenced for around $5,000 (scientists have been aiming for $1,000), and scientists could analyze the DNA of unborn children.

Most notably, the project has made possible new cancer treatments, a step in the direction toward a cure. As with any new product, these services have come at a significant cost—projected upward of $100,000, according to Kolata for the New York Times (4 Nov. 2013)—spurring a debate about income inequality and the cost of medical treatment. Other questions, both ethical and political, have arisen as well. An exhibition at the Smithsonian called Genome: Unlocking Life's Code (June 2013–Sept. 2014), has posed some of these questions to museumgoers. As reported by Edward Rothstein for the New York Times (30 Aug. 2013), the US Supreme Court ruled in June 2013 that human genes cannot be patented, alleviating the concerns of many. However, research into the human genome has continued to raise questions about insurability and personal choice, among other areas of concern.

BROAD INSTITUTE

Lander met Eli Broad in October 2001, when Broad paid a visit to the Whitehead Institute/MIT Center for Genome Research. Broad is the founder of two Fortune 500 companies (Kaufman and Broad, SunAmerica), and he and his wife Edythe have given generously to the arts and education. The Broads were impressed by Lander and his interest in medical research. In 2003, they gave Lander and his team an initial $100 million to establish the Broad Institute of MIT and Harvard, of which Whitehead was the cornerstone. In 2008, the Broad Institute became an independent research institution, and Lander, by this time a professor of systems biology at Harvard Medical School, left his leadership job at Whitehead to direct it.

Since the Human Genome Project, Lander and his colleagues have been finding new ways to implement genetic information. "Think of it this way," Lander told Hilary Parker for the Princeton Alumni Weekly (28 Jan. 2009), "all life on this planet contains in its genomes the record of 3.5 billion years of evolution, the lab notebooks of evolution's experiments, information about exposure to different infectious diseases, and so much more. It's as if life has been keeping notes in its genomes on all these topics for 3.5 billion years, and this is the generation that finally gets to read these lab notebooks."

Hundreds of scientists associated with the Broad Institute work on more than a dozen projects at any one time, but they are particularly interested in how genetic sequencing can be used to cure diseases such as cancer. They have focused on the genetic changes and mutations that occur in different forms of cancer, with the ultimate hope that if doctors know more about each specific disease, they can devise better treatments. Their work contributes to the larger Cancer Genome Atlas Project, which Lander helped found. Like the Human Genome Project, the Cancer Genome Atlas Project will take years of work, but Lander has been optimistic. "It's faith," Lander told Snyder, "a confidence that the way to change the world is to get information and tools into the hands of as many people as rapidly as possible."

PERSONAL LIFE

Outside of the lab, Lander is an avid traveler, reader, and theatergoer. He met his wife, Lori, an artist, in a constitutional law class during his sophomore year at Princeton. The couple married in 1981 and have three children: Jessica, Daniel, and David. In 1999, the Landers bought the former Fayerweather Street School in Cambridge, Massachusetts, and converted it into a modern living space. To the endless fascination of their friends, the Lander children used to attend the school before it became their house. After renovations, it would be difficult for anyone to tell that the family's home used to be an old schoolhouse if it were not for the original gymnasium on the third floor.

SUGGESTED READING

Dawkins, Richard. "How Do You Wear Your Genes?" *London Evening Standard*. Evening Standard, 3 Apr. 2000. Web. 3 Dec. 2013.

Green, Eric D. "Human Genome, Then and Now." Interview by Gina Kolata. *New York Times* 16 Apr. 2013: D3. Print.

Kolata, Gina. "Power in Numbers." *New York Times* 3 Jan. 2012: D1. Print.

Rothstein, Edward. "The ABC's of Your DNA." Rev. of *Genome: Unlocking Life's Code* at Smithsonian Natural History Museum. *New York Times* 30 Aug. 2013: C17. Print.

Snyder, Bill. "Eric Lander: The Great Amplifier." *Lens*. Vanderbilt Medical Center, Feb. 2007. Web. 3 Dec. 2013.

Zitner, Aaron. "The DNA Detective." *Boston Globe Sunday Magazine* 10 Oct. 1999: 17. Print.

—*Molly Hagan*

Yair Lapid

Born: November 5, 1963
Occupation: Politician and celebrity

When journalist Yair Lapid announced that he was running for a seat in the Knesset, Israel's 120-seat parliamentary body, reactions were mixed. Some saw him as a valuable addition to a political system that was bloated, stagnant, and beholden to special interests. Characterizing Lapid as "a charismatic figure and a gifted speaker," Jonathan Rosen wrote in an op-ed for the *Jerusalem Post* (9 Jan. 2012) that "for years, he has weighed in on a broad spectrum of issues that concern all Israeli citizens. . . . [His] appearance on the political scene is a welcome development that has the potential to produce real change." Some, however, considered him a rank dilettante and pointed out that many of his ilk had entered Israeli politics aiming to make a difference but ultimately accomplishing little. Making reference to the fact that Lapid's father, Yosef "Tommy" Lapid, was also a journalist turned politician, Liel Leibovitz wrote in an opinion piece for *Tablet Magazine* (11 Jan. 2012), "Israeli voters are constantly on the lookout for a savior to redeem them from the doldrums of an ossified political system. . . . [The political party Tzomet's] disgruntled voters looked elsewhere for hope,

David Vaaknin/Pool/EPA/Landov

and, in 2003, gave fifteen mandates to Shinui, an anti-religious party led by TV pundit Yosef Lapid, making it the third largest party in the Knesset. By 2008, Shinui, too, was defunct." He continued, "Most likely, [the younger Lapid's] new party will fizzle away just like his father's—and every other recent overnight political sensation."

It remains to be seen which view is correct. In January 2013 the party Lapid founded, Yesh Atid (There Is a Future), became the second largest in the Knesset by winning nineteen seats, and Lapid subsequently joined Prime Minister Benjamin Netanyahu in forming a coalition government, taking the position of finance minister. Soon after his ascension to that position, the editors of *Time* magazine included him in their list of the world's hundred most influential figures that year. Similarly the editors of the *Jerusalem Post* placed him in the number-one spot on their own list of the fifty most influential Jews in the world. Announcing that decision, Gil Hoffman wrote on May 14, 2013, "To go from not on the list to No. 1 in a year is not easy. But in just a year, Lapid, forty-nine, has rocketed his way to the top of the Israeli consciousness."

EARLY YEARS AND EDUCATION

Yair Lapid was born on November 5, 1963, in Tel Aviv, Israel. His mother, Shulamit, is a popular author of short stories, novels, and plays. Lapid's father, Yosef, generally known by the name Tommy, had immigrated to Israel from Hungary with his mother after World War II. (Tommy's father and many of his other relatives had been killed in the Holocaust, and mother and son managed to escape a Nazi roundup only by hiding in an outhouse.) Tommy, whose nickname derives from his original Hungarian name, Tomislav, found work at the daily Hebrew-language newspaper *Ma'ariv*, which Shulamit's father, David Giladi, had helped found. Because Tommy—who would later in life found the secular, anticlerical political party known as Shinui (which means "change")—worked as a foreign correspondent, Lapid spent a portion of his youth in England.

Lapid had two sisters, Merav, who is a psychologist, and Michal, who died in 1984. Writing for the Israeli newspaper *Haaretz* (23 Jan. 2012), Asher Schechter described Lapid as "'a prince,' meaning someone who came from a well-to-do background, went to preppy schools and was destined for great things, given his family's connections and Israel's penchant for nepotism." Despite his relatively privileged upbringing, however, Lapid's youth was far from problem free. He struggled with learning disabilities during a time when such disabilities were not well understood and generally went undiagnosed, and as a result he did not complete his high school education. That lack of academic credentials later caused a flurry of negative attention when it was reported that he had been admitted to a graduate program at Bar-Ilan University based on his professional experience. Although the practice was not unheard of in Israel, in the wake of Lapid's high-profile case, the country's Council for Higher Education called for a ban, and he was barred from pursuing an advanced degree without a bachelor's.

MEDIA CAREER

Like all young Israelis, both male and female, Lapid was required to serve in the Israeli Defense Forces. During that time he worked as a reporter for *Bamahane* (In the camp), the military's weekly magazine. Upon discharge he began writing for *Ma'ariv*, and in 1988 he was hired to edit the local newspaper *Iton Tel Aviv*. In 1991 he began penning a weekly column titled Where's the Money? for the *Ma'ariv* weekend supplement and later supplied the column to *Yedioth Aharonot*, where it became a popular Friday feature.

The title of Lapid's column later became his political slogan. As quoted by Isabel Kershner in the *New York Times* (22 Jan. 2013), he once wrote: "This is the big question asked by Israel's middle class, the same sector on whose behalf I am going into politics. Where's the money? Why is it that the productive sector, which pays taxes, fulfills its obligations, performs reserve duty, and carries the entire country on its back, doesn't see the money?"

In his columns, according to Rosen, Lapid sometimes addressed "the evolution of Israeli society into its current 'tribal' state, the dangers such tribalism poses, and the ways in which society must change if it wishes to survive." Schechter described his work in less lofty terms, asserting, "Lapid would often write about the things that interested him most: boxing, Raymond Chandler, the battle between the sexes, and scotch." (Lapid had been an avid amateur boxer, and detractors once tried to embarrass him by publicizing a video of him being trounced in the ring.)

In 1994 Lapid acted in the romantic comedy *Shirat Ha'Sirena* (Song of the siren), portraying a handsome but obnoxious bachelor. He also began appearing on television, hosting a series of talk shows and news programs that included *Sogrim Shavua* and *Yair Lapid Chai Be'Eser* (Yair Lapid live on ten). From 2000 to 2008 he hosted a highly rated eponymous show that aired during prime time on Channel 2, a major Israeli broadcast station. He became known during this period for closing guest interviews with the question, "What is Israeli in your eyes?" He had hit upon a winning formula. "It was then, during his eight-year tenure hosting the most-watched talk show in Israel, that Lapid became more than just a media personality and more than just a columnist," Schechter wrote. "On air, he was transformed into an icon." Despite the demands of his hosting duties, in 2005 he found time to write and appear in the television drama *Hadar Milhama* (War room).

In 2008 Lapid, who also appeared regularly in ads for Israel's largest financial institution, Bank Hapoalim, began hosting Channel 2's leading news show, *Ulpan Shishi* (Friday studio). While some critics felt that he lacked the journalistic credentials to head a serious news program, he remained in the post until 2012.

BOOKS

In addition to his other pursuits, Lapid has been a prolific author of books, many of which made the best-seller lists in Israel. Among them are the thrillers *Ha-Rosh Ha-Kaful* (The double head, 1989), *Hahida Hashishit* (The sixth riddle, 2001), *Haisha Hashnia* (The second woman, 2006), and *Sheki'ah be-Moskvah* (Sunset in Moscow, 2007). He has also published a collection of his newspaper columns and the occasional children's book. Lapid received the most attention for his 2010 book, *Memories after My Death: The Story of Joseph "Tommy" Lapid*, in which he channels the voice of his father, who died in 2008. While some reviewers were put off by the hybrid autobiography/biography format of the volume, others saw it as a loving tribute.

LAUNCHING A POLITICAL CAREER

Although media observers had long asserted that Lapid harbored political aspirations, he steadfastly denied that he was planning to seek office. So certain did that possibility seem, however, that a bill brought before the Knesset prohibiting journalists from working in media for several months before entering a political race was dubbed the Yair Lapid law. The bill, which was ultimately unsuccessful, reflected the belief that journalists have an unfair advantage because they can use the media to promote themselves during their campaigns.

Despite his prior denials, in January 2012 Lapid officially announced that he was leaving the field of journalism to enter politics. Not wanting to join any of Israel's many existing parties, in April of that year he registered his own, Yesh Atid. In addition to his ambitious schedule of in-person campaign stops, Lapid made ample use of social media—a move some said had been inspired by US president Barack Obama. Other American figures with whom he has been compared include actors-turned-politicians Ronald Reagan and Arnold Schwarzenegger.

In his platform Lapid called for an end to the automatic military exemptions for ultra-Orthodox students that are standard in Israel, better public education, and tax relief for Israel's struggling middle class. He also became the public

face of the so-called Cottage Cheese Revolution, which revolved around economic inequality; the dairy product was invoked because it is often served as part of Israeli breakfasts, and many saw its steadily rising price as a symbol of how hard everyday life could get for ordinary citizens.

On the hot-button issue of the Palestinians, Lapid asserted that he favored negotiations for a two-state solution while leaving the largest of the contentious West Bank settlements under Israeli control and maintaining an undivided Jerusalem. While his father's political party was strictly secular, Lapid told interviewers that he does believe in God, and Yesh Atid counts a few prominent rabbis among its members.

2013 ELECTION AND COALITION

Although most polls indicated that Lapid's party could expect to win about ten seats in the Knesset, when the polls closed on January 22, 2013, Yesh Atid had garnered nineteen seats, second only to the thirty-one seats granted to a group composed of the center-right Likud and the right-wing Yisrael Beytenu, led by Prime Minister Benjamin Netanyahu. That showing, as Kershner wrote, "position[ed] Mr. Lapid as the chief power broker in the formation of the next governing coalition." Pointing out that his base hailed mainly from cosmopolitan Tel Aviv and its bourgeois suburbs, Tamar Hermann, a political scientist, called Lapid "the epitome of the Israeli dream" and described his voters as "the mainstream of the mainstream," as quoted by Jodi Rudoren and Kershner for the *New York Times* (23 Jan. 2013).

In mid-March Lapid and Netanyahu formed a coalition government, and Lapid assumed the post of finance minister. The first months of his tenure were rocky. "As finance minister, Lapid, whose party was catapulted to a second place finish by capitalizing on middle class discontent, has had the unfortunate responsibility of paying the bills in a country where most people and their government live on credit," Jonathan S. Tobin wrote for *Commentary* magazine (20 May 2013). "Having taken on the job of running the economy, Lapid has assumed a post that breaks most politicians." Bringing up a point echoed almost universally by those covering Israeli politics, Tobin concluded that Lapid could very well become "a one-election wonder rather than challenging Netanyahu for prime minister the next time Israelis head to the polls."

In March 2014, the *Jerusalem Post* (1 Mar. 2014) reported that a public opinion poll conducted by Channel 2 News's *Meet the Press* to mark the anniversary of the government's induction showed that Lapid was one of the two least popular government ministers in Israel, tying for last place with Housing Minister Uri Ariel. In April 2014, as peace talks between Israel and the Palestinians broke down, Lapid warned that if the collapse was Prime Minister Netanyahu's responsibility, then Yesh Atid may leave the coalition government. He also said that he would prefer to freeze the growth of settlements in the West Bank over freeing Palestinian prisoners.

PERSONAL LIFE

Lapid's first marriage, to Tamar Friedman, produced one son, Yoav. He met his second wife, Lihi, after his divorce, while both were serving in the military. Lapid was so enamored of Lihi, who was then working as an IDF photographer, that he was inspired to write a pop song, "Gara BeSheinkin" (Living on Sheinkin Street), which was recorded by the band Mango and became a modest hit in the late 1980s. A journalist and novelist, Lihi is perhaps best known for her 2008 memoir-novel, *Eshet Chayil* (*Woman of Valor*, 2013). The Lapids have two children, a son and a daughter, and live in Tel Aviv.

SUGGESTED READING

Hoffman, Gil. "Yair Lapid: From off the List to Number 1." *Jerusalem Post*. Jerusalem Post, 14 May 2013. Web. 10 Mar. 2014.

Kershner, Isabel. "Charismatic Leader Helps Israel Turn toward the Center." *New York Times*. New York Times, 22 Jan. 2013. Web. 10 Mar. 2014.

Lapid, Yair. "Lally Weymouth Interviews Israeli Finance Minister Yair Lapid." Interview by Lally Weymouth. *Washington Post*. Washington Post, 20 June 2013. Web. 10 Mar. 2014.

Leibovitz, Liel. "Israel's Great White Hope." *Tablet Magazine*. Nextbook, 11 Jan. 2012. Web. 10 Mar. 2014.

Rosen, Jonathan. "Inside Out: Yair Lapid and the Potential for Change." *Jerusalem Post*. Jerusalem Post, 9 Jan. 2012. Web. 10 Mar. 2014.

Schechter, Asher. "Who Is Yair Lapid?" *Haaretz*. Haaretz Daily Newspaper, 23 Jan. 2012. Web. 10 Mar. 2014.

—*Mari Rich*

Risa Lavizzo-Mourey

Born: 1954
Occupation: President and CEO of the Robert Wood Johnson Foundation

In 2003 Risa Lavizzo-Mourey took over as CEO and president of the Robert Wood Johnson Foundation (RWJF), the United States' largest philanthropic health organization. The foundation, established in 1972, distributes about $400 million in grants and contracts annually and has an endowment of $9 billion. With her appointment, Lavizzo-

Bloomberg via Getty Images

Mourey became the first woman and the first African American to head the foundation.

Since taking the helm, Lavizzo-Mourey has focused on the needs of elderly patients, increased programs tackling obesity, and introduced measures to eliminate unequal treatment in health care due to ethnicity. Under Lavizzo-Mourey, the RWJF has remained committed to investing in projects aimed at key public health issues, including lowering tobacco, alcohol and illegal drug use; endorsing healthy lifestyles and communities; ensuring that people have access to quality, affordable health care; and improving end-of-life care.

EARLY LIFE

Risa Lavizzo-Mourey was born Risa Lavizzo in 1954 to Blanche and Philip V. Lavizzo. At the time of her birth, her parents were both residents at a hospital affiliated with Meharry Medical College, a historically African American institution. Lavizzo-Mourey's father became a surgeon, while her mother pursued a career in pediatrics.

The family relocated when Lavizzo-Mourey was two, after her father was offered a surgical residency at a public-health hospital in Seattle, Washington. Her mother had the distinction of being the state's first African American female pediatrician. She also served as the inaugural medical director of Seattle's Odessa Brown Children's Clinic, providing quality health care to the state's underserved and underprivileged population.

Lavizzo-Mourey credits her early love of medicine to the time she spent at her parents' joint medical practice. "I grew up with a lot of dinner table conversations about health care and ways in which the system was inadequate for the needs of many of the patients they took care of," she recalled to Dennis Nishi for the *Wall Street Journal* (30 July 2008). "I also grew up with a real appreciation about just how wonderful and intimate the relationship is between a doctor and a patient was and the sense that this was a noble profession."

FOLLOWING IN HER PARENTS' FOOTSTEPS
In 1968, after attending John Muir Elementary and Asa Mercer Junior High, Lavizzo-Mourey entered eighth grade at Helen Bush–Parkside, an all-girls school in Seattle. (The school became coeducational two years later, when it was renamed the Bush School.) By this time, Lavizzo-Mourey had already decided to become a physician. Upon completing high school in 1972, she attended the University of Washington for one year before transferring to the State University of New York (SUNY) at Stony Brook, where her boyfriend and future husband, Robert J. Mourey, was a graduate student in sociology.

In 1975, following her junior year at Stony Brook, Lavizzo-Mourey abandoned her undergraduate studies altogether to attend Harvard Medical School in Boston, Massachusetts. "I've been described as impatient," she joked to Peggy McGlone for the New Jersey *Star-Ledger* (6 Jan. 2013). That year she married Mourey, and the newlyweds both took on the last name Lavizzo-Mourey.

Lavizzo-Mourey's philanthropic interest was initially sparked while studying under Jack Geiger at Harvard. "He became one of the people that illustrated the connection for me between the broader fields of public health and the kind of health care and quality of life that people experience on a day-to-day basis, which really led to a shift in my thinking," Lavizzo-Mourey explained to Mitch Nauffts for the *Philanthropy News Digest* (31 May 2005). "It helped me to see the importance of being able to look at patient populations rather than only looking at the patient in front of me." After earning her medical degree in 1979, Lavizzo-Mourey pursued an internal medicine residency at Boston's Brigham and Women's Hospital, a teaching affiliate of Harvard Medical School.

FURTHER STUDIES AND EARLY CAREER
When Lavizzo-Mourey's residency ended in 1982, she and her husband moved to Philadelphia. She joined the staff at Temple University Medical School as a clinical instructor while studying business at the University of Pennsylvania's (Penn's) prestigious Wharton School. "Since I wanted to get a perspective on populations and analyzing the world in ways broader than the individual patient, I went to business school in health care administration," she recalled to Stephen Isaacs for the 2012 anthology *To Improve Health and Health Care, Volume XV*.

Following her two-year stint at Temple University, Lavizzo-Mourey conducted graduate-level research as a Robert Wood Johnson Clinical Scholar, specializing in geriatric medicine. Also in 1984, she was appointed director of Penn's Institute on Aging. "Given an interest in health policy and the importance of Medicare in setting a national agenda for health policy, it made perfect sense to pursue geriatrics," she told Nishi. "And once I started working with older people, I realized how much I enjoyed the intellectual challenge of taking care of patients who have multiple, complex medical problems."

After receiving her MBA degree in 1986, Lavizzo-Mourey joined the faculty of Penn's School of Medicine as an assistant professor and was promoted to associate professor six years later. During this period she assumed the additional role of associate chief of staff for geriatrics and extended care at the Philadelphia Veterans Administration Medical Center.

Lavizzo-Mourey was granted a leave of absence from Penn in 1992, when she accepted a position in the George H. W. Bush administration as deputy director of the Agency for Health Care Policy and Research, later renamed the Agency for Healthcare Research and Quality. Under President Bill Clinton, Bush's successor, Lavizzo-Mourey joined the White House Task Force on Healthcare Reform, which was aimed at creating a national healthcare system. While in the nation's capital, she sat on the federal Task Force on Aging Research and was codirector of an Institutes of Medicine report that uncovered widespread inequities in health care among people of color.

ROBERT WOOD JOHNSON FOUNDATION
Lavizzo-Mourey returned to Penn in 1994 as an associate professor and director of the Institute on Aging. She also served as chief of geriatric medicine at Penn's medical school, where she was appointed Sylvan Eisman Professor of Medicine and Healthcare Systems in 1997. The following year she conducted house calls as part of a model team program designed to improve care for elderly patients in Philadelphia. In 2001 Lavizzo-Mourey resigned from Penn when Steven A. Schroeder, president and CEO of the New Jersey–based Robert Wood Johnson Foundation (RWJF), offered her the position of senior vice president and director of the foundation's Health Care Group.

At the end of 2002, Lavizzo-Mourey was tapped to succeed the retiring Schroeder at RWJF. "I'd already been at the foundation for a little over a year . . . so I had a good understanding of the organization and its many strengths, as well as some of the potential opportunities," she told Nauffts. "And that familiarity, both with the programs and with the foundation's incredibly passionate and dedicated staff and grantees, really made the transition for me easier than it might have been for someone joining the foundation from the outside." When Lavizzo-Mourey officially assumed her new post in January 2003, she became the fourth president in the foundation's history.

RWJF PRESIDENT

One of Lavizzo-Mourey's first measures involved developing a blueprint that accurately conveyed the beliefs driving the organization. "When I stepped into Steve's shoes, we were in a period of redefining ourselves. We had the Core Values document, but it was not as accessible as it should have been," she told Isaacs. "We had small groups examine the language, and then we had an active discussion throughout the Foundation. The result was our Guiding Principles, a document that represented what we aspired to do and how we aspired to conduct ourselves."

The Guiding Principles emphasized that the foundation would safeguard the private resources received by RWJF and use them for the common good, collaborate with other organizations to achieve its mission, and insist on clear standards for interactions with partners that reinforce the organization's commitment to fairness, transparency, and open communication. The document also underscored the staff's professional and moral standards as well as the foundation's continuous dedication to bettering itself.

GOALS AND STRATEGIES

Lavizzo-Mourey's agenda also involved spearheading a reassessment of the foundation's priorities. "We've always been focused on measuring what we do and having an impact on important health-related issues. So, in that spirit, as I prepared to move into my new role, I asked our grantees as well as experts in the field to send me a short essay . . . about our work," she told Nauffts. "What I learned from that exercise was that the foundation's grantmaking and the way we do our work was quite diverse and spoke to a variety of needs."

Within several months the RWJF had developed a framework identifying the various approaches that are integrated into the foundation's work. The foundation also restructured its grant-making process, creating four investment portfolios, or groups, that allowed them to pinpoint any potential collaborations among the areas they funded while deriving the maximum effect from each area.

While the Human Capital Portfolio supports identifying and fostering future health care leaders to serve as catalysts and creators of change, the Vulnerable Populations Portfolio seeks innovative solutions to health care issues that affect society's at-risk populations, especially those related to social factors such as poverty. Examples of the latter include CeaseFire, a public-health

program to reduce gun violence, and the Nurse-Family Partnership, which focuses on postnatal care for low-income mothers and newborns. The Pioneer Portfolio allocates a portion of the foundation's resources to innovative, surprising discoveries.

With the fourth group, the Targeted Portfolio, Lavizzo-Mourey aims to pinpoint a number of problem areas in which the foundation's resources could bring about the most change in a shorter period of time. In addition to health care coverage, an area of focus since the foundation's beginnings, the organization has dedicated itself to combating and treating addiction, lessening tobacco use and exposure, and fighting childhood obesity, among other initiatives.

CHILDHOOD OBESITY AND AFFORDABLE HEALTH CARE

Lavizzo-Mourey has made the overall well-being and physical health of children one of the RWJF's most critical issues. "About one-third of America's children are obese or overweight," she told Summer Faust for Associations Now magazine (Oct. 2010). "Unless we act quickly and collaboratively, those obese or overweight children will become obese or overweight adults . . . with shorter lifespans and serious chronic conditions, like hypertension and diabetes." To that end, in 2007 the foundation pledged to battle childhood obesity by investing $500 million over five years—its biggest investment to date.

In 2008 the RWJF, under its national Leadership for Healthy Communities program, organized a nationwide summit, assembling state and local leaders to discuss and promote policies that foster an active lifestyle and healthy eating in their communities. That December, Healthy Kids, Healthy Communities, another RWJF program aimed at reaching children who present the greatest risk for obesity, began to confer $33 million in grants to more than forty communities across the United States to fund local programs that would make affordable, healthy foods more accessible and also provide children with the opportunity to engage in physical activities. In December 2009 Lavizzo-Mourey testified before the US House Energy and Commerce Health Subcommittee, identifying ways to remove obstacles to healthy eating.

Following the Obama administration's passage of the Patient Protection and Affordable Care Act (2010), which provides for the expansion of national health care coverage, Lavizzo-Mourey has also been instrumental in helping to implement a reformed health care system modeled somewhat on the successes of Massachusetts, which had instituted a reformed system several years before. "What we are committed to doing at the Robert Wood Johnson Foundation is learning from Massachusetts, but then also expanding that learning to other states," she told *Knowledge@Wharton*, the Wharton School's online business journal (8 June 2011). "So, we're looking to fund states like Alabama and Colorado and New Mexico, Tennessee, Minnesota, Maine . . . which complement the kind of demographics, politics and leadership that Massachusetts has, so that at the end of the day, we have a broad-based understanding of how to actually improve health and health care in this country."

RECOGNITION AND PERSONAL LIFE

Lavizzo-Mourey was named one of *Forbes* magazine's 100 Most Powerful Women in 2008 and one of the 100 Most Powerful People in Healthcare for 2010 by the magazine *Modern Healthcare*. Despite her executive post, she continues to see patients at a community health clinic in New Brunswick, New Jersey. "What continues to energize me is the opportunity to address big problems in the area of health and health care, to make a difference on a large scale, and to touch people directly and change their lives," she told *Wharton Magazine* (2007).

Lavizzo-Mourey and her husband are parents to a daughter, Rel, and a son, Max. She is an avid hiker and also enjoys photography.

SUGGESTED READING

Faust, Summer. "Five Intriguing Association Leaders: Dr. Risa Lavizzo-Mourey." *Associations Now*. American Society of Association Executives, Oct. 2010. Web. 25 Sept. 2013.

McGlone, Peggy. "Robert Wood Johnson Foundation Chief Combines Drive, Dedication and a Warm Heart." *The Star-Ledger*. Advance Publications, 6 Jan. 2013. Web. 25 Sept. 2013.

Nauffts, Mitch. "Dr. Risa Lavizzo-Mourey, President/CEO, Robert Wood Johnson Foundation: Philanthropy in the Service of a Healthier America." *Philanthropy News Digest*. Foundation Center, 31 May 2005. Web. 25 Sept. 2013.

Nishi, Dennis. "Dr. Risa Lavizzo-Mourey President and CEO, Robert Wood Johnson Foundation." *Wall Street Journal*. Dow Jones, 30 July 2008. Web. 25 Sept. 2013.

—*Bertha Muteba*

Libby Leffler

Born: January 29, 1985
Occupation: Internet executive

As strategic partner manager, Libby Leffler forges partnerships with various nonprofit organizations on behalf of the social media giant Facebook. "Facebook is all about sharing and connecting," Leffler told Beth Kanter, the

Johannes Simon/Getty Images

coauthor of *Measuring the Networked Nonprofit: Using Data to Change the World* (2012), for her blog (17 July 2012). "On Facebook, people connect with friends, family, their communities, and the issues and causes they care about most." Her job, she explained, is "to provide causes and nonprofits with the tools that they need to best utilize our open platform." Leffler's job brings together some of Facebook's newer features, such as the Facebook Live program and the company's Non-Profits on Facebook group. Before serving in her current position, Leffler worked as the "business lead" for Sheryl Sandberg, the chief operating officer (COO) of Facebook, for nearly three years. In that capacity, Leffler managed Sandberg's hectic schedule during the launch of her "Lean In" feminist empowerment campaign. Leffler considers Sandberg—named the ninth most powerful woman in the world by *Forbes* in 2014—her mentor. In 2014, *Forbes* named Leffler to its list of "30 under 30" business leaders.

EARLY LIFE AND EDUCATION

Leffler grew up in Modesto, California, where both of her parents, Duke and Paula, run PMZ Real Estate. She has two younger siblings, Duke Jr. and Hilary, and was raised in the Greek Orthodox Church. As a student at Modesto High School, Leffler participated in speech and debate and founded the school's first girl's golf team. She graduated in 2002, enrolling in the Berkeley Haas School of Business at the University of California. (Her parents, both Cal alumni, met at the university.) As a college student, Leffler managed to maintain near-perfect grades while balancing a hectic schedule. She was president of the Berkeley chapter of Tri Delta and also served as the sorority's national spokesperson during her sophomore and junior years. In 2005, she won the sorority's Sarah Ida Shaw Award for leadership. The same year, she won the title of Miss Stanislaus in her home county and went on to compete for the Miss California crown. In the talent portion of the beauty pageant, Leffler performed a monologue. In addition to her hours in class, in meetings, and at the gym, Leffler found time to mentor local elementary school students. "It has taken me a lot of time to develop the crucial skills of time management," she told the college prep website NextStepU. She graduated as an Alumni Leadership Scholar with a BS degree in business administration in 2006.

Leffler worked briefly as a consultant after graduation and, after months of interviews, she landed a job at Google in sales operations. Her official title was strategist, and she worked within an online sales and operations group that had previously been run by Sandberg. In September 2008, she interviewed for a job at Facebook. She was offered a sales job but turned it down. "I was afraid of taking the risk of leaving my comfortable job at a large, established company for something new and unfamiliar," she told Diane Anderson for *CalBusiness* (Fall 2011), the Haas School magazine. A few days later, Leffler changed her mind; she called the recruiter to find out if the position was still available and, finding that it was, accepted the position.

WORK FOR SANDBERG AND "LEAN IN"

Leffler worked in Facebook's inside sales team for eleven months, and in 2009, she was offered a job as Sandberg's business lead. Formerly Google's vice president for global online sales and operations, Sandberg became Facebook's COO in early 2008. Her decision was widely considered a risky one at the time. At Google, Sandberg managed more than four thousand employees, while Facebook was barely profitable. But the match proved successful. In a *New Yorker* profile of Sandberg (11 July 2011), Ken Auletta wrote that Sandberg's job description included overseeing advertising strategy, hiring and firing, management, and political issues—"that stuff that in other companies I might have to do," Facebook chief executive officer Mark Zuckerberg told Auletta. "And she's much better at that." As her business lead, Leffler was Sandberg's "invisible right hand," Matt Lynley wrote for *Business Insider* (29 June 2012), managing Sandberg's public appearances, speaking engagements, and various research projects. "Libby's work was just outstanding," Sandberg told Anderson of her decision to hire Leffler, adding that Leffler "stood out above all of the others."

Sandberg launched the Lean In campaign in 2010. With a TED talk and book called *Lean In: Women, Work, and the Will to Lead* (2013),

she encouraged working women to be more assertive in their careers. The movement, which connects its followers through Facebook groups, made Sandberg a hot commodity on the speaking circuit, which in turn, made Leffler's job quite demanding. The Lean In website invites successful women to share their "lean in" moment—the moment in their lives in which they decided to take control of their future. Writing for the Lean In website, Leffler explained that her "lean in" moment happened during her first week working for Sandberg, when she was asked to join her boss in a partner meeting "that included the CEO and COO of a major media organization." Leffler was nervous because she had not yet worked with Sandberg, but she dutifully set up her own meetings to learn everything she could about the media company with whom they were meeting. "I became an expert on the client's business model and devised several concepts for ways we could work together more effectively," Leffler wrote. "As I briefed Sheryl, she peppered me with tough questions that I tried my best to address."

On the day of the meeting, Leffler arrived at the conference room only to realize, as everyone began taking their seats, that there were not enough chairs at the conference table. Unsure of what to do, Leffler took a seat along the wall. After the meeting Sandberg asked Leffler why she did not find a seat at the table. When Leffler replied that there had not been room, Sandberg chided her saying, "that as her right-hand associate, I had already earned my seat. I realized that it was my responsibility not only to work alongside Sheryl for the many meetings we would take together over the next two and a half years but also to directly engage with our partners, build credibility, and earn their respect."

The episode echoes an anecdote that Sandberg's former coworker Marne Levine recalled to Auletta about Sandberg when she served as the chief of staff to Larry Summers, who was then serving as the deputy secretary of the US Treasury, in the mid-1990s. Summers's office had a large conference table with chairs as well as a seating area behind the table. "The more senior officials, usually men, would sit at the table," Levine told Auletta. "The more junior, several of whom were women, would sit in the seating area. Sheryl was always at the table," loudly encouraging the staffers to join the table, saying "We'll make room." The concept of "finding a seat at the table" is part of the larger bootstrap-feminism ethos of the Lean In campaign. Sandberg wants to see women take control of their careers, but her message of empowerment rests on the idea that the corporate workplace is a true meritocracy, which, her critics argue, is hardly the case.

In 2011, Leffler spoke at the DLDwomen Conference in Munich. (DLD stands for

Digital-Life-Design.) She talked about a concept called "gender fatigue," which, as she later explained to Meredith Lepore for the blog *Levo League* (23 July 2013), "is a phenomenon that suggests people assume gender issues 'no longer matter' because the problems have been solved—or, worse, that individuals lack the energy to tackle something that we no longer see or experience as an obstacle in our daily lives." Taking a page from her former boss's playbook, Leffler suggests reframing the gender problem as a business problem. She argues that diverse teams are more innovative and, as she told Lepore, citing a *Harvard Business Review* study, smarter.

STRATEGIC PARTNER MANAGER

After nearly three years of working for Sandberg, Leffler became the strategic partner manager for Facebook. In 2011 and 2012, she staffed the World Economic Forum in Davos, Switzerland. (The forum brings together state officials and private business owners to discuss world issues.) In 2012, she met Nobel Peace Prize–winner Leymah Gbowee, who led the women's peace movement in Liberia. The same year, Leffler facilitated an interview with Gbowee and Nicholas Kristof of the *New York Times* on Facebook Live, the social network's live-streaming program. The brainchild of Randi Zuckerberg, Facebook's former director of market development and CEO Zuckerberg's sister, Facebook Live was launched in 2010.

In 2011, Facebook launched its Nonprofit Resource Center, ostensibly with Leffler at its helm. The "center" is really a page ("Non-Profits on Facebook") on Facebook's site, but it includes a trove of valuable resources for organizations and charities looking to use Facebook to their best advantage. A how-to guide walks users through creating a page and using discussion boards, while a more in-depth guide offers pointers on effective communication. In her interview with Kanter, Leffler shared her "top five tips" for nonprofits just starting out. Among them, she encourages organizations to find their own voice and to "create a conversation" about their cause. The "Non-Profits on Facebook" page also highlights various organizations using Facebook, and Leffler told Kanter about two such organizations. One of them, a UK-based charitable-giving website called JustGiving, reportedly procured more than £22 million (about $36 million) through Facebook alone in 2012. The company reported a 120 percent rise in donations from the previous year. Of that £22 million, "from September 2011 to April [2012], £925,000 extra was donated via Facebook purely because someone had clicked 'share,'" after making a donation, JustGiving's product manager Jonathan Waddingham told Claudia Cahalane for the London *Guardian* (3 July 2012).

The Blue Cure Foundation found success a little differently. In 2010, Leffler told Kanter, a thirty-five-year-old man named Gabe Canales was diagnosed with prostate cancer. As Canales wrote in an article for the *Huffington Post* (2 May 2012), none of his doctors recommended that he join a cancer support group. Feeling adrift—and unprepared to seek help on his own—Canales shared the news of his diagnosis on his personal Facebook page. To his surprise, he began getting messages from other cancer patients and cancer survivors. Eventually, he set up a separate page called "Journey with Prostate Cancer" and a nonprofit called Blue Cure. Canales wrote that he derived the most satisfaction from facilitating meaningful connections on "Journey with Prostate Cancer." "For some, in-person support groups aren't an option due to time, lack of proximity, and comfort level. In the case of prostate cancer and other men's health issues, men just aren't as emotive and open about their health," he wrote. "But Facebook overcomes such walls and makes it much easier."

Offline, Facebook has sponsored meetups across the country. Since 2012, Leffler's team has presided over a TED-style event at Facebook's Menlo Park headquarters called the Social Media for Nonprofits Conference. Facebook is not the first company to focus on facilitating social good. Google has its own page called "Google for Nonprofits," and in 2013, it launched a mobile donation app called One Today. Meanwhile, Kiva, a microfinancing organization launched in 2010, uses social media technology to connect lenders and borrowers across the globe. In an article for *Forbes* (30 July 2013), Leffler called such endeavors the philanthropy of the future. She wrote specifically about the millennial generation (commonly defined as anyone born between 1980 and 2000), who, she said, "are using our vast networks of friends to connect with the causes that we care about in arguably more personal ways than ever before, using platforms that did not even exist five or ten years ago to organize, raise awareness, and fundraise. . . . Our parents might think we spend too much time with our noses in our phones," she wrote, "but what they don't know is that we just might be making a real difference—and doing it our own way."

PERSONAL LIFE

Leffler met Porter Felton, a tech entrepreneur, at a Spinsters of San Francisco holiday gala. (The Spinsters are a philanthropic social organization. Leffler joined the group after college and has served as its president.) When the couple started dating in 2010, they discovered that their mothers, who both attended the University of California, Berkeley, lived together in the Pi Beta Phi house in the late 1970s. They live in San Francisco.

In her free time, Leffler is an avid golfer and tennis player. In addition to her work for Facebook, she is involved with several nonprofit organizations in San Francisco. Furthermore, she is a member of the board of Symphonix, a young donors group at the San Francisco Symphony.

SUGGESTED READING

Anderson, Diane. "Libby Leffler, BS 06: Business Lead to COO, Facebook." *CalBusiness*. University of California, Berkeley, Fall 2011. Web. 16 Sept. 2014.

Auletta, Ken. "A Woman's Place: Can Sheryl Sandberg Upend Silicon Valley's Male-Dominated Culture?" *New Yorker*. Condé Nast, 11 July 2011. Web. 16 Sept. 2014.

Le Beau, Emilie. "Balancing Act—Time Management Tips for Teens." *NextStepU*. Next Step Education Group, n.d. Web. 16 Sept. 2014.

Leffler, Libby. Interview by Beth Kanter. "An Interview with Facebook's Libby Leffler: Facebook and Nonprofits." *Beth's Blog*. BethKanter.org, 17 July 2012. Web. 16 Sept. 2014.

Leffler, Libby. "Meet the Newest Generation of Philanthropists." *Forbes*. Forbes, 30 July 2013. Web. 16 Sept. 2014.

Lynley, Matt. "Meet Libby Leffler, Sheryl Sandberg's Former Invisible Right Hand Who's Moved On to Greater Things." *Business Insider*. Business Insider, 29 June 2012. Web. 16 Sept. 2014.

—*Molly Hagan*

Jack Lew

Born: August 29, 1955
Occupation: Government administrator

Named as the seventy-sixth secretary of the United States Treasury by President Barack Obama in 2013, Jacob "Jack" Joseph Lew has a long history of political involvement. He has twice served as the director of the Office of Management and Budget (OMB) as well as first deputy secretary of state for management and resources. From 1993 to 1994, as President Bill Clinton's special assistant, he helped to design the national service program AmeriCorps. Admitted to the bar in both Massachusetts and the District of Columbia, Lew spent five years in private practice in Washington, DC. He is also a member of the Council on Foreign Relations and the National Academy of Social Insurance. In addition, he served as executive vice president and chief operating officer at New York University. Lew was also on the Corporation for National and Community Service Board from 2004 through 2008. During that time, he chaired its

Jonathan Ernst/Reuters/Landov

Management, Administration, and Governance Committee. Lew was instrumental in creating the federal Low-Income Home Energy Assistance Program (LIHEAP), a federal program. He has served on several boards, including that of the think tank Center on Budget and Policy Priorities in Washington, DC. As he told Tim Weiner for the *New York Times* (8 Nov. 1999), Lew believes in using his power for good. "The purpose of power is to get things done. Budgets aren't books of numbers. They're a tapestry, the fabric, of what we believe. The numbers tell a story, a self-portrait of what we are as a country."

EARLY LIFE AND EDUCATION

Lew was born in New York City on August 29, 1955, and grew up in the Forest Hills neighborhood of Queens. His father, Irving Lew, was a rare book dealer and a lawyer, and his wife, Ruth (Turoff) Lew, was an office manager. She had completed high school at the age of fifteen, during the Great Depression, and found work to help support her family. Irving Lew immigrated to the United States from Poland in 1916 and learned to speak English at a public school, Boys High School in Brooklyn.

Lew first became involved in politics at the age of twelve, when he volunteered to campaign for Senator Eugene McCarthy's 1968 presidential bid. From that point on, he was hooked on politics. His upbringing influenced his choices. "The idea of making the world a better place was very much a part of my upbringing," Lew told

Weiner. "The most important things in my house were books and ideas. The issues of the world were part of our daily conversations."

Lew graduated from Forest Hills High School in Queens, where he had served as an editor on the school newspaper. He attended Carleton College in Minnesota before transferring to Harvard College, where he graduated magna cum laude in 1978. He earned his JD from Georgetown University Law Center in 1983, attending night classes after working in the capitol.

EARLY POLITICAL CAREER

Lew's political career began in 1973, when he served as a legislative aide to the famed New York Democratic representative Bella Abzug, then to Joe Moakley, a Democratic representative from Massachusetts. Between 1979 and 1987, he was a principal policy advisor on domestic affairs to House Speaker Thomas "Tip" P. O'Neill Jr. Lew secured his job in the speaker's office with the help of his roommate and friend Ari Weiss. Through this connection, Lew was hired as a policy staffer on the House Democratic Steering and Policy Committee. Although Lew did not start out with the intention of becoming a numbers guy, he soon discovered that power and precision lay in budgeting and appropriations, which that committee then handled. As Weiss told Nancy Cook for the National Journal (1 Nov. 2012), "Budgets are places with details. Inescapably, you can't put a budget together on slogans. It appealed to Jack and his nature and his talents because it is something that is essential."

In 1983, Lew became O'Neill's liaison to the Greenspan Commission, which brokered a bipartisan agreement to reform Social Security. Additional domestic and economic areas for which he was responsible include appropriations, the federal budget, health care spending, and taxation. After leaving that position, Lew joined Van Ness Feldman, a Washington, DC, law firm, where he worked from 1988 to 1993.

During the Clinton administration, Lew worked as a special assistant to President Bill Clinton from 1993 to 1994. In 1995, he became the deputy director of the Office of Management and Budget OMB), a position he held until 1998, when he became OMB director. At this time, he was also a member of the National Security Council. During those years at the OMB, the government ran a budget surplus for three years in a row. The Republican chair of the House Appropriations Committee in those years was C. W. "Bill" Young. Of Lew, Young told Weiner for the New York Times, "I enjoy working with Jack Lew. He's a tough negotiator, but he's very nice to work with."

NEW YORK UNIVERSITY

After President Clinton left office, Lew became the executive vice president and chief operating officer of New York University, a position he held from 2001 to 2006. In the latter capacity, he managed the budget, financing, and operations of the university. He also served as a professor of public administration.

When he left his position after five years, he received a handsome severance package of $685,000. The sum was spotlighted during the confirmation hearings for Lew's nomination to the Treasury post, because such a large exit bonus is generally not given by a tax-exempt university, especially when the employee is leaving of his own accord.

Officials of the university, however, defended the bonus, which was not written into Lew's original employment contract. John Beckman, a spokesperson for the university, told Danny Hakim for the New York Times (25 Feb. 2013) that Lew "was instrumental in resolving the structural budget deficit N.Y.U. faced when he arrived, putting in place our current budgeting process, addressing N.Y.U.'s deferred maintenance backlog and—in collaboration with other senior colleagues—addressing the complex challenges of unwinding N.Y.U. Medical Center's merger with Mount Sinai Medical Center."

A second issue regarding Lew's time at New York University that was later raised during his confirmation hearings for the Treasury post was the fact that his subsequent employer, Citigroup, became a preferred lender to NYU students during Lew's time at New York University. According to Hakim, Lew defended himself before Senate Republicans, stating, "I do not recall having any conversations with Citigroup officials regarding Citigroup's selection or actions as a preferred lender for N.Y.U. students. Also, I do not believe that I approved the selection of Citigroup as a preferred lender for N.Y.U. students."

CITIGROUP

In 2006, Lew left New York University to join the financial services company Citigroup, where he served as chief operating officer of the wealth management unit and, later, of the alternative investments unit. Citigroup was one of the major investment firms involved in proprietary trading and the trading of collateralized debt obligations backed by subprime mortgages, which were key factors in triggering the 2008 global financial crisis. Citigroup's high-risk investments amounted to more than $65 billion in losses, write-downs for troubled assets, and charges to account for future losses in 2008. As the financial crisis worsened, Citigroup became a recipient of the federal bailout, accepting $45 billion from the Troubled Asset Relief Program (TARP). Shortly thereafter, Lew received a bonus of almost $950,000 and came in for widespread criticism, particularly from conservatives. Fox News later called his appointment to the State Department a "career bailout."

Lew himself does not line up with other liberals on causality of the financial crisis. He breaks with the official White House line, as well as being in contrast with Democratic leaders such as Nancy Pelosi and Harry Reid. As quoted by David A. Graham for the *Atlantic* (9 Jan. 2013), Lew said he does not "personally know the extent to which deregulation drove [the crisis], but I don't believe that deregulation was the proximate cause." Lew was working for President Clinton when two major laws—the Financial Services Modernization Act of 1999 and the Commodity Futures Modernization Act of 2000—that loosened regulations on banking, securities, insurance, and other financial services companies were signed into law. Lew's close ties to Wall Street have also drawn criticism from liberals, who questioned his ability to implement effective financial reforms.

THE OBAMA ADMINISTRATION

Following President Barack Obama's election, Lew served as deputy secretary of state for management and resources from January 2009 until November 2010 under Secretary of State Hillary Clinton, where he garnered positive notice from both liberals and centrists. Although the secretary of state previously had only one deputy, Clinton and Obama appointed a second deputy. Lew worked predominantly on budgetary and internal matters, while the other deputy secretary, James Steinberg, had a more traditional role, focusing predominantly on policy matters.

In 2010, President Obama asked Lew to resume leadership of the Office of Management and Budget. "If there was a hall of fame for budget directors, then Jack Lew surely would have earned a place for his service in that role under President Clinton, when he helped balance the federal budget after years of deficits," President Obama said when announcing Lew's nomination, as quoted by Linda Feldman for the *Christian Science Monitor* (13 July 2010). "When Jack left that post at the end of the Clinton administration, he handed the next administration a record $236-billion budget surplus." The Senate confirmed Lew as the next OMB director by unanimous consent in November 2010.

BUDGET BATTLES

As director of the Office of Budget and Management in 2011, Lew faced a possible government shutdown when Congress showed no signs of agreeing on a budget. At that time, he was the White House team's only senior member who had weathered the 1983 Social Security crisis, the 1997 budget deal, and the government shutdowns under President Clinton. Although optimistic, as reported by Lori Montgomery for the *Washington Post* (26 Feb. 2011), Lew noted the contrast to previous trials, "We're heading into a more difficult and much more complicated conversation because the size of the problem is so great, and the distance between the parties is pretty great as well."

Lew is a believer in the social safety net and other progressive ideals. As Judd Gregg, a former Republican senator and Budget Committee chair, told Nancy Cook for the *National Journal* (1 Nov. 2012), "He's like a labor-union negotiator. He's not going to give you an inch if he doesn't have to. He's a true believer in the causes."

Speaking in 2011 to a conference for Jewish nonprofit organizations, Lew outlined his idea for budget cutting with a scalpel rather than in the broad sweeps that the sequester involved. As quoted by Cook, Lew explained, "I describe budgets as a tapestry: When it's woven together, the picture amounts to our hopes and dreams of a nation."

CHIEF OF STAFF

In January 2012, Obama named Lew as his chief of staff, replacing William Daley, who had served in the position following Rahm Emanuel's departure. Lew, whom Daley recommended for the post, did not actively begin his new role until work on the 2013 federal budget proposal due to Congress in February was completed. House Minority Leader Nancy Pelosi praised Lew's appointment to the post, commenting that Lew was "a proven leader with extensive House experience, an expert on our nation's toughest economic challenges, a strong voice in addressing our nation's budget deficit, and a dedicated public servant with a long record of achievement inside and outside of government," as quoted by George E. Condon Jr. for the *National Journal* (9 Jan. 2012).

Lew served as the White House chief of staff from January 2012 until his confirmation as secretary of the Treasury in early 2013. As David Rothkopf, a former Clinton administration official, told Nancy Cook for the *National Journal* (1 Nov. 2012), Lew is "the classic kind of successful Obama staffer: He's loyal, he keeps his head down, he's not a headline grabber, he works behind the scenes and is very good at keeping the drama to a minimum."

Lew is highly respected in Washington. "Having Lew on your team is the equivalent, as a coach, of having the luxury of putting someone at almost any position on the team and knowing he will do well," Tom Daschle, a former US representative and Senate majority leader, told Cook.

SECRETARY OF THE TREASURY

President Obama nominated Lew as the secretary of the Treasury on January 10, 2013, and the Senate Finance Committee held Lew's confirmation hearings on February 13. During the hearings, Lew met with forty-one senators and answered more than seven hundred questions on the record as he tried to win support for his nomination. Despite the concerns raised by Senator Charles E. Grassley and other Republicans regarding his time at Citigroup, Lew was confirmed by the Senate for the cabinet position on February 27. The following day, Vice President Joe Biden administered the oath of office in the Oval Office, with Lew's family and President Obama in attendance.

As the threat of a government shutdown seemed ever more likely in the fall of 2013, Lew appeared on several national television news shows to discuss the implications. On October 6, 2013, on CNN's "State of the Union," he discussed the need to raise the debt ceiling. "We've never gotten to the point where the United States government has operated without the ability to borrow. It's very dangerous. It's reckless, because the reality is, there are no good choices if we run out of borrowing capacity and we run out of cash. It will mean that the United States, for the first time since 1789, would be not paying its bills, hurting the full faith and credit, because of a political decision."

Lew also opposed the budget sequestration in 2013, arguing instead for closing tax loopholes and reducing spending. As Damian Paletta reported for the *Wall Street Journal* (24 Oct. 2013), Lew argued in a speech to the Center for American Progress, "If we can agree on sensible medium and long-term policies to replace these short-term cuts, we can do something good for the economy and our national security."

PERSONAL LIFE

Lew, an Orthodox Jew, observes the Sabbath and refrains from working from sundown on Friday until sundown on Saturday. One of the few times he recalls using a telephone on the Sabbath was during the 1979 Social Security talks, when he coordinated the White House announcement after talking to Tip O'Neill and Dan Rostenkowski. Twice he has been invited to help light the National Menorah in Washington, DC, in 1998 and in 2011.

Lew divides his time between an apartment in the capitol and his home in Riverdale, in the Bronx. He and his wife, Ruth Schwartz, have two grown children. His daughter, Shoshana, has followed in her father's footsteps, choosing a political career and working for the Council on Environmental Quality. His son, Danny, lives in New York with his wife, Zahava, and their children, Eliora and Moshe Lew. Family is important to Lew, who keeps on his desk a small ceramic replica of Ellis Island as a gesture to his immigrant father, now deceased.

Lew's has also served on the boards of the Tobin Project and the Kaiser Family Foundation.

SUGGESTED READING

Condon, George E. Jr. "Lew Is New White House Chief of Staff." *National Journal.* National Journal Group, 9 Jan. 2012. Web. 5 Dec. 2013.

Cook, Nancy. "Jack Lew: The Man Who Could Save Obama's Legacy."*National Journal.* National Journal Group, 1 Nov. 2012. Web. 5 Dec. 2013.

Graham, David A. "Who Is Jack Lew, Obama's Nominee for Treasury Secretary?" *Atlantic.* Atlantic Monthly Group, 9 Jan. 2013. Web. 5 Dec. 2013.

Hakim, Danny. "Obama's Treasury Nominee Got Unusual Exit Bonus on Leaving N.Y.U." *New York Times.* New York Times, 25 Feb. 2013. Web. 5 Dec. 2013.

Mahanta, Siddhartha. "Flashback: Lew's Time at Citi and Other Disappointments." *Mother Jones.* Mother Jones and the Foundation for Natl. Progress, 9 Jan. 2012. Web. 5 Dec. 2013.

—*Judy Johnson*

Li Na

Born: February 26, 1982
Occupation: Tennis player

Li Na is widely regarded as a trailblazer for Chinese tennis and a transformative figure in her sport. In 2011, she won the women's singles final of the French Open, becoming not only the first Chinese player to win a Grand Slam singles tournament, but also the first player from Asia to win a major title. For Li, who turned professional in 1999, the victory marked the culmination of a late-blooming career defined by firsts—the most notable of which came in 2008, when, after reaching the women's singles semifinal at the Beijing Olympic Games, Li opted out of China's notoriously rigid state-run sports program. The move was unprecedented in the history of the Chinese Tennis Association (CTA) and led to the creation of the *danfei*, or "fly solo," initiative, which gave Li and other Chinese players the freedom to manage their own careers. Not long afterward, Li emerged to become one of her country's most popular and influential athletes.

Li, who has earned the nickname "Big Sister Na" from adoring Chinese fans, is known for her rebellious nature, fierce independent streak, and mischievous sense of humor. According to Brook Larmer, writing for *New York Times Magazine* (22 Aug. 2013), her baseline style of tennis "blends speed and power" and is characterized by "great foot speed," "thunderous ground-strokes," and "what many consider to be the most cleanly struck backhand in the game." Li cemented her

Rhona Wise/EPA/Landov

legacy in 2014, when she won the Australian Open to claim her second career Grand Slam title. Stacey Allaster, the chairman and CEO of the WTA, told Larmer, "If the Williams sisters had the greatest impact on the first decade this century, then I would say, without a doubt, that Li Na will be the most important player of this decade."

EARLY LIFE AND EDUCATION

Li Na was born on February 26, 1982, in Wuhan, the capital of the Hubei province in central China. An only child, Li grew up in a close-knit, working-class family. Her father, Li Shengpeng, worked in sales at the Wuhan-based Yangtze River Metal Products Factory; her mother, Li Yanping, was a clerk. Li was ushered into sports by her father, a professional badminton player who played for the Hubei provincial badminton team. Li started playing badminton at age five.

She received badminton training at a state-run amateur sports school, which she would attend each day after finishing her classes at Wuhan Dandong Xincun Primary School. It was during the summer of her second year at the sports school that she was spotted by a tennis coach, Xia Xiyao. Impressed by Li's height and forceful swing, Xia persuaded Li's parents to drop badminton in favor of tennis, a sport still relatively unknown in China at the time. "They all agreed that I should play tennis," Li told Larmer, "but nobody bothered to ask me." Li, cautiously following Xia's suggestion, switched to tennis at age seven, and soon thereafter, started boarding at the sports school. Her development in the sport came quickly, thanks to her playing exclusively with and against older and more experienced competition.

At age eleven, Li began training with the Hubei provincial team, which was then coached by Yu Liqiao, a former Asian champion. Yu served as her primary tennis coach for the next nine years. During this time, Li mastered the technical aspects of the game, but also developed a crippling sense of self-doubt, induced by the Chinese tennis system's harsh coaching methods. Although Li has cited Yu as having the greatest influence on her game, she has said that she was berated by the coach on a near daily basis and that she never received one word of praise from her during their nine years together. Despite Yu's unforgiving style, Li continued training to please her father, who dreamed she would join the provincial team and, one day, become a national champion.

OVERCOMING TRAGEDY

By her early teens, Li had already begun representing the Hubei team in amateur tournaments. Tragedy struck her family, however, when she was only fourteen years old. On November 14, 1996, her father died of a rare cardiovascular disease. At the time of his death, Li was playing in a youth tournament in the city of Shenzhen, in southern China, but the tragic news was kept a secret from her until the competition was over. In her autobiography, *Li Na: My Life*, translated by Shelly Bryant (2014), Li described her father, who died before the age of forty, as the "warmest ray of sunlight in my childhood memories," and called his death and the fact that she was unable to see him one last time "the most painful scars buried deep in my heart."

Following her father's death, Li fully dedicated herself to tennis. In December 1996, she became an official member of the Hubei provincial team, and several months later, she captured her first national junior title. Shouldered with the family's financial responsibilities, Li gave all of her prize winnings from tournaments during this time to her mother to help pay off debt incurred by her father's medical costs. Her mother, meanwhile, rented out the family house to further ease the financial burden. "After my father died," Li told Christopher Johnson for CNN (26 Jan. 2011), "my mom had to take care of everything. It was tough for her. I learned a lot from her about working hard for everything."

In the fall of 1997, Li was granted the opportunity to study and train at a Nike-sponsored tennis academy in Texas. She spent ten months there, during which she competed against elite amateur players from other tennis academies around the United States. By the time Li returned to China, in June 1998, her mother had remarried and started a family of her own. Feeling deserted, Li recalled in her autobiography, "I was obsessed with the notion that she'd betrayed my father and me, and that she was responsible for making a virtual orphan of me."

FIRST FORAY INTO THE PROFESSIONAL TENNIS RANKS

Shortly after returning to China, Li told an interviewer that she aspired to make the top ten of the WTA singles rankings. Her journey to realizing that highly ambitious goal began in 1999, when, at age sixteen, she turned professional and made her debut on the lower-tier International Tennis Federation (ITF) circuit. Li quickly moved up in the rankings, winning three singles titles and eight doubles titles on the ITF circuit that year, and capturing another eight singles titles and six doubles titles on the circuit in 2000, the same year she played in her first three WTA main draws. She then fulfilled her father's dream for her in 2001, when she claimed gold in both the women's singles and doubles events on the ITF circuit.

By the start of the 2002 season, Li was the number-one ranked female tennis player in China and had, for a brief time, climbed into the top 135 of the WTA singles rankings. Her fast-rising career stalled, however, when stress-related health issues forced her to stop training. Burnt out from the suffocating pressures of the Chinese tennis program, Li decided to take an indefinite break from her professional tennis career to focus more on personal endeavors with her future husband and coach, Jiang Shan, a former Davis Cup player whom she first met on the Hubei provincial team. "I only wanted to pursue a free, full life," she explained in her autobiography. "I wanted to do as I pleased." Li and Jiang married in 2006.

In the fall of 2002, Li, along with Jiang, who had also retired from tennis, enrolled at the Huazhong University of Science and Technology, where she began studying journalism. She studied there until early 2004, at which point Sun Jinfang, then the newly appointed head of the Chinese tennis program, convinced her to return to professional tennis. Li would eventually complete her bachelor's degree in journalism from Huazhong University in 2009.

COMEBACK AND RISE UP THE WTA RANKINGS

After a twenty-five month hiatus, Li returned to the court reinvigorated and with a more relaxed state of mind. That new mindset proved to deliver immediate results. Returning to competition in May 2004, Li won the five singles tournaments on the ITF circuit, elevating her ranking to number 182 in the world. Then, in October of that year, she defeated Martina Sucha in straight sets (6–3, 6–4) at the inaugural Guangzhou International Women's Open in China, to claim her first career WTA singles title. In the process Li became the first Chinese player to win a WTA singles title. By season's end, she had cracked the WTA top one hundred for the first time, finishing the year ranked at number eighty.

In 2005 Li began playing on the WTA Tour full-time. That year she made her singles debut at two of the four WTA Grand Slam tournaments, reaching the third round at the Australian Open and losing in the first round at the US Open. Despite missing several months of the season due to an injury, Li performed well enough against top-ranked opponents to finish at number fifty-seven in the year-end WTA rankings.

Li continued her upward career trajectory in 2006, when she became the first Chinese player to reach the WTA top twenty. That year also saw her defeat her first top-ten opponent and become the first player from her country to reach the quarterfinals of a Grand Slam, doing so in her debut appearance at the Wimbledon Championships. Li improved her world ranking to sixteen in early 2007, after she reached the semifinals of the Sydney Open in Australia. She would miss the second half of that year, however, due to a right rib injury, resulting in her slipping to number twenty-nine in the WTA rankings.

In Li's first competition back from injury, and first of the 2008 season, the Mondial Australian Women's Hardcourts in Gold Coast, Australia, she overcame future world number one Victoria Azarenka in three sets (4–6, 6–3, 6–4) to capture her second career WTA singles title. Three months after that victory, in March 2008, Li was sidelined again after undergoing surgery for a recurring right knee injury. She recovered in time, however, for the 2008 Olympic Games in Beijing, China, where she unexpectedly reached the semifinals.

During her Olympic semifinal match against Dinara Safina, Li gave the tennis world a glimpse of her fiery personality when she famously told overzealous Chinese fans to "shut up" after they kept on chanting her name in between points. She later apologized for the outburst, telling Larmer, "I used to think tennis was simply a sport, but the craziness of that match made me realize that it was endowed with meanings that are far more significant."

FLYING SOLO

Following the Beijing Games, Li left the Chinese national tennis system with three other top women players to gain more control over her career. "I was tired of playing under the national team," she explains in her autobiography. "I wanted to experience what it was really like to be a professional." Li's departure was granted under the then newly created "fly solo" initiative, which gave her and other individual athletes greater autonomy in managing their own coaches, trainers, schedules, and earnings. Under the initiative, Li was required to give just a small fraction of her earnings (between eight to twelve percent) to the CTA and her provincial team, compared with sixty-five percent in the past.

In late 2008 Li started working with the Swedish-born former Chinese national women's coach Thomas Högstedt. Although she continued to be plagued by problems with her right knee during the 2009 season—problems which ultimately led to two more surgeries—Li enjoyed immediate progress under her new arrangement and ended that season with a then career-high world ranking of fifteenth. She improved her world ranking to number eleven in 2010, when she advanced to her first Grand Slam semifinal at the Australian Open and collected her third career WTA singles title at the Aegon Classic in Birmingham, England, defeating former world number one Maria Sharapova.

GRAND SLAM TITLES

Prior to the 2011 season, Li decided to make Jiang her full-time coach after Högstedt left to coach Sharapova. "I chose my husband because he can understand what I do on the court," she said in her interview with Christopher Johnson. "If I am nervous on the court, or shouting, he can understand." With Jiang as her coach, Li enjoyed a historic season. After defeating Kim Clijsters at the 2011 Medibank International Sydney in Australia to win her fourth singles title, she entered the 2011 Australian Open as the number-nine seed. She defeated world number one and top seed Caroline Wozniacki in the semifinal round to become the first Asian player to reach a Grand Slam final. In the final, Li lost to Clijsters in three sets (6–3, 3–6, 3–6).

Li's most memorable performance came at the 2011 French Open, which she won by defeating defending champion Francesca Schiavone in straight sets, 6–4, 7–6, in the final. With that win, she became the first Asian player to win a Grand Slam title and the first from China to crack the world's top five. Her victory was watched by 116 million television viewers in China, and was credited with changing the global landscape of women's tennis. Li quickly became one of China's most popular and heavily endorsed athletes, achieving a level of fame on par with NBA superstar Yao Ming and the gold medal-winning hurdler Liu Xiang.

In the wake of her historic Grand Slam victory, however, Li struggled. Over the next year and a half, she won only one singles title, the 2012 Western & Southern Open in Cincinnati, Ohio, and suffered early-round defeats in six consecutive Grand Slam tournaments. Li attributed most of her struggles during this time to intense scrutiny and pressure from the Chinese media. "If you make your goal too big, it makes it difficult to actually focus on anything," she said in an interview with Debra Bruno for the *Wall Street Journal* (13 Dec. 2013). "I don't feel I can represent all of China."

After commencing a new partnership with Argentine coach Carlos Rodriguez, the former longtime coach of one-time world number one Justine Henin, Li returned to elite form in 2013. That year saw her win the inaugural Shenzhen Open in China, reach the final of the Australian Open for the second time, and advance to the finals of the year-end WTA Championships. Li's performance in the latter tournament helped her climb to number three in the WTA singles rankings. She surpassed Kimiko Date-Krumm of Japan to become the highest-ranked Asian female player of all time.

At the 2014 Shenzhen Open, Li successfully defended her title by defeating Peng Shuai in straight sets to claim her eighth career singles title. She followed up that victory with arguably the second-greatest performance of her career at the 2014 Australian Open, where she advanced to the final for the second consecutive season and third time overall. In the final, Li recorded a straight-set victory over first-time Grand Slam finalist Dominika Cibulkova, to capture her second career Grand Slam title. At thirty-one, she became the oldest female champion in the tournament's history. Her victory, meanwhile, propelled her to a career-best world number two ranking.

PERSONAL LIFE

Li shares a three-story villa with Jiang in Wuhan. She has received a considerable amount of media attention for a rose tattoo on her chest, which pays homage to her love for Jiang. In her autobiography she called her husband "the one person in my life that I cannot do without."

Li has sponsorship deals with Nike sportswear, the German luxury carmaker Mercedes-Benz, and the Swiss watchmaker Rolex, among others. With $18.2 million (USD) in annual earnings as of June 2013, she ranks among the highest-earning female athletes in the world, according to *Forbes* (2014). In 2013, she was named one of the world's most influential people by *Time* magazine for helping boost the popularity of tennis in China.

SUGGESTED READING

Bruno, Debra. "Li Na Finds It Tough at the Top." *Wall Street Journal*. Dow Jones, 13 Dec. 2013. Web. 8 Apr. 2014.

Johnson, Christopher. "One-on-one with Chinese Tennis Ace Li Na." *CNN*. Cable News Network, 26 Jan. 2011. Web. 8 Apr. 2014.

Larmer, Brook. "Li Na, China's Tennis Rebel." *New York Times Magazine*. New York Times, 22 Aug. 2013. Web. 8 Apr. 2014.

Li, Na. *Li Na: My Life*. Trans. Shelly Bryant. Melbourne: Viking, 2014. Digital file.

—*Chris Cullen*

Andrew Lincoln

Born: September 14, 1973
Occupation: Actor

Although Andrew Lincoln had been working as an actor in the United Kingdom for more than fifteen years, he was little known in the United States prior to 2010, when the television network AMC debuted its gripping postapocalyptic television series *The Walking Dead*. In it, Lincoln portrays Rick Grimes, a no-nonsense former sheriff's deputy who finds himself the de facto leader of a group of humans attempting to survive amid an onslaught of flesh-eating zombies. Unlike many previous zombie tales, *The Walking Dead* focuses less on gore and terror—although those elements are certainly still present—and more on how its characters develop and interact in a world where conventional rules of civilization no longer apply. The show became a huge commercial hit, with an average of 16.16 million viewers in 2013, making it the most-watched television drama for adults on cable television. It has also met with widespread critical acclaim.

A large part of *The Walking Dead*'s appeal is the character of Grimes, whom Lincoln says he modeled after Gary Cooper's marshal in the Western film classic *High Noon* (1952). In the movie, Cooper's character must face down a posse of thugs alone, without the help of any of the townspeople he is trying to protect, even though doing so may cost him his marriage; similarly, Grimes often has to make difficult decisions in order to keep himself and his people alive, with nobody else to turn to for aid. "Rick is kind of an old-fashioned hero," Lincoln told David Peisner in an interview for *Rolling Stone* (10 Oct. 2013). "It ain't cool. It ain't sexy. It's not arch. It's raw. It's grungy. It's all about a visceral reaction because the characters don't get the chance to drink cappuccinos and talk about iPods. . . . I'd always played these sort of renegade, irresponsible, idiotic kind of roles, but this is different. This is the guy that people fall in behind in the show, whether he's right or wrong."

EARLY LIFE AND EDUCATION

Andrew Lincoln was born Andrew James Clutterbuck on September 14, 1973, in the city of Kingston upon Hull in Yorkshire, England. (His agent only agreed to represent him as an actor if he used a different surname.) His father was an English businessman and civil engineer, his mother a South African nurse. He has an older brother, Richard, who is now a teacher. When Lincoln was ten years old, his family moved to Bath, where he attended Beechen Cliff School, a secondary school for boys.

As a child, Lincoln was uninterested in performing onstage, preferring to spend the majority of his time playing sports. This changed at

FilmMagic

age fourteen, when one of his teachers yanked him off the school rugby pitch to play the Artful Dodger in *Oliver!*, a musical based on Charles Dickens's classic novel *Oliver Twist* (1838). The experience not only helped him to meet more girls; it also changed his life. "I loved it," Lincoln told Alice Jones for the *Independent* (26 Mar. 2009). "It just caught me. I was kind of a loud, showy-offy child, which is probably why he thought I'd blag it."

After spending his teen years performing onstage, Lincoln was certain that his future lay in acting, and when he was seventeen, he told his parents of his plans. They were less than convinced, and his father suggested they strike a bargain: if Lincoln could gain acceptance to five drama schools, he could attend one of them. Lincoln rose to the challenge. Although his performance suffered in some subjects, such as science and math, he concentrated so much on perfecting his auditions that he was accepted by the top five drama schools in the country. He decided to enroll in the Royal Academy of Dramatic Art (RADA), a highly competitive school that typically selects only a few dozen students from a pool of thousands each year. In order to support himself during his university days, he worked various odd jobs, including stints as a chef, a bartender, and a laborer in one of his father's factories, where he helped build car exhaust pipes.

FIRST ROLES

Shortly after his graduation from RADA in 1994, Lincoln landed the role of Edgar "Egg" Cooke in the BBC television series *This Life* (1996–97), a drama that followed the lives of five young law school graduates. In 2010 Lincoln, who otherwise never revisits his recorded performances, wound up watching the first episode of the series while putting together a show reel for American film producers. In an interview for the *Scotsman* (28 June 2010), he recalled, "We knew nothing about anything; we were newcomers. And there's something so brilliant and unsullied and open about the performances—the sort of acting that you aspire to a lot longer down the line, we were just doing without thinking. We didn't have all those mannerisms. That's why I try to push myself in different directions and turn the ship, as they say, to trick myself and reinvent myself. It's like a spring clean, to reinvent myself every ten years." Lincoln and his fellow cast members reprised their roles in the 2007 television movie *This Life + 10*.

The success of *This Life* enabled Lincoln to build a career in British television and theater, as well the occasional film. One of his more famous roles was in *Love Actually* (2003), where he played Mark, a man desperately in love with his best friend's wife, played by Keira Knightley. His performance earned him a nomination for *Empire* magazine's Empire Award for best newcomer in 2004. He also starred as Simon Casey in the first three seasons of *Teachers* (2001–3), a British series that aired on Channel 4; it was on the set of this show that he met his future wife, Gael Anderson, daughter of Jethro Tull lead singer and flautist Ian Anderson. Lincoln recalled to Peisner, "She was a PA and was supposed to make a cup of tea. That was her job. She didn't make me a f—— cup of tea that whole job. But I just saw her silhouette—she had this crazy mullet with spiky hair—she looked like Sonic the Hedgehog. I saw this crazy-looking girl with these beautiful green eyes and I just went, 'Who the hell is that?' I was spellbound."

Because Lincoln and his wife decided to put their family first, he was reluctant to move to Hollywood to try to make a name for himself in the US film industry. Instead, he remained in the United Kingdom, appearing in stage plays, television series such as *Afterlife* (2005–6) and *Strike Back* (2010), and films such as *Moonshot* (2009) and *Heartbreaker* (2010). But all that changed when he beat out as many as one hundred rivals for a part that would reinvent his career and introduce him to an entirely new audience.

THE WALKING DEAD

The part: Rick Grimes, a deputy sheriff who awakes from a coma to discover that the world has been overrun by flesh-eating zombies. The series: *The Walking Dead*, adapted from Robert Kirkman's highly acclaimed black-and-white comic book series of the same name. Lincoln still is not certain how he, a Briton, beat out so many other actors, mostly Americans, for the role, but he has a working theory. "I'm convinced I got the part because I looked apocalyptic," he told Benji Wilson for the *Telegraph* (28 Oct. 2010). "My son had just been born and I hadn't slept for twelve days. I put myself on tape and they went, 'He looks haggard enough to play this part: he's the guy.'"

Unlike many postapocalyptic tales, which tend to work toward an end goal, *The Walking Dead* is more about what individual characters are willing to do in order to survive. Rick Grimes becomes the leader of a ragtag group of human survivors who must contend not only with zombies, whom they call "walkers," but also with other human beings who threaten to take what little they have left. The former deputy is often faced with hard decisions that he would not have made under other circumstances, and he struggles to make sense of his circumstances and hold on to what it means to be human. It is this ability to make tough choices and inspire his fellow survivors, whom he tries to give hope as they move from place to place, that makes Grimes a natural leader.

The show was developed for television by Frank Darabont, a respected screenwriter and director best known for films such as *The Shawshank Redemption* (1994), *The Green Mile* (1999), and *The Mist* (2007), adapted from works by author Stephen King. While *The Walking Dead* is based on Kirkman's series, it does not strictly follow the plot of the comic book; however, it does make an effort to get the characters right, starting with Lincoln's flawed-but-noble Grimes. It is as much about what it means to survive as it is about the pulp-fiction gore of scores of undead creatures that crave human flesh. Lincoln noted in the *Scotsman* interview, "You realize it's a horror novel, but it's extraordinarily like *Lord of the Flies*. Forget about the zombie thing. It's like a plague has occurred, and what is left of humanity? It's about society and humanity and family, a love story really, and within that, everything has run riot and the rules no longer apply; people have gone extremely feral."

CRITICAL ACCLAIM

Since taking on the role of Grimes, Lincoln has been earning praise from both critics and his fellow actors. *The Walking Dead* films in and around Atlanta, Georgia, where Lincoln and his cast mates endure ninety-degree heat and thick humidity while being chased by the undead. In order to keep in shape, Lincoln does many of his own stunts and runs when he is not filming. "Andy keeps this show alive," costar Steven Yeun told Steve Fennessy for *Men's Health* (Oct. 2012). "He's always there early and leaves late. He always knows his lines. He's always pumping everyone up when he sees a drop in energy in the scene." Lincoln's performance also received praise from Kirkman, who told the *Hollywood Reporter* (6 Apr. 2010), "Writing Rick Grimes month after month in the comic series, I had no idea he was an actual living, breathing human being, and yet here he is. I couldn't be more thrilled with how this show is coming together." The show's fifth season premiers in October 2014.

PERSONAL LIFE

Lincoln and Anderson married in 2006. They have two children, Matilda and Arthur. Although Lincoln has said that he will play Grimes until the character is bitten and turned into a walker, he is committed to his family and prioritizes their needs over his career. He hopes to follow the example of his parents and his in-laws, who remain married after decades together. In order to provide stability for his children, he has never legally changed his name from Clutterbuck, which is his children's surname as well. While *The Walking Dead* is filming, the Clutterbucks reside in Atlanta, Georgia, but Lincoln intends for them to continue living primarily in the United Kingdom.

When not busy with his family or his acting career, Lincoln has worked with the National Youth Theatre charity in London. He also supports Shelter, a British charity dedicated to ending homelessness and poor housing conditions in England and Scotland.

SUGGESTED READING

Fennessy, Steve. "Andrew Lincoln Kills It." *Men's Health* Oct. 2012: 42–46. Print.

"Interview: Andrew Lincoln, Actor." *Scotsman*. Johnston, 28 June 2010. Web. 13 June 2014.

Lincoln, Andrew. "Andrew Lincoln: I'll Play Rick Grimes until They Bite Me." Interview by David Peisner. *Rolling Stone*. Rolling Stone, 10 Oct. 2013. Web. 13 June 2014.

Lincoln, Andrew. "Andrew Lincoln Keeps His Head." Interview by Hunter Stephenson. *Interview*. Interview, 3 Dec. 2010. Web. 13 June 2014.

Lincoln, Andrew. "Q&A: *The Walking Dead's* Andrew Lincoln." Interview by Mike Ayers. *Esquire*. Hearst Communications, 27 Mar. 2013. Web. 13 June 2014.

McIntyre, Gina. "Among *Walking Dead* Zombies, Andrew Lincoln Brings Emotional Heft." *Los Angeles Times*. Los Angeles Times, 13 June 2013. Web. 13 June 2014.

Wilson, Benji. "Andrew Lincoln on Starring in the TV Adaptation of *Walking Dead*." *Telegraph*. Telegraph Media Group, 28 Oct. 2010. Web. 13 June 2014.

SELECTED WORKS

This Life, 1996–97; *Teachers*, 2001–3; *Love Actually*, 2003; *Afterlife*, 2005–6; *This Life + 10*, 2007; *Moonshot*, 2009; *Heartbreaker*, 2010; *Strike Back*, 2010; *The Walking Dead*, 2010–

—Christopher Mari

Rafael Lozano-Hemmer

Born: 1967
Occupation: Electronic artist

Rafael Lozano-Hemmer is a well-known figure in the world of art and is widely recognized for his large-scale public installations, which incorporate lights, sensors, robotics, projections, and other technical components. The works are generally participatory, requiring, for example, viewers to cast their own shadows onto a surface (as in the piece *Body Movies*), record messages to regulate the color and intensity of light (as in *Voice Tunnel*, a piece staged inside New York City's Park Avenue Tunnel), or operate levers to modify canopies of light (as in *Articulated Intersect*). While the results are typically spectacular, Lozano-Hemmer told Randy Gladman for *Canadian Art* (Winter 2002), "It is performed on a spectacular scale, but it is not a spectacle." He is happy to classify his works alongside conventional forms of public art, he told Gladman, asserting, "I like to compare it more to a public fountain or park bench."

Lozano-Hemmer has also been celebrated for his smaller-scale installation works, which tend to explore themes of surveillance and deception. Among such gallery pieces has been *Vicious Circular Breathing*, a 2013 work consisting of a hermetically sealed apparatus and carbon dioxide sensors that invite the public to breathe air that had already been inhaled and exhaled by previous participants. *Please Empty Your Pockets* allows viewers to place an object on a conveyor

Courtesy of Antimodular Research

belt where it is scanned, and the resulting image is saved in a memory bank. "Some people find my work empowering and fun. Others find it frightening," he told Jori Finkel for the *Los Angeles Times* (17 Oct. 2010). "My works are on the border between being very seductive, inviting, inclusive and being predatory, ominous, Orwellian."

Explaining the importance of the artist's oeuvre, Gladman wrote for *Akrylic* (7 July 2008), "The point of interface, where our bodies meet our machines, is at the heart of Rafael Lozano-Hemmer's art. His works create new interfaces and interfere with communications in order to propose new, unexpected, exquisitely simple purposes for our techno-gadgets, and hint optimistically at the intimate things our machines will do for us in the future." Lozano-Hemmer told Finkel, "I work with technology because it's inevitable. Our politics, our culture, our economy, everything is running through globalized networks of communication."

EARLY YEARS AND EDUCATION

Rafael Lozano-Hemmer was born in 1967 in Mexico City. Later in life he became a Canadian citizen and settled in Montreal. "I am," he quipped to Gladman in 2002, "a Chicanadian, a Mexicanuck." Lozano-Hemmer's parents owned a nightclub in Mexico City, and he has explained that growing up in such a relatively freewheeling environment had a profound effect on his sensibilities. "There's a tradition of light art that's associated very often with an almost spiritual approach to light, the idea of enlightenment," he told Annabel Ross for the *Sydney Morning Herald* (5 June 2004), mentioning artists James Turrell and Robert Irwin as examples of that ethos. "While I very much admire all of that, my work comes from a very different place. I associate lights with artificiality and with parties and with carnivals and with this idea of nightclub life." (Although his work is not often overtly political, he has explained that the searchlights used by US helicopter pilots to hunt for Mexicans trying to cross the border into the United States illegally have also inspired him.)

As a student, Lozano-Hemmer was drawn to science, and some observers have speculated that it was the order and structured nature of the field that proved appealing to him after the somewhat hedonistic backdrop of his formative years. He attended Concordia University in Montreal, Canada, earning a bachelor's degree in physical chemistry in 1989. For a few months after receiving his degree, he worked in the lab of a large, multinational company. He soon discovered, however, that he was unhappy there. "I believe science can be intensely creative and uncertain and exciting and so on, but most of the excitement in science in terms of research happens only after you've done a doctorate and

a post doc and if you're lucky you have your own lab," he explained to Elizabeth Fortescue for the Australian-based website ArtWriter.com.au. (17 Dec. 2011). "At my level of chemistry it was all very much analysis, it was not very exciting."

Many of his friends were composers, performers, artists, and writers, and Lozano-Hemmer began joining them in those pursuits. "It was a very festive, very anarchic kind of environment," he recalled to Stefan Zebrowski-Rubin for *Art 21* magazine (23 Sept. 2010).

EARLY CAREER

Lozano-Hemmer was involved in numerous stage and performance art projects early on and once set himself on fire for an avant-garde presentation, suffering second-degree burns on both arms. Performance art gradually evolved into creating installation pieces. "I still think of my work as closer to the performing arts than the visual arts," he told Ross. "I believe there is this kind of event-based activity, and so there is this performance, almost like theatrical pieces, except instead of the performers you have the public—the public are the performers."

Lozano-Hemmer's big break came in 1997, when he created *Re: Positioning Fear*, a large installation in Graz, Austria, where he used Xenon projectors and a wireless 3D tracking system. The shadows of passers-by were projected onto the outer walls of the Styrian Armory while numerous internationally known artists and theorists used an IRC (Internet Relay Chat) platform to discuss the concept of fear. The text of those conversations was projected inside the shadows.

In 1999, Lozano-Hemmer was commissioned to design a massive light show to celebrate the new millennium in Mexico City's Zócalo Square. To prepare for *Vectorial Elevation*, he invited Internet users to visit a dedicated website to design patterns for eighteen searchlights that would be positioned around the square. The lights, visible throughout a fifteen-kilometer area, were manipulated by an online simulation program, and each participant received a personalized webpage with images, information about themselves and the inspiration for their design, and space for others to comment.

VENICE BIENNALE

At the 2007 Venice Biennale, a major contemporary art exhibition held every two years in Venice, Italy, Lozano-Hemmer became the first artist to represent Mexico at the prestigious event. Mexico's pavilion, the site of his solo show, was located in the fifteenth-century Soranzo-Van Axel palace, not far from the Rialto Bridge. Lozano-Hemmer exhibited several works at the Biennale, including *Pulse Room*, in which a sensor measured the heart rates of visitors and displayed the information in the form of flashing incandescent light bulbs; *Wavefunction*, which used a surveillance camera to detect the presence of a visitor and moved an array of chairs up and down electromechanically in a mesmerizing wave pattern when someone entered the room; *Surface Tension*, in which the image of a human eye that was projected onto a screen followed visitors with eerie precision; and *1,000 Platitudes*, a triptych of photos featuring one thousand terms and catchphrases used by marketers to promote cities to potential investors.

The response to the Mexican pavilion was largely positive. "The highlight of the fair's tech-y art may be Mexico's first official participation in the Biennale, an installation by Rafael Lozano-Hemmer," William Hanley wrote for the online arts magazine *ArtInfo* (18 Nov. 2008), while Marcia E. Vetrocq commented for *Art in America* (8 Sept. 2007), "There is nothing tentative about Rafael Lozano-Hemmer's hardware-heavy and technologically agile works in the Mexican pavilion."

INSTALLATIONS IN THE UNITED STATES

In recent years Lozano-Hemmer has displayed some of his most popular and well-attended large-scale installations in major US cities. *Open Air*, for example, was mounted in Philadelphia in the fall of 2012 and allowed participants to record a voice message via a website. Several high-intensity spotlights, which were positioned over the Benjamin Franklin Parkway, reacted to the frequency and volume of the messages and varied their brightness and position accordingly. During the roughly three-week duration of the project, some sixty thousand people from ninety-two countries left almost six thousand messages in more than twenty languages. (The lights could also be made to follow a visitor around the Parkway by means of a special smartphone app that employed GPS technology.) The eye-catching project was voted one of the fifty best public art projects of the year by the Public Art Network.

For *Voice Tunnel*, New York City's 1,400-foot Park Avenue Tunnel was opened to pedestrians for three consecutive Sundays in 2013. Lozano-Hemmer installed three hundred theatrical spotlights designed to produce striking arches of light along the tunnel's walls and ceiling. Participants controlled the intensity of the lights by speaking into an intercom, which recorded and looped their voices. He also installed more than one hundred loudspeakers so that visitors could hear the messages.

PUBLIC OPPOSITION

As has been the case with many of Lozano-Hemmer's large-scale public works, New York City authorities did not immediately embrace the artist's vision for *Voice Tunnel*. The New York Police Department asked him to institute a six-second delay on all the messages reverberating through the tunnel so that potentially offensive or dangerous messages could be deleted before they were broadcasted. "In authoritarian regimes, that can work," Lozano-Hemmer told Julie Turkewitz for the *New York Times* (28 July 2013). "But not here. This is the place for people to express their views. That's what this project is about. And if you want to censor it—I've never in my life censored a work, and I won't do it." A compromise was ultimately reached, when Lozano-Hemmer agreed to assign a person to monitor each message as it was spoken, with only something clearly dangerous (such as someone screaming "Fire!") being deleted.

Lozano-Hemmer has referred to some of his public works as examples of "relational architecture," a term—according to Jacques Perron for the Daniel Langlois Foundation for Art, Science, and Technology website—that "reflects his desire to create social situations, which combine performances and encounters, by using technology to change how people relate to urban architecture. He emphasizes that the use of the adjective 'relational' seeks to avoid the already hackneyed 'interactive' label."

Sometimes it is not the authorities who try to squelch a project but the residents of the proposed site, who disallow the project altogether. In 2008, for example, residents of the Welsh town of Cardigan began voicing their vehement opposition to Lozano-Hemmer's *Turbulence*, a project in which 127 lighted buoys containing speakers would be floated on the River Teifi. The residents were concerned that wildlife habitats would be damaged; others believed the project would pose a navigational nightmare for boats should the floats get stuck in the river's mud or drift toward the center. In January 2008, the *Tivy-Side Advertiser* printed an open letter from Lozano-Hemmer to the residents of Cardigan in which he addressed their concerns and offered solutions. Despite his willingness to compromise and adjust the project, the plans and the project were rejected.

OTHER ARTWORKS

Some of Lozano-Hemmer's smaller works are in the permanent collections of such notable institutions as the Museum of Modern Art (MoMA) in New York City, which owns the piece *33 Questions per Minute*. For that work, a computer program automatically generates some 55 billion random questions, which are then displayed on monitors throughout the gallery. Visitors can type their own questions, which are immediately displayed on the monitors and added to the computer's memory to be used in rotation.

The Tate Modern, in London, owns *Subtitled Public*, a popular piece that projects a written "subtitle" onto a visitor (detected by a surveillance system when he or she enters the gallery). The word is chosen randomly by computer from a list of verbs conjugated in the third person. When two visitors touch, their subtitles are exchanged, encouraging what Lozano-Hemmer hopes will be thoughtful discussions of the asymmetry of observation, the arbitrary nature of computerized surveillance systems, and the dangers of summarily classifying people. (Because he acknowledges that technology becomes outdated so quickly, he has given museum officials permission to update the projector and programming code when needed.)

Lozano-Hemmer's dozens of other pieces have been shown at museums around the world, and he has been the subject of numerous solo shows. His high-profile private collectors include Mexican beverage magnate Eugenio López Alonso and New York real-estate mogul Jerry Speyer. Individual pieces of Lozano-Hemmer's work have reportedly sold for as much as $700,000.

PRIZES

Although Lozano-Hemmer has occasionally bemoaned the fact that art such as his is not taken seriously because it involves what some critics see as "gadgetry," he has been the recipient of numerous prizes and honors. These include a Golden Nica at the Prix Ars Electronica in Austria (2000), an International Bauhaus Award (2002), two British Academy of Film and Television Arts (BAFTA) Awards for interactive art (2002; 2005), a Rave Award for artist of the year from *Wired* magazine (2003), a Rockefeller-Ford Fellowship (2003), the Trophée des Lumières (2003), a National Endowment for the Arts grant (2011), and a Joyce Foundation Award (2012).

PERSONAL LIFE

Lozano-Hemmer and his Canadian wife have three children, including a set of twins whose gestation provided the basis for some of his art. He explained the impetus behind his *Pulse* series to Miranda Siegel for *New York* magazine (19 Oct. 2008): "When my wife was pregnant with twins and you listened to their hearts beating, there was this beautiful syncopation, like minimalist music. I wanted to expand that into something that could be appreciated visually."

Lozano-Hemmer and his family have homes in Montreal, Canada, and Madrid, Spain. He also maintains studios in each city where he employs a large team of engineers, who help him with the complex programming and equipment needed for his work. "When you are working with technology, you are always in a collaboration," he told Gladman during his 2002 interview. "You are always in a dialog. I like the idea that media arts are compared to performing arts. There are several roles. There is programming, writing, time, music, whatever roles you have. Even if you are alone with Photoshop, you are already collaborating with a bunch of programmers who made some rules."

SUGGESTED READING

Finkel, Jori. "Rafael Lozano-Hemmer Takes the 'Pulse' of Electronic Art." *Los Angeles Times*. Los Angeles Times, 17 Oct. 2010. Web. 14 July 2014.

Fortescue, Elizabeth. "Artwriter Interviews Rafael Lozano-Hemmer." *Artwriter.com*. Artwriter.com.au, 17 Dec. 2011. Web. 14 July 2014.

Gladman, Randy. "Body Movies: A Linz Ars Electronica Festival Award Winner on the State of Interactive Art." *Canadian Art* 19.4 (Winter 2002): 56–61. Print.

Gladman, Randy. "Rafael Lozano-Hemmer: Text Art." *Akrylic*. Gladman, 7 July 2008. Web. 14 July 2014.

Perron, Jacques. "Rafael Lozano-Hemmer." *La foundation Daniel Langlois*. FDL, 2009. Web. 14 July 2014.

Ross, Annabel. "Rafael Lozano-Hemmer Light Show to Create Nightclub in the Sky." *Sydney Morning Herald*. Fairfax Media, 5 June 2014. Web. 14 July 2014.

Turkewitz, Julie. "A Rare Chance to Stroll a Park Avenue Tunnel, in the Name of Art." *New York Times*. New York Times, 28 July 2013. Web. 14 July 2014.

SELECTED WORKS

Vectorial Elevation, 1999; *33 Questions per Minute*, 2000; *Body Movies*, 2001; *Frequency and Volume*, 2003; *Pulse Room*, 2006; *Flatsun*, 2011; *Open Air*, 2012; *Voice Tunnel*, 2013; *Method Random*, 2014

—*Mari Rich*

Jenna Lyons

Born: 1969
Occupation: Fashion executive

"Stand across the street from a J. Crew store and take a moment to survey the windows. More likely than not, you'll recognize in the mannequins some of fashion's archetypal forms," Molly Young wrote for *New York* magazine (14 Aug. 2011). "Move closer, however, and the impression skews. Wherever a look would seem to mimic its cultural referent too closely, some trick of styling swoops in to disrupt the cliché: the slim Jackie O. turtleneck is paired with a larksome faux-fur clutch or an Anna Karina trench with pumps the color of Fanta [orange soda]. None of these items is terribly exciting in its own right, or even recognizably J. Crew, but that is exactly the point. You can find a plain silk blouse at Urban Outfitters and cropped navy pants at Forever 21, but only J. Crew combines those items just so."

Getty Images Entertainment

The person largely responsible for that J. Crew sensibility is the company's iconoclastic executive creative director and president, Jenna Lyons. With her guidance, J. Crew, once known for relatively unadventurous, preppy garments, has developed a fervently fashion-conscious customer base that includes First Lady Michelle Obama. (When Barack Obama was inaugurated as US president in 2009, his wife and daughters sported J. Crew outfits.) In 2013—a year in which the company's annual revenues topped $2 billion—Lyons made an appearance on *Time* magazine's list of the hundred most influential people in the world. "She has made fashion relatable," designer Prabal Gurung wrote for *Time* (18 Apr. 2013), explaining Lyons's inclusion in that selective list. "I buy J. Crew, my mom does, my sister does, my niece and nephew do. She understands our zeitgeist. . . . Jenna has made J. Crew more than a brand or a company—it's a philosophy that believes in style."

EARLY LIFE AND EDUCATION

Jenna Lyons was born in Boston, Massachusetts, in 1969. She moved with her family to Palos Verdes, California, when she was four. Her father, an insurance agent, and mother, a homemaker and piano teacher, divorced when she was seven years old. It was difficult for her to watch her mother struggle to make ends meet after the divorce. "I'll never forget my mother standing in the tuna-fish aisle thinking, 'Are we going to get tuna fish this week?'" Lyons explained to Danielle Sacks for *Fast Company* (May 2013). She

added that experience made her feel "like [she] never wanted to rely on a man."

Her childhood was also made difficult by incontinentia pigmenti also known as Bloch-Sulzberger syndrome, a genetic disorder that causes hair loss, scarring, and malformed teeth. (She is very frank about the fact that she has long worn dentures because of the condition.) "It's amazing how cruel kids can be and super-judgmental and really just downright mean," she told Sacks. The teasing was aimed not only at her patchy hair and conical teeth but also at her unusual physique; she reached her full height of over six feet at an early age. "I know what it's like not to feel beautiful," Lyons said during an emotional acceptance speech when she was named a 2012 Woman of the Year by *Glamour* magazine. "I remember that feeling."

Lyons found some relief from her social problems in seventh grade, when she learned to sew in a home economics class. She crafted a long, bias-cut skirt of yellow rayon printed with large watermelons and received a compliment from the most popular girl in school. "When I put the skirt on, I looked like a totally different person," she told Young. After her grandmother gave her a sewing machine and a subscription to *Vogue*—she vividly recalls her first issue, from 1982, with Italian model Isabella Rossellini on the cover—Lyons began haunting the local fabric store, experimenting with whatever the ill-stocked suburban shop had available. While attending the private school Le Lycée Français de Los Angeles, she delighted in altering her uniforms, shortening the skirts or adding nonregulation buttons to the sweaters. She later moved on to a public Palos Verdes high school, and during her summer vacations she worked as a lifeguard to earn money to buy clothes. (She has recalled ordering several rayon shirts in various colors from J. Crew at one point.)

With her sights set on a career in fashion design, the teenage Lyons began assembling a portfolio of her creations, and after graduating from high school, she was enrolled in the Otis College of Art and Design in Los Angeles. For her sophomore year, she transferred to Parsons the New School of Design in New York City, where her classmates in the school's fashion program included Tom Mora, who went on to design menswear for J. Crew, and Derek Lam. Lyons earned a bachelor of fine arts degree in 1990 and set about finding a job. "I was a poor twenty-something-year-old kid who couldn't afford to buy a single piece from most of the places I wanted to work," she said in an interview for the Parsons website.

JOINING J. CREW

After leaving Parsons, Lyons completed an internship at Donna Karan. She was excited to land an interview at J. Crew, then a small company that branded itself as an all-American purveyor of comfortable wardrobe basics. "When my J. Crew interviewer showed up in jeans, I knew I could be myself at the company," she recalled in her Parsons profile.

While the interviewer was impressed enough by the young Lyons to ask for a copy of her portfolio, there were no actual job openings at the company, so Lyons bided her time waiting tables. Within a few months, however, she was called back to meet with a representative from J. Crew's menswear department. She went, bringing with her a series of sketches that were deemed good enough to show to Emily Woods, J. Crew's cofounder. Upon viewing the drawings, Woods immediately offered Lyons a job. The young designer was so excited by the offer that she forgot to ask what her starting salary would be. Of that first position, Lyons told Lisa Armstrong for the *Telegraph* (18 Nov. 2013), "[I was the] assistant to the assistant to the person in charge of rugby shirts. . . . I agonized over those stripes." Despite that exceptionally modest start, Lyons steadily worked her way up the corporate ladder. She held the title of designer from 1994 to 1995, and from 1996 to 1998 she served as design director. In 1999 she was named senior design director and vice president of women's design.

All was not well at the company during those years, however, and Lyons found the corporate focus on pushing merchandise, rather than on creating desirable fashions, distressing. "[Sales managers] would give us a list beforehand that said they needed three $78 pants, six $58 sweaters and ten $78 sweaters," she told Booth Moore for the *Los Angeles Times* (12 July 2009). The results were predictably bleak. "By the early 2000s, the brand had foundered," Young wrote. "Boxy acrylic cardigans shared catalogue space with poly-cotton sleepwear and chinos lined in flannel. There were stretch velvet pants and sueded football jerseys, and zip-cardigans in a pattern that looked like bathroom tile. Four CEOs had cycled through in five years. The company's credit rating was cut, profits faded, and morale was low enough that Lyons can only describe the time in battle metaphors." Lyons elaborated, "We were lost soldiers—working away, following orders. I was shell-shocked and burned from what was going on. Fried."

GROWING WITH THE COMPANY

In January 2003 J. Crew underwent a major transformation. That month Millard "Mickey" Drexler, recently ousted from the helm of the retail behemoth Gap in the wake of falling stock prices, took over as the new CEO. On his first day, Drexler, a plainspoken Bronx native, announced that everyone at the company would be auditioning to retain their jobs. In front of the entire design team, he asked Lyons to review the fall collection. "At that point I was like, I have to

be honest," Lyons recalled to Sacks. "I can't lie to him because this is sort of a do-or-die situation." When she expressed dissatisfaction with several pieces, including a nondescript pair of stretch pants, a stiff leather jacket, and a boucle sweater that she admitted reminded her of a poodle, he instructed her to drop the offending garments on the floor. "I didn't know if I was going to be fired," Lyons told Sacks. "I was so confused, and I was scared, but I was also a little bit excited, because all the things that I liked and that I thought were [right for the brand] he was leaving up on the wall."

After the entire line had been reviewed, Drexler notified Lyons not only that was she keeping her job but also that he was charging her with filling in the gaps left by the product purge. Impressed by her personal style—she was wearing cargo pants with high heels the day they met—he suggested she design things she herself might like to wear. "The outfit's juxtaposition of hard and soft, casual and dressed up, masculine and feminine, became the foundation for Lyons' J. Crew," Moore explained.

In 2007 Lyons was promoted to the post of creative director. She explained to Tommye Fitzpatrick for the *Business of Fashion* (18 Apr. 2012), "People think being a creative director [means] I'm actually touching everything and getting to create everything. In the end, honestly, what it's about is taking care of all the creative people that work with you, really trying to make sure you're nurturing them to the best of your ability and getting the best out of them. That's the most important part of my role." She asserted, "Ultimately, my job is really to make sure that everything that comes out of this company looks visually unified and looks good, looks like the brand, looks in my opinion beautiful."

In 2010 she was named executive creative director and president of J. Crew. That dual role is an unusual one in the fashion industry. "What it says," Lyons told Sacks, "is that no financial decision weighs heavier than a creative decision. They are equal." Her relationship with Drexler is sometimes described as being akin to a father-daughter one, and each frequently praises the other when speaking to journalists. Many industry observers believe that Lyons will likely take the reins of the company when Drexler decides to step down as CEO.

PERSONAL LIFE

In 2002 Lyons married the artist Vincent Mazeau. The couple lived in a painstakingly restored brownstone in the Brooklyn neighborhood of Park Slope. The home was regularly featured in design magazines, and journalists seemed particularly interested in Lyons's room-size closet, which housed custom-made rolling garment racks, hundreds of pairs of shoes, and a fireplace.

The pair had one son, Beckett. Lyons set off a firestorm of controversy in 2011, when a J. Crew advertisement that featured a picture of her painting Beckett's toenails bright pink was unveiled. "Lucky for me I ended up with a boy whose favorite color is pink," the caption read. "Toenail painting is way more fun in neon." Conservative commentators were outraged, deeming the ad an attack on masculinity.

No sooner had that controversy blown over than another erupted. That summer Lyons and Mazeau divorced, and tabloids were rife with details of their custody battle and financial wrangling. Later, when Lyons confirmed that she was involved in a romantic relationship with jewelry executive Courtney Crangi, rumors circulated that Crangi had been the catalyst for the divorce. (Lyons has insisted that the two did not begin dating until after the marriage was over.) The two women live together in the Manhattan neighborhood of Tribeca.

Despite the tabloid press's sometimes mean-spirited coverage of her personal life, fans of J. Crew often count themselves personal fans of Lyons as well. "With her spindly six-foot-tall stature and signature knack for mixing feminine 'fancy' items like sequin pants, satin floral trousers, and glittery statement jewelry with broken-in basics (chambray shirts, striped tees, crewneck sweaters)," Perrie Samotin wrote for *StyleCaster* (15 Apr. 2013), "it's not an exaggeration to say Lyons has become something of a personal-style deity to legions of women who are, for lack of a better word, obsessed with her and everything she represents."

SUGGESTED READING

Colman, David. "Jenna Lyons, the Woman Who Dresses America." *New York Times.* New York Times, 18 Jan. 2013. Web. 6 May 2014.

Fitzpatrick, Tommye. "Jenna Lyons Says You Have to Make Quick Decisions from the Gut." *Business of Fashion.* Business of Fashion, 18 Apr. 2012. Web. 12 May 2014.

Harris, Sarah. "The Creative Force behind J Crew." *Observer.* Guardian News and Media, 28 Apr. 2012. Web. 6 May 2014.

Samotin, Perrie. "Jenna Lyons: Her 20 All-Time Best Outfits." *StyleCaster.* StyleCaster, 15 Apr. 2013. Web. 12 May 2014.

—*Mari Rich*

Ma Jun

Born: 1968
Occupation: Environmentalist

Ma Jun is the founding director of the Institute of Public and Environmental Affairs (IPE), an independent research organization in China. A

AFP/Getty Images

former journalist, he is the author of the book *China's Water Crisis* (1999). Ma is considered one of China's foremost environmental activists, known for combining old-fashioned detective work and digital media to pressure multinational corporations and state-owned enterprises to reform their business practices. Though IPE has no official regulatory authority, Ma and his team have been able to affect change through the distribution of information. This in itself is revolutionary in China, where the government often obscures or censors information about issues it views to be politically sensitive. According to Chi-Chu Tschang for the blog *Business of Water* (2 Apr. 2011), "[the] Chinese government actually generates voluminous amounts of data [on the environment]." However, "no one had collected the data and put it into a database for everyone to access until the IPE came along."

The IPE's air and water pollution maps have helped to increase public awareness about environmental issues in China. "When I look at China's environmental problems, the real barrier is not lack of technology or money," Ma told Christina Larson for *Fast Company* (27 Apr. 2012). "It's lack of motivation. The motivation should come from regulatory enforcement, but enforcement is weak and environmental litigation is near to impossible. So there's an urgent need for extensive public participation to generate another kind of motivation."

In 2006, Ma was listed in the Time 100, *Time* magazine's list of the world's one hundred most influential people. For his innovative brand of grassroots environmentalism, Ma was awarded the Goldman Prize for Asia—often described as the "Green Nobel Prize"—in 2012.

EARLY CAREER AND *CHINA'S WATER CRISIS*

Ma was born in Qingdao, a large city in China's Shandong province, in 1968. His mother was an administrator and his father was an engineer. They raised Ma in Beijing. "[It] was such a different city," Ma told Larson, recalling the capital's lack of cars and the variety of bugs "swirling" around the city streetlamps. He learned the poems of China's great ancient poets, such as Li Bai and Du Fu, who revered the country's rivers and wildlife. "I also have a vivid memory of dazzling sunlight coming out of the sky," he told Larson. Now, Beijing's skies are clouded with smog from cars, burning coal, construction, and factories. In an article for the bilingual environmental news website *China Dialogue* (13 Mar. 2012), Ma wrote that the city's lung cancer rates have risen by 60 percent over the last ten years. He imagines a day in Beijing without pollution, stating, "On the morning of that day, you won't wake up with a sore throat [and] in the dazzling sunlight of an afternoon, even very ordinary buildings will look beautiful against the blue backdrop of the sky."

After graduating with a degree in journalism from the University of International Relations in Beijing, Ma joined the Beijing staff of the *South China Morning Post* as a researcher and translator in 1993. Travelling for his job, Ma was shocked by the environmental impact of the Three Gorges Dam project and the dried up remains of Dongting Lake; it was not the landscape he remembered from the poems of his childhood. Ma wanted to write a story about water pollution and ill-advised engineering projects like the Yellow River Commission, but realized that he had compiled too much information for just a single news article. Using the archives that were available to him as a journalist, Ma wrote a book called *Zhongguo shui weiji* in 1999. The book's English translation, *China's Water Crisis*, was published in 2004. It took a while for the book to find its audience, but later, the actor and environmentalist Ed Norton (whose father oversaw the Nature Conservancy's Yunnan Great Rivers project in China) wrote in *Time* magazine (8 May 2006) that the book could be considered "for China what Rachel Carson's *Silent Spring* was for the U.S.—the country's first great environmental call to arms."

ENVIRONMENTAL CONSULTANT

In 2000, Ma became the chief representative of the *South China Morning Post* website. Two years later, he joined China's Sinosphere Corporation as an environmental consultant. In this role, he made a startling realization when he was tasked with preparing a corporate social responsibility (CSR) program for the supply chain of a major company. The company was reviewing the practices of its supply chain under pressure from labor and environmental groups, and Ma was surprised by the company's decision to change its business practices in light of public discontent. "When we first identified gaps, and made clear that if [the suppliers] didn't change they were going to lose their business, they changed their behavior in just a few months," Ma told John Haffner for Carnegie Council's online magazine, *Policy Innovations* (11 Feb. 2013). "When you put a multimillion dollar contract at stake, it has big leverage."

Ma was invited to Yale University in New Haven, Connecticut, as a visiting World Fellow in 2004. At Yale, he compared environmental management laws and systems in China with those of the United States. Ma observed that successful environmental agencies in the West took violators to court. However, he knew that in China—where courts were often beholden to local officials sympathetic to polluters—such a route would not be effective. Instead, Ma realized that if he put the information in the hands of the people (or from a business perspective, the customers) they might be motivated to act as a unit, putting pressure on the Chinese government as well as shaming offending companies into cleaning up their act. After struggling to find a publisher for his next book upon returning to China in 2005, Ma decided to use his writing as a guide for establishing an organization devoted to environmental issues.

INSTITUTE OF PUBLIC AND ENVIRONMENTAL AFFAIRS (IPE)

Ma founded the Institute of Public and Environmental Affairs (IPE) in 2006, and the group's first project, the China Water Pollution Map, was launched in September. Ma told Haffner that the IPE and its databases were founded on the idea that "participation requires information." The IPE began with Ma, two staffers, and a network of volunteers rooting out company violations from a mass of records. In 2007, the IPE joined a coalition of NGOs to launch the Green Choice Alliance, a database that allows consumers and companies to search for records of a supplier's violations within the previous nine years. In 2008, the IPE's job got a little easier after the Chinese government passed a law requiring local governments to release pollution data. The same year, Walmart used the database to identify factories within their supply chain that were in violation of China's green laws and worked with the IPE to make changes in those factories. Other international brands like Panasonic, Coca-Cola, GE, Levi's, and Microsoft followed suit—citing the database as evidence for changes in their supply chains.

In 2009, the IPE uncovered a plethora of reports of heavy metal pollution causing health problems, though the source surprised them. "To our surprise, the source wasn't mines or government-operated smelters," Ma told Larson, "but factories manufacturing global IT equipment." As it turned out, IT companies were responsible for several other public health violations. Factory workers in at least one plant were exposed to a chemical called n-hexane, used to clean touch screens, and were suffering from nerve damage. After undertaking an investigation that sought to match the offending factories with the international companies that employed them, the IPE found that Wintek, the company operating the factory where there had been reports of exposure to n-hexane and a subcontractor of the company Foxconn, was a supplier for Apple.

"POISON APPLE" CAMPAIGN

In 2010, the IPE and the Green Alliance contacted Apple's CEO Steve Jobs, as well as the CEOs of twenty-eight other tech companies to report their findings. Siemens, the German electronics conglomerate, was among a number of companies that agreed to work with the IPE. Apple did not. The tech giant refused to confirm its relationship to any of the factories—arguing that, as Gies put it, releasing such information would "jeopardize trade secrets." Though this response was clearly a dismissal, Ma assured Apple that the IPE was not interested in smearing the company, only in improving environmental and working conditions.

This shrewd approach has set Ma apart from other activists. He seeks to work with companies to make a change, appearing to operate under the premise that, if companies only knew what was happening within their supply chain they would work to make it right. "He's naturally cooperative, more of a Paul Newman–style activist than Ralph Nader," Larson wrote of Ma. Still, Ma's attempts to reach out to Apple were met with silence. The same year, Ma sent a letter to Jobs, written with a factory worker named Jia Jingchuan who was hospitalized for n-hexane poisoning. After the letter went unanswered, Ma took a more public tack. What followed is an excellent example of Ma's own efficient use of informed public participation as a tool for activism.

Ma launched a social media "Poison Apple" campaign protesting Apple's lack of oversight. In January 2011, Ma wrote a report called "The Other Side of Apple" that was published widely on the Internet. It chronicles Apple's digressions and subsequent denial of any wrongdoing. It also includes information on twelve employee suicides that occurred at Foxconn in 2010. Ma also produced a video that intercuts footage of factory workers suffering from n-hexane poisoning with images from Apple's celebrated launch events.

APPLE'S RESPONSE TO IPE

Soon after, Apple released its own progress report. The paper confirms reports of n-hexane poisoning in its factories, but fails to address any of the larger issues raised by the IPE. The IPE launched a full investigation into Apple's supply chain, which culminated in a forty-six-page report called "The Other Side of Apple II," published in September 2011. Its release coincided with Tim Cook's official promotion to CEO at Apple, following the death of Jobs in October 2011. Within a week of Cook's tenure, the company contacted the IPE to set up a meeting to discuss issues related to n-hexane exposure. In 2012, Apple issued a supplier-responsibility progress report, citing environmental audits on fourteen of the company's suppliers.

According to a January 2013 report from the IPE, Apple has made significant strides since 2010. Most notably, the company has allowed third-party audits of some of its business practices, overseen by the IPE and the Green Alliance. "Apple and the NGOs [IPE, Friends of Nature, Envirofriends, and Nanjing Greenstone], in a step-by-step process, gradually came to a common understanding to push highly polluting materials suppliers to make real changes," the IPE wrote in a January 29, 2013, press release. Ma has expressed the hope that the IPE's success with Apple will encourage other companies to self-regulate.

THE WORK AHEAD

In 2013, Ma and the IPE launched a social media campaign called "Take a Picture to Locate a Polluter," in which citizens and activists are encouraged to post photos of environmental pollution and offending factories. After a photo is posted, the IPE investigates and verifies the claim. The value of the project is two-fold: the crowd sourcing improves the accuracy of the IPE pollution maps, and it gives the amateur photographer a sense of affectivity—a sense of being a part of something larger.

The availability of clean water in China is an issue that has continued to plague the country. According to a report in the *Economist* in October 2013, the situation has become increasingly dire in the years after Ma's book was first published. China is facing a dangerous water shortage due to the country's unsustainable levels of consumption. In addition, there are significant regional disparities pertaining to water resources—most of China's water is in the south, but half of its population and most of its farmland are in the north. Additionally, pollution from farms and factories present additional environmental problems, making what little water remains largely unusable. According to the *Economist* (12 Oct. 2013), only half of the water sources in Chinese cities are fit to drink: "More than half the groundwater in the north China plain, according to the land ministry, cannot be used for industry, while seven-tenths is unfit for human contact, i.e., even for washing."

To rectify the problem, the Chinese government proposed the South-North Water Diversion Project, a vast linkage of canals and tunnels connecting the Yangzi River in the south with the Yellow River in the north. China has accomplished several large-scale water infrastructure projects—the best known being the Three Gorges Dam on the Yangzi River. Nevertheless, many environmentalists—including Ma—have argued that the water diversion project will do more harm than good. Environmentalists argue that rather than looking for ways to conserve water and ways to crack down on polluters, the Chinese government has focused on increasing water supply in the short term, wreaking more environmental havoc in the process. Ma told Naomi Li for *China Dialogue* (21 Sept. 2006) that local government officials are all too willing to sacrifice clean water for the revenue that regulation-flouting companies bring to the provinces. "Water issues present a dichotomy between development and environmental protection. The central government has adjusted some of its strategies and policies, but at a local level, officials still place too great an emphasis on economic development."

GOVERNMENT ACTION

The Chinese government has become more responsive to the pleas of environmentalists, in part a result of work conducted by organizations like the IPE. The Chinese media has begun to issue more reports on pollution and the environment, and some local authorities are beginning to warm to the idea of tougher regulations. More generally, enthusiasm for environmental action in China has been spurred by abysmal conditions in the country. On October 25, 2013, Edward Wong for the *New York Times* reported that the northeastern city of Harbin was shut down by dangerous smog conditions. The emergency terrified residents who wondered what the coming months might bring. "With winter approaching, cities north of the Huai River are turning on their coal-fired municipal heating systems, whose emissions were found in one study to shorten residents' life spans by an average of five years," Wong wrote.

The city has undertaken an emergency program aimed at decreasing air pollution, but Ma, who was interviewed by Wong for the article, said the program is not enough. "I think people won't be satisfied with just knowing which day to put on face masks or not go to school or keep their children indoors. They really want blue-sky days."

Ma lives in Beijing.

SUGGESTED READING

Foroohar, Rana. "Cleaning Up China." *Time.* Time, 24 June 2013. Web. 18 Dec. 2013.

Gies, Erica. "Advocate Helps Track Polluters on Supply Chain." *New York Times.* New York Times, 22 Apr. 2012. Web. 18 Dec. 2013.

Haffner, John, and Ma Jun. "Ma Jun: Information Empowers." *Policy Innovations.* Policy Innovations, 11 Feb. 2013. Web. 18 Dec. 2013.

Larson, Christina. "Most Creative People of 2012: 1. Ma Jun." *Fast Company.* Mansueto Ventures, 27 Apr. 2012. Web. 18 Dec. 2013.

Ma Jun. "Tackling China's Water Crisis Online." Interview by Naomi Li. *China Dialogue.* China Dialogue, 21 Sept. 2006. Web. 18 Dec. 2013.

"Water: All Dried Up." *Economist.* Economist Newspaper, 12 Oct. 2013. Web. 18 Dec. 2013.

Wong, Edward. "Response to a City's Smog Points to a Change in Chinese Attitude." *New York Times* 25 Oct. 2013: A12. Print.

—*Molly Hagan*

Manny Machado

Born: July 6, 1992
Occupation: Baseball player

Baltimore Orioles third baseman Manny Machado is widely considered to be the most exciting young player his franchise has seen since Hall of Fame shortstop Cal Ripken Jr. Drafted by the Orioles in the first round of the 2010 Major League Baseball (MLB) Draft, Machado, whose Florida upbringing, Dominican roots, physical stature, and baseball skills have prompted comparisons to veteran player Alex Rodriguez, was initially groomed as a shortstop in the minor leagues before being converted to a third baseman. Still, Machado had played only two games at third base when he made his major-league debut with the Orioles in August 2012, at the age of twenty. Despite his inexperience, he quickly proved to be a natural at the position, and during the last months of the 2012 season, he played an important role in the Orioles clinching their first winning season since 1997.

Machado established himself as one of the game's brightest young talents in 2013, his first full season in the majors, when he led the American League (AL) in doubles and earned his first All-Star selection. That year he also received his first Rawlings Gold Glove Award after leading the AL in a number of defensive statistical categories. "Manny's got a chance to hit .300 with twenty-five or thirty home runs and one hundred [runs batted in (RBIs)] every year," Ripken told Molly Knight for *ESPN* (25 Dec. 2012). "He's going to be a superstar."

Getty Images

EARLY LIFE

Manuel "Manny" Arturo Machado was born on July 6, 1992, in Miami, Florida, to Dominican parents. His parents divorced when he was a child. With his older sister, Yasmine, Machado was raised by his mother, Rosa Nunez, and an uncle in the Miami suburb of Hialeah, a working-class enclave known for its predominantly Hispanic population. His mother supported the family by working six days a week at a Miami export company. Machado's uncle, a shipping coordinator who lived across the street, stepped in as a father figure and helped cultivate his love of baseball. "He didn't play [professionally]," Machado said of his uncle to Kevin Van Valkenburg for the *Baltimore Sun* (30 Aug. 2010). "But he really loved the sport. I was rarely outside with my friends growing up. I was always at the field with my uncle."

Machado grew up idolizing the perennial All-Star shortstop and third baseman Alex "A-Rod" Rodriguez, who is a fellow Miami native of Dominican descent. He also rooted for the hometown Miami Marlins (formerly the Florida Marlins), whose games he regularly attended. Machado began playing organized youth-league baseball at the age of six and developed his baseball skills by spending hours each day playing with his uncle at a nearby park. His uncle, who put him at the shortstop position from the time he started playing because of his natural fielding and throwing abilities, recalled to Joe Lemire for *Sports Illustrated* (1 June 2010), "On weekends

when all his other friends wanted to play or go to the pool, all he wanted to do was go to the park and hit and catch ground balls."

HIGH SCHOOL CAREER

Machado attended high school at Brito Miami Private School. Despite the school's small size, it has one of the best baseball programs in the state of Florida and has developed a steady stream of major-league prospects since the mid-1990s, most notably MLB first baseman Gaby Sánchez. Machado made Brito's varsity baseball team as a freshman and immediately offered a glimpse of his potential when, in his first varsity at-bat as a pinch hitter, he delivered a game-winning triple. He impressed Brito's head coach, Pedro Guerra, and the school's athletic director, Lazaro Fundora, not only with his natural talent but also with his work ethic and maturity. "We'd have practice at 3:15, and he was out there before everyone else at 1:30 doing his work," Fundora told Albert Chen for *Sports Illustrated* (29 Apr. 2013). "Later at night he'd hit at the cages, and then go to the park and take more ground balls."

Machado first caught the attention of major-league scouts during his junior year at Brito, when he earned first-team all-state honors and showcased his remarkable fielding ability. During the fall of 2009 he helped lead the US national under-eighteen team to its first ever baseball gold medal at the Pan American Championships in Barquisimeto, Venezuela. In six pool-play games, Machado hit two home runs and drove in nine runs.

During his senior season Machado solidified his status as a five-tool player—a player with strong fielding, throwing, and running abilities as well as a strong batting average and a powerful swing—by hitting .639 with twelve home runs and sixty-eight RBIs in twenty-nine games. By the time Machado graduated, he was one of the most heavily recruited shortstops in the country, with up to three dozen scouts in attendance at each of his games. He signed a letter of intent to attend Florida International University before deciding to forgo college to enter the 2010 MLB Draft. The Baltimore Orioles drafted Machado with the third overall pick in the draft's first round. Two months after the draft, the Orioles awarded him a signing bonus of $5.25 million, the second-largest bonus in club history.

BALTIMORE ORIOLE

Machado's arrival in Baltimore came with high expectations. Despite being one of baseball's most historic franchises, the Orioles were in the midst of their thirteenth consecutive losing season. Since their last winning season in 1997, the Orioles had failed to find a franchise player who could turn around their fortunes. Machado, the first shortstop the Orioles drafted in the first round since 1974, was regarded as a possible successor to Ripken, the iconic shortstop who retired in 2001 after a twenty-one-year career. To many in the organization, the only question was whether Machado would remain at shortstop by the time he entered the major leagues. At the time of his drafting, Machado was a lanky six feet two inches and weighed 180 pounds. Oriole scouts, however, expected him to fill out his frame enough, via weight training and diet, to project a possible long-term switch to the third-base position, which better suited his physical stature.

Projections notwithstanding, Machado immediately became the Orioles' top middle-infield prospect. He ascended through the team's farm system in just two years. After playing two games with the rookie-level Gulf Coast League Orioles, Machado was assigned to the Orioles' short-season A affiliate, the Aberdeen IronBirds of the New York–Penn League, where he finished the 2010 season, hitting safely in all seven games in which he played with the team. He opened the 2011 season with the A-level Delmarva Shorebirds of the South Atlantic League and was selected to participate in the league's midseason All-Star Game. He played the second half of the season with the advanced A-affiliate Frederick Keys, with whom he batted .245 with five home runs, twenty-six RBIs, three triples, and eight stolen bases in sixty-three games.

During the Orioles' 2012 spring training, Machado, who had continued to play shortstop up to that point, began working with the club's then minor-league coordinator, Bobby Dickerson, in preparation for a move to third base. The plan was set in motion by the Orioles to accommodate All-Star Gold Glove Award–winning shortstop J. J. Hardy, who had been acquired from the Minnesota Twins before the 2011 season. Dickerson explained to Chen that "it was supposed to be casual. But [Machado] took it as seriously as if he were [the Orioles'] starting third baseman."

A SEAMLESS TRANSITION

Following the Orioles' spring training, Machado was sent to play with the Bowie Baysox of the AA Eastern League, where he continued to be used almost exclusively as a shortstop. In 109 games with the Baysox, he batted .266 with eleven home runs, twenty-six doubles, and fifty-nine RBIs. Machado had played just two minor-league games at third base when, on August 9, 2012, the Orioles called him up to the majors to fill that position, in what Chen called "the boldest move made by any team during the 2012 season."

At the time of Machado's arrival, the Orioles were a surprising 60–51 and, for the first time in over a decade, firmly entrenched in the AL playoff race. Their defense, however, ranked among the league's worst. Machado, despite his limited time at third, was expected to make an immediate impact. In his major-league debut, a home game against the Kansas City Royals, he collected a single and a triple in an 8–2 Orioles loss. The following day, in his second game, he hit his first and second career home runs off of Royals former number-one pick Luke Hochevar. At twenty years and thirty-five days old, Machado became the youngest player in MLB history to accomplish such a feat that early in his career.

Machado finished his rookie season with a respectable .262 batting average, with seven home runs and twenty-six RBIs in fifty-one games. He ignited the Orioles' offense and helped the team secure its first winning season and first postseason berth since 1997. Though the Orioles lost to the New York Yankees in five games in the AL Division Series, Machado established himself as one of the most exciting young talents in the game.

The highlight of Machado's rookie campaign came on September 12, 2012, in a game against the Tampa Bay Rays. With two outs in the top of the ninth inning and a 2–2 score, Machado fielded a slow-roller hit by Tampa Bay third baseman Evan Longoria and then executed a brilliant pump fake—a move in which the player with the ball pretends to throw it in order to confuse the opposing player—to catch pinch runner Rich Thompson in an inning-ending rundown between third base and home. The defensive gem went viral on the Internet and instantly made Machado a Baltimore folk hero. Machado, who also scored the game's winning run, told Knight that it was "the best play of [his] life." Orioles general manager Dan Duquette recounted to Knight, "It was the moment I knew, 'Wow, this kid's a star.'" Ripken told Knight, "Even with all his physical gifts, Manny's greatest asset might be his mind."

MLB ALL-STAR

Machado followed his promising rookie debut with a breakout year in 2013. Machado made history when he finished the month of May with a total of forty-four hits, which were the most in a calendar month by a player younger than twenty-one since Mickey Mantle's forty-six in 1952. Machado earned his first career All-Star selection, as a reserve infielder for the AL squad, after entering the 2013 midseason break hitting a major league–leading thirty-nine doubles, which was the second-highest total ever hit in the first half of a season.

Machado cooled off during the second half of the season but still finished the year with impressive numbers, hitting .283 with fourteen home runs, seventy-one RBIs, and an

AL-leading fifty-one doubles. Meanwhile, he established himself as arguably the best defensive third baseman in the game. For his remarkable defensive work, Machado received his first Rawlings Gold Glove Award, becoming the first Orioles third baseman to win the award since Hall of Famer Brooks Robinson in 1975. "I don't think there's any way that I could do what he's done," J. J. Hardy, who was that year's AL Gold Glove winner at shortstop, told Manny Navarro for the *Miami Herald* (16 July 2013). "Really not playing any games in the minor leagues, then to come up and . . . play third base and be as good as he has. I don't think people realize how good of an athlete he is to be able to make that transition so easily."

During the final week of the 2013 season, Machado suffered a season-ending knee injury after landing on first base awkwardly in a game against the Tampa Bay Rays. He left the game on a stretcher and was forced to undergo reconstructive surgery on his knee. By that time, the Orioles had already been eliminated from the AL playoff race. They finished tied for third in the AL East with an 85–77 record.

Prior to the 2014 season, Machado had his contract renewed by the Orioles for $519,000. He missed the first month of the 2014 season while undergoing rehabilitation for his knee. On June 1, a month after returning to the Orioles lineup, Machado recorded his first career grand slam in a game against the Houston Astros.

Machado shares a luxury condominium near Baltimore's Inner Harbor with his fiancé, Yainee Alonso, the sister of his best friend, San Diego Padres first baseman Yonder Alonso. The two are set to be married in Paris, France, in December 2014.

SUGGESTED READING

Bizik, Jessica. "Magic Manny." *Baltimore Style.* Clipper City Media, Mar.-Apr. 2013. Web. 10 June 2014.

Chen, Albert. "Mannyball." *Sports Illustrated.* Time, 29 Apr. 2013. Web. 10 June 2014.

Ghiroli, Brittany. "Tireless Effort Fueled Rise of O's Machado." *MLB.com.* MLB Advanced Media, 16 Sept. 2010. Web. 10 June 2014.

Knight, Molly. "Manny Machado's Big Night." *ESPN The Magazine.* ESPN Internet Ventures, 25 Dec. 2012. Web. 10 June 2014.

Navarro, Manny. "Hialeah's Manny Machado a Young All-Star with Poise of a Veteran." *Miami Herald.* Miami Herald Media, 16 July 2013. Web. 10 June 2014.

Van Valkenburg, Kevin. "Orioles' Top Draft Pick Machado Adjusting to Life as a Pro." *Baltimore Sun.* Baltimore Sun, 30 Aug. 2010. Web. 10 June 2014.

—*Chris Cullen*

Macklemore

Born: June 19, 1983
Occupation: Rapper

In the high-testosterone, machismo-filled world of hip-hop, Macklemore has produced music that is "shockingly genuine," Casey Jarman wrote for the Portland, Oregon, *Willamette Week* (7 Sept. 2011), about the white Seattle-based rapper. "Macklemore's lyrics tend toward high-drama cautionary tales," Jarman added, "not cars or sexual conquests." The biggest hip-hop artist to emerge from Seattle since Sir Mix-A-Lot, Macklemore has earned the respect of his peers and the hip-hop community for his unique lyrical style, daring fashion sense, and independent approach to the music industry. He began his career as a solo act, self-releasing one EP, *Open Your Eyes* (2000), and one full-length album, *The Language of My World* (2005), before forming a creative partnership with Ryan Lewis, his full-time producer and business partner, in late 2008. After producing two EPs and a series of online-only singles, the duo were catapulted to fame with the release of their debut studio album, *The Heist,* in 2012. The album featured the international smash hit "Thrift Shop," which topped the Billboard Hot 100 chart. In the process Macklemore and Lewis became only the second independent artists in history to top that chart without a major record deal. *The Heist,* meanwhile, became one of the best-selling

Getty Images

albums of 2013 and earned seven Grammy nominations, winning awards in four categories.

EARLY LIFE AND EDUCATION

Born Ben Haggerty on June 19, 1983, in Seattle, Washington, Macklemore was raised in its Capitol Hill neighborhood, which is known for cultural diversity, thriving nightlife, and a large gay population. He has a brother, Tim, who is four years his junior. His father ran an office furniture company, and his mother was a homemaker and social worker. Macklemore has said that he enjoyed a privileged middle-class upbringing. In the song "Claiming the City," off *The Language of My World* (2005), he raps, "I grew up on Capitol Hill/ With two parents and two cars/ . . . My mom didn't have a job, because my dad made enough money that we could live comfortably and he could support us."

Macklemore first discovered hip-hop music at the age of seven after hearing the song "The Humpty Dance" by the Digital Underground. "I dubbed the tape from a friend who was older than me," he recalled to Marisa Fox for *Billboard* (25 May 2013), "and became obsessed." Influenced by the Digital Underground's lead vocalist, Shock G, best known for wearing a large fake nose as his flamboyant alter ego Humpty Hump, Macklemore immersed himself in the music and culture of hip-hop. He started rhyming on local street corners with his friends and covering hip-hop songs at school talent shows. "I was a weird, creative, extroverted child," he told Simon Vozik-Levinson for *Rolling Stone* (11 Apr. 2013). "And I always had a desire to be on a stage."

Macklemore attended TOPS, an alternative K–8 public school in Seattle's Seward Park neighborhood, before enrolling at Garfield High School in the city's Central District. At Garfield, whose alumni include electric guitarist Jimi Hendrix, martial artist and actor Bruce Lee, and composer-producer Quincy Jones, Macklemore began writing his first rap lyrics. He also started drinking and experimenting with drugs. Macklemore described Garfield to Vozik-Levinson as "this massive school, with no supervision," and recalled being "high every day, all the time" as a freshman. After his freshman year his parents moved him to Nathan Hale High School in north Seattle, in an effort to steer him in the right direction.

COLLEGE YEARS

While attending Nathan Hale High, Macklemore took classes at Seattle Central Community College through the Running Start program, which offers eleventh- and twelfth-grade students the chance to earn high school and college credits simultaneously. During the summer after his junior year, he attended the School of Visual Arts in New York, where he indulged his penchant for thrift shops and outlandish clothing. Around this time Macklemore started going by the moniker Professor Macklemore, which had originated from a project for a high school graphic arts class. In 2000, as Professor Macklemore, he independently released his first EP, *Open Your Eyes*, which was partly inspired by experiences with hallucinogenic psilocybin, commonly known as "magic mushrooms." At that time Macklemore explained to Dan Buyanovsky for *Interview* (9 Oct. 2012), "I was just trying to figure out who I was, and that search is documented on that album."

After graduating from Nathan Hale in 2001, Macklemore enrolled at the College of Santa Fe in New Mexico. He left the college after a year, however, after failing to get into its music program. Afterward Macklemore attended Evergreen State College in Olympia, Washington. During his time at Evergreen, from 2004 to 2005, he conducted music workshops for juvenile offenders at the Green Hill Academic School in Chehalis, Washington, through a school-sponsored program called Gateways for Incarcerated Youth. The experience "gave me a lot to write about," as Macklemore said in an interview with Carolyn Shea for *Evergreen Magazine* (Spring 2013). "It was an intense experience and it gave me a lot to reflect on in my life." He eventually graduated with his bachelor's degree from Evergreen in 2009.

EARLY CAREER AND ADDICTION STRUGGLES

Macklemore's music career took off in 2004, when he released a song called "Welcome to MySpace," a humorous diatribe about the pitfalls of the social-networking service. He e-mailed the song to MySpace founder Tom Anderson, who in turn posted it on the then wildly popular social network, instantly bringing him to the attention of millions of people around the country. Soon afterward Macklemore, who by that time had already made a name for himself on Seattle's local hip-hop scene, dropped "Professor" from his name. In January 2005 he self-released his debut album, *The Language of My World*, which featured twenty tracks that offered a "savvy blend of blue-state politics and self-deprecating humor," as Simon Vozik-Levinson wrote. Though only a modest commercial success, the album helped him attract a strong local following and showcased a deeply honest songwriting style influenced by personal experience and topical issues.

Over the next three years, Macklemore built up his local fan base by performing at venues in and around Seattle. As his popularity surged, however, so did his drug and alcohol abuse. During this period Macklemore not only drank alcohol and smoked marijuana on a daily basis, but also developed problems with cocaine, painkillers, and "lean," a codeine-based drink popular in the hip-hop community. His various addictions stifled his artistic creativity, ate up his earnings, and made him become increasingly withdrawn from friends and family.

Macklemore's downward spiral culminated in 2008, when his father staged an intervention and urged him to go to treatment. After completing a thirty-five day rehab program in Canada, he gave up drugs and alcohol. "I don't have moderation when using drugs and alcohol," he explained to Siam Goorwich for the UK *Independent* (19 May 2013). "It got to the point where it was hurting my life, my potential." (With the exception of a brief relapse with "lean" in 2011, Macklemore has reportedly been clean.)

PARTNERSHIP WITH RYAN LEWIS

By the time he completed rehab, Macklemore's music career had reached a nadir. "I was close to giving up," he admitted to Dan Buyanovsky. "I was broke, unemployed . . . and living in my parents' basement. It was a 'If this doesn't work, I gotta get a real job' time in my life." Determined to salvage his career, Macklemore rededicated himself to songwriting. Around this time Macklemore began his creative partnership with Ryan Lewis, an ambitious, jack-of-all-trades producer, musician, and Spokane native whom he had first met on MySpace in 2006. "I had 'friend-requested' Ben after hearing one of his mixtapes and he responded by sending me a message about a beat," Lewis recalled to Goorwich. "Not long after, we met at my parents' house and became friends." Lewis initially worked as a photographer for Macklemore before becoming his full-time producer and business partner.

The first fruits of Macklemore's partnership with Lewis arrived in September 2009, with the release of a compilation called *The Unplanned Mixtape*. The album's lead single, "The Town," celebrated Seattle's hip-hop history. An accompanying music video for the song, directed by Zia Mohajerjasbi, was released on YouTube and quickly went viral. That same month Macklemore and Lewis released a sample-heavy, seven-song EP called *The Vs.*, which was made available online as a free digital download. One of the EP's songs, "Otherside," sampled the eponymous Red Hot Chili Peppers tune and addressed Macklemore's struggles with drug addiction. "*Vs.* was like coming back to life," the rapper told Andrew Matson for the *Seattle Times* (9 Feb. 2011). "It was like, 'Let me retrace my steps and remember why I liked making music in the first place.'" A fifteen-track version of the EP, called *The Vs. Redux*, was released in October 2010.

In 2010 Macklemore and Lewis formed the independent label Macklemore & Ryan Lewis LLC, which they began using to release all of their own music. The two adopted a do-it-yourself approach to all other areas of their music, from merchandising to video production. Meanwhile, they grew their national fan base through performances at US music festivals, word-of-mouth promotion, and savvy marketing strategies launched on social-networking sites Facebook and Twitter. Macklemore and Lewis's popularity was such that in early 2011, they sold out three consecutive shows at the Showbox, one of Seattle's most storied music venues. Around that time they released videos for two new singles, "My Oh My," a tribute to the longtime Seattle Mariners broadcaster Dave Niehaus (1935–2010), and "Wing\$," a cautionary anthem about Air Jordan sneakers and the perils of consumerism.

BREAKTHROUGH SUCCESS WITH *THE HEIST*

"My Oh My" and "Wing\$" were the first two singles off Macklemore and Lewis's long-awaited first full-length studio album, *The Heist*, released October 9, 2012. Distributed by the Alternative Distribution Alliance, a Warner Music Group company that aids independent artists in shipping and promoting recordings, the album debuted at number two on the Billboard 200 album chart and number one on Billboard's R & B/hip-hop albums and top rap albums charts. *The Heist* sold around 78,000 copies in its first week of release; by mid-September 2013 it had sold over one million copies in the United States.

Macklemore and Lewis's chart position was bolstered thanks to their breakout hit, "Thrift Shop," which was released as *The Heist*'s fifth single in August 2012. The song, an infectious, saxophone-tinged ode to bin-diving featuring a vocal hook from the Seattle-based singer Wanz, became a mainstay on pop radio and reached the top spot on the Billboard Hot 100 chart, where it remained for six consecutive weeks. It became only the second independent single to reach the top spot and the first by a Seattle hip-hop artist since Sir Mix-A-Lot accomplished the feat with his Grammy Award–winning single "Baby Got Back" in 1992. It also reached the top spot in eight other countries. Meanwhile, the accompanying video for the song, codirected by Jon Jon Augustavo, Macklemore, and Lewis, and filmed in various locations around Seattle, became a YouTube phenomenon. "Thrift Shop" was the second best-selling song of 2013 after selling more than six million digital downloads. By February 2014 its video had been viewed nearly a half million times on YouTube.

In addition to "Thrift Shop," *The Heist* included a second number-one hit, "Can't Hold Us," which featured vocals from the gospel and R & B singer Ray Dalton, and the top-twenty single "Same Love," which featured a chorus by the singer-songwriter Mary Lambert. (Both Dalton and Lambert are Seattle-based artists.) "Same Love," a condemnation of hip-hop's traditionally narrow-mind attitude toward homosexuality, was widely acclaimed and garnered considered media attention for its pro–gay marriage stance. "I'm always trying to push the margins," Macklemore explained to Siam Goorwich, referring to the song, which was inspired by his personal experience of having two gay uncles. "I wanna be an artist that writes songs that are different; I don't wanna write the same song that everyone else is writing."

The Heist received widespread praise from critics. In a review for *Filter* magazine (3 Jan. 2013) Jonathan Zwickel wrote, "[Macklemore] and Lewis find balance in extremes. There are no small moments on the record. With anthemic bombast, every song goes all-in on a clear-cut theme, whether quotidian (extolling second-hand fashion in 'Thrift Shop') or crucial (supporting gay marriage in 'Same Love')." Meanwhile, in another review for the *New Zealand Herald* (7 Dec. 2012), Scott Kara described the album as "refreshing," "clever," and "beautiful," and called it "innovative good-time hip-hop and pop music."

2014 GRAMMY AWARDS

In support of *The Heist*, Macklemore and Lewis embarked on a seventy-five show, ten-country world tour, performing to sell-out crowds at venues in the United States, Canada, Europe, Australia, and New Zealand. The tour concluded in December 2013 with a trio of performances in Seattle. The duo's promotion for the album also included appearances on such popular television programs as *The Ellen Degeneres Show*, *Late Night with Jimmy Fallon*, and *Saturday Night Live*.

On January 26, 2014, Macklemore and Lewis gave a special performance of "Same Love" at the Fifty-Sixth Annual Grammy Awards ceremony, in Los Angeles, with Mary Lambert, Queen Latifah, and Madonna. During the performance Queen Latifah, a certified minister in California, performed nuptials for thirty-three couples, both gay and straight. Macklemore and Lewis received seven Grammy nominations for *The Heist*, taking home awards in the categories for best new artist, best rap album, best rap song, and best rap performance, the latter two for "Thrift Shop."

Macklemore and Lewis have remained committed to maintaining their independence from major record labels. Their team includes manager Zach Quillen; Macklemore's fiancée Tricia Davis, who serves as their tour manager and video producer; and a small group of touring musicians and singers. "We're not your typical rap entourage," Macklemore told Simon Vozick-Levinson. "More like a weird little liberal arts school out on a field trip."

Macklemore and Lewis's recording studio is based in Seattle. The two began work on a follow-up album to *The Heist* in 2014.

SUGGESTED READING

Fox, Marisa. "Macklemore & Ryan Lewis." *Billboard* 25 May 2013: 20–23. Print.

Goorwich, Siam. "Macklemore: 'I Don't Have Moderation When Using Drugs and Alcohol. It Was Hurting My Life.'" *Independent*. Independent.co.uk, 19 May 2013. Web. 27 Jan. 2014.

Jarman, Casey. "Mack to the Future." *Willamette Week*. Willamette Week Newspaper & WWEEK.COM, 7 Sept. 2011. Web. 27 Jan. 2014.

Macklemore, and Ryan Lewis. "Macklemore & Ryan Lewis Find Clarity." Interview by Dan Buyanovsky. *Interview*. Interview, 9 Oct. 2012. Web. 27 Jan. 2014.

Matson, Andrew. "Seattle Rapper Macklemore Ready to Take a Shot at Pop Stardom." *Seattle Times*. Seattle Times, 9 Feb. 2011. Web. 27 Jan. 2014.

Sommerfeld, Seth. "A Different Beat." *Inlander*. Inlander, 26 Feb. 2013. Web. 27 Jan. 2014.

Vozick-Levinson, Simon. "Macklemore: Thrift Shop Hero." *Rolling Stone*. Rolling Stone, 11 Apr. 2013. Web. 27 Jan. 2014.

SELECTED WORKS

Open Your Eyes, 2000; *The Language of My World*, 2005; *The Unplanned Mixtape* (with Ryan Lewis), 2009; *The Vs.*, 2009; *The Heist*, 2012

—*Chris Cullen*

Audrey MacLean

Born: 1952
Occupation: Businesswoman and entrepreneur

In an article for *Forbes* magazine (23 May 2013), Meghan Casserly called Audrey MacLean "one of the nation's most seasoned, well-connected, and successful angel investors." Unlike venture capitalists, or VCs, who invest other people's money into various companies at different stages of growth, angel investors invest their own money into young companies looking for their first backers. A veteran angel investor, MacLean was a first-round backer of eBay, Google, Netflix, Twitter, Foursquare, and LinkedIn and has become a mentor to dozens of entrepreneurs. A two-time entrepreneur herself, MacLean kept a cool head through the dot-com fever of the late 1990s and early 2000s. "My motto was, You don't need six fluffy dot-coms when it was questionable whether you even needed one," she told

Courtesy of Tustin Ellison

Casserly. She continues to make money with her pragmatic approach to investing. MacLean is also a consulting professor at the Stanford School of Engineering. "I still look to her for inspiration," Reed Hastings, the CEO of Netflix, told Casserly. One VC was more emphatic in his praise, as quoted by Mary Beth Grover for *Forbes* (2 Nov. 1998): "Angel, nothing! Audrey MacLean walks on water."

EARLY LIFE AND EDUCATION

Audrey MacLean was born in 1952 in the rural town of Warwick, New York. She is one of ten children and understood the financial strain of raising a large family early on. By the time she was eight, she had already decided that she would win a college scholarship. The goal was practical but also necessary; her father didn't believe in sending women to college, and he convinced her that any student loan debt—"a negative dowry," as she referred to it in an interview with Adriana Gardella for the *New York Times* (24 June 2011)—would make her unmarriageable. In 1970, she earned a partial scholarship to the Ivy League Columbia University, but her father refused to cosign on a student loan. She attended Long Island University, where she had a full scholarship, instead. After a time, she dropped out and moved to Paris, France, where she modeled for fashion magazines including *Vogue*.

When MacLean returned to the United States, she settled in California, where she attended the University of Redlands. She wanted to make money, and she was good at math, so MacLean decided that technology would be a good fit. She graduated with a BS in mathematics in 1979. The tech industry was just beginning to take off, and though she was one of a

relative handful of women in the field, she did not see her gender as a barrier. MacLean blames early education for the persistently low number of women in tech. Too many young girls think of computers as toys for boys. "We need to get girls interested in computing by first grade," she told Gardella. "By fifth grade, it's game over." If more women majored in tech-related subjects, she claims, the numbers would be higher, because the jobs are there. Tech is a true meritocracy," she told Gardella. "Either you have the goods or you don't."

ENTREPRENEURIAL CAREER

MacLean got her first job as an engineer for the early Silicon Valley networking company Tymshare. Tymshare rented out its mainframe computer to companies that could not afford to house one. The technology that facilitated the exchange, MacLean told Casserly, "was the precursor to what became the Internet." MacLean became a sales executive but left the company in 1982 to cofound a wide-area networking company called Network Equipment Technologies (NET). As an entrepreneur, MacLean was relentless. She invested $70,000 of her own money—which she earned from the sale of a rental property—and did not take a salary for over a year. She called potential customers after she knew that their secretaries had left for the day, so she would be able to speak to them directly. NET got its first round of funding a year after its launch. The money, over $4.3 million, came because she recruited a manager from Comsat, an international telecommunication company, as the company's chief executive. Over the next four years, MacLean raised another $20 million and won an account with IBM. NET went public in February 1987. Its backers reaped sixteen times their investment, but MacLean ended up with less than one percent of the company, worth about $1 million. It was a lesson she would keep in mind for her next venture.

MacLean's second company, Adaptive, made high-speed switches. She helped found the company in 1988 and was named CEO in 1993, when it merged with NET. This time, MacLean held on to 21 percent of the company, a stake worth over $6 million. MacLean decided to cash out of NET and Adaptive, as she was working eighty-hour weeks and wanted to spend more time with her young daughters. With her earnings, she began her career as an investor.

EARLY INVESTMENTS

MacLean immediately knew that she wanted to put her money into exciting new companies—start-ups, she told Casserly, that she would have "wanted to build [herself]"—but her taste was picky and unusual. In 1987, she invested in a microbrewery called Pete's Brewing Co. She knew the founder, Pete Slosberg, through her husband. Slosberg was a brewing hobbyist turned entrepreneur. His American brown ale, Pete's Wicked Ale, had just won a silver medal at the Great American Beer Festival in Colorado. MacLean worked tirelessly on the brand's behalf, investing $215,000 of her own money and drumming up thousands more through her friends, some of whom did not even know anything about beer. When the company went public in 1995, its first backers saw a hundred-fold increase in their investments. The company was sold to Gambrinus, a Texas beer importer, in 1998 for $69 million. The brand was discontinued in 2011.

MacLean also invested in the newly public Cisco Systems, a hugely profitable enterprise that manufactures and sells networking equipment. Other investments offered opportunities for a quick turn-around. In 1997, MacLean and another investor named Michael Price seeded $2.5 million in Avidia, a company that manufactured low-end switches. Six months later, Avidia was sold to Pair Gain Communications for $94 million, yielding MacLean and Price ten times their initial investment.

MENTOR CAPITALIST

MacLean, who makes only one or two investments each year, is a hands-on investor. "I'm only going to make investments with people that I'd want to spend time with anyway," she told Casserly. She wants to invest in someone who is adversarial but not defensive when she asks challenging questions. "Starting a company is like going to war," she told Grover. "You can't do anything else but be fully engaged. You have to be insanely, passionately, nothing-can-stop-me committed." In many ways, Hastings, the CEO of Netflix, represents MacLean's ideal entrepreneur; he was wildly successful—likely beyond even what he or MacLean had ever envisioned—but he was also creative and open to advice. MacLean told Michael Copeland for the technology business magazine *Red Herring* (1 Aug. 2000) that she thinks of herself as less of an investor and more of a "mentor capitalist."

Hastings worked as an engineer for MacLean at Adaptive in the late 1980s. He approached MacLean with a business idea in 1990, when he was thirty years old, the same age that she had been when she founded NET. Several VCs had already turned him away, but MacLean was intrigued. Hastings proposed a company based around Purify, a program that allowed software designers to identify bugs in their own programs significantly faster than existing technologies. As Grover wrote, and MacLean surely knew, "in software, those who get to market first often win."

MacLean gave Hastings $20,000 and later helped him raise another $6.4 million from VCs. Hastings was an excellent engineer, but he was

less adept at managing his growing company, called Pure Software, which he officially founded in 1991. MacLean was tough on Hastings. She took a seat on the board and recruited a vice president of sales for the company after four did not work out. "Audrey is a hard-a—— coach who draws the best out of people," Hastings told Grover. "She's brutally honest but in a productive way." Pure Software went public in 1995, and MacLean's initial investment, $245,000, was worth about $5 million. The company was sold to Rational Software in 1997, and Rational Software was acquired by IBM in 2003. Hastings founded Netflix in 1997, inspired after returning a copy of the 1995 film *Apollo 13* to a local video store and paying a $40 late fee. The subscription-based company, which lets customers rent DVDs through the mail (without any late fees), went public in 2002, introduced streaming television shows and movies on-demand, and later began creating its own content. It was the first nontelevision entity to win an Emmy Award, receiving the award for the show *House of Cards* in 2013. MacLean was a first-round backer.

STANFORD AND CURRENT INTERESTS

MacLean became a consulting professor at Stanford's School of Engineering in 1994. She teaches her students how to be entrepreneurs, a role, she told Lucy Sanders, Larry Nelson, and Lee Kennedy in an interview for the National Center for Women & Information Technology (NCWIT), that is not for everyone. "It is one of the most demanding feats that anyone can undertake," she said. At Stanford, MacLean coteaches a course called Management Science and Engineering 273 (MS&E 273), also known as "Technology Venture Formation," for graduate students. Over the course of the ten-week class, students work in groups to propose tech companies and develop a sustainable business model for those companies. At the end of the class, students pitch their start-ups to a panel of Silicon Valley business experts. "That whole process"—from inspiration to business model—"is something that's valuable to students, whether they ever start a company or whether they work for a big company," MacLean told Michael Peña for Stanford's website (5 Dec. 2013).

Course founder Michael Lyons reckons that over two hundred start-ups have been launched since the course's inception. Famous examples include Big Switch Networks, founded in 2010, and a GPS company called WiFiSLAM, which Apple acquired for $20 million in 2013. Another Stanford start-up, Skybox Imaging, builds small, high-resolution satellites. Google acquired the company for $500 million in 2014.

MacLean wants her entrepreneurs to be tough with their competitors but kind to their employees. Running a start-up can be a thankless and grueling job, and MacLean told Sanders that it is important to celebrate small victories—and pick up the tab for dinners spent at the office. Adaptive had corporate accounts at local restaurants, so that employees could order food from their desks. The same principle applies to companies such as Facebook, which have their own cafeterias. "So, I jokingly say feed them. Literally, feed them," MacLean said. "[T]hose sorts of things are important." MacLean says that company heads need to recognize that employees have lives outside of work. At Adaptive, her second company, MacLean organized family activities and awarded employees with New Baby stock if they or their spouse gave birth. But nurturing a familial corporate culture also requires day-to-day flexibility. In her conversation with Sanders, MacLean recalled one day when the CFO of Adaptive came into her office distraught. He said that he had a meeting with her in twenty minutes, but his nanny's car had broken down and there was no one to pick up his son from preschool. When MacLean realized that the meeting was just between the two of them, she offered to drive him to the preschool, so that he could present his material and still pick up his son. They were back at the office in time for their next meeting. "It's that type of thing," MacLean told Sanders. "It's giving people the permission to think about what needs to be done that will make their life support the incredible task you're trying to undertake with a startup company."

In addition to teaching, MacLean serves as chair of the board at Coraid, a data storage vendor. She told Sanders that the tech world has never been more exciting and full of possibility. "The potential for innovation that will help change the way we will live on this planet is greater today" than it has ever been, she said.

PERSONAL LIFE

MacLean married Michael Clair in the late 1970s. Clair was an executive at Tymshare and later a cofounder of the LAN switch manufacturer SynOptics. He is also an angel investor. They have two daughters together.

SUGGESTED READING

Casserly, Meghan. "Golden Seeder: How Angel Audrey MacLean Invests Like an Entrepreneur." *Forbes.* Forbes.com, 23 May 2013. Web. 8 July 2014.

Copeland, Michael. "Me & My Mentor: When Youth Starts a Business, It Needs Someone to Trust." *Red Herring.* Red Herring, 1 Aug. 2000. Web. 8 July 2014.

Gardella, Adriana. "Why Women Have an Advantage in Technology." *New York Times.* New York Times, 24 June 2011. Web. 8 July 2014.

Grover, Mary Beth. "Starting a Company Is Like Going to War." *Forbes.* Forbes.com, 2 Nov. 1998. Web. 8 July 2014.

Peña, Michael. "MS&E 273: Turning Stanford Students into Entrepreneurs." *Stanford Technology Ventures Program.* Stanford Univ., 2 Dec. 2013. Web. 8 July 2014.

Sanders, Lucy, Larry Nelson, and Lee Kennedy. "Entrepreneurial Heroes: Interview with Audrey MacLean." *National Center for Women & Information Technology.* National Center for Women & Information Technology (NCWIT), 30 July 2008. Web. 8 July 2014.

—*Molly Hagan*

Hilary Mantel

Born: July 6, 1952
Occupation: Novelist

Award-winning English writer Hilary Mantel is the author of numerous highly acclaimed contemporary and historical novels. She became internationally known following the critical and commercial successes of her books *Wolf Hall* (2009) and *Bring Up the Bodies* (2012)—the first two installments of a trilogy, both of which were awarded the Man Booker Prize—yet Mantel is by no means a newcomer to the British literary scene. Over the course of three decades, she has received a number of prestigious literary awards, and in 2006 she was named a Commander of the Order of the British Empire, one of the United Kingdom's highest honors.

Despite the challenges of a troubled childhood, serious health problems in her young adult life, and early career setbacks, Mantel went on to publish eleven successful novels, a memoir, and a collection of stories. Through her work, she developed a reputation as one of England's most prolific and beloved authors. Known for her attention to detail, dedication to history, and devotion to the craft of writing, Mantel is regarded as a literary treasure, not only in her native country but also worldwide.

EARLY LIFE AND EDUCATION

Hilary Mary Thompson was born on July 6, 1952, in Glossop, a town in England's Derbyshire County. She was the oldest of three children born to Margaret and Henry Thompson and was raised in nearby Hadfield. As a young child, she was aware of her parents' marital troubles and watched as a man named Jack Mantel moved into their home, gradually taking the place of her father. When she was eleven years old her mother and Jack moved the family to the county of Cheshire, leaving Henry behind. Jack became an unofficial stepfather to Thompson, and though he and her mother were not married, she and her younger brothers took on the last name Mantel. Mantel never saw Henry

Luke MacGregor/Reuters/Landov

Thompson again and has described his presence in her childhood as ghostlike.

Mantel told the *Independent* (10 May 2003) that her "childhood seemed very much haunted" and added that she "retreated into being virtually dumb and hardly uttered during the rest of [her] primary education." She went on to note, "School saved my sanity. It was an oasis of civilisation and calm." Though she had attended a local Roman Catholic primary school, Mantel lost her religious convictions at an early age. She went on to attend school at Harrytown Convent in Cheshire County. After graduating she briefly attended the London School of Economics before transferring to the University of Sheffield, from which she graduated in 1973 with a bachelor's degree in law.

FIRST NOVELS
After leaving school Mantel first took a job in hospital social work and then worked briefly as a saleswoman before making her first foray into writing. In the mid-1970s she began working on a book about the French Revolution, though the final work—*A Place of Greater Safety*—would not be published until 1992.

In 1977 Mantel and her husband, geologist Gerald McEwen, moved to Botswana, where Mantel taught English. "I became a teacher under bizarre circumstances, but in retrospect it was one of my better career moves," she wrote in an article for the *New York Times* (2 June 2012), noting that it was the hardest job she has ever had. During this time Mantel began to experience increasing health problems, dealing with near-constant pain and persistent discomfort.

Though she was initially diagnosed with mental health problems and treated with psychotropic and antidepressant drugs, it was later discovered that she was suffering from endometriosis—a serious and incurable gynecological condition. The disease left Mantel unable to have children after a hysterectomy at the age of twenty-seven.

In addition to her long and difficult recovery, Mantel had to cope with the rejection of her manuscript in 1979. On this period of her life, Mantel told the *Independent*, "The rejection of the book and the end of my fertility seemed of a piece. It seemed terribly symbolic, part of the numb misery." However, she also added, "I don't think I would have been a writer if I hadn't been ill," going on to note, "Illness forces you to the wall, so the stance of the writer is forced on you. Writing keeps you still and as long as your brain is working it doesn't matter if your body isn't."

In late 1982 Mantel and her husband continued their life abroad when they moved to Jeddah, Saudi Arabia, where McEwen continued his geological work. Throughout their four years there, Mantel continued writing; the results of her work were the novels *Every Day Is Mother's Day* (1985) and its continuation, *Vacant Possession* (1986), both based on her time as a social worker. In 1986 Mantel and her husband returned to England after nearly nine years abroad. For her next work, Mantel fictionalized her experiences in Saudi Arabia in her 1988 novel *Eight Months on Ghazzah Street*, which was praised by critics.

INCREASING LITERARY SUCCESS
Mantel followed *Eight Months on Ghazzah Street* with the 1989 novel *Fludd*, which began a string of successes that would continue steadily through the 1990s. *Fludd* is set in England in 1956 and addresses religion and faith in a small village. The work was critically praised and won the 1989 Winifred Holtby Memorial Prize from the Royal Society of Literature.

Following the success of this latest work, in 1992 Mantel was finally able to publish *A Place of Greater Safety*—the work she had started nearly two decades earlier. "The novel was my dark secret," she told Sarah O'Reilly for the *Harper-Collins Canada* website when reflecting on having an unpublished first novel. "It had been a long time since I'd looked at it, and I was afraid that it would be unviable." The novel recounts the events of the French Revolution using historical figures, such as Maximilien Robespierre, as one of the characters. Mantel won the Sunday Express Fiction Award for her work.

In 1994 and 1995 Mantel published two of her most successful novels yet: *A Change of Climate* and *An Experiment in Love*. *A Change of Climate* follows an English family in 1980, with portions set nearly thirty years prior in southern Africa; the *New York Times Book Review* named it one of the best books of the year when it was released in the United States in 1997.

BRANCHING OUT

With her next novel, *The Giant, O'Brien* (1998), Mantel returned to historical fiction with a story involving Charles Byrne (a so-called giant who became well known during the 1780s) and surgeon John Hunter. The work was praised by critics and readers, and Mantel also adapted the book into a play for BBC Radio Four.

Mantel's next work was the memoir *Giving Up the Ghost*, which was published in 2003. The work discusses not only the career that had thus far resulted in eight successful novels but also Mantel's tumultuous family and childhood and the health ordeals of her twenties. On the notion of memoirs, Mantel told an interviewer for the *New York Times* (16 May 2013), "The writer has to negotiate with her memories, and with her reader, and find a way, without interrupting the flow, to caution that this cannot be a true record: this is a version, seen from a single viewpoint." She added, "But she has to make it as true as she can. Writing a memoir is a process of facing yourself, so you must do it when you are ready."

That same year she released *Learning to Talk*, a collection of loosely autobiographical stories. The collection draws from Mantel's life, though it occasionally delves into the perspective of a child or features a male narrator. The stories were praised by critics for their effective blend of fact and fiction.

Beyond Black (2005) marked Mantel's return to novels with its dark comedy and harrowing story about clairvoyance. This book, like her others, addresses the notion of a world that lies beyond what is readily apparent to the naked eye. Mantel told O'Reilly, "In virtually all my books there's a slight edge of the supernatural, and a preoccupation with what is hidden, what may be in the locked room. The locked room may be part of the psyche; it may be the part of the imagination that one doesn't dare enter." *Beyond Black* was shortlisted for the Orange Prize for Fiction in 2006. That year Mantel was also awarded the title of Commander of the Order of the British Empire (CBE).

WOLF HALL

In 2009 Mantel published the work that would catapult her into mainstream success. *Wolf Hall* is part of a planned trilogy that fictionalizes the life of Thomas Cromwell, a sixteenth-century Englishman who served as a minister to King Henry VIII. *Wolf Hall* chronicles his life from 1500 to 1535, and the plot includes Cromwell's rise at the side of Cardinal Thomas Wolsey and his growing importance to the king. The title refers to the familial seat—Wolfhall—of the Seymour family, who would come to be major figures in the lives of Cromwell and the king.

Mantel spent years researching English history to align her story and characterization with real-life events. She told Larissa MacFarquhar for the *New Yorker* (15 Oct. 2012), "I know the subject matter's dire, but I was filled with glee and a sense of power, a sense that I knew how to do this. . . . It was as if after swimming and swimming you've suddenly found your feet are on ground that's firm." She added, "I knew from the first paragraph that this was going to be the best thing I'd ever done." The book was widely praised by critics for its narrative and scale, though some took issue with its length of nearly seven hundred pages. Despite any critical misgivings, *Wolf Hall* won the 2009 National Book Critics Circle Award and the 2010 Walter Scott Prize.

Mantel also won the prestigious Man Booker Prize in 2009, with the panel of judges recognizing *Wolf Hall* for its ambition, technique, and detail. When the prize was announced Mantel gave a brief statement, noting that winning the prize had been compared to being in a train crash and remarking, "I can tell you at this moment I am happily flying through the air."

BRING UP THE BODIES

A sequel to *Wolf Hall*, titled *Bring Up the Bodies*, was published in the spring of 2012. The historical novel picks up where its predecessor had left off, following Cromwell over the course of nine months up to the execution of King Henry's wife, Anne Boleyn, which he helped orchestrate so that the king could marry his new interest, Jane Seymour. The title refers to the four men who were executed for supposedly committing adultery with Queen Anne.

Critics again praised Mantel's work for making the well-known life and marriages of Henry VIII exciting and suspenseful while adhering to historical fact. On her attention to detail, Mantel told MacFarquhar, "If I were to distort something just to make it more convenient or dramatic, I would feel I'd failed as a writer. If you understand what you're talking about, you should be drawing the drama out of real life, not putting it there, like icing on a cake." Critics also continued to laud her portrayal of Cromwell and her use of dialogue and pacing. Mantel was awarded the 2012 Costa Book Awards for best novel and best book of the year and the Walter Scott Prize for historical fiction. Most notably, Mantel made headlines when she won the Man Booker Prize for *Bring Up the Bodies*, becoming the first British writer to win the award twice.

When asked about the challenge of sticking with a project as broad in scope as her trilogy, Mantel told Ilana Teitelbaum for the *Huffington Post* (9 May 2012) that she is "built for the long haul" and explained, "I drive my people forward, telling their story in the present tense as it unfolds, and always mindful that if we know the ending, they don't." She added, "Like a historian, I interpret, select, discard, shape, simplify. Unlike a historian, I make up people's thoughts."

ONGOING WORK AND CONTROVERSY

Following the success of *Bring Up the Bodies*, Mantel began work on the final novel in the trilogy, set to be titled *The Mirror and the Light*. This work will follow Cromwell's life from the end of the previous book through his fall from grace and his death in 1540. *The Mirror and the Light* is expected to be published in 2015.

While working on her final Cromwell installment, Mantel also began writing her first historical nonfiction book, provisionally titled *The Woman Who Died of Robespierre*, about Polish playwright Stanisława Przybyszewska and her reported obsession with Maximilien Robespierre, the subject of Mantel's own novel *A Place of Greater Safety*. Mantel has noted that this work is a long-term project.

Mantel made headlines again for entirely different reasons in the winter of 2013, when she made controversial comments at a lecture at the British Museum about Catherine, Duchess of Cambridge—better known as Kate Middleton—the wife of Prince William. In the lecture, later published in the *London Review of Books* (21 Feb. 2013), Mantel observed that most of the attention the duchess received was related to her appearance, fashion, and pregnancy. Discussing the role of the media in the public portrayal of modern royal women, Mantel compared the duchess to a "shop-window mannequin," noting that at times she "appeared to have been designed by a committee and built by craftsmen."

While Mantel intended to critique the media's obsession with image and the royal body, she instead found the scrutiny turned on herself. She was attacked by many members of the media, and even British prime minister David Cameron decried her comments. In turn, many outlets pointed out that Mantel's lecture was taken out of context and that the resulting media furor only served to illustrate a point she made in the lecture: "That's what discourse about royals comes to: a compulsion to comment, a discourse empty of content." While Mantel declined to comment on the incident, sales of her books experienced a strong increase.

PERSONAL LIFE

Mantel met Gerald McEwen when she was sixteen and later transferred from the London School of Economics to Sheffield University to be closer to him. The couple married in 1972, when they were both twenty years old. Mantel's health problems took a toll on her marriage, and the couple divorced soon after her multiple operations resulted in surgical menopause. Three years later, however, Mantel and McEwen reconciled and remarried. McEwen worked as a

geologist when the pair were first married and transitioned to work as a journal editor, then as an information technology consultant, and later as his wife's manager. They live in Budleigh Salterton, a town in the county of Devon.

Though Mantel slowly accepted that she would never have children, she still struggled with other side effects of her treatments; the use of steroids caused a dramatic weight gain in her twenties. Mantel has worked to raise public awareness of endometriosis and served for a time as the patron of the Endometriosis SHE Trust in the United Kingdom.

SUGGESTED READING

Elmhirst, Sophie. "The Unquiet Mind of Hilary Mantel." *New Statesman*. New Statesman, 3 Oct. 2012. Web. 17 Sept. 2013.

"Hilary Mantel: The Exorcist." *Independent*. Independent, 10 May 2003. Web. 17 Sept. 2013.

MacFarquhar, Larissa. "The Dead Are Real." *New Yorker* 15 Oct. 2012: 46–57. Print.

Mantel, Hilary. "*Bring Up the Bodies*: A Review and Interview with Booker Prize–Winning Author Hilary Mantel." Interview by Ilana Teitelbaum. *Huffington Post*. TheHuffingtonPost.com, 9 May 2012. Web. 17 Sept. 2013.

Mantel, Hilary. "Hilary Mantel." *New York Times Book Review* 19 May 2013: 6. Print.

Mantel, Hilary. "Royal Bodies." *London Review of Books* 35.4 (2013): 3–7. Print.

SELECTED WORKS

Every Day Is Mother's Day, 1985; *Vacant Possession*, 1986; *Eight Months on Ghazzah Street*, 1988; *Fludd*, 1989; *A Place of Greater Safety*, 1992; *A Change of Climate*, 1994; *An Experiment in Love*, 1995; *The Giant, O'Brien*, 1998; *Giving Up the Ghost*, 2003; *Learning to Talk*, 2003; *Beyond Black*, 2005; *Wolf Hall*, 2009; *Bring Up the Bodies*, 2012

—*Kehley Coviello*

Michel Martin

Occupation: Journalist and radio host

Michel Martin is an Emmy Award–winning broadcast journalist and, from 2007 to 2014, the host of the National Public Radio (NPR) program *Tell Me More*. Martin came to NPR from ABC, where she served as a correspondent on the television show *Nightline* from 1996 to 2006, specifically to develop *Tell Me More*, which was aimed at African American listeners. Martin, and her executive producer, Carline Watson, will

Courtesy of Stephen Voss/NPR

remain at NPR, but the show's cancellation was a great disappointment for Martin. The decision to bring it to an end was part of a larger budget cut that included twenty-eight jobs at the company. "To be honest with you, I think we've been casualties of executive churn," Martin told David Folkenflik for NPR (20 May 2014). "Every CEO who has been at this network since I've been here—and how many are there now? Six? Seven?—all of them have supported this program, but none of them have stayed around long enough to institutionalize that support."

The cancellation was a blow not only to Martin, but also to NPR's African American listeners. Folkenflik noted that *Tell Me More* is the third NPR program expressly developed for people of color to come to an end. Tavis Smiley, whose show now airs on PBS, left NPR after clashing with executives; *News and Notes*, which featured the staff of the former Tavis Smiley show, was canceled in 2008. In May 2014 the National Black Church Initiative (NBCI) announced a boycott of NPR for canceling *Tell Me More*. NBCI president, the Reverend Anthony Evans, told Bill Chappell for the NPR affiliate, Southern California Public Radio (28 May 2014), that Martin's show is "a shining light for African American broadcasters, and serves a much-needed role of minority voices in the media. NPR has abandoned the African American community, and we must turn a deaf ear to you." NPR countered that it would be able to reach a larger and more diverse audience through its new multimedia initiatives.

A former White House correspondent for the *Wall Street Journal*, Martin was noted for her candor on *Tell Me More*. In the regular "Can I

Just Tell You?" segment, she discussed personal topics such as raising young twins and caring for her elderly father. In 2010, when she spoke about the suicide of her younger brother two weeks earlier, *Tell Me More* was flooded with listener feedback expressing condolences and identifying with Martin's experience.

Martin has been the recipient of numerous awards including the 1992 Candace Award for Communications from the National Coalition of 100 Black Women; the 1995 Joan S. Barone Award for excellence in Washington-based national affairs or public policy broadcasting from the Radio and Television Correspondents' Association; a Silver Gavel Award, given by the American Bar Association, in 2002; and a Hank Meyer Headliner Award in 2014. She won an Emmy Award for a segment of the former newsmagazine program, *Day One*, and has been nominated for an Emmy three additional times.

EARLY LIFE IN BROOKLYN

Martin grew up in the East New York neighborhood of Brooklyn in New York City. She lived in a mixed-income development, and her father, a native New Yorker with Southern roots, spent his life working for the city, first as a police officer and then a firefighter. When she was a child, her father worked an extra job at the department store Abraham & Straus during the Christmas season so, as Martin put it when she spoke about his death on her show (24 Oct. 2012), "he could help Santa out, hint-hint." Growing up in the 1960s and 1970s in Brooklyn, Martin and her brother and sister witnessed a good deal of race-driven violence, bigotry, and protest. On the same episode of *Tell Me More*, Martin recalls that her father always kept his "dress uniform pressed and cleaned to attend the all-too-frequent funerals, at least as I remember it, during the tumultuous days of the urban riots."

Martin's sister is Mari McQueen, who also went on to become a reporter. Her younger brother, Norman McQueen Jr., was a New York City fireman. He suffered from depression after losing one of his closest friends on September 11, 2001, and committed suicide in 2010.

Martin attended elementary school and junior high school in Brooklyn and recalls looking up to journalist, Melba Tolliver, a pioneer black anchor of a WABC-TV network news program in New York. Martin was nine when she watched Tolliver refuse to conceal her Afro while covering the 1971 wedding of Tricia Nixon, then President Richard Nixon's daughter. Tolliver was pulled off the air for what her bosses perceived to be a radical hairstyle. Martin was so impressed by Tolliver's daring that, when allowed shortly thereafter to go to the beauty shop on her own, she got an Afro herself.

Martin was an exemplary student. With Leslie Groves, a friend from her Brooklyn neighborhood, she attended St. Paul's School in Concord, New Hampshire, a college prep boarding school that had only recently begun to enroll girls. In 2008 Martin returned to her old neighborhood with Groves, for her show. They were both struck by the life-changing significance of their decision to attend St. Paul's. Martin explained (30 June 2008) that as an adult she learned that when her father dropped her off at the school for the first time, he stayed in the parking lot for half an hour, waiting for her to look back. "He said, had I looked back, he would have taken me home because he would have taken that as a sign, but I never looked back. And now, of course, I see that as this metaphor. Never did." Neither woman moved back to Brooklyn.

EDUCATION AND EARLY CAREER

Martin graduated from St. Paul's in 1976 and enrolled in Radcliffe College at Harvard University on a work-study scholarship. She began her career in journalism there, as a writer for the *Harvard Crimson*. She graduated cum laude in 1980. Following her years at Harvard, Martin relocated to Washington, DC. She did graduate work at Wesley Theological Seminary and took a job as a staff writer for the *Washington Post*. In 1987 Martin joined the staff of the *Wall Street Journal*, first as a housing and urban affairs reporter, and then as a White House correspondent. Martin told Chip Rowe for *American Journalism Review* (1 Nov. 1992) that her five-year stint at the White House was rewarding, if not exactly the highlight of her career. "It's almost hard to talk about because you sound churlish in describing its drawbacks," a thirty-three-year-old Martin said. "It's a lot like Harvard, you get more credit than you deserve just for being picked. I'm eager to do something where I'm not with two hundred people every day of my life."

CAREER WITH ABC AND *NIGHTLINE*

In September 1992 ABC hired Martin away from the *Journal* to be a Washington-based correspondent for a new Sunday newsmagazine program, modeled after CBS's *60 Minutes*. "You don't often get a chance in an era of shrinking resources to create something," she told Rowe. The program, called *Day One*, was hosted by broadcast journalists Forrest Sawyer and Diane Sawyer and premiered opposite *60 Minutes* on Sunday, March 7, 1993. The show's early ratings were poor; according to Scott Williams for the *Los Angeles Times* (4 July 1993), *Day One* consistently failed to crack the top forty highest-rated television shows and spent a significant part of its early 1993 run ranked as sixty-eighth. The show was pulled off the air for two weeks in May and returned, slightly revamped, in a new time slot on Monday night. Ratings improved and critics began warming to the show. "*Day One* has one great thing going for it: ABC News decided

to make a magazine show, where reporters make 'good stories well-told' and put them on the air," Williams wrote. "That's bucking the trend."

In 1993 Martin reported on the International Campaign to Ban Landmines (ICBL) for *Day One*. Her work earned her and the show an Emmy Award for outstanding coverage of a continuing news story (segment) in 1994. Another report, which she filed with Robert Krulwich, about children's attitudes toward race, was nominated for an Emmy. Despite these and other accolades, *Day One* failed to garner a sizeable audience. It was canceled in 1995.

In 1996 Martin became a correspondent for the award-winning late-night ABC news program *Nightline*. In addition to her wide-ranging regular reports on the show, she contributed to *Nightline*'s series about race called *America in Black and White*, which premiered in 1996. "The series is tapping into a new bluntness about race relations," Caryn James wrote for the *New York Times* (21 May 1996). "Old and formerly cloaked biases on both sides have been raised to the surface by the O. J. Simpson trial, with its great divide between black and white attitudes toward him." Coverage included a story about an African American woman who was so badly harassed that she left her predominantly white neighborhood and another about retail establishments—a shopping mall, a pizza shop—that went to subtle and disquieting lengths to dissuade black patrons. Ted Koppel, who hosted the program, told Lawrie Mifflin for the *New York Times* (15 May 1996) that the program was inspired in part by his African American colleagues, who, he said, "were tired of seeing blacks portrayed as either criminals or victims." *America in Black and White* won an Emmy in 1997. Martin was also a primary contributor to *Nightline*'s short-lived spin-off, *Up Close*, which featured one-on-one interviews.

Martin's other contributions to the network included an hour-long special for the documentary program *Turning Point* about Anita Hill, who testified before Congress in 1991 that she had been sexually harassed by Supreme Court nominee Clarence Thomas. The special, which aired in 1994, was called "Anita Hill vs. Clarence Thomas: the Untold Story." In 1996 Martin joined Barbara Walters to present an annual hour-long special about AIDS; in 1998 she was one of the primary reporters for a special news broadcast, "Cedric's Journey," about an Ivy League student named Cedric Jennings who grew up in inner city Washington, DC.

LIFE 360

In October 2001 PBS premiered *Life 360* with Martin as host. (The series was coproduced by Oregon Public Broadcasting and *Nightline*.) *Life 360* had an unusual format: it was a thematic news-based variety show, featuring short documentary films, musical performances, comedy, and storytelling. Its closest equivalent, and reportedly its inspiration, was the National Public Radio program, *This American Life*. The concept for *Life 360* was developed long before the terrorist attacks on September 11, 2001, but by the time the show premiered in October, its content struck a peculiar chord with audiences. The first episode's theme was six degrees of separation; it featured a performance by the actress and playwright, Anna Deavere Smith and told the story of a soldier who died saving his fellow men in Vietnam. In an added segment, it also paid homage to a firefighter who lost his life on September 11.

"Criticism, like everything else, has fallen into a pattern of before and after," Julie Salamon wrote in her *New York Times* (5 Oct. 2001) less than a month after the attacks. "Before, [*Life 360*] would merely have seemed like a refreshing reinvention . . . but now—this being after—the vibrant braininess and earnest humanity of *Life 360* also feel like a salve. The show allows for a certain kind of escapism, not so much away from care as toward a valuable inner connection." *Life 360* was part of a larger attempt by PBS to attract a younger audience. Though the show was critically well received, it failed to meet ratings expectations and was pulled from the air in early 2002. It returned, briefly, but was officially canceled later that year.

During this time Martin was also a regular panelist on the PBS show *Washington Week* and a contributor to *NOW with Bill Moyers*. From September 2002 to January 2003 she served as a weekly contributor to the ABC Sunday morning news show *This Week with George Stephanopoulos*.

TELL ME MORE

In 2006 Martin joined the staff at National Public Radio (NPR) to develop a show aimed at an African American audience—*Tell Me More*. The show was piloted online (a first for the public broadcaster) in 2006; as part of the pilot, producers asked listeners for feedback. "We want to bring listeners into the mix in unprecedented ways, to go beyond the typical Friday letters segment," former associate producer Lee R. Hill told Jennifer Dorroh for the *American Journalism Review* (1 Oct. 2008). *Tell Me More* was part of a larger initiative at NPR to expand its brand to include multimedia such as photojournalism, Internet reporting, and social media interaction. While developing her show with NPR, Martin also worked as a contributor to other NPR shows, including *Talk of the Nation* and *News & Notes*. *Tell Me More* premiered on local radio stations on April 30, 2007.

In her *Tell Me More* host bio on the NPR website, Martin sums up her interests as a journalist and her strong instinct toward empathy,

which was an integral part of *Tell Me More*: "I wonder what it's like to leave everything and everyone you know for the promise of a better life, to run for President, to be a professional athlete, to parent children of a different race," she writes. "I am fascinated by people who live lives different from my own. And at the same time, I feel connected to all of these lives being a journalist, a woman of color, a wife, and mother."

PERSONAL LIFE

Martin is married to William "Billy" Martin, a high-profile attorney whose clients include the New York Jets quarterback Michael Vick. The couple has school-aged twins, a boy and a girl; Martin is also the stepmother to her husband's two adult daughters. She lives with her family in Washington, DC.

SUGGESTED READING

Dorroh, Jennifer. "The Transformation of NPR." *American Journalism Review*. American Journalism Review, 1 Oct. 2008. Web. 11 June 2014.

Folkenflik, David. "NPR to End *Tell Me More*, Eliminate Twenty-Eight Positions." *NPR*. NPR, 20 May 2014. Web. 11 June 2014.

"Michel Martin: Host, *Tell Me More*." *NPR*. NPR, 2014. Web. 17 June 2014.

"Michel Martin Returns to Brooklyn Roots." Narr. Michel Martin. *Tell Me More*. NPR. NPR, 30 June 2008. Web. 11 June 2014. Transcript.

Mifflin, Lawrie. "TV Notes: Questions of Race." *New York Times*. New York Times, 15 May 1996. Web. 11 June 2014.

Rowe, Chip. "Second Prize: Lunch with Michel." *American Journalism Review*. American Journalism Review, 1 Nov. 1992. Web. 11 June 2014.

Salamon, Julie. "TV Weekend: Endless Connections in the Circle of Life." *New York Times*. New York Times, 5 Oct. 2001. Web. 11 June 2014.

SELECTED WORKS

America in Black and White (*Nightline*), 1996; *Day One*, 1993–95; *Life 360*, 2001–2; *Tell Me More*, 2007–14

—Molly Hagan

Tina Maze

Born: May 2, 1983
Occupation: Alpine ski racer

Tina Maze is one of the world's most successful alpine ski racers. A native of Slovenia, she competed regularly in youth skiing competitions

against Croatian skiing champion Janica Koste-
lic. Maze specializes in a race known as the giant
slalom, which involves skiing downhill between
poles at speeds approaching fifty miles per hour.
The giant slalom is one of most technically demanding events in professional ski racing. Maze
made her International Ski Federation (FIS)
Alpine World Ski Cup debut at age fifteen. The
FIS World Cup, considered the world's penultimate skiing competition, is a series of racing
events held between January and March. World
Cup participants compete on a point system—
race winners are awarded one hundred points,
second place is awarded eighty points, and third
place is awarded sixty points. Points are awarded to fourth place and below based on a sliding
scale, with last place (out of thirty competitors)
being awarded one point. Since her debut in
1998, Maze has amassed over twenty FIS World
Cup race victories. During the 2013 FIS World
Cup, Maze amassed over 2,400 points, breaking the previous record of 2000. Maze made her
Winter Olympics debut in Salt Lake City, Utah,
in 2002. She competed in the 2010 Winter
Olympics in Vancouver, British Columbia, winning two silver medals, and in the 2014 Winter
Olympics in Sochi, Russia, where she won two
gold medals.

Maze has gained a reputation as a fierce
competitor. As former American Olympic champion Julia Mancuso explains to Nathaniel Vinton
for the *New York Daily News* (16 Mar. 2013),
"she's in it for the win. That's why you see her
being a little disappointed when she gets second sometimes. For most of us we think it's a
little crazy to be disappointed when you're on the
podium." Maze's talent and good looks have led
many to compare her to American skiing champion Lindsey Vonn, a racer she has competed

© PCN/Corbis

against at major skiing events throughout the
world. Over the course of her career, Maze has
visited the winner's circle so frequently that she
has developed a signature celebratory move after
winning races: a cartwheel in her ski boots. In
addition to her athletic skills, Maze is also a pop
musician. In October 2012, she released a single
entitled "My Way Is My Decision." The song was
released with an accompanying music video on
YouTube.

CHILDHOOD

Tina Maze was born on May 2, 1983, in Slovenj
Gradec, Slovenia, part of the former Yugoslavia.
She grew up in Črna na Koroškem, a small mining town in the country's north central region.
Her family has roots in the area—years ago,
Maze's grandfather worked in the town's mines.
"It's like a small family," Maze said to Vinton
about her hometown, "Everybody knows everybody. You cannot hide. You are what you are." According to Vinton, nearly a dozen Olympic skiers
have hailed from Črna na Koroškem, which is
located in a mountainous region. Skiing and ski
racing is an indelible part of Slovenia's culture.
Maze's parents, Sonja and Ferdo Maze, began
teaching her to ski in the backyard when she was
three years old. As a child, she also took piano
lessons and played volleyball regularly. As Maze
grew older, she began taking competitive skiing
more seriously and began winning minor league
circuit races.

In support of her passion for the sport, her
family had to make sacrifices. Maze's mother
Sonja described the family to Vinton as "a very
average Slovenian family, without any money to
invest in skiing. . . . we had to decide whether
to buy a car or skis for Tina, that was our life."
When Maze was still an amateur competitor,
her father once promised her that he would quit
smoking cigarettes if she won a minor league skiing even; Maze met the challenge and her father
has since given up the habit. Maze's hard work
and the support of her family paid off. In January 1999, she made her debut at the FIS World
Cup in St. Anton, Italy, at age fifteen. In 2001,
Maze finished sixth place in the giant slalom
at the Junior World Championship in Verbier,
Switzerland. She also competed in Junior World
Championship events in 2002 in Sella Nevea
and Ravascletto, Italy.

EARLY CAREER ACHIEVEMENTS

Maze was selected for the Slovenian Olympic
Ski Team in 2002. At the 2002 Winter Games in
Salt Lake City, Utah, she finished twelfth overall
in the women's giant slalom—the highest finish
on the Slovene team. Following her Olympic
debut, she began working to expand her professional racing repertoire, adding the Super-G (super giant slalom, a higher speed slalom event). In
2003, she finished thirteenth in the giant slalom

event at the FIS World Cup. She competed in both slalom events and the downhill event in the 2005 FIS World Cup, finishing with the highest point total of career (650). Although her FIS World Cup point total was below three hundred in 2007 and 2008, she achieved a new personal best in 2009, competing in five of six events and finishing with 852 points—enough to finish sixth overall.

Maze made her second Olympic appearance at the 2010 Winter Olympics in Vancouver, British Columbia, carrying the flag of Slovenia during the opening ceremonies. She finished ninth in the slalom, eighteenth in the downhill, and fifth in combined events—a score that is calculated by combining a series of race results. Maze's completion of the Super-G run in less than one minute and twenty-one seconds earned her a silver medal. Her combined runs at the giant slalom events earned a second silver medal. Upon her return to Slovenia, she was presented with two commemorative plaques by Miro Cerar, a gymnast who is recognized as one of the most successful Slovene athletes of all time. Maze's success continued at the 2010 FIS World Cup, where she finished fourth overall, earning 943 points, over three times her 2007 total.

CONTINUED TRAJECTORY

Maze's 2011 performance at the FIS World Cup began a remarkable run of ski racing success. For the first time in her career, she finished with more than one thousand points, finishing third overall. In 2012, she again bested her 2011 career high, finishing third in the slalom event, fifth in the giant slalom event, and fourth in Super-G. She also earned a second place in combined events and the city event—a head-to-head giant slalom race—for a total of 1,402 points and a second place overall finish. The skiing season is challenging, requiring competitors to race in regular competitions throughout Europe. Maze explained the test of endurance that World Cup skiing involves to Brian Pinelli of the *New York Times*. "Sometimes you don't feel so well, and it's hard to motivate yourself after so many races," Maze said. She added "It's such a long season, and you need to stay focused."

In January 2012, Maze found herself at the center of controversy after the Swiss ski federation accused her of wearing plastic undergarments in an attempt to improve her aerodynamics on the slopes. FIS officials conducted an investigation of Maze's skiing gear and ruled that the undergarments were permissible in competition. However, they did suggest that wearing certain kinds of synthetic material could cause skin irritation. "The factory explained that it's not plastic, that it's a normal under-suit," Maze is quoted as saying by Kelley McMillian of the *New York Times* (17

Jan. 2012). Maze had another reaction to the incident, which she revealed after a race in the form of a written message on her sports bra: "Not your business."

2013 FIS WORLD CUP

Maze's 2013 FIS World Cup performance made history. She finished first in the giant slalom, first in the Super-G and second in the downhill race, the highest downhill finish of her World Cup career. She also finished first in combined event and second in the city event. Her consistent excellence on the slopes in 2013 earned her 2,414 overall points—breaking the standing FIS World Cup record by over 400 points and earning her the FIS World Cup championship. Maze became the first Slovene in history to win the World Cup. Maze's competition during the 2013 season came not just from other skiers—she also faced issues of gender discrimination. The previous World Cup points record was set by Austrian skier Hermann Maier. According to Paul Gittings of *CNN* (4 Mar. 2013) she was emailed a death threat as she approached Maier's record. "It shouldn't be part of the game," said Maze of the incident, "but life is not perfect. It's not nice for me, it's not nice for my team. They want to ruin your day, ruin the record."

Maze's final point total for the 2013 season was more than double that of the second place finisher, Maria Hoefl-Riesch (1101 points). She dominated her competition for the entire year, becoming the first woman skier in FIS World Cup history to maintain a number one overall ranking all season long. She had eleven wins during the season and became the third woman in history to win all five alpine ski-racing events in one season. "Winning the overall is a dream I've had since being a young skier," Maze told Gittings. Maze's head coach Andrea Massi, himself a former ski racer, inspired her to compete at her highest level by telling her about Italian skier Alberto Tomba, winner of three Olympic gold medals. "I said to Tina, your target is to be like Tomba—to have the power in the legs and also to be strong in the brain," he told Pinelli, "with this combination of technical skiing, mental strength and physical power, we can make great results." During her historic season, Maze did not allow herself to become distracted by the project of completing a record-breaking campaign. "I'm not really concerned about making history when I get prepared for a race," she said in an interview with the FIS World Cup website (Jan. 2013), "but it is always a nice thing to hear once it's done." Maze's twenty-two career FIS World Cup race victories make her the most successful Slovene competitor in FIS history. At the 2013 Alpine Ski World Championships in Schladming, Austria, Maze won a gold medal in the Super-G and a silver medal in the combined event.

OTHER ENDEAVORS

According to Gittings, Maze regularly entertains her fellow professional skiers with her piano-playing abilities at hotels during the competition tours. She took her musical talents a step further in late 2012, teaming up with Slovene music producer Raay and lyricist Charlie Mason to craft the pop song "My Way Is My Decision." "The song is full of energy, it has strong dynamics and a good message," Maze told the *Slovenia Times* (24 Oct. 2012). Following its release, the song's music video garnered over four hundred thousand views on YouTube and reached the number one spot on Slovenia's pop music charts. Maze compares the challenges of music performance to the challenges of professional ski racing. "You need so many talents to be fast and be good at this sport," she tells Gittings, "you [also] need talent and sensibility with music." The success of her music in her home country has made Maze proud. As she told Pinelli, "I've had a lot of compliments in Slovenia, but the most exciting thing was at home to see some five-year-old kids dancing and moving when they heard my song. This was the most beautiful thing I've seen."

One of Maze's longtime sponsors is the Swiss chocolate brand Milka. Her purple skiing helmet with the white Milka logo has become one of her trademarks and it is featured in the music video for her hit single. The German ski glove manufacturer Reusch and the Swiss ski company Stoeckli are also longtime sponsors of Maze. In 2008, she opted to leave Slovenia's national ski team to start her own team—aMaze—with head coach Andrea Massi, physiotherapist Nežka Poljanšek, and administrator Andrea Vianello. In 2010, Italian skiing coach Livio Magoni joined team aMaze. In addition to her music career, she has also done some modeling. In June 2012, Maze appeared on the cover of the Slovene edition of *Cosmopolitan*.

PERSONAL LIFE

Maze has been in a relationship with her head coach Andrea Massi for several years. When she is not traveling for skiing competitions, she resides in Črna na Koroškem. Maze speaks German, Slovenian, and English.

SUGGESTED READING

Gittings, Paul. "Skiing's Pop Queen Maze Did It Her Way." *CNN*. Cable News Network, 4 Mar. 2013. Web. 18 Sept. 2013.

McMillan, Kelley. "Boxers, Briefs, or a Hybrid Sheath?" *New York Times*. New York Times Co., 17 Jan. 2012. Web. 19 Sept. 2013.

Pinelli, Brian. "Skier Closes in on a Breakthrough for Slovenia." *New York Times*. New York Times Co., 5 Jan. 2013. Web. 18 Sept. 2013.

"Tina Maze Ends Historic World Cup Season With GS Win." *CBSSports*. Canadian Broadcasting, 7 Mar. 2013. Web. 18 Sept. 2013.

"Tina Maze Sets World Cup Points Record." *New York Times*. New York Times Co., 2 Mar. 2013. Web. 18 Sept. 2013.

—*Josh Pritchard*

Melissa McCarthy

Born: August 26, 1970
Occupation: Actor

Actor Melissa McCarthy has gone from standup comedy to television to film, along the way earning an Emmy Award for her work in the show *Mike & Molly* as well as nominations for several other awards. She has captured the attention of moviegoers and television viewers with her comedic presence, entertaining characters, and self-confidence in the face of media scrutiny. After a blog post on MarieClaire.com derided the idea of a romance between two overweight people, the premise of *Mike & Molly*, McCarthy commented on her self-image to Karen Valby for *Entertainment Weekly* (20 May 2011), "Please, I don't throw on a dress and go, 'That's perfect!' . . . But I do quite often go, 'Well, it's not changing today, so just go out and have fun and stop worrying about it.'" For McCarthy, having fun has included hosting *Saturday Night Live* on three occasions and costarring in the comedy *Bridesmaids* alongside former *Saturday Night Live* cast member Kristen Wiig. She told Scott Raab for

Wirelmage

Esquire (June/July 2013), "I think the whole reason I act is because it's much more fun to be somebody else. I'm pretty boring."

EARLY LIFE AND EDUCATION

Born in Plainfield, Illinois, Melissa McCarthy grew up on farmland, although her father, Mike, did not farm. Having grown up on the South Side of Chicago, he wanted to raise his children away from the city. He commuted to the city for his job as a railroad arbitrator. McCarthy's mother, Sandy, worked for *World Book Encyclopedia* and later for First Midwest Bank as an executive secretary.

The performing bug bit McCarthy early; as a child she performed in the laundry room for her mother, singing made-up songs that had many verses. Growing up in a rural area without many friends living nearby, she and her sister, Margie, who is three years older, often entertained each other. The downtown Chicago music scene and goth style drew McCarthy during her teen years, a dramatic U-turn from her roles on student council and as a cheerleader at a Catholic high school. As she told Valby for an *Entertainment Weekly* cover story (4 Nov. 2011), "There was a three-year chunk as a teen where I should have been tranquilized and put in a cage."

McCarthy attended Southern Illinois University in Carbondale, where she was bored, for about a year and a half. Although she wanted to attend New York's Fashion Institute of Technology, her parents were leery. Still, they never opposed her career choices. Because her mother fears flying, her parents now take the train from Chicago to Los Angeles for important events.

TRAINING FOR THEATER

At age twenty, after dropping out of college, McCarthy followed her sister to Boulder, Colorado, where she made costumes for a dance company. Her high school friend Brian Atwood, who would later design her shoes for the Academy Awards, convinced her to join him in New York. McCarthy planned to study fashion design. Instead, Atwood saw an ad in the *Village Voice* for an open mike at a comedy club and told her that she was about to become a standup comic. McCarthy performed at the Improv and Standup New York, but within six months she tired of the heckling and instead began to take roles in Off-Off Broadway productions.

In the early 1990s McCarthy moved from New York to Los Angeles, a city she had never visited, with under two hundred dollars. She shared a studio apartment with a friend, working jobs to which she could walk and barely making a living. McCarthy took a bus to audition for the Groundlings, a training group for improvisation and drama that takes its name from Elizabethan working-class spectators who paid a penny to stand on the ground and watch plays. In 1974

Gary Austin founded the group along with fifty founding members, who each paid twenty-five dollars to attend workshops. Eventually the company grew so large that auditions were required and membership capped at thirty actors at a time; the school officially opened in 1979.

McCarthy's aha moment came when she was accepted into the Groundlings. Over the next dozen years of working with the group, she improved her acting and writing skills. She also met actors with whom she would later work in the industry, such as Kristen Wiig. Describing her time with the Groundlings, McCarthy explained to Raab, "You better work like an animal and not b—— about it, because there's . . . people who are dying to get into that company and take that spot. And no one wants to work with a pain in the a——. It's too hard and we all care about it too much, so that kind of personality weeded itself out. So you ended up with a bunch of really funny people with a great work ethic."

A PERMANENT COLLABORATOR

One of the people McCarthy met during her time with the Groundlings was actor, writer, and director Ben Falcone. In her first writing class, McCarthy said she had gone to school in Carbondale, a location she was sure no one knew; Falcone responded that he was from the town. The two began writing together, hanging out at a bar with other Groundlings, and staying after the others left so that they could be together. Falcone told Leah Rozen for *More* magazine, "We decided if we don't start dating, we're going to become alcoholics."

After five years together the couple married in 2005. Falcone had a small role in *Bridesmaids* as the love object of Megan, McCarthy's character. McCarthy considers her husband to be the funniest person alive. They continue to write together, collaborating on film and television projects.

TELEVISION WORK

In the late 1990s McCarthy began her acting career with bit parts, first on her cousin Jenny McCarthy's show on MTV. After a few small roles in films such as *Charlie's Angels* (2000) and *Go* (1999), she won the role of chef Sookie St. James, best friend of Lorelai Gilmore (Lauren Graham) in the television series *Gilmore Girls*, which ran from 2000 to 2007. She claims that needing to memorize ten pages of dialogue, word-perfect, in ten minutes, helped her learn to focus.

McCarthy again played the best friend of the main character in *Samantha Who?* (2007–9). While working on the show McCarthy received validation as a writer when cocreator Donald Todd told her that if she wrote a funnier line than what was scripted, they would use it. It was the first time someone with that level of power had acknowledged that she was a writer. The 2007 writers' strike hurt the show, which lasted only two seasons, but despite their short time working together, McCarthy remains friends with her fellow actors from the series.

Her big break in television came when she was cast in *Mike & Molly* on the strength of her audition tape, which featured her Groundlings character Marbles Hargrove. The CBS comedy, which premiered in 2010, focuses on two people who meet in Overeaters Anonymous and fall in love. Mike, a police officer, and Molly, a teacher, later marry, creating new plot twists as they begin a life together. McCarthy stars opposite Billy Gardell, another actor whose career began in stand-up comedy.

The show's creator, Mark Roberts, has praised McCarthy for "protecting her character and understanding [Molly's] humor and humanity," as quoted by Rozen. He explained, "I've worked with actors who just say, 'I want a better joke.' She wants the whole scene to be better. She likes to watch the other actors score. She wants the show to be good."

McCarthy was stunned when she won the Emmy Award for outstanding lead actress in a comedy series in 2011. The other nominees included Edie Falco (*Nurse Jackie*), Laura Linney (*The Big C*), and Amy Poehler (*Parks and Recreation*), all of whom were considered stronger contenders. The nominees had planned to rush the stage as their names were called and did so. McCarthy was not sure whether the roses and tiara she was given were part of the act and then teared up when the other women began congratulating her.

BRIDESMAIDS

Cast as the misfit in the 2011 comedy *Bridesmaids*, McCarthy stole the show with her portrayal of Megan, the mysterious and macho sister of the groom. Fellow Groundlings alum Kristen Wiig, who cowrote the film, recommended her for the role. For her audition for director Paul Feig and producer Judd Apatow, McCarthy had a clear idea of Megan. She told Valby for *Entertainment Weekly* (20 May 2011), "I kept saying, 'Guy Fieri on the Food Network'. . . . I saw it all: cropped Dockers, athletic sandals, pearls, maybe a carpal-tunnel bandage." When she left the reading, she was certain she had overdone it and had wasted her opportunity to impress Apatow. She was wrong.

McCarthy threw herself into the role, transforming the character, originally written as a nervous and nutty woman, into the confident, quirky Megan. She felt that the character was odd and eccentric but not crazy or creepy. When filming for *Bridesmaids* ended, McCarthy wept. She told Valby (20 May 2011), "I felt like school had ended and I was saying goodbye to all my best friends and it would never be this perfect again." Instead, her career continued to expand.

For her performance as Megan, McCarthy was nominated for the Academy Award for best supporting actress. Her performance won her numerous awards, including the Las Vegas Film Critics Society Award for best supporting actress (2011), the Boston Film Critics Society Award for best supporting actress (2011), and an MTV Movie Award for best comedic performance (2012).

THE HEAT

After appearing in a small role in Apatow's film *This Is 40* (2012), earning praise for her performance as a working-class mother who is insulted by a couple dining at the restaurant where she works, McCarthy was cast in a buddy-cop movie, *The Heat*, alongside Sandra Bullock. Despite her tight schedule—at the time she was filming *Identity Thief* (2013) in Atlanta and was soon due to shoot another season of *Mike & Molly*—McCarthy accepted the role of tough Boston police officer Mullins, excited to work with Feig again and to costar with Bullock. Only a few hours after wrapping *Identity Thief*, she went to Boston to begin filming *The Heat*. She filmed the movie on weekends in Boston, flying back to Los Angeles during the week to film *Mike & Molly*.

Through their work together and shared experiences as mothers of young children, Bullock and McCarthy soon bonded. Bullock told Rozen, "Working with Melissa is like working with a rabid cat. . . . You have no idea where she is going to go, so you need to let go and just enjoy the ride." In 2013 the two shared a Teen Choice Award for choice movie chemistry for *The Heat*.

MOVING FORWARD

McCarthy and Falcone formed a production company, On the Day, after finding that the scripts McCarthy began receiving after *Bridesmaids* were not up to par. The name comes from a phrase McCarthy often utters to express her dislike of overrehearsing: "On the day, on the day, it will be fine." They have been working on a television pilot in addition to writing *Tammy*, a film about a midwestern woman who goes on a road trip to Mount Rushmore with her grandmother. According to Falcone, the script was inspired by the pair's own close connections with their grandmothers. Scheduled for release in July 2014, the cast includes not only McCarthy but also such stars as Kathy Bates, Susan Sarandon, Allison Janney, Toni Collette, and Dan Ackroyd. McCarthy and Falcone not only cowrote the screenplay but also served as the film's codirectors and executive producers.

In *St. Vincent de Van Nuys*, a dramedy slated for an April 2014 release date, McCarthy stars alongside Bill Murray and Naomi Watts. McCarthy plays a single mother to a twelve-year-old son upset by his parents' divorce; Murray, playing a retired war veteran, becomes the boy's unlikely friend.

PERSONAL LIFE

McCarthy and Falcone have two daughters, Vivian and Georgette, who were born in 2007 and 2010, respectively. A fan of HGTV, she has renovated three of the family's homes and a friend's bathroom. McCarthy also loves to cook for and host large groups of friends. She practices Pilates, which she began after her daughters were born, and also plays tennis. McCarthy has mentioned in interviews that she is working on designing a line of flattering clothing for plus-sized women.

SUGGESTED READING

Keeps, David A. "Funny Girl." *Good Housekeeping* Nov. 2012: 134. Print.

Miller, Nancy. "Melissa McCarthy." *Los Angeles Magazine* Feb. 2013: 20. Print.

Newman, Judith. "Funny Girl Melissa McCarthy." *Ladies Home Journal.* Meredith, May 2012. Web. 28 Jan. 2014.

Valby, Karen. "The Bridesmaid Who Steals the Movie." *Entertainment Weekly* 20 May 2011: 52. Print.

Valby, Karen. "The New Queen of Comedy." *Entertainment Weekly* 4 Nov. 2011: 30–34. Print.

SELECTED WORKS

Gilmore Girls, 2000–7; *Samantha Who,* 2007–9; *Mike & Molly,* 2010–; *Bridesmaids,* 2011; *The Heat,* 2013; *Identity Thief,* 2013

—Judy Johnson

Getty Images

Garrett McNamara

Born: August 10, 1967
Occupation: Professional big-wave surfer

The Hawaiian-based big-wave surfer Garrett McNamara has established a reputation for pushing the boundaries of what is possible in his sport. One of the most fearless and respected big-wave riders in the world, McNamara has spent over a decade chasing the biggest waves on the planet, from the famed surf breaks on Hawaii's North Shore to tidal waves created by calving glaciers in Alaska. "Even in the fraternity of big-wave surfers . . . McNamara stands out as a gambler," Bill Gifford declared for *Outside* magazine (May 2014). After an unheralded competitive career in the 1980s and 1990s, McNamara turned his attention to big-wave surfing, and in the early 2000s he emerged as a standout talent, becoming known just as much for his legendary rides as for his death-defying wipeouts. His relentless pursuit of the world's best waves paid off in 2011, when he rode a record-breaking seventy-eight-foot wave in Nazaré, Portugal. He went on to break that record in 2013, again in Nazaré, when he caught an estimated hundred-foot wave, which helped McNamara achieve a level of celebrity on par with iconic surfers such as Laird Hamilton and Kelly Slater. "The ocean is my church and my playground," he told Samantha Sutton for *Men's Fitness* (May 2013). "It's where I belong."

EARLY LIFE

The older of two children, Garrett McNamara was born on August 10, 1967, in Pittsfield, Massachusetts. When he was eighteen months old, his parents, Malia and Laurence, who worked at the prestigious Berkshire School in Sheffield, Massachusetts, moved the family to Berkeley, California. There, McNamara's parents adopted a hippie lifestyle and helped cofound a commune in Sonoma County, "where [McNamara] spent all day running around naked with other kids," Gifford wrote. The commune dissolved after two years, at which point McNamara's parents separated.

Throughout his childhood McNamara's family led a nomadic existence, moving from commune to commune in various northern California towns, Mexico, and Belize. During this time McNamara and his brother, Liam, who is two years younger, were shuttled back and forth between parents. When McNamara was eleven, he and his brother moved with their mother to Hawaii. They settled in Waialua, a coastal town on the North Shore of Oahu, which is home to some of the world's best and most famous surf spots.

Despite Waialua's idyllic surroundings, McNamara and his brother grew up in poverty while their mother struggled to make ends meet. They wore hand-me-down clothes and ate cereal with powdered milk, unable to afford real milk. "We were urban kids," McNamara recalled to Kimball Taylor for *Surfer* magazine (Jan. 2009). "We were alone and living on welfare." McNamara and his brother were treated as social outcasts in school because of their "haole," or non-Hawaiian, status; as a result, the two frequently got into fights with other students. Before moving to Hawaii, the brothers were active in a wide variety of sports, including baseball, football, soccer, and skateboarding. They soon took up surfing to escape their predicament.

A SURFER IS BORN

The McNamara brothers' first surfboards were given to them by a neighbor. Soon McNamara and his brother started surfing at world-class spots such as Haleiwa and Velzyland. Despite their late start in the sport, the boys proved to be natural watermen, entering organized surfing competitions and holding their own in lineups alongside more experienced North Shore surfers their age. While Liam was, by all accounts, the more talented surfer of the two, Garrett was the greater adventure seeker, which led him to seek bigger waves at spots such as Sunset Beach and Waimea Bay, both of which are known to produce waves in excess of twenty feet.

In 1985, at age seventeen, McNamara entered the prestigious Vans Triple Crown of Surfing, which is one of the world's premier series of professional surfing events. The Triple Crown is held annually on the North Shore and includes the Reef Hawaiian Pro at Haleiwa, the O'Neill World Cup of Surfing at Sunset Beach, and the Billabong Pipeline Masters at the Banzai Pipeline. McNamara placed at the Sunset and Pipeline events that first year, thus automatically earning professional status. He explained to Jeff Ho for *Juice* magazine (1 Dec. 2005), "When you won money . . . that made you a professional surfer."

The same year he competed in the Triple Crown series, McNamara, who, by his own admission, was a poor student and routinely skipped school to surf, graduated from Waialua High School. Afterward, he embarked on a professional surfing career. Along with his brother, McNamara won a sponsorship deal with the surfboard shaping company Surfers Alliance,

owned and run by Randy Rarick, who served as the executive director of the Triple Crown of Surfing from its inception in 1983 until 2012. "All of a sudden, I was a pro surfer," McNamara told Ho. "I knew what I was going to do with my life."

EARLY SURFING CAREER

Unlike his brother, who emerged as a standout on the Association of Surfing Professionals (ASP) World Championship Tour, McNamara had a relatively undistinguished competitive surfing career. During the 1980s and 1990s, he regularly competed in the Triple Crown series and other annual events, such as the Excel Pro at Sunset Beach and HIC Pro at Pipeline, but he ultimately failed to break through into surfing's elite. Nonetheless, he and his brother attracted enough attention to win endorsements and sponsorships with a series of prominent brands in Japan, where they became minor celebrities. They traveled to competitions all over the world and both became fluent in Japanese.

In the midst of his competitive surfing career, McNamara continued to cultivate his passion for big-wave riding. His penchant for riding monstrous waves, however, sometimes resulted in disastrous consequences. Early in his career, McNamara shattered a disc in his back while wiping out on a twenty-foot wave at Waimea Bay. The injury, which kept him out of the water for almost a year, took away his competitive spirit, which, as he explained to Taylor, "shattered [him] emotionally." Upon returning to competition, McNamara struggled to regain his competitive drive and confidence in the water.

A turning point in McNamara's life occurred around 1994, when he spotted with big-wave riders Laird Hamilton and Buzzy Kerbox using a Zodiac personal watercraft, which they used to tow each other into the path of massive waves on Oahu's North Shore. Tow-in surfing, which Hamilton and Kerbox helped invent, allowed surfers to catch bigger and faster-moving waves that were previously impossible to paddle into by hand. McNamara became mesmerized by the then-burgeoning sport, which reignited his passion for big waves. He bought a personal watercraft of his own and spent the next several years experimenting.

By the late 1990s, however, McNamara had retired from the competition circuit and started a family with his first wife, Connie. For financial stability, he ran a surf shop in Haleiwa called Epic Sports. He recalled to Taylor, "I barely surfed. I worked the store and it was all about the family, becoming a nine-to-five guy."

BIG-WAVE SURFER AND EXTREME WATERMAN

Unfulfilled by the stifling nature of his life, McNamara left the surf shop in the 2000s in an attempt to revive his surfing career as a big-wave rider. "Riding big waves was my passion," he explained to Gifford. "It's all I wanted to do." McNamara started training regularly at Pipeline and Sunset Beach and came up with a list of goals that included winning the big-wave event the Quiksilver in Memory of Eddie Aikau, regarded as the most prestigious big-wave competition in the world, and the Tow-In World Cup at Jaws, which was established in 2002 as the first official tow-in surfing contest.

McNamara achieved one of his goals in early 2002 when he won the inaugural Tow-In World Cup with Brazilian partner Rodrigo Resende. Despite having never surfed Jaws before, the duo outshone the competition in seventy-foot surf and took home the $70,000 first-place prize. That summer, McNamara performed notably in a tow-in session at Teahupoo, Tahiti, where he was photographed in a dramatic barrel. The image appeared on the covers of several surf publications. Then, in November, he returned to Jaws, where he was towed into a massive, fifty-foot barrel "with more intense fury than God's own washing machine," Gifford wrote. McNamara's ride was featured in the opening scene of the seminal 2004 big-wave documentary *Riding Giants*, and it is considered to be one of the longest and deepest tubes ever ridden.

Over the next several years McNamara traveled the world in search of the biggest waves. By 2007 his thirst for pushing the boundaries of big-wave riding took him to Child's Glacier in Cordova, Alaska, where he and Hawaiian tow-in partner Kealii Mamala surfed tidal waves created by a three-hundred-foot calving glacier. The stunt almost killed the duo and was described by Taylor as "the most dangerous wave-riding attempt ever." A documentary film about the expedition, *The Glacier Project*, was released in 2012.

RECORD-BREAKING WAVES

McNamara's reputation for extreme surfing brought him to the attention of Dino Casimiro, a bodyboarder from Nazaré, a small Portuguese fishing village located an hour north of Lisbon. Casimiro sent McNamara a photo of a giant wave breaking at Nazaré's Praia do Norte beach and invited him to investigate the then relatively unknown surf spot, which is located at the edge of deep undersea canyon that reaches a depth of more than 15,000 feet. Impressed, McNamara traveled to the village for the first time in the fall of 2010, after teaming up with local government officials and Zon, Portugal's largest cable-television provider, on a film project called the *Zon North Canyon Show*. As quoted by Andy Jacobsohn for the *Daily Beast* (30 Jan. 2013), McNamara recalled of his first visit to Nazaré, "I saw waves over one hundred feet the first day I got here, and I was in awe, and couldn't believe what I found."

In November 2011 McNamara returned to Nazaré and made surfing history when he was towed into the path of a wave estimated to be seventy-eight feet tall. The feat was officially verified by the Guinness Book of World Records as the tallest wave ever ridden, surpassing the previous record by one foot, which instantly propelled McNamara to international fame. He received the Biggest Wave Award at the 2012 Billabong XXL Awards, commonly referred to as the Oscars of surfing.

McNamara eclipsed his own record in January 2013, when he rode a wave at Nazaré that measured one hundred feet. Photos and video of his ride were broadcast around the world, and in March 2013, he appeared with American television journalist Anderson Cooper on a segment for the television series *60 Minutes Sports*. McNamara ultimately withdrew his record-breaking ride from consideration for the 2013 Billabong XXL Awards in protest over the event's alcohol beverage sponsor, Pacifico Beer.

While many prominent big-wave riders have dismissed the Nazaré wave as a short-lived novelty wave, "a mountain of mush rather than a majestic curl," as Gifford wrote, McNamara has served as one of its most outspoken advocates. "Praia do Norte is the best secret in the world," he told Maïa de la Baume for the *New York Times* (25 Feb. 2013). "There is nowhere in the world where you can be so close to the giant waves." He added to Gifford, "Here you have a rogue wave that breaks on the beach, which doesn't happen anywhere else."

PERSONAL LIFE

McNamara, who typically wakes up between three and five every morning to track storms and prospective big-wave swells, lives in Haleiwa with his second wife, Nicole, whom he married in November 2012. He has three children from his first marriage, and he and Nicole are expecting their first child in August 2014. McNamara maintains a vegan diet, abstains from drinking alcohol and coffee, and is a practitioner of yoga. He has been involved in philanthropic work, including conducting surfing camps for autistic children across the United States. He has a surfboard sponsorship with the German luxury carmaker Mercedes-Benz and is a global ambassador for WaveJet, an innovative personal water propulsion system. In addition to his brother, Liam, McNamara has five stepbrothers—Bill, Allen, Mike, Joel, and BJ—and a half-brother, Michael.

SUGGESTED READING

Craft, Terri. "Garrett McNamara." *Juice*. Juice Enterprises, 1 Dec. 2005. Web. 17 June 2014.

De la Baume, Maïa. "On Portugal Beach, Riding a Wave That Hits Like a Quake." *New York Times*. New York Times, 24 Feb. 2013. Web. 17 June 2014.

Gifford, Bill. "Ride It Like You Stole It." *Outside* May 2014: 78–127. Print.

Sutton, Samantha. "Go Big." *Men's Fitness* May 2013: 30. Print.

Taylor, Kimball. "The Rush." *Surfer* Jan. 2009: 78–134. Print.

—*Chris Cullen*

Mads Mikkelsen

Born: November 22, 1965
Occupation: Actor

In the United States the Danish actor Mads (pronounced "mass") Mikkelsen is best known for portraying two larger-than-life villains: Le Chiffre, the James Bond villain in *Casino Royale* (2006), and the cannibalistic serial killer Dr. Hannibal Lecter on the NBC series *Hannibal*, which debuted in 2013 and has received such critical and popular acclaim that it was renewed for a second season. In his native Denmark, Mikkelsen has been considered an actor of impressive and diverse range, as well as something of a sex symbol, since his breakout role in the 1996 urban drama *Pusher*. He is also famed for his role as a police officer in the early 2000s Danish television series *Unit 1*.

Since that time Mikkelsen has rotated between acting in Danish art-house films and big-budget American adventure films. His talent for capably playing a variety of film roles—as everything from a queen's lover to a knight to a one-eyed Viking—has helped him garner diverse leading roles in film studios on both sides of the Atlantic. In 2012 he received his greatest accolade to date when he was presented with the best actor award at the Cannes Film Festival for his role in *The Hunt*, a Danish drama in which he portrays a man falsely accused of child abuse. Mikkelsen is grateful that he has never been typecast. He told John Anderson for the *New York Times* (6 June 2010), "Once you do one bad guy, usually all you get offered is bad guys. But I've been able to do different things. I'm not looking for a challenge, necessarily. I'm looking to make a really great film."

EARLY LIFE

Mads Dittman Mikkelsen was born in Copenhagen, Denmark, on November 22, 1965. He is the son of Bente Christiansen, a nurse, and Henning Mikkelsen, a cab driver who later became a union boss at a bank. He has an older brother, Lars Mikkelsen, who is also an actor. From the age of six to age eighteen, Mads was a devoted gymnast. "I was a very focused kid," he recalled in an interview with Chitra Ramaswamy for the *Scotsman* (10 June 2012). "I always had

Hubert Boesl/DPA/Landov

this crazy lifestyle . . . billions of jobs, two hours of gymnastics every day, handball, anything with a ball, really. I must have had ADHD [attention deficit hyperactivity disorder] or something. I was very energetic, and very small. I didn't start growing until the last year of high school."

Upon leaving high school Mikkelsen had no idea about what to do with his life until he spied an advertisement for dancing courses and immediately signed up. Before long he found himself gaining a reputation as a skilled dancer, first in amateur shows and later in professional ones.

DANCE CAREER

After about eight years of working as a professional dancer, Mikkelsen joined Denmark's government-sponsored theater academy and subsequently moved to New York City to study at legendary dancer and choreographer Martha Graham's School of Contemporary Dance. "It was my first trip outside Denmark," he told Ramaswamy. "Martha Graham came in a few times. She was lying about her age and must have been about 102 but she was saying she was 90. Anyway, she was this amazing old woman who would fall asleep in the middle of class, wake up, straighten her back, and show us her moves. She would say, 'Jump boys!' and we would start jumping all over the place. Then we would look at her and she would be nodding off again."

Mikkelsen loved living in New York. At first he shared a basement apartment in Greenwich Village—then a fairly seedy neighborhood—with about twelve other people, mostly fellow dancers and artists. He later moved uptown to

Spanish Harlem, where he spent much of his time off from dancing playing basketball and pool. Upon returning to Denmark, it began to dawn on him that dancing was not his governing passion as much as the performance involved in it. So, at the age of thirty, Mikkelsen decided that he would quit dancing to become an actor. "I was interested in the drama of the dance more than the technique," he told Frazier Moore for the *Huffington Post* (2 Apr. 2013). "I felt that if that was what I was loving, why don't I do that full-on?"

GROWING AS AN ACTOR

After studying at the Aarhus Theater School in Denmark, Mikkelsen got his first big acting break in the gritty crime film *Pusher* (1996), directed by Nicholas Winding Refn. Danish cinema was gaining worldwide recognition at this point in the 1990s, due in large part to earnest directors like Refn, who was looking to produce low-budget films that could be both experimental and popular. *Pusher*, a gritty thriller about Danish street life among criminals and drug addicts, proved to be a breakout work for both its director and lead actor, who have since made three additional films together: *Bleeder* (1999), *With Blood on My Hands: Pusher II* (2004), and *Valhalla Rising* (2009). In the lattermost film, Mikkelsen stars as a one-eyed, mute Viking who is a member of a small group of Danes who sail to the Americas to establish a Christian colony.

Refn and Mikkelsen have admitted to having a combative relationship while working together on the set, but both have also acknowledged that Mikkelsen has done an excellent job of bringing Refn's characters—which both men have claimed are based on the director himself—to life. Typically, after Refn wrote a script, the duo would argue over Mikkelsen's character for at least the first week of shooting. "He's from a part of Copenhagen where they don't have the best of manners," Refn told John Anderson. "There's a lot of profanity involved."

In his native Denmark, Mikkelsen quickly became something of a matinee idol and sex symbol, both through his collaborations with Refn as well as through his portrayal of a police officer on the Danish TV series *Unit 1* (2000–2004). Some of his other Danish films include *Flickering Lights* (2000), *The Green Butchers* (2003), *Adam's Apples* (2004), and *After the Wedding* (2006). *After the Wedding* follows the story of Jacob Pedersen (Mikkelsen), an orphanage manager in India who must face a personal dilemma in Copenhagen. The film was nominated for an Academy Award for best foreign language film of the year at the 2007 Oscars.

RISE TO FAME IN HOLLYWOOD

A career in American films soon blossomed. Mikkelsen first received some attention portraying the knight Tristan in the 2004 film *King Arthur*. His profile saw a significant boost in the United States after that film, however, when he was tapped to play the lead villain in *Casino Royale* (2006), the first James Bond film to feature Daniel Craig as the British superspy codenamed 007 in the long-running film series. Professional critics and fans of the series found *Casino Royale* to be an excellent return to form and Craig to be a perfect fit as an edgier Bond, but Mikkelsen also received serious praise for his turn as Le Chiffre, the ruthless villain who sheds bloody tears.

Critics on both sides of the Atlantic were particularly impressed at the time with the range of Mikkelsen's acting and how he has been able to portray such a wide variety of characters despite having come to acting relatively late in life. Mikkelsen has credited a somewhat cerebral approach to his craft. In an interview with R. Kurt Osenlund for *Slant Magazine* (13 July 2013), he remarked: "When I sit down with [a director] and discuss things, I try to be the devil's advocate, I try to be the scriptwriter, and I try to ask all the questions that I have inside. I try to be fairly intellectual about what we're doing. But once we start shooting, we've been there, and we've done that, and I try to shut that out and go instinctively with the character, and see where it takes us." He added, "But that kind of fore-work is necessary for us both to be on the same page, and then we can start being creative, and fluid, and airy later on. And it depends on the character, of course."

MOVING IN NEW DIRECTIONS

Since the release of *Casino Royale*, Mikkelsen has expanded his already diverse resume by taking on roles in both big-budget movies and in smaller, character-driven films. A sampling of some of his films shows the breadth of his diversity, including *Coco Chanel & Igor Stravinsky* (2009), in which he portrays Stravinsky, considered one of the preeminent composers of the twentieth century; the 2010 remake of *Clash of the Titans*, in which Mikkelsen portrays Draco, the leader of the king's guard; the role of Rochefort in *The Three Musketeers* (2011), a popular film based on Alexandre Dumas's famous novel; and the romantic lead of Johann Friedrich Struensee in *A Royal Affair* (2012).

A Royal Affair is a Danish film detailing a true-life story of an affair between the wife of the eighteenth-century Danish king Christian VII and a royal physician, Johann Friedrich Struensee. As the king was mentally unstable, Struensee eventually consolidated enough personal power to control the government and attempt to carry out widespread reforms. Mikkelsen greatly enjoyed having the opportunity to play a historical figure who also happened to be the romantic lead. "This is the only time I've done it," he told

Ramaswamy. "I'm usually a crazy priest, a junkie or a one-eyed slave. But I didn't see Struensee as a romantic lead. I saw him as this passionate, conflicted, intense, complicated person. But I suppose there were [romantic] moments . . . when we were sitting by a lake in our costumes and I would be making eyes at the queen and saying, 'Oh your Majesty . . .', while she's peeking out from under a little parasol."

ACCLAIM FOR *THE HUNT*

Mikkelsen's other highly regarded film of 2012 was *The Hunt*. The film centers on the character of Lucas (Mikkelsen), a small-town teacher and deer hunter who is falsely accused of pedophilia by the young daughter of one of his good friends. The Danish film, which was directed by Thomas Vinterberg from a screenplay coauthored by the director and Tobias Lindholm, is a brutal psychological exploration of how an innocent man can be tried and convicted in the court of public opinion without justification and be subsequently ruined personally and professionally.

Mikkelsen was lauded for his performance, which earned him the award for best actor at the Cannes Film Festival in May of that year. In the *Hollywood Reporter* (19 May 2012), David Rooney wrote: "Intense, wounded, wrung out and pushed to the brink of insanity, Mikkelsen's Lucas is a devastating characterization, all the more so because his outbursts of rage are so infrequent."

SINKING HIS TEETH INTO TELEVISION

In 2013 Mikkelsen debuted on American television as the lead character in *Hannibal*, a drama based on the series of novels written by Thomas Harris about Dr. Hannibal Lecter, a forensic psychiatrist who is revealed to be a cannibalistic serial killer. Hannibal is depicted as a refined and culturally sophisticated man with considerable skills as a gourmet cook, which he uses to prepare and eat his victims. Hannibal has been portrayed several times on screen, including three times by British actor Anthony Hopkins, most famously in the 1991 film adaptation of Harris's novel *The Silence of the Lambs*. Hopkins's performance in that movie earned him an Academy Award for best actor in a leading role—and made Mikkelsen very reluctant to take on the character for television. "It's been done to perfection," he said of Hopkins's famous portrayal in conversation with Moore. "What could we add?"

After almost saying no to NBC executives, Mikkelsen began to reconsider. His Hannibal would not be locked up inside a jail cell, having already been revealed to the world as a cannibal. His Hannibal would instead be just beginning to go on his bloody rampages, and most of the world would only know him as a refined intellectual working dutifully as a psychiatrist with a troubled criminal profiler named Will Graham (Hugh Dancy) and Special Agent Jack Crawford, head of the Federal Bureau of Investigation's Behavioral Science Unit (Laurence Fishburne). In an interview with the *Independent* (31 Aug. 2013), Mikkelsen told Liam O'Brien: "When I got the first script I couldn't tell what direction it was going in, so I was reluctant. . . . But I realised this was taking place before he's captured. Normally when you're dealing with psychopaths, there's a reason they are how they are, and in Hannibal's case it's non-existent. He kills because he finds people banal. I call him the fallen angel: he finds beauty in things the rest of us find horrible." *Hannibal* was a commercial and critical success in its first season and was renewed for a second season.

PERSONAL LIFE

Although Mikkelsen spends part of the year on location filming, his wife, Hanne Jacobsen, and their two children, Viola and Carl, remain based in Copenhagen. When Mikkelsen is not filming, he can be found at home with them. He told O'Brien, "There's been no real reason to move to LA. The stuff I've done for America has been done in Europe anyway. We made a decision early on that we'd find our base and not shake the children's world as much as mine."

SUGGESTED READING

Anderson, John. "Sex Symbol with an Unearthly Twist." *New York Times* 6 June 2010: AR8. Print.

Hale, Mike. "A Serial Killer Now Prepared for TV Dinners." Rev. of *Hannibal*, created by Bryan Fuller. *New York Times* 4 Apr. 2013: C1. Print.

Mikkelsen, Mads. "The Conversation: Actor Mads Mikkelsen on *Hannibal*, Hollywood Remakes and the Paparazzi." Interview by Liam O'Brien. *Independent*. Independent.co.uk, 31 Aug. 2013. Web. 19 Nov. 2013.

Mikkelsen, Mads. Interview by Kurt R. Osenlund. *Slant*. Slant Magazine, 12 July 2013. Web. 19 Nov. 2013.

Moore, Frazier. "*Hannibal* Star Mads Mikkelsen Almost Said No to NBC Series." *HuffPost TV*. TheHuffingtonPost.com, 2 Apr. 2013. Web. 19 Nov. 2013.

SELECTED WORKS

Pusher, 1996; *Unit 1*, 2000–2004; *After the Wedding*, 2006; *Casino Royale*, 2006; *Coco Chanel & Igor Stravinsky*, 2009; *Valhalla Rising*, 2009; *Clash of the Titans*, 2010; *A Royal Affair*, 2012; *The Hunt*, 2012; *Hannibal*, 2013–

—*Christopher Mari*

Patina Miller

Born: November 6, 1984
Occupation: Actor and singer

Patina Miller first caught the eye (and ear) of the New York theater audience in 2008, when she appeared in the Public Theater revival of the classic 1960s musical *Hair*. Miller went on to star in the Broadway musical comedy *Sister Act*, for which she earned her first Tony Award nomination, in 2011. Two years later she starred in her second Broadway musical, *Pippin*, for which she won the Tony Award for best leading actress in a musical. On the Broadway stage, Miller has proven that she can dance, sing, and act, yet her talents also extend to television and the big screen. Miller appeared in more than thirty episodes of the television soap opera *All My Children* from 2007 to 2008, and she is slated to play Commander Paylor in *The Hunger Games: Mockingjay* films, scheduled for release in 2014 and 2015.

EARLY LIFE AND EDUCATION

Patina Renea Miller was born on November 6, 1984, in Pageland, South Carolina. Growing up in Pageland, Miller and her siblings would sing together, often—and most fortuitously—performing the songs from the musical comedy film *Sister Act* (1992) and its sequel, *Sister Act 2: Back in the Habit* (1993). But Miller's performances were not just for fun around the house. As a youth, Miller attended a performing arts camp, and she decided to pursue a career in musical theater after playing the villainous Miss Hannigan in a camp production of the musical *Annie*. Miller received a great deal of encouragement from her mother, who persuaded her to sing at church and supported her later artistic education, first at a performing arts boarding school and then at college.

Miller attended Carnegie Mellon University in Pittsburgh, Pennsylvania, where she studied in the school's musical theater program. Carnegie Mellon professor Gary Kline, in an interview for the university's website in the winter of 2011, recalled, "Patina auditioned for me in Chicago. I was auditioning the hundreds of high school seniors who applied to our Musical Theater Program." He went on, "It didn't take me long—maybe three notes—to know she was an exceptional talent. She was a keeper." Miller took her first voice lesson—during her sophomore year—with Kline. "My jaw dropped again," Kline recalled. "This young lady could 'belt' up to a high A flat. Unbelievable." Carnegie Mellon drama professor Don Wadsworth, also in an interview for the university's website, said, "Patina was clearly a dynamic young singer. She could always tear up a song and leave the room breathless." He added, "But I must say she also knew

Getty Images

how to handle the acting end of things, too. She is a strong young woman and brings herself into the work which always makes it look authentic and moving." In addition to acting and singing courses, Miller also took dance classes at the university. Miller graduated from Carnegie Mellon's musical theater program in 2006.

ROAD TO BROADWAY

After graduation, Miller became concerned about her future prospects as an actor and singer. "Right after school I panicked, because every college graduate panics, especially in this business," Miller told Gemma Wilson for Broadway. com (6 Sept. 2011). "All my graduation money went to paying for bartending classes so I could have a side gig. I bartended for two months before I was supposed to move to New York." Once in New York, it did not take Miller long to obtain a role in the Off-Broadway production of *Hair: The American Tribal Love-Rock Musical*. The musical, known simply as *Hair*, originally premiered in New York City in 1967, as a kind of exploration and showcase of the new youth generation and its musical tastes and social concerns. It featured such soon-to-be-classic songs as "Aquarius," "Hair," and "Let the Sunshine In." The show was met with both acclaim and controversy for its depiction of sexuality, drug use, antiwar themes, and full nudity.

The 2008 Off-Broadway revival of *Hair*, which was directed by Diane Paulus, received mostly positive reviews. Ben Brantley wrote for the *New York Times* (8 Aug. 2008), "The pure hormonal vitality that courses through the Public Theater's exuberant production of *Hair* . . . is enough to make it the pick-me-up event of New York's dog days this year." Brantley, one of the most prominent theater critics in the United States, went on to call the show "excitingly eye-opening." In a show featuring more than two-dozen performers, Miller—who played the character Dionne—still managed to stand out. In a review for *New York* magazine (8 Aug. 2008), Jeremy McCarter wrote of "the potent, lively voice of Patina Renea Miller" and went on to mention that her "raucous lead vocal for [the song] 'White Boys' ought to put her on the road to stardom."

SISTER ACT

The revival of *Hair* moved to Broadway in the spring of 2009, and Miller could have gone with it, but she did not. Instead, at the age of twenty-four, she traveled to London, England, to star in the stage adaptation of the film musical *Sister Act*. In an interview with Robert Kahn for the NBC New York website (27 Mar. 2013), Miller recalled, "I don't think I missed out (with the Broadway transfer of *Hair*), because I got one of the best experiences out of it. You know, I wanted to lead a show. But then it was like: 'I know *Hair* is going to be successful. What if I go to London and *Sister Act* fails?' . . . I really just had to not be afraid, and believe in myself. It was a big opportunity for me, to lead a show, and I knew it could change my life."

Beginning in the spring of 2009, Miller starred in the West End (London) staging of *Sister Act*, which ran for nearly eighteen months. Miller played Deloris Van Cartier—originally played by Whoopi Goldberg in the *Sister Act* films—a nightclub singer who, after witnessing a crime, is forced to hide away at a convent for her own protection. While in London, Miller, according to various press accounts, indeed lived "like a nun" offstage—meaning she did not go on dates or go out drinking in pubs. She focused her energy solely on the musical, and her hard work paid off. She received generally positive reviews from the London theater press, and she was nominated for the Laurence Olivier Award for best actress in a musical. Miller would go on to be the only London cast member to make the transfer to Broadway.

AT HOME ON BROADWAY

Produced by Whoopi Goldberg, the musical comedy *Sister Act* opened on Broadway in 2011. In addition to having a brand new cast—with the exception of Miller—the musical had gone through extensive revisions prior to its Broadway premiere: the original soundtrack was revised by the award-winning director Jerry Zaks, and playwright Douglas Carter Beane tweaked the original book (the musical's dialogue) by Cheri and Bill Steinkellner. In an interview with Mark Kennedy for Backstage.com (20 Apr. 2011), Miller explained how her character, Deloris Van Cartier, is different in the Broadway version: "Deloris is a lot more grounded. Whereas in London she was very sassy, now she's just cool. I am loud and brassy sometimes, but there is another side to

her as well, which is just cool and laid back. And there's a really serious side to her that you see at the end."

The musical received a good share of positive reviews, although some leaned toward the lukewarm. In a review for the *Hollywood Reporter* (20 Apr. 2011), David Rooney called it an "enjoyable family-friendly musical" but went on to point out that Miller's "comic chops are not quite equal to her powerhouse vocals or knockout looks." He added, "Despite some strong numbers, it takes Miller most of the patchy first act to seize ownership of the role, which she eventually does. In the more assured second act, the musical catches fire, establishing a fresh identity distinct from that of the movie." With regard to the musical, Charles Isherwood for the *New York Times* (20 Apr. 2011) offered a harsher assessment, writing that "when the jubilant choral numbers subside, as inevitably they must, *Sister Act* slumps back into bland musical-theater grooves and mostly lacks the light of invigorating inspiration."

While Isherwood's review of the musical was mixed at best, his review of Miller's performance was glowing. He wrote of her "radiant presence" and "strong voice with a tangy timbre," adding, "Even when Deloris is shimmying in a leopard miniskirt in the show's opening number, Ms. Miller somehow exudes sweetness and sincerity. This makes the heroine's transition from sassy sinner to sympathetic musical instructor less outlandishly funny than it was in the movie. . . . Still, when she is slashing away at the sky with her arms, reaching for heavenly inspiration as she exhorts her flock of gawky nuns to shed their inhibitions and let the spirit put their hips in motion, Ms. Miller is a delight to watch." For her role, Miller received the Theatre World Award and was nominated for the Drama Desk Award for outstanding actress in a musical as well as the Tony Award for best performance by an actress in a musical.

PIPPIN

After ending her run as the star of *Sister Act* in March 2012, Miller went into a sort of depression. In an interview with Michel Martin for National Public Radio (26 Aug. 2013), Miller spoke openly of her doubts: "I started questioning myself and my ability, and luckily I have . . . an amazing mother and an amazing fiancé who really just kind of . . . talked me off the ledge a little bit and was like, stop this, you know, you haven't had a time to rest for a long time, like, this is a good thing." Despite Miller's fears, she would not remain away from the stage for long. A few months after leaving *Sister Act*, Miller got a call from theater director Diane Paulus, who in 2008 had directed Miller in the Off-Broadway production of *Hair*. Paulus wanted to know if Miller was interested in auditioning for her revival of the pop musical *Pippin* at the American Repertory Theater in Cambridge, Massachusetts, where Paulus is the artistic director.

Before premiering on Broadway in April 2013, *Pippin* played at the American Repertory Theater from 2012 to 2013, with Miller in the role of the Leading Player. When *Pippin* premiered on Broadway in 1972, the Leading Player was played by a man. Paulus decided to change that by casting Miller in the role. *Pippin* is the story of a young man who wants to be great but does not know quite how to go about it. In the musical, Pippin searches for meaning, the charismatic Leading Player serving as guide in his journey of self-discovery. Miller's role was very physically demanding and garnered acclaim from many critics. A review that appeared in the *New York Daily News* (25 Apr. 2013) described "the Hula-Hooping, whip-cracking, pelvis-popping Miller" as "soulful, sinewy, and sensationally funny." A few months after the show opened, Miller won the 2013 Tony Award for best performance by an actress in a leading role in a musical.

A number of critics noted the impressive physicality of Miller's performance. Marshall Heyman of the *Wall Street Journal* (7 June 2013) called her performance "arguably one of the more challenging roles on Broadway this season." Heyman pointed out that in the show, Miller sang, acted, and danced—which made her a "triple threat," in theater lingo—and performed complicated moves borrowed from acrobatics and the circus; she even performed on a trapeze, despite her fear of heights. Shortly before and especially after winning the Tony Award, Miller was featured in a variety of articles that went into depth about her fitness routine, which essentially consisted of extensive cardio and weight training and a low-calorie diet rich in lean protein. Miller trained at Mark Fisher Fitness, a Manhattan gym that specializes in training Broadway performers.

Miller lives in Manhattan. In April 2013 she became engaged to investor David Mars, who proposed the night of *Pippin*'s Broadway premiere.

SUGGESTED READING

Isherwood, Charles. "Different Church, More Sequins." *New York Times* 21 Apr. 2011: C1. Print.

Kahn, Robert. "Q&A: Patina Miller Finds the Simple Joys in 'Pippin.'" *NBCNewYork.com*. NBCUniversal Media, 27 Mar. 2013. Web. 10 Apr. 2014.

Martin, Michel. "'Pippin' Star Patina Miller Soars on Broadway." *Tell Me More*. NPR, 26 Aug. 2013. Web. 10 Apr. 2014.

O'Connor, Anahad. "Patina Miller's Broadway Workout." *New York Times*. New York Times, 15 Aug. 2013. Web. 10 Apr. 2014.

SELECTED WORKS

Being Alive, 2007; *Hair*, 2008; *Romantic Poetry*, 2008; *Sister Act*, 2011–12; *Pippin*, 2013–14

—*Dmitry Kiper*

Rutu Modan

Born: 1966
Occupation: Illustrator and comic book artist

Although the state of Israel does not have a long or deep comics tradition, it can claim Rutu Modan—a pioneering presence of Israeli alternative comics and a highly acclaimed comic book writer and artist —as one of its own. Although Modan has worked in numerous genres and illustrated in many styles, she is probably best known internationally for two full-length adult graphic novels, *Exit Wounds* (2007) and *The Property* (2013). Modan's work, particularly the works she has both written and illustrated, have earned numerous awards both inside Israel and outside of it, most notably a Will Eisner Comic Industry Award for best graphic novel of the year in 2008 for *Exit Wounds*.

Modan's artwork is as deceptively simple as her writing is emotionally complex, mirroring in many ways the society in which she lives. Yet, despite the specificity of her subject matter, Modan's work is accessible to readers the world over for its ability to tap into universal human themes of family, loss, longing, and the struggle for understanding. In much of her work, Jewish cultural history, such as the Holocaust or the tensions between Israelis and Palestinians,

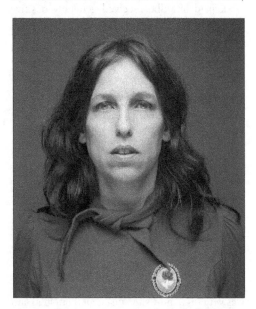

Contour by Getty Images

serves as simply the backdrop to the emotional problems facing her characters. Modan has admitted that much of her fiction is based on her own family and friends in order to provide much of the realism in her comics, but that she also changes her stories just enough to prevent anyone from taking offense. In an interview with the Canadian newspaper the *National Post* (11 May 2013), Modan told Mark Medley, "The great thing about writing fiction, is that it allows you to tell secrets but since they are disguised it's okay."

EARLY LIFE AND EDUCATION
Like many Israelis of her generation, Rutu Modan is the grandchild of European Jews who fled Europe in the years leading up to World War II, when Adolf Hitler's Nazi regime was already menacing the Jewish population. Both sets of Modan's grandparents hailed from Poland, where her father had been born. Because the Nazis had killed so many Jewish people there during the Holocaust, Modan's family never talked about their lives in Poland. In an interview with Marc Sobel for the *Comics Journal* (28 May 2013), Modan remarked: "Growing up, my parents and grandmothers never spoke about Poland. They never spoke about the families that were left behind either. If Poland was mentioned at all, they called it 'the land of the dead' or they'd refer to it as 'one big cemetery.' For me, it wasn't a country."

Rutu Modan herself was born in 1966 in Tel Hashomer, Israel. Her father, Baruch Modan, was a cancer researcher who served as director general of the Israeli Health Ministry in the 1980s; her mother, Michaela Modan, was an epidemiologist who focused on diabetes research. Modan and her two sisters—one older, one younger—were raised in the doctors' residences of the Sheba Medical Center, a neighborhood she has described in interviews as a protected environment of open doors and no roads, where each one of her classmates was the child of a doctor, nurse, or someone on the medical staff.

Modan's parents, both busy with work, were almost never at home; their house was messy and meals were always disorderly except on Fridays, for Shabbat. Modan recalled in an interview with Kobi Ben-Simhon for *Haarezt* (28 Aug. 2008): "Once the electricity broke down and we lived for three weeks by candlelight, only because nobody had the patience to contact the electrician. I always returned home from school to an empty house, but I loved that. I loved the independence and the freedom."

INTRODUCTION TO COMICS
The freedom Modan loved most was what she felt when she took up a pen and began drawing. As a child she snatched pens and pads of paper from her parents' office cabinets and drew whenever she had a spare moment. She continued to draw even after her family moved to Afka, in north Tel Aviv, when she was ten years old. As drawing became a central part of her identity, she sought out as many styles and types of illustration as possible. Although comic books were not particularly popular in Israel, she read them for a time but eventually gave up on them, having only passing interest in superheroes or science fiction—two mainstays of comic books. By thirteen, having begun to develop an interest in classical literature, Modan stopped drawing entirely, believing she had little real talent.

Although a friend encouraged Modan to return to drawing during her third year of required military service in the 1980s, she did not begin drawing again until she was a student at Bezalel Academy of Art and Design in Jerusalem, from which she graduated cum laude in 1992. It was there, in her third year, that she was exposed to comic books once again through a course taught on the subject by illustrator Michel Kishka, who showed her and her fellow classmates that comics could be far more than the narrow slice she had experienced as a child. He showed them many "alternative" comics, including the seminal work *Maus* (1991) by Art Spiegelman and issues of *Raw Magazine* (1980–91). As Modan recalled for Ben-Simhon, "Suddenly I saw that comics can actually be any type of story with any type of drawing. Simply a story told with drawings instead of words." From that point on, Modan knew exactly the kind of artist she wanted to be.

EARLY CAREER AND ACTUS TRAGICUS
Modan swiftly went from writing and illustrating comic strips and stories for student publications to doing the same for several leading Israeli newspapers, including *Maariv*, *Yedioth Ahronoth*, and *Haolam Hazeh*. She did this work for about fifteen years, while at the same time pursuing a career as an indie comic book artist. In 1993— at the beginning of that fifteen-year stretch— thanks to her uncle Oded Modan, a publisher, she was named as an editor for the Hebrew version of *MAD*. Although the magazine ceased publication after just ten issues, it did allow her to work alongside Yirmi Pinkus, a fellow comic artist she met at Bezalel and with whom she would found Actus Tragicus (also called Actus Comics) in 1995.

Actus Tragicus, an artist collective and publishing house that remained active until 2010, sought to bring alternative comics to Israel. In order to broaden their appeal, members of the group published their works in English, a language known to most Israelis and one that would give the group international exposure. In an interview with Grace Bello for *Publishers Weekly* (25 May 2013), Modan described their fan base as "people who liked alternative comics, people who were interested in international stuff—it was a very small circle." Modan's first graphic novel, *Nobody Said It Was Going to Be Fun* (1996), was done in collaboration with Etgar Keret and became an Israeli bestseller. In 1997 the Israeli Ministry of Culture named Modan Young Artist of the Year. The first children's book she illustrated was *Dad Runs Away with the Circus* (2001), which was also written by Keret. Her work on this book earned her the Hans Christian Andersen Award for Illustration from the International Board on Books for Young People. She also served as the illustrator for another children's book, *Where Is?* (2002), written by Tamar Bergman.

MAKING A NAME FOR HERSELF

At the start of the twenty-first century, Modan was dividing her time between producing her own graphic novels and books and illustrating for various periodicals, both Israeli and international. Some of the international periodicals her illustrations have been published in include *Le Monde*, the *New York Times*, and the *New Yorker*. In 2007 Modan experienced a true career breakthrough when she completed *Exit Wounds*, a graphic novel she both wrote and illustrated. Her first full-length graphic novel, it would eventually be published around the world in ten different languages and named to various "best of" lists by such notable magazines and newspapers as *Entertainment Weekly*, the *Mercury News*, *Time*, the *Washington Post*, *Publishers Weekly*, and *New York*, among others. It also won the Will Eisner Comic Industry Award for best graphic novel of the year. "*Exit Wounds* was a big break for me for sure," Modan told Bello. "I was hoping people would like it, but I didn't have this kind of expectation."

Exit Wounds centers on the relationship between Numi, a very tall female Israeli soldier, and a taxi driver named Koby Franco, who set out to discover if a body unidentified after a suicide bombing is that of Koby's father, Gabriel. Koby has not seen his father in many years and Numi has been Gabriel's lover. Together, the pair set out on an emotional journey to discover if Gabriel is still alive or has just abandoned Numi as he had his son. Reviewing the graphic novel for the *New York Times* (2 Dec. 2007), Douglas Wolk wrote that "the real glory of *Exit Wounds* is Modan's artwork. Her characters' body language and facial expressions, rendered in the gestural 'clear line' style of Hergé's Tintin books, are so precisely observed, they practically tell the story by themselves." Wolk also states: "Modan's Israeli landscapes, colored in flat, solid tones, capture the look of the country with spare precision: a few fluid lines describe a dingy bus-station cafeteria or a scrubby beach, echoing the book's treacherous interpersonal terrain, where everything and everyone has sustained collateral damage."

SUCCESS AFTER EXIT WOUNDS

With the critical and commercial success of *Exit Wounds*, Modan found herself as a truly in-demand artist. One of her first works completed after *Exit Wounds* was *Mixed Emotions*, an autobiographical visual blog, which touches on everything from the birth of her first child to her first visit to New York City. *Mixed Emotions* was published in six parts on the website of the *New York Times* throughout 2007. She followed that work with another serial, *The Murder of the Terminal Patient*, published in the *New York Times Magazine* in seventeen chapters through 2008.

In 2009 Drawn and Quarterly, the Canadian publishing house that had published *Exit Wounds*, collected seven short stories Modan had previously published elsewhere under the title *Jamilti and Other Stories*. The stories cover different time periods and different subjects, ranging from political moments to personal revelations. Reviewing the collection for *School Library Journal* (Mar. 2009), Kelliann Bogan calls it "well written and surprising," adding, "In contrast to the author's later work, the character representations here are less refined and often have exaggerated features and expressions that help to illustrate Modan's narrative points. The backgrounds also tend to be less detailed, which helps to draw readers' eyes back to the characters and their emotions."

THE PROPERTY

After completing *Maya Makes a Mess*, the first children's book she both wrote and illustrated, in 2012, Modan returned to full-length adult graphic novels with the publication of *The Property* in 2013. In it, a young Israeli woman named Mica agrees to travel with her grandmother Regina to Warsaw, Poland, supposedly to reclaim a piece of property the family had been forced to give up during World War II. The two women are divided by family secrets as well as the absence of Mica's father, who was Regina's son and died prior to the events of the story.

In writing *The Property*, Modan had to research the history of Poland and mined her own family experiences to imagine a trip she might have taken there with her grandmothers, both of whom served as the basis for the character of Regina. She also employed real-life actors to model the characters during the production of the book. After she had written the script, Modan posed and photographed the actors based on storyboards she had already roughed out. In describing the process to Medley, Modan said, "I even used wardrobe and props. What I tried to achieve is that the characters will feel very much alive, like they were real people. Another benefit this method gave me is that the photos became my sketches, so my first drawing, which many times tends to be the most free and interesting, becomes the final drawing."

Like her previous works, *The Property* met with almost universal acclaim, in large part because the overall simplicity of the plot belies the complicated truths about the characters' family that lie hidden in Warsaw. In an online review of the graphic novel for National Public Radio (25 June 2013), Glen Weldon calls it "wryly funny and ultimately wrenching." He also notes of Modan's work: "Her clean and often brightly colored illustrative style serves in part to lift the fog of war, allowing us to see these conflicts, be they emotional or military, with new eyes."

NOAH'S LIBRARY, TEACHING, AND PERSONAL LIFE

Later in 2013, Modan once again teamed up with Yirmi Pinkus, this time to launch a line of comic books for children. They announced their new project, called Noah's Library, in November, and by early December had released two books for preschoolers. The stories follow two well-known characters of modern Hebrew literature: Uri Kaduri, one of the first Hebrew comic-book heroes, created by illustrator Aryeh Navon in the 1930s; and Mr. Gazma'i Habeda'i, created by Navon's collaborator, writer Lea Goldberg. Modan produced illustrations for Uri Kaduri's adventures, while Pinkus produced illustrations for the adventures of Mr. Gazma'i Habeda'i. Noah's Library announced plans to publish works by a variety of illustrators and has been working with other publishing houses to accomplish that goal.

Modan divides her time between writing, illustrating, and teaching comics and illustration at a number of schools, including the Bezalel Academy of Art and Design, her alma mater. She began teaching two years after graduating from Bezalel. Modan's illustration work is very time consuming; she can spend days at a time doing nothing but drawing, which she does primarily on the computer. She has admitted that her work can put a strain on her family life, especially when she is in a very creative period and working twelve or fourteen hours at a clip. "Comics is very lonely work," Modan explained to Ben-Simhon. "Work suitable for a monk. You sit alone in a room for days on end, writing and drawing, torn between a feeling that you're a genius and a feeling that you're a worthless worm. When the work is finished, the last thin[g] you want to hear is criticism. You only want people to tell you how wonderful your work is."

Modan lives in Tel Aviv with her husband, Ofer, who works with computers, and their two children, Michal and Hillel. Since 2005 she has been an artist of the Israel Cultural Excellence Foundation.

SUGGESTED READING

Bello, Grace. "Rutu Modan: Family Fictions." *Publishers Weekly*. Publishers Weekly, 25 May 2013. Web. 16 Dec. 2013.

Ben-Simhon, Kobi. "Funny Girl." *Haaretz*. Haaretz Daily Newspaper, 28 Aug. 2008. Web. 16 Dec. 2013.

Modan, Rutu. "A Q&A with Rutu Modan, author of *The Property*." Interview by Mark Medley. *National Post*. Postmedia Network, 11 May 2013. Web. 16 Dec. 2013.

Modan, Rutu. "The Rutu Modan Interview." Interview by Marc Sobel. *Comics Journal*. Fantagraphics Books, 29 May 2013. Web. 16 Dec. 2013.

Modan, Rutu. "A Week in Culture: Rutu Modan: Cartoonist." *Paris Review*. Paris Review, 27 June 2013. Web. 16 Dec. 2013.

SELECTED WORKS

Exit Wounds, 2007; *Mixed Emotions*, 2007; *The Murder of the Terminal Patient*, 2008; *Jamilti and Other Stories*, 2008; *Maya Makes a Mess*, 2012; *The Property*, 2013

—*Christopher Mari*

Natalia Molchanova

Born: May 8, 1962
Occupation: Freediver

According to Alec Wilkinson in an article for the *New Yorker* (24 Aug. 2009), freediving "is frequently described as the world's second most dangerous sport, after jumping off skyscrapers with parachutes." Natalia Molchanova, a Russian freediver, is the most decorated woman in the history of the sport, which can involve descending hundreds of feet into the ocean's depths on a single breath, without benefit of supplemental oxygen equipment of any type.

AFP/Getty Images

As of mid-2014, Molchanova held forty world records and some twenty gold medals in sanctioned international freediving competitions. The president of the Russian Freediving Federation, she won special applause in September 2009 when she became the first woman ever to dive deeper than 100 meters in an event known as "constant weight," which requires that a diver not drop any weight during the dive. The 100-meter mark for women, as Wilkinson wrote shortly before the competition, "is a barrier something like the four-minute mile used to be, and the diver who is the first to accomplish the feat will have a prominent place in the annals of the sport."

There is little argument that Molchanova has, indeed, earned an exceptionally prominent place—for that 2009 accomplishment and many others. In 2013, for example, she set three world records in a single day. Her performances have given her a reputation as a juggernaut, and have earned her a formidable nickname: the Russian Monster. Ashley Chapman, a fellow freediver, wrote for the United States Freediving Association website (13 July 2013) that even those who have managed to beat Molchanova's records on occasion do not remain in the top spot for long. "Not only do women like [me] have to earn the record but we have to maintain the record," she asserted. "For us it is a full time job trying to master just one discipline, answering back to Molchanova every time she decides to swab the deck with our efforts and reclaim a record. Hoping all along that she'll have mercy and just break it by a meter, giving us a ghost of a chance to get it back for a split second."

EARLY YEARS AND EDUCATION

Molchanova, about whom little personal information is available from English language sources, was born in Russia on May 8, 1962.

She holds a doctoral degree in pedagogical science, and her years of study sometimes interfered with her participation in the sport. "You know all this research, analysis, and paperwork consume enormous amount of free time leaving too little for traveling and participating in each and every competition," she explained to Katerina Smirnova in an undated interview for the *World of Freediving* website.

When not competing, Molchanova works as an associate professor at the Russian State University of Physical Education, Sport, Youth, and Tourism, founded in 1918 and originally known as the State Central Order of Lenin Institute of Physical Education. Among the school's other notable athletic alumni are several Olympians, including figure skater Irina Slutskaya and hockey player Pavel Bure. Molchanova's area of academic specialty is the theory and methodology of applied sport and extreme activities. She has written two training handbooks related to

freediving and several scientific papers on the topic.

FREEDIVING

The sport's governing body, the Association Internationale pour le Développement de l'Apnée (International Association for the Development of Apnea, or AIDA), asserts on its website, "Freediving is as ancient an activity as humanity itself. More than any other sport, freediving is based on old subconscious reflexes written in the *Homo sapiens* genome. For the first nine months of their lives, humans exist in an aquatic environment very similar to seawater. If a human infant is submerged under water, it instinctively holds its breath for up to 40 seconds while making swimming motions, although we seem to lose this ability as soon as we commence walking." (*Apnée*, or apnea, refers to the suspension of breathing.)

According to AIDA, archeological evidence exists that proves members of a Scandinavian Stone Age culture were practicing freediving as a recreational activity as early as 5400 BCE. Because both Homer and Plato mention the use of natural sea sponges in their writings, scholars surmise that freediving for commercial purposes took place in ancient Greece. The Japanese female pearl divers known as amas, who are still exhibiting their freediving talents to tourists today, are thought to have begun plying their trade some two thousand years ago.

The first modern freediver of note was Giorgios Haggi Statti, a Greek sponge fisherman who was hired in 1913 by the captain of an Italian warship to recover an anchor lost between Crete and Rhodes. Statti, who had heavily damaged both eardrums in the course of his sponge diving, boasted that he was able to descend to a depth of 110 meters and could hold his breath for seven minutes. Diving by holding a stone tied to a rope, he found the anchor within about three minutes at a depth of some 80 meters and was able to tie a rope to it for retrieval. The modern sport of competitive freediving was born in 1949, when a Hungarian-born Italian spear fisher named Raimondo Bucher bet a compatriot that he could descend to 30 meters on one breath.

Founded in 1992, AIDA recognizes eight disciplines under the umbrella of freediving. Three take place in conventional pools: static apnea, a duration contest in which a diver holds his or her breath as long as possible; dynamic apnea with fins, in which the diver travels as far as possible under the water in a horizontal direction in one breath, only by kicking his or her feet wearing fins; and dynamic apnea without fins. The other five, known as the "deep" disciplines, take place in open water and involve a guide rope. These include constant weight, in which a diver ascends and descends under his or her own power, wearing fins; constant weight without fins; free immersion, in which the diver has no fins and is propelled by pulling on the rope during ascent and descent; variable weight, in which the diver descends using a weighted device known as a sled and then swims to the surface; and no limits, in which the competitor descends using a sled and comes up using any method, generally by inflating a balloon.

TRAINING

The physical training involved in freediving includes cardiovascular conditioning as well as exercises for muscular strength and flexibility—many of the same things required for other sports. It also, however, necessitates a more specific set of skills, including equalizing one's ears, holding the breath for long periods of time (with some athletes practicing on dry land during what they call "apnea walks"), adapting one's lungs to handle depth and compression, and mastering precise diving techniques.

Molchanova has pointed out that much of the training is not physical, but mental in nature. She has written academic papers about a method she employs called attention deconcentration, which was developed as a means of managing stressful mental states by a Russian psychologist, Oleg Bakhtiyarov. "It means distribution of the whole field of attention—you try to feel everything simultaneously," she explained to Alec Wilkinson. "This condition creates an empty consciousness, so the bad thoughts don't exist." Attention deconcentration can be compared to meditation, she asserted, "to some degree, except meditation means you're completely free, but if you're in the sea at depth you will have to be focused, or it will get bad. What you do to start learning is you focus on the edges, not the center of things, as if you were looking at a screen. Basically, all the time I am diving, I have an empty consciousness. I have a kind of melody going through my mind that keeps me going, but otherwise I am completely not in my mind."

THE DANGERS

Freediving is an admittedly dangerous sport, and there have been several high-profile deaths among competitors. Among the most infamous incidents occurred in October 2002, when Audrey Mestre, a twenty-eight-year-old from France, attempted a no-limits dive to 171 meters in the Dominican Republic. As she started her ascent, her lift balloon malfunctioned, and she remained submerged for almost nine minutes before her husband, fellow diver Francisco "Pipín" Ferreras, was able to bring her body to the surface, where she was pronounced dead.

Molchanova herself once had a frightening accident during a no-limits dive in the Red Sea. She reached 90 meters of depth, and the balloon that was supposed to inflate and carry her back

to the surface malfunctioned. She told Smirnova, "Suddenly the end of the hose leading into the balloon comes loose and starts flying all over the place making lots of bubbles. I closed the valve, put the hose into its place and opened the tap again." The hose then came loose a second time. "Time keeps running away," she recalled. "I don't know why I stayed there at all, I could very easily come up without the damn thing, but instead I was fixing it. So, I'm still there putting the hose back once more, and this time to prevent it from slipping out I'm holding it with my hand. That worked out and I headed up." After the attempt she suffered decompression sickness, commonly called the "bends," and spent time in the hospital recuperating.

SETTING RECORDS

So numerous are the occasions on which Molchanova sets a new record or wins a gold medal that it is almost surprising when she is bested. As of mid-2014, of the eight freediving categories AIDA recognizes, Molchanova held the women's record in seven of them. Only a handful of women in the world are considered to pose any serious competition to her, including Tanya Streeter of the Cayman Islands (who holds the one AIDA record Molchanova does not, in no-limits diving), Sara Campbell of the United Kingdom, Ilaria Bonin of Italy, and Ashley Futral Chapman of the United States.

From time to time, her accomplishments have rivaled or surpassed those of male divers, such as in 2007, when her winning time in the static apnea event was longer than that of the male champion. Two years later she became the first woman ever to pass the 100-meter mark in constant weight diving, recording a depth of 101 meters in the Red Sea off Sharm el-Sheikh, Egypt. The dive took a total of three minutes and fifty seconds. Previously, Sara Campbell had reached that depth, but had lost consciousness upon surfacing and was disqualified. Although it is not uncommon for divers to black out because of cerebral hypoxia (lack of oxygen to the brain), AIDA rules state that in order for a dive to qualify, the diver must follow a three-step safety check upon breaking the surface: removing their goggles or mask, giving a physical hand signal, and verbalizing that they are all right.

In 2013 in Belgrade, Serbia, Molchanova set an astounding three world records at a single event: recording a dynamic no-fins swim of 182 meters (beating Bonin by one meter); a dynamic (with fins) swim of 234 meters, beating her own previous record by 11 meters; and holding her breath for nine minutes two seconds in the static apnea finals. That last result beat even that of Croatian freediver Goran Čolak, who won the male gold medal, and marked the first time a woman had successfully surpassed the nine-minute mark in competition. (The men's world record in static apnea is held by Frenchman Stéphane Mifsud, at eleven minutes thirty-five seconds.)

Among Molchanova's latest records is one set on May 15, 2014, at Dahab, Egypt, where she descended to a depth of 70 meters in the difficult discipline of constant weight without fins. The dive took three minutes and thirty seconds and broke a record she had set the previous year in Kalamata, Greece.

PERSONAL LIFE

Molchanova lives in Moscow and has a daughter, Oksana, who is studying to be an architect. Her son, Alexey, who has completed his engineering studies, is also a freediver, and shows signs of being as proficient as his mother. The two frequently run classes and training camps together, and in 2013, in Kalamata, Greece, where his mother was also competing, the twenty-six-year-old Alexey set a new men's record of 128 meters in constant weight.

"This was a day to remember," Molchanova wrote on her Facebook page. "I suspect that it is relatively rare in sports to happen, but it did. Imagine that my son, Alexey, and I managed to, both, take first place on the same day at the World Championships in the 'blue ribbon' discipline, Constant Weight. To see Alexey [after his record-setting dive] was a very happy moment that I will carry with me forever."

SUGGESTED READING

Koe, Francesca. "Natalia Molchanova Rules the Pool in Belgrade with 3 World Records." *Deeper Blue*. Deeperblue.net, 29 June 2013. Web. 8 July 2014.

Molchanova, Natalia. "Methods of Freediver Training." *Freedive Central*. Freedive Central, 5 June 2006. Web. 8 July 2014.

Smirnova, Katerina. "Interview with Natalia Molchanova." *World of Freediving*. World of Freediving, n.d. Web. 8 July 2014.

Wilkinson, Alec. "The Deepest Dive." *New Yorker* 24 Aug. 2009: 24–30. Print.

—*Mari Rich*

Yadier Molina

Born: July 13, 1982
Occupation: Baseball player

St. Louis Cardinals catcher Yadier Molina, known affectionately by teammates and fans as "Yadi," is considered by many to be the best all-around Major League Baseball (MLB) player at his position. Writing for *ESPN* magazine (10 Aug. 2009), Lindsay Berra, granddaughter of the legendary Hall of Fame catcher Yogi Berra,

described Molina as baseball's "one true game-changing catcher" and called him "a throwback, a catcher in the grittiest sense of the word."

The younger brother of two other MLB catchers, Molina joined the Cardinals' organization in 2000, straight out of high school in Puerto Rico, and made his major-league debut with the team in 2004. Known for his powerful arm and superior baseball instincts, Molina initially established a reputation as the best defensive catcher in the game before transforming himself into an offensive threat after the 2006 season. He emerged as a top Most Valuable Player (MVP) candidate in 2013, when he finished among the National League (NL) leaders in a number of statistical hitting categories. He has won six Rawlings Gold Glove Awards for defensive excellence, earned five All-Star selections, and played in four World Series with the Cardinals, winning titles in 2006 and 2011. Widely viewed as the face the Cardinals franchise, Molina has already been ranked among the greatest MLB catchers of all time. "He is as great a catcher as anybody that's ever played the game," former Cardinals manager Tony La Russa said to Tyler Kepner for the *New York Times* (18 Mar. 2013).

EARLY LIFE

The youngest of three sons of Benjamin Molina Sr. and Gladys Matta, Yadier Benjamin Molina was born on July 13, 1982, in Bayamón, Puerto Rico. He grew up in a small, two-bedroom home in nearby Vega Alta, a town known for its rich baseball tradition, which had a strong grip on the Molina household. Molina's father was a talented second baseman and outfielder who played for fifteen years in Puerto Rico's amateur league, Liga de Béisbol Superior Doble A. He retired as the league's all-time hit leader, finishing with a .320 career batting average, and was inducted into the Puerto Rican Baseball Hall of Fame in 2002.

Molina and his brothers, Benjamin Jr. (nicknamed "Bengie") and José, who are eight and seven years older, respectively, inherited their love of baseball from their father, who worked ten hours a day as a Westinghouse factory technician. Benjamin Molina Sr. would return home from work each day at around four o'clock in the afternoon, eat a quick dinner, and then take his sons to Jesús "Mambe" Rivera Park, a ramshackle field located across the street from the family home. There, he spent countless hours running his sons through drills that emphasized the fundamentals of the game.

His work and dedication paid off: in 1993, Bengie was signed as an amateur free agent by the California Angels (later the Anaheim Angels, now the Los Angeles Angels of Anaheim) and José was drafted by the Chicago Cubs in that year's MLB amateur draft, both as catchers. Bengie played for four teams during his thirteen-year MLB career (1998–2010), during which he won two Gold Gloves and one World Series title. José, a two-time World Series champion, began his fourteenth MLB season and third season as a member of the Tampa Bay Rays in 2014.

Yadier Molina started catching at the age of five and dreamed of one day joining his brothers in the professional baseball ranks. "When I was a kid, I liked to watch my brothers and learn," he told Berra. "They played the game like I want to play right now, aggressive and confident." Like his brothers, Molina was taught the intricacies of every position on the field, but it was as a catcher that he truly excelled.

A BOY PLAYING WITH MEN

Molina's baseball talent was such that he was often the first player selected in Puerto Rico's youth-league drafts. He was developing at a rapid rate when, at age fifteen, he was suspended from his youth-league team. Fearing the consequences of extended time off, Molina's father had him try out for a top-tier Puerto Rican amateur team, Los Tigres de Hatillo, which featured mostly adult players, some more than twice his age. Despite the wide age gap, Molina was designated the team's starting catcher after one practice session. "He was a kid who was playing with men," his brother Bengie recalled to Jenifer Langosch for MLB.com (21 Oct. 2013). "That right there made Yadi who he is . . . that's when he became a man."

Like his brothers, Molina attended high school at Escuela Superior Maestro Ladi in Vega Alta. During that time, he worked to master the mental aspects of catching, from studying batter tendencies to learning how to strategically direct pitch sequences. As a catcher for Los Tigres,

Molina was responsible for calling his own games, which helped him develop skills far more advanced than most catchers his age—particularly those in the United States, where coaches normally call pitches. Molina has credited his father, who died of a heart attack in 2008 at age fifty-eight, with shaping him into the player he is today. "I play for him," he told Ben Reiter for *Sports Illustrated* (31 Mar. 2014), "by being the way he taught me to be."

ST. LOUIS CARDINALS

Molina first came to the attention of major-league scouts in high school. Among them was Edwin Rodriguez, then a scout for the Minnesota Twins. At the time, Rodriguez recalled to Stan McNeal for *USA Today* (1 May 2013), Molina was known primarily as a "defensive catcher" with a "great arm" but a "weak bat."

Underdeveloped offensive skills notwithstanding, Molina's strong, major-league-caliber defense was enough to get him drafted at age seventeen by the St. Louis Cardinals in the fourth round of the 2000 MLB Draft. Still, the Cardinals were unsure about his skills until he showcased them in several extended spring-training games with the team in Orlando, Florida. In September 2000, the team awarded Molina a contract that included a signing bonus of $325,000. "He had grown up in a catching family that gave him a lot of knowledge before he got to us," Cardinals minor-league operations director John Vuchs told McNeal. "He came into the organization already a lot more polished than the average high-school-aged catcher."

Molina ascended through the Cardinals' farm system in just three and a half seasons, during which he established himself mostly as a singles hitter, batting .278 in 297 games. In the minors, he further advanced his already-polished defensive skills under the guidance of longtime Cardinals catching instructor Dave Ricketts, who died of renal cancer in 2008. While some questioned Molina's offensive ability, the Cardinals were so confident in his defensive prowess—he had a stellar 45 percent caught-stealing percentage in his minor-league career—that the team called him up to the majors at age twenty-one. Molina made his major-league debut on June 3, 2004, in a game against the Pittsburgh Pirates. Filling in as an injury replacement for Mike Matheny, the Cardinals' Gold Glove–winning starting catcher and future manager, he made two hits in four at-bats and caught for five veteran pitchers in a 4–2 win for St. Louis.

DEFENSE-FIRST CATCHER

Molina remained with the Cardinals for the rest of the 2004 season, during which the team captured both the NL Central Division title and the NL pennant and reached the World Series. Serving as Matheny's backup at catcher,

Molina appeared in fifty-one games, the most for a catcher his age since Ivan "Pudge" Rodriguez in 1992. Despite posting only pedestrian offensive numbers—a .267 batting average with two home runs and fifteen runs batted in (RBIs) in 135 at-bats—he immediately established himself as a defensive force, throwing out 47 percent of runners trying to steal. It was Molina's defense that led Cardinals manager Tony La Russa to name him the starting catcher for Game 4 of the World Series against the Boston Red Sox. Though the Red Sox won the game, completing a four-game sweep of the Cardinals and claiming their first World Series title in eighty-six years, Molina's start marked "the beginning of what may be remembered as an era," as Derrick Goold noted for the *St. Louis Post-Dispatch* (22 Oct. 2013).

Following the 2004 season, Molina became the Cardinals' starting catcher after Matheny signed a free-agent contract with the San Francisco Giants. The next two seasons saw him build his reputation as the best defensive catcher in baseball. In 2005 Molina threw out a league-best 64 percent of runners attempting to steal, allowed a major-league low of fourteen stolen bases, and recorded nine pickoffs. Then, in 2006, he retired 44 percent of would-be base stealers, picked off eight runners, and led all NL catchers with seventy-nine assists. The Cardinals successfully defended their NL Central title in both 2005 and 2006.

Molina's defense-first mentality initially had a negative effect on his offensive output, as he batted .216 during the 2006 season, a career low. He redeemed himself with a breakthrough performance during the 2006 postseason, when he batted .358 and led the majors with nineteen hits in sixteen games. One of those hits was a dramatic two-run home run at the top of the ninth inning of Game 7 of the National League Championship Series (NLCS) against the New York Mets. The home run propelled the Cardinals to the World Series, where they defeated the Detroit Tigers in five games to earn the franchise's tenth world championship. Commenting on his early offensive struggles, Molina said to Stan McNeal, "The numbers show different, but I feel like I had a good approach back then but didn't execute."

OFFENSIVE TRANSFORMATION AND MLB ALL-STAR

Over the course of the next several seasons, Molina's offense began to catch up to his elite, game-changing defense. Despite only playing in 111 games in 2007 due to injuries, he finished the year with a then-career-high batting average of .275 and led the majors in caught-stealing percentage, nabbing 54 percent of would-be base stealers. Molina posted even better numbers at the plate during the 2008 season, when he broke his previous records in batting average

(.304), RBIs (fifty-six), on-base average (.349), and slugging average (.392). He also proved to be one of the most difficult players to strike out, doing so just twenty-nine times in 485 plate appearances—the second-fewest strikeouts against a major-league backstop since 1993. While Molina underperformed on defense compared to previous years, throwing out only 35 percent of runners trying to steal, he still led the majors with seven pickoffs, which was enough to earn him his first Gold Glove Award.

Molina bolstered his standing as one of baseball's most durable catchers in 2009, when he started 136 of 138 games behind the plate, a career and major-league best. He produced a solid .293 batting average and hit six home runs with fifty-four RBIs. On the defensive side, Molina threw out 41 percent of runners trying to steal and again led the majors with eight pickoffs. He earned his first career All-Star selection as the starting catcher for the NL squad and won his second straight Gold Glove. Molina helped guide the Cardinals' pitching staff to a team earned-run average (ERA) of 3.66, the fourth highest in the majors that year, which played a significant role in the team capturing their first NL Central title and first postseason berth since 2006.

For the next two seasons, Molina led the majors in games started as catcher, with 130 games in 2010 and 131 in 2011. During the 2010 season, he led the majors in caught-stealing percentage for the third time in his career, blocking 49 percent of base-stealing attempts, and earned his second consecutive All-Star selection and third straight Gold Glove. The 2011 season was a breakout offensive year for Molina, who led the Cardinals and all NL catchers with a .305 batting average. He also ranked first among NL catchers in hits (145), second in doubles (thirty-two), and third in RBIs (sixty-five). In addition to receiving his third consecutive All-Star selection and fourth straight Gold Glove, Molina helped lead the Cardinals to their second World Series title in six years. They defeated the Texas Rangers in a dramatic seven-game series to claim the franchise's eleventh world championship, and Molina set a team record with nine RBIs. "You don't play this game just to play it," he explained to Goold. "You don't play this game just to put up the numbers. You play it to win, to win championships."

MVP CANDIDATE

During the 2012 off-season, Molina signed a five-year, $75 million contract extension with the Cardinals. Commenting on his long-term commitment to the club, he told Reiter, "To be around good people, to be on a good team, to have a chance to play in the playoffs—that was the main thing for me." That same off-season saw longtime Cardinals manager Tony La Russa retire and three-time MVP first baseman Albert Pujols leave the team to sign with the Los Angeles Angels. La Russa was replaced by Molina's former mentor, Mike Matheny, who had previously served as an instructor in the Cardinals' minor-league system.

Under Matheny, the Cardinals continued to enjoy success. In 2012, they finished second in the NL Central with an 88–74 record and advanced to the NLCS, where they lost to the San Francisco Giants in seven games. Molina rewarded the Cardinals' faith in him by producing an MVP-caliber season. He again led the team in batting average (.315) and posted the best power numbers of his career, hitting a career-high twenty-two home runs with seventy-six RBIs. He achieved another personal best with twelve stolen bases, a single-season franchise record for a catcher, and continued his elite defensive play, finishing second in the majors in caught-stealing percentage (48 percent). He was named to his fourth consecutive All-Star team, earned his fifth straight Gold Glove, and finished fourth in the NL MVP vote.

Molina cemented his status as one of baseball's best all-around players in 2013, when he established career highs in batting average (.319), hits (161), doubles (forty-four), RBIs (eighty), and runs scored (sixty-eight), earning him his fifth consecutive All-Star selection. His batting average led the Cardinals for the third consecutive season, and his double total was the second-highest single-season total for a catcher in MLB history. More remarkably, due to injuries to several Cardinals starting pitchers, Molina shepherded a pitching staff mostly made up of rookies to the World Series. Though the Cardinals lost the World Series to the Boston Red Sox in six games, Molina was widely recognized for his achievements during the regular season, receiving his first Silver Slugger Award and sixth straight Gold Glove and finishing third in the NL MVP vote.

By the 2014 season, Molina had become the undisputed face of the Cardinals franchise and one of the game's most respected players. According to many baseball observers, his value as a player is unquantifiable, as he possesses numerous on-field attributes that are not measured by statistics. This includes the ability to manage the pitching staff, call games, frame and block pitches, and orchestrate the team's defensive alignments. Cardinals general manager John Mozeliak told Goold that "the trajectory that [Molina's] career is on could end up in Cooperstown" and that "his baseball IQ is off the charts."

In addition to playing for the Cardinals, Molina represented his home country of Puerto Rico in the first three World Baseball Classics (2006, 2009, and 2013), leading his team to a second-place finish in the tournament in 2013.

He lives in Jupiter, Florida, with his wife, Wanda, and their two children, Yanuell and Adriana.

SUGGESTED READING

Berra, Lindsay. "Yadier Molina Knows Squat." *ESPN*. ESPN Internet Ventures, 10 Aug. 2009. Web. 5 Apr. 2014.

Goold, Derrick. "Molina Joining Elite Group of Cardinals." *St. Louis Post-Dispatch*. Stltoday. com, 22 Oct. 2013. Web. 10 Apr. 2014.

Langosch, Jenifer. "Following Yadi: Cards Have Best of Best behind Plate." *MLB.com*. MLB Advanced Media, 21 Oct. 2013. Web. 10 Apr. 2014.

McNeal, Stan. "Rock of St. Louis: Cardinals Catcher Irreplaceable." *USA Today*. Gannett, 1 May 2013. Web. 10 Apr. 2014.

Reiter, Ben. "The Molina Way." *Sports Illustrated* 31 Mar. 2014: 42–47. Print.

—*Chris Cullen*

Chloë Grace Moretz

Born: February 10, 1997
Occupation: Actor

Though just seventeen years old, American actor Chloë Grace Moretz has been compared to Jodie Foster and Natalie Portman, two former child actors who successfully made the transition to critically acclaimed adult performers. Since Moretz's first significant role, as one of the children in the 2005 remake of 1979's *The*

Sebastien Nogier/EPA/Landov

Amityville Horror, her ability to take on often complex and dark material has wowed many film critics, and her remarkable poise and professionalism from a very young age have impressed interviewers and film fans alike.

Moretz, who has accumulated more than forty film and television credits since the age of six, attributes her success to her supportive family, including her four older brothers, who have helped her hone her innate talents and with whom she makes all her important career decisions. Moretz's breakout role came in 2010, when she appeared as foul-mouthed kid vigilante Mindy Macready, a.k.a. Hit-Girl, in the film adaptation of Mark Millar's comic book series *Kick-Ass*. In addition to reprising her role as Hit-Girl in *Kick-Ass 2* (2013), she has since taken on other formidable roles, including a centuries-old child vampire in *Let Me In* (2010), a troubled telekinetic teenager in *Carrie* (2013), and a teenage prostitute in *The Equalizer* (2014), starring Oscar winner Denzel Washington.

Moretz understands that many people might be uncomfortable with the idea of her playing a prostitute in *The Equalizer* after seeing her in such kid-friendly films as *Diary of a Wimpy Kid* (2010) and *Hugo* (2011). "When you do a lot of kid movies, that can be a problem. You were a little sister type, and then all of a sudden you're a prostitute, and people don't like it," Moretz said to Andrea Hubert for the *Guardian* (9 Aug. 2013). "Unless, like Jodie Foster, that's how you start off. And I'm similar because the first time anyone really saw me was in *Kick-Ass*, killing people. . . . I guess maybe we veer towards darker roles because we want to stretch ourselves. I'm a well-rounded girl from a normal family; I'm not a psychopath. So it's fun to be those characters that have all these dark undertones, because it's just acting."

EARLY LIFE AND CAREER

The only daughter and youngest of McCoy "Mac" Moretz and Teri Duke Moretz's five children, Chloë Grace Moretz was born on February 10, 1997, in Atlanta, Georgia. The Moretz family lived in Atlanta until 2005, when Mac Moretz decided to move his plastic-surgery practice from Atlanta to Beverly Hills, California, just as his daughter's acting career was beginning to take off. Moretz's four older brothers—Brandon, Trevor, Colin, and Ethan—have always been protective of her, but she is especially close to Trevor, who, in addition to working as an actor and producer, also serves as her acting coach. Her mother reads all of the scripts she gets and helps her choose parts.

Moretz's parents divorced when she was still very young, soon after the family's move to California, and Teri Moretz raised her children as a single parent. She homeschooled Moretz from the age of six, when she landed her first major film role, in the 2005 remake of *The Amityville Horror*. About being homeschooled, Moretz told Ethan Sacks for the New York *Daily News* (11 Aug. 2013), "I miss out on some silly stuff, but at the end I've learned fifteen times more than things I could have learned just by going to school."

Although *The Amityville Horror* was not well received by critics, Moretz's performance was recognized as a standout, leading to roles in television series such as *My Name Is Earl* in 2005, *Desperate Housewives* in 2006 and 2007, and *Dirty Sexy Money* in 2007 and 2008. She also appeared in numerous films, including *Big Momma's House 2* (2006), *Wicked Little Things* (2006), and *(500) Days of Summer* (2009). Additionally, she provided the voice for recurring character Darby in a number of Winnie the Pooh cartoons, including the television series *My Friends Tigger & Pooh*, from 2007 to 2009.

BREAKING OUT

Shortly before landing what would become her breakout role, Moretz, then age eleven, saw a poster of Angelina Jolie's character in the action film *Wanted* (2008) and realized that she, too, wanted to take on such a role. "I really want to do an Angelina Jolie–type character," she told her agents, according to Dave Itzkoff for the *New York Times* (8 Apr. 2010). "You know, like an action hero, woman empowerment, awesome, take-charge leading role." Within a month her mother was reading the script for a film adaptation of Mark Millar's comic book series *Kick-Ass*, a superhero parody about a teenager who dresses up in costume and tries to fight crime, with mixed results. "My mom was like, 'It's exactly what you've been wanting to do,'" Moretz recalled to Itzkoff.

Moretz plays Mindy Macready (spelled McCready in the comic book), an eleven-year-old costumed vigilante whose father, portrayed by Nicholas Cage, trained her to be a lethal combatant from a very young age. The character, who is better known by the pseudonym Hit-Girl, drew criticism for her frequent use of profanity; after an R-rated trailer for *Kick-Ass* showed Moretz using an obscene word before brutally taking down a drug gang, film fans and professional critics were divided over whether or not child actors such as Moretz should be allowed to say such things in films. The film's director, Matthew Vaughn, condemned the hypocrisy of a public that seemed more outraged by the language than the ultraviolence. "I was like, 'Does it not bother you that she killed about fifty-three people in this film?'" Vaughn told Itzkoff. "I'm like, 'Would you rather your daughter swore, or became a masked vigilante killer?'"

Not all of Moretz's roles during this time were so controversial; she and her family sought out roles that would showcase various aspects of her talent. A year prior to taking on the mantle of Hit-Girl for the first time, Moretz portrayed the gifted younger sister of Joseph Gordon-Levitt's character in (500) Days of Summer, and she later appeared in Diary of a Wimpy Kid, a film based on the satirical young-adult novel by Jeff Kinney. In 2011 she costarred in Hugo, the first children's movie from legendary film director Martin Scorsese, about a boy who lives alone in a Parisian railway station and has extraordinary adventures with his friend Isabelle (Moretz).

MORE CHALLENGING ROLES

Moretz continued to explore dark material in Let Me In (2010), in which she played Abby, a centuries-old vampire who, despite her age and experience, still looks like a young girl. When Abby meets and befriends a bullied twelve-year-old boy, she must balance their growing relationship with her relationship with the man pretending to be her father, who protects her during the day and helps her feed. Two years later, Moretz returned to the vampire world in Dark Shadows (2012), directed by Tim Burton and starring Johnny Depp, based on the 1960s television series of the same name. She then returned to her signature role of Hit-Girl in the 2013 sequel Kick-Ass 2, which is set several years after the first and portrays Mindy adjusting to high school while at the same time trying to train wannabe-superhero Dave Lizewski, a.k.a. Kick-Ass, to fight crime. Although the film, which also starred comedian Jim Carrey, was not as much of a commercial success as the original, Moretz again received high praise for her take-no-prisoners approach to Hit-Girl.

One of Moretz's most challenging roles during this period was the titular character in the 2013 remake of Carrie, played by Sissy Spacek in the 1976 original. The film, based on Stephen King's acclaimed first novel, focuses on the coming-of-age of a bullied teenage girl who is also developing telekinetic abilities. The remake was directed by Kimberly Peirce, best known for Boys Don't Cry (1999) and Stop-Loss (2008), and also starred award-winning actor Julianne Moore as Moretz's deranged, religiously obsessed mother. Although the movie met with mixed reviews, with many critics believing the film to be an unnecessary remake, viewers and critics alike were generally impressed with Moretz's performance. She also impressed her fellow actors, including Moore. "I was really struck by her emotional maturity and her willingness to explore the complications of the role," Moore wrote in an e-mail to Dave Itzkoff for the New York Times (9 Apr. 2014). "Often, young actors have anticipated their responses or have been coached into a performance. Chloë is available, emotional, and present."

Moretz herself believes that the long hours she spent as Carrie improved her skills as an actor. "I would come home from the set just drained," she said to Gina McIntyre for the Los Angeles Times blog Hero Complex (17 Oct. 2013). "I would have to stay for eighteen hours and just be in that mind-set of Carrie, which is just the darkest, most suicidal area that you could be in. It's hard to stay there your entire day. I would look in the mirror and be like, I don't know who I am right now."

THEATER DEBUT

In 2014 Moretz took on her first theater role in an Off-Broadway production of The Library, a drama about the aftermath of a school shooting. The play, written by Scott Z. Burns and directed by famed film director Steven Soderbergh, centers on Moretz's character, who is a survivor of the shooting. The play begins while the audience members are still finding their seats; Moretz is already on stage, lying motionless on a table, shortly before awakening in a hospital after the shooting.

In The Library, Burns seeks not to take sides on the issue of gun control but rather to reflect on what such a violent incident does to the survivors. The power of the play was not lost on Moretz, even during rehearsals. She told Itzkoff, "I came home one day, and I just couldn't stop crying. I've never been that affected by a movie. It's only a play that can affect you that much."

PERSONAL LIFE

Moretz has faced a number of challenges in her young life, even aside from her parents' divorce. She learned to confront homophobia from an early age; two of her four brothers are gay, and they "were treated horrifically until they grew up and understood how to deal with it," she told an interviewer for Seventeen magazine (Oct. 2013). In addition, at age ten, Moretz learned that before she was born, her parents had had another daughter, who died after two days. "We light a candle for her birthday every year," she told Harvey Marcus for InStyle UK (Aug. 2013).

Moretz has also had to contend with her mother's battle with kidney cancer, which began when she was just ten years old. "It made me realize, along with everything that happened with my dad, that your parents aren't these godly figures," she said to Marcus. "They're not chosen by the heavens. They're humans. Their bodies can fail and they can die at any moment. They make mistakes. They cry. They fight. It definitely, from a young age, put everything into perspective for me."

Shortly before Carrie premiered in October 2013, Moretz reached out to her fans on Twitter, asking them to pray for her mother. While she did not elaborate, many assumed the request was related to her mother's cancer. The following week, her mother accompanied her to the Carrie premiere, along with the rest of their family, and

Moretz told reporters that she was doing well. "She's here and she's looking hot," she assured a reporter for *People* (9 Oct. 2013). "Teri is looking hot."

SUGGESTED READING

Hubert, Andrea. "*Kick-Ass 2* Star Chloë Moretz on *Carrie*, Controversy and Other C-Words." *Guardian*. Guardian News and Media, 9 Aug. 2013. Web. 10 July 2014.

Itzkoff, Dave. "Just a Sweet Young Actress? $&@# Right!" *New York Times*. New York Times, 8 Apr. 2010. Web. 10 July 2014.

Itzkoff, Dave. "A Young Star, Poised and Grounded." *New York Times*. New York Times, 9 Apr. 2014. Web. 10 July 2014.

Marcus, Harvey. "Teenage Kicks." *InStyle UK* Aug. 2013: 100–109. Print.

McIntyre, Gina. "*Carrie* Star Chloe Grace Moretz Plays a Hit-Girl of a Higher Power." *Hero Complex*. Los Angeles Times, 17 Oct. 2013. Web. 10 July 2014.

Pols, Mary. "Young Blood." *Time*. Time, 11 Oct. 2010. Web. 10 July 2014.

Sacks, Ethan. "*Kick-Ass 2* Star Chloe Grace Moretz Has Grown Up Since Her Breakout Turn as Hit Girl in 2010 Original." *Daily News*. NYDailyNews.com, 11 Aug. 2013. Web. 10 July 2014.

SELECTED WORKS

The Amityville Horror, 2005; *(500) Days of Summer*, 2009; *Diary of a Wimpy Kid*, 2010; *Kick-Ass*, 2010; *Let Me In*, 2010; *Hugo*, 2011; *Dark Shadows*, 2012; *Kick-Ass 2*, 2013; *Carrie*, 2013; *If I Stay*, 2014; *The Equalizer*, 2014

—*Christopher Mari*

Alex Morgan

Born: July 2, 1989
Occupation: Soccer player

One of the best-known American soccer players both at home and the world over, Alex Morgan is also likely to be recognized by some for her extracurricular activities: posing nude (in body paint) for *Sports Illustrated*, authoring three children's books, and appearing in ads for ChapStick, Nike, Panasonic, and other products. Morgan's is not just a case of a sculpted body and television-ready good looks, however. At age twenty, while still playing soccer for the University of California, Berkeley (Cal), she became the youngest member of the US women's national soccer team. In 2011 the team was the runner-up at the FIFA Women's World Cup. The following year the team won the gold medal at

Getty Images

the 2012 Olympic Games in London. Leading up to the 2012 Olympics, Sam Borden for the *New York Times* (22 July 2012) dubbed Morgan "the next face of women's soccer," and her plays during that event and subsequently have solidified her position as the presumptive heir to US soccer legend Mia Hamm.

EARLY DAYS

Alexandra "Alex" Patricia Morgan was born on July 2, 1989. She grew up in Diamond Bar, California, outside Los Angeles, along with two older sisters. Morgan was always a competitive child, and she and one of her sisters would often run on the track to see who was fastest. From a young age Morgan played a variety of sports, including soccer, softball, basketball, and volleyball. Her parents encouraged her to play all kinds of sports and did not pressure her to focus on any one in particular. Although her father was a baseball enthusiast and initially made his preference known, he respected his daughter's wishes when she eventually decided to focus on soccer. He even began to study the sport, about which he initially knew little, so that he could help her improve. Although Morgan did not begin to focus on soccer until her early teens, her first big impression of it came in 1999, the so-called golden summer for women's soccer, when she was only ten years old. She watched the US national team play in the televised finals of the Women's World Cup, which, coincidentally enough, was held at the Rose Bowl, about thirty miles from her home. The most memorable moment of the game came when Brandi Chastain scored the game-winning goal on a penalty kick and stripped off her jersey, revealing a sports bra underneath, to celebrate the shot. In addition to Chastain, Morgan also looked up to the US women's team soccer players Hamm and Kristine Lilly.

As a young teenager, while still playing multiple sports—sometimes she had soccer, basketball, and softball practices all on the same day—Morgan began to consider making soccer her primary focus. She was already successfully playing for the American Youth Soccer Organization (AYSO); however, she soon began to consider the next step—club soccer. In an interview with Joe Curley for Cal South Soccer (9 June 2011), the website for the youth and adult state soccer association for Southern California, Morgan recalled, "When I was around 13 years old, I was heading into high school the next year, I kind of decided that soccer was my thing. I was actually pretty good at it, better than softball and basketball, I kind of narrowed it down."

SERIOUSLY KICKING IT

Morgan's decision to join club soccer at fourteen—a little later than some of her peers—was based on the demands such teams place on players. "I knew girls who had taken the leap and had gone to club teams a lot earlier, when they were 10, 11, 12. I just felt like still having fun with soccer and other sports," she explained to Curley. "I didn't want to take such a big commitment on myself . . . jump[ing] from AYSO to club, so I kind of waited until I knew youth soccer was the sport I wanted to pursue." A more serious pursuit than AYSO, club soccer taught Morgan a great deal about the game that would one day be her livelihood. Only half a year into club she had her first Olympic Development Program (ODP) camp. Speaking of that experience, she told Curley, "Being a young player, it opened my eyes to the game. It helped me learn a lot about myself, about confidence and having a positive attitude . . . because ODP took up a lot of time on the weekends, it helped me balance my time a lot better." She added, "On the field, the best girls in Southern California were coming together to play, so my game improved every time I played with them."

Although she was clearly talented, Morgan was not noticed as an outstanding player for about two years. Thus, at the age of sixteen, she extended her commitment to soccer. The hard work paid off: at age seventeen, Morgan landed a spot on the US Under-20 Women's National Team. However, she injured her knee, tearing her right anterior cruciate ligament (ACL), which led her to miss most of the season during her senior year in high school. The setback only increased her passion for the sport. She was determined to continue and was sure she would go on to play college soccer—and perhaps, one day, turn pro.

COLLEGE AND BEYOND

In 2007 Morgan received a scholarship to attend Cal. In college she not only played for the university team but also joined the US women's national soccer team. During her freshman year she starred in fifteen of seventeen games, led the school in goals (eight), and earned various honors, including honorable-mention All-Pacific-10 selection and a Pacific-10 all-freshman pick. The following year she again led the school in goals (nine), was named to the Soccer Buzz All-West Region second team, received a Pacific-10 All-American honorable mention, and she scored the game-winning goal at the 2008 FIFA Under-20 Women's World Cup.

By her junior year Morgan became Cal's female soccer player to watch. She again led the team in goals (fourteen), three of which were game winning, and earned a Pacific-10 all-academic honorable mention. She was also placed on the watch list for the Hermann Trophy, an annual award given to the best male and female college soccer players, and joined the senior national team for several offseason games. As a senior Morgan again led the team in scoring (fourteen goals), was named to the All-Pacific-10 first team, and was a candidate for player of the year. She also helped the US women's national team qualify for the World Cup. During her senior year Morgan played only twelve games for Cal because she was also playing for the US team. She graduated a semester early, in December 2010, with a bachelor's degree in political economy. She was able to graduate early because, after deciding she was going to pursue soccer on a professional level, she took on a substantial course load in summers and off-seasons.

WORLD CUP RUNNER-UP

In December 2009, while still in college, Morgan became the youngest member of the US women's national soccer team. She was twenty years old at the time. As a member of the team, under the leadership of Coach Pia Sundhage, Morgan participated in the FIFA Women's World Cup in Frankfurt, Germany, in the summer of 2011. She played the position of forward, and even though she was not a starter, she was no ordinary substitute: she was designated a "super sub," which meant that she usually entered late in the game and was given the task of continually pressuring the opposing team and seeking every goal-scoring opportunity. She earned the nickname Baby Horse because of her speed.

On July 13, 2011, in the closing minutes of the FIFA Women's World Cup semifinal match between the United States and France, Morgan scored a goal that gave the United States a 3–1 lead and, soon after, the victory. The US team went on to play Japan in the finals. In the sixty-ninth minute of the match, Morgan scored the first goal of the game; later in the game, she assisted Abby Wambach, who headed in a goal. However, the US team could not hold on, losing to Japan and becoming the tournament's runner-up.

About six months before the World Cup, Coach Sundhage spoke to Jordan Conn of *Sports Illustrated* (27 Jan. 2011) about Morgan. "She's fast, she's strong, and she goes straight for goal," Sundhage said. "She comes in with the confidence and the expectation that she's going to change the game." For the same article, Morgan's teammate Wambach told Conn: "Alex has come on and really been like a sponge. . . . I see a lot of myself in her in the way I related to Mia (Hamm). It will be an exciting couple of years for her to see how she grows, but she's already made it this far, and she totally deserves all the things that are coming to her."

OLYMPIC GOLD

Soon after the 2011 World Cup, the US women's national team began preparing for the following summer's Olympic Games. By the time of the Games, Morgan had progressed from being a "super sub" to being a starter. Despite being under plenty of pressure—the greater responsibility of starting, the potential rematch against Japan, her first Olympic Games—Morgan was poised and ready to play. In August of that year, in an Olympics semifinals match against Canada, she scored what has become one of the most famous goals in the history of American soccer. In the 123rd minute of the match, she headed in a goal, effectively sending the US team to the finals. (Fittingly, Coach Sundhage had previously told Morgan that she needed to improve her heading, advice not lost on her.) The US team faced Japan in the Olympic finals. The match took place at London's Wembley Stadium in front of a crowd of more than eighty thousand people, the largest soccer crowd in the history of the Olympic Games. The US team scored first, in the eighth minute of the game, and then again in the fifty-fourth minute. Japan scored ten minutes later, but it would not score again. The US team held on for a 2–1 victory, and Morgan and teammates received the gold medal.

SOCCER IN THE STATES

In addition to playing soccer for the US national team, Morgan plays professionally in the United States. About a month after graduating from Cal, she was drafted in the first round in the now-defunct Women's Professional Soccer (WPS) draft by the Western New York Flash. In 2012, after the WPS folded, she signed with the Seattle Sounders of the United Soccer League's W-League. The next year she switched teams again, staying in the Northwest but moving to the Portland Thorns of the National Women's Soccer League (NWSL). According to a July 27, 2013, article on *Oregon Live*, the website of

the *Oregonian* newspaper, Morgan has not only helped increase attendance at Thorns matches—the team is the leader in attendance in the NWSL—but also helped "boost attendance around the league, where attendance will be at or near a season-high when the Thorns visit." The 2013 season was somewhat of a struggle for the Thorns—especially given the expectations placed on Morgan and her teammate Christine Sinclair—but the team powered through, doing well in away games, and went on to play in the finals against the Flash. Months after winning the league championship, Morgan injured her left ankle; it eventually became a stress reaction. Though not as bad as a stress fracture, the injury prevented Morgan from playing in early 2014.

PERSONAL LIFE

Morgan enjoys doing yoga and attending spin classes. She loves listening to music when practicing or cleaning the house. Katy Perry and Rihanna are her favorites. She is also a fan of 1990s hip-hop and rhythm and blues as well as modern bands such as fun. In December 2013 she became engaged to professional soccer player Servando Carrasco.

Starting in 2013 she published *Kicks*, a three-book series about soccer for middle school children. The books—*Sabotage Season* (2013), *Saving the Team* (2013), and *Win or Lose* (2014)—became best sellers.

SUGGESTED READING

Arnold, Geoffrey C. "Thorns' Alex Morgan Embraces Stardom and Role as Face of Women's Soccer." *Oregon Live*. Oregonian, 27 July 2013. Web. 8 May 2014.

Borden, Sam. "Rising as Fast as Her Feet Will Take Her." *New York Times*. New York Times, 22 July 2012. Web. 8 May 2014.

Conn, Jordan. "Huge Expectations for Cal's Morgan." *Sports Illustrated*. Time, 27 Jan. 2011. Web. 8 May 2014.

Roenigk, Alyssa. "Alex Morgan Makes Most of Moment." *ESPN.go.com*. ESPN Internet Ventures, 7 Aug. 2012. Web. 8 May 2014.

—*Dmitry Kiper*

Andy Murray

Born: May 15, 1987
Occupation: Tennis player

When Scotland native Andy Murray defeated Novak Djokovic in the men's final of the 2012 US Open, he became the first British man in seventy-six years to win a Grand Slam singles tournament. That victory marked Murray's first Grand Slam title in five attempts and helped him

WireImage

break through the barrier of the so-called Big Three of men's tennis—Djokovic, Roger Federer, and Rafael Nadal. The Big Three had captured twenty-nine of the previous thirty Grand Slam titles. Five weeks before his US Open victory, Murray captured the gold medal in men's singles at the 2012 Olympic Games in London, England. Murray firmly solidified his status among the men's tennis elite in 2013, when he won his second Grand Slam title at that year's Wimbledon Championships in England, the world's oldest and most prestigious tennis competition.

Since he turned professional in 2005, Murray has amassed twenty-eight singles titles and fourteen runner-up finishes on the Association of Tennis Professionals (ATP) World Tour. Murray has established himself as an elite player with a dynamic all-around game, one that is characterized by crafty on-court tactics, speed, and athleticism. "He appears to have no distinctive weapon, because his entire game constitutes one huge one," Bill Dwyre wrote for the *Los Angeles Times* (8 July 2013). "The serve is big, the ground strokes off both sides are big and his movement is deceptively smooth and quick. He lands few big knives to the opponent's heart, just hundreds of sharp needles."

EARLY LIFE

The younger of two sons, Andrew "Andy" Barron Murray was born on May 15, 1987, to William and Judy Murray in Glasgow, Scotland. He and his brother, Jamie, who is fifteen months older,

were raised in Dunblane, a small country town located about forty miles from Glasgow. Murray comes from an athletic family. His maternal grandfather, Roy Erskine, was a professional soccer player who played for the Scotland-based Hibernian, Stirling Albion, and Cowdenbeath football clubs in the 1950s. His mother was a champion tennis player who became the top-ranked player in Scotland in the 1970s. Judy Murray played briefly on the professional tennis circuit in her late teens before turning to coaching. She served as Scotland's national tennis coach from 1995 to 2004 and became captain of the British Fed Cup team in 2011.

Murray first picked up a tennis racket at the age of two and by age three, he was regularly competing against his brother in matches held in the family living room. The two would hit sponge balls or balloons to each other over a net made from various household items. By all accounts, when Murray was growing up, his brother was the superior tennis player and athlete. "He was cleverer than me, better at tennis, a better runner . . . he did most things better than me," Murray recalled to Simon Hattenstone for the *Guardian* (8 June 2007). Murray's overwhelming desire to beat his brother helped to spur his development as a tennis player.

Murray's mother was a major influence on his tennis development, serving as his primary coach until he was twelve years old. Judy Murray spent hours each day practicing with her sons at the Dunblane Sports Club, which was located only two hundred yards from their home. Early on, she taught her sons to play from a tactical standpoint, rather than a technical one, stressing the importance of such things as shot strategy and placement. "I'd never been coached," Murray's mother told Christopher Clarey for the *New York Times* (26 Jan. 2011), "so I tried to teach them how to make it difficult for an opponent."

DUNBLANE TRAGEDY

Murray won his first tournament at age eight, at an age ten and under event in Solihull, England. The same year, he endured an experience that irrevocably altered his perspective on life. Along with his brother, he attended Dunblane Primary School and was present on March 13, 1996, when Thomas Hamilton, a forty-three-year-old former Scout leader, entered the school and murdered sixteen children and a teacher before killing himself. The Dunblane school massacre became known worldwide and spawned stringent anti-gun legislation across Great Britain. Murray has since rarely spoken about the incident in interviews, claiming that he was too young at the time to understand what was going on.

Not long after the Dunblane tragedy, Murray's parents separated, largely due to his mother's hectic schedule as a tennis coach. (They divorced in 2005 after a nine-year separation.) Afterward, Murray and his brother went to live with their father, who managed a Scottish newsagent chain. Judy Murray nonetheless remained intimately involved in her sons' upbringing and continued to play a major role in their tennis careers. Though his mother has received the lion's share of publicity throughout his tennis career, Murray has credited his father with helping him "mature as a person," as he told Hattenstone.

JUNIOR CAREER

Disheartened by his parents' separation, Murray found an escape from his grief on the tennis court. At age twelve, he won his age group at the prestigious Orange Bowl tournament in Miami, Florida. Scottish tennis coach Leon Smith, who coached Murray from age eleven until age seventeen, said of the victory to Hattenstone, "That's when it hit home, that we were dealing with one of the world's best talents." According to Smith, Murray stood out among his peers not only for his competitiveness but also for his tennis acumen. By that time, he was regularly defeating his brother, who had become one of the world's top junior players in his own right. The Murray brothers would later become occasional doubles partners.

Murray attended Dunblane High School but left the school without graduating. Instead, he opted to focus on his burgeoning tennis career. At age fifteen, he moved to Barcelona, Spain, to study and train at the Sánchez-Casal Academy, directed by former champion doubles partners Emilio Sánchez and Sergio Casal. Murray remained there for over a year, during which he learned how to play effectively on both clay and hard courts by increasing his speed, strength, and stamina. To fund his stint at the academy, which cost approximately £30,000 per year, Murray's parents took on extra jobs. Murray told Paul Henderson for GQ (July 2013) that attending the academy "was probably the best decision I have made in my career."

Murray's time at the academy paid immediate dividends. In 2003, he won the Canadian Open junior title and claimed his first title on the ITF Futures circuit, the lowest tier of professional tennis. The following year he won four Futures tournaments and became the first British winner of the junior US Open title. That latter victory helped propel Murray to number two in the world junior rankings and number 411 in the year-end ATP singles rankings, prompting the British Broadcasting Corporation (BBC) to honor him with the 2004 Young Sports Personality of the Year Award.

TURNING PROFESSIONAL AND RISE UP THE ATP RANKINGS

Murray announced his arrival on the world tennis stage in 2005, when he turned professional and cracked the top one hundred of the ATP rankings for the first time. That year he became the youngest Briton ever to play in the Davis Cup, the foremost annual international team competition in men's tennis. During the course of his career, Murray has played in a handful of other matches for Great Britain's Davis Cup team. Murray also made his professional singles debut at both Wimbledon and the US Open, and advanced to his first ATP final at the Thailand Open, where he lost to future nemesis Roger Federer, then the world's number one in straight sets. He ended 2005 with an ATP singles ranking of sixty-four, making him, at eighteen, the first teenager from Great Britain to finish in the year-end top one hundred since 1974.

Murray continued his steady climb up the men's world tennis rankings in 2006, which marked his first full season competing on the ATP circuit. After losing in the first round of his maiden Australian Open, Murray captured his first ATP title at the SAP Open in San Jose, California. The victory moved him ahead of fellow British players Tim Henman and Greg Rusedski in the ATP rankings to become Britain's number-one player. Henman, a six-time Grand Slam semifinalist who mentored Murray during the early stages of his career, said to Henderson that Murray "always seemed to play the right shot at the right time, and was a great competitor who knew how to win even at such a young age." Murray finished the year in the top twenty of the ATP rankings, with a ranking of seventeen, thanks to fourth round finishes at both Wimbledon and the US Open.

CHALLENGING THE BIG THREE OF MEN'S TENNIS

Prior to the 2007 season, Murray started working with renowned American tennis coach Brad Gilbert, known for coaching such tennis champions as Andre Agassi and Andy Roddick. Despite being hampered by injuries throughout the season, Murray improved both his game and his ranking under Gilbert. He successfully defended his title at the SAP Open and added another title at the St. Petersburg Open in Russia, while notching runner-up finishes at tournaments in Qatar and France. He reached number eight in the ATP singles rankings and spent nine weeks in the top ten before finishing the year at number eleven.

Murray parted ways with Gilbert in late 2007, after which he began working with British coach Miles Maclagan. He worked with Maclagan for the next two and a half years, during which he firmly established himself as the world's fourth-best player, behind Roger Federer, Rafael Nadal, and Novak Djokovic, a trio that came to be known as the "Big Three" of men's tennis for their dominance in Grand Slam events. During the 2008 season, Murray won five ATP titles, including a victory over Djokovic at the Cincinnati Masters. He reached his first ever Grand Slam final at the US Open, where he lost to Federer in straight sets. That season he also reached the quarterfinals at Wimbledon, but lost to Nadal in straight sets. He finished 2008 with a world number four ranking.

Murray continued to build on his success in 2009, when he led all players on the ATP Tour with six victories. That year he achieved a career-high singles ranking of number two before finishing the year at number four for the second straight year. Murray would also finish 2010 and 2011 as the world's number-four ranked player. During those years, he added seven more ATP titles to his resume, as well as two more runner-up finishes in Grand Slam events. Murray lost to Federer in straight sets at the 2010 Australian Open and then to Djokovic in straight sets at the 2011 Australian Open. Meanwhile, he lost to Nadal in the semifinals of four Grand Slams, the 2010 and 2011 Wimbledon Championships, the 2011 French Open, and the 2011 US Open.

OLYMPIC GLORY

Prior to the 2012 season, in his effort to break through the seemingly impenetrable barrier of the Big Three, Murray hired the Czech-born eight-time Grand Slam champion Ivan Lendl as his new coach. Lendl, a former world number one who himself had lost four Grand Slam finals before winning his first, immediately began working on improving Murray's mental toughness, which had long been seen as a weakness in his game. Lendl also pushed Murray to learn more from his losses and to play more aggressively, urging him to go for his shots rather than wait for them.

Murray's newfound mental approach under Lendl proved to have an immediate impact on his tennis game. He opened the 2012 season with a victory at the Brisbane International and then reached the semifinals of the Australian Open, where he narrowly lost to Djokovic in a grueling five-set match. After reaching the finals of the Dubai Tennis Championships and the Miami Masters—where he finished as the runner-up to Federer and Djokovic, respectively—Murray advanced to his first ever Wimbledon final, becoming the first British man to do so since Bunny Austin in 1938. In the final, he lost to Federer in four sets. Afterward, Murray broke down in tears in his on-court interview, which, as US Davis Cup captain and former world number one Jim Courier told S. L. Price for *Sports Illustrated* (8 July 2013), made people "realize how much he cared."

Following the heartbreaking loss, Murray bounced back to represent Great Britain at the 2012 Olympic Games in London. There, he lost only one set in five matches en route to the men's singles final, where he again faced Federer, defeating him convincingly in straight sets to claim Olympic gold. With the win, Murray became the first British man to win an Olympic singles title since Josiah Ritchie in 1908. At the London Games, he also captured a silver medal in the mixed doubles event with partner Laura Robson.

FIRST GRAND SLAM TITLES

Five weeks after his Olympic triumph, Murray silenced his critics by winning his first career Grand Slam singles title at the 2012 US Open. In the final, he defeated Djokovic in a hard-fought five-set battle to become the first British man to capture a Grand Slam title since Fred Perry in 1936. He also became the first male player in tennis history to win an Olympic gold medal and a US Open title in the same calendar year. The feat established a place for Murray in the "Big Four" of men's tennis. "The grand slam tag is something that our country had been waiting on for so long, and maybe winning a slam was something I wanted too much," Murray told Shaun Assael for *ESPN* magazine (3 Dec. 2012). "I became so obsessed with it that I wasn't focusing on all my other matches . . . winning the US Open and the Olympics was a massive weight off my shoulders."

Murray entered the 2013 season as the number-three ranked player in the world. That season he successfully defended his Brisbane International title and reached the finals of the Australian Open for the third time in his career. In the Australian Open final, he was defeated by Djokovic in four sets. Murray went on to advance to the finals at Wimbledon for the second straight year, where he and Djokovic squared off again. He won his second Grand Slam title in decisive fashion, defeating Djokovic in straight sets to become the first British man since Fred Perry in 1936 to win the prestigious tournament. Based largely on that victory, Murray was named an Officer of the Order of the British Empire (OBE) and honored with the 2013 BBC Sports Personality of the Year Award.

At the 2014 Qatar Open, the first event of the 2014 season, Murray lost to Florian Mayer in the second round. Nevertheless, in January 2014 he was ranked number four in the world. He has amassed more than $30 million in career prize earnings.

PERSONAL LIFE

British actor and comedian James Corden, a close friend of Murray, described him to Henderson as "exceptional in every way" and "the most unassuming, polite and honest elite sportsman I have ever met." Murray is well known for his aversion to the cult of celebrity and has largely abstained from the party scene. Instead, in his spare time, he enjoys watching boxing, soccer, and basketball, riding go-karts, and playing video games. He and his longtime girlfriend, Kim Sears, daughter of the British tennis coach Nigel Sears, live in Surrey, England.

SUGGESTED READING

De Jonge, Peter. "Ivan Lendl Gets Back to Tennis." *New York Times*. New York Times, 20 June 2012. Web. 14 Jan. 2014.

Dwyre, Bill. "With Andy Murray, the Sum Is Greater Than the Parts." *Los Angeles Times*. Los Angeles Times, 8 July 2013. Web. 14 Jan. 2014.

Hattenstone, Simon. "Boy on the Brink." *Guardian*. Guardian News and Media, 8 June 2007. Web. 14 Jan. 2014.

Henderson, Paul. "Man on Fire." *GQ*. Condé Nast UK, 28 May 2013. Web. 14 Jan. 2014.

Murray, Andy. "Andy Murray Finally Breaks Through." Interview by Shaun Assael. *ESPN*. ESPN Internet Ventures, 3 Dec. 2012. Web. 14 Jan. 2014.

—*Chris Cullen*

Rita Ora

Born: November 26, 1990
Occupation: Singer-songwriter

Rita Ora, who sports peroxide blond hair, is a British singer-songwriter and actor of Kosovar Albanian descent. Signed by rapper Jay-Z to his Roc Nation Records when she was only eighteen years old, she waited four years to release her first studio album, *Ora* (2012). The album hit number one on the UK charts—as did her first three singles—and went platinum in the United

FilmMagic

Kingdom. Though she was only twenty-two years old when she released *Ora*, the album was the culmination of years of work for the singer. In March 2014, Ora released the lead single from her second album, "I Will Never Let You Down," which was produced by the successful Scottish DJ Calvin Harris. The song also rose to number one on the UK charts, making Ora the second British female solo artist to have four singles reach the number-one ranking on the UK charts after pop star Geri Halliwell. A superstar in the United Kingdom, Ora continues to establish herself alongside similar pop artists in the United States. "I kinda think, when your ball is rolling, you don't stop it," Ora told Simon Mills for the *London Evening Standard* (1 Feb. 2013). "You keep it rolling. You have to make yourself . . . unforgettable."

EARLY LIFE AND EDUCATION

Born Rita Sahatçiu on November 26, 1990, in the city of Pristina, then in the former state of Yugoslavia and now in Kosovo, Ora began singing at the age of six, and by fourteen she had already appeared in a major motion picture. Her paternal grandfather was the well-known Yugoslavian film director Besim Sahatçiu, and she is named after his favorite film star, Rita Hayworth. Ora's family long held ties to intellectuals and artists in their hometown, but in the early 1990s, ethnic Kosovar Albanians like the Sahatçius were being oppressed by the Serbian majority, and more than eight hundred thousand ethnic Albanians fled their homes in Kosovo during this time.

In 1991, when Ora was just one year old, Ora's family—her father, Besnik; her mother, Vera; and her older sister, Elena—moved to London, England, where they settled in a one-room flat in Earls Court. The family spoke Albanian in the house and worked to overcome the stigma of being refugees. Eventually, Ora's mother, a doctor in her native country who had been working as a waitress, learned English and found a job as a psychiatrist. Ora's younger brother Don was born in 1998, the same year that the family moved to a larger flat in Kensal Rise and Besnik opened a pub called the Queens Arms at Kilburn. The year 1998 was also when war broke out among the splintering factions of the former Yugoslavia, and Ora recalls her parents worrying about relatives back home. "I couldn't figure it out. All the arguments, all the tension—I knew it was coming from something," she told Ed Caesar for *British GQ* magazine (1 Aug. 2013).

Growing up, Ora delighted in perusing her parents' record collection and idolized Canadian songstress Celine Dion. Ora won a place at the Sylvia Young Theatre School, a performing-arts school in London, when she was eleven. Around that time—and with Rita's future stage career in mind—her father decided to add "Ora" to the family surname, making it easier to pronounce. When Ora was fifteen, her mother was diagnosed with breast cancer, and Ora stopped going to school. Her mother soon recovered—and her older sister, Elena, prodded Ora to return to class—but the experience left an impression on Ora. "My mum had always been one of those free-spirited women and her being ill was really confusing for me," she told Mills. "I couldn't understand why my mum wasn't a superhero, why she wasn't, you know, unbreakable. I'd sit around the house for days. I was really down."

EARLY CAREER

When Ora was not in class or working at her dad's pub or at a shoe store, she was hustling to be recognized as a singer. She performed in clubs, bars, and even in a few musicals, though she admitted to Mills that musical theater is not her style. Navigating both gigs and school was taking its toll, however. "It was a really weird time in my life but it was also amazing because I had to grow up fast," Ora told Lauren Nostro for *Complex* magazine (23 Apr. 2012).

In 2004, at the age of fourteen, she was cast as an Albanian youngster in the British film *Spivs*, an experience she told Nostro was "good fun." The same year, Ora landed a production deal with Swedish record producer Martin Terefe. The deal was not a lot of money, Ora told Nostro, and the stipulations of the contract were loose. "I used to go there after school and just sit there, work with him and just kind of get the vibe of it," she recalled to Nostro. In 2007, Terefe was working with British R & B star Craig David, and he asked Ora to complete a demo for David's new record. Terefe and David liked Ora's take so much that they kept her on the song "Awkward," Ora's first official appearance on a record. She also appeared on David's next album *Greatest Hits* (2008), on a single called "Where's Your Love," featuring rapper Tinchy Stryder.

After two years, Ora felt that the partnership with Terefe had run its course and elected not to extend her contract. She was only sixteen but felt the pressure to jump-start her career. She auditioned for *Eurovision: Your Country Needs You!*, a BBC program looking for a British vocalist to compete in the 2009 Eurovision Song Contest. It was not how Ora wanted to start her career, but she took the opportunity anyway. "I just felt like I didn't know what was going to happen to me," she told Nostro, "so I thought that was my last chance." At the audition Ora sang for judges, including Andrew Lloyd Weber, the composer of *Cats* and *The Phantom of the Opera*, but, as she relayed to Mills, as soon as she entered the room she had a bad feeling. "Right from the start I was, like, 'What am I doing here?'" she recalled. Without waiting for feedback, Ora walked out of the audition immediately after finishing her song. The judges were shocked and even tried calling her agent to bring her back, but Ora refused to return. The same year, as she told Mills, she was walking down Kensington High Street in London when she received an incoming international call on her cell phone. She thought it was her grandmother, but instead it was someone at Roc Nation, the record label owned by Jay-Z.

SIGNING TO ROC NATION

Ora's brief professional relationship with Terefe had put her on the radar of record-label talent scouts, including an A&R at Universal named Brynee. Brynee contacted Jay Brown, the co-founder (along with Jay-Z and Ty Ty Smith) and president of Roc Nation Records, on Ora's behalf. Meanwhile, Ora received offers from labels such as Universal and Island Records, but no deal seemed imminent. She sent Brown a rough demo of a song she composed called "I'll Be Waiting," which she recorded using the Apple software GarageBand. Two days later, she received a call from Roc Nation; Brown offered to fly her to New York City for a meeting. As soon as she got off the plane, the representatives from Roc took her to a club where Rocawear, a clothing manufacturer that is also owned by Jay-Z, was having a Christmas party. She met Brown, Smith, and—unexpectedly—Jay-Z himself. "I'm happy I didn't know," Ora told Nostro of the encounter, "because if I knew, I would've freaked out."

The group took Ora to Roc the Mic, Jay-Z's recording studio in Manhattan, and played some of her songs. Jay-Z offered to sign her on the spot. The eighteen-year-old Ora was excited but also restless to make it big. "I got signed and I was like 'Cool, Oprah next week,'" she recalled to Nostro. "But obviously not. I knew I was going to record the album or whatever but I was so eager to put everything out that I didn't think about the long run." Jay-Z advised her to be patient and told her to take her time recording her first album. "They told me to go find myself and do what I do," she said. The process ultimately took much longer than Ora had anticipated. Roc Nation sent her on an exhausting tour in the United States and, in 2008, she recorded an album, only to scrap the entire project. During this time, she wrote songs with singer and rapper Drake, who asked Ora to appear in the music video for his single "Over" in 2010. In 2012, Ora met DJ Fresh, who was looking for a vocalist for a single. Ora, who was putting the finishing touches on her debut album, jumped at the chance. The turnaround was quick—"We did it and the next week it was on the radio," she told Nostro. The song, "Hot Right Now," was released in February 2012 and quickly became the number-one song on the UK singles chart.

ORA'S DEBUT ALBUM

Alongside Jay-Z, Ora officially released her first US solo single "How We Do (Party)" at New York City's Z100 radio station in February 2012. Ora told Nostro that after the release she cried with relief and happiness. The song, which samples the 1993 song "Party & Bulls——" by the late rapper Notorious B.I.G. (then known as Biggie Smalls), became a summer anthem. It also hit number one in Britain, just after her first UK single "R.I.P.," featuring English rapper Tinie Tempah, did the same. Ora became the first artist of 2012 to have three consecutive number-one hits in the United Kingdom.

Drake had written "R.I.P." for Barbados-born R & B singer Rihanna, but she turned it down. When Ora heard "R.I.P." she knew she had to record it. "It was such a banger that I was like, 'I don't care who it's been through, I want that song. And I will own it,'" Ora recalled to Nostro. Ora said the song is about a young woman taking ownership of herself. The video, which "oozes confidence," Ora told Nostro, garnered 2.5 million hits on YouTube in the two days after it was posted.

Incidentally, Ora bears a striking resemblance to Rihanna and has been accused of being a Rihanna-copycat since the beginning of her career. Some critics have been unable to resist the comparison when reviewing Ora's music. In fact, though a commercial success, Ora was not a critical favorite. Michael Cragg wrote in a review of the album for the Guardian (30 Aug. 2012) that Ora feels "more like a collection of other people's songs than a cohesive album." Ryan Copsey's review for Digital Spy (28 Aug. 2012) was more positive, and he acknowledged the less-than-flattering Rihanna comparison. "She rarely colors outside the lines," he wrote, "but when she does—in the case of gentle ballad 'Hello, Hi, Goodbye'—it points to an artist with brighter prospects than a sub-par Rihanna."

Ora's second US single was "Radioactive," written by the Australian singer-songwriter Sia Furler, better known simply as Sia. Best known for her appearance on DJ David Guetta's 2011 hit "Titanium," Sia has collaborated with everyone from Beck to Beyoncé. Long before working with her, Ora counted Sia as one of her musical idols.

Ora's third single, the empowering anthem "Shine Ya Light," also performed well in the United Kingdom, though it did not rise to number one. Ora shot the video in her hometown of Pristina, Kosovo, where her extended family still lives. "The whole country was outside," she told Caesar of her arrival. "I got off the plane, it was like millions of heads. I couldn't see the floor." The moment was captured at the beginning of the video. When she walked on stage, the fans were chanting her name. "It was the most surrealest [sic] experience I've ever felt. It was more than a music video. [It] was a moment in our history as Kosovo, it was a moment for people to see us: how we live, our landscape."

PERSONAL LIFE AND ACTING ROLES

Ora made a cameo appearance in the 2013 movie Fast and the Furious 6 and was cast as Christian Grey's sister in the film adaptation of the 2011 erotic novel Fifty Shades of Grey. The role, for which Ora had to perfect an American accent, was hard-won: It took her eight callbacks to secure the part. The film is scheduled for a 2015 release.

Ora briefly dated Scottish DJ Calvin Harris, with whom she collaborated on "I Will Never Let You Down," but the couple parted in June 2014. In August, Ora said that Harris would not allow her to perform the song live for the Teen Choice Awards. Also in 2014, Ora teamed with Australian rapper Iggy Azalea on the song "Black Widow," for which the pair made a music video that pays homage to Quentin Tarantino's Kill Bill films (2003–4). Ora lives in London.

SUGGESTED READING

Caesar, Ed. "The Golden Ora." British GQ. Condé Nast, 1 Aug. 2013. Web. 18 Aug. 2014.

Gannon, Emma. "The Improbable Rise of Rita Ora: A Guide for the Modern-Day Celebrity." Daily Beast. Daily Beast, 5 May 2014. Web. 18 Aug. 2014.

Godwin, Richard. "Elevating Rita." Vogue UK. Condé Nast, 20 Dec. 2012. Web. 18 Aug. 2014.

Mills, Simon. "Rita Ora: 'You Have to Make Yourself . . . Unforgettable.'" London Evening Standard. London Evening Standard, 1 Feb. 2013. Web. 18 Aug. 2014.

Nostro, Lauren. "Who Is Rita Ora?" Complex. Complex Media, 23 Apr. 2012. Web. 18 Aug. 2014.

—Molly Hagan

Neri Oxman

Born: 1976
Occupation: Designer

Neri Oxman is an Israeli-born artist, architect, ecologist, computer scientist, and a designer, who Anya Kamenetz describes for Fast Company (8 May 2009) as someone "who is not just making new things but also coming up with new ways to make things." She is the Sony Corporation Career Development Professor and Assistant Professor of Media Arts and Sciences at the Massachusetts Institute of Technology (MIT) Media Lab, where she founded the Mediated Matter research group in 2010. Oxman studied

medicine and architecture and researches ways in which digital design and architecture function and interact with organic forms such as the human body.

EARLY LIFE AND INFLUENCES

Oxman was born in 1976 and raised in the Mount Carmel region of the coastal city of Haifa, Israel. Her parents, Rivka and Robert Oxman, are well-known architectural theorists and professors at the Technion–Israel Institute of Technology in Haifa, and the pair recently coedited *Theories of the Digital in Architecture* (2014). They also published *The New Structuralism: Design, Engineering and Architectural Technologies* in 2010. Oxman has a younger sister, Parisa, who is an artist.

As a child, Oxman spent countless daytime hours in her grandmother's garden, and at night she spent time in her parents' architectural studio building balsa wood airplanes and being surrounded by the modernist designs that her parents favored. Oxman explained to the Vilcek Foundation (3 Feb. 2014) that in dividing her time this way, she grew up "between nature and culture" and believes that the dichotomy of nature and culture is present in her current work.

EDUCATION

Oxman recalls sitting in on her father's design classes at Technion, but after completing the mandatory three years of military service in Israel, she chose to study medicine at the Hebrew University Hadassah Medical School in Jerusalem. She left medical school after two years to study town planning and architecture at Technion, but her interest in anatomy and biology remained. "I realized that 99 percent of this work consisted of analysis and only one percent was

reflection," Oxman told Hubertus Breuer for the German magazine *Gaggenau New Spaces* (2010), and she "wanted to reverse these proportions in [her] life."

During her fourth year at Technion, Oxman transferred to the Architectural Association School of Architecture in London where she completed her degree. It was while working in various London architectural offices that she was first introduced to digital design. Oxman moved to the United States in 2005 to earn her master's degree at MIT, where she studied under the late architect William J. Mitchell. She remained at the school to work toward a PhD in design computation, which she completed as a Presidential Fellow in 2010.

DESIGN PHILOSOPHY

Oxman was already interested in objects that looked like natural forms, but as she completed work for her PhD, she also became interested in the processes that *make* natural forms. Could a designer create in much the same way that nature creates? The concept is known as biomimicry, which is a developing science that uses designs found in nature to solve human dilemmas, and it is gaining momentum as scientists and architects look for ways to make products more sustainable. In nature, each part of an organism serves a specific purpose, as does the organism as a whole. Through evolution, the design of each living thing is optimized for the organism to perform a particular function and to survive. "The most beautiful products, or the most elegant or seductive products, in my mind are those that tell a story of a process," Oxman told Humphries for *MIT Technology Review* magazine. Oxman coined the term *material ecology* to describe her design philosophy. She wants to change the way designers think about the process of making things so that a finished product will adapt and continue to adapt to the environment, to humans, and to other products. Energy efficiency is only a part of Oxman's ultimate aim. She envisions a world in which complex man-made objects interact and grow like organisms in nature as a part of a larger ecosystem.

3-D PRINTING AND DESIGN

Oxman developed what she calls Material-based Design Computation at MIT. Some artists work with paints or clay, but Oxman works with various materials to fabricate her designs. She is able to design an object on a computer and generate it using 3-D printing. When objects are traditionally manufactured, they are made up of many different parts, and those parts are made by cutting and shaping fixed materials such as metal. The use of 3-D printers, also known as "additive manufacturing," manufactures an object by adding layer upon layer of material—each layer being a fraction of a millimeter in width—until the finished three-dimensional object emerges. The object that eventually emerges from the 3-D printer leaves no excess material because it uses only the amount of material it needs, unlike manufacturing traditionally fabricated objects, which involves wasted material that is unable to be reused.

The relatively new technology of 3-D printing makes customization and optimization of products much easier because designers are able to control every facet of an object's composition, including, as Oxman has found, programming new materials within an object to serve a desired purpose. Nuit Banai for *Icon* magazine wrote on April 24, 2013, that "at the heart" of Oxman and her team's mission is engendering "a radical shift in the world of 3-D printing, with the machine becoming a form-giver rather than merely a form-replicator."

BEAST AND CARPAL SKIN

Beast is the title of an early work created by Oxman in collaboration with MIT materials science professor W. Craig Carter between 2008 and 2010. The piece is a prototype for a chaise lounge that responds to the shifting weight of its sitter, and the chair, which John Ortved for *Interview* magazine (1 May 2009) described as resembling a praying mantis, is made of eight different materials chosen to respond to a person's shape and distribution of weight so that the chair can behave and adapt to the body like human skin, what Oxman described in an interview with Andrew Dent for *Matter* magazine (9 Sept. 2009) as "responsive architecture" where "form follows force not unlike the way Mother Nature has it."

Another of Oxman's projects, *Carpal Skin*, is a hybrid splint and glove that she created between 2009 and 2010 for sufferers of carpal tunnel syndrome, which Oxman also suffers from and which is caused by a compressed nerve in the wrist. The texture of *Carpal Skin*'s glove resembles the surface of a brain, and its ingenious composition—a complex distribution of hard and soft materials based on a patient's specific physiology and "pain profile"—is inspired by animal coating.

Ortved relates that both *Beast* and *Carpal Skin* exemplify the "living-synthetic constructions" that Oxman has become known for creating because they behave like living organisms, but they are constructed using a computer and a 3-D printer. "We are creating a new language that is directly influenced by the behavior of nature," Oxman told Noam Dvir for Israel's *Haaretz* newspaper (7 June 2011). The technology allows Oxman to assemble multiple materials and make composite materials within each work. Though her works suggest a practicality, they are also sculptural and can be found at some of the world's top art institutions. Although pieces

such as *Carpal Skin* resemble familiar objects and material, others are more alien. "A recurring theme for her work," Carter told Humphries "is something that's creepy and beautiful at the same time." Humphries noted that though Oxman's works are created with machines, "they seem almost perversely alive."

THE MEDIATED MATTER GROUP

After earning her PhD in 2010, Oxman developed a research group called the Mediated Matter group at MIT's Media Lab. Professor Craig Carter, a mainstay of the group, first worked with Oxman when she was a doctoral student and they created *Beast*, and they continue to work in tandem. Before Oxman begins a project, she will send Carter an image of a project she has begun to imagine. Carter then develops algorithms that would generate an object similar to that image, and Oxman interprets the algorithms, allowing, as Humphries explains, "the algorithm [to] create the form. It is this final step that elevates Oxman's work above a mere imitation of nature and creates "new artifacts that are more than the sum of their parts."

In 2012 Oxman collaborated with Carter, Joe Hicklin of the software company MathWorks, and the Israeli 3-D printing company Object to create the series *Imaginary Beings: Mythologies of the Not Yet*, inspired by Argentinean poet Jorge Luis Borges's *The Book of Imaginary Beings* (1957). The series, which explores the intersection of design and mythology through prototypes for human bodies, debuted at the Centre Pompidou in Paris, France, in May 2012. *Imaginary Beings* suggests the possibilities that await us through new technology. One piece, *Arachné*, was inspired by the mythical figure of the same name. The goddess Athena transformed Arachne, a mortal, into a spider after Arachne challenged her to a weaving contest. *Arachné* is a corset that functions as body armor, though it is made of soft and flexible materials. The corset forms a web over the wearer's ribcage. Another piece, *Leviathan 1*, is also an armored corset, modeled after descriptions of the Leviathan, Hell's gatekeeper, in the Book of Job. *Pneuma 1* is a helmet. The ancient Greek word *pneuma* means "air in motion," but it was used to describe the airy soul housed in the human body. Resembling a porous ocean sponge, the helmet is made of hard and soft materials to be strong and comfortable and to let air circulate freely. In January 2013 Oxman collaborated with the Dutch designer, Iris van Herpen, to create *Anthoza*, a 3-D printed dress and cape "that acted like a 'second skin'" Banai wrote, for Paris Fashion Week.

SWARM MANUFACTURING

Oxman is fascinated by the world's natural weavers. Describing *Arachné* and the eight different types of thread that can be produced by one spider, Oxman told Banai, "In more ways than one, spider spinnerets are the antecedents of multimaterial printers." In 2013 Oxman and the Mediated Matter group conducted an architectural experiment they called the Silk Pavilion. Oxman found she could control the spinning patterns of silkworms by altering their environment. The Mediated Matter group constructed an aluminum scaffold resembling a tent and used a robot to string silk starter threads across it. They hung the pavilion at MIT and released 6,500 live silkworms on it to spin more thread, constructing a webbed dome. The result was a living scaffold, a human-sized cocoon. Oxman and her team called the hybrid fabrication method, CNSILK (Computer Numerically Controlled Silk Cocoon Construction). The experiment supported a theory that Oxman has been working on regarding 3-D printers and large-scale objects. (It was also suggested that similar silk structures might be useful in creating shelter for refugees after a natural disaster.) Rather than using the traditional layering approach, Oxman believes that entire buildings can be erected using what she calls the "swarm approach," in which small robots spin material like a silkworm. "The project [Silk Pavilion] speculates about the possibility in the future to implement a biological swarm approach to 3-D printing," Oxman told Joseph Flaherty for *Wired* magazine (11 July 2013). "Imagine thousands of synthetic silkworms guided by environmental conditions such as light or heat—supporting the deposition of natural materials using techniques other than layering. . . . Google is for information what swarm manufacturing may one day become for design fabrication."

AWARDS AND RECOGNITION

In 2008, Oxman was named a Revolutionary Mind by SEED magazine and received a Graham Foundation Carter Manny Award. In 2009, she was named to *Fast Company*'s list of the year's one hundred most creative people and to *Icon*'s list of the twenty most influential architects to shape the future. That year she also won the International Earth Award for Future-Crucial Design, and a Metropolis Next Generation Award. Since then, she has also received a Building Design + Construction 40 Under 40 award (2012), a Design Futures Council Award (2013), and the Vilcek Prize in Design (2014), which is given to foreign-born scientists and artists who have made outstanding contributions to US society.

Oxman's work has been exhibited at many institutions around the world, including the Museum of Modern Art (MoMA), New York (2008), which commissioned her *Natural Artifice* series; the architectural biennial at the World Art Museum, Beijing, China (2010); and the Smithsonian Institute, Washington, DC (2013). In 2009

Oxman had a solo show, *Neri Oxman: At the Frontier of Ecological Design*, at the Museum of Science in Boston, Massachusetts; the show is now part of the museum's permanent collection. Her work may also be found in permanent collections at the Centre Pompidou Museum, Paris, France; the FRAC Collection for Art and Architecture, Orléans, France; and the Museum of Fine Arts, Boston, among others. In 2014, Oxman has shows at the Victoria and Albert Museum, MoMA, New York's Museum of Art and Design, and Paris's Le Laboratoire.

SUGGESTED READING

Banai, Nuit. "Feature: Neri Oxman." *Icon*. Iconeye, 24 Apr. 2013. Web. 7 Apr. 2014.

Dvir, Noam. "'Nature is a brilliant engineer.'" *Haaretz*. Haaretz Daily Newspaper, 7 June 2011. Web. 7 Apr. 2014.

Flaherty, Joseph. "A Mind-Blowing Dome Made by 6,500 Computer-Guided Silkworms." *Wired*. Condé Nast, 11 July 2013. Web. 10 Apr. 2014.

Humphries, Courtney. "Redesigning Product Design." *MIT Technology Review*. MIT Technology Review, 18 June 2013. Web. 9 Apr. 2014.

Kamenetz, Anya. "Most Creative People 2009: 43. Neri Oxman." *Fast Company*. Mansueto Ventures, 8 May 2009. Web. 8 Apr. 2014.

Ortved, John. "'It's Alive!': The Work of Neri Oxman." *Interview*. Interview, 1 May 2009. Web. 8 Apr. 2014.

—*Molly Hagan*

Luca Parmitano

Born: September 27, 1976
Occupation: Astronaut

Luca Parmitano is an astronaut of many firsts. In 2013, at the age of thirty-six years and eight months, he became the youngest astronaut ever to participate in a long-duration mission. During that mission, to the International Space Station (ISS), he also became Italy's first space-walking astronaut. A former decorated pilot in the Italian Air Force, Parmitano is perhaps best known for the near-fatal mishap that occurred on his second space walk, during which the cooling system in his spacesuit leaked and his helmet began to fill with water. Thanks to his quick thinking, he was able to return to the station safely and continue his mission, as well as produce some widely praised photographs of Earth from the station's Cupola module, which he disseminated via social media.

In an interview for NASA.gov (Apr. 4, 2013), conducted prior to his mishap, Parmitano

Maurizio Brambatti/EPA/Landov

discussed the potential dangers of being an astronaut. "The risks, yes, of course, there are risks. I think that our engineers and our technicians do an incredible job of minimizing those risks. I like to think that the chances of those risks becoming real are very small. Of course the consequences are enormous in most cases." He added, "Is it worth it? Yes, it's worth it because that's who we are. That's what makes us humans. That is what makes us different from all, from the rest of the animal kingdom. And if we don't follow our nature of being explorers, of being thinkers, then we are denying a part of ourselves that is incredibly important."

EARLY LIFE AND EDUCATION

Luca Parmitano was born in Paternò, Sicily, Italy, on September 27, 1976, and grew up in the nearby town of Catania. His childhood memories are happy ones. In his preflight interview for NASA.gov, he recalled: "I feel that I was privileged because I grew up in a beautiful city. . . . It's a place filled with sun, close to the beach. Every day going to school I would see the Italian sea in front of my eyes and I remember sunny days in the mild Italian weather, especially in the south." His family was incredibly close. As he explained in his preflight interview, "I grew up in a very loving family, typical Italian family with the expanded family. Every Sunday or every time there was any kind of celebration we would always be together. So with my brother and my cousins, we grew up together, sort of like brother and sisters, really."

The son of teachers, he grew up understanding that getting a good education was a necessary

component of leading a fulfilling life. As a high school student, Parmitano earned a scholarship to study for a year abroad in California. Upon returning to Italy, he completed his high school degree at the Liceo Scientifico Statale Galileo Galilei in Catania in 1995. He then studied at the University of Naples Federico II, completing a bachelor's degree in political science in 1999. A year later, he graduated from the Italian Air Force Academy in Pozzuoli, Italy.

FIGHTER PILOT, TEST PILOT

Parmitano had long wanted to earn his pilot's wings, which he saw as a steppingstone to his ultimate goal: becoming an astronaut. From the age of three or four, he had dreamed of exploring outer space. He remarked in his preflight interview: "I was born in 1976 . . . [just before] the time that the very first shuttle flights were happening . . . those were highly televised, even in Europe, even in Italy. So I remember seeing the first astronauts floating around the space shuttle doing their job, and I think that even [as] a kid, small as I was, I just thought that must be the greatest job in the world to be able to do those things and call it a living."

In 2001, Luca trained with the United States Air Force (USAF) at the Euro-NATO Joint Jet Pilot Training Program at Sheppard Air Force Base in Texas. The following year, he completed further training with the US Air Force in Sembach, Germany. He continued to advance in the Italian Air Force, qualifying as an electronic warfare officer in Italy in 2003 and completing a tactical leadership program in Belgium in 2005. From 2001 to 2007, he flew AMX ground-attack aircraft out of Amendola Air Base in Italy, eventually earning all available aircraft qualifications. He has flown more than forty different types of aircraft and is qualified to fly more than twenty types of military airplanes and helicopters. As of May 2014, he has logged more than two thousand hours as a pilot.

He became a test pilot for the Italian Air Force in 2007, rising to the rank of major, and earned his master's degree in experimental flight test engineering at the Institut Supérieur de l'Aéronautique et de l'Espace in Toulouse, France, in 2009.

JOINING THE EUROPEAN SPACE AGENCY

That same year, he got the call he had long dreamed of receiving: he had been selected to join the European Space Agency's 2009 class of astronauts, along with Timothy Peake of Great Britain, fellow Italian Samantha Cristoforetti, Thomas Pesquet of France, Alexander Gerst of Germany, and Andreas Mogensen of Denmark. Parmitano joined the astronaut corps during a period of transition in manned space exploration. The US space program was in the process of retiring its fleet of space shuttles, which had been NASA's sole means of transporting American astronauts into space since 1981. (The US government hopes to have a replacement manned spacecraft, the Orion Multi-Purpose Crew Vehicle, ready for crewed flight by 2020.) The Chinese space program was underway with its Shenzhou spacecraft but remained separate from American and European efforts. After the US shuttles were retired in 2011, the only way to reach the ISS was via the Soyuz spacecraft, which have been the backbone of the Russian space program since 1967. Thanks to an agreement between NASA and the Italian Space Agency, Parmitano was fast-tracked to fly to the ISS in exchange for the Italians building containers to store the retired US shuttles.

In February 2011, Parmitano received his assignment as a flight engineer on Italy's first long-duration mission to the ISS. After additional training, he and two crewmates, Russian Fyodor Yurchikhin and American Karen L. Nyberg, were launched from Baikonur, Kazakhstan, to the station aboard a Soyuz spacecraft on May 28, 2013. The crew arrived at the station via a "quick-rendezvous," which allows a spacecraft to dock with the ISS after just six hours (or four orbits around Earth) instead of waiting in orbit for two days.

THE INTERNATIONAL SPACE STATION

Parmitano spent 166 days aboard the International Space Station, returning to Earth on November 11, 2013, after having participated in more than twenty experiments, two space walks, and the docking of four spacecraft. Parmitano has described astronauts as having to wear various hats during a mission to the space station. Once the spacecraft is docked, astronauts must remove their pilot hats and put on their scientist hats, in order to conduct various experiments. They must also be adept mechanics and plumbers in order to provide maintenance to the station's systems. Finally, they must serve as inventory managers, not only knowing exactly where various parts are stowed on the station but also which parts have recently arrived and which have been discarded via supply crafts.

During Parmitano's stay aboard the ISS, the crew oversaw between 130 and 150 active experiments. The experiments in which he participated included, among others, ongoing experiments into osteoporosis, a form of bone loss common among the elderly that also occurs in astronauts on long-duration flights due to periods of immobility and the effects of zero gravity; a study looking into how sarcomeres, the basic structural units of muscle cells, are affected by abnormal conditions, such as being weightless or bedridden; and the Italian Combustion Experiment (ICE) Green Air, which, as the name suggests, sought to reduce the amount of toxic chemicals in combustion fuels to produce more environmentally friendly fuels. Each of these

experiments, Parmitano has emphasized, has real-world applications and is not just important to continuing the advancement of spaceflight.

Although work aboard the ISS is intense, astronauts are required by mission protocols to take some downtime in order to avoid burnout. One of the ways Parmitano enjoyed his downtime aboard the station was by taking photographs of Earth inside the Cupola, a seven-window observatory module added to the ISS in February 2010. Peering at Earth through the Cupola's windows inspired Parmitano to take up photography, something he had not previously done. Describing his photography, he told Meredith Rizzo for NPR (5 Nov. 2013): "I wish that through these pictures people could realize our planet is unique in its beauty and fragility, that it is our only home, and it is for us to keep healthy, preserve, and share—not only with other humans, but with all the innumerable species that inhabit it."

THE HELMET INCIDENT

On July 16, 2013, Parmitano faced his greatest challenge as an astronaut during a space walk outside the ISS. He had already successfully completed his first space walk on July 9 with fellow astronaut Chris Cassidy. During that space walk, the duo installed power cables, conducted routine maintenance, and collected material research samples as part of the effort to prepare the station for the installation of a new Russian multipurpose module. Ninety minutes into his second space walk, however, (also conduced with Cassidy), Parmitano ran into trouble: more than 230 miles above Earth, he found that his head was wet. Water was leaking into his helmet. At first the water was covering the front of his visor. Before long, it was cutting off his audio contact with his fellow astronauts. When he shifted positions in order to get into a position to allow his safety cable to rewind and bring him closer to the airlock, water began to cover his nose. "By now, the upper part of the helmet is full of water and I can't even be sure that the next time I breathe I will fill my lungs with air and not liquid," as he described the incident in his blog post "EVA 23: Exploring the Frontier" on the European Space Agency website ESA.int (20 Aug. 2013): "To make matters worse, I realize that I can't even understand which direction I should head in to get back to the airlock. I can't see more than a few centimeters in front of me, not even enough to make out the handles we use to move around the Station."

Since space-walking is physically very taxing, astronauts need to stay hydrated via little drink bags inside their suits. They also need to stay cool, and to do that, space suits have built-in radiators that circulate water around an astronaut's body while he or she is conducting a space walk. The problem, however, arises when water is exposed to weightless conditions. Geoff Brumfiel explained the odd properties of water in outer space on the National Public Radio program *All Things Considered* (17 July 2013): "Surface tension causes [water] to sort of glom together like mercury does. . . . Little beads of mercury will tend to clump up. And so what potentially could have happened is he would have this big floating blob of water in his helmet that he couldn't clear away. . . . He could've choked or drowned. So it was potentially, actually, a pretty dangerous situation."

Although Parmitano was quickly brought inside the ISS with Cassidy's help and suffered no lasting ill effects, people at NASA were concerned about the potential dangers of a leaking spacesuit. Ultimately the leak was traced to contamination that had clogged a filter in the suit, but it remains unknown as to what caused the contamination. Taking no chances, NASA engineers devised a low-tech snorkel system made of tubes that will extend from the helmet to the suit's chest area so astronauts can get fresh air in case the helmet does fill with water. Additionally, they have added absorbent pads in the backs of the station's spacesuit helmets, which astronauts can periodically check by tilting their heads back to see if they have become saturated. The spacesuit Parmitano used during his ill-fated space walk has been repaired and remains in operation aboard the space station.

PERSONAL LIFE

Luca Parmitano and his wife, Kathy Dillow, have two daughters, Maia and Sarah. Parmitano met Dillow when he was just sixteen, while studying as an exchange student with the American Field Service at a high school in Mission Viejo, California. When he returned to Italy to complete his high school degree after his yearlong fellowship, they maintained a long-distance relationship. He recalled in his preflight interview: "I like to say that we are probably the last generation of people that would write letters, which were not in electronic form. We still have our packages of letters that we sent to each other." In his spare time, Parmitano enjoys reading, music, scuba diving, snowboarding, swimming, skydiving, and weight training. In 2007 he was awarded the Silver Medal for Aeronautical Valor by the president of Italy.

SUGGESTED READING

Amos, Jonathan. "Rookie Astronaut Luca Parmitano Gets His Chance." *BBC News*. BBC, 18 Feb. 2011. Web. 16 Sept. 2014.

Chang, Kenneth. "NASA Solves Helmet Leak with Makeshift Snorkels." *New York Times*. New York Times, 20 Dec. 2013. Web. 16 Sept. 2014.

"Helmet Scare Shuts Down Spacewalk." *NPR. org*. NPR, 17 July 2013. Web. 16 Sept. 2014.

"Luca Parmitano." *ESA.int*. European Space Agency, 27 May 2014. Web. 16 Sept. 2014.

Parmitano, Luca. "EVA 23: Exploring the Frontier." *ESA.int*. European Space Agency, 20 Aug. 2013. Web. 16 Sept. 2014.

Parmitano, Luca. "Preflight Interview: Luca Parmitano." *NASA*. NASA, 4 Apr. 2013. Web. 16 Sept. 2014.

Rizzo, Meredith. "The View from the Largest Window in Space." *NPR*. NPR, 5 Nov. 2013. Web. 16 Sept. 2014.

—*Christopher Mari*

Rajshree Pathy

Born: April 15, 1956
Occupation: Entrepreneur

Indian entrepreneur Rajshree Pathy is the chairperson and managing director of Rajshree Sugars and Chemicals Ltd., a conglomerate located in Coimbatore, India. She founded her first company at the age of eighteen and took over Rajshree Sugars and Chemicals after the sudden death of her father in 1990. Though originally trained in the textile trade, Pathy quickly learned the sugar business and made the company profitable within a year. She served as the president of the South India Sugar Mills Association from 1995 to 1997 and from 2007 to 2009. She also served as the first female president of the Indian Sugar Mills Association (ISMA) in 2004–2005. Pathy is a former chair of the Confederation of Indian Industry (CII) committee on textiles and was named a Global Leader for Tomorrow at the

India Today Group/Getty Images

World Economic Forum in 1996. In 2013, Pathy received the Padma Shri, a national civilian honor, for her work in trade and industry.

Pathy is no ordinary entrepreneur. A pleasure seeker who loves design and travel, she began collecting art when she was seventeen years old. In 2012 Pathy and her daughter, Aishwarya, founded the India Design Forum (IDF), an annual design conference. They have also worked to establish the Coimbatore Centre for Contemporary Arts (CoCCA) in an old textile mill. CoCCA, which was set to be completed in phases over the course of several years, will serve as both a museum and an arts education facility. To some observers, the realms of business and art might seem at odds, but Pathy believes otherwise. "For me, business is creative and the sugar business is perfect," she told Aparna Piramal Raje for the *Financial Times* (10 May 2013). "Because from one cane of sugar, you get power, you produce organic fertilizer, you produce sugar, and you produce alcohol. For me, that is very creative."

EARLY LIFE AND CAREER

Rajshree Pathy was born on April 15, 1956, in Coimbatore, a city in the southern Indian state of Tamil Nadu. Her father, G. Varadaraj, was a famous Indian industrialist and parliamentarian and an active participant in his family's charitable trust, PSG & Sons. In addition to building educational and medical facilities across Coimbatore, Varadaraj ran two textile businesses, Ganga Textiles and Rajshree Spinning Mills. Pathy's mother was an artistic woman who decorated the family's home in the modernist Bauhaus style and inspired Pathy's early love of art and design. As the children of a prominent business leader, Pathy and her younger sister, Jaishree, were granted access to an unusual world. "A lot of interesting people—politicians, business personalities and foreign diplomats—frequented our house," Pathy told Nischinta Amarnath and Debashish Ghosh for the book *The Voyage to Excellence: The Ascent of 21 Women Leaders of India Inc* (2005). An active and curious child, Pathy played tennis and studied music and dance.

Pathy wanted desperately to study architecture at the University of Mumbai's prestigious Sir Jamsetjee Jeejebhoy School of Art, but her parents insisted she remain in Coimbatore and marry. Pathy obliged, studying commerce at Avinashilingam University in Coimbatore and marrying S. Pathy, the son of an industrialist, after her second year. At eighteen the newlywed Pathy founded her first company, Aloha Tours and Travels. Her company enabled her to travel the world without financial help from her parents, a particular success in the restless Pathy's eyes. Over the following years she also completed her degree and gave birth to two children, a daughter named Aishwarya and a son named Aditya.

RAJSHREE SUGARS AND CHEMICALS

In the mid-1980s Pathy began working at her father's textile mill after studying textile technology and cotton testing. "Dad needed help," Pathy recalled to Shonali Advani for India's *Entrepreneur* magazine (20 July 2013). "I had cousins running the business and I found that things were out of control." In the 1980s, Tamil Nadu chief minister M. G. Ramachandran asked Varadaraj to build a sugar factory in Theni, a district populated largely by poor farmers. Pathy began helping her father with his new enterprise—Rajshree Sugars and Chemicals (RSCL). Varadaraj died unexpectedly in 1990, leaving Pathy devastated. "My personal growth happened because I was determined to be the son my father never had," Pathy told Priya Kanungo for the magazine *Power Women* (9 Jan. 2011). "People used to write off the future of my father's business because he didn't have a son." Despite her grief, Pathy was "determined to carry the family name forward," she said.

As the new head of RSCL, Pathy faced countless challenges. The company's investors were wary of her because she was a woman, as were the sugarcane farmers. She was a new mother as well as new to the sugar business, having worked for years in textiles. Money was running low, and Pathy had to "run from bank to bank," she told Kanungo, to secure funds. To make matters worse, the sugarcane crop that season was poor. It was a difficult year, but Pathy managed to turn the company around in that time. Indeed, she had no other choice; Narayanan Vaghul, the head of one of India's largest banks, gave her exactly twelve months to prove herself as chair of RSCL. Pathy attributes much of her success to building relationships with the sugarcane farmers and factory workers who formed the company's backbone. "I would spend hours with sugarcane farmers, who were apprehensive about putting their future in my hands," she told Kanungo. "I would sit late into the night with workers in the factory trying to understand the way things worked."

AN INDUSTRY LEADER

In 1994, Pathy enrolled in Harvard University's Owner-President Management program, in which students learn business strategies and connect with other executives. Pathy learned valuable lessons from her classmates, including the importance of taking risks. "Only in India people think failure is something to be ashamed of," she told Advani. "Anywhere else in the world if you say you haven't tried and failed with businesses, no one takes you seriously." In 1999, Pathy took a course on strategic alliances and corporate ethics at the Fontainebleau, France, branch of INSEAD, an international business school, and the following year, she was awarded an Eisenhower Fellowship.

When Pathy took over as chair and managing director of RSCL, critics argued that she would be unable to learn the ins and outs of the politically driven sugar industry. By 2014, however, she was one of the industry's most powerful players. RSCL has interests in distilleries, bioproducts and bagasse-generated power, and pesticides. The publicly held company has three sugarcane-based integrated biorefineries in Tamil Nadu and one, acquired in 2006, in Andhra Pradesh. Pathy is a vocal figure in the movement to relax government regulation of the sugar industry, a movement that has achieved some success and bolstered Pathy's plans for RSCL. She hopes to invest in the sugar industry, diversify RSCL's brand, and continue to expand the company's reach to other industries, including the green energy sector, through its cogeneration division. Pathy's strategy focuses heavily on her company's workers. "I invest in technical people and cane people," Pathy explained to Advani. "Without cane you cannot do anything; without the best machines and technology you cannot be efficient."

COCCA AND THE INDIA DESIGN FORUM

An avid art collector, Pathy bought her first piece, a painting by Indian artist M. F. Husain, for 18,000 rupees (about 300 US dollars) when she was seventeen. It took her two years to pay off the loan she took out to purchase it. For Pathy, art became an instinctual mode of communication—even if she was only supporting the work and not making it herself. When her daughter turned twelve, Pathy began buying artwork each year for Aishwarya's birthday. "Art isn't something I have to keep under lock and key," she told Deepika Khatri for *India Today* (10 Jan. 2008). "It's rewarding intellectually, emotionally, and financially." Pathy and her daughter, who is an artist, later founded an arts initiative called Contemplate. "My greatest regret is that I am not a performing artiste," Pathy told Rana Siddiqui Zaman for the *Hindu* (30 July 2011). "So I promote performing arts through Contemplate and feel good."

Through Contemplate, the two women founded an art institute in Coimbatore called the Coimbatore Centre for Contemporary Arts (CoCCA) as well as a partnered art museum that will feature many pieces from Pathy's personal collection. Pathy hopes that CoCCA, which was planned to be built in stages, will eventually offer advanced programs in art, design, and architecture in addition to hosting exhibitions and workshops for Coimbatore residents. Through Contemplate and CoCCA, Pathy and her daughter brought another ambitious idea to fruition in 2012: the India Design Forum (IDF).

The first annual IDF took place in New Delhi in February and March 2012; the second IDF was held in Mumbai in March 2013. The first event of its kind in India, the IDF consists of two parts: Design Week, which was open and free to the public, and Design Forum, a two-day private event featuring talks by noted figures in design, such as French shoe designer Christian Louboutin. Although products such as Louboutin's shoes, instantly recognizable by their signature bright red soles, are luxury items available only to the elite, Pathy is working to dispel the notion that art and design are only for the upper classes. "Design is not elitist," she told Dibeyendu Ganguly for the *Economic Times* (15 Mar. 2013). "It's an intervention meant to add value, provide solutions, and make life easier for the consumer." She hopes that the IDF will change minds in India. Meanwhile, Pathy is developing outreach programs to bring the residents of Coimbatore to CoCCA.

PERSONAL LIFE

Pathy separated from her husband in the early 1990s. She loves to travel, is a certified deep-sea scuba diver, and drives a 1963 convertible. "If I enjoy wearing a business suit and being serious, [that] doesn't mean I can't let my hair down and dance all night," she told Raju Narisetti for the Indian business newspaper *Live Mint* (7 Sept. 2007). "It doesn't make Rajshree two different people. I don't think a damn what people think of me. I want to be remembered as a good person who did what she wanted to do in her own way. I don't want to be defined just by my company's balance sheet." In this endeavor, Pathy cites British entrepreneur Richard Branson, the founder of the Virgin Group, as her career inspiration.

Pathy divides her time between her apartment in bustling New Delhi and her house, located on a coconut plantation, in provincial Coimbatore. Continuing her family's philanthropic legacy, Pathy funds a free school for children in Tamil Nadu.

SUGGESTED READING

Advani, Shonali. "Rajshree Pathy Leans In on Breaking Through in One of the Most Male-Dominated Industrial Sectors." *Entrepreneur*. Network 18 Media and Investments, 20 July 2013. Web. 8 Apr. 2014.

Amarnath, Nischinta, and Debashish Ghosh. *The Voyage to Excellence: The Ascent of 21 Women Leaders of India Inc*. Delhi: Pustak Mahal, 2005. Print.

Ganguly, Dibeyendu. "Women Entrepreneurs Aren't Always Thinking about Profit: Rajshree Pathy." *Economic Times*. Bennett, 15 Mar. 2013. Web. 8 Apr. 2014.

Kanungo, Priya. "You Can't Be Limited by Other People's Limitations." *Power Women*. Planman Media, 9 Jan. 2011. Web. 8 Apr. 2014.

Khatri, Deepika. "An Acquired Taste." *India To-day*. India Today, 10 Jan. 2008. Web. 8 Apr. 2014.

Raje, Aparna Piramal. "At Home: Rajshree Pathy." *Financial Times*. Financial Times, 10 May 2013. Web. 8 Apr. 2014.

—*Molly Hagan*

Aaron Paul

Born: August 27, 1979
Occupation: Actor

When Aaron Paul took on the role of the meth-amphetamine-dealing Jesse Pinkman on the AMC hit series *Breaking Bad*, which began airing in January 2008, many observers described him as "an overnight success." In reality, his acting career had been more than a decade in the making. Paul's previous roles had been easy to miss, however, and included multiple commercials on network television; a couple of music videos; a handful of guest turns on such series as *ER*, *Guiding Light*, and *Veronica Mars*; and a minor role in the poorly received film *Van Wilder* (2002), in which he is credited as "Wasted Guy." His most high-profile role prior to *Breaking Bad* was on the HBO drama *Big Love*, in which he portrays a devoted young husband who helps his wife break free of her family of practicing polygamists.

Breaking Bad catapulted Paul to an unexpected level of fame, as millions of viewers tuned in each week to follow the adventures of Jesse and his murderous partner Walter White (played by Bryan Cranston), Jesse's former high school chemistry teacher turned drug kingpin. Much of the award-winning show's phenomenal success has been attributed to Paul's abilities to make Pinkman relatable and sympathetic even as he descends deeper into a life of crime. In an interview with Dave Itzkoff for the *New York Times* (21 Mar. 2010), Vince Gilligan, the creator of the series, described Jesse Pinkman as "the moral center of the show," despite the fact that he is a meth addict, manufacturer, and dealer, who at one point kills a man by shooting him point-blank in the face. Cranston admiringly said in an interview on the late-night talk show *Last Call with Carson Daly* (27 May 2010), "Aaron's capacity to convey someone who is daring and vulnerable, to bring likeability to an unsympathetic character, is astonishing."

CHILDHOOD AND EARLY INTEREST IN ACTING

Aaron Paul Sturtevant was born on August 27, 1979, in Emmett, Idaho. (He dropped his last name early in his acting career because casting directors had difficulty pronouncing it.) His

Wirelmage

mother, Darla, gave birth to him at home because she went into labor unexpectedly, a month early. His father, Robert, is a retired Baptist minister, and journalists have often commented on the irony of Paul's religious upbringing given his nuanced portrayal of a drug addict and criminal on *Breaking Bad*. Paul has credited his father with instilling in him a love of the dramatic. "Throughout my entire life growing up in Idaho, we would go to his congregation every week, and he would preach," Paul told Terry Gross for the NPR show *Fresh Air* (19 Sept. 2011). "It was inspiring, really. I mean he would get up in front of all these people and kind of just get lost in the moment as well. And I think that's where I take—not that I'm saying he was really standing up there acting—but he would just really get lost into these stories." Paul himself participated in several church programs and plays, even portraying the baby Jesus in a church Nativity play as an infant.

Paul is the youngest of five children, and he consistently describes his family as close-knit and supportive. Following that first Nativity play, Paul was often called upon to appear in theatrical productions at his father's church, including one performance called *Dinky the Donkey* in which he played the title character at the age of six, and he found that he enjoyed the exercise a great deal. When he was in eighth grade, he announced his intention to become a professional actor one day.

HIGH SCHOOL YEARS

Paul attended Centennial High School, in Boise, where he became a devoted member of the drama department and studied with a teacher named Nancy Link. "She was such a huge support system for me," Paul told Christine Fall for AMC's official *Breaking Bad* website (13 Apr. 2010). "I was the first freshman ever in our school to make it to the advanced theater group that they would only allow juniors and seniors to be a part of. When she found out I wanted to graduate early and move to LA—I talked to her about it all the time—she applauded me and said, 'Yeah go for it. You can do this.' And she never once said, 'What's your backup plan?'"

Paul worked hard to graduate a year early, at age seventeen, so that he could move to California and begin pursuing his ambition. To that end, he took extra classes early in the morning before school and also completed supplementary correspondence courses. He rarely attended parties or dated, so focused was he on his goal. He earned money for the trip by working as a costumed mascot for a local radio station, making promotional appearances as both a toucan and a frog. Although they naturally worried, his parents were consistently encouraging. "We're from a small town and are a very close-knit family, and it was really frightening when Aaron was going to Los Angeles, to the big bad world," Darla Sturtevant told Josh Gajewski for the *Los Angeles Times* (30 May 2009). "But we would have never been able to say no."

MOVING TO LOS ANGELES

Upon arriving in Los Angeles, Paul optimistically entered the International Modeling and Talent Association's twice-yearly competition in 1996, a "cattle call" that regularly attracts thousands of would-be performers. Paul prepared a monologue to use at his audition, but seeing the high caliber of the competition, he decided against using it and quickly set about preparing something else. His loud and histrionic rehearsal caused the guest in the next hotel room to call security, and Paul found himself explaining to the security guard that he was not mentally ill or suicidal. When he performed for the judges, he was named runner-up, and his efforts caught the attention of a manager who signed him and helped him find an agent.

To pay the rent on the tiny studio apartment he had settled upon with his mother's help, he took a job as a movie theater usher at Universal CityWalk. During his second week there, he saw director Steven Spielberg, who was attending a premiere, and although the two did not speak, Paul considered the sighting a sign that he was in the right milieu. At one point, he appeared on the popular game show *The Price Is Right*, hosted by Bob Barker. In clips that went viral on the Internet after Paul, by then famous, mentioned the incident on a late-night talk show, he can be seen whooping excitedly and jumping around. While he won a desk, he ultimately lost the big-ticket "Showcase Showdown," as the final contest on each episode of *The Price Is Right* is called, by overestimating the showcase's price by less than two hundred dollars.

A FLEDGLING CAREER

Soon, Paul began to land parts in commercials for products such as Vanilla Coke, Juicy Fruit gum, 1-800-COLLECT, and Corn Pops cereal. In 1999 he appeared in an episode of *Beverly Hills, 90210*, and was subsequently a guest on a steady stream of television shows, including *Melrose Place, Suddenly Susan, 3rd Rock from the Sun, The X-Files, Judging Amy, ER, Guiding Light*, and *NYPD Blue*. He also earned small parts in various films, including the sci-fi drama *K-Pax* (2001), starring Kevin Spacey and Jeff Bridges, and the campus comedy *Van Wilder* (2002), starring Ryan Reynolds as a hard-partying dropout.

In 2002, Paul was also featured in the music video for the song "Thoughtless," by Korn; in it he portrays a high school student who is mercilessly beaten and ridiculed by a group of jocks but who gets a gut-wrenching revenge at his prom. He starred in a second music video in 2004, this one for the single "White Trash Beautiful," by Everlast. He continued acting in minor roles on television, making appearances in *Veronica Mars, Joan of Arcardia*, and *Point Pleasant* in 2005 and *Bones* and *Ghost Whisperer* in 2006.

BIG LOVE

After portraying the brother-in-law of Ethan Hunt (Tom Cruise) in the 2006 action picture *Mission: Impossible III*, Paul got an even bigger break in 2007 when he was cast as Scott Quittman in the drama series *Big Love*, which aired on HBO for five seasons beginning in 2006. The show revolves around Bill Henrickson (played by Bill Paxton), a polygamist fundamentalist Mormon who has three wives and several children. Paul's character—who appears in fourteen episodes, including the 2011 series finale—is a straight-laced young man who courts Henrickson's oldest daughter (played by Amanda Seyfried) and eventually marries her, convincing her that the polygamist lifestyle undertaken by her parents is not the only choice open to her. While *Big Love* never enjoyed the critical or commercial success of other HBO dramas such as *The Sopranos* or *The Wire*, it garnered a solid fan following. (By way of comparison, the premiere of *Big Love* had an audience of 4.6 million people, while the episode of *The Sopranos* that aired that same week drew 9.5 million viewers.)

BREAKING BAD

While he was still appearing in *Big Love*, Paul received a pilot script for a proposed AMC series by Vince Gilligan, a television writer known for his work on *The X-Files*. "I was like, this is the best thing I have ever read," Paul recalled to Itzkoff, "and also there's no way that this show will ever see the light of day. It was so intense from the very first page."

The series—titled *Breaking Bad*—stars Bryan Cranston, best known up until then for playing the befuddled dad on the Fox sitcom *Malcolm in the Middle*. Somewhat ironically, Paul had unsuccessfully auditioned to play one of the sons on that show, which ran from 2000 to 2006. Cranston's character on *Breaking Bad*, Walter White, is a seemingly mild-mannered chemistry teacher who turns to cooking crystal meth after he discovers that he has terminal lung cancer. Initially determined to do so only until he has enough funds to leave his family comfortable, he instead devolves into a criminal mastermind—and in the process involves his protégé and partner, Jesse Pinkman (Paul), in a downward spiral of drug dealing and violence.

Gilligan had fully intended to kill Jesse off at the end of the show's first season, but Cranston and Paul worked so well together that he instead changed the story arc and deepened the relationship between the two characters. "It was all good on the page, but I think once they saw it brought to life by us, they just were like, 'Huh. That's interesting. We should roll with it,'" Paul explained in an interview with Daniel Riley for *GQ* (Aug. 2012). "They loved the whole butting-head element, the odd-couple tug-of-war relationship that we had, and they wanted to keep going."

A CULTURAL PHENOMENON

Despite the show's dark humor and its complicated morality, Paul remained committed to portraying his character's descent into the drug world honestly. "I love that I'm able to actually portray this role now, and I hope to God I'm doing it justice, because it needs to be genuine, it needs to be true," Paul told Gajewski. "This show absolutely does not glamorize crystal meth. It shows the dark, devastating side." Over the course of five seasons, from 2008 to 2013, *Breaking Bad* became a cultural phenomenon, with the series finale attracting more than 10.3 million viewers. That much-watched finale was bittersweet for Paul. "For the past six years I've been breathing through [Jesse's] skin," he explained to Rob Tannenbaum for *Rolling Stone* (16 Sept. 2013). "It was the roughest day of my career, my final day of shooting on *Breaking Bad*, knowing that I will never be able to kind of zip on that skin again."

Breaking Bad has earned numerous awards, including a Primetime Emmy Award for outstanding drama series in 2013 and a 2014 Golden Globe for best television series drama. Paul's performance on the series earned him four Emmy Award nominations for outstanding supporting actor in a drama series; he won twice, in 2010 and 2012. He also won two Saturn Awards, also in 2010 and 2012, for best supporting actor on television for his portrayal of Jesse Pinkman.

OTHER PROJECTS

While shooting *Breaking Bad*, Paul appeared in the well-received horror remake *The Last House on the Left* (2009) and in the independent feature *Smashed* (2012), in which he and actor Mary Elizabeth Winstead play a married couple struggling with alcoholism, whose relationship becomes strained when the wife announces her intention to get sober. *Smashed* won the Special Jury Prize at the Sundance Film Festival in 2012.

Paul's other projects include *Decoding Annie Parker* (2013), about the efforts to cure breast cancer; *A Long Way Down* (2014), an adaptation of a Nick Hornby novel; and *Need for Speed* (2014), a big-budget picture set in the world of high-stakes auto racing.

PERSONAL LIFE

As one of five siblings, Paul has more than a dozen nieces and nephews. When *Breaking Bad* was on the air, the entire Sturtevant clan reportedly gathered each Sunday night to watch the show.

Paul married Lauren Parsekian, an activist known for her work with the Kind Campaign, an anti-bullying program, on May 26, 2013, in Malibu, California. The two, both avid music fans, had met at the Coachella Valley Music and Arts Annual Festival in Indio, California. In 2013, Paul helped raise nearly two million dollars for the Kind Campaign, which Parsekian cofounded with her friend Molly Thompson in 2009, through a contest that offered the chance to meet the *Breaking Bad* cast and to attend a finale-viewing party in Los Angeles.

Paul, who has more than 1.5 million followers on Twitter, often tweets sweet, romantic messages to his wife on the site. By all reports he is friendly and attentive to his fans, coming out to greet them when he notices tour buses driving by his home in Los Angeles.

SUGGESTED READING

Gajewski, Josh. "Aaron Paul Catches a Couple of Breaks in *Big Love* and *Breaking Bad*." *Los Angeles Times*. Los Angeles Times, 30 May 2009. Web. 8 Jan. 2014.

Itzkoff, Dave. "Character and Career, Both Alive." *New York Times* 21 Mar. 2010: AR18. Print.

Myers, Andrew. "The Good Fella." *Manhattan*. Modern Luxury, 1 Oct. 2012. Web. 8 Jan. 2014.

Paul, Aaron. "Aaron Paul: *Breaking Bad* Dealer Isn't Dead . . . Yet." Interview by Terry Gross. *Fresh Air.* NPR, 19 Sept. 2011. Web. 8 Jan. 2014.

Paul, Aaron. "The Dirt on Aaron Paul." Interview by Daniel Riley. *GQ.* Condé Nast, Aug. 2012. Web. 8 Jan. 2014.

Paul, Aaron. "I Miss Jesse Pinkman Terribly." Interview by Rob Tannenbaum. *Rolling Stone.* Rolling Stone, 16 Sept. 2013. Web. 8 Jan. 2014.

SELECTED WORKS

Mission Impossible III, 2006; *Big Love*, 2007–11; *Breaking Bad*, 2008–13; *The Last House on the Left*, 2009; *Smashed*, 2012; *Decoding Annie Parker*, 2013

—*Mari Rich*

Francis Specker/CBS/Landov

Pauley Perrette

Born: March 27, 1969
Occupation: Actor

Pauley Perrette is an activist and actor who is best known for her role as Abby Sciuto, a smart and sweet lab assistant with a goth style, on the long-running CBS procedural *NCIS*. The show, which premiered to lackluster ratings in 2003, was named the most watched drama series in the world at the fifty-fourth Monte-Carlo Television Festival in 2014. The organization, which selects winners based on data culled from nearly three billion viewers, reported that *NCIS* garnered an impressive 57.6 million viewers worldwide in 2013. The success is in no small part thanks to Perrette, who, in 2010, topped the list of most likeable television stars according to her Q Score, a rating by which the familiarity and appeal of a certain show, brand, or celebrity is measured. Her Q Score puts her in the company of such well-loved Hollywood icons as Morgan Freeman and Tom Hanks.

For all of her celebrity, however, Perrette remains incredibly down-to-earth. She drives a beat-up station wagon, buys her red carpet attire at charity thrift stores, and quipped to reporter Jon Steely in an interview for the *Huffington Post* (11 Sept. 2013), "I don't have a publicist. I have dogs." Known for her black pigtails and Bettie Page–style bangs on *NCIS*, Perrette is a natural blonde from the South. (She even co-owns a Southern-style Manhattan bakery named Donna Bell's Bake Shop after her late mother.) But like her character, Perrette studied science—not acting. "Even without having any acting training whatsoever, I spent my time studying human behavior through psychology, sociology and

criminal science," she told Frazier Moore for the Associated Press (12 Dec. 2011). "I was a voracious student, and I ended up with the best background to be an actor ever, because I'd been studying human behavior in science for years and years."

EARLY LIFE AND EDUCATION

Laura Pauline "Pauley" Perrette was born on March 27, 1969, in New Orleans, Louisiana, but she was raised in various states across the South, including Alabama, North Carolina, Tennessee, and Georgia. Growing up, Perrette underwent a series of surgeries on her leg and eye, after which she was required to wear a body cast and an eye patch. Of her lifelong desire to help others, Perrette explained to Ken Knox for the *Advocate* (27 Oct. 2008), "I knew what it was like to be discriminated against and for people to be mean." Perrette's family was religious and did not allow her to watch many movies or television shows. She was an avid reader, however. Perrette has always had a wide range of interests, but she was focused on studying sociology and criminal psychology from an early age, prompted by a slew of child murders in Atlanta, Georgia, in the late 1970s and early 1980s. "I feel like life on planet Earth is incredibly hard," she explained to Moore. "There are things we just can't stop: floods and fires and earthquakes and tsunamis—crushing events for people to deal with. But I don't understand someone making the world more difficult on purpose, to harm people with no empathy whatsoever, saying, 'I'm going to make things even worse. Watch me!' That's the motivation for me wanting to be a crime fighter."

As a teenager, Perrette went by her first name, Laura, and worked at a car lot. She graduated from Crestwood High School in Dunwoody, Georgia, a suburb of Atlanta, where she was once named homecoming queen. Perrette studied sociology, psychology, and criminal science at Valdosta State University in Valdosta, Georgia. She graduated in 1990 and moved to New York City to work on a master's degree at the John Jay College of Criminal Justice. Perrette worked several jobs to support herself and pay for her education. She moonlighted as a bartender in the city's thriving club scene, wearing a bra, combat boots, and white Mohawk. She also recalls wearing a sandwich board and passing out fliers for the fast-food chain Taco Bell while on roller skates. "And I worked on one of these boats that go around Manhattan—way down in the galley, knee-deep in fish water, cooking food for the rich people upstairs," she recalled to Moore.

It was an exciting but rough time for a twenty-something in New York City. Drug use was rampant—"I've done everything. Everything! I can't believe I survived," Perrette told Moore. She was also witness to the HIV/AIDS epidemic that struck the city in the 1980s and early 1990s. During one of her first winters in New York, Perrette decided to visit the HIV ward at St. Vincent's hospital, where she passed out Christmas ornaments. "What struck me the most was that everyone in there was alone, and that really broke my heart," Perrette told Diane Anderson-Minshall for *HIV Plus* magazine (22 Oct. 2012).

EARLY CAREER

Desperate and broke, Perrette heard one of the customers at the bar where she worked say that she had made three thousand dollars after appearing in a commercial and became interested in pursuing an acting career herself. Soon after, another worker at the bar introduced her to a director who liked her unusual look. "I started booking commercials like craaazy," Perrette told Moore. She made her television debut in 1996 on the short-lived drama *Murder One* (1995–97), on which she had a recurring role.

For the next seven years, Perrette appeared in a number of television shows and movies. Highlights from her early career include two episodes on the hit comedy *Frasier* in 1996 and 1997, followed by a string of episodes on *The Drew Carey Show*, in which she played Carey's girlfriend Darcy in 1998. She also had recurring roles on the short-lived series *That's Life*, which aired for one season on ABC in 1998, and *Jesse*, which ran for two seasons on NBC between 1998 and 2000. In 2000, she landed a small part in the hit film *Almost Famous*. The same year, she joined the female punk rock band Lo-Ball as lead vocalist. Their song "Can't Get Me Down" appeared on the soundtrack for the 2001 film *Legally Blonde*. From 1999 to 2000, Perrette appeared on the short-lived *Party of Five* spin-off *Time of Your Life*, and in 2002, she appeared in

the horror movie *The Ring*. She landed her role as Abby Sciuto on *NCIS* in 2003.

NCIS

NCIS, or Naval Criminal Investigative Service, was originally intended as a spin-off to the successful CBS military legal drama *JAG* (1995–2005). The show was the brainchild of writer and producer Donald P. Bellisario. Bellisario, who had created *JAG*, was also the creator behind such successful prime-time shows as *Magnum, P. I.* (1980–88) and *Quantum Leap* (1989–93). Bellisario, however, fought CBS when they pressured him to make *NCIS* more like *JAG*. The network wanted to call the show *Navy NCIS*, to highlight its relationship to the military. Bellisario, on the other hand, chose the NCIS as his subject because of its tangential relationship to the military; criminal investigators in the Navy do not report to naval officers. "I fought that idea all the way," Bellisario told Bill Carter for the *New York Times* (25 Oct. 2005). "I did not want the show to be just a stopgap for CBS. I foresaw CBS saying this is good for now and always looking for something better." Bellisario was likewise against making the show too much like *CSI: Crime Scene Investigation*, the network's other megahit. He did not want *NCIS* to be a run-of-the-mill procedural. He wanted it to be funny, and he wanted the characters to be complex.

Bellisario was also determined to reel in young viewers—*JAG*'s viewership had skewed toward an older demographic—so he populated *NCIS*'s cast with young characters like Perrette's Abby Sciuto. The show's star is veteran actor Mark Harmon, but in practice the weight of the show is supported by its ensemble cast, including Perrette, Michael Weatherly, David McCallum, Sean Murray, Rocky Carroll, and Cote de Pablo. *NCIS* premiered in September 2003. Reviews of the early episodes were poor, as were the show's ratings, but *NCIS* started to build a following after reruns began airing on the USA Network. By October 2005, viewers were tuning in to the live show in droves, making *NCIS* one of the most watched shows on Tuesday nights. Its popularity skyrocketed from there, though Bellisario was fired from the show in 2007. *NCIS* was named the most popular drama in the United States for five consecutive years from 2009 to 2014. The show, which has far outpaced its popular predecessor, has even launched several spin-off series of its own. In 2009, CBS premiered *NCIS: Los Angeles*, and in 2013 the network announced plans for another location-based spin-off called *NCIS: New Orleans*, which is scheduled to premiere in September 2014.

In 2014, Perrette began her twelfth season on the show as the brainy, beautiful, and off-beat Sciuto. "It's hard to pull them apart," Perrette's longtime friend Kevin Lawson told Rodney Ho for the *Atlanta Journal-Constitution* (16 Apr.

2010) of Perrette and Sciuto's striking similarity. "I think she got the job as Abby because she walked in and they said, 'That's her!'" Sciuto is a forensic scientist with a sad and complicated past. She flaunts her tattoos and wears a dog collar, yet her personality is surprisingly sweet. As one fan described her appeal to Ho, saying Sciuto "is subversive with a smile." To say that Sciuto is a fan favorite would be an understatement. "People adore Abby," Perrette, who occasionally receives fan mail from aspiring female scientists, told Ho. "I love her. I think she's awesome. I want to be her."

ACTIVISM

The sociologist in Perrette is drawn to finding ways to help others. As of 2012, she was involved in more than thirty charity organizations dealing with issues such as civil rights, marriage equality, global disaster assistance, animal rights, and HIV research. She sits on the board of Project Angel Food, a Los Angeles–based organization that prepares and delivers meals to people with HIV/AIDS and other life-threatening illnesses. She has also been active in encouraging Christian organizations to support HIV research efforts. (Perrette, a devout Christian, attends the Hollywood United Methodist Church.) "A lot of bigotry [against gay and HIV-positive people] started at the church level, and we have a responsibility to combat that," she explained to Anderson-Minshall.

In 2013, Perrette screened *Citizen Lane*, a documentary that she had written, directed, and produced about the life of attorney and civil rights activist Mark Lane. Perrette spent eight years interviewing and filming Lane, who had been the only elected official to participate in the Freedom Rides to protest racial segregation in the South in the 1960s. Lane also wrote a best-selling critique of the Warren Commission (the report filed after President John F. Kennedy's assassination), titled *The Last Word: My Indictment of the CIA in the Murder of JFK* (1966).

PERSONAL LIFE

In her spare time, Perrette writes poetry and music. One of her songs, "Fear," is available on the official *NCIS* soundtrack. In 2011, Perrette and her longtime friend Darren Greenblatt opened Donna Bell's Bake Shop in the Hell's Kitchen neighborhood of New York City—the same neighborhood in which Perrette and Greenblatt had met nearly twenty years earlier. Greenblatt, whose family lived in New York, recalled visiting Perrette's mother and watching her cook. "She had a grace about her and a hospitality that I loved," he told Scott Huver for CNBC.com (10 Feb. 2012). Perrette grew up cooking with her mother, and, after Donna Bell died of breast cancer in 2002, she decided to use her mother's recipes to honor her. Perrette and Greenblatt

convinced another friend, food specialist Matthew Sandusky, to join them as a partner in the venture. Securing the midtown Manhattan real estate for the bakery was a tough hurdle for the trio, who insist that the bakery is not some kind of vanity project. The walls of the bakery feature Bell's handwritten recipes as well as a note that has become the shop's unofficial motto, Huver wrote. "You're gonna love this," it says. "It's a lot of trouble, but it's worth it." Perrette spends most of her time in Los Angeles, but is, by all accounts, a hands-on partner in the business, which has been a success with locals and tourists. She is considering opening a Donna Bell's Diner, though no official plans have been made.

Perrette married Francis "Coyote" Shivers, a musician, in 2000. They separated in 2004 and officially divorced in 2006 after a bitter legal battle. Following their separation, Perrette filed a restraining order against Shivers, which a judge granted based on Shivers's history of emotional abuse.

Explaining why she had stayed in the toxic relationship, Perrette told Steely, "My worth as a human being had been chiseled down by several people along the course of my life, in my childhood and my upbringing." Perrette was previously engaged to cameraman Michael Bosman, but the couple parted ways in 2008. In December 2011, Perrette announced her engagement to Thomas Arklie, a former British Royal Marine. In an article for *Us Weekly* (26 Jan. 2014), Perrette called Arklie "the kindest person I've ever known."

SUGGESTED READING

Anderson-Minshall, Diane. "Fearless and Selfless: NCIS's Pauley Perrette." *HIV Plus*. Here Media, 22 Oct. 2012. Web. 13 Aug. 2014.

Carter, Bill. "Behind a Quiet Little Hit, a Reliable Hit Maker." *New York Times*. New York Times, 25 Oct. 2005. Web. 13 Aug. 2014.

Ho, Rodney. "Interview with Former Atlantan and 'NCIS' Star Pauley Perrette, Coming to the Atlanta Film Festival Monday, April 19." *Atlanta Journal-Constitution*. Cox Media, 16 Apr. 2010. Web. 13 Aug. 2014.

Huver, Scott. "Pauley Perrette's Southern Bakery a Hit in Manhattan." *CNBC.com*. CNBC, 10 Feb. 2012. Web. 13 Aug. 2014.

Knox, Ken. "NCIS Star Pauley Perrette Takes on Prop 8." *Advocate*. Here Media, 27 Oct. 2008. Web. 13 Aug. 2014.

Moore, Frazier. "Pauley Perrette: Goth Go-To Gal on Drama 'NCIS.'" *Associated Press*. Assoc. Press, 12 Dec. 2011. Web. 13 Aug. 2014.

Perrette, Pauley. "Pauley Perrette: 25 Things You Don't Know About Me." *Us Weekly*. Us Weekly, 26 Jan. 2014. Web. 13 Aug. 2014.

—*Molly Hagan*

Anne-Sophie Pic

Born: July 12, 1969
Occupation: Chef and restaurateur

In the male-dominated world of fine dining, a female chef who achieves fame is relatively rare. The owner of her family restaurant, Maison Pic, Anne-Sophie Pic is one of those few women whose career as a chef has brought her recognition both within and beyond the culinary community. In 2003 she was named a chevalier, or knight, of France's Order of Arts and Letters, an honor granted to individuals who have made significant contributions to French culture. The following year she published the cookbook titled *Au nom du père* (In the name of the father), which received the Gourmand World Cookbook Award. In 2007 Pic became one of the few French women to earn three stars from the prestigious Michelin restaurant guide since the rating's introduction in 1931. The award, Michelin's highest rating, also marked the first time that three successive generations of a family have held the honor. As Pic told Julien Bissen for *France Today* (1 Mar. 2008), winning the third star "was fabulous." She added, "This is what I've worked so hard for all these years."

Throughout her career as a chef, Pic has faced many challenges, specifically gender-related criticism and the pressure of living up to her familial predecessors. She told Euan Ferguson for the *Observer* (24 Mar. 2007), "My main difficulty, the thing I had to find strength for, was to impose upon myself the idea that I didn't care what people said. I told myself I didn't care what they were saying, every day, behind my back." As the years have gone on and she has garnered increasing success and accolades, Pic has continued to push herself. "The most important thing is to stay creative, whatever it is you're cooking," she told Bissen.

EARLY LIFE AND EDUCATION

Pic, born July 12, 1969, is a member of the third generation to own the Pic family restaurant, Maison Pic, in Valence, France. She has described the restaurant's founder, her grandfather André, as outgoing and someone who never charged his many friends for their meals. Her father, Jacques, was shy in comparison but respectful of others. Speaking to James Graff for *Time* (14 Aug. 2007), Pic said, "My father had a cuisine of generosity, and I try to do the same, but by reducing things. . . . Where we used to use a ladle for our sauces, now we use a spoon." Growing up in a restaurant, Pic developed an excellent palate. The treats that children usually enjoyed were denied her in favor of more sophisticated sweets. Her father forbade her from purchasing processed foods. Instead, she had cookies and "Piccakes" made in the restaurant for her

Wirelmage

afternoon tea. She then went into the kitchen to learn how these delicacies and other menu items were made from scratch.

As a young woman, Pic was interested in the world of fashion design. At her mother's suggestion, she attended a business school, the Institut Supérieur de Gestion (ISG) in Paris, though her father wanted her to enroll in a restaurant school in Switzerland. Via an exchange program, she studied in the United States and Japan; during her three months in the latter nation, she gained an appreciation for Asian flavors. After completing internships at the luxury-goods companies Cartier and Moët & Chandon, her desire to cook grew. Pic told the trade magazine *Caterer and Hotelkeeper* (19 July 2007), "I took a step back, pictured the marketing career that was mapped out for me, and told myself, this isn't me. I want to do something concrete." She does not regret the five years away, however, and has referred to them as a necessary piece of her education.

A FAMILY TRADITION

Beginning in 1889, Sophie Pic headed L'Auberge du Pin, a highly regarded restaurant in France's Ardèche area. In 1934 her son André became the first in the family to be awarded three Michelin stars. Two years later he founded the restaurant and hotel Maison Pic in Valence on Route Nationale 7, the main highway from Paris to Côte d'Azur. The choice of location proved to be prescient; during the 1950s and 1960s, many Parisians took that route to the Mediterranean Sea. Like Route 66 in the United States, Route Nationale 7 became legendary. Maison Pic is in

France's Drôme region, an area noted for both its proximity to the sea and its fresh food. André's son, Jacques, initially desired the life of an automobile mechanic but was drawn to the kitchen. The restaurant had slipped to one star by the time he took over in 1951, but Jacques won his own three stars in 1973.

Pic returned to the kitchen of Maison Pic to work with her father after graduating in 1992. Her father died three months later from heart disease, creating a crisis for the restaurant. Only twenty-three and an apprentice at the time of her father's death, Pic worked with her older brother, Alain, to keep the restaurant going. She found it difficult to work with her brother and switched to the management end of the business after nine months. After disagreements, Alain left Pic to start the restaurant Les Mesanges-Alain Pic in Grenoble, located in southeastern France.

After Alain left in 1997, Pic returned to the kitchen to teach herself to be a chef. During this time Pic sensed the prejudice against female chefs. She credits her tenacity for her success, and she learned to remain calm during her period of training, when men in the kitchen did not take kindly to taking orders from or being critiqued by a woman, especially one they had known since she was a child. She told Emma-Kate Symons for the *Wall Street Journal* (30 July 2010), "When you are a self-taught woman and you start out in this milieu of cooking which is very masculine and even until a few years ago, was hardly open to women, you always feel guilty and are always trying to prove yourself." Despite the prejudice, Pic and her mother, Suzanne, kept the family restaurant in business. "Those were very difficult years, for the family and for the restaurant, which was unfairly attacked," Pic told Bissen. After Pic's father died, Maison Pic lost its third star. At that point, Pic made it her goal to recover the third star in her father's memory. The restaurant underwent a makeover, moving from a typical Provençal feel to a modern design.

OVERCOMING OBSTACLES

Women have traditionally been rare in the world of haute cuisine, and this rarity is evident within the Michelin restaurant guide, which since the early twentieth century has been widely regarded as the most prestigious of its kind. Originally distributed for free as a means of promoting Michelin tires to motorists, the guide began assigning stars to fine-dining restaurants in the 1920s and in 1931 introduced two- and three-star ratings. As of 2014, only twenty-six restaurants in France hold the coveted three stars, and Maison Pic is the only woman-helmed restaurant among them. In fact, Pic was the first French woman to receive three stars since 1951, when Marguerite Bise earned a third star for the restaurant L'Auberge du Père Bise. "For a long time women didn't try to make it as chefs. They were drawn to other careers," Pic told Bisson. "The profession itself became more technical and closed its doors to women cooks." She noted, however, that "it seems the French culinary world is evolving."

After earning a third Michelin star in 2007, Pic received an increasing number of applications from women hoping to apprentice with her. She finds that working with women softens the atmosphere in the kitchen, and, as she has hired more women at the restaurant, she has noted that men tend to be better behaved in their presence. Pic does not approve of what she calls "feminine cuisine"; however, she does think that women perhaps bring a different sensibility to cooking. "Every chef has a personal style, quite apart from gender. Maybe there are a few differences from men," she told Bisson, citing the different taste perceptions of female sommeliers, who are in charge of selecting and serving wine, as an example. With chef and restaurateur Hélène Darroze, Pic founded Nouvelles Mères Cuisinières (new mothers of cuisine), an organization for top female chefs. The name honors the mères cuisinières of the late nineteenth and early twentieth centuries, women who cooked in family restaurants.

Like many professionals who work long hours, Pic at times struggles to balance work and family life. Though she is often able to eat supper with her husband, David Sinapian, and son, Nathan, she returns to the restaurant for the evening rush, generally not getting home until long after her son is in bed. In an article about Pic and other female chefs for the London *Times* (15 Aug. 2008), Fiona Sims wrote, "Women chefs, like women in any other demanding and time-consuming profession, have to make loaded decisions when it comes to having a family. Restaurant hours are hardly child-friendly, and taking a year off to have a baby is deemed to be career suicide. The solution, say those who have managed to pull it off, is to focus on your career first, then have a family (or make sure you have a great sous chef)."

EXPANDING THE PIC BRAND

In addition to regaining Maison Pic's third Michelin star, Pic has focused on establishing a number of related businesses. Pic's husband developed the idea of Le 7, a bistro next to the main restaurant that offers good food at a fraction of the cost of a meal at Maison Pic. Named for Route Nationale 7, the bistro reflects car culture in its decor: the menu is printed on a folded map, and checks are delivered in baskets made of recycled tires. The bistro opened in 2006.

Pic opened Scook, a cooking school down the street from Maison Pic, in 2008. In addition to holding half-day to multiple-day training sessions for adults, Scook offers classes for children and young people. For ages six to ten, there is Scookid; Scookado targets those from eleven to sixteen. Scook also offers specialized classes, such as a pastry class and a course to train sommeliers.

In 2009 Pic opened a restaurant in the renovated Beau-Rivage Palace in Lausanne, Switzerland, placing chef Guillame Rainex in charge of the kitchen. Together, the two have earned two Michelin stars for the restaurant, one of several in the historic structure. Pic also opened a restaurant in Paris, Le Dame de Pic, in October 2012. She based the menu on three distinct fragrances: the sea, spices, and vanilla. A scented strip of each aroma, created in conjunction with noted perfumer Philippe Bousseton, arrives at the table with the fixed-price menus, allowing diners to choose their meal based on scent. Designer Bruno Borrione created the decor, which evokes that of a feminine boudoir. On the restaurant's website, Pic describes it as "an elegant place that encourages sharing, pleasure, and the enjoyment of food."

Pic has published several cookbooks, including *Au nom du père* (2004), for which she earned the Gourmand World Cookbook Award, and *Le livre blanc* (2013; The white book), a cookbook for professionals and passionate home cooks. The first half of the latter book is composed of photographs of lovely food, with references to the fifty recipes included. In homage to her father, Pic includes as her first recipe in the book his sea bass with caviar.

PERSONAL LIFE

Pic met her husband while in Japan; he is also a graduate of ISG. They married in 1993. Sinapian serves as the business manager for Maison Pic and president of Groupe Pic. He was also a key contributor to the redecoration of Maison Pic. Their son, Nathan, was born in 2005. Pic has said that she will not force Nathan into the family business, but she does take him to local farms to help her gather fresh produce.

SUGGESTED READING

Bisson, Julien. "Pic Season." *France Today*. France Media, 1 Mar. 2008. Web. 11 Mar. 2014.

Ferguson, Euan. "Michelin Women." *Observer*. Guardian News and Media, 24 Mar. 2007. Web. 11 Mar. 2014.

Graff, James. "Anne-Sophie Pic." *Time*. Aug. 2007: 34. Print.

Pic, Anne-Sophie. "How I Make It Work." Interview by Stephanie Theobald. *Sunday Times*. Times Newspapers, 24 July 2011. Web. 11 Mar. 2014.

Symons, Emma-Kate. "Maison Pic's Breath of Fresh Air." *Wall Street Journal*. Dow Jones, 30 July 2010. Web. 11 Mar. 2014.

—Judy Johnson

Julia Pierson

Born: 1959
Occupation: Law enforcement official

On March 27, 2013, Julia A. Pierson was sworn in as the twenty-third director of the US Secret Service, making her the first woman to head the agency since its formation in 1865. Prior to Pierson's swearing in, the Secret Service's reputation suffered greatly due to a 2012 incident in Cartagena, Colombia, where Secret Service agents had solicited prostitutes while preparing for a presidential state visit. "During the Colombia prostitution scandal, the Secret Service lost the trust of many Americans and failed to live up to the high expectations placed on it," Senator Charles E. Grassley of Iowa said in a statement, as quoted by Tabassum Zakaria and Steve Holland in an article for Reuters (26 Mar. 2013). "Ms. Pierson has a lot of work ahead of her to create a culture that respects the important job the agency is tasked with. I hope she succeeds in restoring lost credibility in the agency."

In announcing Pierson's appointment, President Barack Obama praised Pierson's strong leadership skills and thirty years of experience at the agency, stating, "Julia has had an exemplary career, and I know these experiences will guide her as she takes on this new challenge to lead the impressive men and women of this important agency." As the first woman to head the historically male-dominated agency, Pierson's appointment "[represented a milestone for law enforcement, putting a woman at the top of an agency with a storied past and a Hollywood-fueled image of Clint Eastwood–style men with sunglasses and earpieces stoically guarding the commander in chief at home and abroad," as

Getty Images

Peter Baker wrote in an article for the *New York Times* (26 Mar. 2013). "Mr. Obama has also installed women as directors of the Marshals Service and Drug Enforcement Administration, but the Secret Service has a unique visibility."

EARLY LIFE

Little information has been made public about Julia Pierson's earliest years. Most reputable sources agree that she was born in 1959, and some sources claim that her exact date of birth was July 21, 1959. She is a native of Orlando, Florida.

As a teenager, Pierson took part in the Exploring program, a lesser-known co-ed program affiliated with the Boy Scouts of America that enables young people (aged fourteen to twenty-one years) to discover which of their interests might lead to fulfilling employment later in life. As stated on the program's website, the program's mission is "to provide positive and meaningful real-world career experiences and leadership development opportunities for all teenagers and young adults in their chosen field of interest." The participants, who are known as "Explorers," can gain experience in such fields as agriculture, architecture, business management, teaching, government service, health science, hospitality and tourism, information technology, or law enforcement.

Pierson presciently chose to pursue law enforcement and joined an Explorers unit attached to the Orlando Police Department. Most of the law-enforcement posts in the Exploring program are managed by local police departments, while federal agencies such as the Drug Enforcement Administration, the Federal Bureau of Investigation, the Federal Air Marshal Service, the US Army Military Police, the Customs and Border Protection Service, the Postal Inspection Service, the Secret Service, and the Bureau of Tobacco, Firearms and Explosives offer support in the form of scholarships and workshops. In 1978, when she was about eighteen years old, Pierson served in a leadership position as the National Law Enforcement Exploring youth representative. "As I became more involved, first at a state and then a national level, I met some Secret Service agents," Pierson said in an interview with Siobhan Roth for *Smithsonian Magazine* (1 June 2007), explaining her experiences with the Exploring program. "It was through this exposure to special agents that I thought this might make an interesting career."

As a teen, Pierson also found work at Disney World. She began as a parking-lot attendant before being assigned to operate one of the theme park's watercraft rides and later toiled in the Florida heat as a costumed character in the twice-daily spectacle "America on Parade," which was mounted in celebration of the 1976 US bicentennial. "To this day, I think the experience of dealing with large crowds at the park had a good influence on my ability to do that sort of work with the Secret Service," she told Roth.

EDUCATION AND EARLY CAREER

Pierson attended the University of Central Florida (UCF), where she majored in criminal justice. She earned her bachelor's degree in 1981. (With its 1,415-acre main campus outside of downtown Orlando and its typical enrollment of nearly sixty thousand students, the University of Central Florida is among the largest universities in the nation.) In 2013, shortly after her appointment as the head of the Secret Service, the university honored her with the Michelle Akers Alumni Award, named for a fellow UCF graduate and renowned professional soccer player.

Pierson later completed graduate-level studies in public policy at the George Washington University in Washington, DC. She began her career in law enforcement with the Orlando Police Department, the same department with which she had been affiliated as an Explorer. By all accounts she had been well liked there, even as a teenager. One of the first female officers on the force to be placed on street patrol rather than in a less dangerous assignment such as the youth division, she patrolled the northeast section of the city, where she became known for verbally defusing tense situations in a calm and careful manner. "She got people to do what she wanted to do without violence," Mike McCoy, a former colleague, told Henry Curtis for the *Orlando Sentinel* (26 Mar. 2013). Remarking on Pierson's appointment to the directorship of the Secret Service, McCoy added, "They couldn't have made a better choice in terms of quality of the person. . . . She was certainly on the cutting edge of women in law enforcement."

After three years as an officer with the Orlando Police Department, Pierson decided to pursue her childhood interest in joining the Secret Service, and in 1983, she began her training to join the agency.

THE SECRET SERVICE

The United States Secret Service was founded in 1865, in the wake of the American Civil War. Originally a division of the US Department of the Treasury, the Secret Service was given the mission of suppressing counterfeit currency, as an estimated one-third of all US currency circulating at that time was thought to be counterfeit. Soon after its founding, however, the Secret Service was called upon to investigate criminal acts such as murder and illegal gambling because the US Marshals, which then comprised one of the only federal law-enforcement groups in existence, did not have the manpower needed to investigate all crimes that fell under federal jurisdiction.

Following the assassination of President William McKinley in 1901, Congress informally asked the Secret Service to provide presidential protection, and the following year the agency assumed full-time responsibility for protecting the president. In 1951 legislation was enacted that permanently authorized Secret Service protection of the president, his immediate family, the president-elect, and the vice president. Those protection duties have since expanded to include former presidents and their spouses, major presidential and vice presidential candidates and nominees, the widows of presidents until death or remarriage, the children of former presidents until they reach the age of sixteen, and visiting heads of a foreign state or government.

Because of the popular image of the Secret Service in movies and television shows—with black-suited agents running alongside the presidential motorcade or whispering into high-tech communications devices—many people do not realize that the scope of the agency still encompasses a wide variety of duties beyond presidential protection. "[The most common misconception is] that it's all protection work. People don't realize the investigative duties that we have," Pierson explained to Roth. "Besides counterfeiting, we investigate cyber crime and electronic access device fraud. We have joint jurisdiction with the FBI for bank fraud. We're responsible for providing communications support for the president and those at the White House. We also have an intelligence group, and maintain liaisons with the military and state and local law enforcement to keep pace with any potential threats."

At the outset of her training for the Secret Service, Pierson was among the approximately 50 percent of all Secret Service rookies who had previous law-enforcement experience. She embarked on an intensive twenty-seven-week course that began at the Federal Law Enforcement Training Center in Glynco, Georgia, where she and her fellow aspirants studied basic law, constitutional law, investigative techniques, and basic firearm tactics, among other topics. The trainees then moved on to the James J. Rowley Training Center in Beltsville, Maryland, where they focused on counterfeiting, cybercrime, and protection duties. When her training was complete, she was assigned to the Miami field office and placed on a credit card fraud investigative team. Somewhat ironically, her first paycheck from the Secret Service was stolen, because criminals had intercepted her new ATM card and password in the mail and emptied her bank account.

CLIMBING THE LADDER
Since joining the Secret Service as a special agent in 1983, Pierson has steadily advanced through the ranks. In 1985 she left the Miami field office for a post in the Orlando field office, and three years later, in 1988, she transferred to the Presidential Protective Division in Washington, DC, where she was assigned to the security detail of President George H. W. Bush. From 1992 through 1994, she served as the coordinator of the agency's drug program and, in 1996, she took on an upper-level administrative post in the Office of Protective Operations. After briefly returning to Florida, where she served as the assistant special agent in charge of the Tampa field office and helped establish a cutting-edge cybercrime task force, she was promoted to special agent in charge of the Office of Protective Operations in 2000. She was serving in that capacity during the terrorist attacks of September 11, 2001. She has described that day, when she was responsible for immediately accounting for every person under Secret Service protection, as the tensest and most dangerous of her career.

From 2001 to 2005 Pierson worked as the deputy assistant director of the Office of Administration and oversaw not only the agency's budget but all its administrative operations, including strategic planning, procurement, and property management. She then returned to the Office of Protective Operations, serving as the deputy assistant director and supervising the presidential and vice presidential protective details until 2006, when she was named assistant director of the Office of Human Resources and Training.

Given Pierson's wealth of administrative experience—including her successful oversight of a $250 million project to modernize the agency's communications and data-management networks—few were surprised when she was named chief of staff in the Office of the Director in 2008, where she worked directly under Director Mark J. Sullivan, whom she would later succeed. That year, she was also given the Presidential Meritorious Executive Award in recognition of her superior management skills.

DIRECTOR OF THE SECRET SERVICE
In late March 2013, President Barack Obama announced Pierson's appointment to the post of director of the agency, making her the first woman to head the Secret Service. (Just over 10 percent of the Secret Service's agents and uniformed officers are women.) The Secret Service—and Sullivan himself—had been under fire since April 2012, when several Secret Service agents had hired prostitutes in Cartagena, Colombia, where they had been preparing for Obama's upcoming trip for the sixth Summit of the Americas. (Their actions came to public attention when one of the agents was seen by a fellow hotel guest loudly arguing with his sexual partner about payment.) More than a dozen male agents were involved, and while Sullivan immediately implemented new rules restricting the use of alcohol in the hours before officers report

to duty and instituting a curfew on international trips, the policy changes did little to staunch the flow of bad press, with many journalists reporting that married Secret Service agents had long held an unofficial motto of "[airplane] wheels up, [wedding] rings off" while traveling.

Pierson's appointment was thus seen by many as a welcome antidote to the machismo of the Secret Service, and Obama himself asserted at her swearing in that she was "breaking the mold." Some, however, felt that she was not qualified to take charge of an agency that encompasses a $1.6 billion annual budget, approximately seven thousand personnel, and more than 150 domestic and international field offices. "She's not done her time in the trenches," one unidentified agent told David Nakamura and Scott Wilson for the *Washington Post* (26 Mar. 2013). "She's mostly been riding a desk." W. Ralph Basham, a former director of the Secret Service and Sullivan's predecessor, defended Pierson's appointment, stating, "Julie has proven herself to be a leader, as an assistant director and chief of staff. . . . I'd match her up against anyone in the organization."

Obama had interviewed other candidates, including David O'Connor, a recently retired assistant director of investigations for the agency who was heavily favored to win the job by the press. O'Connor's candidacy was scuttled, however, when he was tied to a lawsuit that charged agency officials with condoning racial discrimination. By the time Pierson was sworn in, however, there was little evidence at the White House that she had been anything but the front-runner. "We have the greatest confidence in the wonderful task that lies ahead and great confidence she's going to do a great job," Obama said at Pierson's swearing-in ceremony. "I could not be placing our lives in better hands than Julia's."

PERSONAL LIFE

Pierson rarely gives interviews and when she does they tend not to be of a personal nature. She explained to Roth that being in the Secret Service can make juggling work and family life very difficult. "Agents will spend 21 days out, come back for 21 and then go out again," she said. "These trips can be very exciting and interesting, but life continues to happen around them. If you have a sick family member or other family matter, it can be very awkward to manage. And on protective assignments, you and the other agents are living with each other, traveling with each other, eating lunch with each other, spending your lives with each other. It can be challenging."

Still, she has found her work exceptionally fulfilling and encourages young people to consider a similar career. "Whether you're an English major or studying a foreign language or getting a fitness or sports-type degree, there could be a niche for you here," she said to Roth. "You don't have to be 6-feet-4-inches, 300 pounds and built like a linebacker."

SUGGESTED READING

Nakamura, David, and Scott Wilson. "Obama Names Julia Pierson as Secret Service Director." *Washington Post*. Washington Post, 26 Mar. 2013. Web. 12 May 2014.

Terry, Allison. "Obama Appoints First Female Director of Secret Service. Why Julia Pierson?" *Christian Science Monitor*. Christian Science Monitor, 27 Mar. 2013. Web. 12 May 2014.

Zakaria, Tabassum, and Steve Holland. "Obama Appoints First Woman Secret Service Director." *Reuters*. Thomson Reuters, 26 Mar. 2013. Web. 12 May 2014.

—*Mari Rich*

Aubrey Plaza

Born: June 25, 1984
Occupation: Actor and comedian

Aubrey Plaza is an actor and comedian best known for her breakout role as the sullen and sarcastic April Ludgate in the Amy Poehler–helmed NBC comedy *Parks and Recreation*. Plaza played a slew of similarly disaffected characters until 2013, when Mark Byrne for *GQ* magazine (Aug. 2013) wrote that Plaza's starring role as the overachieving Brandy Klark in *The To Do List* was the first time "in which she finally plays a character who doesn't totally hate everything." In person, Plaza appears to be far from an April Ludgate type, though her unusual sense of humor occasionally falls flat. On a ho-hum Hollywood interview circuit rife with polished prima donnas, Plaza is refreshingly offbeat—though some might describe her in different terms. At the MTV Movie Awards in 2013, for example, Plaza famously walked onstage (a la Kanye West at the 2009 VMA Awards) while *Saturday Night Live* (SNL) alum Will Ferrell was accepting an award and tried to take it from him. The bit turned awkward, and Plaza sat down. "It's better to go out there and do something interesting than to just do what everybody expects," she later told Byrne. Spontaneously strange has always been Plaza's brand of comedy, which she exhibited as an outspoken kid growing up in Delaware and honed with the Upright Citizen's Brigade improv group before landing a role in Judd Apatow's *Funny People* (2009), Edgar Wright's *Scott Pilgrim vs. the World* (2010), and *Parks and Recreation* (2009–), all in one week of auditions at age twenty-four. "I went literally from doing nothing," Plaza told Mark Olsen for the *Los*

Getty Images

Angeles Times (3 Aug. 2009), to landing three career-making roles. "It's kind of a crazy story, how all this stuff happened to me."

EARLY LIFE AND EDUCATION

Aubrey Plaza was born on June 25, 1984, in Wilmington, Delaware. "I was a very big mistake," Plaza told Jada Yuan for *New York Magazine* (21 May 2012) of her birth. Plaza's Irish Catholic mother, Bernadette, was a twenty-year-old student at Westchester College when she gave birth, and her Puerto Rican father, David, was delivering pizzas. During her early years, she was passed among relatives as her parents, who were both working at convenient stores, found careers in finance and law. Bernadette Plaza became a lawyer with the firm Goldfein and Joseph, and David Plaza became senior vice president of wealth management at the Plaza Thompson Group. Plaza has two younger sisters, Natalie and Renee. As a young child she was shy around strangers but thrived performing skits for her family. "For as long as I can remember I wanted to be an actor and comedienne," she told John Micklos Jr. for the magazine *Delaware Today* (Mar. 2012). "I don't know why."

Growing up Plaza performed with the Wilmington Drama League. Her first role was in the Christmas musical *Here's Love*. After that she considered the theater her second home, and

director Kathy Buterbaugh became her mentor. She landed her first big part as a stepsister in *Cinderella* and later played a chicken in *The Ugly Duckling*. "She spent all of her free time at the theater—building, painting, helping in any way she could," Buterbaugh told Micklos. Plaza auditioned for a production outside of the drama league, but she did not get the part. Her mother was afraid that she would be crushed, but Plaza took it in stride. "It was then that I started to realize that if she could handle the rejection and loved doing it that much, then maybe things would work out," Bernadette Plaza told Micklos.

Plaza attended the Catholic all-girls Ursuline Academy for high school, where she demonstrated the bizarre sense of humor that would make her famous. According to Micklos, Plaza once climbed up in the scaffolding of the school gym wearing a cape and mask after she decided that the basketball team needed a mascot. Yet another time she encouraged all of her classmates to wear fake mustaches to class. But Plaza was no mere class clown; she was class president and student council president. She also worked at a video store and played volleyball and softball. (Plaza still plays softball—on the *Parks and Recreation* team.) She graduated from Ursuline in 2002.

COMEDIC BEGINNINGS

Like many future comedians, Plaza was obsessed with the sketch comedy show *SNL*. At fifteen she convinced her parents to sign her up for improv classes at ComedySportz Philadelphia. When she enrolled in New York University (NYU)'s Tisch School of the Arts to study filmmaking, she was determined to work for *SNL* and take classes at the city's legendary Upright Citizens Brigade Theatre (UCB). She did both. After sending her resume around to every department at *SNL*, Plaza landed an internship in the art department in 2005. She actually worked there while Amy Poehler was still on the show, though they never met. (She auditioned for the show in 2008 but failed to make the cut.)

Plaza worked other odd jobs and internships, including one at Post-it. She was a host at Joe's Crab Shack in Wilmington (until a fellow employee robbed her) and wore a sleazy uniform as a server at an expensive New York City bowling alley. She also worked as an NBC page, though, by her own admission, she was not a very good one. Her life could have been that of any other aspiring New York actor until July 2005, when she suffered a stroke. For several days she lost all movement on her right side as well as her ability to speak. Plaza briefly moved home and received speech therapy. She regained all of her faculties within a few weeks and does not experience any residual effects, though she did suffer anxiety attacks. In the fall her parents wanted her to remain in Delaware and rest, but the incident only made Plaza more determined to return to New York. "If anything," Plaza told Karina Longworth for the *Guardian* newspaper (14 Dec. 2012), the stroke "made me more aggressive about getting things that I want. Maybe subconsciously I was feeling it was . . . not a near-death experience, but it put things in perspective." She graduated from NYU in 2006, and the next year she guest-starred in the NBC comedy *30 Rock*.

Plaza made a name for herself during her four years at UCB. Countless comedic hopefuls take classes at the theater, but relatively few of those hopefuls become regular performers. In 2008 she performed an impression of stand-up comedian Sarah Silverman and uploaded the video on YouTube. As of July 2014 the video had over 1.1 million views. (Plaza has done some stand-up herself. She taped her first open-mic at a club in Queens as a part of her audition for *Funny People*.) She also shared the stage with Rob Riggle of *The Daily Show*; John Mulaney, who went on to become *SNL*'s head writer; and Aziz Ansari, a stand-up comic who would become her costar on *Parks and Recreation*. In 2007 an agent saw her on the web series *The Jeannie Tate Show*, a faux talk show hosted by a soccer mom, and contacted Plaza to meet for coffee. By her own account, Plaza pestered the agent until she sent her on some auditions.

TRIPLE THREAT

On her first professional trip to Los Angeles in spring 2008—"I was wearing jean shorts and wishing I could get out of there," she recalled to Yuan—she landed three major roles that would change the course of her career. The first audition, which was a call-back, was for the Judd Apatow comedy *Funny People*, starring Adam Sandler. In *Funny People*, Plaza plays a stand-up comedian loosely based on Janeane Garofalo. After Plaza won the part, however, Apatow incorporated more of her personality into the role. "Judd kind of made that character me," she told Olsen. "I was playing myself, not myself, but she's an up-and-coming stand-up just figuring out stand-up. And that's who I was at the exact time we were shooting it, because I dove into this world I didn't know," Plaza said of Apatow's insistence that she perform stand-up for packed crowds. (Ever game for anything, Plaza obliged.) Her character was even from Delaware. When she improvised a scene with costar Seth Rogen, Plaza told him she was from Delaware and was surprised when her home state got a laugh from Apatow, who kept the exchange—which also incorporates Delaware's most famous resident, Vice President Joe Biden—in the final cut.

The second role was in the comedy *Scott Pilgrim vs. the World*, an adaptation of the graphic novel of the same name, starring Michael Cera and directed by Edgar Wright of *Shaun of the Dead* (2004) fame. Plaza plays Scott's rude friend Julie Powers. It was a small and largely unremarkable role, but the third gig Plaza scored during that fateful week of auditions would make her career.

Greg Daniels, cocreator of the mockumentary sitcom *Parks and Recreation*, which starred Poehler, was auditioning women to play Poehler's intern assistant on the show. Poehler plays Leslie Knope, the deputy director of the Parks and Recreation Department in Pawnee, Indiana, and Daniels wanted what Plaza described to Yuan as a "dumb-blonde" type as her intern. "I was like, 'Your idea is stupid,'" Plaza recalled to Yuan. Why not make her smart and apathetic—against Knope's enthusiastic zeal—instead? Daniels ended up taking Plaza's advice, casting her as the supremely disaffected April Ludgate. *Parks and Recreation* was met with a lukewarm reception during its first two seasons, but in 2011 the show had finally found its legs. As the show progressed, the ambitious Knope became a councilwoman and the show's dopey view of local politics sharpened. "'Parks' is not an overtly ideological show," television critic Emily Nussbaum wrote for the *New Yorker* (22 Oct. 2012). "But buried within it are thoughtful, complex political themes that extend into the larger world in a way that's rare for modern network shows." *Parks and Recreation* since has become one of the most popular shows on network television.

A STAR ON THE SILVER SCREEN

In 2012 Plaza landed her first starring role in the film *Safety Not Guaranteed*. The indie comedy is a critique of the culture of irony—in it Plaza plays Darius, a cynical magazine intern who writes an article poking fun at a man who puts out a classified ad looking for a time-traveling companion. She ends up falling for him. In his tentatively positive review of the film for the *New York Times* (7 June 2012), Stephen Holden called the movie a potential "career catapult" for Plaza, whom he called "a compelling screen presence who suggests the next generation's Janeane Garofalo, but much softer edged."

Plaza landed her second starring role in *The To Do List* (2013). The film, which was written and directed by Maggie Carey, is a classic gross-out, coming-of-age tale a la *American Pie* (1999), but told from a female perspective. Plaza plays Brandy Klark, an overachieving high school valedictorian in Boise, Idaho. When Brandy develops a crush on a popular undergraduate played by Scott Porter, she realizes that she knows nothing about sex and, in characteristically methodical fashion, sets out to discover intercourse and every other sexual act she can. The type-A Klark devises a sexual checklist for herself and vows to complete it during the summer before she goes away to college. The movie is set in 1993 but, as Ryzik wrote for the *New York Times* (11 July 2013), "presented with a 21st-century feminist point of view." Carey, whose husband is *SNL* alum Bill Hader, developed the film around Plaza. "You see her in a room or onstage or on set, and she's not afraid of making someone else uncomfortable," Carey told Ryzik. "But the tension is comedic, and it works. It's a very specific Aubrey quality." Carey and Plaza met at UCB, and Plaza starred in Carey's 2007 web series, *The Jeannie Tate Show*, in which Plaza played Tate's bellicose teenage stepdaughter Tina Tate.

The To Do List also features Hader, Clark Gregg, Connie Britton, Donald Glover, and Andy Samberg. Neil Genzlinger, a film critic for the *New York Times* (25 July 2013), wrote that it was "smarter and better acted and just plain funnier than most of its predecessors in the my-first-time genre, no matter which sex is losing what." Plaza's next film, *About Alex* (2014), a dramedy about seven college friends who reunite after one of them suffers a nervous breakdown, has been billed as a version of the classic 1983 film *The Big Chill* for children of the nineties.

PERSONAL LIFE

Plaza lives in Los Angeles with her longtime boyfriend, screenwriter and director Jeff Baena, who, along with director David O. Russell, cowrote the film *I Heart Huckabees* in 2004. In 2014 Plaza and Baena collaborated on the zombie comedy *Life after Beth*, starring John C. Reilly and also directed by Baena.

SUGGESTED READING

Holden, Stephen. "Looking for Themselves in Fading Dreams from the Past and Present." Rev. of *Safety Not Guaranteed*, dir. Colin Treverrow. *New York Times*. New York Times, 7 June 2012. Web. 9 July 2014.

Longworth, Karina. "Aubrey Plaza: 'I'm a Poster Child for Irony.'" *Guardian*. Guardian News and Media, 14 Dec. 2012. Web. 9 July 2014.

Micklos, John, Jr. "Aubrey Plaza of NBC's *Parks and Recreation*: Wilmington Native Is Building a Buzz in Hollywood." *Delaware Today*. Today Media, Mar. 2012. Web. 9 July 2014.

Nussbaum, Emily. "I Love Leslie." *New Yorker*. Condé Nast, 22 Oct. 2012. Web. 9 July 2014.

Olsen, Mark. "Aubrey Plaza: Funny Person." *Los Angeles Times*. Los Angeles Times, 3 Aug. 2009. Web. 9 July 2014.

Ryzik, Melena. "Aubrey Plaza Is Dangerously Funny." *New York Times*. New York Times, 11 July 2013. Web. 9 July 2014.

Yuan, Jada. "Aubrey Plaza's Perfect Game: From Bowling-Alley Waitress to Romantic Lead in the Roll of an Eye." *New York*. New York Media, 21 May 2012. Web. 9 July 2014.

SELECTED WORKS

Parks and Recreation (2009–); *Funny People* (2009); *Safety Not Guaranteed* (2012); *The To Do List* (2013)

—*Molly Hagan*

Laura Poitras

Born: 1964

Occupation: Documentary filmmaker and producer

Laura Poitras is a Pulitzer Prize–winning documentary filmmaker and journalist. Her first feature film, *Flag Wars* (2003), about the gentrification of an African American neighborhood in Ohio, won a Peabody Award, and her second film, *My Country, My Country* (2006), about an Iraqi family living in US–occupied Baghdad, was nominated for an Academy Award in 2007. Poitras received a MacArthur "genius" grant in 2012 and the Courage Under Fire Award from the International Documentary Association in 2013. Despite her numerous accolades as a filmmaker, Poitras is perhaps best known as one of the two journalists that broke the National Security Agency (NSA) surveillance scandal that made Edward Snowden a household name in 2013. The story, which continues to unfold, began in 2010, when Poitras met journalist Glenn

Courtesy of the John D. & Catherine T. MacArthur Foundation

Greenwald. At the time, Poitras was making a film about government surveillance after having been placed on a government watch list because of her work in Iraq. Poitras and Greenwald, working with veteran journalist Ewen Macaskill, earned a Pulitzer Prize for the London *Guardian* and the *Washington Post* for their work on the Snowden story, and in 2014, Poitras and Greenwald jointly received a George Polk Award for national security reporting.

EDUCATION AND EARLY CAREER

Laura Poitras was born in Boston, Massachusetts, in 1964. After graduating from high school, she moved to San Francisco, where she worked as a chef at several upscale French restaurants over the course of about ten years. Eventually, she enrolled in a film class at the San Francisco Art Institute. Her first teacher was Ernie Gehr, a central figure in the structural film movement of the 1970s and a legend in avant-garde film. She shot her first footage on Super 8 film. "Using that camera was a way for me to interpret this new landscape for myself," Poitras told a reporter for the film website *Still in Motion* (19 Apr. 2008). "I picked up this camera and sort of fell in love with it." Poitras also studied with the late George Kuchar, another experimental filmmaker, who championed lo-fi, campy films. Eventually, Poitras quit her job as a chef and began working for a nonprofit media organization. She moved to New York City in 1992, where she pursued filmmaking and studied political theory in the graduate program at the New School in Manhattan.

FLAG WARS

While working as an assistant film editor, Poitras met an experimental filmmaker named Linda Goode Bryant. The two women wanted to make a feature-length documentary about Bryant's hometown in Columbus, Ohio, focusing on a traditionally low-income African American neighborhood that, in the late 1990s and early 2000s, had an influx of wealthy, white gay and lesbian residents. It was an interesting project for Poitras, a white lesbian then living with her girlfriend in the predominantly black Harlem neighborhood of New York. Through a few carefully drawn characters, *Flag Wars* examines the complicated intersection of race, class, and homophobia. It shows not only that well-to-do couples are not immune to homophobic crimes but also, as Poitras said on the film's website, as quoted by Gerald Peary for the weekly *Boston Phoenix* (23–29 Apr. 2004), that sexual orientation does not erase the privileges afforded by being white and rich. "I especially want *Flag Wars* to be seen by queer audiences and to raise debate around class and race in the queer community," Poitras wrote. The four-year process of filming was an exhilarating experience for

Poitras, who discovered one of the fundamental truths of documentary filmmaking while working on the film. "You go in with one idea and then you're confronted with something that's so much more complicated, so much more exquisite, so much more heart-breaking," she told *Still in Motion*. "You have to re-think everything."

They received about $400,000 in state grants, most of which came from the Independent Television Station (ITVS). *Flag Wars*, which does not feature any voice-over narration or "talking head" interviews, is a classic example of Poitras's cinema verité documentary style. She prefers viewers to experience the events in her films in real time without backstory. *Flag Wars* aired on PBS as a part of the network's Point-of-View documentary series in 2003, was nominated for an Emmy Award, and received a Peabody Award in 2004.

MY COUNTRY, MY COUNTRY

In a 2003 issue of *New Yorker* magazine, Poitras read a twenty-thousand-word article called "War after the War," by the award-winning author and journalist George Packer. Poitras was frustrated that the George W. Bush administration had used the outpouring of support and unity following the terrorist attacks on September 11, 2001, to bolster its case for a war in Iraq, and further, that any discussion of the war was filtered through American ideological viewpoints. She had no experience filming in a conflict zone, but Poitras felt compelled to travel to Iraq in 2004 and document the US occupation. "I anticipated that the film would focus on the U.S. presence in Iraq, particularly those who were conducting the elections and nation-building. But I quickly realized I couldn't tell a meaningful story from that perspective only," Poitras said in an interview with EPIC (Education for Peace in Iraq Center) in September 2006. "I needed to have an Iraqi perspective, otherwise I would replicate the ideological ping-pong game I had already witnessed, and I knew that wouldn't be helpful."

Poitras gained clearance to film members of Baghdad's City Council inspecting Abu Ghraib prison shortly after the release of damning photos depicting American soldiers abusing and humiliating prisoners. One council member, an English-speaking Sunni doctor and politician named Riyadh al-Adhadh (Dr. Riyadh in the film), was furious about the incarceration and began shouting that there was no reason for the prisoners, a few of whom were as young as nine years old, to be there. Poitras caught it all on camera. She befriended al-Adhadh, who invited her to his clinic in Adhamiyah and into his home. The footage she captured of his family's life in occupied Baghdad between June 2004 and February 2005 became the documentary *My Country, My Country*, which premiered in 2006.

Shuttling between al-Adhadh's house and the American Green Zone, Poitras had access to completely different worlds between which she was able to move with almost total freedom; the respect that Dr. Riyadh commanded within his community afforded her some protection as well. Poitras did not conduct interviews with her subjects, and even though she has talked about her own experiences in Iraq at length in interviews, she is totally absent from the film itself. "Without comment but with unusual sensitivity, Ms. Poitras, exposes the emotional toll of occupation on Iraqis and American soldiers alike," Jeannette Catsoulis wrote in her review of the film for the *New York Times* (4 Aug. 2006). *My Country, My Country* was nominated for an Academy Award for best documentary in 2007.

THE OATH

From 2007 to 2010, Poitras shot footage for a documentary called *The Oath*. She had set out to make a film about the homecoming of a prisoner from the Guantánamo Bay detention center. Instead, Poitras stumbled upon a very different story—one that focused on a man who had never been to Guantánamo at all. In Yemen, she met a Saudi-born cab driver—and former bodyguard of Osama bin Laden—named Nasser al-Bahri, better known by his nom de guerre, Abu Jandal. Jandal joined bin Laden in Afghanistan in 1996, and several years later, recruited his friend, a Yemeni man named Salim Hamdan. Hamdan was bin Laden's driver, and after September 11, he was captured by Afghan forces and handed over to the US government. He was sent to Guantánamo in 2002.

The story of *The Oath* revolves around Hamdan's incarceration and possible release, but as Mike Hale for the *New York Times* (6 May 2010) noted, the film is dominated by Jandal. "He's a natural, a bearish, handsome man with bottomless brown eyes who projects earnestness and (perhaps) remorse, the onetime terrorist as reformed bad boy," Hale wrote. "And his current life, as he presents it to Ms. Poitras, is the stuff of best sellers: a father struggling to support his young son by driving a cab in the chaotic streets of Yemen's capital, Sana; a former jihadi role model who renounces terrorist tactics and may die because of it; a free man racked by guilt over . . . [Hamdan's] imprisonment."

Except for one blurry scene, Hamdan never appears on camera. In 2008, Hamdan was the first detainee to be sentenced by a US military commission. His story is told in part by the two American military lawyers, Commander Brian Mizer and Lieutenant Commander Charles Swift, who fought to exonerate him. Hamdan was released from Guantánamo, after serving seven years, in 2009. *The Oath*, which was praised for its rich portrayal of a complicated man, was critically acclaimed in its festival run

and aired on PBS in 2010. The film was partially funded by a Guggenheim fellowship and was nominated for an Emmy Award in 2011.

GOVERNMENT SURVEILLANCE FILM

In November 2004, while Poitras was still living with Dr. Riyadh and his family, an American raid of a mosque in Adhamiyah killed several Iraqis. The next day, Poitras bore witness to the eruption of violence in the doctor's neighborhood. Her presence there—she watched the fighting with the family from al-Adhadh's roof—spawned allegations that she had known about an insurgent attack that killed an American soldier later that day. She denied the accusation, but it followed her from airport to airport as she hopscotched the globe to show *My Country, My Country*. According to Peter Maass for the *New York Times* (13 Aug. 2013), she had been placed on a terrorist watch list in 2006. Poitras told Maass that she was detained for extra searches and interrogation more than forty times while trying to enter or leave a country. "Because the interrogations took place at international [border] crossings, where the government contends that ordinary constitutional rights do not apply, she was not permitted to have a lawyer present," Maass wrote. She was even forbidden to take notes, and when she asked why, her interrogators told her that her pen could be used as a weapon. When she asked for a crayon, they refused. Sometimes, armed security agents would confiscate her cell phone or her laptop, or demand that she show them her working notes. "It's a total violation," Poitras told Maass. "That's how it feels. They are interested in information that pertains to the work I am doing that's clearly private and privileged. It's an intimidating situation when people with guns meet you when you get off an airplane."

Poitras began giving her notes to a traveling companion and clearing her phone and computers before traveling. She encrypted the data on her electronic devices, so that authorities could not see it, but even as she took such painstaking precautions to travel, it occurred to her that the government was likely already surveilling her e-mail, phone calls, and web activity. Her Kafkaesque journey inspired her film project, a film about government surveillance. The interviews she conducted for the film only added fuel to her fears, and her security measures became even more complex.

MEETING EDWARD SNOWDEN

Greenwald was intrigued by Poitras's story of detention and surveillance, and in April 2012, he published an article for *Salon* called "U.S. Filmmaker Repeatedly Detained at Border." After the article went live, Poitras's security troubles abruptly stopped. In August of the same year, Poitras filmed a short documentary for the *New*

York Times website called *The Program*. It featured a former NSA mathematician and code breaker turned whistle-blower named William Binney, who worked for the NSA for nearly thirty-two years, spending much of his tenure developing a foreign spying program during the Cold War. He contends that his program, which was designed to cull information from individuals through phone calls and other electronic activity, was used to create a nearly identical top-secret, US domestic spying program called Stellar Wind in September 2001. In her accompanying article for the *New York Times* (22 Aug. 2012), Poitras reported that the program was so controversial that several top Justice Department officials almost resigned in 2004. The video, and Binney's allegations, were damning, but it was only the tip of the iceberg for Poitras.

In January 2013, a stranger who had read Greenwald's article and seen *The Program*, contacted her and asked to send her an encrypted email. She agreed; she was working on a documentary about surveillance, so the request in and of itself was not unusual. But when she decrypted the message, Poitras was floored. The stranger offered her proof of a number of secret surveillance programs run by the US government to spy on its own citizens. "I thought, O.K., if this is true, my life just changed," Poitras told Maass. The stranger turned out to be a twenty-nine-year-old former CIA employee named Edward Snowden, and Poitras and Greenwald's subsequent meeting with him in Hong Kong in June 2013 would spawn a number of revelations, some that are still being brought forth. For example, in May 2014, Poitras and James Risen of the *New York Times* broke a story about sophisticated facial recognition programs, detailed in documents from 2011 provided by Snowden.

Snowden was a security guard at an NSA facility and then worked in IT security for the CIA, where he rose through the ranks quickly because of his talent for computer programming. By 2007, he was stationed in Geneva, Switzerland, with a high security clearance, and was growing disillusioned with the CIA. He left the organization in 2009 to work for the private defense contractor Booz Allen Hamilton, which was working with the NSA. Snowden was making more than $200,000 a year and living in Hawaii but, he told Greenwald, Poitras, and journalist Ewen MacAskill for the *Guardian* (9 June 2013), he felt compelled to act on the information that was at his disposal. "The government has granted itself power it is not entitled to," he said. "There is no public oversight. The result is people like myself have the latitude to go further than they are allowed to."

Snowden left his job, copying the last of his trove of NSA documents, in late May 2013. A few weeks later, he asked the journalists to meet him in Hong Kong, where he believed he would be safe to tell them his story. The now famous meeting—Snowden told them to look for a man carrying a Rubik's Cube—took place in early June. The interview in Snowden's hotel room lasted for several hours. To Maass, Poitras recalled the moment she took out her video camera. Greenwald and Snowden were nervous, but Poitras saw their consent as a bond of trust. "There is something really palpable and emotional in being trusted like that," she said.

The Hong Kong meeting was, until very recently, the last time Poitras saw Snowden. However, in May 2014, Greenwald's partner David Miranda posted a photograph of himself, Greenwald, Poitras, and Snowden on his Facebook page. No other information about the meeting has been made available.

Snowden gave Poitras and Greenwald thousands of highly classified NSA documents, but not all of those documents have been made available. Unlike WikiLeaks, which tends to release a huge volume of documents at once, Poitras and Greenwald have been combing through the NSA documents and releasing them piecemeal. A larger bulk of information is expected to appear in Poitras's untitled and unfinished documentary.

PERSONAL LIFE AND OTHER WORK

Poitras directed a short experimental film, comprising images shot in the days after September 11, 2001, in New York City, called *O'Say Can You See*. Poitras also served as an executive producer on the films *The Law in These Parts* (2011), *Evaporating Borders* (2014), and *1971* (2014). Poitras has taught film studies at Yale University and lived, for many years, in New York City. After the Snowden story broke, she relocated to Europe—specifically to Berlin, as was last reported in 2013—to edit her upcoming film.

SUGGESTED READING

Greenwald, Glenn, Ewen MacAskill, and Laura Poitras. "Edward Snowden: The Whistleblower Behind the NSA Surveillance Revelations." *Guardian*. Guardian News and Media, 9 June 2013. Web. 4 June 2014.

Hale, Mike. "Two Paths from Al Qaeda in the Post-9/11 World." *New York Times*. New York Times, 6 May 2010. Web. 4 June 2014.

Maass, Peter. "How Laura Poitras Helped Snowden Spill His Secrets." *New York Times*. New York Times, 13 Aug. 2013. Web. 29 May 2014.

Poitras, Laura. Interview. "Interview: Laura Poitras, Director *My Country, My Country*." *Still in Motion* 19 Apr. 2008. Web. 29 May 2014.

Poitras, Laura. Interview. "Laura Poitras: Exploring the Iraqi Perspective." *EPIC*. Education for Peace in Iraq Center, 1 Sept. 2006. Web. 29 May 2014.

Poitras, Laura. "The Program." *New York Times*. New York Times, 22 Aug. 2012. Web. 5 June 2014.

Risen, James, and Laura Poitras. "N.S.A. Collecting Millions of Faces from Web Images." *New York Times*. New York Times, 31 May 2014. Web. 5 June 2014.

SELECTED WORKS
Flag Wars, 2003; *My Country, My Country*, 2006; *The Oath*, 2010

—*Molly Hagan*

Yasiel Puig

Born: December 7, 1990
Occupation: Baseball player

Yasiel Puig is a Cuban-born outfielder for the Los Angeles Dodgers. The young athlete has been compared to the famous right fielder Sammy Sosa as well as football and baseball All-Star Bo Jackson, who was named the greatest athlete of all time by ESPN. Puig is an aggressive player with a divisive personality; following his major-league debut in June 2013, he led the last-place Dodgers to a precarious position as the number-one team in the National League West division at the start of the 2014 season.

But Puig's story began in a small town in Cuba, where he learned to play baseball on a makeshift baseball diamond behind a sugar factory. By the time he was a teenager, he was playing in Cuba's top national league, the Cuban National Series, or Serie Nacional, and earning seventeen dollars a month. Puig tried to flee Cuba at least five times, only to be detained by the Cuban authorities or the United States Coast Guard. Finally, in the spring of 2012, he left his home in the province of Cienfuegos, on the southern coast of Cuba, for the last time. After a harrowing escape from the island and a near hostage situation with his smugglers in Mexico, Puig officially defected in June 2012 and signed a seven-year, $42 million contract with the Dodgers. In 2013 he was the National League Rookie of the Year runner-up.

According to Cuban immigration laws, defectors are citizens who leave the country of their own free will. Defectors are officially banned from returning to Cuba for eight years, though many never return at all. For most Cuban migrants, defection is a one-way ticket. The United States has a number of convoluted policies that both make it easier for Cubans to defect and make it more difficult for them to do so. The 1995 US–Cuba Migration Accord, familiarly known as "wet foot, dry foot," says

Getty Images

that any Cuban who is caught traveling by sea between the island and the United States will be sent back to Cuba or sent to a third country. Those who make it to land—"dry foot"—are allowed to stay, and after one year, they are allowed to apply for an immigrant visa. Major League Baseball (MLB) further complicates the process of defection by requiring prospective Cuban players to establish residence in Mexico, or any other third country, if they want to avoid the amateur draft. "In doing so, they become free agents—able to sell their talents to the highest bidder—and can land better-paying contracts," Linda Robertson, Jay Weaver, and David Ovalle reported for the *Miami Herald* (20 Apr. 2014). Many blame the MLB's policy for the uptick in the kind of smuggling exemplified in Puig's story. The league is so ravenous for Cuban talent that when it comes to the trafficking of athletes, former federal prosecutor Ben Daniel told the *Herald*, baseball teams "are looking the other way."

EARLY LIFE IN CUBA
Puig was born on December 7, 1990, in the tiny sugar mill town of Elpidio Gómez in Cienfuegos, Cuba. Both of his parents worked in sugarcane. His mother, Maritza Valdes Gonzalez, headed one of the town's subsidiaries, and his father worked as an agronomist. He grew up in an apartment building on the edge of the factory's grounds, a stone's throw from a makeshift baseball diamond installed by the state. Journalist Jesse Katz broke the story of Puig's harrowing

escape from Cuba for *Los Angeles Magazine* on April 13, 2014. For his article, Katz traveled back to Puig's hometown, where he described the grounds on which Puig cut his teeth as a player. The outfield was "a scorched patch of earth, the grass reduced to straw," he wrote. The bleachers were crumbling, and the bases were merely "frayed swatches of burlap, salvaged from old flour bags." Due to the US embargo, the town, like much of Cuba, unpleasantly recalls a bygone era; vendors travel in horse-drawn carts, and a pint of pressed sugarcane juice costs about eight cents in local pesos.

Early on, Puig was asked to play baseball at a nicer ballpark in nearby Palmira. Sports are an important morale booster for the Cuban regime, and the government grooms its young athletes into champions of and for the state. A mural, Katz noted, in the Palmira park says, "Sports has to do with the life of the country, with the future of the country, with the survival of the country!" Like many Cuban athletes—including Puig's younger sister, Yaima, who threw the shot put and javelin—Puig attended one of Cuba's Schools for Sports Initiation, or EIDEs, followed by one of the country's High Schools of Athletic Perfection, or ESPAs. He made the junior national team when he was seventeen years old.

ELEFANTES DE CIENFUEGOS
Baseball has a long tradition in Communist Cuba, one that is rooted in the country's close relationship with Major League Baseball before the 1959 revolution. Katz wrote that the country "was practically an extension of MLB's farm leagues." But Fidel Castro viewed professional baseball as an industry akin to slavery. In its place, he instated a sixteen-team amateur league called the National Series, or Serie Nacional, in 1962. Players are required to play for their home province, so Puig began his career with the Elefantes de Cienfuegos. The eighteen-year-old Puig quickly developed a reputation as an unreliable player, a rabble-rouser, and a flirt. Several old schoolmates and friends described him to Katz as "crazy." Michel Hernandez, a former bartender who hung out with Puig on the boardwalk after games said, "He was just such a *jodedor* [a screw-around] not in a bad sense but like a joker. Beer and girls, beer and girls, always a party!"

Katz suggested that Puig's carefree sense of time kept him on the bench for most of his second season with the Elefantes, but Puig was a breakout star during his third season. His stats earned him a spot on the national team at the World Port Tournament in the Netherlands. Reports are split on the cause of Puig's troubles after the games. Some say that he attempted to defect and was rebuked—at the same games, Gerardo Concepción, a left-handed pitcher, defected in Rotterdam and signed a $6 million contract with the Chicago Cubs—but Peter

Bjarkman, the coauthor of *Smoke: The Romance and Lore of Cuban Baseball* (1999), told Katz that he believes that Puig shoplifted a pair of tennis shoes from a Dutch mall. Cuban players, Bjarkman said, "buy what they can," though they "have different amounts of money. They're allowed to bring cigars to sell. Some try to sell their uniforms. But some guys don't have much of anything." Whatever the case, Puig's name did not initially appear on the 2011–12 roster. In March 2012 Cuba's National Baseball Commission said only that Puig was a "bad example" to other players. After some maneuvering, he was reinstated as a reserve and cleared to play twenty-five games.

FAILED ATTEMPTS TO ESCAPE
In Cuba, the temptation to defect is strong, particularly considering that players are routinely approached with offers to facilitate their defection. In 2010—during Puig's uneventful second season with the Elefantes—he claims that he was approached by a couple who lured him into a waiting car where a foreigner offered him a large sum of money if he would agree to defect to the United States. Puig informed the Cuban authorities. An alleged intermediary in the scheme, Miguel Angel Corbacho Daudinot, was sentenced to seven years in prison and later sued Puig and his mother for $12 million. According to Katz, Puig's claim is questionable: Corbacho Daudinot's lawsuit reveals that Puig conspired to send at least three others to prison on similar charges and suggests that Puig wanted to appear trustworthy in the eyes of the Cuban government as he planned his own escape. Katz wrote that it was possible to characterize Puig's dilemma this way: "If you are being hounded with offers to flee, how do you know whom to trust and when to do it—without landing in jail yourself?"

Despite Puig's reputation as a snitch, the Cuban boxer Yunior Despaigne approached him with an offer from a Miami businessman and petty thief named Raul Pacheco. Katz reported that in 2009, twenty defectors signed MLB contracts, totaling over $300 million; Pacheco was well aware of the financial opportunities Puig would bring in the United States, and he wanted to cash in. Through Despaigne, he offered to pay for Puig's trip. According to Katz, it costs an average Cuban citizen about $10,000 to flee the country. When Puig arrived in Mexico, he would be required to pay Pacheco back in full and provide him with 20 percent of any future MLB contract.

Pacheco advanced Puig nearly $30,000 before Puig was able to defect successfully. Puig and Despaigne first tried to escape in 2011 but were thwarted when the Cuban police stopped their car. Two subsequent attempts were blocked as well. Then, in April 2012, they boarded a boat and made it out to sea, only to be stopped by the US Coast Guard near Haiti. Jeff Passan for *Yahoo Sports* (2 July 2013) first reported the story in 2013. Those aboard the Coast Guard cutter *Vigilant* were cruising the Windward Passage between Cuba and Haiti. When they first spotted Puig's boat, they thought it was smuggling drugs. The crew stopped the boat and, in accordance with standard protocol, welcomed Puig and his codefectors onboard to await instruction from the Cuban authorities. Puig carried all of his belongings in a garbage bag. Carlos Torres, the boat's interpreter, befriended Puig, who asked him if he had a big house and what his life in Florida was like. Puig told him, "Somebody is going to take a chance on me, and I'll be rich someday. That someday will be pretty soon," Passan wrote. Two weeks later, the *Vigilant* returned Puig and his group to a waiting boat in Cuban waters. Torres asked Puig to autograph two tennis balls—the only sports-related items he could find.

ESCAPE AND OFFICIAL DEFECTION

With each foiled attempt at defection, Puig risked being imprisoned and losing his career, but Passan and Torres described him as determined, if a bit naive. Describing his unglamorous time on the cutter, Passan wrote of Puig's undeterred optimism, "If it meant surviving under the tarp on slop and sleeping on a pebbled deck and waking up at 0700 hours with the rest of the Coasties, that was merely a precursor to his eventual success." Within two months of his run-in with the Coast Guard, Puig was in Mexico. The story of how he got there is its own saga—one that involves Puig, Despaigne, Puig's then-girlfriend Yeny, and a Santeria priest named Lester, who performed a ceremony before they embarked on the treacherous journey. The group drove three hours from Cienfuegos to the northern province of Matanzas. They walked to the shore in the middle of the night, where they met their shepherds: four men with links to drug cartels. The smugglers left them at the docks of Isla Mujeres, an island not far from Cancún on the Yucatán peninsula. The four defectors shared one room in a shabby motel.

The problem, Despaigne later told Katz, was that the smugglers wanted cash immediately—they didn't want to wait for Puig to win a major-league contract and then take a cut. Each day, their demands rose, ultimately approaching $400,000. They decided to call sports agents and effectively auction Puig off to the highest bidder—a surprisingly frequent practice. "What the players go through to get here, it's not correct, it's not fair," one agent, Gus Dominguez, told Katz. Meanwhile, Pacheco, Puig's sponsor, was growing restless. As the stand-off entered its third week, he hired a team of fixers to raid the motel and effectively kidnap Puig and his

cohorts. Days after the raid, Puig was performing for MLB scouts in Mexico City.

Puig met sports agent Jaime Torres in Cancún. Due to a new MLB rule that was about to go into effect, the two had less than a month to secure permanent residency in Mexico for Puig and a license to play in the major leagues, a process that usually takes months. Torres announced Puig's official defection on June 19 and invited scouts out to Mexico to watch him play. They were largely disappointed. Puig was out of shape—he had not played in a year—so observers were shocked when the Dodgers signed him for a staggering $42 million on June 28, 2012.

ROOKIE SEASON

One of the Dodgers' scouts, Cuban American Mike Brito, knew of Puig. He had watched him play in Canada as a young teenager. Brito, Katz wrote, "vowed not to lose track of the kid," and invited Logan White, the Dodgers' vice president of amateur scouting, down to Mexico to watch him play. Even out of shape, White recalled, Puig was impressive. "I was like, 'Oh, my gosh, this guy's special,'" he told Katz. The two men knew the clock was ticking, and they were determined to craft an offer that was impossible for either Puig or Torres to reject. They settled on a seven-year contract for $42 million.

The Dodgers put Puig on their Arizona Rookie League squad and assigned him a mentor and cultural guide named Tim Bravo. Puig embraced American life. He learned how to tip and how to use an ATM; he learned to love Denny's steak and eggs and the Three Stooges. Bravo taught him English and how to drive. Puig's exploits, then and now, reflect the sloppy verve of a teenager. Off the field, he has been arrested several times for speeding, and his teammates and mentors work to keep him out of trouble. Mike Poole, the Dodgers' clubhouse manager, even assigned him the number 66 because Puig reminded him of the Tasmanian Devil cartoon character.

During his debut month in June 2013, Puig batted .436 with seven home runs and sixteen runs batted in (RBIs). "The last player with as many as forty-four hits in his first major league month—Joe DiMaggio in 1936," Passan wrote, referring to the legendary center fielder. His rookie season was equally stunning. Puig "changed the atmosphere" of the lackluster Dodgers, Billy Witz wrote for the *New York Times* (11 June 2013). Though the team did poorly in the playoffs, the Dodgers entered the 2014 baseball season ranked number one in their league.

But even as Puig dominated in the ballpark in 2013, winning both fans and detractors, he was being hounded by the smugglers whom he had already paid, Katz reported. Months after Puig's defection, Leo, the Cuban American mafioso who brought him to Mexico and held him captive, was murdered. The imbroglio—with all of its players, accusations, and lawsuits—has yet to be resolved.

In 2013, Puig's mother left Cuba, and that December, Puig's new girlfriend gave birth to his first child, a boy named Diego.

SUGGESTED READING

Katz, Jesse. "Escape from Cuba: Yasiel Puig's Untold Journey to the Dodgers." *Los Angeles Magazine.* Los Angeles Magazine, 13 Apr. 2014. Web. 7 July 2014.

Passan, Jeff. "Coast Guard Crew Reflects on Time with Yasiel Puig during Attempt to Defect to the US" *Yahoo Sports.* Yahoo Sports, 2 July 2013. Web. 7 July 2014.

Robertson, Linda, Jay Weaver, and David Ovalle. "From Cuba to the Majors: Yasiel Puig's Harrowing Story." *Miami Herald.* Miami Herald, 20 Apr. 2014. Web. 7 July 2014.

Witz, Billy. "Puig Brings Vigor to Lifeless Dodgers." *New York Times.* New York Times, 11 June 2013. Web. 7 July 2014.

—*Molly Hagan*

NHLI via Getty Images

Jonathan Quick

Born: January 21, 1986
Occupation: Hockey player

Jonathan Quick experienced an impressive rise to elite goalie status in the National Hockey League (NHL) after just four full years as a starter for the Los Angeles Kings. Drafted by the Kings in 2005 at the age of nineteen, he played two seasons with the University of Massachusetts Amherst (UMass Amherst) and two seasons with the Kings' affiliate teams in developmental leagues before becoming a starter in the middle of the 2008–9 season. In his first full season as a starter, 2008–9, he led the team to its first playoff berth since 2002. Two years later, he shepherded a low-scoring offense to a winning season and was a main architect of the team's first Stanley Cup win. He led the league with ten shutouts during the season, notched a postseason record of 16–4 and a .956 save percentage, and secured the Conn Smythe Trophy, honoring the most valuable player of the postseason.

Quick is known as a highly athletic goalie with a natural quickness who has worked hard to develop a restrained technique at the net. "Quick is a terrific athlete whose unorthodox style is better explained than defined," Bucky Gleason wrote for the *Buffalo News* (2 June 2012). "He crawls around the crease like a crab combing the seashore, with limbs going in different directions but covering the territory just the same. He might look out of control, but he's usually very much in command." Quick—called

"Quickie" by his teammates and coaches—is also known for his steady demeanor on the ice. "He's always in his own little zone," Kings defenseman Matt Greene told the *Los Angeles Daily News* (23 Mar. 2010). "He's got it all figured out. Look at him after a big save, he's got the same expression as if he missed one he should have got. That's what you want in a goaltender back there—never too high, never too low." Quick signed a ten-year $58-million contract with the Kings in June 2012.

CHILDHOOD AND EARLY EDUCATION

One of four children of Doug and Lisa Quick, Jonathan Douglas Quick was born in Milford, Connecticut, on January 21, 1986. He grew up in Hamden, a suburb of New Haven. A New York Rangers fan who idolized former goalie John Vanbielsbrouck, Quick spent much of his youth playing pickup hockey with friends on his neighborhood streets. As a street hockey player, he wanted to play forward, not goalie, and he had to be coaxed to play at the net.

Quick played in Hamden's youth league and two seasons with the Hamden High School team. He played junior varsity as freshman and then beat out a senior for the starting goalie position on the varsity team as a sophomore. Quick's skill—and work ethic—stood out to his Hamden High coaches, including head coach Bill Veneris and assistant coach Todd Hall. "Jon had something," Hall told Gleason. "He was never interested in the newspaper articles or any of the interviews. All he cared about was stopping the puck. When you scored on him, he would grab the same puck, the exact same puck, throw it back and say, 'Do it again.'" Quick's first job was at a dry cleaning business owned by Veneris called Rainbow Cleaners.

After his sophomore year at Hamden High, Quick transferred to Avon Old Farms, a private preparatory school known for its hockey program, which boasts such notable alumni as NHL Hall of Famer Brian Leetch. Avon Old Farms head coach John Gardner noticed Quick's athleticism and his aggressiveness with shooters. "I told him, 'You got it all going in the right direction,'" Gardner told Chris Hunn for the *New Haven Register* (19 May 2012). "The only person that could stop him is him. I had a feeling he'd be a really great player." Quick excelled at Avon Old Farms, leading the team to two New England regional titles. Quick's records for the 2003–4 and 2004–5 seasons were 20–1 and 25–2, respectively.

COLLEGE AND EARLY PRO CAREER

After graduating in 2005, Quick enrolled at UMass Amherst. As the starting goalie for the Minutemen, Quick was named Hockey East Defensive Player of the Week twice in his freshman season. He was also Hockey East Goaltender of the Month in November 2005. In 2006–7, Quick's single season totals of wins, appearances, saves, and minutes were the highest in the school's history. That season, Quick was a Hockey East Second Team All Star and National Collegiate Athletic Association (NCAA) East Second Team All Star. Quick finished his Amherst career with a 23–22–6 record in 54 appearances, as well as three shutouts, a 2.39 goals-against-average (GAA), and a .925 save percentage. During his tenure at Amherst, Quick led the team to its only NCAA tournament appearance.

Quick was selected seventy-second overall in the third round of the 2005 NHL Draft by the Los Angeles Kings. However, he didn't sign with the team until 2007 after completing his sophomore season at UMass Amherst. Meanwhile, Quick spent the majority of his first professional season playing with the Kings' affiliate teams in developmental hockey leagues, in the American Hockey League (AHL) and the East Coast Hockey League (ECHL). In 2007–8, he racked up records of 11–8 and 23–11 playing for the AHL's Manchester Monarchs and the ECHL's Reading Royals, respectively. Terry Murray, the Kings' head coach from 2008 to 2012, believes the experience of playing in the NHL's developmental leagues helped Quick develop the ability to bounce back from a loss. "When you spend some time in the ECHL traveling on buses, and you're playing three games in three nights in the American Hockey League, you have to get on top of yourself, push yourself and demand lots," Murray told the *Los Angeles Daily News* (23 Mar. 2010). "Forget about that game Saturday night because now you're traveling ten hours on the bus back home and you're playing the four o'clock game on Sunday."

The young goalie's first season with the Kings' organization was widely viewed as part of a "rebuilding period" for a team that had not advanced to the playoffs since the 2002 season. The year before, the Kings had hired a new head coach, Marc Crawford, and acquired a new goalie from the Vancouver Canucks, Dan Cloutier. However, the team struggled with their goaltending throughout that season before settling on Jason LaBarbera as the starting goalie in 2007–8. Quick made his NHL debut with the Kings on December 6, 2007, contributing fifteen saves in a win over the Buffalo Sabres. Quick's other starts that season—in which the Kings finished with a 32–43 record—resulted in losses. The season ended with Quick sitting on the bench.

BECOMING A STARTER—AND AN OLYMPIAN

Quick began the 2008–9 season as a backup goaltender behind LaBarbera and Erik Ersberg. He unexpectedly gained the starting position midseason when LaBarbera was traded to the Canucks and Ersberg was placed on injured reserve. Quick earned his first career shutout on December 23, 2008, in a game against the Columbus Bluejackets. He finished the season with a record of 21–18, the third highest win total for a rookie in club history and third among that year's NHL rookie goalies. He also boasted a 2.48 GAA, a .914 save percentage, and four shutouts. The Kings, however, failed to make the playoffs, finishing the season with a record of 34–37.

In practice, Quick focused on developing his technical skills at the goal. "He's worked hard," Bill Ranford, Quick's goaltending coach, told the *Waterloo Chronicle* (26 Jan. 2010). "He's always had the athletic ability, but it was just basically trying to reel that in a little bit and get some control in his game." "He'd have success in a game, enjoy that success and then kind of get off the game plan that gave him that success," says Ranford, "and when things were going well, he became loosey-goosey in practice, instead of realizing that there's got to be that constant attention to detail." Quick's hard work was rewarded in October 2009, when he signed a three-year contract extension with the Kings worth $5.4 million.

In June 2009, Quick was one of thirty-four players invited by USA Hockey—the sport's national governing body—to participate in a camp for prospective members of the United States Olympic team at the 2010 Winter Games in Vancouver, Canada. In January 2010, Quick was named to the final Olympic roster. He was the youngest of the three goaltenders, which included the league's top goaltenders—Tim Thomas of the Boston Bruins and Ryan Miller of the Buffalo Sabres. Serving as a backup, Quick saw no action during the Olympic Games. Nonetheless, the American team exceeded expectations, going undefeated in the preliminary rounds. The team defeated Switzerland in the quarterfinals and Finland in the semifinals before falling to Canada in an exciting final game that went into overtime. The United States team returned with the silver medal, while the bronze medal went to Finland.

RAPID RISE TO HOCKEY STARDOM

In his first full season as a starter, Quick set Kings single season records with thirty-nine wins and seventy-two appearances, ranking sixth in wins among NHL goaltenders. Upon breaking the team record set in 1981 by Mario Lessard, Quick—who is known for his modesty—acknowledged the contributions of his teammates. "I believe the record that was set was more of a team record than a personal record," Quick told the *Los Angeles Daily News* (23 Mar. 2010), "I can't take too much credit."

Quick led the Kings—which boasted one of the youngest average roster age of any team in the league—to a 46–27 record and their first playoff berth since 2002. In fact, it was the first playoff appearance for the entire Kings' roster. The team, however, lost in the conference quarterfinals to the Vancouver Canucks. Their loss was due in part to uneven goaltending by Quick, which resulted in a number of "soft goals," or goals that should have been routine saves.

The year after his first full season with the Kings, Quick established himself as one of the team's indisputable leaders. In sixty-one games, he notched a record of 35–22, leading the Kings to a season record of 46–30–6. Quick gained significant media attention for a seemingly miraculous save in a March 2011 game against the Calgary Fire, in which a shot from Calgary's captain Jarome Iginla appeared to take a strange right turn as it was headed toward the goal. "It's no secret that I have mind control," Quick joked about the save, as quoted in the *Nanaimo Daily News* (31 Mar. 2011). The Kings finished the season tied with the New Jersey Devils for the fewest power play goals scored, with forty. Advancing to the playoffs for the second year in a row, the Kings lost in the quarterfinals to the San Jose Sharks.

ROAD TO THE STANLEY CUP

The Kings struggled offensively for much of the 2011–12 season. Observers noted that the team's low-scoring offense was saved mainly by Quick's consistent goalkeeping. In October 2011, Quick recorded his hundredth win in the NHL in a shutout over the Phoenix Coyotes, becoming the third Kings' goalie in history to record 100 victories—and doing so quicker than anyone before him, in just 185 games. Quick allowed just 1.41 goals per game, posted a .946 save percentage, and led the league with ten shutouts. He also set a club record for the fewest goals allowed in

a season (179). In January 2012, he was one of six goalies selected to play in the NHL All-Star game. The Kings—which had replaced head coach Terry Murray with Darryl Sutter in December and traded for power forward Jeff Carter—finished the season with a 40–27–15 record. They advanced to the playoffs as the eighth seed in the Western Conference.

After struggling during the regular season, the Kings accelerated through the playoffs, defeating the Vancouver Canucks in the conference quarterfinals and the St. Louis Blues in the conference semifinals. Quick was a major part of the team's success. "We don't make that many mistakes, but when we do he always seems to come up with the big save," Kings captain Dustin Brown told Dan O'Neill for the *St. Louis Post Dispatch* (28 Apr. 2012). "The difference between a good goalie and a great goalie is a good goalie will make all the saves he's supposed to, a great goalie will make all the saves he's supposed to and a few he's not supposed to. That's what he's given us."

The Kings next faced the Phoenix Coyotes in the Western Conference Finals. After going up 3–0 on the Coyotes, the Kings lost Game 4, but came back strong in Game 5, which they won in overtime. The win made the Kings the first team to go undefeated en route to the Stanley Cup Finals. The team had not appeared in the finals since 1993. Upon entering the Stanley Cup, Quick had a 13–2 record in the playoffs, with a 1.49 goals-against average, a .946 GAA, a .929 save percentage.

In the run-up to the finals against the New Jersey Devils, the Kings received significant media attention and Quick's discomfort with speaking with reporters was evident. At press conferences, the soft-spoken Quick gave one and two word responses and deflected questions about his own thoughts and playing by crediting his teammates. "Uh, well, I don't, to be honest, really enjoy this," Quick said at one prefinals press conference, as quoted by Cam Cole for the *Calgary Herald* (30 May 2012). "When I think of the finals, I don't think of being here in front of you guys. I think of going to play in a hockey game at the highest level, that's all I think about."

The Kings won the first three games against the Devils before losing Game 4 at home and then breaking their on-the-road winning streak with a loss in Game 5. The Kings went on to win Game 6 at the Staples Center by a score of 6–1. Quick won the Conn Smythe Trophy as the most valuable player of the playoffs. Earlier in the playoffs, he had received a nomination for the Vezina Trophy, which honors the highest performing goalie. On the night Quick and the Kings won the Stanley Cup, fireworks were set off on Tanglewood Drive in Hamden, the street where he grew up. Rainbow Cleaners, where Quick had worked as a teenager, draped a marquee congratulating him. Quick's hometown officially declared the Thursday after the Stanley Cup win as Jon Quick Day.

RECENT PLAYING

Shortly after the Stanley Cup victory, Quick signed a ten-year contract with the Kings worth a reported $58 million. The deal marked the first ten-year contract the organization had ever awarded. In August 2012, Quick underwent minor back surgery for an inflammatory cyst and disc fragment. The beginning of the 2012–13 NHL season was delayed for four months because of contract disputes between the players association and management. In the shortened 48-game season, which began in mid-January, the Kings finished second in the Pacific Division, with a 27–16 record. Quick finished the regular season with an 18–13 record and a save percentage of .902.

Entering the playoffs, the Kings sought to defend their Stanley Cup title and Quick aimed to replicate his stellar performance in the 2012 playoffs. The Kings managed to defeat the St. Louis Blues in the conference quarterfinals and the San Jose Sharks in the semifinals. However, they lost in the conference finals to the Chicago Blackhawks, the eventual Stanley Cup winners. Though his performance in the series was generally strong—with a save percentage .934 and a GAA of 1.86—Quick was pulled from the second game of the Blackhawks' series after allowing four goals out of seventeen shots. That marked the first time he had been pulled from a game in forty-one consecutive playoff starts. In interviews after the game, however, his teammates were supportive. "Quickie's given us a chance to win in almost every single game he's played in since I've been in Los Angeles," Kings defenseman Rob Scuderi told the *St. Louis Post-Dispatch* (4 June 2013). "Nobody thinks any less of him," added Scuderi, "sometimes it happens. Sometimes it's not your night, and as a goalie it's a little more obvious."

Quick began the 2013–14 season as the Kings' starter but after injuring his groin in a November game against the Buffalo Sabres, the Kings announced that he would be on injured reserve until December. His replacement, Ben Scrivens, formerly of the Toronto Maple Leafs, excelled as Quick's replacement. In January of 2014, Quick was selected to participate on the United States men's hockey team for the 2014 Winter Olympics in Sochi, Russia.

PERSONAL LIFE

Early in his pro career, Quick was known for his tendency to oversleep. He would often fall asleep on the team bus only to be woken up after they had reached their destination and the bus had been emptied. Quick began taking precautions to ensure he woke up on time. "You sleep through a couple of practices, you learn from it," Quick told the *Waterloo Chronicle* (26 Jan. 2010). "Now, I have two or three alarm clocks set every morning."

Quick lives in Connecticut with his wife, Jaclyn, and his young daughter, Madison. Jaclyn's sister, Alicia, is married to New York Islander forward Matt Moulson, who served as Quick's youth coach. The two hockey couples are long-time friends and spend significant time together in the offseason.

In 2011, Quick and Moulson founded the 326 Foundation—a reference to their respective jersey numbers, 32 and 26. The organization donates to their teams' charities, the Kings Care Foundation and the Islanders Children's Foundation, which benefit nonprofit groups in their respective cities. Through the 326 Foundation, Quick donates $500 for each one of his wins, and Moulson donates $500 for each one of his goals.

According to his official team biography, Quick enjoys the television shows *Dexter*, *Entourage*, and *Jersey Shore*, and his favorite sports are hockey, football, and basketball.

SUGGESTED READING

Gleason, Bucky. "Kings Goalie in Command." *Buffalo News*. Berkshire Hathaway, 2 June 2012. Web. 17 Dec. 2013.

Hoornstra, J.P. "Quick Study; Level-headed Approach Has Worked Wonders for Kings Goaltender." *Los Angeles Daily News*. LA Daily News, 23 Mar. 2010. Web. 17 Dec. 2013.

Hunn, Chris. "NHL: Hamden Celebrates Stanley Cup Win by Jonathan Quick." *New Haven Register*. Journal Register, 13 June 2012. Web. 17 Dec. 2013.

Hunn, Chris. "NHL PLAYOFFS: Hamden's Jonathan Quick Is King of the Rink." *New Haven Register*. Journal Register, 19 May 2012. Web. 17 Dec. 2013.

"Jonathan Quick, An Admittedly Heavy Sleeper, Is Among NHL's Busiest Goalies." *Waterloo Chronicle*. Metroland Media Group, 26 Jan. 2010 Web. 17 Dec. 2013.

—*Margaret Roush Mead*

Christine Quinn

Born: July 25, 1966
Occupation: Politician

In 2013, Christine C. Quinn, the Speaker of New York's City Council, ran in the Democratic primary to become the party's candidate for mayor of New York City. Although she appeared to be in the lead, she garnered only 15.5 percent of the vote, losing to Bill de Blasio, who went on

Getty Images

to win the mayoralty. Her push to extend term limits during her time on the city council was seen as a mark against her. As she told Jonathan Van Meter for *New York* (4 Feb. 2013), "[F]or people who really believe that was a mistake, I respect their decision not to support me. What I would tell them is that I voted in a way that I thought was in the best interest of the City of New York. Even though I knew that the majority of the electorate disagreed with me. And at the end of the day, we want elected officials who do what they think is right, notwithstanding the political consequences." Had she won, Quinn would have been the first female and first openly gay mayor of the city. Questions about the effect her sexual orientation had on the race abound. Quinn remained upbeat, despite the loss. At the post-primary election gathering, according to Jodi Kantor for the *New York Times* (11 Sept. 2013), Quinn stated, "This may not be the outcome you wanted, but there's a young girl out there who was inspired by the thought of New York's first woman mayor."

EARLY LIFE AND EDUCATION

Quinn grew up in Long Island. Ellen Shine Callaghan, her maternal grandmother, left Ireland and became a maid in the United States, sailing on the *Titanic*. She fought her way from the steerage area below and became one of the last people to get a seat in a lifeboat. Her mother, Mary Callaghan Quinn, was a social worker for Catholic Charities. Diagnosed with breast cancer when Quinn was in second grade, Quinn's mother died, and was buried on the Christmas Eve of Quinn's sixteenth year. Her father, Lawrence, was a union electrical engineer and union shop steward. Quinn told Meryl Gordon for *New York* (12 June 2006), "He is devoted to me and my sister [Ellen]. At my swearing-in ceremony, I kissed a row of people and I shook his hand. In thirty-nine years I've never kissed him. He's a

tough Irish guy." Still, Quinn senior had an office in the basement of City Hall, where he made calls to voters on behalf of his daughter.

Raised in a devotedly Democratic family, Quinn's interest in politics began early. Her older sister says that Quinn was always bossy, so much so that a neighbor had a T-shirt made for Quinn emblazoned with the words "Mayor of Libby Drive." She was a voracious reader of political autobiographies. In seventh grade, she lobbied for school band uniforms. She attended Catholic schools in Glen Cove. Quinn has detailed her struggles with bulimia as a teenager and her alcohol dependency in her 2013 memoir, *With Patience and Fortitude*.

She graduated from Trinity College, Hartford, in 1988, with a dual degree in urban studies and education. She had so many political internships in college that Trinity later changed its policies about the number of credit hours a student could earn from them.

Quinn had a college crush on another woman, but told herself she was not going to allow anything to happen. With her life's ambitions already set, she expected to remain single. She dated a few men, with unsatisfactory results. It was only after she began working for gay politician Tom Duane that she allowed her sexual orientation to be known.

According to Quinn, one of her most difficult challenges was coming out to her father. He first told her to never again say the words "I'm gay." However, he realized he could lose Quinn over the issue and gradually accepted her lifestyle. He has even marched in the city's gay pride parades.

EARLY POLITICAL CAREER

After college, Quinn headed New York City's Housing Justice Campaign for the Association of Neighborhood and Housing Development. It was during this time that she met Thomas K. Duane, who would become the first openly gay, openly HIV-positive member of City Council. She left her job to manage his 1991 campaign, and then served as his chief of staff following his successful run.

In 1996, she became executive director of the New York City Anti-Violence Project. She left that job three years later to run for the City Council seat vacated after Duane was elected to the State Senate. Because she was filling out the remainder of his term, she was eligible to run twice more, due to term limits rules. Quinn beat three other contenders, including two other gay politicians.

Quinn was elected to City Council representing New York's Third District, the liberal West Side, in 1999. She served as chair of the Health Committee, and in that role supported Bloomberg's smoking ban in restaurants. She also led in addressing issues such as crystal methamphetamine abuse and HIV/AIDS. She advocated for zoning rules that favored small business owners and tenants in her district.

Quinn was not unilaterally in favor of all of Mayor Bloomberg's ideas. She was one of the few to buck the mayor's 2004 plan for a football stadium on Manhattan's West Side.

MADAM SPEAKER

In 2006, Quinn was elected Speaker of the City Council, a position created in 1990 when the city's charter was rewritten. Winning required her to gain fifty votes among her colleagues as well as support throughout five boroughs of the city. She beat out six other contenders, including then councilman Bill de Blasio. Although de Blasio was favored to win, in the final weekend before the election, Quinn gained some crucial support from two Democratic Party bosses, showing her political savvy. She was the first woman and first openly gay person to hold the position.

The Speaker is considered the second most powerful office, after mayor, in the city. As Matt Foreman, the executive director of the National Gay and Lesbian Task Force, explained to Winnie Hu for the New York Times (4 Jan. 2006), "In terms of raw political power, the size of the city budget and the Council's powers, she will become the most powerful openly lesbian or gay official in the country."

COLLABORATING WITH THE MAYOR

Working with Mayor Michael Bloomberg brought its own set of challenges, especially given that the previous Speaker, Gifford Miller, had had an adversarial relationship with the mayor. Quinn was determined to get things done by working with Bloomberg, as she explained to Rebecca Mead for the New Yorker (2 Apr. 2012), "I decided that the Mayor and I would have a good working relationship. We are going to be respectful; we are going to be forthright; we are going to be forward-moving. You have a limited time in life, and to waste time posturing and chiding each other and stabbing each other in the back when you have the opportunity to make each other's lives better—it's just dumb."

This strategy did not preclude disagreements. Under Quinn's leadership, the City Council sued the administration in December 2011 over a new policy on homelessness. Quinn termed the mayor's suggestion of fingerprinting those who received food stamps meanspirited.

Quinn had promised in 2005 to work toward securing a term limits extension. However, when public opinion polls showed a negative attitude toward that extension a year later, she opposed the idea. By 2008, her staff was working closely with Mayor Bloomberg's office to craft an extension, apparently signaling another change in her position, explained by that year's financial crisis.

Critics called the move self-serving—Quinn would be allowed to run for another term, postponing a run for mayor. The extension passed, giving Bloomberg another term, but tarnishing Quinn's credibility in the process.

FOR THE RECORD

Quinn used her power soon after taking office to fire sixty-one people, change the way money is allotted, and limit lobbyists' influence. She also set new rules for Friday dress, banning casual sweats, baseball caps, jeans, and T-shirts for a more professional look. When interviewed by Sean Kennedy for Advocate (14 Mar. 2006) about her victory, she commented, "I think it sends a great message to particularly young women and young LGBT people that in the city of New York—they say if you can make it here, you can make it anywhere—being a woman, being LGBT is not a hindrance. If you have great dreams and you work very hard, you can make those dreams reality."

In her final State of the City address in 2013, Quinn laid out a vision for aiding the financially squeezed middle class. She presented four points to consider: preserving existing housing, restoring rental units that had become unsafe, funding new housing construction, and making units more affordable through property tax caps and other measures.

In addition, Quinn brought to the fore the expense of child care as another factor hurting the shrinking middle class; the average cost was $19,000 annually. She suggested a child-care tax credit with a higher income ceiling than currently existed.

Quinn also proposed an expansion of adult education opportunities, citing a waiting list and 16,000 immigrants in the city who would face deportation if they could not enroll. Furthermore, in light of the damages from Hurricane Sandy, she suggested for New York a path to better protect the city.

RUNNING FOR MAYOR

Almost as soon as she became Speaker, others began to speak of Quinn making a bid for the mayor's seat or the governorship. She downplayed her ambition for either job. When she decided to run in the 2013 mayoral race, she focused on her record, which she described to Jonathan Van Meter for New York (4 Feb. 2013) as "Productive, practical, pragmatic, and progressive." She went on to point out the laws that the City Council passed during her tenure as Speaker, which included pro-immigration, pro-choice, environmental, and living-wage legislation.

Under New York's public-financing system, Quinn was allowed to raise as much as $4.9 million for her campaign, which she had on hand by the beginning of 2013. She polled high early in the year and was considered the favorite, with an endorsement from Emily's List.

In July 2013, more than twenty women leaders met with Quinn to try to make her comprehend the struggles she would face as a woman striving to win an election in a society still challenged by sexism. The qualities that had brought success, the group said, were also liable to defeat her, because powerful women are feared. While ambition, a tough stance, and drive to succeed are socially accepted in men, in many cases they still are not accepted in women.

Quinn maintained at this meeting that she looked at the issues not as a woman or a lesbian, but as a politician. Wanting to be judged on her record, critics said she missed the point. As she told Jonathan Van Meter for *New York* (4 Feb. 2013), "I try to not think too much about how stuff gets seen as it's being done by a woman. Because if you think about it, then you end up thinking about how you're acting, and if you are thinking about how you're acting, then you are preoccupied and you're going to end up being insincere. You're kind of not present."

Voters are notoriously vague in their responses to questions about why they didn't vote for a particular candidate. Criticisms of Quinn were a bit more pointed, however. She was attacked for her voice, for the color of her hair, and for her clothing choices. Feminist activist Gloria Steinem commented to Jodi Kantor for *New York Times* (11 Sept. 2013), "Wherever there is more power, there is more opposition. If you're tough enough to run New York City, you're too tough to be considered acceptably feminine."

PERSONAL LIFE
In May 2012, Quinn married Kim M. Catullo, an attorney. The two met on a blind date after the World Trade Center attack in 2001. Catullo also lost her mother to cancer, on Christmas Day, when Catullo was seventeen. They reside in the Chelsea neighborhood of New York with their dog, Sadie, and have a weekend house in New Jersey.

Quinn has refused to march in New York's renowned St. Patrick's Day parade, sponsored by the Ancient Order of Hibernians, which is not in favor of gay rights. She maintains that she will participate only when the event includes LGBT Irish Americans.

Quinn, who is known for her bold personality and loud voice, told Jonathan Van Meter for *New York* (4 Feb. 2013), "[I]f I tried not to be loud, I would be unable to do it. My late mother was very clear to my sister and I that we were to be strong women; that we were to be effective; that we were to be heard. My mother was also extraordinarily hard of hearing—and toward the end of her life was almost totally deaf—so I think part of the loudness is left over from me yelling,

'Maaa!'" Her sister, Ellen, a geologist, is ten years older than Quinn and lives in Connecticut.

Raised as a Roman Catholic, Quinn has not considered leaving the church that considers gay relationships a sin. As she said to David Greene on NPR's *Weekend Edition* (24 June 2012), "How can you leave a faith? A faith is who you are. It's what's inside of you. It's how you see the world. It's what inspires you. It's what comforts you. It's what uplifts you in the dark days. So you can't leave a faith; the faith is who you are. It's what you have. Why should I leave the church? It's my church. They're the ones who have the wrong perspective."

SUGGESTED READING
Gordon, Meryl. "Boss Quinn." *New York* 12 June 2006: 28–104. Print.
Kantor, Jodi, and Kate Taylor. "In Quinn's Loss, Questions About Role of Gender and Sexuality." *New York Times*. New York Times, 11 Sept. 2013. Web. 9 July 2014.
Kennedy, Sean. "Q&A: Christine Quinn." *Advocate* 14 Mar. 2006: 4. Web. 3 July 2014.
Mead, Rebecca. "Mayor Presumptive." *New Yorker* 2 Apr. 2012: 24–29. Print.
Quinn, Christine C. "A Discussion On New York City and Its Future: A Conversation With New York City Council Speaker Christine Quinn." *New York Law School Law Review* 58.1 (2013): 55–69. Print.
Van Meter, Jonathan. "Madam Would-Be Mayor." *New York* 4 Feb. 2013: 26–93. Print.
"'Who I Am': NYC Council Speaker On Politics, Faith." *Weekend Edition*. NPR, 24 June 2012. Web. 9 July 2014.

—*Judy Johnson*

Zachary Quinto

Born: June 2, 1977
Occupation: Actor and producer

Zachary Quinto is probably best known for his celebrated turn as the half-human, half-Vulcan emotionless Mr. Spock in J. J. Abrams's revitalization of the classic television and film series *Star Trek*, but he is also becoming widely recognized as a very accomplished stage actor in New York theater. In 2013 he garnered critical acclaim for his portrayal of the leads in Tony Kushner's *Angels in America* and Tennessee Williams's classic *The Glass Menagerie*. The willingness to take on such diverse characters stems in large part from his wide-ranging experience in the theater (going back to childhood) and on television (going back to shortly after his graduation from drama school), including, most famously, his star-making turn as the lead villain in NBC's smash

Robert Pitts/Landov

hit *Heroes*, which ran for four seasons between 2006 and 2010. Despite his numerous successes Quinto remains unsatisfied with simply being an actor and has begun producing several critically acclaimed independent films, including *Margin Call* and *All Is Lost*, both released in 2013, while maintaining a full acting schedule. What drives him—whether in big-budget films like *Star Trek* (2009) and *Star Trek into Darkness* (2013) or in smaller, more character-driven works—is an enduring commitment to his character and helping to tell a good story. He remarked to Patricia Sheridan for the *Pittsburgh Post-Gazette* (7 Apr. 2014), "I am interested in pursuing projects that fulfill me creatively, that fulfill me personally and my professional ambitions and that I can feel good about the people I'm working with and the work that I'm doing. I have been really lucky to have that be the case."

EARLY LIFE AND CAREER

Zachary John Quinto—who is part Italian and part Irish—was born in Pittsburgh, Pennsylvania, on June 2, 1977, the second of Joseph and Margo Quinto's two sons. After Zachary's father, who had worked as a barber, died of cancer when Zachary was seven, Margo returned to work full time to provide for him and his older brother, Joe. For Zachary, acting was both a childhood passion—he was featured in productions for the Pittsburgh Civic Light Opera as a child—and an escape. "I think losing my father put me in a position where I needed an outlet for this trauma," he explained to Elizabeth Day for the British newspaper the *Guardian* (4 May 2013). "It started as a hobby and within a year

or two of starting to perform, I felt completely at home and comfortable."

At Central Catholic High School, Quinto was deeply involved with his school's theater program. In 1994 he earned a Gene Kelly Award for his performance as the Major General in his high school's production of Gilbert and Sullivan's *The Pirates of Penzance*. A year later he was nominated for the same award for his performance as John Adams in his school's production of *1776*. Although he enjoyed his time in the theater, he was never quite sure about making acting his career until he survived a serious car accident at sixteen. From that point he was determined to become a working actor. Upon graduation, he entered Carnegie Mellon University in Pittsburgh, Pennsylvania, where he studied theater and earned his bachelor of fine arts degree in 1999. Although he loved stage work, Quinto decided instead to attempt to make his mark as an actor in the film industry of Los Angeles, California, rather than on stage in the theaters of New York City.

THEATER AND TELEVISION

Almost immediately, Quinto's decision to move to the West Coast paid off when he began finding guest-starring roles on a wide variety of television series, including *The Others* (2000), *Touched by an Angel* (2001), *CSI* (2002), *Lizzie McGuire* (2002), *Haunted* (2002), *The Agency* (2002), *Six Feet Under* (2003), *Joan of Arcadia* (2004), and *Crossing Jordan* (2006). He also found parts in multiple theater productions, including *Gross Indecency* with the City Theater Company, *A Lonely Impulse of Delight* at the Vineyard Playhouse, *The Bear* with the Tintreach Company in Ireland, *Much Ado about Nothing* at the LA Shakespeare Festival, and *Lonesome Hollow* at the Ojai Playwright's Conference, among others.

Quinto landed his first steady television work in 2003 when he was cast in the role of computer analyst Adam Kaufman on the 2003–4 season of Fox's edge-of-your-seat dramatic series *24* (2001–10). In 2006 Quinto received acclaim for his role as Tori Spelling's flamboyant best friend Sasan on the comedy *So NoTORIous*, which was not picked up after its first season. Beginning in 2011 Quinto also appeared as a recurring character on the television anthology series *American Horror Story*.

Although these roles and others enabled Quinto to call himself a working actor, he was unsatisfied with the direction of his career and, at one point, contemplated giving it up. That all changed in 2006 when he secured the role of Sylar, a super-powered serial killer, on the NBC hit series *Heroes* (2006–10), in which ordinary people have been granted amazing abilities similar to those possessed by comic-book super heroes like Superman and Spider-Man. A critic for *TV Guide* wrote of Quinto's performance, "With his icy stare and monotone delivery, Quinto proved to be a breathtaking villain." Initially a recurring character in the first season, Sylar would become a mainstay of the critically acclaimed series for its final three seasons. He told Sheridan, "'Heroes' really changed my trajectory in a significant way. [The year] 2007 was a big year because I was made a series regular on 'Heroes' at the same time I was cast in 'Star Trek' and I turned thirty."

STAR TREK

At the 2007 Comic-Con International: San Diego, which is an annual comic-book fan convention, longtime science-fiction fans learned that *Star Trek*, Gene Roddenberry's pioneering 1960s sci-fi television series that spawned five spin-off television series and ten big-budget films, would be rebooted by director and producer J. J. Abrams. Abrams was recasting with younger actors the iconic roles of Captain James T. Kirk and Science Officer Mr. Spock, who were played by William Shatner and Leonard Nimoy in the original series and films. Chris Pine would take on the mantel of Captain Kirk, while Quinto would portray Spock. Quinto was particularly pleased to learn that Nimoy, who had casting approval, would be helping him prepare for the role in the film. In fact, Nimoy also appears as Spock in the 2009 movie and is central to its plot.

Abrams's *Star Trek* was a box-office smash and is credited with resurrecting the franchise. However, it also divided critics and longtime fans who felt the sincerity and reflection found in the original series had been jettisoned in favor of the kind of special effects extravaganza more generally associated with the *Star Wars* films. Critics and fans, however, were not divided on Quinto's performance as Spock, which was singled out time and again as a highlight of the film. In the *New Yorker* (18 May 2009), Anthony Lane wrote that Quinto "is the most commanding reason to see this film. . . . Quinto is the one person here who may leave teen-aged viewers more perplexed than puffed up; he somehow rebukes the movie's whole obsession with backstory and immaturity by seeming riper and wiser than the charmless folly that is spun around him."

STAR TREK INTO DARKNESS

Quinto returned to the Spock role in the film's first sequel, *Star Trek into Darkness* (2013), also directed by Abrams. In the new film, Kirk, Spock, and the crew of the starship *Enterprise* must match wits with a genetic superman who is part of a plot to undermine all of Starfleet. Like its predecessor, the movie relies on many plot points from old *Star Trek* films and, as a result, also split fans and critics. Writing for the *Atlantic* (17 May 2013), reviewer Christopher Orr was more impressed by Quinto than the film itself. Orr opined, "Zachary Quinto continues to

find wit and nuance within the tight characterological constraints of Mr. Spock."

Because of the films' popularity at the box office, it is likely that Quinto will continue to portray Spock on the big screen for some time to come, even though he finds the role a serious acting challenge. "The reality is Spock has emotion but he just doesn't express it," he told Day. "For me, playing Spock was really about cultivating an inner life. As an actor, your nature is to emote, so it's a little counterintuitive."

AWARD-WINNING STAGE ACTOR

Since achieving stardom on *Heroes*, Quinto has found himself an in-demand stage actor, appearing both on and off Broadway in New York City. He received accolades in 2010 and 2011 during an Off-Broadway revival of Tony Kushner's *Angels in America*, in which he played the lead role of Louis Ironson, who leaves his AIDS-wracked boyfriend during the course of the play. In an interview with Benjamin Wallace for *New York* (17 Oct. 2011), Quinto described his eight months in the role as "the most challenging thing I've ever done as an actor and the most rewarding." The revival earned numerous awards; Quinto himself won the 2011 Tina Award for Best Actor as well as the 2011 Theatre World Award for outstanding Off-Broadway debut performance.

In 2013 he again earned critical acclaim, this time in the lead role of the son, Tom Wingfield, in the Broadway revival of Tennessee Williams's 1944 family drama and memory play *The Glass Menagerie*. Starring alongside Quinto were Cherry Jones as Tom's mother, Amanda, and Celia Kennan-Bolger as his sister, Laura. Numerous critics were captivated by this revival of an American classic, but perhaps none more so than Ben Brantley, who in his review for the *New York Times* (26 Sept. 2013) described Jones and Quinto's work as "career-defining performances." Brantley added that Quinto "plays Tom with more than a touch of the author who conceived him. This kinetically charged, purple-prose-spouting Tom is an angry young man who, in his way, is as self-dramatizing as Amanda and as much of an outcast as Laura. No wonder he feels he has to run away; at home, there are too many mirrors." Quinto and his cast mates received several Tony Award nominations and won the 2013 Elliot Norton Award for outstanding ensemble for their work on *The Glass Menagerie*.

FILM PRODUCER

Since 2008 Quinto has also been working behind the scenes as a film producer. In 2008 he formed the production company Before The Door Pictures with Corey Moosa and Neal Dodson, two friends from Carnegie Mellon. Their first full-length movie was *Margin Call*, a 2011 independent film about the real-life financial crisis that triggered the worldwide economic recession, which began in late 2007. Quinto costarred in the film with Kevin Spacey, Stanley Tucci, and Jeremy Irons. He also helped cast the film and raise the three million dollars needed to make it. In his interview with Wallace, Quinto explained, "The point of this movie is not to judge or to vilify or to place blame on any one company or individual. It's really to examine the emotional impact that the decisions these people had to make along the way had on them." *Margin Call* won the 2012 Independent Spirit Award for best first feature and the 2012 Robert Altman Award. Other films from Before The Door include the Robert Redford solo drama *All Is Lost*, the comedy *Breakup at a Wedding*, and the horror film *Banshee Chapter*, all released in 2013.

PERSONAL LIFE

In 2011, during a magazine interview, Quinto came out as a gay man—a rare admission among leading Hollywood actors. In interviews following his revelation, he said that he had been debating whether to admit his homosexuality for a long time, but he decided to do so after learning of the suicide of a fourteen-year-old boy named Jamey Rodemeyer, who was openly homosexual and fought against homophobia. Despite Jamey's strong stand against discrimination, the constant bullying overwhelmed him and he committed suicide in September 2011. Reacting to Jamey's death, Quinto wrote in a post on his official website (16 Oct. 2011), "In light of Jamey's death—it became clear to me in an instant that living a gay life without publicly acknowledging it—is simply not enough to make any significant contribution to the immense work that lies ahead on the road to complete equality." Quinto was in a relationship with fellow actor Jonathan Groff from 2010 to 2013.

A self-described "left-leaning Democrat," he is active in politics and publicly supported Barack Obama during the 2008 and 2012 presidential campaigns. He lives in Los Angeles but visits New York City often.

SUGGESTED READING

Day, Elizabeth. "Zachary Quinto: Boldly Going Where Other Actors Fear To." *Guardian*. Guardian News and Media, 4 May 2013. Web. 29 Apr. 2014.

Lane, Anthony. "Highly Illogical." *New Yorker*. Condé Nast, 18 May 2009. Web. 29 Apr. 2014.

Sheridan, Patricia. "Patricia Sheridan's Breakfast with . . . Zachary Quinto." *Pittsburgh Post-Gazette* [PA]. PG Publishing, 7 Apr. 2014. Web. 2 May 2014.

SELECTED WORKS

24, 2003–4; *So NoTORIous*, 2006; *Heroes*, 2006–10; *Star Trek*, 2009; *Margin Call*, 2011;

American Horror Story, 2011–13; *Star Trek into Darkness*, 2013

—Christopher Mari

Ben Rattray

Born: June 16, 1980
Occupation: Founder and CEO of Change.org

In 2007 Ben Rattray, a graduate of Stanford University, founded Change.org, a social media network that enables people to become activists by clicking in support of a petition. As of 2014, the company, which has its technology headquarters in California's Silicon Valley, boasted more than sixty million users and had offices in eighteen nations. Rattray is not content with this success, however; he wants the network to have a greater social impact. "The question is: How do we turn these remarkable, momentary victories into longer-term social movements?" he said to Eilene Zimmerman for the *New York Times* (6 June 2013). "We are focused on building tools to enable that."

Rattray was included in *Time* magazine's 2012 list of the world's one hundred most influential people. "If we're not touching billions of lives or at least aspiring to do so," he told Noah Rayman for *Time* (11 Nov. 2013), "then we're underselling our opportunity." He hopes that people will come to associate his website with activism the same way that they associate Amazon.com with books.

EARLY LIFE AND EDUCATION

Rattray was born on June 16, 1980, in Santa Barbara, California, the second of five children. His mother, Judy, sold title insurance for real estate; his father, Michael, was an executive at Raytheon, a defense and aerospace company, as well as the head of a Boys and Girls Club. Each summer, Rattray visited grandparents in Scottsdale, Arizona, where he gathered autographs from San Francisco Giants team members who were in town for spring training. As a child, Rattray showed an early aptitude for making money, trading baseball cards with fellow second-graders who knew baseball stats but not card values.

According to Rattray, he was a typical golden child. In addition to being homecoming king, the head of both the debate team and the track team, student-body president, and sports editor of the school newspaper, he still found time to go water-skiing five days a week. He initially set his sights on Wall Street, planning to start an online sports-betting website until he discovered that such a site would be illegal.

The idea for Change.org began during the holiday break of Rattray's senior year at Stanford,

Getty Images Entertainment

when his younger brother Nick came out as gay and spoke about his experiences with bullying and homophobia. "He told me about the pain he experienced as a closeted and confused young gay man," Rattray recalled to Bora Chang and Jessica De Jesus for *Good* magazine (9 Nov. 2012). "But what hurt the most weren't the people who were actively anti-gay, but the people who passively stood by and refused to stand up and speak out against them—people like me." The conversation inspired Rattray to shift his focus from a career in law or investment banking to one that would create positive social change. Within three days he had roughed out a business plan for what would become Change.org.

After graduation, Rattray attended the London School of Economics and Political Science and earned his master's degree. He then returned to the United States and worked as a consultant in Washington, DC, where he helped start a social-entrepreneurship group that aided nonprofit organizations in low-income areas in identifying and applying for grants.

STARTING A MOVEMENT

Rattray had originally planned to attend New York University to study public-interest law, but when he encountered Facebook for the first time in 2005, he realized the potential for social media to effect change. Three weeks before he was to begin classes, Rattray decided to forgo further education. Instead, he persuaded Mark Dimas, a former roommate from Stanford, to join his efforts and borrowed a thousand dollars to develop the site. Change.org debuted nearly two years later. After experimenting with different platforms, such as volunteerism, social fundraising, and political action committees, Rattray

discovered petitions to be the most effective. "This merging of old-school advocacy with social media made the petition much more effective," he said to Zimmerman.

In the early days of the site, Rattray relied on contributions from family and friends to stay afloat, intending to repay them once he began to make a profit. As recently as 2012, Rattray was still living with three friends and driving the 1996 Toyota Camry he had bought from a friend's mother. Any money that the company makes goes into expanding internationally.

MAKING PROFITS AND DOING GOOD

Change.org is a certified benefit, or B, corporation, a relatively new designation that allows for-profit companies to place social benefit over shareholder profits. It does not accept funds from venture capitalists because Rattray does not intend to take the company public, sell it, or otherwise relinquish control. "We aren't in the business of optimizing and maximizing profits," he told Zimmerman. "We're in the business of impact." Even if he were so inclined, venture capitalists would be unlikely to back a company aimed at initiating social change, where the window of success can be fifteen to twenty years—especially when that company has vowed to never be sold or traded publicly. Instead, the site generates revenue by charging companies and organizations to post petitions (individuals can post for free). The target size of the company's audience determines the cost of the petition.

Within five years of its founding, the company had revenues of $15 million. In 2013 it gained that same amount of funding from the Omidyar Network, a philanthropic investment company established by eBay founder Pierre Omidyar and his wife. Rattray had approached Omidyar when he first began Change.org, but Omidyar, like many investors, preferred to wait for the company to build a track record. Another investor is the San Francisco–based Uprising. Such investors are most likely to receive returns in the form of stock buybacks or dividends over time.

Rattray believes that his generation is interested in social causes, but the public perception is that one must choose between making a profit and doing good works. By changing the website's status to that of a B corporation, Rattray wants to upend this accepted dictum. "If we're going to build real tools that help people create change, we need to generate revenue," he said to Rip Empson for *TechCrunch* (21 May 2013). "Although many of my friends told me I was crazy not to seek traditional venture capital, that doesn't mean investment wouldn't be important—I still knew that if we wanted to be fast, to build an innovation-focused business and create the kind of scale you find in the for-profit world, we would need mission-driven capital to help us get there."

MAJOR VICTORIES

The turning point for Change.org came in 2010, when a woman in Cape Town, South Africa, launched a petition to combat "corrective" rape of lesbians, a widespread problem in South Africa. After the petition garnered 170,000 signatures from people around the world, the Parliament of South Africa created a national task force to examine the issue. "There's no person on Earth with seemingly less power than a poor, lesbian South African woman," Rattray said to Meredith May for *SFGate* (12 Aug. 2012), "but she can change the history of an entire country."

Within a few weeks, Change.org began to focus exclusively on petitions. In contrast to petitions begun by professional activists targeting organizations such as the United Nations or the president of the United States, the petitions on Change.org are personal and require a specific response. As Katie Bethell, Change.org's director of campaigns, told Adam Bluestein for *Fast Company* (Sept. 2013), "The campaigns that rise to the top are based in strong stories of individuals standing against injustice that anyone can understand."

Other victories soon followed. In 2011 a twenty-two-year-old nanny, frustrated by a new five-dollar surcharge that Bank of America planned to levy on low-income customers for using their debit cards, turned to Change.org. A month later, more than three hundred thousand people had signed a petition asking the company to remove the fees. The story made national news, members of Congress weighed in, and the bank backed down. The win put corporations on notice that they were being monitored in a new way.

One remarkable aspect of this new order is the degree to which young people have become involved. Jamba Juice exchanged its Styrofoam cups for a more environmentally friendly option as a result of a ten-year-old's petition, while a fourteen-year-old successfully convinced *Seventeen* magazine to stop using Photoshop to digitally enhance photographic images of the models depicted in its pages. In May 2014, clothier Abercrombie & Fitch was targeted for its lack of clothing in larger sizes and the cavalier attitude of a spokesman. After a petition started by an eighteen-year-old collected seventy-five thousand signatures, executives met to consider how they might be more inclusive.

One of Change.org's more notable successes came in 2013, when a young Indian woman named Laxmi petitioned her government to regulate the sale of acid after a rejected suitor threw acid in her face. Within days, more than twenty-seven thousand people had signed; less than a week later, India's Supreme Court issued a ruling that would require shopkeepers to obtain a license to sell acid and buyers to present identification. In March 2014, Laxmi was one of ten women to receive an International Women of Courage Award, presented by US First Lady Michelle Obama.

SEEKING FAIRNESS

While Change.org permits all varieties of petitions as long as they do not incite violence or espouse hate, the site does tend to skew politically left, especially on social issues. At times, petitions in direct conflict have been mounted at the same time, which does not upset Rattray. The company's communications director, Benjamin Joffe-Walt, explained to Ylan Q. Mui for the *Washington Post* (23 Jan. 2012), "People who want to create positive social change don't always agree on the best way to do that. We are very aware of that and are interested in all people finding a home on our platform."

To counter charges of bias from its critics, in 2013 Change.org added a new section called Decision Makers, which permits those who are the targets of petitions to respond directly. Rattray explained to Nick O'Malley for the *Sydney Morning Herald* (23 Nov. 2013), "I think a world in which people can free-flow express their opinions and have the capacity for public communication is really powerful. I will say that I do think it's the case that people that are being petitioned should be able to respond to those. Give them the capacity, then it's a war of ideas."

Staff members monitor the website for petitions that meet several criteria. Is the petition gaining a lot of attention? Are its goals focused and reasonable, and can they be attained? Could it move other groups to act? If so, the company offers petitioners training in how to handle media and organize community support. After a plea to allow women in Saudi Arabia to drive gathered more than seventy-five thousand signatures, staff members organized protests, drafted press releases, and sent massive amounts of e-mail to State Department officials, including then US secretary of state Hillary Clinton.

In Rattray's opinion, the lack of focus or designated leaders found in movements such as Occupy Wall Street are deficits that prevent success. "The power unlocked when people have the capacity to more rapidly and effectively organize with others is unprecedented in human history," he told his staff in an e-mail, as reported by Mui. "But what's needed for this to be truly transformational is a solution that turns people-power from a force that is episodically realized to one that is deeply embedded in our political and social lives—something that makes people-power pervasive and sustained."

During 2011, the site boasted some eight hundred victories on a variety of issues, most of them local, where change is more likely to occur. In fact, the use of petitions for local issues has caught the attention of members of Congress; Massachusetts senator Elizabeth Warren and Wisconsin representative Paul Ryan have both created their own Change.org landing pages to respond directly to issues that pertain to their constituents.

THE CRITICS

Change.org has come under fire from critics who consider it to be another manifestation of what is often called "slacktivism" or "clicktivism." During the 1990s and 2000s, many online campaigns promised global change but generated few real results. "Social media tools can be very effective if they complement offline campaigns," Jillian C. York, the Electronic Frontier Foundation's director of international freedom of expression, said to Gerry Shih for the *New York Times* (1 July 2011). "But I don't think signing a petition does anything useful."

Despite this widespread perception, other sites have also begun offering the option of signing online petitions. Both Facebook and Google have added these features, and Moveon.org has started the service Signon.org. However, the woman who started the petition against the ban on Saudi women drivers believes that Change.org is different. "On Twitter and Facebook there are all these people who don't know anything; they're just people who are concerned but they don't have any experience or background in how to get the word out," she told Shih. "Change.org is more empowering. They assign people to campaigns who know the ins and outs."

PERSONAL LIFE

In 2012 Rattray was named one of *Forbes* magazine's top forty business leaders under the age of forty. He identifies as politically independent, having been both a Republican and a Democrat at various points in his life—the former until he was eighteen, the latter while in college. He claims not to have time for a social life, although he has dated several women. Rattray remains passionate about the nature of his organization. "We're not in the business of raising awareness; we're in the business of creating change," he told Issie Lapowsky for *Inc.* magazine (May 2013). "If things don't really change, then we haven't done our jobs."

SUGGESTED READING

Bluestein, Adam. "You Sign, Companies Listen." *Fast Company* Sept. 2013: 34–36. Print.

Lapowsky, Issie. "The 25 Audacious: Social Impact." *Inc.* May 2013: 70–72. Print.

Mui, Ylan Q. "Change.org Emerges as Influential Advocate on Issues from Bullying to Bank Fees." *Washington Post.* Washington Post, 23 Jan. 2012. Web. 25 July 2014.

O'Malley, Nick. "Just Sign Here: How Change.org Is Helping People to Make a Difference." *Sydney Morning Herald.* Fairfax Media, 23 Nov. 2013. Web. 25 July 2014.

Rayman, Noah. "Power to the People." *Time* 11 Nov. 2013: 16. Print.

Shih, Gerry. "Online Activism Finds a Home in San Francisco." *New York Times* 1 July 2011: A17. Print.

Zimmerman, Eilene. "Company Makes a Business of Selling Social Change." *New York Times* 6 June 2013: B6. Print.

—*Judy Johnson*

Kelly Reilly

Born: July 18, 1977
Occupation: Actor

Although she has appeared alongside such stars as Johnny Depp, Robert Downey Jr., and Denzel Washington, Kelly Reilly says that she has little interest in achieving their level of renown. "Fame and celebrity don't interest me at all," she told a reporter for the *Scotsman* (1 Jan. 2005). "I've acted with a lot of very famous people, so I've seen their world and all the stuff that comes with it. I don't want to be doing fashion shoots and being interviewed about where I shop. Who cares? I act because I have to, because I need to find out whether I can do it or not—that's what drives me and excites me and lights me up." Speaking even more bluntly, she told Chloe Fox for the London *Telegraph* (20 Oct. 2007), "I really can't be arsed

Francis Specker/Landov

with the whole red carpet thing. To be totally honest, it brings me out in a bit of a rash."

Reilly may soon have little choice in the matter. She is already well known to London theatergoers—in 2004 she became the youngest actor to date to be nominated for an Olivier Award for best actress—and fans of British television have seen her in several popular series, including the prime-time crime drama *Above Suspicion*, which aired from 2009 to 2012. Her more recent big-budget Hollywood movies, such as *Flight* (2012) and *Heaven Is for Real* (2014), have introduced her to an even wider audience, and critics have asserted that she is destined for stardom—whether or not that is her aim. In a review of *Flight*, for example, Mick LaSalle wrote for the *San Francisco Chronicle* (1 Nov. 2012), "[Director Robert] Zemeckis deserves praise for casting her. She has been [acting] for years, but this is the first time she has ever gotten to bat with the bases loaded. Under Zemeckis' direction, when Reilly and [Denzel] Washington are onscreen, the eyes go to Reilly."

EARLY YEARS

Kelly Reilly was born on July 18, 1977, in Surrey, England, and was raised in an area of Greater London known as Chessington. Her father, Jack, now retired, worked for more than two decades as a police officer. "You hear that people hate the police, like during the recent student protests [in London], and I think: 'Well, they're doing their job and they have kids who want to go to university too,'" Reilly told Ursula Kenny for the London *Observer* (1 Jan. 2011). "My dad is such a good man." Her mother was a homemaker who took part-time administrative jobs at hospitals and factories to help support the family. Reilly has one brother, Neil, who is a professional golfer.

Although she is Catholic, Reilly "knew very early on that I'd not be taking communion," as she explained to Julia Llewellyn-Smith for the London *Telegraph* (9 Apr. 2014). "All that doctrine didn't resonate with me. I didn't need it to feel the relationship with my spiritual beliefs." She credits her parents with keeping her level-headed and grounded. "I was taught to be humble, not to make a noise about myself, so I still get embarrassed when someone pays me a compliment," she admitted to the *Scotsman*.

A NEWFOUND PASSION

By her own account, Reilly was far from a stellar student, and she was placed on an undemanding academic track at Tolworth Girls' School in Surbiton. She has noted with chagrin that her curriculum did not include much literature: "I didn't even go near a Shakespeare play or anything that, God forbid, might have inspired me," she told Fox. She found unlikely champions, however, in a pair of drama teachers who discerned something special about her. The first play she ever read and performed was *The Cherry Orchard* by Anton Chekhov. "Suddenly, the lights went on," she told Fox. "I just loved everything about it." Her parents were puzzled by her newfound passion, she recalled to Fox: "Theater was a world very far removed from the world they knew and they feared for me. But they knew I was very strong-willed and that I would do exactly what I wanted anyway."

Reilly began attending professional stage productions as often as possible. "It was Antony Sher in *The Resistible Rise of Arturo Ui* that did it for me," she told Stuart Jeffries for the *Guardian* (27 Nov. 2007). "It was 1994 and the first time I'd been to the Olivier [part of the National Theatre in London]. I remember the stage revolved and the whole atmosphere: it was so . . . theatrical. My jaw was on the floor. I don't think I completely understood what was going on but I wanted to be in it."

With the encouragement of her drama teachers, Reilly performed a monologue at the Casting Couch, a small venue on London's Tottenham Court Road. There, she was seen by an agent, who subsequently helped her win a role in a 1995 episode of *Prime Suspect*, a long-running police procedural starring Helen Mirren. Mirren reportedly counseled Reilly to see the world or get a university degree rather than attending drama school; Reilly took her advice, leaving home soon after finishing secondary school and supporting herself as a waiter while seeking other acting jobs. "I have a very close, very loving relationship with my parents, but I've always lived in my head a lot, creating my own world in my imagination, and I must have driven my parents mad," she told the *Scotsman*. "I wasn't an easy teenager. I'm rather strong-minded, so I needed to go and to spread my wings."

EARLY TV AND STAGE CAREER

Reilly's faith in herself and her decision to forgo drama school were soon justified. In 1996 alone, she appeared as a guest in another television crime series, *The Ruth Rendell Mysteries*; the period drama series *Bramwell* and *Poldark*; and the Clive Owen detective series *Sharman*. Director Terry Johnson, who had seen Reilly in *Prime Suspect*, subsequently cast her in his 1997 production of the farcical *Elton John's Glasses* at the Palace Theatre, Watford. Over the next several years, steady work continued to come her way, both on the stage and in television.

Among Reilly's highest-profile early stage roles was a 2001 production of *Blasted*, a play by Sarah Kane that included scenes of cannibalism and rape. The work had been pilloried by critics when it premiered in 1995, but many later came to appreciate its moral themes, and a 2010–11 production earned an Olivier Award. "When my parents came to see *Blasted*, I was really worried, but they were great about it," Reilly told Jeffries. "My dad loved it. I admired him for that reaction because I didn't expect it."

In 2000 Reilly played the ingenue in Johnson's stage version of *The Graduate*, the hit 1967 film starring Dustin Hoffman, and in early 2003 she appeared alongside American sitcom star Matthew Perry in the David Mamet play *Sexual Perversity in Chicago*. "This was the bloke I'd watched on Friday night with a bottle of wine!" she said to Noam Friedlander for the London *Telegraph* (9 Dec. 2009). "Chandler from *Friends* turns up at rehearsal. Right in the same room!"

CRITICALLY ACCLAIMED PERFORMANCES

While Reilly's theater reviews had been consistently good, she received an extraordinary amount of praise for her next work, a production of Patrick Marber's *After Miss Julie* that ran at the Donmar Warehouse from November 2003 to February 2004. Based on the classic 1888 play *Miss Julie* by August Strindberg, Marber's work takes place on the estate of an English peer in 1945. The man's daughter, Miss Julie (Reilly), surreptitiously sleeps with the family chauffer, and the relationship brings to light long-simmering class tensions and resentments. "Kelly Reilly brilliantly captures the spoilt hauteur and louche sensuality of Miss Julie, but, as she faces the prospect of public shame, she also makes you feel genuine concern for this sexually voracious yet emotionally frigid woman, driven to the point of no return by her passion and her class," Charles Spencer wrote in a review for the London *Telegraph* (27 Nov. 2003). "There is a trembling, barely contained hysteria in Reilly's performance as she fluctuates between desperate panic, impossible dreams, and ludicrously inappropriate hauteur that keeps you on the edge of your seat. . . . An unforgettable night of white-hot theatrical intensity."

Spencer's sentiments were almost universally echoed, and Reilly's performance earned her a 2004 Olivier Award nomination for best actress of the year—the youngest actor ever nominated in the category at the time. She was nominated for the same award again, in 2008, for her portrayal of Desdemona in an acclaimed 2007–8 staging of *Othello* at the Donmar Warehouse. The play also starred Chiwetel Ejiofor and Ewan McGregor.

In addition to being in demand in the West End theater scene, Reilly could be seen regularly in such television productions as *Wonderful You* (1999), *Sex 'n' Death* (1999), *The Safe House* (2002), *A for Andromeda* (2006), *Joe's Palace* (2007), and *He Kills Coppers* (2008). From 2009 to 2012 she starred in *Above Suspicion*, a television crime drama written by Lynda La Plante, who wrote the novels the series was based on and was also responsible for the popular *Prime Suspect*. In *Above Suspicion* Reilly played Anna Travis, an ambitious but flawed police detective. Her parents were pleased when she won the role. "Dad was very excited when I told him about it and, initially, I couldn't understand why," she told Tim Oglethorpe for the *Daily Mail* (26 Dec. 2008). "I'd underestimated the effect it had on him—and on my mum—of seeing me playing characters who are slightly dodgy. . . . So Anna Travis is a breath of fresh air, especially for my dad. The chance to see me playing not only someone decent but somebody in the same profession as he was in delights him."

FILM CAREER

Reilly had, indeed, portrayed several less-than-admirable characters, many of them on the big screen. She appeared as a harlot alongside a licentious Johnny Depp in *The Libertine* (2004) and as a dancer in an all-nude revue in the 2005 film *Mrs. Henderson Presents*. (Discussing the former, she joked to interviewers that she had telephoned her friends to gossip like schoolgirls after being called on to kiss Depp in a scene.) In *Eden Lake* (2008), Reilly starred as a young woman named Jenny who falls into the clutches of a murderous band of teens, and while her character was a sympathetic one, most reviewers found the film brutal and horrifying.

In 2009 and 2011 Reilly played Mary Morstan (later Mary Watson), John Watson's love interest, in two action-oriented reboots of the Sherlock Holmes franchise, directed by Guy Ritchie and starring Robert Downey Jr. Although the part was relatively small, critics enjoyed watching Reilly on the screen, and many credited her character with adding a needed fillip of tension and jealousy to the relationship between Holmes (Downey Jr.) and Watson (Jude Law).

HOLLYWOOD

In 2012 Reilly, who had moved to the United States after marrying an American, appeared in the movie *Flight*, which starred Denzel Washington as an alcoholic airline pilot. In the film she portrays Nicole, a beautiful heroin addict who tries to aid Washington's character in his recovery. In a review for the online film magazine *Cinema Blend* (21 Nov. 2012), Robert O'Connell wrote, "The two names you heard over and over prior to the release of *Flight* were Denzel Washington and Robert Zemeckis. Understandably. . . . Yet now that the Oscar contender is out, a name people hear repeatedly is Kelly Reilly, who holds her own alongside Washington in a remarkably complicated role and—in some ways—steals a spotlight away from her pedigreed co-star."

While an Oscar nomination for Reilly's performance never materialized, she did win a 2012 Spotlight Award at the Hollywood Film Festival. She also appeared with Greg Kinnear in the movie *Heaven Is for Real* (2014), and while most reviewers dismissed the picture's heavy-handed religious themes, they had kind words for Reilly's portrayal of a mother whose young son has had an out-of-body experience that heartens the members of his small community.

Among Reilly's more recent projects is *Black Box*, an ABC series that debuted in April 2014. In the series, she plays Catherine Black, a famed neuroscientist secretly struggling with bipolar disorder. Before filming began, Reilly spent months interviewing neurologists, psychologists, and other mental health professionals to learn about their work and the disorder. "I feel very protective of making sure that we tell this story truthfully," she explained to Rick Bentley for the *Fresno Bee* (22 Apr. 2014). "There's no point in making it if we don't honor it and we don't ignite it with truth and with all aspects of truth."

PERSONAL LIFE

Reilly, who enjoys horseback riding and cooking in her spare time, married financier Kyle Baugher in 2012. The couple live in New York and have homes in Manhattan and the Hamptons. They are rarely photographed together in the entertainment press, as Reilly believes strongly in not revealing details of her personal life.

Before her marriage Reilly had been romantically involved with American-born British actor JJ Feild and Israeli actor Jonah Lotan. While it was rumored that she had dated *Sherlock Holmes* director Guy Ritchie and was responsible for his divorce from pop star Madonna, all parties firmly denied the rumor, and Reilly evinced horror that reporters had turned up on her parents' doorstep during the resulting tabloid frenzy.

SUGGESTED READING

Bentley, Rick. "New Doctor Drama *Black Box* Vows Not to Be Like Any Others." *Fresno Bee.* Fresno Bee, 22 Apr. 2014. Web. 10 July 2014.

Fox, Chloe. "Kelly Reilly: From the Heart." *Telegraph.* Telegraph Media Group, 20 Oct. 2007. Web. 14 July 2014.

Friedlander, Noam. "Kelly Reilly Interview." *Telegraph.* Telegraph Media Group, 9 Dec. 2009. Web. 14 July 2014.

"The Life of Reilly." *Scotsman.* Johnston, 1 Jan. 2005. Web. 10 July 2014.

Llewellyn-Smith, Julia. "Kelly Reilly Interview." *Telegraph.* Telegraph Media Group, 9 Apr. 2014. Web. 14 July 2014.

Reilly, Kelly. "Actress Kelly Reilly Lets Loose about Her Very Controversial Character." Interview by Elizabeth Luisi. *Huffington Post.* TheHuffingtonPost.com, 5 May, 2014. Web. 14 July 2014.

SELECTED WORKS

The Libertine, 2004; *Pride & Prejudice*, 2005; *Mrs. Henderson Presents*, 2005; *Eden Lake*, 2008; *Above Suspicion*, 2009–12; *Sherlock Holmes*, 2009; *Sherlock Holmes: A Game of Shadows*, 2011; *Flight*, 2012; *Black Box*, 2014; *Heaven Is for Real*, 2014

—*Mari Rich*

Willie Robertson

Born: April 22, 1972
Occupation: Television personality and CEO of Duck Commander

In an article for the *New York Times* (25 Aug. 2013), Bill Carter called Willie Robertson and his family "the subjects of the biggest reality show hit in the history of cable television." That show, *Duck Dynasty*—which premiered in 2012 and consistently draws millions of viewers to each episode—introduced the Robertsons to a wide mainstream audience, but, as Carter explained, "in the more contained world of ducks, guns and camouflage gear, the Robertsons were already celebrities thanks to the family's core business: sales of duck gear, especially duck calls."

Reviewers almost universally agree that the show's appeal is evident. "We just can't seem to get enough of the hairy Robertson clan from West Monroe, Louisiana—their beards, their bandannas, their zany adventures trying to dynamite the local beaver dam," Rob Sheffield wrote for *Rolling Stone* (28 Aug. 2013). "It's easy to see why *Duck Dynasty* has gotten so huge—it's an old-school sitcom in reality drag, loaded with folksy charm and cozy family shenanigans. . . . Multiply *Home Improvement* by *The Beverly Hillbillies*, then subtract any sense of fancy-pants production values, and *Duck Dynasty* is what you get." Echoing those sentiments, Kate Storey wrote for the *New York Post* (18 Aug. 2013), "*Duck Dynasty* is praised for its authenticity, its charismatic characters, its

Bill Greenblatt/UPI/Landov

quirky setting. But the show's runaway success has much to do with its wholesomeness. It's G-rated, family-friendly programming that's mostly absent from television today." By all accounts, the program, which ends each episode with the clan praying around the dinner table, is an accurate reflection of the Robertsons' values. "For as long as I can remember, my life has centered around three building blocks: faith, family, and food," Robertson wrote in his 2012 memoir, *The Duck Commander Family: How Faith, Family, and Ducks Created a Dynasty.*

EARLY YEARS

Willie Robertson was born on April 22, 1972, in Bernice, Louisiana, to Phil and Kay Robertson. He was the third of the couple's four sons. His older brothers are Alan, who was born when Kay was just sixteen years old, and Jason, who is generally known as Jase; his younger brother is Jeptha.

In what has become an integral part of Robertson family legend, Phil, always an avid hunter, was tapped as the starting quarterback for two seasons at Louisiana Tech University, but quit the team when it interfered with duck hunting. Fellow student Terry Bradshaw replaced him and ultimately went on to stardom in the NFL.

A heavy drinker as a young man, Phil tried a variety of careers, including teaching gym, commercial fishing, and managing a bar. Then, in 1972, he hit upon the idea of making and selling duck calls, officially starting the Duck Commander Company in 1973. Although the calls were among the most realistic sounding on the market, the business took several years to get off the ground, and the family often struggled financially. "When we were growing up with nothing more than an idea in Dad's head for a duck call that sounded exactly like a duck, folks would sometimes look at us with pity and wonder why Dad [who already had his distinctive facial hair] didn't shave his beard and get a regular job," Robertson wrote in his memoir. "Some would even poke fun of us. We made it through some really tough times."

Meals sometimes consisted of only rice and beans or fried bologna sandwiches, and for years the boys qualified for free school lunches. Gradually, however, word spread about the quality of the double-reed calls made by Phil, who dubbed his fledgling enterprise Duck Commander. "Over the next few years, I noticed that our family was beginning to make more money," Robertson wrote. "When we went from receiving free lunches to getting reduced lunches, I thought that was a sign that Duck Commander was taking off. When we started paying for our own lunches, I thought, 'Man, we must be rich now!'"

EDUCATION AND EARLY CAREER

Robertson attended West Monroe High School, a large Louisiana public school. Upon graduating, he entered a local seminary but after he got married, on January 11, 1992, he transferred to Harding University, where his new wife, Korie, was studying. At Harding, Robertson majored in kinesiology. During his final year, in 1995, he transferred to Northeast Louisiana University (now known as University of Louisiana at Monroe) to undertake a program in health and human performance. As part of the program, he was required to take business courses. Despite that training, he did not yet entertain the idea of joining his parents at Duck Commander full-time. He helped out a great deal, particularly when Phil set up booths at trade shows, but his main source of income was a job at Camp Ch-Yo-Ca, the Bible-based camp where he and Korie had originally met.

At the time, the camp was deeply in debt, and the savvy Robertson found that he was able to generate additional revenue by renting the facilities to churches and youth groups during the off-season. He also improved the amenities on the property, adding hiking trails and tennis courts, and had soon rescued Ch-Yo-Ca from its sea of red ink. He found running the camp gratifying, but as his family grew, he realized that he needed to do work that would be both more lucrative and more secure.

JOINING THE BUSINESS

By that time, Duck Commander was relatively successful, and Robertson approached his father about joining the enterprise. Phil unhesitatingly agreed, although there was no formal role into which he could easily step. Within a few months, thanks to his business courses, Robertson recognized that Duck Commander was not being run in an efficient manner, and he had ideas that he believed would help.

Phil had noticed by the early 1980s that many of the mom-and-pop sporting-goods stores that had agreed to carry his duck calls were going out of business, and he managed to sell his wares in bulk to the retail behemoth that was causing the smaller stores to shut down: Walmart. From selling about $8,000 worth of duck calls his first year, Phil was soon selling $500,000 worth to Walmart alone each year. As Robertson wrote in his memoir, "It was always a big day around the Robertson house when Walmart wired its money to our account to pay for its products." Still, he realized, "By the time you shipped the products the way Walmart wanted them shipped, you weren't really making much money. Those big checks that came in always seemed to get spent before we knew it, because there wasn't much profit in them, which created a big cycle of debt for years."

Kay and Phil agreed to let their son take over the financial operations of Duck Commander, and later that year Robertson and Korie mortgaged their home in order to buy half of the business. Among his first moves was making the enterprise less dependent on Walmart by courting large retailers that focused year-round on sporting goods and hunting equipment. In 2005, Robertson assumed the title of CEO.

TELEVISION

In addition to making duck calls, Phil had branched out into making hunting videos. The first, released in 1988, had been made with rented camera equipment and sold only about one hundred copies. By the time the third came out in 1997, however, the quirky hour-long videos, backed by Phil's favorite classic-rock tunes, had won a sizable cult following. Fans often told family members that they were funny enough to have their own television show; the banter among Phil and his sons as they sat in their duck blind was as popular as the footage of waterfowl being blown from the sky.

Robertson liked the suggestion but had little idea of how to go about getting a television deal. Then, one day, a representative from Benelli Shotguns approached the family with an offer to make and sponsor a duck-hunting show. Called *Duck Commander*, the show premiered on the Outdoor Channel in 2009 and won several prizes at the 2010 Golden Moose Awards, an Oscar ceremony of sorts, aimed at sporting and nature shows.

After taping two seasons of the program, the Robertsons were approached by a producer who offered to make what is known as a "sizzle reel," in an attempt to pique the curiosity of a major network. A&E was interested, and the first episode of the new show, called *Duck Dynasty*, aired on March 20, 2012. "Very little duck-call making actually takes place in any given episode," Neil Genzlinger wrote for the *New York Times* (7 Oct. 2012). "Instead the focus is likely to be some harebrained project instigated by Willie's older brother Jase, or Phil's obsession with ridding his land of beavers, or Kay's determination to open a restaurant, or Uncle Si's efforts to give driving pointers to a young member of the clan, or some similar bit of frivolousness. Willie, the only man with obvious business acumen, is forever exasperated by his inability to get Jase and the rest of the Duck Commander staff to stop goofing off, although he too has been known to shirk certain duties."

The formula was an immediate success. That first year, the season finale was the highest-rated non-sports cable program that night, with more than 2.5 million viewers. When season four premiered, that number climbed to more than twelve million. Sales of the company's duck calls mirrored that increase. In 2011, Duck

Commander had shipped 60,000 units, and while that was admittedly an impressive figure, the following year, after the show began airing, that number shot to 300,000—the vast majority of which went to non-hunters, who wanted the calls simply as mementos. In addition to the duck calls themselves, the family licensed a staggering array of other merchandise. "I knew I had a Chia Pet and a bobblehead and an action figure," Robertson told Bill Carter. "I didn't know [until recently that] I had a garden gnome. That's awesome. I guess Pez dispenser is the last weird thing I have to see myself on."

The show's fifth season, which began airing in January 2014, suffered a noticeable drop in viewership, with episodes drawing less than five million viewers by the season finale. Many observers attributed the phenomenon to a controversy that arose in December 2013, when Phil Robertson was interviewed by *GQ* magazine and made comments that were widely considered to be homophobic and racist. After much posturing on all sides—with A&E threatening to fire Phil permanently, Robertson and the rest of the family rallying around their patriarch, some retailers announcing their intention to pull Duck Commander items from the shelves, and loyal fans threatening to boycott anyone who did so—a decision was made to continue filming and airing the show as normal. Pundits pointed out that five million viewers—while not as remarkable as the twelve million who had watched just months before—were still more than most cable shows could ever hope to attract.

POLITICAL ASPIRATIONS

In 2013, rumors swirled that Robertson would be running for a seat in Louisiana's Fifth Congressional District. The post had been left vacant by Republican representative Rodney Alexander, who had stepped down during his sixth term to join the administration of Governor Bobby Jindal. "A new political dynasty might soon be joining the Kennedys, Clintons, and Bushes: Duck Dynasty, that is," Paul Bedard wrote for the *Washington Examiner* (12 Aug. 2013). "Some key Republican operatives are eager to woo one of the hit show's stars—Willie Robertson—to run."

While the rumor proved unfounded, Robertson did endorse Vance McAllister, who ultimately won the race. In gratitude, McAllister invited Robertson to Washington, DC, as his guest, to hear President Barack Obama give the 2014 State of the Union address. Although the reality star wore a suit jacket, as a nod to the formality of the occasion, he did not wear a tie and still sported his trademark bandana around his head. Describing the scene as "surreal" and "bizarre," CNN reporter Dana Bash said, "You're sitting there with members of the Supreme Court, the majority leader, the vice president and a lot of members are just interested in coming and taking a picture with . . . a star of *Duck Dynasty*. It is definitely something I have not seen in my many years of covering state-of-the-union address."

PERSONAL LIFE

Robertson met his wife, Korie Robertson, at a Christian summer camp when he was in third grade, and the two had begun dating seriously when they were teens. John Luke, the couple's oldest son, was born in 1995, and their daughter Sadie followed two years later. In 2001, they adopted a boy they named Will, and their fourth child, Bella, was born in 2002. The family now also includes a foster daughter, Rebecca, who had originally come to Louisiana as an exchange student from Taiwan.

SUGGESTED READING

Carter, Bill. "A Calculated Push into Entertainment Lifts *Duck Dynasty* Family's Fortunes." *New York Times.* New York Times, 25 Aug. 2013. Web. 6 May 2014.

Genzlinger, Neil. "Lured In by a Family Just Being Itself on TV." *New York Times.* New York Times, 7 Oct. 2012. Web. 6 May 2014.

Robertson, Willie, Korie Robertson, and Mark Schlaback. *The Duck Commander Family: How Faith, Family, and Ducks Created a Dynasty.* New York: Howard, 2012.

SELECTED WORKS

Benelli Presents Duck Commander, 2009–11; *Buck Commander: Protected by Under Armour*, 2010–11; *Duck Dynasty*, 2012–

—Mari Rich

Saoirse Ronan

Born: April 12, 1994
Occupation: Actor

Saoirse Ronan first came to the widespread attention of audiences at the age of thirteen, when she appeared in the acclaimed 2007 film *Atonement.* Her performance earned her an Oscar nod in the category of best supporting actress, and although she did not ultimately win, she took her place in Academy Award history as one of the youngest people ever nominated for one of the coveted statuettes. She has since had roles in several other films, including *The Lovely Bones* (2009), *Hanna* (2011), and *The Host* (2013), earning almost widespread praise for her acting ability and magnetic screen presence. "To describe her as a former 'child star' sounds wrong," Sophie Wilson wrote for the *Telegraph* (29 Mar. 2013). "Her work is mature, timeless,

FilmMagic

unflashy—always has been." In a piece for the online arts magazine *Slant* (7 Nov. 2013), R. Kurt Osenlund agreed with those views, writing: "While it's tempting to describe a young actor as precocious, such a term would be grossly underselling Ronan at this point. She's an established, bona fide actress in her own right—one of very few leading ladies under twenty who can carry a film, and one of fewer still who can confidently look forward to a lengthy, prestigious career."

EARLY YEARS

The pronunciation of Saoirse Ronan's first name has been the source of much fascination and confusion in the American press. "'Searsha' is how Irish people pronounce it, but I would pronounce it 'Sersha,' like 'inertia,'" Ronan explained to Ed Symkus for the *Leesville Daily Leader* (7 Apr. 2011). "It's got a beautiful meaning. It's Irish for 'freedom.' I recently found out that my middle name, Una, means 'unity' in Ireland. And I think my last name means 'seal.' So I'm a free, unified seal."

The actor was born on April 12, 1994, in the New York City borough of the Bronx, in a heavily Irish enclave known as Woodlawn. Ronan's mother, Monica, was a nanny, and her father, Paul, did seasonal construction jobs and tended bar when they first arrived in the United States from Ireland. The bar in which Paul worked was popular with a group of Irish actors, and one of them, Chris O'Neill, suggested that he try his hand on the stage. Paul Ronan began winning occasional roles, and the bar's owner soon gave him an ultimatum: focus on serving drinks or quit. Although money was tight, Paul decided to quit, and in 1997 he appeared alongside Brad Pitt and Harrison Ford in *The Devil's Own*, a thriller about the militant (some say terrorist) Irish Republican Army. One widely circulated story tells of Ronan visiting her father on the set and being carried around by Pitt, but she has no real memory of the incident. "[I remember mainly] unimportant things," she told Xan Brooks for the *Guardian* (22 Jan. 2010), speaking about her childhood. "I remember my dad's friend showing me a little spider in a box that shook its legs, and me getting scared. That, and going to Toys R Us. My mam used to drive me to this huge Toys R Us store outside town. Not to buy anything, but just as an outing, to look at things."

When Ronan was three years old, the family moved back to Ireland, to county Carlow, reasoning that it would be easier for Paul to find acting jobs on his home turf. He did, indeed, find a relatively steady stream of small parts, but the family still struggled financially on occasion.

Ronan proved to be an exceptionally inventive child. "I used to make up stories," she told Yvonne Villarreal for the *Los Angeles Times* (10 Dec. 2009). "Little soap operas. Polly Pocket's boyfriend was Woody from *Toy Story*. They were together for a very long time—since high school, actually. In college, he had an affair. It was very complex—things that probably a seven-year-old shouldn't have been imagining. I was a weird gal."

EARLY CAREER

At the age of eight, Ronan won a recurring role on the prime-time medical drama *The Clinic* in 2003 and 2004, which portrayed the soap opera–like lives of the staff at a Dublin health center. She followed that with a stint on the 2005 television crime thriller *Proof*, which also aired during prime time. As her fame grew, Ronan found it problematic to attend school and instead embarked on a course of home study. "The reason was teachers giving me a hard time," she recalled to Brooks. "Some of the students were, you know, mean. But I only stayed a while. It wasn't really working out. You know, the school is a good school and the people who go there are good people. But when your schoolmates recognize you before they've met you, and the teachers do, too, it can make things very awkward and difficult."

Ronan made her Hollywood debut in the Michelle Pfeiffer vehicle *I Could Never Be Your Woman*, a romantic comedy shot in 2005 and released straight to video in 2007. While critics were united in their dismissal of the formulaic picture, many mentioned Ronan's naturalistic portrayal of a young teen and devoted a portion of their reviews to describing her luminous blue eyes. Others marveled at her uncanny ability to mimic an American accent, despite the heavy Irish brogue in which she normally speaks.

GETTING SERIOUS

While the much-delayed release of *I Could Never Be Your Woman* proved something of a disappointment, 2007 marked a turning point

for Ronan. That year she appeared in the award-winning romantic drama *Atonement*, directed by Joe Wright and starring Keira Knightley and James McAvoy. The film was nominated for best picture at the Academy Awards and won the best film award from the British Academy of Film and Television Arts (BAFTA). Ronan played Briony Tallis, a wealthy thirteen-year-old British girl who sets in motion a tragic series of events when she misconstrues the relationship between her older sister and the son of the family housekeeper. Based on the novel by Ian McEwan, *Atonement* received enthusiastic reviews, including raves for Ronan. In an assessment for *Rolling Stone* (14 Dec. 2007), for example, Peter Travers wrote that in an early scene viewers "learn that the film will be seen entirely through Briony's eyes. And what eyes!" He added: "Ronan is the film's glory. Note to Oscar: This is acting of the highest order. Ronan simply takes your breath away." The Academy did, indeed, take note, and Ronan joined the ranks of Tatum O'Neill, Keisha Castle-Hughes, and Abigail Breslin as one of the youngest actors ever to receive an Oscar nomination at the time. Ronan ultimately lost the Academy Award for best supporting actress to Tilda Swinton.

Later that year Ronan was featured in *Death Defying Acts*, an Australian film that tells the story of famed magician Harry Houdini's improbable love affair with a duplicitous psychic. Ronan returned to Hollywood in 2008 to star in *City of Ember*, based on a dystopian novel of the same name and costarring Harry Treadaway. Even those critics who had reservations about the source material—a popular but by-the-numbers work of science fiction geared toward teens—found no fault with Ronan. "The young actors, Ronan (*Atonement*) and Harry Treadaway, couldn't be better," Mick LaSalle wrote for the *San Francisco Chronicle* (10 Oct. 2008). "If you have any reservations about going to a movie starring two teenagers, put them aside."

Notices were similarly favorable for Ronan in her next outing, *The Lovely Bones* (2009), which was also based on a best-selling book. Ronan portrayed Susie Salmon, a fourteen-year-old Pennsylvania girl who has been raped and murdered by a neighbor. She narrates from a heaven-like place she calls the "in-between" as her family and friends attempt to deal with their grief and track down her killer. While many reviewers disliked the premise, they had copious praise for Ronan. Stephanie Zacharek cited her as an example of "perfect casting" in *Salon* (10 Dec. 2009), and in *Rolling Stone* (11 Dec. 2009), Peter Travers lauded her "remarkable performance." Although *Atonement*'s subject matter had been far from light-hearted, Ronan felt that this was her most serious, important role to date. "This was the first time I felt like a grown-up and really absorbed the material," she told Scott Bowles for *USA Today* (8 Dec. 2009).

MORE MATURE ROLES

After providing the voice of the main character for the British release of the animated Japanese film *The Secret World of Arrietty* (2010), Ronan played a young Polish orphan in *The Way Back*, a little-seen 2010 film about a group of escapees from a Siberian gulag.

The following year she had the lead in *Hanna*, the story of a girl who has been trained as an assassin by her father, a former intelligence operative, played by Eric Bana. Ronan underwent a grueling course of physical conditioning for the role, including martial arts and weight lifting. The thriller also saw her once again working with director Joe Wright. *Hanna* received generally positive reviews and was praised for its action and performances. When she subsequently starred as a killer in *Violet & Daisy* (2011), Anthony Breznican wrote for *Entertainment Weekly* (7 Apr. 2011), "What is it about this starry-eyed young actress that makes directors see a monster? . . . [She has become] the go-to actress for sinister characters with a sweetheart veneer."

Ronan's next sinister character was that of a vampire in the stylish horror film *Byzantium* (2012), and the following year she took on a difficult dual role in *The Host*, based on a book by Stephenie Meyer of *Twilight* fame. On the prospect of becoming as well known as the actors from Meyer's earlier franchise, Ronan told Sophie Wilson, "If you're in a place you're going to get that kind of attention it would be too much, but I think because of where I live . . . hopefully it will be OK." *The Host*, a film about an alien race whose members dislodge humans from their bodies and erase their memories, did not prove to be a blockbuster on par with the *Twilight* films and grossed a relatively disappointing $26 million in the United States. Expectations were more reasonable for Ronan's next effort, *How I Live Now*, a British coming-of-age drama shown on the festival circuit.

In early 2014 Ronan appeared as part of an ensemble cast in Wes Anderson's film *The Grand Budapest Hotel*. She was also cast in actor Ryan Gosling's directorial debut, *How to Catch a Monster*, which is slated for release in 2014.

RESPONSE FROM DIRECTORS

In addition to being a darling of film critics, Ronan is consistently praised by her coworkers and directors. "The amazing thing about Saoirse is that she acts from her imagination," Joe Wright told Peter Debruge for *Variety* (4 Oct. 2007). "She isn't involved in emotional recall. I like actors who work with their imagination rather than their own crap."

"She was only thirteen years old when we filmed," Stanley Tucci, who played the murderer in *The Lovely Bones*, told Yvonne Villarreal. "How someone acquires that kind of maturity as an actress at such a young age is remarkable. I can't imagine it. She handles herself as well as any seasoned actor. I wouldn't even be able to finish a sentence at her age." Peter Jackson, the director of the film, agreed, explaining to Scott Bowles, "We honestly assumed it would be an American actress. Then we get this beautifully shot DVD of a girl with a perfect American accent, doing dialogue from the book. There wasn't much point in continuing the search." He concluded, "In a way, I like to think that Susie Salmon found us."

PERSONAL LIFE

Ronan discourages journalists who ask about her love life. "My personal life is private and the thing for me is that people know me for the films that I'm in, more so than who I am," she told Alexandra Ryan for the *Irish Evening Herald* (28 Dec. 2011). Ronan, who only recently began traveling to movie sets without the supervision of one of her parents, does not mind being considered a role model for young fans and has asserted that she will never behave in a way that would invite negative tabloid attention.

While she will not talk about possible love interests, Ronan is happy to speak about her border collie, Sassie. The actor is an ardent supporter of the Irish Blue Cross, an animal-care philanthropy known for its mobile clinics. She credits the group with reuniting her with her pet, who once ran away and was taken to a Blue Cross facility.

Discussing her choice of profession, she told Martyn Palmer for the *Daily Mail* (6 May 2011), "I don't feel I've had to grow up faster because of my job. In a way, it helps to be a child, because children always act—it's natural to pretend. Being around adults and involved in in-depth stories and thinking about characters has certainly helped me to mature. But I've always been kind of mature anyway, without forgetting that I'm still young."

Ronan would one day like to study film or art history at New York University.

SUGGESTED READING

Brooks, Xan. "Saoirse Ronan: A Name to Reckon With." *Guardian*. Guardian News and Media, 22 Jan. 2010. Web. 28 Jan. 2014.

Debruge, Peter. "Atonement Actress Creating 'Lovely' Buzz." *Variety*. Variety Media, 4 Oct. 2007. Web. 28 Jan. 2014.

Johnston, Sheila. "Saoirse Ronan: On Set with Brad, Keira and Michelle." *Telegraph*. Telegraph Media Group, 2 Feb. 2008. Web. 28 Jan. 2014.

Osenlund, R. Kurt. "Interview: Saoirse Ronan." *Slant Magazine*. Slant Magazine, 7 Nov. 2013. Web. 28 Jan. 2014.

Palmer, Martyn. "Actress Saoirse Ronan." *Daily Mail*. Associated Newspapers, 6 May 2011. Web. 17 Mar. 2014.

Villarreal, Yvonne. "Saoirse Ronan of The Lovely Bones Stays on Balance." *Los Angeles Times*. Los Angeles Times, 10 Dec. 2009. Web. 28 Jan. 2014.

Wilson, Sophie. "Saoirse Ronan Interview for The Host." *Telegraph*. Telegraph Media Group, 29 Mar. 2013. Web. 28 Jan. 2014.

SELECTED WORKS

I Could Never Be Your Woman, 2007; *Atonement*, 2007; *City of Ember*, 2008; *The Lovely Bones*, 2009; *The Way Back*, 2010; *Hanna*, 2011; *Violet & Daisy*, 2011; *Byzantium*, 2012; *The Host*, 2013; *How I Live Now*, 2013; *The Grand Budapest Hotel*, 2014

—*Mari Rich*

Robert Pitts/Landov

Hans Rosling

Born: July 27, 1948
Occupation: Global health expert and statistician

Since Hans Rosling became popular on the video-sharing website YouTube with his eye-catching and thought-provoking presentations on global socioeconomic trends, journalists have been commenting on the unlikelihood of his fame. "The concept of a 'celebrity statistician' might sound as though it must be—and should forever remain—an oxymoron," Edwin Smith wrote for the London *Telegraph* (7 Nov. 2013). "But watch Prof. Hans Rosling in full flow, commentating on a moving hologram that illustrates the health, wealth, and population of two hundred countries over two hundred years in less than a minute, and you may change your mind."

Rosling prepares his presentations—which sometimes involve Lego blocks, coffee cups, and other props—with Trendalyzer, the data-visualization software that he helped develop. Trendalyzer, which was purchased in 2007 by Google, employs moving bubbles, bright colors, and flowing curves to compellingly illustrate reams of data that might otherwise be described as dry. Now the self-styled "edutainer" of the nonprofit Gapminder Foundation, which promotes itself not as a think tank but as a "fact tank that promotes a fact-based world view," Rosling believes that understanding global data is essential for everyone and that having accurate data can change a person's entire perspective. The data prove, he asserts, that the idea of a planet divided into "us" and "them" is wrong. "The old concept of the Western world and developing world is very strong," he told Ray Suarez for *PBS NewsHour*

(30 Jan. 2012). In fact, he asserted, Asia and Africa "are customers. These are partners. And prosperity in the rest of the world means more peace. . . . So it's sort of a new vision about the world we must have."

Whether they are ready to embrace that new vision or not, millions have viewed Rosling's videos, and his appeal is often compared to that of famous figures in the entertainment world. As Kate Allen wrote for the *Financial Times* (17 Jan. 2014), "Rosling has been described as . . . the closest thing statisticians have to a rock star."

EARLY YEARS AND EDUCATION

Hans Rosling was born on July 27, 1948, and raised in Uppsala, a Swedish city about forty miles north of Stockholm. His father had a blue-collar job roasting coffee beans, which helped Rosling develop an interest in global issues from an early age. "This all started when I was four," he told Annie Maccoby Berglof for the *Financial Times* (26 Apr. 2013). "My father . . . came home with coins in his pocket that people had dropped in by accident while drying the coffee beans in Guatemala, Brazil, east Africa. And he would open an atlas and tell me about the conditions of the coffee-pickers across the world." Years later, at fifteen, Rosling would set out to see more of the world for himself, biking across England and Denmark.

Rosling, the first in his family to receive higher education, attended Uppsala University and earned an undergraduate degree in statistics in 1967. He remained at the university to pursue a medical degree but had something of a rude awakening when he traveled to

Bangalore, India, in 1972 as a guest student taking a monthlong course in public health at St. John's Medical College. "That changed my mindset forever," he said during a November 2009 TEDIndia talk titled "Asia's Rise: How and When." Rosling explained, "It was not the course content in itself that changed the mindset. It was the brutal realization, the first morning, that the Indian students were better than me. . . . Indian students studied harder than we did in Sweden. They read the textbook twice, or three times or four times. In Sweden we read it once and then we went party[ing]." He concluded, "That personal experience was the first time in my life that the mindset I grew up with was changed. And I realized that perhaps the Western world will not continue to dominate the world forever."

Rosling earned his medical degree from Uppsala in 1974. In 1977 he took an intensive yearlong course in international aid and disaster relief in Sandö, Sweden. His other degrees include a diploma in nutrition, public health, and tropical medicine (1978) and a PhD in medical sciences (1986), both from Uppsala University.

PHYSICIAN AND EDUCATOR

From 1979 to 1981 Rosling worked as a district medical officer in Nacala, on the northern coast of Mozambique. He and a colleague "were only two doctors for three hundred thousand people in my district," he recalled to Berglof. "One year I was alone. [At the same time] in Sweden there were eight hundred doctors for three hundred thousand. I'm still recuperating from the numerical trauma."

One day Rosling heard from a remote clinic about a large group of women and children suffering from an unidentified disease whose symptoms included paralysis of the lower body. He and a team of Swedish scientists discovered that the condition, which they called "konzo," was the result of eating improperly prepared bitter cassava root, which has toxic effects if not carefully processed. Outbreaks occurred during times of famine, when the hearty crop provided virtually the only source of nutrition for some of Africa's inhabitants. Over the next decade Rosling investigated several more outbreaks of the disease in poor, rural areas of the continent. (He explained to Berglof that he is one of only a handful of "toxico-nutritional neuro-epidemiologists" in the world, referring to those who apply epidemiological methods to study neurological disorders that arise from exposure to toxins and from malnutrition.)

Rosling's travels have not been confined to Africa; in 1993, for example, he was approached by officials at the Cuban embassy in Sweden and asked to visit the island nation to investigate a major outbreak of neuropathy, a condition involving damage to the nerves. Once there Rosling personally met Communist leader Fidel Castro, who quizzed him on his qualifications and methodologies. He ended up staying for three months at the invitation of the minister of health and the head of the armed forces.

In addition to his global medical research, Rosling has held several academic posts. From 1983 to 1996 he was a lecturer in international health at Uppsala University, and in 1997 he became a professor of international health at Sweden's Karolinska Institutet, a world-renowned medical school. He has also advised the World Health Organization (WHO) and the United Nations Children's Fund (UNICEF) and helped establish the Swedish arm of the humanitarian group Médecins Sans Frontières (Doctors Without Borders).

DATA VISUALIZATION

While teaching at Uppsala, Rosling sometimes became frustrated by the difficulties of conveying important information to his classes. "I used to make huge photocopied sheets of UNICEF statistics for the students on income, life expectancy, and fertility rates around the planet," he recalled to Mark Harris for the Economist Technology Quarterly (11 Dec. 2010). "But it didn't change their world view, it didn't create another mindset. They still insisted that we [in the West] were different."

Inspired in part by the nurse Florence Nightingale, who had devised a new type of pie chart to illustrate how many soldiers were dying in the Crimean War from wounds sustained in battle and how many were dying of infections that could be prevented with proper hospital hygiene, Rosling set about trying to find a way to convey large sets of data in a compelling way. The first chart he designed featured bubbles, with income displayed on one axis and health on the other. He then approached his son, Ola Rosling, and his daughter-in-law, Anna Rosling Rönnlund, both technically adept art students. Together they came up with software to animate the bubbles and to create "trails" for them that somewhat resemble footprints in snow. They dubbed the program Trendalyzer. "It was a conscious intent to make the data look alive," Rosling explained to Harris. "You can see how countries have changed. And we could overlay countries historically so that it's clear that, for example, China today is like Sweden in 1948 and people in Vietnam now have the same life expectancy as Americans did in 1985. Every country has a graphical path that describes its development." Colors, shapes, and sizes, he has pointed out, are much less cognitively demanding to absorb than lists of numbers. "I call our approach 'fact-based vulgar simplification,'" he quipped, as reported by Fast Company (18 May 2011). "We look like a tabloid newspaper from the front but a university from the back."

GAPMINDER FOUNDATION

On February 25, 2005, the trio founded the Gapminder Foundation, basing the name on the London Underground announcement to "mind the gap"—in this case, the gap between a well-informed view of the world and an outdated one built on misconceptions. Their aim was to collate huge amounts of data from multiple sources, analyze it for patterns, and present it in a format that anyone could understand using Trendalyzer. Not every source they wanted to use was cooperative; the World Bank, for example, threatened legal action against Rosling were he to publicize their global development data and relented only after years of lobbying. "Most public data was not made available in a license where you were allowed to redistribute it. Neither was it in a unified structure or technological format," Rosling told Harris. "I had to become the Robin Hood for free data. At the Gapminder Foundation, we won't display any data that is not freely available to everyone."

Despite his passionate social views, Rosling avoids advocacy work on other issues, preferring that his audience draw their own conclusions from his data. "We are not for or against nuclear power, we are not for or against carbon capture, we are not for or against this or that," he told Allen. "We do not say that HIV is a bigger problem than female illiteracy. We show how much HIV there is, and how much female illiteracy there is." He reiterated the point for Harris, stating emphatically, "I produce a road map for the modern world. Where people want to drive is up to them. But I have the idea that if they have a proper road map, they'll make better decisions."

BECOMING AN EDUTAINER

In 2006 Rosling was invited to speak at the annual Technology, Entertainment, and Design (TED) conference, dedicated to presenting lectures from innovative thinkers in a variety of fields. His talk, "The Best Stats You've Ever Seen"—in which he discussed recent global changes in fertility, life expectancy, child survival, and poverty by nation and debunked several myths about the so-called third world—quickly went viral and has since been seen by more than eight million people.

Many observers have attributed the large viewership not only to Rosling's compulsively watchable animations but also to his enthusiastic manner of speaking. In a piece for the National Institutes of Health's online newsletter, the *NIH Record* (2 Apr. 2010), Valerie Lambros wrote of one performance, "Starting the graph, he called the action like an announcer at Churchill Downs: 'Vaccinations being applied in Asia. . . . That is the great leap forward by Mao Zedong which caused the famine . . . now China is getting it into order with family planning and the family size is decreasing, and India is trying

to follow there and see the miracle of Bangladesh! Bangladesh is coming there and they are going." By the time the bubbles stopped, in a total time of about thirty seconds, Rosling had "traversed a half-century of data and displayed the reality of today's life-expectancy figures," Lambros noted.

After working closely with Google on Trendalyzer for some time, Rosling reached an agreement with the company in March 2007. Google acquired the software, and a new version, Google Motion Chart, is now available free of charge on the web. The deal enabled Gapminder to become nonprofit and freed Rosling to focus on education. Rosling has since given several other TED talks, each of which attracted millions of viewers, and has also appeared in the BBC documentaries *The Joy of Stats*, which aired in 2013, and *Don't Panic: The Truth about Population*, which aired in March 2014. He hopes his audiences appreciate that he is neither an optimist nor a pessimist but what he calls a "possibilist." He told Harris, "We can stop population growth, we can eradicate poverty, we can solve the energy and the climate issues, but we have to make the right investments. I know a good world is possible if we leave emotion aside and just work analytically."

PERSONAL LIFE

Rosling is married to Agneta Thordeman, a child and adolescent psychiatrist. They divide their time between homes in Uppsala and Stockholm. (Their Stockholm apartment was once occupied by famed Swedish director Ingmar Bergman.) In addition to their son, Ola, the couple have two other children.

When he was thirty, Rosling had metastatic testicular cancer, and although he recovered, his brush with mortality changed him. "I spent a year of my life preparing for dying," he told Shanna Carpenter for *TED Blog* (15 May 2009). "That made me more relaxed with other people and kinder. I was quite nasty with people when I was young. This helped. It calmed me down."

In medical school, Rosling once saw an x-ray of a sword-swallower and became determined to learn the trick. He is one of only five member of the Sword Swallowers Association International and sometimes swallows his 1815 Swedish Army bayonet during his presentations.

SUGGESTED READING

Allen, Kate. "Hans Rosling: Data Rock Star." *Financial Times*. Financial Times, 17 Jan. 2014. Web. 15 July 2014.

Berglof, Annie Maccoby. "At Home: Statistician Hans Rosling." *Financial Times*. Financial Times, 26 Apr. 2013. Web. 15 July 2014.

Harris, Mark. "Making Data Dance." *Economist Technology Quarterly* 11 Dec. 2010: 19–20. Print.

Katiyar, Arun. "Do Your Numbers Tell a Story?" *Livemint.* HT Media, 20 Aug. 2013. Web. 15 July 2014.

Provost, Claire. "Hans Rosling: The Man Who's Making Data Cool." *Guardian.* Guardian News and Media, 17 May 2013. Web. 15 July 2014.

Rosling, Hans. "Hans Rosling Brings Life, Humor, Sword-Swallowing to Global Health Statistics." Interview by Ray Suarez. *PBS NewsHour.* NewsHour, 30 Jan. 2012. Web. 15 July 2014.

Singer, Natasha. "When the Data Struts Its Stuff." *New York Times.* New York Times, 2 Apr. 2011. Web. 15 July 2014.

—*Mari Rich*

Renzo Rosso

Born: September 15, 1955
Occupation: Fashion entrepreneur

For those born after the 1970s, it might be hard to believe that denim jeans were once purchased pristine and stiff and that achieving a raggedy state of soft comfort required wearing them repeatedly. The phenomenon of predistressed denim, with its faded spots, rips, and fraying, is widely credited to Renzo Rosso, the head of the popular brand Diesel. Rosso—who is often quoted as saying, "Diesel is not my company, it's my life"—explained to Meredith Bryan for the *New York Observer* (7 Feb. 2008) that "we spend a lot of money on the treatment. The treatment is sometimes two times more expensive than the fabrics and the manufacturing. Denim is the only fabric you can transform with the treatment. So denim for me is special, and very unique."

© Alessandra Benedetti/Corbis

Famously referred to as the Jeans Genius by influential fashion critic Suzy Menkes, Rosso has built Diesel and its holding company, Only the Brave (OTB), into a multibillion-dollar concern that encompasses such products as sunglasses, perfume, and home furnishings. "Thirty years ago we were the first brand to introduce the premium denim concept," Rosso told Mark Patiky for *Forbes* (14 Mar. 2013), adding, "We proposed a new way to wear denim—in any occasion. We didn't just sell a new product, we choose to sell a new lifestyle."

EARLY YEARS

Renzo Rosso was born on September 15, 1955, in the village of Brugine, in the northeastern Italian region of Veneto. His father, Vittorio, and mother, Fortunata, earned their living as farmers. The youngest child of three, he has a brother, Giuseppe, and a sister, Gianna. The entire village reportedly had only two television sets and one car during the years in which Rosso was a child. There was an American army base nearby, and he has recalled the kindness of its personnel. "One day, in front of my house, some soldiers in a big Cadillac started to do a picnic," he told Lauren Collins for *W* magazine (22 Aug. 2013). "I looked at them like they were coming from the moon. I remember they gave me a box of rice pudding—that, for me, was the American Dream."

Another oft-repeated tale of his childhood holds that one day when Rosso was about twelve years old, a generous classmate named Walter, whose father bred rabbits, provided him with a plump one meant to be slaughtered and eaten. Within a short time it became evident that the animal was not simply heavy but pregnant. A less entrepreneurial youngster might still have turned the rabbit over to his mother for a family dinner, but Rosso saw a business opportunity. He purchased chicken wire, built cages, and rigged up a rudimentary feeding-and-watering system using old plastic bottles. Over the next year he raised hundreds of rabbits, which he regularly sold at a local marketplace.

EDUCATION

Despite that entrepreneurial zeal, Rosso was not an especially motivated student. He was more concerned with meeting girls, playing the electric guitar in an amateur rock band, and immersing himself in American pop culture whenever possible. Not wanting to become a farmer like his father and older brother, however, he knew he needed to remain in school. Fortuitously, he heard about a technical school in Padua called the Instituto Marconi, which offered courses in becoming a manufacturing consultant. The region had many textile companies, and the courses were being taught by industry professionals rather than ivory-tower academics—a factor

Rosso found appealing. He has also admitted that he had heard that the course of study was an easy one, and that clinched the decision. At the institute he learned how to make patterns, cut fabric, and assemble the pieces into finished garments.

When he was fifteen years old, another event that has become a part of his legend occurred. A friend obtained a good quantity of denim imported from the United States and gave it to Rosso, who decided to make himself a pair of pants. Using his mother's Singer sewing machine, he crafted a pair of tight-fitting bell-bottom jeans, with hems that flared out almost seventeen inches. (He forgot to sew a flap behind the zipper, making fastening the pants a harrowing experience each time he wore them.) Finding the denim uncomfortably stiff, he rubbed them on a piece of concrete he found in the yard of the family farmhouse, a move that foreshadowed his later work.

His friends and classmates loved the jeans, and Rosso found himself running something of a cottage industry, selling his creations for 3,500 lire a pair (equivalent to about €1.8 or $2.50 in 2014).

ENTRY INTO THE PROFESSIONAL FASHION INDUSTRY

After finishing his classes at the Instituto Marconi in 1975, Rosso, then twenty years old, found a job with Moltex, a manufacturing company owned by Adriano Goldschmied. With no practical experience aside from making jeans for his friends, Rosso floundered in the job, which involved overseeing a production line with eighteen workers. He eventually improved somewhat under the tutelage of a more experienced friend in the industry, but Rosso has admitted that he preferred having fun to working and never gave the job his full attention. Unsurprisingly, within two years Goldschmied decided to fire him.

A contrite Rosso pleaded to keep his job and promised that he would turn matters around. Goldschmied's wife was fond of the young employee and persuaded her husband to give him a second chance. As a precaution, Goldschmied decided to tie Rosso's salary to his performance. True to his word (and spurred on by the financial incentive), Rosso doubled production within a week.

In 1978 Goldschmied offered Rosso a 40 percent stake in the company, which Rosso accepted, with the help of a loan from his father. Although Moltex already had several popular brands under its umbrella, including Daily Blue and Replay, the two conceived of a bold new brand, which they dubbed Diesel. "I liked the name Diesel because it was short, international, and it was pronounced the same way almost everywhere in the world," Rosso wrote in his book *Be Stupid: For Successful Living*, a combination

memoir and business advice book published by Rizzoli in 2011. "Also this was during the oil crisis, and diesel, more economical than gasoline, was the true alternative energy at the time."

In 1985 Rosso offered to buy out Goldschmied's share of Diesel for $500,000 plus his interest in the company's other brands. The older man, wanting to focus on his more established brands and reportedly still unconvinced of Diesel's promise, readily agreed.

DIESEL TAKES OFF

Since abandoning his youthful tendency to ignore work in favor of partying, Rosso had gained a reputation as a solid businessman and had developed several valuable commercial relationships. He was thus able to borrow the money he needed to push Diesel to global prominence. "I was ready for anything, even failure, and I figured in the worst-case scenario I'd just run off to a deserted island," he wrote in *Be Stupid* (2011). "Up until 1985 I'd just been responsible for managing the brand, but now I owned it and could make exactly the product I wanted. As I was convinced that I was going to go bankrupt in less than a year, I decided to indulge all my crazy ideas—including my passion for vintage jeans."

Retailers sometimes returned the distressed denim garments, thinking that their shipments had somehow been damaged en route. Even once it had been made clear to them that the faded spots and rips had been made intentionally, many were reluctant to stock Diesel items; consumers, they felt, would not find the jeans appealing—particularly not at the price Rosso was asking. At a time when a luxury brand like Ralph Lauren was selling for about fifty dollars a pair, the cheapest Diesel jeans cost one hundred.

Rosso bargained with distributors and store owners: if the jeans did not sell, he assured them, he would be happy to take them back. He was never called upon to do so, however. Contrary to predictions, the jeans flew off store shelves, and Rosso's revenue skyrocketed from $2.8 million to $10.8 million in the first year alone. In 1987 that figure jumped to more than $25 million. "Denim was once casual, a working-class, down-and-dirty product," Marshal Cohen, a respected apparel-industry analyst, explained to Clare O'Connor for *Forbes* (25 Mar. 2013). "All of a sudden [in the mid-1980s] it was the antithesis. It could be sexy and special. Ralph Lauren himself wore a sports jacket with denim. What Diesel did was create the quest for the perfect pair of jeans. As other designers entered the market, it only propelled it."

BE STUPID AND OTHER AD CAMPAIGNS

Diesel's growth was fueled in part by its edgy, provocative advertising. In 2001, for example, the company launched a print campaign in the form of a fictitious newspaper called the *Daily African*, in which denim-clad black models posed under such headlines as "African Expedition to Explore Unknown Europe by Foot." The ad campaign took home that year's grand prize at the International Advertising Festival in Cannes. Another campaign encouraged consumers to "Save yourself (drink urine)," presumably a cynical comment on the lengths to which people will go to remain young, while others featured a man sawing a female mannequin in half (eliciting protests that Rosso was encouraging violence toward women) and a trio whipping each other so that the welts formed tic-tac-toe patterns.

Among the company's most talked-about campaigns was Be Stupid, first mounted in 2010. The ads featured, among other images, a woman standing in the road with her vision obscured by the traffic cone she is wearing on her head and a bikini-clad woman obliviously taking a photo while a lion creeps up behind her. The Be Stupid campaign earned Rosso another Cannes grand prize.

BUILDING A CONGLOMERATE

The Diesel brand began major international expansion in the early 1990s, opening its New York City flagship store in 1996. Diesel also expanded its line outside of jeans in the mid-1990s, first producing sunglasses in 1995 and then wristwatches shortly after. While denim remains a cornerstone of the Diesel brand, consumers can purchase these Diesel accessories as well as perfume, sofas, and many other products. There are approximately four hundred stand-alone stores in eighty countries around the globe, including India, China, and Israel. Rosso employs more than six thousand people, and in 2012 Diesel generated approximately $1.7 billion in sales. (Rosso's personal wealth is said to be $3 billion.)

Rosso's holding company oversees not only Diesel but also a number of other prestigious brands he has acquired over the years, including DSquared (2000), Viktor & Rolf (2008), and Marni (2012). Among his most-buzzed about acquisitions was that of the Belgian designer Martin Margiela's line in 2002. Rosso responded criticisms of the acquisition by telling Robert Murphy for *Women's Wear Daily* (5 Sept. 2002), "I'm not buying a fashion company like other groups have done. I'm investing in Margiela so two friends can work together to grow a very special brand." Nevertheless, Murphy wondered about the impetus behind the move, noting in a November 4, 2002, article the disparities between the two companies: "Diesel creates crazy, controversial advertisements with creepy masked models and kissing clergy, while the ever-ephemeral Margiela doesn't even put his name on the label." On Rosso's advice, Maison Martin Margiela added accessories and perfume to its offerings, and revenues burgeoned; the line had been worth $20 million in 2002, and within a decade that number grew to $100 million. (Margiela himself left the company in 2009. The line has since been designed by a large roster of young talent but retains its cult following.) All told, Rosso owns a reported fifteen lines, twelve licenses, and nineteen subsidiaries.

BOOKS AND WINE

In addition to writing *Be Stupid: For Successful Living*, Rosso contributed to *Fifty*, a book published in 2005 to celebrate his fiftieth birthday. The book features key moments in Diesel's history, an examination of the company's retail philosophy, a profile of Rosso, and interviews between him and a group of iconoclastic figures, including the Dalai Lama, singer Bono, and designer Alexander McQueen.

Besides dabbling in writing, Rosso is something of a vintner. In the mid-1990s he purchased a 260-acre vineyard in the Marostica hills of Italy, and a few select restaurants serve his wines. He has joked that his late father, unconvinced that his son could really make millions of dollars a year selling jeans, was relieved upon learning of the vineyard.

PERSONAL LIFE AND STYLE

Rosso, who is by all accounts exceptionally family-oriented, has been married twice and has six children: Andrea, Stefano, Alessia, twins Asia and Luna, and India. Andrea and Stefano work for Only the Brave and are slated to take over the company if Rosso retires.

Rosso is known for his unruly blond curls (which have been graying) and luminous blue eyes. He has several tattoos, including the Mohican face that serves as the Only the Brave logo, the distinctive Margiela four-stitch motif, and the lowercase initials rr (on two fingers of his right hand). He can often be found in T-shirts and Diesel jeans, although, as Collins wrote, "A few years back, at the Cannes Film Festival, he was photographed welcoming some models for lunch on the deck of his yacht . . . wearing sunglasses, a ski cap, a muscle shirt, and what were either gym shorts or hot pants."

In addition to the vineyard, Rosso owns an antique-filled seventeenth-century villa in the heart of Bassano del Grappa, not far from his childhood home. His outside interests include soccer (he plays in an over-fifty league) and cars—he collaborated with Fiat to design a special-edition Diesel-branded sports model, a version of the Fiat 500 released in 2008. Rosso considers himself a relatively down-to-earth person despite his immense wealth and told Collins, "I hate this thing, the people who are going around with bodyguards, just because they think it looks cool. I vomit against that."

Rosso's philanthropic activities are conducted under the auspices of his Only the Brave

Foundation, which funds a wide variety of social, health care–related, and educational causes. In December 2012 he pledged to donate €5 million ($6.5 million) to the city of Venice to aid in the restoration of the Ponte di Rialto, an important sixteenth-century bridge.

SUGGESTED READING

Collins, Lauren. "Renzo Rosso: Rags to Riches." *W.* Condé Nast, 22 Aug. 2013. Web. 29 Jan. 2014.

McCormack, Nicola. "Fueller of Fashion." *Herald*. Herald & Times Group, 3 June 2006. Web. 29 Jan. 2014.

Menkes, Suzy. "Renzo Rosso, Jeans Genius." *International Herald Tribune*. New York Times, 30 Sept. 2003. Web. 29 Jan. 2014.

O'Connor, Clare. "Blue Jean Billionaire: Inside Diesel, Renzo Rosso's $3 Billion Fashion Empire." *Forbes*. Forbes, 25 Mar. 2013. Web. 22 Dec. 2013.

Rosso, Renzo. "CEO Talk: Renzo Rosso, Chairman, Only the Brave." Interview by Imran Amed. *Business of Fashion*. Business of Fashion, 4 Apr. 2013. Web. 29 Jan. 2014.

—*Mari Rich*

Carlos Ruiz Zafón

Born: September 25, 1964
Occupation: Novelist

Carlos Ruiz Zafón is the author of seven novels, including the best-selling Cemetery of Forgotten Books series. His books for adults and young adults have been translated into more than forty languages and have sold tens of millions of copies around the world. The Spanish novelist believes that much of his success stems from the fact that he is a devotee of great nineteenth-century authors such as Émile Zola, Honoré de Balzac, and Charles Dickens, for whom narrative drive and full-bodied characters were as important as impeccably beautiful writing. He has little regard for authors who prefer verbal gymnastics to genuine storytelling. "The entire world you are stepping into as a reader must feel real. It must have resonance, you must be able to touch the light; smell the smells," Ruiz Zafón told Nigel Farndale in an interview for the *Telegraph* (27 Nov. 2005). "You have to work hard to create this illusion. You have to seduce the reader, manipulate their mind and heart, listen to the music of language." Asked what elements he believes have made his books so widely popular, Ruiz Zafón added, "We want an intense experience, so that we can forget ourselves when we enter the world of the book. When you are reading, the physical object of the book should

Robert Marquardt/Getty Images

disappear from your hands. The writer must subjugate his ego: not advertise himself by saying 'look how clever this sentence is.'"

In his own writing, Ruiz Zafón seeks to combine such nineteenth-century novelistic characteristics with the skills he mastered while working as a screenwriter in Hollywood, striving to ensure that what he writes can be seen in the most cinematic way possible. He is particularly fascinated with the atmospheric films of Orson Welles, with which his novels have been compared, as well as the period of the early to mid-twentieth century, in which a great deal of his fiction takes place. He believes that much of that era says a great deal about human nature. "There's something about that period that's epic and tragic. There's a point after the industrial period where it seems like humanity's finally going to make it right," he explained to Gilbert Cruz in an interview for *Time* magazine (30 June 2009). "There were advances in medicine and technology and education. People are going to be able to live longer lives; literacy is starting to spread. It seemed like finally, after centuries of toiling and misery, that humanity was going to get to a better stage. And then what happens is precisely the contrary. Humanity betrays itself."

EARLY LIFE

The youngest of three brothers, Carlos Ruiz Zafón was born on September 25, 1964, in Barcelona, Spain, during the dictatorship of Francisco Franco, who ruled Spain from the end of the Spanish Civil War in 1939 until his death in 1975. Growing up under an oppressive regime that suppressed any and all dissent left an indelible imprint on the future author. "Franco's regime is interesting because it was the only Fascist dictatorship that survived in Europe. Franco was ruthless. He was a man interested in power; he was not an ideological man," he remarked to Christian House for the *Independent* (24 June 2012). "He died in bed. How many dictators in the 20th century have died in bed? Most of them end up in apocalyptic scenes of horror."

Ruiz Zafón's father, an insurance salesman, grew up impoverished during the Spanish Civil War and spent much of his life struggling financially—although he admitted to his son that he once wanted to be poet. Like his father, Ruiz Zafón was also interested in language and writing from an early age. "My childhood was surrounded by books and writing. From a very early age I was fascinated by storytelling, by the printed word, by language, by ideas. So I would seek them out," he explained to Cruz. "Even before I learned to read and write, I was telling stories. I always knew that I was going to be a writer because there was no other choice. I was always fascinated by the fact that you could take paper and ink and create worlds, images, characters. It seemed like magic." Yet despite this similarity to his father, the author often felt isolated as a child because he believed his parents and two older brothers did not know what to make of him. "The things that interested me were different. I was interested in books, music and films. They were an escape for me, from an environment that I found boring and where I didn't feel I fitted in," he explained to Farndale.

LITERARY ASPIRATIONS

Ruiz Zafón felt like an outsider, both at home and in school. He did, however, feel particularly comfortable in the literary worlds created by such authors as J. R. R. Tolkien, Charles Dickens, Gustave Flaubert, and Stephen King, as well as in the cinematic worlds of directors such as Orson Welles, Steven Spielberg, Ridley Scott, and Francis Ford Coppola. He has also cited the novels of classic noir authors Raymond Chandler and James M. Cain as major sources of inspiration. As a teenager, he produced a seven-hundred-page Gothic-style novel. It pleased him so much that he sent it around to a number of publishers, none of whom accepted it.

After completing his education, he worked in television advertising for seven years, first as a copywriter and then as a creative director, producing and directing television commercials. In 1993, he published his first young adult novel, *El príncipe de la niebla*, which won the 1994 Edebé Prize for young adult fiction. The novel was later translated into English as *The Prince of Mist* in 2010. Also in 1993, he decided to move from Spain to California. There he found work as a screenwriter in Hollywood. It earned him a steady income, but he did not enjoy the work because he was always writing for someone else and not what he wanted to write. One benefit of living in the United States, however, was having easy access to an enormous number of bookstores. He particularly liked visiting secondhand ones whenever he traveled. "You could wander inside and get these treasures for 50¢," he told Andrew Stephens for the *Sydney Morning Herald* (23 June 2012). "They had most likely not been opened for decades. I also found this shocking because these were treasure troves of beauty and knowledge." This experience of finding all this hidden knowledge in out-of-the-way bookshops later served as the inspiration for the Cemetery of Forgotten Books, his best-selling series.

THE CEMETERY OF FORGOTTEN BOOKS SERIES

In the series, the Cemetery of Forgotten Books is the most phenomenal library imaginable. Hidden inside an old palace in Barcelona, it contains hundreds of thousands of books throughout its various sections. Traveling through the library's numerous bridges and tunnels, one can find any book ever printed and any one ever thought to be lost, suppressed, or destroyed. The secret society that maintains the Cemetery has few members, including some associated with the Sempere & Sons bookstore, but those who discover their way into the library are allowed to select one from its endless shelves—provided that the volume is never lost to time or destroyed.

In the first volume of Ruiz Zafón's series, published as *La sombra del viento* in 2001 and as *The Shadow of the Wind* in Lucia Graves's English translation in 2004, a young boy named Daniel Sempere is taken to the Cemetery by his father, a bookseller. Daniel chooses a book from its shelves by an unknown Spanish writer who died under mysterious circumstances during the Spanish Civil War. The boy's fascination with the author ultimately shapes his life into adulthood as he comes ever closer to unraveling the mystery of the late author's life. The novel, which became an international best seller, was also critically lauded. Reviewing *The Shadow of the Wind* for the *New York Times* (25 Apr. 2004), Richard Eder remarked, "Ruiz Zafón gives us a panoply of alluring and savage personages and stories. His novel eddies in currents of passion, revenge and mysteries whose layers peel away onionlike yet persist in growing back."

The second installment of the series, *El juego del ángel* (2008; *The Angel's Game*, 2009), chronicles the life of a hack writer named David Martín who, in securing himself steady work, may have signed a deal with the devil when he accepted a commission from a mysterious Parisian editor. Unlike the previous volume in the series, this one met with more mixed reviews, but many critics were still caught up in Ruiz Zafón's twisting and complex tale. Terrence Rafferty, in a review of *The Angel's Game* for the *New*

York Times (24 June 2009), wrote: "'The Angel's Game' has emotional truth to burn because Carlos Ruiz Zafón uses every narrative technique in the book, high and (mostly) low. Whatever other ideas may impinge on his consciousness from time to time, he always falls back on storytelling."

The third book in the series, *El prisionero del cielo* was published in 2011 and in English translation as *The Prisoner of Heaven* in 2012. In a review for the *Guardian* (28 June 2012), Steven Poole wrote of *The Prisoner of Heaven*: "Melodrama succeeds when there is no embarrassment in its execution, and Zafón is a splendidly solicitous craftsman, careful to give the reader at least as much pleasure as he is evidently having."

YOUNG ADULT FICTION

Before beginning work on the Cemetery series, Ruiz Zafón wrote four young adult novels. In interviews he has described them as being the four books he needed to write before he could embark on his ambitious multivolume project chronicling the Cemetery of Forgotten Books. Despite the author's modesty, each of these young adult novels has proven widely popular and has met with considerable praise. Following the remarkable success of Ruiz Zafón's Cemetery of Forgotten Books series in the United States and the United Kingdom, his first four novels were translated into English to widespread acclaim. His award-winning first novel, *The Prince of Mist*, first published in 1993, was translated into English in 2010. Of *The Prince of Mist*, a reviewer for *Publishers Weekly* (12 Apr. 2010) remarked: "Ruiz Zafón maintains a sweet, believable relationship among the characters when dealing with mundane concerns . . . but still conveys a sense of adventure and danger. The bittersweet ending suits the theme and setting, offering both hope and tragedy without any pretense of fairness."

The Midnight Palace, originally released in Spain as *El palacio de la medianoche* in 1994, was published in the United States in 2011. Set in Calcutta, India, in 1932, the novel follows two twins as they seek to unravel the story behind their parents' death in an effort to keep themselves alive. In a review of *The Midnight Palace*, a critic for *Kirkus Reviews* wrote (1 May 2011): "Though the villain's motives and origins are muddy and the secondary characterizations thin in this sensationalistic gothic tale, the steamy atmosphere of Calcutta is palpable and the confrontations between the twins and their malevolent nemesis truly terrifying. Perfect for readers who value mood over all else."

Ruiz Zafón's 1995 novel *Las luces de septiembre* was published in English in 2013 as *The Watcher in the Shadows*. Again the mystery involves a pair of young children, Irene and her younger brother Dorian, as they and their mother settle in a French costal village in 1937. Shortly upon their arrival in a secluded mansion called Cravenmoore, where their mother will start work as a housekeeper for a retired toymaker and his sickly wife, a murder occurs in a nearby forest, dragging Irene and Dorian into the mix.

First published in 1999, *Marina* received its English-language publication in 2014. Of *Marina*, a reviewer for *Publishers Weekly* wrote (12 May 2014): "On a rational level, the tale, like many Gothic thrillers, is preposterous, but readers are never given time to think rationally. Unlikely discoveries in mysterious, half-ruined mansions alternate with spine-tingling action sequences to create a grotesquerie that will delight horror fans."

PERSONAL LIFE

Carlos Ruiz Zafón was married in 1993. He met his wife while they were both working in television advertising. His wife, a translator, is (like him) a night owl who prefers to work late into the evenings and enjoys traveling. For these lifestyle reasons, among others, he believes they made the right decision not to have children. He told Farndale for the *Telegraph*: "We don't feel a void. I don't think [children] would give my life meaning. I do think of the books as my children, though. . . . The way I like to live, working at night, hopping from country to country, disappearing for six months, it doesn't suit children. When you decide to become a writer, you have to accept that you will have to be a bit selfish."

Ruiz Zafón splits his time between homes in Los Angeles, California, and Barcelona, Spain. Although he grew up in Barcelona and much of his fiction is set there, he admits he feels more comfortable in Los Angeles. He believes what he sees as the open-mindedness of Los Angeles is in sharp contrast to the provinciality of his native city and much of Spain. There are other differences as well. "Barcelona is a very old city in which you can feel the weight of history; it is haunted by history. You cannot walk around it without perceiving it," he noted to Andrew Stephens for the *Sydney Morning Herald*. "In Los Angeles, it is quite the opposite: it is an older city than it might seem to be, but you don't perceive this—every day you get out of your home, you are driving somewhere and sometimes you get this impression that everything was put there the night before."

SUGGESTED READING

Eder, Richard. "In the Cemetery of Forgotten Books." Rev. of *The Shadow of the Wind*, by Carlos Ruiz Zafón. *New York Times*. New York Times, 25 Apr. 2004. Web. 12 Aug. 2014.

Farndale, Nigel. "The Shadow Maker." *Telegraph*. Telegraph Media Group, 27 Nov. 2005. Web. 12 Aug. 2014.

House, Christian. "Carlos Ruiz Zafón: 'I'm Haunted by the History of My City.'" *Independent*.

Independent.co.uk, 24 June 2012. Web. 12 Aug. 2014.

Ruiz Zafón, Carlos. Interview by Paul Blezard. "An Interview with Carlos Ruiz Zafón." *CarlosRuizZafon.co.uk*. Orion Publishing Group, n.d. Web. 12 Aug. 2014.

Ruiz Zafón, Carlos. Interview by Gilbert Cruz. "Author Carlos Ruiz Zafón." *Time*. Time, 30 June 2009. Web. 12 Aug. 2014.

Stephens, Andrew. "Interview: Carlos Ruiz Zafón." *Sydney Morning Herald*. Fairfax Media, 23 June 2012. Web. 12 Aug. 2014.

SELECTED WORKS

The Shadow of the Wind, 2004; *The Angel's Game*, 2009; *The Prince of Mist*, 2010; *The Midnight Palace*, 2011; *The Prisoner of Heaven*, 2012; *The Watcher in the Shadows*, 2013; *Marina*, 2014

—Christopher Mari

Roll Call/Getty Images

Raul Ruiz

Born: August 25, 1972
Occupation: Doctor and politician

US Congressman and doctor Raul Ruiz was elected to serve California's Thirty-Sixth Congressional District in November 2012. Though he had never before run for public office, Ruiz, a Democrat, unseated the seven-term incumbent, Republican Mary Bono Mack. Ruiz's stunning victory could be attributed to his hometown popularity. He was raised in the Coachella Valley, and after earning three degrees from Harvard—becoming the first Mexican American to do so—he returned to the rural community to work as an emergency-room doctor in the area's lone not-for-profit hospital, Eisenhower Medical Center. Ruiz is a physician with deep concern for social justice. (His other two degrees are in public health and public policy.) Coachella Valley has only one doctor for every nine thousand low-income residents, and is significantly deficient when compared to the national standard of one for every two thousand people. In an effort to expand access to health care to residents who cannot afford it, Ruiz founded the Coachella Valley Healthcare Initiative in 2010. For Ruiz, who has spent time working in Mexico, Serbia, El Salvador, and Haiti, such efforts are a natural extension of his work as a physician. "I always knew, even when I was in medical school, that in order to make a larger impact in a community I would have to leave the exam room," he told Daniel Lovering for Harvard School of Public Health's online magazine (Spring 2013).

When Ruiz announced his candidacy for Congress, he said, as quoted by Kate Nocera for *Politico* (18 Nov. 2012), that he was entering politics to address the "social determinants of health," including jobs and access to health care and education. He felt that Bono Mack, a moderate Republican, had failed to adequately represent the area's growing Hispanic population. Though he was effectively a hometown hero, few people thought Ruiz could best the popular incumbent, and indeed, his victory was by the slimmest of margins. The race garnered national attention, with outside groups pouring hundreds of thousands of dollars into each campaign, but beyond money, the race seemed to point to a larger shift in the state, both ethnic and political.

In 2012, California gave four seats to Democrats. Those elections put into effect the state's 2010 referendum requiring a new primary structure, which found several districts running candidates of the same party against each other in the general election, and redistricting by bipartisan committee. (The Thirty-Sixth Congressional District was among those districts that were redrawn.) After the election, minority leader and California congresswoman Nancy Pelosi noted that the Senate Democratic Caucus counted more women and minorities combined than white men. "More than anything, it's a reflection of America," Ruiz told Nocera. "It's a reflection of changing times that people are electing folks they feel are competent and will represent the issues and values of the country as a whole."

EARLY LIFE AND EDUCATION

Ruiz, who is of Mexican and Native American descent, was born on August 25, 1972, in Zacatecas, Mexico. Months after his birth, his biological mother died in Mazatlan, and Ruiz was adopted by his biological father's sister, Blanca, and her husband, Gilbert Ruiz. The causes of his mother's death are unknown. Ruiz sees his biological father occasionally, but considers Blanca and Gilbert (who died in 2004) his true parents; he joined his new family in Coachella Valley in Southern California when he was still an infant. He has two siblings, Robbin and Star. Early in Ruiz's childhood, his family lived in a trailer in Coachella, where his mother picked crops and his father repaired farm equipment and later became a foreman and manager at Sun World. Just before Ruiz was born, Coachella Valley played an instrumental role in the rise of the United Farm Workers. The association, founded by Cesar Chavez, demanded better wages and working conditions for farm laborers. Still, Ruiz's parents could not afford health insurance when he was growing up. The family relied on herbal remedies and a healthy diet to stave off illness.

The Ruiz family moved into a small home in a working-class neighborhood in the late 1970s. Ruiz played Little League baseball and later attended Coachella Valley High School, where he served as class president for three years and student body president during his senior year. He also played baseball and football, though he was committed to becoming a doctor—an ambition he voiced at the age of four. With the financial help of a family friend, Ruiz was able to apply to the University of California, Los Angeles (UCLA). He was accepted but did not have enough money to pay tuition. So, the resourceful Ruiz went to neighbors and local businesses with a contract he had drawn up himself. He asked people to contribute to his college fund, Lauren Dickinson wrote for the *National Journal* (6 Nov. 2012), "in exchange for his future medical service to the community." He raised nearly two thousand dollars, and years later, he made good on his promise.

MEDICAL EDUCATION AND ACTIVISM

Ruiz graduated from UCLA in 1994 and enrolled in Harvard Medical School. During his time at Harvard, he decided also to pursue two master's degrees in public policy and public health. He completed his medical and public policy degrees in 2001 and his master's in public health in 2007. He is the first Mexican American to complete three degrees from Harvard. Ruiz spent his third year of medical school working with the international aid group Partners in Health in Chiapas, Mexico. "I went in romanticizing the poor and their struggle and issues with social justice," Ruiz said, as quoted by Marcel Honoré for the Palm Springs *Desert Sun* (9 Dec. 2012). "But I

came out of there realizing the tremendous nature of poverty and how real policies can actually affect human lives." Later, he also served as a consultant to the Ministries of Health in Serbia and El Salvador. As a medical student, he trained as an emergency-room doctor, and at the Harvard School of Public Health, he focused on humanitarian and disaster aid. He volunteered in Haiti following the devastating earthquake that occurred there in 2010, and became the founding medical director for the Jenkins-Penn Haitian Relief Organization. His efforts earned him the Commander's Award for Public Service from the US Army's 82nd Airborne.

He also volunteered for the nonprofit North American Indian Center of Boston and began participating in the United American Indians of New England's annual "National Day of Mourning." The event has taken place near Plymouth Rock on Thanksgiving Day since 1970 to protest the abysmal treatment of American Indians by the United States. Ruiz attended the event for six years without incident, but in 1997, the protest turned violent. Ruiz, who by his own account was protecting an older protestor from a policeman's club, was arrested and charged with disorderly conduct and tumultuous behavior. He pled not guilty, and the charges were later dropped. The incident and Ruiz's 1998 statement that Thanksgiving is "the glorification of an incident in history which has a direct link to the . . . poverty and oppression which (Latinos and American Indians) experience today," (from the *Harvard Crimson*, quoted by Honoré) were used as ammunition against him during his 2012 campaign versus Bono Mack. In response to Bono Mack—who labeled his work on behalf of American Indians as, ironically, "un-American"—Ruiz invited the congresswoman, during a live television debate, to spend Thanksgiving with his family. He also distanced himself from his earlier activism, including his support for Leonard Peltier, an American Indian activist convicted of killing two FBI agents in the 1970s, telling Honoré that now he seeks change "through consensus and understanding [rather] than confrontation."

COACHELLA VALLEY HEALTHCARE INITIATIVE

Ruiz completed his residency work in Pittsburgh, Pennsylvania, and was an international emergency medicine fellow at Brigham and Women's Hospital in Boston in 2006 and 2007. After completing his final degree, he moved back to Coachella Valley and began working in the emergency room of Eisenhower Medical Center in Rancho Mirage. Ruiz gained a reputation for calm under pressure. "He took his time. He was always very thorough and calm," Dr. Samuel Ko, one of Ruiz's colleagues, told Honoré. Working in the emergency room "can be very hectic and intense (but) he walks slow. Everything was purposeful with him." He also became the senior associate dean at the University of California, Riverside School of Medicine.

With an aim to provide health care to low-income residents, Ruiz founded the Coachella Valley Healthcare Initiative in 2010. The area of California that Ruiz represents in Congress is notable for its striking disparities. It encompasses most of wealthy Palm Springs and most of Coachella Valley, where Ruiz has said, a medical crisis is occurring. Poverty, rising health care costs, and a population boom resulting from an increasing number of migrant workers coming from nearby Mexico have contributed to the crisis. In 2010, the Emergency Medicine Physicians (29 Nov. 2010) noted that the Flying Doctors, a nonprofit group that administers aid to developing nations, "makes its *only American stop*" in the Coachella Valley.

Ruiz also founded the Dr. Ruiz & Partners Future Physician Leaders program in 2009. The program mentors premed students and encourages them to work and become leaders in low-income areas. Essentially, the program nurtures career paths that closely resemble the one upon which Ruiz embarked; even within Harvard's Kennedy School of Government, where Ruiz studied public health, he was an anomaly. Erwin Cho, a former classmate of Ruiz, told Honoré that of the estimated sixty students studying public health at the time, most were hoping for jobs in Washington, DC, or other big cities. "Very few talked about going back to their smaller hometowns." Even then, Cho said, Ruiz "saw a great need, not just for him to return" but also for others to follow the similar path.

CONGRESSIONAL CAMPAIGN AND EARLY CAREER

Though Hispanics account for about 47 percent of the population in the Thirty-Sixth Congressional District, Ruiz was the first Hispanic challenger Bono Mack had faced during her fourteen years as a congresswoman. Bono Mack, a Republican, is the widow of the late entertainer and congressman Sonny Bono. She won her husband's seat in a special election after his death in a skiing accident in 1998. She won handily in subsequent elections until 2012. The 2012 election was colored by both California's new top-two primary system, in which the top two candidates from a multiparty primary face off against one another, and Proposition 20, which passed with more than 60 percent of the vote in 2010. The proposition gave the Citizens Redistricting Commission, a body composed of Democrats, Republicans, and Independents, the authority to redraw California's congressional districts. (That authority was previously held by the state legislature.) The district had been reconfigured before—Bono Mack served it as the Forty-Fourth Congressional District from 1998 to 2003 and as the Forty-Fifth from 2003 to 2013—but the district as it was drawn after 2010 boasted more Democrats and Hispanics than ever before. Still, in the June 2012 primary, Bono Mack won with 58.1 percent of the vote. Ruiz became her official challenger after garnering 41.9 percent.

In the general election, Ruiz attacked Bono Mack's support for Representative Paul Ryan's plan to reform Medicare through vouchers and her apparent lack of empathy toward the Hispanic, largely impoverished sector of her constituency. Ruiz campaigned in support of President Barack Obama's Affordable Care Act and called for a 30 percent tax on millionaires. Bono Mack attacked Ruiz for his participation in the "Day of Mourning" and, more damningly, for his support of Peltier. Ruiz was endorsed by former President Bill Clinton and his campaign received hundreds of thousands of dollars from the Democratic Congressional Campaign Committee and the Democratic, House Majority PAC. Bono Mack still managed to raise more campaign funds than Ruiz, however.

On election day, Ruiz claimed a narrow victory, by three percentage points. He was sworn into office in January 2013. In November of the same year, he broke with members of his own party to vote for a GOP-sponsored bill to delay the Affordable Care Act's individual mandate. The bill's sponsors argued that, in light of the Obama administration's announcement that large employers would not be required to offer health insurance until 2015, individuals should be given the same flexibility. Detractors argued that the bill would allow insurance companies to keep expensive-selling policies that did not comply with the Affordable Care Act's new rules. Ruiz was one of the thirty-nine House Democrats that voted for the bill, to the ire of party hard-liners. Ruiz defended his position, saying that his decision was based on the Obama administration's promise that people would be able to keep their own policies under the Affordable Care Act, a guarantee that turned out to be not entirely true. Ruiz told Jeff Horseman for California's *Press-Enterprise* (15 Nov. 2013): "One of the ways that we need to improve the Affordable Care Act is by making sure that people can keep their existing health care policies if they choose to do so. That's why I voted today for a bipartisan bill that would allow people to maintain their existing healthcare plan. . . . Many people may find that there are better, less expensive alternatives available through . . . Covered California. But with this bill, all Californians would be free to choose any options available, including their current policies."

PERSONAL LIFE

Congressman Ruiz plans to keep his medical license and has considered practicing medicine part time in addition to his duties on Capitol Hill. In October 2013, he made headlines for stabilizing a fellow passenger who had lost consciousness on a flight from Washington, DC, to Dallas-Fort Worth. The plane was diverted to Raleigh, North Carolina.

In 2009, Ruiz received the Latino of the year award from the Inland Empire Hispanic Image Awards. In 2010, the Rancho Mirage Chamber of Commerce and San Gorgonio Pass Hispanic Chamber of Commerce named him humanitarian of the year, and in 2011, he was named person of the year by *Desert Magazine*, a publication of the Palm Springs *Desert Sun*.

SUGGESTED READING

Dickinson, Lauren. "Calif., 36th House District: Raul Ruiz (D)." *National Journal*. National Journal Group, 6 Nov. 2012. Web. 5 Jan. 2014.

Honoré, Marcel. "A Look into Raul Ruiz." *Desert Sun* [Palm Springs]. Gannett, 9 Dec. 2012. Web. 5 Jan. 2014.

Horseman, Jeff. "Affordable Care Act: Raul Ruiz Votes for GOP Bill." *Press-Enterprise* [Riverside]. Enterprise Media, 15 Nov. 2013. Web. 6 Jan. 2014.

Lovering, Daniel. "Dr. Ruiz Goes to Washington." *HSPH Magazine*. Harvard School of Public Health, Spring 2013. Web. 5 Jan. 2014.

Nocera, Kate. "Raul Ruiz Win Tells Story of Election 2012." *Politico*. Politico, 18 Nov. 2012. Web. 6 Jan. 2014.

"Raul Ruiz Leads Campaign for Healthcare in Rural California." *Emergency Medicine Physicians*. Emergency Medicine Physicians, 29 Nov. 2010. Web. 6 Jan. 2014.

—*Molly Hagan*

Donald Sadoway

Born: March 7, 1950
Occupation: Materials scientist

Donald Sadoway is the coinventor of the liquid-metal battery, which has the potential to revolutionize how people use and store energy. The liquid-metal battery could also significantly reduce the world's dependence on oil and natural gas, thereby curtailing a substantial amount of pollution that is created and emitted by their acquisition and use. One of the key challenges in harnessing renewable energy sources such as wind and solar power is they are only intermittently available—on cloudy or windless days, the amount of solar and wind energy that can be harnessed is often insufficient. Sadoway's goal is to make batteries that are capable of storing the energy gathered by wind or solar farms—or any other environmentally friendly means of

Courtesy of Ethan Gordon

gathering energy—so that it can be used when needed. In 2012 Sadoway was named to the Time 100, *Time* magazine's annual list of the world's hundred most influential people.

Sadoway is a professor of materials chemistry in the Department of Materials Science and Engineering at the Massachusetts Institute of Technology (MIT). But what exactly is materials science? That is the question Sadoway received when he appeared on the satirical comedy program the *Colbert Report* in October 2012. "It's the science of inventing new materials—materials that involve new mixes of atoms in ways that give us properties that we haven't had before," Sadoway explained to host Stephen Colbert, as quoted by Lynne Robinson for *JOM* (18 Jan. 2013). "I think a peaceful and prosperous world rests on the invention of modern, cost-affordable batteries."

In April 2014, Ambri, the company Sadoway cofounded in 2010, announced that it had raised $35 million from new and existing investors, including Bill Gates, the oil company Total, and the venture capital firm Khosla Ventures. "The willingness of investors to pony up that kind of cash confirms what many already know: that storage is going to be a big deal in the years to come," wrote Peter Kelly-Detwiler for *Forbes* (14 May 2014). "Research firm Navigant projects that the global market for storage will increase from under $150 million to $10.3 billion over the next decade. This group of backers is betting that Ambri is going to grab a significant stake of that overall purse."

EARLY LIFE
Donald Robert Sadoway was born on March 7, 1950, in Toronto, Ontario, and raised in Oshawa, a town just northeast of Toronto. For the first three or four years of his life, he did not speak English: he was raised by his parents and grandparents, who all spoke Ukrainian to him at home.

During his high school years, Sadoway excelled at math, physics, and chemistry. But chemistry in particular appealed to him. "I've always wanted to be at the interface between theory and practice, and I always felt that chemistry, for me, was the subject that helped me position myself at that interface," Sadoway told Hessenbruch. "I always wanted to be not a chemical engineer, I always bristled at the word engineer. But I didn't want to be a scientist, I wanted to be someone at that interface." Explaining how he was drawn to materials science as a student, he told Hessenbruch, "Oddly enough at the University of Toronto, the school of engineering is called the Faculty of Applied Science and Engineering, and I read that, and said, 'That's it! Applied science.' Science and application, science in service of humanity."

UNIVERSITY EDUCATION
For his undergraduate and graduate studies, Sadoway attended the University of Toronto. He received his bachelor's degree in engineering science in 1972 and his master's degree in chemical metallurgy the following year. His master's thesis was titled "Thermodynamic Properties of Manganese Dichloride in Ternary Solutions with Sodium Chloride and Cesium Chloride." From 1972 to 1976, he served as a teaching assistant in the university's Department of Metallurgy and Materials Science, teaching undergraduate courses on metallurgical thermodynamics, electrochemistry, and the kinetics of metallurgical processes. In his interview with Hessenbruch, Sadoway recalled his university education: "When I went to the University of Toronto, I thought I would be in the chemical engineering department doing applied chemistry. And, fortunately, I was in an honors program called Engineering Science, which was actually modeled on MIT. And the first two years were general, very rigorous, a lot of math." However, his chemistry courses were taught by a chemical engineer instead of by faculty in the chemistry department. "I hated it," he told Hessenbruch. "Chemical engineering, this is 1968, was very much still petroleum. I didn't like organic chemistry, and I had no desire to learn how to push liquids through pipes. I loved chemistry, and [decided on] metallurgy, which was basically high temperature physical chemistry. . . . I went in

there thinking I was doing chemical metallurgy and before I knew it I was exposed to this entire world of metals, ceramics, and so on." Sadoway's doctoral thesis was titled "Thermodynamic Properties of Some Alkali-Metal Hexachloroniobates and Hexachlorotantalates, and the Separation of Tantalum from Niobium." Sadoway completed his PhD in chemical metallurgy in 1977.

POSTDOCTORAL FELLOWSHIP
After earning his PhD, Sadoway decided to leave Canada for the United States. "I knew I wanted to be in academics, but by the mid 70s, the Canadian university system was very much constipated, there were very few vacancies," Sadoway explained to Hessenbruch. "The average age [of] the faculty was such that there weren't a lot of retirements on the imminent horizon. So one of my faculty advisors in Toronto took me aside and said, 'You know I can see you're interested in academics, you really ought to postdoc and fatten up your resume, and eventually something will break loose here.'" Following this advice, Sadoway applied for and received a research fellowship from the North Atlantic Treaty Organization (NATO), for which he was able to go anywhere within the NATO alliance. Sadoway chose to complete his postdoctoral research at the prestigious Massachusetts Institute of Technology in Cambridge, Massachusetts. He had been inspired to attend MIT after reading the four-volume series *Structure and Properties of Materials* (1964–66) by John Wulff, a former professor there.

Sadoway's faculty advisor at the University of Toronto, Alex McLean, gave Sadoway another piece of advice that would soon help his career a great deal; McLean advised Sadoway to get the proper immigration papers to live and work in the United States, arguing that because the US economy is so much larger than Canada's, the United States would likely have more university teaching opportunities available. Sadoway took that advice to heart and applied for permanent-resident status in the United States at the US consulate in Toronto. In his interview with Hessenbruch, Sadoway described his green card as a "godsend." From 1977 to 1978, Sadoway spent one year at MIT working on his postdoctoral studies. During that time, a vacancy opened up in the MIT faculty—a teaching job that he would never have considered applying for if he had come to the United States on only a student visa. "There was no way that they would have fought to get a J visa commuted," Sadoway explained to Hessenbruch. "So I'm here largely because there were a few people who took a critical interest in me in a critical stage in my career."

JOINING THE MIT FACULTY
In 1978 Sadoway became an assistant professor in the Department of Materials Science and

Engineering at MIT. In 1982 he became an associate professor, and in 1992 he was again promoted, this time to the tenured position of professor. Since 1999, Sadoway has served as the John F. Elliott Chair in Chemical Metallurgy. Sadoway has taught a variety of courses at MIT, including Introduction to Solid State Chemistry (freshman level), Chemical Metallurgy (senior level), and Kinetic Processes in Materials (graduate level). His courses are some of the most popular classes in the history of MIT.

In the early to mid-1990s, Sadoway taught a class in the Technology and Policy Program, and his students were interested in studying the batteries of electric cars. Sadoway began researching and lecturing on the various applications of batteries. He did not know very much about batteries at the time, and no one at MIT was doing battery research. In his interview with Hessenbruch, Sadoway explained why he thought that was the case: batteries were not biotechnology, nanotechnology, nor semiconductors; in other words, they were viewed as something of the past and not of the future. Batteries were not considered a sexy or compelling area of research. But to Sadoway they were. To Sadoway batteries held the answer to one of humankind's biggest problems: the fact that the earth's reserves of oil and natural gas are limited and dwindling and that the use of those resources creates huge amounts of carbon dioxide emissions, which contribute to global climate change, putting the well-being of the environment and future generations at risk. Furthermore, as Sadoway explained in a March 2012 TED (Technology, Entertainment, Design) Talk, "The way things stand today, electricity demand must be in constant balance with electricity supply. If . . . some tens of megawatts of wind power stopped pouring into the grid, the difference would have to made up from other generators immediately. But coal plants, nuclear plants can't respond fast enough. A giant battery could."

LIQUID-METAL BATTERIES

After studying batteries for ten years, Sadoway first thought of using batteries for grid storage in 2005. Sadoway selected magnesium and antimony for electrodes because they are cheap and domestically available and separate easily in liquid form. In 2007, David Bradwell, a student at MIT working in Sadoway's lab, helped Sadoway invent a liquid-metal battery (using the combination of magnesium and antimony) that was about the size of a tall shot glass. In 2009, Bradwell and Sadoway received almost $7 million in funding from the United States Department of Energy's Advanced Research Projects Agency–Energy (ARPA-E) and $4 million from the French oil company Total. Microsoft founder Bill Gates was also an early supporter. In a statement announcing the project's funding (26

Oct. 2009), ARPA-E praised the potential of Sadoway and Bradwell's invention: "If successful, this battery technology could revolutionize the way electricity is used and produced on the grid, enabling round-the-clock power from America's wind and solar power resources, increasing the stability of the grid, and making blackouts a thing of the past."

The funding allowed Sadoway to hire more staff and to move his research along at a faster pace. The batteries Sadoway is working on, it is important to point out, are stationary, so they could not be used in cars. The batteries have three liquid layers, so they cannot be disturbed. If, for example, a home is using such a battery and an earthquake occurs, the resident could restart the battery after the initial disturbance; however, restarting a battery in a moving vehicle would not be practical.

The electrodes of the liquid-metal battery could operate at electrical currents "tens of times higher than any [battery] that's ever been measured," Sadoway told Kevin Bullis for the MIT Technology Review (Mar./Apr. 2009). Most significantly, wrote Bullis, the materials used in the battery are fairly cheap and the overall design relatively simple, making the batteries easy to manufacture. In an interview with Josie Garthwaite for GigaOm.com (18 Mar. 2011), Sadoway said his plan was to scale the size of the battery's diameter from that of a shot glass (1 amp) to that of a hockey puck (20 amps), a pizza (200 amps), and ultimately a ping-pong table. Such technology "will enable grid-level storage in the extreme," Sadoway explained to Garthwaite. "There are a variety of applications. You could imagine batteries about the size of a small refrigerator in the basement of every home, where people can take energy off the grid in the wee hours of the morning, then draw upon that stored energy throughout the day and maybe even sell it back to the grid during peak demand times."

AMBRI

In 2010, Sadoway and Bradwell founded the Liquid Metal Battery Corporation, which was later renamed Ambri. The company's slogan, "Storing Electricity for Our Future," reflects its primary goal of making batteries for grid storage. Wind and solar farms—alone, without the backing of a natural-gas plant—cannot fully power even a majority of a grid because they do not have a steady supply of energy to meet peak demand. According to Martin LaMonica for the MIT Technology Review (18 Feb. 2013), the significance of what Ambri is doing could have enormous consequences: "If Ambri or anyone else can make grid storage cheap and dependable, it will change the way we get electricity." If Ambri's battery grid storage becomes successful, there may be no need to build more power plants, and some existing plants could be closed.

When asked by Garthwaite what he sees as Ambri's biggest competitors, Sadoway said there are none. The goal of his company at the time was to bring down costs to below $100 per kilowatt-hour; sodium sulfur in stationary installations runs at about $600 per kilowatt-hour and lithium-ion at about $800 per kilowatt-hour. That is simply too expensive for widespread practical applications, said Sadoway, which is why he maintained that his company has no real competitors.

In an interview with Anirban Sen for Live-Mint.com (2 Apr. 2013), Sadoway elaborated on the issue of cost, which he considers the "big problem with batteries." The batteries used in cell phones and computers are mostly lithium ion, which is very expensive yet manageable for those devices because of their small size. However, when it comes to cars and especially grid-level storage, lithium ion batteries are prohibitively expensive. Furthermore, even though digital devices have evolved at a very fast pace with regard to memory, speed, and other features, the improvement in lithium ion batteries has been slight. The alternative to lithium, said Sadoway, is magnesium and aluminum. The latter is especially abundant in the earth's crust, so it could be produced cheaply. The battery industry, he told Sen, is "conservative" in that it tries to improve upon something that works but is very expensive instead of trying to invent something new that is "designed from the beginning to be cost-effective."

HONORS AND SOCIETY MEMBERSHIPS

Sadoway has received many honors and awards for his teaching methods and groundbreaking research, including the Alcoa Foundation Professional Development Award, the Professor T. B. King Memorial Award, the MIT Graduate Student Council Teaching Award, the Bose Award for Teaching in the School of Engineering at MIT, the Everett Moore Baker Memorial Award for excellence in undergraduate teaching, the Lightspeed Venture Partners Professional Development Award for research on grid-level energy storage, and the Minerals, Metals, and Materials Society Distinguished Lecturer Award.

Sadoway is a member of multiple scientific societies, including the American Association for the Advancement of Science, the Iron and Steel Society, the International Society of Electrochemistry, the Materials Research Society, the Electrochemical Society, and the Minerals, Metals, and Materials Society. Sadoway also served as the principal editor of the *Journal of Materials Research* from 1996 to 2001 and as a member of the editorial board for the *Journal of Light Metals* from 2001 to 2002.

SUGGESTED READING

Armstrong, David. "Power in Your Hands." *Forbes*. Forbes.com, 26 Dec. 2005. Web. 16 June 2014.

"Bold, Transformational Energy Research Projects Win $151 Million in Funding." *ARPA-E*. US Dept. of Energy, 26 Oct. 2009. Web. 16 June 2014.

Bullis, Kevin. "Liquid Battery." *MIT Technology Review*. MIT Technology Review, Mar./Apr. 2009. Web. 16 June 2014.

LaMonica, Martin. "Ambri's Better Battery." *MIT Technology Review*. MIT Technology Review, 18 Feb. 2013. Web. 16 June 2014.

Robinson, Lynne. "Donald Sadoway Delivers the Good News about Materials Science." *JOM*. Minerals, Metals & Materials Soc., 18 Jan. 2013. Web. 16 June 2014.

Sadoway, Donald. Interview by Arne Hessenbruch. *Materials Research*. Dibner Institute for the History of Science and Technology, 2 Aug. 2002. Web. 16 June 2014.

—*Dmitry Kiper*

Kira Salak

Born: September 4, 1971
Occupation: Adventurer and journalist

Kira Salak is that rare kind of adventurer able to survive punishing journeys into isolated parts of the world and gifted enough to write compelling tales of her travels. A solo traveler since the 1990s, she has visited parts of the world few Americans have heard about, let alone seen. She has also made history, becoming the first woman to backpack across Papua New Guinea alone. The award-winning author of two books of nonfiction and a novel, Salak has published her writing in many respected newspapers and magazines, including *National Geographic*, the *Washington Post*, the *New York Times Magazine*, *Travel & Leisure*, *Backpacker*, and *National Geographic Adventure*, serving as a contributing editor for the latter.

Salak has often been described as gutsy, tough, and resilient—even crazy—for her adventures, particularly because she is a woman and travels alone. After enduring numerous challenges, she has come to understand why she embarks on such arduous treks. In an interview with Michael Finkel for *National Geographic Adventure* (Aug. 2008), she explained, "By going to unfamiliar or even hostile areas, I discovered parts of myself I didn't know were there. It was a way for me to be reborn, in a sense, to discover who I was and what I was capable of."

Wirelmage for Roberson PR

EARLY LIFE

Kira Salak was born on September 4, 1971, in Illinois, to parents who believed in self-sufficiency and who raised her as a "strict Ayn Randian atheist," according to her 2001 book, *Four Corners: Into the Heart of New Guinea—One Woman's Solo Journey*. Her parents' emphasis on self-reliance did not improve her confidence, however. She has said that she suffered from depression and low self-esteem from an early age and escaped by writing fiction. She also challenged herself physically, becoming a state champion in cross-country and track in high school and pursuing her interest in hiking, mountain climbing, and camping. Her father taught her to shoot a Walther P38 handgun at the age of eleven, and trips to the local firing range became common.

Salak earned her BA from Emerson College in Boston, Massachusetts, in 1993 and went on to receive an MFA in fiction writing from the University of Arizona. In 2004, she earned her PhD in English literature and writing from the University of Missouri–Columbia. She became fascinated with traveling while studying abroad as an undergraduate in the Netherlands. At the time, the nineteen-year-old Salak bought a Eurail ticket and explored the European continent on her own to overcome some of her fears. On her official website, she recalled, "That was when I realized how exciting travel was and how much I loved it. I was completely hooked. I worked in a crouton factory to save up money, then I backpacked alone around eastern and central Africa and Madagascar when I was twenty."

Even though she feared being raped while traveling through Mozambique's war zone to Zimbabwe, Salak's solo trip to Africa gave her the confidence she had long sought. Despite the difficulty of traveling through a foreign continent entirely on her own, the trip empowered her. She returned to the crouton factory to save up more money with a new goal in mind: a solo backpacking trip across Papua New Guinea, a nation in the South Pacific considered one of the most dangerous places in the world for tourists and a known hotspot for sex trafficking.

PUBLISHING *FOUR CORNERS*

Despite the danger the country presented, Salak embarked on her trip to Papau New Guinea because she wanted to explore a part of the world rich in culture (the country is home to more than seven hundred unique tribes) and little known to Westerners. In order to make the trek, she decided to follow in the footsteps of Ivan Champion, a British explorer who successfully crossed the country in 1927. Salak became the first woman to make the same sojourn, during which she came into contact with everything from various tribes to missionary families, all while dodging gangs of unemployed men looking for trouble and discovering refugee camps filled with people who had fled strife in neighboring Irian Jaya. "Traveling could allow me to be reborn," she remarked, as quoted by Karen Karbo for the *New York Times* (2 Dec. 2001). "I knew that Papua New Guinea had a reputation for being especially dangerous. . . . So here again was the challenge: Get yourself out of the place. I would have to toughen up like never before. No fear. I would be forced to have confidence in myself, and to trust in my capabilities."

Salak recorded the details of her trip in *Four Corners*, which is equal parts travelogue and self-exploration. In the book she reflects on everything from her unhappy childhood to the growing self-acceptance that had come to her via her travels, particularly her trip to Papua New Guinea. A critic for *Kirkus Reviews* (15 Aug. 2001) called her debut a "luminously written, thoughtful account."

WORKING FREELANCE

Four Corners found its way onto the desk of an editor at *National Geographic Adventure*. Intrigued by her story, the editor asked if she would like to contribute to the magazine by making additional solo journeys and writing about them. Before long, in the pages of *National Geographic Adventure* and other periodicals, she would describe the solo trips she made to some of the remotest places on Earth. Her notable achievements include becoming the first person to kayak solo down the Niger River to Timbuktu, Mali, in 2002; cycling 800 miles across Alaska to the Arctic Ocean in 2003; and completing the harsh Snowman Trek, a 216-mile high-altitude sojourn across the Himalayas, in 2007.

As a freelance journalist Salak also has covered war-torn countries. In 2004, her article on the civil war in the Democratic Republic of the Congo (DRC) garnered her a PEN Award for journalism. A year later, she received the 2005 National Geographic Society Emerging Explorer Award. All told, she has traveled alone to countries on nearly every continent and led expeditions to politically forbidding states such as Burma, Iran, and Libya. In an article for the *Wall Street Journal* (26 July 2008), she explained to Jeffrey A. Trachtenberg how her desire for travel and exploration has evolved: "When I discovered solo travel it was a way of uncovering parts of myself I didn't know were there. Then I broke into magazine writing and found I liked adventure-travel trips, an arena mostly filled with male writers. I needed to prove I could do those trips, and on another level I was challenging my own inner fears."

Her kayaking trip down the Niger River, funded by *National Geographic Adventure*, inspired her to pen her second nonfiction book, *The Cruelest Journey: Six Hundred Miles to Timbuktu* (2004). In it, she describes how she modeled her trip on the ill-fated expedition of Scottish explorer Mungo Park, who died attempting to find the end of the Niger in 1806. Before leaving, Salak prepared her parents for the possibility that she also might die in the attempt. The book provides a harrowing account of her journey, as well as vivid descriptions of traditional villagers' lifestyles, including the practices of bodily mutilation and slavery. A reviewer for *Publishers Weekly* (18 Oct. 2004) wrote, "The book juxtaposes Salak's physical strength with delicate prose. . . . Though tough as nails, she's easy with her feelings, especially her constant fear of not knowing if the villagers near where she camps will be like the friendly Fulani herders, who embrace her as a wayward traveler, or like the Bozos, 'young toughs' who mock and threaten her."

EXPERIENCE WITH AYAHUASCA
Despite her robust physical capabilities and her mental determination to tackle difficult trips and assignments, Salak remained troubled by the depression she had endured since childhood, as well as the migraines and post-traumatic stress disorder (PTSD) she developed after covering the war in the DRC, during which she saw great barbarity. That wartime experience took two years to recover from, but her recovery was aided in part by her experience with ayahuasca healing in Peru. In April 2004, she traveled to the South

American country to cover a "shamanic tour" for an American publication. She knew little about ayahuasca, other than that it was a special tea made from several Amazonian plants and was used by religious groups. The concoction was said to possess healing properties, curing those who drank it of various mental, physical, and spiritual disorders. Yet, because those who have consumed ayahuasca experience visions, it is banned in the United States.

During that trip, Salak participated in five ayahuasca ceremonies; after the third she realized her lifelong depression had disappeared. She described on her website, "It was as if a water-logged wool overcoat had been removed from my shoulders. There was a tangible, visceral feeling of release. I noticed that the nature of my thoughts had completely changed. There were no more morbid, incessant desires to die. Gone was the 'suicidal ideation' that had made joy seem impossible for me, and made my life feel like some kind of punishment. I actually woke up in that hut in the jungle of Peru desiring only to live. Wanting to live. Feeling hope for the first time in my life. It was, without a doubt, miraculous." According to Salak's website, the depression has never returned in the years since that healing ceremony.

Salak continued to participate in ayahuasca ceremonies in Peru, and in short order, her PTSD, migraines, knee joint pains, anxiety disorders, and other ailments disappeared. The first article she wrote about the experience was trimmed to remove most of the explanatory section about ayahuasca because the editor felt the subject was too controversial. The editor at *National Geographic Adventure*, however, accepted another article describing another trip to Peru, which also contained the background information on ayahuasca. That article, "Hell and Back," published in the March 2006 issue, became the most popular piece published in the magazine's history.

ACCLAIMED NOVELIST
In 2005, Salak's only sibling, Marc, drowned while trying to swim across a river on the border of Namibia and Angola. The loss of her brother inspired her to write a novel, *The White Mary* (2008). Unemployed and living in a small basement apartment in Columbia, Missouri, Salak wrote the book over the course of a year. She recalled in her interview with *National Geographic Adventure*, "I didn't tell anyone what I was doing. It was a very private experience. I almost feel that the book wasn't so much written by me, but rather channeled through me."

In many ways, the novel is autobiographical, informed by Salak's experiences covering the civil war in the DRC, her trip through Papua New Guinea, and her personal experiences with malaria and dysentery. *The White Mary* focuses on a young journalist and war correspondent named Marika Vecera, who travels to Papua New Guinea in search of the highly esteemed reporter Robert Lewis, who has gone missing and reportedly has committed suicide following the murder of his son in Africa. Marika, however, does not think this sounds much like the man she has respected for so long, and she decides to follow a rumor that he faked his own death in order to hide himself in the jungle. Led by Tobo, a local witch doctor, through the jungle of Papua New Guinea, Marika is confronted with both horrific brutality and her own secrets.

The novel was named a "Pick of the Week" in *Publishers Weekly* (1 Aug. 2008), the editors of which called it a "gripping debut novel, a blend of *Heart of Darkness* and *Tomb Raider*." In the *Washington Post* (14 Sept. 2008), Elizabeth Hand remarked, "Marika's friendship with the sorcerer Tobo is depicted with remarkable delicacy and, in its final pages, helps her achieve something close to rapture. . . . In *The White Mary*, Salak shows the courage of facing down . . . darkness and the inescapable price it exacts upon one's soul."

PERSONAL LIFE AND ACCOMPLISHMENTS

Salak has been awarded the Writers@Work fellowship in nonfiction, the AWP/Prague Fellowship award in creative nonfiction, and Lowell Thomas gold awards for best foreign article, best adventure article, and best environmental reporting. Her fiction and nonfiction have been included in several anthologies, including *Best New American Voices*, *Adrenaline 2002: The Year's Best Stories of Adventure and Survival*, *The Best Women's Travel Writing*, and *Nixon under the Bodhi Tree and Other Works of Buddhist Fiction*.

Salak continues to enjoy hiking, camping, kayaking, mountain climbing, and kickboxing. She lives in the Bavarian Alps with her husband and daughter.

SUGGESTED READING

"About Kira Salak." *Kirasalak.com*. Kira Salak, 2008. Web. 11 Feb. 2014.

Karbo, Karen. "Travel." *New York Times*. New York Times, 2 Dec. 2001. Web. 11 Feb. 2014.

Salak, Kira. "Ayahuasca Healing in Peru." *Kirasalak.com*. Kira Salak, 2008. Web. 11 Feb. 2014.

Salak, Kira. "Here There Be Monsters." Interview by Michael Finkel. *National Geographic Adventure* Aug. 2008. Web. 11 Feb. 2014.

Salak, Kira. "The Vision Seekers." *New York Times*. New York Times, 12 Sept. 2004. Web. 11 Feb. 2014.

Trachtenberg, Jeffrey A. "Imaginary Journey." *Wall Street Journal*. Wall Street Journal, 26 July 2008. Web. 11 Feb. 2014.

SELECTED WORKS
Four Corners: Into the Heart of New Guinea—One Woman's Solo Journey, 2001; *The Cruelest Journey: Six Hundred Miles to Timbuktu*, 2004; *The White Mary*, 2008

—Christopher Mari

Joel Salatin

Born: 1957
Occupation: Farmer, author

Joel Salatin is the proprietor of a small family farm in rural Virginia. Though Salatin limits delivery of his grass-fed beef, pork, rabbit, and poultry to customers living within a 250-mile radius of his farm, he is one of the most famous farmers in the United States. Fred Walters, the editor of the sustainable farming magazine *Acres USA*, called Salatin "the high prophet of sustainable family farming," telling Todd S. Purdum for the *New York Times* (1 May 2005), he "aims for low-tech, simple systems. While conventional agriculture is trying to make agriculture a factory or a physical system, in the end it's a biological system: there's life involved. Joel recognizes the life behind the system. And in doing so, he's created a model that can save the family farm, where people don't have to have thousands of acres and millions of dollars of debt." Many can agree on the evils of industrial farming, but Salatin told Purdum that even large government-certified organic farms have "compromised the movement's values" to produce food on a massive scale. He describes his own innovative set-up on Polyface Farm—located in bucolic Swoope, Virginia, on the edge of the Shenandoah Valley—as "beyond organic."

AFP/Getty Images

Salatin was made famous as the hero of Michael Pollan's nonfiction book, *The Omnivore's Dilemma: a Natural History of Four Meals* (2006), and also appeared in the popular documentary *Food, Inc.* in 2008. Both reports were influential in the burgeoning sustainable food movement, but *Food, Inc.* might have been the more alarming. The film revealed that the handful of gargantuan plants producing meat in the United States were subject to fewer health inspections than ever before and that the use of chemicals and hormones on mistreated animals was making Americans sick. Several reviewers compared the film to Upton Sinclair's groundbreaking work of muckraking journalism, *The Jungle*, published in 1906. *The Jungle* revealed poor conditions in American meat-packing plants and put pressure on the Roosevelt administration to create a new federal agency, which ultimately became the Food and Drug Administration (FDA), but *Food, Inc.* appealed directly to consumers. "The very banality of it," Gaby Wood wrote of the film for the *Guardian* (30 Jan. 2010), "the fact that we could, the filmmakers suggest, change the world with every bite yet somehow refuse to—is horrifying."

Opinions about how to change the way Americans eat, of course, are divided. Salatin, a former newspaper reporter and an author, educator, and motivational speaker who famously described himself to Pollan in an article for *Mother Jones* (1 May 2006) as a "Christian-libertarian-environmentalist-lunatic farmer," proposes a total return to the land. He believes that urbanization has led to a disconnect between humans and the animals they eat. Animals that are raised to be eaten are often treated cruelly, which leads to misconceptions, Salatin told Wood, about eating meat at all. "[P]eople are not now connected to their ecological umbilical, so that the only connection anyone has to an animal is a pet cat or a pet dog," he said. "And that really gives you a very jaundiced view of cycles of life—death, regeneration."

Elsewhere, Salatin is more radical; his writing is deeply rooted in homespun, evangelical, antigovernment values. His disciples are myriad and his disdain for what he called (as quoted by Pollan) the "multi-national global corporate techno-glitzy food system" is absolute. According to Salatin, nature is telling us what the corporate food lobbies will not. "What happens is all these things we're seeing—campylobacter, E. coli, mad cow, listeria, salmonella, that weren't even in the lexicon thirty years ago—that is the industrial paradigm exceeding its efficiency," he told Wood. "[N]obody is listening to the pleadings of nature saying: 'Enough.'"

EARLY LIFE AND EDUCATION
Salatin's farming roots run deep. His grandfather, Frederick Salatin, was an organic gardening

enthusiast and beekeeper in Indiana in the 1940s, around the time that the term *organic farming* was coined. Salatin was born in the United States to parents William and Lucille in 1957, but the family moved to Venezuela when he was just six weeks old. They started a farm there but lost it in 1961 during the country's political upheavals, so they returned to the United States and purchased 550 acres of land in Swoope, Virginia, founding what would later become known as Polyface Farm. The land had been ravaged by years of intermittent farming, but by implementing Frederick Salatin's chemical-free farming principles, the Salatins were able to turn it around and raise beef cattle. To supplement their income from the farm, William Salatin worked as an accountant, and Lucille Salatin taught high school physical education.

While in high school, Salatin started his own business raising chickens and rabbits and met his future wife, Teresa, who grew up on a nearby farm. Together they attended the South Carolina fundamentalist Christian college, Bob Jones University, where he majored in English and she studied home economics. They graduated in 1979 and were married the following year. Salatin got a job as a reporter for the Staunton, Virginia, *News Leader*, while his wife took a job at a local fabric store. Salatin spent most of his time writing obituaries and police reports. "I didn't really see a way to make a living on the farm," he told Purdum of his decision to become a journalist. "I always loved writing. I was the guy who won the D.A.R. [Daughters of the American Revolution] essay contest and things like that, and it was the era of Watergate, and I decided I would be the next Woodward and Bernstein, and then retire to the farm." Salatin's reporting days were short-lived, however. He told Purdum that he chafed against the political mores of the paper—he sardonically refers to it as the "Daily Misprint"—and quit to try his hand at farming full-time when he was twenty-five years old.

POLYFACE FARM
Salatin and his wife, who were living in an attic apartment in his parents' farmhouse for $300 a month, were already largely self-sufficient. They produced their own meat, milk, and butter on the farm. Teresa canned applesauce and made bread, and she also homeschooled the couple's children. The little money they made at their jobs was spent on thrift store clothing and toiletries. "I always said if I could figure out a way to grow Kleenex and toilet paper on trees, we could pull the plug on society," Salatin told Purdum. On the farm, Salatin was equally devoted to his principles. While he has been praised for his innovative ideas about farming, in his own view he set out with a few core values and built his farm from there. Because he did not want to use chemicals, Salatin was forced to devise methods

to deal with fertilization, insects, thistles, and weeds. He also wanted to continue to improve the quality of his soil, and to do that, he looked to nature.

Biomimicry, or the practice of imitating processes found in nature and applying them to the human world, is a large part of Salatin's philosophy. "[W]e're trying to use nature as a template in a commercial domestic production model," he told Patrick Alan Coleman for the *Portland Mercury* (12 Aug. 2009). When it comes to raising beef cattle, for instance, Salatin looks to wild herbivores like the African wildebeest and Cape buffalo or the American bison. He told Laura McCandlish for the *Oregonian* (22 Sept. 2009) that he learns from the very specific behaviors that those animals exhibit: "They're always moving. They don't stay in the same spot. They're always mobbed up, for predator protection." At Polyface, Salatin herds his cows to a new patch of grass every day, where they act as natural lawn mowers and fertilizers. Salatin refers to his lush fields as a "salad bar" (hence his signature "salad bar beef") where every square yard contains at least forty varieties of plants. The chickens, meanwhile, contribute to the Polyface ecosystem by picking insects out of the previous day's cow patties and scratching the fresh manure into the dirt. The pigs forage for acorns, hickory nuts, herbs, and grubs in the mountainside forest. Over the years, Salatin has built a complex system that is totally reliant on the foraging and composting skills of the animals themselves. He does not use any standard farming equipment. "There's a big difference between industrializing production of tractors and industrializing production of food," he told Purdum. "We like technology, but we really like technology that allows us to do better what nature does itself."

PARTNERSHIPS AND BUSINESS MODEL

Over time, the farm has built a legion of individual shoppers but has also developed relationships with local restaurants including outposts of the national Mexican fast food chain, Chipotle, in Charlottesville (since 2008) and Harrisonburg (since 2010). Salatin writes about his partnership with Chipotle in his 2012 book, *Folks, This Ain't Normal: a Farmer's Advice for Happier Hens, Healthier People, and a Better World*. Steve Ells, the restaurant's founder, was willing to negotiate with Salatin, though the deal only worked because Salatin was able to find buyers for the parts of the animal that Chipotle did not want. "The bottom line is that the lack of variety in the fast food simple-menu model creates an inherent inaccessibility to small-scale local producers who need to move the whole animal," he wrote, as excerpted by *Grist* on February 14, 2012. Like his farming methods, Salatin's business model is driven by a larger philosophy. Salatin does not set sales goals, welcome outside investors, or hire employees. A handful of people work on the farm—including interns, apprentices, and Salatin's own adult children—but Salatin refers to them as "autonomous collaborators," as he put it to McCandlish. Still, Polyface Farm manages to fare more than well for such a small outfit. Though he refuses to engage in long-distance shipping and delivers his goods only within a 250-mile radius of the farm, in 2009, he estimated that the farm would hit almost $2 million in gross sales.

LIFE OFF THE FARM

A prolific writer, Salatin released his first self-published book in 1993. Among his subsequent titles are *Salad Bar Beef* (1996); *Pastured Poultry Profit$* (1996); *You Can Farm: the Entrepreneur's Guide to Start and Succeed in a Farming Enterprise* (1998); *Family Friendly Farming: a Multi-Generational Home-Based Business Testament* (2001); *Holy Cows and Hog Heaven: the Food Buyer's Guide to Farm Friendly Food* (with a foreword by Michael Pollan) (2005); and *Everything I Want to Do Is Illegal: War Stories from the Local Food Front* (2007). The last title is inspired by Salatin's favorite gripe. His dream of living free from any regulation is, in practice, against the law, but Salatin also takes issue with a number of specific US Department of Agriculture (USDA) regulations. For instance, Salatin has a special exemption from the regulatory body to process *fewer* than twenty thousand chickens each year, and according to the laws of the state of Virginia, Salatin's open-air farm is unsanitary simply because it does not have walls. Such regulations, Salatin argues, are designed to prevent contamination in industrial-sized farms but threaten the very existence of smaller outfits like Polyface.

Salatin travels around the country and abroad to speak about Polyface and encourage people to start their own organic farms. His educational video series, *Polyface Primer*, is available on DVD and is streamed on the Polyface website. When it comes to farming, Salatin is an evangelist, and a true agrarian in the mold of the citizen-farmers that founding father Thomas Jefferson once envisioned. But in the twenty-first century, Salatin's views on government and food are radical, Bryan Walsh reported for *Time* magazine (14 Oct. 2011). For Salatin, organic-friendly supermarkets like Whole Foods might as well be Walmart. (Salatin used to sell eggs to the Whole Foods store in Charlottesville but terminated the relationship when they asked him to upgrade his packaging.) He believes in a total return to the land so that consumers might get to know their local farmers. "Salatin doesn't just want to change your dinner plate—he wants to change the country," Walsh wrote.

Unsurprisingly, this absolutist rhetoric doesn't fly with everyone—particularly city-dwellers or those who barely earn enough money to put food on the table at all regardless of where it comes from. Additionally, there are problems with so-called sustainable farming. There is evidence to suggest that grass-grazing cows and pastured chickens actually have adverse affects on the environment, and as environmental historian James E. McWilliams wrote for the *New York Times* (12 Apr. 2012), if all of the farms in the United States were to raise their cows on grass, the cows would require about half of the country's land. "Nothing about this is sustainable," McWilliams wrote.

Salatin and his wife, Teresa, have two children, Daniel and Rachel, and two grandsons. When Salatin is away, Daniel takes over day-to-day operations of the farm.

SUGGESTED READING

Coleman, Patrick Alan. "Everything Joel Salatin Does Is Illegal." *Portland Mercury*. Index Newspapers, 12 Aug. 2009. Web. 8 Aug. 2014.

McCandlish, Laura. "Growing Greener Acres." *Oregonian*. Oregonian, 22 Sept. 2009. Web. 8 Aug. 2014.

Pollan, Michael. "No Bar Code." *Mother Jones*. Mother Jones and the Foundation for Natl. Progress, 1 May 2006. Web. 8 Aug. 2014.

Purdum, Todd S. "High Priest of the Pasture." *New York Times*. New York Times, 1 May 2005. Web. 8 Aug. 2014.

Salatin, Joel. "Protein: We Only Serve White Meat Here [excerpt]." *Grist*. Grist Magazine, 14 Feb. 2012. Web. 9 Aug. 2014.

Walsh, Bryan. "Can Joel Salatin Save America's Food?" *Time*. Time, 14 Oct. 2011. Web. 8 Aug. 2014.

Wood, Gaby. "Interview: Joel Salatin." *Guardian*. Guardian, 30 Jan. 2010. Web. 8 Aug. 2014.

SELECTED WORKS

Holy Cows and Hog Heaven: the Food Buyer's Guide to Farm Friendly Food (with a foreword by Michael Pollan), 2005; *Everything I Want to Do Is Illegal: War Stories from the Local Food Front*, 2007; *Folks, This Ain't Normal: A Farmer's Advice for Happier Hens, Healthier People, and a Better World*, 2012

—Molly Hagan

Indira Samarasekera

Born: April 11, 1952
Occupation: President and vice-chancellor of the University of Alberta

Indira Samarasekera became president and vice-chancellor of the University of Alberta in 2005. The first woman to hold the position, Samarasekera has spent a good deal of time and effort promoting the cultural and economic importance of education, particularly science education, in Canada, which she has called home since 1977. After receiving her PhD in metallurgical engineering from the University of British Columbia in 1980, she remained at the school to teach and in 2000 became its vice president of research. Because of her success in networking and fundraising, she began to attract the attention of other universities, including the University of Alberta. Under her leadership, the University of Alberta has received millions of dollars in investment and contributions. However, Samarasekera has also had to deal with ongoing budget cuts and several controversies, such as those surrounding her high salary and her comments about the need to attract more men to universities.

EARLY LIFE

Samarasekera was born Indira Vasanti Arulpragasam on April 11, 1952, in Ceylon, now Sri Lanka, an island nation off the coast of southern India. The oldest of four children, Samarasekera did well in school, particularly in mathematics and physics. According to a profile of her by Gordon Laird for the *Walrus* (Sept. 2010), her father decided that his sons and daughters would all receive a university education; this was particularly notable because none of the

Associated Press

female members of the family had ever attended university.

Samarasekera's multicultural education started long before she attended college or pursued graduate studies in the United States and Canada. Her father was a surgeon, and around the time Samarasekera was three years old, he took his entire family to the United Kingdom while he was completing postgraduate work. Even though Samarasekera was very young, the experience would prove to be a life-changing one—especially upon her return to Sri Lanka. "Her early impressions were very different from those of her peers back home: ballet, English gardens, very proper schooling, and the full gamut of Western technology, including television," Laird wrote. "But with this worldliness came challenges. Returning home three years later, she had to become trilingual in order to reintegrate into postcolonial Sri Lanka's complex and divided society." Around the time the family returned to Sri Lanka in the late 1950s, the country was experiencing violent social instability and was well on its way to civil war. As part of the Tamil ethnic minority, Samarasekera's family feared for their safety after the anti-Tamil riots of 1958. They escaped the violence by moving to Jaffna, in the northern part of Sri Lanka, where Tamils were the majority.

EDUCATION
In school, Samarasekera excelled at math and physics and was passionate about their potential applications, particularly with regard to technology that could improve people's lives. For her undergraduate studies, she attended the University of Ceylon, where she studied mechanical engineering—an opportunity she had to fight for. "I wanted to do mechanical [engineering], and they hadn't allowed any women up to then," she told Laird. "I went in and said, 'I want to do mechanical, and you are going to have to let me.'" She received her bachelor's degree in 1974, becoming the first female mechanical engineer in the country, and went on to work as a maintenance engineer for a Shell oil refinery. During this time, Sri Lanka began to pass laws that discriminated against Tamils, and an early version of the Tamil Tigers guerilla group was starting to carry out bombings and engage in other methods of violent protest and resistance. Samarasekera, for personal and academic reasons, decided it would be best to leave Sri Lanka.

In 1975, a year after earning her bachelor's degree, she married Sam Samarasekera, who was also a mechanical engineer, and together they moved to the United States, where they both pursued master's degrees at the University of California, Davis (UCD). Samarasekera, who was on a Fulbright scholarship at UCD, completed her master of science degree in 1976. In January of the following year, the couple moved to Vancouver, Canada, where Samarasekera began her doctoral studies at the University of British Columbia (UBC) and her husband worked as a nuclear engineer at the Swiss engineering company Sulzer. Samarasekera's PhD supervisor was J. Keith Brimacombe, whom she considered a true mentor. "He taught me how to think critically and uncover my talent and apply it for the greater good," she told Marina Jimenez in an interview for the Globe and Mail (7 Oct. 2010). "He taught me how to be inquisitive, creative, and to never be satisfied." In fact, according to Laird, Samarasekera had considered quitting her doctoral studies due to the difficulty of balancing her family life with her academic pursuits, but Brimacombe told her not to let her talents go to waste and to finish her degree. Samarasekera received her PhD in metallurgical engineering from the University of British Columbia in 1980, the same year she became a Canadian citizen.

THE THREE RS
After earning her PhD, Samarasekera quickly secured a teaching post in UBC's Department of Materials and Materials Engineering. Although the job was temporary at first, she eventually graduated to a tenured position, becoming only the second female member of the university's engineering faculty. According to Laird, she "went on to have a major influence on the international steel industry, using mathematical models to predict and correct subtle defects, which facilitated major advances in quality and efficiency."

In 2000 Samarasekera was named vice president of research at UBC—a somewhat unusual move by the university, according to some, as she had not previously held any executive positions, such as dean or provost. Nevertheless, Samarasekera excelled in her new role, playing a large part in augmenting the university's three Rs: revenue, research, and reputation. In the space of four years, she increased UBC's research funding from $149 million to $377 million.

Samarasekera's networking, vision, and fundraising abilities did not go unnoticed. Various universities began reaching out to her, and her career options opened up. In 2005 she accepted an offer to become president and vice-chancellor of the University of Alberta (U of A), where her passion for education, fundraising, international connections, and the relationship between industry, politics, and universities became her trademark. She began to spend about a third of the year traveling, making connections and raising funds, primarily for research. She was keenly aware of the significance of emerging markets, such as Mexico and China, and managed to obtain funds from international contributors, including Chinese billionaire Li Ka-shing. She also helped found the Canada Excellence Research Chairs initiative, a significant effort by the government to bring some of the world's biggest names in science and technology to Canada. In 2010, the U of A received approximately $40 million from the initiative, more than any other Canadian university.

CONTROVERSIES
Samarasekera has faced her fair share of controversies. In 2008 Keith Gerein reported for the *Edmonton Journal* (4 Apr. 2008) that she had earned almost $600,000 in salary and benefits the previous fiscal year, compared to the $430,000 earned by David Naylor, president of the University of Toronto, Canada's largest university. Gerein added, paraphrasing director Alex Usher of the Education Policy Institute's Canadian office, that "it would not be wildly out of line for Samarasekera to be at or near the top of the list, considering the U of A is now one of the country's leading institutions." At the time of the article, the university had a budget of $1.3 billion, 37,000 students, and 9,700 full-time employees.

Two years later, the issue of Samarasekera's high salary and benefits, which amounted to $936,000 during the 2009–10 fiscal year, took on new significance when it was reported that in 2009, she had sold her house to the U of A for $930,000 as part of her contract negotiations. The university also paid for renovations on the house, which Samarasekera had bought for around $750,000 in 2005. "The university has a very strategic advantage of owning a house for their president, which is really, really beneficial when you're recruiting a president," said Brian Heidecker, chair of the U of A's board of governors, as reported by CTV Edmonton News. Heidecker also said that Samarasekera would continue to live in the house and pay rent. According to an article by Erin Millar for *Maclean's On Campus* (6 Aug. 2010), it is not unusual for a university to own the house in which the president lives—such is the case at UBC and the University of Toronto, among others—but it is unusual that the U of A bought the house from their current president and that it is not on campus.

The previous year, Samarasekera had stirred up controversy with her remarks on the fact that female undergraduates were outnumbering males in Canada, at the time making up 58 percent of undergraduate enrollment. "I'm going to be an advocate for young white men, because I can be," she told Gerein for the *Edmonton Journal* (20 Oct. 2009). "No one is going to question me when I say we have a problem." Some, including an on-campus group calling itself the Samarasekera Response Team, took issue with her apparent lack of concern about the relatively low number of women and minorities in certain departments and faculty positions, particularly the higher-paying ones; others expressed concern over the fact that low-income earners were underrepresented in the student body. A few days after the article was printed, the Samarasekera Response Team posted flyers with slogans such as "WOMEN: STOP! DROP! MEN: ENROLL!" and "WOMEN ARE ATTACKING CAMPUS!" More controversy ensued after campus security took down the posters and threatened the group with disciplinary action. Making matters worse was the combination of a struggling economy, rising student expenses, and a reduction in the number of full-time staff. When reports about Samarasekera's high earnings and the university's purchase of her home came out the following year, more backlash followed.

ONGOING CHALLENGES
Samarasekera's biggest challenge in recent years has been to keep the university running well despite ongoing budget cuts. In an effort to produce a balanced budget by the spring of 2015, the U of A announced in 2013 that it would cut $56 million in two years to meet a deadline set by the provincial government of Alberta, and that more cuts could follow. Samarasekera said she would limit her international travel in order to reduce costs. She has expressed concern about how detrimental budget cuts could be to her university, universities in general, and Canada as a whole; in an interview with Dawn Calleja for the *Globe and Mail* (28 Feb. 2013) about Canada falling behind other countries in research and development, Samarasekera said that Canada's "innovation ecosystem is not functioning well," a problem that should be "address[ed] . . . at a systemic level." One of the causes of this phenomenon, she asserted, is that "Canada produces an insufficient number of science and engineering graduates, as a percentage of our overall graduation rates, compared to other, more successful countries." She appealed to Canadian companies to "hire the brightest and best coming out of our universities. And learn to be patient."

EXTRACURRICULARS AND AWARDS
In addition to her position as president and vice-chancellor, Samarasekera contributes her time to various national and international organizations, including Canada's Science, Technology and Innovation Council and the Worldwide Universities Network, of which she is chair. She served as an adviser to the Canadian minister of environment at the 2009 United Nations Climate Change Conference in Copenhagen and as a moderator and speaker at several of the annual World Economic Forum meetings in Davos, Switzerland. She also participated in the 2008 and 2009 Global University Summits in Sapporo, Japan, and Turin, Italy, respectively, as well as in Prime Minister Stephen Harper's round table on Canadian-Indian cooperation in higher education in New Delhi, India, in 2009. Samarasekera became the first female president

of the Canadian Institute of Mining, Metallurgy and Petroleum's Metallurgical Society in 1995; served on the board of the Minerals, Metals, and Materials Society of the American Institute of Mining, Metallurgical, and Petroleum Engineers (AIME); and was chair of the board of directors of Genome British Columbia.

Samarasekera was made an officer of the Order of Canada in 2002 for her outstanding contributions to steel process engineering. In 2012, she received the Queen Elizabeth II Diamond Jubilee Medal and the Peter Lougheed Award for Leadership in Public Policy and was named Canada's Outstanding CEO of the Year. The following year, she received an AIME Honorary Membership, one of the highest honors awarded by that institution. She is a fellow of the Royal Society of Canada, the Canadian Academy of Engineering, and the Canadian Institute of Mining, Metallurgy and Petroleum.

Samarasekera lives in Edmonton, Alberta, and also maintains a condo in Vancouver. She is divorced and has two grown children.

SUGGESTED READING

Gerein, Keith. "More Women Than Men Making the Grade." *Edmonton Journal* 20 Oct. 2009: A1. Print.

Laird, Gordon. "Office of the President." *Walrus*. Walrus Fndn., Sept. 2010. Web. 14 Jan. 2014.

Samarasekera, Indira. "Indira Samarasekera: 'There Is No Other Country in the World Where Immigrants Have Had So Much Opportunity.'" Interview by Marina Jimenez. *Globe and Mail*. Globe and Mail, 7 Oct. 2010. Web. 14 Jan. 2014.

Samarasekera, Indira. "U of A's Indira Samarasekera: Canada's R&D Lag Costs Us." Interview by Dawn Calleja. *Globe and Mail*. Globe and Mail, 28 Feb. 2013. Web. 14 Jan. 2014.

—*Dmitry Kiper*

Yoani Sánchez

Born: September 4, 1975
Occupation: Blogger

Yoani Sánchez is an award-winning Cuban blogger and dissident. Her blog, *Generación Y*, chronicles her day-to-day life under Cuba's totalitarian regime. (The blog's title refers to the fact that many Cubans born in the 1960s and 1970s, like Sánchez, have Russian-sounding names that begin with the letter *y*—an homage to the Soviet Union.) "This country is so saturated with contaminated, corrupted political discourse, with empty pamphleteering, that I wanted to explore other areas," she told Larry Rohter for the

Grzegorz Jakubowski/EPA/Landov

New York Times (5 July 2011) of her blog in a phone interview. "I write about my interior life, the intimate sphere. It's the sentiments of one person but sums up the reality of many people and shows just how sick this society is." The blog is available in eighteen different languages and, as of 2011, received more than fourteen million visits a month. Her book, *Cuba Libre* (free Cuba), was censored by the Cuban government, but it was published as *Havana Real: One Woman Fights to Tell the Truth about Cuba Today*, in the United States in 2011.

Sánchez met with Nobel Peace Prize winner and former president Jimmy Carter when he visited Havana in 2008. The same year, she was named one of *Time* magazine's hundred most influential people in the world. In 2009 she interviewed President Barack Obama for *Generación Y* and became the first blogger to win a Maria Moors Cabot Prize for journalism from Columbia University. Sánchez has also been the recipient of the Ortega y Gassett award in Spain (2008), the Prince Claus award in the Netherlands (2010), and the World Press Freedom Hero award from the International Press Institute (2010). In May 2014 Sánchez and her journalist husband launched *14ymedio*, Cuba's first independent digital newspaper. The name translates to "fourteen and a half" in English, a nod to the year of its birth (2014) and her fourteenth floor apartment in Havana. The *y* is for *Generación Y*.

The Cuban government claims that Sánchez is a counterrevolutionary who receives support in her effort to slander Cuba from the United States government. Former Cuban president Fidel Castro himself, Rohter reported, accused her of conducting a "cyberwar" against the Cuban government. The state blocked local access to *Generación Y* until 2011, and authorities have detained and beaten Sánchez in the past.

In many ways, technology—blogs, social media, satellite television, cell phones—poses the biggest threat to the outmoded Cuban regime. Despite a largely effective campaign to censor state media, the government is at a loss when it comes to stemming the tide of something as seemingly innocuous as Miami television. In one essay published in the *New York Times* (27 May 2014), Sánchez reported that the government had attempted to demonize modern means of communication. Referring to a well-known Communist mouthpiece, she wrote, "A few days ago, the newspaper *Juventud Rebelde* ran a cartoon of the Statue of Liberty holding a cellphone instead of a torch. The message was clear: information and communication technology are the tools of the enemy."

EARLY LIFE AND EDUCATION

Yoani Sánchez was born in Cuba's capital city of Havana on September 4, 1975, to William Sánchez and Maria Eumelia Cordero. Her father was trained as an engineer and, like the men in his family before him, worked for the state's railroad system. After the system crumbled, he became unemployed, eventually finding a job as a bicycle repairman. Sánchez attended and boarded at a revolutionary high school in the countryside that encouraged a return to farm life. The school was named for the Socialist Republic of Romania; she entered the school in 1990, a year after the Socialist Republic of Romania ceased to exist.

After the collapse of the Soviet Union, Cuba fell into a period of economic crisis. In 1991 Castro drastically reduced food rations, and diseases caused by poor nutrition plagued the island. Sánchez recalls swallowing spoonfuls of sugar to stave off hunger pains. She observed her parents' desperation as they were unable to feed her and her sister, and it seeded her cynicism toward the regime. At school, she longed for privacy and escaped into the world of J. R. R. Tolkien's *Lord of the Rings* trilogy.

Sánchez majored in Spanish literature at the Instituto Pedagógico (Pedagogical Institute) before transferring to the arts department at the University of Havana in 1995, where she studied to become a philologist (a linguist focused on the relationships among human speech, literature, and cultural history). Her thesis was titled "Words under Pressure: A Study of the Literature of Dictatorship in Latin America." Unsurprisingly, it was viewed as a criticism of the Cuban government. "On finishing at the university I realized two things," Sánchez wrote in her profile on her blog, "first, that the world of the intellectual and high culture is repugnant to me and, most painfully, that I no longer wanted to be a philologist."

According to the same profile, in September 2000 she went to work for a publisher called Gente Nueva. Her salary, like that of many Cubans, was not enough to support her family, she wrote. She asked to be dismissed from the job so that she could teach Spanish to German tourists in Havana for more money. By her own account, highly educated Cubans clamored for jobs in the service industry, in part so that they might encounter wealthy tourists. In 2002 Sánchez immigrated to Switzerland, where she learned HTML and founded, with a group of island-based Cubans, a magazine focused on reflection and debate, *Consenso*, in 2004. That year she returned to Cuba—against the advice of her friends, she wrote—for unspecified "family reasons." From Cuba, in 2007, she served as the webmaster and editor of a German-based website called *Desde Cuba* (from Cuba).

GENERACIÓN Y

In April 2007 Sánchez launched her blog, which she described in her profile as "an exercise in cowardice": online she was free to say the things that she was not allowed to say in public. She wrote about her frustrations with Cuba's bureaucracy and the absurdity of the regime, but she also wrote about the mundanities of receiving daily rations—a shortage of lemons and a schoolyard where parents smuggled food to their children. In doing so, she became a digital practitioner of the essayistic genre known as *crónica*, or "chronicle." "With her focus on the quotidian, she is very much a part of that tradition," Enrique Del Risco, a Cuban exile who teaches contemporary Latin American literature at New York University (NYU), told Rohter. "It's precisely that grounding in the domestic and personal plane that allows her to show how exhausting and crushing daily life can be."

Sánchez wrote her essays by hand and posed as a tourist in order to make use of Internet cafes. (Spotty Internet service was available at these rare cafes; the few that existed catered to a foreign clientele.) During her few precious minutes of Internet time, she uploaded her posts and copied a few articles onto a memory stick. In 2008 James C. McKinley Jr. wrote for the *New York Times* (6 Mar. 2008) that an underground market existed for the memory sticks themselves—which were mostly obtained through European tourists—as well as the information they contained.

Generación Y was remarkable for its almost poetic detail but also for its identity. Unlike the handful of other Cuban bloggers writing at the time, Sánchez refused to remain anonymous.

She posted her name, photo, and biography on her site along with direct criticisms of the government—no small feat in a country where, a journalist for the *Wall Street Journal* (22 Dec. 2007) wrote, most Cubans were too afraid to utter the name "Fidel Castro" in public. "Instead, they silently pantomime stroking a beard when referring to their leader," the journalist wrote. It is also remarkable that Sánchez managed to avoid jail time for her activities, a fact that baffled many Cuban exiles and led some of them to believe that she was part of an elaborate scheme concocted by the regime. It's funny, but it seems that the only way some people will believe I am authentic is if I am thrown in jail," she told the *Wall Street Journal*. "I'm not sure I want to provide that kind of proof." Then, after gaining international acclaim, she was beaten by thugs in 2009. She suffered no permanent physical damage, but the experience was traumatic. "I really thought they were going to kill me," she told Andrew Hamilton for the *Telegraph* (28 Nov. 2009). In 2012 she and her husband were detained on their way to a political trial. They were released thirty hours later.

TRAVELING OUTSIDE CUBA

In January 2013 the Cuban government discontinued the requirement that citizens obtain an exit permit to leave the country. Sánchez had chronicled her own quest to obtain this document—known as a "white card"—on her blog. The permit cost $200, the amount of an average Cuban's annual salary, and reasons for denial were plentiful and arbitrary. Sánchez herself was denied nineteen times between 2008 and 2012. The change in policy was celebrated internationally, although Cubans still had to apply for a passport to leave the country. After years of waiting, Sánchez finally received her passport in February 2013. As reported by Natalie Kitroeff for the *New York Times* (22 Mar. 2013), Sanchez reckoned that the government eventually decided that the mounting pressure and publicity were worse than letting her leave the country. (The same day, Angel Moya, another Cuban dissident, had his passport request denied, causing Sánchez to tweet that it was both a happy and a sad day for her.)

In March she embarked on a whirlwind, eighty-day international tour that included stops in South America, Europe, and the United States. In the United States she urged lawmakers to reconsider their trade embargo with Cuba. In 1960, one year after Castro seized power in Cuba, the United States placed an embargo on the island that stands to this day. Discussions about lifting the embargo are rare; a writer for the *Economist* (5 Apr. 2014) called it a "part of the furniture of American foreign policy." Most Cuban exiles actually support it, but Sánchez says that it has not worked and that the government has found it easy to blame the embargo for the country's woes. "If there aren't potatoes, it's because of the embargo. If there aren't tomatoes, it's the embargo. If there aren't freedoms, it's the embargo's fault," she told Kitroeff of the government's position.

Critics say that any new cash would flow directly to the government—an argument that Sánchez does not deny, though she still thinks the money would, at least indirectly, help the Cuban people. During his first term in office, President Obama eased travel restrictions between the United States and Cuba, but Sánchez says that more can be done. "I believe we are in times of change," she told Gizelle Lugo for the *Guardian* (16 Mar. 2013). "We need the United States to acknowledge these changes occurring in Cuba—changes that transcend politics and are expanding across the digital world."

CURRENT LIFE IN CUBA

Things are indeed changing in the island country—in the past several years, the government has issued about half a million licenses for people to work in the private sector, which reopened during the economic crisis in 1993—but overall, the path to progress in Cuba is arduous and slow. As the country inches toward the twenty-first century, news on the island follows a circuitous path. Most Cubans still do not have access to a computer, much less the Internet. According to Kitroeff, "an hour of wireless connection" in Cuba "can cost ten dollars—half of the average monthly salary." Blog posts are saved on thumb drives, tweets are texted, and exiled family members call their Cuban relatives' newly permitted (though not Internet-equipped) cell phones. "We find out about something that happened a few meters away after the news has left the country and come back like a boomerang," Sánchez told Kitroeff.

Many cite the eventual death of the octogenarian Castro as a possible turning point, but there is no evidence to support the notion that a regime without him would be remarkably different from the one that exists now, which is publicly run by his younger brother Raúl. "Since taking power in 2008, Raúl Castro has granted a series of concessions that spin the island's compass toward a system without paternalism, but also without rights," Sánchez wrote of what she calls the "Raúlist reforms" in an essay published in the *New York Times* (27 May 2014). While some Cubans received permission to open private businesses, hundreds of thousands of government workers were laid off. They are not "unemployed" according to the official lexicon, Sánchez observed, but instead labeled "available" for work. "This way no one can say they have lost their job in the proletarian paradise," she wrote. According to Sánchez, as reported by Lugo, the reforms stem not from a position of strength or goodwill but rather from the international (and economic) pressure that the regime feels. With each new step toward autonomy for Cuban citizens, the regime loses a bit of its control—a pattern that the Castros are not in any rush to accelerate.

PERSONAL LIFE

Sánchez married Reinaldo Escobar, a journalist nearly thirty years her senior, in 1993, when she was eighteen years old. Escobar was barred from journalism after he published some articles deemed critical of the government in the 1980s. For much of their early married life, he taught Spanish to European tourists. Sánchez gave birth to their son, Teo, in 1995. They live in Havana.

Sánchez is not a part of any political organization in Cuba, and she does not vote, an activity she views as pointless. "There are many ways to pretend in Cuba: you can say things that you don't believe, or you can stay quiet about the things you don't like," she told the *Wall Street Journal* in 2007. "I have the tranquility of being able to look at my son and he knows that I don't fake it."

SUGGESTED READING

"Cuban Revolution: Yoani Sánchez Fights Tropical Totalitarianism, One Blog Post at a Time." *Wall Street Journal*. Dow Jones, 22 Dec. 2007. Web. 9 July 2014.

Hamilton, Andrew. "Yoani Sánchez, Cuba's Popular Blogger, Has Been Beaten Up for Describing Life." *Telegraph*. Telegraph, 28 Nov. 2009. Web. 9 July 2014.

Kitroeff, Natalie. "Interview with Cuban Blogger Yoani Sánchez." *New York Times*. New York Times, 22 Mar. 2013. Web. 9 July 2014.

Lugo, Gizelle. "Yoani Sánchez: Dissident Cuban Blogger Hopeful of Digital Change." *Guardian*. Guardian, 16 Mar. 2013. Web. 9 July 2014.

Rohter, Larry. "In Cuba, the Voice of a Blog Generation." *New York Times*. New York Times, 5 July 2011. Web. 9 July 2014.

Sánchez, Yoani. "My Profile." *Generación Y*. Sánchez, 2008. Web. 9 July 2014.

Sánchez, Yoani. "The Castros in Their Labyrinth." *New York Times*. New York Times, 27 May 2014. Web. 9 July 2014.

—*Molly Hagan*

Emeli Sandé

Born: March 10, 1987
Occupation: Singer and songwriter

Journalists often seize upon two interesting facts about singer-songwriter Emeli Sandé: she sports distinctive platinum blond hair, and she attended medical school for a time before deciding

© Rune Hellestad/Corbis

to focus solely on her music career. Relying on those catchy details to engage readers presumably makes less evident the difficulties that arise when trying to categorize Sandé's musical style, which is as distinctive as her coiffure.

"Sandé's songs carry a distinct edge," Jess Righthand wrote for the *Washington Post* (11 Jan. 2013). "They fall somewhere between Rihanna's in-your-face party fare and [Alicia] Keys's neo-soul piano ballads. Her style is mature, both compositionally and lyrically, but without too much melodrama." As for where Sandé finds inspiration for her musical style, she told Righthand, "The writers that I really look up to and admire are those that can really say so much and resonate with a lot of people without too many words and without being too self-indulgent. So I try my best to kind of walk within those lines."

At the 2013 BRIT Awards, which are considered the United Kingdom's equivalent of the US Grammy Awards, Sandé was named best British female artist, and her debut album, *Our Version of Events* (2012), took best album of the year honors. What was undeniably a banner year for Sandé also proved to be a record-breaking one: in April 2013 *Our Version of Events* marked its sixty-third week in a top-ten spot on the British album chart, the longest run ever enjoyed by a debut effort. It had, as observers marveled, shattered a record held by the Beatles for fifty years.

EARLY YEARS

Adele Emeli Sandé was born on March 10, 1987, in Sunderland, a city in northeast England. She does not use her first name professionally to avoid confusion with fellow Brit Adele Adkins, the wildly popular singer better known as simply Adele. Sandé's father, Joel, is a native of Zambia, and her mother, Diane, hails from Cumbria, in northwest England. The two met while attending college in Sunderland. After Sandé's father completed a sponsored training course in mechanical engineering, the couple traveled to Zambia, but when a pregnant Diane became ill with malaria, they moved to Aberdeen, Scotland. When Joel Sandé finished training to become a technical teacher, the family settled in the small village of Alford.

The Scottish village was so insular that the family's arrival occasioned a story in the local paper headlined "African Teacher Comes to Alford!" "We were seen as very different, certainly," Sandé told Alan Jackson for the London *Daily Mail* (3 Feb. 2012). "But as a family we experienced nothing negative; nor did I encounter bullying or racism, despite being both the youngest pupil and the only black one until my sister Lucy, who's two years younger, joined me at school."

Sandé's father, a teacher at the secondary school in Alford, has also served as its choirmaster. Sandé, by all accounts a serious, well-behaved student, has said that she was deeply influenced by her father's musical tastes, particularly his love of jazz and soul singer Nina Simone. From an early age she delighted in belting out songs from the Disney film *The Little Mermaid* and power ballads by Whitney Houston and Mariah Carey.

TALENT COMPETITIONS

While she initially took recorder and clarinet lessons, Sandé later switched to piano, wanting to learn an instrument she could play while she sang. (Her sister has told journalists that the neighbors sometimes complained about how loud she was.) When she was eleven years old, Sandé wrote a song that was performed by a group of classmates at a school show, and her talent, according to those in attendance, was evident even then. The following year, however, she failed in the preliminary audition stage of a talent competition held at the local town hall. She fared much better the year after that, coming in third and winning £150. Later, as part of an a cappella trio called Celeste, she finally took first place in the annual event but had to share the £500 prize with her two bandmates.

When Sandé was sixteen, her parents took her to an Alicia Keys concert—a pivotal moment for the budding singer. "I'd read about her background and identified with her on so many levels," she recalled to Jackson. "[Keys] was mixed race like me, a great student who'd been top of her class, who played piano and loved Nina Simone. And there she was in the pop charts, yet with songs that had a message. I saw 16,000 people hanging on her every word and thought, 'I want this kind of attention.'"

That year Sandé entered a talent contest sponsored by Trevor Nelson's BBC radio show *Rhythm Nation*. First prize, which she won, was a short-term record deal. After close consultation with her parents, however, she declined to sign the contract, reasoning that it did not provide her with enough security or future artistic support. Although she turned down the opportunity to launch her professional music career, she retained the interest of music manager Adrian Sykes, who vowed to wait until she was ready.

COMBINING MUSIC AND MEDICINE

Sandé's parents considered education a priority and always insisted that attending college was nonnegotiable. While music might have seemed a natural course of study for her, she opted not to pursue it. "I've always kept music and school very separate because I knew that music was something very natural to me and I didn't want it to become a science," she explained to Jade Wright for the *Liverpool Echo* (30 Mar. 2012). "I had a lot of friends who studied music and by the end of it, they'd lost that magic and the spark for it, so I definitely wanted to protect that." She chose medicine and entered Glasgow University in 2006, intending to focus on neurology. "I just find the whole human body so fascinating, and the brain in particular, the mystery of it," she told Greg Kot for the *Chicago Tribune* (17 May 2012).

Even while devoting herself to her medical studies, Sandé found time to perform. "Her work ethic was remarkable," Adrian Sykes, her music manager, told John Dingwall for the Glasgow *Daily Record* (17 Feb. 2013). "Monday to Thursday, she would be . . . doing what young trainee doctors do. Then she would fly down to London on Thursday night and be in the studio until Sunday night. She'd fly back up to Glasgow on Monday morning . . . and start all over again." One weekend, while showcasing a set of songs she had written at a club in London, she caught the attention of Shahid Khan, a Pakistani-born British producer and musician known professionally as Naughty Boy. Impressed, he suggested they work together, and in 2009 they collaborated on the track "Diamond Rings" by British rapper Chipmunk. The single from Chipmunk's debut album, produced by Naughty Boy and featuring vocals by Sandé, became a hit, reaching number six on the UK Singles chart.

That year Sandé left Glasgow University to concentrate on her songwriting. "I got to a point where I was trying to balance both things at the same time and I really missed being creative," she told Emily Laurence for *Seventeen* magazine (June 2012). "I was giving 50 percent to medicine and 50 percent to music and I wasn't being the best I could be in either of them." (In June 2013 the school awarded Sandé an honorary doctoral degree.)

CAREER BREAKTHROUGH

Sandé continued to collaborate with Naughty Boy, and in 2010 the two had another success with "Never Be Your Woman," produced by Naughty Boy and featuring vocals by Sandé and rapper Wiley. Demand for Sandé's work—her songwriting as well as her singing—escalated, and she was soon being called upon to write songs for a wide variety of other singers and rappers. Among those she has collaborated with are Cheryl Cole ("Boys," 2009), Tinie Tempah ("Let Go," 2010), and Susan Boyle ("This Will Be the Year," 2011). She believes that writing songs for other artists was a wise method of breaking into the business. "You get the industry on board a little bit more," she told John Doran for music website the Quietus (8 Feb. 2012). "They know who you are . . . and you know a lot more about the industry."

In February 2012 Sandé released her debut solo album, *Our Version of Events*, which features more than a dozen tracks, including "Heaven," "Daddy," "My Kind of Love," "Mountains," "Clown," "Breaking the Law," and "Next to Me." It also includes "Hope," a tune she penned with the help of Alicia Keys, whom she has so long admired. "It was an incredible experience for me—someone's who has really been a great inspiration to me—sitting at a piano with her," Sandé told a reporter for British network STV (6 June 2012). "We wanted to really get back to the real bones of songwriting, the real craft of songwriting just on an instrument."

Our Version of Events, which was released by Virgin Records, sold a reported 1.4 million copies before the end of 2012, according to figures from the Official Charts Company. It spent ten weeks at the number-one spot on the Official Album Chart and eventually racked up a total of sixty-six consecutive weeks in the top ten, thus breaking a record set by the Beatles; their 1963 debut album, *Please Please Me*, had spent sixty-two weeks there. On three separate occasions during its first year of release, *Our Version of Events* sold more than 100,000 copies in a single week, and the hit single "Next to Me" was among the most-played pop songs of 2012, according to record industry data.

ACCOLADES FOR *OUR VERSION OF EVENTS*

The album received largely positive reviews. "What's magical about this album is how Ms. Sandé's stance remains unmistakable regardless of what the backdrop is," Jon Caramanica wrote for the *New York Times* (6 June 2012). "It's not a flawless album, but rather one with a number of flawless moments. When she chooses to unleash it, Ms. Sandé has a perspective-altering voice, clear and brassy and weapons-grade." Another critic, Ernest Hardy for the *Los Angeles Times* (4 June 2012), said: "*Our Version of Events* lives up to the hype," adding, "It's filled with finely crafted, expertly produced love songs about complex, complicated emotions . . . as well as songs thickly peppered with social consciousness."

Sandé, who has also written for the singer Rihanna, won critics' choice at the 2012 BRIT Awards. She was nominated in the category of British breakthrough act as well. The following year she garnered BRIT laurels as best British female solo artist, and *Our Version of Events* was named British album of the year. Her songs "Next to Me" and "Beneath Your Beautiful" were nominated for best British single that year as well. Sandé's other accolades include three Music of Black Origin (MOBO) Awards won in 2012: for best female act, best R & B/soul act, and best album. In 2013 she won two Ivor Novello Awards from the British Academy of Songwriters, Composers, and Authors (BASCA) for "Next to Me," which was deemed best song (musically and lyrically) and most performed song.

Sandé performed at the opening and closing ceremonies of the 2012 London Olympic Games as well as at a 2013 White House celebration honoring Carole King. She told Kot of her artistic goals: "I want to put the poetry back into pop music," adding, "Melody is a way to get people to listen, and maybe to encourage them to sing along. But the words have to say something. I try to look at an ordinary event and take a different angle on it."

PERSONAL LIFE

In addition to her platinum hair, Sandé is known for her chic but edgy fashion sense. She attributes her love of distinctive clothing to the fact that when she was a medical student, she was required to dress in an understated, traditional manner. She has a large tattoo bearing the likeness of Mexican artist Frida Kahlo, whose life and work she considers inspiring.

In mid-2012 Sandé wed longtime boyfriend Adam Gouraguine, a native of Montenegro. Even as her fame spread during the later years of their courtship, Gouraguine, a marine biologist, shunned the public eye, preferring to focus on his studies. The singer has reportedly taken his surname but will continue to use the moniker Emeli Sandé professionally.

Sandé, whose next full album is scheduled for release in mid-2014, has said that when her recording career winds down, she will put her medical training to use and work in the field of music therapy. She has been known to donate a portion of her ticket sales to the music therapy organization Nordoff Robbins.

SUGGESTED READING

Jackson, Alan. "Emeli Sandé: Meet Music's New Darling, Who Is Living Her 'Dream Come True.'" *Daily Mail* [London]. Associated Newspapers, 3 Feb. 2012. Web. 29 Jan. 2014.

Kot, Greg. "Emeli Sande: A Neuroscientist with Pop-Star Talent." *Chicago Tribune*. Chicago Tribune, 17 May 2012. Web. 29 Jan. 2014.

Righthand, Jess. "Pop Stardom Trumps Plan B." *Washington Post*. Washington Post, 11 Jan. 2013. Web. 29 Jan. 2014.

Rothman, Lily. "50 Years Later, A Beatles Record Is Broken." *Time*. Time Inc., 30 Apr. 2013. Web. 29 Jan. 2014.

Stevenson, Jane. "Emeli Sande Is Her Own Adele." *Toronto Sun*. Canoe Sun Media, 20 July 2012. Web. 29 Jan. 2014.

Topping, Alexandra. "Read All about It . . . Emeli Sandé Reigns at the Brit Awards 2013." *Guardian*. Guardian News and Media, 20 Feb. 2013. Web. 29 Jan. 2014.

—*Mari Rich*

George Saunders

Born: December 2, 1958
Occupation: Writer

George Saunders has been heralded as one of the greatest living American authors, a satirist skilled at capturing the most absurd aspects of modern life but generous enough that compassion animates and informs his often luckless characters. His stories often take place in a surreal, near-future America that is strung out on corporate buzzwords, starved for kindness, and clearly meant as a reflection on the contemporary world. Though his stories are often dystopian, his characters take stabs at hope and act as somewhat cartoonish heroes seeking a bit of redemption from the world around them—their dead-end jobs, their unsavory relationships, and their own moral ruin. Yet Saunders admits to no agenda, apart from trying to craft a well-told story that is a true reflection of his own inner self. "The assumption trickles down that artists have this viewpoint we want to ram down your throat. I'm not really trying to say anything. Most people assume you have an intention and then you execute. There are some writers like that," Saunders said to Jon Niccum in an article published in the *Kansas City* (Missouri) *Star* (11 Jan. 2014). "But for me, I'm trying to not have an intention. I just have a little fragment and start working with it to see where it goes. When I'm done, sometimes I go, 'Wow, I said that? I didn't know I thought that.'"

EARLY LIFE
The oldest of three children, George William Saunders was born on December 2, 1958, in Amarillo, Texas, but raised in Chicago, Illinois. Having owned restaurants in both Amarillo and Chicago, Saunders's father became a salesman after losing his business in a fire. As a child Saunders loved to read and to listen to stories, particularly ones his father told around the dining room table after working in Chicago all day. "This was during the '60s, so he'd come back with all these tales of riots and slumlords," Saunders remarked in an interview with Laura T. Ryan and Peter Schaffer for the *Syracuse* (New York) *Post-Standard* (24 July 2005). "And as I'm getting older, I'm realizing more and more what an influence he was. Because he tells these funny, fast stories that kinda maybe incline a bit toward the dark side."

Saunders fell in love with literature in the third grade, when he was given a copy of *Johnny Tremain*, the 1943 historical children's novel by Esther Forbes that won the 1944 Newbery Medal. Something about the language in the book captured him and sparked his lifelong love of reading. Though fond of reading, he was a mediocre student and cruised through high school with no career goal in mind, apart from joining a rock band. Two teachers in his senior year, Joe and Sheri Lindbloom, each believed he should continue his education after high school. Joe, who taught English, suggested liberal arts colleges; Sheri, who taught geology, suggested something in her field. After attempting to get into schools far above his grade point average, including Notre Dame, he eventually was accepted into the Colorado School of Mines, from which he earned his bachelor's degree in geophysical engineering in 1981.

Robert Pitts/Landov

LITERARY INFLUENCES

With an oil boom occurring at the time of his graduation, Saunders quickly found work as a field geophysicist. The job brought him to Sumatra, Indonesia, where his schedule permitted him to work for four weeks, then have two weeks off, all while living in a jungle camp that was a helicopter ride away from the nearest city. During this period he loaded up bags full of books and read whenever he found time. He also traveled during his weeks off, to countries such as Afghanistan, Cambodia, Malaysia, Pakistan, and Russia. "At the time, I had this whole [Ernest] Hemingway idea," Saunders told Ryan and Schaffer. "That I was going to use that, to go have some experience and write about it. And I sort of did." He also fell under the spell of Ayn Rand's objectivist philosophy, which is held in high regard by libertarians who support a completely free-market system. After witnessing abject poverty across Asia, however, he became convinced that Rand's thinking did not account for those who suffered needlessly, and he has since repudiated his libertarian leanings.

GRADUATE STUDIES

Saunders left his job after about a year and a half, following a severe illness that he contracted from swimming in a river polluted with monkey feces. He returned to the United States and spent about two years attempting to emulate another of his literary heroes, Jack Kerouac, by traveling the country and taking odd jobs. During this period he worked as a knuckle-puller at a slaughterhouse, a doorman in Beverly Hills, and a landscaper. After a spell in Los Angeles, he returned to his hometown of Chicago completely broke. He lived in his aunt's basement while working as a roofer. He had hit bottom.

Then in 1985 Saunders stumbled across an article about the American author Jay McInerney that described how he had earned a master's of fine arts degree at Syracuse University in New York. Having never heard of such a program, Saunders was intrigued and applied to several schools, including Syracuse, where the short story he submitted came across the desk of noted American author Tobias Wolff, who was then teaching creative writing at the university. That story, "A Lack of Order in the Floating Object Room," got Saunders into the program, where he studied under both Wolff and Douglas Unger.

TECHNICAL WRITER

While at Syracuse he also met his future wife, Paula Redick, to whom he became engaged after just three weeks. Seven months later they were on their honeymoon; shortly thereafter they found out they were expecting their first child. Their older daughter, Caitlin, was born in 1988; their younger daughter, Alena, was born in 1990.

The couple had no money, and their plans of becoming bohemian writers seemed far removed from the reality of having to feed and clothe a young family. After earning his MFA from Syracuse in 1988, Saunders took a job as a technical writer at the Radian Corporation. He would later work for Eastman Kodak Company. "I was so terrified by that LA experience," he told Joel Lovell for the *New York Times* (3 Jan. 2013), "I couldn't imagine getting to that place with Paula and the girls. So I took the Radian job, and it was a very liberating thing. If I can provide for them, then in my writing time I can be as wild as I want. Having felt that abyss, I basically said, 'OK, capitalism, I have seen your gaping maw, and I want no trouble with you.'"

DEBUT COLLECTION

Saunders worked as a technical writer from 1989 to 1995, a period in which he failed to finish three books before finally being able to complete a fourth, *CivilWarLand in Bad Decline* (1996), a collection composed of a novella and several stories that became a PEN/Hemingway Award finalist that year. One of the stories in that first book, "Offloading for Mrs. Schwartz," had been published in the *New Yorker* in 1992; since that time he has published numerous stories in that prestigious magazine. The critical and commercial success of that first book enabled Saunders to return to Syracuse in 1996, this time as a teacher of creative writing, a position he holds to this day. In interviews Saunders has said he takes immense satisfaction from his teaching, both in helping young authors to find their literary voices and in how those same students inspire his own work. "At a certain age, you start to calcify a little bit," he told Jon Niccum. "You have your shtick and your ideas and your rules. Teaching at that level keeps knocking the scale off your tank."

CELEBRATED AUTHOR

Since *CivilWarLand in Bad Decline* was first published, Saunders has been hailed as one of the greatest short-story writers working in the United States today. In 2000 he published two new books, *The Very Persistent Gappers of Frip*, a children's book that became a *New York Times* best seller, and *Pastoralia*, another highly regarded collection of stories. These works further burnished his reputation as an up-and-coming author and garnered him additional accolades. In 2001 *Entertainment Weekly* named him to its list of the top one hundred most creative people in entertainment; a year later the editors of the *New Yorker* named him among America's twenty best fiction writers under forty.

Saunders next published *The Brief and Frightening Reign of Phil* (2005), a fable about a nation so small it could accommodate only one citizen at a time. Illustrated by Lane Smith, the novella received widespread praise from such noted critics as Michiko Kakutani of the *New York Times* and famed American author Thomas Pynchon. The book also helped Saunders earn two prestigious fellowships, the Guggenheim and the MacArthur, in 2006. Around the time of the book's publication, Saunders reflected on the remarkable changes his creative life had undergone in just a few short years. "When I was first writing *CivilWarLand*, I was just so struck about how hard life could be. And how quickly out of nowhere it could be difficult," he noted in his *Syracuse Post-Standard* interview. "And now, at 46, having had so much good fortune, you have to say, 'Well, on the other hand, wow. Life can be pretty beautiful.' So the trick is to get both things in there. And I'm trying to get the second one in there, but it's harder to write that."

TENTH OF DECEMBER

Although Saunders regularly publishes short fiction in the *New Yorker* and travel pieces in *GQ*, he has described himself as an "obsessive reviser" in several interviews, which is why he says he has never published a full-length novel and can take years to finish a single short story. "The Semplica Girl Diaries," one of the stories in his most recent collection, *Tenth of December* (2013), is just twenty-four pages long but required hundred of drafts and took him a dozen years to finish. When asked by Jacki Lyden in a January 20, 2013, interview on NPR why he preferred to write short stories, he replied, "Well, a kind of dumb answer is I just find it so beautiful. And I have not figured it out yet. I started maybe in my middle 20s trying a crack at it, and it's just a deep, deep well, you know? So when you get it right, it can be such a beautiful explosion of submerged meaning."

Tenth of December's reception was remarkable, even for an author whose previous books have been highly regarded in critical circles. Book reviewers loved the tales in this, his fourth story collection, both for the humorous way he presents surreal situations and also for the way his regular-guy characters meet moral challenges with remarkable courage, all in the hopes of at least taking a shot at redemption for their unfulfilled lives. In a review of *Tenth of December* for the *Washington Post* (7 Jan. 2013), Jeff Turrentine wrote: "Each one of these is as funny and off-kilter and formally ingenious as you want a Saunders story to be, but each one is also something else: unabashedly tender. The author has often been compared to Kurt Vonnegut, whom he regards as a major influence. . . . But even Vonnegut's biggest fans acknowledge his cynicism. . . . Saunders, by contrast, hasn't given up on us all—not yet." He elaborated, "As one particularly despondent character says about the value of staying alive, of remaining connected to those he loves: 'There could still be many—many drops of goodness.'"

AWARDS AND HONORS

In April 2013, just months after *Tenth of December*'s publication, Saunders learned that he had been chosen as the winner of the 2013 PEN/Malamud Award, which recognizes authors for their success in the field of short fiction. The award, which carries a stipend of five thousand dollars, has been handed out each year since 1988; past recipients include Edward P. Jones, Nam Le, Joyce Carol Oates, Grace Paley, John Updike, and Saunders's former writing professor Tobias Wolff. Later that month Saunders was named to *Time*'s annual list of the hundred most influential people in the world. In a piece praising Saunders, Mary Karr, a fellow author and colleague at Syracuse, wrote in *Time* (18 Apr. 2013): "For more than a decade, George Saunders has been the best short-story writer in English—not 'one of,' not 'arguably,' but the Best. . . . George's work is a stiff tonic for the vapid agony of contemporary living—great art from the greatest guy."

Saunders is also the recipient of the 2009 Arts and Letters Award for literature from the American Academy of Arts and Letters and has appeared on numerous television programs, including *The Charlie Rose Show*, *The Colbert Report*, and *Late Night with David Letterman*.

PERSONAL LIFE

Raised Roman Catholic but now a practicing Buddhist, Saunders received accolades for a commencement speech he gave at Syracuse University in May 2013, in which he told the assembled graduates that his greatest regret in life was not being as kind as he could have been. "I've been thinking about this kindness idea for most of my life, I guess," Saunders said, as quoted by Chris Baker for the *Syracuse* (New York) *Post-Standard* (8 Aug. 2013). "[I] was raised Catholic and always loved that part of the tradition. [I] was very taken with, and moved by, the idea of Jesus being infinitely patient and loving. And my wife and I have been studying Buddhism since our kids were little. And kindness—and the reasons for our unkindness—[are] at the center of those practices."

Saunders lives in the Catskill Mountains and teaches at Syracuse University.

SUGGESTED READING

Brunner, Rob. Rev. of *Tenth of December*, by George Saunders. *Entertainment Weekly*. Entertainment Weekly, 11 Jan. 2013. Web. 14 Feb. 2014.

Karr, Mary. "The 2013 Time 100: George Saunders." *Time*. Time, 18 Apr. 2013. Web. 14 Feb. 2014.

Lovell, Joel. "George Saunders Has Written the Best Book You'll Read This Year." *New York Times*. New York Times, 3 Jan. 2013. Web. 14 Feb. 2014.

Lyden, Jacki. "George Saunders on Absurdism and Ventriloquism in *Tenth of December*." *All Things Considered*. NPR, 20 Jan. 2013. Web. 14 Feb. 2014.

Turrentine, Jeff. "George Saunders Unleashes More Satirical Stories in *Tenth of December*." *Washington Post*. Washington Post, 7 Jan. 2013. Web. 14 Feb. 2014.

SELECTED WORKS

CivilWarLand in Bad Decline, 1996; *The Very Persistent Gappers of Frip*, 2000; *Pastoralia*, 2000; *The Brief and Frightening Reign of Phil*, 2005; *In Persuasion Nation*, 2006; *The Braindead Megaphone*, 2007; *Tenth of December*, 2013

—*Christopher Mari*

Associated Press

Eugenie Scott

Born: October 24, 1945
Occupation: Physical anthropologist

Dr. Eugenie Scott is a physical anthropologist and the former executive director of the National Center for Science Education (NCSE), a California-based nonprofit group that supports the teaching of evolution in schools and advises parents and teachers fighting local efforts to add creationism and intelligent design to school curriculums. (Creationism is the theory that the world was created as literally described in the Bible, while intelligent design is the theory that the complexity of life suggests the existence of a divine creator.) The NCSE was founded in 1981, and Scott joined the organization in 1987. She was lauded for her patient approach to a contentious conversation as well as for her ability to forge partnerships with religious communities. When Scott announced that she was stepping down as the executive director of the NCSE in 2013, Kenneth Miller, a biology professor at Brown University and a former NCSE board member, told Jeffrey Mervis for *Science* magazine (6 May 2013), "She's incomparable, irreplaceable, and indispensable." He added that she consistently transformed heated debate with her ability "to bring people together around the goal of defending the integrity of science education."

Legislative efforts to ban the subject of evolution from school curriculum in favor of creationism have been deemed unconstitutional, and in 1987, in *Edwards v. Aguillard*, the United States Supreme Court ruled that it was likewise unconstitutional to require schools to give equal time to the teaching of creationism. Thus, Scott told Sandra Blakeslee for the *New York Times* (29 Aug. 1999), creationists have since opted

to present "evidence" against evolution, hoping to undermine it. The plethora of theories offered up by antievolution forces have kept the NCSE busy for years; many arguments even bear scientific-sounding names such as *creation science* and *intelligent design* as well as *abrupt-appearance theory* and *irreducible complexity theory*. For Scott and the chronically underfunded NSCE, the amount of financial and ideological support for these biblically inspired theories can be daunting. But Scott reminds her supporters that the evolution "debate" is a matter not of belief or disbelief but of good science. "I won't defend evolution," Wilgoren explained, as quoted by Jodi Wilgoren for the *New York Times* (6 Oct. 2005). "We don't defend the spherical Earth. We need to stop defending, as they put it, Darwinism, and just make [the creationists] show they have a scientific view."

EARLY LIFE AND EDUCATION

Eugenie Carol Scott was born on October 24, 1945, in La Crosse, Wisconsin. After sneaking a peek at her older sister's anthropology textbook, the ten-year-old Scott decided on her future profession. Growing up, she was an enthusiastic science student despite attending high school during an era in which evolution was absent from most school textbooks. In a short essay for the online magazine *Spiked*, Scott wrote about the first time she encountered an explanation of Darwinian natural selection. She and a friend asked their biology teacher why there were so many animals. "He said: 'Well, some people believe that some animals are better able to live in an environment than others, and they have more offspring and that kind comes to dominate in that environment, and the population gradually becomes different through time,'" she wrote. "My head reeled. This was such a wonderful, simple explanation, and it made so much sense."

Scott did not formally study evolution until she was an anthropology student at the University of Wisconsin–Milwaukee. She earned her bachelor's degree in 1967 and her master's in 1968. She enrolled at the University of Missouri–Columbia to earn her doctorate, and it was there that she first encountered the term *creation science* in 1971, when her professor and mentor Jim Gavan handed her a stack of brightly colored pamphlets produced by the Institute for Creation Research (ICR). The organization, which was founded in 1970, is now a multimillion-dollar enterprise, but at the time, Scott was fascinated by what she considered to be a peculiar fringe movement and began collecting creationist literature.

In 1974, the year Scott earned her doctorate, Gavan agreed to debate Duane Gish, a biochemist and leader in the creationist movement. (Gish, who died in 2013, was a former vice president of the ICR.) In an interview with Cornelia Dean for the *New York Times* (2 Sept. 2013), Scott said that the debate was the first time she recognized the seriousness of the creation movement—and what it would mean for future generations of scientists. Scott, who had just begun teaching at the University of Kentucky at Lexington, took some of her students to Missouri to hear her mentor speak. "We were greatly dismayed," she recalled. "The scientist [Gavan] talked science, and the creationist [Gish] connected to the audience and told good jokes and was really personable. And presented a lot of really bad science."

TEACHING CAREER

Scott was still a professor at the University of Kentucky in 1980, when a group of citizens proposed that Lexington's schools should add creationism to their curriculum. Scott, by her own account, was the only "one on campus with a box of creationist literature," she told Myrna Watanabe for the *Scientist* (27 May 2002), and thus she was put in charge of formulating a response. She became the leader of the opposition group and even engineered a partnership between university professors and local religious figures. After two years, Scott and her team prevailed, and the proposal to teach creationism in Lexington schools was dropped. But in a larger sense, the battle was just beginning. The same year Lexington considered adopting the creationism proposal, the ICR promoted the so-called Ellwanger bills in a number of states. The bills called for both evolution and creationism to be given "equal time" in science classrooms. "Equal time" became law in Arkansas and Louisiana but was declared unconstitutional by the US Supreme Court in 1987 in *Edwards v. Aguillard*. The case was a victory for scientists, but it set the stage for the pseudoscientific intelligent design debates that would come to a head in the 2000s.

NCSE AND *KITZMILLER V. DOVER*

In 1986, Scott saw that the NCSE, which was founded in 1981, was looking for an executive director. She decided to apply for the position and was soon hired, filling the post in 1987. The organization has grown over the years, but it remains a small operation. According to Dean, the Oakland, California, headquarters of the NCSE employ fourteen staff members—some of whom are part-time workers—and has an annual budget of $1.5 million. The center publishes reports and a weekly newsletter for its five thousand members, but fielding daily phone calls from concerned teachers and parents around the country is its primary function. Miller, the Brown biology professor and former NCSE board member, likened Scott and her team to a "national fire department." "Whenever the scientific integrity of biology teaching is under fire or compromised, the center goes there to provide support and lend resources to people who are actually fighting the fire," he told Blakeslee.

In the early 2000s, Scott and the NCSE became aware of a school board in Dover, Pennsylvania, that included a handful of creationists. The state of Pennsylvania requires biology classes to teach evolution, but in 2004, that board proposed adding to the curriculum the intelligent design textbook *Of Pandas and People: The Central Question of Biological Origins* (1989). The board passed a policy requiring teachers to teach intelligent design in late 2004, but, as Scott told D. J. Grothe for the Center for Inquiry podcast *Point of Inquiry* (20 Jan. 2006), that policy was "watered down," requiring that each teacher only read a disclaimer that said that there were problems with the theory of evolution as well as competing and equally valid theories—including intelligent design. The disclaimer encouraged students to seek out *Of Pandas and People* on their own in the school library.

Unhappy with the actions of the board, a group of parents and teachers contacted the NCSE. Scott and her colleagues provided them with resources explaining intelligent design and why it is not a viable scientific theory. When the group of citizens decided to sue the school board, the NCSE brought in the American Civil Liberties Union (ACLU) and found them a lawyer who took the case pro bono. The NCSE advised the legal team and even recommended expert witnesses. It was the first time intelligent design had gone to trial, and the judge, a Republican appointed by President George W. Bush, criticized the "breathtaking inanity" of the creationists' arguments, Dean reported. The 2005 case, known as *Kitzmiller v. Dover*, was a landmark victory for the NCSE.

EVOLUTION VS. CREATIONISM

In 2004, Scott published a textbook titled *Evolution vs. Creationism: An Introduction*. "Its main virtue is to explain the scientific method, which many invoke but few describe vividly," Judith Shulevitz wrote in an essay for the *New York Times* (22 Jan. 2006). Scott's focus on the scientific method—the steps that form the foundation of scientific inquiry—is purposeful. Her frustration with creationism and intelligent design primary lies in the inability of those theories to follow any coherent line of questioning; they flout the very tenets of science itself, asking students to have faith instead of teaching them to look for evidence. (Scott works hard to rid her arguments of vague words such as *believe*, and requires those around her to say that they accept evolution, not that they believe in it.)

Some have argued that Scott lends credence to intelligent design by engaging in and patiently refuting theories such as abrupt appearance theory, which contends that life, in all of its present-day complexity, simply appeared out of thin air. But Scott told Liza Gross for *QUEST* (22 Aug. 2012) that she aims her arguments at a group she calls the "big middle": "the people who are not conservative Christians, who don't have a religious or ideological reason to object to evolution but who just don't know very much about it and who are reachable." In this vein, Scott and fellow NCSE employee Glenn Branch edited a collection of essays about evolution and intelligent design, titled *Not in Our Classrooms: Why Intelligent Design Is Bad for Our Schools* and published in 2006.

CLIMATE CHANGE

In 2012, Scott announced that the NCSE would add supporting the teaching of climate change to its mission. Just as many schools teach students that creationism is a viable alternative to evolution, a growing number are also denying the existence of human-induced climate change. "As a scientist, I know the process that scientists go through to come up with the conclusions," Scott told Katherine Bagley for *Inside Climate News* (2 July 2013). "It is not like we wake up one morning and say, 'I think it is getting warmer.' There is a long process of data collection and analysis, constant questioning from your colleagues, and the back and forth of disputes, and presentations of more data and more models. Finally you reach a consensus. That is the way it was with evolution. That is the way it was with climate change."

Climate change deniers, Scott has asserted in several interviews, make many of the same arguments that creationists do. Creationists seize on gaps in the fossil record, for instance, while climate change deniers look for specific occurrences that, taken out of context, appear to support their claim. As Scott told Gross, 1998 was an unusually warm year, so a graph measuring temperature data between 1998 and 2008 appears to suggest that temperatures are getting cooler; thus, deniers assert, global warming is not happening. Scott calls this tactic "anomaly mongering." This fixation on random pieces of evidence, Scott says, suggests a larger confusion about the role of science and what it means to view the world through a scientific lens. "I think so much of what people misunderstand about science is this balance between science being very reliable in explaining the natural world yet it's expandable," she told Gross.

Scott stepped down from the position of executive director in January 2014 and was succeeded by biologist Ann Reid. She remains active with the NCSE, serving as the chair of the organization's advisory council. She has also told interviewers that she hopes to embark on a speaking tour and write a new book.

Scott is married to Thomas C. Sager, a lawyer. They have one daughter and live in Berkeley, California.

SUGGESTED READING

Blakeslee, Sandra. "In Schools Across the Land, a Group Mounts Counterattacks on 'Creation Science.'" *New York Times*. New York Times, 29 Aug. 1999. Web. 7 Jan. 2014.

Dean, Cornelia. "Standard-Bearer in Evolution Fight." *New York Times*. New York Times, 2 Sept. 2013. Web. 7 Jan. 2014.

Gross, Liza. "In Defense of Science: An Interview with NCSE's Eugenie Scott." *QUEST*. KQED, 22 Aug. 2012. Web. 7 Jan. 2014.

Mervis, Jeffrey. "Eugenie Scott to Retire from US Center That Fights Antievolution Forces." *Science*. American Association for the Advancement of Science, 6 May 2013. Web. 7 Jan. 2014.

Shulevitz, Judith. "When Cosmologies Collide." *New York Times*. New York Times, 22 Jan. 2006. Web. 7 Jan. 2014.

Wilgoren, Jodi. "Seeing Creation and Evolution in Grand Canyon." *New York Times*. New York Times, 6 Oct. 2005. Web. 7 Jan. 2014.

—*Molly Hagan*

Tim Scott

Born: September 19, 1965
Occupation: United States Senator

Tim Scott gained national attention in 2010 as the first black Republican to be elected to the US House of Representatives from the Deep South in more than a century. In addition, he was the first black Republican to serve in the House since the retirement of Oklahoma's J. C. Watts in 2003. He was then appointed to the Senate in 2012—only the fourth black Republican member of that body since 1870. Speaking of learning his way around the Senate to Schuyler Kropf

Joshua Roberts/Reuters/Landov

for *Charleston Post and Courier* (26 May 2014), Scott said, "To make progress you certainly have to be willing to understand that persistence and patience will lead to progress." Both then House majority leader Eric Cantor and Speaker John Boehner attended his birthday party in 2011, indicating that Scott is a man to watch in Washington. As an Evangelical Christian, Scott appeals to the many conservative voters in his home state of South Carolina.

EARLY LIFE AND EDUCATION

Scott's parents divorced when he was seven. His mother, a nurse at a hospital in Charleston, worked long days to keep herself and her two sons off the welfare rolls. Scott began working at thirteen, serving popcorn at a movie theater and wiping windshields at a gas station. However, he was disruptive in class, and by ninth grade, was in academic trouble.

Enter John Moniz, who owned a Chick-fil-A fast-food restaurant next to the movie theater, where Scott would often go on breaks to buy fries and flirt with the girls. Moniz, a graduate of the Citadel and a conservative Christian, noted that Scott bought only fries—it was all he could afford. He began giving Scott sandwiches for free, and the two soon became close, with Moniz mentoring Scott on the importance of structure and discipline.

In addition, Moniz introduced Scott to motivational writings of men such as Zig Ziglar. As Scott told Katherine Q. Seelye for *New York Times* (25 June 2010), "To know my story is to

understand that there were people who had no reason to step up to the plate and help me, but who did. I want to serve the community because the community helped me."

Moniz died of a heart attack when he was only thirty-eight years old; Scott was seventeen. In the wake of that loss, Scott wrote a personal mission statement—to positively affect a billion people before his own death. Moniz himself had hoped to reach a million people.

From that statement came a series of five-year goals and plans. He related to Seelye, "I have financial goals, the number of lives I want to impact, the number of speeches to give to nonprofits and to faith community organizations, the number of dollars to invest back into the community, the number of speeches to kids like me in high school who are dropping out."

Scott improved his grades and went to Presbyterian College on a partial football scholarship, playing tailback. He spent the first year of college reading the Bible as well as playing football. As a result, he felt God had plans for him other than playing ball and transferred to Charleston Southern University, earning a degree in political science in 1988.

EARNING HIS WAY

Following his graduation, Scott worked as a partner in Pathway Real Estate Group and headed Tim Scott Allstate Insurance. He had five employees at the insurance agency, where he worked his way up to a net worth of more than $750,000.

After deciding to become a Republican as Moniz had been, Scott spent thirteen years in county government; he also worked for Republican Mark Sanford's campaign for governor. Friends counseled him that he would need to wait to gain recognition as a Democrat; Scott was not content to wait. The Republican Party donated the maximum amount, $5,000, to his campaign.

After his 1995 election to the Charleston County Council with 80 percent of the vote, Senator Strom Thurmond sent a handwritten note to welcome him to the Republican Party. Given that Thurmond had been a prominent supporter of segregation in the past, this gesture seemed significant. The following year, Scott became cochair of Thurmond's last senatorial campaign. The senator died, at 100, in 2003, the year he retired. The strangeness of an African American working with Thurmond did not occur to Scott. As he told Katherin Seelye for *New York Times* (25 June 2010), "The Strom Thurmond I knew had nothing to do with that. I don't spend much time on history."

From Charleston County Council, Scott moved in 2008 to the South Carolina House of Representatives. There he cosponsored a bill on immigration that called for measures similar to those taken by Arizona (most of which the US Supreme Court later struck down). The anti-immigration Minutemen Project endorsed him as a result.

Although he submitted five bills in South Carolina, within six months, he was running for the US House of Representatives. He was backed by Tea Party sympathizers, including Sarah Palin, and by members of the Republican establishment, such as Virginia's Eric Cantor. The Club for Growth, a fiscally conservative political action committee dedicated to limited government, donated to his campaign. Scott promised that if elected, he would not serve longer than four terms, citing other goals.

US REPRESENTATIVE

Scott won the 2010 election to the United States House of Representatives with sixty-nine percent of the vote. He represented the First Congressional District, which included Charleston and areas along the coast. Unlike many African Americans in Congress, he declined to join the Congressional Black Caucus, commenting that race isn't part of his identity as a politician. J. C. Watts, of Oklahoma, who retired from the House in 2003, likewise did not join. As he told Zev Chafets for Newsweek (2010), "What I am eager to do is be an ambassador to all groups on my issues. Sure, I'll go if they want to send me to the Urban League or black business groups to talk about economic empowerment and the importance of fiscal responsibility, but I'm not going to be their black Republican."

Of the eighty-seven newly elected Republicans in the lower chamber, Scott was one of only two African Americans—the other being Florida's Allen West. Scott became a House deputy whip and the liaison to the leadership for the freshman class of House members as a member of the Elected Leadership Committee. He also was assigned to the Rules Committee, a powerful position. Like many with Tea Party leanings, Scott sought to repeal the Affordable Care Act, stop tax increases, and fight amnesty for illegal aliens. He is opposed to affirmative action programs, which he considers unnecessary, and favors school choice and voucher programs.

FORMING ALLIANCES

Scott was one of four Republican newcomers from South Carolina elected in 2010. The men quickly bonded, meeting for dinner many nights and playing basketball in the House gym. Three of the men already knew one another from serving in the South Carolina legislature. In an effort to cut costs, Scott and Duncan shared an apartment. Scott was the man to whom the others turned for tactics and energy.

As a body, they voted against a deal in April 2011 that the Speaker John Boehner and President Obama put together to avoid a government shutdown. Scott supported then House majority leader Eric Cantor when the latter walked out of debt-ceiling negotiations. Scott sponsored a bill that proposed cutting corporate taxes from 35 to 23 percent. In his thinking, this was a first step toward completely rewriting the tax code, an easier bill to pass than one on capital gains or the so-called death tax. Like many fiscal conservatives, Scott viewed lowering corporate taxes as a means to job creation.

Traditionally conservative, South Carolina voters often elect candidates with small-government views. At the time of Scott's appearance on the national stage, the state suffered from a poor reputation in light of ex-governor Mark Sanford's cover-up of his extramarital affair. As Scott explained to Jennifer Steinhauer for New York Times (11 Apr. 2011), "We have a poor reputation nationally. And I think sometimes when you feel like an underdog, the troops coalesce."

Support for Scott within the black community is lacking, however, because most blacks are Democrats. Scott has expressed that he has no interest in the past, preferring to focus on the future. Thus, removing the Confederate flag from the South Carolina capitol building is a nonissue for him. The NAACP gave Scott an F for his politics, citing, among other things, his vote to delay funding a settlement between the federal government and black farmers who claimed their requests for loans were denied because of their race. He also voted to repeal the Affordable Care Act and opposed the budget put forth by the Congressional Black Caucus. Speaking to Zev Chafets for Newsweek (2010), Conquestrina White, an art student in Charleston said, "He comes across to black people as someone we can't trust. I especially don't appreciate the way he bashes Obama."

US SENATOR

In December 2012, South Carolina governor Nikki Haley tapped Scott to replace Jim DeMint in the Senate. DeMint was leaving to head the Heritage Foundation, a conservative think tank. Scott was sworn into office on January 3, 2013 to serve as an interim senator until either he or a new senator are elected by constituents and sworn in to finish the rest of DeMint's term, due to end in 2016.

As a US senator, Scott has promoted a balanced budget and has been willing to vote against his party. When Republicans came into power, they banned pork in the budget, but several members of Congress have continued to push for projects in their states or districts.

Scott himself pushed for what would have been considered an earmark by any other name—a harbor-dredging project in his hometown of Charleston. As he told Ron Nixon for New York Times (19 July 2011), "This was a merit-based project that was open and transparent." His rationale was that dredging would allow larger ships to use the port, thus creating more jobs and boosting the economy. Scott secured $150,000 for the first segment of what is projected to be a $300 million dollar project. Although President Obama did not greenlight the project for the Army Corps of Engineers, the corps added the project to their budget after Scott and Senator Lindsey Graham threatened to obstruct congressional progress. "Persistence pays off," Scott told Nixon. "We knew dredging the Port of Charleston was a worthy project, and we were persistent in ensuring that the corps knew that, too."

Scott commented in light of the 2012 school shooting in Newtown, Connecticut, that he might vote against further gun control measures. As he said on CNN's *Starting Point with Soledad O'Brien*, as quoted by *CNN Newswire* (19 Dec. 2012), "I think the solutions are not necessarily in new legislation. Perhaps the solution starts with us examining the mental condition of the person and the persons in the past that have had the desire to create the atrocities we have seen recently."

In June 2014 Scott won the Republican special election primary for the vacant Senate seat with 90 percent of the vote. His landslide victory was unsurprising given that his primary opponent did not campaign. Scott will face Democratic candidate Joyce Dickerson in the November 2014 special election.

A DIFFERENT KIND OF TEA PARTY MEMBER

Although Scott was tapped to temporarily replace Senator Jim DeMint, sometimes considered one of the Tea Party's fathers, he has a more moderate approach than many in the party. Scott is certainly in favor of repealing the Affordable Care Act, and supports other Tea Party–aligned initiatives. However, he is looking at the long term, and is seemingly content to keep a low profile in the early days of what he hopes will be a long Senate career.

One of Scott's areas of focus is education. He is in favor of dismantling the Common Core objectives put forth by the Department of Education, with input from many stakeholders. He has been a speaker at historically black colleges, where he has gained an audience despite his lack of support among many African American voters and organizations.

Trying to introduce himself to voters throughout South Carolina, Scott began a listening tour, traveling incognito, wearing blue jeans. He volunteered at Goodwill, worked at a shoe shop, and rode the bus through Charleston's low-income neighborhoods. As he told Ben Terris for *Washington Post* (7 May 2014), "If you want to build a relationship and build a rapport, then you don't talk about specific issues first. This is about becoming credible. It's hard to have a conversation with someone who lacks credibility." He likens these actions to being a salesman, referring to his past efforts selling vacuum cleaners and Amway products door-to-door.

PERSONAL

Before Scott was elected to the US House of Representatives, he lost thirty pounds over a two-year period. He helped develop a heart-healthy program for the hospital where his mother works, and maintained a regular Sunday lunch date with her. After his election to the House, he continued to speak to her three times a day. A firm believer in individual initiative over government intervention, he told Seelye, "I need to invest my time, my talent and my treasure in getting things done. That's my ambition." While driving in the car, Scott listens to Hootie and the Blowfish and motivational tapes. He has served as a trustee on the board of suburban Charleston's Seacoast Church, a nondenominational, Evangelical megachurch. He counts Chief Justice John Roberts and Justice Clarence Thomas among his intellectual heroes.

SUGGESTED READING

Chafets, Zev. "Tea For Tim." *Newsweek* 15 Nov. 2010: 39–41. Print.

Kropf, Schuyler. "Tim Scott Running Full-bore Campaign Against Minimal Opposition." *Charleston Post and Courier*. Post and Courier, 26 May 2014. Web. 12 June 2014.

Nixon, Ron. "Cost-Cutters, Except When the Spending Is Back Home." *New York Times*. New York Times, 19 July 2011. Web. 12 June 2014.

Peterson, Kyle. "Great Scott! South Carolina's Junior Senator on Race, Education, and Growin' Up Po'" *American Spectator* 46.8 (2013): 4–5. Print.

Seelye, Katherine. "S. Carolina Candidate Shrugs off History's Lure." *New York Times*. New York Times, 25 June 2010. Web. 3 June 2014.

Steinhauer, Jennifer. "Close-Knit, New to the House, And Resistant to Blending In." *New York Times* 11 Apr. 2011: A1(L). Print.

Terris, Ben. "The Undercover Senator: Tim Scott Goes Anecdote Shopping in S.C." *Washington Post*. Washington Post, 7 May 2014. Web. 12 June 2014.

—*Judy Johnson*

Sara Seager

Born: July 21, 1971
Occupation: Astrophysicist

There are approximately fifty billion planets in the Milky Way galaxy. Roughly five hundred million of these planets are thought to orbit in the

Courtesy of the John D. & Catherine T. MacArthur Foundation

so-called "habitable zone," the region of space that scientists believe is the right distance from a parent star for liquid water—and possibly life—to exist. Sara Seager, an astrophysicist and professor of planetary science and physics at the Massachusetts Institute of Technology (MIT), has made it her life's goal to find an Earth-like planet among these millions of worlds. Although such a discovery may appear to be a long shot, she believes that humanity is on the cusp of finding just such a planet, as scientists now have the tools to not only detect exoplanets but to categorize their compositions and atmospheres.

Scientists first confirmed the existence of planets orbiting stars other than the sun in the mid-1990s, using a method called radial velocity, which measures minute changes to a parent star's spectral lines caused by the gravitational pull of an orbiting planet due to the Doppler effect. Since then, astronomers have catalogued more than seventeen hundred such exoplanets and have been developing increasingly advanced techniques to directly observe such planets. However, most of the exoplanets discovered so far have been gas giants like Jupiter, incapable of supporting life as we know it, or planets that orbit too closely to their stars to support a viable atmosphere or liquid water—two key factors in the development of life on Earth. Today, planet hunters such as Seager are using ever-more refined tools to find smaller, Earth-like worlds and to study their atmospheres through techniques Seager herself has pioneered. "We want to change the way people see their place in the universe," she said to John Allemang for the *Globe and Mail* (25 Feb. 2011) of herself and her fellow exoplanet hunters. "My aim is to take people and point at a star you can see with the naked eye in a really dark sky and say, 'That star has a planet like Earth.'"

EARLY LIFE AND EDUCATION

Sara Seager was born in Toronto, Ontario, on July 21, 1971. Her parents divorced when she was in grade school. During her childhood, she spent most weekdays with her mother, siblings, and stepfather and most weekends and summers with her father, a general practitioner who later became an expert on hair transplants. In interviews, Seager has admitted that her father was an enormous influence on her continuing development. "My Dad really pushed me to be a successful person," she told Allemang for the *Globe and Mail*. "He was constantly doing things to make me uncomfortable, to push my boundaries, then push them again." Her father's attention was particularly necessary to Seager as a child, when she felt isolated from the rest of her family and very much an outsider. She had a strained relationship with her stepfather, which caused difficulty with her mother and siblings. Since her father's death from cancer in 2007, Seager has described herself as an orphan because she is no longer on speaking terms with the rest of her family.

Seager first realized that she wanted to become an astrophysicist as a high school student at the Jarvis Collegiate Institute, a public high school in Toronto known across Canada for its science program. When she was sixteen years old, she attended an Astronomy Day opening house at the St. George campus of the University of Toronto and came home captivated by the cosmos and aspiring to become an astrophysicist. Her father, however, was not entirely convinced. As she recalled in an interview with Corey S. Powell for *Smithsonian* magazine (May 2014), "He gave me a long, harsh lecture, 'You can't do that, you need a real job.' But after that, every few months, he'd ask, 'So what does a physicist do?' He couldn't get his head around the idea, what is their job?" Undaunted, she entered the University of Toronto in the fall of 1990 to study mathematics and physics. Upon earning her bachelor of science degree in 1994, she entered the doctoral program in the Department of Astronomy at Harvard University in Cambridge, Massachusetts. There, under the guidance of Dimitar Sasselov at the Harvard-Smithsonian Center for Astrophysics, she tackled the problem of modeling how radiation collided with hot gases following the big bang.

PIONEERING GRADUATE SCHOOL WORK

Despite her love of astronomy, Seager was admittedly uncertain whether she truly wanted a career in science during the time she was working toward her PhD. When she heard the first substantiated reports of planets orbiting distant stars, however, she became more certain she was on the right path. The first exoplanet to be discovered, dubbed 51 Pegasi b and confirmed in 1995, was a gas giant as large as Jupiter that orbited very closely to its parent star—a phenomenon scientists had not anticipated because all of the gas giants orbiting the sun are in the outer reaches of the solar system. (Since that time, other exoplanet discoveries—including planets that orbit in the opposite direction of their parent star's rotation and planets that have tilted orbits—have forced scientists to rethink previously accepted theoretical models of planetary formation.) Seager and Sasselov quickly realized that the modeling work they had been doing with hot gases could be applied to understanding the atmospheres of these distant gas giants, where temperatures could reach upwards of 2,000 degrees Fahrenheit. They became convinced that they could study the starlight passing through the atmosphere of a distant world to learn important facts about the atmosphere's composition.

Seager's subsequent work wowed her fellow researchers. Two years after the existence of an exoplanet was first confirmed, she modeled the appearance of starlight reflecting off the atmosphere of an exoplanet, laying the foundation for other astronomers in her field. Furthermore, as Powell noted in Seager's profile for *Smithsonian*, "In 1999, she predicted that the element sodium should leave a prominent fingerprint in light shining through the atmosphere as a planet transits in front of its star, a finding soon confirmed when a colleague at the Center for Astrophysics (and a fellow University of Toronto alum), David Charbonneau, observed just such a transiting planet." As Seager recalled to Powell, "People were really impressed, to make a prediction at that level that led to an observation."

In 1999, Seager completed her doctoral degree with her thesis *Extrasolar Planets under Strong Stellar Irradiation*. She immediately accepted a postdoctoral appointment at the Institute for Advanced Study in Princeton, New Jersey, where she worked under the guidance of astrophysicist John Bahcall from 1999 to 2002, becoming the institute's resident expert on exoplanets. Her work there ultimately led her to her current specialty—searching for a small terrestrial planet with an atmospheric composition and liquid water similar to Earth.

SEARCHING FOR AN EARTH-LIKE PLANET

From 2002 to 2006, Seager served as a senior research staff member at the Carnegie Institution of Washington in Washington, DC, and in January 2007, she became an associate professor of planetary science at MIT, earning tenure in July 2007. During this period of her career, she sought ways to improve astronomers' chances of detecting Earth-like planets. Because terrestrial planets tend to be smaller and have less mass than gas giants, they are more difficult to detect through radial velocity and even less likely to be directly observed. That said, a number of promising terrestrial planets have been located in the nearly twenty years since the first exoplanets were discovered. Yet, as the list of confirmed exoplanets continues to grow, Seager remains confident that researchers will be able to find telltale signs of life by analyzing the atmospheric composition of an Earth-like planet. "If an alien civilization is looking at us from far away, and it knows something about chemistry, it will know that we have millions to billions of times more oxygen than we should [if there were no life on Earth]. It's hard to come up with any other process that can produce that amount of oxygen, other than the activity of living things," she explained in an interview with Phil Plait for *Discover* magazine (Nov. 2010). "So we're looking for an atmosphere with chemicals in it that should not be in it by any stretch of the imagination."

The process, however, remains daunting. She remarked to Allemang, "If I were to take a harsh look at reality, and say, 'What are my chances of finding another Earth?'—that's not a pretty picture. So in order to get up every day and do my job and get excited about it, I have to believe we're going to do it—and do everything in my power to bring it about." But she also stresses that what she is looking for is not necessarily proof of the existence of an advanced civilization like humans on Earth but rather for the signs of life in general—even the existence of single-celled organisms such as bacteria. In order to narrow down the candidate planets that could potentially host living organisms, Seager and her fellow planet hunters need to locate the best possible candidates to look for chemical signs of life in their atmospheres, improve their detection of biochemical processes in faraway atmospheres, and improve the ways in which scientists can observe those planets directly. To those ends, the primary focus of her research involves refining the theoretical models of exoplanet atmospheres and developing an unmanned space mission for the US National Aeronautics and Space Administration (NASA) to carry out using a fleet of nanosatellites called ExoplanetSats, which are small, space-based telescopes that will be able to view exoplanets much more clearly than ground-based telescopes.

UPCOMING PROJECTS

As of 2014, Seager has a number of projects in development. The first is NASA's Transiting Exoplanet Survey Satellite, better known as TESS, which is due to launch in 2017. TESS will search the cosmos for planets circling about a half million M stars, red dwarfs that are smaller than the sun and therefore more likely to show the shadows of their orbiting planets. She is also anticipating the projected 2018 launch of the James Webb Space Telescope, which is set to replace the pioneering Hubble

Space Telescope that has been orbiting Earth since 1990. The Webb Telescope will be able to directly observe the atmospheres of planets found by TESS and analyze if they indicate signs of life. Seager explained their methods in an interview with Adam Hadhazy for *Discover* (6 Jan. 2014): "When a planet travels in front of its star, some of the starlight passes through the atmosphere, and some of the atmospheric gases leave telltale signatures on that starlight. By separating out the starlight from the planet light, we can identify molecules in the planet's atmosphere and look for gases produced by life, like oxygen, ozone and ammonia."

Seager is also the chair of NASA's science and technology definition team for the starshade project, which is developing a giant, flower-petal-shaped screen that could be deployed in front of a space telescope to block the light from distant stars so that astronomers could observe any orbiting planets without interference. The target date for launch is 2022. In addition to these NASA-related projects, Seager has partnered with a private company called Planetary Resources, which is looking to mine near-Earth asteroids for precious metals, in the hopes that her potential share of the profits will fund further efforts in her search for an Earth-like planet. She is also cofounder of the nonprofit Nexterra Foundation, which seeks to map planets in neighboring star systems.

PERSONAL LIFE AND AWARDS

Sara Seager has received many awards throughout her professional life, including the 2004 Bok Prize in Astronomy from Harvard University, the 2007 Helen B. Warner Prize from the American Astronomical Society, the 2012 Raymond and Beverly Sackler Prize in the Physical Sciences, and a 2013 MacArthur Foundation fellowship. She has been a member of the American Physical Society and the American Astronomical Society since 1999 and was a member of the American Geophysical Society from 2007 to 2011. In 2012, she was named a fellow of the American Association for the Advancement of Science (AAAS), and the following year she became an honorary member of the Royal Astronomical Society of Canada.

She has also received considerable media attention in recent years. In 2006, *Popular Science* placed her on the magazine's fifth annual "Brilliant Ten" list. In 2008, she was named to *Discover* magazine's list of the "Best 20 under 40." In 2012, she was named one of the "25 Most Influential in Space" by the editors of *Time* magazine. Seager has spoken at dozens of international conferences and public lectures throughout her career, and her findings have been published in numerous scientific journals. She also wrote *Exoplanet Atmospheres: Physical Processes* (2010), which is considered to be an essential book in her field, and she served as the editor of *Exoplanets* (2010).

A US citizen since July 2010, Seager was married to Michael Isaac Wevrick, a Canadian editor of science and mathematics textbooks, until his death from cancer of the small intestine on July 23, 2011. Together, they had two sons, Maxwell and Alexander. The couple met at a skiing event in 1994, when she was twenty-two and he was thirty. Six months into their relationship, they embarked on a two-month canoe trip, exploring the Northwest Territories in Canada. Even then, all they needed was one another's company. "When I was married I only had my husband, who was my best friend," she remarked to Powell. "I'm not your average person, and it's really hard for me to integrate with the real world. . . . The most important thing that ever happened to me was my husband dying. Everything else was meaningless."

SUGGESTED READING

Allemang, John. "A Space Pioneer Aims to Prove We're Not Alone." *Globe and Mail*. Thomson Reuters, 25 Feb. 2011. Web. 14 Aug. 2014.

Hadhazy, Adam. "Worlds without End: Q&A with Exoplanet Hunter Sara Seager." *Discover*. Kalmbach, 6 Jan. 2014. Web. 14 Aug. 2014.

Plait, Phil. "Is Anybody Out There?" *Discover*. Kalmbach, 27 Jan. 2011. Web. 14 Aug. 2014.

Powell, Corey S. "Life in the Cosmos." *Smithsonian*. Smithsonian.com, May 2014. Web. 14 Aug. 2014.

—*Christopher Mari*

Christine Sinclair

Born: June 12, 1983
Occupation: Soccer player

Canadian professional soccer player Christine Sinclair is considered to be one of the greatest athletes in the sport. "She is the undisputed face of women's soccer in this country," Patrick Kennedy wrote for Ontario's *Kingston Whig-Standard* (29 Nov. 2008), "a shining, selfless example to tens of thousands of young female players, a bona fide star with a stunning list of past achievements."

A fixture on the Canadian national squad since her debut in 2000, Sinclair is both the team's current captain as well as its all-time leading scorer. By March 2014 she had netted 148 goals in international competition, which placed her third on the all-time list behind the Americans Mia Hamm, with 158 goals, and Abby Wambach, with 165 goals. Her valiant efforts on the pitch at the 2012 Summer Olympics

Getty Images

By the age of eleven, Sinclair was playing on the under-fourteen all-star team. Her coaches soon recognized her potential and developed lofty expectations. All-star coach Keith Puiu told her she'd one day represent Canada in international competition and that she would play for the national team before she was twenty-five. Sinclair still remembered the talk years later, explaining to Kennedy, "Even though I was a pretty good player, to have your coach tell you something like that when you're so young, it can't help but stay with you. After that, I really started to focus on that goal."

In addition to soccer, Sinclair also played baseball. After getting her start at tee-ball as a five-year-old, she went on to play second base in a boys' league, earning a spot on the local under-eleven all-star team. Among her early athletic heroes was Toronto Blue Jays second baseman and future hall-of-famer Roberto Alomar, whose poster hung in her bedroom and whose retired number 12 she has worn in tribute throughout her athletic career.

Sinclair helped guide her youth league team to six league championships and five provincial championships. During her time with the team they were twice ranked among the top five in all of Canada. Sinclair then led her high school team to three provincial championships.

INTERNATIONAL DEBUT AND THE UNIVERSITY OF PORTLAND

At the age of sixteen, Sinclair lived up to Puiu's expectations and joined the Canadian national team. She made her international debut on March 12, 2000, at the Algarve Women's Cup in Portugal in a match that Canada lost to China 4–0. Two days later Sinclair scored her first goal in a game against Norway. "I intercepted a pass from one of their centre-backs," Sinclair recalled to Lori Ewing for the *Canada Press* (11 Dec. 2013), "and I went in on a breakaway and scored, and it was crazy. It was obviously a goal I'll never forget." She notched two more goals on March 18 against Denmark.

After graduating from high school in 2001, Sinclair matriculated at the University of Portland in Oregon on an athletic scholarship. Joining the school's soccer team, she quickly emerged as one of the best collegiate players in the country. During her freshman year she tallied 23 goals and 8 assists, was the top scorer among all NCAA Division I freshmen, and was named freshman of the year by *Soccer America* magazine. She played even better the following year, achieving an NCAA Division I best with 26 goals and 3 assists, which helped propel the Portland Pilots to their first NCAA championship. In the finals in Austin, Texas, Sinclair scored twice, including a title-clinching overtime game winner—a so-called golden goal—to seal the 2–1 victory over Santa Clara University.

in London helped earn her team the bronze medal. Based on that performance, Sinclair won both the 2012 Lou Marsh Trophy honoring Canada's athlete of the year and the 2012 Bobbie Rosenfeld Award for Canada's female athlete of the year. She is also counted among the greatest college players, having led the University of Portland in Oregon to two national championships.

Though she favors privacy over celebrity, eschewing the glamour often associated with top female athletes, Sinclair has emerged as a national icon in Canada. "She is at the Michael Jordan level," Canadian national team coach John Herdman told Dave Feschuk for the *Toronto Star* (10 Dec. 2012). "That's a reality."

EARLY LIFE AND EDUCATION

The younger of two children, Christine Margaret Sinclair was born June 12, 1983, in Burnaby, British Columbia, to Bill and Sandra Sinclair. Soccer was in Sinclair's blood: her father competed as a Canadian amateur and two of her maternal uncles, Brian and Bruce, both played in the now defunct North American Soccer League (NASL) during the 1970s and 1980s. Brian Sinclair also competed on the Canadian national team.

Sinclair did not immediately take to the sport. "My first memory of her with soccer is that she didn't want to play," older brother Michael told Stephanie Ip for the Vancouver *Province* (13 Aug. 2012). "She was four- or five-years-old and playing on a team with seven- or eight-year-olds. She was tiny and it wasn't fun." But the early difficulties failed to hold her back, and before long her natural talent and dedication paid off.

During the tournament, Sinclair tallied 10 goals and 1 assist. This broke the all-time NCAA record of 16 points set in 1993 by Mia Hamm.

In addition to competing for the national team, Sinclair also played for Canada's under nineteen (U-19) national squad in the FIFA U-19 World Cup, which was hosted by Canada. The Canadian team fell to the United States in the finals, but individually Sinclair dominated the tournament. She earned the Golden Ball and Golden Foot trophies, which respectively recognized her as the competition's MVP (most valuable player) and, with 10 goals, its top scorer.

FIRST WORLD CUP, SECOND NCAA TITLE

To play for the Canadian national team in the 2003 FIFA World Cup, Sinclair did not compete for the Pilots in 2003, choosing to take a break from college play while preserving her fourth year of eligibility. (According to NCAA bylaws college athletes can only play for four years). At the competition hosted by the United States in September and October, the Canadian squad played well, finishing fourth overall behind the United States, runner-up Sweden, and world champion Germany. In the six matches Canada played, Sinclair scored three times, contributing Canada's only goal in the third place game, a 3–1 loss to the United States.

Sinclair returned to the Pilots for the 2004 season, notching 22 goals and 11 assists. Based on her accomplishments, the Missouri Athletic Club awarded her the Hermann Trophy. The prize is given annually to the top male and female collegiate soccer players in the country. But Sinclair saved her best performance for her final season. In 2005, she scored a record 39 goals and assisted on 10 others. In the NCAA finals, Sinclair netted two goals as the Pilots captured their second title, shutting out the University of California at Los Angeles (UCLA) 4–0 in College Station, Texas, on December 4. The game marked the end of Sinclair's college career, but she had more than left her mark. She held the all-time record for goals in NCAA tournament play with 25. All told, Sinclair racked up 110 goals and 32 assists; she was among only six women in NCAA history with more than 100 goals and 30 assists in their college careers. In honor of her achievements during her final season, she earned another Hermann Trophy and the 2005–6 Honda-Broderick Cup, which recognizes the country's best female collegiate athlete. Sinclair was the third soccer player to earn the Honda-Broderick Cup, following Mia Hamm and Cindy Daws. Sinclair graduated in the winter of 2005 with a bachelor's degree in life science and a stellar 3.75 grade point average.

WORLD CUP AND OLYMPIC COMPETITION

In the FIFA Women's World Cup in 2007, Sinclair and the Canadian team headed to China, and in their first game they fell to Norway 2–1. Three days later they earned a 4–0 victory over Ghana in which Sinclair scored twice. Sinclair netted another goal in a 2–2 draw against Australia, but it was not enough to help Canada advance to the quarterfinals.

Sinclair returned to China in 2008 to compete in her first Summer Olympics. The Canadians made it out of the first round, defeating Argentina 2–1 and then tying China 1–1, and then losing to Sweden 2–1. The Canadians were stopped 2–1 in overtime in the quarterfinals by the United States, and Sinclair netted the Canadians lone goal in the losing effort. Overall, the Canadians came in eighth with the Americans advancing to win the gold medal.

At the next major international competition, the 2011 World Cup, which was held in Germany, Sinclair put in a truly gutsy performance. Early in the second half of Canada's first match against Germany, Sinclair suffered a severely broken nose due to an errant elbow from an opposing player. On the sideline, she brushed off the doctors who tried to examine her. The medical team recommended she stay out of the game, but Sinclair insisted she be put back in. She returned to score Canada's only goal of the tournament in the 2–1 loss. After the game, she was taken to the hospital where her nose was reset. "She's fantastic. Not every player can do what she did," Team Canada's coach Carolina Morace said afterwards as quoted by Cathal Kelly for the Toronto *Star* (26 June 2011). "That's why she is a champion." Despite her inspiring performance, the Canadians were shut out in their next two games and were eliminated. "The opening game of the World Cup, you break your nose, it's like uh-oh," Sinclair remarked to Richard Poplak for the *Walrus* (June 2013). "I mean, you plan for things, but never for that. I broke my nose, I scored a goal. Maybe it's just going to add to the story of our team doing well. But no. Didn't happen."

OLYMPIC HAT TRICK

Seeking redemption from their disappointing showing at the World Cup, Sinclair and Team Canada put in a sterling effort at the 2012 Olympic Games in London. After dropping their first match 2–1 against Japan, Canada rebounded three days later and shut out South Africa 3–0, with Sinclair scoring two of the goals. The Canadians followed that up with a 2–2 tie against Sweden to qualify for the quarterfinals. Playing Great Britain three days later, Sinclair contributed a goal to Canada's 2–0 shutout of the host country.

In the semifinals against the United States, Sinclair put in a now-legendary performance. With over ten million Canadians watching on television, Sinclair scored the opening goal to give Canada the lead. The United States came back with one of their own. So Sinclair netted another. After the Americans tied it up a second time, Sinclair rocketed a third ball past American keeper Hope Solo for the hat trick.

But then, in an unusual call that outraged the Canadians, the referee penalized Canadian goaltender Erin McLeod for holding the ball too long, violating the so-called "six-second rule." This set up an American indirect kick that resulted in a handball by one of the Canadian players. Awarded a penalty shot, the Americans tied up the game and ultimately sent it into sudden-death overtime, which ended in just over two minutes with a header by American Alex Morgan that clinched the victory for Team USA. The Americans would go on to defeat Japan in the finals to claim the gold medal.

THE BRONZE MEDAL
Afterward, Sinclair, her coach, and teammates criticized the officiating. "We feel like we didn't lose," Sinclair remarked according to Poplak. "We feel like it was taken from us." But it was what she supposedly said to the referee in the tunnel following the game that would lead to an official reprimand. Her precise words remain in dispute. On the heels of an investigation that concluded after the Olympics, FIFA suspended her for four games and fined her over $3,500 "for displaying unsporting behaviour towards match officials after the match," according to Sean Fitz-Gerald for the *National Post* (12 Oct. 2012).

Rather than allow the heart-wrenching loss and the ensuing controversy to drag her team down, Sinclair gave an inspiring pep talk in the locker room. She reminded her teammates that they still had a bronze medal to win. Subsequently, Team Canada defeated France 1–0 at London's Wembley Stadium to claim the bronze. The third-place finish helped eased the pain of their defeat in the semifinals. The medal ceremony marked the fulfillment of a lifelong goal for Sinclair. "To actually reach one of your childhood dreams," Sinclair told Ewing, "not many people can say they actually get to do that, and I was just completely overwhelmed by . . . winning a bronze medal, and then stepping onto the podium and seeing the Canadian flag rise. It's pretty special." In the closing ceremonies of the Olympics, Sinclair was chosen to bear the Canadian flag. Back home, she was widely celebrated for her performance, winning both the Lou Marsh Trophy and Bobbie Rosenfeld Award. "Canada needed a hero at these Olympics," Andrew McKay wrote for Yahoo! Sports, Canada (6 Aug. 2012). "Now, our home and native land has one—Christine Sinclair."

WHAT'S NEXT?
In 2013 Sinclair was inducted into Canada's Walk of Fame, which honors the nation's greatest

achievers. In December she played in her two-hundredth game for the Canadian team and the next day was named Canada's women's soccer player of the year for the tenth consecutive time and the eleventh time overall.

In addition to international and collegiate competition, Sinclair has competed in various women's professional soccer leagues. Prior to games, Sinclair insists on listening to Michael Jackson's "Man in the Mirror" and always puts her left cleat on first. One of her favorite luxuries after a workout is a glass of chocolate milk.

Regarding her future plans, Sinclair is focused on soccer, setting her sights on the 2015 World Cup, which will be hosted by Canada, and the 2016 Summer Olympics in Rio de Janeiro. She doesn't expect those competitions to be her swansong on the soccer pitch either. "I can't imagine only playing for two more years," she told Ewing. "Assuming I can stay healthy, obviously I want to keep going."

SUGGESTED READING
Feschuk, Dave. "Lou Marsh Award: Christine Sinclair's Remarkable Talent Matched by Her Humility." *Toronto Star*. Toronto Star Newspapers, 10 Dec. 2012. Web. 11 Mar. 2014.
Granger, Grant. "Burnaby's Christine Sinclair Helps Canada Chase Olympic Soccer Dream." *Burnaby News Leader*. Black Press, 25 Jan. 2012. Web. 2 Mar. 2014.
Ip, Stephanie. "'Go, Auntie Canada, Go!' Christine Sinclair Makes Family Proud." *Province*. Postmedia Network, 13 Aug. 2012. Web. 11 Mar. 2014.
Kennedy, Patrick. "From Strikes to Striker." *Whig*. Kingston Whit-Standard, 29 Nov. 2008. Web. 11 Mar. 2014.
Poplak, Richard. "The Game Not Played." *Walrus*. Walrus Foundation, June 2013. Web. 11 Mar. 2014.

—Paul McCaffrey

Kyrsten Sinema
Born: July 12, 1976
Occupation: Politician

Kyrsten Sinema, a member of Congress representing Arizona's Ninth District, is known for her tenacious personality and intriguing life story. She spent a part of her childhood homeless, graduated from college at the age of eighteen, and went on to earn a master's degree in social work, a law degree, and a doctorate in justice studies. She served for six years in the Arizona House of Representatives and another year in the Arizona Senate before running for Congress as a Democrat in 2012. Since her election,

The Washington Post/Getty Images

Sinema has also made headlines for being the first openly bisexual person to serve in Congress.

Sinema began her political career as an outspoken leftist but later rejected harsh partisan rhetoric in favor of coalition building. "We've seen a decline in civility and bipartisanship, and a rapid increase in hostility between those who have differing opinions," she told an interviewer for *Time*, which included her in its "40 under 40: New Civic Leaders" feature in October 2010. Her book *Unite and Conquer: How to Build Coalitions That Win and Last*, published in 2009, discusses forwarding progressive ideals through bipartisan action.

As a liberal representative in Arizona's conservative state legislature, Sinema led a coalition called Arizona Together to defeat Proposition 107, a 2006 ballot initiative that proposed a ban on same-sex marriage. In 2010, she fought tirelessly—though ultimately in vain—to defeat Arizona's anti-immigration Senate Bill 1070, which would allow police to check a person's immigration status if they had reason to believe that person was an illegal immigrant. The bill has been strongly criticized for encouraging racial profiling. Sinema debated the bill's sponsor, state senator Russell Pearce, for hours on the House floor; Pearce was later recalled by voters. Also in 2010, Sinema worked to pass bipartisan legislation to crack down on human trafficking.

Despite overwhelming opposition, Sinema has consistently found ways to reach across the aisle to accomplish her goals, and her talent for bipartisanship in spite of her less-than-bipartisan ideology was not lost on voters in 2012. When the editors of the *Arizona Republic* (10 Oct. 2012) endorsed her campaign, they wrote, "In the polarized politics far too common in Washington, the other side is the enemy. That is not Sinema's approach, and this attribute strongly favors her. For Sinema, it's always about the issue, not the personalities. She could argue

passionately during floor debate, then enjoy a beer with political adversaries after hours."

EARLY LIFE

Kyrsten Sinema was born on July 12, 1976, in Tucson, Arizona. She has an older brother and a younger sister. Books and learning became a refuge for Sinema during her sheltered childhood, and she borrowed extensively from the Tucson public library.

Sinema's parents divorced when she was a child, and she moved to Florida with her mother, who later married Sinema's elementary school vice-principal. After her stepfather lost his job, Sinema and her family were homeless for two years, during which time they squatted at an abandoned gas station outside of Defuniak Springs. She considers this period to be the defining experience of her life. "I was old enough to know something was wrong," she told Ann Friedman for *Elle* magazine (22 May 2013). "We didn't have electricity. My stepdad built a bunk bed for me and my sister. We separated our bunk bed from the kitchen with one of those big chalkboards on rollers. I knew that was weird. A chalkboard shouldn't be a wall. A kitchen should have running water. We didn't have a toilet."

EDUCATION

Sinema's stepfather eventually found another job, and her family found a home. Despite the hardships she faced, Sinema graduated from high school at age sixteen as valedictorian of her class and, with the aid of a Pell Grant and various scholarships, including a Ezra Taft Benson Scholarship, went on to attend Brigham Young University, a predominantly Mormon institution in Salt Lake City, Utah. While she had a conservative Mormon upbringing, she chose to leave the faith after college. Journalists have variously characterized Sinema as a nontheist, an atheist, and a nonbeliever, but she waves away all three descriptors. She has said that she claims no religion and makes policy decisions based on her own experiences and secular judgment. When she was sworn into office in 2013, she placed her hand not on the Bible but on a copy of the United States Constitution.

Thanks to the sixty community-college course credits she had earned over the course of her high school career, Sinema was able to earn her bachelor's degree in social work in two years. She subsequently earned a master's degree in social work from Arizona State University (ASU) in 1999 and took a job with an elementary school in the low-income Sunnyslope neighborhood near Phoenix. She told Friedman that her office was in the school gym and that she used the former girls' locker room and shower area as a family resource center and clothing bank. In 2000, the school district's budget was threatened, and Sinema was nominated by her colleagues to lobby on its behalf at the state capitol. "I was scared I wasn't knowledgeable enough," she told Friedman. She was surprised to find herself at home in the political setting. "I realized I was way overeducated. I had the skill level. And I realized there weren't people like me inside the building. At that moment, I decided to run for office."

ARIZONA STATE LEGISLATURE

Sinema ran unsuccessfully for Phoenix City Council in 2001 and waged her first campaign for state legislature the following year, while she was attending law school at ASU. She ran in both elections as an independent supported by the Green Party; a friend of Sinema suggested to Manuel Roig-Franzia for the *Washington Post* (2 Jan. 2013) that this was because Sinema did not think Democrats were bold enough in their environmental policies. She later characterized that decision as a mistake. "Here's the thing: you can't win that way," she told Friedman. Sinema ran for state legislature as a Democrat in 2004 and won, taking office a month before she took the bar exam. At twenty-eight years old, she was Arizona's youngest lawmaker.

Sinema found herself at odds with the ultra-conservative statehouse, which voted to restrict abortion rights for women and pass harsh anti-immigration policies. Sinema sought to set herself apart. She described her former persona to Roig-Franzia as a "bomb thrower" in the legislature, giving fiery speeches on the floor only to see conservative legislation passed anyway. She was frustrated, she told Friedman, working away in her "lonely corner." She realized that ideology alone was not enough.

Sinema soon exchanged her combative style for political savvy, which allowed her to push a number of measures with bipartisan support. At the same time, she was working as a criminal defense attorney and teaching as an adjunct professor at ASU, where she was also pursuing her doctorate in justice studies. As the chair of the Arizona Together coalition, Sinema led an effort to block a ban on same-sex marriage in Arizona in 2006. It was the first time such a measure had ever been blocked at the state level. Her approach was controversial among some activists because her arguments had nothing to do with sexual orientation; rather, she and other opponents of the proposition warned that it would hurt unmarried heterosexual couples as well. Phoenix mayor Greg Stanton told Roig-Franzia that Sinema was instrumental in defeating the ban and defended her tactics, saying, "She had to change the conversation." In 2008, Sinema led another campaign against a similar proposed ban, this time without success.

BIPARTISAN EFFORTS

In 2007, Sinema decided, as she later wrote in *Unite and Conquer*, that she "was going to do something about Darfur." The Sudanese government had been committing genocide against the non-Arab population of Sudan's Darfur region since 2003, and while many people knew about it, very little action was being taken against it. Sinema, who was writing her dissertation on the 1994 Rwandan genocide, teamed up with the Sudan Divestment Task Force, a nonprofit organization that aided governments in divesting funds from companies that helped perpetuate the genocide. With the help of the task force, Sinema crafted legislation that would prohibit Arizona from contracting any corporation that was materially helping the Sudanese government kill its own people. She held fundraisers and invited Darfuri refugees to speak at the capitol. The bill passed in 2008 with bipartisan support and, a few months later, became the first state law of its kind. Also in 2008, Sinema chaired another coalition, Protect Arizona's Freedom, which was devoted to keeping an anti–affirmative action measure off the state ballot. The campaign was successful, but the measure made it to the ballot in 2010 and passed.

Sinema was elected to serve District Fifteen as state senator in 2010, replacing Democrat Ken Cheuvront, who had reached his term limit. Her victory speech on election night was less than victorious, but it garnered attention across the state. Republicans had gained a supermajority in Arizona, which left Democrats in an awkward position in terms of policy making. "I said we might not be able to stop [the Republicans]," Sinema told Craig Outhier for *Phoenix Magazine* (Feb. 2011) of her speech, "but we could make sure that every last Arizonan knows what their policies mean to our future. And provide alternative solutions."

CONGRESSIONAL CAMPAIGN

On January 3, 2012, Sinema announced that she would resign her state senate post and run for US Congress. In the Democratic primary, Sinema faced Arizona Democratic Party chair Andrei Cherny and state senate minority leader David Schapira. The race was tight and, by some accounts, vicious. Sinema claimed that Cherny told union leaders that she would not be able to win a general election because she was a single bisexual woman. True to form, the outspoken Sinema fired back, as quoted by Michelle Garcia of the *Advocate* (22 Aug. 2012), "It's true that I'm openly bisexual, I have been my entire adult life, and I've managed to win four elections, and, meanwhile, [Cherny]'s lost two, so perhaps it was being straight that was the problem here." Sinema won the primary with a plurality of the vote.

In the general election, Sinema faced Vernon Parker, a Tea Party Republican who had served in both Bush administrations. Despite each candidate's partisan credentials, the hard-fought race became about which candidate was more moderate; the Ninth District is divided almost evenly among Republican, Democrats, and independents. Both Sinema and Parker made jobs and the plight of the middle class their battle cry while trying to paint the other as impractical and extreme. Parker released ads calling Sinema a socialist, quoting a quip she had once made to a fashion magazine in which she described herself as a "Prada socialist." Despite the attacks, Sinema received the endorsement of the *Arizona Republic* in October. Following the election, it took fifteen days for all the votes in the Ninth District to be counted, but in the end, Sinema narrowly defeated Parker by ten thousand votes. She earned her PhD from ASU the same year.

Sinema was sworn in as a member of the 113th Congress in January 2013. She serves on the Housing and Insurance and the Oversight and Investigations subcommittees within the House Committee on Financial Services. She has sponsored and cosponsored numerous bills in support of veterans' issues, including H.R. 357, the GI Bill Tuition Fairness Act. The bill, which is similar to legislation Sinema pushed into law in Arizona, would allow veterans to attend any state-run college or university at in-state tuition rates, whether or not they are residents of that state. In a press release on her website, Sinema cited the College Board's report that average in-state tuition fees in 2012–13 were slightly less than $8,655 per year, while average out-of-state fees were $21,706 per year. In addition, in January 2014, Sinema and Colorado senator Mark Udall joined forces to campaign for the reversal of cuts to military retirement benefits instituted by Congress's two-year budget agreement the previous month.

PERSONAL LIFE

Sinema does not publicly discuss her romantic or family life. She has never officially come out as bisexual but told Friedman that she has "always been out." Her first public comment about her sexuality, made in 2005 in reaction to an insult from a Republican lawmaker directed at the LGBT community, occurred almost as an afterthought; when asked by reporters about her response—"We're simply people like everyone else who want and deserve respect"—and why she included herself, she replied, as quoted by Friedman, "Duh, I'm bisexual."

Sinema puts in long hours at her congressional office and returns to Arizona on the weekends, where she trains for triathlons and marathons. She completed an Ironman Triathlon in November 2013, becoming the first serving member of Congress to do so. She has a close-knit group of friends in Arizona with whom she runs; while in Washington, she is occasionally joined on her morning runs by US Marines. Sinema also loves fashion and once admitted to owning over one hundred pairs of shoes. She almost always wears a pair of designer eyeglasses, which have become one of her trademarks.

SUGGESTED READING

Friedman, Ann. "America's Most Colorful Congresswoman: Kyrsten Sinema." *Elle*. Hearst Communications, 22 May 2013. Web. 11 Feb. 2014.

Garcia, Michelle. "House Hopeful Claims Opponent Is Using Biphobic Tactics." *Advocate*. Here Media, 22 Aug. 2012. Web. 11 Feb. 2014.

Outhier, Craig. "Phoenix Democrat Kyrsten Sinema." *Phoenix Magazine*. Phoenix Magazine, Feb. 2011. Web. 11 Feb. 2014.

Roig-Franzia, Manuel. "Kyrsten Sinema: A Success Story Like Nobody Else's." *Washington Post*. Washington Post, 2 Jan. 2013. Web. 11 Feb. 2014.

"Sinema a Good Fit for District." *Arizona Republic*. Azcentral.com, 10 Oct. 2012. Web. 11 Feb. 2014.

Sinema, Kyrsten. "40 under 40: New Civic Leaders—Kyrsten Sinema." *Time*. Time, Oct. 2010. Web. 11 Feb. 2014.

—Molly Hagan

Shane Smith

Born: 1970
Occupation: Journalist and entrepreneur

In naming Shane Smith, the cofounder of *Vice* magazine (an enterprise that has expanded into multiple media formats), one of 2014's thirty-five most powerful people in New York media, the editors of the *Hollywood Reporter* (16 Apr. 2014) explained, "With an HBO newsmagazine show, a YouTube channel with nearly 4.5 million subscribers, a record label with artists like Snoop Dog [sic], a film division . . . and an in-house ad agency tapped by AT&T for a smartphone campaign for millennials . . . Vice is expected to post $500 million in revenue this year, with Smith promising the company will hit the billion-dollar mark by 2016." Known in some circles for his bombastic manner (and his tendency to pepper conversations with obscenities), Smith told the *Hollywood Reporter*, "If money is the modern-day report card, we get an A-plus."

Describing the edgy mix that makes Vice Media's content so compelling to its young target audience, Tim Adams wrote for the *Guardian* (23 Mar. 2013), "There is above all a sort of attention-deficit quality to Vice's output, shifting abruptly between tones and sensibilities. . . . There is a voyeuristic *Dazed and Confused* edge to a lot of it, done with the production

Frederick M. Brown/Getty Images

values of *National Geographic*, and occasionally the kind of easy misogyny that has seen the magazine banned from campuses." Among the regular features Smith publishes are a dos and don'ts column, which includes snarky commentary on photos of anonymous people, and "Vice Guides" on such disparate topics as travel, sex, and adulthood.

The mixture does not appeal to everyone. A widely quoted piece in *US News & World Report* (28 Feb. 2013) called some of Vice's news coverage "more *Jackass* than journalism," and in the *New Yorker* (8 Apr. 2013), Lizzie Widdicombe opined, "Vice has never been celebrated for good taste." Smith dismisses that type of criticism. "Every time mainstream media says we are not doing it correctly, we say 'Sure. We are doing it our own way,'" he told Miguel Helft for *Fortune* (14 Oct. 2013). "If that doesn't satisfy the old guard, they can go to hell quite frankly."

EARLY YEARS AND EDUCATION

A native of Canada, Shane Smith was born in 1970. He was raised in Ottawa, Ontario. He has expressed contradictory views on his home country, asserting in a 2014 episode of HBO's *Real Time with Bill Maher* (quoted on the Canadian news website *Global News*) that it had been a pleasant, clean place but that it stifled creativity and rewarded conformity. "One of the shocking things when I go back to Canada is they cut off the tall trees—it's sort of like everyone's the same," he said.

Smith's mother was a paralegal, and his father was a computer programmer whose work

has been described as pioneering. "My dad has always been like me but on steroids, a lot smarter than I am, a lot tougher than I am," Smith recalled to Adams. "When I was a kid my dad told me two things. . . . Life isn't fair and you have to be both the strongest guy and the smartest guy." He mentions that he helped his dad build a house and that on weekends they would select a car from the junkyard to try to get it into working order. These tasks exemplify his dad's philosophy that Smith had to learn to do things for himself.

Smith's parents divorced when he was young. Though Smith has told journalists that he ran away and lived independently at the age of thirteen, family friends have refuted that; they assert that Smith did indeed leave his mother's home because he did not get along with his stepfather but that he readily found a comfortable home with his father. No one has refuted Smith's assertions that he was a troublesome teen who drank copiously, ingested alarming amounts of illegal substances, and hung out with a bad crowd. Despite those tendencies, he did well at Lisgar Collegiate Institute, a highly regarded Ottawa public school, and then attended Carleton University, where he earned a degree in political economy.

LIVING IN EUROPE

After graduating, Smith was intent on seeking excitement. "When you're eighteen, nineteen, you want to live fast and leave a beautiful corpse behind. It's kind of romantic," he told Matthew Garrahan for the *Financial Times* (28 Dec. 2012). "I thought I was going to die anyway so I might as well go out there and suck the marrow from the bone of life." He decided to travel around Europe. A fan of such towering literary figures as Samuel Beckett and Aleksandr Solzhenitsyn, Smith was eager to amass fodder for his own writing. "I thought I was a pretty good writer but I didn't have anything to write about," he explained to Garrahan. "I wanted to go out in the world, have some adventures and then write about them."

He visited war-torn Yugoslavia and then Hungary, where he claims to have freelanced for the *Budapest Sun* and Reuters. Longtime acquaintances have told journalists that those claims are overblown and that Smith was merely teaching English. He also asserts that he had a lucrative sideline trading currency at youth hostels. "Real cowboy capitalism," he told Garrahan. "I was hanging out with lots of seedy dudes. I had a car and driver and lived in the same building as the Hungarian prime minister. But I couldn't take any of the money out of the country." As to the exact amounts of money, he told Alex Williams for the *New York Times* (16 Aug. 2010), "Doctors there were making like $200 a month, and I was making $2,000."

STARTING *VICE*

In the early 1990s, Smith returned to Canada, settling in Montreal and earning a meager living by canvassing for the environmental group Greenpeace. He also reunited with a childhood friend, Suroosh Alvi, a recovering heroin addict. In 1994, Alvi and Gavin McInnes, an unemployed cartoonist, had been charged with starting a magazine under the welfare-to-work program in which they were participating. Distributed free, the *Voice of Montreal*, as it was called, covered the city's punk and rap scenes. Alvi tapped Smith to sell ad space in the publication. "He could sell rattlesnake boots to a rattlesnake," Alvi told Widdicombe.

By 1996, the trio had begun distributing the publication throughout Canada and had even persuaded some US record stores to carry it. They ultimately dropped the *o* in *Voice*, calling their brainchild *Vice*. Smith has been widely acknowledged as the most ambitious of the three, sometimes calling his partners late at night to crow about the money he believed they would soon be making.

Prone to exaggeration (and sometimes outright fabrication), Smith granted an interview to a Canadian newspaper in which he falsely claimed that a dot-com millionaire named Richard Szalwinski had offered to buy *Vice*. Amused by Smith's bravado, Szalwinski agreed to make a relatively modest investment, building an eye-catching website at ViceLand.com; the URL Vice.com was then owned by a pornography company, but Smith was eventually able to secure the URL after the porn producers went out of business. Szalwinski also financed a 1999 move to New York City for *Vice* staffers. Smith explained to Maher, "If you're big in Toronto, you're big in Canada. But if you're big in New York, you're big in the rest of the world."

After the dot-com bubble burst at the beginning of the twenty-first century, Szalwinski's backing became uncertain, and soon Smith and his cohorts became deeply mired in debt. They moved from Manhattan to less expensive space in the neighborhood of Williamsburg, Brooklyn, an area that has subsequently experienced gentrification; negotiated with creditors; and made a concerted push to sell more ad space. Within a year, the magazine was turning a profit and becoming an entrenched part of life in the borough. "A certain type of downtown denizen likes to talk about his first encounter with *Vice*," Widdicombe wrote. "The magazine presented an aggressive hedonism—early covers featured lines of cocaine—combined with a love of everything taboo. . . . Bylines were often made up. Articles tended to launch directly into rants."

GROWING A MEDIA EMPIRE

In subsequent years, as Williams wrote, "the magazine started to grow a social conscience."

Smith began instituting more serious stories, covering the 2007 troop surge in Iraq, for example, from the point of view of Iraqi citizens or embedding himself with mujahideen jihadists. "In the beginning," Smith admitted to Adams, "there was this era online of let's just be cool and criticize everything, and we were very guilty of that. . . . [But] we have been trying to say, 'OK we are going to go out and actually do stuff, get involved.'"

Smith has called his brand of journalism "immersionism," and his methods are often compared to those of gonzo reporter Hunter S. Thompson. "We have local stringers, we dress the part [of the locals], and we try not to be intrusive," Smith explained during a 2013 panel discussion hosted by the Television Critics Association. "We also try to be smart about it. We aren't action junkies. We just try to get a good story."

VICE-INDUCED CONTROVERSIES

While the results are generally acknowledged to be compelling, there has been some media backlash against *Vice*'s approach. Setting off one widely publicized contretemps, Smith visited Liberia in 2009 to report on a vicious warlord, child soldiers, and cannibalism. "Most of the time when the mainstream media reports on something, it never tells the whole story," he asserted at one point. In response, *New York Times* reporter David Carr confronted him, saying, "Before you ever went there, we've had reporters there reporting on genocide after genocide. Just because you put on a f—— safari helmet and looked at some poop [a reference to Smith reporting from a feces-strewn beach] doesn't give you the right to insult what we do." (The confrontation can be seen in the 2011 documentary *Page One: Inside the New York Times*.)

In 2012, *Vice* editors unwittingly revealed the location of fugitive millionaire John McAfee, who was fleeing a murder investigation in Belize, because GPS data was embedded in the picture featured in its coverage. (The article was headlined, "We're with John McAfee, Suckers.") Other media outlets mocked *Vice* for getting a source arrested; McAfee asserted that they had done so on purpose so that they could obtain exclusive footage of his capture.

In 2013, Smith sent controversial basketball player Dennis Rodman, along with members of the Harlem Globetrotters, to North Korea, where they played an exhibition game and Rodman bewilderingly befriended infamous dictator Kim Jong-un. While Smith defended his actions in arranging the trip as an attempt at "basketball diplomacy," he was almost universally derided for cooperating with North Korea's propaganda machine.

OTHER MEDIA VENTURES

Despite the occasional backlash, Smith has been avidly courted by investors from the world of mainstream media. In 2007, he teamed with Tom Freston, the former CEO of Viacom, to launch VBS.tv, an online network featuring documentaries and news. (The stories about Liberia and Rodman's trip to North Korea aired on the network.) He has also partnered with HBO to air a documentary series and hired director Spike Jonze as creative director.

Furthermore, Vice Media encompasses record and film units as well as an ad agency, and Rupert Murdoch's 21st Century Fox owns a 5 percent stake in the enterprise. (After first meeting with Smith, Murdoch tweeted, "Who's heard of VICE media? Wild, interesting effort to interest millennials who don't read or watch established media. Global success.")

Smith has announced his intention to transform Vice Media, which operates in more than thirty countries, into the next CNN or ESPN. "[I] realized that given the digital revolution that is not only within my grasp, but I am frontrunner to get there," he told Adams.

PERSONAL LIFE

Smith is typically described as "burly" or "bear-like," and reporters often comment on the zeal with which he eats and drinks alcohol. According to Widdicombe, he has called himself "the poor man's Hemingway" and summarized his lifestyle thusly: "Bon vivant, storyteller, drunk. Let's have fourteen bottles of wine at dinner, roast suckling pig, and a story about chopping a dude's head off in the desert."

Smith is married to Tamyka Booth. They have two children, Martina and Piper. After Martina was born at home with the help of a midwife in 2010, Booth was featured in the media as an advocate for home birthing.

SUGGESTED READING

Adams, Tim. "Shane Smith: I Want to Build the Next CNN with Vice." *Guardian*. Guardian News and Media, 23 Mar. 2013. Web. 25 May 2014.

Garrahan, Matthew. "Lunch with the FT: Shane Smith." *Financial Times*. Financial Times, 28 Dec. 2012. Web. 25 May 2014.

Pompeo, Joe. "What Is Vice Media's Shane Smith Really Selling? It's Hard to Say, but Everyone's Buying." *Capital*. Capital, 18 May 2012. Web. 25 May 2014.

Staley, Willy. "Vice's Shane Smith: Have We Unleashed a Monster?" *New York Times*. New York Times, 21 Mar. 2014. Web. 25 May 2014.

Widdicombe, Lizzie. "The Bad-Boy Brand." *New Yorker*. Condé Nast, 8 Apr. 2013. Web. 25 May 2014.

Williams, Alex. "A Wild Man Grows Up (Just Enough)." *New York Times*. New York Times, 16 Aug. 2010. Web. 25 May 2014.

—*Mari Rich*

Jason Smyth

Born: July 4, 1987
Occupation: Sprint runner

Irish sprint runner Jason Smyth is known as the world's fastest Paralympian. He has been widely referred to as the Usain Bolt of Paralympic runners—referring to the Jamaican multi–gold medal sprinter—for his sustained dominance in individual sprint events at the Paralympic level. Diagnosed with the genetic visual impairment Stargardt disease as a child, Smyth gained worldwide recognition in 2008, when he won the 100- and 200-meter sprint events in the T13 classification at the Paralympic Games in Beijing, China, with world-record times. Following the 2008 Games, Smyth made the crossover to mainstream competition, and in 2010 he became the first Paralympic athlete ever to compete in the able-bodied European Athletics Championships. Despite failing to achieve his goal of qualifying for and competing in the 2012 Olympic Games in London, Smyth successfully defended his 100- and 200-meter T13 titles at

Bongarts/Getty Images

the 2012 Paralympic Games, also held in London, with world-record times, cementing his legacy as "the fastest Paralympian of all time," according to Barry Egan for the *Irish Independent* (2 Oct. 2013). One of the "faces" of the Paralympics, Smyth told Egan, "I very much believe I have been blessed with a talent. . . . Everybody has their own gifts in everything and in the many different aspects of life. Mine is running."

EARLY LIFE

The oldest of Lloyd and Diane Smyth's five children, Jason Smyth was born on July 4, 1987, in Derry, the second-largest city in Northern Ireland. He has three sisters, Leeza, Laurajayne, and Jessica, and a brother, Justyn. His father is a partner in a kitchen business, and his mother is a homemaker and former nurse. Smyth's paternal grandparents were among the first converts to the Mormon faith in Derry, which has a largely Catholic population, and he and his siblings grew up immersed in the teachings of the Church of Jesus Christ of Latter-day Saints.

Smyth's parents taught him "to do things properly, not half-heartedly," as he told Trent Toone for the Salt Lake City, Utah, *Deseret News* (25 July 2012). They also stressed the importance of family and helping others, which helped him remain grounded from an early age. Keeping with Mormon tradition, Smyth's parents encouraged him and his siblings to lead a healthy lifestyle by participating in sports and other physical activities and eschewing vices such as alcohol and cigarettes. Growing up, Smyth's first love was soccer, which he began playing as a child.

SEEING THROUGH ADVERSITY

For Smyth, sports empowered him to overcome a debilitating physical condition. He was eight years old when his parents noticed that his vision seemed to be impaired, and he was diagnosed with Stargardt disease, a genetic condition that gradually reduces a person's central vision. Smyth, whose vision is about 10 percent that of a person with normal eyesight, learned to adjust to life with his impairment. He can see only shapes and outlines of people and objects and cannot drive or perform some everyday activities because of his limited vision. Smyth has said that he becomes most frustrated when he is not able to see people trying to wave at or talk to him on the street. "It's unfortunate that I have bad eyesight, but everybody has problems," he explained to Toone. "There's not an awful lot you can do about things, apart from get on with it and make the best of the opportunities put in your path."

In spite of his condition, Smyth continued to play sports with and against able-bodied children. While soccer remained his passion, it was running in which he truly excelled. Smyth fell into the sport by accident when, at age sixteen, a physical education teacher saw him running and suggested he give track a try. Initially reluctant, he relented only after the teacher provided him with information about a local track club. Fellow Northern Irishman and former long jumper Stephen Maguire quickly recognized Smyth's natural running ability and became the young athlete's coach and mentor, helping him develop the strength and power necessary to become a sprinter.

Smyth attended the selective, coed Limavady Grammar School. After teaming up with Maguire, he competed in able-bodied races for the school and won three consecutive Irish Schools Championships. Smyth has credited his parents with pushing him to stick with running, despite his initial ambivalence toward the sport. "They really encouraged me with the building blocks that I would be able to build on as I improved," he told Egan.

ENTRY INTO PARALYMPIC COMPETITION

Smyth's first major running competition was in Bendigo, Australia, at the 2004 Youth Commonwealth Games. He ran the 100- and 200-meter sprint events, clocking in at 11.10 and 22.27 seconds, respectively, but failed to medal. Not long afterward, Smyth became involved in Paralympic competition, with the 100- and 200-meter sprints becoming his signature events. His father first contacted UK athletics officials about him joining the UK Paralympic squad, but after failing to get a reply, he reached out to the Irish team, who willingly took Smyth on.

Despite initial apprehensions, Smyth quickly realized that the Paralympics, which primarily features athletes with physical and visual impairments, offered him the best chance to succeed athletically. In 2005 he participated in his first major Paralympics competition, the International Paralympic Committee (IPC) Athletics European Championships, held in Espoo, Finland. There, he placed first and set world records in the 100- and 200-meter sprint events in the T13 classification, which includes visually impaired athletes who can make out shapes between six and eighteen feet away. (The T13 class is one of three classifications for athletes with visual impairments.)

In 2006 Smyth competed in the IPC Athletics World Championships in Assen, Netherlands, where he again swept the field and set world records in the 100- and 200-meter sprints. That year he also ran at the able-bodied World Junior Under-20 Championships in Beijing, China, where he barely missed making the semifinal in the 100-meter sprint. Later in 2006 Smyth ran at the World Indoor Paralympic Championships in Bollnäs, Sweden, where he placed first in the sixty-meter sprint with a time of 6.92 seconds. His time broke a fourteen-year-old Irish able-bodied junior record in the event.

FASTEST PARALYMPIAN ON EARTH

By the end of 2006, Smyth had already started receiving financial support from the Irish Sports Council, which contracted him at ☒31,500 (about $53,000) per year, the maximum amount for a top-level athlete in Ireland. He spent all of 2007 training in preparation for the 2008 Paralympic Games in Beijing, China. As part of his training, Smyth began an intensive physiotherapy and strength and conditioning regimen at the Sports Institute of Northern Ireland (SINI), based at the University of Ulster in Jordanstown.

In Beijing, Smyth defeated his T13 field in the 100- and 200-meter sprint events to claim his first two Paralympic gold medals. He established new world records in both events, running the 100-meter in 10.62 seconds, 0.26 seconds ahead of runner-up Alexey Labzin, and the 200-meter in 21.43 seconds, 0.44 seconds ahead of Labzin, who again claimed second place. "The best was the relief, the joy, and the satisfaction of winning," Smyth told Toone. "All the hard work I had put in to that point paid off."

Winning his races in front of thousands of spectators at Beijing National Stadium, known as the Bird's Nest for its iconic design, Smyth left China as one of the new faces of the Paralympics and with the undisputed title of fastest Paralympian on Earth. Many observers began referring to Smyth as the Paralympian equivalent of Jamaican sprinter Usain Bolt, who made history at the 2008 Olympic Games, held in Beijing one month prior to the Paralympics, when he became the first man to win both the 100- and 200-meter races in world-record times.

PARALYMPIC TRAILBLAZER

Following the 2008 Paralympic Games, Smyth began pursuing a long-term goal of qualifying for the 2012 Olympics in London. The first step toward achieving that goal involved moving his training base to the National Training Center Track and Field Complex in Clermont, Florida. There, Smyth began intensive training with a group of world-class sprinters under renowned American track coach Lance Brauman. Maguire, meanwhile, was brought on as a member of Brauman's coaching team. Among Smyth's training partners were American 100- and 200-meter world champion Tyson Gay, Jamaican world relay champion Steve Mullings, and Olympic gold medalists Aleen Bailey of Jamaica and Debbie Ferguson-McKenzie of the Bahamas. Though his first day training in Florida was "daunting," Smyth, who initially kept his visual impairment a secret from the group, explained to Anna Kessel for the *Guardian* (23 May 2010), "There's no better way to learn than learning from the best. If you want to improve you need to see how they do it."

Smyth's new approach to training paid immediate dividends, as his improved strength and power helped him qualify for and perform well in a series of prestigious able-bodied competitions. At the 2009 European Athletics Under-23 Championships in Kaunas, Lithuania, Smyth placed third in his 100-meter heat with a time of 10.60 seconds. He then competed in the 2010 European Team Championships in Budapest, Hungary, where he claimed first place in the 100-meter sprint with a personal-best time of 10.27 seconds.

A month after the European Team Championships, Smyth became the first Paralympic athlete to compete in the European Athletics Championships. At the 2010 championships in Barcelona, Spain, he competed in the 100-meter sprint and reached the semifinals, placing fourth with a time of 10.46 seconds. He planned to defend his 100- and 200-meter world titles at the 2011 IPC Athletic World Championships in Christchurch, New Zealand, but withdrew from the competition after suffering a stress fracture in his back that sidelined him for three months.

DEFENDING HIS TITLES

In May 2011, Smyth achieved a personal best and the Olympic B standard in the 100-meter sprint in Clermont, Florida, with a time of 10.22 seconds. His time was a mere 0.04 seconds short of the Olympic A standard required for admission into the Irish Olympic team. Smyth continued to try to reach the Olympic A standard in the 100- and 200-meter events in competitions leading up to the 2012 Olympics.

At the 2011 World Track and Field Championships in Daegu, South Korea, Smyth clocked a 10.57 in his 100-meter heat, narrowly missing out on a place in the semifinals. He then reached the semifinals in the 100-meter sprint at the 2012 European Athletic Championships in Helsinki, Finland, placing seventh with a time of 10.52. Shortly after that competition, Smyth ran a 10.38 in the 100-meter sprint at the 2012 Irish Championships, finishing just 0.01 seconds behind first-place finisher Paul Hession.

Despite his promising performances, Smyth failed to qualify for the Olympics. "I never felt I got everything right in a race," he explained to John Haughey for BBC Sport (22 Aug. 2012). "In a sprint you have no room for error." Disappointed but not defeated, Smyth focused on retaining his Paralympic 100- and 200-meter titles in the T13 classification. "For each individual athlete—not only athletes, but people, it's about trying to achieve what you're capable of," he later told Ros Dumlao in an interview for the International Paralympic Committee's website (7 Sept. 2013).

In the London Paralympic Games, Smyth easily defended his 100- and 200-meter titles to solidify his status as the fastest Paralympian of all time. After setting a world record in the 100-meter T13 heats with a time of 10.54 seconds, he broke his own world record in the 100-meter T13 final, claiming his second straight gold in the event with a time of 10.46 seconds, 0.56 ahead of runner-up Luis Felipe Gutiérrez of Cuba. He then earned another gold-medal victory in the 200-meter T13 event, breaking his third Paralympic world record in the final with a time of 21.05 seconds, 0.90 ahead of second-place finisher Labzin.

In 2013 Smyth competed in the IPC Athletics World Championships in Lyon, France, and reclaimed his 100- and 200-meter sprint world titles. At the end of that year, he relocated from Florida to London, where he began training under British Olympic medalist Clarence Callender. Smyth has announced that he hopes to qualify for and race in the 2016 Olympics and Paralympics in Rio de Janeiro, Brazil. "I want to, by the time I've come to finish, realize and look back and think: 'I did everything I could to be the best I could, he told Egan."

Smyth married Elise Jordan in Salt Lake City, Utah, in December 2012.

SUGGESTED READING

Dumlao, Ros. "Seven Year Itch for World's Fastest Paralympian." *IPC.* International Paralympic Committee, 7 Sept. 2013. Web. 12 May 2014.

Kessel, Anna. "Jason Smyth Aims for Olympic and Paralympic Double in 2012." *Guardian.* Guardian News and Media, 23 May 2010. Web. 12 May 2014.

Toone, Trent. "Running on Faith: Mormon Who Just Missed Olympics Will Compete in Paralympic Games." *Deseret News.* Deseret News, 25 July 2012. Web. 12 May 2014.

—*Chris Cullen*

Kseniya Sobchak

Born: November 5, 1981
Occupation: Television personality and political activist

Kseniya Sobchak is often likened to American socialite Paris Hilton, but considering Sobchak's lucrative business career and unexpected embrace of Russia's protest movement in 2012, the comparison hardly seems fair. The only daughter of a respected Russian politician who died in 2000, Sobchak has successfully parlayed her famous surname into a media empire. She is the former host of *Top Model po-Russki*, an adaptation of the modeling competition program *America's Next Top Model*, and *Dom-2* ("House 2"), a show reminiscent of Britain's popular reality series *Big Brother*. In 2011, she became the star of the independent television network Dozhd,

Prokofyev Vyacheslav/ITAR-TASS/Landov

where she hosts a political talk show called *Sobchak Live*. Her father, the late Anatoly Sobchak, was a law professor and politician who gave Russian president Vladimir Putin his first job in politics in 1990. (There is a rumor that Putin is Sobchak's godfather, but she denies it.) The family history and Sobchak's individual fame make her work in the opposition all the more significant—and all the more surprising.

Sobchak's unlikely turn as protest leader began on YouTube. In the fall of 2011, she encountered a man named Vasily Yakemenko at an expensive Moscow restaurant. Yakemenko is a politician and former leader of a Kremlin-sponsored "of-the-people" youth group called Nashi, which translates as "ours" or "our own." In an article about the organization's role in the 2008 presidential campaign for the *New York Times* (8 July 2007), Steven Lee Myers wrote that Nashi seemed more like a former Communist Party youth group than the Boys and Girls Club: "Its main role . . . is the ideological cultivation—some say indoctrination—of today's youth, the first generation to come of age in post-Soviet Russia." When Sobchak saw Yakemenko, she ambushed him with her cell-phone camera. "Look who's here!" she says in the video, as quoted by Andrew Meier for the *New York Times* (3 July 2012). With relish, she zooms in on the restaurant's pricey menu and reads some of it aloud with mock surprise: "Bellini Champagne for 1,300 rubles [$40] a glass!" Yakemenko looks uncomfortable. "I mean, it's not surprising for me to be here, I'm a socialite," she says, "but you!" A spokesperson for Nashi responded to the video by calling Sobchak a "cheap prostitute."

In 2012, Sobchak saw herself as a full-fledged member of the opposition, even if the opposition did not. "They see a threat: 'Sobchak will blacken the image of the opposition.' And they may be right," Sobchak told Meier. "But I can't change what I've done, any more than I can change my biography." Sobchak has a huge fan base and the cachet of her family name, and she exploits these advantages easily and without scruple. Masha Gessen, a Russian journalist and author of *The Man without a Face: The Unlikely Rise of Vladimir Putin* (2013), told Elisa Lipsky-Karasz for *Harper's Bazaar* (21 May 2012) that Sobchak's involvement in the protest movement is "very significant." Gessen added, "Obviously her name and celebrity are massive, and when she speaks about Putin as someone who knows him, it has resonance."

A POLITICAL FAMILY

Kseniya Sobchak was born on November 5, 1981, in Leningrad (now Saint Petersburg). Her father, Anatoly Sobchak, was a leader in Russia's democratic movement who rose to power in the post-Soviet era of the early 1990s. He was the first democratically elected mayor of Leningrad, taking office in 1991, and led the campaign to restore the city's original name. In August of that year, he successfully—and crucially—rallied Leningrad citizens against a Communist-backed coup. His role in quelling the uprising made him one of the country's most popular politicians.

Putin had been one of Anatoly Sobchak's law students in the 1970s and became his adviser for international affairs in 1990, when Sobchak was still the city chairman of Leningrad. After being elected mayor, Sobchak made Putin a top deputy despite the latter's long history with the KGB, the former Soviet Union's secret police force. Sobchak seemed poised to run for president, but tensions between him and then-president Boris Yeltsin, formerly an ally, took their toll. A smear campaign against Sobchak—which, his family claims, came directly from the Kremlin—cost him his reelection in 1996.

In 1999, Yeltsin appointed Putin to the position of prime minister, the head of the executive branch and second-in-command to the president; when Yeltsin unexpectedly resigned on New Year's Eve, Putin became Russia's acting president. In 2000, Putin ran for his first official term as president and asked Sobchak to work on his campaign. "He was a friend and mentor to me," Putin said, as quoted by Meier. Sobchak, who had been ill for several years, died of a heart attack while campaigning for Putin in Kaliningrad in February 2000. There are photos of Putin huddled together with Sobchak and her mother, Lyudmila Narusova, at Anatoly's funeral. There is one point, at least, on which Putin and Sobchak agree: they both maintain that Anatoly

Sobchak was killed by the stress he endured after falling from the Kremlin's good graces.

Narusova, who was Anatoly's second wife, was a politician as well, joining the State Duma in 1995. In 2002 she was elected senator for the Tuva Republic, and she represented the region in the Federation Council, the upper house of Russia's parliament, for eight years. She was elected again in 2010, this time by her native region of Bryansk, and held the position until October 2012, when she was recalled from the council after criticizing the government's crackdown on protesters.

Sobchak was eighteen when her father died, and the event, she told Meier, "was the end of my first life." She sank into a deep depression and refused to leave her family's Saint Petersburg apartment for months. Eventually she came out of it, telling her mother, "I've got to start a new life—on my own." She transferred from Saint Petersburg State University to the Moscow State Institute of International Relations, where she earned a bachelor's degree in political science in 2002 and a master's degree in 2004.

Despite her prestigious degrees and her family connections, Sobchak initially turned away from politics, instead seeking out a career in show business. In an interview with the independent Russian magazine *New Times*, as quoted by Nataliya Vasilyeva and Laura Mills for the Associated Press (14 June 2012), she said the decision "was a conscious choice, to build my own career, to make a name for myself. . . . I used all means to build it and was ready to pay any price for it." Off-camera, she embraced the hedonistic lifestyle of Russia's elite during the oil-boom years.

RUSSIA'S "IT GIRL"

Russia was in financial ruins after the fall of the Soviet Union in 1991, but an oil and real-estate boom in the early 2000s flooded the Russian elite with cash. After decades of deprivation, Russia's nouveau riche flaunted their money with abandon, and Sobchak, a beautiful young woman in her early twenties, became their mascot. She was a flashy dresser who went clubbing with celebrities and oligarchs in Moscow and posed for Russian *Playboy* and *Maxim*. She developed a requisite disdain for the poor; in an interview with Sabrina Tavernise for the *New York Times* (29 July 2003), a twenty-one-year-old Sobchak described her insulated existence in "little oases of normal Western lifestyle," avoiding Russia's less privileged classes. "Home, the car, the health club, entertainment," she said. "You go out on the street and it's dirty. There are people and their envy. It's a lot of negative energy." Russia's burgeoning tabloid culture tracked her every romance, exploit, and drunken altercation, making her the country's flawed "it girl." It was a role Sobchak embraced, and when comparisons to Paris Hilton were drawn, she courted them, even providing the voice-over for Hilton's role in the Russian-language version of the 2006 National Lampoon movie *Pledge This!*

In 2004, Sobchak starred in a movie called *Thieves and Prostitutes* and began hosting the reality television show *Dom-2*, Russia's version of Britain's *Big Brother*. On the show, contestants build a house and then compete to win the house by coupling up. Meier quotes a British critic who wrote that *Dom-2* "manages to make *Big Brother* look like a model of taste and humanity." In 2005, Moscow politicians condemned the show as exploitative and petitioned to have it shut down; they even accused Sobchak, in her role as host, of "organizing prostitution acts" and "pimping." The show, which is the longest-running reality show in history, remains tremendously popular.

In 2006, Sobchak and fellow socialite Oksana Robski published a book titled *Zamuzh za millionera ili brak vysshego sorta* (To marry a millionaire; or, the best marriage) and released a perfume by the same name. The how-to guide, which includes such timeless advice as not dressing like a "Ukrainian prostitute," cashed in on a publishing trend that in turn was capitalizing on Russia's growing population of wealthy bachelors. But the coup de grâce of Sobchak's era of debauchery was her 2007 reality series *The Blonde in Chocolate*. The show's aesthetic was tacky and over the top, and Sobchak was petulant, seductive, and often drunk. Sobchak insisted that it was a parody of Russian excess and that she was playing a character. "I like this idea that what we are doing on my program is taking an image like Paris Hilton, like this dumb blond doing nothing, but we are showing it in a fun way—absurdly," she told Peter Savodnik for *W* magazine (Nov. 2007).

Character or not, Sobchak managed her show-business career with surprising ease. Journalists who conflated Sobchak and Hilton underestimated Sobchak's intelligence and shrewdness. In addition to her work in television, Sobchak makes millions from her stake in a Russian telephone company and is coowner of a chic Moscow restaurant called Tverbul.

THE SNOW REVOLUTION

Putin won Russia's presidential election in 2000, the year Sobchak's father died, and was reelected in 2004. A two-term limit prevented him from running for office again, so Putin stepped down, and Dmitry Medvedev was elected president in 2008. Medvedev immediately appointed Putin as his prime minister, an arrangement that made many Russians uneasy. In September 2011, Putin announced that the Kremlin was voting to extend the presidential term from four years to six years. Because of the change, he said, he had decided to run for a third, nonconsecutive term as president. Parliamentary elections were held on December 4, and candidates from Putin's party won a majority of the seats—victories that were widely believed to be fraudulent.

Less than a week after the election, tens of thousands of Russians gathered in Bolotnaya Square in Moscow to demand Putin's resignation, launching what many in the media dubbed the "snow revolution." Most of the protesters were young members of the middle class who, as Andrew E. Kramer and David M. Herszenhorn wrote for the *New York Times* (11 Dec. 2011), had actually benefited under Putin due to Russia's ongoing boom. "This is not a protest of empty pots," Viktor A. Shenderovich, a Russian radio commentator, said, as quoted by Kramer and Herszenhorn. "This is political, not economic. . . . These are people protesting because they were humiliated. They were not asked. They were just told, 'Putin is coming back.'"

Sobchak spoke at a rally on December 24, 2011. When she got up in front of the crowd of eighty thousand Russians, she was greeted with a chorus of jeers. "I'm Kseniya Sobchak, and I've got something to lose," she said, according to Vasilyeva and Mills. "But I'm here."

VOICING DISSENT

Sobchak had remained politically aware even during what she has referred to as her "Paris Hilton years"; in 2006, she tried to start a youth movement called All Free, although the idea never got off the ground. By early 2012, Sobchak was a familiar, if unlikely, face of the opposition, though she maintained her relatively moderate political stance. She was not calling for an overthrow of the government, she insisted. In her *New Times* interview, as quoted by Vasilyeva and Mills, she explained, "I'm against this system. I'm against bureaucratization, corruption, seeing the same people in power. But I'm not personally against Putin."

In the run-up to the presidential election in March 2012, Sobchak threw herself into her new role as dissident, launching the political talk show *GosDep* on MTV Russia in February. The show was canceled after one episode despite high ratings, a decision Sobchak publicly attributed to the fact that she had invited leading anticorruption campaigner Alexei Navalny to appear in the second episode. Her new show, *GosDep-2*, is hosted on the website Snob.ru, and Sobchak freely discusses topics such as the Orthodox Church and gay rights. She even spoofed Putin's campaign videos, which featured sexy women endorsing him; she starred in her own version, as reported on the BBC News website (12 June 2012), in which she looked "bedraggled and abused." "Now is not the time to rock the boat, and we should rally round one leader," she says in the video, before being tied up, gagged, and spirited away by thugs.

Putin won reelection in March, and the so-called snow revolution was dwindling by the time the real snow melted in May. Putin began mercilessly cracking down on dissent—Sobchak's mother lost her Federation Council seat when she argued that he had acted too harshly toward protesters—and the police began making arrests. Many in the opposition movement were angry that Sobchak seemed to glide above the law, but in June 2012, this turned out not to be the case: an armed team from the newly created Investigative Committee of the Russian Federation raided her apartment, confiscating her passport and more than $1.5 million in assorted currencies. Both passport and money were later returned, but the raid cost Sobchak her job hosting both *Top Model po-Russki* and *Dom-2*.

PERSONAL LIFE

In 2012, Sobchak began a public romance with Ilya Yashin, a leader of the People's Freedom Party. The two made such an unlikely pair that Anna Nemtsova, writing for the *Daily Beast* (17 Dec. 2012), dubbed them "the Russian opposition's Romeo and Juliet." But Sobchak surprised her followers and the press in February 2013 when she announced via her Twitter account that she had married actor and television producer Maksim Vitorgan in a private ceremony. The two had started dating in late 2012 following Sobchak's little-publicized breakup with Yashin. Vitorgan, who is widely known in Russia for his role in the satirical 2007 film *Den vyborov* (Election day), is also a supporter of the opposition movement and was among the thousands of independent volunteers monitoring the March 2012 election.

SUGGESTED READING

Ioffe, Julia. "The Price of Opposition in Russia." *New Yorker*. Condé Nast, 14 June 2012. Web. 15 May 2014.

Meier, Andrew. "Ksenia Sobchak, the Stiletto in Putin's Side." *New York Times*. New York Times, 3 July 2012. Web. 15 May 2014.

Vasilyeva, Nataliya, and Laura Mills. "Russian It Girl's Path from Parties to Protests." *Big Story*. Assoc. Press, 14 June 2012. Web. 15 May 2014.

—*Molly Hagan*

Erik Spoelstra

Born: November 1, 1970
Occupation: Basketball coach

In April 2008, Erik Spoelstra—essentially unknown outside basketball circles, but the handpicked successor of Hall of Fame coach and team president Pat Riley—became the head coach of

David Santiago/MCT/Landov

the Miami Heat. At thirty-seven, Spoelstra was the youngest head coach at the time, unseating New Jersey Nets coach Lawrence Frank for the distinction; he also was the first Asian American to be hired as a head coach in any of the four major American sports leagues. Because of Spoelstra's relative anonymity, his hiring confounded those unfamiliar with his rise through the Heat organization, but Riley's decision was a calculated one, based on Spoelstra's wide range of basketball experience, his impeccable work ethic, and his National Basketball Association (NBA) pedigree. "I believe Erik Spoelstra is one of the most talented young coaches to come around in a long time," Riley said at the time (*NBA.com* 28 Apr. 2008). "This game is now about younger coaches who are technologically skilled, innovative and bring fresh new ideas. That's what we feel we are getting with Erik."

As a head coach, Spoelstra has weathered his share of criticism. Initially, members of the media were skeptical of his lack of head-coaching experience, especially at the beginning of the 2010–11 season, after a summer in which the Heat acquired all-star free agents LeBron James and Chris Bosh to complement superstar Dwyane Wade. Spoelstra remained above the fray, amid reports of a contentious relationship with James, to lead the team to three consecutive NBA Finals, guiding the Heat to championships in 2012 and 2013.

EARLY LIFE AND EDUCATION

Spoelstra was born on November 1, 1970, in Evanston, Illinois, to parents Jon Spoelstra, an

NBA marketing executive, and Elisa Celino, who was born in the Philippines. Spoelstra's father met his mother while stopped in Manila on his way to Australia. The two returned to the United States, marrying two years later and having their first child, Monica, soon after.

Because of his father's occupation, Spoelstra spent his childhood in several locations, including New York, until the family settled in Portland, Oregon, when his father began working for the Trail Blazers basketball team. Given that Spoelstra's father was a sports executive and that his grandfather, Watson Spoelstra, had been a long-time sports journalist for the *Detroit News*, it seems logical in hindsight that Spoelstra would pursue a career in the business of sports, but his family connections were not enough to predict his dramatic rise within the industry. He was "just a normal neighborhood kid," insists his father, as reported by Linda Robertson for the *Miami Herald* (16 June 2013), but he became obsessed with basketball. Spurred by his father's instruction, Spoelstra channeled his obsession, practicing relentlessly, even taking thirty thousand jump shots the summer before his freshman year in high school. Spoelstra was also afforded the unique opportunity of attending any Trail Blazer's home game he chose and interacting with some of the players on the team. His father told Robertson that attending games together "was a way for me to bond with Erik," but the experience exposed Spoelstra to the professional game, fostering his intuitive ability to analyze and dissect the game.

Spoelstra started at point guard for Jesuit High School in Beaverton, Oregon, eventually opting to stay close to home to attend and to play basketball for the University of Portland. He was named the West Coast Conference freshman of the year during the 1989–90 season, and was even on the court for the tragic in-game death of Loyola Marymount star Hank Gathers. "When he fell to the ground it was like time ran in slow motion," Spoelstra told Kevin Arnovitz for *ESPN.com* (1 June 2011). "I still remember how eerie the sound of an absolutely silent gym sounded. The piercing silence. . . . It's something I won't forget." During his college career, Spoelstra averaged 9.2 points and 4.2 assists, and he finished with more than one thousand points in his career while earning a bachelor's degree in communications.

FROM GERMANY TO THE DUNGEON

Following his career at the University of Portland, Spoelstra took a job as a player-coach for a professional team in Westphalia, Germany. As it turned out, his primary duties were coaching a youth team sponsored by the Westphalia club. Spoelstra's first practice was chaotic. "I don't even know what kind of offense I'm going to run

and how to organize a team," he recollected to Arnovitz. "Everybody was out of control, running and bumping into each other." Spoelstra's work ethic and ability to communicate despite the language barrier eventually made the endeavor successful, however, and gave him the coaching experience he greatly desired. As his two years in Germany wound down, he searched for a coaching position at an American college, but was unsuccessful.

Though Spoelstra was content to spend more time in Germany to gain additional experience, his circumstances changed in 1995; that year his father used his connection with Chris Wallace, the Heat's director of player personnel at the time, to persuade general manager Dave Wohl to grant an interview to Spoelstra. Wohl was impressed: "Sometimes you just get a really good feeling about somebody," Wohl explained to Amalie Benjamin for the *Boston Globe* (3 June 2012). Spoelstra's family connections had paid off, but he still had to prove himself. He was hired initially to assist with the 1995 NBA draft, a temporary position, but was then asked to initiate the development of a video department, something that he knew nothing about but an opportunity he eagerly accepted. "I was kind of like the concierge-slash-video coordinator my first year," Spoelstra explained to Arnovitz. "I just figured I wanted them coming to me with as many different things as possible to lean on, whether it was basketball-related or not. I wanted to be the guy who they'd pick up the phone and say, 'He'll get it done.'" In another fortuitous happenstance, Spoelstra was close to being replaced as the video coordinator before the project even got off the ground: Riley, the incoming coach, wanted to bring the video team from his New York Knicks staff, but was contractually obligated to maintain the Heat's video department, securing Spoelstra's job and introducing Riley to a new protégé.

Spoelstra's role as the video coordinator required him to log countless hours in a windowless basement room below the Miami Arena called the Dungeon. "It wasn't even part of the offices," he reported to Arnovitz. "It was probably an old storage room." He often slept in his office and sometimes made middle-of-the-night treks to the Miami airport to ship packages to the team when traveling. Sequestered in the Dungeon, separated from staff and friends, Spoelstra could have easily decided to leave the Heat in pursuit of a coaching position but instead worked his way up through the organization through ingenuity, a willingness to contribute, and a work ethic that was visible to everyone within the organization, including Riley.

UP THE LADDER

After two years as the video coordinator, Spoelstra began his steady ascent toward head coach.

In 1997, the Heat promoted him to assistant coach, though he still headed the video department. In 1999, he left the video department behind, maintaining his title as assistant coach and becoming an advanced scout for the team. In 2001, barely out of his twenties, he was named the Heat's director of scouting. Each of these experiences added to his resume, and his broad work experience eventually translated into a perspective that few head coaches possess. As Riley told Arnovitz, "Sometimes I think being a video coordinator and an advance scout prepares you better to be a head coach than just becoming an assistant coach. You're forced to look at X's and O's and so many things. He had such a great reservoir of basketball knowledge."

Riley had groomed several of his previous assistant coaches, including the Van Gundy brothers (Stan and Jeff), to be head coaches; it became apparent to members of the Heat organization that he was priming Spoelstra for a similar transition. From 2001 until 2008, Spoelstra brought his unique experience and perspective to the Miami bench; there, he bonded with Heat players and personnel, including Dwyane Wade. Wade, who entered the NBA in 2003 and won his first championship with the team in 2006, underlines the faith he has in Spoelstra, despite the latter's age and initial lack of head coaching experience: "We worked a lot of hours. . . . You saw that he knew the game of basketball. You knew he was a hard worker. He gave me the confidence to think, 'I can do it,'" he told Arnovitz. When Riley decided to step down as coach of the Heat to concentrate on his role as president of the team, he had only one person in mind to replace him.

HEAD COACH
When Spoelstra took over as head coach of the Heat at the end of the 2007–8 season, he became not only the youngest head coach in the NBA, but also the first of Asian descent in the NBA, National Football League (NFL), Major League Baseball (MLB), or the National Hockey League (NHL). Spoelstra inherited a team that finished with a 15–67 record, a league worst and a key reason for Riley's departure. Riley was not abandoning a bad situation, however, but handing over the reins to someone he felt was capable of leading the Heat into its next decade. Spoelstra is "a man that was born to coach," Riley stated in his press release regarding the coaching change (NBA.com).

Spoelstra spearheaded a rapid turnaround, leading the team to a 43–39 record and a fifth-place finish in the Eastern Conference. The Heat lost in the first round of the playoffs to the fourth-place Atlanta Hawks, but Spoelstra had defied those who thought he was unprepared to be a head coach and instilled confidence in his players. Other than Wade and rookie Michael

Beasley, acquired with the second pick in the 2008 draft, the Heat had no standout players, and the team's finish was a testament to both Spoelstra's ability and the system that Riley had put in place.

In 2009–10, the Heat improved again, posting a 47–35 record and again finishing fifth in the Eastern Conference. The team reached the playoffs for a second consecutive year, but again lost in the first round, this time to the Boston Celtics, who eventually advanced to the NBA Finals. Despite the team's improvement and Spoelstra's increasing abilities, major changes were in store.

JAMES AND COMPANY ARRIVE
The 2010 free-agency class was one of the most anticipated in NBA history, and at the top of every team's wish list was forward LeBron James, widely considered the best player in the game. The primary critique of James was that he had been unable to win a championship, reaching the NBA Finals once, in 2007. Another of the top-tier free agents was Chris Bosh, a power forward–center from the Toronto Raptors, who was known for his rebounding ability. James and Bosh were friends with Wade, as the three had appeared on several Eastern Conference all-star teams together as well as the 2008 gold-medal–winning US Olympic basketball team.

After intense media speculation as to where the two free agents would sign, James made his announcement during a live event broadcast by ESPN on July 8, 2010; James reported that he, along with Bosh, would join Wade in Miami to compose a team many predicted would compete for championships throughout the following decade.

The Heat began the 2010–11 season sluggishly, posting a 9–8 record to begin the season, and reports surfaced that James and Spoelstra were having trouble communicating. The situation seemed to come to a head during a game on November 28, when James bumped into his coach during a timeout. Spoelstra told the media, as reported by the Sun Sentinel (29 Nov. 2010), "I didn't even notice it until people mentioned it after the game. Often, coming out of the timeout, it's a pinball game. I'm colliding into a lot of people. So it's probably a perfect case of over-speculation from this team." James gave a similar response, but, for some, the incident seemed to confirm the rift between the two; for others, it was a clear indication of the overbearing media scrutiny that the team would have to endure, regardless of whether rumors were based on substance.

The early part of the 2010 season was rocky, but Riley never lost faith in Spoelstra, reminding him to communicate with his players. Discussing the rough patch, Spoelstra told Arnovitz "There's an integrity to my intentions. I probably look at this more simplistic than you want. It doesn't matter whether you're a former player or you come up through the video room. . . . You have to earn that trust from NBA players every day. . . . at some point, they believe you can help them achieve what they want to achieve." By season's end he had rallied his troops, leading them to the NBA Finals. However, the Heat was defeated by the Dallas Mavericks, and Spoelstra faced scrutiny once again.

NBA CHAMPIONS

Riley squashed speculation that he would return to coach the Heat for the 2011–12 season, instead extending Spoelstra's contract by two seasons. Spoelstra was not the only one to receive criticism from fans and the media for failing to guide the team to a championship. More than anyone else associated with the franchise, James was lambasted for his inability to secure a trophy. Therefore, the 2011–12 season represented a chance for both player and coach to dispel the criticism that followed in their wake.

The Heat began the season 19–6, the best twenty-five game start in franchise history, and did not slow down afterward, earning the second playoff position in the Eastern Conference. The team defeated the Knicks, Pacers, and Celtics to reach the finals once again. "I don't know of another coach that has been under a microscope as much as Erik without really a whole lot of time to develop," Wohl told Benjamin, during the team's matchup with the Celtics. Though the finals series against the Oklahoma City Thunder featured a number up-and-coming players, such as Kevin Durant, James stole the show; the Heat won the series in five games.

After proving that he could helm a championship team, Spoelstra eyed a repeat in 2012–13. During the season, the Heat compiled a twenty-seven-game winning streak, the second longest in NBA history, cruising to an Eastern Conference regular-season championship and record of 66–16. Repeating as champions was not an easy task, as the Heat took the full seven games to defeat the Pacers in the Eastern Conference Finals and the San Antonio Spurs in the NBA Finals, clawing back from a double-digit deficit in the sixth game of the finals to capture a second championship.

The accolades began to stream in for Spoelstra and his team after the victory. "I definitely think he's a Hall of Famer," Stan Van Gundy told Chris Tomasson for *Fox Sports Florida* (7 July 2013), which Spoelstra called "ridiculous." However, only thirteen coaches have won multiple championships in the NBA, and only four coaches have won three or more, a group Spoelstra could easily join in the future with James, Wade, and Bosh under contract. Spoelstra signed a contract extension with the Heat in September 2013.

Spoelstra lives in Miami. Known for keeping his personal life private, Spoelstra made his relationship with former Heat dancer Nikki Sapp public in March 2013.

SUGGESTED READING

Abrams, Jonathan. "Spoelstra Raised to Be in N.B.A., and Rising to Challenge." *New York Times*. New York Times Co., 28 May 2011. Web. 17 Sept. 2013.

Amalie, Benjamin. "On the Hot Seat, Erik Spoelstra Has Stayed Cool for Miami Heat." *Boston Globe*. New York Times Co., 3 June 2012. Web. 17 Sept. 2013.

Arnovitz, Kevin. "The Mystery Guest Has Arrived." *ESPN.com*. ESPN Internet Ventures, 1 June 2011. Web. 17 Sept. 2013.

Richards, George. "Miami Heat Coach Erik Spoelstra Earning His Due Respect." *Miami Herald*. Miami Herald Media, 25 June 2013. Web. 17 Sept. 2013.

"Riley Steps Down, Spoelstra Named Head Coach." *NBA.com*. NBA Media Ventures, 28 Apr. 2008. Web. 17 Sept. 2013.

Smith, Chris. "Miami's Erik Spoelstra Could Take Step Closer to Hall of Fame with Finals Win." *Forbes*. Forbes.com, 20 June 2013. Web. 17 Sept. 2013.

Winderman, Ira, and Michael Cunningham. "Spoelstra Has Been around the Game since Childhood." *Sun Sentinel*. Sun Sentinel, 29 Apr. 2008. Web. 17 Sept. 2013.

—*Christopher Rager*

Peter Stamm

Born: January 18, 1963
Occupation: Writer

There are few modern continental European authors whom American critics have praised as much as Peter Stamm, a Swiss novelist and short story writer who was nominated for the Man Booker International Prize in 2013. Five of his novels, including the forthcoming *All Days Are Night* (2014), and many of his short stories have been translated into English by the respected German-born poet Michael Hofmann. His stark, deliberate, and restrained writing, centering on the internal struggles of his emotionally detached characters, has earned him comparisons to such literary giants as Albert Camus and Franz Kafka.

The struggles Stamm's characters, who often appear to have a lack of empathy, contend with often appear commonplace at first glance—marriage and work, relationships and family—but underneath their seeming ordinariness, these characters are charged by an existential turmoil

about the very meaning of their lives. In an interview with Deborah Treisman for the *New Yorker* (7 May 2012), Stamm said of his work, "It has always been my goal to make literature out of ordinary people's lives. I don't like the extremes; I don't think that they teach us much about ourselves. And very often extreme or willfully original stories are just trying to make up for a lack of empathy on the part of the author. Writers can learn from painters. No great painter would ever choose an original subject for his paintings. Cézanne, for example, needed only a few apples and some old pots and jugs to prove his artistry."

EARLY LIFE AND CAREER

Peter Stamm was born on January 18, 1963, near Lake Constance, in northeastern Switzerland. Stamm, who is fluent in both German and his native Schweizerdeutsch (Swiss German) but writes in German, recalled his childhood hometown in his interview with Treisman: "It's very nice, with lots of apple orchards, vineyards, forests, and little lakes, where we used to go swimming." Although he grew up in a prosperous, postwar Switzerland—which today is internationally renowned not only for its powerful banking sector but also for its production of high-quality goods such as textiles and watches—his native country was poor well into the 1800s. He wrote in an essay for the *New York Times* (22 Nov. 2013), "My great-grandmother, who grew up in an Alpine valley, often went hungry; occasionally, she was forced to eat grass to fill her belly."

In college Stamm studied accounting, as his father had done, and he spent the first five years of his working life in his father's profession. But accounting did not suit Stamm, and he quit, deciding to return to school for additional studies. He then traveled for a time, visiting cities in the United States and Europe, before returning home to pen his first novel, *Agnes*, which was published in German in 1998. The novel's title character, a young woman living in Chicago who is both a science student and a cellist, has fallen in love with a very detached young Swiss journalist, who is researching a history of Pullman train cars. Agnes decides to ask her boyfriend to write a story about her. The result is somewhat surreal: Agnes is both the title character of the novel and a character in the story her boyfriend is writing. When she gets her literary wish, however, she discovers that he has more control over her than she could have ever possibly imagined. An English edition of the novel, translated by poet Michael Hofmann, was published in 2000.

UNFORMED LANDSCAPE AND ON A DAY LIKE THIS

The success of Stamm's first novel across Europe helped transform him into a respected literary figure. His next novel, *Unformed Landscape* (*Ungefähre Landschaft*, 2001), was published in English translation in 2004 and received considerable acclaim when it was published in the United States. In it, a woman named Kathrine, who is living in Narvik, Norway, wants to escape her dull life in her town above the Arctic Circle. Although she eventually travels south, Kathrine's personal journey, which involves relationships with a number of men, does more to help her abandon her illusions about the outside world than to fulfill any fantasies she may have had about it. In a review of *Unformed Landscape*, a critic for the *New Yorker* (23 May 2005) wrote, "If Albert Camus had lived in an age when people in remote Norwegian fishing villages had e-mail, he might have written a novel like this. . . . In Stamm's portrait, a scenario that could have been half-baked captures what seems a particularly Nordic view of adult life: austere pragmatism mixed with mordant wit."

In Stamm's third novel, *On a Day Like This* (*An einem Tag wie diesem*, 2006), which was published in English translation in 2007, a Swiss man named Andreas has been a German teacher at a school outside Paris for about eighteen years. He has two romantic relationships going at the same time—one with a divorcee named Nadia, whom he has been dating for some time, and another with a married woman named Sylvie. Both women mean nothing to him despite their physical intimacy. His sense of detachment also extends to his own family. Upon returning to Switzerland to attend his father's funeral, he finds himself emotionless and unable to mourn.

Over the course of the story it is revealed that the only person who ever mattered to him was a Frenchwoman named Fabienne, but he never told her he loved her. A chronic cough, which hints at a more serious illness, prompts Andreas to quit his job, leave the women in his life, and sell his apartment. After embarking on a road trip, he finds himself back in his hometown, trying to have a relationship with a young woman named Delphine while at the same time seeking to reconnect with the now-married Fabienne. Unlike Stamm's prior novels, *On a Day Like This* met with mixed reviews. In a review of the novel, a critic for *Kirkus Reviews* (15 May 2008) wrote, "In this study of anomie there are echoes of *The Stranger*, though Stamm's novel has none of the power or the eventfulness of the Camus classic. . . . There is an upbeat ending which doesn't ring true. Andreas's condition does not seem authentic in this mannered treatment."

SEVEN YEARS

Stamm's novel most recently translated into English, *Seven Years* (*Sieben Jahre*, 2009), had been inspired by *Ivona, Princess of Burgundia* (1935; English translation, 1969), a little-known play by the Polish writer Witold Gombrowicz, and was highly regarded upon its publication in the United States in 2011. Set in Germany in the 1980s, it depicts the development of a relationship of a "beautiful couple"—architects Alex and Sonia—from first romance to maturing boredom. Alex attempts to relieve his boredom through an affair with Ivona, an unattractive bookstore worker with whom he has an on-and-off affair for several years. Like many of Stamm's narrators and protagonists, Alex is aloof emotionally and cares little for anyone beside himself. He is disconnected from his wife, with whom his life develops as a series of projects (get married/make a home/start a business/have children), and has little affection for his mistress, apart from his need to use her as a mirror with which to adore himself.

Reviewing *Seven Years* for the *New York Times* (25 Mar. 2011), Sarah Fay remarked, "With its understated descriptions and cool perceptions, Stamm's fiction . . . explores the tendency to experience two incongruous emotions or sensations simultaneously: attraction and disgust, warmth and estrangement, anxiety and liberation. . . . Stamm's talent is palpable, but what makes him a writer to read, and read often, is the way he renders contemporary life as a series of ruptures. Never entirely sure of their position, his characters engage in a constant effort to establish their equilibrium."

SHORT STORIES

Although Stamm has garnered international acclaim as a novelist, he is also esteemed as a master of short fiction. During his career, he has published several collections of stories, two of which have been published in English. Of his affection for the short story form, Stamm remarked in his interview with Treisman, "My novels usually sell about twice as well as my story collections, but to me the story form has always been important. I sometimes compare stories to chamber music, where you have only a few instruments but you can hear every single note. I like reduction, concentration, clarity."

Stamm's first English-language collection was published in 2006 under the title *In Strange Gardens and Other Stories*. In this collection of twenty tales originally published in German, Stamm's characters are typically strangers who find themselves meeting as, for example, passengers on a train, or as campers, or as visitors to New York City. Many of the characters are shallow and drift through the stories, simply reacting to what has been going on around them. A reviewer for *Publishers Weekly* (12 Dec. 2005) praised *In Strange Gardens*, writing, "The stories are narrated with clinical detachment, and are often hauntingly impressionistic. . . . Stamm derives his narrative power from absence and void."

Stamm's most recent collection, *We're Flying*, was published in English in 2012. As in the previous collection, much of what occurs in these stories happens internally, within the minds of the characters. All of the stories relate to what it means to be human—adolescent awkwardness, sexual relations, falling in love, struggling with belief, facing death. Again, critics found themselves comparing Stamm's work to that of Kafka and Camus, particularly when reviewing stories such as "Children of God," in which a minister falls in love with a pregnant girl who claims to have experienced an immaculate conception, and "Go Out into the Fields . . . ," a story written in the second person viewpoint of a landscape painter who is indifferent to his own work. Writing of *We're Flying*, a critic for *Kirkus Reviews* (22 July 2012) proclaimed, "Beneath the surface placidity of Swiss life, undercurrents of spiritual turmoil and existential despair charge this powerful collection of provocative stories. . . . The American publication combines two separate story collections, the first published in 2008, the second in 2011, yet the stories themselves are timeless, like fables or parables, with the plainspoken translation reinforcing the stark, spare essence of the fiction."

RECOGNITION AND FORTHCOMING WORK

Since gaining a considerable fan base in the United States following the publication of *Seven Years* in 2011, Stamm has published his short fiction and essays in English translation in a number of major US publications, including the *New Yorker* and the *New York Times*. In the *Times*, he has written opinion pieces about issues facing his native Switzerland, including his support for its national efforts to limit excessive compensation for executives as well as his criticism of a national ban on the building of new minarets, an architectural feature associated with Islamic houses of worship, particularly mosques. Other Press, Stamm's American publisher, will publish an English translation of Stamm's most recent novel, *All Days Are Night* (*Nacht ist der Tag*, 2013), in November 2014. In the novel, a popular and beautiful television host named Gillian must rebuild her life after she awakes in a hospital following a horrific car accident to learn that her husband has been killed and she has been severely disfigured.

Stamm, whose works have been published in more than thirty languages, was a finalist for the 2013 Man Booker International Prize. He lives outside Zürich, Switzerland.

SUGGESTED READING

Boylan, Roger. "Debts: In Peter Stamm's World, We All Have Them." *Boston Review*. Boston Review, 19 Aug. 2013. Web. 10 July 2014.

Fay, Sarah. "A Cheating Husband's World." Rev. of *Seven Years*, by Peter Stamm. *New York Times*. New York Times, 25 Mar. 2011. Web. 10 July 2014.

"In Strange Gardens and Other Stories." *Publishers Weekly*. Publishers Weekly, 12 Dec. 2005. Web. 10 July 2014.

"On a Day Like This." *Kirkus Reviews*. Kirkus Reviews, 15 May 2008. Web. 10 July 2014.

Treisman, Deborah. "This Week in Fiction: Peter Stamm." *New Yorker*. New Yorker, 7 May 2012. Web. 10 July 2014.

"Unformed Landscape." *New Yorker*. New Yorker, 23 May 2005. Web. 10 July 2014.

"We're Flying." *Kirkus Reviews*. Kirkus Reviews, 22 July 2012. Web. 10 July 2014.

SELECTED WORKS

Agnes, 2000; *Unformed Landscape*, 2004; *In Strange Gardens and Other Stories*, 2006; *On a Day Like This*, 2007; *Seven Years*, 2010; *We're Flying: Stories*, 2012; *All Days Are Night*, 2014

—*Christopher Mari*

Nina Stemme

Born: May 11, 1963
Occupation: Opera singer

Many consider Swedish soprano Nina Stemme one of the finest contemporary operatic sopranos. Known for her interpretations of operas by German composers Richard Wagner and Richard Strauss, she diversifies with Italian opera as

Joshua Gunter/The Plain Dealer/Landov

well. Fittingly enough, in both the Norwegian and Danish languages, her last name, *stemme*, means "voice." Director Francesca Zambello told Cori Ellison for the *New York Times* (20 May 2012), "Who she is offstage is so different from who she is onstage. In life, she often seems so understated. Then she gets onstage, and some sort of primal creature takes over. She's an absolutely fearless singing actress for whom no challenge is too much." Booked for five years in advance, Stemme notes that she feels privileged to have a full calendar at a time when opera houses throughout Europe are closing because of financial difficulties. She has been a guest performer for many companies, including the New York Metropolitan Opera, Milan's La Scala, the Paris Opera, and the Royal Opera House in London. In addition, she has sung at many music festivals, such as the BBC (British Broadcasting Company) Proms in London, Germany's Bayreuth Festival, and the Salzburg Festival in Austria. Unlike some famous performers, Stemme does not knit or do other things backstage while waiting for long periods of time between entrances. Rather, she follows the show, attempting to remain in character, and claims never to be bored. In describing her process to Jessica Duchen for *Opera News* (2012), Stemme said, "Normally I use the first rehearsals to take in as much information as possible and to see what the director wants and sometimes they don't really know what I'm capable of doing until I get onstage. It all comes out in the performance—more or less out of control!"

EARLY LIFE AND EDUCATION

Nina Stemme was born on May 11, 1963, and grew up in Stockholm, Sweden, in a family of amateur musicians. She began piano lessons at age six, after she auditioned for and was accepted into the Adolf Fredriks Musikklasser (Music School). She studied both violin and viola before cultivating her voice. The first record she ever bought was a collection of Franz Schubert compositions performed by Dame Janet Baker, a mezzo-soprano. Choral music plays a large role in the Scandinavian countries. However, Stemme told Ellison, "Music was a big part of my life. But there was no thought of a career. In Sweden, nobody is supposed to stick out from the crowd."

Stemme, who was shy and more comfortable as a member of the chorus than in solo roles, came to McLean, Virginia, for a year as an exchange student at Langley High School. Despite her initial shyness, Stemme's ability as a vocal soloist in the chorus won her awards. She received the second highest marks overall at her audition for the Virginia All-State Chorus, which gave her more confidence.

Upon her return to Sweden, Stemme pursued studies in economics and business administration at the University of Stockholm, planning to become an auditor. She was also singing and acting, and it soon became apparent where her true desires would lead. She attended a two-year program of study at Stockholm Opera Studio in her mid-twenties, beginning as a mezzo-soprano and making her 1989 debut in Wolfgang Amadeus Mozart's *Nozze di Figaro* as Cherubino. She often sang in churches and hospitals to earn some money on the side.

After further vocal coaching, she switched to lyric soprano roles at the age of twenty-seven. Doing so meant starting over and facing her fear of failure. From 1990 to 1994, she studied at Stockholm's University College of Opera. Even before her graduation, Stemme was singing minor roles with the Royal Swedish Opera. She remains a member of the company, even though she now has an international career.

COMPETITIONS LEAD TO A CAREER

In 1993 Stemme was a finalist in the Cardiff Singer of the World competition. The same year she entered the operatic tenor Plácido Domingo's first Operalia contest, held in Paris. Despite a bout of food poisoning before the competition, she won. Domingo later asked her to sing with him in concerts in Paris and Munich. Domingo and Stemme later recorded Wagner's *Tristan und Isolde* with the two of them in the title roles. Stemme commented to Ellison, "Those competitions opened the door to the opera world. I got an audition for

the Vienna State Opera and was offered a contract right away. But I felt I wasn't really ready yet. My technique was not settled enough."

Leery of burning out too quickly or ruining her voice by beginning a career at the Vienna level too soon, Stemme instead went to the smaller Cologne Opera for four years. There she learned the music of Giacomo Puccini and Giuseppe Verdi. As a resident member of the company—one not so demanding or prestigious as Vienna—she was able to start her family and develop her talent over time. At Cologne, she portrayed the title role in Puccini's *Madama Butterfly* for a matinee Red Cross benefit concert. Her portrayal led to an offer to do the role the following season, and eventually to Wagnerian opera.

Her decision to refuse the job at the Vienna State Opera proved beneficial to her growth as a vocalist, as Antonio Pappano, the music director of Covent Garden's Royal Opera House, told Jessica Duchen for *Opera News* (2012). "One thing that has enhanced her career is the fact that she's done so many different types of repertoire," he explained. "I think this also gives her a breadth and makes her a much more interesting artist than if she were singing only Wagner every day."

In 1996 Stemme received a personal scholarship from the famed Swedish soprano Birgit Nilsson. The two remained in contact, though Stemme did not fulfill her dream of singing the role of Wagner's Isolde for the older woman.

OPERA'S LYRIC ROLES

The word *opera*, meaning "works," is Italian, because the art form originated in Italy during the end of the sixteenth century. In 1637, the first opera house opened in Venice. Opera combines many aspects of the arts—music, dance, spoken text, costumes, and stage sets. Because words are sung rather than said, operas typically take longer to perform than plays. An early composer of operas described the dramatic singing style as being more than speech, but less than song.

Two types of opera soon developed as the form spread throughout Europe. *Opera buffa* was a comic, light opera. *Opera seria* was a dramatic opera, often concerned with stories of the gods. The former lends itself to lyrical voices and a light touch. The latter demands strong voices.

Working with the Cologne Opera, Stemme initially sang lyric opera roles, such as the Countess in Mozart's *Marriage of Figaro*, and light Italian works such as Verdi's *Suor Angelica*. She explained to Cori Ellison, "Italian opera requires a different approach, a different temperament, and I really want to find the color of it, which is a stretch for me. It helps the Wagnerian singing to do Italian repertoire."

Additional lighter roles included Verdi's *Tosca*. She also began singing Wagner's more lyric roles, such as Elisabeth in *Tannhäuser* and Elsa in *Lohengrin*. These were steps on her path to becoming a dramatic soprano. She explained the change in her voice to Duchen, noting, "I do know that it has grown and stabilized a bit, and since the size has increased I don't have a huge problem sounding through an orchestra. I've never heard my own voice! But this is what others tell me, and I think it must be true."

A DRAMATIC SOPRANO
In 2000 Stemme took on the dramatic role of Senta in Wagner's *The Flying Dutchman*. Although she had expected the role to test the limits of her vocal ability, she found that her voice developed further during the experience. Other singers had warned Stemme that once she took on the roles of Isolde and Brünnhilde, she would be unable to go back to other roles, simply because singing Wagner strengthens the voice so much that it becomes overpowering in other, lighter roles. She found their warning to be accurate. As Stemme told Kate Molleson for *Scotland Herald* (7 Nov. 2012), "My heart is still with Puccini and Verdi but my voice is with Wagner and Strauss. Verdi was the music that opened my heart and soul to opera. Whereas Wagner has to come to you; you can't force yourself on to Wagner."

Stemme was initially hesitant to accept the offer to sing the female lead in Wagner's *Tristan und Isolde*. Commenting on its length—the three-act opera runs about five hours—she has likened filling the role of Isolde, which she first performed in 2003 at the Glyndebourne Festival and which brought her public acclaim, to running a marathon. Other noted sopranos, such as Linda Esther Gray and Helga Dernesch, damaged their voices performing the role. She has since performed Isolde more than sixty times, finding something new in the role each time she sings it.

In 2011 Stemme sang Wagner's complete *Der Ring des Nibelungen*, a sixteen-hour, four-opera cycle that is generally performed over the course of several days, for the first time. She took the challenging role of Brünnhilde, which she initially did not feel competent to undertake. That San Francisco Opera production, under Francesca Zambello, proved her wrong. It was the first of several performances leading to the celebration of Wagner's two-hundredth birthday on May 22, 2013. Describing Stemme's talent for *Opera News* (2012), Jessica Duchen referred to its "irresistible magnetism" and noted that it is "a combination of purity, magnitude, and steely strength, built on a foundation of intelligence, focus, good sense, and absolute musicality."

Stemme fears that Wagnerian opera is becoming an endangered species in an age of declining patronage and tight budgets. The pieces are massive and expensive to produce. Indeed, the Washington (DC) National Opera delayed a production of the complete *Ring* cycle due to budget shortfalls. Stemme is contracted to perform the third of the four operas with the company, however, for a 2016 production, to be directed by Zambello.

Swedish singers have historically gravitated toward the notoriously difficult Wagner repertoire. Stemme explained this multigenerational tradition to Duchen, saying it is likely driven by that fact that Swedes are "well grounded in our relationship to nature and in our ability to relax and not take in the stress of city life. When you're grounded, you can tackle these extremely demanding parts without destroying yourself."

CRITICAL RECEPTION AND AWARDS
From the beginning of her operatic career, Stemme has impressed critics both in live performances and on recordings. As Marc Mandel wrote for *Fanfare* (1 Sept. 2007) of her recording of Richard Strauss's *Capriccio*, he "was particularly startled and impressed by Stemme's delivery of the harp-accompanied sonnet embedded in the scene. She's not just singing it through: she seems actually to be thinking hard about the sonnet, and weighing the difficulty of her position, at every step along the way." According to Anthony Tommasini, writing for *New York Times* (5 Feb. 2010), when Stemme performed the title role in Strauss's *Ariadne auf Naxos* with New York's Metropolitan Opera, she was "in excellent voice here, singing with earthy colorings, ample power, and vivid character."

In 2012, the recording Stemme made of Ludwig von Beethoven's *Fidelio* with Jonas Kaufmann and the Lucerne Festival Orchestra, under the direction of Claudio Abbado, won a Gramophone Award. Stemme has done extensive recording, including three recordings of Wagner's *Tristan und Isolde*, first with Domingo as Tristan, then in 2008 with Robert Gambill on DVD, and again with Stephen Gould in 2012. Among her other recordings are Verdi's *Aida* and Strauss's *The Flying Dutchman*.

In 2006, Stemme was appointed Swedish Court Singer. Her performance of Isolde at London's Royal Opera House in 2010 earned her the Laurence Olivier Award for best role interpretation. Twice, in 2005 and 2012, the German magazine *Opernwelt* named her Singer of the Year. She also received *Opera News*'s 2013 Opera News Award, which honors those who have made a significant contribution to that musical art form. SWEA International, a global network for women of Sweden, named Stemme Swedish Woman of the Year in 2014. She has three times been nominated for the Stockholm Prize.

PERSONAL
Stemme is married to Bengt Gomer, a stage designer, with whom she has three teenage children.

According to Stemme, they provided her with an understanding of how the character of Salome in Strauss's opera was innocent, yet sending out sexual messages she did not understand. She also feels that Wagner's music—with its overwhelming emotion—speaks to teenagers. Stemme travels for performances and is attracted to new works. Speaking of her family, she explained to Richard Speer for *Opera News* (2007), "I can't complain, because they're incredibly supportive. But we do have to plan differently. We live in Stockholm, so I go do new productions and then try to be home between the productions." When apart, family members rely on the Internet phone service Skype to stay in touch.

Although she most enjoys performing Wagner, Stemme prefers to listen to Mozart. Her favorite soprano, to whose recordings she always returns, is the twentieth-century Norwegian Kirsten Flagstad. She refers to dark chocolate and malt whiskey as her guilty pleasures. Stemme takes seriously her responsibility to her talent. She told Molleson, "At the end of the day I'm the only one who's responsible for my voice. People will just try to use it. They tried to get me to sing dramatic repertoire too early, but I said no. And one no gives you more respect than one yes too many." Her personal creed is "hurry slowly."

SUGGESTED READING

Duchen, Jessica. "Woman of the Year." *Opera News* Nov. 2012: 24–29. Print.

Ellison, Cori. "A Drama Queen with Her Head on Straight." *New York Times* 20 May 2012: 11(L). Print.

Molleson, Kate. "The Essential Isolde." *Scotland Herald*. Herald & Times Group, 7 Nov. 2012. Web. 4 June 2014.

Moss, Stephen. "Nina Stemme: I Am Always Questioning Myself: Could It Be Better?" *Guardian*. Guardian Media, 2 May 2013. Web. 4 June 2014.

Serinus, Jason Victor. "Frank Talk from Nina Stemme." *San Francisco Classical Voice*. San Francisco Classical Voice, 2011. Web. 4 June 2014.

Tommasini, Anthony. "The Opera in an Opera Overcomes Illnesses." *New York Times*. New York Times, 5 Feb. 2010. Web. 4 June 2014.

Wasserman, Adam. "Nina Stemme." *Opera News*. Apr. 2014: 24–25. Print.

SELECTED WORKS

Tristan und Isolde, 2003; *Rosenkavalier*, 2004; *Jenufa*, 2007; *Aida*, 2007; *Die Walküre*, 2010; *Der Ring des Nibelungen*, 2011

—Judy Johnson

P. K. Subban

Born: May 13, 1989
Occupation: Hockey player

Widely considered to be among the best defensemen in the National Hockey League (NHL), the Montreal Canadiens' P. K. Subban possesses "natural speed, brute strength and footwork as elegant as Patrick Chan's," as Matthew Hague wrote for *Toronto Life* (11 Dec. 2013). Known for his hard-nosed style of defense, exceptional offensive skills, and flashy personality, the six-foot, 217-pound Subban has taken the hockey world by storm since making his debut with the Canadiens during the 2009–10 season. In his first four full NHL seasons, Subban amassed 165 points (42 goals and 123 assists), seventh best among the league's defensemen. He has also tallied 30 points in forty-three career playoff games. Subban enjoyed a breakthrough season in 2012–13, when he led all NHL defensemen in points. He earned his first career All-Star selection and won the James Norris Memorial Trophy as the league's top defenseman. Though his on-ice antics have made him one of the NHL's most polarizing players, Subban, a Canadian citizen of Caribbean descent, has been credited with reenergizing the Canadiens' languishing fan base and with helping to broaden the appeal of hockey for minorities.

EARLY LIFE

Pernell Karl "P.K." Subban was born on May 13, 1989, in Toronto, Ontario, Canada, to a Jamaican father, Karl, and a Montserratian mother, Maria. (His mother named him after the actor Pernell Roberts, best known for his role on the television western *Bonanza*.) Both of his parents had emigrated from the Caribbean in the 1970s. They raised P. K. and his four siblings—older sisters Nastassia and Natasha and younger brothers

Malcolm and Jordan—in a four-bedroom home in the Toronto neighborhood of Rexdale. His father taught and served as principal at a succession of Toronto schools before retiring in 2013; his mother is a quality control analyst at CIBC Mellon.

P. K. Subban comes from an athletic family. His father played basketball at Lakehead University in Thunder Bay, Ontario, and his mother ran track at Bathurst Heights Secondary School. His eldest sister, Nastassia, who is now a teacher, played basketball at Toronto's York University, where she scored the most points in Ontario university basketball history. Though he played basketball, Karl Subban was a zealous hockey fan who spent his youth rooting for the Montreal Canadiens and playing pickup hockey games with children from his mostly French-speaking neighborhood. His passion for hockey was passed down to all of his children, but none more so than P. K., who started skating at the age of two.

P. K. had his father enroll him in his first house-league hockey team at age four, after being mesmerized by the popular weekly sports program *Hockey Night in Canada*. When P. K. was six, Karl, recognizing his son's potential, began devoting all of his scant free time to developing P. K.'s hockey skills. Each weeknight, Karl would return home from a moonlighting vice-principal job, wake up his son, and drive him downtown to Toronto's Nathan Phillips Square outdoor skating rink, where they would spend countless hours skating and practicing. Before heading home he would treat his son to a slice of pizza. "A lot of times, as a kid growing up, there were times when I didn't want to go and play, I didn't want to go skate," P. K. Subban explained to Dave Feschuk for the *Toronto Star* (24 Dec. 2007). "But my dad encouraged me to do it, 'If you want to play in the NHL, that's what it takes.'"

AN OFFENSIVE DEFENSEMAN
By age ten Subban was already showing glimpses of his star potential. "He was bigger than other players and had more depth in his abilities, and more guts," Hague noted. Armed with a blistering slap shot that could lift the puck off the ice, Subban initially played forward before being converted into a defenseman by his father, who felt he would thrive in the less flashy and often overlooked position. Commonly referred to as "blueliners" in reference to their lining up and playing near the blue line on the ice rink that indicates the boundary of the offensive zone, defensemen are primarily responsible for preventing the opposing team from taking shots on their goal. Unlike traditional defensemen, Subban worked to cultivate an aggressive, offensive style of defense that would complement his elite skating and puck-handling abilities, one that not only

allowed him to block shots and prevent goals on the back end but also contribute on offense.

In 2004, at age fifteen, Subban began playing for the Markham Islanders in the Greater Toronto Hockey League, where he met and befriended the future NHL star John Tavares. In sixty-seven games with the Islanders, he recorded fifteen goals and twenty-eight assists. Subban's journey toward becoming a professional hockey player accelerated in 2005, when he was drafted in the sixth round of the Ontario Hockey League (OHL) draft by the Belleville Bulls. The OHL is a major junior league in Canada for players aged fifteen to twenty and one of three that make up the Canadian Hockey League, the world's largest development hockey league.

BELLEVILLE BULLS AND NHL DRAFT
After being drafted Subban left home and relocated to the Bulls' home base in Belleville, a city in southeastern Ontario, so he could train and practice with the team on a full-time basis. He attended Quinte Secondary School and resided with a Belleville city employee, Amy McMillan, who took on the role of surrogate mother. Because he was a sixth-round pick, Subban, who at the time was regarded as nothing more than a raw talent, arrived in Belleville with little fanfare. Nevertheless, he immediately impressed the Bulls' head coach and general manager, George Burnett, with his strong desire to play, work ethic, and confidence, which presented itself on the day of his draft, when he declared he would make the team as a rookie. Determined to make good on that brash declaration, Subban spent the summer of 2005 overhauling his diet and adding muscle to his frame through an intensive training regimen. His hard work paid off, as he earned a Bulls roster spot after proving himself in his first training camp with the team. "He took advantage of an opportunity and we were happy to provide it," Burnett told Stu Cowan for the *Montreal Gazette* (10 Jan. 2014). "He ran with it."

During the 2005–6 season Subban tallied five goals and seven assists in fifty-two games. He made significant improvement the following season, when he was paired with veteran defenseman Geoff Killing. He amassed fifteen goals and forty-one assists in sixty-eight games. One month after he turned eighteen, Subban entered the 2007 NHL Entry Draft. Despite initially being projected to be a middle-round pick, he was selected by the Montreal Canadiens in the draft's second round, as the forty-third overall pick. In an interview with Luke Fox for the Canadian website Sportsnet (6 Sept. 2012), Subban called his drafting "the most special day of [his] life." In his conversation with Cowan, George Burnett said that it was Subban's fierce competitiveness that ultimately helped him move up in the draft. "That competitiveness is something that I think a lot of people underestimate . . . how hard he is to play against and how much pride he takes in winning the battles."

MONTREAL CANADIENS

Subban remained with the Bulls for two more seasons, after which he signed for three years (and $2.6 million) with the Canadiens, commonly referred to as the Habs, short for *Les Habitants*, the name given to the original French settlers of Quebec. During the 2007–8 season he posted forty-six points (eight goals and thirty-eight assists) in fifty-eight games, leading the Bulls to a runner-up finish in the 2008 J. Ross Robertson Cup. Then, in 2008–9, he recorded a junior career high: seventy-six points in only fifty-six games. Subban was also a two-time member of Canada's junior national team, winning consecutive gold medals at the 2008 and 2009 World Junior Ice Hockey Championships.

Subban was assigned to the Hamilton Bulldogs, the Canadiens' American Hockey League (AHL) affiliate, to begin the 2009–10 season. He displayed his all-around talent in his first professional season and was selected to play in the 2010 AHL All-Star Game in Portland, Maine. A few weeks after that game, on February 11, 2010, Subban earned his first call-up to the Canadiens. The following day he made his NHL debut in a game against the Philadelphia Flyers, in which he registered his first career point on an assist. Subban went on to appear in one more game for the Canadiens before returning to the Bulldogs.

Subban first made his presence felt around the league during the 2010 Stanley Cup playoffs, when he was recalled to the Canadiens for their first-round matchup against the Washington Capitals. He notched his first career playoff point on an assist in his NHL postseason debut and added seven more points (one goal and six assists) in thirteen other playoff appearances with the Canadiens, who advanced to the Eastern Conference finals. Subban's performance was key in the Canadiens' playoff run, and his hard-nosed and exciting style of play immediately won over the team's rabid fan base.

Subban returned to the Bulldogs after the Canadiens' playoff exit and played for them in the 2010 Calder Cup playoffs, helping them reach the Western Conference finals. For his achievements with the team during the 2009–10 season, Subban was honored with the AHL's President Trophy.

MAKING HIS MARK

Subban earned a permanent spot on the Canadiens' roster in 2010–11, his first full season in the league. He entered that season as a top contender for the Calder Memorial Trophy, bestowed annually to the NHL's Rookie of the Year. However, his patented "brashness" and "all-out

persona," as Charlie Gillis noted for *Maclean's* (22 May 2014), quickly made him a lightning rod for controversy.

Just months into his rookie season, Subban became more known for his trash talking and showboating than for his performance on the ice. Around this time Michael Farber, writing for *Sports Illustrated* (20 Dec. 2010), described Subban as "a one-man on-ice filibuster" who "harangues opponents with a playground you-can't-beat-me braggadocio." Subban's unpredictable and risk-taking nature led Canadiens head coach Jacques Martin to bench him for three games in December 2010, following a dismal fifteen-game stretch in which he recorded only one goal and two assists. Nevertheless, he bounced back to put up solid overall numbers as a rookie, tallying thirty-eight points (a career-high fourteen goals and twenty-four assists) in seventy-seven games.

In January 2011 Subban was among a select group of rookies chosen to participate in that year's NHL All-Star Game festivities in Raleigh, North Carolina. The highlight of Subban's rookie campaign, however, came on March 20, 2011, when he recorded a hat trick (at least three goals in a single game) in an 8–1 Canadiens victory over the Minnesota Wild. He became the first rookie defenseman in team history to accomplish such a feat. For his regular-season performance, he was named to the NHL All-Rookie Team, becoming only the second Canadiens defenseman ever to receive the honor (after Chris Chelios in 1984–85). The Canadiens, meanwhile, finished second in the Northeast Division with a record of 44–30–8. In the first round of the playoffs, the Canadiens lost to the eventual 2011 Stanley Cup champion Boston Bruins in a hard-fought seven games.

NORRIS TROPHY WINNER

High expectations surrounded Subban and the Canadiens in 2011–12, but the team grossly underperformed. Two months into the season, after leading the team to a subpar 13–12–7 record, Jacques Martin was replaced by interim coach Randy Cunneyworth. The former assistant coach did not fare much better, and the Canadiens finished last in both their division and conference with a 31–35–16 record. Subban again put up impressive numbers, notching seven goals and twenty-nine assists in eighty-one games, but was ultimately disappointed with the team's results. "I learned right away that momentum is not carried season-to-season," he told Fox. "It's built from Game 1 to Game 82—not individually but as a team."

After the 2011–12 season Subban became a restricted free agent. Afterward he and his agent, Don Meehan, engaged in a lengthy contract dispute with the Canadiens that held him out of training camp and the first four games of the 2012–13 season, which was shortened to forty-eight games due to a lockout. Despite being perceived by fans and teammates as greedy and selfish, Subban, who ultimately agreed to a two-year, $5.7 million deal, silenced many of his detractors in his return by establishing himself as arguably the best defenseman in the league. In only forty-two games he led all NHL defensemen in points (thirty-eight) and finished second and third among league blueliners, respectively, in goals (eleven) and assists (twenty-seven). He earned his first selection to an NHL All-Star Team and won that year's James Norris Memorial Trophy, recognizing the league's best defenseman.

Thanks to Subban's stellar play, the Canadiens, under new head coach Michel Therrien, had an impressive bounce-back season, winning the Northeast Division with a 29–14–5 record. Though the Canadiens lost to the seventh-seeded Ottawa Senators, four games to one, in the first round of the playoffs, the season was regarded as a success.

TO SOCHI AND BACK
During the 2013–14 season Subban finished second on the Canadiens and fifth among NHL defensemen with fifty-three points (ten goals and a career-high forty-three assists) in eighty-two games, which tied for the league lead. In February 2014 Subban traveled to Sochi, Russia, to compete in the 2014 Winter Olympics, as a member of Team Canada. Despite not receiving any playing time in the six games Canada played, he won a gold medal after Canada defeated Sweden, 3–0, in the final.

Once NHL play resumed Subban helped lead the Canadiens to a third-place finish in the newly formed Atlantic Division with a record of 46–28–8. In the first two rounds of the playoffs, the Canadiens swept the Tampa Bay Lightning and upset the top-seeded Bruins, respectively, before facing the New York Rangers in the Eastern Conference finals. They lost to the Rangers in six games. Subban led all Canadiens with fourteen points (five goals and nine assists) in seventeen postseason games.

In August 2014 the Canadiens expressed their faith in Subban by signing him to an eight-year contract extension worth $72 million. The deal makes him the highest-paid defenseman in the NHL and the league's third highest–paid player.

A POLARIZING TALENT
Despite being one of the Canadiens' most popular players, Subban is arguably the most polarizing figure in the NHL, so much so that he was named the league's most hated player in an article by *Sports Illustrated* in 2013. Subban has been known to pose as an archer after scoring goals, share triple low-five handshakes with teammates after victories, and refer to himself as the Subbanator, antics that some NHL players, coaches, analysts, and pundits have interpreted as being disrespectful to the game and its traditions. Other hockey observers, however, have embraced Subban as a breath of fresh air in a conservative sport. In an interview with Joe O'Connor for the *National Post* (11 Apr. 2014), Canadian senator and former Canadiens coach Jacques Demers described Subban as "the kind of player you want to pay to see . . . he is good for the game."

Subban's younger brothers, Malcolm and Jordan, have also been drafted into the NHL. Malcolm is a goaltender in the Boston Bruins' system, and Jordan is a defenseman in the Vancouver Canucks' organization. "All three of us playing in the NHL is a product of us working hard," Subban explained to Luke Fox. "It's work ethic."

Subban owns a condominium in downtown Toronto. He spends much of the offseason training and spending time with his family.

SUGGESTED READING
Farber, Michael. "Montreal's Mighty Mouth." *Sports Illustrated*. Time, 20 Dec. 2010. Web. 26 Aug. 2014.
Fox, Luke. "P. K.: 'It was the Most Special Day of My Life.'" *Sportsnet*. Rogers Media, 6 Sept. 2012. Web. 26 Aug. 2014.
Gillis, Charlie. "Who Does P. K. Subban Think He Is?" *Maclean's* 2 June 2014: 40–43. Print.
Hague, Matthew. "Can This Family Produce Three NHL Stars? The Unlikely Rise of Team Subban." *Toronto Life*. Toronto Life, 11 Dec. 2013. Web. 26 Aug. 2014.

—*Chris Cullen*

Kevin Systrom

Born: December 30, 1983
Occupation: Entrepreneur, CEO of Instagram

Kevin Systrom is the cofounder and chief executive of Instagram, an online photo-sharing application. He founded the popular social media app, which allows users to customize and post photos and follow friends, with Mike Krieger in 2010. Facebook acquired Instagram for $1 billion in 2012 with Systrom netting $400 million in the deal. He was only twenty-eight, but he had already cut his teeth at some of the tech industry's biggest companies including Google and Odeo, the precursor to Twitter. While he was a student at Stanford University, he was offered a job at Facebook but turned it down to finish his degree. Systrom's original idea for Instagram—a website called Burbn—boasted several functions, but he ultimately decided, after partnering

Lucas Jackson/Reuters/Landov

with Krieger, to pare down his vision and make an app that simply shared photos. As the two men developed Instagram, they added filters so that users, like real photographers, could manipulate the color or mood of their images.

Systrom is a lifelong photography enthusiast. He told Allie Townsend for *Time* magazine (4 Apr. 2012) that growing up, he would receive a new camera every Christmas. He studied photography abroad in Florence, Italy, during his junior year of college, where his professor took away his prized Nikon, and made him use a plastic Holga instead. It had a "terrible lens," Systrom recalled to Townsend, but "I was blown away by what it could do to photos." With his professional camera, Systrom had been "focused on being meticulous with these really beautiful, complex architectural shots," but with the Holga, he was able to "see the world through a different lens." The experience would later inform Instagram's design as well as its mission. "We wanted to give everyone the same feeling of discovering the world around you through a different lens," he said.

EARLY LIFE AND EDUCATION

Systrom was born on December 30, 1983, in the upper middle class Boston suburb of Holliston, Massachusetts. His father, Douglas Systrom, is a vice president in human resources at TJX Companies Inc., a department store chain. His mother, Diane, is a marketing executive at Zipcar,

though she worked for Monster.com during the early Internet boom years. Systrom attended Holliston High School where he ran cross-country, but transferred to Middlesex School, a private academy in Concord, Massachusetts, when he was in tenth grade. He graduated in 2002 and enrolled at Stanford University in California.

At Stanford, Systrom studied management science and engineering, though he remained an avid photographer. In 2005 he did an internship for a company called Odeo. It was arranged through the Mayfield Fellowship Program, a Stanford-run entrepreneurial leadership program that pairs students with mentor companies. Odeo was a podcast directory and the original home of Twitter, which launched in 2006 and was a novel text-messaging application and only one component of the larger Odeo. At Odeo, Systrom met Jack Dorsey, one of Twitter's founders who would later play an important role in the early development of Instagram.

Systrom graduated from Stanford in 2006. He had already turned down a job offer from Facebook while still at Stanford, and after graduation he moved to Mountain View, California, to work for Google. For almost three years he worked in product and corporate development on such products as Gmail and Google Reader. He then worked for Nextstop, a travel-tip site run by a handful of former Google employees, where he stayed for over a year; the site was purchased by Facebook in 2010 for $2.5 million.

BURBN

In early 2010, Systrom came up with an idea for a website called Burbn, which allowed users to share their location with friends and post accompanying pictures of what they were doing. Systrom was excited about the idea, but he was having trouble getting it off the ground despite having a prototype and at least one interested investor: Steve Anderson, the founder of Baseline Ventures. Anderson advised Systrom to find a business partner, so Systrom approached Brazilian born Mike Krieger, a talented programmer who blended coding with psychology. Soon after Krieger came on board, Anderson invested $250,000 in Burbn, and another venture capitalist firm, Andreessen Horowitz, also invested $250,000.

It wasn't long before Systrom and Krieger began to feel that the vision for Burbn was a bit muddy and without clear focus. It had too many functions, and it was a little too close in intent to the already established and popular location-based application Foursquare. Systrom and Krieger decided to scratch Burbn and salvage the most popular aspect of the site: the photos. Systrom recalled to Kara Swisher for *Vanity Fair* (June 2013), "Instead of doing a check-in that had an optional photo, we thought, 'Why don't we do a photo that has an optional check-in?'" In

Silicon Valley jargon, Systrom and Krieger "pivoted" the aim of their business.

THE ORIGINS OF INSTAGRAM

In June 2010, Apple released the iPhone 4 with a high-performing camera and able to display higher resolution images—the perfect complement to a mobile photo-sharing app. Systrom told Dan Schawbel for *Forbes* magazine (27 June 2012) that he and Krieger wanted an app that would allow users to communicate visually as if they were sending an instantly visual telegram. "We realized that we'd be taking all these photos with our iPhones that would sit on our camera roll, and it felt like they should be seen—not necessarily because they were good photos, but because a photo that no one sees isn't really that interesting," he explained to Schawbel. "Every photo you take communicates something about a moment in time . . . where you were, who you were with, and what you were doing."

Systrom and Krieger put in thousands of hours throughout 2010 developing Instagram and working out of Dogpatch Labs, which was located inside an old pier in San Francisco. Systrom recalled to Swisher that during the summer of 2010, he and girlfriend Nicole took a short vacation to Todos Santos, a small artists' village in Baja California Sur, Mexico. Walking on the beach one day, Nicole said she didn't think her future Instagram photos would look as good as the photos of a mutual friend who was a photographer. Systrom explained that the friend used filtering applications on his photos to make them look the way they did, and that Nicole then replied, "Well, you guys should probably have filters too, right, then?"

When they got back to the hotel, Systrom began work on Instagram's first filter, X-Pro II. He used it to take the first Instagram: a picture of a dog lying next to Nicole's foot.

INSTAGRAM IS LAUNCHED

After Systrom and Krieger decided they would create optional filters for the app, they set a launch date for the fall. They prepared a beta version of Instagram to show Silicon Valley bigwigs. Jack Dorsey, an early fan, told Swisher, "From the start, Instagram was a simple application and a joy to use." Crucially, Dorsey posted his early Instagram photos to his Twitter feed, stirring up demand for the app before its release. Instagram officially launched on October 6, 2010. Thousands of people—25,000 before the day was over—were downloading the free app, and the server kept crashing. Unsure how to handle the traffic, Systrom made an emergency late night phone call to Adam D'Angelo, former chief technology officer at Facebook. D'Angelo, who was also a Stanford grad and like Systrom a member of the Sigma Nu fraternity, talked Systrom and Krieger through the problem.

Within the first week, over 100,000 people had downloaded Instagram. Systrom and Krieger began taking their laptops with them everywhere so that they could troubleshoot problems. The user base continued to grow, and Systrom and Krieger garnered larger investments, including sizeable ones from Dorsey and D'Angelo. Systrom recalled another early milestone in Instagram's history: The company's staff—which numbered only thirteen including Systrom and Krieger—was listening to the roar of the crowd at the San Francisco Giants baseball game from the nearby AT&T Park. They wondered if anyone was using Instagram at the game and a quick search revealed that nearly 140 photos had been taken there in two hours. "That was the moment we realized Instagram could be far more than photo sharing," Systrom told Swisher. He and his staff were able to be a part of an experience without directly participating in it.

CORPORATIONS COURT INSTAGRAM

Keeping up with Instagram's rapid growth was a Herculean task for its small staff. Though Systrom had previously denied interest in selling the company, he began to gauge the interest of larger tech companies. Mark Zuckerberg of Facebook and Dorsey were Instagram's most ardent suitors, followed by a young venture capitalist named Roelof Botha at Sequoia Capital, who committed $50 million in new funding for Instagram in early 2012. Shortly after Botha made his offer, Twitter's then chief financial officer, Ali Rowghani, made Systrom an offer to buy Instagram for about $500 million in restricted and common stock.

Systrom claims that Twitter never formalized the offer, and in early April, he called Twitter's CEO, Dick Costolo, to tell him that he had decided to take Botha's investment and keep Instagram independent. Systrom also called Zuckerberg to share the news, but Zuckerberg was determined and two days later invited Systrom to his house in Palo Alto and offered him a staggering $1 billion for the company, which included over $300 million in cash. (After a drop in Facebook's stock, the final value of the offer was $736.5 million.) The offer was more than double Twitter's offer and larger than anything Facebook had previously paid to acquire a company.

The offer was also appealing to Systrom because it would allow Instagram to operate independently within Facebook with few changes in appearance or functionality. "Most of the other things we bought [prior to acquiring Instagram] were talent acquisitions," Zuckerberg told Swisher, "but in this case we wanted to keep what it was and build that out."

After leaving Zuckerberg's house, Systrom called Krieger to discuss the offer and the two men made the decision to sell. Systrom reasoned that he liked Zuckerberg and he liked Facebook, but on a deeper level, Facebook was a Silicon Valley mainstay. The company had achieved so much where so many others had failed; Instagram was still so new, and it was entirely possible, both founders realized, that it could be another casualty.

FACEBOOK ACQUIRES INSTAGRAM

The landmark deal was carried out over Easter weekend in 2012. Systrom and Krieger returned to Zuckerberg's house on Saturday to sign the agreement. Although, according to Swisher, negotiations paused for a *Game of Thrones* viewing party, Systrom spent a great deal of time on the phone with lawyers and investors. Steve Anderson, Instagram's earliest investor, recalled his shock at the call he received. "I sat back and thought, 'What just happened?'" he told Swisher. "Holy sh——, *what just happened?*" His reaction echoed what many in Silicon Valley were thinking (and some continue to think) about the sale of the young company: Did they sell too soon?

The deal was officially announced on Monday, April 9, the same day it was announced to Instagram's tiny staff. Dorsey heard about it from an employee, and Dorsey and Systrom's personal relationship reportedly soured over the snub. Later, a regulatory hearing would take place over the validity of Twitter's original offer. As for Botha, Systrom had already made the investment deal, therefore earning Sequoia, as Swisher put it, an "instant windfall."

Instagram employees work out of Facebook's headquarters in Menlo Park, California, a stone's throw from Zuckerberg's office. Its user base continues to grow: in just over three years after it first launched in 2010, Instagram reported over 150 million registered users. Instagram became available to Android users about a week before the Facebook deal, and over one million people downloaded the app in the first twelve hours. In December 2012, Instagram users revolted over a new terms of agreement that would allow Instagram to use any photo posted on the site for advertising purposes without permission or credit. Systrom quickly removed the clause and later called the controversy a learning experience. In June 2013, Instagram introduced video capabilities on the heels of the more popular six-second video app Vine Videos. Instagram videos can be up to fifteen seconds.

PERSONAL LIFE

While at Stanford, Systrom met his longtime girlfriend and fellow undergraduate, Nicole Schuetz, who has since returned to Stanford to complete an MBA. Outside of his work, Systrom collects rare liquors and champagne and occasionally cooks with professional chef Jamie Oliver. His Instagram handle is @kevin.

SUGGESTED READING

Kiss, Jemima. "Kevin Systrom, Instagram's Man of Vision, Now Eyes Up World Domination." *Guardian.* Guardian News and Media, 11 Oct. 2013. Web. 3 Mar. 2014.

Schawbel, Dan. "What Gen-Y Entrepreneurs Can Learn from Kevin Systrom [Interview]." *Forbes.* Forbes, 27 June 2012. Web. 15 Feb. 2014.

Swisher, Kara. "The Money Shot." *Vanity Fair.* Condé Nast, June 2013. Web. 15 Feb. 2014.

Townsend, Allie. "Kevin Systrom Says Comparing Instagram to Photography Is Like 'Comparing Twitter to Microsoft Word.'" *Time.* Time, 4 Apr. 2012. Web. 15 Feb. 2014.

—*Molly Hagan*

Chris Thile

Born: February 20, 1981
Occupation: Bluegrass musician

"Google the word 'mandolinist' and take a look at the suggestions that drop down in the search bar," David Weininger wrote for the *Boston Globe* (19 Oct. 2013). "The name 'Chris Thile' is sure to be at, or near, the top." He explained, "It's a convenient shorthand for the fact that Thile has revolutionized his instrument—not only by furthering the evolution of bluegrass but by bringing the mandolin out of its niche and making it a viable contributor to a variety of styles."

Yet some musical purists do not believe that the mandolin needed to be brought out of its niche. As a result, Thile—who was named a national mandolin champion at age twelve, earned the title of Mandolin Player of the Year from the International Bluegrass Music Association at age twenty, and won a 2012 MacArthur Foundation "genius grant" at age thirty-one—has not been fully embraced by certain segments of the music community. His detractors assert that he has veered too far away from the traditional bluegrass music that was pioneered by the legendary Bill Monroe in the late 1940s, with which the mandolin is most often associated. In response, Thile told Cameron Matthews for the country-music website *The Boot* (17 Feb. 2012), "We [the Punch Brothers] have a tremendous amount of respect for our predecessors on this group of instruments, which is commonly associated with bluegrass, but we're not interested in being museum curators of their work. Rather, we want them to influence our work." Addressing the same issue, he later told Cormac Larkin for the *Irish Times* (13 July 2012), "To me, it's always made sense to look forward when it comes to making music of any kind. . . . Bill Monroe and those guys weren't trying to sound like anyone.

Courtesy of the John D. & Catherine T. MacArthur Foundation

They were trying to create something new, and that's why their music is so important to so many people. I just think it's so funny when people decide that what we do isn't good because it doesn't sound like Bill Monroe. It's like saying that a zebra isn't a very good rhinoceros."

Thile has even recorded an album of Bach sonatas, written his own ambitious forty-minute, four-movement suite, and collaborated with celebrated cellist Yo-Yo Ma. Explaining why he feels comfortable transcending musical boundaries, he told Geoffrey Himes for the folk-music magazine *Sing Out!* (2008), "Genre distinctions are only good for record stores. It's all the same notes. In Western music there are twelve notes to choose from; [classical composer Gustav] Mahler used the same twelve as [bluegrass musician] Jimmy Martin."

EARLY YEARS
Chris Thile was born on February 20, 1981, in Oceanside, California. He has an older brother, John, and a younger brother, Daniel. Commenting on the unlikelihood of a West Coast native taking an interest in bluegrass music and the mandolin, which are typically associated with Kentucky, Thile told Ralph Berrier Jr. for the *Roanoke Times* (20 Oct. 2006), "I'm from Southern California. My 'roots' are more likely the Beach Boys. I've always been a bluegrass outsider. I don't identify with moonshining or coal mining."

Thile's father, Scott, was a professional piano tuner, and Thile remembers being surrounded

by music from the time he was in diapers. When he was still a toddler, his parents regularly took him to That Pizza Place, a Carlsbad-area restaurant that hosted evenings of live bluegrass music. There he became fascinated by the sound of the mandolin, a stringed instrument belonging to the lute family. After his parents found a cassette tape of the Foggy Mountain Boys' *Flatt & Scruggs' Greatest Hits* in a drugstore bargain bin, he listened to it incessantly.

Almost immediately after being introduced to the instrument, Thile began pestering his parents for a mandolin of his own. Finally, when he was five years old, they agreed, allowing him to have a relatively inexpensive model handed down by a family friend. (One of the instruments he now plays, by contrast, is said to be worth $200,000.) They hired John Moore, a highly respected mandolin player who often performed at That Pizza Place, to teach him. "When he was a little kid, just learning, we'd sit down and I'd gauge how he was feeling," Thile's mother, Kathy, told Caroline Wright for *Bluegrass Now* magazine (Aug. 2002). "Some days he'd have more ability to stick to something than on other days. At only five, they're different from day to day! . . . We'd go for however long he could do it." She continued, "When he was a little older, he set himself up with a little star chart with his songs on it, and he'd do the song, then grade himself. I still have one where he wrote, '*Pritty Good!*'"

NICKEL CREEK
In 1989, when Thile was eight years old, he and two other youngsters—fiddler Sara Watkins, who was also eight, and her older brother, Sean, a twelve-year-old mandolinist and guitarist—formed the band Nickel Creek. The two families had met while attending shows at the pizza parlor, and the trio began playing their own gigs there, with Scott Thile on bass. Throughout the 1990s the band proved a popular feature at bluegrass festivals all over the country, and their busy touring schedule required the young members to be homeschooled.

Early on, Thile, who moved with his family to Kentucky in 1995 so his father could work as a musical instrument technician at Murray State University, recorded both with Nickel Creek and as a solo artist. Of his first solo effort, *Leading Off . . .* (1994), Stanton Swihart wrote for the AllMusic website, "According to the liner notes, in most ways Chris Thile was a typical thirteen-year-old when he put out this debut album. . . . From the musical evidence, though, he was a typical teenager in the way that, say, Mozart was probably a typical teenager. The level of playing and compositional skill, not to mention the imagination, displayed on *Leading Off . . .* is no less than virtuosic."

Although Nickel Creek released *Little Cowpoke* in 1993 on the tiny label Choo Choo

Records and followed it in 1997 with the self-released *Here to There*, most sources refer to their eponymous 2000 album as their debut. It was, more accurately, their major-label debut. Produced by the popular bluegrass and folk artist Alison Krauss, who had met the young musicians at a festival, and released by Sugar Hill Records, known for its seminal catalog of roots music, the album quickly went platinum. The recording also earned the group two Grammy Award nominations, in the categories of best bluegrass album and best country instrumental (for the song "Ode to a Butterfly"). Nickel Creek was nominated for a Country Music Association (CMA) Award for best vocal group and named one of the "Five Music Innovators of the Millennium" by the editors of *Time* magazine.

Despite the accolades, Thile, who at age twelve had become the youngest winner in the history of the National Mandolin Championships, is not especially proud of his earliest recordings. "Having come of age on record, it comes down to that classic cliché: the more you know, the more you don't know," he admitted to Matthews. "And I definitely thought I knew everything when Nickel Creek's first record came out. I was seventeen when we recorded it and eighteen when it was released. That music . . . just sounds unbearably smug to me. The know-it-all kid in class . . . it's hard for me to listen to it."

Nickel Creek released other well-regarded albums, including *This Side* (2002) and *Why Should the Fire Die?* (2005), before disbanding in 2006 to pursue other projects. Their farewell tour extended into 2007.

THE EVOLUTION OF THE PUNCH BROTHERS
After leaving Nickel Creek, Thile, who had studied music at Murray State University for a few semesters before dropping out to focus on his professional career, joined fiddler and longtime friend Gabe Witcher, banjo player Noam Pikelny, guitarist Chris "Critter" Eldridge, and bassist Greg Garrison to form a new group, initially called Chris Thile and the How to Grow a Band. "The acoustic-music scene we all come from is really small," Eldridge told Dan Bolles for the Vermont alternative weekly newspaper *Seven Days* (5 Feb. 2008). "After a while you kind of get to know everyone else. It's a small community. So the band sort of formed through these mutual relationships. We're all guys around the same age who are on the same wavelength musically and as far as what our aspirations were." The group released their first album together, *How to Grow a Woman from the Ground*, in 2006 to positive reviews. In a review for *Sing Out!* (2007), Stephanie P. Ledgin called it "a colorful panorama of [Thile's] expansive creativity" and said of the band, "Each player is a perfectly matched complement to the others."

For a time, the group changed its name to the Tensions Mountain Boys (the pun becomes apparent when the name is said quickly). They ultimately settled on the Punch Brothers, a reference to a Mark Twain story, under which name they recorded such albums as *Punch* (2008), *Antifogmatic* (2010), *Who's Feeling Young Now?* (2012), and *Ahoy!* (2012). Signaling Thile's determination to push musical boundaries, *Punch* includes a genre-bending four-movement composition called "The Blind Leaving the Blind." "It's part modern chamber music and part song cycle—an impressionistic picture of a young marriage gone sour," Craig Havighurst wrote for National Public Radio (29 Feb. 2008). "It owes a debt to Bach, Bob Dylan, even the Beach Boys. And, of course, bluegrass."

Actor and comedian Ed Helms summed up the Punch Brothers' appeal in an article for *Paste* magazine (10 Aug. 2010), writing, "Their music is an impossibly perfect mixture of down-home charm and staggering sophistication"—a sentiment almost universally echoed by other music journalists. (Helms also concluded that the band members must be aliens, observing, "Frontman Chris Thile's mandolin playing defies the laws of physics. It is my belief that he has an additional six fingers on his left hand which are invisible.") In an interview with Hal Bienstock for *American Songwriter* (9 Jan. 2012), record producer T Bone Burnett called the Punch Brothers "one of the most incredible bands this country has ever produced" and described Thile as "probably a once-in-a-century musician, like Louis Armstrong was a once-in-a-century musician."

OTHER COLLABORATIONS AND PROJECTS
Thile has performed as a backup musician with a wide variety of other artists, including country-music stars Dolly Parton and Dierks Bentley. He teamed up with fellow mandolinist Mike Marshall for *Into the Cauldron* (2003) and *Live: Duets* (2006) and paired with bassist Edgar Meyer for a category-defying album titled simply *Edgar Meyer & Chris Thile* (2008). Additionally, he was joined by guitarist Michael Daves on *Sleep with One Eye Open* (2011), a collection of traditional tunes from such bluegrass legends as Jimmy Martin and the Foggy Mountain Boys.

One of the most unusual collaborations Thile has ever undertaken came in 2011, when he, Meyer, fiddler Stuart Duncan, and acclaimed cellist Yo-Yo Ma recorded *The Goat Rodeo Sessions*. (In colloquial terms, a "goat rodeo" is a chaotic event that defies efforts to impose order on it—a reference to the seeming impossibility of four such disparate artists reaching any musical consensus.) "It's more of a little Frankenstein music monster. . . . I think what you have is a broad range on the spectrum of formal to informal music making," Thile told Gary Graff for *Billboard* (27 Oct. 2011). "Everyone complements each other nicely. I think it's the kind of thing that maybe classical music listeners will think is bluegrass and bluegrass listeners will think it's classical. Hopefully it lands in the nebulous zone where it can't really be named." The quartet was featured on several late-night talk shows and also performed live in concert. In 2013 the recording earned Grammy Awards for best folk album and best engineered nonclassical album.

Thile reunited with Sara and Sean Watkins in 2014 to record a new Nickel Creek album, *A Dotted Line* (2014), and to tour in celebration of the group's twenty-fifth anniversary. "Now we can look back and have a good laugh at ourselves—like looking at your baby pictures," Thile told Jim Farber for the *New York Daily News* (25 Apr. 2014).

PERSONAL LIFE
Thile married fashion designer Jesse Meighan in 2003. The marriage was brief, ending in divorce the following year. Thile has said that his pain over the breakup was his inspiration for composing "The Blind Leaving the Blind." In December 2013 Thile married Claire Coffee, an actor best known for playing villain Adalind Schade on the hit television series *Grimm* (2011–). The wedding took place on a picturesque farm resort in the Great Smoky Mountains of Tennessee.

Thile lives in the New York borough of Manhattan. In 2012 he won a John D. and Catherine T. MacArthur Foundation Fellowship, commonly called the "genius grant," for "his adventurous, multifaceted artistry as both a composer and performer" and for "creating a distinctly American canon for the mandolin and a new musical aesthetic for performers and audiences alike."

SUGGESTED READING
Farber, Jim. "Nickel Creek, One of the Youngest Bands to Ever Celebrate a 25th Anniversary, Returns with Album and Tour." *New York Daily News*. NYDailyNews.com, 25 Apr. 2014. Web. 1 July 2014.

Graff, Gary. "Yo-Yo Ma Trades Bach for Bluegrass in *Goat Rodeo Sessions*." *Billboard*. Billboard, 27 Oct. 2011. Web. 1 July 2014.

Helms, Ed. "The Slobbering Rave: Beware the Punch Brothers." *Paste*. Paste Media, 10 Aug. 2010. Web. 1 July 2014.

Himes, Geoffrey. "Punch Brothers: A Little of Everything Makes a Lot." *Sing Out!* Autumn 2008: 34–39. Print.

Thile, Chris. "Chris Thile, Youngest MacArthur Genius of 2012, on His 'Dauntingly Lofty' New Status." Interview by Mallika Rao. *Huffington Post*. TheHuffingtonPost.com, 4 Oct. 2012. Web. 1 July 2014.

Thile, Chris. "Punch Brothers' Chris Thile Embraces 'Relative Incompetence.'" Interview by

Cameron Matthews. *The Boot*. Townsquare Media, 17 Feb. 2012. Web. 1 July 2014.

Weininger, David. "Not Enough Music in the Day for Mandolinist Chris Thile." *Boston Globe*. Boston Globe, 19 Oct. 2013. Web. 1 July 2014.

SELECTED WORKS
Leading Off . . . , 1994; *Nickel Creek* (with Nickel Creek), 2000; *Into the Cauldron* (with Mike Marshall), 2003; *Why Should the Fire Die?* (with Nickel Creek), 2005; *How to Grow a Woman from the Ground*, 2006; *Edgar Meyer & Chris Thile* (with Edgar Meyer), 2008; *Antifogmatic* (with the Punch Brothers), 2010; *Sleep with One Eye Open* (with Michael Daves), 2011; *The Goat Rodeo Sessions* (with Stuart Duncan, Yo-Yo Ma, and Edgar Meyer), 2011; *A Dotted Line* (with Nickel Creek), 2014

—*Mari Rich*

Riccardo Tisci
Born: 1974
Occupation: Fashion designer

Riccardo Tisci, the creative director of the high-fashion company Givenchy, creates designs that are often characterized as Gothic or excessively dark, but he eschews those descriptions. "My way of showing [my collections] is very melancholic," he explained to Cathy Horyn for the *New York Times* (28 Feb. 2007). "People call me a Gothic designer—I don't think I am. I love romanticism and sensuality. . . . I'm also a person who is very emotional. I like black, I like white. I never like what's in the middle. And the runway is where I try to transmit this."

Then a relatively unknown designer, Tisci seemed an unlikely choice to most industry insiders when he was appointed to his post in 2005. The iconic company, founded by Hubert de Givenchy in 1952, had long been known for its elegant, feminine designs and was closely associated with its most well-known couture client, the actress Audrey Hepburn, who wore Givenchy's little black dresses and chic gowns in *Sabrina* (1954), *Funny Face* (1957), and—perhaps most famously—*Breakfast at Tiffany's* (1961), among other classic films. Tisci was chosen in part because he promised to invigorate the then-struggling fashion house. "He was the only [candidate] who didn't make a single reference to Audrey Hepburn," company president Marco Gobbetti recalled to a reporter for Agence France-Presse (10 July 2005).

Despite a less-than-enthusiastic welcome from the fashion media—one headline read

Wirelmage

"Riccardo *Who*-sci?"—Tisci has since found many fans and has been praised for breathing new life into the venerable brand. "Sometimes you need to see a movie three times before you understand it," he told J.J. Martin for *Harper's Bazaar* (1 Oct. 2008) as more favorable reviews of his collections began to appear. "I think [my clothing is] the exact same style it always was, but now everyone is used to it."

EARLY LIFE

Riccardo Tisci was born in 1974 in Taranto, an atmospheric coastal city in southern Italy that dates back to 706 BCE, when it was established as a Greek colony. Despite the beauty and rich history of his surroundings, Tisci's youth was far from charmed. His father, a greengrocer, died when Tisci was four years old, leaving his widowed mother, Elmerinda, to raise him and his eight older sisters. His octet of female siblings had a deep influence on him, as he often explains to journalists. "I grew up amongst these women: they are my greatest inspiration and my biggest fans," he told Andrew O'Hagan for the *New York Times* fashion supplement *T* (12 Apr. 2013). He recalled to Diane Solway for *W* magazine (Sept. 2010), "I would sit on the little bidet watching them put on makeup and dress up for the club, and I was so attracted by the metamorphosis they were making."

The family lived in Cermenate, in the province of Como, and Tisci was often keenly aware that they had far fewer financial resources than others in their town. As a preteen he began working with his uncle, a plasterer, to earn money to help support his mother and sisters. Intensely shy as a teen, he routinely secluded himself in

his room, where he listened to music by Iron Maiden, the Cure, and Alice Cooper, among other artists, and made collages with images he had cut from magazines.

During one phase, Tisci echoed the style of his favorite musicians, sporting long black hair, purposely ripped jeans, and ghostly pale makeup and causing consternation among his conservative neighbors when he ventured out. Elmerinda steadfastly defended him whenever anyone made comments. (She continues to be a source of great support, regularly attending his shows and excitedly wearing the Givenchy gifts he gives her for each birthday.) Of his love for the punk ethos, he told O'Hagan, "Punk is an attitude—it is being free, it is being honest. When I was young, I felt punk was like me dreaming. I was attracted to all these sounds and to the look of these people. I felt that I had something to say that people didn't understand. Emotions come from reality, not fakeness."

EDUCATION IN FASHION

In 1990 Tisci won an internship at Faro, a textile company based in Como, and the following year he earned a diploma from an art institute in Cantù, Italy. Having dreamed for years of living in Paris, New York, or London, Tisci chose to move to England after his graduation. There he worked as a retail clerk, and after seeing an advertisement for the London College of Fashion while on the train, he enrolled in a few basic courses. Recognizing his talent, his professors encouraged him to apply to the prestigious Central Saint Martins (CSM), a constituent college of London's University of the Arts. He was admitted, and although money was constantly in short supply, he was able to attend thanks to a state-sponsored scholarship.

The invitation to Tisci's graduation show in 1999 featured the up-and-coming Italian model Mariacarla Boscono, who became a good friend as well as a muse. The pair was soon something of a fixture in London's bustling nightclub scene, and Tisci particularly delighted in spotting high-profile figures such as the singer Boy George and the supermodel Naomi Campbell in the same clubs the struggling young fashionistas frequented. He often styled outfits for Boscono to wear while club-hopping; one particularly eye-catching ensemble consisted of a fur skirt (made from fur he had found in a secondhand store) and a fishnet top adorned with tulle and fragments of military hardware.

A FLEDGLING CAREER

After graduating from CSM, Tisci returned to Italy. He settled in Milan and began working for designer Stefano Guerriero, who had begun his career in fashion as a model before deciding to create a ready-to-wear clothing line. (In the fashion world, *ready-to-wear* refers to clothing that is purchased off the rack and not custom fitted for individual clients; *haute couture*, in contrast, refers to very exclusive, custom-fitted, high-end garments.)

Concurrently, Tisci began receiving orders for his own designs from the trendy London boutique Kokon To Zai, whose creative director, Marjan Pejoski, had been a fellow CSM student. Having no start-up capital with which to hire employees or rent a workspace, he called upon his mother and sisters for help. In the evenings, the entire family would gather to watch television and sew. Kokon To Zai provided Tisci with much-needed exposure; among the first customers to purchase a Tisci design at the boutique was the singer Björk, who is known for her quirky personal style, and other fashion-forward figures soon followed her lead.

By 2002, Tisci had become a womens wear designer for the large company Puma, which is known for its sportswear, and shortly thereafter he was named creative director of the Marchese Coccapani label. In early 2004 Tisci signed on to work at Ruffo, a company specializing in leather clothing. Charged with overseeing the cutting-edge Ruffo Research line, he was dismayed when the line was discontinued just months after his hiring.

FIRST PROFESSIONAL SHOW

Next, at the suggestion of a designer friend who maintained an embroidery workshop there, Tisci traveled to India, where he rededicated himself to his own line. By then Boscono, whose modeling career had taken off, had made several contacts in the fashion world, and she helped organize Tisci's first professional showing, convincing her model friends to participate for free and inviting several influential fashion editors to attend. While preparing for the show Tisci used Lea T., a friend from Brazil, as a fit model—an individual who serves, in effect, as a living mannequin, allowing a designer to check the appearance of a garment-in-progress on a live human being. This collaboration marked the beginning of a long and productive working relationship; in addition to becoming Tisci's muse, Lea T. would go on to become one of the world's first high-profile transgender models and serve as the face of Givenchy.

Tisci mounted the show in an abandoned Milan warehouse, decorating the space with hundreds of candles and cars he had found in a demolition yard. Rather than sending the models down a runway, he instead posed them in a series of tableaux vivants. It was a startlingly original choice, and many of the editors assembled found the tactic pretentious or ineffective. "They didn't get it," he recalled to Martin. "You know, at the beginning there was just a lot of misunderstanding with the outside world. [The presentations were] the opposite of pretentious! I was

showing respect for women. I didn't want to see them walking around like robots."

GIVENCHY

Soon after his first show, rumors that Tisci would be tapped to become creative head of Givenchy began to circulate. The label's founder, Hubert de Givenchy, had retired to his estate in the French countryside in 1995, and a series of designers, including Alexander McQueen, John Galliano, and Julien Macdonald, had stepped into the post—none for very long.

The rumors, spread in large part by the influential publication *Women's Wear Daily*, proved to be correct. Marco Gobbetti, Givenchy's president, offered the nearly unknown designer the coveted job after slipping unannounced into his second show, held in an incense-filled factory decorated with a massive wooden cross and featuring models garbed in flowing black dresses and beaded coats.

Thinking that he would not be a good fit for the storied couture house, Tisci almost turned down the offer. "I wasn't interested," he recalled to Ella Alexander for *Vogue* (21 Mar. 2011). "I was going to say no. But the week before, my mother called me and said to me, 'I am going to tell you something I haven't even told your sisters: I think I am going to sell our house because your sisters are struggling, they're having children, they need the money. I will go to a retirement home.' When I heard that it was like a knife in my heart. . . . And then I went to Paris, and they showed me a contract with all these zeros on it, and it was like help from God. I thought 'If I sign this, my mother will never have to worry again.' So I signed it."

FACING THE CRITICS

Tisci was correct in his prediction that he would not immediately fit in at Givenchy; even being addressed as *monsieur* by his overly formal staff made him uncomfortable. Worse, his earliest shows were not considered rousing successes by most observers. "Tisci's debut collection for Givenchy . . . was no triumph," Suzy Menkes wrote for the *New York Times* (6 Oct. 2005). Still, the influential fashion critic saw reason for anticipation. "The designer had the delicacy and the humility to look to the soul of the brand, and he came up with fine elements on which to build for the future," she wrote, praising Tisci's white blouses, which she deemed "beautifully done with fine details."

The following year, Menkes again found reasons for complaint, opining for the *New York Times* (31 May 2006) that Tisci "surely must have been dragooned into mounting a fast-paced hard-edged show that looked like Hubert (as in Givenchy) had collided with Helmut (as in Lang)." She continues, "Exactly what he was drawing from the Givenchy archives to project into the present and the future did not come through." In an otherwise favorable review for the *New York Times* (8 Dec. 2008), Menkes characterizes a shirt imprinted with an image of the Virgin Mary as "more bling than beatific." (Tisci, raised a Roman Catholic, often draws on religious imagery for his designs.) Of receiving such negative or mixed reviews, Tisci told Martin, "I've been through so much [stuff] in my life, you think I go home and cry for a review? No way. I don't cry for fashion."

Despite early reservations, critics eventually began warming to the designer. Martin, an unabashed fan of Tisci, notes in his 2008 article that public favor was turning the designer's way, asserting, "Times have certainly changed at Givenchy, where, against stacked odds, Italian designer Riccardo Tisci has pulled off the feat of resuscitating a barely breathing fifty-six-year-old brand, leaving it not just in a stable postoperative state but vigorously kicking."

RUMORS ABOUT DIOR

By 2011, Tisci, who had also been given responsibility for Givenchy's menswear line, was garnering nearly rhapsodic reviews on a regular basis. Even the hard-to-please Menkes wrote in a *New York Times* review headlined "Pure Is Beautiful" (5 July 2011), "His collection is the link to those few, rare customers who are searching for the exceptional." Others were equally impressed; a *Women's Wear Daily* (5 July 2011) reviewer called the collection "both provocative and elegiac," and *Vogue* (5 July 2011) characterized it as "contained but sublime." *Interview* magazine (2011) went so far as to call Tisci's 2011 presentation "one of the best things to happen to haute couture in a long time."

That year rumors circulated that Tisci was in talks with rival fashion house Dior to replace ousted creative director John Galliano, who had been fired after making anti-Semitic comments on multiple occasions. While Tisci had been considered a less-than-stellar choice to take over a major fashion house in 2005, his star had risen so much that many outlets were reporting the move to Dior as a foregone conclusion. However, while Tisci professed to feel sorry for Galliano, whose actions were being attributed to alcohol and drug addiction, he stressed that he was happy at Givenchy and intended to stay. He had learned, as he told Mark Holgate for *Vogue* (Jan. 2010), that he had much in common with Hubert de Givenchy: "[We] actually share many of the same codes: He was all about severity, aristocracy, irony, and couture craftsmanship, too."

HIGH-PROFILE CLIENTS AND PROJECTS

Tisci has a large circle of celebrity fans. Among them are Queen Rania of Jordan; Rihanna, who wore a dramatic Tisci-designed black silk cape with an embroidered collar while on tour;

Madonna, whom he dressed for her 2012 Super Bowl halftime performance; and Kim Kardashian, who donned a Tisci-designed flowered gown with attached gloves for the Metropolitan Museum of Art Costume Institute's 2013 benefit. Tisci cochaired the punk-themed benefit and dressed several other guests in addition to Kardashian, including Madonna, who caused a stir by arriving in a tartan jacket with spikes, ripped fishnet stockings, and no pants.

In addition to clothing, Tisci designed the covers for rappers Kanye West and Jay-Z's collaborative 2010 single "H.A.M." as well as their album *Watch the Throne*, released in 2011. The album's cover features geometrical prints, animal motifs, and religious iconography—all imagery that Tisci often incorporates into his couture clothing.

PERSONAL LIFE

Tisci considers West and Kardashian, who became engaged in October 2013, close personal friends, and when he was photographed holding the pair's child, the image quickly went viral. Others in his inner circle include the artist Marina Abramović, fashion editor Carine Roitfeld, singer Courtney Love, and stylist Marcelo Burlon, who has Tisci's initials tattooed on his elbows. Tisci was named designer of the year in 2012 by the editors of *GQ* and was also the recipient of the 2013 Council of Fashion Designers of America (CFDA) International Award.

Although Tisci's designs have rekindled Givenchy's popularity among celebrities, the designer is also proud to have democratized the company to an extent. "I make sure that in every collection there is stuff for kids with less money. They might have to save up but it is reachable," he told O'Hagan. "My sisters still work in factories, and why shouldn't normal people have the chance to dream, to wear the Givenchy label? I want my sister, my nephew, my niece to be able to go to a Givenchy store and buy something, not just a princess, you know?"

SUGGESTED READING

Holgate, Mark. "Already Famous." *Vogue*. Condé Nast, Jan. 2010. Web. 4 Dec. 2013.

Martin, J.J. "What's Hot Now." *Harper's Bazaar*. Hearst Digital Media, 1 Oct. 2008. Web. 4 Dec. 2013.

O'Hagan, Andrew. "Man of the Moment." *T*. New York Times, 12 Apr. 2013. Web. 4 Dec. 2013.

Solway, Diane. "Riccardo Tisci: Tisci's Tribe." *W*. Condé Nast, Sept. 2010. Web. 4 Dec. 2013.

Tisci, Riccardo. "The Q & A: Riccardo Tisci." Interview by Cathy Horyn. *New York Times*. New York Times, 28 Feb. 2007. Web. 4 Dec. 2013.

—Mari Rich

Christina Tobin

Born: 1981
Occupation: Political activist

The founder and president of the Free & Equal Elections Foundation, Christina Tobin focuses on energizing young voters and pushing back against the entrenched two-party US political system. She also ran as a Libertarian candidate for secretary of state for California in 2010, but garnered only 2.3 percent of the vote, finishing fourth in a field of five candidates. Additionally, she served as the campaign manager for New York Democratic congressional candidate Dan O'Connor and has verified ballot petitions for a number of third-party candidates. She is an executive of Taxpayers United of America, a nonprofit organization started by her father. Tobin was a board member of Californians for Electoral Reform and the founder of StopTopTwo.org, which targeted the setup of primary election ballots in which only the top two vote getters are featured on the final ballot for elective office. Her political career has been focused on helping third-party candidates and citizens outside the political mainstream be heard and supported. As she told Carl Gibson for Occupy.com (11 Sept. 2013), "I want a new generation of young leaders to get inspired to take their government back, starting at the local level."

Courtesy of Free & Equal Network and RT America

EARLY LIFE AND EDUCATION

Born in Texas, and raised in Texas and Illinois, Tobin grew up in a political family. She attended Fenwick High School in Oak Park, Illinois, and in 2004, she graduated from St. Mary's University of Minnesota, where she played on the women's varsity tennis team. Her father, James, ran for governor of Illinois as a Libertarian Party candidate in 1998; the events surrounding his candidacy galvanized Tobin politically. At the time, candidates from Republican and Democratic parties needed only five thousand signatures to qualify for a slot on the ballot, while third-party candidates required twenty-five thousand signatures. Although James Tobin gathered sixty thousand signatures, he was left off the ballot—a result, Tobin claims, of the political influence of the Daley family in Chicago. Witnessing firsthand the machinations of the Chicago political clique emboldened Tobin to fight for a more inclusive political system, driven more by the people and less by the interests of corporations and wealthy individuals. Tobin explained to Tom Mullen for the *Washington Times* (4 Nov. 2012), "It's the money in politics, Democrats and Republicans alike, the money in media and so on that has got us where we are today." As a result, Tobin has devoted her life to changing the political landscape.

TAKING ON RETIREMENT PLANS

In 1976, Christina's father James founded Taxpayers United of America, a nonprofit company based in Chicago. The group is dedicated to cutting taxes and led a property-tax strike in Illinois the year after its founding. Christina Tobin serves as the organization's vice president. In 2011, Tobin toured the Midwest ahead of the 2012 general elections, raising awareness of the retirement provisions for state employees. Educators—particularly those in administrative positions—and public employees such as judges topped the list of those with the biggest retirement payouts. As she explained in a statement reported by Kevin Leininger for Fort Wayne, Indiana's *News-Sentinel* (16 Nov. 2011), "Government employees really rake it in while they are employed and then when retired. Taxpayers not only foot the entire bill for the lush salaries, but 100 percent of these government employee pensions are funded by the taxpayer. In many cases, even the lump-sum annuity savings account is also completely funded by the taxpayers, who will have to work until they drop to fund their neighbors' retirement."

Instead of the current system, Taxpayers United favors a defined-contribution plan, such as a 401(k), for new employees. As Tobin told David Hunn for the *St. Louis Post-Dispatch* (22 Aug. 2011), "If the system stays the way it is, it will collapse." According to Tobin's figures at least one hundred current or former school district leaders would have earnings exceeding $4.3 million after retirement, with more than one hundred Missouri state workers making more than $2.3 million over a lifetime (the report set the average length of service at thirty-five years, retirement age at about sixty, and a life span into the eighties).

Rae Ann McNeilly, executive director for Taxpayers United of America and responsible for explaining the data the group used, told Chris Hunter for *Salina (Kansas) Journal* (23 Feb. 2012), "Every tax increase is to keep the pension system alive. We can say it is for all of these other purposes, but . . . It is to take more and more from taxpayers." There has been criticism of the Taxpayers United of America's calculations, however. For example, Jason Gage, the city manager of Salina, Kansas, believes the organization's methods of determining payouts is flawed. As he told Hunter, "If you torture numbers long enough, they will confess to anything. . . . I think they tortured those numbers quite a lot." Mary Vanek, executive director of the Public Employees Retirement Association of Minnesota, also disagrees with the numbers that Taxpayers United used. As she told Peter Passi for *Duluth News-Tribune* (22 Apr. 2012), "They've picked a demographic that clearly skews the facts."

WORKING FOR THIRD-PARTY CANDIDATES

Tobin has made a career of ensuring ballot access, most often for third-party candidates. Elections in Pennsylvania are one of the toughest for third-party or independent candidates because of the number of signatures needed to get a candidate's name on the ballot. In 2004, for example, Ralph Nader was challenged by Democrats in that state and did not remain on the ballot; the Commonwealth Court regarded some of the signatures as invalid. In Illinois, Tobin worked for Nader defending signatures his campaign gathered, even though she was still in college at the time. Also in 2004, she defended signatures for Rich Whitney, the Green Party candidate for governor of Illinois. She became Nader's national ballot access coordinator in 2008, when Nader gained 500,000 signatures, more than double the number needed. As she told Amy Worden for the *Philadelphia Inquirer* (2 Aug. 2008), "One hundred percent of the signatures are valid. . . . I was watching them very closely myself."

Since 1988, televised presidential debates have been under the auspices of the privately funded nonprofit Commission on Presidential Debates. According to Tobin, wealthy and conservative interests such as JPMorgan Chase have funded the group to keep the two-party system intact because it favors their business interests. Thus, during the 2008 presidential election, Tobin organized the sole nationally televised debate for third-party candidates. CSPAN-2 broadcast the event live and in prime time, with journalist Chris Hedges as moderator. Tobin also put together a vice presidential debate and two Illinois gubernatorial debates. Her vision includes hosting panel discussions to provide a free flow of ideas.

FREE & EQUAL ELECTIONS

In 2008, Tobin founded the Free & Equal Elections Foundation, a nonprofit organization whose motto is "more voices, more choices." Tobin had been running a business, which she sold for $250,000; she used the proceeds as seed money to begin the foundation. Several years later the group was offered a half-million-dollar donation by a corporation; Tobin refused to accept it, fearing that her vision would be compromised.

In 2012, Free & Equal Elections sponsored televised presidential debates for third-party candidates, with Larry King and Tobin comoderating. As Tobin told Jennifer Harper for the *Washington Times* (18 Oct. 2012), "The previous debates between Obama and Romney have failed to address the issues that really concern everyday Americans. . . . From foreign policy, to the economy, to taboo subjects like our diminishing civil liberties and the drug war, Americans deserve a real debate, real solutions, and real electoral options."

More than twenty million people viewed the debates. Four candidates from third parties took part: Justice Party's Rocky Anderson, Virgil Goode of the Constitution Party, Libertarian Gary Johnson, and Green Party nominee Jill Stein. Tobin had high hopes that the debate would affect the election, as she told Mullen that the various third-party candidates "do have a different take on things such as healthcare and so on, but my feeling is that the two-party system has been playing us for over a century now and they've made us quite divisive. I do foresee, after this election, a huge movement of independents running for office and finding, well, we do have a lot in common across the spectrum."

FIGHTING TOP-TWO PRIMARIES

As Tobin told Dennis Trainor Jr. for the website Popular Resistance (11 June 2014), "We believe that freedom is enhanced when voters are presented with all the sides to an issue and have a chance to fairly evaluate all the candidates running in an election. However, the incumbent political parties like to define the parameters of the debate by presenting only two choices, or two versions of the same idea." Part of Tobin's efforts to include third-party candidates is her work with StopTopTwo.org, a subdivision of Free & Equal Elections. Started as a committee effort to halt California's Proposition 14 in 2010, StopTopTwo.org takes issue with the practice of primary elections in which candidates select their own ballot labels, rather than being nominated by a party. In every other nation that uses both a primary and general election, the party must nominate the candidate. All names appear on the primary election ballot, but only the top two vote getters are permitted to run in the November elections. After California voters passed Proposition 14 in 2010, StopTopTwo.org began to coordinate a national campaign to make voters aware of what StopTopTwo.org describes on the Free & Equal website as "the flaws in the Top Two election system."

Begun in Louisiana in the 1970s as a way of ensuring continued Democratic control, the top-two primary system spread to Washington in 2008 and California in 2010. Tobin views top-two primaries as violating the Constitution in two major ways. First, by allowing candidates to run who have not been nominated by the party, thus removing control of who uses party labels, the process violates the right of free association. Second, voters wishing to elect a third-party candidate are disenfranchised by this system.

In 2012, voters in Arizona rejected the top-two primary system after Tobin swung through the state to warn of the dangers of Arizona's Proposition 121. As she told Mara Knaub for the *Yuma (Arizona) Sun* (23 Oct. 2012), "Arizona is a gateway. If it passes here, it would spread across the country." Tobin additionally maintained that voter turnout was lower in top-two primaries. In March 2014, the Montana Supreme Court rejected the right of a legislative referral on the top-two primary to appear before voters. Colorado and Oregon were scheduled to vote on a top-two system in 2014.

Not everyone agrees with Tobin's arguments, however. In 2008, the US Supreme Court upheld Washington's new process. In addition, Senator Charles E. Schumer, a New York Democrat, decries the political polarization that had led to gridlock in Congress and believes the adoption of top-two primaries would be beneficial. As he wrote in the *New York Times* (21 July 2014), "While there are no guarantees, it seems likely that a top-two primary system would encourage more participation in primaries and undo tendencies toward default extremism."

UNITED WE STAND FEST

In May 2014, United We Stand, an initiative of Free & Equal Elections, planned an event to kick off a university bus tour; the group enlisted the aid of musicians such as Immortal Technique, Chuck D of Public Enemy, and founders of the Wu-Tang Clan. Author and candidate Marianne Williamson was one of the keynote speakers, and several businesses noted for being socially responsible, such as Dr. Bronner's Magic Soaps and Ben and Jerry's, contributed to the cost of the event. Originally to be held at Pauley Pavilion, on the campus of University of California, Los Angeles (UCLA), the event was relocated to the Belasco Theater in downtown Los Angeles when UCLA canceled because of a lack of payment. Originally priced at about eighteen dollars, tickets were subsequently offered for free.

The campaign sought to energize young voters and encourage them to run for elective office in 2014. As Tobin told Gibson, "We want people to rise above the two-party system and take our government back. We need a mass uprising of honest people—solution-based, led by youth who are most open-minded . . . There's nothing wrong with recognizing there's something wrong with the system, but we need to help train and inspire people to rise up and take leadership."

The event reached its goal of $25,000 in only ten days through crowdfunding. A second effort to finance a United We Stand Fest in 2015 began after the success of the first event.

PERSONAL LIFE

Tobin serves on the boards of StopTopTwo.org and the Coalition for Free and Open Elections. She is a self-described "realistic optimist." She told Mullen, "We're here for the long haul. I'm 31 years of age and I'll be doing this full-time for the rest of my life. I'm the luckiest girl ever. I love this. It's so much fun."

SUGGESTED READING

Gibson, Carl. "Christina Tobin: Reforming Politics to Make 'All Elections Free and Equal.'" *Occupy.com.* Occupy.com, 11 Sept. 2013. Web. 11 Aug. 2014.

Harper, Jennifer. "Inside the Beltway: Prurient and Presidential." *Washington Times.* Washington Times, 18 Oct. 2012. Web. 28 July 2014.

Hunter, Chris. "Taxpayer Group Takes Issue with Pensions." *Salina Journal* [Kansas] 23 Feb. 2012. Web. 16 July 2014.

Knaub, Mara. "Prop 121 Foe Makes Her Case in Yuma." *Yuma Sun* [AZ] 23 Oct. 2012. *Regional Business News Plus.* Web. 11 Aug. 2014.

Schumer, Charles. "End Partisan Primaries, Save America." *New York Times.* New York Times, 21 July 2014. Web. 28 July 2014.

—*Judy Johnson*

Eric Topol

Born: June 26, 1954
Occupation: Cardiologist and digital medicine advocate

Dr. Eric J. Topol is a cardiologist, author, and digital medicine advocate. Since 2007 he had been the director of the Scripps Translational Science Institute in La Jolla, California, where he serves as professor of genomics at the Scripps Research Institute and chief academic officer of Scripps Health. Topol, who is an outspoken critic of medicine's conservative culture, published a book in 2012 titled *The Creative Destruction of Medicine: How the Digital Revolution Will Create Better Health Care.* "The field has resisted a truly remarkable digital infrastructure to the nth degree," Topol told Ron Winslow for the *Wall Street Journal* (14 Feb. 2013). According

Courtesy of Eric Topol

to Topol, the marriage of genetic sequencing and new technology opens up all kinds of digital possibilities for treating patients. From simple smartphone apps to biosensors (wearable sensors) that measure blood pressure or glucose and wirelessly connect to your doctor, Topol thinks that the "digitization" of humans will transform, and indeed improve, the future of medicine. "The digital world has been in a separate orbit from our medical cocoon," he told Winslow, "and it's time the boundaries be taken down."

As a tireless public advocate for the use of mobile devices in health care—known as mobile health or mHealth—Topol has garnered both supporters and critics. Many physicians bristle at his blunt rhetoric. Describing his general feelings about the medical community to Robbins, Topol quoted Voltaire: "Doctors prescribe medicine of which they know little, to cure disease of which they know less, in human beings of which they know nothing." But his provocative tone has also inspired countless people; Topol believes in the possibility of great change in an era when the term *health care* itself sparks political debate. In 2012, two major health care magazines named him the most influential physician executive in the United States, and the Institute of Scientific Information crowned him "Doctor of the Decade." In 2009, he was featured as one of *GQ* magazine's eleven "Rock Stars of Science," and he promoted his book on the television talk show *The Colbert Report* in 2013. Even his detractors admit that, as Robbins wrote, he has become "too famous to ignore."

Topol is also vice-chairman of the West Health Institute, which he helped found in 2009. He was elected to the prestigious Institute of

Medicine in 2004. In 2011, the University of Michigan introduced an honorary position called the Eric Topol Professor of Cardiovascular Medicine, and the University of Rochester, his graduate alma mater, awarded him the school's Hutchinson Medal. Topol founded the informational website *TheHeart.org* in 1999 and served as the editor in chief of a genomic website before taking on his current role as editor in chief of *Medscape*, a medical news website for physicians, in 2007. He was named chief medical adviser to AT&T in 2014.

EARLY LIFE AND EDUCATION

Topol was born on June 26, 1954, and grew up on Long Island in New York. He lost relatives to cancer when he was young, and his mother, who was a smoker, died of leukemia in her early fifties. His father went blind from diabetes when he was forty-nine. Topol attended the University of Virginia, where he worked a night shift at the campus hospital in the intensive care unit. "What I saw was really sick people getting better," Topol told Robbins of the experience. "All I had prior to that was watching my relatives die. That was a real inflection point for me. I decided I wanted to go to medical school." He earned his bachelor's degree in biomedicine in 1975. For his undergraduate thesis, the budding geneticist wrote a paper titled "Prospects for Genetic Therapy in Man." In it, he speculated about the ways in which genetics might one day aid in identifying inherited diseases.

Topol attended medical school at the University of Rochester in Rochester, New York, and received his MD in 1979. He began a residency in internal medicine at the University of California, San Francisco, the same year. During his cardiology fellowship at Johns Hopkins University, which he began in 1982, Topol became the first doctor to give a patient t-PA (tissue plasminogen activator), a protein that helps break down blood clots and is now in wide use for that purpose. He also introduced an improved probe for heart surgeons; he even gave a talk about it at a conference, but Bernadine Healy, a Johns Hopkins professor who would later become head of the National Institutes of Health (NIH), was resistant about putting it into practice. "I was ready to quit my fellowship that day," Topol recalled to Robbins. Healy's dismissal represented what would become a familiar scenario: Topol pushing one way and the medical community pushing back.

In 1985, Topol left Johns Hopkins and joined the faculty at the University of Michigan. He taught, became a tenured professor, and worked on a number of important studies. In 1989, Topol became the first doctor to give a patient the blood thinner Angiomax. The same year, he helped develop another blood thinner, Plavix. The US Food and Drug Administration

(FDA) approved the sale of Plavix in 1997, the same year it approved another drug Topol helped develop called ReoPro. Plavix was a top-selling drug worldwide by 2011.

CLEVELAND CLINIC

Topol was hired as head of the cardiology department at the Cleveland Clinic in 1991, at the age of thirty-six. The Cleveland Clinic was one of the world's best heart care facilities at the time, and during his time there, Topol improved upon its already sterling reputation. In 1991, the clinic's cardiology department was ranked fourth in the nation by *US News and World Report*; four years later it was ranked first, a ranking it held for nineteen consecutive years as of 2013. In 1996, Topol founded the first cardiovascular gene bank, which allowed researchers to identify genes associated with heart disease.

Outside of his work with the clinic, Topol was asked to be an adviser for CardioNet, the first mHealth company, in 1999. "They were basically trying to transmit heart rhythms over the Internet," Topol told Shiv Gaglani for the American College of Cardiology's *CardioSource* website (Sept. 2013). "I became an adviser and brought along other cardiologists to form a whole clinical advisory group. It was a success at least initially, and for a number of years was really the only technology that allowed real-time collection and transmission via the web of heart rhythms." Competitors such as AliveCor and iRhythm have since entered the market, reducing CardioNet's stature, but CardioNet played an important role in Topol's career: it was his first encounter with the burgeoning digital health movement.

In the late 1990s, Topol helped persuade Cleveland philanthropist Al Lerner to donate $100 million to found a medical school, the Cleveland Clinic Lerner College of Medicine, which enrolled its first students in 2004. He was named chief academic officer at the Cleveland Clinic in 2001.

VIOXX CONTROVERSY

In 2001, Topol was the primary author of a paper published in the *Journal of the American Medical Association* (*JAMA*) that argued that the popular painkiller Vioxx increased a patient's risk of heart attack or stroke. In the ensuing years, Topol was criticized for his relationships with various drug and medical device companies and a hedge fund that shorted Vioxx manufacturer Merck. (Topol was a paid consultant for the hedge fund, which created the appearance of a conflict of interest should the fund benefit from a fall in Merck's fortunes.) In the wake of the controversy (which Merck worked hard to fuel), Topol announced in 2005 that he would sever most of his corporate ties, in order to protect his "academic credibility."

Merck removed Vioxx from the market in 2004 due to the safety concerns Topol had brought to light, but in 2005, Merck was taken to court for the 2001 death of a Florida man who took Vioxx, and Topol was asked to provide testimony. "Less than a week after his videotaped lambasting of Merck was played in a Houston federal courtroom," Alex Berenson reported for the *New York Times* (10 Dec. 2005), Topol "lost his title as chief academic officer of the Cleveland Clinic's medical college." The demotion did not affect his salary—he was still chief of cardiology—but it removed him from the clinic's governing board. In the tape, Topol accused Merck of irresponsible marketing and "scientific misconduct." He believes that his testimony cost him his job. A representative for the Cleveland Clinic told Berenson that Topol's testimony was not a factor, and that the clinic was simply scrapping Topol's position altogether. "It was the most difficult period in my life," Topol told Gary Robbins for the *San Diego Union-Tribune* (15 Sept. 2012) of the episode.

In 2006, Scripps Health in La Jolla, California, recruited Topol to be chief academic officer of the health system and to lead the new Scripps Translational Science Institute and the Scripps Genomic Medicine program. In this position, he raised money from local philanthropists to found the Gary and Mary West Wireless Health Institute (now known simply as West Health) in 2009.

THE CREATIVE DESTRUCTION OF MEDICINE

Topol published *The Creative Destruction of Medicine: How the Digital Revolution Will Create Better Health Care* in February 2012. The phrase "creative destruction" in the book's title comes from the twentieth-century economist Joseph Schumpeter, who used it to describe increased efficiency through innovation, seen as a core process of capitalism. In the book, Topol describes his vision for the future of medicine. Topol is in favor of technologies that he says would effectively "digitize" humans: biosensors and DNA sequencing will soon provide troves of individual patient data for physicians, digitized and available at the click of a mouse or the swipe of a finger. Topol argues that technology can address real problems in a health care system that is inefficient and often ineffectual, delivering care to populations rather than individuals. "What constitutes evidence-based medicine today is what is good for a large population," he wrote in *The Creative Destruction of Medicine*, "not for any particular individual." Doctors prescribe—overprescribe, according to Topol—medicines that do little to treat the ailments people actually suffer from.

If patients are better able to monitor their own physiological metrics, the more information a doctor has to interpret, according to Topol. The more information a doctor has to interpret, the more precise his or her diagnosis, and the more effective the prescribed treatment. The data available through individual DNA sequencing further augments this store of patient information. Doctors could preventatively diagnose any number of ailments before they occur. For Topol, mobile health is about aggregating data, removing unnecessary barriers between doctor and patient, and giving people more control over their own health care. Answering criticisms that technology will make medicine less personal in terms of human interaction, Topol told Winslow, "I use a portable pocket ultrasound device instead of a stethoscope to listen to the heart, and I share it with the patient in real time. 'Look at your valve, look at your heart-muscle strength.' So they're looking at it with me. Normally a patient is tested by an ultrasonographer who is not allowed to tell them anything. They have to call the doctor and ask, 'What did it show?'"

WIRED FOR HEALTH

In 2013 Topol and his colleagues at the Scripps Translational Science Institute launched a new study called Wired for Health to determine the efficacy and overall outcome of using mobile health devices. Their first randomized controlled trial will test the Withings blood pressure monitor, AliveCor heart monitor, and iBGStar blood glucose meter. One criticism regarding mobile health that Topol has entertained is the potential of a "digital medical divide" in which new technologies are accessible only to the educated and affluent. "I think this is an issue which we have to deal with but if we can come up with better ways to prevent diseases in the future then it should hopefully [affect] all individuals," he told Franz Wiesbauer in an interview for the website *MedCrunch* (2 Mar. 2012).

CHIEF MEDICAL ADVISER FOR AT&T

In 2014, Topol was named the chief medical adviser for AT&T. He began working for the wireless company in 2013 when it introduced a mobile emergency-response device for elderly people called EverThere. AT&T hopes that Topol can bolster the company's mobile health programs. According to Gary Robbins and Bradley J. Fikes for the *San Diego Union-Tribune* (9 Feb. 2014), the mobile health industry is poised to reach $26 billion in sales by 2017. That number translates to an annual growth rate of 61 percent. "AT&T has the pipes to move information between connected devices," Topol told Robbins and Fikes regarding his appointment. "This is the future of medicine."

Topol has a wife named Susan and two adult children named Sarah and Evan.

SUGGESTED READING

Berenson, Alex. "Doctor Suggests Merck Trial May Have Led to Demotion." *New York Times*. New York Times, 10 Dec. 2005. Web. 11 Apr. 2014.

Gaglani, Shiv. "Wired for Health: An Interview with Dr. Eric Topol." *CardioSource*. American College of Cardiology, Sept. 2013. Web. 11 Apr. 2014.

Holt, Matthew. "Eric Topol: Too Clever by Three-Quarters." *The Health Care Blog*. THCB, 22 Feb. 2012. Web. 11 Apr. 2014.

Robbins, Gary. "Eric Topol's Tough Prescription for Improving Medicine." *San Diego Union-Tribune*. San Diego Union-Tribune, 15 Sept. 2012. Web. 11 Apr. 2014.

Robbins, Gary, and Bradley J. Fikes. "Topol Named AT&T's Chief Medical Advisor." *San Diego Union-Tribune*. San Diego Union-Tribune, 9 Feb. 2014. Web. 11 Apr. 2014.

Wiesbauer, Franz. "MedCrunch Interview with Eric Topol MD: The Cardiologist Who Wants to Digitize You and Your Patients." *MedCrunch*. MedCrunch, 2 Mar. 2012. Web. 11 Apr. 2014.

Winslow, Ron. "The Wireless Revolution Hits Medicine." *Wall Street Journal*. Dow Jones, 14 Feb. 2013. Web. 11 Apr. 2014.

—Molly Hagan

Yani Tseng

Born: January 23, 1989
Occupation: Professional golfer

Taiwanese golfer Yani Tseng, as Karen Crouse wrote for the *New York Times* (6 Dec. 2011), is "the Arnold Palmer of women's golf, increasing the sport's visibility with her genial nature and go-for-broke playing style." Like Palmer, the American golfing legend and seven-time major champion who helped popularize golf in the 1950s, Tseng has enjoyed phenomenal career success that has made her an icon in her native Taiwan and a global ambassador for women's golf.

Turning professional in 2007 at the age of eighteen after a decorated amateur career, Tseng burst onto the scene in 2008, when she won her first major title and was named the Ladies Professional Golf Association (LPGA) Rookie of the Year. She then followed up a respectable 2009 season with one of the most remarkable two-year stretches in the history of women's golf. From 2010 to early 2012 she captured thirteen LPGA Tour titles, including four major championships. In 2011 the twenty-two-year-old became the youngest player, male or female, to win five majors, and in the following year she set a new LPGA time record in career earnings. During her run of dominance, she held the top ranking in women's golf for 109 weeks straight, won

Danny Moloshok/Reuters/Landov

back-to-back Rolex Player of the Year awards in 2010 and 2011, and made *Time* magazine's 2012 list of the world's one hundred most influential people.

Tseng's rapid ascension to the top of women's golf, however, was followed by an equally spectacular fall from grace. Plagued by self-doubt and mounting pressure, she struggled mightily during the 2013 and 2014 seasons, in which she failed to win a single LPGA title and plummeted from the top fifty in the world rankings.

EARLY LIFE

The middle of three children, Yani Tseng was born on January 23, 1989, in Guishan Township, in the northwestern region of Taoyuan County, Taiwan. She has an older brother and a younger sister. Both of Tseng's parents, Mao-Hsin "Charlie" and Yu-Yun Yang, are golf enthusiasts. Her father, now an oil-company distributor, was a distinguished amateur golfer in Taiwan, and her mother worked as a caddie. Tseng was introduced to golf at the age of five, after her parents began taking her to the driving range they owned. There, she practiced for hours at a time alongside her parents and other adults.

Tseng first competed at age six, and by ten she was training under her first coach, Tony Kao, an accomplished amateur Taiwanese golfer. Under Kao, who coached her until she turned eighteen, she developed her golf swing and learned how to have fun with the sport. "For the first year or so," Tseng recalled to Josh Sens for *Golf Magazine* (Jan. 2012), "the only thing he told me was to just swing as hard as I can and not worry where it goes."

At age eleven Tseng was good enough to beat her father, who played a major role in her development as a golfer. Charlie Tseng took her to the course nearly every day, both after school and on the weekends, and taught her the importance of setting goals. Also, in order to maintain his daughter's interest in the sport, he encouraged her to place bets with other golfers, a practice that gave her an early desire to succeed.

Tseng's progress was such that at age twelve she resolved to become the number-one player in the world, fostering dreams of following in the footsteps of her idol, the Swedish golfer Annika Sörenstam, arguably the greatest female golfer of all time. It was at that age that Tseng's parents sent her to the United States to further her golf skills. By then, she had already developed the ability to shape shots and was driving the ball 240 yards.

AMATEUR CAREER

Beginning in 2001 Tseng summered in San Diego, California, where she was hosted and mentored by Ernie Huang, a local businessman and junior golf booster. She started practicing at private clubs and traveling with Huang to US Asian Junior Golf Association and US Golf Association events. A turning point for Tseng came in July 2002, when she got the opportunity to attend the US Women's Open in Hutchinson, Kansas. Despite being just thirteen at the time, Tseng expressed the belief that her game was good enough to beat some of the players she saw, prompting Huang to investigate how she could qualify for the tournament, considered to be the most prestigious in women's golf.

Tseng's road to playing in the US Women's Open began to take shape in 2003, when she came in first place at the Callaway Junior Golf Championship and captured her first of three consecutive Asia-Pacific Junior Championship titles. She first drew the public's attention in 2004, when, at fifteen, she defeated American golfing prodigy Michelle Wie in the final of the US Women's Amateur Public Links Championship. "You could tell right away you were seeing something special," Gary Gilchrist, Tseng's swing coach who was instructing Wie at the time, told Sens.

In 2005 Tseng overtook another young American phenom, Morgan Pressel, to win the North and South Women's Amateur Championship. Also that year, she won the Joanne Winter Arizona Silver Belle Championship and reached the semifinals of the Amateur Public Links Championship. Tseng's performance in the latter event helped her qualify for the 2005 US Women's Open in Cherry Hills Village, Colorado. Though she failed to make the cut, Tseng said the experience of playing in the tournament for the first time was "one of my best memories ever," as she told Katie Ann Robinson for the LPGA website (2 July 2012).

Tseng held the top spot among amateurs in Taiwan from 2004 to 2006, during which time she was regarded as the best women's amateur in Asia. During her amateur career she amassed a total of nineteen victories, notching fifteen internationally and four on US soil.

TURNING PRO AND FIRST LPGA TITLES

Tseng performed well as a newcomer to the professional circuit in competition at the 2007 Ladies Asian Golf Tour and Canadian Women's Tour, leagues that serve as proving grounds for golfers aspiring to play on the LPGA Tour. After winning once in each, Tseng placed sixth in the LPGA Qualifying Tournament, also known as LPGA Q School, which ensured her a LPGA Tour card for the 2008 season.

Tseng opened the 2008 season in dominant fashion by winning her fourth professional title, the Royal Ladies Open on the LPGA of Taiwan Tour, by a resounding seventeen strokes. She then recorded a pair of second-place finishes in her first ten starts on the LPGA Tour before playing in her first career LPGA Championship. Despite shooting a one-over-par seventy-three in the opening round, Tseng rebounded to shoot a second-round seventy and third-round sixty-five, leaving her only four shots off the lead going into the final round. She then shot a sixty-eight in the final round to force Maria Hjorth into a four-hole sudden-death playoff. After birdying the fourth hole, Tseng claimed her first LPGA victory and first major title. She also became the first rookie in a decade to win a major golf championship. At nineteen she also became the youngest player ever to win the tournament, which came with a $300,000 purse.

Tseng continued to impress in her rookie season, recording three more runner-up finishes, the most notable of which came at the 2008 Women's British Open. She finished the year ranked third on the LPGA Tour earnings list, with more than $1.75 million, and won the Louise Suggs Rolex Rookie of the Year award, named in honor of the LPGA founder Louise Suggs. Throughout her rookie season, Tseng exhibited aspects of her game that ultimately propelled her to the top of women's golf. Known for her aggressive approach off the tee and on the greens, she led the tour in birdies (388) and finished sixth in driving distance average (266.1 yards). "She is so aggressive, you could almost say she plays more like a man," Gilchrist said of his pupil to Josh Sens.

TOP FEMALE GOLFER IN THE WORLD

During the 2009 season Tseng captured her second career LPGA title at the LPGA Corning Classic, where she shot a career-best sixty-two in the third round. Despite encountering some rough patches during the season, she led the tour in birdies (381) for the second consecutive year and finished seventh on the earnings list, with more than $1.2 million.

In 2010 Tseng began working with Gilchrist, who helped correct flaws in her overall game and increase her positivity. She returned to the golf course with a refined swing, improved accuracy, and a more unflappable demeanor

that paid immediate dividends. In the 2010 Kraft Nabisco Championship in Rancho Mirage, California, she edged Suzann Pettersen with an eagle (two under par) on the last hole to win her third career LPGA major title. She then won the 2010 RICOH British Open in Southport, England, after outlasting Katherine Hull in the final round with another narrow one-shot victory. With that win Tseng, at twenty-one, became the youngest player ever to win three major championships.

One month after the British Open, Tseng won her fifth career LPGA title at the Northwest Arkansas Championship in Rogers, Arkansas, defeating her rival Michelle Wie by one stroke. She finished the year ranked fourth on the earnings list, with more than $1.5 million. For her performance during the season, Tseng received the LPGA's coveted Rolex Player of the Year award, a first for a Taiwanese golfer. Moreover, Tseng was second only to Nancy Lopez, the 1978 recipient, for youngest winner.

A HISTORIC SEASON

Tseng built on her success in a historic way in 2011, when she ascended to the top of women's golf and emerged as a global icon. Tseng topped the LPGA rankings in just about every measurable category, including victories (7 in 22 starts), top-ten finishes (14), birdies (368), scoring average (69.66), driving distance (269.2 yards), rounds under par (54 of 77), and rounds in the sixties (41). Two of Tseng's victories came in majors: in June 2011 she won the LPGA Championship by ten strokes to claim her fourth major title, and in the following month, she successfully defended her British Open title, winning by four strokes to secure her fifth career major. At twenty-two years old, Tseng became the youngest golfer, male or female, to win five majors. Around this time Hall of Fame golfer Juli Inkster said of Tseng to Crouse for the *New York Times* (9 July 2011): "She can bomb the ball. She's got a lot of passion for the game. She wants to be the best. She wants to get better. So she could be here for a while."

During the 2011 season Tseng took home some $2.9 million in prize earnings, more than double the amount of the next highest earner on tour, and again earned Rolex Player of the Year honors. She became the youngest player to receive the honor in consecutive years. Tseng's remarkable season also included winning international events on the LPGA of Taiwan Tour and the Ladies European Tour.

BEATEN BUT NOT BROKEN

Tseng carried her dominance into 2012, when she won three of the first five tournaments on the LPGA Tour: the Honda LPGA Thailand, the RR Donnelley LPGA Founders Cup, and the Kia Classic. With her victory in the RR Donnelley

LPGA Founders Cup, she surpassed $8 million in career earnings, making her the fastest LPGA player to ever hit that mark. That milestone notwithstanding, Tseng struggled the rest of the year and failed to win another title. Still, she finished fourth on the earnings list, with more than $1.4 million.

Tseng continued to struggle during the 2013 and 2014 seasons, in which she went winless and earned just six top-ten finishes. In March 2013 Tseng relinquished the top spot in the world golf rankings to Stacy Lewis, after holding the spot for 109 consecutive weeks. Her 109-week run at the top was the second-longest in history, behind only Lorena Ochoa's 158 weeks. As of September 2014, she ranked ninth all-time on the LPGA Tour career money list, with more than $9.6 million, but had plummeted to number sixty-four in the world rankings. This slump in professional golfing has inspired the Buddhist-raised Tseng to attend Bible studies on tour and pray with and for fellow players. Despite her recent struggles, Tseng, who has also changed her practice habits and sought the treatment of a sports psychologist, has expressed confidence that she will regain her championship form. "Yani is still in there somewhere," she said, as quoted by Steve DiMeglio for *USA Today* (15 Aug. 2014). "My skill is still inside me. I just have to trust myself and let it out."

PERSONAL LIFE

Tseng lives in the gated community of Lake Nona Golf and Country Club, in Orlando, Florida, in a house formerly owned by Annika Sörenstam, whom she considers a friend and mentor. Known for her warm smile and affable personality, Tseng has developed a reputation for being one of the most accessible players on the LPGA Tour, which has helped to win her thousands of supporters around the world. Those attributes have also helped her land endorsement deals with such brands as Adams Golf, Titleist, Lacoste, and Oakley.

In 2012 Tseng was listed among that year's one hundred most influential people in the world by *Time* magazine for her contribution to increasing the popularity of golf in her native Taiwan, where she is regarded as an icon. Sörenstam, in a commendation for *Time* (18 Apr. 2012) that recognized Tseng and her golf achievements, described her friend as a "rare talent with the ability to energize a new generation of LPGA fans . . . Yani's blend of skill, grace, and work ethic will be a powerful force on the LPGA tour for years to come."

SUGGESTED READING

Crouse, Karen. "Celebrated in Asia, Little Known in America." *New York Times*. New York Times, 6 Dec. 2011. Web. 18 Sept. 2014.

DiMeglio, Steve. "Yani Tseng, Former No. 1, Tries to Push Doubts Aside." *USA Today*. USA Today, 15 Aug. 2014. Web. 18 Sept. 2014.

Nichols, Beth Ann. "Tseng an Inspiring and Joyful Force." *Golf Week*. Turnstile, 28 Mar. 2012. Web. 18 Sept. 2014.

Sens, Josh. "So Why Don't You Know Her Name?" *Golf Magazine* Jan. 2012: 74. Print.

—*Chris Cullen*

Masai Ujiri

Born: 1970
Occupation: Basketball executive

Masai Ujiri became the general manager of the Toronto Raptors basketball team in 2013. He joined the team after a successful, if abbreviated, run as the general manager of the Denver Nuggets. Ujiri's tenure as Denver's general manager began in the fall of 2010, and in early 2011 he presided over a gutsy three-team deal that sent superstars Carmelo Anthony and Chauncey Billups to the New York Knicks in exchange for Raymond Felton, Wilson Chandler, Danilo Gallinari, and Timofey Mozgov from the Knicks and Kosta Koufos from the Minnesota Timberwolves. "The Trade," as it became known in Denver, launched Ujiri's career and earned him a reputation as a general manager with a particular vision. Despite being one of the youngest general managers in the National Basketball Association (NBA) and managing one of the youngest teams in the league, he defied expectations and was named the NBA Executive of the Year in 2013. Under Ujiri's guidance and direction, the Nuggets made it to the first round of the 2011 NBA Playoffs without Anthony, and the team enjoyed an explosive winning streak during the 2012–13 season. Unfortunately, the Nuggets lost in the first round of the 2013 NBA Playoffs, and Ujiri left the franchise shortly thereafter.

Mark Blinch/Reuters/Landov

Ujiri, who was raised in Zaria, Nigeria, is the first African general manager of a major American sports franchise. He spent more than six years playing professional basketball in Europe and several more years as an international scout. He is a leader within the NBA's outreach program Basketball without Borders, where he serves as the director of the organization's annual camp in Africa. As Donnovan Bennett explained for *SportsNet* (14 Feb. 2014), Ujiri's athletic and philanthropic interests "work in perfect harmony." In 2003, Ujiri founded an outreach organization in Nigeria called Giants of Africa, which runs two camps designed to teach African youth the fundamentals of basketball and life skills to utilize off the court. "There are a lot of good, smart kids there who just need an opportunity," Ujiri told William C. Rhoden for the *New York Times* (12 Mar. 2011). "I represent a great continent. People ask, Is there pressure on me? I don't feel pressure at all. It's an unbelievable challenge for me, but I feel like I carry the weight of my continent on my shoulders. I want to help the next generation in Africa."

EARLY LIFE

Ujiri grew up in Nigeria and England, where his Nigerian parents studied abroad. His mother, Grace Paula, is a doctor, and his late father, Michael Ujiri, was a hospital administrator. He has three siblings. Growing up, Ujiri played soccer "until I stepped on a basketball court for the first time and fell in love with the game," he told Woody Paige for the *Denver Post* (28 Aug. 2010). He soon decided that he wanted to move to the United States and play for the NBA like his idol, Hakeem Olajuwon, the league's first Nigerian star.

As a teenager, Ujiri attended a prep school in Seattle, Washington, where he lived with a Nigerian family. While in Seattle, he met Nigerian player Godwin Owinje, and both men decided to attend Bismarck State College (BSC) in North Dakota to play for the school's basketball team. Buster Gilliss, who was the BSC basketball coach at the time, told Paige that the two seasons Ujiri and Owinje were on the team (1993–94 and 1994–95) were some of the school's best ever. Ujiri "was a slasher-type, a runner, a jumper," Gilliss said. "He hit a game-winning shot in the playoff to go to nationals, but the officials ruled it came after the buzzer. We got a drawer full of letters about those two players."

EUROLEAGUE BASKETBALL

Owinje received a scholarship to play for Georgetown University in Washington, DC, and Ujiri enrolled at Montana State University Billings (MSUB), but he only stayed at the school for one semester. After leaving MSUB, Ujiri set his sights on a professional career. He secured an agent and went to play professional basketball in Europe. Since he held a British passport, he was not subject to the limits that teams within the Euroleague set on the number of foreign players allowed.

Ujiri joined the (now defunct) Derby Storm in the British Basketball League (BBL), and he remained in Europe for six years, playing for BBL teams in Watford and Solent and eventually joining a team in Belgium. After several years of playing for B-level teams across Europe, Ujiri began to realize that he did not have the skill level to play for the NBA in the United States and that perhaps playing professional basketball was not what he was meant to do. "At some point I started chasing this thing that is not there anymore," he explained to Rhoden. He knew, however, that he wanted to stay involved in the sport, and he had "made some money, learned a lot about basketball and introduced myself to everyone," as Ujiri told Paige. He had also collected a number of contacts in the NBA. "When my playing career ended, I got out my black book and starting making calls."

SCOUTING CAREER

Ujiri had met David Thorpe, the executive director of the Pro Training Center in Florida and an employee of Scouts Inc., in 2000 at a summer-league game in Boston, Massachusetts. In 2002, as Ujiri was wrapping up his pro career in Europe, he sent Thorpe an e-mail looking for other work in basketball. Thorpe agreed to introduce him to several contacts at the college championships a few weeks later, and when they met again, Thorpe was charmed by Ujiri's intelligence and warmth—as were a legion of others with whom he came in contact at the championships. "You know how people talk about videos spreading virally on the Internet?," Thorpe remarked to Henry Abbott for ESPN.com (26 Aug. 2010). "Masai spread virally that weekend. By the time Sunday rolled around, he had meetings set up with all kinds of coaches. People I had never met. Everyone wanted him to help them find good players at every level." The Orlando Magic hired him as an unpaid European scout in the fall of 2002, and the Denver Nuggets hired him as a paid scout in 2003. He was named the director of international scouting for the Nuggets for the 2006–07 season.

Far from glamorous, the life of an international scout is extremely demanding and allows little time for sleep. (Ujiri may have been uniquely qualified for the job in that regard. He told Benjamin Hochman in an interview for the *Denver Post* (19 Feb. 2012) that he typically sleeps less than five hours a night.) Mark Titus, a writer for the sports website *Grantland* (30 July 2014), reported that scouts are always on the move—making it hard to maintain relationships and families back home. "In truth, being an international scout in the NBA means taking the red-eye from Bulgaria to Estonia so you can watch a 6-foot-9 fourteen-year-old Estonian with back hair and try to figure out if he'd average 0.5 or 2.5 points per game in the league in seven years. Then you write your report on him as you fly to Turkmenistan, rinse, and repeat pretty much every day of the year." Titus also remarked that only two non-American players—French point guard Tony Parker and German power forward Dirk Nowitzki, both nearing the end of their careers—made the 2014 NBA All-Star Game, begging the question as to whether the brutal nature of the job is worth it. Ujiri believed it was, explaining in an interview with Eric Weinstein for NBA.com (10 Aug. 2005), "You cannot miss [international basketball]. There's no running away from it. You have to cover everywhere. Basketball globally has gotten better, the skill level has gotten better."

In 2007, Ujiri left the Nuggets to take a position as the director of global scouting for the Toronto Raptors. Former president and general manager of the Raptors Bryan Colangelo promoted him to assistant general manager with the team in 2008.

GENERAL MANAGER FOR THE DENVER NUGGETS

In 2010, Ujiri was offered the chance of a lifetime. After David Griffin, a former assistant general manager with the Phoenix Suns and the current general manager of the Cleveland Cavaliers, turned the job down, Ujiri was offered the general manager position with the Denver Nuggets. He was officially named executive vice president of player operations for the Nuggets on August 27, 2010. At thirty-nine, he was one of the youngest general managers in the league. When he was hired, his colleagues praised his work ethic and positive attitude. Former Nuggets coach George Karl said at the press conference announcing Ujiri as the new general manager, "I think Masai has a personality that fits the problems that we have," Karl told Aaron J. Lopez for NBA.com (31 Aug. 2010).

Indeed, Ujiri had his work cut out for him. Morale was low; many of the players were suffering from injuries and coach Karl was recovering from throat and neck cancer. But perhaps most immediate among Ujiri's woes was finding a way to hold on to the team's star player, Carmelo Anthony. The Nuggets had selected Anthony with the third overall pick in the 2003 NBA Draft, and in his rookie year he led the once-losing team to the 2004 NBA Playoffs. Though they lost in the first round, the Nuggets appeared in the postseason every year Anthony was on the team, and in 2009, he and the 2004 NBA Finals MVP Chauncey Billups (who signed with the Nuggets in 2008) led the team to the Western Conference Finals. In Toronto, Ujiri had watched as Chris Bosh, the star power forward

for the Raptors, left the team to join superstars LeBron James and Dwyane Wade on the Miami Heat. When Ujiri returned to Denver, Anthony was eyeing a similar opportunity in New York.

"THE TRADE"

In February 2011, Ujiri oversaw a three-team trade with the New York Knicks and the Minnesota Timberwolves that Nuggets fans referred to as "the Trade." The Nuggets sent Anthony, Billups, Anthony Carter, Renaldo Balkman, and Shelden Williams to the New York Knicks in exchange for four young players: Danilo Gallinari, Raymond Felton, Wilson Chandler, and Timofey Mozgov, as well as New York's first-round 2014 draft pick and three million dollars. Center Kosta Koufos came to Denver from the Minnesota Timberwolves. In one fell swoop, Ujiri had changed the character of the entire franchise. The team had succeeded with Anthony, but their play was unevenly weighted—Anthony was the undisputed superstar and he rarely shared the ball. With a fresh, young group, coach Karl was given an opportunity to build a more cohesive team from scratch.

Anthony left the team midseason, and despite a revolving starting lineup, the Nuggets still managed to make a postseason appearance in 2011, but they lost to the Oklahoma City Thunder in the first round. The new team gained momentum during the 2011–12 season. Though the Nuggets gave the Los Angeles Lakers a run for their money in the first round of the 2012 NBA Playoffs, they lost to the Lakers in game seven. The Nuggets really hit their stride in the 2012–13 season, finishing the regular season with fifty-seven wins and twenty-five losses, marking the team's best record since the Nuggets joined the NBA in 1977. However, the Nuggets were eliminated from the first round of the 2013 NBA Playoffs by the Golden State Warriors. It was just the first blow for the team that had enjoyed a winning streak earlier in the year: Ujiri, who was named the 2013 NBA Executive of the Year, announced that he was leaving the team to return to the Raptors as their general manager. A few days later, Karl, who was named the NBA Coach of the Year in 2013, was fired.

GENERAL MANAGER FOR THE RAPTORS

Ujiri's departure appeared to surprise Nuggets executives, particularly president Josh Kroenke, but as Hochman reported for the *Denver Post* (31 May 2013), the decision was a financial one. The Raptors had offered Ujiri a five-year contract worth $15 million, a price that the Nuggets were unable to match. Ujiri was officially named general manager of the Raptors in late May. As the new general manager, Ujiri replaced his old boss and friend Colangelo. In December 2013, the Raptors cut a crucial trade deal with the Sacramento Kings. The seven-player deal involved sending Rudy Gay, Aaron Gray, and Quincy Acy to the Kings in exchange for Chuck Hayes, John Salmons, Greivis Vásquez, and Patrick Patterson.

The reenergized Raptors met the Brooklyn Nets in the first round of the 2014 NBA Playoffs. The Raptors gave a strong showing, but they lost to the Nets in game seven. Fans were disappointed but upbeat, and as James Herbert wrote for CBSSports.com (10 Aug. 2014). "At the end of it all, Toronto general manager Masai Ujiri found himself presiding over a franchise on the rise rather than one mired in mediocrity."

OUTREACH PROGRAMS IN AFRICA AND PERSONAL LIFE

The NBA and the International Basketball Federation (FIBA) have jointly operated a global outreach program called Basketball without Borders (BWB) since 2001. Ujiri has served as a camp director for the BWB Africa program since its inception, and each year he heads to the BWB camp in Johannesburg, South Africa.

In 2003, Ujiri cofounded the Nigeria-based organization Giants of Africa in order to use basketball as a means to help educate African youth and enhance their lives. Through the group's Top 50 Camp and Big Man Camp, Giants of Africa provides players with quality coaching and the facilities to learn and practice the sport. For Ujiri and Giants of Africa, basketball is not just a sport but rather a tool to enable players to further their education and broaden their world experiences.

Ujiri speaks five languages, including two dialects. His wife, Ramatu, is a model. Together, they have one daughter, who was born in 2013.

SUGGESTED READING

Abbott, Henry. "Masai Ujiri through David Thorpe's Eyes." *ESPN.* ESPN Internet Ventures, 26 Aug. 2010. Web. 15 Aug. 2014.

Hochman, Benjamin. "Masai Ujiri Leaves Nuggets to Take Job as Toronto GM." *Denver Post.* Denver Post, 31 May 2013. Web. 15 Aug. 2014.

Lopez, Aaron J. "Newly Named VP of Basketball Ops Set to Meet with Melo." *NBA.com.* NBA Media Ventures, 31 Aug. 2010. Web. 15 Aug. 2014.

Paige, Woody. "Paige: Ujiri in Nuggets' Jungle." *Denver Post.* Denver Post, 28 Aug. 2010. Web. 15 Aug. 2014.

Rhoden, William C. "Journey to NBA, via England and Nigeria." *New York Times.* New York Times, 12 Mar. 2011. Web. 15 Aug. 2014.

Titus, Mark. "My Trip to NBA Scout School." *Grantland.* ESPN Internet Ventures, 30 July 2014. Web. 15 Aug. 2014.

—*Molly Hagan*

Chika Unigwe

Born: 1974
Occupation: Writer

African literature has experienced a renaissance in the first decades of the twenty-first century, with authors such as A. Igoni Barrett of Nigeria, NoViolet Bulawayo of Zimbabwe, Lauren Beukes of South Africa, Teju Cole of Nigeria, Beatrice Lamwaka of Uganda, and others receiving international critical acclaim for their groundbreaking work. Among those celebrated writers is Chika Unigwe, a Nigerian-born author who writes in Dutch and English. Lauded both in Europe and in her birth country for her work, she has begun to make a distinct impression on American critics as well.

Initially drawn to poetry, Unigwe has since made her reputation as a fiction writer of considerable depth and warmth, with an uncanny ability to tackle difficult subjects—ranging from prostitution to prejudice and xenophobia— with seeming ease. Writing for *Life & Times* magazine (17 May 2013), Jude Akudinobi remarked, "Chika Unigwe's Africa and Africans are not framed in simplistic and specious pulls between 'tradition' and 'modernity,' often proffered in the West, nor are they governed by some kind of anthropological determinism. With spry strokes, bold but sensitive sketches of African womanhood, and assured control of challenging

© Colin McPherson/Corbis

narrative strands, she weaves evocative worlds rich in insight and nuance."

Two of Unigwe's novels in particular, *On Black Sisters Street*, which was published in English in 2009, and *Night Dancer*, published in English in 2012, were greeted warmly by critics in both the United Kingdom and the United States. In 2012, her reputation as a first-rate artist was cemented when it was announced that she had won the Nigeria Prize for Literature. Her novel *De zwarte messias* (The black messiah), about the African explorer, writer, merchant, and abolitionist Olaudah Equiano, was published in Dutch in 2013.

EARLY LIFE AND EDUCATION

Chika Unigwe was born in Enugu, Nigeria, in 1974. The sixth of seven children, she had little privacy or quiet time in her large, boisterous household. She quickly learned how to concentrate on her writing in the middle of a crowd, and even as an adult Unigwe prefers to write on a laptop inside a loud café. She earned her bachelor's degree in English language and literature from one of the best schools in her home country, the University of Nigeria, Nsukka, graduating with honors. While still an undergraduate she published her first collection of poetry, *Tear Drops*, in 1993, and followed it two years later with a second collection, *Born in Nigeria*.

The year of her graduation, Unigwe married Jan Vandenhoudt, a Belgian man she had known for two years. Many of her friends and relatives were concerned that the marriage had come too soon, particularly because Vandenhoudt was from another country. Unigwe, however, did not share their worries, and when Vandenhoudt told her that he wanted to return to Belgium shortly after their marriage, she readily agreed to accompany him. She recalled in an essay published in the online magazine *Aeon* (14 Mar. 2013), "I was certain that I would love [Belgium] and make it mine too, for the simple reason that it was his. Moreover, I did not mind veering off the beaten path. Armed with a brand-new degree from one of the top universities in Nigeria then, and an arsenal of phrases from a *Teach Yourself Dutch* book, I was confident that the only way to go was up. I was eager to begin writing this new chapter of my life."

LIFE IN BELGIUM

The newlyweds first settled in the Belgian city of Turnhout, Flanders, where Unigwe's husband had grown up. They lived with Vandenhoudt's parents for a time while he looked for employment. Although Unigwe found her husband's family friendly, the family's routines were not. Unigwe was immediately thrown off by the strictly regulated household, in which meals were rituals, conducted at specific times and in a specific manner. The quiet of her new

hometown was also disconcerting, as was her inability to communicate in a meaningful way with anyone other than her husband. Even more distressing was the sense that her muse, the force that inspired her to write poetry, had left her.

Little by little, Unigwe retreated from the world around her. Unable to find work, write as she once did, or even speak more than a few phrases in Dutch, she found herself scarcely ever leaving the small house into which she and her husband had settled. After several months of putting on a brave face for her husband, she decided to follow his suggestion that she enroll in intensive courses in Dutch at the Catholic University of Leuven. She recalled in her essay in *Aeon*, "That became my saving grace. The seven hours I spent in class each day, with other newcomers, trying to come to grips with this guttural language, which sometimes sounded deceptively like English but that made no sense at all, began to pay off. . . . And only then was I free to write again. Not poetry. The Muse, alas, never returned, but fiction came in its stead."

Unigwe later earned a master's degree from the Catholic University of Leuven and continued her studies at the University of Leiden in the Netherlands, earning her PhD in literature in 2004.

EARLY WRITING CAREER

Unigwe began publishing short fiction around the time she was completing her PhD. Her work, both fiction and nonfiction, has since appeared in numerous literary journals and anthologies, and her short stories have been broadcast on radio stations such as BBC World Service and Radio Nigeria. Several of her short stories have won awards, including "Borrowed Smile," which won the 2003 BBC Short Story Competition, and "De smaak van sneeuw" (The taste of snow), her first published short story written in Dutch, which earned a Flemish literary prize. In 2004, her story "The Secret" was nominated for a Caine Prize. In addition to writing short fiction and essays, Unigwe authored two children's books published in the United Kingdom by Macmillan: *A Rainbow for Dinner* (2002) and *Ije at School* (2005).

Unigwe's debut novel, *De feniks* (2005), was the first novel published in Dutch by a Flemish author of African ancestry. In 2007 it was published in English as *The Phoenix*. The novel, which draws heavily from Unigwe's personal experiences, follows a Nigerian-born woman as she struggles to adjust to life in Belgium and cope with her loneliness and grief.

ON BLACK SISTERS STREET

The breakout moment of Unigwe's writing career came in 2007, when her second novel, *Fata Morgana*, was published in Dutch. Published in English two years later under the title *On Black*

Sisters Street, the novel depicts the lives of four African-born prostitutes living on Zwartezusterstraat (literally "Black Sisters Street") in Belgium. Although they are housemates brought together by the same pimp, a man named Dele who sells African women to brothels across Europe, the four women know little of each other's backgrounds until one of them, Sisi, is murdered. As they exchange histories, the surviving women learn of the tragic and brutal circumstances that brought each of them to Zwartezusterstraat. The murdered Sisi, however, in many ways emerges as the most tragic figure because she drifted into prostitution not because of brutalities she suffered but because she was simply unable to find a job in her home country.

Upon its publication in English, *On Black Sisters Street* garnered impressive reviews. A critic remarked in *Publishers Weekly* (10 Jan. 2011) that Unigwe gives "powerful voice to women of the African Diaspora who are forced to use sex to survive. The author's raw voice, unflinching eye for detail, facility for creating a complex narrative, and affection for her characters make this a must read." Writing for the *New York Times* (29 Apr. 2011), novelist Fernanda Eberstadt agreed with that assessment, remarking, "Despite the horrors it depicts, *On Black Sisters Street* is also boiling with a sly, generous humor. Unigwe is as adept at conveying the cacophony of a Nigerian bus as she is at suggesting the larger historical events that propel her characters. *On Black Sisters Street* marks the arrival of a latter-day Thackeray, an Afro-Belgian writer who probes with passion, grace and comic verve the underbelly of our globalized new world economy." In 2012 Unigwe received the Nigeria Prize for Literature for *On Black Sisters Street*.

NIGHT DANCER

Unigwe's next novel, *Nachtdanser* (2011), which was published in English as *Night Dancer* in 2012, explores the relationship between a mother and daughter across decades, in a plot that moves back and forth through time. As the novel opens, Mma has just buried her mother, Ezi, for whom she feels little love. Throughout her life her mother, an educated woman, had kept her apart from the rest of her family, including her father, for reasons Mma did not know. After unearthing a box of letters her mother left for her, Mma learns the truth about why she was raised in isolation. As the plot drifts back to the 1970s, the reader learns that Ezi and her husband had tried to have children, to no avail. After a time, the family began to turn against her, because traditional Nigerian Igbo culture specified that it was a wife's duty to produce a male heir. Ezi finally became pregnant, but her daughter, Mma, was not as highly regarded as the son Ezi's husband conceived through an affair with his teenage maid, Rapu. Ezi was expected to accept Rapu as her husband's second wife, but she refused and instead deserted her husband, taking Mma with her. In the process, she was disowned by the entire family, including by her own parents and her younger sister, who was unable to find a husband of her own because her family was tainted by her sister's scandal. A social pariah, Ezi became unable to find work, and Mma, although conceived in marriage, was considered an illegitimate child. Mma's discovery of these events sheds light on her complicated relationship with her mother and calls attention to the role of women in Nigerian society.

Upon its publication in English, *Night Dancer* was met with considerable praise. A reviewer for *New Internationalist* (Nov. 2012) wrote, "This is a story of discovery, of a truth which unfolds for the reader and the protagonist at the same time. . . . Emotions bubble under the surface of this simply told story; the ending is at once cathartic yet strangely frustrating." Bernardine Evaristo, writing for the *Guardian* (3 Aug. 2012), proclaimed, "Chika Unigwe is one of the most probing, thought-provoking writers of the recent renaissance in African fiction. Many of these are female, bringing hitherto submerged stories about African women to the fore. . . . With *Night Dancer*, she continues her project of tackling big issues through superb portrayals of complex female characters, and immersing us in the dramas of their lives." Unigwe's next novel, *De zwarte messias* (The black messiah), was published by the Belgian publisher De Bezige Bij Antwerpen in 2013.

Unigwe and Vandenhoudt have four children. The family lived in Turnhout, Belgium, for many years and also spent time in the United States.

SUGGESTED READING

Eberstadt, Fernanda. "Tales from the Global Sex Trade." *New York Times*. New York Times, 29 Apr. 2011. Web. 11 Apr. 2014.

Evaristo, Bernardine. "*Night Dancer* by Chika Unigwe—Review." *Guardian*. Guardian, 3 Aug. 2012. Web. 11 Apr. 2014.

"*Night Dancer* by Chika Unigwe." *New Internationalist* Nov. 2012: 36. Print.

"*On Black Sisters Street*." *Publishers Weekly*. Publishers Weekly, 10 Jan. 2011. Web. 11 Apr. 2014.

Unigwe, Chika. "Losing My Voice." *Aeon*. Aeon Media, 14 Mar. 2013. Web. 11 Apr. 2014.

SELECTED WORKS

A Rainbow for Dinner, 2002; *Ije at School*, 2005; *The Phoenix*, 2007; *On Black Sisters Street*, 2009; *Night Dancer*, 2012

—*Christopher Mari*

Lucy Walker

Born: ca. 1970
Occupation: Filmmaker

The British filmmaker Lucy Walker has "found a niche directing documentaries that feel like the film equivalent of extreme sports," David Gritten wrote for the *Telegraph* (7 Feb. 2011). Widely regarded as one of Britain's leading documentarians, Walker is known for making highly stylized, cinema verité documentaries that deftly explore inaccessible subjects and places. "I like to take people into places they can't access on their own," she explained to Gritten. "If you can get inside worlds that are closed to people, then it's an opportunity to give audiences a window they can't get somewhere else."

A graduate of New College, Oxford, and the Tisch School of the Arts at New York University (NYU), Walker began her career in the late 1990s as a television director before branching out to the nonfiction realm in 2002 with her first feature-length documentary, *Devil's Playground*, about Amish teenagers. Walker has directed several subsequent feature-length documentaries—*Blindsight* (2006), *Waste Land* (2010), *Countdown to Zero* (2010), and *The Crash Reel* (2013)—as well as a handful of short films, including *The Tsunami and the Cherry Blossom* (2011) and *The Lion's Mouth Opens* (2014). Walker received Academy Award nominations for *Waste Land* and *The Tsunami and the Cherry Blossom* and has won more than eighty film awards, making her one of the most recognized female filmmakers in the film industry. "In a world packed with excellent documentaries," Anne Thompson wrote for *Indiewire* (11 Nov. 2013), "Walker's tend to rise to the top."

EARLY LIFE AND EDUCATION

Lucy Walker was born in London, England, where she also grew up. Her late father, Norman, held executive roles at several British advertising agencies before becoming the CEO and president of K'Nex, a construction toy company based in Hatfield, Pennsylvania. She has three sisters, all of whom have launched successful careers, two as teachers and the other as a lawyer. Walker was born blind in one eye, which sparked an early fascination with film and other visual media, such as photography and painting. She told Liz Hoggard for the London *Evening Standard* (10 Feb. 2011), "Everything visual became so precious and intriguing to me that I saw things with different eyes." Her favorite films as a child included two Disney animated features: *The Jungle Book* (1967) and *The Aristocats* (1970), both of which were directed by famed Disney animator Wolfgang Reitherman.

A precocious, inquisitive, and overachieving adolescent, Walker was, by all accounts, a

Wirelmage

standout student. After graduating from the prestigious Westminster School in London, she studied English literature at New College, one of the oldest and best-known constituent colleges of the University of Oxford. While there she began directing stage plays, one of which was an acclaimed outdoor musical production of *The Jungle Book*. While videotaping a performance, Walker "realized what motion pictures were capable of," she said in an interview with *Indiewire* (7 Mar. 2008). Still, she gave little thought to filmmaking as a realistic career option.

MAKINGS OF A FILMMAKER

In 1992, after graduating from New College with first-class honors, she won a prestigious Fulbright scholarship to pursue graduate film studies at NYU's Tisch School of the Arts. However, her arrival at Tisch was humbling: "I had never made a film before, I hadn't even seen a film camera, and I discovered that everyone else in my class had made several films in order to get in," Walker recalled to Kelly Leow for *MovieMaker* magazine (12 Dec. 2013). Undaunted, she immersed herself in all aspects of the filmmaking process, experimenting with anything that piqued her interest without trepidation.

While at Tisch, Walker won a contest to direct a music video for the Canadian alternative-country band Cowboy Junkies. She has cited two of her teachers, legendary American filmmaker Barbara Kopple—who won Academy Awards for her documentaries *Harlan County, USA* (1976) and *American Dream* (1990)—and acclaimed Latvian director Boris Frumin, as mentors. Walker has said that Kopple taught her everything she knows about documentaries, and Frumin, her fiction-directing teacher, encouraged her to make "strange, soulful, lyrical, never-before-seen films," as she explained in an interview for *Film Independent* (16 June 2013).

Walker supported herself in New York by working as a DJ and was a member of the experimental electronic music ensemble Byzar. The ensemble is credited with inventing a genre known as illbient, which combines elements of ambient music and hip-hop. While performing at clubs in and around New York, she met and befriended the Grammy Award–winning American DJ and musician Moby, who later contributed music to several of her documentaries.

BLUE'S CLUES AND DEVIL'S PLAYGROUND

After earning an MFA degree in film from Tisch in 1998, Walker landed a job directing episodes of *Blue's Clues*, a highly acclaimed children's show that aired on the cable-television network Nickelodeon. She served as a director for the show for the following three years, receiving Daytime Emmy Award nominations in 2001 and 2002 for outstanding directing. "It was an ideal show to work on," she recalled to Robert Goldrich for *Shoot* (28 Mar. 2011), "a great first break for me, mixing live action and animation, learning about blue screen and other effects, working on a tight television schedule—and most importantly being involved in a show that was a positive learning experience for children."

Walker's yearning to explore new terrain led her to leave what she described to Goldrich as "a comfortable gig" at *Blue Clues* to make long-form documentary films. For her first such venture, *Devil's Playground*, she spent three years trying painstakingly to gain access to and trust within an Old Order Amish community in La-Grange County, Indiana. Shot with a skeleton crew consisting of only Walker and cinematographer Daniel Kern, the seventy-seven-minute film follows a group of Amish teenagers as they experience a pivotal rite of passage known as *rumspringa* (meaning "running around" in Pennsylvania Dutch), which gives them the freedom to enjoy the lures of the outside world before deciding whether they want to return to their families and community. The film focuses particularly on an eighteen-year-old named Faron Yoder, an Amish minister's son who turns to selling drugs in order to support a crippling addiction to crystal methamphetamine.

Premiering in January 2002 at the Sundance Film Festival, *Devil's Playground* was well received by critics. Despite little promotion, the film enjoyed a successful festival run, winning several awards and honors, including the audience award for best film at the 2002 Sarasota International Film Festival and a nomination for best documentary at the 2003 Independent Spirit Awards. It debuted on television in May 2002 and earned Emmy Award nominations for best documentary, best director, and best editing.

BLINDSIGHT

Walker's next long-form documentary, *Blindsight*, centers on six blind Tibetan teenagers who attempt to climb to the top of Lhakpa Ri, a 23,000-foot mountain peak on the north side of Mount Everest in the Himalayas. Producers recruited Walker to direct the privately financed film based on her ability to persuade teenagers to open up in front of the camera, and her own personal experiences with blindness drew her to the project. *Blindsight* tells each of the teenagers' stories and that of their teacher, Sabriye Tenberken, a blind woman from Germany who cofounded Braille Without Borders, the first blind school in Tibet. The film follows them on their dangerous three-week expedition, led by the famous blind American mountaineer Erik Weihenmayer, noted for being the first, and currently only, blind person to summit Everest. While filming the expedition in 2004, Walker suffered myriad injuries, including a broken leg, amebic dysentery, and altitude sickness.

Blindsight premiered at the Toronto International Film Festival in September 2006 and won audience awards at the American Film Institute, Berlin, Ghent, and Palm Springs film festivals. It was also nominated for best documentary at the 2006 British Independent Film Awards and short-listed for the best documentary feature Academy Award. Universally acclaimed by critics, the film "is not only a touching and beautifully shot movie about the exceptional courage and determination of its principal subjects, but also gives a fascinating insight into the contrasting ways in which different cultures deal with the perceived impediments of blindness," Nick Dawson observed for *Filmmaker* magazine (5 Mar. 2008).

WASTE LAND

Walker's fourth feature-length documentary, *Waste Land*, became the biggest hit of her career. Codirected by João Jardim and Karen Harley, the film offers a portrait of the internationally acclaimed Brazilian artist Vik Muniz, whom Walker first met in 2007 while attending several film festivals in England. A longtime fan of Muniz's work, which is characterized by the creative use of found objects and materials, Walker wanted the artist to serve as a catalyst for a "narrative nonfiction story, a beautiful filmic piece, a work of cinema," as she explained to Thompson.

After discovering they shared a mutual interest in the role of garbage in society, Walker and Muniz focused their attention on the *catadores*, or recyclable materials collectors, at Jardim Gramacho, a 321-acre open-air landfill on the outskirts of Rio de Janeiro, Brazil. Subsequently, Walker spent three years filming Muniz as he collaborated with a disparate group of *catadores* on an ambitious social art project that involved creating massive portraits with recyclable materials found at Gramacho, which was the largest landfill in the world before closing in 2012. In addition to highlighting the life and work of Muniz, *Waste Land*, which features original music by Moby, profiles six *catadores*, who defy "every stereotype imaginable about people who sift rubbish for a living," Gritten wrote.

Premiering at the 2010 Sundance Film Festival, *Waste Land* garnered rapturous praise from critics, who dubbed the film "the *Slumdog Millionaire* of documentaries" (referring to the 2008 Academy Award–winning British film directed by Danny Boyle) because of its crowd-pleasing rags-to-riches story. "On paper, a film about pollution, waste-management failures, and the gap between the rich and poor in Brazil sounds painfully worthy," Hoggard commented. "But in Walker's hands, it's a thrilling and uplifting journey." *Waste Land* screened at festivals all over the world and became the first film ever to win the audience awards at both Sundance and Berlin. The film won more than thirty other awards, including the International Documentary Association's best documentary award, and it earned Walker her first career Academy Award nomination for best documentary feature.

COUNTDOWN TO ZERO AND THE TSUNAMI AND THE CHERRY BLOSSOM

Walker's fifth feature-length documentary, *Countdown to Zero*, an exposé about the state of nuclear weapons in the twenty-first century, also premiered at the 2010 Sundance festival. Described by Walker as a "nonfiction horror movie," the film chronicles the history of nuclear weapons, from the development of the first atomic bomb in the 1940s to the resultant nuclear arms race, and it highlights their potentially calamitous effects on humanity in the age of global terrorism. The film features interviews with numerous former world leaders, including Jimmy Carter, Tony Blair, and Mikhail Gorbachev, as well as with a host of CIA experts and physicists, all of whom make a strong case for complete nuclear disarmament. Praised by critics for its unsettling immediacy, *Countdown to Zero* screened as the official selection at the 2010 Cannes Film Festival and was released in theaters in the United States by Magnolia Pictures. It made its television broadcast premiere on the History Channel in 2011.

Walker next made the forty-minute short film *The Tsunami and the Cherry Blossom*, a visual poem that juxtaposes survivor accounts of the 2011 Japanese earthquake and tsunami against the backdrop of the cherry blossom season. Walker originally intended to make a short,

personal film about cherry blossoms and had already set in motion plans to film in Japan in March 2011, when a massive 9.0 earthquake struck off the Pacific coast of the country's Tōhoku region. She initially thought of canceling the trip altogether, but her longtime collaborator, cinematographer Aaron Phillips, ultimately persuaded her to continue the project. "I couldn't help thinking that maybe this was the most important time of all to go to Japan," she explained on her website, "that this cherry blossom season—with its spirit of renewal, and its symbolism of the fragility of life—would be the most important one ever."

The Tsunami and the Cherry Blossom, which features another original soundtrack by Moby, debuted at the Toronto International Film Festival in September 2011. The film received a number of awards and honors, including the short film jury prize in the nonfiction category at Sundance and an Academy Award nomination for best documentary short subject. It premiered on HBO in July 2012.

THE CRASH REEL AND OTHER PROJECTS

Walker's sixth feature-length documentary, *The Crash Reel*, tells the story of American snowboarder Kevin Pearce, whose promising career ended abruptly after he suffered a traumatic brain injury in the run-up to the 2010 Winter Olympics in Vancouver, Canada. Featuring a mixture of archival material from more than two hundred sources—from official snowboarding broadcasts to amateur home video footage and personal interviews—the film offers a visual time line of events leading up to Pearce's near-fatal injury and then chronicles his long road to recovery under the watchful eye of his doctors and close-knit Vermont family. It also delves into larger questions about traumatic brain injuries and safety in extreme sports.

The Crash Reel premiered as the opening-night film at Sundance in January 2013. It also premiered at that month's Winter X Games in Aspen, Colorado, becoming the first film to play as a featured part of the event. It screened at other top festivals around the world and received numerous awards, including the audience award at the 2013 South by Southwest Film Festival. It also brought Walker her first Directors Guild of America Award nomination for outstanding directorial achievement in documentaries. In a review for *NPR* (4 July 2013), Ian Buckwalter wrote, "Few documentaries manage to show character arcs as full as the one Walker captures here."

In 2013, Walker released a six-minute short, *David Hockney IN THE NOW*, which honors the famed British artist and painter. Her film *The Lion's Mouth Opens* screened at Sundance in 2014. Described by the *Los Angeles Times* as "an espresso shot to the heart," the fifteen-minute short follows the Scottish-born writer-director Marianna Palka as she undergoes tests for the gene that causes Huntington's disease, an incurable neurodegenerative disorder that killed her father.

In addition to her short- and long-form documentaries, Walker has made commercials and branded content via Supply and Demand Integrated and Pulse Films. She holds membership in the Academy of Motion Picture Arts and Sciences, the Academy of Television Arts and Sciences, the British Academy of Film and Television Arts, the International Documentary Association, the Directors Guild, and the Writers Guild.

Walker lives in Venice Beach, California.

SUGGESTED READING

Dawson, Nick. "Lucy Walker, Blindsight." *Filmmaker*. Filmmaker Magazine, 5 Mar. 2008. Web. 31 Mar. 2014.

Gritten, David. "Lucy Walker on Her New Documentary, Waste Land." *Telegraph*. Telegraph Media Group, 7 Feb. 2011. Web. 31 Mar. 2014.

Hoggard, Liz. "Waste Land Is the Slumdog Millionaire of Documentaries." *Evening Standard* [London]. Evening Standard, 10 Feb. 2011. Web. 31 Mar. 2014.

Walker, Lucy. "'Crash Reel' Documentarian Lucy Walker Knows Where She's Going." Interview by Anne Thompson. *Indiewire*. SnagFilms, 11 Nov. 2013. Web. 31 Mar. 2014.

SELECTED WORKS

Devil's Playground, 2002; *Blindsight*, 2006; *Waste Land*, 2010; *Countdown to Zero*, 2010; *The Tsunami and the Cherry Blossom*, 2011; *The Crash Reel*, 2013; *The Lion's Mouth Opens*, 2014

—*Chris Cullen*

Wang Shu

Born: November 4, 1963
Occupation: Architect

In 2012, Wang Shu became the first Chinese architect to win the Pritzker Architecture Prize, the most prestigious prize in architecture. Since 1997, he and his wife, architect Lu Wenyu, have worked out of Amateur Architecture, a small design studio in the eastern city of Hangzhou, China. Wang has completed about fifty projects, including many museums, academic campuses, public spaces, and a handful of residences. He is known for designing modern structures that embrace Chinese history and traditions through embedded references in design and materials.

© Alexander F. Yuan/AP/Corbis

Deeply influenced by the years he spent working as an artisan, Wang endeavors to use recycled, local, and sustainable materials and employ local, skilled artisans.

The Pritzker website's 2012 jury citation for Wang notes that his work "opens new horizons while at the same time resonates with place and memory. His buildings have the unique ability to evoke the past, without making direct references to history." Wang's constructions stand in stark contrast to the rapid urbanization taking place in China, which has led to the destruction of entire historic villages. Wang has been outspoken in his criticism of the "professionalized, soulless architecture, as practiced today" in China, as he told Robin Pogrebin for the *New York Times* (28 Feb. 2012). Wang—who has described himself a part-time architect—also serves as dean of the architecture school at Hangzhou's Academy of Art. He was named by *TIME* magazine as one of the one hundred most influential people of 2013.

EARLY LIFE AND EDUCATION

Wang Shu was born on November 4, 1963, in Urumqi, the capital of the Xinjiang region of northwest China. Wang's father was a musician and amateur carpenter, and his mother was a teacher and a school librarian. Wang spent much of his youth at his grandmother's large house in Beijing, which sat on a traditional narrow brick alley called a *hutong*, the walls of which he has recalled drawing on as a young boy. Though he grew up during some of the most tumultuous years of the Cultural Revolution—the period of China's history when Communist Party Chairman Mao Zedong was aggressively ridding the country of outside cultural and political influences—Wang has fondly recalled his own limited experience of the Cultural Revolution as a boy. Wang told Edwin Heathcote for *Financial Times* (29 Mar. 2013), "For a child it was wonderful. School was stopped and, apart from having to spend two hours each day reading the works of Chairman Mao, we could play all day and read books. I read all the classics, Chinese and western, Balzac, Zola Dickens." Wang's mother accompanied him to libraries and encouraged his reading, while he taught himself to draw and paint.

As a student, Wang was initially attracted to art and literature, but his parents encouraged him to pursue science and engineering in college. As a compromise, he studied architecture at Nanjing University of Technology, located in the eastern province of Jiansu. He received an undergraduate degree in 1985 and a master's degree in 1988. During that time, Wang expanded his understanding of art history outside of China and Europe, to Africa, India, and the United States. He also became acquainted for the first time with contemporary art, philosophy, and pop culture. In 2000, he received a PhD from the School of Architecture of Tongji University in Shanghai.

EARLY CAREER

Wang's first job after earning his master's degree was as a researcher at Zhejiang Academy of Fine Arts, a top-ranked arts university located in the eastern city of Hangzhou, long regarded as one of China's most beautiful places. In that job, he was tasked with conducting research in preparation for the renovation of some of the school's oldest buildings. Wang completed his own first architectural project in 1990, a 3,600-square-foot youth center for the town of Haining, located in Zhejiang Province.

For much of the next decade, however, Wang received no commissions. Supported by the work of his wife, also an architect, Wang spent those years working on construction sites. As the head of a crew of craftsmen, he gained a hands-on understanding of construction materials and methods, as well as a respect and affection for the personal contributions that are made by artisans to a building. "We worked on the site from 8:00 in the morning [until] midnight every day," Wang told Heathcote, "and I could become familiar with every level of construction, with every part of the process."

After receiving his PhD in 2000, Wang established the architecture department at Hangzhou's Academy of Art. There he designed a unique program requiring students to gain hands-on experience with all parts of the building process. Students learn carpentry, bricklaying, and general construction work—just as Wang had done earlier in his career. Wang also became the architecture school's dean, a position he continues to hold. The competitive program admits only 120 students per year from an applicant pool of more than 10,000.

FOUNDING AMATEUR ARCHITECTURE STUDIO

Meanwhile, in 1997, Wang and his wife founded their own studio based in Hangzhou, named Amateur Architecture Studio. The name was chosen to convey Wang's support for the amateur, artisanal spirit of untrained architects and artists. Wang also intended the name—and the studio itself—as a challenge to the rapid construction being completed by most professional architecture firms in China. "'Amateur' has many different levels of meaning," he told Heathcote. "First there is anger at the professional, at what they are doing. . . . The architects and urban planners who are rebuilding China have no understanding of tradition, no understanding of life. Their buildings are abstract, pure—amateur work is more rough and . . . dirty."

Wang begins his creative process by immersing himself in the site. He spends an enormous amount of time researching its history, culture, and geography. To clear his mind, he begins each morning by practicing calligraphy, and he does all of his designing by hand. Wang has said that both he and his wife are essential parts of his design firm but that he handles more of the design and she mostly works on the design's implementation. During construction, Wang often leaves room for his skilled laborers and craftspeople to improvise as they are building.

The first project that garnered Wang and his studio significant attention was the Wenzheng College library at Suzhou University. Because the project's site is located between a mountain range and lake, Wang adhered to feng shui principles, which dictate that buildings sitting between those two landforms should not challenge the importance of either. As a result, Wang designed the library as a low cluster of cube-shaped buildings, partially surrounded by water. One of the three floors of the main library sits partially underground. Completed in 2000, the library was widely praised. In 2004, it won China's Architecture Arts Award.

CHINA ACADEMY OF ART, XIANGSHAN CAMPUS

One of Wang's next major projects was the China Academy of Art's campus in Xiangshan, located on the outskirts of Hangzhou and home to the academy's School of Design, School of Architecture, Public Art Institute, and Media and Animation Institute. In creating Phase I of the project—ten buildings as well as two bridges and an athletic field, all on a 67,000–square meter campus—Wang drew inspiration from the shape of the Chinese character that means "enclose" as well as from traditional Chinese courtyard homes. Indeed, the U-shaped gardens and courtyards recall traditional Chinese dwellings, and many of the enclosed spaces echo that character's shape. According to *Chinese-Architects. com* (n.d.), the entire design is meant to convey a sense of freedom and improvisation. The buildings, completed in 2004, also reference the area's history and culture in its use of local materials. The campus's base was made by craftspeople who employed traditional, local methods used in tea field construction. Perhaps most strikingly, the roofs were constructed with more than two million pieces of tile salvaged from recently demolished traditional houses.

Phase II of Wang's work at the China Academy of Art's Xiangshan campus, completed in 2007, shares some traits with Phase I, such as the wooden shutters, winding ramps, and gray brick walls, but its overall aesthetic is not similar. It consists of white concrete box buildings that appear to be stacked on one another, with varying rectangle-shaped windows asymmetrically arranged. Like many of Wang's buildings, the campus is a stark contrast to the uniformity of mainstream contemporary Chinese architecture. "Unlike the rigidly ordered superblocks of Chinese mega cities, expanding in endless grids of wide, noisy boulevards, Wang's buildings . . . cling to a slope in a closely spaced jumble," James Russell wrote for *Bloomberg* (13 June 2012). "I want the campus to feel as if it is more than one person's vision," Wang told Russell.

MAJOR PROJECTS IN NINGBO
Wang has completed several projects in the port city of Ningbo, one of the oldest cities in China. The first of those projects was the Ningbo Contemporary Art Museum, located at the site of a former harbor. Wang had initially intended to preserve the old structure, but after learning that it did not meet construction standards, he decided to demolish it, leaving only its beacon tower. However, he took care to incorporate references to the original structure into the new one. For instance, as is noted on *Chinese-Architects.com*, the relationship between the old port and the ships that would dock there is echoed in the building's high platform, where visitors enter. Among other nods to the historic port, its role as a place for pilgrims to set off on journeys to Putuoshan (Mount Putuo), a Buddhist holy land, is reflected in a series of Buddha figures along the river.

Wang won an acknowledgement prize from the Holcim Awards for Sustainable Construction in 2005 for his next project in Ningbo. Called "Five Scattered Houses," the project was begun in 2004 and completed in 2008. Wang's goal was to design simple, beautiful residences using local, inexpensive materials in order to set an example for future development. His five residences are each located in a different area of Ningbo. In addition to being sustainable, the structures also incorporate traditional elements of Chinese design and are considered both modern and comfortable for an average family.

NINGBO HISTORY MUSEUM
In 2004, Wang received a commission to design what many people consider his signature project, the Ningbo History Museum. Wang has said that the design for the museum, which contains artifacts about the arts and humanities of Ningbo's long history, came to him in a dream: he burst from his bed and began drawing the structure. His goal was for the structure itself to communicate what life was like in Ningbo's past. Local officials initially opposed Wang's design because it did not use modern materials, such as glass and steel. Wang instead used recycled building materials from the area, including pieces of rubble from farmers' homes that had been destroyed to make room for the project.

The finished building is an imposing, severe structure that from the outside looks mountainous. Its exterior walls appear layered like the earth, and it is composed of Wang's signature rectangular windows. Jane Perlez wrote for the *International Herald Tribune* (12 Aug. 2012), "The museum looks bulky from a distance; up close the recycled ceramic tiles and vintage bricks in hues of gray, orange and blue lend a feeling of earthiness."

HIGH-RISE BUILDINGS AND VERTICAL COURTYARDS
In writings and speeches, Wang has explicitly criticized China's penchant for destroying community-focused designs of the past and replacing them with sterile, isolating structures. In a spring 2013 lecture delivered at a public forum in Singapore, Wang blasted the tendency of Asian cities to construct residential buildings that emulate European and American architecture, "whose building designs are based on the concepts of jails," he said, as quoted by the Singapore *Straits Times* (7 May 2013). Referring to high-rise apartments, Wang said, "The isolated individuals closed up in their own apartments are all like prisoners—they come out to do some work, have some food and entertainment and then go back to their jails. And they're happy with it." Given his aversion to high-rise buildings, it is not surprising that he has largely avoided constructing one.

The architect did, however, make one exception when he accepted a commission to create residential high-rise buildings in Hangzhou. He decided to do so because the developer was interested in breaking conventions. Wang came up with the idea to try to create buildings that incorporate the traditional Chinese arrangement of homes around a central courtyard. The resulting design is essentially a stack of courtyards that the residents can customize in ways not possible in a traditional high-rise. "Usually, in a high-rise building people can't tell which window is their own," Wang told Rowan Moore for the *Guardian* (15 Dec. 2012). "Here you can plant a pine tree and say that the flat with a pine tree is mine." The six completed eight-story high-rises of the Vertical Courtyard Apartments—designed from 2001 to 2003 and built from 2004 to 2006—have room for eight hundred residents. The apartments were bought by families rather than investors, which Wang considers a positive outcome. The Vertical Courtyard design was nominated for the 2008 German-based International Highrise Award.

ZHONGSHAN ROAD AND OTHER PROJECTS
Over the years, Amateur Architecture has continued to add to its idiosyncratic list of projects—all of them in China. In 2009 Wang oversaw the completion of the conservation and renovation project of Zhongshan Road, a historic imperial road in Hangzhou. A variety of architects were each assigned a section of the road; Wang himself designed one of the buildings, the Exhibition Hall of the Imperial Street of the Southern Song Dynasty. For this project, he made use of "a chunky wooden roof loosely based on ancient bridges, and some curious zoomorphic towers in rough concrete," according to Moore.

In 2010, as part of that year's Shanghai Expo, Wang completed the Ningbo Tengtou Pavilion, a 1,500–square meter ecofriendly event space that resembles a folk house found in the village of Tengtou, one of China's greenest communities. It makes use of devices powered by water, wind, and solar panels, as well as open walls and roof gardens. Also in 2010, Wang won praise for an installation for the 2010 Venice Architecture Biennale called *Decay of a Dome*, which received special mention. Inspired by Western-style domes but created with traditional Chinese methods, the structure is described in the Pritzker Prize biography of Wang as a "light, mobile and utterly simple structure" that "can be speedily constructed or returned to nothingness."

Wang has exhibited his work at numerous major international shows, among them the 2002 Shanghai Biennale at the Shanghai Art Museum, the 2003 "Alors, la Chine?" exhibit at the Centre Pompidou in Paris, the 2007 Shenzhen and Hong Kong Bi-City Biennale of Urbanism/Architecture, and a solo exhibition at the BOZAR Centre for Fine Arts in Brussels called "Architecture as Resistance."

In 2010, Wang and his wife were awarded the Schelling Architecture Prize, which honors individuals who have responsibly advanced architecture's development with significant designs and who have contributed to architectural history and theory. The following year, Wang became the first Chinese Kenzo Tange Visiting Professor at the Harvard Graduate School of Design.

2012 PRITZKER PRIZE
Wang's February 2012 selection as the winner for the 2012 Pritzker Architecture Prize was a surprise to many. The award, which is accompanied by a $100,000 prize, recognizes a living architect whose work shows talent and vision and who has also "produced consistent and significant contributions to humanity and the built environment through the art of architecture," according to the prize's website. While few people questioned Wang's talent, he did not seem to fit the mold of the "starchitects" who had won the award in the past. Wang has not sought out high-profile projects around the world. His small firm has only undertaken about fifty projects, and they are all in China.

Many people considered Wang's selection, at least in part, a political statement against the architecture that has accompanied China's rapid urbanization. The Pritzker jury citation states: "The question of the proper relation of present to past is particularly timely, for the recent process of urbanization in China invites debate as to whether architecture should be anchored in tradition or should look only toward the future. As with any great architecture, Wang Shu's work is able to transcend that debate, producing an architecture that is timeless, deeply rooted in its context and yet universal."

The award was presented to Wang in May 2012; Li Keqiang, then China's vice premier, attended the ceremony and congratulated Wang. When accepting the award, Wang criticized the architecture establishment of China. As quoted by Perlez, Wang asked whether China needed to "resort to gigantic symbolic and iconic structures" and whether there were "smarter ways to address environmental and ecological challenges."

Wang was pleased with the award but expressed his view that his wife should have also received it, because his studio is a partnership and none of the buildings would have been designed without her.

PERSONAL LIFE
Wang and his wife, Lu Wenyu, met in architecture class at the Nanjing Institute of Technology. Perlez describes them as "an inseparable couple, "with an around-the-clock working partnership that seems easy, sometimes jokey and truly

collaborative." Wang, who does not use e-mail or drive, lives quietly in Hangzhou near the Amateur Architecture studio with his wife and son. He and his wife spend time with their friends, many of whom are poets and musicians.

SUGGESTED READING

Heathcote, Edwin. "Building Society: Wang Shu." *Financial Times*. Financial Times, 29 Mar. 2013. Web. 16 Dec. 2013.

Perlez, Jane. "An Architect's Vision: Bare Elegance in China." *International Herald Tribune* 12 Aug. 2012 New York ed.: AR1. Print.

Pogrebin, Robin. "For First Time, Architect in China Wins Field's Top Prize." *New York Times* 28 Feb. 2012: C1. Print.

Russell, James S. "Pritzker-Winning Architect Bucks China's Megacity Trend." *Bloomberg*. Bloomberg, 13 June 2013. Web. 16 Dec. 2013.

Volner, Ian. "Made on the Mainland." *Wall Street Journal*. Dow Jones, 25 Oct. 2012. Web. 16 Dec. 2013.

—*Margaret Roush Mead*

WireImage

Jetsun Pema Wangchuck

Born: June 4, 1990
Occupation: Queen Consort of Bhutan

Jetsun Pema Wangchuck is the queen of Bhutan, a small country located on the eastern end of the Himalayas, bordered by China and India. In contrast to its heavily populated neighbors, Bhutan numbers only around 730,000 citizens. Yet Pema—an airline pilot's daughter who married the King of Bhutan, Jigme Khesar Namgyel Wangchuck, in a celebration that lasted for three days in October 2011—is known around the world for her grace and charm. Gardiner Harris for the *New York Times* (14 Oct. 2013) also reports that she is a formidable basketball player. She has played since she was nine years old, and as queen, she plays every day with a group of young women. Her statistics are impressive, only partially aided by a Bhutanese custom that forbids commoners from touching royals without invitation. She invites the girls to check her, Harris reported, but they are often too afraid. Regardless, Pema relishes her time on the court. "For me now, basketball is a great way of meeting girls and interacting with them in an informal way," she told Harris.

Wangchuck, who assumed the throne from his father in 2006, quickly cast himself as a king of the people. Handsome and young, nearby Thailand dubbed him "Prince Charming," according to Hillary Brenhouse for *Time* magazine (23 May 2011). Wangchuck and Pema, whose own family, though commoners, has always enjoyed connections to the royal family, were both educated in London, she at Regents College and he, ten years her senior, at Oxford. Various Western publications have called the couple the "Will and Kate" of Bhutan, referring to the United Kingdom's Prince William and his wife Catherine, Duchess of Cambridge. Indeed, like Will and Kate, Wangchuck and Pema represent an encroaching modernity amid staid traditions: they are a well-educated, happily married twosome. Wangchuck's love of his wife and praise for her intellect has been breathlessly noted in celebrity magazines across Asia and Europe. "He really loves her," a sixteen-year-old guest at the couple's thirty-thousand-spectator wedding celebration told a journalist for Britain's *Hello* magazine (17 Oct. 2011). "Wherever he goes, he holds her hand," he said—a reminder that Wangchuck's father often walked several steps in front of his own four wives, all sisters. "Now young people are starting to copy."

But Pema and Wangchuck's union is significant in other ways, too. Their egalitarian marriage makes them the dual face of Bhutan, a nascent democracy noted for its innovative "gross national happiness index," which measures the overall contentment of its citizens rather than their material wealth. As king, Wangchuck has embraced the Bhutanese practice of *kidu*, which Simon Denyer for the *Washington Post* (12 Oct.

2011) wrote roughly translates to "his majesty's welfare." The concept is best described as an initiative to put Bhutanese people first; under *kidu*, the king may grant government land to poor and homeless citizens, and citizens may approach the king to air their grievances. Wangchuck—and now also Pema, whom he routinely has by his side—enjoys mixing with his subjects, and has said his goal is to meet each of them. It is an attempt to bridge generations of absolute rule and a violent recent history with the future promise of democracy. "This is not a photocopy of the Western form of democracy; neither is it a celebration of the past," Dorji Wangchuck, the king's press secretary, told Denyer of the changes in Bhutan. "But it is a genuine attempt to see how Western democratic practices can be merged with traditional forms of governance, where the king and the government are seen to be more caring and at the service of the people."

Wangchuck was initially concerned that the Bhutanese people would be slow to accept his commoner bride, but within months of their engagement, she became a nationally beloved figure. The country declared October 13–15 a national holiday in honor of the wedding. Citizens were euphoric regarding the union, Karma Tshiteem, the head of the Gross National Happiness Commission, told a journalist for *Hello* (13 Oct. 2011). "You can be sure that our happiness is increasing," he said.

EARLY LIFE AND EDUCATION
Pema was born on June 4, 1990, in Thimphu, Bhutan's capital city. Though she is technically a commoner (not from a noble background), her family has close ties to the Bhutan monarchy. Her father, Dhondup Gyaltshen, is an airline pilot whose grandfather was the governor of the eastern province of Tashigang. Her mother is Aum Sonam Chuki, whose father was a halfbrother of the two wives of Bhutan's second king (the current king's great-grandfather). Pema is the second oldest of five children. She has an older sister named Yeatso Lhamo, as well as two brothers, Thinley Norbu and Jigme Namgyal, and a younger sister, Serchen Doma. She attended Little Dragon Montessori School and Sunshine School as a child, and later, Changangkha Lower Secondary School and Lungtenzampa Middle Secondary School in Thimphu, and St. Joseph's Convent school in Kalimpong, West Bengal, India.

Pema began attending high school at Lawrence School, Sanawar, in Himachal Pradesh, India, in 2006. She studied English, history, geography, and economics, and developed a love for painting and art. She was active outside of her studies as well, her teacher and house mistress Neelam Tahlan recalled to Anand Bodh for the *Times of India* (22 May 2011). "She was a good athlete and basketball player," Tahlan said of Pema, who was captain of the school's team. Tahlan also recalled a cultural event in which Pema had to learn a Punjabi folk dance. "When she had to learn the bhangra she turned out to be good at it," she said. Pema graduated in 2008.

Pema speaks Dzongkha, the national language of Bhutan, but she is also fluent in English and Hindi. After graduating high school, she enrolled at Regent's College in London, where she majored in international relations with a double minor in psychology and art history. She was a student there when Wangchuck announced the couple's engagement. Her college education is currently on hold.

WANGCHUCK DYNASTY
Jigme Khesar Namgyel Wangchuk is the oldest son of Jigme Singye Wangchuk, the fourth Druk Gyalpo, or "Dragon King," of Bhutan. The elder Wangchuck, who introduced the concept of gross national happiness (GNH) in 1971, abdicated the throne to his son in 2006 (although his coronation was delayed until 2008). The royal shift marked Bhutan's transition from an absolute monarchy to a constitutional monarchy in 2008, when a new constitution took effect. Bhutan's first democratic elections were held in 2008; the current and fifth Dragon King rules as a constitutional monarch. The elder Wangchuck was also a beloved king, but he was far more reserved than his son. He rarely interacted with the Bhutanese people, which might explain the lengths to which the naturally gregarious younger Wangchuck goes to appear friendly and approachable. "The fourth king was another world, another time," Francoise Pommaret, an author and expert on Bhutan told Denyer, "but this is another generation, another country."

Bhutan's focus on its citizens' spiritual, physical, and environmental well-being continues under the current government. Once considered a novelty, Bhutan's GNH index is gaining popularity in the wake of the global financial crisis of 2007–8 and the ongoing threat of climate change. Bhutan, Annie Kelly wrote for the London *Guardian* (1 Dec. 2012), has long put conservation and sustainability at the center of its domestic policy. Additionally, "Bhutan has doubled life expectancy, enrolled almost 100% of its children in primary school and overhauled its infrastructure" over just two decades, Kelly wrote. The GNH policies even extend to education, where students learn about agriculture and environmental protection in addition to their regular subjects. To aid the students' well being, Bhutan schools also offer daily meditation sessions. "People always ask how can you possibly have a nation of happy people? But this is missing the point," Thakur Singh Powdyel, Bhutan's minister of education, told Kelly. "GNH is an aspiration, a set of guiding principles through which we are navigating our path towards a sustainable and equitable society. We believe the world needs to do the same before it is too late."

The GNH policies address very real problems in Bhutan, where most citizens are poor farmers, and many lack electricity. (Bhutan is in the midst of a period of rapid modernization; television and the Internet were only introduced into the country in 1999.) In the early 1990s, the Bhutanese government expelled tens of thousands of Bhutanese who were ethnic Nepalis. The refugees amounted to nearly one-sixth of the country's population. Wangchuck's father carried out this policy of ethnic cleansing—though the Bhutanese government denies this characterization—for the stated purpose of preserving Bhutan's cultural heritage. The dominant ethnic group in Bhutan descend from Tibetan migrants to the region; they adhere to a school of lamaistic Tibetan Buddhism. As of 2007, there were still over 100,000 Bhutanese refugees living in refugee camps maintained by the United Nations at the border of Nepal. Around half of those have since, through diplomatic arrangements initiated by Nepal, immigrated to Western countries, as Bhutan has refused to repatriate them. Writing for the *Nation* (7 Mar. 2012), Kai Bird suggests that Wangchuck's father "escaped any real censure from the international community" by carrying out his policies at a time when ethnic cleansing was happening on a much larger scale in Rwanda and Bosnia. Still, Bhutan has yet to reckon with this part of its history. "Bhutan is not a pure Shangri-La," said Bhutanese educator Karma Pedey, as reported by Andrew C. Revkin for the *New York Times* (4 Oct. 2005), "so idyllic and away from all those flaws and foibles."

ENGAGEMENT AND ROYAL WEDDING

The reigning Wangchuck's personal history is a combination of Eastern and Western influences: he was largely educated abroad. He played varsity basketball at Wheaton College in Massachusetts—he and Pema are big NBA fans—and graduated from Oxford University in England. The two are longtime sweethearts. One widely told version of their story has them meeting at a family gathering when Pema was seven and Wangchuck was seventeen. Whenever and wherever they met, it was "love at first sight," Wangchuck told a group of Bhutanese students as quoted by a journalist for the *Washington Post* (14 Oct. 2011). The two bonded over their love of basketball, art, and photography. They had already been living together for eight months when Wangchuck announced their engagement to Bhutan's parliament in May 2011. Before revealing Pema's name, Wangchuck said that he had found a woman that fit the traditional mold of a queen, in that she was "uniquely beautiful, intelligent and graceful." He added of the twenty-one-year-old Pema, "While she is young, she

is warm and kind in heart and character. These qualities together with the wisdom that will come with age and experience will make her a great servant to the nation."

The royal wedding, which generated the same levels of excitement among the Bhutanese people as the British royal wedding did among Britons earlier the same year, began with a five-hour private ceremony on October 13, 2011. Bhutan declared October 13–15 a national holiday to mark the occasion, and Wangchuck and Pema's engagement photo was plastered on billboards and hung on lampposts across the country. The ceremony itself took place at Punakha Dzong (palace of great happiness), a Buddhist monastery and administrative center in Punakha, Bhutan's ancient capital. It was a traditional Buddhist marriage ceremony that also culminated in Pema's coronation as queen. At one point, Wangchuck, his father, and Je Khenpo, the country's chief abbot, sought blessings from the embalmed body of Shabdrung Namgyel, a seventeenth-century lama, who is kept in a small chamber at the dzong. Pema was not allowed to participate in the sacred ritual.

On October 16, Pema and Wangchuck held a public celebration at Changlimithang Stadium in Thimphu; thirty thousand Bhutanese citizens were in attendance. They played to the crowd—at one point, Wangchuck asked those assembled if he should give Pema a kiss, and the resulting chaste peck on the lips made headlines. The Bhutanese monarchy is hereditary, but Wangchuck and Pema have no immediate plans of starting a family—perhaps because they are so busy. The couple spent their would-be honeymoon working. "We start[ed] working right after the day we were married," Wangchuck told a journalist as quoted by *Hello* (17 Oct. 2011). "And if we travel we'll travel around the country. We like to meet more people."

SUGGESTED READING

"Bhutan Royal Wedding: Who Is the Young Beauty Who Has Captivated the King and a Nation?" *Hello.* Hello, 13 Oct. 2011. Web. 13 Mar. 2014.

Bird, Kai. "The Enigma of Bhutan." *Nation.* Nation, 7 Mar. 2012. Web. 13 Mar. 2014.

Bodh, Anand. "Bhutan King to Wed Sanawar Girl." *Times of India.* Bennett, Coleman, 22 May 2011. Web. 13 Mar. 2014.

Brenhouse, Hillary. "Another Monarch Off the Market: Bhutan's King to Wed a Commoner." *Time.* Time, 23 May 2011. Web. 13 Mar. 2014.

Denyer, Simon. "Bhutan's Modern 'Dragon King' Weds Longtime Girlfriend." *Washington Post.* Washington Post, 13 Oct. 2011. Web. 13 Mar. 2014.

Harris, Gardiner. "In Bhutan, a Bid to Turn Basketball from a Royal Sport to a National One."

New York Times. New York Times, 14 Oct. 2013. Web. 13 Mar. 2014.

Kelly, Annie. "Gross National Happiness in Bhutan: The Big Idea from a Tiny State That Could Change the World." *Guardian.* Guardian News and Media, 1 Dec. 2012. Web. 13 Mar. 2014.

Revkin, Andrew C. "A New Measure of Well-Being from a Happy Little Kingdom." *New York Times.* New York Times, 4 Oct. 2005. Web. 13 Mar. 2014.

—*Molly Hagan*

Jesmyn Ward

Born: April 1, 1977
Occupation: Novelist

© Tina Fineberg/AP/Corbis

Writer Jesmyn Ward has received accolades for her two novels and one memoir detailing life for young African Americans in the modern South. Based on her life and friendships, her books indict American culture's treatment of African Americans as a group.

Her decision to write stems from the early, violent death of her brother Joshua. To her, this traumatic incident seemed rooted in racism: a white man, with a history of drunk driving, killed her brother but was charged only for leaving the scene of the car accident. As she wrote for the *New York Times* (7 Aug. 2013), "There is power in naming racism for what it is, in shining a bright light on it, brighter than any torch or flashlight. A thing as simple as naming it allows us to root it out of the darkness and hushed conversation where it likes to breed like roaches. It makes us acknowledge it. Confront it. And in confronting it, we rob it of some of its dark pull. Its senseless, cold drag. When we speak, we assert our human dignity. That is the worth of a word."

At the 2011 National Book Awards, while accepting the award for fiction for *Salvage the Bones* (2011), Ward explained, "I wanted to write about the experiences of the poor and the black and the rural people of the South, so that the culture that marginalized us for so long would see that our stories were as universal, our lives as fraught and lovely and important, as theirs." Ward was the 2010–11 Grisham Writer in Residence at the University of Mississippi. She is the Stokes Fellow of Creative Writing at University of South Alabama and serves as a columnist for *Oxford American*.

EARLY LIFE AND EDUCATION
Ward was born April 1, 1977, in Alameda, California, though her family relocated to the South when she was five years old. She grew up in Chaneaux, a poor section of DeLisle, Mississippi.

Her father abandoned the family of four children, which included her siblings Nerissa, Charine, and Joshua.

Ward's mother, a maid, supported the family alone. Her employer provided a scholarship for Jesmyn to attend predominately white schools under the auspices of the Episcopal Church. Ward was subjected to racist comments and bullying. As she wrote for *New York Times*, "In the end, I learned that all I could do against something so great and overwhelming, all those histories and years and lives and deaths and threats secreted like seeds, was to open my mouth and speak. I could not let it silence me as it had done when I was younger."

The first in her family to attend college, Ward was admitted to Stanford University, where she earned both her bachelor's degree in English in 1999 and master's degree in media studies and communication in 2000. She considered a career in law, working a holiday retail job in Mississippi before turning to New York.

EARLY WRITING CAREER MARKED BY TRAUMA
While interviewing for publishing jobs in 2000, Ward received news that her brother Joshua had died in an accident when a drunk driver struck his car. Devastated, she questioned what she could do that would give her life meaning. Though she was working in the publishing

industry at Random House, she felt she could create more meaning for her own life and contribute more to society by writing.

Ward was working in Manhattan on September 11, 2001, and saw the planes strike the World Trade Center. She walked four hours back to her home in Brooklyn; she would require therapy before being able to fly again. When she made trips back to the South to look for jobs, she rode on Amtrak or drove.

In 2003, she left New York for graduate school at the University of Michigan, intent on becoming a writer of fiction. While there she earned five Hopwood Awards for her drama, essays, and fiction while completing a master's degree in fine arts in 2005.

On August 29, 2005, Hurricane Katrina made landfall in Louisiana, and Ward's family had to evacuate their home. Experiencing Katrina firsthand effectively silenced Ward in its aftermath; during that time she wrote only a brief essay about the storm. As she wrote on her blog on October 14, 2011, while looking back on that time, driving to work through Katrina-damaged New Orleans "subdued me so thoroughly I didn't write a new sentence for three years. *Fine*, I thought, *I'll shut up now*. I told despair: *You win*. I began looking up the prerequisite courses I'd need to enter a nursing program, began plotting my return to school, my leave from writing." Furthermore, Ward's agent was not having success selling her work, and both her first novel and her stories were rejected by publishers.

STEGNER FELLOWSHIP AND FIRST NOVEL
Ward's writing career began to turn around in 2008, when she began a two-year Stegner fellowship in the creative writing program at Stanford University. The fellowship is highly competitive and Ward was one of nine hundred applicants competing for five spots. That same year, Ward's first novel, *Where the Line Bleeds* (2008), was picked up for publication by Agate, a publisher of African American authors.

Set in Bois Sauvage, a fictional version of DeLisle, *Where the Line Bleeds* tells the story of twin brothers, raised by a grandmother, who choose different paths after graduating from high school. One becomes a drug dealer, while the other finds work on the docks. Their paths inevitably diverge further, and additional conflict is created by the arrival of their parents.

For Ward, writing in a male voice was made simpler because of her closeness to her brother and his friends. As Brad Hooper wrote for *Booklist* (15 Nov. 2008), "Ward credited her keen awareness of male points of view to her friendships with boys when she was growing up; as she revealed, more boys than girls lived in her neighborhood, so understanding young men became natural for her."

Ward gained recognition around the country for *Where the Line Bleeds*. It was an *Essence* magazine book-club selection and the Black Caucus of the National Book Awards selected it for an honor award. In addition, the novel was a finalist for both the 2009 Virginia Commonwealth University Cabell First Novelist Award and for the 2009 Hurston/Wright Legacy Award.

A SECOND NOVEL
Based on Ward's experiences of Hurricane Katrina, *Salvage the Bones* is an award-winning portrayal of life in and around the violence of the storm. In addition to winning the 2011 National Book Award, an honor that surprised many because Ward was not well known at the time, *Salvage the Bones* won an Alex Award for Young Readers from the American Library Association's Young Adult Library Services division. Discussing the difficulties of writing truthfully in her novels, Ward told Kevin Nance for *Poets and Writers* (Sept./Oct. 2013, 44), "I realized I had to be honest. If I'm going to write the truth about this place, I'm going to have to be honest about the realities of it. I can't act like some benevolent god when, you know, no one is spared." She alluded to her desire in her first novel to protect her characters from harm, which desire she had to abandon in *Salvage the Bones*.

The novel has a female narrator: teenage girl Esch, who has just discovered that she is pregnant; Esch is fascinated by the myth of Medea. Ward told Elizabeth Hoover for *Paris Review* (30 Aug. 2011), "It infuriates me that the work of white American writers can be universal and lay claim to classic texts, while black and female authors are ghetto-ized as 'other.' I wanted to align Esch with that classic text, with the universal figure of Medea, the antihero, to claim that tradition as part of my Western literary heritage." The other main characters of *Salvage the Bones* are three male siblings, an alcoholic father, and a pit bull named China. Several of the characters surfaced in her first novel, in particular, Skeetah, China's owner.

MEN WE REAPED
Ward's third book, *Men We Reaped* (2013), is a memoir about five young African American men whom Ward knew, including Joshua, who died violently in the first few years of the twenty-first century. Ward realized that although the deaths seemed unconnected, they were all in some way related to modern society's view of young black men as disposable entities.

Shortly after the fourth death, Ward met her agent, Jennifer Lyons, who suggested the idea of a memoir. Not yet ready for that change in direction, Ward sabotaged her own proposal. However, the idea of writing a long piece of creative nonfiction never completely died, despite the difficulties the topic presented. Writing memoir reopened wounds that had begun to heal—Ward has said that most days while writing the book, she wept at her keyboard.

The book's title comes from words of Harriet Tubman, as quoted by Nance, "We saw the lightning and that was the guns; and then we heard the thunder and that was the big guns; and then we heard the rain falling and that was the blood falling; and when we came to get in the crops, it was dead men that we reaped." Ward chose her book's title even before she began writing the memoir.

Structurally, the work creates a dual tension, because Ward tells two stories with two chronologies. One story—about growing up in a rural Southern community—moves forward in time. She interweaves the stories of the deaths of five young men she knew, working with a reverse chronology, because she was determined to end the book with her brother's death.

Knowing that her memoir is also an indictment of life in the United States for African Americans, Ward defended her work to Nance, "In all kinds of ways, the society is telling us that we're worth less—that we're worth nothing, in fact—and that informs our choices. So, yes, I have a responsibility to tell this story. And yes, I can't apologize for indicting this system. Because if I don't do it, who will?"

THE CHALLENGES OF WRITING MEMOIR

Although Ward's teachers had encouraged her to write creative nonfiction, she deferred doing so to write fiction, not wanting to confront her own or her family's past. After her brother's death, however, she decided it was time to tell some truths. She was acutely sensitive to the difficulties of writing *Men We Reaped*, given that she has returned to live in DeLisle, a close-knit community, and that the stories involve her own family. One of her sisters had been romantically involved with one of the young men who died. Ward chose to tell the truth that her brother had at one time dealt drugs, although at the time of his death, he was working as a car valet. Nevertheless, she committed to telling the full story. As she told Joanna Scutts for *Biographile* (3 Oct. 2013), "My understanding of memoir is that it's based in fact, and my job was to tell the truth, in the hope that in telling the truth there's some result in the end, that I'm working for something."

Ward admits to finding it difficult to tell this story, both because of the personal connection and because she had to create herself as a character in the narrative. Discovering who she was as a person at the time of the events in the memoir and creating a central character from her discoveries was difficult. Yet she chose memoir rather than fiction, as she explained to Rachel Martin for NPR's *Weekend Edition* (15 Sept. 2013) because "I didn't think that it would

be successful as fiction because I didn't think that people would believe it because it was so awful and large and horrendous. And I felt like their stories were powerful enough that I thought that they would be better served in creative nonfiction, when I could just tell the truth about them."

Predictably, the response in her local community has been mixed; some did not appreciating all the truth telling while others were glad that the story had been told. With this work, Ward hopes to shake people from complacency about the war against young African Americans, particularly men. The book came at a cost, however; she admits to many tears, and she plans to return to fiction for her fourth book.

PERSONAL LIFE

Ward acknowledges a sense of responsibility to DeLisle, living in a suburb with her longtime boyfriend and their young daughter. In doing so, she is going against the path that many other Southern writers have chosen, whose goal was to succeed and leave the region. As she wrote in *Oxford American* (11 June 2012), discussing why she had moved in with her mother even though she had been working in northern cities, "Something about the South feels as familiar as family, as true as blood." She also explained to Carolyn Kellogg of the *Los Angeles Times* (22 Apr. 2012), "People ask me about staying here. I think they assume that I wouldn't want to come back to a place like Mississippi, which is so backward and which frustrates me a lot. . . . The responsibility that I feel to tell these stories about the people and the place that I'm from is what pulls me back."

She has taught at University of New Orleans and University of Mississippi in Oxford. She is an assistant professor at the University of South Alabama in Mobile, even though the job requires a two-hour commute each way. She teaches classes in both fiction and nonfiction. She cites William Faulkner, Harlem Renaissance writer Jean Toomer, the Bible, and hip-hop as her inspirations.

SUGGESTED READING

Kellogg, Carolyn. "Jesmyn Ward (*Salvage the Bones*) writes of Mississippi." *Los Angeles Times*. Los Angeles Times. 22 Apr. 2012. Web. 29 Dec. 2013.

Nance, Kevin. "Where the Writing Will Take Her: A Profile of Jesmyn Ward." *Poets & Writers* Sept./Oct. 2013: 43–48. Print.

Ward, Jesmyn. "Against All Good Sense." *Oxford American*. Oxford American, 11 June 2012. Web. 2 Jan. 2014.

Ward, Jesmyn. Interview with Elizabeth Hoover. "Jesmyn Ward on *Salvage the Bones*." *Paris Review*. Paris Review, 30 Aug. 2011. Web. 2 Jan. 2014.

Ward, Jesmyn. Interview by Carolyn Kellogg. "An Interview with National Book Award Winner Jesmyn Ward." *Los Angeles Times.* Los Angeles Times, 19 Apr. 2012. Web. 29 Dec. 2013.

SELECTED WORKS
Where the Line Bleeds, 2008; *Salvage the Bones,* 2011; *Men We Reaped,* 2013; "A Cold Current." *New York Times* 7 Aug. 2013

—*Judy Johnson*

Benjamin Warf
Born: February 26, 1958
Occupation: Neurosurgeon

Courtesy of the John D. & Catherine T. MacArthur Foundation

In 2011 Dr. Benjamin C. Warf, the director of the Neonatal and Congenital Anomaly Neurosurgery Program at Boston Children's Hospital, was asked to testify before a US House subcommittee about the treatment of hydrocephalus in Uganda. In his testimony, he said of the opportunity to speak to the subcommittee, "[This] is the kind of thing that I never thought I would have a chance to do, so I am very honored and humbled." Greater honors were yet to come, however. The following year Warf was awarded a fellowship from the John D. and Catherine T. MacArthur Foundation, the so-called genius grant, for his pioneering work in pediatric medicine.

For more than two decades, Warf has specialized in the treatment of children suffering from hydrocephalus, a condition affecting the brain. Hydrocephalus occurs when excessive cerebrospinal fluid (CSF) accumulates, exerting pressure on the brain and potentially causing severe cognitive and physical impairments or even death. While traditional treatment had been to insert a shunt, which diverts the flow of CSF to another area of the body to be absorbed naturally as part of the circulatory process, shunts often clog or malfunction. In the United States and other parts of the world where medical treatment is just an ambulance ride away, a malfunctioning shunt is a frightening but correctable occurrence; in developing countries with fewer resources, such a problem might prove deadly.

While working in Uganda, Warf developed a minimally invasive surgical technique that reduces the production and retention of CSF. Using the procedure, he saved thousands of lives during his six-year tenure in Africa; since his return to the United States, the procedure has become the standard of care at Boston Children's Hospital. Despite his many accolades and honors, which include a 2007 Humanitarian Award from the American Association of Neurological Surgeons, Warf is reluctant to accept all the credit for his extraordinary capabilities. One patient, commenting on an article by Katherine Lutz for the Boston Children's Hospital blog *Vector* (4 Feb. 2011), wrote that when he thanked the doctor, who is a devout Christian, for saving his life, Warf pointed upward and said, "Direct your praise where it is deserved."

EARLY YEARS AND EDUCATION
Benjamin C. Warf was born on February 26, 1958, and grew up in the Appalachian region of Kentucky. His father, Curtis H. Warf, is a clergyman and the pastor emeritus at the First Baptist Church of Richmond. In addition to teaching public school in the Pikeville, Kentucky, education system, Warf's late mother, Jean Warf (née Akin), taught Sunday school, played the piano during services, and sang in the choir. Warf has one sister, Beth Warf Prassel, who attended the Southern Baptist Theological Seminary and is a writer and teacher.

Warf's own ambitions crystallized early on. "I knew when I was a young person," he recalled to Lutz, "that medical mission work was something I was meant to do." In 1980 he earned his bachelor of science degree from Georgetown College, a Christian school in Kentucky that was founded in 1829 as the first Baptist college west of the Allegheny Mountains. Although it emphasizes a liberal arts curriculum, the school has a strong religious component; its mission statement reads, "Georgetown College pursues and cultivates a knowledge of and commitment to the Christian faith. Faculty, staff and students are called to embrace their role in our community, which is characterized by God's redemptive grace for all people and traditions."

Upon graduating from Georgetown College, Warf entered Harvard Medical School, in

Boston, Massachusetts. After earning his medical degree in 1984, he moved to Ohio and embarked on an internship in general surgery at Case Western Reserve University/University Hospitals of Cleveland. He completed his residency in neurosurgery there in 1991. Warf then returned to his native state, joining the staff of the hospital system affiliated with the University of Kentucky. By 2000 Warf was the chief of pediatric neurosurgery.

HYDROCEPHALUS

Warf's particular area of expertise, hydrocephalus, derives its name from the ancient Greek words *hydro*, meaning water, and *cephalus*, meaning head; although the fluid in question is actually CSF, decades ago patients were said to have "water on the brain." In normal amounts, CSF serves important functions: it protects the brain from blows; it delivers nutrients to the brain and removes waste; and it flows between the cranium and the spine, helping to compensate for changes in intracranial blood volume. Because the body continuously produces CSF, anything that blocks its regular flow or rate of absorption causes excess fluid to accumulate. When this happens, the spaces in the brain known as ventricles widen, exerting potentially harmful pressure.

Hydrocephalus can be either congenital, in which case the child is born exhibiting symptoms, or acquired, in which case it occurs sometime after birth as a result of trauma or infection. Sometimes hydrocephalus is caused by another condition, such as spina bifida or intraventricular hemorrhaging. Because the bones of an infant's skull have not fully closed, excess CSF, no matter its origin, causes the entire head to enlarge, often to an extent alarming to lay observers. If untreated, half of all infants with hydrocephalus will die before the age of two, and the other half will have severe cognitive and physical disabilities.

In the United States hydrocephalus is more common than Down syndrome or deafness. According to the National Institutes of Health, it occurs in one out of every five hundred births, with another six thousand children under the age of two developing it each year.

MOVING TO UGANDA

While practicing in Kentucky and holding the post of chief of pediatric neurosurgery, Warf did not forget his desire to be of service in the developing world. He took periodic trips to Kenya to work with CURE International, a Christian nonprofit organization that operates hospitals in ten countries around the globe and programs in at least twenty more.

In 2000 Warf sold his house and farm in Kentucky and moved his family to Uganda, where more than four thousand new cases of

infant hydrocephalus are reported each year. Once there he became the director of a new pediatric hospital opened by CURE in the eastern Ugandan city of Mbale. "It was the beginning of an extraordinary six-and-a-half-year journey, fraught with violence, racism and difficult living conditions," Lutz wrote. "Warf, at the age of 42, quickly went from being a respected neurosurgeon with many friends to being the strange white man people pointed to and laughed at on the street."

Warf's family often lacked what had been considered necessities of life in the United States, including electricity (they read to each other by candlelight at night), running water, and phone service. Crime against expatriates was common, and one day a close family friend was murdered. The situation was particularly difficult for Warf's daughter, Sarah, who has neurofibromatosis, a syndrome that can cause the growth of benign tumors on nerve tissue, which in turn results in abnormalities in the skin and bones. In certain segments of Ugandan culture, disabilities are viewed superstitiously as curses or punishments from the gods, and disabled children are sometimes hidden away by their embarrassed parents or even, in extreme cases, surreptitiously killed. Because of these attitudes, Sarah was often taunted or subjected to various other cruelties when she was out in public.

ACHIEVEMENTS IN UGANDA

Despite the hardships, Warf set about making the hospital into a leader in the treatment of hydrocephalus across the African continent. As reported by Lutz, at the time of Warf's arrival, "there were no pediatric neurosurgical hospitals and few trained neurosurgeons in all of Africa—where high birth rates, poor perinatal care and very large numbers of children create an extraordinary need for qualified pediatric specialists."

Because of the facility's reliance on donations, much of the medical equipment there was old and in disrepair; Warf has recalled that in the absence of a modern CT scan machine, he used an outdated obstetrical ultrasound unit. Additionally, many of the nurses lacked knowledge considered basic in other parts of the world, such as how to perform CPR. Still, Warf was fulfilling his long-held desire to use his medical training in the service of his religious beliefs.

He learned to make use of whatever supplies and equipment were available. Once, when he received a shipment of low-cost shunts, he undertook a randomized trial and discovered that the devices, at thirty-five dollars each, worked about as well as models used back in the United States that cost more than six hundred dollars.

Shunts, however, posed significant problems. A child in the United States whose shunt fails is in life-threatening danger but probably has ready access to an emergency room; there are no such guarantees in sub-Saharan Africa. Warf realized that circumventing the problem would require devising a treatment that did not involve a shunt at all.

His solution was a revolutionary two-part surgical procedure. The first part, endoscopic third ventriculostomy (ETV), creates a new pathway through which the excess fluid can escape the brain's ventricles; the second part consists of endoscopic choroid plexus cauterization (CPC), which cauterizes a portion of the tissue responsible for the fluid, significantly slowing the rate of production. Warf was the first to ever try the combined procedure, now generally known by its acronym, ETV/CPC.

Warf also trained other doctors, who came from all over Africa, to perform the surgery; this had an immediate impact not only on the health of the patients but on the continent's economy. "Detailed economic analysis estimates a lifetime treatment cost of around $90 per disability-adjusted life year averted, with a minimum benefit-to-cost ratio of 7:1," Warf explained in an article for *Vector* (9 Aug. 2011). "This cost compares very favorably to the few other surgical interventions that have been studied in developing countries."

RETURNING TO THE UNITED STATES

Warf and his family left Uganda in 2006. One of the doctors he had trained, John Mugamba, took over as medical director of the CURE Children's Hospital there. "I worked myself out of a job," Warf quipped to Lutz. CURE now estimates that more than 11,300 surgeries have been performed at the facility since its founding in 2000. In addition, its mobile clinics regularly reach remote areas of the country for follow-up care and to identify other children for treatment. Upon his return home, Warf joined the faculty of Philadelphia's Thomas Jefferson University School of Medicine and became a member of the neurosurgery department at the Nemours/Alfred I. duPont Hospital for Children in Wilmington, Delaware.

Warf has never been content to rest on his laurels. He wrote in his *Vector* article, "Our work isn't done. Post-infectious hydrocephalus, even when treated, leads to premature death or severe disability in the majority of infants. It is imperative that we identify the organisms that infect these babies so that public health strategies for prevention can be constructed and millions of lives saved."

Great strides have been made in that regard. While in Uganda, Warf had noted that a few months after suffering an infection such as neonatal sepsis, many infants would return to the hospital exhibiting symptoms of hydrocephalus. He later helped a colleague, Steven Schiff of the Penn State Center for Neural Engineering, track nearly seven hundred cases and correlate them with rainfall data from the National Oceanic and Atmospheric Administration. They found that the number of cases rose dramatically during certain times in the weather cycle. "Hydrocephalus is the first major neurosurgical condition linked to climate," Schiff said, as reported in *Penn State News* (3 Jan. 2013). "This means that a substantial component of these cases [is] almost certainly driven from the environmental conditions, and that means they are potentially preventable if we understand the routes and mechanisms of infection better."

Thanks to Warf's influence, ETV/CPC is now becoming more common in US hospitals. He has pointed out that even in the West, shunts are sometimes less than optimal. "I have parents who are afraid to go to Disney World because they worry about a shunt failure," he told Josh Goldstein for the *Philadelphia Inquirer* (4 Aug. 2008). "Every time the kid has a headache, they are worried about a failure. Every time she has a fever, they are worried about a shunt infection."

The John D. and Catherine T. MacArthur Foundation fellowship that Warf received in 2012 was awarded to him for displaying extraordinary creativity and making noteworthy contributions to society. In its citation, the foundation provided this fitting summary of his work: "Through his research, practice, teaching, and organizing activities, Warf is demonstrating that standards of health care can be improved alongside access to that care, in both the developing and the developed world."

PERSONAL LIFE

In 2010 Warf accepted a professorship at Harvard Medical School, one of his alma maters, and subsequently assumed his position at Boston Children's Hospital as the director of the Neonatal and Congenital Anomaly Neurosurgery Program. He lives in Lexington, Massachusetts, with his wife, Cindy. They have six children: Joanna, Micah, Naomi, Sarah, Asa, and Ezra.

Warf returns regularly to Uganda to help train additional surgeons, "increasing exponentially the number of children who can now be treated using his method," according to the MacArthur Foundation.

SUGGESTED READING

Conaboy, Chelsea. "Lexington Neurosurgeon, 54, Earns 'Genius Grant.'" *Boston Globe*. Boston Globe, 1 Oct. 2012. Web. 4 June 2014.
Goldstein, Josh. "A Better Way? Neurosurgeon Ben Warf's New Approach to Brain Surgery for Hydrocephalus Offers an Alternative to the Risky Standard Treatment of Installing a Shunt." *Philly.com*. Philadelphia Media Network, 4 Aug. 2008. Web. 4 June 2014.

Lutz, Katherine. "Building Neurosurgical Care in the Heart of Africa: One Doctor's Story." *Vector*. Boston Children's Hospital, 4 Feb. 2011. Web. 4 June 2014.

"Rainfall, Brain Infection Linked in Sub-Saharan Africa." *Penn State News*. Pennsylvania State U, 3 Jan. 2013. Web. 4 June 2014.

Warf, Benjamin. "Hydrocephalus: Tackling a Global Health Problem." *Vector*. Boston Children's Hospital, 9 Aug. 2011. Web. 4 June 2014.

—*Mari Rich*

Padmasree Warrior

Born: 1961
Occupation: Business executive

Between 2012 and 2013, Cisco Systems, one of the United States' largest technology companies, completed fifteen acquisitions in just fifteen months. Bringing new companies into Cisco's fold is just one of Padmasree Warrior's many responsibilities. As the $48 billion networking company's chief technology and strategy officer, she is in charge of developing and implementing the company's global business and technology strategy, mergers and acquisitions, equity investments, and innovation. Warrior first joined Cisco in 2007 as its chief technology officer and cohead of its engineering organization; the role of chief strategy officer was added to her responsibilities in 2012. Over the past five years or so, the product categories she has managed have grown in market share, and her visionary strategies have been a key factor in the company's growth.

In May 2013 *Forbes* magazine ranked Warrior fifty-seventh on its list of the world's hundred most powerful women, and she was ranked ninth out of its 2013 list of the fifteen most powerful women in technology. She has achieved such rankings in similar lists compiled by the *Wall Street Journal, Fast Company*, the *Economic Times*, and *Business Insider*. Noting that he views her as a potential successor, Cisco Systems chair and CEO John Chambers told the *Economic Times* (18 Apr. 2013), "Warrior is among the sharpest technology persons in the world." She is reportedly on the Cisco board's list of ten possible replacements for Chambers upon his departure, a list that the board reviews quarterly.

Warrior is a dedicated and passionate advocate of the advancement of women and minorities. Her advocacy is based on her personal experience, first when she was one of only a few women in her college engineering classes and later when she found a similar dearth of women at work as she entered the tech industry.

© Rick Friedman/Corbis

EARLY LIFE AND EDUCATION

Padmasree Warrior was born in 1961 in Vijayawada, Andhra Pradesh, India. She wrote in her biography for the professional networking site LinkedIn (22 July 2013) that her love of science, which has motivated her since her youth, led her to conduct numerous home experiments as a child. "Curiosity about how things worked got me out of bed and kept me going every day, growing up. And it still does," she explained in her biography. "Science has always been the true inspiration in my work. As a young girl, I wanted to be an astronomer and was fascinated by space travel."

In Vijayawada, Warrior attended the Children's Montessori School and Maris Stella College. When it came time to apply to universities, the Indian Institute of Technology Delhi (IIT-Delhi), one of the top-ranked engineering schools in the nation, seemed like a natural choice to Warrior. Though she originally intended to study physics, she eventually chose to focus on chemical engineering. After graduating in 1982, she left India and went on to study at Cornell University in Ithaca, New York, from which she earned her master's degree in 1984.

MOTOROLA

Warrior was working on her doctorate when she left her studies to begin her career at Motorola, Inc., headquartered in Schaumburg, Illinois, as a research engineer in one of the company's semiconductor factories. During her twenty-three years at Motorola, she rose through the ranks, becoming the corporate vice president and chief technology officer (CTO) of Motorola's semiconductor products sector and then the corporate vice president and general manager of the company's energy systems group, which offered a variety of products in the global mobile phone, portable computing, and handheld electronics market.

Warrior was promoted to Motorola's CTO position in January 2003. The promotion put her in charge of a $4 billion research and development budget, twenty-six thousand engineers across the world, and Motorola Labs, and made her the highest-ranking woman in the company's history at that time. She was also responsible for the company's early-stage accelerators, which functioned like separate start-up companies within Motorola and were agile enough to develop, produce, and market products based on innovative ideas within short time frames. One of the new products developed by Motorola Labs during Warrior's tenure was Ming, a 2006 smartphone with the ability to read handwritten Chinese characters and scan business cards.

SEAMLESS MOBILITY

In early 2004, Warrior and Motorola's new CEO, Ed Zander, were on a transatlantic flight to attend a conference where they were to present their vision of the company's future—no small feat, considering that Motorola was the world's number-two mobile phone maker at the time. Frustrated with their presentation, Warrior and Zander devised the concept of seamless mobility, the idea that as more and more people around the world gain access to mobile phones, the phones will allow users to do more—send e-mails, watch videos, surf the web, access their bank accounts—wherever they might be. The concept was novel at the time and was launched that July as Zander's key focus for the company, one that aimed to introduce a more user-driven approach and make the company's devices easier to use. As CTO, Warrior was responsible for implementing the strategy in the company's research and development of new technology offerings.

Seamless mobility and connectivity became influential and widely adopted concepts throughout the tech industry. While she was CTO, Motorola was awarded a 2004 National Medal of Technology for "over seventy-five years of achievement and leadership in mobile communications, and for the development of innovative technologies that allow people to seamlessly connect with their world," according to the US Patent and Trademark Office website. Warrior accepted the honor on behalf of Motorola from President George W. Bush.

Warrior resigned as Motorola's CTO and executive vice president on December 3, 2007, just a few days after Zander's imminent departure as CEO was announced. Industry analysts did not know if the two departures were linked, but InfoWorld's Nancy Gohring (3 Dec. 2007)

reported that according to Motorola spokesperson Jennifer Erickson, the move was "the final step in redefining the CTO responsibilities" and was "entirely consistent" with the company's new direction. The changes in leadership came at a time when Motorola faced declining revenue, profits, and market share.

JOINING CISCO

The day after she left Motorola, Cisco Systems, a large networking equipment company located in San Jose, California, announced that it was hiring Warrior as its CTO and as cohead of its engineering organization. In this role Warrior and her colleague Pankaj Patel were accountable for roughly two-thirds of Cisco's revenues and oversaw more than twenty-two thousand engineers. Warrior was the first executive to be hired from outside of Cisco's ranks. As the company's tech visionary, she devised and implemented the company's strategies for dealing with market transitions based on ever-changing developments in technology, such as cloud computing. "I spend a lot of time with customers understanding what their future needs are going to be, where they see the future heading, sharing with them our view of the future, how things are going to transition and then translating that back into what our strategy should be," Warrior said in an interview with John Boudreau for the San Jose Mercury News (10 Mar. 2009). Her other responsibilities included communicating Cisco's strategy and innovation to networking industry analysts, financial analysts, the media, and other stakeholders.

Warrior has embraced what she sees as Cisco's entrepreneurial spirit and willingness to take risks—qualities that she attributed to Cisco being made up of smaller companies that it had acquired. She told Boudreau that at Cisco "there is a willingness to try new things, to listen to people with different ideas"—even if those new ideas came from someone who, like her, was hired from outside of the company.

NEW RESPONSIBILITIES

In June 2012, Ned Hooper, Cisco's chief strategy officer (CSO), left the company. Warrior replaced him as CSO while retaining her position as CTO, taking the new title of chief technology and strategy officer. In addition to her CTO responsibilities, her duties include overseeing Cisco's growth agenda, technology direction, and acquisition team. According to the Cisco corporate website, Warrior is tasked with "aligning technology development and corporate strategy to enable Cisco to anticipate, shape, and lead major market transitions. She helps direct technology and operational innovation across the company and oversees strategic partnerships, mergers and acquisitions, the integration of new business models, the incubation of new technologies, and the cultivation of world-class technical talent."

As chief technology and strategy officer, Warrior has added to Cisco's growing portfolio. In particular, she led the acquisition of fifteen companies within fifteen months between 2012 and 2013. In July 2013, Cisco announced its $2.7 billion acquisition of Sourcefire, a cyber-security company based in Maryland. The rapid pace of the company's growth caused some skeptics to wonder if Cisco was growing too quickly. The company also came under fire for laying off close to twelve thousand employees between 2011 and August 2013—at around the same time that the mergers were taking place and profits were up.

All the same, some industry analysts have speculated that Warrior may be tapped to replace CEO John Chambers when he is ready to step down. Andrew Butler, vice president and distinguished analyst at Gartner, told the *Economic Times* (30 June 2012) that "Cisco's culture favors promoting from within, and Warrior brings a grace and style that would be popular with most audiences." This sentiment was echoed by William Kreher, senior technology analyst for financial services firm Edward Jones, also quoted by the *Economic Times*: "We believe that the traits [Warrior] brings to the table include strong presentation skills and a holistic understanding of the technology landscape." Butler concluded, however, by saying that there is no obvious frontrunner as yet for Chambers's position and that the succession will depend on how long Chambers remains at Cisco.

HONORS AND ACHIEVEMENTS

Warrior has received many honors in recognition of her accomplishments and leadership. *Forbes* magazine named her to its list of the world's hundred most powerful women in 2012 and 2013. In 2012, *Business Insider* deemed her one of the twenty-five most influential women in wireless. In 2008 the *Wall Street Journal* designated her as one of its top fifty women to watch, and *Fast Company* identified her as one of the hundred most creative people in business. The Women in Technology International Hall of Fame inducted her in 2007. Warrior's myriad awards include the World of Difference Award, presented by the International Alliance for Women, and the Visionary Award, given by Silicon Valley's SVForum. Additionally, Warrior has been a board member for several technology organizations, including the Singapore Agency for Science, Technology, and Research; the White House Fellowships Selection Board; and the National Science Foundation's Advisory Committee for Computing and Information Science and Engineering. In September 2013, she was elected to serve on the board of directors for Gap Inc.

ADVOCATE FOR WOMEN AND MINORITIES IN STEM

Many of Warrior's honors and achievements reflect her commitment to advancing women and minorities in the fields of science, technology, engineering, and mathematics (STEM). Her advocacy is grounded in her own experience as a college engineering student at IIT-Delhi. She wrote in her LinkedIn biography, "To my dismay . . . I found very few women in my class. Well, we girls stuck together and helped each other. I guess it is this first experience of being a minority that taught me the importance of a support network and made me passionate about paying it forward." Warrior found the same gender disparity when she entered the tech workforce. As an advocate, Warrior has "paid it forward" not only by setting an example within the companies where she has worked but also by contributing her own time and leadership to several community and nonprofit organizations. She has sat on the board of trustees for the Museum of Science and Industry and has been a sponsor for Motorola's CTO Diversity Council.

PERSONAL LIFE

Despite being connected to 1.4 million Twitter followers, Warrior has learned the importance of taking time out from the connection that she has helped to foster. "While technology empowers us to remain connected all the time," she told *Forbes*, "it's up to us as people to decide when it is not appropriate to be connected . . . to opt out when you need to." Saturdays are reserved for her other interests, which include painting, photography, and haiku.

In 1984 Warrior married Mohandas Warrior, her classmate from IIT-Delhi and the CEO and president of the Madison, Wisconsin, laser manufacturing company Alfalight. They have a son, Karna Warrior.

SUGGESTED READING

"Could an Indian Succeed John Chambers at Cisco?" *Economic Times*. Bennett, Coleman & Co., 18 Apr. 2013. Web. 11 Oct. 2013.

Duffy, Jim. "Cisco's CTO Talks First Impressions." *Network World* 30 June 2008: 14. PDF file.

Forbes, Moira. "Cisco's CTO: Do Women in Business Give Up Their Power?" *Forbes*. Forbes.com, 9 July 2013. Web. 11 Oct. 2013.

Hamblen, Matt. "Padmasree Warrior." *Computerworld* 10 May 2010: 14–16. PDF file.

Lawson, Stephen. "Cisco Hires Former CTO at Struggling Motorola as Its CTO." *Network World*. Network World, 5 Dec. 2007. Web. 11 Oct. 2013.

Singh, Shelley. "Padmasree Warrior among Favourites for CEO Job in Cisco." *Economic Times*. Bennett, Coleman & Co., 20 June 2012. Web. 11 Oct. 2013.

Warrior, Padmasree. "What Inspires Me: Discovering What Makes Me Tick." *LinkedIn*. LinkedIn, 22 July 2013. Web. 11 Oct. 2013.

—*Lisa Phillips*

Carrie Mae Weems

Born: April 20, 1953
Occupation: Photographer and artist

In 2013, photographer Carrie Mae Weems was among the twenty-four people to be awarded a grant from the MacArthur Foundation (the so-called "genius award"). A prize of $625,000, to be paid out over five years, is awarded in light of prior work, with no restrictions as to its use. Announcing Weems's win, the MacArthur Fellows Program released a statement praising her decades-long career (25 Sept. 2013), stating, "Her intimate depictions of children, adults, and families in simple settings document and interpret the ongoing and centuries-old struggle for racial equality, human rights, and social inclusion in America. In images that are lyrical and evocative, Weems unites critical social insight with enduring aesthetic mastery."

To add to the excitement of that year, the University of Massachusetts Amherst commissioned Weems to create a project to mark the fiftieth anniversary of the death of sociologist and civil rights activist W. E. B. Du Bois; with landscape architect Walter Hood, Weems co-designed a memorial garden in his honor. She also named a new variety of peony after him—the Du Bois Peony of Hope.

Although her work is often focused on social and historical issues, Weems is interested in moving the artistic conversation beyond the contexts of race, gender, or class. As she told Charmaine Picard for *Modern Painters* (Jan. 2014), "African-American artists are still considered outliers, and people don't really know how to integrate them into broader themes. People frame my work in terms of race and gender and don't integrate it into broader historical questions, and I think that limits the possibilities of what the public is allowed to understand about our production in the country." Much of Weems's work is focused on reexamining the historical record to bring forward the voices of marginalized people.

EARLY LIFE

Carrie Mae Weems grew up as the second of seven children in Portland, Oregon. Her father, Myrlie Weems, was a laborer and a church singer, and her mother, Carrie Polk, ran a barbeque restaurant. After giving birth to her only child, Faith C. Weems, at age sixteen in 1969, Weems

© Terrence Jennings/Retna Ltd./Corbis

relied on the help of her mother, aunt, and sister to raise her daughter. After graduating from high school, Weems moved to San Francisco in 1970, where she met celebrated dancer Anna Halprin, who invited her to join the esteemed San Francisco Dancer's Workshop. After a year and a half in San Francisco, Weems moved with Faith to New York City, but she returned to California after she was unable to find work in New York.

In 1973, on her twentieth birthday, Weems's boyfriend gave her a Nikon camera. As Weems told Hilarie M. Sheets for the *New York Times* (12 Sept. 2012), "Suddenly this camera, this thing, allowed me to move around the world in a certain kind of way, with a certain kind of purpose." To improve her skills, she studied the works of classic photographers and those featured in the *Black Photographers Annual*. Noted photographers Henri Cartier-Bresson and Roy DeCarava were early influences. "I took to it like a fish to water. I knew at the moment that this was the thing I would be doing," she explained to Kristin Braswell for *Ebony* (5 Feb. 2014). "Photography has this amazing ability to describe things in a way that I might be at a loss of words for; there are some things we cannot point to, but a photo can."

EDUCATION

Weems's first camera inspired her to pursue studies in photography and design at San Francisco City College. In 1976, Weems returned to New York, where she attended photography classes at the Studio Museum in Harlem and worked as an office temp as a side job. Weems then enrolled at the California Institute of the Arts in Valencia, earning her bachelor of fine arts degree there in 1981. Recalling her time at CalArts in her interview with Picard, Weems said, "They didn't always know what to do with this brown woman taking brown photographs. . . . The field was more limited then."

Weems went on to attend the University of California, San Diego. Her first photographic series debuted in 1984 as part of her master's thesis, which was a reaction to the Moynihan report that was issued by the US government in 1965. The report asserted that black families were inherently flawed because of the default matriarchal structure in the absence of men. *Family Pictures and Stories* features a series of photographs depicting Weems's own family functioning perfectly well. The photographs are accompanied by audio recordings of Weems's family members describing their lives, particularly her parents' migration from Mississippi to Oregon. "I knew that I wanted to be involved with work that had to do with a shift in perception, not only of black people, but of women and aspects of humanity that have been essentially denied in the canon generally," Weems stated, explaining her inspiration to Aaron Scott for the *Portland Entertainment Monthly* (18 Jan. 2013).

Weems completed her master of fine arts degree in 1984. She continued her studies at the graduate program in folklore at University of California, Berkeley, where she studied African, American, Irish, and Russian oral traditions from 1984 to 1987.

BREAKTHROUGH

From 1987 to 1991, Weems served as an assistant professor in photography at Hampshire College, a private liberal arts college in Amherst, Massachusetts. Each evening, she returned to her own studio to work on what became the *Kitchen Table Series*, completed in 1990. Using herself as a model, Weems stood in as an American Everywoman in a series of photographs depicting her at the kitchen table with her friends, children, or a romantic male partner, or by herself. The series grew out of her earlier work with documentary photography. She included fourteen text panels to accompany the photographs and offer a brief narrative. "The simplicity and universality of these staged photographs let viewers read a variety of meanings in them," art critic Cathy Curtis wrote of the series for the *Los Angeles Times* (21 Oct. 1991). "There remains plenty of room to conjecture about what it means to be a woman—specifically, but not exclusively, a black woman—in the 1990s: how a domestic setting is both confining and nurturing; how human nature doesn't really change, despite well-meaning theories; and how one's best friend often turns out to be oneself."

This project became her breakthrough moment; she was both subject and photographer, which continued to be the case in many of her future works. Weems has not only used herself as a model in her photography but also has provided voiceovers for her later videos and installations. Upon winning the 1996 Herb Alpert Award in visual arts, Weems stated, "The focus of my work is to describe simply and directly those aspects of American culture in need of deeper illumination. My responsibility as an artist is to work, to sing for my supper, to make art, beautiful and powerful, that adds and reveals; to beautify the mess of a messy world, to heal the sick and feed the helpless; to shout bravely from the roof-tops and storm barricaded doors and voice the specificity of our historical moment." Other series created by Weems at this time include *Ain't Jokin* (1987–88), which examines outlandish racial stereotypes about African Americans, and *American Icons* (1988–89), a series of still-life photographs showing vintage, racist knick-knacks in peaceful, domestic settings.

NEW DIRECTIONS

In the early 1990s, Weems visited the Peabody Museum of Archaeology and Ethnology at Harvard University, where she found daguerreotypes of slaves that had been commissioned by Harvard professor of zoology Louis Agassiz in the nineteenth century to support the "son of Ham" theory, which posited separate biological origins for the different races. Despite having signed a contract promising not to use the museum's images without permission, Weems felt compelled to include the daguerreotypes in her series *From Here I Saw What Happened and I Cried* (1995–96). She photographed and enlarged the images, tinted them red, and emblazoned them with provocative phrases such as "you became a scientific profile" and "an anthropological debate." Harvard University threatened to sue Weems for defying her contractual agreement and violating copyright, but Weems was willing to take her case to court to defend her right to use the images. Harvard ultimately abandoned its case against Weems and purchased the images for the university's art museum.

With her 1998 series *Ritual and Revolution*, Weems began printing her images on translucent scrims made of muslin. Photographs were developed on the scrims and hung so that the viewers had to walk through them, becoming part of the exhibit themselves. The series featured images of Greek sculpture, Assyrian steps, and Mayan courtyards, expanding Weems's historical and geographical reach. As Weems explained to curator Kathryn Delmez for the catalog *Carrie Mae Weems: Three Decades of Photography and Video*

(2012), "By moving into and through the work, I wanted to give the viewer permission to invade the work of art, to invade history, and thereby claim it as one's own; to feel that one is a part of history and, therefore, one makes history. In this way, the viewer is transformed from audience to participant/observer."

Following the confirmation, based on DNA samples, that the third president of the United States, Thomas Jefferson, had a sexual relationship with and children by Sally Hemings, one of his slaves, Weems created *The Jefferson Suite* (2001). It consisted of seventeen semitransparent muslin banners of varying sizes along with Weems's voice overlaying a musical score, with photographs of Charles Darwin and the sheep Dolly, the first mammal to be cloned. The series was both a study of biotechnology and DNA and an examination of male-female relationships.

EXPANDING TO OTHER MEDIA

Weems began creating video in 1982, with a piece about black photographers that highlighted the work of Roy DeCarava. Other film projects followed, in addition to her photographic work. "At a certain point, I realized that I didn't know how to make photographs sing in a certain way, and I was becoming increasingly interested in composers and music and how one uses the voice," Weems explained to James Estrin in an interview for the *New York Times* (25 Sept. 2013). "Film and video really allowed me to work across all of those interests in a single project. I could use voice and rhythm and work with the composers and use music to effect a certain visual image." Despite the difficulties and complexities in making a film, Weems loves the form and is committed to it. She cites Lars von Trier and Federico Fellini as important influences on her work.

Weems received the Joseph H. Hazen Rome Prize Fellowship in 2006. The prize, which allows fellows to stay at the American Academy in Rome, is given annually to an international group of artists, scholars, and writers. While in Italy, she created photographs that became the 2006 series *Roaming*. Dressed in a long black dress, with her back to the camera, Weems stands in front of and views iconic structures. Weems explained to A. M. Weaver for *Aperture* (Winter 2009), that this solitary woman, present in many of her works, is "a witness . . . my muse, my leader, my object and subject."

While in Rome, Weems also made a video, *Italian Dreams* (2006), which relies on a fragmented, Fellini-like style. A repeated image is that of a young woman near a window, apparently writing at a table in a darkly lit room with paper strewn around her. The film suggests that its various unconnected sequences may be the woman's imaginings.

RETROSPECTIVE

As early as 2008, art critic Holland Cotter called for a retrospective of Weem's work, writing an article for the *New York Times* (29 Feb. 2008), "I don't know why Carrie Mae Weems hasn't had a midcareer museum retrospective. No American photographer of the last quarter-century . . . has turned out a more probing, varied and moving body of work. None has made more adventurous use of the photographic medium, adding performance, film and installation to the serial print format." Subsequently, Kathryn E. Delmez became the curator of Weems's first major retrospective, which toured from 2012 through 2014. The traveling exhibit included more than two hundred photographs, videos, and installations, beginning with work from the 1970s that had never before been shown. As Delmez told Sheets for the *New York Times* (12 Sept. 2012), "When you're talking about Carrie Mae Weems, you're going to talk about race and gender and classism. But I really think it goes beyond that to her desire to insert all marginalized people into the historical record, as she says, to tell the stories that have been ignored or forgotten or erased. Through Carrie's lens she's looking at who's writing history, who has the power to influence other people's lives."

Weems had high hopes for the retrospective, which began at Nashville's Frist Center for the Visual Arts and ended at the Solomon R. Guggenheim Museum in New York City, making her the first black woman to have a solo exhibition at the Guggenheim. Noting that the Guggenheim did not generally attract African American or Latino visitors, Weems told Robin Cembalest for *Art News* (1 Oct. 2013), "I want to make sure I have a dynamic presence of people of color flowing through the space. There could be a night around art and activism, with people who are troubling the waters, as they say."

In conjunction with the retrospective, "Carrie Mae Weems: The Museum Series" was shown at the Studio Museum in Harlem. In this series of photographs, Weems positions herself, back to the camera, in front of some of the world's most iconic museum facades: the British Museum, the Tate Modern, the Louvre, and the Philadelphia Museum of Art, among others. Her pose is typical of that of many of her works, in which she appears in a plain black dress to represent the muse, or in a simple cotton dress evoking the clothing of slaves. Standing outside of and dwarfed by these temples to art, Weems reminds the viewer that women and African American artists are underrepresented and often excluded from the canon of Western art.

PERSONAL LIFE

Weems is married to Jeffrey Hoone, whom she met in 1986 while holding a residency at the

Visual Studies Workshop in Rochester, New York. They married in 1995. Hoone is the executive director of Light Work, a nonprofit organization that provides support to up-and-coming artists through residencies, publications, and exhibitions. Hoone and Weems live in Syracuse, New York, although Weems also has a studio in New York City, near the Pratt Institute.

Weems is also active in Syracuse's Institute of Sound + Style, which she founded in 2012 to work with young people in the area. The program offers a weekly stipend to young artists for a four-week summer program that trains them for careers in fashion and the arts. Training is offered in practical aspects of the music and film world, such as sound engineering, graphic design, and videography. Weems told Estrin, "It's really a fabulous project, and I tell you, I get as much out of it as the kids. So that's what I'm working on, that's my heart's desire."

In addition to the MacArthur Fellowship, Weems's many honors include the Congressional Black Caucus Foundation's Lifetime Achievement Award (2013), the Gordon Parks Foundation Award (2013), and the US State Department's Medal of Arts Award (2012).

SUGGESTED READING

Cembalist, Robin. "Chatting with MacArthur Winner Carrie Mae Weems." *Art News*. ARTnews, 1 Oct. 2013. Web. 8 Mar. 2014.

Cotter, Holland. "Testimony of a Cleareyed Witness." *New York Times*. New York Times, 24 Jan. 2014. Web. 4 Mar. 2014.

Sheets, Hilarie M. "Photographer and Subject Are One." *New York Times*. New York Times, 16 Sept. 2012. Web. 4 Mar. 2014.

Weaver, A. M. "Carrie Mae Weems: History and Dreams." *Aperture* 197 (2009): 24–29. Print.

Weems, Carrie Mae. "The 'Genius' of Carrie Mae Weems." Interview by James Estrin. *Lens*. New York Times, 25 Sept. 2013. Web. 3 Apr. 2014.

Weems, Carrie Mae. "Artist Carrie Weems on 30 Years of Genius." Interview by Kristin Braswell. *Ebony*. Ebony Magazine, 5 Feb. 2014. Web. Apr. 2014.

Weems, Carrie Mae. "A Q&A with Carrie Mae Weems." Interview by Charmaine Picard. *Modern Painters* 26.1 (2014): 66–69. *Academic Search Complete*. Web. 8 Apr. 2014.

SELECTED WORKS

Family Pictures and Stories, 1981; *Ain't Jokin*, 1987; *American Icons*, 1988; *The Kitchen Table Series*, 1990; *From Here I Saw What Happened and I Cried*, 1995; *Ritual and Revolution*, 1998; *The Jefferson Suite*, 2001; *Roaming*, 2006; *Italian Dreams*, 2006; *The Obama Project*, 2012

—Judy Johnson

Jess Weiner

Born: October 31, 1973
Occupation: Entrepreneur and self-esteem expert

Jess Weiner has engaged in many occupations throughout her career—from playwright and theater troupe founder to advice columnist and social media strategist. A singular goal has connected all of those pursuits: to empower young women, encourage their self-esteem, and help them process the deleterious messages with which they are constantly bombarded. An outspoken leader in the body-acceptance movement—which encourages women to be more tolerant of themselves, to use positive language when referring to their bodies, and to value health before media-driven notions of conventional beauty—Weiner sometimes calls herself an *actionist*, a word she uses to indicate her hands-on approach and passionate mission.

"Throughout my career, I've had one foot planted in the Heartland, working with women and girls across America to strengthen their self-confidence, and I've had one foot in Hollywood, working with media executives to develop more empowering, honest stories that truly speak to the girls I've come to know," she wrote on the website of Dove, a beauty-products company for which she serves as a global ambassador. "No matter where I travel or whom I speak with, the core issue we end up addressing is always the same: today's young woman is feeling more conflicted and concerned about her image than ever before."

Getty Images

EARLY LIFE

Jessica Weiner was born on October 31, 1973, and raised in Florida. Her father, Michael, was a businessman, and her mother, Jane, was a teacher. "Thanks to my parents, a combination of entrepreneurship and education is in my DNA, and those are the foundations on which I've built my career," she explained to *Current Biography*. Weiner's parents were exceptionally supportive, as were her maternal grandparents, Michael and Molly Marcus, who were both educators as well. She credits her grandfather, in particular, with encouraging her to write down her experiences and thoughts in a journal. He persisted in reminding her to "write it down!"— even when she disregarded the advice, preferring to sing, watch the popular sitcoms of the day, or engage in imaginative role-playing games with her sister instead. (She did pick up the habit in later years, amassing more than eighty completed journals.)

Despite the incredibly strong web of support her family provided for her, Weiner was plagued by doubts about her appearance from an early age. "I'd pray extra hard that when I woke up in the morning I'd look like Barbie," she wrote in her first book, *A Very Hungry Girl: How I Filled Up on Life . . . and How You Can, Too!* (2003). "Every morning I was disappointed."

INTEREST IN THEATER

While she may have lacked Barbie's straight, blonde hair and tiny waist, Weiner was a bright and verbal student. She delighted in making up stories and performing. In *A Very Hungry Girl*, she recalls a pivotal moment in her fifth-grade classroom: "[One day] when [my teacher] called on me to read my homework assignment, something came over me, and an accent flew out of my mouth—the origin of which I'm not quite sure, but it sounded funny and it made people laugh," she wrote. "I fell more in love with performing than ever before. But better than that, they were laughing at what I wrote, what I'd created, and the power to move them with my words had me hooked."

Weiner won admission to Southwood, a performing arts middle school in South Florida, an incredible achievement that was tainted for her when a harsh drama teacher there criticized her looks and opined that she would only ever play "Ethel Merman–type" character roles. She nevertheless persevered, and after graduating from Southwood, she was accepted into the highly competitive New World School of the Arts, a high school in Miami. There, during her teenage years, Weiner's battle with body image and dieting intensified. "Being satisfied with my appearance was an oxymoron," she wrote in *A Very Hungry Girl*. "All I wanted to do [at age seventeen] was shrink, and mold myself into what I thought I should be: an empty, pretty vessel, one

who ignored her smarts, wit, and passion and instead focused on how many fat grams were in a whole-grain bagel." She regularly allowed herself only baked chicken—even for breakfast—and crammed in an occasional candy bar when no one was watching. Given the milieu in which she found herself, that behavior did not appear extreme: binging and purging were common practices among her classmates, so ingesting only poultry and sneaking candy bars seemed like relatively benign practices.

STUDIES IN THE PERFORMING ARTS

After graduating from high school, Weiner settled upon Pennsylvania State University, which had a well-regarded theater program and satisfied her ideas (formed by watching years of network television) of what a campus should look like. The only freshman cast in both main shows mounted by the theater department that year, she later wrote in *A Very Hungry Girl*, "I guess these professors didn't get the memo sent from my earlier teachers that I wasn't pretty enough to be a leading lady."

In addition to her theater courses, Weiner studied the classics, which gave her insight into the art of public debate, and she incorporated women's studies into her program as well, learning about the female pioneers often left out of the literary and historical canon. "That might seem like an unusual combination," she admitted to *Current Biography*, "but you have to study what you love, and those subjects all 'lit me up' like nothing else. And, not incidentally, they've all proven invaluable to my career."

During her time at Penn State, Weiner appeared in such productions as *Trojan Women* and *Peer Gynt*, but it was an educational production called *Not Just Fooling Around*, which examined a variety of socially relevant issues, including homosexuality, sexually transmitted disease, and date rape, that provided her with an epiphany about her acting career. After the show, the actors, remaining in character, took questions from the audience. Weiner was stunned when one young woman took the microphone and said that she had been particularly moved by the vignette about date rape because it had happened to her. Others chimed in in agreement, and a dialogue ensued. "I felt as if I'd done more than recite someone else's lines—I'd acted my way into [the audience's] hearts by speaking their words and telling their stories," Weiner recalls in *A Very Hungry Girl*. "That night I felt that I was a part of something greater than myself."

BEGINNINGS AS A PLAYWRIGHT

While many of her college friends regularly binged and purged, Weiner resisted the urge to do so. Realizing that her relationship with food was disordered and unhealthy, however, she joined a support group on campus. "Every

Thursday for the next four years I entered a space where lives were changed forever," she wrote. While still in college, Weiner penned a performance piece called *Wake Up World* that consisted of monologues, dance, music, and slides. In it she explored such issues as drug use, eating disorders, sexual relationships, and abortion. It met with applause when she mounted it in a tiny black-box theater on campus, and afterward a spirited discussion broke out. Weiner found it transformative to hear the audience reacting to words she had penned herself, and her career as a professional playwright had its seeds in that moment.

Weiner received experience in a different type of performance when she became a correspondent for the television program *MTV News: Unfiltered*, reporting on a now-defunct Penn State tradition in which male students rampaged through the campus one night a year, verbally harassing and terrorizing the female students, who were forced to take refuge in their dorms until the mob had dispersed.

Weiner graduated from Penn State in 1995 and moved to Indianapolis to live with her boyfriend. She found work at a mall clothing store, and while she enjoyed helping women find flattering items that made them feel better about themselves, she did not intend to work in retail for long.

THEATER WITH A MISSION
Weiner was unsuccessful, however, in convincing theater companies in the region to share her vision of mounting productions centered on social issues relevant to young people. In response, she took a class in grant writing at a local community college and soon won five thousand dollars with which she founded a summer arts program for at-risk youth. That first year twelve participants registered, but within the next few years, the number had grown to forty, and more than eighty had added their names to a waiting list for admission.

Making the rounds of local colleges and drama programs, Weiner subsequently signed on eight actors, who formed what she called her A.C.T. OUT Ensemble. Paying each of them about ten dollars per show plus meals, she mounted nine productions during her first season, generally at student-activism or eating-disorder conferences. Word spread, and the group was soon performing one hundred times a year. Weiner traveled with the company from 1995 to 2001. Among their most requested offerings was the play Weiner had started while at Penn State, *Body Loathing/Body Love*, which she expanded to reflect not only her own experiences but also the stories of others. Sometimes she was called upon to create plays specifically for school systems plagued by gang violence, suicides, or homophobia, among other issues. (The ensemble played at Columbine High School in the wake of the 1999 shooting there.) Weiner estimates that she visited more than two hundred cities and engaged with some 300,000 young audience members during her tenure with the troupe, which is now run by a former assistant and continues on without her.

IN THE BELLY OF THE BEAST
Wanting to take her message to a wider audience and having slowly grown apart from her boyfriend, Weiner decided to leave Indianapolis for Los Angeles, a locale she has referred to as "the belly of the beast," because so many of the hypersexualized images and troubling messages aimed at young girls originate with the entertainment industry there. Although she knew only two people in the entire city, she was soon scheduling meetings and learning all she could.

Thanks to a large dose of personal charisma and perseverance, soon after she arrived on the West Coast, Weiner was hired by Warner Bros. to host a talk show centered on the youth-oriented issues that were important to her. It was an era in which almost every talk show on the air was hosted by a big-name celebrity, however, and her show, not fitting that mold, was never picked up by a network. Still, taping it provided her with valuable experience both in front of and behind the camera.

As word of her expertise spread, Weiner was booked as a guest on various programs, including the *Today Show* and the *Oprah Winfrey Show*, and she appeared regularly on the *Tyra Banks Show*, giving advice on how to have healthy self-esteem.

PRINT OUTLETS
In addition to *A Very Hungry Girl*, a combination memoir and advice book, Weiner is the author of the motivational volume *Do I Look Fat in This? Life Doesn't Begin Five Pounds from Now* (2005). "Are you waiting to be skinnier, thinner, more toned, more tanned, better dressed, more lovable, sexier, nicer, smarter, funnier, or wealthier before you really begin your life?" she asks in the first chapter. "Millions of us are. And it's a complete waste of time. Body obsession and the quest for perfection are destroying our lives, and we are willing partners in this destruction."

Weiner's writing has appeared in such publications as *Glamour*, *Redbook*, and *CosmoGirl*, and for several years, beginning in 2005, she wrote the popular "Body Peace" column for *Seventeen* magazine, for which she continues to serve as a contributing editor. (The column is now penned by a rotating roster of writers.) Additionally, another column, "Ask Jess," appeared on the website run by actresses Mary Kate and Ashley Olsen.

DOVE BRAND AMBASSADOR

In 2004 Dove launched its "Campaign for Real Beauty" with a controversial ad featuring everyday women whose appearances do not meet the conventional standards of beauty. In 2006 the company produced a much-buzzed-about short film, *Evolution*, depicting the machinations required to transform an average woman into a model, thus promoting awareness of how unrealistic images of beauty are created by the media. They also launched the Dove Self-Esteem Fund, intending to inspire and educate girls and women about a wider definition of beauty, and hired Weiner as a global self-esteem ambassador.

The job entails making media appearances on behalf of the company, giving lectures on confidence, shaping the brand's messaging, and helping to develop the curriculum used in Dove's self-esteem workshops. As of 2013 the workshops have been held in countries around the world, including the United Kingdom, Germany, and France, and have reached well over 12.5 million girls. "If you spend the time helping a girl build a positive relationship with beauty, identifying her strengths, and creating an open and supportive dialogue, you can really make a world of difference," Weiner told a reporter for *Entertainment Close-Up* (26 Sept. 2010).

SOCIAL MEDIA STRATEGY

In 2003, realizing that traditional forms of personal protest such as letter-writing campaigns could do little to affect corporate, media, and cultural consciousness, Weiner formed Talk to Jess, a consulting firm that specializes in helping companies craft campaigns that will send positive messages to girls and women. "This is a little different from marching on Washington," she told *Current Biography*. "But in the current climate, real change has to happen from within. That's the only way." Her clients have included Mattel, the Disney Channel, Walmart, and Lifetime Television Networks, among others. "We're helping some of the biggest stakeholders on the planet reach millions of people," she explained, "and if we influence the corporate conversation, we can have an enormous impact on the personal conversation. Above all, we want those conversations to be curious, compelling, and graceful."

PERSONAL LIFE

In 2003 Weiner received the Penn State School of Theatre's Alumni Achievement Award, and in 2009 she was invited back to her alma mater to deliver that year's commencement address. In addition to her other activities, she works as an adjunct professor at the University of Southern California's Annenberg School for Communication and Journalism, where she teaches personal branding and entrepreneurship. An in-demand public speaker, she also lectures on a variety of topics, including the impact social media has on self-esteem and how entrepreneurs and small business owners can realize their dreams. In 2013 Weiner married a man she describes as "the love of her life." She and her husband are looking forward to starting a family together.

SUGGESTED READING

Hesse, Monica. "At Girls' Summit, an Image Betwixt and Be Tween." *Washington Post*. Washington Post, 13 Oct. 2009. Web. 9 Dec. 2013.

Stepp, Laura Sessions. "What Happens When Mean Girls Grow Up?" *Washington Post*. Washington Post, 20 Feb. 2011. Web. 9 Dec. 2013.

Weiner, Jess. "Jess Weiner: 'Did Loving My Body Almost Kill Me?'" *Glamour*. Condé Nast, Aug. 2011. Web. 9 Dec. 2013.

—Mari Rich

Edith Widder

Born: 1951
Occupation: Marine biologist

Edith Widder is CEO, president, and senior scientist at the Ocean Research and Conservation Association (ORCA). An inventor and a scientist, she uses her abilities to not only strengthen our knowledge of the oceans, but also to protect them and their extraordinary biodiversity. In her more than thirty years of exploratory experience, Widder has made numerous discoveries about the planet's marine environment. She is perhaps best known for developing the technology that recorded the first ever video of the elusive giant squid in its natural habitat—more than one thousand feet below the ocean's surface—in 2012. Widder maintains that by conserving marine ecosystems, we stand a better chance of protecting ourselves from the worst effects of climate change, which most scientists believe will greatly impact the planet over the next century.

Widder thinks that bioluminescence—the light produced by numerous organisms living in the deepest parts of the oceans to attract mates and prey and frighten off predators—could provide insight into how pollution and climate change are recalibrating the marine environment. Widder has studied bioluminescence throughout her career. She recalled in an interview with the PBS program *Nature* (Nov. 2007) how she first grew fascinated with the subject: "I had questions . . . Who's making the light? How much light? How many organisms? Why? And, most importantly, why aren't more scientists studying this? . . . and I wanted answers. I knew how much energy—the currency of life—that was required for an organism to produce

Courtesy of the John D. & Catherine T. MacArthur Foundation

light, so my subjective impression was that this has to be one of the most important processes in the ocean." ORCA, the nonprofit association she cofounded in 2005, has used biolumines-cence to better understand how pollution has affected the Indian River Lagoon, long thought to be the most diverse estuary in North America. With ORCA, she has also designed monitors to assess health in bodies of water. She believes a worldwide network of such monitors would help scientists to better track packets of water and to determine what pollutants are present therein.

EARLY LIFE AND EDUCATION

The daughter of mathematicians, Edith "Edie" Widder was born in 1951. She decided to be-come a marine biologist at age eleven, when her father, then head of Harvard University's mathe-matics department, took a yearlong sabbatical to travel with his family around the world. During the family's first stops in Europe, she was awed by the continent's art museums and decided to become an artist. Upon seeing the pyramids of Egypt, she was convinced she would become an archeologist. While tramping through Australia, she again altered her career aspirations—she would be a biologist. In the coral reefs of Fiji, however, she finally found her calling. "I just was mesmerized by all of this life everywhere," she told Neil deGrasse Tyson for the PBS program *Nova* (23 July 2008). "And so I wanted to be a marine biologist. . . . So the family joke is, 'If we'd gone from west to east instead of east to west, would I have ended up as an artist?' But I think the total lack of talent might have been somewhat of a drawback."

In 1973, Widder earned her bachelor's de-gree (magna cum laude) in biology from Tufts University in Medford, Massachusetts. She

received her master's of science degree in bio-chemistry from the University of California, Santa Barbara, in 1977, and then took a sum-mer program in experimental neurobiology at the Catalina Marine Science Center in 1979. She completed her doctoral degree in neurobiology at the University of California, Santa Barbara, in 1982. It was there, as a doctoral student, that she received an opportunity to pursue her longstanding dream of becoming a marine biolo-gist. She recalled in her interview with *Nature*: "For my PhD thesis I was measuring the elec-trical activity that triggers light emission from a bioluminescent dinoflagellate. As I was nearing the completion of my degree, my major profes-sor wrote a grant for an instrument for measur-ing the color of very dim light flashes from bio-luminescent animals. . . . I kept tinkering with this instrument, until I became the lab expert. At that point, he suggested I tag along on some marine biology trawling cruises and measure the colors emitted by different bioluminescent organisms. I was thrilled. Suddenly, I was doing what I had always dreamed of doing: going to sea on exploratory expeditions!"

In 1982, Widder was part of a team organized by Bruce Robison for what would be a landmark exploratory mission to test WASP, a diving suit developed by oil companies to fix underwater rigs. Robison and his crew wanted to repurpose WASP to study the bioluminescence of deep-dwelling sea creatures. Previously, scientists had employed nets to study these animals, which proved so delicate that they often disintegrated upon being brought out of their natural environ-ment a thousand or more feet below the surface. Because Widder was not qualified to dive, she remained on the ship monitoring the divers as they took turns. Sensing her enthusiasm, Robi-son suggested that she train as a WASP pilot for the next trip. She earned her certification as a pilot for atmospheric diving system submersibles in 1984.

EARLY CAREER

That same year, in the Santa Barbara channel, Widder made her first dive. Hoping to see a bit of bioluminescence at about 880 feet, a point at which sunshine was only a faint haze above her, she decided to kill her running lights—and was overwhelmed by brilliance. "There were explo-sions of light all around, and sparks and swirls and great chains of what looked like Japanese lanterns," she recalled to Abigail Tucker for *Smithsonian* (Mar. 2013). "I was enveloped. Ev-erything was glowing. I couldn't distinguish one light from another. It was just a variety of things making light, different shapes, different kinetics, mostly blue, and just so much of it. That's what astonished me."

She desperately wanted to know what made all of this light and why. Sunlight is rare in the deep ocean; it disappears at around three thousand feet below the surface, yet these animals were expending considerable energy to communicate via bioluminescent light. She, like many of her fellow scientists, believes that any bioluminescent message must be vitally important if the animal is willing to transmit it in the pitch-black deep. "It's the basic stuff of survival," Widder told Abigail Tucker for *Smithsonian*. "There's incredible selective pressure on the visual environment, where you have to worry about what's above you if you're a predator and what's below you if you're prey. Often you're both."

Between 1989 and 2005, Widder served in various capacities at the Harbor Branch Oceanographic Institute. Much of her early research funding in the bioluminescent field came from the United States Navy. For the US Navy, she built the HIDEX, a now-standard device on submarines that helps keep them hidden from enemy ships by measuring the amount of bioluminescence in the water. She also built a deep-sea light meter called the LoLAR, which measures both sunlight and bioluminescence in the deep ocean. She then began constructing devices that would differentiate between the light signatures of different sea creatures. She believed that such equipment would help scientists better understand these creatures in their natural environments, since any attempt to study them in submersible crafts—even with the running lights off—had tended to scare them off.

DEEP SEA EXPLORATIONS WITH EITS
Widder knew the key to accurately observing these creatures and their complex ecosystems would be to design a camera that could sit unobtrusively on the ocean bed. In the mid-1990s, she envisioned a battery-powered red-light camera that would be undetectable to fish, as they cannot see red light. At the same time, she wanted an electronic "lure" of blue lights that would mimic the distress response of an *Atolla* jellyfish and could be remotely operated to attract predators to the camera. Piecing together funding, a prototype was constructed and first deployed in June 2004 in the Gulf of Mexico. Widder dubbed the camera Eye-in-the-Sea (EITS) and the lure e-Jelly. Eighty-six seconds after the equipment was deployed and turned on, a six-foot squid, of a species previously unknown to science, came toward the camera. "I couldn't have asked for a better proof of concept," Widder told Erik Olsen for the *New York Times* (19 Dec. 2011).

Since that first outing, EITS has produced footage of jellyfish and rare sharks, including a variety of six-gilled shark that was exhibiting unusual behavior. She told Neil deGrasse Tyson: "They were doing something nobody's ever seen before. They were rooting on the bottom and apparently sucking up, in the sand, these little pill bugs, these isopods. And it's a possible explanation for how these behemoths survive in what seems like a desert sometimes." On an expedition to the Bahamas, Widder and her crew observed nine different species of shark, including an unusual seven-gilled shark. Because of the sheer amount of bioluminescence she has encountered with EITS, she has become convinced that bioluminescent creatures communicate through light; the key now is to unlock their meanings. She told *Nature*: "As humans reach deeper into the ocean to feed a hungry planet, many of these deep dwellers are in danger of being wiped out. Their growth and reproduction are often too slow for them to be fished sustainably. We need to know about their life histories and behaviors in order to protect them."

MEDUSA AND THE GIANT SQUID
Widder adapted EITS into a floating version she dubbed Medusa, which she hoped to use to capture a giant squid in its native habitat for the first time. No mission prior to Widder's had ever captured or recorded a live giant squid, despite their being described by sailors for centuries. Scientists have caught glimpses of dead ones, floating on the surface of the ocean, but in order to find out about its habits, it was necessary to film one undetected.

In the summer of 2012, near the Ogasawara Islands, six-hundred miles south of the Japanese mainland, Widder deployed the Medusa for the first time alongside her e-Jelly optical lure. The device was lowered to a depth of about 2,300 feet from a buoy on the surface and left to drift for hours. Reviewing the recordings later, a colleague discovered that Widder's device had hit the jackpot: three enormous tentacles had tried to snatch up the blue light lure. In her interview with Jacki Lyden for *NPR* (13 Jan. 2013), Widder recalled her first reactions to the giant squid: "The excitement was incredible. It's just amazing to be able to have a moment like that and realize you've done something people have been trying to do for decades. That's what got me into science in the first place—this opportunity to explore a new frontier. But I never, never imagined that I'd get an opportunity like this."

The Medusa device would go on to have five contacts with giant squid, including one in which the animal came into full view. Although pleased with the encounters, Widder wanted to capture the giant squids in living color, and the Medusa was only capable of recording in black and white. So her team sent their Triton submersible down with a smaller diamondback squid tied to the sub, along with Widder's electronic bait. At 2,000 feet, a giant squid took hold of the bait, with the crew recording the encounter the whole time. The sub and squid continued to descend together for another 1,000 feet—just 300 feet above the sub's maximum safe depth of 3,300 feet—when the squid abruptly slid off.

Widder told Jacki Lyden that the squid was "a spectacular silver and gold . . . it looks like it was carved out of metal. It's just absolutely breathtaking and completely unexpected."

ENVIRONMENTAL WORK WITH ORCA

Following two disturbing government reports in 2003 and 2004 describing the overall health of the world's oceans, Widder decided to leave the Harbor Branch Oceanographic Institute in 2005 to cofound ORCA, a nonprofit that strives to help protect and restore marine habitats through public education, conservation, and innovative new technologies designed to better monitor and assess damage caused by pollution and climate change. At the center of ORCA's work is bioluminescence, which Widder believes can fight pollution by helping to identify its sources and the places where it is most present.

An ongoing ORCA project is studying pollution in the Indian River Lagoon in Florida. About 156-miles long, it is one of the state's most endangered estuaries and one of its most biologically diverse. Widder and her team have used bioluminescent bacteria to determine the toxic levels in the lagoon's sediment—the more quickly the light dims as the bacteria is killed, the greater the level of pollution. Studying the level of pollution in sediment is key to understanding the level of contamination. "Pollution in the water is transient," Widder told Erik Olsen for the *New York Times*, "but in sediment it's persistent." She and her team have also placed sensors around the lagoon, which can send back real-time data about the water that can help trace the source of the pollution.

PERSONAL LIFE AND AWARDS

Edith Widder is married to her high school sweetheart, David Smith, a developer of high-tech instruments. Widder is the recipient of numerous awards including the 2006 Wings Worldquest Sea Award and a 2006 MacArthur Fellowship. She was inducted into the Women Divers' Hall of Fame in 2005, was named an Aspen Environment Forum Fellow in 2008, and was named both Environmentalist of the Year by the Conservation Alliance of St. Lucie County, Florida, and Blue Friend of the Year by the Loggerhead Marine Life Center in 2009. She has published extensively on her findings and is a member of numerous professional societies, including the American Academy of Underwater Sciences and the Explorers Club, among others.

SUGGESTED READING

Broad, William J. "Giant Squids Ready for Small-Screen Debut." *New York Times*. New York Times, 14 Jan. 2013. Web. 14 Aug. 2014.

Lyden, Jacki. "The Kraken Is Real: Scientist Films First Footage of a Giant Squid." *NPR. org*. NPR, 13 Jan. 2013. Web. 14 Aug. 2014.

Olsen, Erik. "Illuminating the Perils of Pollution, Nature's Way." *New York Times*. New York Times, 19 Dec. 2011. Web. 14 Aug. 2014.

Schrope, Mark. "The Giant Squid Stalker." *Slate*. Slate Group, 25 Jan. 2013. Web. 14 Aug. 2014.

"The Beauty of Ugly; Interview: Dr. Edith Widder." *Nature*. THIRTEEN Productions, Nov. 2007. Web. 14 Aug. 2014.

Tucker, Abigail. "Bioluminescence: Light Is Much Better, Down Where It's Wetter." *Smithsonian*. Smithsonian, Mar. 2013. Web. 14 Aug. 2014.

Tyson, Neil deGrasse. "Profile: Edith Widder." *Nova*. WGBH Educational Foundation, 23 July 2008. Web. 14 Aug. 2014.

—*Christopher Mari*

Mo Willems

Born: February 11, 1968
Occupation: Writer and animator

Calling Mo Willems "the most famous man in the literary world, if you are under three feet tall," Monica Hesse wrote for the *Washington Post* (7 Jan. 2012), "Willems is doo-doo funny for kids, but he's witheringly funny, almost sad-funny, for their parents. . . . His works, say the people who deeply believe in him, *mean* something—something both very basic and very complex that has been distilled into cartoons and monosyllabic words."

Willems, who began his career writing for the PBS children's television series *Sesame Street*, published his first book, *Don't Let the Pigeon Drive the Bus!*, in 2003. Its obstreperous avian protagonist was an immediate hit with readers, and he has since written several other books about the bird, as well as a popular series featuring a pig and an elephant who are friends and another series about a small girl and her beloved stuffed rabbit, whom she calls Knuffle Bunny. His books have won numerous awards for children's literature.

Willems explained to Michele Norris for the National Public Radio show *All Things Considered* (22 May 2008) that although his books might help children better understand the world and the emotions it evokes in them, he "balk[s] at the word instructive." He added, "I want to be real and I want to act in the same way as kids and adults do. I really feel that the difference between kids and adults is that kids are shorter. You know, they live on planet Earth, and they have the same emotions that we do and they react in the same way that we do. So I don't want to preach. . . . I just want to show and let the kids figure out what the books mean for them."

John Suchocki/The Republican/Landov

EARLY YEARS AND EDUCATION

An only child, Mo Willems was born on February 11, 1968, in Chicago, Illinois, just a few months after his parents emigrated from Holland. "There's no way around the eccentricity of having heavily accented parents . . . in a conservative town," he told Hesse. "But I think that it's helped me write with great empathy." When they were in their mid-thirties, Willems's parents took a pottery course together. His father, Casey, enjoyed the craft so much that he left his job in the hotel industry to become a potter full time, while his mother, Constance, discovered that she had such a love of learning that she eventually earned a law degree and went on to a career that included a tenure as a counsel for the Dutch government.

The family moved to New Orleans, Louisiana, when Willems was young, and he has recalled his childhood as a lonely one. The biggest mistake children's writers can make, he believes, is to depict childhood as an unremittingly happy or blissful time. He took great solace in looking at books illustrated by the Dutch artist Fiep Westendorp, known for her fanciful and colorful drawings. He was also an avid fan of the *Peanuts* comic strip, written and drawn by Charles Schulz, whom he counts as a major influence. One anecdote that Willems often relates to interviewers involves his childhood fan letter to Schulz, asking if he could have the famed cartoonist's job upon his death. Yet despite his love of comics, he "was not considered a reader," he told Amy Joyce in an interview for the *Washington Post* (4 Dec. 2013), because he "didn't gravitate to *Little House on the Prairie*"—a fact he considers "completely unfair, if the only books are going to be about a dog you know is going to die in the middle of Wisconsin." "For my generation," Willems explained, "reading comic strips was like smoking or something."

As a teen, Willems attended the Isidore Newman School, a private institution in New Orleans for gifted and talented students, where he took part in several stage productions and was convinced at various times that he should pursue a career in acting or directing. After finishing high school in 1986, Willems decided to travel to the United Kingdom to try his luck as a stand-up comedian. He found some degree of success in London clubs and even won a spot performing at the famed Edinburgh Fringe Festival.

Upon his return to the United States the following year, Willems entered New York University's Tisch School of the Arts, where he joined a sketch-comedy troupe called the Sterile Yak. He also discovered during this time that he had a talent for animation; in an interview with Greg Cook for the Boston public radio station WBUR (25 June 2013), he joked that he became interested in animated films because "in order to make live-action films you had to have friends, weather, location, and money, and I had none of those things." Willems graduated from Tisch cum laude in 1990 and subsequently took a job writing for *Sesame Street*.

WORK IN TELEVISION

Willems has told interviewers that he was hired by the *Sesame Street* producers because he was a comedian and they found it easier to teach someone funny to write for children than to teach educators how to be funny. Part of his work involved making short animated films, "essentially as an independent filmmaker," he told Cook. "They would contract me and I would shoot it and do everything and whatnot." Among his most popular animated characters was Suzie Kabloozie, a young girl prone to breaking into song.

Willems also contributed to the show as a scriptwriter. "Here's the great thing about *Sesame Street*," he said to Cook. "I was really a young guy when I was a writer there. I really was learning, it was like going to graduate school. The great thing is you could write a script that wasn't perhaps the best script in the world and these Muppeteers would make it funny. There's something to be said about the anonymity of television and there's also something to be said about writing stuff for people who are really talented." Willems ultimately won six Emmy Awards for his writing on the show. While still working for *Sesame Street*, he also produced a series of animated shorts called *The Off-Beats*, which aired between segments of the Nickelodeon television series *KaBlam!* from 1996 to 1999.

In 2000 Willems created a show for Cartoon Network called *Sheep in the Big City*, which follows the adventures of the titular animal as it tries to evade military operatives who want to capture it to fuel their sheep-powered death ray. (Among the military characters are General Specific, Major Pain, and Private Public.) The show attracted a fervent cult following but was canceled after two seasons. In 2002 Willems became the head writer for another Cartoon Network show, *Codename: Kids Next Door*, about a group of ten-year-olds who fight for the rights of children everywhere by fending off adult villains such as Gramma Stuffum, Knightbrace, and Mr. Fibb. He remained with the popular show until 2005.

CHILDREN'S BOOKS

Willems had long dreamed of writing children's books, reasoning that it would give him greater creative freedom than writing for television. He was interested in themes such as failure, sadness, and anger—concepts he has noted that producers of children's television are sometimes reluctant to explore. Additionally, he wanted to spend more time at home with his family than being the head writer for a television show allowed.

He quickly found that his previous success counted for little in the publishing world. "My experience in animation, the Emmys I had won, meant nothing," he told Delia O'Hara for the *Chicago Sun-Times* (21 Feb. 2010). "I sent *Don't Let the Pigeon Drive the Bus* to something like twenty-eight editors. They all said it was 'unusual,' but the twenty-eighth didn't think 'unusual' was a pejorative." That book, the first in what would become a series, was published in 2003. It remained on the New York Times Best Sellers list for several weeks and garnered a prestigious Caldecott Honor for illustration from the American Library Association. Other books in the series include *The Pigeon Finds a Hot Dog!* (2004), *The Pigeon Has Feelings, Too!* (2005), *Don't Let the Pigeon Stay Up Late!* (2006), and *The Pigeon Needs a Bath!* (2014), all featuring a simply drawn bird whose desires are consistently thwarted. The pigeon has exceptionally wide appeal; in his 2011 Zena Sutherland Lecture, Willems recalled reading two separate reviews of his first book: "The first one said, 'I love this book because it teaches perseverance. It teaches kids never to give up. To fight on.' The second review said, 'I love this book because it teaches kids to value the word 'no,' to know when to stop.'"

Willems is also the author of the Elephant and Piggie series, which debuted in 2007 and features two unlikely friends who find themselves in situations to which children might relate. Books in the series are refreshingly nondidactic and generally employ no more than fifty different words each; as Willems told Norris, "they are easy readers—or as I like to call them, hard writers." The twenty-first Elephant and Piggie book, *My New Friend Is So Fun!*, was published in June 2014.

Among Willems's most popular books are the three that explore the changing relationship between a young girl and her stuffed rabbit: *Knuffle Bunny: A Cautionary Tale* (2004), *Knuffle Bunny Too: A Case of Mistaken Identity* (2007), and *Knuffle Bunny Free: An Unexpected Diversion* (2010). Based in part on his own daughter, the books, the first two of which garnered Caldecott Honors, employ carefully modified photos of New York City and other locales as backdrops for his simply drawn characters. (Willems removes any window air-conditioning units, for example, to preserve the timeless feel of the pictures.) "It is one of Mo Willems's many achievements to be, if not the first, then certainly the best author to present the dread heartbreak of the lost stuffed animal," Pamela Paul wrote in a review for the *New York Times* (17 Dec. 2010). She added, "Willems has a Pixar-esque knack for speaking to parents and children at the same time, without over- or underestimating either."

FURTHER SUCCESS IN PUBLISHING

In addition to his various series, Willems has penned several stand-alone books, including *You Can Never Find a Rickshaw When It Monsoons: The World on One Cartoon a Day* (2006), which contains work he did while backpacking around the world after college. In early 2009 he published *Naked Mole Rat Gets Dressed*, in which the protagonist, Wilbur, horrifies his fellow naked mole rats by insisting on wearing clothes. Although he has not hinted that Wilbur will be a recurring character, critics felt that a sequel featuring the iconoclastic mammal would be welcome. "Willems tackles the old it's-OK-to-be-different genre with his customary chutzpah and subversive charm," one wrote for *Kirkus Reviews* (1 Dec. 2008). "[He] eschews a black-and-white encouragement to stand out from the crowd, offering instead a story that makes a case for different opinions to operate side by side."

Willems's work has spawned a multitude of videos, toys, and apps, and both the Knuffle Bunny and Elephant and Piggie series inspired plays that toured the country after opening at the Kennedy Center in Washington, DC. "My hope is that my books and my apps and other platforms of entertainment engender a desire by a large number of kids to write and draw on their own," Willems told Jeff Labrecque for *Entertainment Weekly* (27 Oct. 2011). "The day that they discover that they're not going to be an artist for real in their lives is probably the day they discover they're not going to be basketball players for real. Yet the kids keep playing basketball, but they stop drawing. So if I can create work that sparks kids to create their own stuff . . . and they keep doing it, that would be a phenomenal achievement."

Willems's work has been the subject of major retrospectives at the Eric Carle Museum of Picture Book Art in Amherst, Massachusetts, and the Seongnam Arts Center in Seoul, South Korea. He also sculpts, and his fifteen-hundred-pound steel sculpture *The Red Elephant* is on long-term loan to the Eric Carle Museum, where it is exhibited in the courtyard.

PERSONAL LIFE

In 1997 Willems married Cheryl Camp, a television production manager. They have one daughter, Trixie, who was the inspiration for the young girl in the Knuffle Bunny books. Willems has said that although Trixie is much older now, she still believes that they are the best books in his oeuvre. Willems and his family moved to Massachusetts from the New York City borough of Brooklyn in 2008.

SUGGESTED READING

Hesse, Monica. "Mo Willems Is the Go-To Author for Children—and Their Parents." *Washington Post*. Washington Post, 6 Jan. 2012. Web. 4 June 2014.

Willems, Mo. "Author Mo Willems on 'Elephant and Piggie.'" Interview by Michele Norris. *National Public Radio*. Natl. Public Radio, 22 May 2008. Web. 4 June 2014.

Willems, Mo. "Don't Pigeonhole Him: An Interview with Kids Book Author Mo Willems." Interview by Glen Cook. *WBUR*. Boston U, 25 June 2013. Web. 5 June 2014.

Willems, Mo. "'Elephant and Piggie' Author Mo Willems on His Latest Best-Seller and His New Pigeon App." Interview by Jeff Labrecque. *Entertainment Weekly*. Entertainment Weekly, 27 Oct. 2011. Web. 5 June 2014.

Willems, Mo. "Mo Willems on Writing for the Reluctant Reader." Interview by Amy Joyce. *Washington Post*. Washington Post, 4 Dec. 2013. Web. 4 June 2014.

Willems, Mo. "Mo Willems Talks about His Animal Friends." Interview by Delia O'Hara. *Delia O'Hara*. O'Hara, 21 Feb. 2010. Web. 4 June 2014.

SELECTED WORKS

Don't Let the Pigeon Drive the Bus! (Pigeon #1), 2003; *Knuffle Bunny: A Cautionary Tale* (Knuffle Bunny #1), 2004; *Leonardo, the Terrible Monster*, 2005; *Edwina, the Dinosaur Who Didn't Know She Was Extinct*, 2006; *You Can Never Find a Rickshaw When It Monsoons: The World on One Cartoon a Day*, 2006; *Today I Will Fly!* (Elephant and Piggie #1), 2007; *Naked Mole Rat Gets Dressed*, 2009; *City Dog, Country Frog*, 2010

—*Mari Rich*

Rebel Wilson

Born: February 3, 1986
Occupation: Actor and comedian

While she was still a young law student in Australia, Rebel Wilson was already making a name for herself as an actor known for her fearless approach to comedy. Though she originally took up acting lessons as a remedy for her shyness, an illness as a teenager provided her with a vision of stardom that she spent the next years struggling to realize.

After finding work in local theater and television, Wilson eventually moved to the United States and saw her career skyrocket following her appearance in the 2011 comedy hit *Bridesmaids*. From her small, scene-stealing role, Wilson found herself immediately cast in a series of films, including the black comedy *Bachelorette* and the musical comedy *Pitch Perfect*. With her near-ubiquitous presence on late-night television and the 2013 debut of her sitcom, *Super Fun Night*, Wilson is poised to become one of the most prominent female voices in comedy. "It was hard work," she told Thomas Gut for *GQ Australia* (25 Jan. 2013). "I did a lot of stand-up, I had to prove myself." Wilson added, "It's not like I was plucked out of nowhere to get in these movies. When I was just a girl in Sydney, no one thought, 'Oh, she's going to be a movie star.' No one. I had to get by with actual skill and talent."

EARLY LIFE AND EDUCATION

Rebel Melanie Elizabeth Wilson was born in Sydney, Australia, on February 3, 1986. Her parents named her after a woman who sang at their wedding. Like younger siblings Ryot, Annachi, and Liberty, Wilson was given a middle name based on English royalty—Elizabeth—which she went by in school. Wilson's mother bred beagles and worked as a dog show judge, and Wilson and her siblings frequently attended competitions.

Wilson attended her first acting class when she was fourteen years old, in an attempt to overcome her shyness. In school she excelled in mathematics and played sports such as tennis, hockey, and basketball. She also appeared in musical productions of *Grease* and *Fiddler on the Roof* and sang in an a cappella group. After high school, Wilson traveled to southern Africa to work as a Rotary International Youth Ambassador. While there, she contracted malaria and was hospitalized in Johannesburg, where she

Doug Peters/PA Photos/Landov

had a dream in which she won an Academy Award. This vision sparked a drive to become an actor. "I just always thought I'd be good, even at the first," she told Jeremy Kinser for the *Advocate* (28 Sept. 2012). "I was so nervous to get in front of people and whatever, but there was just something inside of me that I just thought, *No I will be good. Just keep going and keep trying.* And then weirdly now it's kind of become true, but I think if you just stay true to yourself and just show people who you are, then, hopefully, they'll like it."

After returning to Australia Wilson began work in Sydney-area theaters and the Australian Theatre for Young People (ATYP). Reflecting on one musical in which she appeared, she told Christina Radish for *Collider* (2 Oct. 2012), "I remember, very clearly, that I was in the chorus and they made me stand right at the back of the stage because I pulled focus. . . . Sometimes I even had to turn around and face away because, for some reason, and I don't know what it is, they said I pulled focus and that I was distracting from the real people playing the real characters." She went on to note, "I was just trying to give really good energy and be really passionate when I sang. It's funny how it happens." Wilson also performed at the National Institute of Dramatic Art (NIDA) but was denied admission to train there. Instead, she enrolled at the University of New South Wales, where she majored in arts and law. In addition to her course load, Wilson continued to act, working at the Push Up Theatre Company as a performer, writer, and director. In an act that would change her career path, Wilson wrote

a play called *The Westie Monologues*, in which she starred at the 2002 Sydney Fringe Festival.

EARLY TELEVISION CAREER

In 2002 Wilson was granted an ATYP scholarship and traveled to New York to train with the Second City improvisational comedy group and study at the New York Film Academy. In 2003 she began appearing in the Australian television series *Pizza*, which aired on the SBS network from 2003 to 2007; Wilson also worked on the show's spin-off film, *Fat Pizza* (2003). She next appeared in the Australian sketch show *The Wedge*, in which she played various characters in 2006 and 2007.

For her next role on Australian television, Wilson created and starred in the SBS series *Bogan Pride*, in which she plays teenager Jennie Cragg. The show aired for one season in 2008. During this period she was also a cast member of the series *Monster House*, though the show was also short-lived.

Wilson looks back fondly on these early television experiences and has commented on their differences from her later work in the United States. "On the first TV show I did, I would have to go and buy my own costumes and bring my own props," she told Marshall Heyman for the *Wall Street Journal* (28 Sept. 2012). "For lunch we would go to a McDonalds drive through." In a break from television, Wilson starred in the 2009 short film *Bargain!*, for which she won a best actor award at the Tropfest film festival. She made small appearances in series including *Thank God You're Here*, *Talkin' 'Bout Your Generation*, and *City Homicide* before moving to Los Angeles in 2010.

AMERICAN FILM DEBUT

In 2010, after dozens of failed auditions, Wilson was cast in the film *Bridesmaids*, a comedy directed by Paul Feig, produced by Judd Apatow, and starring Kristen Wiig, Maya Rudolph, Rose Byrne, and Melissa McCarthy. Wilson auditioned for the role that ultimately went to McCarthy but impressed Feig so much with her energy and presence that he created a character specifically for her. In the film Wilson plays Brynn, an obnoxious and off-putting Englishwoman who is a roommate of the protagonist, played by Wiig. Though she appears in only four scenes, Wilson received significant attention for her role, for which she drew heavily from her training in improvisational comedy.

Bridesmaids was released in the United States on May 13, 2011, and became a hit with critics and audiences. The film grossed over $288 million internationally and was nominated for numerous awards, including the Golden Globe for best motion picture and the Academy Award for best original screenplay. With the success of *Bridesmaids*, Wilson suddenly found herself an in-demand actress. She told Radish, "It was just like, 'Bang!' I booked five movies within a week or two."

FOLLOW-UP ROLES

The following year Wilson appeared in the black comedy *Bachelorette*, written and directed by Leslye Headland. In the film Wilson plays Becky, a woman who is getting married and must celebrate her bachelorette party with three women who tormented her in high school, played by Kirsten Dunst, Lizzy Caplan, and Isla Fischer. The film received generally poor reviews, but Wilson was praised for her work. Director Headland told Sandy Cohenap for the Associated Press (7 Sept. 2012), "Becky is a very difficult character to cast. You need really, really adept and fearless actors. I met Rebel and I saw her work and I was like, 'I have to have her.'"

In 2012 Wilson took on small roles in the comedy *Small Apartments* and the coming-of-age film *Struck by Lightning*. She also appeared in the comedy-drama *What to Expect When You're Expecting*, based on the famous pregnancy guide and starring A-list actors Cameron Diaz, Jennifer Lopez, and Elizabeth Banks. In her first animated film role, Wilson voiced Raz, a prehistoric kangaroo, in *Ice Age: Continental Drift*, the fourth installment of the popular *Ice Age* film franchise.

PITCH PERFECT

Wilson took on her next major role in the film *Pitch Perfect*, a musical comedy about a collegiate a cappella group. She was the first actor cast for the film, securing her role months before her costars. For her audition, she sang the Lady Gaga song "The Edge of Glory." She told Kinser, "I did my own body percussion just to add that extra little flavor and just belted it out because I knew they really wanted to see whether I could sing or not." In the end she easily won the role of Amy, a brassy and funny student from Tasmania who nicknames herself "Fat Amy" so that other people will not do it behind her back.

The film involves numerous musical numbers and choreographed dance routines, and much of Wilson's scene-stealing performance was improvised. She told Heyman, "That was often my job, to come up with certain little things to say and I was surprised when a lot of things made it into the movie." Wilson has noted in interviews that her favorite performance was her solo during the song "Turn the Beat Around." The film's director, Jason Moore, has praised her fearless performance, telling Cohenano, "There's this beautiful openness to the way Rebel approaches everything."

Pitch Perfect premiered on September 28, 2012, and was met with positive reviews. Critics praised the film's music and the performances of Wilson and her costars, Anna Kendrick,

Skylar Astin, Anna Camp, and Brittany Snow. The film's soundtrack, *Pitch Perfect: Original Motion Picture Soundtrack*, became a best seller. A sequel was announced in the spring of 2013, with an anticipated release date in 2015. Wilson has confirmed that she will reprise the role of Fat Amy in the sequel.

RETURN TO THE SMALL SCREEN

In 2013 Wilson was given the opportunity to try a new style of performance when she was asked to host the MTV Movie Awards, which aired on April 14, 2013. Wilson was the first woman to emcee the event since comedian Sarah Silverman in 2007. Her turn as host received mixed responses from viewers and critics, with mild reactions to her sense of humor, which is often described as being uncomfortable or crass. Nevertheless, she was applauded for the scope of what she was asked to do on stage. In addition to hosting she performed a medley with the cast of *Pitch Perfect* and accepted an award for best breakthrough performance. In an interview with the press after the show she admitted, "I don't know if I'd ever host again. It's pretty nerve-wracking because it's not like doing a movie where if you stuff up, you can get many takes. I just had one chance." That same month she appeared in the Michael Bay–directed film *Pain & Gain*.

Wilson's other major project in 2013 was her first American sitcom, *Super Fun Night*. The show, produced by television host Conan O'Brien, was originally developed for CBS as a multicamera sitcom. O'Brien was impressed by Wilson's turn in *Bridesmaids* and her subsequent appearance as a guest on his show. "She has an incredible will, but she's completely unselfconscious in how she presents herself," O'Brien told Lynn Hirschberg for *New York Magazine* (15 Sept. 2013). "That willingness to be bold and her innate likability is contagious: even during our first meeting, I found that I couldn't take my eyes off her." Over time the show evolved into a single-camera comedy and was picked up by ABC after CBS passed on the project. In addition to serving as creator, Wilson stars as lawyer Kimmie Boubier, who gets together with two friends, played by Lauren Ash and Liza Lapira, every Friday night. The show was scheduled to premiere on October 2, 2013. Wilson has noted that she is most excited to depict characters who are generally underrepresented on television. "The bigger purpose in all of this," she told Hirschberg, "is to inspire girls who don't think they're socially all that—who don't think they're pretty and popular. To let them know they can have fun and exciting lives."

PERSONAL LIFE

Wilson has noted in interviews that her weight has always been an important part of her life, both on and off camera. From 2011 to 2013 she served as a spokesperson for the Jenny Craig weight loss company. She is noted for being extremely open about her body type and for embracing her trademark size and image. "Some actresses who are bigger say, 'I don't want to get famous for playing a fat character,'" she explained to Josh Rottenberg for *Entertainment Weekly* (11 May 2012). "But the size I am, you can't just ignore it and try to go for skinny roles. In comedy you have to use what you've got."

Wilson lives in Los Angeles with roommate Matt Lucas, the British actor and her *Bridesmaids* and *Small Apartments* costar. Wilson has described Lucas as a big brother and a close friend.

SUGGESTED READING

Cohenap, Sandy. "Rebel Wilson's Popularity Just Keeps Growing in Hollywood." *news.com.au*. News, 7 Sept. 2012. Web. 19 Sept. 2013.

Heyman, Marshall. "Rebel Wilson on Playing the Comic 'Button.'" *Wall Street Journal*. Dow Jones, 28 Sept. 2012. Web. 19 Sept. 2013.

Hirschberg, Lynn. "The Misfit: Can Rebel Wilson Create the American Sitcom's First Genuine Outcast?" *New York*. New York Media, 15 Sept. 2013. Web. 19 Sept. 2013.

Kinser, Jeremy. "Rebel Wilson: Big Fun." *Advocate*. Here Media, 28 Sept. 2012. Web. 19 Sept. 2013.

Rottenberg, Josh. "Beyond *Bridesmaids*." *Entertainment Weekly* 11 May 2012: 46–49. Print.

Wilson, Rebel. "Rebel Wilson Talks *Pitch Perfect*, Her Career Post-*Bridesmaids*, and Her ABC Show *Super Fun Night*." Interview by Christina Radish. *Collider*. Collider, 2 Oct. 2012. Web. 19 Sept. 2013.

SELECTED WORKS

Pizza, 2003–7; *Fat Pizza*, 2003; *The Wedge*, 2006–7; *Bogan Pride*, 2008; *Bridesmaids*, 2011; *Bachelorette*, 2012; *What to Expect When You're Expecting*, 2012; *Ice Age: Continental Drift*, 2012; *Pitch Perfect*, 2012; *Pain & Gain*, 2013; *Super Fun Night*, 2013–

—*Kehley Coviello*

Lennox Yearwood

Born: 1969
Occupation: Minister and activist

Most often seen publically clad in clerical clothing (black pants and shirt with a white collar) and a black baseball cap resting slightly askew atop his head, activist Lennox Yearwood Jr.

Alexis C. Glenn/UPI/Landov

embodies the seemingly incongruent intermingling of religion and hip-hop. An ordained minister with a master of divinity degree, Yearwood has embraced hip-hop as not only an expression of cultural identity, but also as a tool to raise social and political awareness among young people. As president of the Hip Hop Caucus—a nonprofit organization that focuses on increasing political involvement by integrating hip-hop music and culture into its public campaigns—Yearwood promotes an agenda that encompasses racial, environmental, and social issues through the lens of peaceful nonviolence.

Yearwood's purpose is twofold: to attract a young voting base that may feel like the political process is out of its hands, and to influence those in power to account for the young, primarily urban, voting bloc. "We're non-partisan," he told Arielle Loren for *BET.com* (17 Sept. 2012). "We want people to make [a voting] decision. We want an educated voter." On the other hand, he encourages politicians to engage young, specifically minority, voters. "[Do not] disregard a base of people because the numbers don't show they voted in the past, but figure out what we have to do to make sure they can vote." As a civil rights leader, Yearwood sees an increasing encroachment on basic rights, and his message is essentially that for freedom to be protected, people must understand the issues confronting policy makers and engage in the process of policy making by voting.

EARLY LIFE AND EDUCATION

Yearwood was born in 1969 in Shreveport, Louisiana, and was the first of his family, who mostly hail from Trinidad and Tobago, to be born in the United States. As an African American from a family of immigrants, he had a unique perspective on race relations that has informed his career arc.

In 1990, as a student at the University of the District of Columbia (UDC), in his first foray into activism, Yearwood organized a student sit-in that lasted ten days. He and the other students were protesting both budget cuts and a proposed relocation of the campus; the school did eventually close its downtown campus, moving to the North Cleveland Park area of the capital city. Yearwood graduated from UDC in 1998. Four years later, he earned a master of divinity degree from Howard University. He also spent time in the US Air Force Reserve, joining in 2000 in order to help pay for his education. He entered the Chaplain Candidates program, finishing in 2003, at which point he decided not to become an Air Force chaplain, though he remained a reservist.

HIP-HOP AND POLITICS

Yearwood came to prominence as an advocate for the importance of youth culture. Though he has been described by many as a radical, he has spent more than a decade as a political activist focused on empowering African Americans and other minorities, as well as exposing what he deems to be the political corruption of the federal government. In 2004, Yearwood partnered with rap superstar Sean Combs (perhaps better known by his monikers Puff Daddy and Diddy) to create the "Vote or Die" campaign, encouraging young people and minorities to play a part in the political process. "We have to grow our power within politics to be able to break down . . . barriers," Combs said at the time (*NBCNews.com* 29 Oct. 2004). "Vote or Die" was one of several campaigns in 2004 that focused on the youth vote, which accounted for 18.4 percent of the total vote and set a precedent for future voter campaigns.

Yearwood began the Hip Hop Caucus nonprofit organization in 2004; his goal was to integrate hip-hop culture and political campaigns to increase public involvement. He linked his agenda with that of Combs and rap mogul Russell Simmons, who, with Yearwood, embarked on the Hip Hop Team Vote Bus Tour. Yearwood's work with rap luminaries coincided with the general mission of the Hip Hop Caucus. Addressing the reason for his involvement with the hip-hop generation, in an interview with Martha van Gelder for *Green America* (Jan./Feb. 2013), Yearwood said, "I think that there's an idealistic viewpoint that this world can be something better. I think there's a hope, there's an energy. But

most importantly, for students everywhere, it's about their future."

Continuing what he started in 2004, Yearwood initiated "Respect My Vote!" for the 2008 election cycle to target young adults between the ages of eighteen and twenty-nine without college experience. The "One Day Vote" campaign headed by the Hip Hop Caucus registered more than thirty thousand people on September 30, 2008, and featured performers such as Nelly. "This one day event proves that we can make an impact in this election, and that working together to get out the vote is the only way to see results," Yearwood said at the time (*Common Dreams* 3 Oct. 2008). Because of its success in 2008, Yearwood insists that the hip-hop generation was a primary force behind the election of President Barack Obama. "Respect My Vote" resurfaced for the midterm elections of 2010. Registering young people to vote has been a much publicized aspect of the Hip Hop Caucus's mission, but its overarching goal has been to help young people identify the connections between poverty, racism, and the environment, among other issues.

PROTEST AND ARREST

As a minister of Church of God in Christ, a Pentecostal and largely African American denomination, Yearwood has been a spokesman for peace; he was particularly outspoken about the US invasion of Iraq in 2003, at which time he was training to be a chaplain in the Air Force. A February 2003 sermon that he delivered at Andrews Air Force Base (entitled "Who Would Jesus Bomb?") aligned him with the interpretation of the biblical Jesus as a promoter of peace. Over the following years, Yearwood began a vociferous campaign against the Iraq War, one that pitted him against the establishment in which he was entrenched; he conflated events such as the federal government's handling of Hurricane Katrina in New Orleans with military action in the Middle East and the country's history of oppressing minorities. In a July 2, 2007, press release from the Hip Hop Caucus, Yearwood insisted, "This moment in history is our generation's lunch-counter moment—Iraq is our Vietnam and New Orleans is our Birmingham. Our generation could be the generation to defeat racism, poverty and war, but only if we come together as people of conscience."

Soon after launching the "Make Hip Hop Not War" tour in 2007, Yearwood received notice that he was to be discharged from the Air Force, ostensibly because of his antiwar stance. He issued the July 2007 press release to inform the general public of the campaign being waged against him. Because of Yearwood's resistance to being discharged, the Air Force reportedly considered deploying him to Iraq or sentencing him to jail. With pressure from the public, the Air

Force eventually decided to grant him an honorable discharge. "I will end my service with the honorable discharge that I earned," Yearwood stated, as quoted by Ken Butigan on the website *Waging Nonviolence* (7 Feb. 2013). "I am eternally grateful, and evermore committed to taking on the powers that be for the powers that ought to be."

Only months after his letter, in September 2007, Yearwood was at the center of another controversy when he was arrested while trying to enter the hearing room where General David Petraeus was testifying about the Iraq War. A widely circulated YouTube video shows Yearwood trying to regain his place in line after exiting to conduct an interview (according to him, with permission from the police) and then being denied entrance to the hearing. After he and the officer who denied him access spoke for a brief period, a group of officers surrounded him, handcuffed him, and dragged him to the ground. On September 12, after his arraignment for charges that included assaulting an officer and disorderly conduct, he released a statement via the Hip Hop Caucus (and quoted on the website *Common Dreams*) in response to his arrest: "My role is to make government more transparent to the people, especially people of color. How am I supposed to convince other African-Americans to come to Capitol Hill to participate in democracy, when Capitol Police will go so far as to jump me when I question my exclusion from a hearing that is open to the public?" His arrest only served to affirm his belief in an unjust system that sought to exclude minorities and those who questioned the machinations of the federal government.

HIP-HOP AND ENVIRONMENTALISM

Yearwood has used hip-hop to connect to a young generation that is increasingly politically aware, a development for which he is at least partially responsible, and as he has gained more political footing within the community, he has begun to shift his focus to environmental issues, specifically climate change. Yearwood was a key participant in the "Forward on Climate" rally held in Washington, DC, in February 2013; he also served as the host of the event. Yearwood has established himself as a unique personality in the environmental movement, lending a perspective to a cause that has been primarily a white middle-to-upper-class undertaking.

"This year is the 150th anniversary of the Emancipation Proclamation, and we're celebrating that from the standpoint that slavery was an institution, just like Big Oil, that we were able to get rid of. It took a lot, but we were able to get rid of that," Yearwood explained to Van Gelder for *Green America*. By conflating race issues with the environment, Yearwood hopes both to expose what he perceives to be

the establishment's resistance to change even in the face of overwhelming evidence and to remind the public, specifically minority communities, that institutions can be altered. To push his environmental agenda, he and the Hip Hop Caucus have reached out to black colleges—where issues concerning the environment have not always been at the forefront—and to others in minority communities that usually set issues of race, poverty, and education above environmentalism. He told Van Gelder: "They need to understand that while there is clearly a need to address poverty and education and issues of imbalance, if we don't correct the situation involving our planet, all those problems will cease to exist."

Yearwood first began to see how climate issues impact underprivileged communities during Hurricane Katrina, creating the Gulf Coast Renewal Campaign, and he continues to focus on the role young people can play in the debate over climate change and its effects. "[They] have always been at the core of every single movement that has created change in this country, and it cannot stop now," he said to Van Gelder. As he told Alexander Zaitchik for *Rolling Stone*, "What we're seeing now—young people willing to get arrested . . . is what we need, because the situation is critical. For me, if that means literally putting my body against the gears of the machine to stop the madness, that's what I'll do." Yearwood's radicalism, sparked by both the power imbalance he experienced as an African American youth and his understanding of the Christian gospel as a mechanism for peaceful change, has made him a key figure in the environmental movement, one of the most pressing ongoing political issues.

WALKING IN KING'S FOOTSTEPS

Yearwood has garnered comparisons to Martin Luther King Jr., a spokesman for justice and peace at a critical juncture in the history of the United States. The underlying connections are obvious: like King, Yearwood is a minister and civil rights leader who employs nonviolent resistance to engender political change. Though King and his ideas entered the mainstream long ago, Yearwood insists that the radical nature of King's mission is often glossed over. "His message was neutered," Yearwood claimed in an interview with Michael Cooper Jr. for *Generation Progress* (23 Jan. 2013). "In his last speech he linked up with the striking sanitation workers in Memphis. He was against the [Vietnam] war, and even called out his country as one of the greatest purveyors of violence in this world. It is almost intentional to neutralize his message." Despite feeling that King's radicalism has been neutralized, however, Yearwood is emboldened by the stances taken by King and is clearly influenced by him.

He points to King as an early purveyor of the intermingling of politics and culture, which is the foundation of the Hip Hop Caucus. "Culture comes before politics," he told Cooper. "Using artists like 2 Chainz or Immortal Technique allows us to create a drum beat to march to, which makes our work easier. Even Dr. King worked with Harry Belafonte. Every movement needs cultural game changers to make a difference." To Yearwood, linking entertainment and politics is not counterintuitive, but, contrarily, is essential to provoking change, and he uses King as an example of the ways religion, culture, and politics can mingle to incite people to think about broad issues that affect entire communities.

Named in 2010 as one of *Ebony* magazine's one hundred most powerful African Americans, Yearwood, through the Hip Hop Caucus, has promoted politics as cool, collaborating with Combs, Jay Z, and many others in the hip-hop community to raise awareness in schools and among youth in general. "I believe that we are the most important generation this country has ever had," he said to Cooper. "If we fight for justice, and equality, and fairness, we can change this country and the world." Saint Paul's College in Virginia granted him an honorary doctorate degree in 2011. Yearwood is the father of two boys and lives in the Washington, DC, area.

SUGGESTED READING

Butigan, Ken. "Rev. Lennox Yearwood, Jr.'s Forward Motion for a World That Works for All." *Waging Nonviolence*. Waging Nonviolence, 7 Feb. 2013. Web. 20 Sept. 2013.

Gerken, James. "'Forward on Climate' Rally Brings Climate Change Activists to National Mall in Washington, D.C." *Huffington Post*. TheHuffingtonPost.com, 17 Feb. 2013. Web. 20 Sept. 2013.

Loren, Arielle. "Respect My Vote: The Hip Hop Caucus Merges Community and Politics." *BET.com*. BET Interactive, 17 Sept. 2012. Web. 20 Sept. 2013.

Yearwood, Lennox. "Five Minutes With: The Hip Hop Caucus' Rev. Lennox Yearwood." Interview by Michael Cooper Jr. *Generation Progress*. Generation Progress, 23 Jan. 2013. Web. 20 Sept. 2013.

Yearwood, Lennox. "Green or Die." Interview by Brentin Mock. *American Prospect*. American Prospect, 26 Nov. 2008. Web. 20 Sept. 2013.

Yearwood, Lennox. "The Hip-Hop Activist: Rev. Lennox Yearwood." Interview by Martha van Gelder. *Green America*. Green America, Jan./Feb. 2013. Web. 20 Sept. 2013.

Zaitchik, Alexander. "The Reverend." *Rolling Stone* 25 Apr. 2013: 47. Print.

—*Christopher Rager*

Yi So-yeon

Born: June 2, 1978
Occupation: Scientist

Yi So-yeon is a scientist and biotech engineer who has the distinction of being the first Korean to go to space. If Yi were a man, her journey to the International Space Station (ISS) in 2008 would undoubtedly have been less complicated. From her studies at the Korean Advanced Institute of Science and Technology (KAIST)—where the faculty buildings don't even have women's bathrooms—to her subsequent work in a totally male-dominated field, Yi has achieved success based on a lot of hard work and one stroke of good fortune.

In 2006 she beat out some 36,200 applicants to become one of the two finalists in a national contest for the honor of being Korea's first astronaut and riding aboard a Russian Soyuz rocket to the ISS. Although she lost the contest to former military officer Ko San, they both went to Russia to train with the cosmonauts—Ko as an astronaut and Yi as his understudy. After a year of intense training and less than a month before the launch, Yi was informed that she would be replacing her colleague, who had broken several rules, and she would be going to space. At twenty-nine, she would become the first astronaut to travel to space before the age of thirty.

Growing up, Yi loved watching science fiction movies, but she never dreamed she would be an astronaut. Now, Yi has something else she didn't bargain for: celebrity. "When I returned, thousands of people waited for me and shouted my name. I began to feel like my life was not my life anymore," she told Asher Schechter for the Israeli website *Haaretz* (2 Sept. 2012). "It wasn't easy. I am just a scientist that unexpectedly became a celebrity. I am now more accustomed to it, but it's still a huge burden. If you ask me what's harder, being famous or flying to space, I'd say fame is much harder."

Yi is the second Asian woman to go to space, after Chiaki Mukai of Japan. In 2011, she was named in "The Ultimate List of Fifteen Asian Scientists to Watch" by Juliana Chan for *Asian Scientist*. One of her life goals is to encourage women to pursue careers in science.

EARLY YEARS AND EDUCATION

Yi was born on June 2, 1978—nearly ten years after Neil Armstrong and his crew landed on the moon and seventeen years after Russian cosmonaut Yuri Gagarin first orbited Earth—to parents Yi Kil-su and Jung Kum-sun. She grew up in Gwangju, South Korea, with her brother, Yi Ki-baek.

Traditionally, South Korea is a male-dominated society, but Yi's parents were not conservative in terms of gender roles. When her father, who was trained as an engineer but worked as a banker, engaged in household projects like fine-tuning the family car, he always asked Yi to be his special assistant.

South Korea is a very different place than it was when Yi's parents were growing up. Her mother, she told Lopez-Alegria, "couldn't even go to middle school." Thanks in part to her father, Yi was interested in science from a young age; she graduated from Gwangju Science High School in 1997. She completed her undergraduate and postgraduate studies in mechanical engineering, in 2001 and 2002 respectively, at Korea Advanced Institute of Science and Technology (KAIST) in Daejeon, where according to Andrea Galvez for *Haps* magazine (8 Jan. 2012), "she lived in the lab." This is unsurprising considering that Yi completed her PhD in biological science in February 2008 at twenty-nine, while at the same time training for her journey to space. When she couldn't attend her doctoral graduation, her mother stepped in to take her place.

Yi's work ethic, according to numerous sources, is brutal even if it is rewarding. Rachel Lee, writing for the *Korea Times* (24 Aug. 2012) wrote a review of Yi's 2012 autobiography (available only in Korea), *The Eleventh Endeavor: The First Astronaut in Korea, Yi So-yeon's Full Story*, in which she reports that Yi struggled to overcome her fear of failure. "She now thinks that failure is like a vaccine that helps people become successful," Lee wrote.

DECISION TO ENTER THE ASTRONAUT PROGRAM

In 2006 South Korea and the Korea Aerospace Research Institute (KARI) announced plans for a contest to select one Korean to go to the International Space Station aboard a Russian Soyuz rocket. For the privilege of sending the first Korean national to outer space, the South Korean government paid Russia about 26 billion won (about 27 million dollars)—a figure that remains controversial with South Koreans. But the nation was anxious to go to space, in part to catch up with China and Japan and thereby to join a second space race reverberating through Asia.

The country launched its first satellite in 1992; that same year Japan was already sending its first professional astronaut into space—on board the US space shuttle *Endeavor*. Eleven years later China sent Yang Liwei to space aboard its own *Shenzhou 5* spacecraft. During this time South Korea's space dreams were stymied due to lack of funds and ongoing restrictive agreements with the United States (stemming from US fears of igniting an arms race with totalitarian North Korea). In the meantime, the price of sending a shuttle to space had become so expensive that, to alleviate some of that cost, Russia began selling space flights to other countries like South Korea that did not have their own functioning space programs.

When South Korea held an open call for astronauts through its South Korean Astronaut Program, the stipulations were loose. Any Korean older than nineteen was eligible to apply. Nonetheless Yi was realistic about her chances. As quoted by Amy Daybert for the Everett *Herald* (29 Dec. 2012), Yi recalled her decision to apply this way at a meeting of the South Everett–Mukilteo Rotary Club in Everett, Washington: "I told my friends, 'I know I will not make it, but when I am a grandma or a mom . . . I might be able to tell my children I knew the first Korean astronaut.'" Secretly, she hoped to be among the 245 candidates who would advance to the second round of the selection, but even the chances of that were looking slim as 36,206 Koreans applied.

SELECTION AS KOREA'S FIRST ASTRONAUT

The astronaut selection process began in earnest in April 2006, and Yi was among the finalists announced in November. She didn't even tell her family until the list had been reduced to thirty-six candidates. On Christmas Day 2006 Yi received the news that she was one of only two finalists remaining in the contest. The other, Ko San, was a male mathematician and roboticist.

Yi and Ko were sent to a cosmonaut training center in Russia where they began a "series of physical, mental, intellectual and publicity tests," Cho Jin-seo of the *Korea Times* (8 Apr. 2008) reported, and where they learned Russian. Back in South Korea, their personalities were being evaluated by the media; Ko reportedly even released his diaries. The South Korean government wanted the best person for the job, but they also wanted their chosen astronaut to serve as a likeable spokesperson, drumming up support for a planned space program and rocket launch. On September 5, 2007, the South Korean government announced that Ko had won the contest. Yi remained in Russia as his understudy and continued her training with the backup crew. Of Ko's selection and future plans, Cho wrote, "one thing is clear—he will be the nation's most eligible bachelor."

From the perspective of the South Korean people, everything seemed to be going smoothly until March 2008, less than a month before Ko was scheduled to launch. On March 7 Yi began training with the primary flight crew; on March 10 it was announced that she would be taking Ko's place on the mission. According to the Russian Federal Space Agency, Ko had repeatedly violated the agency's strict regulations, including borrowing training materials from the training center library without permission. In her book *Women in Space: Twenty-three Stories of First Flights, Scientific Missions, and Gravity-Breaking Adventures* Karen Bush Gibson writes that Ko sent sensitive materials home to Korea. (Both countries denied what some suspected and stated that Ko was not working as a spy.) Choe Sang-Hun of the *New York Times* (11 Mar. 2008) reported that the South Korean government "appeared unhappy" about the switch, especially as it happened so close to the launch. She quotes statements given by Lee Sang-mok, an official at the Ministry of Education, Science and Technology, during a nationally televised news conference: "The Russian space agency has stressed that a minor mistake and disobedience can cause serious consequences in space. So the honor of becoming South Korea's first astronaut now goes to a woman."

SOYUZ ROCKET LAUNCH

Although she discovered that she would go to space only a month before the scheduled launch, Yi was already physically prepared to cope with zero gravity and the wild fluctuations in pressure that occur when a spacecraft leaves or reenters the atmosphere. She was also prepared for the experiments she would need to complete once she was aboard the ISS and she was even familiar with surviving in extreme climates in the event of an emergency landing.

Yi relocated to the Baikonur Cosmodrome, the launching site in Kazakhstan, and five days before the launch, she moved into a "clean room" to prevent viral infections. On April 8, 2008, two hours before launch time, Yi said good-bye to her family (who had travelled to Kazakhstan to see her off) and joined two Russian cosmonauts, Sergey Volkov and Oleg Kononenko, to board the Soyuz TMA-12 spacecraft. The shuttle launched as planned and docked with the ISS, as scheduled, two days later. For some fifty hours, Yi and her colleagues had to remain seated with no access to food or toilet facilities. The successful launch made South Korea the thirty-fifth country in the world to send a national to space.

Back in South Korea, citizens from across the nation watched the launch. In anticipation, young students at Yi's alma mater, the Gwangju Science High School, launched their own powder rockets in the school's playground. "Students feel proud of Yi," one teacher told Kim Rahn for the *Korea Times* (8 Apr. 2008). She "has helped them believe their dreams can come true."

LIFE ABOARD THE ISS

Once aboard the ISS, Yi experienced several physical problems, including facial bloating and acute motion sickness as she adjusted to zero gravity. Perhaps most disturbing were the severe back pains she suffered—due to her youth and the flexibility of her spine, upon arrival she instantly grew three centimeters in height.

But Yi had little time to adjust to her new surroundings. Russian space officials had given Yi the title of "participant," suggesting that her role was merely that of a tourist. Despite the characterization and determined to make the most of its time on the ISS, South Korea assigned Yi a tremendous amount of work. "They gave me eighteen experiments to complete in my ten days in the ISS. That's a lot," she told Schechter. She studied the effects of pressure in space on her heart, her eyes, and the shape of her face, which got puffier during her stay. She also monitored the one thousand fruit flies she had brought with her, observing them for any changes in behavior. Some of the recorded experiments were educational and were later distributed to schools. Others, like the observations of her own body, proved valuable in compiling a training manual for future South Korean astronauts. "Everyone told me I didn't have to complete all of [the experiments], that it wasn't expected of me," she told Schechter. "But I knew everyone was watching me, so I gave up meals and sleep and completed all eighteen experiments. It's a very Korean thing to do." South Korea became the eleventh country to carry out experiments on the ISS.

Before her stay was over, Yi was able to complete a more personal task. She sang her favorite song, Frank Sinatra's "Fly Me to the Moon," in space.

BACK TO EARTH

Yi was scheduled to return to Earth, along with American astronaut, Peggy Whitson, and Russian flight engineer, Yuri Malenchenko, on a Soyuz capsule on April 19. Unlike the launch, the landing did not go as planned. Officials told a reporter for the Associated Press (20 Apr. 2008) that the capsule followed a ballistic reentry, a "very steep trajectory that subjects the crew to extreme physical force." The capsule landed twenty minutes late and nearly 260 miles off its mark. Yi, Whitson, and Malenchenk were unhurt though they had been subjected to gravitational forces nearly ten times of those on Earth. Yi was hospitalized for her previously sustained back injuries upon her return.

For the next four years, Yi worked as an ambassador and researcher for KARI and served as an adjunct professor at KAIST where she lectured on space experiments, biosystems, and human space flight. In the fall of 2012, Yi enrolled at the Haas School of Business, University of California, Berkeley, to pursue her MBA degree. Her decision caused a bit of a controversy in South Korea, where some lawmakers blamed waning interest in the country's space program on her departure. Getting an MBA, she told the Yonhap News Agency as quoted by the *Korea Herald* (23 Oct. 2013), "was a decision I made after realizing that I can't live the rest of my life talking about what I did in space for eleven days. I chose to pursue an MBA because I want to be someone who connects science with investors." She received her diploma in 2014.

PERSONAL LIFE

Yi married Jung Jae-hoon, a Korean American ophthalmologist, in Long Beach, California, on August 1, 2013. She retains her position as adjunct professor at KAIST.

SUGGESTED READING

Cho Jin-seo. "Yi Ready for Blasting Off into Space." *Korea Times*. Korea Times, 8 Apr. 2008. Web. 7 June 2014.
Choe Sang-Hun. "Woman Replaces Colleague for South Korea's First Space Mission." *New York Times*. New York Times, 11 Mar. 2008. Web. 7 June 2014.
Daybert, Amy. "First Korean Astronaut Addresses Controversy over MBA Studies in US." *Korea Herald*. Korea Herald, 23 Oct. 2013. Web. 9 June 2014.
Galvez, Andrea. "Feature: The First Lady of Space, Yi So-yeon." *Haps* [Busan, Korea]. Haps, 8 Jan. 2012. Web. 6 June 2014.
Gibson, Karen Bush. *Women in Space: Twenty-three Stories of First Flights, Scientific Missions, and Gravity-Breaking Adventures.* Chicago: Chicago Rev. P, 2014. Print.
Schechter, Asher. "Yi So-Yeon, S. Korea's First Astronaut, Who Didn't Mean to Be One at

All." *Haaretz* [Israel]. Haaretz, 2 Sept. 2012. Web. 4 June 2014.

—*Molly Hagan*

Bassem Youssef

Born: March 21, 1974
Occupation: Television host and doctor

Bassem Youssef, familiar to many Americans as the "Egyptian Jon Stewart," is the host of Egypt's television show *Al Bernameg* (sometimes transliterated as *El Bernameg*), or "The Program"—though CBC, the Egyptian network on which it aired, suspended the program in late 2013, deeming it too politically offensive. The satirical news show is based on the popular American program *The Daily Show with Jon Stewart*, in which Stewart, a comedian, offers insight through humor, reporting current events with the structure of the nightly news program but with a tone that is both irreverent and illuminating. Youssef was a practicing heart surgeon when, amid Egypt's uprising in 2011, he took to YouTube to record a series of short videos called "The B+ Bassem Youssef Show." The show, which was recorded in Youssef's Cairo apartment, premiered in March 2011 and mocked the Egyptian media coverage of the revolution. Within a few weeks, his videos had more than one million views, and less than two months after that, Youssef was offered a television deal with the network ONTV, owned by Egyptian billionaire, Naguib Sawiris.

In the more than two years since he began his show, Youssef has become much more than a popular entertainer; he has become an icon of the country's desire to speak out. "The voice of the Egyptian individual has been suppressed for nearly 60 years, but now, for the first time in many years, Egyptians feel this voice matters," Rasha Abdulla of the American University in Cairo told Miral Fahmy for Reuters (27

© Asmaa Waguih/Reuters/Corbis

Apr. 2011) during the uprising. "There's a thirst to speak out, an infatuation with the idea that we can actually make a difference, so now everybody's talking politics. Nobody's afraid anymore." However, Youssef's arrest in 2013—he was charged with insulting the president and Islam, released on bail, and fined—shows that the fight for freedom of speech in Egypt is ongoing. "This is by far the most important issue that everybody should fight for," Youssef told Ian Lee and Teo Kermeliotis for CNN.com (28 June 2013). "If you start to suppress people's freedom of speech under whatever excuse you want—'it's not good for the country, it's not good for the building of the country'—so every time they say this, we raise the ceiling, we raise the roof, we push it further. And I'm going to do this until the ceiling is broken or we are shut down."

EARLY LIFE AND MEDICAL CAREER

Bassem Raafat Muhammad Youssef was born in Cairo, Egypt, on March 21, 1974. His mother was an education specialist and a professor at the University of Cairo; she died in 2013. In a heartfelt article about her death for the Egyptian newspaper *Al Shorouk* (translated into English by Nadine Hafez for the website *Tahrir Squared*), Youssef wrote that, despite his mother's well-meaning pressure on him to marry at a young age, he pursued a medical career. He graduated from Cairo University's Faculty of Medicine in 1998, and spent time working for a medical equipment company in the United States and Europe. After earning his doctorate in Cairo, he performed heart- and lung-transplant surgeries in Germany, and in 2005, he was awarded his practitioner's license as a cardiothoracic surgeon.

REVOLUTION IN EGYPT

Youssef was a practicing surgeon and a faculty member at the University of Cairo in 2011, the year of Egypt's history-altering revolution. On January 25, Egyptian citizens gathered in Cairo's Tahrir Square to protest the repressive regime of President Hosni Mubarak. The protest, which turned violent after police tried to quell the growing crowd with tear gas and water cannons, was inspired by a similar uprising in Tunisia, which overthrew that country's authoritarian government less than two weeks before. The Egyptian Revolution ended the rule of Mubarak, but it also was the catalyst in a chain of unrest throughout the Arab world known as the "Arab Spring." The significance of what protesters called "the day of rage" was not immediately clear to all of the country's citizens—Youssef did not join the protests until several days after they began. He collected donations and delivered blankets to protestors, and in early February, he was among a group of doctors and nurses tending to the wounded after government henchman launched an attack on the square, an event that

came to be known as the Battle of the Camel. Later, the Battle of the Camel would be considered the decisive moment of the revolution, the moment that fueled Mubarak's ouster soon after. After thirty years in power, Mubarak resigned on February 11.

If the events of the revolution were not confusing enough—less than a month passed between the first sit-in and Mubarak's resignation—the reports of the revolution in the Egyptian media were awash with lies and conspiracy theories. Mubarak had lorded over the media for decades, and most newspapers and television stations were either run by the state or at least sympathetic to the state out of fear. Later, a handful of privately owned news outlets appeared that were willing to criticize the regime, Joshua Hersh wrote for the *New Yorker* (21 Aug. 2013), and "their encouragement and reporting helped pave the way for the revolution." But even in the days following Mubarak's resignation, reports were full of distortions—some of them downright outlandish, such as the rumor that protestors were being paid in American dollars and Kentucky Fried Chicken (KFC). (The idea was that those who were protesting were perpetuating foreign interests at Egypt's expense.) Youssef was frustrated by the idiocy of such theories, though he chose his words carefully. "Let's just say I'm annoyed at how the ignorance of the people is being used against them," Youssef told Willem Marx for *Bloomberg Businessweek* (29 Mar. 2012).

YOUTUBE SENSATION

To remedy what he saw as a lack of reason, Youssef teamed up with his friend Tarek AlQazzaz, the general manager of the production company Baraka One Web and a partner in YouTube, to produce a series of short videos modeled after the American television show *The Daily Show with Jon Stewart*. Youssef was (and is) a huge fan of Stewart, particularly the comedian's lucid takedowns of American new networks such as Fox News. Stewart has accused Fox of distorting facts to fit a conservative narrative and likes to use clips from the network to serve his punch lines and to expose the network's hypocrisy. Of such fodder for jokes Youssef told Brooke Gladstone for National Public Radio's (NPR's) *All Things Considered* (15 Apr. 2011) that the reportage surrounding the Egyptian revolution was "a gold mine." With the structure of *The Daily Show* in mind, Youssef began writing five- to fifteen-minute episodes of a show called *The B+ Bassem Youssef Show*, hoping to provide some much-needed clarity through satire.

Youssef spent hours viewing footage in preparation for each short episode and bought a plastic backdrop that was a collage of images from the revolution. With a video production crew, he shot eight short videos in a spare room in his apartment. The total cost of production was about $5,000. Youssef posted the first video—which took specific aim the KFC issue—on YouTube on March 8, 2011. He later told a reporter for the online magazine *Cairo 360* (27 Mar. 2011) that he had hoped the video would garner about ten thousand views within the week. Instead, he pulled in millions of viewers in Egypt and around the world. By April, he was fielding inquiries from Western media outlets such as the *New York Times* and NPR, and after his ninth episode, he was offered a television deal. On the same day, he received a work visa to take a job as a pediatric heart surgeon in Cleveland, Ohio. "That would have been the job of my life," Youssef told Benjamin Barthe for the London *Guardian Weekly* (11 June 2013), "but I chose TV and up to now I haven't regretted it."

AL BERNAMEG

A number of television stations, including Al Jazeera's satellite network, offered Youssef a contract, but in May 2011, he signed a year-long deal with Egypt's privately owned ONTV. *Al Bernameg* premiered during Ramadan, the Muslim holy month of fasting. During Ramadan, families tend to stay home in the evening and watch television together. *Al Bernameg* initially aired three nights a week, and despite a competitive slate of programming, became the most popular television show during Ramadan. Youssef continued to run the operation out of his apartment; he and his team of writers—most of whom were unpaid interns—wrote episodes that were filmed back-to-back on Saturdays at ONTV's studio outside of Cairo. The schedule was grueling, but for Youssef, the work was rewarding. The aims of *Al Bernameg* were the same as *The B+ Bassem Youssef Show* before it: to inspire positivity for Egypt's future (thus the "B+" or "be positive" in the old title), to promote tolerance in a time of dangerous division, and to inspire viewers to think critically about the news. "I want people not to be spoon-fed," Youssef told Molly Hennessy-Fiske and Amro Hassan for the *Los Angeles Times* (5 June 2011).

Comparisons between Youssef and Stewart abound, but Hennessy-Fiske and Hassan point out that Youssef's satire bears a stronger artistic resemblance to that of Stephen Colbert, a former correspondent for the *Daily Show* who hosts a show in which he plays a perpetually outraged conservative. Youssef has been known to play the part of the conservative or to throw around conservative buzzwords—"infidel," "traitor"—to humorous effect. His antics have been tremendously effective against those he targets, such as the ultraconservative Salafis. "You could write a Ph.D. dissertation on the contradictions in Salafi discourse, or I could write a human rights report about its bigoted rhetoric," Hossam Bahgat of the Egyptian Initiative for Personal Rights told

David D. Kirkpatrick and Mayy El Sheikh for the *New York Times* (30 Dec. 2012), "but none of this is half as effective as one of Bassem's weekly shows."

IMPACT AND AN UNCERTAIN FUTURE

Al Bernameg moved to Egypt's CBC network in November 2012. Segments for the show are taped in front of a live audience, and a two-hour program, *Al Bernameg*, aired on Friday nights. Stewart appeared on the show as a guest in June 2013. It was a year after Youssef first appeared on the *Daily Show* and several months after Egypt's public prosecutor ordered Youssef's arrest for insulting the newly elected President Mohamed Morsi and denigrating Islam. News of the arrest warrant made headlines across the globe and cast Morsi's faltering government in an unflattering light. Morsi claimed that he did not order the arrest—and, according to Egypt's unusual legal setup, that seemed to be the case—though Youssef was among a handful of Egyptians arrested on similar charges brought by Morsi supporters. Youssef submitted to a five-hour interrogation but wore a comically oversized version of a hat worn by Morsi that he had parodied on his show. He was released on bail and fined the equivalent of twenty-two hundred dollars. In July 2013, Morsi was overthrown by the Egyptian military, and *Al Bernameg* abruptly went on hiatus.

Youssef has acknowledged that *Al Bernameg* and the political turmoil in Egypt have changed his life forever; in a short letter to his one-year-old daughter published in *TIME* magazine, he worried about the kind of future that awaits her, and in his article about his mother, he writes about how the television show (and its numerous conservative detractors) put stress on his relationships with his family. Many were uncertain about the future of *Al Bernameg*, but Youssef insisted that the show would return in fall 2013. On Friday, October 25, *Al Bernameg* aired for the first time post-Morsi; by most accounts, Youssef tread lightly during the premiere, though he predictably enraged supporters of the new regime. Longtime fans seemed to be satisfied with Youssef's return, however cautious he appeared. "Bassem Youssef didn't explicitly say that the king is naked," journalist Dina Samak wrote, as quoted by Kareem Fahim for the *New York Times* (26 Oct. 2013), "but advised people to look at his clothes." However, CBC removed Youssef's show after only one episode of the new season, citing the inability of Youssef and his production team to follow the station's editorial guidelines and for not adhering to financial commitments. In November 2013, Youssef's production company, QSoft, announced it was leaving CBC and would take legal action against the network for what it deemed to be the unjust removal of *Al Bernameg*.

Youssef still occasionally practices medicine despite the demands of his television show. He lives in Maadi, a wealthy suburb of Cairo, with his wife, Hala, and their daughter, Nadia, who is named after his mother.

SUGGESTED READING

Fahim, Kareem. "Egyptian Satirist Returns to TV with Careful Barbs." *New York Times*. New York Times, 26 Oct. 2013. Web. 31 Oct. 2013.

Gladstone, Brooke. "Egypt Finds Its Own 'Jon Stewart.'" *All Things Considered*. NPR, 15 Apr. 2011. Web. 18 Oct. 2013.

Hennessy-Fiske, Molly, and Amro Hassan. "Cultural Exchange: Bassem Youssef Is a Kind of Egyptian Jon Stewart." *Los Angeles Times*. Los Angeles Times, 5 June 2011. Web. 21 Oct. 2013.

Hersh, Joshua. "Egypt's Media Counter-Revolution." *New Yorker*. Condé Nast, 21 Aug. 2013. Web. 21 Oct. 2013.

Kirkpatrick, David D., and Mayy El Sheikh. "For Liberals in Egypt, a Champion Who Quips." *New York Times*. New York Times, 30 Dec. 2012. Web. 21 Oct. 2013.

Lee, Ian, and Teo Kermeliotis. "Bassem Youssef: 'Sarcasm Is a Weapon.'" *CNN.com*. Cable News Network, 28 June 2013. Web. 18 Oct. 2013.

—*Molly Hagan*

Sports Illustrated/Getty Images

Gideon Yu

Born: 1971
Occupation: Sports executive, technology investor

Gideon Yu, the former chief strategy officer for the San Francisco 49ers, was named president and co-owner of the NFL team in February 2012. With a long and lucrative history with various Silicon Valley companies, including You-Tube and Facebook, Yu was hired to oversee the financing of the new Levi's Stadium in Santa Clara, California, in 2011. Yu's career trajectory has intersected with the turbulent history of the Silicon Valley tech industry, but his job with the 49ers made him a key force in revitalizing the region's troubled football team. The 49ers made it to the Super Bowl in 2013 and won the bid to host the fiftieth Super Bowl—Super Bowl L—in 2016. "My job here is the perfect mix of my passions for football, entrepreneurship, business management, and technology. Being at my favorite team in my favorite sport is a dream come true," Yu told Mike Florio for *NBC Sports* (10 Feb. 2012). But the stadium itself, slated for completion in late 2014, is Yu's real achievement; it is a marriage of his two favorite things,

football and new technology. Yu and Jed York, the young franchise owner, have reimagined the stadium, and increasingly the football team itself, as a start-up. "User experience," unusual words to use in conjunction with a live event, is a phrase the two men have used to describe Levi's. The stadium will have full WiFi coverage, but beyond that, York and Yu are partnering with a number of Silicon Valley firms to develop technologies specifically for the venue, including a smartphone application that would allow fans to order concessions from their seats. The stadium is also sustainably designed, with a green roof and solar panels. "Not many people in Silicon Valley see sports as a bastion of innovation," Yu told Brian O'Keefe of *Fortune* magazine in an interview for *CNN Money* (24 July 2013), "but this team being led by Jed is really one of those bastions."

EDUCATION AND EARLY CAREER

Yu, who is Korean American, was born in 1971 and grew up in Nashville, Tennessee. He attended the University School of Nashville, where math teacher Debbie Davies fostered his love of math, science, and technology. (He established the Debbie Davies Endowed Chair for Excellence in Teaching at the school in her honor in 2011.) He graduated in 1989, the same year that he won the First Place Grand Award at the Fortieth International Science and Engineering Fair in Environmental Science with a project called "In Situ Surfactant Flushing," which modeled remediation of groundwater contaminated by compounds such as polychlorinated biphenyl

(PCB). The accolade earned him admittance to the Association of Groundwater Scientists and Engineers at the age of seventeen. Yu went on to earn a bachelor of science degree in industrial engineering management from Stanford University in 1993 but ultimately decided to pursue a career in finance.

During the 1990s, Yu was a financial analyst for Donaldson, Lufkin & Jenrette. He chose the investment firm, he told Susan Kelly for the online finance magazine *Treasury & Risk Management* (1 Nov. 2003), because he wanted to gain experience in making deals. He later handled billions of dollars in a financial position with the Walt Disney Company, where he worked on a merger with Capital Cities/ABC. After Disney, he became the director of corporate finance for the Hilton Hotels Corporation. He was the youngest person ever to hold a corporate directorship in the company's history. During a brief hiatus from the finance world, Yu earned an MBA from Harvard Business School in 1999.

SILICON VALLEY CAREER

Yu left Harvard just as the dot-com bubble was reaching its zenith. Investors were pouring millions into young tech companies, and Yu went west to get in on the action. He became the CFO and vice president of corporate development of a start-up called TheMan.com, a commerce and content site devoted to male interests outside the realm of the more common sex- and sports-focused men's magazines. Its founders hoped that TheMan.com would garner success just as the similarly configured MarthaStewart.com and Women.com had, but by April 2000, market shares in all three companies were falling fast. Along with hundreds of other companies, TheMan.com closed its doors in November 2000. Despite the fallout, Yu gained valuable experience. "The great thing and perhaps the scary thing about the dot-com era is that it allowed people like me to get senior-level experience quickly," Yu told Kelly. In August 2000, he was hired as the CFO and vice president of finance and administration of NightFire Software. For the young broadband company, which was acquired by Neustar in 2003, Yu brokered deals and raised capital.

"Yu seems to have an amazing ability to get a sweet job at the hot web company of the moment at just the right time," Kara Swisher wrote for the *Wall Street Journal* (16 Aug. 2007). And indeed, Yu was spirited away by an ascendant Yahoo shortly before NightFire's acquisition. He was named Yahoo's treasurer and vice president of corporate finance in May 2002, and in 2003, he played a key role in the company's acquisition of the search companies Overture Services and Inktomi for $1.63 billion and $235 million, respectively.

YOUTUBE

In September 2006, Yu became the CFO and senior vice president of finance at the video-sharing site YouTube. The site was less than two years old and, like Yahoo before it, just beginning its rise. In an article announcing Yu's hiring, Kevin J. Delaney for the *Wall Street Journal* (2 Sept. 2006) called YouTube "a poster child for a new generation of startups, which is surging thanks to the growth in usage of the Internet and online advertising. . . . Such small, fast-growing firms have long attracted recruits [like Yu], in part because of the possibility of receiving equity that could dramatically increase in value if the start-ups were to eventually be bought or go public. In the 90s, Yahoo was in a similar position, wooing staff from older technology concerns whose growth and buzz it was eclipsing."

Yu's move to YouTube had been in the works for nearly a year, and a month after he joined the company, he played an instrumental role in its sale, for $1.65 billion, to Google. (The search giant reportedly outbid Yahoo for the online video company.) It was a major coup for YouTube, and though it was considered a risky investment on Google's part at the time, a reporter for the *New York Times Dealbook* (17 May 2010) later lauded it as "one of Google's smartest acquisitions." By at least one account—that of John Cloud, who wrote a major article about the YouTube founders for *TIME* magazine (25 Dec. 2006)—Yu was a shrewd negotiator in the sale of the company. He reportedly smooth-talked his way out of sharing budgetary information with Google executives in an effort to retain some control during the integration process. It may not have been the most honest tactic, but Yu's way of doing business appealed to Sequoia Capital, a major Silicon Valley venture capital firm. Sequoia's Pierre Lamond, an early investor in YouTube, became a mentor to the site's founders. Yu made plans to become a partner in the firm in 2007, but before he got the chance, he was scooped up by the next big thing—a social network called Facebook.

FACEBOOK

Yu replaced Mike Sheridan as the CFO of Facebook in the summer of 2007. "I consider it kind of a coup that we were able to recruit him here," Facebook founder and CEO Mark Zuckerberg told Kevin J. Delaney for the *Wall Street Journal* (25 July 2007). "He's just excellent." The match seemed to be made in heaven; Yu was wildly successful when it came to raising capital, and Facebook, which continued to draw millions of users into its network, was looking for ways to capitalize on its popularity. There were rumors at the time, though Zuckerberg denied them, that Facebook was preparing an initial public offering, or IPO. (Ultimately, this would not take place until 2012.) Within his first year as finance chief, Yu secured a major investment from Microsoft that placed Facebook's value at a whopping $15 billion. But in the major recession year that followed, raising money at that valuation became much more difficult.

Facebook, a site that had begun in Zuckerberg's Harvard dorm room in 2004, had captured the public imagination and was growing at an astounding rate. When Yu was hired, the site counted more than 20 million users. By the time he left in 2009, it had just under 200 million. To accommodate all of that growth, the company needed huge amounts of cash, but Zuckerberg, the young wunderkind behind the site, was hesitant to relinquish any creative control to investors or advertisers. On that point, as it later became clear, Yu and the CEO clashed. Yu left the company—other accounts say that he was forced out—in late March 2009. He was not the first high-level executive to leave the company after a rumored dust-up with Zuckerberg. One employee, echoing other reports about the Facebook hierarchy, told Swisher for the *Wall Street Journal* (31 Mar. 2009), "At Facebook, you're either with Mark or you're not. And, if you're not, you leave."

In August 2009, Yu joined former Sequoia venture capitalist Pierre Lamond as a partner with the firm Khosla Ventures. His first investment was in a mobile payment company called Square, which allows users to take credit card payments with their smartphones. He worked at the company's office once a week until about 2011 and continued to advise the company for another year. He also invested in a company called Meebo, a social media platform that was acquired by Google in June 2012.

SAN FRANCISCO 49ERS

Yu was hired by the San Francisco 49ers football team in 2011. At the time, the franchise's ownership history was marked by scandal, and the team, once iconic within the NFL, struggled just to compete. On top of it all, the franchise had been in desperate need of a new stadium since the late 1990s, when Eddie DeBartolo Jr., the former owner, was charged with fraud, in part for trying to finance one. He resigned in disgrace. DeBartolo's nephew, Jed York, is the owner and CEO of the franchise. His father tapped him for the job in 2010—when York was only twenty-nine—in the hope that York could give the team a fresh start. York's first task was selling the residents of Santa Clara, a city located thirty-eight miles south of San Francisco, on building a new stadium. The state of California had not built a professional football venue in about fifty years, and the country was still in the midst of the great recession. So York went door to door for an entire year, lobbying for Measure J, a proposal that would allot the team land for a new stadium. Miraculously, the measure passed. In

the meantime, York had done a tremendous job turning the team around, but he still faced one major obstacle: to build, he needed the banks to loan him $1.3 billion.

This predicament led him to Yu, whom Seth Wickersham described for *ESPN* magazine (14 Oct. 2013) as "tall and skinny, a fast talker and an even faster thinker." Together, they hatched a risky plan. York wanted to open the stadium a year earlier than the agreed-upon 2015 deadline. He needed to sell season tickets and believed moving the opening to 2014 was the only way to do it. Yu was cautious; according to Wickersham, if they were to embark on York's new plan, they would need to raise $850 million within one month for construction costs. Despite the huge risk, they decided to do it and set up fifty meetings with major banks across New York City. At one early meeting, a bank offered to give them the full $850 million if the bank was also given naming rights. York said no. Yu was shocked but ultimately impressed. He told Wickersham that York's confidence reminded him of his previous boss, Zuckerberg.

RETHINKING LIVE SPORTS

Yu and York found banks to finance the stadium, and construction crews broke ground in April 2012, a few months after Yu was named president and co-owner of the team. With construction at Levi's Stadium well under way, Yu has focused on other ways of bringing new technologies to the business of football. He is looking for ways to streamline the drafting and scouting process, but he has even talked about ways to use smartphones to organize fan chants and noise during games. According to Kevin Clark for the *Wall Street Journal* (11 Dec. 2012), most of the innovations will be announced on opening day. As the 49ers franchise continues to draw former tech execs such as Yu into its ranks, the sky seems to be the limit. Yu has been pleased to see people from all over the valley clamoring to pitch him new ideas. He told Clark that the team is "fundamentally trying to rethink everything about live sports."

PERSONAL LIFE

Yu and his wife, Susie, have two children, Jonathan and Emily. After Jonathan, their firstborn, suffered a medical scare as an infant, Yu became a member of the board at the University of California San Francisco Medical Center Foundation. He and his wife are active philanthropists and founders of the Susie and Gideon Yu Foundation.

SUGGESTED READING

Clark, Kevin. "Silicon Valley Straps on Pads." *Wall Street Journal*. Dow Jones, 11 Dec. 2012. Web. 9 Jan. 2014.

Delaney, Kevin J. "Facebook Hires Yu as Finance Chief." *Wall Street Journal*. Dow Jones, 25 July 2007. Web. 8 Jan. 2014.

Delaney, Kevin J. "YouTube Taps Yahoo Treasurer Yu." *Wall Street Journal*. Dow Jones, 2 Sept. 2006. Web. 8 Jan. 2014.

Swisher, Kara. "Facebook CFO Gideon Yu Out; Fast-Growing Social Network Says It's Doing Fine Financially." *Wall Street Journal*. Dow Jones, 31 Mar. 2009. Web. 8 Jan. 2014.

Wickersham, Seth. "The Hail Mary in Santa Clara." *ESPN the Magazine*. ESPN Internet Ventures, 14 Oct. 2013. Web. 8 Jan. 2014.

York, Jed, and Gideon Yu. "Video and Transcript: San Francisco 49ers." Interview by Brian O'Keefe. *CNN Money*. Cable News Network, 24 July 2013. Web. 8 Jan. 2014.

—Molly Hagan

OBITUARIES

Claudio Abbado

Born: Milan, Italy; June 26, 1933
Died: Bologna, Italy; January 20, 2014
Occupation: Conductor

Italian conductor Claudio Abbado was a champion of contemporary music and was considered to be one of the most accomplished conductors of the twentieth century. In addition to serving as music director of La Scala in Milan, Italy, Abbado worked with many of the world's leading orchestras, including the London Symphony Orchestra, the Berlin Philharmonic, and the Vienna State Opera.

Abbado was born in 1933 into a musical Milanese family. Abbado's father Michelangelo was a professional violinist and teacher at Milan's Giuseppe Verdi Conservatory, while his mother, Maria Carmela, was a pianist and author. Abbado's brother, Marcello, was also a musician who later became musical director of the Verdi Conservatory. Abbado said that his inspiration to pursue a career as a conductor came after a visit to the Milan's famed Teatro alla Scala at age eight.

Abbado learned to play piano as a child and performed piano-violin duets with his father around Milan. After studying piano at the Verdi Conservatory until 1955, Abbado was accepted to the Vienna Academy of Music in 1956, and studied conducting under Hans Swarowsky. That same year, Abbado married Giovanna Cavazzoni, with whom he had two children.

In Vienna, Abbado became friends with Zubin Mehta, who also became a world-renowned conductor later in life. Abbado and Mehta both competed at the 1958 Tanglewood Festival in Massachusetts, where Abbado won the highest honor, the Serge Koussevitzky Prize. In 1963, Abbado was one of three young conductors to win the Dimitri Mitropoulos prize in New York, and won a yearlong assistant position at the New York Philharmonic under Leonard Bernstein. In 1965, conductor Herbert von Karajan invited Abbado to lead the Vienna Philharmonic at the Salzburg Festival.

In 1968, Abbado became music director of Teatro alla Scala, where he remained until 1986. The same year he took up that position, Abbado and his first wife divorced and he later married dressmaker Gabriella Cantalupi, with whom he had a son. In 1979, Abbado became principal conductor of the London Symphony Orchestra, serving as the orchestra's music director from 1983 until 1988. Abbado also served as music director of the Vienna State Opera from 1986 to 1991, and in 1989, replaced Karajan as chief conductor of the Berlin Philharmonic after Karajan's death. Though he was still married, Abbado began a relationship with Russian violinist Viktoria Mullova around 1986, resulting in the birth of a son.

The Berlin Philharmonic was Abbado's home until the end of his career, and his tenure was controversial at times because of his increasing focus on promoting contemporary music within the historically traditional orchestra. Abbado had surgery in 2000, after being diagnosed with stomach cancer, and decided not to extend his contract at the Berlin Philharmonic at the end of the 2001–2 season. Abbado retired to Italy, where he died at his home in Bologna on January 20, 2014. He was eighty years old. In addition to two brothers and a sister, Abbado is survived by his four children and his second wife, Gabriella.

See Current Biography Illustrated 1973.

Fouad Ajami

Born: Arnoun, Lebanon; September 19, 1945
Died: Maine; June 22, 2014
Occupation: Scholar

Fouad A. Ajami was a Middle Eastern scholar from Lebanon who advocated for the US invasion of Iraq and wrote books about Middle Eastern history and government.

Ajami, a Shiite Muslim, was born in Arnoun, Lebanon, in 1945. His family was originally from Iran and came to Lebanon in the 1850s to work in the tobacco farming industry. When Ajami was four years old, his family moved to Beirut, where he attended school. In his teenage years, Ajami was a supporter of Arab nationalism, though he later came to reverse his position on the issue. Ajami moved to the United States in 1963 and became a US citizen in 1964. Ajami attended Eastern Oregon College to earn his bachelor's degree and then earned a doctorate in international relations in 1973 from the University of Washington, writing his thesis on world government.

In 1973 Ajami joined the faculty of Princeton University, where he taught political science and international relations. He was asked to join Johns Hopkins University as director of Middle East studies at the School of Advanced International Studies (SAIS) in 1980. The following year, Ajami published his first book, *The Arab Predicament*, about the history of the Arab world surrounding the 1967 Six Day War. Ajami won a five-year grant from the MacArthur Foundation to pursue research into Middle East politics in 1982. His next book, *The Vanishing Imam: Musa al Sadr and the Shia of Lebanon* (1986) described the history of Muslim cleric Sayyid Musa al Sadr, who disappeared in 1978 but helped to transform the Shia faith in Lebanon. Ajami followed this success with the collaborative book *Beirut: City of Regrets* (1988), a historical, political, and artistic investigation of Beirut, Lebanon, through the photographs of Eli Reed.

Ajami's controversial 1998 book, *The Dream Palace of the Arabs: A Generation's Odyssey*, revealed his changing political attitudes; some readers felt that the book had an anti-Arab tone, though many of the essays within celebrated Arab writers and intellectuals of the past. After the terrorist attacks of 2001, Ajami was one of several US Middle Eastern scholars called upon to advise state leaders on the conflict and how best to address terrorism. Ajami advised officials of the George W. Bush presidential administration on the issue and became known as one of the most outspoken supporters of the US invasion of Iraq in 2003. Ajami frequently appeared on television in support of the invasion, earning praise and criticism for his role in the controversial military operation.

In 2006 Ajami was awarded the National Humanities Medal in recognition of his contributions to international relations. He joined the Hoover Institution at Stanford University in 2011 as a senior scholar. His book, *The Syrian Rebellion* (2012), discussed the history and political issues surrounding the Syrian political uprising of 2011. In his later life, Ajami suffered from cancer, eventually leading to his death on June 22, 2014, age sixty-eight, at his home in Maine. Ajami's survivors include his wife, Michelle Ajami. In July 2014 the Hoover Institution published Ajami's long essay, *The Struggle for Mastery in the Fertile Crescent*, in book form as part of its essay series, The Great Unraveling: The Remaking of the Middle East.

See Current Biography 2007.

John F. Akers

Born: Boston, Massachusetts; December 28, 1934
Died: Boston, Massachusetts; August 22, 2014
Occupation: Technology executive

John Fellows Akers was the sixth chief executive officer of IBM and worked with the company for over three decades during the transition from mainframe computers to personal computers.

Akers was born in Boston, Massachusetts in 1934 and graduated from Needham High School before going on to Yale University, where he obtained an undergraduate degree in business in 1956. Akers then enlisted in the Navy where he rose to the rank of lieutenant and served as a naval carrier pilot before leaving the military in 1960 to return to the private sector. That same year, he married Susan Davis, with whom he would have three children.

Akers's career with IBM began just after returning from the Navy, when he joined the company as a sales trainee in the company's San Francisco offices in 1960. He started out as a salesman in Vermont, and climbed through the ranks in the sales department during a time when IBM's focus was on producing and selling mainframe systems. In 1971, he was promoted to the position of executive assistant to Senior Vice President Frank T. Cary, and relocated to IBM's headquarters in Armonk, New York. In 1974, he became president of the company's data processing division where he remained for nine years. During this time, IBM was a pioneer of the personal computer, releasing the IBM PC model in August of 1981.

In 1983, Akers was elected president of IBM, and in 1985, he succeeded John R. Opel as the sixth CEO of the company. The following year, Akers also became chairman of the board of directors. While he worked at IBM, he also became a trustee of the California Institute of Technology and served on the board of directors for the New York Times Company, beginning in 1985.

Akers had been a key figure in helping IBM to grow and develop its mainframe computer market, but took the CEO position during a transitional time when the company needed to adjust to the growing personal computer market. As IBM lost profitability in the late 1980s, the board of directors was divided on how to increase the company's competitiveness in the changing market. Akers refused to resort to massive layoffs, believing strongly that the company should endeavor to take care of its career employees. After the company suffered more than $7 billion of losses in the early 1990s, the board of directors asked Akers to step down as CEO in 1993. Leadership was turned over to Lou Gerstner, a company outsider, who cut about $9 billion from the budget and laid off thousands, bringing IBM back to profitability over the next decade.

Akers served on the boards for many prominent companies, including PepsiCo and Hallmark. He remained on the board for the New York Times Company from 1985 to 2006, making him one of the longest serving members in the history of the company. Akers retired to Boston, Massachusetts, where he died on August 22, 2014, after suffering a stroke. He was seventy-nine. He is survived by his wife Susan; their son, Scott; two daughters, Pamela Sjodin and Annie Klyver; and ten grandchildren.

See Current Biography 1988.

Licia Albanese

Born: Bari, Italy; July 22, 1909
Died: New York, New York; August 15, 2014
Occupation: Opera singer

Licia Albanese was an operatic soprano who became one of the most celebrated opera singers of the twentieth century. Albanese gave more than one thousand performances during her career and was often a featured performer at the New York Metropolitan Opera (Met) where she performed more than four hundred times.

Albanese was born Felicia Albanese in Bari, Italy, one of seven children born into a musical family. Albanese and her siblings were all given music lessons and she began taking voice lessons at twelve on the recommendation of her piano teacher. Albanese studied opera with soprano Giuseppina Baldassarre-Tedeschi who was known for her portrayal of Cio-Cio-San in Giacomo Puccini's *Madama Butterfly*—a role for which Albanese herself would become famous.

Albanese had her debut in 1934 during the second half of a performance of *Madama Butterfly* at the Teatro Lirico in Milan when the lead soprano took ill and Albanese, who was then employed as an understudy, was called in to complete the performance. The following year, at the prestigious Teatro alla Scala in Milan, Albanese performed the role of Lauretta in Puccini's *Gianni Schicchi*. She became a featured performer at La Scala, and also gave an acclaimed performance as Micaela in Georges Bizet's *Carmen*. Albanese had her debut at England's Covent Garden in 1937, performing the part of Liù in Puccini's *Turandot*, another role that she became known for during her career.

In 1939 Albanese made her first trip to the United States and made her American debut at New York's Metropolitan Opera in February 1940, performing the role of Cio-Cio-San in *Madama Butterfly*. Albanese went on to perform in the famous role more than three hundred times during her career. She became a regular at the Met, becoming known for her powerful performance as Violetta in Giuseppe Verdi's *La Traviata*. Critics praised her singing, but also noted her ability to perform well in dramatic, tragic roles and she became known for her ability to stage a convincing death scene.

In 1945 Albanese married Joseph Gimma, a Wall Street stockbroker, with whom she had a son. Albanese became a US citizen in the 1940s and spent much of her career performing at the Met and other American theatres. Albanese also became known for the roles of Mimi in *La Bohème* and Susanna in *Marriage of Figaro*. In 1946 she recorded her performance of *La Bohème*, with Arturo Toscanini conducting, to commemorate the fiftieth anniversary of the opera.

When the Met left its old location to relocate to Lincoln Center in 1966, Albanese tried to save the old building, unsuccessfully, and refused to perform at the new location. She conducted master's classes in New York and elsewhere around the world after retiring from performance. In 1974, she and her husband established the Licia Albanese–Puccini Foundation, which provides scholarships and grants for young opera singers. In 1995 she received the National Medal of Arts from President Clinton. Albanese died at her home in Manhattan on August 15, 2014. She was 105. Predeceased by her husband in 1990, Albanese is survived by her son, Joseph; two grandchildren; and three great-grandchildren.

See Current Biography Illustrated 1946.

Maya Angelou

Born: St. Louis, Missouri; April 4, 1928
Died: Winston-Salem, North Carolina; May 28, 2014
Occupation: Writer and poet

Maya Angelou is one of the most celebrated American authors and poets of the twentieth century, known largely for her autobiographical memoir *I Know Why the Caged Bird Sings*.

Angelou was born Marguerite Johnson in St. Louis, Missouri, and at the age of three was sent to live with her grandmother in the impoverished and racially divided Stamps, Arkansas, after her parents divorced. At age seven or eight, shortly after returning to St. Louis to live with her mother, Angelou was raped by her mother's boyfriend. Her rapist was arrested, tried and convicted, but was found murdered before he was imprisoned. Angelou suspected that her mother's brothers killed the man for his crime and, believing that her voice had killed the man, Angelou refused to speak for five years. She was finally coaxed out of her silence by a teacher who also inspired her interest in classical literature and poetry.

In 1940 Angelou moved to San Francisco with her mother, where, shortly after graduating from high school at the age of seventeen, she gave birth to a son, Clyde "Guy" Johnson. To care for her son, Angelou became a waitress and dancer, and also worked as a prostitute and madam. Angelou's skill as a singer and dancer allowed her to escape from poverty and she became an in-demand calypso singer. In the early 1950s, Angelou married Enistasious "Tosh" Angelos, a former sailor. Though they divorced a few years later, Angelou kept a modified version of his surname as her own. She was offered a role on Broadway in the play *House of Flowers*, but turned it down to tour Europe as a dancer with the Everyman Opera Company's production of *Porgy and Bess* in 1954 and 1955.

In 1959, Angelou moved to New York, where she worked as an organizer for Martin Luther King's Southern Christian Leadership Conference. A relationship with a black South African civil rights activist took her to Cairo, Egypt, where she became an editor for the English-language *Arab Observer* newspaper. When the relationship ended, Angelou and her son moved to Accra, Ghana, where she taught at the University of Ghana. Angelou met Malcolm X in Ghana and returned to the United States to work with him in 1964, though he was assassinated not long afterward.

Angelou published *I Know Why the Caged Bird Sings* in 1969, the first in a series of autobiographical memoirs documenting her life to age forty. The book became an international best seller and Angelou began publishing books of poetry as well, beginning with *Just Give Me a Cool Drink of Water 'fore I Diiie*, in 1971, which was nominated for a Pulitzer Prize. Each of her memoirs became a best seller and she also published a screenplay and appeared in the 1977 television series *Roots*. In 1982 Angelou became the first Reynolds Professor of American Studies, a lifetime appointment, at Wake Forest University in North Carolina, one of more than twenty institutions to grant her honorary degrees over the course of her career.

Angelou was asked to read a poem at the 1993 inauguration of Bill Clinton, inspiring a resurgence of interest in her writings and role in African American history. In 1998, wanting to utilize her fame and influence for philanthropic purposes, she founded the Maya Angelou Institute for the Improvement of Child and Family Education under the auspices of Winston-Salem State University. To commemorate her contribution to American culture, President Barack Obama presented Angelou with the Presidential Medal of Freedom in 2011. Angelou died in Winston-Salem, North Carolina, on May 28, 2014, at age eighty-six. She is survived by her son, two grandchildren, and two great-grandchildren.

See Current Biography Illustrated 1974, 1994.

Reubin Askew

Born: Muskogee, Oklahoma; September 11, 1928
Died: Tallahassee, Florida; March 13, 2014
Occupation: Governor

Reubin O'Donovan Askew became a progressive governor of Florida in the 1970s, championing racial equality and governmental ethics in an era where politicians of the "New South"

became a driving force in American politics. Askew was also a prominent scholar of political science, teaching at several prominent Florida universities.

Askew was born in Muskogee, Oklahoma, the youngest of six children. His father, Leon, was a carpenter, and his mother, Alberta, worked as a seamstress and waitress. After his parents divorced in 1937, Askew and his five siblings lived in his mother's hometown, Pensacola, Florida. Askew graduated from Pensacola High School in 1946 and joined the US Army serving as a paratrooper until his discharge in 1948.

Using assistance from the GI Bill, Askew attended Florida State University in Tallahassee, where he earned his BS in public administration in 1951. He then reentered the armed forces, serving with the Air Force during the Korean War. Returning to civilian life, Askew attended law school at the University of Florida in Gainesville, earning his LLB in 1956. Following his graduation, Askew married Donna Lou Harper, with whom he would later have two children, and became an assistant county solicitor for Escambia County, Florida.

In 1958, Askew won election to the Florida House of Representatives, serving for four years while simultaneously working as a lawyer. In 1962, Askew was elected to the Florida Senate, where he served for eight years, including serving as president pro tempore from 1968 to 1970.

In 1970, Askew campaigned in the state's gubernatorial elections, despite being a relative unknown outside his home district. Askew ran on a populist platform, promising higher taxes on business profits, and was able to defeat incumbent Claude Kirk. As the state's thirty-seventh governor, Askew championed desegregation and racial equality, and appointed the first African American justice to the Florida Supreme Court. Though liberal by some measures, Askew's devotion to his Presbyterian faith and focus on morals and family values gave him traction with some facets of the conservative population. Askew also overhauled the state's ethics regulations and created new regulations for former government lobbyists. He served two terms and left office in 1979.

That year, President Jimmy Carter, a fellow New South Democrat, appointed Askew to serve on his cabinet as a trade representative. Askew became a leading figure of the Southern Democrats, and announced his decision to run for the presidency in 1983. However, Askew's more conservative views, including his opposition to abortion, prevented him from building sufficient support to win the nomination at the 1984 Democratic primary. In 1988, Askew attempted to return to political office again, making a bid for the US Senate, but abandoned his campaign due to lack of funds.

After retiring from politics, Askew turned to education, becoming a visiting professor at Florida International University. He also taught politics and international affairs at Florida Atlantic University, the University of Florida, Gainesville, and Florida State University. During his career, Askew was awarded with fifteen honorary doctorate degrees, as well as numerous awards from the state of Florida for his teaching and public service. Askew died on March 13, 2014, at the age of eighty-five, after suffering from pneumonia and a stroke. He was survived by his wife; his son, Kevin; and daughter, Angela.

See Current Biography 1973.

Richard Attenborough

Born: Cambridge, England; August 29, 1923
Died: London, England; August 24, 2014
Occupation: Actor, director, and producer

Lord Richard Samuel Attenborough was an Academy Award–winning actor, director, and producer who began in the British theater in the 1940s and '50s and became an internationally known director in the 1980s. In recognition of his contributions to British film, Attenborough was made a Commander of the Order of the British Empire in 1967, knighted in 1976, and made a life peer in 1993.

Attenborough was born in 1923 in Cambridge, England, the eldest of three sons born into an upper-class liberal family. He later described himself as a struggling student who took an early interest in performance and left school at sixteen after earning a scholarship to the Royal Academy of Dramatic Art (RADA). Not yet out of school, Attenborough made his professional stage debut in the play Ah, Wilderness! and was cast by famed director Noël Coward to appear in the patriotic 1942 war drama In Which We Serve. Enlisting in the Royal Air Force (RAF) during World War II, he served as an aerial photographer for three years, taking photographs of RAF bombing targets before and after key strikes. In 1945 he married Sheila Sim, a fellow student at RADA, who became a well-known stage actress in England before retiring to care for the couple's three children.

Attenborough appeared in a number of successful plays in the 1940s and '50s, but was relatively unknown outside of England until he appeared in the 1963 film The Great Escape alongside American film star Steve McQueen, playing the role of squadron leader Roger Bartlett. His first major award came for the 1964 films Séance on a Wet Afternoon and Guns at Batasi, for which he was honored with a British Academy of Film and Television Arts Award for best British actor.

Attenborough's directorial debut was the 1969 musical Oh! What a Lovely War, featuring John Gielgud, Vanessa Redgrave, and Maggie Smith. In 1977 he directed the acclaimed World War II film A Bridge Too Far, starring Gene Hackman and Michael Caine. Attenborough's 1982 film Gandhi—a project two decades in the making—cemented his status as one of Britain's most prominent directors. The film won eight Academy Awards, including best director, best picture, and best actor for star Ben Kingsley. Attenborough's other films varied in success and genres. Among his best-known films were the 1985 adaptation of A Chorus Line, the 1987 drama Cry Freedom with Denzel Washington and Kevin Kline, and the 1992 biopic Chaplin, starring Robert Downey Jr.

After a long hiatus, Attenborough returned to acting, appearing in a supporting role in Jurassic Park in 1993 and as Kris Kringle in a remake of Miracle on 34th Street the following year. Other supporting roles followed, including Hamlet (1996) and Elizabeth (1998). Attenborough also continued directing throughout the 1990s, with mixed success. His final film as a director was a romantic drama called Closing the Ring, which premiered in 2007.

In his later life, Attenborough and his wife sold their estate and relocated to a nursing home in London. Attenborough was predeceased by his daughter, Jane Holland, and granddaughter, Lucy, who died in the 2004 Indian Ocean tsunami, along with Holland's mother-in-law. Attenborough died on August 24, 2014, age ninety, in London. He is survived by his wife and the couple's two surviving children, Michael and Charlotte.

See Current Biography Illustrated 1984.

Tony Auth

Born: Akron, Ohio; May 7, 1942
Died: Philadelphia, Pennsylvania; September 14, 2014
Occupation: Editorial cartoonist and children's book illustrator

William Anthony Auth Jr., known professionally as "Tony Auth," was a Pulitzer Prize–winning cartoonist known for his political cartoons published in the Philadelphia Inquirer.

Born in Akron, Ohio, in 1942, Auth took an early interest in sketching and drawing. Later relocating to Southern California with his family, he graduated from the University of California, Los Angeles (UCLA), with a degree in biological illustration in 1965. Auth published his first cartoons in the Daily Bruin, a student newspaper published at UCLA, but he did not initially pursue cartoon illustration as a career.

After graduation, Auth worked as a medical illustrator at Rancho Los Amigos Hospital in Downey, California, eventually publishing political cartoons in an alternative newspaper circulated by college friends in the late 1960s. These cartoons came to the attention of publishers in the mainstream news industry and, in 1971, the *Philadelphia Inquirer* employed Auth as an editorial cartoonist.

For more than forty years, Auth's cartoons were a familiar feature of the *Philadelphia Inquirer's* editorial page, usually providing political or social commentary on the issues of the day. Though Auth lampooned and criticized politicians and policies from both sides of the ideological divide, he took a largely liberal stance on politics and drew sharp criticism from the conservative community. Over the course of his career, the Republican Party and the Catholic Church were among the many organizations that complained to *Philadelphia Inquirer* editors about how they were depicted in Auth's cartoons, but the newspaper remained firm in its support of his art and social commentary.

Auth won a Pulitzer Prize for editorial cartooning in 1976, which was largely attributed to his cartoon commentary on American and Russian relations. Also nominated for a second and third Pulitzer Prize in 1983 and 2010 respectively, he finished as a finalist on both occasions. While working for the newspaper, Auth illustrated eleven children's books, working with authors such as Chaim Potok and Daniel Pinkwater. In 1989, Pinkwater and Auth collaborated on a Sunday comic for King Features Syndicate titled *Norb*, which received critical acclaim but was cancelled after fifty-two weeks of publication. In 2005, Auth won the Herblock Prize from the Herb Block Foundation and said, in his acceptance speech that he considered himself part of a "reality-based community" that was under attack from both the left and the right and that he viewed it as his role to promote independent thought through his work.

Following a major buyout of the paper and subsequent shift in management, Auth left the *Philadelphia Inquirer* in 2012 and began working for WHYY's NewsWorks website, producing syndicated cartoons for the national press. That same year, Pennsylvania's James A. Michener Art Museum produced a retrospective of his work, titled *To Stir, Inform and Inflame: The Art of Tony Auth*, with a companion book compiled by Auth and writer David Leopold. After battling brain cancer, Auth died on September 14, 2014, in Philadelphia, at age seventy-two. Survivors include his wife of thirty-two years, artist Eliza Drake Auth, and two daughters, Katie and Emily.

See Current Biography 2006.

Lauren Bacall

Born: New York, New York; September 16, 1924
Died: New York, New York; August 12, 2014
Occupation: Actor

Lauren Bacall was an American actor famous for a string of sultry performances in 1940s films and for her on- and off-screen relationship with Humphrey Bogart.

Bacall was born Betty Joan Perske in the Bronx in 1924. Although she was raised in relative poverty by her mother after her parents divorced, a wealthy uncle paid for her to attend Highland Manor, an excellent private school. She also took acting lessons at the New York School of Theater. In 1940, Bacall entered the American Academy of Dramatic Arts, but she was forced to leave after a year when her family could no longer afford her education.

In 1941, Bacall started modeling and working as an usher at Broadway theaters and hoped to catch the eye of a producer. The following year, *Harper's Bazaar* fashion editor Diana Vreeland met Bacall and featured her on the cover of the March 1943 issue. This photo attracted the attention of producers, and Bacall received offers from Howard Hawks, Howard Hughes, and David O. Selznick. Accepting Hawks's offer, Bacall left for Hollywood at eighteen. She had her screen debut as Lauren Bacall (changing her name on Hawks's advice) in the 1944 film *To Have or Have Not* alongside Bogart. Bacall's most famous lines from the film, "You know how to whistle, don't you, Steve? You just put your lips together and blow," became an iconic moment in American film history, and she and Bogart developed an off-screen attraction that developed into an affair.

Though Bogart was married and twenty-five years older than Bacall, he obtained a divorce and married her in 1945, while the pair was filming *The Big Sleep* (1946). Hawks had warned Bacall that the relationship would stall her career, and this warning proved apt, as she never recaptured the buzz that surrounded her first two films with Bogart. She appeared with Bogart again in *Dark Passage* (1947) and *Key Largo* (1948) but to lesser acclaim.

Bacall and Bogart had two children and, as her career halted, she dedicated herself to her role as a mother and a wife, often traveling with Bogart when he filmed on location. After her husband's death in 1957, Bacall had a short but widely publicized affair with Frank Sinatra, who was a longtime friend of both. In 1961, Bacall married Jason Robards Jr., with whom she had a son, though their marriage ended in divorce in 1969. Along with minor roles in a string of films in the 1960s, she returned to the stage with successful Broadway appearances in the comedies *Goodbye, Charlie* (1959) and *Cactus Flower* (1965).

In 1978, Bacall wrote *Lauren Bacall: By Myself*, a best-selling autobiography about her career and relationships that won a National Book Award in 1980, and continued acting into the 2000s. She won a Golden Globe Award for her supporting role in the 1996 Barbra Streisand film *The Mirror Has Two Faces* and received an honorary Oscar for her lifetime contributions to film in 2009. Bacall died in Manhattan on August 12, 2014, at the age of eighty-nine. She was survived by her two children with Bogart, Stephen and Leslie, and her son with Robards, Sam.

See Current Biography 1970.

Howard H. Baker

Born: Huntsville, Tennessee; November 15, 1925
Died: Huntsville, Tennessee; June 26, 2014
Occupation: Politician

Howard Henry Baker Jr. was a Republican senator and former senate leader from Tennessee. He was known as a skilled negotiator and speaker for the moderate, centrist Republican Party coalitions of the 1960s and '70s. Before entering politics, Baker was a lawyer in his hometown of Huntsville, Tennessee.

Baker was born on November 15, 1925, in Huntsville to Howard Baker Sr. and his first wife, Dora (Ladd) Baker. Baker graduated from the McCallie School, a military academy in Chattanooga, in 1943 and completed a naval officer training program, for which he studied at Tulane University and the University of the South. After a brief tour in the South Pacific during World War II, Baker attended the University of Tennessee, where he earned his bachelor of laws degree. Baker's father was elected to the US Senate in 1951. That same year Baker married Joy Dirksen, the daughter of Senator Everett McKinley Dirksen of Illinois.

Baker worked in private practice in both civil and criminal law. He was also a successful investor in the banking and real-estate markets. His first attempt to win public office came in 1964 when he ran against Ross Bass and lost by a wide margin. In 1966 he ran again against Governor Frank G. Clement for a vacant seat, adopting a more moderate stance, and won the election. Baker's campaign received a major boost when Richard Nixon campaigned on his behalf as part of his attempt to gain public support for his 1968 presidential campaign.

Baker campaigned twice to become Senate Republican leader in 1969 and 1971, losing both times. In 1972, Baker was asked to represent the party in the committee to investigate the Watergate scandal. His appearances on the news and in press conferences in 1973 and 1974 cemented Baker as a nationally recognized figure and allowed him to present a moderate voice for the Republican Party amid the scandal. Baker became the Republican minority leader in 1977 and was one of the leading Republican candidates for the presidency in 1980, coming in third after Ronald Reagan and George H. W. Bush.

Baker resigned in 1984, with Democrat Al Gore taking the majority leadership role in the Senate. That same year Baker received the Presidential Medal of Freedom. In 1987 President Reagan asked Baker to become his chief of staff, stepping into the position open after the resignation of Donald T. Regan. The Reagan administration was suffering from the Iran Contra affair and needed a moderate voice like Baker's to help address the situation. He clashed with the president's advisers over key issues, however, and left in 1988.

Baker's first wife, Joy, died in 1993. In 1996, he married former senator Nancy Landon Kassebaum, a colleague and friend he had known since 1978. Baker returned to private law practice but served as US ambassador to Japan from 2001 to 2005 under President George W. Bush. He then worked as an international adviser to Citigroup and helped found the Bipartisan Policy Center along with long-time colleague Bob Dole in 2007. Baker died on June 26, 2014, age eighty-eight, of complications from a stroke. He was survived by his wife, Nancy; siblings Mary Stuart and Beverly Patestides; son, Darek, and daughter, Cynthia, from his first marriage; and four grandchildren.

See Current Biography Illustrated 1974, 1987.

Ian G. Barbour

Born: Beijing, China; October 5, 1923
Died: Minneapolis, Minnesota; December 24, 2013
Occupation: Physicist, theologian

American scholar Ian Graeme Barbour was a pioneer in the process of integrating science and theology and achieved recognition as one of the world's preeminent religious scholars. Barbour authored nine books on the subject and is often credited with creating the field of interdisciplinary science and religion research.

Blending scholarly research and faith was a family tradition for Barbour, whose parents were both academics and Christian missionaries. Barbour was born in 1923 in Beijing (Peking), China, where his parents—George Barbour, a Scottish Presbyterian geologist who helped discover Peking Man, and Dorothy Dickinson, an

American Episcopalian schoolteacher—were teaching at Yenching University. After leaving China in 1931, Barbour's family lived in the United Kingdom before settling in the United States, where Barbour attended college, earning his bachelor's degree in physics from Swarthmore College in 1943.

A conscientious objector during World War II, Barbour joined the Civilian Public Service (CPS), through which he aided public welfare projects around the United States. While working with the CPS in North Carolina, Barbour enrolled at Duke University, where he completed his MS in physics in 1947. Barbour then continued his training in physics at the University of Chicago, where he worked under renowned nuclear physicist Enrico Fermi and finished his PhD in 1950. Between 1949 and 1953 he rose through the ranks of the physics department at Kalamazoo College in Michigan to become its chair.

In interviews Barbour would later report that his life changed when he became concerned about working on research contributing to atomic weapons technology. He enrolled in Yale University's Divinity School in 1953, studying ethics and religion, and graduated with a bachelor's degree in divinity in 1956. A year before he completed his divinity training, Barbour was offered a position as chair of a newly created religion department at Carleton College in Northfield, Minnesota. There, Barbour taught both science and religion and began to develop a system for blending the scientific and religious worldviews, long considered by many scholars on both sides to be incompatible. Barbour's experiments in this regard resulted in his groundbreaking *Issues in Science and Religion* (1966), one of the first books that recommended a conciliatory approach toward integrating religion and science for mutual benefit. In 1967 he was awarded both a Guggenheim and a Fulbright fellowship.

In 1972 Barbour created one of the nation's first interdisciplinary academic programs for the study of science and religion at Carleton College. Barbour remained at Carleton, becoming professor emeritus in 1986 when he formally retired. In 1989 Barbour was chosen to become a Gifford Lecturer, one of the highest theological honors in Scotland. Barbour published *Religion in an Age of Science* (1990) and *Ethics in an Age of Technology* (1993) based on the content of his Gifford Lectures. In 1999 Barbour received a Templeton Prize, given to individuals who have made important contributions to global spiritual life.

Barbour had a stroke on December 20, 2013, and died on December 24, at age ninety. Barbour was predeceased by his wife, Deane Kern Barbour, in 2011, and is survived by their four children, John, David, Blair, and Heather;

his brother Hugh; and three grandchildren and one great-grandson.

See Current Biography 2000.

Tony Benn

Born: London, England; April 3, 1925
Died: London, England; March 14, 2014
Occupation: Politician, member of Parliament

Anthony Neil Wedgwood Benn was a controversial political leader in the British Parliament who became a spokesman for the radical faction within the nation's Labour Party. Benn was known as a passionate defender of union rights, the antiwar movement, and nuclear disarmament.

Benn was born in Marylebone, London, in 1925, the second of four sons born to William Wedgwood Benn, a Liberal member of Parliament (MP) and Royal Air Force (RAF) veteran, and Margaret Holmes, a theologian and advocate for gender equality in religious leadership. Benn was born into a political dynasty, as both his father and grandfather served as MPs. In 1942, William Wedgwood Benn was ennobled, receiving the hereditary title of Viscount Stansgate.

Benn attended the Westminster School and then went to New College, Oxford, where he studied political philosophy, before leaving the university to join the RAF during World War II. Benn returned to Oxford after the war and completed his degree in 1949. That same year, Benn married American-born Caroline Middleton DeCamp, who was a fellow student at Oxford. The following year, Benn became an MP representing the Labour Party.

Due to the death of his older brother in World War II, Benn was in line to inherit his father's peerage, which, according to British law, would have made him ineligible to serve in Parliament's House of Commons. In 1955, Benn introduced the Peerage Bill, which would allow the inheritor of a peerage to renounce the title for his or her lifetime. Benn was the first MP to lobby for the right to renounce peerage and his efforts gained him a reputation as a constitutional reformer and a critic of the British nobility system. Though he was elected as a member for Bristol in 1961, an election court ruled the vote invalid and his seat went to his Conservative opponent. The bill officially passed in 1963, allowing Benn to run for office as a member of the House of Commons.

The Labour Party came to power in 1964 and Benn served in a number of prominent positions within the administration of Prime Minister Harold Wilson. While serving as postmaster general, Benn made global headlines when he campaigned to have the Queen's image removed from national stamps. Benn was also known for his service as minister of technology in 1966, where he led a campaign to reinvigorate the nation's auto industry.

During the 1970 elections, Benn's increasingly radical views brought him into conflict with the party mainstream. Benn was responsible for writing the "Belsen speech," in which he compared Conservative Party candidate Enoch Powell's policies to those of the Nazis. The speech was widely criticized and some believed it to be a contributing factor in the Labour Party's loss to the Conservative Party. Benn was also known for his distrust of the media, which led him to record all of his interviews and to keep detailed personal diaries. Benn began publishing his diaries in 1987, as a memoir of his life in politics.

Benn spent much of his later life campaigning with his wife on antiwar and antiviolence issues. The year after the death of his wife in 2000, Benn retired from Parliament, though he remained an active political advocate. After the invasion of Iraq in 2003, Benn was a leader in the nation's Stop the War Coalition. Benn died on March 14, 2014, age eighty-eight, after suffering from a stroke. He is survived by three sons and a daughter.

See Current Biography Illustrated 1965, 1982.

Polly Bergen

Born: Knoxville, Tennessee; July 14, 1930
Died: Southbury, Connecticut; September 20, 2014
Occupation: Actor

Nellie Paulina Burgin, better known by her stage name, Polly Bergen, was an Emmy Award–winning actor and singer who also became a successful entrepreneur, with a best-selling series of fashion books and her own line of cosmetics.

Bergen was born in Knoxville, Tennessee, in 1930, and moved to Los Angeles as a teenager. Her father was a musician and singer, and Bergen began singing with him on radio and nightclub appearances when she was around fourteen years old. Bergen's appearances as a singer attracted the attention of Paramount Pictures executives, and she signed a contract, making her debut portraying a barroom singer in the 1949 film *Across the Rio Grande*. She then had bit parts in a series of three Dean Martin and Jerry Lewis comedies over the next few years.

Bergen made a few hit song recordings, beginning with the 1955 radio hit "Little Girl Blue." Dissatisfied with her opportunities for the big screen, Bergen turned to television, appearing on the panel show *To Tell the Truth* (1956–61), and was then offered her own variety series, *The Polly Bergen Show*, which aired for a

single season from 1957 to 1958. Bergen won an Emmy Award for her portrayal of an ailing singer in the 1957 television film *The Helen Morgan Story*, part of the *Playhouse 90* series.

In the early 1960s, Bergen began selling her own line of cosmetics. The entire line was later purchased by the Fabergé company. Bergen also produced a line of shoes and jewelry and wrote a best-selling self-help book, *The Polly Bergen Book of Beauty, Fashion, and Charm*, published in 1962. That same year Bergen returned to the big screen in the thriller *Cape Fear*, starring alongside Gregory Peck and Robert Mitchum; her performance as Peggy Bowden won her critical and audience praise. She was also one of the first actors to play a female president on screen, in the critically panned 1964 comedy *Kisses for My President*. Over the next twenty years, Bergen rarely returned to the big screen, opting for smaller roles in a variety of television films and series. She also published two more books in the 1970s, *Polly's Principles* (1974) and *I'd Love To, But What'll I Wear?* (1977).

By the late 1970s, Bergen's entrepreneurial activities had made her a millionaire. Having already married and divorced twice previously, Bergen married investor Jeffrey K. Endervelt in 1982, which proved disastrous to her finances. The couple divorced in 1990. Bergen returned to television in the 1980s, earning an Emmy nomination for her performance in the 1988 drama miniseries *War and Remembrance*. Her return to stage, in a 2001 production of Stephen Sondheim's *Follies*, won her critical praise. She had a recurring role on *Desperate Housewives* from 2007 to 2011, resulting in another Emmy nomination.

Having had an abortion that left her unable to have children when she was a teenager, Bergen was active in campaigning for reproductive rights for most of her career. She also took part in campaigning for Hillary Clinton's bid for the presidency in 2008. Bergen died at her home in Southbury, Connecticut, on September 20, 2014, age eighty-four. She is survived by a daughter, P. K. Fields; a son, Peter Fields; stepdaughter, Kathy Lander; and three grandchildren.

See Current Biography 1958.

Thomas Berger

Born: Cincinnati, Ohio; July 20, 1924
Died: Nyack, New York; July 13, 2014
Occupation: American novelist

Thomas Louis Berger was an American novelist whose witty and insightful explorations of middle-class American culture made him a favorite among critics. Berger wrote twenty-three novels, exploring a variety of genres from Westerns to science fiction.

Berger was born in 1924 in Cincinnati, Ohio, the son of Thomas and Mildred (Bubbe) Berger. After graduating from Lockland High School in 1942, Berger enlisted in the US Army, joining the Medical Corps and serving in England and Germany during World War II. Returning home, Berger attended the University of Cincinnati, where he earned a bachelor's degree in 1948. Berger began but never finished a graduate program in English at Columbia University. While there, he met and married his wife, painter Jeanne Redpath Berger, in 1950.

Berger's experiences in World War II provided the inspiration and setting for his first novel, *Crazy in Berlin*, which was published in 1958 and was the first of four books developing the character of Carlo Reinhart, an aimless everyman who many critics called Berger's alter ego. Berger turned to the Western genre with his third novel, *Little Big Man* (1964), which became his most popular and iconic book. In the novel, Berger's protagonist Jack Crabb, a white drifter adopted by the Cheyenne tribe, meets and has often-humorous interactions with many famous historical figures of the American West while en route to an emotional showdown with General George Custer. Berger's *Little Big Man* has been favorably compared to the works of Mark Twain and won the Richard and Hinda Rosenthal Award and an award from the National Institute of Arts and Letters in 1965. A 1970 film version, staring Dustin Hoffman, was one of four films adapted from Berger's novels.

Berger explored many different genres, including horror in the 1967 book *Killing Time* and dystopian furturism in *Regiment of Women* (1973). Many of his books were set in middle America and explore seemingly banal events that transform people's lives into slapstick violence. His 1975 novel, *Sneaky People*, about a murder plot involving a used-car salesman, is considered one of his best novels in this vein. Berger also explored the pulp detective genre with *Who is Teddy Villanova?* (1977) and took a humorous look at chivalry and honor in his take on the King Arthur legend, *Arthur Rex: A Legendary Novel* (1978). The second most successful film adaptation of a Berger novel was the 1981 film *Neighbors*, based on Berger's 1980 novel of the same name. Berger's 1983 book *The Feud* was another of his most popular books and was a finalist for the 1984 Pulitzer Prize.

In his youth, Berger was an eager participant in the New York literary scene, but he became increasingly reclusive in the 1970s and 1980s and rarely gave interviews to the press. Berger died on July 13, 2014, at the age of eighty-nine. Berger is survived by his wife, Jeanne.

See Current Biography 1988.

Carlo Bergonzi

Born: Vidalenzo, Italy; July 13, 1924
Died: Milan, Italy; July 25, 2014
Occupation: Opera singer

Carlo Bergonzi was an Italian operatic tenor who was widely considered to be one of the greatest interpreters of the tenor roles in the operas of Giuseppe Verdi, Gaetano Donizetti, and Giacomo Puccini. Often praised for the emotive quality of his voice and his skill with subtle phrasing, Bergonzi remained one of the top opera tenors for more than forty years.

Bergonzi was born in 1924 in the town of Vidalenzo in northern Italy, the son of a prominent Parmesan cheese maker. Bergonzi took to singing in his youth, performing in his church choir and later attending the Parma Conservatory. Due to his opposition to the Nazi Party and the Italian alliance with Nazi Germany, Bergonzi was jailed for three years in a concentration camp during World War II. When he was released, he resumed his studies and made his professional debut in 1948, singing as a baritone and appearing as Figaro in a production of Gioachino Rossini's *The Barber of Seville*. In 1950, Bergonzi married Adele Aimi, with whom he later had two children.

While he was trained as a baritone, Bergonzi found that his voice and personal tastes were more suited to tenor roles and decided to retrain in hopes of transitioning to a career as an operatic tenor. After a couple years of practice, Bergonzi made his tenor debut in Umberto Giordano's *Andrea Chénier* in Bari, Italy, in 1951. After his 1953 performance at La Scala in Jacopo Napoli's opera *Mas'Aniello*, critics began recognizing Bergonzi as one of the best emerging tenors in Europe.

In 1955, Bergonzi made his first visit to the United States, performing with the Lyric Opera of Chicago (then the Lyric Theater of Chicago) in Puccini's *Il Tabarro*, and the following year he was invited to perform at the Metropolitan Opera of New York, performing the part of Radames in *Aida*. This was the first of more than three hundred performances that Bergonzi gave at the Met over the next thirty years. Bergonzi's first appearance at the famed Royal Opera House in London's Covent Garden came in 1962, with a performance as Don Alvaro in Verdi's *La Forza del Destino*. Bergonzi returned many times to Covent Garden over his career as well, often performing in Verdi and Puccini compositions.

In interviews, Bergonzi admitted that while his short stature and extra weight made him ill suited to physically portray the romantic heroes of the great operas, he attempted to make up for physical limitations by acting with his voice. In addition to live appearances, Bergonzi recorded dozens of performances, capturing every stage of his career from the 1950s to the 1990s. Many of Bergonzi's recordings were of his favorite roles, which included Pinkerton in *Madama Butterfly* and Nemorino in Donizetti's *L'Elisir d'Amore* in addition to the works of Verdi and Puccini.

Bergonzi gave a critically praised farewell performance in 1994, at age seventy, at Carnegie Hall, though he reemerged from retirement for an unsuccessful staging of Verdi's *Otello* with the Opera Orchestra of New York in 2000. After retirement, he continued working as a teacher and opera coach. Bergonzi died on July 25, 2014, at the age of ninety, at a hospital in Milan, Italy. He is survived by his wife, Adele, and the couple's two sons, Maurizio and Marco.

See Current Biography 1992.

Shirley Temple Black

Born: Santa Monica, California; April 23, 1928
Died: Woodside, California; February 10, 2014
Occupation: Actress, diplomat

Shirley Temple Black was a Hollywood icon and one of the most successful child actors in the history of American film. After retiring from acting, Black became a prominent Republican spokeswoman and served as a US Ambassador to both Ghana and Czechoslovakia.

Shirley Temple Black was born Shirley Jane Temple in Santa Monica, California. Her mother, Gertrude, decided early on to promote her daughter as a performer and enrolled her in Mrs. Meglin's Dance Studio at three years of age. Black had her film debut in a 1932 series of short films known as Baby Burlesks, and soon attracted the attention of the major movie studios. Black's feature film *Stand Up and Cheer* in 1934, a droll, Depression-era comedy, brought her into the Fox studios lineup of actors.

Black, then known as Shirley Temple, was often cast as an orphan whose charm and good nature saved her from poverty and suffering. Many of Black's films featured songs that also became major hits on the radio and through the sheet music market. Among these musical successes was the song "On the Good Ship Lollipop," from the 1934 film *Bright Eyes,* and the popular children's song "Animal Crackers in my Soup," from the 1935 film *Curly Top.* Black appeared in dozens of films, but only a few became major box office hits, including *Captain January* (1936), *Heidi* (1937), and *The Little Princess* (1939).

Fox did not renew Black's contract after the 1940 film *The Blue Bird* failed at the box office. Black, unemployed, finished her high school education at Westlake School for Girls. She made a brief return to films as a teenaged actress, but was unable to recapture her earlier success. In 1945 she married John Agar, with whom she had a daughter in 1948. The couple divorced in 1949, and the following year, Black retired from acting. That same year, she married Charles Alden Black, a navy intelligence officer with whom she had two children. Black began to take an interest in politics in the 1960s, becoming a member of the California Republican Party. Black's celebrity made her attractive as a spokeswoman for the party, and President Nixon appointed her as a delegate to the United Nations General Assembly in 1969.

In 1974, President Gerald Ford appointed Black to become the US Ambassador to Ghana, where she served until 1976, earning distinction for her humanitarian efforts. Black then became the first woman to serve as US Chief of Protocol, helping to organize diplomatic functions for visiting foreign dignitaries. Black retired after hosting the inaugural ball for President Carter in 1977, but was invited by President George H. W. Bush to rejoin the government in 1989, becoming the US Ambassador to the former nation of Czechoslovakia. Black retired from the position in 1992, the year before Czechoslovakia was dissolved. Black died in her home in Woodside, California, on February 10, 2014. She was eighty-five. Predeceased by her second husband in 2005, Black is survived by her three children, Linda, Charles, and Lori.

See Current Biography Illustrated 1970.

Edgar M. Bronfman

Born: Montreal, Canada; June 20, 1929
Died: New York, New York; December 21, 2013
Occupation: Business executive, philanthropist

Billionaire beverage mogul and noted philanthropist Edgar Miles Bronfman helped to build the Seagram Company into one of Canada's most successful liquor producers. Bronfman was also widely recognized for his efforts to promote Jewish political and philanthropic projects that had a positive impact on Jewish communities around the world.

Bronfman inherited control of Seagram Company from his father, Samuel Bronfman, who immigrated to Canada, along with his wife, Saidye Rosner Bronfman, from eastern Europe. Samuel Bronfman entered the liquor business with his brother Allan in 1915 and bought out rival Joseph E. Seagram & Sons in 1928. The company retained the Seagram name and opened a US Seagram subsidiary in 1933, after the end of Prohibition. Edgar Bronfman joined the family business in 1951, after completing a degree from McGill University in Montreal. In

1953 Bronfman's father made him head of the US division. In that capacity he helped the company to expand its portfolio with investments in oil, chemical, and other interests. Following the death of his father in 1971, Edgar Bronfman became chair and CEO of the company.

In 1981 Bronfman was elected president of the World Jewish Congress (WJC), an international organization that works to protect Jewish communities and interests. In the 1980s Bronfman played a major role in advocating for Jewish rights in the Soviet Union, where Jews were prohibited from immigrating to Israel and where teaching Hebrew had effectively been prohibited. Bronfman was the first WJC president to meet with Soviet officials, and played a major role in changing Soviet policies under President Mikhail Gorbachev toward the end of the decade. In 1986 Bronfman led the WJC to accuse Austrian president Kurt Waldheim of hiding past connections to the Nazi Party. During this same period Bronfman regularly utilized his personal wealth to fund philanthropic causes, including founding the Bronfman Youth Fellowships in Israel and North America in 1987.

In 1989 Bronfman turned the presidency of Seagram over to his second son, Edgar Jr., who also became CEO in 1994. Bronfman then concentrated on his work with the WJC and his charitable interests. In 1995 Bronfman spearheaded a campaign to obtain restitution from Swiss banks on the basis that the banks had kept money deposited by Jews who were murdered during the Holocaust. In 1998 these efforts resulted in a $1.25 billion settlement, and in 1999 Bronfman was awarded the Presidential Medal of Freedom by President Bill Clinton in recognition of his humanitarian achievements. Bronfman stepped down as WJC president in 2007. On December 21, 2013, Bronfman died at his Manhattan home, at age eighty-four. He is survived by his fourth wife, artist Jan Aronson; brother Charles Bronfman and sister Phyllis Lambert; sons Samuel Bronfman II, Edgar Bronfman Jr., Matthew Bronfman, and Adam Bronfman; daughters Holly Bronfman Lev, Sara Igtet, and Clare Bronfman; twenty-four grandchildren; and two great-grandchildren.

See Current Biography 1974.

Jim Brosnan

Born: Cincinnati, Ohio; October 24, 1929
Died: Park Ridge, Illinois; June 28, 2014
Occupation: Athlete and author

James "Jim" Patrick Brosnan was a major-league pitcher, remembered as one of best relievers of the early 1960s. His autobiographical books about his baseball career are often credited with inspiring a new genre of sports writing.

Brosnan was born in Cincinnati, Ohio, in 1929. He later credited his interest in baseball to his father, John, a milling machinery worker, while his mother, Rose, a nurse, introduced him to literature and music. Playing for the Bentley Post American Legion team, Brosnan made the 1946 national finals and was drafted by a Chicago Cubs farm team that year. In 1950 he joined the US Army, spending two years at Fort Meade in Maryland. There he met Anne Stewart Pitcher, whom he married in 1952.

The Chicago Cubs brought Brosnan to the major leagues in 1954. Teammates described him as a loner, and he earned the nickname the Professor for his tendency to smoke a pipe and read literature in the bullpen. Brosnan kept a journal of his time in the major leagues and published a few pages of it in Sports Illustrated in 1958. That year Brosnan was traded to the St. Louis Cardinals and, the following year, to the Cincinnati Reds.

In 1959 Harper & Row editors, liking the Sports Illustrated pieces, asked Brosnan to write a book about his experiences. The result was the controversial behind-the-scenes book The Long Season (1960), which provided what critics called the first realistic account of life in professional baseball. However, some felt the diarial book betrayed the privacy of the clubhouse, though Brosnan did not focus, as later writers have, on colleagues' sexual exploits or personal foibles. The book won praise from critics, many of whom highlighted the fact that Brosnan, as an athlete-intellectual, was a rarity in the world of professional athletics.

Brosnan wrote a second book about his time with the Reds during the 1961 season, which was also one of Brosnan's most successful seasons as a pitcher, with a record of 10–4. Brosnan's 1962 book, Pennant Race, became another best seller, largely because of Brosnan's irreverent and honest approach to sports writing. Brosnan was traded to the White Sox in 1963. When the Sox contract for 1964 prohibited him from writing about baseball during the season, Brosnan chose instead to retire to focus on his writing.

In retirement Brosnan worked as a sportscaster and contributed articles to numerous magazines, including Chicago Tribune Magazine, Sports Illustrated, and Playboy. He also wrote a series of baseball-themed books for young readers, including Little League to Big League (1968). Brosnan's wife predeceased him in 2013, and Brosnan died in June 2014, age eighty-four. He was survived by his brother Michael; children Timothy, Jamie, and Kimberlee; and four grandchildren.

See Current Biography 1964.

Louise Brough

Born: Oklahoma City, Oklahoma; March 11, 1923
Died: Vista, California; February 3, 2014
Occupation: Tennis player

Althea Louise Brough Clapp, better known by her professional title Louise Brough, was one of the greatest tennis players of the mid-century era, winning thirty-five grand slam tennis championships in the 1940s and '50s and becoming the top-ranked women's tennis player in 1947. Brough and her longtime partner and friend Margaret Osborne DuPont were also a formidable force in doubles tennis, winning twelve women's doubles championships at the United States Nationals.

Brough was born in Oklahoma City, Oklahoma, where her father was a wholesale grocer, on March 11, 1923, and relocated with her family to Beverly Hills, California, during her youth. An enthusiastic child athlete, Brough began taking tennis lessons on public courts and, at age fourteen, became a pupil of Dick Skeen, regarded as one of the best women's tennis coaches of the era. Brough and fellow women's tennis star Gertrude "Gussie" Moran competed for the top spot in California's teen tennis leagues and Brough won the girls' national junior championships in 1940 and 1941.

As a professional, Brough rose quickly through the ranks, from being named the twelfth-best women's tennis player in 1940 to attaining the second-place ranking in 1942. That same year, Brough partnered with Margaret Osborne DuPont to win the US National Doubles Championship. Brough and Osborne retained the title from 1942 until 1950, constituting the longest winning streak in women's doubles history to that point.

Though she and Osborne were nearly unbeatable in doubles, Brough had more difficulty in singles play, competing against a host of some of the most formidable players in the history of women's tennis, including Shirley Fry, Pauline Betz, Doris Hart, Althea Gibson, and her doubles colleague Osborne. Brough only won the US National Singles Championship once in her career, after a hard-fought 1947 victory over Osborne. She fared better at the UK–based Wimbledon Championships, winning singles championships for three years from 1948 until 1950. In 1950, Brough also became a singles champion at the Australian Championship. Brough was also a force at the Wightman Cup, an annual challenge between US and British champions, in which she played a total of twenty-two matches and won all of them.

In the early 1950s, Brough said in interviews she felt she had lost her edge due to the pressure of competition. She continued to play, however, and had a resurgence in 1955, winning the Wimbledon singles championship for the fourth time. She and Osborne also returned to supremacy in doubles play, winning the US National Championships from 1955 to 1957.

In 1958, Brough decided to retire, settling into married life with her husband, dentist Alan Clapp. Over the next twenty years, Brough regularly taught tennis to juniors players. She was formally inducted into the International Tennis Hall of Fame in 1967.

Brough was predeceased by her husband in 1999 and spent the remainder of her life in Vista, California, where she died on February 3, 2014, at age ninety.

See Current Biography 1948.

Gyude Bryant

Born: Monrovia, Liberia; January 17, 1949
Died: Monrovia, Liberia; April 16, 2014
Occupation: Interim leader and businessman

Charles Gyude Bryant was a leader of the moderate Liberia Action Party (LAP) who was appointed to lead the transitional government in 2003 following the end of the Liberian civil war, which began in 1999. Bryant was also a businessman, involved in the equipment import industry, and a lay leader of the Episcopal Church of Liberia.

Bryant was born on January 17, 1949, in Monrovia, Liberia. While many of the nation's future political leaders were descended from the former American slaves who founded Liberia in the mid-nineteenth century, Bryant's family was of the native Grebo ethnic group. Bryant completed a bachelor's degree from Monrovia's Cuttington University College in 1972, and married Rosielee Williams, who worked for US–based United Airlines, in 1974. Bryant built a business importing and selling heavy equipment for construction and, starting in 1996, served as chair of the board of trustees for the Episcopal Church of Liberia.

Bryant became one of the founding members of the moderate LAP in the 1980s and was seen as instrumental in helping the party to come to national prominence. Political analysts have speculated that governmental corruption prevented the LAP from taking the presidency in the 1985 elections. Bryant was elected chairman of the LAP in 1992 and was one of the politicians vocally opposed to the authoritarian policies and corrupt practices of President Charles Taylor, who came to power in 1997. In 1999, Liberians United for Reconciliation and Democracy (LURD) staged a militant uprising against Charles Taylor's government. This set off several years of intense fighting between political factions, resulting in thousands of deaths. While many of the nation's political leaders, including Taylor, fled to Nigeria and neighboring countries, Bryant remained in Liberia, where the LAP adopted a conciliatory approach to the conflict and called for peace between the warring factions.

In 2003, representatives of the major political parties met in Accra, Ghana, to discuss terms for a peace agreement. In a development that surprised many political analysts, Bryant, though largely a political unknown was chosen to serve as Chairman of the Transitional Government and tasked with paving the way for democratic elections. While rival candidate Ellen Johnson Sirleaf was the politician most analysts felt would be appointed to the position, Bryant was chosen because he represented a neutral position between the more politically polarized candidates.

In the Liberian presidential elections of 2005, Sirleaf won a contested and controversial election while Bryant was prohibited from running for the presidency under the terms of the 2003 peace agreement. In 2007, Bryant and several other members of his administration were accused of embezzling more than $1 million while in office. The controversy resulted in a 2009 trial in which Bryant was acquitted of some of the charges; the rest were dropped in 2010 due to lack of proof.

Bryant died in Monrovia on April 16, 2014, age sixty-five, after suffering from a protracted illness. The details of his illness were not released to the press. Bryant is survived by his wife and the couple's three children.

See Current Biography International Yearbook 2005.

James MacGregor Burns

Born: Melrose, Massachusetts; August 3, 1918
Died: Williamstown, Massachusetts; July 15, 2014
Occupation: Author and political scientist

James MacGregor Burns was a Pulitzer Prize–winning historian known for his books exploring the nature of leadership and the American presidency. In addition to political biographies, Burns was also a professor of political science at Williams College for nearly forty years.

Burns was born in Melrose, Massachusetts, a suburb of Boston, to Mildred Bunce and Robert Burns. He was raised in Burlington, Massachusetts, after his parents divorced. Burns attended Williams College in Williamstown, Massachusetts, where he majored in political science and graduated in 1939. He then began work as a congressional aide in Washington, DC. During World War II, Burns served in the US Army as a combat historian and received a Bronze Star for

his service. After the war, Burns earned a PhD in government from Harvard University and, in 1947, he began teaching political science at Williams College. In 1949, Burns published his first book, *Congress on Trial*, a critical look at the history of the US Congress and its role in making laws.

While a student, Burns became fascinated with President Franklin Roosevelt's role in initiating the New Deal and spent years conducting research on President Roosevelt's life and work. This effort resulted in Burns's first major publishing success, his 1956 book *Roosevelt: The Lion and the Fox*, which covered the early years of Roosevelt's life and became a critically acclaimed best seller. Burns briefly considered entering politics and ran for a seat in Congress in 1958, but he lost the race to Republican Silvio O. Conte. During his brief entrée into politics he met John F. Kennedy, who was then running for reelection to the US Senate. Burns wrote the first biography of Kennedy, *John Kennedy: A Political Profile* (1960), in which he praised Kennedy's potential as president.

Burns's greatest success came with the 1970 publication of *Roosevelt: The Soldier of Freedom*, his second biography of Franklin Roosevelt covering the president's middle and later years. The book won high praise from critics and readers largely due to Burns's unconventional biographical approach. While he presented a detailed historical analysis of Roosevelt, Burns also provided an insightful exploration of Roosevelt's failings and personality that some reviews called almost psychoanalytical in nature. Burns won both the National Book Award and the Pulitzer Prize in history and biography in 1971.

In 1978 Burns published *Leadership*, a theoretical exploration of leadership through examinations of some of the world's greatest leaders. The book was a critical success and its influence also extended to academia where the book has been a seminal text in political science and history studies. Burns published more than twenty books during his career, many of which were published after his retirement from Williams College in 1986. His last book, *Fire and Light: How the Enlightenment Transformed Our World*, was published in 2013.

Burns was married and divorced twice in his life, and he had four children. He spent many of his later years with his companion and fellow professor Susan Dunn, with whom he co-authored the 2001 book *The Three Roosevelts* and the 2004 biography *George Washington*. Predeceased by his son David in 2010, Burns died on July 15, 2014, at the age of ninety-five, at his home in Williamstown, Massachusetts. He is survived by his companion Susan Dunn and three children.

See Current Biography 1962.

Sid Caesar

Born: Yonkers, New York; September 8, 1922
Died: Beverly Hills, California; February 12, 2014
Occupation: Comedian

Comedian and writer Sidney "Sid" Caesar played a pioneering role in redefining American comedy. He became one of America's best known comedic personalities in the 1950s, and his television programs propelled the careers of some of the twentieth century's most revered comedy writers.

Caesar took an early interest in performing, and began playing saxophone for touring bands when he was fourteen years old. Caesar met and married Florence Levy in 1943, while he was touring clubs in the Catskills. He served in the Coast Guard during World War II, and began writing comedy in his free time. His comedy writing won him a spot performing for troops in the production *Tars and Spars*, under the direction of Max Liebman.

Caesar starred in a film version of *Tars and Spars* in 1946, and Liebman, realizing he had found a great talent in Caesar, produced a Broadway review program, *Make Mine Manhattan* in 1948, built around Caesar's comedy. In 1949, Caesar got his television break in *The Admiral Broadway Revue*, which was also produced by Liebman and became a major hit. The series also featured comic actor Imogene Coca, who was the perfect foil for Caesar's unique blend of character-based humor.

In 1950, Liebman brought Caesar and Coca together for a National Broadcasting Company (NBC) television sketch comedy program, *Your Show of Shows*, which was an immediate success and quickly became one of the most popular programs in America. Caesar helped to redefine American comedy, moving away from pratfalls and slapstick humor, and creating a character-focused comedic style. The series also featured the talents of some of the era's visionary comedy writers, including Mel Brooks, Woody Allen, and playwright Neil Simon. In 1954, NBC executives decided to capitalize on their success by splitting up Caesar and Coca to create two separate series. Caesar's follow up, *Caesar's Hour,* was not as successful as *Your Show of Shows*, and audiences dwindled until NBC cancelled the series in 1957.

Caesar developed an addiction to alcohol and pills following the cancellation of *Caesar's Hour* and the subsequent decline in his career. He worked sporadically throughout the 1960s and 1970s, appearing primarily in bit parts on television and in films. Among his memorable film roles, Caesar appeared in the Mel Brook's film *Silent Movie* in 1976, and played the role of the coach in the popular comedy *Grease* in 1978. That same year, Caesar felt he hit rock bottom, and decided to seek treatment for substance abuse.

In recovery, Caesar began trying to rejuvenate his career, appearing in a variety of television and film roles. He also wrote a best-selling biography of his life, *Where Have I Been?* in 1982. In 1985, Caesar was inducted into the Television Academy Hall of Fame in recognition of his pioneering work in the industry. Caesar died at his Beverly Hills home on February 12, 2014, at the age of ninety-one, after suffering from a brief illness. He was predeceased by his wife Florence in 2010, and is survived by his three children, Michele, Karen, and Richard.

See Current Biography 1951.

Nigel Calder

Born: London, England; December 2, 1931
Died: Crawley, England; June 25, 2014
Occupation: Author

Nigel David Ritchie Calder was an influential British science writer, television producer, and author. One of the founding members of the science journal *New Scientist* and the producer of several popular BBC science specials, Calder later became one of the most outspoken British scientists in the global climate change debate.

Calder was born in London, England, in 1931 to Mabel and Peter Ritchie Calder, a journalist and science editor for the *News Chronicle*. Born into an intellectual family, Calder enjoyed a privileged education and attended Sidney Sussex College, Cambridge, where he obtained his bachelor's degree in 1954 and his master's degree in 1957. From 1954 to 1956, Calder worked as a research physicist at Mullard Research Laboratories before leaving to pursue science writing as a career.

In 1956, Calder joined the editorial staff of the fledgling science news publication *New Scientist* as a science editor. The magazine enjoyed high initial sales but was unsuccessful in obtaining significant advertising revenues until 1957, when the Russian government launched Sputnik 1, the first artificial earth satellite. That event ushered in the space age and initiated the international race to develop and implement space exploration technology and defensive systems. *New Scientist* was at the cutting edge of these developments, feeding a growing public demand for popular science news. In 1962, after the death of the magazine's first editor, Percy Cudlipp, Calder became the editor of *New Scientist*. In addition to his work at *New Scientist*,

Calder also began writing and editing books about science for general audiences.

In 1966 Calder developed a script for a special BBC science documentary called *Russia: Beneath the Sputniks*. The program won critical praise, and Calder decided to quit his job at *New Scientist* to pursue work as a freelance writer and television producer. His next major success was the 1969 television special *The Violent Universe*, for which he also wrote a companion best-selling book. Calder's popularity was partially the result of his ability to identify and explore key areas of scientific inquiry of interest to the general public. His 1972 *The Restless Earth*, which explored the concept of plate tectonics and continental drift, was among the earliest popular books and television specials to cover the subject.

Calder authored and produced television specials on a variety of other subjects, including Albert Einstein's contributions to science in the 1979 book and television special *Einstein's Universe*. He was also a recreational sailor and wrote several books and articles about sailing, including *The English Channel* (1986), which won the Best Book of the Sea Award. In the 1990s, Calder became an outspoken supporter of controversial climate change theories. His 1997 book on the subject, *The Manic Sun*, became a best seller and helped to popularize the issue.

Calder continued writing and editing until his death in June 2014 at his home in Crawley, West Sussex. He was survived by his wife of sixty years, Elisabeth Palmer; their five children, Simon, Jonathan, Sarah, Penny, and Kate; and seven grandchildren.

See Current Biography 1986.

Anthony Caro

Born: New Malden, United Kingdom; March 8, 1924
Died: London, United Kingdom; October 23, 2013
Occupation: English sculptor

Anthony Caro was hailed as one of the greatest contemporary sculptors in history and was one of the most internationally acclaimed artists of the twentieth century. Caro was also a prolific teacher, whose students have gone on to make major contributions to contemporary sculpture around the world.

Caro was born on March 8, 1924, in New Malden, United Kingdom. As a child, Caro's father didn't approve of a career in art, comparing it to working as a professional gambler. In an effort to appease his father, Caro earned his degree in engineering in 1944 at Christ's College, Cambridge. Though he had an early interest in sculpture, Caro didn't begin training in the art until he returned to England after serving in the

Fleet Air Arm of the Royal Navy during World War II. In 1946 he started studying art at Regent Street Polytechnic and in 1947 he continued his studies at the Royal Academy Schools in London. In 1949 Caro met and married the painter Sheila Girling.

Caro worked as a part-time assistant to Henry Moore, an acclaimed English sculptor, starting in 1951. He worked with Moore for two years before returning to London to develop his own artistic style. In 1952, he accepted a position as a part-time instructor at St. Martin's School of Art in London, where he taught from 1953 to 1979. The inspiration for the abstract steel creations that later made Caro famous came partially from a 1959 trip to the United States, where Caro met a number of innovative American painters and sculptors, including David Smith, who was known for his abstract steel sculptures. Returning to London in 1960, Caro, who was influenced by Smith's technique, embarked on a new path, producing a series of painted metal abstractions still considered masterpieces, such as the yellow steel sculpture *Midday* (1960).

In the 1960s, Caro's work appeared in a number of individual exhibitions in New York City and London, including a notable 1963 exhibition at the Whitechapel Gallery in London, where Caro's work began to attract public acclaim. In his review of Caro's work at the Whitechapel Gallery in the *London for Arts* magazine, Gene Baro, a prominent organizer of art exhibitions, said Caro, "achieved with rigid and austere materials the warmth, sensuousness, spatial variety, romantic feeling and monumentality that are qualities of sculpture in stone and bronze."

In addition to larger works, Caro is also known for his smaller home sculptures of the 1960s and 1970s, including his *Writing Piece "Other"* (1979) and *Table Piece CCLXVI* (1975). Caro's work continued to evolve, and he later abandoned painting the metal he used in his work, opting to preserve the natural hues of the rusted metal. This led to Caro's larger works that he called "sculpitecture," which he felt blended the lines between architecture and sculpture by inviting visitors to physically interact with the sculptures. A notable example is the *Tower of Discovery* (1991), which he made for an exhibition at the Tate Gallery in 1991.

Caro won numerous awards over his career and became known as one of England's premier artists and teachers. In 1987 he was knighted by Queen Elizabeth II and in 2000 he received the Order of Merit, considered one of the highest royal honors. Caro was productive until his death on October 23, 2013, from a heart attack. He was eighty-nine years old. Caro is survived by his wife, Shelia; his two sons, Timothy and Paul; and his three grandchildren.

See Current Biography Illustrated 1981.

Rubin Carter

Born: Clifton, New Jersey; May 6, 1937
Died: Toronto, Canada; April 20, 2014
Occupation: Boxer and legal rights advocate

Rubin "Hurricane" Carter was a middleweight professional boxer who spent nearly twenty years in prison after being falsely accused and convicted of murder in 1966. After his conviction was overturned in 1985, Carter relocated to Toronto, Canada, where he founded an organization that lobbies for the investigation of cases in which individuals have been wrongly convicted.

Carter was born in 1937, in Clifton, New Jersey, the son of Lloyd, a church deacon and owner of an ice delivery business, and Bertha Carter. Carter spent much of his youth in state homes and juvenile incarceration centers for various crimes. When he was eleven, Carter was convicted of assault for stabbing a man Carter later accused of having attempted to sexually abuse him. Carter fled juvenile custody to join the Army at seventeen, serving in Germany, where he took up boxing. Discharged from the Army in 1956, Carter returned to New Jersey where he again took up crime. In 1957, he was jailed on several charges of mugging. Upon his release in 1961, Carter began working towards a professional boxing career.

Though not a major prospect, a surprise knockout of welterweight champ Emile Griffith made him a major draw for the next three years. Carter lost a close decision to middleweight Joey Giardello in his only fight for a middleweight title in 1964. In 1966, Carter and friend John Artis were arrested in connection with the murder of three individuals in a Paterson, New Jersey, bar and grill. Testimony by two petty criminals at the scene to commit an unrelated burglary resulted in Carter and Artis's conviction.

From prison, Carter published a biography, *The Sixteenth Round* (1974), which he sent to a host of celebrities hoping to build support for his professed wrongful conviction. Carter was released in 1975 when the criminals who placed him at the scene recanted their testimony. Bob Dylan recorded a song, "Hurricane," about the case, while other celebrities, including Muhammad Ali, rallied to the defense. At the retrial, however, one of the witnesses recanted his recantation and the prosecution alleged a racial motive for the murders, resulting in both men being convicted a second time.

Carter's first wife, Mae Thelma Basket, filed for divorce shortly after his return to prison, alleging that he had been unfaithful with female supporters during his nine-month release. From prison, Carter worked towards an appeal, aided by the Toronto-based Association in Defence of the Wrongly Convicted (AIDWYC). In 1985, a federal judge overturned Carter's conviction on the basis of prosecutorial misconduct and lack of evidence.

Carter relocated to Toronto, where he married AIDWYC head Lisa Peters, and eventually became chairman of the organization. Carter's life was the subject of a 1999 biopic, *Hurricane*, starring Denzel Washington, for which Washington was nominated for an Academy Award, though the film was criticized as highly inaccurate. In 2004, Carter and Peters divorced and he left the AIDWYC to form his own group, Innocence International, lobbying for prisoners considered wrongly convicted. Carter was diagnosed with prostate cancer in 2011 and died on April 20, 2014, age seventy-six, in Toronto. Carter is survived by a son and daughter from his first marriage.

See Current Biography 2000.

Chryssa

Born: Athens, Greece; December 31, 1933
Died: December 23, 2013
Occupation: Artist

Greek-born artist Chryssa was an avant-garde sculptor known for pioneering the use of neon in her installations. Chryssa displayed her abstract sculptures, using steel, acrylic glass, and neon-light media in Greece, Paris, and the United States, and became a major figure in the New York art scene of the 1950s and 1960s.

Chryssa was born Chryssa Vardea-Mavromichali on December 31, 1933, to a prominent family from Greece's Mesa Mani region. Throughout her career, she preferred to use the mononym "Chryssa" professionally. In a 1966 interview with the *New York Herald Tribune*, Chryssa said that her interest in "textual" art was inspired partially by the messages scrawled on buildings by the Greek underground in Athens during the Nazi occupation of mainland Greece between 1941 and 1944. Chryssa studied social work as a youth and spent a period on Zakynthos, aiding victims of the 1953 earthquake. That same year, a local art critic saw Chryssa's paintings and encouraged her family to provide her with artistic training. Chryssa spent part of 1953 and 1954 in Paris studying at the Académie de la Grande Chaumière.

In 1954, Chryssa traveled to the United States, and spent part of a year in San Francisco, California, where she attended the California School of Fine Arts. Chryssa moved to New York, where she began working in sculpture. Soon after her arrival, Chryssa produced her first now famous sculptural series, a group of plaster relief sculptures known as the *Cycladic Books*. The series was the first of many of her works that utilized typographic elements, including punctuation marks, letters, and other linguistic symbols. In interviews, Chryssa said she was inspired by both her experiences with Greek street writing and her experience of New York itself, which she described as "the new Byzantium," with Times Square as "the kingdom of light."

In 1961, the same year she had her first professional exhibit, Chryssa achieved a rare honor for a young artist, when she was invited to hold a solo exhibit at the Guggenheim. In the early 1960s, Chryssa began using neon lighting in her work, such as her famous 1962 *Times Square Sky*, which combined steel, aluminum, and neon lighting. Chryssa's 1966 *The Gates to Times Square*, a large ten-foot cube sculpture consisting of plexiglass, blue neon tubes, and steel, became one of her most famous works, and has been described as one of the most important works of American sculpture. By the late 1960s, Chryssa was considered one of the finest contemporary American sculptors and was invited for numerous solo and group exhibitions. Her work appeared at the Museum of Modern Art, the Whitney Museum of American Art, and the Leo Castelli Gallery among many other locations.

Though she gained her American citizenship, Chryssa decided to return to Athens in 1992, closing her New York studio to establish a new studio in an abandoned cinema called the Oasis. Chryssa later returned to New York and then divided her time between homes in New York and Athens. Though famous as an artist, Chryssa's private life was kept from the press. Chryssa died on December 23, 2013, at age seventy-nine, and was buried in Athens.

See Current Biography 1978.

Arthur Coleman Danto

Born: Ann Arbor, Michigan; January 1, 1924
Died: New York, New York; October 25, 2013
Occupation: American philosopher and art critic

The American philosopher and art critic Arthur Coleman Danto is considered to be one of the most well-known and influential art critics of the postmodern era. He published more than thirty books during his career, including *The Philosophical Disenfranchisement of Art* (1986), *Beyond the Brillo Box: The Visual Arts in Post-Historical Perspective* (1992) and *What Art Is* (2013). He was an early patron and promoter of avant-garde artists, including Andy Warhol, in the United States and was one of the architects of modern art commentary.

Danto was born on January 1, 1924, in Ann Arbor, Michigan. In 1942, Danto volunteered for the US Army and served during World War

II as a guard on trains running between Casablanca, Morocco, and Oran, Algeria, and also as a driver for the military postal service in Italy. After his discharge in 1945, he studied art and history at Wayne University (now Wayne State University) in Detroit, and did graduate work in philosophy at Columbia University, earning a master's degree in 1949 and a doctorate in 1952. Between earning his master's and his doctorate, Danto studied with Maurice Merleau-Ponty, a renowned phenomenologist, in Paris for a year on a Fulbright grant. Danto taught briefly at the University of Colorado before taking a teaching position in 1951 at Columbia, where he remained for the majority of his career. He retired from Columbia in 1992, after which he was named Johnsonian professor emeritus of philosophy.

While in graduate school, Danto also became an artist in his own right, producing a series of prints and woodcuts that were displayed at galleries, such as the National Gallery of Art in Washington, DC, and at the Art Institute of Chicago in the 1950s. By the early sixties, however, Danto's prominence as a critic largely overshadowed his own artistic career. The turning point in his career came in 1964, when he first saw Andy Warhol's innovative sculpture *Brillo Box* (1964). The sculpture intrigued Danto and led him to question why this sculpture, which was visibly the same as an ordinary object (a cardboard soap-pad container), was considered art. After his first encounter with Warhol, Danto wrote extensively on the subject of how to define art and proposed what came to be known as the institutional theory, which essentially asserts that art is defined by a general agreement of people in the artistic community, such as artists, critics, and art historians, rather than by a set of objective aesthetic qualities.

Danto wrote a number of essays about the nature of art, beginning with "The Artworld" in 1964. In the 1960s and 1970s Danto became a champion of abstract and avant-garde art and promoted innovative works through his philosophical analyses.

Danto's views on art are perhaps best known from his long tenure as the art critic for the *Nation* from 1984 to 2009. While his criticism was contemporary, Danto's views were informed by his philosophical training especially in the work of Georg Wilhelm Friedrich Hegel, a nineteenth century German philosopher. His essays covered the careers of modern masters like Damien Hirst and Gerhard Richter, but also contemporary views on the classic works of Pablo Picasso, Alberto Giacometti, and Kazimir Malevich. In 1990, he won the National Book Critics Circle prize for criticism for *Encounters and Reflections: Art in the Historical Present* (1990).

Danto continued writing until he died from heart failure on October 25, 2013, in New York

City. He was eighty-nine years old. Danto was married twice, first to Shirley Rovetch, who passed away in 1978, and then to Barbara Westman Danto in 1980. He is survived by his wife and two daughters, Elizabeth and Ginger.

See Current Biography 1995.

Ruby Dee

Born: Cleveland, Ohio; October 27, 1922
Died: New Rochelle, New York; June 11, 2014
Occupation: Actor

Ruby Ann Wallace, better known as Ruby Dee, was an African American actor and activist who won critical praise for her appearances on stage, screen, and television in a career that spanned more than seventy years.

Dee was born in Cleveland, Ohio, in 1922 but grew up primarily in New York's Harlem neighborhood. There she lived with her father, Marshall Wallace, and his second wife, Emma Amelia Benson, who introduced Dee to music and dance. Though she described herself as a shy child, Dee felt drawn to the stage and, in 1940, she apprenticed with the American Negro Theatre. The next year she married singer Frankie Dee Brown and adopted his middle name as her stage name. She also earned her bachelor's degree in French and Spanish at Hunter College in 1944. The following year, Dee and Brown divorced, though she continued using Dee as her working name.

In 1943, Dee made her first Broadway appearance in *South Pacific* (a play unrelated to the later Rodgers and Hammerstein hit musical), which flopped after only five performances. She returned to Broadway in 1946 as an understudy for the lead role of Libby in the play *Jeb*. Dee was asked to replace the original female lead before opening night and performed alongside Ossie Davis, who starred in the title role. Dee and Davis became romantically involved during the production and married in 1948. Over fifty-six years together, Dee and Davis costarred in dozens of plays as well as in television and film roles.

Dee made the transition to film with a series of noteworthy roles in such films as *The Jackie Robinson Story* (1950) and *Edge of the City* (1957), in which she appeared alongside Sidney Poitier. Her most famous stage appearance was as Ruth Younger in the original Broadway cast of *A Raisin in the Sun* in 1959. Davis and Dee were also politically active, participating in the March on Washington in 1963 and becoming close friends with Malcolm X. Dee was later inducted into the National Association for the Advancement of Colored People (NAACP) Hall of Fame in 1989 for her civil-rights activism.

Dee won the 1971 Obie Award for best actress for her performance in the play *Boesman and Lena*, about a couple dealing with racism during the apartheid era in South Africa. Dee appeared in many television roles throughout the 1970s and became increasingly in demand for supporting film roles. Dee and Davis appeared together in director Spike Lee's early films *Do the Right Thing* (1989) and *Jungle Fever* (1991). In 1991 Dee won the Emmy Award for outstanding supporting actress in a miniseries or special for her performance in the television film *Decoration Day*.

In 1998 Dee and Davis marked their golden wedding anniversary with a memoir, *With Ossie and Ruby: In This Life Together*. Dee continued delivering acclaimed performances into her seventies and eighties, among them her one-woman show, *My One Good Nerve*. She earned an Academy Award nomination for best actress in a supporting role for her performance, alongside Denzel Washington, in the 2007 film *American Gangster*. Predeceased by her husband in 2005, Dee died on June 11, 2014, at her home in New Rochelle at the age of ninety-one. She was survived by her sister Angelina, son Guy, daughters Nora and Hasna, and seven grandchildren.

See Current Biography 1970.

Paco de Lucía

Born: Algeciras, Spain; December 21, 1947
Died: Playa del Carmen, Mexico, February 26, 2014
Occupation: Musician

Guitarist and composer Paco de Lucía was one of the most internationally well-known flamenco musicians, helping to bring this distinctive Spanish tradition to music aficionados around the world. De Lucía is also credited with modernizing the flamenco by blending traditional and modern sounds in his recordings and performances.

De Lucía was born Francisco Sánchez Gómez in Algeciras, a small city in Andalusia, Spain. De Lucía's father, Antonio Sánchez, was a laborer who supplemented his income by performing guitar in local venues. Though de Lucía's family was not part of the ethnic Gitano group typically credited with creating flamenco music, the family lived in a heavily Gitano neighborhood where de Lucía was exposed to flamenco performance at a young age. De Lucía began studying guitar at age seven, and learned the fundamentals of flamenco from family friend Niño Ricardo, a prominent local musician. De Lucía developed his stage name by combining the common diminutive of Francisco, "Paco," with his mother's name, Lucía.

In 1959, de Lucía won first prize at the International Flamenco Competition in Jerez, and was invited to tour the United States with the famous José Greco Dance Company for the next several years. After returning to Spain, de Lucía began performing and recording with his brothers Ramón and Pepe, a collaboration that would continue intermittently for the next thirty years.

De Lucía released his first solo album, *La fabulosa guitarra de Paco de Lucía*, in 1967, by which time he was one of Spain's most acclaimed flamenco guitarists. Around this same time, he began recording and performing with Gitano singer Camarón de la Isla, and the duo continued recording together until the singer's death in 1992, releasing ten albums over the course of their collaboration.

Beginning in the late 1970s, de Lucía increasingly gravitated towards a modern, unique sound, combining flamenco with elements from a variety of musical genres. De Lucía and his brothers, performing in a popular sextet, championed the use of Peruvian cajón, a South American wooden percussion instrument that has since become common in flamenco music. Among de Lucía's most famous experimental projects was the 1981 album *Friday Night in San Francisco* with American guitarists John McLaughlin and Al Di Meola, which featured jazz fusion with flamenco elements. Though traditionalists sometimes criticized him for "polluting" flamenco, de Lucía was celebrated around the world for his skill and inventiveness. In 1992, he received the Gold Medal of Merit from the government of Spain for his contributions to Spanish music.

De Lucía won his first Latin Grammy Award in 2004 for his album *Cositas buenas* and that same year was the recipient of the Prince of Asturias Award for the arts, the government of Spain's highest artistic honor. De Lucía won a second Latin Grammy Award in 2012 for a double album consisting of recordings of his live performances.

De Lucía died suddenly on February 2014 at the age of sixty-six from a suspected heart attack in Playa del Carmen, Mexico, where he had a vacation home. De Lucía is survived by his second wife Gabriela Carrasco; their two children, Diego and Antonia; and three children from his first marriage, Casilda, Lucy, and Curro.

See Current Biography International Yearbook 2004.

Felix Dennis

Born: Kingston-upon-Thames, England; May 27, 1947
Died: Dorsington, England; June 22, 2014
Occupation: Publisher

Felix Dennis was a British writer and magazine-industry innovator who became one of Britain's richest self-made entrepreneurs. Dennis became known for his work on *Oz* magazine in the 1970s and later published a wide variety of news and entertainment publications, including the popular men's magazine *Maxim*.

Dennis was born in Kingston-upon-Thames in southwest London. Growing up under the care of a single mother, Dennis was an unenthusiastic student, leaving school and home at fifteen and working a series of odd jobs. He sent a magazine review to the editor of the controversial *Oz* magazine, Richard Neville, and landed a job selling copies of the magazine on the street in 1967. Impressed by Dennis's industriousness and inventiveness, Neville made him a coeditor of the magazine in 1969. A 1970 issue of *Oz*, for which the editors accepted submissions from adolescent readers, became the subject of the longest obscenity trial in British history due to a sexually explicit comic of Rupert the Bear featured in the issue. Dennis and two other editors were arrested and charged with conspiracy to corrupt public morals. The highly visible 1971 trial resulted in convictions for all three defendants, though they were released pending appeal, which they won in 1973.

After *Oz* folded, Dennis and *Oz* colleague Dick Pountain launched *Cosmic Comix*, a magazine collecting short comic features from alternative artists. Failing to find success in the comics field, Dennis founded Dennis Publishing in 1973. In 1974 Dennis was inspired by a growing interest in Chinese martial arts movies within Britain and began publishing *Kung-Fu Monthly*. The magazine spread to seventeen countries, becoming one of the cornerstones of Dennis's publishing empire. Dennis later expanded by taking advantage of the emerging computer market, purchasing and publishing computer weeklies and monthlies aimed at both the PC and Macintosh markets, including *PC World* and *MacUser*.

In 1995 Dennis launched a new men's magazine, *Maxim*, which was an immediate success in Britain and became the best-selling men's magazine in the United States. Bolstered by this new arm of his publishing business, in 1996 Dennis purchased the *Week*, a publication that provided aggregate news stories culled from other publications. Presaging the popularity of this form of news in Internet media, the *Week* became a major success in the United States after it was introduced to American readers in 2001.

Dennis began writing and publishing poetry in 1999 while recovering from a hypothyroid condition and crack-cocaine addiction. His poetry became popular, and Dennis performed readings around the world. Having become a multimillionaire, Dennis invested money in a wide variety of unusual ventures, including constructing an enormous, contiguous deciduous forest on his Warwickshire estate, called the Heart of England Forest Project. Dennis also published the autobiographical *How to Get Rich* (2006), in which he expounded on his business acumen and methods. In 2013, he received a lifetime achievement award from the British Media Awards. Dennis was diagnosed with throat cancer in January 2012 and died in June 2014, at the age of sixty-seven, at his home in Dorsington, England. Dennis neither married nor had children. He was survived by his brother, Julian, and longtime companion Marie-France Demolis.

See Current Biography 2000.

Jeremiah Denton

Born: Mobile, Alabama; July 15, 1924
Died: Virginia Beach, Virginia; March 28, 2014
Occupation: US senator and naval admiral

Jeremiah Denton became famous for covertly revealing the use of torture by his Vietnamese captors while being held as a prisoner of war from 1965 to 1973. Denton became an admiral in the Navy and later served as a Republican senator representing Alabama.

Jeremiah Andrew Denton Jr. was born in Mobile, Alabama, in 1924, the oldest of three children born into a devout Catholic family and raised by their mother after their parents divorced in 1938. Denton attended the United States Naval Academy at Annapolis, Maryland, graduating with honors in 1946. That same year, he married Kathryn Jane Maury, with whom he would have seven children. Denton served as a naval flight instructor, squadron leader, and test pilot in the 1940s and '50s. He eventually returned to school, graduating from George Washington University in 1964 with a master's degree in international affairs.

On July 18, 1965, while Denton was serving as a commander in the Vietnam War, he and several of his squad were shot down and captured by North Vietnamese forces. For seven years and seven months, Denton and his fellow soldiers were tortured and starved in a series of Vietnamese war prisons, including the infamous "Hanoi Hilton" detention center. About ten months after his capture, Denton was forced to appear in a propaganda video that was taped by a Japanese crew and broadcast on American television on May 17, 1966. While being interviewed, Denton blinked his eyes in a pattern that spelled out "T-O-R-T-U-R-E" in Morse code. The interview became famous when Denton's hidden message was deciphered. In the accompanying interview, Denton said that, while he was unaware of the progress of the war, he remained a loyal supporter of his government.

Denton was one of the highest-ranking POWs captured in Vietnam and was one of the first to be released after Nixon signed the peace agreement in 1973. Having been awarded the Navy Cross and promoted to captain during his confinement, Denton returned to military service after his release. He was appointed commandant of the Armed Forces Staff College in 1974 and was eventually promoted to the rank of rear admiral. In 1976, Denton published a best-selling memoir of his experiences as a POW, *When Hell Was in Session*, which became the basis for a 1979 television movie.

In 1977, Denton retired from the military and started the Coalition for Decency, an organization for promoting family values and citizenship. He began working as a consultant for the Christian Broadcasting Network, working closely with evangelist Pat Robertson. Denton capitalized on his celebrity to win an election to the Senate in 1980, representing his native state of Alabama. Denton was the first Republican to be elected to the Alabama senate since Reconstruction and represented a highly conservative wing of the Republican Party. Remaining in office until 1987, Denton supported abstinence-only sex education and a number of other conservative issues popular among the Christian conservative movement.

Denton was predeceased by his first wife in 2007 and later married Mary Belle Bordone. Denton died on March 28, 2014, age eighty-nine, from complications arising from a heart ailment. He is survived by his second wife, a brother, six children from his first marriage, fourteen grandchildren, and six great-grandchildren.

See Current Biography 1982.

Jean-Claude Duvalier

Born: Port-au-Prince, Haiti; July 3, 1951
Died: Port-au-Prince, Haiti; October 4, 2014
Occupation: Former president of Haiti

Jean-Claude Duvalier was a former president of Haiti who took the reins of his father's (François "Papa Doc" Duvalier) violent regime in Haiti in 1971 and was expelled from the nation in 1986 during a populist uprising. At the time of his appointment, Duvalier was also the youngest president in the world, having come to power at age nineteen as the nation's "president for life."

Born in the capitol city of Port-au-Prince in 1951, Duvalier was educated by private tutors and never finished a university education. His father, François "Papa Doc" Duvalier, was a ruthless dictator who ruled Haiti from 1957 to 1971, using a private militia (the Tonton Macoutes) to imprison or kill political opponents. After becoming ill, the elder Duvalier appointed his son, Jean-Claude, to succeed him as president for life in 1971. When his father died later that year, Duvalier, nicknamed "Baby Doc" by the press, reduced governmental controls, temporarily allowing the country to recover from the economic stagnation that persisted under his father's regime. With foreign aid, the economy began to stabilize and unemployment rates dropped. Duvalier also allowed small political parties and private media outlets to form, cultural institutions that had been curtailed or eliminated under his father's rule. He was also able to gain unprecedented foreign support, as his ascension marked the end of the nation's most violent period to that point.

In 1980, Duvalier controversially married Michèle Bennett, an upper-class, light-skinned woman, in an opulent private ceremony. Some saw Duvalier's marriage as a violation of his father's focus on black nationalism and objected to his marrying a woman from the elite class. When liberals protested his marriage, Duvalier had reporters and journalists ejected from the country. Over the next four years, Duvalier faced opposition from within the regime's Macoutes militia, as well as from liberal dissidents and an increasingly influential foreign media. Among many other complaints, the media and dissidents criticized the president for his wife's lavish lifestyle while so many continued to live in abject poverty.

Antigovernment protests spread around the nation in 1984 and hundreds were killed or executed by the Macoutes militia. It is estimated that more than thirty thousand died under both Duvaliers' regimes. When Haitian soldiers killed three schoolchildren at a 1985 protest, the opposition became stronger, and it became clear that Duvalier could not maintain control. The US government arranged to smuggle Duvalier, his wife, and his mother to France, thus ending the regime. Duvalier's departure left a vacuum of power in Haiti that resulted in a decade of instability and violence. Bennett and Duvalier divorced in 1993. Duvalier returned to Haiti in 2011 after the election of Michel Martelly, a former supporter of the Duvalier regime, who allowed him to return without the threat of being arrested.

Several attempts were made to initiate legal proceedings against Duvalier after his return, but corruption within the judiciary system prevented criminal charges from coming to fruition. Duvalier died on October 4, 2014, age sixty-three, after suffering from a heart attack. He is survived by his companion, Véronique Roy, and his son and daughter, François-Nicolas and Anya.

See Current Biography 1972.

Gerald M. Edelman

Born: New York, New York; July 1, 1929
Died: San Diego, California; May 17, 2014
Occupation: Immunologist and neuroscientist

Gerald Maurice Edelman was a Nobel Prize–winning immunologist and physician known for his groundbreaking research into the structure and function of antibodies in the immune system. Edelman later became one of the primary proponents of neural Darwinism and helped to elucidate the evolution and development of the brain.

Edelman was born in 1929 in Queens, New York, and grew up on Long Island, the son of a physician and an insurance agent. Edelman married Maxine M. Morrison in 1950, the same year he graduated from Ursinus College in Pennsylvania. Edelman earned his medical degree from the University of Pennsylvania in 1954 and served in the Army Medical Corps in Paris from 1955 to 1957. Returning from his term in the army, Edelman began focusing on immunological research and entered a doctorate program at Rockefeller Institute, which later became Rockefeller University.

Edelman completed his PhD in 1960 and became a professor at Rockefeller University. Founding his own laboratory at the university, Edelman began a decade of antibody research that elucidated the chemical structure of antibody molecules for the first time. Specifically, Edelman's research demonstrated the chemical structure of the immune system molecules known as immunoglobulins. As a result of this research, Edelman was recruited to take part in the National Institutes of Health study section on biophysics and biophysical chemistry from 1964 to 1967, and he won the 1965 Eli Lilly Award from the American Chemical Society for his research into antibody structure. The culmination of Edelman's research in antibodies came when he and British immunologist Rodney R. Porter shared the 1972 Nobel Prize in Physiology or Medicine for their separate but simultaneous discovery of immunoglobulin molecules.

Beginning in the mid-1970s, Edelman became interested in the physiological and philosophical study of consciousness and the relationship between the mind and brain, and, in 1981, he started Rockefeller University's Neurosciences Institute. Edelman became the primary proponent of the "neural Darwinism" theory, which says that the development of the brain follows a pattern in which groups of neurons compete within the brain for resources in the form of chemical nutrients. Edelman theorized that as the brain encounters new stimuli, certain groups of neurons grow faster than others, thus gradually refining the design of the brain through a process analogous to differential survival in the evolution of species. Edelman published a number of books on the subject including *A Universe of Consciousness* (2000) and *Wider than the Sky: A Revolutionary View of Consciousness* (2004). While his theories on brain development were initially viewed with skepticism, in the 2000s experimental research confirmed some of these ideas.

Edelman died on May 17, 2014, age eighty-four, at his home in San Diego, California. According to reports given by his children, Edelman had been suffering from prostate cancer and Parkinson's disease. In addition to his wife, Edelman is survived by the couple's three children, David, a neuroscientist; Eric, an artist; and Judith, a bluegrass recording artist.

See Current Biography Illustrated 1995.

Márta Eggerth

Born: Budapest, Hungary; April 17, 1912
Died: Rye, New York; December 26, 2013
Occupation: Singer, actor

Hungarian-born operetta star and actor Márta Eggerth became a teenage singing sensation during the interwar period, often called the silver age of Viennese operetta. She went on to become an international star of both stage and screen, appearing in over three dozen films and giving thousands of performances in many of the world's most famous venues.

Eggerth began singing as a child in Budapest, where her mother, a retired professional opera singer, encouraged her singing career. She was performing professionally by her early teens and gained a reputation as a coloratura, a soprano specializing in pieces that demonstrate dynamic vocal range. Eggerth eschewed a career in traditional opera for operetta, a lighter genre that became wildly popular during the interwar period in Europe. Among her first major performances was a role in Johann Strauss II's famous *Die Fledermaus* in 1929.

Eggerth began appearing in films in 1930 and by 1932 had become a major film star in Europe, largely due to her appearance in the 1932 films *Where Is This Lady?* and *Es War Einmal Ein Walzer* (*Once There Was a Waltz*), which was based on a script by famed playwright Billy Wilder and featured music by Franz Lehár, one of the founders of Viennese operetta. Eggerth could perform in about a half-dozen languages, including German, Italian, and English, and often appeared in multiple versions of the same films in different languages. It was while performing in the 1934 film *Mein Herz ruft nach Dir* (*My Heart Is Calling*), with music by Robert Stoltz, that Eggerth met and fell in love with Polish tenor and matinee star Jan Kiepura. The couple wed in 1936 and became one of the most famous celebrity couples in Europe, performing together in several popular films.

In 1938 Eggerth and Kiepura, both of whom were part Jewish, fled to the United States to avoid the Nazi regime. Kiepura joined New York's Metropolitan Opera, while Eggerth continued to pursue her film career. Though she had minor roles in *For Me and My Gal* (1942), alongside Gene Kelly and Judy Garland, and *Presenting Lily Mars* (1943), Eggerth was unable to reclaim her celebrity status with US film producers. Eggerth and Kiepura returned to the stage for a 1943–44 Broadway run of Franz Lehár's *The Merry Widow*, and Eggerth became known for her association with this famous operetta, performing selections of *The Merry Widow* more than two thousand times in the United States and across Europe.

After Kiepura's death in 1966, Eggerth retired briefly but began appearing in small venues during the 1970s. Eggerth returned to large-scale public performance occasionally, beginning with the 1982 production of the Tom Jones musical *Colette*. In 1999 Eggerth was asked to sing selections from *The Merry Widow* at the Vienna State Opera. In 2005, Eggerth collaborated with son and pianist Marjan Kiepura, to compile and release a double CD of her performances, *My Life My Song*. For her remaining years Eggerth continued performing in small venues, including New York's Café Sabarsky. She gave her final public performance in 2011, at age ninety-nine. Eggerth died at her home in Rye, New York, on December 26, 2013, at age 101, and is survived by two sons, Marjan Kiepura and John Thade.

See Current Biography 1943.

John S. D. Eisenhower

Born: Denver, Colorado; August 3, 1922
Died: Trappe, Maryland; December 21, 2013
Occupation: Historian, diplomat

John Sheldon Doud Eisenhower, son of former president Dwight D. Eisenhower, was a prominent military historian who wrote several acclaimed books on US military history. Eisenhower also served as a White House adviser and as US ambassador to Belgium.

Following in his father's footsteps, Eisenhower entered the United States Military Academy at West Point in 1941. He graduated on June 6, 1944, the very day that his father was leading American forces in the invasion of Normandy during World War II. Though he asked to be placed in active duty, army commanders feared the danger of his being killed or captured, given that his father was the supreme Allied commander in Europe, and so assigned him to administrative and intelligence assignments.

Following the war Eisenhower attended Columbia University, where he earned a master's degree in English literature in 1950. He then taught English at West Point before he was called into active duty to serve in an infantry battalion in Korea, shortly before his father's inauguration as president of the United States in 1953. Eisenhower later wrote in a 2008 *New York Times* op-ed that he felt presidential children should not be allowed to engage in combat out of the danger that the child's death or capture might affect the president's duties.

Following his tour in Korea, Eisenhower became a White House adviser on national security for the remainder of his father's administration. Eisenhower retired from active duty in 1963, with the rank of lieutenant colonel, but remained in the Army Reserve until 1974, rising to the rank of brigadier general. Eisenhower began writing soon after he left the White House and published his first book, *The Bitter Woods*, in 1969, a historical description of the 1944–45 Battle of the Bulge. After the death of his father in 1969, Eisenhower briefly served as the US ambassador to Belgium, leaving the position in 1971.

Eisenhower's second book, *Strictly Personal* (1974), was a memoir that drew strongly on recollections of his father. He followed this with the 1982 book *Allies, Pearl Harbor to D-Day* about the Allied war effort, which was based partially on his father's unpublished memoirs. While his books were successful, Eisenhower told interviewers he felt he had been living in his father's shadow and wanted to achieve recognition as a historian in his own right. Eisenhower achieved this goal with his bestselling 1989 book *So Far from God*, about the Mexican-American War, and *Intervention!* (1993), which deals with American involvement in the Mexican Revolution.

In 2001 Eisenhower and his second wife, Joanne Thompson, collaborated on the book *Yanks: The Epic Story of the American Army in World War I*, which became one of Eisenhower's most popular and acclaimed books. Among his final works were a military biography of his father, *General Ike: A Personal Remembrance* (2003), *They Fought at Anzio* (2007), and *Soldiers and Statesmen: Reflections on Leadership* (2012).

Eisenhower died at his home in Trappe, Maryland, on December 21, 2013, at age ninety-one. He was survived by his wife, Joanne; four children (from his first marriage to Barbara Jean Thompson), Dwight David II, Anne, Susan, and Mary; and eight grandchildren.

See Current Biography 1969.

Jack Fleck

Born: Bettendorf, Iowa; November 1921
Died: Fort Smith, Arkansas; March 21, 2014
Occupation: Professional golfer

Golfer Jack Donald Fleck achieved one of the greatest upsets in golf history when he defeated renowned champion Ben Hogan to win the 1955 US Open. Fleck also helped to establish the Champions Tour circuit and became a respected golf instructor and golf course designer.

Fleck was born in Bettendorf, Iowa, a small city near Davenport, and was one of five children born into a poor farming family. As a child, Fleck worked as a caddie and played on the golf team at Davenport High School. Fleck then joined the Navy and served aboard a British ship during the invasion of Normandy. Returning to Iowa, Fleck became a club pro and, in 1949, married Lynn Burnsdale, a Chicago native whom he met while working at his Davenport golf club.

When Fleck entered the US Open in 1955, he qualified with only two pro victories to his name and was largely unknown to international golf fans. Fleck's opponent, Ben Hogan, was a four-time champion and fan favorite considered one of the greatest golfers of the era. Fleck was trailing in the fourth round when the media began congratulating Hogan on what they considered an inevitable triumph. In the playoff of the final day, Fleck outshot Hogan, winning by three strokes to become the surprise US Open champion. Fleck became an overnight celebrity, and was interviewed hundreds of times on his victory. He appeared on NBC's *Today* with Dave Garroway and was invited to meet President Dwight Eisenhower, a dedicated golf aficionado.

Fleck, whose weakness had always been his short game, was never able to recapture the US Open title. He won the 1960 Phoenix Open and the 1961 Bakersfield Open, and played against Hogan again in the 1960 Open at Cherry Hills, where both he and Hogan lost to up-and-coming golf star Arnold Palmer. Fleck retired from competition briefly after his wife's suicide in 1975. In interviews, Fleck expressed the opinion that his wife's suicide was related to the negative press he received after his failure to recapture the success of his 1955 win.

Fleck won the first Senior PGA Championship in 1979 while he was becoming a prominent golf instructor in Iowa, and married his second wife, Mariann, in 1980. Fleck is credited with helping to create and develop the Champions Tour, in which he played from 1980 to 1988. After relocating to Arkansas, Fleck designed a small golf course in Magazine, Arkansas, called Lil' Bit a Heaven Golf Club, which opened in 1992. Fleck reported later that he was forced to sell his US Open medal to pay for repairs after the course flooded.

After the death of his second wife in 2000, Fleck married a third time, to Carmen Hall Fleck of Fort Smith, Arkansas, where he lived for the rest of his life. Fleck wrote three books about golf and his experiences winning the championship and he continued appearing in seniors' tours into his nineties. Fleck died on March 21, 2014, at age ninety-two. He is survived by his wife, Carmen, and his son, Craig, from his first marriage.

See Current Biography 1955.

Eileen Ford

Born: New York, New York; March 25, 1922
Died: Morristown, New Jersey, July 9, 2014
Occupation: Modeling agency executive

Eileen Cecile Otte, better known by her married name, Eileen Ford, was a modeling industry pioneer and executive famous as the creative force behind the influential Ford Models for more than fifty years. Ford also wrote six books on modeling and helped launch the careers of numerous prominent models and actresses.

Ford was born in Manhattan in 1922. Her mother, Loretta Marie Otte, was a model who worked for Best & Company. Ford followed her mother into the industry, working as a model for the Harry Conover agency while she attended Barnard College; she earned a bachelor's degree in psychology in 1943. Ford married Navy officer Jerry Ford in 1944, eloping to San Francisco where he was stationed. While her husband was serving overseas, Ford began acting as an informal agent for local models. Upon her husband's return, in 1946, Ford and her husband worked together to transform Ford's side business into a competitive agency.

Ford Models officially launched in 1947 and opened its first office on Second Avenue in 1948. Ford was the official scout and recruiter for the company, and within a year, the company was grossing more than $200,000 annually and was able to compete with industry leaders like Conover Modeling. With an eye for talent, Ford recruited some of the most successful models of the era, including Suzy Parker, Mary Jane Russell, Carmen Dell'Orefice, and Dorian Leigh. By 1960, Ford Models was the leading agency in the United States. Building on this success, Ford began publishing books about modeling, beginning with *Eileen Ford's Book of Model Beauty* in 1968.

Over the years, Mrs. Ford received both praise and criticism for her micromanaging approach to working with her models and for her blunt criticism of would-be models' weight and other imperfections. Though seen as dictatorial, Ford found great success with her approach and kept Ford Models at the top of the industry for more than forty years. In addition to promoting hundreds of successful models, Ford Models also became a stepping stone for models looking to transition to film and television, including Jane Fonda, Brooke Shields, Ali MacGraw, Martha Stewart, and Kim Basinger. During the 1970s and '80s, modeling industry competition grew more intense with the emergence of new international competitors like John Casablancas's agency, Elite Model Management. This period, colloquially known as the "model wars," almost removed Ford Models from their position as the leading US agency. However, Ford responded by becoming more innovative, including creating an international competition, known as the Ford Models Supermodel of the World, which is partially credited with inventing the concept of the "supermodel."

The Fords sold their modeling agency to investment bank Stone Tower in 2007, and Jerry Ford died the following year. In retirement, Ford lived in Califon, New Jersey, and continued contributing to articles and books about modeling. Ford died on July 9, 2014, age ninety-two, while in treatment at Morristown Memorial Hospital. She is survived by her four children, and eight grandchildren.

See Current Biography 1971.

Mavis Gallant

Born: Montreal, Quebec; August 11, 1922
Died: Paris, France; February 18, 2014
Occupation: Writer

Mavis Gallant was an acclaimed and prolific writer of short stories, publishing over one hundred works in the *New Yorker* over the course of about sixty years. Her carefully observed portraits of the dispossessed, exiled, and abandoned, often leavened with a sly sense of humor, won much praise from critics, and she received numerous literary awards over the course of her decades-long career.

Shunted from boarding school to boarding school after her father died and her mother remarried, Gallant often returned to the themes of absent or neglectful parents and children in precarious situations in her writing, especially in the semi-autobiographical "Linnet Muir" stories, published as a section in *Home Truths* (1981).

Gallant began her writing career as a journalist with the *Montreal Standard* in the 1940s, and published several of her early short stories in the paper as well. In 1950 she left her job with the *Standard* and moved to Europe to pursue fiction writing full-time. While she struggled at first, and feared that her passion for writing might outstrip her talent, she found success in 1950 when she sold the short story "Madeline's Birthday" to the *New Yorker*, which published the story in its September 1, 1951, issue. In addition to the many pieces which appeared in the *New Yorker* and other magazines, Gallant published nine short story collections, the first of which, *The Other Paris*, came out in 1956, and the last, *Across the Bridge*, in 1993.

Though the short story remained her favorite form, Gallant also tried her hand at other types of writing. Her two novels, *Green Water, Green Sky* (1959) and *A Fairly Good Time* (1970), are two different takes on the theme of North

American expatriates in Paris, and her early 1980s play, *What Is to Be Done?*, deals with the Franco regime in Spain. She did not fully abandon her journalistic roots, either, and continued to write nonfiction pieces on current events in Paris, many of which were published in the collection *Paris Notebooks* (1986). Her skill with nonfiction writing led Random House to commission from her a biography of Alfred Dreyfus, the French Jewish army officer falsely convicted of treason in the late nineteenth century. But though Gallant conducted extensive research, including interviews with Dreyfus's daughter and the children of other key players in the affair, the book was never finished.

For her contribution to literature, Gallant was named an Officer of the Order of Canada in 1981 and won the prestigious Governor General's Literary Award in 1982. She also received the Prix Athanase-David, which had never before been given to an English-language author, from the government of Quebec in 2006. Other literary awards Gallant received include the Writer's Trust of Canada's Matt Cohen Prize in 2000, the Rea Award for the Short Story in 2002, and the PEN/Nabokov Award in 2004.

Gallant died on February 18, 2014, at her home in Paris. She has no immediate survivors. At the time of her death, she was preparing her private journals for publication in the United States and Canada in 2015.

See Current Biography 1990.

Gabriel García Márquez

Born: Aracataca, Colombia; March 6, 1927
Died: Mexico City, Mexico; April 17, 2014
Occupation: Novelist and journalist

Gabriel José de la Concordia García Márquez was a Nobel Prize–winning Colombian novelist credited with contributing to the birth of the genre of magical realism and helping to inspire a renaissance in Latin American literature. García Márquez also spent much of his life working as a journalist and investigative reporter.

García Márquez was born in 1927 in Aracataca, a small town on the Caribbean coast of Colombia; he was the eldest of twelve children born into a poor family. As García Márquez's father traveled to pursue work as a telegraph operator, García Márquez was left in the care of his maternal grandparents, whom he later credited with inspiring his fiction. After the death of his grandfather, García Márquez was sent to a Jesuit boarding school and then entered the National University of Colombia at Bogotá in 1946 as a law student. In 1948, a military coup and the eruption of violence resulted in the university's closure, and García Márquez began working as a journalist.

In 1954, the liberal newspaper *El Espectador* hired García Márquez as an investigative reporter and he was branded as an agitator after publishing a series of articles revealing government corruption. The newspaper sent García Márquez to Europe as a foreign correspondent, but the paper was shut down while García Márquez was on assignment in Paris, leaving him in dire financial straits. García Márquez continued pursuing a career in fiction writing, however, and his first novel, *Leaf Storm*, was published in 1955. *Leaf Storm* introduced the fictional town of Macondo, to which he would return in many of his subsequent novels, including the acclaimed *One Hundred Years of Solitude*.

In 1958, García Márquez returned to Colombia to marry Mercedes Barcha Pardo, his fiancée of more than twelve years, and over the next several years the couple moved to Venezuela, New York, and finally Mexico City. García Márquez published his first award-winning novella, *In Evil Hour*, in 1962 and began to gain renown as a novelist.

After a four-year dry spell, García Márquez began writing his next book, *One Hundred Years of Solitude*, in 1965. For eighteen months he dedicated himself solely to working on this novel, which he published in 1967. Taking the history of Colombia and condensing it into a multigenerational saga set in a surreal fictional village, the novel was an immediate success in Latin America and became an international bestseller. Literary analysts use *One Hundred Years of Solitude* as an archetypal example of magical realism and the novel's success inspired international interest in Latin American literature.

In 1982, García Márquez became the first Colombian to win the Nobel Prize for Literature. García Márquez's 1985 novel *Love in the Time of Cholera* was the second of his books to win widespread international acclaim. The novel, which covers decades in the life of two lovers who are separated and eventually reunite in their old age, enjoyed enduring popularity and was adapted into a film in 2007. García Márquez went on to publish two more novels, a novella, a short story collection, and an autobiography, all of which were well received by critics, although none had the mainstream success of *One Hundred Years of Solitude* and *Love in the Time of Cholera*.

The financial success of his fiction enabled García Márquez to spend the rest of his life living in comfort, with homes in Barcelona, Paris, and Mexico City. García Márquez was diagnosed with lymphatic cancer in 1999 and suffered from senile dementia in his later years. García Márquez died on April 17, 2014, age eighty-seven, at his home in Mexico City. He is survived by his wife and two sons.

See Current Biography Illustrated 1973; Current Biography International Yearbook 2002.

James Garner

Born: Norman, Oklahoma; April 7, 1928
Died: Los Angeles, California; July 19, 2014
Occupation: Actor

James Scott Bumgarner, better known by his stage name James Garner, was an American actor who appeared in more than fifty films and dozens of television roles and became an American screen icon in the 1960s.

Garner was born in 1928 in Norman, Oklahoma, and grew up in Denver, Oklahoma, with his father and two brothers, after the untimely death of his mother when Garner was four years old. Garner left school at sixteen to join the merchant marine. In 1950 he was drafted to serve in the Korean War, where he earned two Purple Hearts after being wounded in action. After leaving the military, Garner drifted through a series of odd jobs in Los Angeles. He was working with a carpet installation business when, on a whim, he walked into an acting agency and applied for work.

Garner's first speaking role on television came when he was cast in the Western series *Cheyenne* in 1955. From there, he was employed by Warner Brothers, and appeared in minor roles in a number of films. Garner married his wife Lois Clarke in 1956, after a two-week courtship, and, the following year, got his first leading role in the World War II film *Darby's Rangers*, released in 1958. Later in 1957, Garner was cast as the lead in the Western television series *Maverick*, playing a professional gambler who toured the Mississippi poker circuit engaging in a variety of adventures. The series was a major hit, and Garner became a household name for portraying the iconic antihero Bret Maverick. Despite this success, Garner left the series in 1960 due to a contract dispute.

Garner had a string of high profile film roles in the 1960s, including two romantic comedies alongside Doris Day, *The Thrill of It All* and *Move Over, Darling*. Another of Garner's best-known roles was captured Air Force pilot Bob "the Scrounger" Hendley in the World War II film *The Great Escape*. Garner delivered a critically acclaimed performance as Lieutenant Commander Charles Edward Madison in the 1964 film *The Americanization of Emily* alongside Julie Andrews, which he later listed as one of his favorite performances. In 1974, Garner returned to television when he was cast in the lead role in the series *The Rockford Files;* he played the title character, a roguish private detective, until the series ended in 1980. Garner's Rockford became a television icon and he was identified with the role for the rest of his career.

Garner was particularly skilled as a romantic lead, often earning his most enthusiastic critical praise for romantic comedy films. These included the 1982 film *Victor/Victoria* with Julie Andrews and the 1985 romantic comedy *Murphy's Romance* alongside Sally Field, for which Garner received his first and only Academy Award nomination.

Garner continued appearing in cameo roles throughout the 1990s and the 2000s, including episodes of the medical drama *Chicago Hope* and numerous other series. Garner wrote and published an autobiography about his career, entitled *The Garner Files*, in 2011. Garner died on July 19, 2014, age eighty-six, at his home in Los Angeles. He is survived by his wife Lois, daughter Greta, and stepdaughter Kimberly.

See Current Biography 1966.

H. R. Giger

Born: Chur, Switzerland; February 5, 1940
Died: Zurich, Switzerland; May 12, 2014
Occupation: Artist

Hans Reudi Giger was a Swiss surrealist artist known for designing the fictional extraterrestrial species featured in the *Alien* movie franchise. Giger's self-described "biomechanical" art and designs inspired a host of later artists and movie creators.

Giger was born in Chur, Switzerland, in 1940. As a child he suffered from night terrors, a sleeping disorder characterized by frequent, intense nightmares. Giger was enrolled in an art therapy program to combat this disorder and this inspired his interest in painting and drawing. An unenthusiastic student, Giger enrolled in the School of Applied Arts in Zurich, Switzerland, to study industrial design and worked as an interior designer for several years before quitting to concentrate on his art.

As an artist, Giger often focused on the union of biological and mechanical elements. Many of his works were controversial because of their overt sexuality and morbidity. Giger first gained international attention as a designer of album covers, including a painting for Emerson, Lake and Palmer's album *Brain Salad Surgery* (1973). In 1975, cult director Alejandro Jodorowsky asked Giger to design landscapes, costumes, and alien species for a film adaptation of the science fiction epic *Dune* by Frank Herbert. While working on the film, Giger met Salvador Dalí, one of his greatest artistic inspirations, who was to play a leading role. Though Jodorowsky's film failed before he reached the production stage, much of Giger's artwork for the film was featured in the 2013 documentary *Jodorowsky's Dune*.

In 1977, Giger published his first book, *Necronomicon*, which featured a collection of extraterrestrial and fantasy-themed designs.

Director Ridley Scott found Giger's work and asked Giger to design what became known as the "xenomorph," an alien based on the painting *Necronom IV* from his book. In addition to the xenomorph, Giger designed the alien planet LV-426 and the species later known as the "space jockey" featured in Scott's 1979 hit film *Alien*. Because his artwork was central to the film, Giger shared in the film's 1980 Academy Award for special effects.

Gaining worldwide fame as a result of his involvement in *Alien*, Giger was hired to design several prominent album covers, including the cover for Debbie Harry's 1981 album *Koo Koo*. Another of Giger's paintings, a sexually themed work entitled *Penis Landscape*, became the subject of a 1986 obscenity lawsuit against the band Dead Kennedys when the artwork was included as a poster in the band's album *Frankenchrist* (1985).

Giger collaborated on designs for several other science fiction films, including *Alien 3* (1992) and the *Alien*-inspired science fiction film *Species* (1995). In 1988, Giger opened the first in a series of Giger Bars, drinking establishments with décor based on Giger's artwork. From the first Giger bar in Tokyo, Japan, Giger opened others in Chur, New York, and finally a bar and museum in Gruyères, Switzerland, in 1998. For his last film collaboration, Giger designed several xenomorph-like species for Ridley Scott's *Alien* prequel, *Prometheus* (2012).

Giger died in Zurich, Switzerland, on May 12, 2014, age seventy-four, from injuries suffered after a fall. Giger was married twice during his life. His first marriage, to Mia Bonzanigo, ended in divorce in the early 1980s. His second marriage was in 2006 to Carmen Scheifele-Giger, director of the H. R. Giger Museum in Gruyères, who survives him.

See Current Biography International Yearbook 2002.

Nadine Gordimer

Born: Springs, South Africa; November 20, 1923
Died: Johannesburg, South Africa; July 13, 2014
Occupation: Author

Nadine Gordimer was an author and Nobel laureate whose novels and short stories helped to demonstrate the racial injustice and complicated consequences of South African apartheid to a global audience. Gordimer wrote fifteen novels and several volumes of short stories and became one of South Africa's most renowned literary figures.

Gordimer was born in 1923 in South Africa, the daughter of immigrant parents who inspired her interest in the arts. Gordimer was privately tutored at her home and began writing around the age of nine, publishing her first short story at fifteen. In 1945, Gordimer studied at the University of Witwatersrand in Johannesburg, and she published her first book of short stories, *Face to Face*, in 1949. That same year, Gordimer married dentist Gerald Gavron, with whom she had a daughter before the couple divorced in 1952.

Gordimer published her first novel, *The Lying Days*, in 1953. This novel established Gordimer's characteristic politically charged style of fiction with a lens aimed at the racial stratification she saw in her native South Africa. The following year, Gordimer married art dealer Reinhold Cassirer, with whom she had her second child in 1955. Gordimer's second novel, *A World of Strangers*, was published in 1958, and told the story of a British immigrant to South Africa observing the injustice of the apartheid system. The South African government banned the novel for twelve years, though it was published abroad and helped to draw global attention to the political landscape of South Africa. Gordimer's 1966 novel, *The Late Bourgeois World*, was also banned for nearly ten years. Despite the controversy surrounding her books, however, Gordimer was never detained or jailed.

Gordimer had already made a significant name for herself in the literary world when she published *The Conservationist* in 1974. Told from the perspective of a white South African antihero struggling to hold onto power and privilege that are beginning to slip away from him, the novel won the Booker Prize in 1974. A string of novels followed, including the acclaimed *Burger's Daughter* in 1979, which was also banned, though only for a matter of months. Nelson Mandela, a friend of Gordimer's since the 1960s, had a copy of the book smuggled to him in prison.

Throughout the 1980s, Gordimer continued to explore the apartheid system and to write about the potential future of South Africa after the inevitable abolishment of the system. In 1991, Gordimer was awarded the Nobel Prize in literature for her life's work to that point. Gordimer continued writing after the end of apartheid, exploring the new South African society that was emerging. She also continued her involvement in political activism, with a particular focus on South Africa's AIDS pandemic, which she felt the government was handling poorly. Her last novel, *No Time Like the Present*, was published in 2012.

Gordimer remained in Johannesburg and died in her sleep on July 13, 2014, age ninety. Predeceased by her second husband in 2001, Gordimer is survived by their son, Hugo, and a daughter, Oriane, from her first marriage.

See Current Biography Illustrated 1959, 1980.

Tony Gwynn

Born: Los Angeles, California; May 9, 1960
Died: Poway, California; June 16, 2014
Occupation: Athlete

Anthony "Tony" Keith Gwynn was a career San Diego Padres outfielder, winning eight National League batting championships in twenty professional seasons, and election to the Baseball Hall of Fame. His death, from oral cancer, has raised concerns over the use of smokeless tobacco in professional baseball.

Gwynn was born in 1960 in Los Angeles, the middle of three children. He grew up in Long Beach and attended Long Beach Polytechnic High School, where he earned the attention of recruiters. In 1981 Gwynn graduated from San Diego State University, where he had been point guard for the basketball team and also become an All-American outfielder. That year Gwynn was a third-round draft pick for the San Diego Padres and a tenth-round pick for the San Diego Clippers in the NBA draft. Gwynn chose baseball over basketball, believing that he was better suited physically to play baseball.

Gwynn began playing in the Class A Walla Walla Padres minor-league team and was promoted to the triple-A Hawaii Islanders in 1982. In July 1982 he joined the Padres major-league roster, earning his first major-league hit, a double, against the Philadelphia Phillies in his fourth outing. In later interviews Gwynn revealed that Pete Rose, all-time MLB leader in hits, came up to congratulate him on his hit that night. Gwynn won his first batting championship in 1984, hitting .351, and helped the Padres to win the National League West title, a first in the club's history. Though the Padres lost to the Detroit Tigers in the World Series, Gwynn also made his first appearance in an All-Star Game, the first of fifteen All-Star appearances.

Gwynn went on to play twenty seasons with the Padres, eschewing higher pay from larger baseball markets in favor of remaining in his adopted hometown. He was known for his habit of taping his own batting performances and studying them to improve his swing. Gwynn hit .300 or better for nineteen seasons straight and won eight batting championships, coming in only behind Ty Cobb's twelve American League batting titles. Gwynn also won five Gold Glove Awards for superior fielding abilities. Gwynn was again the standout star when the Padres won their second pennant race in 1998, and he performed well against the Yankees in the World Series, though the Padres lost in four games. Gwynn retired in 2001 and coached for the next twelve years at his alma mater, San Diego State.

Over the years Gwynn acquired the nickname Mr. Padre and came to be a symbol for the team. The Padres' ball field, PETCO Park, has a listed address of 19 Tony Gwynn Drive (his jersey number) and features a statue of Gwynn. In 2007 Gwynn was elected to the Baseball Hall of Fame.

Gwynn was diagnosed with salivary gland cancer in 2010, which Gwynn attributed to the use of chewing tobacco throughout his career. Gwynn underwent surgery and aggressive treatments but died in June 2014, at age fifty-four, from complications related to the disease. He was survived by his wife, Alicia; brothers, Chris and Charles; and children, Anisha and Tony Jr., an outfielder for the Philadelphia Phillies.

See Current Biography 1996.

Charlie Haden

Born: Shenandoah, Iowa; August 6, 1937
Died: Los Angeles, California; July 11, 2014
Occupation: Musician

Charlie Haden was an influential bassist who became an important figure in the 1960s free jazz scene.

Charles Edward Haden was born in 1937 in Shenandoah, Iowa, where his parents and siblings performed together as the Haden Family on their own country music radio program. Haden began performing as Cowboy Charlie on his parents' radio show and later became the bassist for the family band. Although he was a singer in his early youth, at fifteen Haden contracted bulbar polio, which affected the nerves of his face and throat and effectively prevented him from singing.

Haden's interest in jazz was inspired by a trip to Omaha with his father to see saxophonist Charlie Parker in 1951. Haden relocated to Los Angeles and enrolled in Westlake College of Music to pursue his burgeoning interest in jazz. One of Haden's first jazz groups was with saxophonist Art Pepper and pianist Hampton Hawes. In the late 1950s, Haden met saxophonist Ornette Coleman, who was experimenting with a radical new approach to jazz composition. In 1959 Haden joined the Ornette Coleman Quartet, consisting of Haden, Coleman, drummer Billy Higgins, and trumpeter Don Cherry, and recorded the groundbreaking album *The Shape of Jazz to Come* (1959). Though not universally loved, Coleman's free jazz was a major force in jazz evolution, and within a few years established jazz artists were adapting and imitating Coleman's style. In 1969, Haden and pianist Carla Bley formed the Liberation Music Orchestra, an ensemble performance group whose compositions were often dedicated to social justice and other global human rights issues.

In 1982, Haden helped to establish the jazz program at the California Institute of the Arts, where he served as the director of jazz studies for most of the remainder of his career. In 1984, Haden married singer Ruth Cameron, who became the stepmother to his four children from a previous marriage. In 1986, Haden, pianist Alan Broadbent, saxophonist Ernie Watts, and drummer Larence Marable formed the Quartet West jazz ensemble, with music based on the nostalgic jazz of the 1930s and 1940s. In addition to performing with the Liberation Music Orchestra and Quartet West, Haden was in high demand as an accompanist in the 1980s and 1990s and recorded with a host of famous jazz artists including Wayne Shorter, Stan Getz, Chet Baker, Herbie Hancock, and Joe Henderson. Haden won his first Grammy Award for his collaboration album *Beyond the Missouri Sky* with Pat Metheny in 1997 and won two additional Grammys for his two collaboration albums with Cuban pianist Gonzalo Rubalcaba, *Nocturne* (2001) and *Land of the Sun* (2004).

Haden joined with his four children and his wife to record a country music album in 2008, featuring a variety of guests artists, including Elvis Costello and Rosanne Cash. In 2011, Haden was diagnosed with degenerative post-polio syndrome linked to his childhood illness. Haden died of complications from post-polio syndrome on July 11, 2014, at the age of seventy-six, in Los Angeles. He was survived by his wife, Ruth; his son, Josh; his triplet daughters, Petra, Tanya, and Rachel; and three grandchildren.

See Current Biography 2000.

Jim Hall

Born: Buffalo, New York; December 4, 1930
Died: New York, New York; December 10, 2013
Occupation: Musician

Guitarist Jim Hall was one of the most respected jazz musicians of the twentieth century, known for his minimalist approach and skill with subtle improvisation. Hall was also a composer and teacher whose approach to music inspired many modern guitarists.

Hall grew up in Cleveland, Ohio, and began playing guitar at age ten. By thirteen he was performing professionally. His interest in jazz resulted from listening to recordings of Charlie Christian, often hailed as the father of improvisational jazz guitar. Hall graduated from the Cleveland Institute of Music in 1955 with a degree in music theory and began a master's degree program, before deciding that he needed to leave Cleveland to pursue his interest in jazz. Toward that end Hall moved to Los Angeles, where the budding "cool jazz" scene was being developed by such innovators as trumpeter Miles Davis and pianist Dave Brubeck.

Hall's first break was as a rhythm guitarist for drummer Chico Hamilton's cool jazz ensemble. While some guitarists specialized in fast, agile soloing, Hall found that he lacked similar speed and so concentrated on developing his own minimalist method of soloing using sparse collections of notes. His soloing technique, he told interviewers, was based on imitating piano and tenor saxophone as much as guitar. This style fit in well with the mellow cool jazz style, and Hall was soon in demand as a performer. His second major break came in 1957, when he left Hamilton's group to play with renowned saxophonist Jimmy Giuffre in New York.

Through Giuffre's group Hall traveled to Europe in 1958, where he performed several times as a backup guitarist for French singer Yves Montand. He later toured South America with Ella Fitzgerald. Back stateside Hall played with legendary tenor saxophonist Ben Webster and then recorded two albums with pianist Bill Evans.

In the early 1960s Hall returned to New York, where he was invited to play with Sonny Rollins, one of the era's greatest saxophone players. Hall and Rollins began playing together in 1961 and released a hit recording, *The Bridge*, in 1962. After a hiatus from the club scene in the mid-1960s, Hall resumed playing in jazz trios and quartets and recording with trumpeter Chet Baker, saxophonist Paul Desmond, guitarist Bill Frisell, and bassist Ron Carter, among other jazz greats. In the 1990s Hall taught performance and composition at the New School for Jazz and Contemporary Music in New York.

In 1995 Hall was given an honorary doctorate of music from Boston's Berklee School of Music. Among the many awards given to Hall were the JAZZPAR Prize, one of the international jazz community's highest distinctions, in 1998, and a Jazz Masters Award from the National Endowment of the Arts in 2004. Despite suffering from health problems and having back surgery in 2008, Hall continued playing until the end of his life and appeared at the 2013 Newport Jazz Festival in Rhode Island. Hall died on December 10, 2013, age eighty-three, of heart failure at his home in Greenwich Village. He is survived by his wife, psychoanalyst Jane Yuckman Hall, and daughter, Devra Hall Levy, who also served as his manager.

See Current Biography 2001.

Walter J. Harrelson

Born: Winnabow, North Carolina;
November 28, 1919
Died: Winston-Salem, North Carolina;
September 5, 2012
Occupation: Biblical scholar

Walter Joseph Harrelson was a religious scholar and dean of the Divinity School at Vanderbilt University. Harrelson was also one of the founders of the divinity program at Wake Forest University in the 1990s.

Harrelson was born in Winnabow, North Carolina, an unincorporated suburb in Brunswick County, where he and his siblings were raised on a family farm. Harrelson had an early interest in divinity studies and entered Mars Hill College in 1940, at twenty years old. Harrelson left before finishing his degree and enlisted in the US Navy during World War II, serving for four years. Upon his return to civilian life, Harrelson decided to complete his education and earned a bachelor's degree from the University of North Carolina at Chapel Hill before enrolling in a doctorate program at Union Theological Seminary, which he completed in 1953. Harrelson completed postdoctoral work at Switzerland's University of Basel and Harvard University, where he gradually became an Old Testament specialist.

Harrelson's first teaching position was at Andover Newton Theological School in Newton Centre, Massachusetts. In 1955, he became the dean of the University of Chicago Divinity School, where he served for the next five years. In 1960, Vanderbilt University offered Harrelson a full professorship, focusing on Old Testament studies, and Harrelson accepted. At Vanderbilt, Harrelson specialized in Biblical interpretation, Jewish-Christian relations, and Biblical law and helped to make Vanderbilt's divinity school one of the foremost in the nation for Old Testament studies. In 1967, he was named dean of the Vanderbilt Divinity School, a position he held until 1975, when he decided to resign to spend more time teaching and conducting research.

Harrelson remained a distinguished professor at Vanderbilt University until 1990, conducting research on the Hebrew Bible and the Church of Ethiopia. Harrelson's research and papers published during this time became part of an important collection of documents relating to the spread of the Hebrew Bible. Harrelson worked with Rabbi Randall Falk on two publications regarding Jewish-Christian relations called *Jews and Christians: A Troubled Family* (1990), and *Jews and Christians in Pursuit of Social Justice* (1996). In 1994, Harrelson was called out of retirement to aid in the creation of a new divinity school at North Carolina's Wake Forest University. Over the next five years, Harrelson recruited professors and helped to develop a modern curriculum for the university.

In retirement, Harrelson continued writing and publishing books on religion and religious scholarship. His last book was *The Ten Commandments for Today* (2006), which examines the core meaning of the Ten Commandments and their relevance to modern culture. Harrelson was predeceased by his wife of nearly seventy years, Idella Aydlett Harrelson, in 2009. He died in Winston-Salem, North Carolina, on September 5, 2012, at the age of ninety-two. Harrelson was survived by his daughter, Marianne Harrelson McIver, and two sons, David Aydlett Harrelson and Robert Joseph Harrelson.

See Current Biography 1959.

Richard D. Heffner

Born: New York, New York; August 5, 1925
Died: New York, New York; December 17, 2013
Occupation: Broadcaster, historian

Richard Douglas Heffner was a television commentator, historian, and educator who helped to shape educational public television programming in the United States. Heffner also became a successful popular author, often writing about the history of American culture.

Heffner graduated from New York's Columbia University in 1946 with his AB and completed his master's degree there in 1947, with a thesis on the public perception of former president Theodore Roosevelt. Heffner then taught political science and history at Rutgers University, Columbia, and Sarah Lawrence College.

In 1952 Heffner published his first book, *A Documentary History of the United States*, which became a best seller and a classic in popular history writing. Believing that serious historians should play a role in news analysis, he attempted to pitch this concept to the television networks. Though television stations refused, New York radio station WMCA agreed to broadcast Heffner's planned interview with former First Lady Eleanor Roosevelt to commemorate the eighth anniversary of the death of her husband.

The Roosevelt interview was a critical success, and in 1953 Heffner left teaching to host a regular radio program, *History in the News*. In 1955 the NBC television network hired Heffner as a writer-producer, and among other programs, he led the weekly discussion series *Man of the Year*, which profiled a prominent figure each week. The following year Heffner began airing *The Open Mind*, a weekly discussion program in which Heffner spoke with noted experts about seminal issues in American culture. Among many other issues, *The Open Mind* held discussions on feminism, homosexuality, race relations, and anti-Semitism, and featured guests including Martin Luther King Jr., Thurgood Marshall, Gloria Steinem, Margaret Mead, Elie Wiesel, and Malcolm X.

In 1957 Heffner became director of the Metropolitan Educational Television Association (META). Then in 1959 he transitioned from NBC to CBS, where he supervised the network's educational and special products. A couple of years later Heffner led META to purchase WNTA-TV, at a cost of $6.2 million, which resulted in the formation of Channel 13, New York's first public television station and a model for educational television programming. There Heffner served as founding general manager for its first couple of years.

In 1964 Heffner returned to teaching at Rutgers, though he remained active with *The Open Mind*, which had been moved to Channel 13. In 1974 Heffner was approached to work with the Motion Picture Association of America (MPAA), helping to assign ratings to films. Heffner remained the MPAA chair until 1994 and was credited with strengthening ratings for violence while reducing ratings restrictions for sexuality and nudity.

Heffner again served as host of *The Open Mind* from 1967 until his death and also continued writing and publishing, including *As They Saw It* (2004), a collection of interviews from the program. He received honorary doctorates from the State University of New York and Long Island University, as well as Columbia's Medal for Distinguished Service to Education. Heffner died in Manhattan on December 17, 2013, at age eighty-eight, from a cerebral hemorrhage. He is survived by his second wife, psychotherapist and professor Elaine Segal Heffner; their sons, Daniel and Andrew, and their spouses, Beth and Carla and four grandchildren.

See Current Biography 1964.

Roger Hilsman

Born: Waco, Texas; November 23, 1919
Died: Ithaca, New York; February 23, 2014
Occupation: Educator and presidential adviser

Presidential adviser Roger Hilsman Jr. was an educator and military officer famous for his role in advising President John F. Kennedy during the early developments of the Vietnam War. Hilsman also became a respected author and a professor of international relations at Columbia University.

Hilsman was born in 1919 in Waco, Texas, the son of Army officer Roger Hilsman Sr. and Emma Prendergast. Hilsman spent much of his youth living on military bases and followed his father's example by attending the United States Military Academy at West Point. Hilsman served with a now famous Army commando unit Merrill's Marauders, operating in Japanese-occupied Burma (now Myanmar). Hilsman was wounded in action, and upon recovery transferred to the Office of Strategic Services (OSS), where he took part in a parachute mission to rescue his father and a number of other soldiers from a Japanese POW camp in China. After returning to the United States, Hilsman married Eleanor Willis Hoyt, with whom he would have four children.

Hilsman continued his involvement in the OSS and its successor, the CIA, until he entered Yale University in 1947. After earning his doctorate in international relations in 1951, Hilsman spent several years working in a variety of positions with the North Atlantic Treaty Organization (NATO) in Europe. In 1956, Hilsman joined the Congressional Research Service for the Library of Congress and, in this capacity, conducted research on behalf of Senator John F. Kennedy. Hilsman became friends with Kennedy and helped to draft speeches for the senator's 1960 presidential campaign. After Kennedy won the election, Hilsman became a member of the State Department, serving as Director of the Bureau of Intelligence Research.

Hilsman played an important role in advising Kennedy during the Cuban Missile Crisis in 1962, including becoming a crucial link in communications between the US and Soviet officers. As the U.S. military became involved in the Vietnam conflict, Hilsman favored a combination of covert operations and counterinsurgency that contrasted to the traditional military approach favored by the Joint Chiefs of Staff and the State Department. Hilsman was one of several architects of a controversial cable sent to the US ambassador in Vietnam, suggesting that the United States should not support then South Vietnamese president Ngo Dinh Diem unless Diem dismissed his brother Ngo Dinh Nhu, who was involved in controversial persecution of Vietnamese Buddhists. Analysts later blamed Hilsman's cable for providing implicit support for the assassination of President Diem and his brother in a November 1963 coup, which was a contributing factor in the escalation of the conflict.

Following Kennedy's assassination, Hilsman had few supporters in the State Department and resigned under pressure in February 1964. That same year, Hilsman became a professor of international relations at Columbia University where he remained until his retirement in 1990. Hilsman also became a respected author of historical nonfiction and his 1967 book, *To Move a Nation*, explained his views on Kennedy's foreign policy and asserted controversially that, had Kennedy lived, he would not have escalated US involvement in Vietnam. Hilsman published thirteen books during his life, the last of which, a cookbook of Chinese recipes, appeared in 2005. Hilsman and his wife lived in retirement in Ithaca, New York, until his death on February 23, 2014, age ninety-four, from complications after suffering a series of strokes. Hilsman is survived by his wife, four children, and six grandchildren.

See Current Biography 1964.

Philip Seymour Hoffman

Born: Fairport, New York; July 23, 1967
Died: New York, New York; February 2, 2014
Occupation: Actor

Philip Seymour Hoffman was an Academy Award–winning actor who appeared in over fifty films and garnered widespread acclaim for bringing complexity to a variety of leading and supporting roles. Hoffman was also a talented director, who had just begun to explore this aspect of his career in the years before his death.

Hoffman's interest in acting began at Fairport High School, after he auditioned for a part in a school production of Arthur Miller's *The Crucible*. Hoffman attended New York University's (NYU) Tisch School of the Arts, where he cofounded the Bullstoi Ensemble theater company with his friend and future collaborator Bennett Miller. Hoffman graduated from NYU with a BFA in drama in 1989 and had his professional acting debut in 1991, appearing in an episode of the crime procedural *Law & Order*. That same year, Hoffman had his film debut in the independent crime drama *Triple Bogey on a Par Five Hole*, written and directed by Amos Poe.

A host of minor roles followed for Hoffman, and the first role for which he was widely recognized was as the classmate of Chris O'Donnell's character in the Al Pacino film *Scent of a Woman* (1992). In addition to television and film, Hoffman remained active in stage productions throughout his career. In 1995, Hoffman joined Labyrinth Theater Company, an Off-Broadway theater group founded by actors looking to explore all aspects of theatrical production. Hoffman later served as artistic director for the company.

Hoffman's rise to fame came in part through his collaborations with director Paul Thomas Anderson, beginning with a minor role as a gambler in the 1996 film *Hard Eight*. Hoffman received critical and popular acclaim for his appearance in Anderson's 1997 *Boogie Nights*. Hoffman had the ability to portray comical characters, such as a goofy sidekick storm chaser in the action

thriller *Twister* (1996), as well as complex, dramatic performances, such as his role in the 1998 Todd Solondz film *Happiness*.

In 2005, Hoffman took on a challenging role portraying writer Truman Capote in the film *Capote*, delivering one of the most lauded performances of the year and winning the Academy Award, Golden Globe Award, and BAFTA Award for best actor. The following year, Hoffman gave another memorable performance in *Mission: Impossible III*, demonstrating his versatility as an actor in the role of a menacing villain.

In addition to winning the Oscar for his performance in *Capote*, Hoffman was nominated for three additional Academy Awards during his career, for his supporting roles in the 2007 film *Charlie Wilson's War*, the 2008 film *Doubt*, and Paul Thomas Anderson's 2012 film *The Master*. In 2010, Hoffman had his directorial debut with *Jack Goes Boating*, a comedic romance that was well received by critics and in which he also played the title role. And, in 2012, he made his last Broadway appearance starring as Willy Loman in *Death of a Salesman*. He also appeared in the film adaptations of *The Hunger Games* book series as Plutarch Heavensbee, and was completing his work on the last films in the series when he died.

On February 2, 2014, Hoffman died unexpectedly of an apparent heroin overdose at the age of forty-six, in a Manhattan apartment. Hoffman was survived by his parents, Gordon and Marilyn (Loucks), who are divorced; three siblings, Gordon, Jill Hoffman DelVecchio, and Emily Hoffman Barr; his long-time partner, costume designer Mimi O'Donnell; and their three children.

See Current Biography 2001.

Richard Hoggart

Born: Leeds, England; September 24, 1918
Died: London, England; April 10, 2014
Occupation: Author, historian

Richard Hoggart was an academic who became famous for his penetrating analyses of British working-class culture. Hoggart famously participated in a 1960 obscenity trial that helped to institute major changes to British censorship laws.

Richard Herbert Hoggart was born in Leeds, England, in 1918, one of three children in a poor family. His father died while Hoggart was still in infancy and his mother died when he was eight years old, after which Hoggart lived with a widowed grandmother in Hunslet. In 1936, Hoggart won one of forty-seven scholarships given for students to study at the University of Leeds, where he earned his bachelor's (1939) and master's (1940) degrees in English.

Hoggart served with the Royal Artillery during World War II and spent time teaching cultural history on military bases. In 1942, Hoggart married Mary France, with whom he would have three children.

After the war, Hoggart became a lecturer at the University of Hull. He published a first book, an analysis of W. H. Auden's poetry, in 1951 and spent several years working on his follow-up, *The Uses of Literacy* (1957), which is generally considered his seminal work. In the book, Hoggart explores the British working class in the period following World War II and addresses issues such as advertising, mass media, and the evolution of language. *The Uses of Literacy* has been hailed as one of the great social commentaries of the twentieth century and brought Hoggart significant renown as a cultural critic. Following the publication of the book, Hoggart became a senior lecturer of English at the University of Leicester.

In 1960, Hoggart was one of several prominent literary figures asked to testify at a now-famous censorship trial after Penguin Books was charged with violating obscenity laws by publishing D. H. Lawrence's controversial novel, *Lady Chatterley's Lover*. While Hoggart was not the most famous person invited to testify, his eloquent and persuasive exposition on the importance of Lawrence's work is often credited as the turning point in the trial, which resulted in significant changes to British law and was seen as a great victory for freedom of literary expression. The trial was dramatized in a celebratory 2006 television film, *The Chatterley Affair*, in which Hoggart was played by actor David Tennant.

In 1962, Hoggart became a professor of English at the University of Birmingham, where he founded the university's Center for Contemporary Cultural Studies in 1964 and became its first director. From 1969 to 1975, Hoggart worked as a cultural advisor for UNESCO, but found himself at odds with the organization's administration. After leaving this position, Hoggart wrote a critical account of UNESCO, *An Idea and Its Servants* (1978). Hoggart then took a position at the University of London, where he remained until his retirement in 1984. Hoggart published more than fifteen books over the course of his career, including an autobiography, *A Measured Life*, in 1993.

Hoggart died on April 10, 2014, age ninety-five, at a nursing home in London. He is survived by his wife of sixty-two years, Mary; his children, Nicola and Paul, and eight grandchildren. Another son, Simon, died of pancreatic cancer in January 2014.

See *Current Biography 1963.*

Christopher Hogwood

Born: Nottingham, England; September 10, 1941
Died: Cambridge, England; September 24, 2014
Occupation: Conductor and musicologist

Christopher Jarvis Haley Hogwood was an English conductor and scholar known for his involvement in the historic music movement and as the founder of the Academy of Ancient Music (AAM).

Born in Nottingham, England, in 1941, into a music-loving family, Hogwood took interest in the harpsichord as a child, eventually studying at Pembroke College with musical talents such as Rafael Puyana. Beginning in 1967, Hogwood performed with the Early Music Consort (of which he was also a founder), an orchestra specializing in performances of baroque compositions. The second founder of the group, David Munrow, became one of England's most notable experts on ancient music and the baroque chamber music revival of the 1960s and '70s. The group came to national fame after performing the soundtrack for the BBC series *The Six Wives of Henry VIII* (1970), and Hogwood built on this fame, creating and producing the music magazine program *The Young Idea* (1972–82) for BBC Radio 3.

In 1973, Hogwood founded the AAM, an organization dedicated to the study and performance of ancient music from the baroque and later the classical age. Under Hogwood's leadership, the AAM produced new arrangements of many important classical pieces, gradually becoming one of the most respected orchestras in the historic music revival. The AAM was a pioneer in "period-instrument" performance, attempting to perform ancient compositions as close as possible to the way that they were initially performed, and with the same instrumentation. By 1980, Hogwood was a star within England's classical music community, and was being invited to perform around the world. Hogwood's AAM performed at the Hollywood Bowl during the Los Angeles Olympics in 1984, and they were also asked to perform with the Chicago Symphony Orchestra and at New York's Lincoln Center. Hogwood remained a dedicated music historian, publishing a well-received biography of George Frideric Handel in 1984.

After being appointed artistic director of the Handel and Haydn Society in Boston, Massachusetts, in 1986, Hogwood was dually appointed director of music for the Saint Paul Chamber Orchestra of Minnesota two years later, a position he held until 1992. From 1989 to 1993, Hogwood was also an artistic adviser to the Australian Chamber Orchestra. Remaining with the AAM, as director and later emeritus director, for the rest of his career, he later shared conducting duties with Paul Goodwin and Andrew Manze. He supplemented his conducting, directorial, and performance duties with work as a scholar and publisher, producing volumes of work from historic artists. From 1992 to 2008, he was a visiting professor at the Royal Academy of Music, which was one of several honorary academic posts held during his later career.

Hogwood died at his home in Cambridge on September 24, 2014, age seventy-three, after suffering from a brief illness. Survivors include his four younger siblings, Frances, Charlotte, Kate, and Jeremy.

See Current Biography 1985.

Geoffrey Holder

Born: Port of Spain, Trinidad and Tobago; August 1, 1930
Died: New York, New York; October 5, 2014
Occupation: Actor, dancer, and choreographer

Geoffrey Lamont Holder was a Trinidadian actor, dancer, painter, and choreographer who became internationally famous as a spokesman for the 7UP soft drink brand in the 1970s.

Holder was born in 1930 in the Port of Spain, on the island of Trinidad. His elder brother, Arthur Aldwyn "Boscoe" Holder, was a dancer who first introduced his younger brother to dancing and painting. Holder joined his brother's dance group, the Holder Dancing Company, when he was seven years old, and became director of the troupe in 1948, after his brother left Trinidad to pursue his dancing career in England.

Holder was invited to bring the Holder Dancing Company to New York for a performance, and was captivated by the New York art and dance scene when he arrived in 1954. He remained in the city and, made his Broadway debut in the Truman Capote musical *House of Flowers* later that year. During the show, Holder met dancer Carmen de Lavallade, whom he married in 1955. Holder also took a position teaching at the Katherine Dunham dance school and was a featured dancer for the Metropolitan Opera Ballet. As his dance career flourished, Holder also gained recognition as a painter. He won a Guggenheim Fellowship to pursue painting in 1956, and had solo art shows in many of New York's most prestigious galleries.

Throughout his life, Holder was a dedicated ambassador for Caribbean culture. He coauthored a 1959 book on Caribbean folklore, *Black Gods, Green Islands*, which he also illustrated. Having gained fame as a dancer, Holder began receiving offers to appear in films in the late 1950s. One of his first film roles was in the 1962 British production *All Night Long*, a remake of *Othello*. In the 1970s Holder was asked to become the spokesman for the 7UP soft drink brand, then owned by Philip Morris, and appeared in the brand's Uncola campaign. Holder said in later interviews that he was more often recognized as the 7UP spokesman than for any other film, television, or theater performance during his career.

Bit parts in films followed, including the role of a sorcerer in Woody Allen's *Everything You Always Wanted to Know about Sex* but Were Afraid to Ask* (1972). Perhaps his most recognizable film role was in the 1973 James Bond film *Live and Let Die*, alongside Roger Moore, in which Holder played a henchman named Baron Samedi (Lord Saturday), a character based on a role he had played in *House of Flowers* and which was inspired by a mythical folk deity from the Haitian voodoo religion.

In 1975, Holder won a Tony Award for directing *The Wiz*, an all-black Broadway musical based on *The Wizard of Oz*. In addition to directing, Holder designed costumes for the production, winning a Tony for that work as well. The show ran for four years and became an iconic production in black theater history. Holder directed, choreographed, and designed costumes for the 1978 Broadway musical *Timbuktu!* and earned another Tony nomination for best costume design. He had a supporting role in the 1982 musical film *Annie*. In 1986, he published a book of his photography, entitled *Adam*. Holder continued performing and painting for the rest of his life. Recognizable later roles included a bit part in the 1992 film *Boomerang* alongside Eddie Murphy, and a voiceover performance as the narrator in Tim Burton's *Charlie and the Chocolate Factory* (2005).

Holder died in Manhattan on October 5, 2014, from complications of pneumonia. He was eighty-four. Holder is survived by de Lavallade and their son, Léo.

See Current Biography 1957.

Bob Hoskins

Born: Bury St. Edmunds, England; October 26, 1942
Died: London, England; April 29, 2014
Occupation: Actor

Bob Hoskins was a BAFTA-winning English actor known for his roles in *Mona Lisa* and *Who Framed Roger Rabbit*. Hoskins also appeared in a number of acclaimed stage and television productions during his career.

Robert William Hoskins was born in 1942 in Bury St. Edmunds, Suffolk, but his family relocated to London shortly after he was born. Hoskins's father worked as a truck driver and bookkeeper and his mother worked as a nursery school teacher. Hoskins left school at the age of fifteen and took a variety of temporary jobs, including stints as a seaman in the Norwegian navy and as a camel herder in Syria. In 1969, while accompanying a friend to an audition at the Unity Theatre in London, Hoskins was mistaken for an actor and asked to audition for a part in the play. Hoskins's audition impressed the casting director sufficiently that he was offered the lead role in the play *The Feather Pluckers*. Following the opening night of the play, a theatrical agent signed Hoskins as a client.

Hoskins appeared in a number of television roles before being cast as Arthur Parker in the innovative television serial *Pennies from Heaven* (1978), in which the actors lip-synced and danced to 1930s music to represent the lead character's Broadway fantasies. Hoskins became an international star thanks to his portrayal of a mob boss in the film *The Long Good Friday* (1980), which won him a BAFTA nomination for best actor. Hoskins then appeared in a number of minor film roles, including scene-stealing performances in *The Cotton Club* (1984) and *Brazil* (1985). In 1986, Hoskins was cast as a prostitute's driver in *Mona Lisa*, alongside Michael Caine, delivering a performance that received an Oscar nomination and won him a BAFTA for best actor.

To American audiences, Hoskins is most famous for his role in *Who Framed Roger Rabbit* (1988), after which he increasingly received offers to act in American films. Over the course of his career, Hoskins appeared in more than a hundred productions, playing a wide range of characters. Other notable films include *Mermaids* (1990), *Hook* (1991), *The Secret Agent* (1996), and *Enemy at the Gates* (2001). In 2009, Hoskins appeared on the British television series *The Street*, which gained him a best actor award at the International Emmy Awards.

Hoskins retired from acting in 2012, reporting to the press that he had been diagnosed with Parkinson's disease. Hoskins was married twice, to Jane Livesey, with whom he had two children, until 1978, and then to Linda Banwell in 1982, resulting in the birth of a son and daughter. Hoskins died on April 29, 2014, age seventy-one, after suffering from a bout of pneumonia. He is survived by his second wife and his four children.

See Current Biography 1990.

B. K. S. Iyengar

Born: Bellur, India; December 14, 1918
Died: Pune, India; August 20, 2014
Occupation: Yogi

Bellur Krishnamachar Sundararaja Iyengar was an Indian teacher and author credited with helping to popularize yoga in Western Europe and North America. Iyengar wrote fourteen books on yoga theory and practice during his career.

Iyengar was born in 1918, the eleventh of thirteen children born into a poor family living in the southern Indian state of Karnataka. A sickly child, Iyengar contracted typhoid, tuberculosis, and malaria when he was young. Iyengar began studying yoga at sixteen as a way to strengthen his body and immune system, and he became one of the most advanced students of the yoga school at Jaganmohan Palace in Mysore. Iyengar became one of the school's instructors and was often chosen to demonstrate the school's yoga methods to visiting dignitaries.

Iyengar married in 1943, and he said in later interviews that his wife, Ramamani, was the one who encouraged him to expand his teaching to broader audiences. In 1952, Iyengar gave a specialty class to violinist Yehudi Menuhin, who saw something special in Iyengar and decided to fund a program to bring Iyengar's yoga methods to students outside of India. With Menuhin's support, Iyengar began visiting Europe regularly to give workshops in yoga. Among the celebrities who studied with Iyengar during this time were author Aldous Huxley and Belgium's Queen Elisabeth, who Iyengar famously taught to perform a headstand, though the queen was eighty-five at the time.

Iyengar first visited the United States in 1956, when popular interest in yoga was minimal. Iyengar gradually developed his own teaching style based on 216 yoga postures that served as the basis for what later came to be called Iyengar yoga. Iyengar's style was so popular that he wrote a book on the subject, *Light on Yoga*, in 1966, which became an international best seller and was later translated into seventeen languages. Interest in Iyengar yoga spread rapidly in the United States in the late 1960s as interest in India spread throughout the youth counterculture.

In 1975, Iyengar established the Ramamani Iyengar Memorial Yoga Institute in Pune, India, named in honor of his wife. Iyengar eventually opened more than seventy institutes on six continents. As his fame and influence spread, Iyengar continued publishing as well, following up his initial success with *The Art of Yoga* and *The Tree of Yoga*, published in 1985 and 1988, respectively. Other books followed, including the 1993 *Light on the Yoga Sutras of Patanjali*. In the 2000s, Iyengar's writings took on a more autobiographical character, exploring his life as a yoga teacher and the broader culmination of yoga's joint physical and spiritual focus. Iyengar's 2005 book, *Light on Life: The Yoga Journey to Wholeness, Inner Peace, and Ultimate Freedom*, delved into the psychology of yoga practice.

Iyengar continued practicing yoga into his nineties and retired to Pune, India, in his final years. Iyengar died on August 20, 2014, at the age of ninety-five. He was predeceased by his wife in 1973 and was survived by six children, five grandchildren, and three great-grandchildren.

See Current Biography 2007.

Wojciech Jaruzelski

Born: Kurów, Poland; July 6, 1923
Died: Warsaw, Poland; May 25, 2014
Occupation: Polish president and military leader

Wojciech Witold Jaruzelski was the last Communist leader of Poland. He became notorious for his role in the declaration of martial law to defeat the native democratic movement of the early 1980s. However, at the end of that decade he helped to negotiate the orderly end of Communism in Poland.

Jaruzelski was born on July 6, 1923, in Kurów, a city in eastern Poland, into a powerful family that was part of Poland's aristocracy. After the 1939 German and Russian invasion of Poland, the Jaruzelski family fled to Lithuania where they survived by working on a farm owned by a Polish immigrant. In 1941 Jaruzelski's family was arrested as part of a larger movement to purge former members of the Polish aristocracy. Jaruzelski, his mother, and younger sister were sent to a Siberian village. His father was imprisoned in a labor camp where he later died.

When the Soviets turned against the Nazis, Jaruzelski joined a Polish Communist militia and was sent to an officers' training school in Ryazan in the Soviet Union. He returned to Poland in 1944 and took part in the liberation of Warsaw. After the end of the war, Jaruzelski led a branch of the newly established Communist army to suppress the remaining freedom fighters who resisted the imposition of Communist control.

In 1956, at thirty-three, Jaruzelski became the youngest general in the Polish army. He joined the parliament in 1961. From 1962 to 1968 he served as deputy minister of defense. One of his first actions upon assuming the position of minister of defense in 1968 was the authorization of the use of Polish forces in the Soviet invasion of Czechoslovakia. In the later 1960s anti-Communist sentiment grew. It erupted in 1970 in a series of workers' strikes across the country, resulting in military suppression against the labor movement. Jaruzelski's role in this response remained unclear, though many felt that he had directly ordered the attacks, resulting in at least forty-four deaths, against his fellow Polish citizens.

Labor unrest peaked again in 1980. The administration of Edward Gierek attempted to solve the crisis through negotiation, but delays in promised reforms led to another round of strikes in 1981. The Communist faction of the Polish government chose Jaruzelski to serve as prime minister. The activist group Solidarity initially met with Jaruzelski to organize a new system for economic recovery in return for promises to suspend the strikes. However, the Soviet Union increased pressure on Jaruzelski, and in December he declared martial law, claiming that Soviet invasion was imminent otherwise. Over the next two years, Jaruzelski's government was strongly criticized both domestically and internationally for using violence to control its people. Several governments, including the United States, either threatened or imposed economic sanctions against Poland. Under pressure, Jaruzelski lifted martial law in 1983; thousands of prisoners were released and the harshest measures were ended.

In 1988 Jaruzelski opened talks with Solidarity, a move that was opposed by hard-line Communist leaders. The first genuinely free elections in a Communist state resulted. Although Jaruzelski was elected president, he served only one year of a six-year term and stepped down to allow a second election in which the Solidarity leader Lech Wałęsa was popularly elected. In 1993 he wrote the book *Why Martial Law?* in an effort to explain his actions over the years to the populace.

In 2000 Jaruzelski was charged with ordering the shooting of striking workers in 1970, and he was charged in 2007 with illegally imposing martial law in 1981. He avoided trial due to illness; the courts ultimately dismissed these and other charges. Jaruzelski remained a controversial figure until his death in 2014, at ninety, from complications of a stroke. He is survived by his wife, Barbara, whom he married in 1961, and a daughter, Monika, born in 1963.

See Current Biography 1982.

James Jeffords

Born: Rutland, Vermont; May 11, 1934
Died: Washington DC; August 18, 2014
Occupation: Politician

James Merrill Jeffords was a Vermont senator and former Republican legislator most famous for his controversial shift away from the Republican Party in 2000, when he became an independent and gave the Democratic Party a temporary lead in the Senate.

Jeffords was born on May 11, 1934, in Rutland, Vermont, the son of Olin M. Jeffords, who served as the chief justice of the Vermont Supreme Court from 1955 to 1958. Jeffords earned his bachelor's degree from Yale University in 1956 and enlisted in the US Navy, serving as a gunnery officer on the Navy destroyer *McNair*. Jeffords's naval regiment was famously involved in reopening the Suez Canal in 1957. Jeffords served three years of active duty and retired from the Naval Reserve as a captain in 1990. He married Elizabeth Daley in 1961 and, the following year, completed his law degree at Harvard Law School. He subsequently returned to Vermont, going into private practice in Rutland.

Jeffords won election to the Vermont State Senate in 1966 and, in 1969, successfully ran to serve as the state's attorney general, a position he held until 1973. Jeffords won election in 1974 to the US House of Representatives, holding the seat until 1989. While a representative, Jeffords occasionally showed a willingness to go against the standard party position, as when he was the only Republican in the House to vote against President Ronald Reagan's tax package in 1981. Jeffords spent fourteen years in the House before succeeding Robert Stafford as the US senator from Vermont.

While he aligned with the official Republican stance on military matters, Jeffords took a more liberal stance on social issues, bringing him into conflict with the more conservative elements of the Republican Party. Jeffords voted for the 1991 Civil Rights Act, supported abortion rights, and was one of a minority of Republicans in favor of ending the ban on openly gay service members in the military. Jeffords was also a strong supporter of the Clinton administration's effort to establish a national health care system and was also one of the most outspoken opponents to President George H. W. Bush's decision to nominate Clarence Thomas to the US Supreme Court.

After the 2000 election of George W. Bush, Jeffords became increasingly dissatisfied with elements of the Republican Party platform. In 2001, Jeffords announced that he was leaving the Republican Party and became an independent. Though he did not officially join the Democratic Party, Jeffords caucused with the Democrats and gave the Democrats a temporary advantage in the Senate.

Jeffords published a book about his controversial departure from the Republican Party, *My Declaration of Independence* (2001), in which was highly critical of the social conservatism that he felt had come to be characteristic of the Republican platform. After becoming an independent, Jeffords continued voting along more liberal lines. He was one of only twenty-three senators to vote against the US invasion of Iraq and voted against the establishment of the Department of Homeland Security in 2002, a demonstration of his political transformation during his time in office. In 2007, Jeffords retired in Washington, DC, with his wife, who died later that year. Jeffords died on August 18, 2014, at the age of eighty. He was survived by two children, Laura and Leonard, and two grandchildren.

See Current Biography Electronic 2001.

Alison Jolly

Born: Ithaca, New York; May 9, 1937
Died: Lewes, England; February 6, 2014
Occupation: Primatologist

Alison Jolly was a renowned American primatologist whose pioneering research into the behavior of lemurs in Madagascar helped to redefine commonly held notions about male dominance in primates. Jolly was one of the world's preeminent experts on primate behavior and a former president of the International Primatological Society.

Born Alison Bishop in Ithaca, New York, Jolly attended Cornell University, where her father worked as a professor, and obtained her bachelor's degree in biology before going on to complete a PhD in zoology at Yale University in 1962. It was while a student that Jolly first visited the island nation of Madagascar, where millions of years of evolutionary isolation created a unique group of primates known as lemurs, which represent an ancient branch of the primate evolutionary tree.

In 1962, Jolly began studying the ring-tailed lemur (*Lemur catta*), a unique species that is active during the day, while most lemurs are predominantly nocturnal. Jolly catalogued hundreds of hours of observation, which became dozens of scientific papers on the structure of ring-tailed lemur society. In 1963, Jolly married economist Richard Jolly and relocated to England, where, in 1966, she became a research associate at Cambridge University.

Jolly compiled her field studies into the 1967 book *Lemur Behavior: A Madagascar Field Study*, which remains the most comprehensive examination of lemur behavior. Her observations became the foundation for a new theory of social behavior called the social intelligence hypothesis, which says that social integration was the driving force in the evolution of intelligence, rather than the development of tool use, which is a popular competing theory to explain this phenomenon.

Among Jolly's most notable accomplishments was her discovery of female dominance in ring-tailed lemurs, contradicting the traditional belief that all primate societies were male dominated. In her 1972 book, *The Evolution of Primate Behavior*, Jolly proposed that the female dominance emerged when females needed the bulk of the available food to ensure successful reproduction in a species with low birth rates. Jolly also advocated the belief that female-dominated societies, which were based on social structure integration, evolved in a different way from societies that were dominated by males.

Jolly divided her time between raising her four children and returning to Madagascar to continue her research and advocate for the conservation of the rapidly decaying Madagascar forests. She also wrote a series of popular science books and articles, including *A World Like Our Own: Man and Nature in Madagascar* (1980), in which she introduced the social intelligence theory to general audiences. From 1992 to 1996, Jolly was president of the International Primatological Society, and, in 1998, she was inducted to the National Order of Madagascar for her contributions to Malagasy conservation. Her 1999 book, *Lucy's Legacy: Sex and Intelligence in Human Evolution*, represents the culmination of many of her theories and applies the social intelligence hypothesis to human physiology and psychology.

Though never reaching the level of public renown awarded to Jane Goodall and other primatologists working with the charismatic "great apes," Jolly's contributions established her as among the foremost field biologists of the twentieth century. In 2006, Jolly received one of science's highest honors when a newly discovered lemur species, *Microcebus jollyae*, was named in her honor. Jolly died at her home in England on February 6, 2014, age seventy-six, after being diagnosed with breast cancer. She is survived by her husband and four children.

See Current Biography 2009.

Ahmad Tejan Kabbah

Born: Pendembu, Sierra Leone; February 16, 1932
Died: Freetown, Sierra Leone; March 13, 2014
Occupation: Sierra Leonean president

Ahmad Tejan Kabbah became president of Sierra Leone during the nation's civil war of the 1990s and has been credited with playing a major role in the reestablishment of a democratic government. Prior to his presidency, Kabbah had been a high-ranking government minister and a United Nations advisor.

Kabbah was born in Pendembu, in the eastern part of Sierra Leone, where his father was a scholar of the Qur'an. Kabbah was raised in the capital city of Freetown, where he attended St. Edwards Catholic School. He then went abroad to attend Aberystwyth University in Wales, graduating in 1959 with a degree in economics.

Sierra Leone achieved independence in 1961, and Kabbah became a civil servant with the Sierra Leone People's Party (SLPP). By 1963, he had risen through the ranks to become minister of trade and industry. In 1965, Kabbah married Patricia Tucker, a lawyer and educator. When the rival All People's Congress (APC) party took power in a 1967 coup, Kabbah and other SLPP leaders were forced from their positions and had their possessions confiscated. Kabbah fled to Britain in 1968 and completed his degree in law, passing the bar exam in 1969.

Kabbah joined the United Nations Development Program in 1970 and spent twenty-two years with the UN traveling throughout Africa and the United States. In 1992, revolutionary leader Valentine Strasser led a military coup to remove the APC from power, and established an interim government to pave the way for elections. Kabbah returned to Sierra Leone to take part in the National Advisory Council, but elections stalled under Strasser's lead until another coup in 1996 removed Strasser and allowed the elections to proceed. Kabbah was selected as the SLPP presidential candidate and won nearly 60 percent of the vote in the elections to become the nation's first elected leader since before the civil war.

In 1997, the Revolutionary United Front (RUF) toppled Kabbah's government, installing Johnny Paul Koroma as head of state. Kabbah escaped to Guinea with the aid of soldiers from the Economic Community of West African States Monitoring Group (ECOMOG), a multinational armed force based in Nigeria. In February of 1998, after months of bloody conflict, ECOMOG forces removed the RUF junta and temporarily restored Kabbah's government, but another RUF attack in January 1999 forced Kabbah back into exile. In July, Kabbah and RUF leader Foday Sankoh signed a peace agreement after United Nations peacekeepers entered Sierra Leone.

The peace agreement failed in May 2000 and the RUF took five hundred peacekeepers hostage as part of a bid to regain power. The British military sent armed forces into Sierra Leone to back Kabbah's government, eventually toppling the RUF junta and imprisoning Sankoh. With his government in a more stable position, Kabbah began negotiations with rebel groups, and the government was able to declare an official end to the war in 2002.

Kabbah won about 70 percent of the vote to serve a second five-year term from 2002 to 2007. Leaving office in accordance with the two-term limit imposed by the constitution, Kabbah was replaced by APC candidate Ernest Bai Koroma. Kabbah died on March 13, 2014, age eighty-two, at his home in the Jubah Hill neighborhood. He was predeceased by his wife in 1998 and is survived by five children and three grandchildren.

See Current Biography 2002.

Justin Kaplan

Born: New York, New York; September 5, 1925
Died: Cambridge, Massachusetts; March 2, 2014
Occupation: Biographer

Justin Daniel "Joe" Kaplan was a Pulitzer Prize–winning biographer known for his insightful and innovative biographies of Mark Twain and Walt Whitman. Kaplan was also an editor of *Bartlett's Familiar Quotations* and became a leading figure of the informal literary community of Cambridge, Massachusetts.

Kaplan was born in Manhattan in 1925, the son of clothing manufacturer Tobias Kaplan and Anna Rudman. Kaplan was orphaned as a child, as both parents died of cancer, and was thereafter raised largely by his older brother and the family's housekeeper. Kaplan later credited the tribulations of his early life with inspiring his curiosity in the lives of others, which led him to biographical writing. Kaplan obtained a bachelor's degree in English from Harvard University in 1944 and began graduate studies at the university, though he left before completing his doctorate.

Kaplan spent several years as a freelance writer and book editor before he was hired by Simon & Schuster, where he worked under anthology editor Louis Untermeyer and edited books by a number of elite intellectual authors, including philosophers Bertrand Russell and Will Durant and sociologist C. Wright Mills. In 1954, Kaplan married novelist Anne Bernays, with whom he had three children.

In 1959, Kaplan quit his job to begin working on a biography of Mark Twain, and moved his family to Cambridge, Massachusetts, where he could conduct research at Harvard University. Kaplan's biography of Twain, *Mr. Clemens and Mark Twain: A Biography*, was published in 1966 and became one of the most critically acclaimed books of the year, winning the 1967 National Book Award in arts and letters and a Pulitzer Prize for nonfiction. Many reviewers were captivated by Kaplan's then unusual structural approach to the story of Twain's life, which began when Twain was thirty-one and just gaining fame as a writer before retracing the story of Twain's childhood.

After publishing a well-received biography of journalist Lincoln Steffens in 1974, Kaplan spent several years writing his next biography, *Walt Whitman: A Life*, which was published in 1980 and became an international best seller, winning Kaplan his second National Book Award. Kaplan and his wife also organized a literary social circle that became a cornerstone of greater Boston's intellectual community. In 1988, Kaplan was asked to become the general editor for *Bartlett's Familiar Quotations*, and worked on the publication's sixteenth and seventeenth editions, in 1992 and 2002 respectively. Kaplan reviewed more than twenty-five thousand quotations in deciding on content for the sixteenth edition and was the first editor to include a variety of pop culture quotations.

Kaplan and his wife collaborated on two books, the first of which was a history of proper names entitled *The Language of Names*, which was published in 1997. In 2002, the couple published a joint memoir, *Back Then: Two Lives in 1950s New York*, which also received critical praise. Kaplan's final book, *When the Astors Owned New York: Blue Bloods and the Grand Hotels in a Gilded Age*, was published in 2006. Kaplan died on March 2, 2014, at age eighty-eight, from complications arising from Parkinson's disease. Kaplan is survived by his wife and the couple's three daughters, Susanna, Hester, and Polly.

See Current Biography 1993.

Casey Kasem

Born: Detroit, Michigan; April 27, 1932
Died: Gig Harbor, Washington; June 15, 2014
Occupation: Radio personality

Kemal Amen Kasem, better known as Casey Kasem, was a radio DJ and television personality who became one of America's best-known voice talents in the 1980s. Kasem also had a side career as a voice actor for animated television series and was a passionate activist for Middle East peace and cooperation, beginning with the First Lebanon War in 1982.

Kasem was born in 1932 in Detroit, Michigan, where his parents, Lebanese immigrants of the Druze faith, were proprietors of a small grocery store. Kasem enrolled in Wayne State University, before being drafted in 1952 and sent to Korea, where he worked as a broadcaster for the Armed Forces Radio and Television Service. After the war Kasem returned to school and finished his degree in education in 1958.

After working briefly in Detroit and several other cities, in 1963 Kasem got a major break when he was hired as an announcer for KRLA in Los Angeles. He also became a voice actor in 1969 when he was cast to play the character of Shaggy on the long-running *Scooby-Doo* cartoon. Kasem began hosting *American Top 40*, the series that made him into a radio icon, in 1970. Though radio was moving away from the single-song format, Kasem chose to retain the "old-fashioned" approach and the show gained a broad audience. Listeners also identified with Kasem's characteristic style of introducing artists via biographical snippets, a habit that Kasem likened to the Lebanese storytelling traditions he learned through his family. Within a few years Kasem's radio series was carried on more than one thousand radio stations across the country.

As his fame grew, he was increasingly asked to appear in bit parts in television and films. For instance, Kasem played himself in the 1984 film *Ghostbusters*. Kasem's *American Top 40* television series ended over a contract issue in 1988, and Kasem started his own rival show, *Casey's Top 40*. In 1998 Kasem regained the rights to the original series and resumed his role as host until 2004, when he ceded the position to Ryan Seacrest.

In 2007 Kasem was diagnosed with Lewy body dementia and legally authorized his adult children from his first marriage to Linda Myers to act in his behalf in determining health care decisions. In 2013 Kasem's second wife, actress Jean Thompson Kasem of *Cheers* fame, and his three elder children engaged in a highly publicized court dispute over conservatorship. Kasem, eighty-two, died in 2014 in Gig Harbor, Washington. Survivors include his wife, Jean; brother, Mouner; and children, Julie, Kerri, Mike, and Liberty.

See Current Biography 1997.

Ralph Kiner

Born: Santa Rita, New Mexico; October 27, 1922
Died: Rancho Mirage, California; February 6, 2014
Occupation: Baseball player and sportscaster

Despite his relatively short ten-year career, Ralph McPherran Kiner made a lasting name for himself as a batter, leading the National League in home runs in each of his first seven seasons and racking up a ratio of 7.1 home runs to 100 at-bats, which few players have managed to top. After being forced to retire at the age of thirty-two due to a back injury, Kiner went on to become an announcer for the New York Mets, calling their games for over fifty years.

Kiner played for the Pittsburgh Pirates from 1946 to 1952. Though as a fielder he was slow and had a weak throwing arm, his skill as a batter was unquestionable: he twice hit more than fifty home runs in a single season, and was the second player in history to hit at least forty in five consecutive seasons. He played for the Chicago Cubs in 1953 and 1954, but his career was already on the decline due to worsening back problems. He played one more season for the Cleveland Indians in 1955, and then retired with a lifetime batting average of .279 and a total of 369 home runs, which was enough to gain him election to the Baseball Hall of Fame in 1975.

He was not done with baseball, however: in 1961 he began calling games on the radio for the Chicago White Sox, and in 1962 was offered a job broadcasting for the New York Mets. He also began hosting a show called *Kiner's Korner*, in which he interviewed members of the Mets and their opposing teams after games. As a broadcaster, Kiner was known for his malapropisms—he once introduced himself on the air as Ralph Korner—but also for his intentional wit, insight, and knowledge of baseball history. Though health problems in the early 2000s left him with slurred speech, he continued broadcasting, and at the time of his death was the oldest active announcer in Major League Baseball.

Kiner died of natural causes on February 6, 2014, at his home in California. He is survived by two sons, Ralph and Scott; three daughters, Kathryn Chaffee Freeman, Tracee Kiner Jansen, and Kimberlee Kiner; and twelve grandchildren.

See Current Biography 1954.

Doris May Lessing

Born: Kermanshah, Persia; October 22, 1919
Died: London, United Kingdom; November 17, 2013
Occupation: British novelist and Nobel laureate

Doris May Lessing was one of the most respected and prolific British authors of the twentieth century, having published more than fifty books over the course of her career. Lessing received the Nobel Prize in 2007, becoming the oldest Nobel laureate (at eighty-eight years old) to win the award for literature. Though she published in a variety of genres, Lessing is best known for her poignant social commentary on feminism and racism.

Born Doris May Taylor in Kermanshah, Persia (now Iran), and raised in the colonial regime of early twentieth century Rhodesia (now Zimbabwe), Lessing experienced the racial inequity of British colonialism firsthand. Her two-volume autobiography, *Under My Skin* (1994), which won the James Tait Black Memorial Prize in 1995, and *Walking in the Shade* (1997), provided insight into her fiction by revealing details about her troubled childhood. Having left school at the age of fourteen, Lessing was largely self-educated, gaining a feeling for writing by reading the great Indian, Russian, and British novelists and essayists. Her experiences through a variety of minor jobs, from stenographer to nursemaid, helped inspire the characters and situational dramas she later explored in many of her novels.

Lessing married Frank Wisdom in 1939; they had a daughter, Jean, and a son, John. She left her husband and children, however, in 1943, explaining later that she felt stifled by the relationship and the role of wife and mother. In 1944 she married Gottfried Lessing, the father of Lessing's son, Peter, and the leader of a leftist political group. Lessing ended her second marriage in 1949, and decided to leave Africa, relocating with her son to Britain.

Lessing's first novel, *The Grass is Singing* (1950), addressed the African environment that Lessing lived in through a tragic set of fictional characters whose lives were affected by racial prejudice and class struggles. One of Lessing's most popular and critically lauded works was *The Golden Notebook* (1962), which became a favorite among feminist theorists. Many of Lessing's novels were controversial both in Europe and her former home in Africa. In response to her criticisms of the apartheid government and racial injustice, the governments of Southern Rhodesia and South Africa declared her a prohibited alien in 1956.

Lessing did not limit herself to a single genre; in 1979 she published a science fiction novel, *Shikasta*, in which she explored social themes through a hypothetical world marked by accelerated evolution. In the 1990s, Lessing began writing about her own life, beginning with the 1992 memoir *African Laughter: Four Visits to Zimbabwe*. Lessing returned to Africa to visit her daughter in 1995, after the fall of the apartheid government. She was too late to reunite with her first son, John, who died of a heart attack in 1992. Lessing also continued writing novels, including the bestselling *The Sweetest Dream* (2001).

In interviews, Lessing said she was pleased by the reach of her work but was not fond of ceremonial recognition. For example, she refused a 1999 offer to become a Dame of the British Empire and repeatedly rejected being honored as a feminist icon, saying that she never intended her work specifically to address feminist issues. In addition to the Nobel Prize, Lessing also won many of the world's most prestigious literary awards and received an honorary doctorate from Harvard University in 1995. Lessing died in London on November 17, 2013. She was ninety-four years old. Lessing is survived by her daughter, Jean, and two grandchildren.

See *Current Biography Illustrated 1976, 1995.*

Yuri Lyubimov

Born: Yaroslavl, Russia; September 30, 1917
Died: Moscow, Russia; October 5, 2014
Occupation: Theater director and actor

Russian theater director Yuri Lyubimov was world renowned as the director and founder of the Taganka Theatre in Moscow, which opened in 1964 and became a focal point for alternative theater in Eastern Europe as well as one of the most famous theaters in the Soviet Union.

Yuri Petrovich Lyubimov was born in Yaroslavl, a small town in northeastern Russia. His father was a grocery merchant and his mother was a music teacher. Taking an early interest in theater, Lyubimov joined the Second Studio of the Moscow Art Theatre, under the direction of Michael Chekhov. He graduated from the Vakhtangov Theatre, a studio for actors established by famed Russian actor Yevgeny Vakhtangov, before being drafted into the army in 1941. Assigned to the NKVD, the Soviet Union's secret service, Lyubimov served as a director of the secret service's dance troupe and choir.

When World War II ended, Lyubimov rejoined the Vakhtangov Theatre as a featured performer. His breakthrough as a director came in 1963 with an acclaimed production of Bertolt Brecht's *The Good Person of Szechwan*. This play established Lyubimov as a symbol of the Russian avant-garde theater movement. The following year, in 1964, he and his students founded the Taganka Theatre in Moscow, which quickly became the most controversial and popular theater in the city.

Due to government monitoring, some of Lyubimov's productions were banned or heavily censored, but he cultivated productions that skirted the edge of rebellion, staging innovative and unusual productions of popular works and plays by up-and-coming playwrights. Among the most famous productions at the Taganka were a 1976 performance of *Hamlet* and a 1977 staging of *The Master and Margarita*, by Russian author Mikhail Bulgakov. In 1965, the Taganka also staged a famous production loosely based on the book *Ten Days That Shook the World* (1919), by American journalist John Reed, which reflected on the Bolshevik revolution.

In 1984, when Lyubimov gave a performance of *Crime and Punishment* in England, his criticisms of the Soviet government, published in British newspapers, resulted in the Soviet government revoking his citizenship and removing him as director of the Taganka. Lyubimov spent several years in exile, taking a position at the La Scala in Milan, Italy, and also serving as a guest director at the Royal Opera House in London. He staged productions of *Crime and Punishment* at the Arena Stage in Washington, DC, and visited the Lyric Opera of Chicago in 1987 to direct a production of *Lulu*.

Invited to return to the Soviet Union in 1988, Lyubimov resumed his leadership of the Taganka Theatre after a successful Moscow staging of *Boris Godunov*. He remained in that position until 2011, when he resigned from the Taganka following disagreements with performers. He returned to the Vakhtangov Theatre to direct for the last part of his career. Lyubimov died on October 5,

2014, age ninety-seven, in Moscow. Survivors include his wife, theater critic Katalin Koncz, and the couple's son, Peter Lyubimov.

See Current Biography Illustrated 1988.

Lorin Maazel

Born: Paris, France; March 6, 1930
Died: Castleton, Virginia; July 13, 2014
Occupation: Conductor

Lorin Varencove Maazel was an orchestral conductor who held prominent posts in the United States and across Europe. Maazel was also a composer and violinist who wrote and performed violin concertos around the world.

Maazel was born in 1930, in the Neuilly-sur-Seine suburbs of Paris, France, where his parents, who were both American music students, had been living while finishing their degrees. Maazel was a musical prodigy who began studying violin, piano, and conducting by the age of seven. After the family returned to Los Angeles, Maazel studied conducting with private tutors and was enrolled in the Interlochen Center for the Arts in Michigan. At age nine, Maazel was asked to conduct the Interlochen Orchestra at the 1939 World's Fair in New York and, on the strength of this performance, he was invited to sit in as guest conductor for the Pittsburgh Symphony the following year. Over the next five years, orchestras across the United States invited Maazel to sit in as guest conductor. He performed with the New York Philharmonic and with the NBC Symphony at Radio City Music Hall.

At fifteen, Maazel enrolled at the University of Pittsburgh, where he studied languages, mathematics, and philosophy. In 1948, he joined the Pittsburgh Symphony as a violinist and then won a Fulbright fellowship to study Italian music in Rome in 1951. In 1953, Maazel returned to conducting when he was asked to sit in as guest conductor for the Teatro Bellini in Catania, Italy. Maazel spent the next decade touring Europe as a guest conductor, performing with more than twenty European orchestras. In 1962, Maazel returned to the United States as guest conductor for the New York Philharmonic.

In 1965, Maazel accepted his first directorship at the Deutsche Opera in West Berlin. He remained in this position until 1971, when he accepted a position as music director for the Cleveland Orchestra, which was to begin in 1972. In 1982, he returned to Europe to take over as general manager of the Vienna State Opera but parted ways with the company in 1984, two years into a four-year appointment. That same year, he became a music consultant for the Pittsburgh Symphony Orchestra and took

a position as its music director in 1988. During the 1990s, Maazel returned to composition, producing a series of well-regarded concertos for the violin and often performing his own compositions at featured concerts.

In 2002, while touring the world for his seventieth birthday, Maazel learned that the New York Philharmonic was looking for a new conductor. He applied for the position and was hired, remaining with the orchestra until 2009. In his last professional position, from 2010 to 2013, Maazel was music director of the Munich Philharmonic. He also organized the Castleton Festival for classical music in his home town of Castleton, Virginia. Maazel was married three times, the final time to German actor Dietlinde Turban in 1986. Maazel died in 2014, at the age of eighty-four, after contracting pneumonia. He was survived by his wife, their three children, and four children from his previous marriages.

See Current Biography Illustrated 1965.

Nelson Mandela

Born: Mvezo, South Africa; July 18, 1918
Died: Johannesburg, South Africa;
December 5, 2013
Occupation: South African president

Nelson Mandela was the first black president of South Africa and one of the most important figures of the African independence movement in the twentieth century. Known primarily for his role as the symbol of South Africa's struggle against the white apartheid government, Mandela became a global icon of racial unity, liberation, and justice. Through his example, diplomatic efforts, and presidency, Mandela helped to build South Africa into one of the most stable democratic states in Africa.

Mandela was born Rolihlahla Dalibhunga Mandela on July 18, 1918, in the village of Mvezo, South Africa. In 1939, he enrolled in the University College of Fort Hare, South Africa, where he met fellow activist Oliver Tambo and became involved in a radical student group. Mandela and Tambo were expelled from the university in 1940 for their roles in a student protest over poor food quality. He later completed his bachelor's degree in 1943 through the University of South Africa, although he returned to Fort Hare for graduation. Mandela married his first wife, Evelyn Mase, in 1944, and they had four children. In 1944, Mandela joined the African National Congress (ANC), a leftist political organization founded in 1912 that played an important role in the antiapartheid movement.

In 1952, the ANC launched the Defiance Campaign, a nonviolent mass resistance effort that protested unjust laws against blacks. In June 1955, Mandela began organizing an armed campaign under the ANC's Freedom Charter. The government cracked down on the growing resistance movement, arresting Mandela and 155 other insurgents on December 5, 1956, and charging them with high treason. Mandela, who was released on bail while awaiting trial, continued to build the ANC. During this time he divorced Mase and married his second wife, Winifred (Winnie) Madikizela, with whom he went on to have two children. (The couple later divorced in 1996.) As government pressure grew, Mandela retreated into the underground, participating in covert protests and attempting to organize a resistance militia.

When the treason case was finally brought to trial in 1959, the government was not able to prove Mandela guilty of plotting violent acts and acquitted on March 29, 1961. However, on August 5, 1962, he was arrested on charges of leaving the country without valid documents and inciting workers to strike. Consequently, he was sentenced to five years without parole on November 7, 1962.

Less than a year after his imprisonment, the government raided ANC headquarters and discovered documents that allegedly revealed the organization's plans to implement guerilla warfare. Mandela and other top ANC leaders were convicted of treason, a crime punishable by death. Thus began the famous Rivonia Trial (1963–64), which resulted in Mandela being sentenced to life in prison.

Mandela's reputation continued to grow during his incarceration, and he eventually became the most prominent symbol of black independence in Africa. In 1989, while still in prison, he obtained a bachelor of laws (LLB) degree through the University of South Africa. He remained in prison until his release on February 11, 1990.

On several occasions, the South African government offered Mandela conditional release from prison if he would publically disavow the liberation movement or speak out against violent rebellion, but Mandela repeatedly refused until he was finally offered a complete and unconditional pardon in February 1990. After his release, Mandela was thrust directly back into the political spotlight and began working with then South African president F. W. de Klerk to form a new democratic government to replace the apartheid system. On June 3, 1993, it was declared that the first elections open to all South African citizens would be held on April 27, 1994. Mandela and de Klerk shared the 1993 Nobel Peace Prize for their role in ending apartheid and forming the first democratic government in South Africa.

Mandela won election as the first black president of South Africa and was subsequently inaugurated on May 12, 1994. He served one term, choosing to retire in 1999. Mandela's presidency was, for many South Africans, the pinnacle of the long independence struggle and the symbolic beginning of a new era in the country's history.

Mandela died at his home in Johannesburg on December 5, 2013, after suffering from a prolonged infection in his lungs. He was ninety-five years old. Mandela was predeceased by a daughter and two sons. He is survived by his third wife, Graça Machel, whom he married on July 18, 1998; three daughters, Pumla Makaziwe Mandela, Zenani Dlamini, and Zindziswa (Zindzi) Mandela; seventeen grandchildren; and fourteen great-grandchildren.

See Current Biography 1984, 1995.

Peter Matthiessen

Born: New York, New York; May 22, 1927
Died: Sagaponack, New York; April 5, 2014
Occupation: Novelist and nature writer

Peter Matthiessen was a talented author who wrote both fiction and nonfiction fluently and to great acclaim. The only author to win National Book Awards for both fiction and nonfiction, he is particularly known for his nonfiction books about ecology and wildlife. He is also heralded as a founder of the *Paris Review,* the influential literary journal.

Matthiessen was born in New York City in 1927, where his father Erard worked as an architect and was a leading member of the National Audubon Society. Matthiessen attended private schools and served in the Navy during World War II. He graduated from Yale University in 1950 with a degree in English. In the early 1950s he lived in Paris where he led two different lives. He was both a CIA agent, assigned to keep abreast of the activities of expatriates, as well as an aspiring writer. In 1953 Matthiessen and Harold L. "Doc" Humes founded the *Paris Review* and recruited his friend George Plimpton to become its first editor.

After leaving the CIA and returning to New York, Matthiessen published his first novel, *Race Rock,* in 1954, followed by two others in quick succession. He also began contributing essays and articles to *Sports Illustrated.* His first nonfiction book, a collection of articles on nature and ecology titled *Wildlife in America,* was published in 1959. Matthiessen then began writing for the *New Yorker,* which funded his trips to South America, New Guinea, and Asia. A series of books, including *Under the Mountain Wall* (1962), *The Shorebirds of North America* (1967), and *At Play in the Fields of the Lord* (1965)—Matthiessen's first major success as a novelist—followed from these exploits. During this period, Matthiessen also became involved with LSD (which was not yet illegal) and Zen Buddhism, influences that appeared in much of his later writing.

Matthiessen's crowning nonfiction achievement was *The Snow Leopard* (1978), which blended autobiography with the search for an elusive Himalayan feline; it was widely praised and won the 1979 National Book Award for nonfiction writing. Matthiessen also developed an interest in American Indian activism. His 1983 book, *In the Spirit of Crazy Horse*, chronicles the history of the Sioux people and the 1975 conviction of Leonard Peltier. In the 1990s, Matthiessen returned to fiction. A trilogy of novels set in the Florida Everglades, released together as *Shadow Country* in 2008, won the National Book Award in fiction, thus making Matthiessen the first author to win the award in both categories.

Matthiessen was married three times, first to Patsy Southgate, with whom he had two children, Lucas and Sara, and then to writer Deborah Love, with whom he had a son, Alex, and a daughter, Rue. Love died of cancer in 1972. In 1980 he married Maria Eckhart and they settled on Long Island. Matthiessen died in April 2014, at age eighty-six, from complications arising from leukemia. In addition to his wife, Maria, and his four children, he is survived by two stepdaughters and six grandchildren. Matthiessen's last novel, *In Paradise*, was published just after his death.

See Current Biography Illustrated 1975.

Tadeusz Mazowiecki

Born: Plock, Poland; April 18, 1927
Died: Warsaw, Poland; October 28, 2013
Occupation: Polish political leader

Tadeusz Mazowiecki was best known as the prime minister of Poland and the first non-Communist to lead an Eastern bloc nation since the late 1940s. Known as a champion of free trade and a conciliatory leader who mended the deadlock between the liberal and conservative coalitions in Poland's government, Mazowiecki also made a mark serving in the Polish Parliament and with the United Nations.

Mazowiecki was born in Plock, Poland, on April 18, 1927. Mazowiecki studied law at the University of Warsaw, but he did not graduate and left in 1953 to become the editor of *Wroclawski tygodnik Katolicki*, a weekly Catholic publication. He was eventually fired from the publication due to his opposition to the Communist government. He then started a new Catholic monthly publication, *Wiez*, which he edited until 1981. In 1956, Mazowiecki was one of the founders of the Warsaw Club, an organization of Catholic intellectuals that supported trade reforms. Mazowiecki's involvement in this club helped him win election to the Polish Parliament in 1961, where he served as a Catholic opposition member until 1972.

Mazowiecki's call for an investigation of the 1971 police massacre of workers on strike at the Gdansk shipyards resulted in his being banned from running in the 1972 election to the Polish parliament. Mazowiecki played a role in writing the historic agreement of August 31, 1980, that ended the Gdansk strike and was the genesis of the Solidarity, the first free trade union in the region, which Mazowiecki helped form with the union's leader, Lech Walesa.

The growing influence of Solidarity provoked the Communist regime to declare martial law on December 13, 1981. Consequently, many members of the Solidarity leadership, including Mazowiecki and Walesa, were arrested. After being held for more than a year, Mazowiecki was released from prison on December 24, 1982. A final wave of labor strikes in 1988 convinced Communist leaders to meet with the opposition and discuss a path to democratic elections. Mazowiecki won formal election as prime minister of Poland on August 24, 1989. Not long after his election, the Berlin Wall fell on November 9, 1989, when Communist-controlled East Germany allowed citizens to cross the border into West Germany.

Mazowiecki inherited a nation with an inflation rate of more than 300 percent, and he, along with his deputy prime minister and finance minister, Leszek Balcerowicz, initiated a series of liberal economic reforms that helped to grow free market enterprise and slash inflation. Mazowiecki failed, however, to keep public support toward the end of the year as his administration was blamed for the country's continuing economic issues, including high unemployment rates. Mazowiecki and Walesa differed regarding the role of the government and Walesa ran against Mazowiecki in the nation's 1990 presidential elections. After losing the election by a large margin, Mazowiecki resigned as prime minister. He remained active in the Polish government and on the world stage after this defeat, however, serving in the Polish parliament (1991–2001) and as a special rapporteur on human rights in Yugoslavia for the United Nations (1992–95).

Mazowiecki passed away on October 28, 2013, in Warsaw, Poland. He was eighty-six years old. Mazowiecki was twice married and widowed. He is survived by three sons, Wojciech, Adam, and Michal.

See Current Biography 1990.

Paul Mazursky

Born: New York, New York; April 25, 1930
Died: Los Angeles, California; June 30, 2014
Occupation: Director and screenwriter

Paul Mazursky was an American screenwriter and director known for his hit films that provided a satirical look at American culture of the 1960s and 1970s. In addition to directing, Mazursky was also an actor who appeared in supporting roles in film and television.

Mazursky was born Irwin Mazursky in Brooklyn in 1930. He attended Brooklyn College, where he got his start acting in student stage production before earning his bachelor's degree in 1951. Mazursky was cast in director Stanley Kubrick's first feature film, *Fear and Desire* (1953), and changed his first name to Paul. Mazursky married Betsy Purdy in 1953 and studied method acting with famed instructor Lee Strasberg.

After a string of film and television appearances, Mazursky moved to Los Angeles in 1959, where he joined the improv group Second City. In the 1960s, Mazursky transitioned to screenwriting, often working with fellow Second City performer Larry Tucker. Mazursky and Tucker cowrote the 1966 pilot for the television series *The Monkees* and in 1968, they sold their first screenplay, *I Love You, Alice B. Toklas*, which was produced that year and starred Peter Sellers. Critics have called the film one of the first satires of 1960s hippie counterculture.

Mazursky made his directorial debut with the comedy *Bob & Carol & Ted & Alice*, which he cowrote with Tucker and which starred Elliott Gould, Natalie Wood, Dyan Cannon, and Robert Culp. The film, which explored countercultural sexual freedom and wife swapping, was a major success and won Mazursky and Tucker an Academy Award nomination for best original screenplay. After his second film, *Alex in Wonderland* (1970), failed at the box office, Mazursky left directing and moved briefly to Italy with his family. He returned to directing with *Blume in Love* (1973), starring George Segal, which became one of the most critically acclaimed films of the year. His next film, *Harry and Tonto* (1974), was a dramatic comedy about an elderly man who takes a road trip after being evicted. The film was a success, and the film's star Art Carney won the Academy Award for best actor for his performance.

Mazursky's next major success was *An Unmarried Woman* (1978), starring Jill Clayburgh as a woman coping with the varied life changes brought about by her divorce. The film was nominated for three Academy Awards, including best picture and best screenplay. Mazursky made several films in the 1980s, but his biggest commercial successes were *Moscow on the Hudson* (1984), starring Robin Williams, and *Down and Out in Beverly Hills* (1986), starring Bette Midler and Richard Dreyfuss.

Mazursky cast himself in bit parts in many of his own films and played supporting roles in dozens of other films and television series. As an actor, Mazursky is known for recurring roles in the series *Curb Your Enthusiasm* and *The Sopranos*. Mazursky died in Los Angeles on June 30, 2014, at the age of eighty-four. He was survived by his wife of thirty years, Betsy, and their daughter Jill. Another daughter, Meg, died of cancer in 2009.

See Current Biography 1980.

Joe McGinniss

Born: New York, New York; December 9, 1942
Died: Worcester, Massachusetts; March 10, 2014
Occupation: Journalist, author

Controversial author Joe McGinniss is known for his best-selling, and often debated, books on Richard M. Nixon and the murder trial of Jeffrey MacDonald. Before becoming an author, McGinniss worked as a journalist in Massachusetts and Philadelphia, Pennsylvania.

Joseph McGinniss was born in 1942 in Manhattan, the only child of travel agent Joseph A. McGinniss and secretary Mary Leonard. When McGinniss was young, he chose Ralph as his middle name. He attended the College of the Holy Cross in Worcester, Massachusetts, graduating in 1964 with a degree in journalism. McGinniss then worked as a reporter for the *Worcester Telegram* and a sports columnist for the *Philadelphia Bulletin* before accepting a position as an investigative reporter for the *Philadelphia Inquirer* in 1966.

In 1968, an encounter with the advertising team for presidential candidate Hubert Humphrey inspired McGinniss to investigate the relationship between advertising and politics. McGinniss's book on the subject, *The Selling of the President, 1968* (1969), explored the advertising strategies behind president Richard Nixon's campaign, and was acclaimed for helping to reveal how manipulative advertising affected politics. Though his book was a best seller, McGinniss was criticized for allowing his admittedly anti-Nixon personal views to affect his exposition.

McGinniss quit the *Inquirer* after his first book's success and published his only novel, *The Dream Team*, in 1972 to mixed reviews. His 1976 memoir, *Heroes*, documented McGinniss's struggle with alcoholism, his divorce from his first wife Christine Cooke, and his romance with and marriage to his second wife Nancy Doherty.

In 1979, McGinniss returned to journalism as a reporter for the *Los Angeles Herald Examiner*.

While in Los Angeles, McGinniss met Jeffrey MacDonald, a former US Army Green Beret doctor who was accused of the 1970 murder of his wife and two daughters. MacDonald agreed to allow McGinniss to write a book about his trial, and McGinniss then spent three years researching the case. In the resulting book, *Fatal Vision* (1983), McGinniss traced his own transforming ideas about the case, from being a sympathizer to his eventual belief that MacDonald was guilty and was attempting to manipulate him and the public into supporting his claims of innocence. MacDonald was convicted, and sued McGinniss for breach of contract. Some in the media and among MacDonald's supporters criticized McGinniss for violating principles of journalistic integrity, most famously the journalist Janet Malcolm, whose 1990 book *The Journalist and the Murderer* condemned McGinniss's professional ethics.

McGinniss followed with two additional true crime books, *Blind Faith* (1989) and *Cruel Doubt* (1991), before returning to political biography with his 1993 book *The Last Brother*, about the life of Ted Kennedy. McGinniss's 2011 book *The Rogue: Searching for the Real Sarah Palin* caused a scandal when McGinniss rented a house next door to Palin's family while finishing the book, leading to accusations that he was stalking the Palin family. The book became a best seller, though critics questioned the validity of many of the allegations he made regarding Palin's youth and behavior.

After being diagnosed with prostate cancer, McGinniss spent the last years of his life documenting his treatment and working on an unpublished memoir. McGinniss died on March 10, 2014, age seventy-one, at a hospital in Worcester. He is survived by his wife, Nancy; the couple's two children; and three children from his previous marriage.

See Current Biography 1984.

Joan Mondale

Born: Eugene, Oregon; August 8, 1930
Died: Minneapolis, Minnesota; February 3, 2014
Occupation: Arts advocate and wife of American vice president Walter Mondale

When her husband was appointed to the United States Senate in 1964, Joan Mondale took the opportunity to speak up on behalf of the fine arts. She served on the board of a number of arts organizations, wrote a book on the connections between art and politics, gave guided tours at the National Gallery, and helped to organize public art installations in both Washington, DC, and Tokyo. Her tireless efforts earned her the nickname "Joan of Art" and made her an influential figure in her own right.

Mondale, herself an accomplished amateur potter, worked at the Boston Museum of Fine Arts and the Minneapolis Institute of Arts before moving to Washington, DC, with her husband in 1964. In Washington, Mondale volunteered at the National Gallery of Art, and in 1972 she published *Politics in Art*, a book for young people based on her lectures about the use of art for political commentary. When her husband was elected vice president in 1977 as the running mate of Jimmy Carter, Mondale turned the vice-presidential residence into a gallery of American art and gave tours, curating a collection of works loaned from museums to highlight the work of contemporary artists. Carter also made her honorary chair of the Federal Council on the Arts and Humanities. Mondale used her position to promote other causes as well: a staunch supporter of women's rights, she spoke in favor of the Equal Rights Amendment and equal pay for women.

When Walter Mondale was appointed ambassador to Japan by Bill Clinton in 1993, Mondale took her art advocacy overseas. She filled the ambassador's residence with paintings on loan from an American museum and persuaded McDonald's to fund a public art installation in a Tokyo subway station. She also studied Japanese pottery styles and frequently gave the pieces she made as gifts to Japanese politicians. After her return to the United States in 1996, she published a book, *Letters from Japan* (1997), about her experiences as an ambassador's wife.

After her return to Minnesota, Mondale served on the boards of various arts organizations, including the Minnesota Orchestra, the Northern Clay Center, and the Walker Art Center. In 2004, the Textile Center in her home city of Minneapolis endowed an exhibition space, the Joan Mondale Gallery, in her honor.

Mondale died at a hospice in Minneapolis on February 3, 2014, and is survived by her husband; her two sons, Ted and William; and four grandchildren. She was predeceased by her daughter, Eleanor Mondale Poling, who died of brain cancer in 2011.

See Current Biography 1980.

Gerard Mortier

Born: Ghent, Belgium; November 25, 1943
Died: Brussels, Belgium; March 8, 2014
Occupation: Opera manager and director

Gerard Alfons August Mortier was an opera director and manager known for his work with the Salzburg Festival and the Théâtre de la Monnaie. Mortier is often credited with modernizing contemporary opera and of supporting emerging directors and innovative versions of popular opera.

Mortier was born in 1943 in the city of Ghent, where his parents owned a modest neighborhood bakery. Mortier studied law and journalism at Ghent University, where he also formed, in 1968, a student protest group known as Jeugd-Opera that disrupted what the group saw as overly conservative productions by throwing fruit on the stage and distributing flyers. After completing his degrees, Mortier was selected by Christoph von Dohnányi as assistant administrator for the Frankfurt Opera. Mortier went on to work at Hamburg State Opera from 1977 to 1979, and then worked as an assistant to Rolf Liebermann at the Paris Opera from 1979 to 1981.

Mortier's work with Liebermann won him sufficient prestige that he was offered a position as general director of the Théâtre de la Monnaie in Brussels in 1981. Mortier helped to transform the small theater into a world class opera company, creating an innovative chorus and orchestra while premiering works by emerging, alternative directors. His notable successes included an acclaimed production of Wagner's *Der Ring des Nibelungen* and a production of *Death of Klinghoffer* by John Adams. Mortier also strained the theater's budget to make extensive renovations, including the purchase of a lavish marble foyer floor designed by minimalist artist Sol LeWitt. Mortier's spending became the subject of a government inquiry, but he was able to push his renovations through before he was asked to replace famed director Herbert von Karajan as director of the Salzburg Festival in 1992.

At Salzburg, faced with a conservative public and administration, Mortier continued to favor modernization and innovative productions. Mortier hired director Peter Sellars for productions of Ligeti's *Le grand macabre* and Messiaen's *St. François d'Assise*, and Mortier's productions helped establish these operas among the general repertoire. Mortier was successful in maintaining profitability and in attracting a younger audience to the theatre, but was criticized by some of the theatre's more traditional supporters.

Mortier left Salzburg in 2001 and accepted a position as director of the famed Paris Opera in 2004. In Paris, Mortier introduced new works by now famous director Christoph Marthaler and commissioned Sellars to direct an imaginative production of *Tristan und Isolde*, using video montages to enhance the performance. In 2007, Mortier was offered a $60 million budget to take over as director of the New York City Opera (NYCO). However, due to the economic downturn of 2008, the NYCO board reduced the budget to $36 million, and Mortier declined the offer. That same year, Mortier took up a position as the Teatro Real in Madrid,

where he staged an innovative operatic interpretation of the Annie Proulx short story *Brokeback Mountain* and also produced an acclaimed performance of Philip Glass's *Perfect American*. Mortier was diagnosed with pancreatic cancer in September 2013 and died on March 8, 2014, age seventy, at his home in Brussels. On April 8 of that year, Mortier received a posthumous lifetime achievement award at the International Opera Awards.

See Current Biography 1991.

Farley Mowat

Born: Belleville, Ontario; May 12, 1921
Died: Port Hope, Ontario; May 6, 2014
Occupation: Author and environmentalist

Farley McGill Mowat was a Canadian environmentalist and writer known for pioneering wolf conservation in Canada. During his career Mowat published forty-five books, many of which focused on the environmental decline and need for protection of the northern wilderness in Canada and the United States.

Mowat was born in Belleville, Ontario, in 1921, where his father worked as a librarian. The family moved several times, eventually settling in Saskatoon, Saskatchewan. An only child, Mowat spent a great deal of time exploring the outdoors and developed an interest in wildlife and nature. He kept a variety of exotic pets as well, including a live rattlesnake and a gopher.

Mowat entered the Canadian army during World War II and served in the Hastings and Prince Edward regiment, rising to the rank of captain during a 1943–44 tour in Italy. In 1945 Mowat served in an intelligence unit in the Netherlands organizing supply missions to help Dutch refugees. Mowat experienced directly some of the worst brutality of war; this became an important factor in his increasing disaffection for the human world and his growing attraction to the world of nature and animal life.

Attending the University of Toronto after his years in the military, Mowat visited the Inuit tribes of Canada. He wrote his first novel, *People of the Deer*, about the Ihalmiut, a group of inland Inuit people, and their mistreatment within the colonial system. Though this was a work of fiction, Mowat became passionate about Inuit rights and returned to this issue repeatedly in his later writings as a social activist.

Throughout his career, Mowat experimented with many different types of writing. He wrote children's books, humorous fiction, and nonfiction accounts of conservation, indigenous tribes, and the northern wilderness. Mowat's most famous and popular book was the 1963 *Never Cry Wolf*, a fictionalized account of his experiences studying and living near the Arctic wolf populations in

Canada. The success of *Never Cry Wolf* created widespread interest in wolf conservation. The book also stirred controversy: some wolf experts argued that Mowat misrepresented aspects of wolf behavior to promote his belief that wolf populations should be preserved. The book was later made into a 1983 film by the Walt Disney Company, bringing Mowat international attention.

Mowat also took a keen interest in the preservation of ocean life. Living in a remote fishing village in Newfoundland for nearly eight years, he became acutely aware of the plight of whales and the need for the preservation of all marine life. Later he wrote several books on the subject including *A Whale for the Killing* (1972). Mowat's 1984 book, *Sea of Slaughter*, also focused on the effects of whaling and hunting other oceanic creatures. The book was seen as a threat to the commercial fishing industry, and Mowat was denied entrance to the United States when he attempted to visit in 1985.

Later in his life, Mowat wrote an autobiographical account of his early years and his time in the military, *Otherwise* (2008). He wrote as well about the life and career of Dian Fossey. Mowat received a number of awards for his writing and was made an officer of the Order of Canada in 1981. Throughout his career, he was one of the most popular authors in Canada. Mowat died on May 6, 2014, six days shy of his ninety-third birthday. He is survived by his wife, Claire, whom he married in 1965, and two sons from an earlier marriage.

See Current Biography Illustrated 1986.

Ivan Nagy

Born: Debrecen, Hungary; April 28, 1943
Died: Budapest, Hungary; February 22, 2014
Occupation: Ballet dancer and director

Ivan Nagy was a Hungarian ballet dancer who became one of the major stars of international ballet and the American Ballet Theatre during the 1970s. After retiring from performance, Nagy became a prominent artistic director working with ballet companies across the United States and in his native Hungary.

Nagy was born in 1943 in Debrecen, one of the largest cities in Eastern Hungary. Nagy's mother, ballet instructor Viola Nagy (née Sarkozy), gave her son his first lessons in ballet and, at age seven, Nagy competed with four thousand other students for a spot in the prestigious Budapest State Opera House School, winning one of forty-eight positions awarded that year. Nagy was one of only six students who completed the intensive nine-year intensive program, and he joined the Budapest State Opera Ballet Company as a professional performer in 1960.

Nagy won a prestigious silver medal at the 1965 International Ballet Competition in Varna, Bulgaria, where his performance garnered the attention of Frederick Franklin, director of the National Ballet of Washington, DC. Nagy accepted an invitation from Franklin to relocate to the United States and perform with the National Ballet and within a year had become one of the company's featured soloists. Nagy's performances in *Legend of the Pearl* and George Balanchine's *Serenade* and *Concerto Barocco* won him praise as one of American ballet's most promising performers.

In 1968, Nagy applied for resident alien status in the United States, which was considered a defection from Soviet-occupied Hungary, though he insisted that his decision was not politically motivated. Around this time, Nagy married Australian ballet dancer Marilyn Burr. Nagy and Burr appeared together in a 1968 performance of *Giselle*, which became one of Nagy's most critically acclaimed performances.

Nagy spent a year with the New York City Ballet, under Balanchine, in 1968, but left the following year to join the American Ballet Theatre as a soloist. During ten years with the American Ballet Theatre, Nagy became known for his ability to partner successfully with a range of dynamic dancers, including Natalia Makarova, Carla Fracci, and Marianna Tcherkassky.

In 1978, Nagy surprised the dance world when he announced his retirement at age thirty-five, citing the stress of the performing life as the motivation for his decision. Though he appeared sporadically in limited engagements, including dancing with Makarova at the Metropolitan Opera House in 1980, Nagy spent the rest of his life developing a reputation as a prominent artistic director. Nagy headed the New Orleans Ballet Company from 1986 until 1989 and then worked for the English National Ballet in the early 1990s.

Nagy spent much of his later life living in semi-retirement in Valldemossa, Spain. Nagy died February 22, 2014, age seventy, after suffering from a sudden undisclosed illness while in Budapest working on an upcoming production of *La Sylphide*. Nagy is survived by his wife; a sister; two daughters, Aniko Nagy and Tatjana Harper; and a granddaughter.

See Current Biography 1977.

Magda Olivero

Born: Saluzzo, Italy; March 25, 1910
Died: Milan, Italy; September 8, 2014
Occupation: Opera singer

Magda Olivero was an Italian opera singer who became famous in Italy in the 1930s and rose to become an international star in the 1970s.

Maria Maddalena Olivero was born in 1910 in Saluzzo, a town in Italy's Piedmont region, where her father worked as a judge. She was given piano and music lessons at a young age, eventually gravitating toward opera. After auditioning to sing on Turin radio, she was famously criticized by conductor Ugo Tansini, who claimed she lacked a good voice or any measurable talent. Undeterred, Olivero auditioned for Turin radio again in 1932, giving a performance that won her a spot as a student of renowned voice instructor Luigi Gerussi.

Though she knew that she lacked the natural vocal talents of some of her contemporaries, Olivero worked at developing her voice, and acquired superior skills in the key areas of voice control and dynamics. She also became known for her dramatic flair during operatic death scenes. Olivero's first professional appearance occurred in 1933 when she performed as Lauretta in Giacomo Puccini's *Gianni Schicchi*; from there, she became a well-known figure in the Italian opera scene. Olivero sang alongside some of the biggest stars of the 1930s and also added refined dance skills to her repertoire. This allowed her to perform the challenging dance scenes in operas like Armando La Rosa Parodi's *Cleopatra*.

Olivero married Italian business leader Aldo Busch in 1941, and retired from performing full time in hopes of having a family. As the couple did not have any children, however, Olivero occasionally returned to performing at charitable events. In 1950, composer Francesco Cilea entreated Olivero to return to the stage for a final performance as the lead in his opera *Adriana Lecouvreur*, as he considered her the most suitable performer for this challenging role. Although Cilea died late that year, missing Olivero's return performance as Adriana in 1951, her resurgence garnered major acclaim and she resumed performing across Europe. Despite being older than most opera stars, Olivero's career flourished and she appeared on the US stage for the first time in 1967 at the Dallas Civic Opera. In 1975, at the age of sixty-five, Olivero debuted at the New York Metropolitan Opera in a celebrated performance as Tosca. She followed this with her first appearance at Carnegie Hall in 1977, and she continued performing on stage regularly until 1981, when she gave a farewell performance in Verona.

Renowned for her role as Lecouvreur and for her dramatic flair, Olivero earned a dedicated and, at times, fanatic fan base that kept her in high demand into the 2000s. In 1993, at age eighty-three, she recorded excerpts from her famous Lecouvreur performance. Olivero was predeceased by her husband in 1983. She retired to Italy, where she was often interviewed and visited by fans. Olivero died on September 8, 2014, age 104, in Milan.

See Current Biography Illustrated 1980.

Ian R. K. Paisley

Born: Armagh, Northern Ireland; April 6, 1926
Died: Belfast, Northern Ireland; September 12, 2014
Occupation: Religious leader and politician

Ian Richard Kyle Paisley was a Protestant religious leader from Northern Ireland who served as a member of the UK parliament and was the leader and cofounder of the Democratic Unionist Party (DUP).

Paisley was born in Armagh, Northern Ireland, in 1926, the son of a Baptist minister. After high school, Paisley worked briefly in the farming industry before deciding to join the Protestant clergy. He entered the Barry School of Evangelism and was ordained by his father in 1946. In 1951, Paisley split off from the primary wing of the church, forming his own congregation, the Free Presbyterian Church of Ulster, which developed into a radical conservative faction marked by their opposition to Catholic civil rights and Irish independence.

Paisley came to national attention in 1963 when he organized a protest at the Belfast city hall against the government's decision to lower the flag after the death of the pope. In 1966, after a series of marches that turned into riots between Catholics and Protestants, Paisley was jailed for three months for unlawful assembly. In 1970, Paisley was elected to the House of Commons as an MP for the Protestant Unionist Party. However, Paisley was more vehemently anti-Catholic and loyalist than the main faction of the Protestant Unionist Party, which led him to cofound the DUP in 1971.

Known as a vitriolic and openly bigoted man, Paisley was also a gifted organizer who played a major role in uniting the anti-Catholic factions of Northern Ireland. He began publishing books on his position in the 1970s, including the 1972 inflammatory manifesto *United Ireland—Never!* Paisley's refusal to work with Catholic or Republican factions contributed to the decades-long deadlock in the peace process. Though he was invited to participate in the talks that led to the peacemaking Good Friday Agreement, he refused in protest of the participation of Sinn Féin, the political branch of the IRA. Public opinion turned toward the peace process despite Paisley, and the overwhelming support for the Good Friday Agreement in 1998 left the DUP on the outside of Ireland's political evolution.

Over the next several years, Paisley softened his position, and began working with Catholic politicians. He agreed to the 2006 St. Andrews Agreement, which produced a power-sharing executive branch with both unionist and Sinn Féin ministers. In the elections, Paisley became leader of the province's largest party and then first minister, working alongside former IRA leader Martin McGuinness as his deputy. In creating this power-sharing government, Paisley is credited with helping to cross an important barrier to future peace between the factions.

Paisley gave up leadership of the Free Presbyterian Church in 2008 and stepped down as first minister and DUP leader later that year, citing health concerns. He retired as an MP in 2010 and, upon resignation, was given the lifetime peer title of Baron Bannside. Paisley died on September 12, 2014, age eighty-eight, at his home in Belfast. Survivors include his wife Eileen Cassells, whom he married in 1956, two sons, and three daughters.

See Current Biography Illustrated 1971, 1986.

Mel Patton

Born: Los Angeles, California; November 16, 1924
Died: Fallbrook, California; May 9, 2014
Occupation: Athlete

Melvin Emory "Mel" Patton was an Olympic sprinter and gold medalist considered one of the fastest humans in the world in the 1940s. In addition to his performance in the 1948 Olympics, Patton raced for the University of Southern California as a representative of the National Collegiate Athletics Association (NCAA).

Patton was born in Los Angeles in 1924 and began running track under the coaching of Jim Pursell at University High School in West Los Angeles. After Patton graduated from high school in 1943, he spent two years in the Navy serving as both a seaman and an aviation cadet. In 1945, Patton resigned from the navy and married his girlfriend of several years, Shirley Ann Roos, with whom he later had two children. That same year, he enrolled at the University of Southern California (USC), supporting himself and his new wife on a GI bill allowance of approximately ninety dollars per month.

Patton earned his bachelor's degree at the university while becoming the most celebrated athlete on the USC track team. Under USC coach Dean Cromwell, Patton beat the standing 100-yard dash record of 9.4 seconds on May 15, 1948. In articles covering his achievement, Patton was informally called the "world's fastest man." For three years, from 1947 to 1949, Patton was among the most celebrated collegiate athletes in the nation and held the NCAA 100-yard title. Patton's 100-yard dash record of 9.3 seconds stood until 1961, when American sprinter Frank Budd was able to beat Patton's time by 0.1 seconds.

Patton won the honor of competing at the 1948 Olympic Games in London, where he finished fifth in the 100-meter dash, losing to his teammate Harrison Dillard. Patton credited his disappointing performance to the heat and stress of adjusting to the competition. Patton rebounded from his failure in the 100-meter dash to win the gold in the 200-meter race. The American team also won the gold in the 4×100-meter relay with Patton running in the anchor leg of the race. At a 1949 track meet, Patton broke Olympic star Jesse Owens's record for the 220-yard dash, achieving a record time of 20.2 seconds.

Patton ended his racing career after finishing college and stated in interviews that he was troubled by corruption he witnessed among athletes in the Amateur Sports Association. Patton later earned a master's degree in physical education from USC and became a coach at Long Beach City College from 1949 to 1955. He then relocated his family to Kansas, where he coached track at the University of Wichita from 1955 to 1956. Patton took a number of other jobs as well, including a consulting job in Saudi Arabia as the director of a national sports program. Patton was inducted into the National Track and Field Hall of Fame in 1985.

Patton died on May 9, 2014, age eighty-nine, at his home in Fallbrook, California. He is survived by his wife, the couple's son and daughter, five grandchildren, and a great-grandchild.

See Current Biography 1949.

Otis Pike

Born: Riverhead, New York; August 31, 1921
Died: Vero Beach, Florida; January 20, 2014
Occupation: American congressman

Former New York congressman Otis Grey Pike served nine terms in congress and became one of the legislature's most outspoken critics of military excess and wastefulness. Pike was also famous for conducting one of the first governmental investigations into the Central Intelligence Agency.

Pike was born in Riverhead, New York, on August 31, 1921, and attended Princeton University in 1939, but signed up for naval pilot training with the Marines in 1942. Pike served as a World War II fighter pilot in the Pacific theatre, completing more than 120 missions and earning 5 air medals, before being discharged in 1946, at which point he was awarded his degree from Princeton. That same year, Pike married Doris A. Orth, with whom he would have three children, and enrolled in Columbia University Law School, completing his degree in 1948.

Pike joined a local law firm after graduation, where he worked until he won a 1953 election and became a justice of the peace. In 1958, Pike ran as a Democrat against incumbent Stuyvesant Wainwright II for the House of Representatives seat from New York's First Congressional

District. Though he lost his first race, Pike narrowly unseated his opponent in 1960 to become the district's representative. Pike was considered several times for advancement to higher offices, but was repeatedly passed over for alternative candidates.

Pike became a member of the House Armed Services Committee and grew into one of the legislature's chief critics of military spending. In 1967, Pike was instrumental in demonstrating inflated aircraft construction costs, resulting in a series of reforms to military equipment policies. In 1973, Pike played a major role in defeating a spending bill that would have provided $14 million in flight pay for nonflying military officers. Pike also participated in efforts to protect New York's agricultural and manufacturing industries and these efforts helped him to continue winning elections, despite running as a Democrat in a heavily Republican district.

In 1975, Pike was asked to join a thirteen-member Select Committee on Intelligence, the counterpart to a similar group within the Senate. The legislative committee examined spending and policies within the National Security Agency, Central Intelligence Agency, and Federal Bureau of Investigation in light of international events including the 1968 Tet offensive and the Yom Kippur War of 1973. The committee marked the first time Congress had examined the secret policies of the CIA since the agency was founded in 1947. Pike's committee released their full report in 1976, but the House voted to keep the report secret. Nevertheless, the report was leaked to CBS News and published in the *Village Voice*. Pike was critical of intelligence agency policies, accusing intelligence leaders of ineptitude and of leaving America vulnerable to foreign threats.

Pike left Congress in 1979 to become a columnist for Newhouse Newspapers, publishing hundreds of articles on public and current affairs before retiring from the newspapers in 1999. The death of his first wife Doris, in 1996, left Pike a widower until he met and married Florida resident Barbe Bonjour in the early 2000s. Pike died on January 20, 2014, after an illness left him in hospice care. Pike was predeceased by his son Robert Pike in 2010, and is survived by his wife, Barbe; his son, Douglas, his daughter, Lois Pike Eyre; and two grandchildren.

See Current Biography 1976.

Jean Redpath

Born: Edinburgh, Scotland; April 28, 1937
Died: Arizona; August 21, 2014
Occupation: Musician

Jean Redpath was a Scottish folk singer who helped to revive interest in the traditional folk music of Scotland in the 1960s and '70s. Redpath recorded more than forty albums during her career and performed for dignitaries including Queen Elizabeth II.

Redpath was born in Edinburgh, Scotland, in 1937 and raised primarily in the seaside community of Leven in the county of Fife. Music was an important feature of the Redpath household and she said in later interviews that her father played the hammered dulcimer while her mother taught her the traditional songs of Scotland. Though she was drawn to music, Redpath never formally studied music theory and sang in pubs for extra income while she attended the University of Edinburgh as a student of medieval history. While there, Redpath became versed in the music archive of folklorist Hamish Henderson, who created a collection of recordings of the songs of traveling Scottish singers. Many of these songs became part of Redpath's professional repertoire. Redpath never completed college, however, and decided to travel abroad for experience.

She visited the United States in 1961 and ended up in New York's Greenwich Village folk scene, where she became friends with Bob Dylan. Redpath performed at free concerts around the city until a November 1961 performance at Gerde's Folk City brought her an enthusiastic review in the *New York Times*, launching her career. She recorded her first album, *Skipping Barefoot through the Heather*, the following year for the independent label of folklorist Kenneth Goldstein from Philadelphia. Redpath signed with Elektra Records and later Philo Records, releasing a series of acclaimed albums of traditional Scottish songs through both labels. She also released albums via her own independent label, Jean Redpath Records.

In 1972, Redpath was honored with an appointment as artist in residence at Wesleyan University in Middletown, Connecticut. She also became a regular performer on Garrison Keillor's *A Prairie Home Companion* radio program, which vastly increased the popularity of her music across the country. Redpath's most famous series of albums was made in collaboration with composer Serge Hovey, who had compiled 323 songs written or collected by Scottish poet, lyricist, and folk song collector Robert Burns. Redpath and Hovey released the first album of their collaboration in 1976 and continued working together until Hovey's death in 1989, by which time they had recorded seven out of a planned twenty-two albums of Burns's music. Redpath and Hovey's collaborations are among her most critically acclaimed work. After Hovey's death Redpath recorded four more a cappella albums of Burns's music.

Over the years, Redpath was recognized as one of the most important figures in traditional Scottish music. She performed for Queen Elizabeth II in a 1977 celebration at Edinburgh

Castle, and from 1979 to 1989, Redpath worked at Stirling University, where she taught Scottish song. In 1987, she was appointed a Member of the Most Excellent Order of the British Empire. She returned to Edinburgh University as an artist in residence in the Celtic and Scottish studies department in 2011. Redpath died on August 21, 2014, age seventy-seven, while living in Arizona. Redpath suffered from cancer in her later years and had been admitted to a hospice program shortly before her death.

See Current Biography 1984.

Paul Reichmann

Born: Vienna, Austria; September 27, 1930
Died: Toronto, Ontario; October 25, 2013
Occupation: Canadian real estate developer

Canadian real estate developer Paul Reichmann was responsible for dramatically altering the skylines of some of the world's great urban environments, including Toronto, London, and New York City. Reichmann's most notable projects include the now famous World Financial Center in New York City and the Canary Wharf complex in London.

Born in Vienna, Austria, on September 27, 1930, Reichmann's Orthodox Jewish family fled Austria after it was annexed by Nazi Germany, and they relocated to Paris in 1938, and then to Tangier, Morocco, before finally settling in North York, a suburb of Toronto, in the mid-1950s. Reichmann and his brothers, Albert and Ralph, started a small family business called Olympia Tile, which produced tiles and other building materials. In 1958, they transformed Olympia Tile into Olympia & York Developments, a real estate development firm.

Olympia & York was perfectly placed to take advantage of Toronto's development into the nation's financial capital and became one of the city's largest developers by concentrating on offices and commercial property. In 1973, the company completed the seventy-two-story First Canadian Place, which was the largest building in Canada and became a focal point of the city's skyline.

Olympia & York's success in Canada encouraged the company to expand into New York City's real estate market. In 1977, they took advantage of the city's world financial slump and purchased the Uris buildings, which consisted of eight office towers in Manhattan, from the National Kinney Corporation. In 1980, Olympia & York won the right to build six million square feet of office and retail space near Battery Park, a project that would become the World Financial Center, one of the company's most visible accomplishments.

In 1988, Olympia & York began the development of London's Canary Wharf complex, now one of the city's primary business districts containing the United Kingdom's second-tallest building, One Canada Square. The project consisted of twenty-four buildings and was a gamble at the time, with an estimated cost of $8 billion.

By 1991, the Reichmanns were ranked the fourth-richest family in the world by *Forbes* magazine, with an estimated net worth of $12.8 billion. In 1992, however, Olympia & York collapsed with more than $20 billion in debt resulting largely from the failure of the Canary Wharf project. Consequently, the Reichmanns, in a dramatic turn of events, were left with a net worth of less than $100 million.

Over the next decade, Reichmann slowly rebuilt and eventually regained control of Canary Wharf in 1995. The family's net worth grew from a low of approximately $100 million to more than $1 billion by 2000. Reichmann retired in 2005 after Morgan Stanley and a group of developers acquired Canary Wharf. Upon his retirement, Reichmann, then seventy-four years old, turned over his private property company, Reichmann International, to his son, Barry.

Reichmann became engaged to Lea Feldman when he was just fifteen, meeting the young woman through his family. They married in 1955, shortly before relocating to Canada. Reichmann's faith was an important part of his life, and his companies helped to build a network of Jewish schools and learning centers throughout Canada. Reichmann died on October 25, 2013, in Toronto. He was eighty-three years old. Reichmann is survived by his wife, Lea, and his five children, Barry, Henry, Vivian, Rachel, and Libby.

See Current Biography 1991.

Alain Resnais

Born: Vannes, France; June 3, 1922
Died: Paris, France; March 1, 2014
Occupation: Director

Alain Resnais was a French film director known for his complex, experimental films representing the emergence of the new wave film movement in France. Resnais's unorthodox approach to narrative structure is credited with inspiring a generation of art-house filmmakers around the world.

Resnais began making films when he was twelve years old, and his interest endured into adulthood, motivating him to move to Paris in 1939 to study acting. In 1943, Resnais was accepted at the newly founded L'Institut des hautes études cinématographiques (IDHEC), where he studied filmmaking.

Resnais left IDHEC before graduating to serve in the military during the closing years of World War II. Returning to Paris, he directed a series of acclaimed documentaries, several of which caught the attention of professional producers. Resnais's first major success was the 1955 documentary *Nuit et brouillard* (*Night and Fog*), a combination of newsreel footage and color photography of liberated Nazi concentration camps. The film became an international hit and is still considered one of the most successful explorations of the subject.

Resnais's first feature film was *Hiroshima, mon amour* (1959), the story of a French actress's affair with a Japanese architect, told through flashbacks and memories of the American bombing of Hiroshima. The film was successful but critically divisive, with some critics hailing it as an artistic masterpiece while others called it cold and confusing. Resnais worked with avant-garde authors for many of his screenplays, which both set the tone for his experimental filmmaking style and established him as one of the new generation of new wave filmmakers.

In 1961, Resnais won the Golden Lion award at the Venice Film Festival for his international hit *L'année dernière à Marienbad* (*Last Year at Marienbad*), in which he used flashbacks to slip between the past and present in an examination of memory. His follow up film, *Muriel* (1963) was another major hit, for which his star actress Delphine Seyrig won a best actress award at the Venice Film Festival. In 1969, Resnais married Florence Malraux, who worked as his assistant director on many of his films until the couple divorced in the 1980s.

Resnais's early success made him famous in the French film community and allowed him to embark on more ambitious projects with leading actors. Though he made more than fifty films in his life, few were as well received as his earlier, more experimental works. Among his later successes was the 1977 *Providence*, starring legendary actor John Gielgud, and the 1980 hit *Mon oncle d'Amérique* (*My American Uncle*), which won a Grand Prix at the Cannes Film Festival and was nominated for an Academy Award for best screenplay. From 1986 onward, many of Resnais's films featured Sabine Azéma, who would become his second wife in 1998, in leading roles.

Resnais continued to produce films throughout the 2000s, including *Coeurs* (2006; *Private Fears in Public Places*) and *Les herbes folles* (2009; *Wild Grass*). In 2009, Resnais received a lifetime achievement award at the Cannes Film Festival. Resnais died in Paris on March 1, 2014, age ninety-one, after suffering from a brief illness. He is survived by his wife.

See Current Biography 1965.

Albert Reynolds

Born: Rooskey, Ireland; November 3, 1932
Died: Dublin, Ireland; August 21, 2014
Occupation: Politician

Albert Reynolds was a former food industry executive who became prime minister (taoiseach) of Ireland in the 1990s and helped to forge a peace agreement in Northern Ireland.

Reynolds was born in Rooskey, a town in central Ireland, where his father worked as a coach builder. Reynolds was educated at Summerhill College in Sligo and had his first professional job as a clerk with the state transport company Córas Iompair Éireann. Reynolds and his brother Jim started a side business promoting Irish bands at dancehalls. Using the money he earned from this promotion business, Reynolds invested in a series of companies, including a seafood export business and C & D Foods, a pet food manufacturer.

Reynolds became quite wealthy through the pet food industry and, in the mid-1970s, decided to enter local politics. Reynolds was elected to the Dáil Éireann (Ireland's lower house of parliament) in 1977, representing the center-right party Fianna Fáil, and was a supporter of Charles Haughey's rise to the party leadership. Reynolds held a number of posts within the Fianna Fáil, including minister for industry and commerce and minister for finance. Reynolds developed a reputation as a conciliatory politician and was one of the leaders in an alliance between his party and the Progressive Democrats in the late 1980s. However, due to his rural roots, some members of the administration dismissed Reynolds and his cohorts as representatives of a less cosmopolitan side of the Irish government.

In 1992 Haughey was ousted after a series of scandals and Reynolds succeeded him as prime minister. The coalition with the Progressive Democrats fell apart during Reynolds's first year in office, but Reynolds formed a historical union with the social-democratic Labour Party in February of 1993, marking the first coalition between the Labour Party and the Fianna Fáil in Ireland's history. Reynolds's coalition ushered in a series of progressive legislative developments, including the decriminalization of homosexuality and the passage of a referendum allowing Irish women to travel outside of Ireland to receive abortions. However, Reynolds was also accused of using the position to benefit his political and corporate cronies. In what many historians saw as his greatest achievement, Reynolds partnered with John Major, then the British prime minister, to organize and mediate a historical set of meetings that resulted in a 1994 ceasefire with the Irish Republican Army, and then a Loyalist cease fire the next year. The framework of this agreement became the foundation of the Good Friday Agreement established in 1998.

Despite some success, Reynolds's term as prime minister was one of the shortest in Irish history, as an increasing number of scandals connected to his administration weakened his alliance with the Labour party. One of the most controversial issues was Reynolds's nomination of Harry Whelehan, a conservative attorney general, to become president of the high court. Whelehan played a controversial role in blocking efforts to extradite pedophile priest Brendan Smyth and took a hard line on abortion rights that some felt violated national laws. Reynolds's refusal to stand aside on Whelehan's nomination resulted in the dissolution of Reynolds's government and he stepped down in November 1994.

In his later years, Reynolds suffered from poor health and Alzheimer's disease. Reynolds died on August 21, 2014, age eighty-one, in Dublin. He is survived by his wife, Kathleen (nee Coen), and seven children.

See Current Biography 1994.

Joan Rivers

Born: New York, New York; June 8, 1933
Died: New York, New York; September 4, 2014
Occupation: Comedian and actor

Joan Alexandra Molinsky, better known by her stage name, Joan Rivers, was a pioneering American comedian and actor known for her acerbic wit and tendency to explore risqué subjects in her comedy.

Rivers was born in 1933 to Meyer and Beatrice Molinsky, Russian immigrants who relocated to Brooklyn, New York, where Meyer was a physician. Rivers, the younger of two daughters, went to private schools and graduated from Barnard College in 1954. With an early interest in becoming an actor, she began working in the fashion industry and became a publicist at Lord & Taylor in the 1950s. She then began performing stand-up comedy in clubs around New York, eventually joining the esteemed Chicago improvisational comedy troupe Second City in the early 1960s. Rivers married Jimmy Sanger in 1957, but the marriage was annulled the following year. In 1965, Rivers married producer Edgar Rosenberg, with whom she later had one daughter, Melissa Rivers.

A major break came in 1965 with Rivers's appearance on *The Tonight Show* with Johnny Carson. Because of the success of this appearance, she was often asked to return as a featured performer. Rivers had her film debut in the 1965 movie *Once upon a Coffee House,* which led to other bit parts in films and television. She

also began writing and publishing semiautobiographical books and novels, beginning with the 1974 book *Having a Baby Can Be a Scream.* Rivers wrote and directed her own film, *Rabbit Test* (1978), though it was a flop with both critics and viewers. She followed up with a best-selling novel, *The Life and Hard Times of Heidi Abromowitz* (1984).

In the 1980s, Rivers was regularly asked to guest host for Carson during the host's annual vacations. When Fox approached Rivers to host her own talk show in 1986, her departure from Carson's program caused a rift between them and she later reported that they never reconciled. Just months after Rivers finished heading *The Late Show Starring Joan Rivers* from 1986 to 1987, her husband committed suicide, a subject she addressed in her later writings. From 1989 to 1993, she hosted the daytime talk program *The Joan Rivers Show,* which earned her a Daytime Emmy Award in 1990 for outstanding talk/service show host. She and her daughter starred together in a television feature regarding her husband's suicide, titled *Tears and Laughter: The Joan and Melissa Rivers Story,* in 1994. From the early 1990s to the end of her life, Rivers was a featured guest on numerous television shows and became famous as a red-carpet host for E! Entertainment Television, using her sarcastic wit to critique outfits at celebrity events. A documentary of her life, *Joan Rivers: A Piece of Work,* was released in 2010. Beginning in 2011 she and her daughter also starred in their own WE channel reality series, *Joan & Melissa: Joan Knows Best?*

Rivers died in a Manhattan hospital on September 4, 2014, age eighty-one, after suffering from an unexpected cardiac arrest while undergoing minor surgery on her throat. She is survived by her daughter and a grandson.

See Current Biography 1970, 1987.

Mickey Rooney

Born: Brooklyn, New York; September 23, 1920
Died: Los Angeles, California; April 6, 2014
Occupation: Actor

During his long career, Mickey Rooney appeared in hundreds of film, television, and stage roles. At the age of nineteen, he was the world's leading box office star. A multitalented singer, dancer, comedian, and actor, he was nominated for four Academy Awards, received two special Oscars for his contributions to film, and earned two Golden Globe Awards as well as an Emmy Award.

Born Joseph Yule Jr. in 1920 in Brooklyn, Rooney first performed onstage when he was a toddler. His parents were both vaudevillians—his mother a burlesque dancer and his father a comedian. His parents divorced when he was five, and his mother took him to Hollywood where Rooney was cast to appear in a series of short films as Mickey McGuire, a popular comic book character. He played this role in dozens of the McGuire shorts between 1927 and 1936, and, in 1932, adopted the stage name "Mickey Rooney." At thirteen, he was cast as Puck in the 1935 film *A Midsummer Night's Dream*, which won him a lucrative feature-film contract.

Rooney soon became a major star for his portrayal of Andy Hardy, the lead character in a series of family-friendly films that ran from 1937 to 1944 and that were huge box office draws. By 1939 Rooney had become Hollywood's leading box office star and was awarded a special Academy Award to commemorate his contribution to the portrayal of youth on screen. In 1939, as well, Rooney costarred with Judy Garland in *Babes in Arms*, which was the first of several extremely popular Rooney-Garland musicals and garnered Rooney an Academy Award nomination.

He was nominated for a second Academy Award for his role in the 1943 film, *The Human Comedy*, a movie he filmed just before joining the US Army. He served with the army for two years, traveling to entertain the troops in combat zones in Europe and earning the Bronze Star for this work.

When Rooney returned to Hollywood, his career stalled, as he was now too old to play the teenage roles for which he had become known. He entered the television world, making frequent guest appearances, hosting his own series for a year in the 1950s, and trying his hand at directing. In this period he also began to reinvent himself in the film world and earned a third Academy Award nomination for his role in the 1956 movie *The Bold and the Brave*. Though he filed for bankruptcy in 1962 and suffered a series of personal tragedies, Rooney continued performing and gradually regained financial security.

Rooney received a fourth Oscar nomination for his portrayal of aged jockey Henry Dailey in *The Black Stallion* (1979) and that same year made his Broadway debut in the musical revue *Sugar Babies*. In 1981, he received a Golden Globe and an Emmy for his role in the television movie *Bill*, playing a mentally handicapped man.

Rooney published an autobiography, *Life Is Too Short*, in 1991, in which he gave an honest account of his tumultuous personal life. Rooney was married eight times during his career. His first marriage, to Hollywood star Ava Gardner in 1942, lasted only until 1943. His marriage to Barbara Thomason in 1958 ended in tragedy when the actress was murdered in 1966. Rooney's final marriage to Jan Chamberlin in 1978 ended in separation in 2012; it involved a court case in which Rooney charged Chamberlin's son from

a previous marriage of elder abuse. Rooney had nine children, including one stepson whom he adopted. He was predeceased by his son Tim Rooney in 2006. Rooney died at his home in Los Angeles at the age of ninety-three.

See Current Biography 1942, 1965.

Janet D. Rowley

Born: New York, New York; April 5, 1925
Died: Chicago, Illinois; December 17, 2013
Occupation: Geneticist

Geneticist Janet Davison Rowley, a pioneer in genetics, was the first to demonstrate the genetic link to cancer in leukemia. A longtime professor at the University of Chicago, Rowley's research was a breakthrough in the development of chromosomal translocation research.

Rowley was born in New York City to Hurford and Ethel Davison, both of whom worked as teachers. In 1940, at age fifteen, she won a scholarship for early admission to the University of Chicago, graduating in 1944 with her bachelor's degree and receiving her MD in 1948. The day after graduation, she married fellow medical student Donald Rowley, who became a professor of pathology, and the couple both completed their residencies at the United States Public Health Service's Marine Hospital in Chicago.

The Rowleys had four children, beginning with the birth of their son Donald in 1952, and Rowley spent much of the next couple of decades raising her children and working three days a week outside the home. From 1955 to 1961 Rowley assisted at Chicago's Cook County Hospital, working with children with Down syndrome and other developmental disorders. From 1957 to 1961 she worked as an instructor of neurology at the University of Illinois School of Medicine.

In 1961 Rowley visited Oxford University while her husband was in England on sabbatical and used the opportunity to study emerging methods of chromosomal analysis. Upon her return, Leon Jacobson, a pioneer in hematology, provided Rowley a small stipend and laboratory space and equipment to conduct chromosomal research, and she began investigating the chromosomal links to leukemia.

Rowley made her first major discovery in 1972 while conducting supplemental research in her home, noticing distinct chromosomal differences in patients that suffered from acute myeloid leukemia. Rowley linked this to a genetic abnormality called a translocation, which involves the breaking and reconnection of chromosomes. In 1973 Rowley published her initial results, which linked chromosomal translocation to two types of leukemia. While promising, many in the medical community were not convinced of the chromosomal link until 1977, when Rowley and her team linked translocation with a third type of leukemia. Given this discovery, the chromosomal basis of leukemia became broadly accepted and Rowley was promoted to full professor in recognition of her discovery.

Beginning in the 1980s researchers used the translocation theory to develop new treatments for leukemia, eventually resulting in drugs such as imatinib (Gleevec), which remains among the most promising anticancer drugs. Recognition of Rowley's achievement began with the 1982 Dameshek Prize, the highest honor from the American Society of Hematology. The American Cancer Society presented her with its Medal of Honor in 1996, and in 2009 she received the Presidential Medal of Freedom. Rowley was also awarded honorary doctorates from fourteen institutions, including the University of Pennsylvania and Harvard University. Rowley died at her home in Chicago on December 17, 2013, age eighty-eight, of complications from ovarian cancer. She was predeceased by her husband in February 2013 and son Donald in 1983, and is survived by sons David, Roger, and Robert, and five grandchildren.

See Current Biography 2001.

Julius Rudel

Born: Vienna, Austria; March 6, 1921
Died: New York, New York; June 26, 2014
Occupation: Conductor

Julius Rudel was the long-time director and conductor for the New York City Opera and is credited with renovating and invigorating the opera during his tenure. Rudel also served as artistic director for the Kennedy Center in Washington and as conductor for the Buffalo Philharmonic Orchestra in the 1980s.

Rudel was born in Vienna, Austria, in 1921 to a Jewish family and began formal violin training at age five. Rudel's father died in 1938, the year that the Nazi army annexed Austria. Rudel, his mother, and his brother immigrated to New York, where Rudel helped to support the family by working delivery and clerical jobs. In 1942 he married Rita Gillis, an author and neuropsychologist. Two years later he became an American citizen.

Rudel joined the City Opera in 1943, the same year he completed conducting training at the Mannes School of Music. Rudel started out at City Opera as an unpaid auditions pianist and then moved up to rehearsal pianist. The management gradually allowed Rudel to handle casting and to fill in as a conductor. After financial disaster in 1956, the board selected Rudel to succeed Erich Leinsdorf as conductor and director for the 1957 season. His dual role gave him complete control, which he used to help the City Opera remain relevant and active despite shrinking budgets and diminishing audiences. He also guest conducted in many cities in the United States and across Europe. His production of *Brigadoon* earned him a 1963 Tony Award nomination.

Rudel presided over the City Opera's 1966 move from the former Mecca Temple at 131 West Fifty-Fifth Street to its renovated location at Lincoln Center. Though it struggled financially for decades, Rudel strove to maintain the theater's central mission to produce opera for the general public. To that end the City Opera kept ticket prices low and concentrated on producing innovative interpretations of classic works and fostering the careers of budding writers and singers.

Rudel served as artistic adviser for the Kennedy Center for the Performing Arts in Washington, DC, from 1968 to 1975. Rudel left the City Opera in 1979, becoming the principal conductor for the Buffalo Philharmonic Orchestra in Buffalo, New York, where he remained until 1985. He also had the opportunity to conduct in Copenhagen, Vienna, Rome, and Munich, among many other locations. During his career he guest-conducted at the New York Metropolitan Orchestra more than two hundred times.

Rudel won praise for his even temper and his ability to work harmoniously with performers and theater staff, though some critics found his work inconsistent. In 2013 Rudel and collaborator Rebecca Paller published a book about his career, *First and Lasting Impressions: Julius Rudel Looks Back on a Life in Music*. Rudel, ninety-three, died at his Manhattan home in June 2014. Predeceased by his wife in 1984, he was survived by his brother, Ludwig; children, Anthony, Joan, and Madeleine; seven grandchildren; and seven great-grandchildren.

See Current Biography Illustrated 1965.

Frederick Sanger

Born: Rendcomb, England; August 13, 1918
Died: Cambridge, England; November 19, 2013
Occupation: British chemist and Nobel laureate

British chemist Frederick Sanger was a pioneer in the study of DNA and proteins and developed groundbreaking methods for determining amino acid sequences in the late 1950s, one of the critical breakthroughs in genetic research of the late twentieth century. Sanger is the only person to win two Nobel Prizes in Chemistry (1958 and 1980), and he is one of only four people in history to have achieved the honor of winning two Nobel Prizes.

Sanger was born on August 13, 1918, in Rendcomb, England. He received a science scholarship to attend Cambridge University's St. John's College, and graduated in 1939 with his bachelor's degree in natural sciences. Sanger, a conscientious objector for religious reasons, continued graduate studies at the university during World War II. After earning his PhD in 1943, he began to take an interest in the amino acid structure of proteins. In 1944, he received the Beit Memorial Fellowship for medical research, and he joined the protein chemist Albert C. Chibnall to study the molecular structure of proteins. At the time, scientists were uncertain how proteins were structured or how many amino acids were contained within a protein matrix. Sanger decided to study the protein insulin, which was readily available and important in the treatment of diabetes.

One of Sanger's breakthroughs was the use of a novel chemical, now known as Sanger's reagent, which allowed him to break insulin molecules into shorter chains of amino acids. Over the next ten years, Sanger perfected several methods for determining the amino acid sequence in these short molecular fragments and was gradually able to reconstruct the amino acid of the entire insulin molecule. In addition, Sanger showed how insulin molecules differed between species because of relatively minor changes in amino acid arrangement. Sanger was awarded the 1958 Nobel Prize in Chemistry for these discoveries.

In 1962, Sanger relocated to the British Medical Research Council Laboratory of Molecular Biology. In 1977, Sanger, in collaboration with a team of researchers, became the first to decode a full genome sequence of an entire organism when they pieced together a virus with more than five thousand nucleotides in its sequence. This same year, Sanger was awarded the Copley Medal from the Royal Society for his contributions to chemical research. The team followed this success by determining the genome of human mitochondria, unique structures within cells that have their own genomic compliment. This was the first human DNA ever sequenced. As these discoveries required new methods of splitting and analyzing molecular fragments, Sanger's team pioneered the method of using base terminators to investigate nucleotide chain structure. In 1979, his work with DNA earned him the Albert Lasker Basic Medical Research Award. Sanger then shared the 1980 Nobel Prize in Chemistry with chemists Walter Gilbert of Harvard University and Paul Berg of Stanford University; Sanger and Gilbert were recognized for their respective DNA sequencing methods, while Berg was honored for being the first scientist to move a gene between organisms.

Sanger retired from the British Medical Research Council in 1983, but he remained active and founded the Sanger Centre (now the Wellcome Trust Sanger Institute) in 1993 to support scientists continuing in the fields of protein and gene structure chemistry and research. In 1986, he was awarded the Order of Merit from the British government.

Sanger died in Cambridge, United Kingdom, on November 19, 2013. He was ninety-five years old. His wife, Margaret Joan Howe, predeceased him; he is survived by the couple's two sons, Peter and Robin, and a daughter, Sally.

See Current Biography 1981.

Maximilian Schell

Born: Vienna, Austria; December 8, 1930
Died: Innsbruck, Austria; February 1, 2014
Occupation: Actor

Maximilian Schell was an Academy Award–winning actor who later became a critically acclaimed director. Known for his portrayal of German characters in World War II–era films, Schell appeared in more than one hundred films and television productions during his career.

Most of Schell's family was involved in the theatrical world. His father was a playwright, his mother ran a local acting school, and his older sister Maria was an award-winning actor. Schell's family fled Austria following the Nazi occupation of Vienna in 1938, and Schell enrolled at the University of Zurich before transferring to the University of Munich after the war. Schell began acting professionally in 1952 and made his German film debut in the 1955 film *Kinder, Mütter und ein General*. In 1958, he followed Maria to the United States, where she was already a prominent film star.

Schell began acting on the American stage and was soon scouted for film roles. He made his American film debut alongside Marlon Brando in *The Young Lions* (1958). Schell's breakout role was in the 1961 drama *Judgment at Nuremberg*, in which he portrayed a German attorney defending former Nazi officers accused of war crimes. Among an all-star cast that included Montgomery Clift and Spencer Tracy, Schell delivered the most critically acclaimed performance of the film and won that year's Academy Award for best actor.

Schell also wrote and directed independent films; two of his early films, *First Love* (1970) and *The Pedestrian* (1973), were nominated for the Academy Award for best foreign language film. Schell was nominated for his second Academy Award for his starring performance in the 1975 film *The Man in the Glass Booth*. He was also nominated for the Academy Award for best supporting actor for his performance in the 1977 film *Julia*.

Though known for his roles in Nazi-era films, Schell appeared in a wide variety of movies, including the 1979 science fiction film *The Black Hole*. He also continued making independent films, and his 1984 film biography of Marlene Dietrich, *Marlene*, was nominated for the Academy Award for best documentary. Schell married Russian actress Natalya Andreychenko in 1985, with whom he had a daughter, Anastasia Schell (also known as Natassja Schnell), in 1989. He continued acting throughout the 1980s and 1990s, occasionally winning parts in blockbuster films such as the 1990 comedy *The Freshman* and the 1998 science fiction film *Deep Impact*. He won the Golden Globe Award for best performance by an actor in a supporting role for his portrayal of Vladimir Lenin in the 1992 television movie *Stalin*. In his later life, he increasingly spent time in Austria, appearing in a number of German-language films and television roles.

Schell divorced his first wife in 2005, and in 2008 he began a relationship with German Croatian opera singer Iva Mihanovic, marrying her in 2013. Schell died on February 1, 2014, at the age of eighty-three. He is survived by his wife and daughter.

See Current Biography 1962.

André Schiffrin

Born: Paris, France; June 14, 1935
Died: Paris, France; December 1, 2013
Occupation: French American publisher

André Schiffrin, former editor and publisher for Pantheon Books, was a pioneer in nonprofit publishing and a major figure in the debate over the commercialization of the publishing industry. During his more than fifty years in the publishing industry, Schiffrin is credited with having cultivated the careers of some of the most respected writers of the twentieth century, including Jean-Paul Sartre, Günter Grass, Simone de Beauvoir, Michel Foucault, Studs Terkel, Marguerite Duras, and Gunnar Myrdal.

Schiffrin was born on June 14, 1935, in Paris, France. His father, Jacques Schiffrin, founded La Bibliothèque de la Pléiade, a series of reference editions of classic literature. The family fled France and immigrated to the United States in 1941 to escape the increasingly anti-Jewish laws of the Vichy regime in France. In 1943, Schiffrin's father became an editor at New York's Pantheon Books, where he eventually rose to the position of vice president and remained until his death in 1950.

Schiffrin attended Yale University, where he graduated with a bachelor's degree in history in 1957. He earned his master's degree at Cambridge University's Clare College in 1959. While at Clare College, he became the first American to edit *Granta*, the school's literary journal, which was first published in 1889 by Cambridge University students. In 1961, Schiffrin married Maria Elena de la Iglesia. The following year the couple relocated to New York City and Schiffrin joined Random House's recent acquisition, Pantheon Books.

Schiffrin was promoted to editor in chief of Pantheon in 1963 and became managing director in 1969. During his time with Pantheon, Schiffrin developed a reputation for cultivating relationships with innovative new writers and also for bringing talented European authors to American audiences. Schiffrin was the first American publisher to publish the works of groundbreaking theorist Michel Foucault and also introduced many readers to the work of Noam Chomsky.

In 1990, Schiffrin was asked to resign from Pantheon Books, reportedly because he refused to alter his publishing strategy to stem monetary losses. Schiffrin later described his dissatisfaction with the company as a result of the fact that the management at Random House was increasingly focusing on profit as the only meaningful measure of success. More than two hundred authors, including Kurt Vonnegut and Studs Terkel, protested outside Random House headquarters against Schiffrin's dismissal.

In 1992, Schiffrin joined with former Pantheon editor Diane Wachtell to found New Press, a nonprofit publisher. New Press was an immediate success as Schiffrin was able to attract many of his former clients and the press published numerous bestsellers, including Studs Terkel's *Race: How Blacks and Whites Think and Feel About the American Obsession* (1992) and James W. Loewen's 1995 hit *Lies My Teachers Told Me: Everything Your American History Textbook Got Wrong*. While heading New Press, Schiffrin authored a number of books himself, beginning with his controversial *The Business of Books: How the International Conglomerates Took Over Publishing and Changed the Way We Read* (2000), in which Schiffrin blamed the publishing industry for reducing the quality of American publishing in favor of profit.

Schiffrin died of pancreatic cancer on December 1, 2013, in Paris, France. He was seventy-eight years old. Schiffrin is survived by his wife, Maria, his two daughters, Anya and Natalia, and three grandchildren.

See Current Biography 2000.

James R. Schlesinger

Born: New York, New York; February 15, 1929
Died: Baltimore, Maryland; March 27, 2014
Occupation: Economist, government official

James Rodney Schlesinger was a Republican presidential adviser, economist, and former CIA chief who served under three American presidents. Among a number of high-profile government positions, Schlesinger was a former secretary of defense and became the nation's first secretary of energy.

Schlesinger was born in 1929 in New York City, into a middle-class Jewish family and attended Harvard University, where he obtained a bachelor's degree in economics in 1950. He remained at Harvard to complete his master's in 1952, and married Rachel Mellinger, a Radcliffe College student, in 1954. Schlesinger began teaching economics at the University of Virginia in 1955, a year before he completed his doctorate in economics.

Schlesinger wrote and published his first book, *The Political Economy of National Security* (1960), while at the University of Virginia, and this drew the attention of the RAND Corporation, a nonprofit think tank providing research to the US Armed Forces. Schlesinger accepted a position with RAND in 1963 and became their director of strategic studies in 1967.

In 1969, President Richard Nixon asked Schlesinger to serve on the Bureau of the Budget, where he worked to create new guidelines for military spending. Nixon promoted Schlesinger in 1971 to chair of the Atomic Energy Commission. While in this position, Schlesinger instituted dramatic environmental overhauls to address safety issues in the nuclear power industry.

Schlesinger replaced Richard Helms as director of the Central Intelligence Agency in 1973. After examining the agency, Schlesinger instituted major departmental changes, dismissing more than one thousand employees. He also uncovered evidence of widespread illegal activities that were not made public until 2007. That same year, Nixon appointed Schlesinger to serve as secretary of defense, as the military was slowly pulling troops away from the Vietnam War. Schlesinger suggested major changes to nuclear defense policies that were unpopular with other military leaders. Though President Gerald Ford retained Schlesinger as secretary of defense after Nixon's resignation, Schlesinger clashed with Ford over issues including amnesty for draft evasion and the military budget. Due to ongoing personality conflicts, Ford dismissed Schlesinger from the position in 1975.

In 1976, Schlesinger met with Jimmy Carter during the governor's presidential campaign and Carter asked Schlesinger to serve as the nation's first secretary of energy, a new branch of the government formed through the consolidation of fifty formerly separate departments and agencies. Carter and Schlesinger agreed that nuclear power was a better option than reliance on fossil fuels, but congressional and media criticism of Schlesinger's performance led Carter to dismiss Schlesinger from the position in 1979.

Following his departure from Carter's administration, Schlesinger wrote a number of books on politics and the economy, including *American Security and Energy Policy* (1980) and *America at Century's End* (1989), while also serving as an informal presidential adviser. Schlesinger testified to Congress on the disposal and storage of nuclear weapons and later on the controversial prisoner abuse scandal at Abu Ghraib Prison in 2004. He also became involved in private industry, serving as a chairman for the MITRE Corporation. Schlesinger died on March 27, 2014, age eighty-five, from complications due to pneumonia. He was predeceased by his wife, who died of cancer in 1995, and is survived by the couple's eight children and eleven grandchildren.

See Current Biography Illustrated 1973.

Pete Seeger

Born: New York, New York; May 3, 1919
Died: New York, New York; January 27, 2014
Occupation: Musician and activist

Pete Seeger played a major role in the American folk music revival of the 1960s and helped to popularize and preserve a wide variety of regional American music styles, including country, blues, and Appalachian folk music. Seeger was also a dedicated antiwar and civil rights activist who used his music to spread the message of peace throughout his career.

Seeger was born into a musical family with a long history of social activism. Seeger's father was a prominent musicologist who worked with folklorist Alan Lomax and his mother was a teacher and concert violinist. Seeger studied sociology at Harvard University, where he briefly became involved in the Young Communist League, but left the university in 1938 after a transformative visit to a North Carolina music festival where he discovered Appalachian music. Seeger learned to play the five-string banjo and developed a repertoire of folk and country songs from the 1920s and 1930s. Seeger began collaborating with folksinger Woody Guthrie in 1940, later forming a band called the Almanac Singers. During World War II, the Almanac Singers gained fame singing patriotic songs with antifascist themes.

Seeger was drafted in 1942 and served with Army Special Services, entertaining troops at US bases in the South Pacific. In 1943, Seeger married Toshi Aline Ohta, with whom he later had three children. In late 1948, Seeger, Lee Hays, Fred Hellerman, and Ronnie Gilbert formed a new folk band called the Weavers, which became nationally famous for performing a repertoire of cover songs and political protest music. One of the band's biggest hits was a 1950 cover of the song "Goodnight, Irene" by blues guitarist Lead Belly (Huddie Ledbetter).

In 1952, the Weavers disbanded, partially due to negative press suggesting that Seeger had Communist associations. In 1955, Seeger was called before the House Un-American Activities Committee, where he protested the committee's persecution of American citizens. Seeger was convicted of contempt of Congress and sentenced to one year in prison, though the conviction was overturned before Seeger was incarcerated.

Many of Seeger's songs became famous through other artists, such as "We Shall Overcome," an adaptation of old spirituals which became a staple of the civil rights movement, and "If I Had a Hammer," which became a major hit for the folk group Peter, Paul and Mary. He was one of the founding board members of the Newport Folk Festival, which was first held in 1959. In 1965, Seeger had a short-lived television series, *Rainbow Quest*, which featured live performances by folk musicians such as blues singer Mississippi John Hurt and country star Johnny Cash. In the late 1960s, Seeger took an interest in environmentalism, initiating the Hudson River cleanup project, which remained active into the twenty-first century.

After decades of influence, Seeger began to receive national recognition in the 1980s and 1990s. He received a Grammy for lifetime achievement in 1993, the National Medal of Arts from the National Endowment for the Arts in 1994, and was inducted into the Rock and Roll Hall of Fame in 1996 for his role as an early influence on the genre. *Pete* (1996) and *At 89* (2008) each won the Grammy for best traditional folk album, and in 2011 *Tomorrow's Children* won the Grammy for best children's music.

Seeger remained active until shortly before his death, releasing recordings and giving live performances into his nineties. Seeger died on January 27, 2014, at the age of ninety-four, after a sudden illness and hospitalization. He was predeceased by his wife, Toshi, in 2013. Seeger is survived by two half-sisters, Peggy and Barbara; his son, Daniel; his two daughters, Tinya and Mika; eight grandchildren; and four great-grandchildren.

See Current Biography Illustrated 1963.

Ariel Sharon

Born: Kfar Malal, Palestine; February 26, 1928
Died: Tel Hashomer, Israel; January 11, 2014
Occupation: Israeli politician

Former Israeli prime minister Ariel Sharon was an important architect of the modern Israeli government and one of the nation's most respected military leaders. Toward the end of his life, Sharon helped to orchestrate a plan for the creation of a Palestinian state.

Sharon was born Ariel Scheinerman on the Kfar Malal moshav, a semicollective farming community outside of Tel Aviv. His parents immigrated to Israel from Russia following the Russian Revolution and became farmers. Sharon joined the Haganah, an underground paramilitary group that later became part of the Israeli Defense Forces. Following a trend within the Zionist movement, Sharon abandoned his foreign surname Scheinerman and took the Hebrew name Sharon.

Sharon served in the 1948 war and was wounded in a battle against the Jordanian Arab Legion. That same year, he married Romanian immigrant Margalit Zimmerman, with whom he had a son, Gur. In 1952, Sharon moved with his family to Jerusalem where he took classes in Middle Eastern studies at the Hebrew University. The following year, Sharon was integral in the formation of the country's first elite special operations division, Unit 101. After his first wife died in a tragic car accident in 1962, Sharon married his former wife's younger sister, Lily, with whom he had two children. Sharon became nationally famous for his military leadership during the Yom Kippur War of 1973, partially for his daring tactics that helped to defeat the Egyptian army.

Sharon was one of the architects of the Likud Party, which emerged from a political union between the Liberal Party and the Herut Party and won election to the Knesset, Israel's parliament, in 1973. In 1977, Sharon became the agricultural minister under Prime Minister Menachem Begin, where he played a role in the 1979 Israeli-Egyptian Peace Treaty. Sharon became the defense minister in 1981 and sanctioned the invasion of Lebanon in 1982. Sharon's role in the conflict was controversial, with some praising his actions and others accusing him of using military force to exact retribution for Palestinian attacks. Due to this controversy, Sharon was removed from his post as defense minister in 1983.

Sharon gradually restored his political reputation and, as the country shifted toward strong military leadership, he was able to win the election to the premiership in 2001. That same year, Sharon contributed to the Road Map for Peace plan, organized through the United States and the European Union, which set out a plan for the creation of a Palestinian state. Sharon surprised many of his constituents when he announced plans for a withdrawal of Jewish settlers from the Gaza Strip in 2003. Sharon also left the Likud party to form a centrist party known as Kadima in 2005.

Sharon had a long history of high blood pressure and suffered a stroke in 2006 that resulted in his being incapacitated and hospitalized. Sharon remained in a long-term care facility for the next eight years or so in a comatose state until his death on January 11, 2014, at the age of eighty-five. Sharon was predeceased by his wife, Lily, in 2000, and his son Gur, who died in a firearms accident in 1967. He was survived by two sons, Omri and Gilad, from his second marriage.

See Current Biography 1981, 2002.

Eduard Shevardnadze

Born: Mamati, Georgia; January 25, 1928
Died: Tbilisi, Georgia; July 7, 2014
Occupation: Georgian politician

Eduard Amvrosiyevich Shevardnadze was a politician in the eastern European nation of Georgia who served as foreign minister to USSR president Mikhail Gorbachev. A controversial leader, Shevardnadze was the second president of Georgia following the country's split from the Soviet Union.

Shevardnadze was born in 1928 in Mamati, Georgia, a small village near the Black Sea. In interviews Shevardnadze revealed that his parents hoped he would become a doctor, but Shevardnadze became interested in politics and gravitated toward the Communist Party as a teenager. Shevardnadze joined the Georgian branch of the Soviet Communist Party in 1948 as a member of Komsomol, a youth organization for young Communist leaders. There Shevardnadze served as political instructor. In 1951 Shevardnadze met and married Nanuli Tsagareishvili, a camp counselor for the Pioneers preteen Communist organization.

Shevardnadze became a minister of public order for the party in 1965 and, three years later, was promoted to interior minister. In both positions Shevardnadze worked closely with the KGB and was rumored to have gained a reputation as a tough negotiator and interrogator of political prisoners. In the early 1970s Shevardnadze reported corruption among Georgian leaders to the Communist Party leaders in Russia and was rewarded with an appointment to first secretary of the Georgian branch of the party. By 1978 he had been promoted to the Politburo, the highest level of Soviet government. In 1985

General Secretary Mikhail Gorbachev, Shevardnadze's former colleague in the Komsomol, chose him to serve as foreign minister, a decision that shocked many analysts. Shevardnadze took a moderate stance as foreign minister, and Gorbachev was pleased with his performance. He and Gorbachev ended the Soviet-Afghan War, allowed the Berlin Wall to fall, and facilitated rapprochement with the West, actions that variously drew praise and condemnation. However, political infighting convinced him to leave the position in 1990. Gorbachev repeatedly attempted to convince him to return to the office, which he did for the final month of the Soviet Union, from November through December 1991.

The Soviet Union's collapse led to independence for Georgia in April 1991, and Shevardnadze was summoned to Georgia to help bring order to the country after the ouster of democratically elected president Zviad Gamsakhurdia. Shevardnadze became interim prime minister, and political opponents attempted to assassinate him in 1992 with a car bomb. He survived the attempt without serious injury and became the president of Georgia in 1995. Political opposition to his presidency did not stop, and Shevardnadze survived another car bomb in 1995. The third attempt on his life came in 1998, when he and his entourage were ambushed, resulting in the deaths of one of the attackers and two presidential guards.

Shevardnadze was reelected in 2000, but the economic collapse was imminent and a series of armed conflicts between police and political opponents weakened the government. In November 2003 Shevardnadze resigned in the midst of widespread accusations of fraud in the nation's 2002 and 2003 elections. Shervardnadze's wife died in 2004, and he remained in Georgia, occasionally commentating on politics in news reports. Shevardnadze died in 2014 at age eighty-six. His survivors are thought to include his son, Pata; daughter, Monana; and four grandchildren.

See Current Biography Illustrated 1986.

Dick Smith

Born: Larchmont, New York; June 26, 1922
Died: Los Angeles, California; July 30, 2014
Occupation: Makeup artist

Richard Emerson "Dick" Smith was an Academy Award–winning makeup artist known for his work on The Exorcist and Amadeus. Smith was a mentor to a generation of makeup artists active in the 1980s and 1990s.

Smith was born in 1922 in Larchmont, New York, and attended Yale University, where he was enrolled in a premed program with hopes of becoming a dentist. Smith later said that a chance encounter with the book *Paint, Powder and Makeup* (1938) inspired his interest in makeup artistry. Smith graduated from Yale in 1943 and enlisted in the army during the last years of World War II. In 1945 he applied to WNBC Television as a makeup director.

Smith worked with WNBC for fourteen years, during which time he pioneered new ways of using foam latex to create more flexible, realistic effects. Smith's innovations later spread throughout the field and he became known as one of the most innovative makeup artists of his era. Smith received critical acclaim for his makeup for the 1959 television adaptation of *The Moon and Sixpence*, in which he transformed Laurence Olivier into a leprosy sufferer.

Smith gradually transitioned into film, beginning with *Requiem for a Heavyweight* (1962), in which Smith transformed Anthony Quinn into an aging boxer. Smith also published a book on the subject, *Do It Yourself Monster Makeup Handbook* (1965), which inspired a generation of young makeup artists. Smith won an Emmy Award for the television film *Mark Twain Tonight* in 1967, where he made actor Hal Holbrook into an aged Mark Twain. His next major challenge was the 1970 film *Little Big Man*, for which Smith needed to make Dustin Hoffman appear to be 121 years old. Smith said later that he spent weeks researching and sculpting test pieces for the project, and his work on the film made him the most sought-after makeup artist in Hollywood.

For the 1972 film *The Godfather*, Smith radically changed Marlon Brando's face using a device called a dental plumper that gives the mouth and cheeks an engorged appearance. He was also responsible for making the actors appear to bleed when shot. Among his most challenging and memorable jobs was creating the illusion that actor Linda Blair was possessed by an evil spirit in the 1973 film *The Exorcist*. Another memorable effect came in the 1980 film *Altered States*, in which Smith used a full-body latex suit to transform William Hurt's body into a grotesque blob.

Smith won an Academy Award for the 1984 film *Amadeus*, in which he created a detailed aging effect to make actor F. Murray Abraham look like an elderly Salieri. Smith also created a text- and video-based self-study makeup course, from which many professional makeup artists learned their skills. Smith's final film credit was the 1999 movie *House on Haunted Hill*, which he completed shortly before retiring. In 2011, Smith received an honorary Academy Award for his lifetime contribution to makeup arts. Smith was predeceased by his wife Jocelyn De Rosa in 2003 and died on July 30, 2014, age ninety-two, after suffering a fractured hip. He is survived by his two sons, Douglas and David.

See Current Biography 1959.

Gregory White Smith

Born: Ithaca, New York; October 4, 1951
Died: Aiken, South Carolina; April 10, 2014
Occupation: Biographer and lawyer

Gregory White Smith was a Pulitzer Prize–winning biographer best known for his controversial account of the life of artist Jackson Pollock and the definitive biography of Vincent van Gogh. He also coauthored sixteen other books, five of which were best sellers; created an annual ranking of American lawyers that has had widespread readership for three decades; and partnered with New York's Juilliard School to create an ambitious music program in South Carolina and Georgia.

Smith was born in 1951 in Ithaca, New York, but spent most of his youth in Columbus, Ohio, where his parents, William and Kathryn, operated a small chain of motels. In 1973 he received a bachelor's degree in English literature from Colby College in Maine. He attended law school at Harvard University where he met his future spouse, Steven Naifeh, a fellow law student. While in law school, Smith was diagnosed with a hemangiopericytoma, a rare type of brain tumor, but was told that it appeared to be benign.

After earning law degrees in 1977, Smith and Naifeh moved to San Francisco. For a brief time, Smith wrote and edited legal briefs, but within a few months both men decided to leave the legal profession and returned to Harvard. Smith obtained a master's degree in education in 1978, while Naifeh received a master's in fine arts.

Together, they began collaborating on writing projects, starting with a self-help fashion guide, *Moving Up in Style* (1980). In 1983 they published *The Best Lawyers in America*, the first of their successful book series Best Lawyers Inc., which rates and describes the careers of prominent American lawyers. The latest edition of the series was published in 2014.

In 1987, after suffering from facial paralysis, Smith learned that his tumor had grown and was told that he might have only a few months to live. He pursued experimental treatment options and was eventually able to have surgery to remove most of the tumor. During this time, Smith and Naifeh published a best-selling true-crime book, *The Mormon Murders* (1988). The couple's next book, published in 1990, was an eight-year enterprise, involving thousands of interviews. The book, *Jackson Pollock: An American Saga*, won the 1991 Pulitzer Prize for biography and was a finalist for the 1990 National Book Award.

While a critical success, Smith and Naifeh's biography was highly controversial within the art history community. Several of the nation's leading Pollock scholars criticized Smith and Naifeh for sensationalizing the life of the artist. They defended their book, speculating that professional art analysts felt threatened by outsiders intruding on their domain.

The couple continued to write and publish regularly, including a largely well-received biography of the artist van Gogh. In 1990 they moved to Aiken, South Carolina, where they purchased and renovated a sixty-room Vanderbilt-Whitney mansion. From this base, they partnered with New York's Juilliard School and cofounded, with Dr. Sandra Field, an annual series of concerts and educational programs, which is known as the Juilliard-in-Aiken Festival.

Throughout his life, Smith continued seeking aggressive treatment for his tumor, undergoing more than a dozen separate surgeries. In 2011 Smith and Naifeh married in New York. In April 2014 Smith died at his Aiken home from complications arising from the tumor. He is survived by his husband; a sister, Linda Hirata; a niece; and two nephews.

See Current Biography 1998.

Clyde Snow

Born: Fort Worth, Texas; January 7, 1928
Died: Norman, Oklahoma; May 16, 2014
Occupation: Forensic anthropologist

Clyde Collins Snow was a forensic anthropologist who investigated the remains of famous historical figures and helped to bring murderers and perpetrators of genocide to justice.

Snow was born in Fort Worth, Texas, in 1928, the only child of Wister Clyde Snow, a community doctor, and Sarah Isabel Snow, her husband's clinic assistant. He earned an associate's degree from the New Mexico Military Institute in 1947; a bachelor's degree from Eastern New Mexico University in 1951; and a master's degree in zoology from Texas Tech University in 1955. Uncertain which direction to go in his career, Snow spent three years in the US Air Force before returning to his education at the University of Arizona, where he earned a PhD in anthropology in 1967.

Snow began working as a forensic anthropologist for the Federal Aviation Administration's laboratory in Oklahoma City, Oklahoma, in the 1960s. From examining the remains of airline accidents, Snow was able to help the FAA refine aircraft safety and escape procedures. By the late 1970s, Snow was considered one of the leading experts in his field. In 1978 he testified before the US Congress to confirm the identity of the remains of John F. Kennedy. In the late 1970s Snow was consulted to identify the bodies of victims murdered in a Chicago suburb by serial killer John Wayne Gacy. In 1979 he investigated the remains of the Chicago American Airlines crash that resulted in the deaths of 271 passengers and two people on the ground. Snow managed to identify twelve passengers from the badly damaged remains, and his role in the investigation gained national attention.

In 1980 Snow retired from the FAA and began teaching classes in investigative archaeology at the University of Oklahoma. In 1983 Snow and facial reconstruction artist Betty Pat Gatliff collaborated to reconstruct the face of Egyptian pharaoh Tutankhamun. Photos of the resulting image were published in a variety of magazines, and their work made international news. In 1984 Snow traveled to Argentina where he took part in investigations aimed at discovering the fate of thousands of political dissidents killed by the military junta that ruled from 1976 to 1983. Snow's evidence was used to help convict five military leaders responsible for ordering the murder of civilian opponents.

In 1985 Snow was contracted to investigate a set of remains found in an unmarked grave in Sao Paulo, Brazil. Snow's investigation was the key in confirming the remains as those of Nazi war criminal Joseph Mengele who had fled to Brazil and assumed a new identity after the fall of the Nazi regime. The discovery of Mengele's remains became international news.

In the 1990s Snow continued investigating cases of genocide and war crimes, including the exhuming and identifying of remains in South America and Africa. In 1995 he was one of the specialists called in to identify the bodies of those killed in the Oklahoma City bombing and he also helped to identify victims of the World Trade Center attacks that occurred on September 11, 2001. In 2006 Snow was one of the witnesses at the trial of Saddam Hussein; he provided evidence from his investigation of mass Iraqi graves that was used to prove Hussein's involvement in war crimes.

Snow died in May 2014, at eighty-six, in a hospital in Norman, Oklahoma, after suffering from lung cancer and emphysema. Snow married Jerry Whistler, his fourth wife, in 1970. In addition to his wife, Snow is survived by four daughters and a son from his previous marriages, eight grandchildren, and eight great-grandchildren.

See Current Biography 1997.

Larry Melvin Speakes

Born: Cleveland, Mississippi; September 13, 1939
Died: Cleveland, Mississippi; January 10, 2014
Occupation: Journalist

Larry Melvin Speakes was a journalist who worked in the press departments of Richard Nixon, Gerald Ford, and Bob Dole. In the 1980s, Speakes became the acting White House press secretary under President Ronald Reagan.

Speaks grew up in Merigold, Mississippi, and attended the University of Mississippi in Oxford, where he studied journalism. While an undergraduate, Speakes worked as an assistant editor at the *Daily Mississippian* and, after graduation, he transferred to the *Oxford Eagle*, where he became news editor in 1961. In 1965, Speakes became managing editor of the *Bolivar Commercial* newspaper in Cleveland, Mississippi, and then worked as general manager and editor for Progress Publishers from 1966 to 1968.

In 1968, Speakes was offered a position working as press secretary for Senator James O. Eastland of Mississippi, who was the chair of the Senate Judiciary Committee at the time. Speakes spent six years working for Eastland, handling the press for the confirmation of four Supreme Court justices and Eastland's 1972 reelection campaign.

In 1974, Speakes was hired as a staff assistant in Richard Nixon's administration. Speakes had the difficult duty of working as the press secretary for the special counsel to President Nixon during the Watergate hearings. Following Nixon's resignation, Speakes remained at the White House, becoming assistant press secretary to President Gerald R. Ford. Speakes later worked as press secretary for Bob Dole during his unsuccessful 1976 vice presidential campaign with Ford.

From 1977 to 1981, Speakes served as vice president of the public relations firm Hill and Knowlton. After Reagan's election to the presidency in 1980, Speakes was hired as deputy press secretary under Jim Brady. On March 30, 1981, Brady was gravely wounded in a failed assassination attempt on President Reagan. Brady was permanently disabled by the attack, and Speakes became the acting press secretary for the remainder of Reagan's presidency; despite carrying out all the duties of the press secretary, Speakes retained the title of deputy press secretary in deference to Brady. Speakes remained with Reagan until 1987, and he had the difficult duty of attempting to defray growing public dissatisfaction with the president surrounding the Iran-Contra affair.

In 1988, Speakes published his memoir, *Speaking Out*, in which he admitted to falsely attributing two quotations to President Reagan that were widely cited by the media. The controversy led to Speakes's resignation from his position as senior vice president for communications at Merrill Lynch.

Speakes retired to Mississippi where he married his third wife, Aleta Sindelar Speakes, in 2001. Speakes died at the age of seventy-four on January 10, 2014, in Cleveland, Mississippi. Speakes was survived by his daughter, Sondra "Sandy" Speakes Huerta; sons Scott and Jeremy; six grandchildren; and one great-grandchild.

See Current Biography 1985.

Thomas Richard St. George

Born: Simpson, Minnesota; November 23, 1919
Died: Rochester, Minnesota; July 29, 2014
Occupation: Journalist and author

Thomas Richard St. George was a journalist and author known for his semiautobiographical accounts of his experiences as a US soldier abroad during World War II.

St. George was born in Simpson, Minnesota, in November 1919, the only child of John and Cecelia (née Kennedy) St. George. Nicknamed "Ozzie" as a child, St. George took an early interest in writing and journalism and enrolled in the University of Minnesota's School of Journalism, where he studied until he was drafted into the army and served in the Thirty-Second Infantry. Due to his experience with journalism, St. George was assigned to work with *Yank* magazine, providing coverage of the war from stations in Australia, New Guinea, and the Philippines.

While serving in the army, St. George wrote the book *C/O Postmaster*, which provides a semiautobiographical account of his experiences in Australia in 1942. The book became a best seller and was a Book-of-the-Month Club selection in 1943. St. George met Amelia "Mimi" Vitali, a Philadelphia native who had become a staff sergeant in the Women's Army Corps in Australia, and the couple married while stationed together in the Philippines. After returning to the United States, they had a second wedding in Philadelphia. In 1945, St. George published the sequel to *C/O Postmaster*, *Proceed without Delay*.

St. George then moved to Southern California, where he worked as a screenwriter briefly before returning to journalism, which included stints writing for newspapers in San Diego and Philadelphia. Returning to his home state of Minnesota, he was hired at the *Pioneer Press*, where he wrote a Sunday column titled Slice of Wry. A talented cartoonist as well, he published a number of cartoons during his career. After suffering a heart attack in 1979, he began working at the newspaper's copy desk.

Following his retirement from journalism in 1994, St. George became a novelist, writing a series of short satirical novels around the character of Edward Temperance Devlin. The novels were later published in a collected format as the *Eddie Devlin Compendium*. St. George's first wife, Mimi, died in 1994; he then married Silvana Hickey of Minnesota. He was predeceased by his son, Dennis, in 2004, and by Silvana in early 2014. St. George died on July 29, 2014, age ninety-four, at Saint Marys Campus of the Mayo Clinic Hospital in Rochester, Minnesota. He is survived by his daughters Diane,

Andrea, and Lisa; seven grandchildren; and six great-grandchildren.

See Current Biography 1944.

Jesse L. Steinfeld

Born: West Aliquippa, Pennsylvania; January 6, 1927
Died: Pomona, California; August 5, 2014
Occupation: Surgeon general

Jesse Leonard Steinfeld was a former US surgeon general known for his campaign against tobacco and his opposition to television violence during President Richard Nixon's first term.

Steinfeld was born in 1927 in West Aliquippa, Pennsylvania. A gifted student, Steinfeld finished high school at sixteen and enrolled at the University of Pittsburgh, where, motivated by his father's premature death due to heavy smoking, he entered a premedical program. When he finished his bachelor's degree in 1945, he enrolled in what is now Case Western Reserve University, earning a medical degree in 1949 with a focus on oncology.

Steinfeld completed an internship at Cedars of Lebanon Hospital (now known as Cedars-Sinai Medical Center) in Los Angeles, California, and had a medical residency in oncology at the University of California, San Francisco. In 1954, Steinfeld took a position at the National Cancer Institute of the National Institutes of Health in Maryland, where he remained until 1959, when he moved back to California to teach at the University of Southern California.

Steinfeld returned to the National Institutes of Health in 1968. Bob Finch, an organizer for Nixon's administration, approached him about becoming the new surgeon general. Although he was planning on moving back to California, Steinfeld agreed and took office in December of 1969. Among the first public health officials to caution against the dangers of secondhand smoke, he famously removed all of the ashtrays from his offices and replaced them with signs thanking others for not smoking. Also refusing to meet with tobacco lobbyists, he promoted the 1972 surgeon general's report that linked smoking with lung disease and cancer. Steinfeld's campaign resulted in larger warning labels from cigarette manufacturers that were less ambiguous regarding the links between smoking and illness.

In addition to his antismoking crusade, Steinfeld was active and outspoken on a number of other issues. He produced public service announcements regarding fluoridation of water and the use of the pesticide DDT. Steinfeld also spoke out against violence on television, which he believed was harmful to children, creating opposition to his role as surgeon general within television corporations. During these heated times, Nixon ultimately asked for Steinfeld's resignation shortly after he won reelection in 1972. After Steinfeld's resignation, Nixon allowed the surgeon general position to remain vacant throughout the rest of his term in an effort to avoid further conflicts with powerful commercial industries.

Steinfeld was one of only two surgeons general to ever be forced out of office. Following his resignation, Steinfeld and his family moved to Rochester, Minnesota, where he directed the Mayo Clinic Comprehensive Cancer Center for several years. Steinfeld then returned to teaching and retired as the president of the Medical College of Georgia. Following complications resulting from a stroke, Steinfeld died on August 5, 2014, age eighty-seven, in Pomona, California. He was survived by his wife of more than sixty-one years, Gen; three daughters; and two grandchildren.

See Current Biography 1974.

Michael A. Stepovich

Born: Fairbanks, Alaska; March 12, 1919
Died: San Diego, California; February 14, 2014
Occupation: Lawyer and governor

Lawyer and politician Michael Anthony Stepovich was the last governor of the Territory of Alaska and is considered an instrumental figure in the territory's 1959 transition to statehood. Stepovich remained active in Alaska state politics and led a prominent Fairbanks law firm until his retirement in 1978.

Stepovich was born in Fairbanks, Alaska, in 1919, the only child of Olga and Marko Stepovich, a miner who emigrated from Montenegro to follow the Klondike gold rush into the Alaska territory. After his parents divorced, Stepovich moved with his mother to Portland, Oregon, and he later attended Gonzaga University in Spokane, Washington, graduating in 1941. Stepovich then enrolled in law school at Notre Dame University, graduating in 1943.

Stepovich served in the navy during World War II and was discharged in 1947, returning to Fairbanks, Alaska, to establish a legal practice as a defense attorney. That same year, Stepovich married Matilda Baricevic, with whom he would have thirteen children over more than fifty years of marriage. Stepovich joined the territorial Republican Party and was elected to the territorial house of representatives in 1950. In 1952, he was elected to the territorial senate, where he became minority leader of the senate in 1955.

In the 1950s, the question of Alaskan statehood was contentious both in the US Congress, where some feared the financial obligation of adding another state to the union, and in Alaska, where some preferred the relative freedom of territorial independence. Upon the recommendation of the Secretary of the Interior Fred Seaton, President Dwight D. Eisenhower chose Stepovich, who did not lobby for the office, as the new governor of the territory in 1957, after the resignation of the former governor.

Stepovich was the territory's first native-born elected governor and became one of the most visible proponents of statehood. Stepovich traveled throughout the territory and appeared before Congress on numerous occasions as part of his statehood campaign. He also famously addressed the issue when he appeared on a 1958 episode of the television game show *What's My Line?* In June of that year, Stepovich was featured on the cover of *Time* magazine in an article addressing the Alaska debate. On July 7, 1958, President Eisenhower signed the Alaskan Statehood Bill, officially making Alaska the forty-ninth state as of January 1959.

Stepovich then campaigned for one of the state's two seats on the US Senate, running against Democrat Ernest Gruening, who had served as Territorial Governor for thirteen years. Despite strong Republican support, including Vice President Richard M. Nixon's visit to Alaska to lobby on behalf of Stepovich, the Democrats swept the elections and Stepovich lost his bid for the Senate. Stepovich ran in the gubernatorial elections of 1962, challenging incumbent governor William A. Egan, and lost a close race to Egan, who retained his seat.

Stepovich retired from politics in 1978, and relocated his family to Medford, Oregon. In 2009, Stepovich received an honorary doctorate from the University of Alaska Fairbanks for his contributions to the state. Stepovich was predeceased by his wife in 2003, and died on February 14, 2014, age ninety-four, after suffering a head injury from a fall while visiting his son in San Diego, California. Stepovich is survived by thirteen children and thirty-seven grandchildren.

See Current Biography 1958.

Robert S. Strauss

Born: Lockhart, Texas; October 19, 1918
Died: Washington, DC; March 19, 2014
Occupation: Ambassador and political lobbyist

Robert Schwarz Strauss was a Democratic Party chief who served as a presidential adviser and a US ambassador to Russia. Strauss was also a founding partner of a prosperous law firm and worked as a lobbyist in Washington.

Strauss was born in 1918 in Lockhart, Texas, where his father Charles, a German immigrant, and his mother Edith owned a general store. In interviews, Strauss said that his mother hoped

he would become the first Jewish governor of Texas. Strauss attended the University of Texas, graduating with his law degree in 1941 and marrying Helen Jacobs of Dallas the same year. While in college, Strauss also volunteered for the congressional campaign of Hubert Humphrey and worked as a clerk in the state capitol.

Rather than serve in the military during World War II, Strauss opted to become a special agent with the FBI, where he worked until 1945. That same year, Strauss and his friend Richard Gump formed the law firm of Strauss and Gump, specializing in energy law, which later grew into the powerful international firm Akin Gump Strauss Hauer & Feld.

In 1962 Strauss became a fundraiser for his college friend John Connally's successful Texas gubernatorial campaign. Connally appointed Strauss to the Democratic National Committee in 1966. In 1968 Strauss worked on Humphrey's presidential campaign. Though Nixon defeated Humphrey in the election, Strauss became a respected party leader, and was named national chair of the Democratic Party in 1972.

Strauss appointed Jimmy Carter chair of the Democratic National Committee's 1974 congressional campaign and then supported Carter's bid for the presidency in 1976. In 1977 Carter appointed Strauss trade negotiator for his administration and Strauss was instrumental in the completion of the Trade Act of 1979. Carter then selected Strauss to be his personal representative in the Middle East peace talks. Strauss was chair of Carter's 1980 campaign; after Carter lost to Reagan, Strauss became one of Reagan's unofficial advisers. In this capacity, Strauss famously advised the president to make major changes to his administration in response to the Iran-Contra scandal. In 1981 Carter awarded Strauss the Presidential Medal of Freedom.

In 1991 President George H. W. Bush chose Strauss as the US ambassador to Russia, hoping that Strauss's experience with forging political relationships across party lines could help the United States to develop stronger ties to various parties within Russia's changing political landscape. Strauss became a mentor to Russian business leaders and had meetings with Boris Yeltsin and Mikhail Gorbachev. He also sponsored the Freedom Support Act (1992), which gave $24 billion in US aid to Russia and Eastern Europe.

Strauss resigned in 1992 and returned to his law practice. In addition to his work as a lawyer, Strauss often traveled as a public speaker and lecturer and was deeply involved in property brokering as a side business. Strauss and his wife maintained homes in Dallas, Florida, and California, but had their primary home in Washington, DC. Strauss died on March 19, 2014, age ninety-five, in Washington. He was predeceased by his wife in 2006, and is survived by his brother, Theodore; two sons, Robert and Richard; his daughter, Susan Breen; seven grandchildren; and six great-grandchildren.

See Current Biography Illustrated 1974, 1992.

Elaine Stritch

Born: Detroit, Michigan; February 2, 1925
Died: Birmingham, Michigan; July 17, 2014
Occupation: Actor

Elaine Stritch was an actor and singer who appeared on stage for more than sixty years and became famous for her unique approach to stage comedy and acerbic wit. Over the course of her career, Stritch received numerous Tony Award nominations and won Emmy and Tony Awards for one-woman shows in which she combined biographical reflections, humor, and musical performance.

Stritch was born in Detroit, Michigan, in 1925, the youngest of three daughters born into a middle-class Catholic family. Stritch left home at seventeen and moved to New York, where she enrolled in a drama program at the New School for Social Research. Stritch made her stage debut in 1946, and had her first role in a Broadway musical in the 1947 revue *Angel in the Wings*. Stritch first gained widespread media attention for her scene-stealing role in the 1952 revival of the Rogers and Hart musical *Pal Joey*, in which she sang the song "Zip," which became a standard in her singing appearances. Stritch's unique, gravelly singing voice made her stand out among other singers of the era, and she was increasingly in demand for appearances in comedic musical roles throughout the 1950s and '60s. Stritch garnered her first Tony Award nomination for her appearance in the 1955 play *Bus Stop*, and in 1958 had her first starring role on Broadway in the musical *Goldilocks*.

In the late 1950s Stritch befriended writer Noel Coward, who wrote his 1961 musical *Sail Away* around a character he created for Stritch. Though the musical was not an overall success, Stritch's performance won praise from critics and earned her another Tony Award nomination. Her next nomination came in 1970 for her role as a jaded society lady in Stephen Sondheim's *Company*.

Stritch continued appearing on stage into the 1980s. After the death of her husband John Bay in 1982, Stritch developed a serious drinking problem that led her to leave the stage until the 1990s. During this period, she acted in several films, beginning with an acclaimed performance in Woody Allen's film *September* (1987). Supporting roles in a variety of films followed as well as appearances in television series including *Law & Order* and *The Cosby Show*.

Stritch returned to Broadway in the mid-1990s, and won another Tony nomination for her appearance in Edward Albee's *A Delicate Balance* in 1996. Stritch finally won her first Tony Award for her critically acclaimed one woman show *Elaine Stritch at Liberty*, which began Off-Broadway in 2001 and moved to Broadway in 2002. The show was later broadcast on HBO where it won an Emmy Award. In 2007, Stritch was cast for her recurring role as Colleen Donaghy in the popular television series *30 Rock*, further contributing to a resurgence in her popularity. Still performing regularly in her eighties, Stritch was the subject of an award-winning 2014 documentary, *Elaine Stritch: Shoot Me*, in which she discusses her life on the stage and experience with aging. Suffering from increasing health problems, Stritch returned to Birmingham, Michigan, to be close to her remaining family. Stritch died on July 17, 2014, age eighty-nine, at her home in Birmingham.

See Current Biography 1988.

Adolfo Suárez

Born: Cebreros, Spain; September 25, 1932
Died: Madrid, Spain; March 23, 2014
Occupation: Spanish prime minister, politician

Despite facing prodigious odds as well as cynicism from apprehensive critics upon his appointment as prime minister in 1976, Adolfo Suárez made a profound impact on Spain's new government in the wake of Francisco Franco's era of totalitarianism. Tasked with the ambitious goal of steering the country toward democracy, Suárez began by holding the first egalitarian election in over forty years. Although he was in office for less than five years, Suárez is credited with such reformative measures as aiding in the implementation of a new constitution and legalizing the previously unsanctioned Communist Party in an effort to promote political autonomy.

Suárez was trained as a lawyer and got his first real political experiences as part of Franco's government. After ascending through different roles within the National Movement, he also served as the governor of Segovia. Aside from his democratic triumphs as prime minister, he further proved his devotion to his country during an event that occurred shortly after his resignation in 1981. Trapped in the midst of a military coup on parliament, Suárez refused to acquiesce to the officers' commands. In recognition of Suárez's service, King Juan Carlos granted him the title of Duke of Suárez that same year; he continued to receive various honors, titles, and awards throughout the remainder of his life.

After a failed attempt to regain some authority as the leader of a newly formed political party, Suárez ultimately withdrew from politics in 1991, appearing in public for the last time in 2003. Following a long battle with Alzheimer's disease—which eventually robbed him of his memories of his place in Spanish history—and a bout of pneumonia, Suárez died at a hospital in Madrid at the age of eighty-one on March 23, 2014. He is survived by four of his five children: Adolfo, Laura, Sonsoles, and Javier.

See Current Biography 1977.

William H. Sullivan

Born: Cranston, Rhode Island; October 12, 1922
Died: Washington, DC; October 11, 2013
Occupation: Diplomat

William Healy Sullivan was an American diplomat who played a central role in the tense negotiations surrounding American involvement in the secret war in Laos and in the Vietnam War. Sullivan was also the last American ambassador to Iran, leaving just before the Iranian hostage crisis of 1979.

After receiving his bachelor's degree from Brown University, Sullivan served as a naval officer during World War II and was educated at Harvard University and Tufts University's Fletcher School of Law and Diplomacy, where he met his future wife, Marie Johnson. Building on his military connections, Sullivan attained a position in the State Department in 1947. He served under General Douglas MacArthur in Tokyo (1950–52) and as a NATO political officer in Rome (1952–55). From 1960 to 1963 Sullivan was a United Nations adviser to the Bureau of Far Eastern Affairs, and he served under Ambassador at Large W. Averell Harriman during the tense Cuban missile crisis in 1961.

In 1964, under the Lyndon Johnson administration, Sullivan became ambassador to Laos. Sullivan's appointment came at the height of the Laotian Civil War, often called the "secret war," and he helped to coordinate with the Laotian government as US military forced began conducting bombing raids against communist targets moving through the country. Sullivan attempted to use his inside knowledge of Laos to help the military avoid civilian casualties when conducting aerial attacks. He played a key role in organizing the first negotiations with North Vietnamese forces and served as deputy for National Security Adviser Henry Kissinger during the Paris Peace Accords from October 1972 to January 1973, which resulted in the US withdrawal from Vietnam. In 1973 Sullivan was named ambassador to the Philippines, where he served until 1977. In that capacity Sullivan was responsible for negotiating with Philippine president

Ferdinand Marcos to allow South Vietnamese refugees asylum in the wake of the Vietnam War.

In a somewhat surprising turn to his career, President Jimmy Carter assigned Sullivan to take over as ambassador to Iran in 1977. Sullivan's relationship with the Carter administration gradually deteriorated, as Sullivan's advice on dealing with the Iranian Revolution of 1979 went unheeded. In February 1979 Sullivan and the embassy staff were briefly taken hostage by guerillas before being rescued by the Iranian forces led by Ayatollah Ruhollah Khomeini. In the wake of this event and due to his strained relationship with Carter advisers, Sullivan left public service in late 1979, just before militants captured the US embassy in Tehran. Sullivan was the last American ambassador to the country.

From 1979 to 1986 Sullivan was president of the American Assembly, a nonpartisan public policy research forum associated with Columbia University. After retiring from this position, Sullivan and his wife relocated to Cuernavaca, Mexico, where they lived for several years before returning to Washington, DC, in 2000. Sullivan's wife died in 2010, and Sullivan lived the remainder of his life in a Washington retirement community. He died on October 11, 2013, at age ninety. Sullivan is survived by his four children, Anne, John, Peggy, and Mark, and six grandchildren.

See Current Biography 1979.

John Tavener

Born: London, England; January 28, 1944
Died: Child Okeford, England; November 12, 2013
Occupation: Musician, composer

English composer John Tavener was one of the most popular classical composers of the twentieth century, basing much of his work on his spiritual and religious beliefs. Tavener's music was featured in a number of high-profile concerts and British governmental events, including the September 6, 1997, funeral of Princess Diana of Wales.

Tavener's introduction to music came through the Presbyterian Church, where in his youth he worked as an organist. He won his first award for composition while still a student at the Royal Academy of Music, for his 1966 cantata *Cain and Abel*. Tavener's professional career began in 1968 with the release of his now famous cantata *The Whale*, an experimental piece inspired by the biblical story of Jonah and the whale. The British rock group the Beatles brought Tavener's music to national attention when they decided to release *The Whale* and several other compositions through their record label, Apple Records.

A devoutly religious man, Tavener converted to the Eastern Orthodox faith in 1977 and credited this conversion with inspiring many of his later compositions. In interviews Tavener espoused the belief that music was originally meant as a form of spiritual devotion and that Western musicians had unfortunately abandoned this central aspect of musical expression. Despite a stroke in 1979 that left him partially paralyzed, Tavener continued composing. He released a choral composition entitled *The Lamb*, based on a William Blake poem, in 1982, which became popular in Britain for Christmas performances. Among Tavener's most famous compositions is his 1988 composition *The Protecting Veil*, based on a miracle of the Virgin Mary, which became a best seller due to a 1989 performance of the piece by cellist Steven Isserlis.

In 1990 Tavener, a thin six-feet-six, was diagnosed with Marfan syndrome, a genetic disorder that affects the joints, tendons, heart, and brain. Throughout Tavener's career, his health issues became part of his artistic inspiration, and he often used death and redemption as themes in his work. Tavener's greatest commercial success was his 1993 four-part choral composition *Song for Athene*, which became internationally famous when it was featured as the closing music in the 1997 televised funeral of Princess Diana.

Tavener was knighted in 2000 in recognition of his contributions to British artistic culture. His 2003 *The Veil of the Temple*, an experimental seven-hour work, was hailed as one of the most daring compositions of the century. In 2007 Tavener produced another experimental piece, entitled *The Beautiful Names*, based on the ninety-nine names of Allah in the Qur'an, which caused a public controversy when it debuted at Westminster Cathedral. Shortly after its release, Tavener suffered a heart attack that nearly ended his life. Gradually Tavener recovered and began producing new compositions. His last major work was the 2012 *The Death of Ivan Ilyich*, based on a novel by Russian author Leo Tolstoy. Tavener died on November 12, 2013, aged sixty-nine, in Child Okeford, Dorset. He is survived by his second wife, Maryanna Schaefer, and their three children, Sofia, Orlando, and Theodora.

See Current Biography 1999.

Charlie Trotter

Born: Wilmette, Illinois; September 8, 1959
Died: Chicago, Illinois; November 5, 2013
Occupation: Chef, restaurateur

Celebrity chef Charlie Trotter made Chicago one of America's premier dining cities through his eponymous Lincoln Park restaurant, established in 1987. Trotter was a pioneer who helped to create a new take on American cuisine both through his restaurant and through his numerous cookbooks and appearances on television.

Born in the Wilmette suburb of Chicago, Trotter learned to cook by working his way through a series of restaurant jobs after graduating from the University of Wisconsin in 1982 with a degree in political science. By Trotter's own estimation, he worked in forty restaurants in Illinois, California, and France, before he felt he was ready to open his own restaurant. Trotter is often credited with inventing a unique type of American gourmet cooking, based on sourcing fresh, seasonal ingredients. This approach became characteristic of the "local food" and "farm fresh" dining movements of the twenty-first century.

Trotter partnered with his father, Bob Trotter, a wealthy businessman, to open his first restaurant, Charlie Trotter's, in 1987 on West Armitage Avenue in Chicago. The restaurant was an immediate success and received rave reviews from local and national restaurant critics. In 1992 the James Beard Foundation named Trotter the best chef in the Great Lakes, among the first of many accolades bestowed on Trotter and his restaurant. Trotter's flagship restaurant received a five-star rating from the Mobil Guide in 1996 and maintained that rating until closing in 2012.

Trotter capitalized on the success of his restaurant with a series of more than a dozen cookbooks based both on the cuisine of his restaurant and his approach to cooking in general. Trotter's first publication was *Charlie Trotter's* (1994), a book featuring recipes from the restaurant. He then authored, or coauthored, more than a dozen cookbooks, including *Charlie Trotter's Vegetables* (1996), *Charlie Trotter's Desserts* (1998) and *Home Cooking with Charlie Trotter* (2008). In 1998 Trotter was asked to host a television series on PBS, *The Kitchen Sessions with Charlie Trotter*, which also became a major success. In 2000 the James Beard Foundation named it the best cooking show on national television.

Trotter also expanded his business through a number of subsidiary ventures, including a takeout restaurant based on the cuisine at Charlie Trotter's, called Trotter's To Go. In 2004 Trotter opened a seafood restaurant, called C, in Mexico, and in 2008 he opened Restaurant Charlie in Las Vegas, which, although considered another major culinary success, was shuttered in 2010.

In 2012, the mercurial, often critical chef announced that he would be closing his restaurants for a sabbatical to travel and pursue a graduate education. On November 5, 2013, Trotter, aged fifty-four, died of a stroke. Trotter's physician had advised him not to fly because of medication he was taking for high blood pressure and seizures. Days before his death, he had flown to Wyoming to deliver a series of lectures, and early media reports, later disproven, linked this to the chef's death. Trotter is survived by his third wife, Rochelle; his mother, Dona-Lee; two brothers, Thomas and Scott; his sister, Anne Hinkamp; and his son, Dylan.

See Current Biography 1997.

Eli Wallach

Born: New York, New York; December 7, 1915
Died: New York, New York; June 24, 2014
Occupation: Actor

Eli Wallach was a celebrated American actor known for his versatility as a practitioner of the method school of acting and for memorable performances in a variety of film, television, and stage productions. The award-winning Wallach was also honored with a lifetime achievement Oscar in 2010.

Wallach was born New York and raised in the Red Hook neighborhood of Brooklyn in 1915. He earned a bachelor's degree at the University of Texas, Austin, in 1936 before earning a master's degree in education at City College in 1938 in the hope of becoming a teacher. Drawn to the theater, Wallach also studied acting at New York's Neighborhood Playhouse before being drafted for World War II service, spending five years in the Army Medical Corps. Returning to New York, Wallach was a founding member of the Actors Studio and studied with famed method-acting instructor Lee Strasberg. Wallach made his Broadway debut in 1945, and the following year he met actor Anne Jackson at a production of *This Property Is Condemned* and started a romantic relationship. The couple married in 1948 and often starred together in stage productions over the next sixty years. Wallach won a Tony Award for his performance in the 1951 production of *The Rose Tattoo*.

Wallach's first film appearance was in the 1956 film *Baby Doll*, for which he won critical praise and received a Golden Globe nomination for his complex portrayal of an unscrupulous adulterer. Though already well regarded among Hollywood critics, Wallach rose to national fame for his appearance as the Mexican gang leader Calvera in the 1960 film *The Magnificent Seven*. Wallach also won praise for a scene-stealing supporting role in the 1961 John Huston film *The Misfits*. In 1966 Wallach appeared alongside Audrey Hepburn in *How to Steal a Million* and also performed in another iconic role as the con man–gunfighter Tuco in the western *The Good, the Bad, and the Ugly*. The following year Wallach won an Emmy Award for his role in the ABC television film *The Poppy Is Also a Flower* (1966).

In between film and television productions, Wallach returned to the stage often acting alongside his wife. Among Wallace's most acclaimed stage appearances was the 1978 production of *The Diary of Anne Frank*, alongside his wife, and a critically acclaimed performance in the 1979 production of the Tom Stoppard play *Every Good Boy Deserves Favour*. Though he rarely starred in films, Wallach remained in demand for key character and supporting roles throughout the 1980s and '90s. Wallach portrayed a psychiatrist in *Nuts* (1987) and a mafioso in *The Godfather: Part III* (1990). He continued acting into his nineties, and one of his last roles came in the 2010 film *Wall Street: Money Never Sleeps*. Wallach died at his home in Manhattan, New York, in June 2014, at age ninety-eight. He was survived by his wife, Anne; sister Shirley; children Roberta, Katherine, and Peter; and three grandchildren.

See Current Biography 1959.

Lawrence E. Walsh

Born: Port Maitland, Nova Scotia; January 8, 1912
Died: Oklahoma City, Oklahoma; March 19, 2014
Occupation: Lawyer, federal judge

As a corporate litigator, federal judge, and counsel in both the private and public sectors, Lawrence E. Walsh had a lengthy and sometimes controversial legal career. Among his varied roles in the legal arena, the most illustrious became his involvement as the independent counsel during the notorious Iran-Contra affair at the age of seventy-four. After the government scandal first broke in 1986, Walsh came out of retirement and devoted more than six years and millions of dollars to investigating the covert sale of arms to Iran and the forbidden channeling of proceeds to a rebel group. Walsh's relentless efforts, simultaneously commended and criticized, engendered a debate around the judicial practice of appointing a special prosecutor. Battling myriad obstacles, Walsh managed to win some convictions, but many were overturned.

Throughout his career, Walsh's work ranged from defeating organized crime units corrupting New York and New Jersey docks as general counsel for the Waterfront Commission of New York Harbor, to mounting a heavily contentious defense of the drug company Richardson-Merrell. He also spent several years of his career at the prestigious private firm of Davis Polk & Wardwell. In 1975, he was named president of the American Bar Association. Approaching retirement age, he settled in Oklahoma City and joined the firm Crowe & Dunlevy in 1981. Walsh released his memoir *Firewall: The Iran-Contra Conspiracy and Cover-Up* in 1997 and his autobiography *The Gift of Insecurity: A Lawyer's Life* in 2003.

Just over two years after celebrating his one hundredth birthday, Walsh died at his home in Oklahoma City on March 19, 2014. He is survived by Barbara and Janet, his two daughters from his first marriage to Maxine Winton. He is also survived by a daughter, Elizabeth, from his second marriage to Mary Alma Porter, as well as two stepchildren, Sara and Dale.

See Current Biography 1991.

Murray L. Weidenbaum

Born: New York, New York; February 10, 1927
Died: St. Louis, Missouri; March 20, 2014
Occupation: Economist, educator, government official

An authoritative and balanced economist, Murray L. Weidenbaum is best known for his years spent as an advisor for White House revenue and budgetary policies—serving five different presidents throughout his career. Shifting between roles in academia and government throughout his life, in 1969 Weidenbaum began a two-year position as assistant secretary of the Treasury during President Richard Nixon's first term, during which Weidenbaum played a major role in developing and championing Nixon's revenue-sharing strategy. In 1981, President Ronald Reagan chose him to head his Council of Economic Advisers (CEA). In this role, he worked to further the goal of government deregulation while facing an economic recession and impending budget deficits. Weidenbaum also provided sound economic counseling for the Lyndon Johnson and George H. W. Bush administrations.

Weidenbaum spent the majority of his professional career outside of the government in an academic setting, however. From 1964 to 1969, he was a professor of economics and subsequently the chair of the economics department at Washington University in St. Louis. He became the first director of the university's Center for the Study of American Business in 1975—which was renamed in 2001 the Weidenbaum Center on the Economy, Government, and Public Policy. Upon his resignation as leader of the CEA in 1982, he returned to Washington University while continuing to offer government and international guidance and writing several books, including *One-Armed Economist: On the Intersection of Business and Government* (2004) and his memoir *Advising Reagan: Making Economic Policy, 1981–82* (2005).

Not long before his passing, Washington University informed Weidenbaum of its decision to create the Murray Weidenbaum Distinguished Professorship in Economics. Weidenbaum died at the age of eighty-seven on March 20, 2014. He is survived by his wife, Phyllis; their three children, James, Laurie, and Susan; and six grandchildren.

See Current Biography 1982.

Robin Williams

Born: Chicago, Illinois; July 21, 1951
Died: Tiburon, California; August 11, 2014
Occupation: Actor and comedian

Robin McLaurin Williams was an Academy Award–winning actor known for his ability to shift between light comic roles and more serious dramatic performances. Williams began as a stand-up comedian before transitioning to film and television.

Williams was born in Chicago, Illinois, and attended Claremont Men's College in California, where he studied political science. Williams was later accepted to the Julliard School in New York, where he studied acting before withdrawing from the program in 1976. After a few years as a stand-up comedian, Williams began receiving offers for small parts on television. His big break came when he was cast as the comedic extraterrestrial Mork in an episode of the series *Happy Days*. Williams reprised the role of Mork in the spinoff series *Mork and Mindy*, which ran from 1978 to 1982 and was a major hit with audiences.

Williams made his film debut in Robert Altman's musical version of *Popeye* (1980), which became a cult classic. He then gave an acclaimed performance in the 1982 adaptation of the John Irving novel *The World According to Garp*. Williams's films varied in critical appeal, and he built a reputation for heartfelt comedies, such as the 1984 *Moscow on the Hudson*. Williams's first hit film was *Good Morning, Vietnam* (1987), in which he displayed a talent for blending dramatic and comedic elements in his acting. Williams's performance earned him his first Academy Award nomination.

Williams earned another Academy Award nomination for his performance as an innovative English professor in the 1989 film *Dead Poets Society*. Two years later, Williams appeared in innovative director Terry Gilliam's *The Fisher King*, in which he played an emotionally troubled homeless man who goes looking for the Holy Grail. The role earned Williams a third Academy Award nomination for best actor in a leading role. Among other celebrated roles, Williams voiced the Genie in Disney's 1992 film *Aladdin* and, that same year, appeared in Steven Spielberg's film *Hook* as the literary hero Peter Pan.

Williams remained active throughout the 1990s. Frenetic comic roles such as those in *Mrs. Doubtfire* (1993) and the children's adventure *Jumanji* (1995) remained his standard fare, though he continued to branch out occasionally for more dramatic parts. His 1997 supporting role as a psychiatrist trying to help a troubled genius played by Matt Damon in *Good Will Hunting* won Williams the Academy Award for best supporting actor. In the 2000s, Williams took on some of his most unusual parts, including an uncharacteristically malevolent character in Christopher Nolan's 2002 film *Insomnia*. While he delved into his darker side, Williams returned to comedy often, such as in his supporting role in *Night at the Museum* (2006) and in subsequent sequels in 2009 and 2014.

Williams suffered from addiction and depression throughout his career. He had two marriages, to Valerie Velardi and Marsha Garces, that ended in divorce. Williams took his own life by asphyxiation on August 11, 2014. He was sixty-three. Williams was survived by his third wife, Susan Schneider, whom he married in 2011, and three children, Zak, Zelda, and Cody, from his earlier marriages.

See Current Biography 1997.

Colin Wilson

Born: Leicester, England; June 26, 1931
Died: St. Austell, England; December 5, 2013
Occupation: Author

English novelist Colin Henry Wilson was an acclaimed author known for his 1956 novel *The Outsider*. Though he never managed to match the critical success of his debut, Wilson published until the end of his life, with more than one hundred publications to his credit, including plays, novels, and nonfiction books.

Wilson was born into a working-class family in Leicester, England, and began writing at age nine. His first published book, *The Outsider* (1956), was a critical and commercial success upon its release, selling over twenty thousand copies within two months. In the book, Wilson examines the qualities that led some individuals, such as Franz Kafka, Albert Camus, and Friedrich Nietzsche, to achieve greatness, and concluded that geniuses necessarily became critics and outsiders, viewing mainstream culture from the fringe. A host of critics initially hailed *The Outsider* as a work of genius and predicted a brilliant career for Wilson, who became an overnight star in Britain, achieving fame atypical of nonfiction writers.

Wilson soon fell out of favor with the press, beginning with a scandal in which newspapers leaked a collection of writings rumored to be from Wilson's personal journals, containing descriptions of deviant sexual behavior and violence. Though the pages were actually intended for a novel, the event damaged Wilson's reputation, and his 1957 follow-up book, *Religion and the Rebel*, was less well received. Critics also scrutinized *The Outsider* more carefully and found it skewed, inaccurate, and lacking in genuine analysis.

In 1960 Wilson published his first novel *Ritual in the Dark*, which was the source of the papers mistakenly thought to be from his journal. While his first novel received mixed reviews, his 1961 *Adrift in Soho*, was better received. Wilson never recaptured his initial level of critical success, thought he continued writing and publishing prolifically for the rest of his life, eventually building a catalog of more than one hundred published works. Wilson occasionally enjoyed commercial success, such as with the 1998 *Alien Dawn*, in which Wilson argues that extraterrestrials have already visited Earth. Wilson published two memoirs of his life, *Voyage to a Beginning* (1969) and *Dreaming to Some Purpose* (2004), the latter of which was one of his last publications.

A stroke in June 2012 left Wilson speechless. He died on December 5, 2013, age eighty-two, of complications from pneumonia. He is survived by his second wife, Joy; their children, Rowan, Damon, and Sally Dyer; his son, Roderick, from his first marriage to Dorothy Betty Troop; and nine grandchildren.

See Current Biography Illustrated 1963.

Saul Zaentz

Born: Passaic, New Jersey; February 28, 1921
Died: San Francisco, California; January 3, 2014
Occupation: Producer

Music and film producer Saul Zaentz was one of the most successful movie executives of the twentieth century, winning multiple Academy Awards for films usually based on prizewinning books and plays. Having made his fortune through the music industry, Zaentz funded films without the backing of major Hollywood studios and was therefore a pioneer in independent film production.

A World War II army veteran, Zaentz briefly studied animal husbandry at Rutgers University before moving to St. Louis, where he studied business. In 1950 Zaentz relocated to San Francisco and began working for jazz record distributor Norman Granz, whose clients included such luminaries as Count Basie and Ella Fitzgerald. In 1955 Zaentz was hired by Max and Sol Weiss, who launched Fantasy Records, where Zaentz produced records by jazz artists Dave Brubeck and Stan Getz and poet Allen Ginsberg. In 1967 Zaentz and several colleagues bought Fantasy Records and began producing folk-pop band Creedence Clearwater Revival and front man John Fogerty. Though Zaentz and Fogerty eventually fell out, with a series of legal disputes between Fogerty and the Fantasy Records label, the partnership was lucrative for Zaentz and enabled him to pursue other interests.

Already in his fifties, Zaentz decided he wanted to produce films and started his own production company. Zaentz's first film was the 1972 independent film *Payday*, starring Rip Torn, that was largely overlooked but later gained a cult following. Next Zaentz partnered with Michael Douglas in 1975 to produce a film version of the Ken Kesey novel *One Flew over the Cuckoo's Nest*, starring Jack Nicholson. Zaentz and director Milos Forman were forced to work with a limited budget ($4.4 million), as they lacked backing from a major studio, but the film was a commercial and critical success, winning five Academy Awards, including best picture, and grossing some $120 million.

Zaentz purchased the film and merchandising rights to J. R. R. Tolkien's Lord of the Rings series and produced the Ralph Bakshi animated film *The Lord of the Rings* in 1978. He later negotiated with Peter Jackson, who undertook live-action versions of Tolkien's books. In 1984 Zaentz and Forman collaborated again on a film version of the Peter Schaffer play *Amadeus*, which won eight Academy Awards, including Zaentz's second best-picture win. Zaentz also produced film adaptations of *The Mosquito Coast* (1986) and the love story *The Unbearable Lightness of Being* (1988), both also critically acclaimed. After a string of financial failures, Zaentz invested a significant portion of his personal assets to produce *The English Patient* (1996), adapted from the book by Michael Ondaatje, which became his next major success, winning nine Academy Awards, including best picture. That year he also received the Academy of Motion Picture Arts and Sciences' Irving G. Thalberg Memorial Award for lifetime achievement.

Zaentz died in his home in San Francisco on January 3, 2014, of complications from Alzheimer's disease. He was ninety-two. Twice married and divorced, Zaentz is survived by his children, Athena, Joshua, and Jonathan; his stepson, Dorian; his nephew and business partner, Paul Zaentz; and seven grandchildren.

See Current Biography 1997.

Efrem Zimbalist Jr.

Born: New York City, New York; November 30, 1918
Died: Solvang, California; May 2, 2014
Occupation: Actor

Efrem Zimbalist Jr. was an actor known for his work in crime dramas, including 77 *Sunset Strip* and *The FBI*. Zimbalist was also a supporter of opera and produced the Pulitzer Prize–winning production of *The Consul* in 1950.

Zimbalist was born in 1918 in New York City, the son of prominent Russian violinist Efrem Zimbalist Sr., who became the director of Philadelphia's Curtis Institute of Music. His mother was soprano Alma Gluck, who was one of America's most famous singers at the turn of the century. Zimbalist attended Yale University but did not graduate, as he could not maintain interest in his schooling. He then studied acting at the Neighborhood Playhouse School of the Theatre in New York before being drafted to join the army in 1941. Wounded in the battle of Hürtgen Forest during World War II, Zimbalist received the Purple Heart and was discharged. He then returned to New York to seek work as an actor. In 1945 he married his first wife, Emily McNair, with whom he had two children, Nancy and Efrem III.

Zimbalist first appeared onstage in the Broadway production of *The Rugged Path*, alongside Spencer Tracy. Zimbalist also became involved in stage production and produced three operas by Gian Carlo Menotti. Zimbalist's staging of *The Consul* won the Pulitzer Prize for music in 1950. That same year, Zimbalist's wife died of cancer and he left New York for Philadelphia to work for his father at the Curtis Institute.

Returning to New York in 1954, Zimbalist appeared in a number of television roles and attracted film producers who offered him a contract with Warner Brothers. In 1956, Zimbalist was married again to Loranda Stephanie Spalding, with whom he had a daughter, Stephanie. Zimbalist's big break came in 1958 when he was cast in the lead role as a private detective on the television series 77 *Sunset Strip*. The series ran until 1964 and was a major success with audiences, making Zimbalist a well-known television personality.

His follow up series, *The FBI*, was even more successful, making Zimbalist one of the best-known television actors of the 1960s. The series aired for nine seasons, from 1965 to 1974, and the show's commitment to realism earned praise from J. Edgar Hoover, who was then the director of the FBI. After the series ended, Zimbalist's well-known face made him a popular choice for minor roles in films and television.

In the 1990s, Zimbalist became a voice actor, portraying characters in a number of animated series including *Spider-Man* and *Batman*. Zimbalist published an autobiography, *My Dinner of Herbs*, in 2003. In 2009, Zimbalist was named an Honorary Special Agent of the FBI, the organization's highest civilian honor, in recognition of his influence on and inspiration of a generation of FBI employees. Zimbalist was predeceased by his second wife in 2007 and his daughter Nancy in 2012. Zimbalist died at his ranch in Solvang, California, on May 2, 2014, age ninety-five, of natural causes. He is survived by his son, Efrem III, and daughter Stephanie.

See Current Biography 1960.

CLASSIFICATION BY PROFESSION

ACTIVISM
Berman, Tzeporah
Chen Guangcheng
Ma Jun
Perrette, Pauley
Tobin, Christina
Yearwood, Lennox

AGRICULTURE
Dalrymple, Jack
Salatin, Joel

ARCHAEOLOGY
Carriger, Gail

ARCHITECTURE
Oxman, Neri
Wang Shu

ART
Abramović, Marina
Downes, Rackstraw
Grimes
Lozano-Hemmer, Rafael
Weems, Carrie Mae

ASTRONAUTICS
Parmitano, Luca

BUSINESS
Bhargava, Manoj
Braun, Scooter
Breyer, Jim
Callum, Ian
Chen, Perry
Chesky, Brian
Christensen, Clayton
Dangote, Aliko
Diamandis, Peter
dos Santos, Isabel
Dyson, James
Fake, Caterina
Ferdowsi, Arash
Friedman, Andrew
Hughes, Chris
Iger, Bob
Jackley, Jessica
Leffler, Libby
Lyons, Jenna
MacLean, Audrey
Pathy, Rajshree
Robertson, Willie
Rosso, Renzo
Smith, Shane
Systrom, Kevin
Ujiri, Masai

Warrior, Padmasree
Weiner, Jess
Yu, Gideon

COMEDY
Farsad, Negin

EDUCATION
Aslan, Reza
Christensen, Clayton
Cummings, Missy
Derricotte, Toi
Diaconis, Persi
Hrabowski, Freeman A., III
Lander, Eric
Samarasekera, Indira

FASHION
Burton, Sarah
Chopra, Priyanka
Conrad, Lauren
Lyons, Jenna
Rosso, Renzo
Tisci, Riccardo

FILM
Adebimpe, Tunde
Al Mansour, Haifaa
Boal, Mark
Chastain, Jessica
Chopra, Priyanka
Cranston, Bryan
Cumberbatch, Benedict
Cuoco-Sweeting, Kaley
Dunham, Lena
Farsad, Negin
Frei, Christian
Garfield, Andrew
Gomez, Selena
Hardy, Tom
Jalade-Ekeinde, Omotola
Junger, Sebastian
Kahn, Michael
Kikuchi, Rinko
Lincoln, Andrew
McCarthy, Melissa
Mikkelsen, Mads
Moretz, Chloë Grace
Paul, Aaron
Plaza, Aubrey
Poitras, Laura
Quinto, Zachary
Reilly, Kelly
Ronan, Saoirse
Walker, Lucy
Wilson, Rebel

GASTRONOMY
Arzak, Elena
Atala, Alex
Basso, Paolo
Bayless, Rick
Humm, Daniel
Pic, Anne-Sophie

GOVERNMENT & POLITICS, FOREIGN
Lapid, Yair
Wangchuck, Jetsun Pema

GOVERNMENT & POLITICS, U.S.
Cohen, Jared
Dalrymple, Jack
de Blasio, Bill
Dimunation, Mark
Greene, Jehmu
Haot, Rachel
Harris, Kamala
Hirono, Mazie K.
Johnson Cook, Suzan
Lew, Jack
Pierson, Julia
Quinn, Christine
Ruiz, Raul
Scott, Tim
Sinema, Kyrsten

HEALTH
Bauer, Joy
Rosling, Hans
Topol, Eric
Warf, Benjamin

HEALTH & MEDICINE
Insel, Thomas R.

JOURNALISM
Boal, Mark
Boo, Katherine
Demick, Barbara
Greenwald, Glenn
Hessler, Peter
Junger, Sebastian
Lapid, Yair
Martin, Michel
Poitras, Laura
Salak, Kira
Sánchez, Yoani
Smith, Shane
Sobchak, Kseniya

LAW
Harris, Kamala

LITERATURE
Anderson, Laurie Halse
Carriger, Gail
Derricotte, Toi

Finney, Nikky
Gabaldon, Diana
Goldsmith, Kenneth
Hamid, Mohsin
Kinney, Jeff
Mantel, Hilary
Modan, Rutu
Ruiz Zafón, Carlos
Saunders, George
Stamm, Peter
Unigwe, Chika
Ward, Jesmyn
Willems, Mo

MATHEMATICS
Diaconis, Persi

MILITARY
Cummings, Missy

MUSIC
Adams, John Luther
Adebimpe, Tunde
Avicii
Azalea, Iggy
Bird, Andrew
Braun, Scooter
Bryan, Luke
Gomez, Selena
Gotye
Grimes
Harris, Calvin
Heap, Imogen
Jalade-Ekeinde, Omotola
Jónsi
Keating, Zoë
Lamar, Kendrick
Macklemore
Miller, Patina
Ora, Rita
Sandé, Emeli
Stemme, Nina
Thile, Chris

NONFICTION
Aslan, Reza
Balog, James
Bayless, Rick
Boo, Katherine
Hessler, Peter
Junger, Sebastian
Salak, Kira
Salatin, Joel

ORGANIZATIONS
Bokova, Irina
Brown, Nancy
Diamandis, Peter
Insel, Thomas R.
Jackley, Jessica

Lavizzo-Mourey, Risa
Ma Jun
Tobin, Christina

PHILANTHROPY
Jalade-Ekeinde, Omotola
Lavizzo-Mourey, Risa

PHOTOGRAPHY
Balog, James
Weems, Carrie Mae

RADIO
Martin, Michel

RELIGION
Yearwood, Lennox

SCIENCE
Barbosa, Marcia
Bargmann, Cornelia
Cummings, Missy
Diamandis, Peter
Helgen, Kristofer
Knowlton, Nancy
Lander, Eric
Rosling, Hans
Sadoway, Donald
Scott, Eugenie
Seager, Sara
Warf, Benjamin
Widder, Edith
Yi So-yeon

SOCIAL SCIENCE
Cuddy, Amy

SPORTS
Ainslie, Ben
Amla, Hashim
Burnquist, Bob
Douglas, Gabby
Franklin, Missy
Friedman, Andrew
Griffin, Robert, III
Johnson, Calvin
Jones, Jennifer
Jurek, Scott
Kershaw, Clayton
Kim, Yuna
Li Na
Machado, Manny
Maze, Tina
McNamara, Garrett
Molchanova, Natalia
Molina, Yadier
Morgan, Alex

Murray, Andy
Puig, Yasiel
Quick, Jonathan
Sinclair, Christine
Smyth, Jason
Spoelstra, Erik
Subban, P.K.
Tseng, Yani
Ujiri, Masai
Yu, Gideon

TECHNOLOGY
Breyer, Jim
Chesky, Brian
Cohen, Jared
Dean, Jeffrey
Dyson, James
Fake, Caterina
Hughes, Chris
Jackley, Jessica
Leffler, Libby
Lozano-Hemmer, Rafael
MacLean, Audrey
Rattray, Ben
Systrom, Kevin
Sánchez, Yoani
Topol, Eric
Yu, Gideon

TELEVISION
Bauer, Joy
Bayless, Rick
Chopra, Priyanka
Conrad, Lauren
Cranston, Bryan
Cumberbatch, Benedict
Cuoco-Sweeting, Kaley
Dunham, Lena
Farsad, Negin
Greene, Jehmu
Lincoln, Andrew
McCarthy, Melissa
Paul, Aaron
Perrette, Pauley
Plaza, Aubrey
Quinto, Zachary
Reilly, Kelly
Robertson, Willie
Smith, Shane
Sobchak, Kseniya
Willems, Mo
Wilson, Rebel
Youssef, Bassem

THEATER
Cumberbatch, Benedict
Miller, Patina